POEMS ON AFFAIRS OF STATE

AUGUSTAN SATIRICAL VERSE, 1660–1714

Volume 7: 1704–1714

Queen Anne, Prince George of Denmark, and the duke of Marlborough, an anonymous engraving

Poems on Affairs of State

AUGUSTAN SATIRICAL VERSE, 1660–1714

VOLUME 7: 1704–1714

edited by

FRANK H. ELLIS

New Haven & London

YALE UNIVERSITY PRESS

1975

Designed by John O.C. McCrillis
and set in Baskerville type.
Printed in the United States of America by
The Murray Printing Co., Forge Village, Mass.

Published in Great Britain, Europe, and Africa by
Yale University Press, Ltd., London.
Distributed in Latin America by Kaiman & Polon,
Inc., New York City; in Australasia and Southeast
Asia by John Wiley & Sons Australasia Pty. Ltd.,
Sydney; in India by UBS Publishers' Distributors Pvt.,
Ltd., Delhi; in Japan by John Weatherhill, Inc., Tokyo.

Published with assistance from the foundation
established in memory of Oliver Baty Cunningham
of the Class of 1917, Yale College.

PREFACE

"The Necessity of a Preface here" is not simply "that People generally expect it," as William Shippen said. The real reason is that a scholarly undertaking of this kind becomes almost a group activity, and it is necessary at last to identify the group.

The General Editor and two Associates in the *Poems on Affairs of State* project have been extraordinarily generous. The largess of George deF. Lord and Basil Duke Henning does not show on the surface, but it informs the whole volume. And no one who even glances at the critical apparatus can fail to see how heavily this volume draws on the resources of the Osborn MSS. in the Yale University Library. Four other friends have been almost equally helpful: Margaret C. Crum, of the Department of Western Manuscripts in the Bodleian Library; David F. Foxon, Reader in Textual Criticism, Oxford University; David M. Lloyd, Keeper of Printed Books, the National Library of Scotland; and Reginald Williams, Department of Prints and Drawings, the British Museum. Crum and Foxon, of course, are already on the way to becoming household words (in bibliographical households).

Work on the text of Swift's verse was enormously facilitated by the Teerink Collection in the University of Pennsylvania Library and the unfailing assistance and good humor of Neda M. Westlake and her staff. The commentary throughout the volume has benefited from the special competence of Bruce T. Dahlberg in the literature of the Bible and Claude M. Simpson in the music of the broadside ballad. In a hundred other ways the volume has profited from the special competences of John Alden, B. M. Austin, R. A. G. Carson, Dr. Eveline Cruickshanks, Henry Grunthal, Henry Horwitz, Felix Hull, Carolyn Jakeman, George P. Mayhew, N. Frederick Nash, John M. Pinkerton, P. W. J. Riley, Anne C. Snape, Henry L. Snyder, G. L. Taylor, Elizabeth von Klemperer, and David Woolley.

The Portland MSS. in custody of the University of Nottingham Library and on loan to the British Museum are quoted by permission of His Grace the Duke of Portland and the Keepers of Manuscripts of the two libraries. The documents at Blenheim Castle are quoted by permission of His Grace the Duke of Marlborough. The Marquess of Bath has given permission to quote from the Prior MSS. and others at Longleat. Quotations from the Holkham MSS. are made with permission of the Earl of Leicester. Lord Downshire has given his consent for extracts to be made from the Trumbull MSS. in the Berkshire Record Office. The kindness of Sir Berwick Lechmere, Bart., has made it possible to quote from the Lechmere MSS. in the Worcestershire Record Office. The Cowper MSS. formerly at Panshanger are quoted by permission of the late Lady Salmond, Lady Ravensdale, and the Hertfordshire Record Office. Mrs. O. R. Bagot has very kindly given permission for the Bagot MSS. at Levens Hall, Westmorland, to be quoted. Permission to publish manuscript material in the British Museum, the Bodleian, and the Houghton Library has very generously been granted by the trustees of those institutions.

"In the middle of the journey" of this volume Dr. William A. Speck, Lecturer in Modern History at the University of Newcastle-upon-Tyne, spent the academic year 1969–70 in New Haven. From the Madan collection of Sacheverelliana, which he brought with him intact, and from his own unequaled knowledge of the manuscript sources for the history of the period, Dr. Speck was able to contribute abundantly to the annotation of this volume.

In the last stages of the work, Barbara Lauren, now assistant professor of English literature at Bowdoin College, and Nancy R. Woodington, now a graduate student of divinity at Yale University, provided research assistance of such high quality that it amounted to virtual collaboration. For the errors that remain I can thank no one but myself.

Ocellus Lucanus is well-known to have written "these words, *Anarchon ara kai atelutaion to pan,* which imply that all things have neither beginning nor end." But the *Poems on Affairs of State* project ends here and the editor of this volume may be allowed to dismiss himself in Joseph Addison's words (*POAS,* Yale, *6,* 33):

> . . . freed at length, he lays aside the weight
> Of publick Business, and Affairs of State:
> Forgets his Pomp, Dead to Ambitions Fires,
> And to some peaceful Brandy-Shop retires.

CONTENTS

LIST OF ILLUSTRATIONS

xiii

ABBREVIATIONS AND
WORKS FREQUENTLY CITED

In bibliographical references the place of publication is London unless otherwise stated. Classical texts are quoted from the Loeb Classical Library, William Heineman Ltd. and Harvard University Press. Shakespeare is quoted from *The First Folio,* ed. Charlton Hinman, New York, Norton, 1968.

Account of the Conduct: *An Account of the Conduct of the Dowager Duchess of Marlborough, from Her First Coming to Court, to the Year 1710. In a Letter from Herself to My Lord — ——, 1742.*

Addison, *Letters:*   *The Letters of Joseph Addison,* ed. Walter Graham, Oxford, Clarendon Press, 1941.

Ailesbury: *Memoirs of Thomas, Earl of Ailesbury Written by Himself,* 2 vols., 1890.

Alumni Oxonienses: Joseph Foster, *Alumni Oxonienses. The Members of the University of Oxford, 1500–1714,* 4 vols., Oxford, 1891–92.

APS: *The Acts of the Parliaments of Scotland,* 11 vols. in 12, plus index, Edinburgh, 1844–75.

Arber: Edward Arber, *The Term Catalogues 1668–1709,* 3 vols., Edward Arber, 1903–06.

Atterbury, *Works:*   *The Miscellaneous Works of Bishop Atterbury with Historical Notes by J. Nichols,* 5 vols., 1789–98.

Aubrey: John Aubrey, *Brief Lives,* ed. Andrew Clark, 2 vols., Oxford, 1898.

Baker: David E. Baker, *Biographia Dramatica,* 3 vols. in 4, 1812.

Beatson: Robert Beatson, *A Political Index to the Histories of Great Britain and Ireland,* 3rd ed., 3 vols., 1806.

Bibliotheca Lindesiana: *Bibliotheca Lindesiana. Catalogue of a Collection of English Ballads of the XVIIth and XVIIIth Centuries,* Privately Printed, 1890.

BIHR: *Bulletin of the Institute of Historical Research,* 45 vols., University of London, 1923–.

Biographia Britannica: *Biographia Britannica: Or, The Lives of the Most Eminent Persons,* 6 vols. in 7, 1747–66; 2nd ed., ed. Andrew Kippis, and others, 5 vols., 1778–93.

BM: British Museum, London.

Bodl.: Bodleian Library, Oxford University.

Bolingbroke, *Letters: Letters and Correspondence, Public and Private, of The Right Honourable Henry St. John, Lord Visc. Bolingbroke; During the Time he was Secretary of State to Queen Anne,* ed. Gilbert Parke, 4 vols., 1798.

Boyer, *Annals:* Abel Boyer, *The History of the Reign of Queen Anne, Digested into Annals,* 11 vols., 1703–13.

Boyer, *History:* Abel Boyer, *The History of the Life and Reign of Queen Anne,* 1722.

Boyer, *Political State:* Abel Boyer, *Quadriennium Annae Postremum; or the Political State of Great Britain,* 2nd ed., 8 vols. in 5, 1718–20.

BPL: Boston Public Library

Brodrick: Thomas Brodrick, *A Compleat History of the Late War in the Netherlands,* 2 vols., 1713.

Browning: Andrew Browning, *Thomas Osborne, Earl of Danby and Duke of Leeds,* 3 vols., Glasgow, Jackson, Son & Co., 1944–51.

Burnet: Gilbert Burnet, *History of His Own Time,* 2 vols., 1724–34.

Burnet, 1823: *Bishop Burnet's History of His Own Time: With the Suppressed Passages of the First Volume, and Notes by the Earls of Dartmouth and Hardwicke, and Speaker Onslow,* 6 vols., Oxford, 1823.

Calamy, *Abridgement:* Edmund Calamy, *An Abridgement of Mr. Baxter's History of His Life and Times, With an Account of the Ministers who were Ejected after the Restoration of King Charles II,* 2nd ed., 2 vols., 1713.

Calamy, *Historical Account:* Edmund Calamy, *A Historical Account of My Own Life,* ed. John T. Rutt, 2nd ed., 2 vols., 1830.

Case: *A Bibliography of English Poetical Miscellanies 1521–1750,* ed. Arthur E. Case, Oxford, Bibliographical Society, 1935.

CBEL: The Cambridge Bibliography of English Literature, ed. Frederick W. Bateson, 5 vols., Cambridge, Cambridge University Press, 1940–57.

Chamberlayne: Edward and John Chamberlayne, *Angliae Notitia: Or, The Present State of England,* 36 vols., 1669–1755.

Chappell: William Chappell, *Popular Music of the Olden Time,* 2 vols. [1855–59].

Cibber, *Lives:* Theophilus Cibber and Robert Shiels, *The Lives of the Poets,* 5 vols., 1753.

CJ: The Journals of the House of Commons.

CJ Ireland: The Journals of the House of Commons of the Kingdom of Ireland, 31 vols. in 27, Dublin, 1782–84.

Collins, 1741: Arthur Collins, *The Peerage of England,* 2nd ed., 4 vols., 1741.

Collins, 1812: *Collins's Peerage of England,* ed. Sir Egerton Brydges, 9 vols., 1812.

Congreve, *Letters:* William Congreve, *Letters and Documents,* ed. John C. Hodges, New York, Harcourt, Brace & World, 1964.

Cowper, *Diary:* *The Private Diary of William, First Earl Cowper, Lord Chancellor of England,* Eton, 1833.

Coxe, *Memoirs:* William Coxe, *Memoirs of the Duke of Marlborough with his Original Correspondence,* revised ed., 3 vols., 1847–48.

CSPD: *Calendar of State Papers, Domestic Series, 1660–1704,* ed. Mary Anne E. Greene, and others, 44 vols., H. M. Stationery Office, 1860–1972.

CTB: *Calendar of Treasury Books, 1660–1718,* ed. William A. Shaw, 32 vols., H. M. Stationery Office, 1904–62.

CTP: *Calendar of Treasury Papers, 1557–1728,* ed. Joseph Redington, 6 vols., 1868–89.

Cunningham: Alexander Cunningham, *The History of Great Britain: From the Revolution in 1688, to the Accession of George the First,* 2 vols., 1787.

Dalrymple: Sir John Dalrymple, Baronet, *Memoirs of Great Britain and Ireland,* 3rd ed., 3 vols., 1790.

Dalton: *English Army Lists and Commission Registers, 1661–1714,* ed. Charles Dalton, 4 vols. in 2, Francis Edwards Ltd., 1960.

Defoe, *Letters:* *The Letters of Daniel Defoe,* ed. George Harris Healey, Oxford, Clarendon Press, 1955.

Defoe, *A True Collection:* *A True Collection of the Writings of the Author of the True Born Englishman,* 1703.

Dennis, *Critical Works:* *The Critical Works of John Dennis,* ed. Edward N. Hooker, 2 vols., Baltimore, The Johns Hopkins Press, 1939–43.

DNB: *The Dictionary of National Biography,* ed. Sir Leslie Stephen and Sir Sidney Lee, 22 vols., Oxford University Press, 1949–50.

Dryden, *Poems:* *The Poems of John Dryden,* ed. James Kinsley, 4 vols., Oxford, Clarendon Press, 1958.

Dryden, *Prose:* *The Critical and Miscellaneous Prose Works of John Dryden,* ed. Edmond Malone, 3 vols. in 4, 1800.

Dryden, *Works:* *The Works of John Dryden,* ed. Sir Walter Scott and George Saintsbury, 18 vols., Edinburgh, 1882–93.

Dunton: John Dunton, *The Life and Errors of John Dunton,* 1705.

Dunton, 1818:   *The Life and Errors of John Dunton,* ed. John Nichols, 2
       vols., 1818.

Echard: Laurence Echard, *The History of England from the Restoration of
       King Charles the Second to the Conclusion of the Reign of King James the
       Second,* 3 vols., 1707–18.

EHD: *English Historical Documents 1660–1714,* ed. Andrew Browning,
       Eyre & Spottiswoode, 1953.

Evelyn: *The Diary of John Evelyn,* ed. Esmond S. deBeer, 6 vols., Oxford,
       Clarendon Press, 1955.

Feiling: Keith Feiling, *A History of the Tory Party, 1640–1714,* 2nd ed.,
       Oxford, Clarendon Press, 1950.

Foss: Edward Foss, *The Judges of England,* 9 vols., 1848–64.

Foxon: David F. Foxon, "Defoe: a specimen of a catalogue of verse
       1701–1750," *The Library, 20* (December 1965), 277–97.

GEC: George E. Cokayne, *The Complete Peerage,* ed. Vicary Gibbs, 13
       vols. in 14, St. Catharine Press Ltd., 1910–59.

GEC, *Baronetage:*   *Complete Baronetage,* ed. George E. Cokayne, 5 vols.,
       Exeter, William Pollard & Co., 1900–06.

Goldsmith, *Collected Works:*   *Collected Works of Oliver Goldsmith,* ed. Arthur
       Friedman, 5 vols., Oxford, Clarendon Press, 1966.

Granger: James Granger, *A Biographical History of England,* 4 vols., 1769.

Grimblot: *Letters of William III and Louis XIV . . . 1697–1700,* ed. Paul
       Grimblot, 2 vols., 1848.

Halkett and Laing: Samuel Halkett and John Laing, *Dictionary of
       Anonymous and Pseudonymous English Literature,* ed. James Kennedy,
       W. A. Smith, and A. F. Johnson, 9 vols., Edinburgh, Oliver and
       Boyd, 1926–62.

Harbottle: Thomas B. Harbottle, *Dictionary of Quotations,* New York,
       1897.

Hardwicke: *Miscellaneous State Papers from 1501 to 1726,* ed. Philip Yorke,
       2nd earl of Hardwicke, 2 vols., 1778.

Hearne: *Remarks and Collections of Thomas Hearne,* ed. C. E. Doble and
       others, 11 vols., Oxford, Clarendon Press, 1884–1918.

HMC *Athole MSS.:*   Historical Manuscripts Commission, *Twelfth Report,
       Appendix, Part VIII, The Manuscripts of the Duke of Athole, K.T., and
       of the Earl of Home,* H. M. Stationery Office, 1891.

HMC *Bagot MSS.:*   Historical Manuscripts Commission, *Tenth Report,
       Appendix, Part IV, The Manuscripts of Captain Josceline F. Bagot,* H. M.
       Stationery Office, 1885.

HMC *Bath MSS.:*   Historical Manuscripts Commission, *Calendar of the*

Manuscripts of the Marquis of Bath Preserved at Longleat, Wiltshire, 3 vols., H. M. Stationery Office, 1904–08

HMC *Beaufort MSS.:*   Historical Manuscripts Commission, *Twelfth Report, Appendix, Part IX, The Manuscripts of the Duke of Beaufort,* H. M. Stationery Office, 1891.

HMC *Buccleuch & Queensberry MSS.:*   Historical Manuscripts Commission, *The Manuscripts of the Duke of Buccleuch & Queensberry,* 2 vols. in 3, H. M. Stationery Office, 1897–1903.

HMC *Cowper MSS.:*   Historical Manuscripts Commission, *The Manuscripts of the Earl Cowper, K.G., Preserved at Melbourne Hall, Derbyshire,* 3 vols., H. M. Stationery Office, 1888–89.

HMC *Dartmouth MSS.:*   Historical Manuscripts Commission. *Eleventh Report, Appendix, Part V, The Manuscripts of the Earl of Dartmouth,* H. M. Stationery Office, 1887.

HMC Downshire MSS.:   Historical Manuscripts Commission, *The Manuscripts of the Marquess of Downshire. Papers of Sir William Trumbull,* 1 vol. in 2, H. M. Stationery Office, 1924.

HMC *Egmont MSS.:*   Historical Manuscripts Commission, *Report on the Manuscripts of the Earl of Egmont,* 2 vols. in 3, H. M. Stationery Office, 1905–09.

HMC *Frankland-Russell-Astley MSS.:*   Historical Manuscripts Commission, *Report on the Manuscripts of Mrs. Frankland-Russell-Astley,* H. M. Stationery Office. 1900.

HMC *Hope Johnstone MSS.:*   Historical Manuscripts Commission, *The Manuscripts of J. J. Hope Johnstone, Esq. of Annandale,* H. M. Stationery Office, 1897.

HMC *Inner Temple MSS.:*   Historical Manuscripts Commission, *Eleventh Report, Appendix, Part VII, The Manuscripts of the Inner Temple, &c.,* H. M. Stationery Office, 1888.

HMC *Lonsdale Mss.:*   Historical Manuscripts Commission, *The Manuscripts of the Earl of Lonsdale,* H. M. Stationery Office, 1893.

HMC *Lords MSS.:*   Historical Manuscripts Commission, *The Manuscripts of the House of Lords, 1678–1714,* 4 vols., 1887–94, New Series 10 vols., H. M. Stationery Office, 1900–53.

HMC *Mar and Kellie MSS.:*   Historical Manuscripts Commission, *Report on the Manuscripts of the Earl of Mar and Kellie,* H. M. Stationery Office, 1904.

HMC *Marlborough MSS.:*   Historical Manuscripts Commission, *Eighth Report of the Royal Commission on Historical Manuscripts . . . Report & Appendix,* 2 parts in 4 vols., H. M. Stationery Office, 1881.

HMC *Ormonde MSS.:*   Historical Manuscripts Commission, *The Manu-*

scripts of the Marquis of Ormonde, 2 vols., 1895–99, New Series 8 vols., H. M. Stationery Office, 1902–20.

HMC *Polwarth MSS.:*   Historical Manuscripts Commission, *Manuscripts of Lord Polwarth formerly preserved at Mertoun House, Berwickshire, and now in the Scottish Record Office, Edinburgh,* 5 vols., H. M. Stationery Office, 1911–61.

HMC *Portland MSS.:*   Historical Manuscripts Commission, *The Manuscripts of the Duke of Portland,* 10 vols., H. M. Stationery Office, 1891–1931.

HMC *Round MSS.:*   Historical Manuscripts Commission, *Fourteenth Report, Appendix, Part IX, Manuscripts of the Earl of Buckinghamshire, the Earl of Lindsey, the Earl of Onslow, Lord Emly, Theodore J. Hare, Esq. and James Round, Esq. M. P.,* H. M. Stationery Office, 1895.

HMC *Rutland MSS.:*   Historical Manuscripts Commission, *The Manuscripts of His Grace the Duke of Rutland, G.C.B., Preserved at Belvoir Castle,* 4 vols., 1888–1905.

HMC *Stuart MSS.:*   Historical Manuscripts Commission, *Calendar of the Stuart Papers Belonging to His Majesty the King,* 7 vols., H. M. Stationery Office, 1902–23.

Holkham MSS.:   Manuscripts of the Earl of Leicester at Holkham Hall, Wells, Norfolk.

Holmes: Geoffrey Holmes, *British Politics in the Age of Anne,* London, Macmillan, 1967.

Horwitz: Henry Horwitz, *Revolution Politicks: The Career of Daniel Finch, Second Earl of Nottingham, 1647–1730,* Cambridge, Cambridge University Press, 1968.

Howell: *A Complete Collection of State Trials,* ed. Thomas B. Howell, 33 vols., 1816–26.

Jacob, *Historical Account:*   [Giles Jacob], *An Historical Account of the Lives and Writings of our Most Considerable English Poets,* 1720.

Jacob, *Poetical Register:*   [Giles Jacob], *The Poetical Register: Or, The Lives and Characters of the English Dramatic Poets,* 1719.

JHM: *Journal of the History of Medicine.*

Johnson, *Lives:*   Samuel Johnson, *The Lives of the English Poets,* ed. George Birkbeck Hill, 3 vols., Oxford, Clarendon Press, 1905.

Kenyon: John P. Kenyon, *Robert Spencer, Earl of Sunderland, 1641–1702,* Longmans, Green, 1958.

Key: [1st t.p.] *The Genuine Works of Mr. Daniel D'Foe, Author of The True-born English-Man, A Satyr . . . To which is added A Complete Key to the Whole, Never before Printed. Vol. I* [2nd t.p.] *A True Collection of* *the Writings of the Author of the True-born English-Man* . . . *Vol. I. The Third Edition*, [1710?], sig. *1–4 (Yale copy: Ik.D362.C703c).

Klopp: Onno Klopp, *Der Fall des Hauses Stuart*, 14 vols., Vienna, 1875–88.

Lady Cowper, *Diary:*   *Diary of Mary Countess Cowper, Lady of the Bedchamber to the Princess of Wales*, 1864.

Lamberty: Guillaume de Lamberty, *Mémoires pour servir à l'Histoire du XVIII Siècle*, 2nd ed., 14 vols., Amsterdam, 1734–40.

Lee: William Lee, *Daniel Defoe: His Life, and Recently Discovered Writings*, 3 vols., 1869.

Le Neve: *Le Neve's Pedigrees of the Knights*, ed. George W. Marshall, Harleian Society, 1873.

Letters of Queen Anne: *The Letters and Diplomatic Instructions of Queen Anne*, ed. Beatrice C. Brown, Cassell & Co., 1935.

Levens MSS.:   The manuscripts of Mrs. O. R. Bagot, Levens Hall, Kendal, Westmorland.

LJ: *The Journals of the House of Lords.*

Lockhart: [George Lockhart], *Memoirs concerning the Affairs of Scotland, from Queen Anne's Accession to the Throne, To the Commencement of the Union of the Two Kingdoms*, 1714.

Longleat MSS.:   The manuscripts of the Marquess of Bath, Longleat, Warminster, Wiltshire.

Lucas: Theophilus Lucas, *Memoirs of the Lives, Intrigues, and Comical Adventures of the Most Famous Gamesters and Celebrated Sharpers in the Reigns of Charles II. James II. William III. and Queen Anne* (1714), ed. Cyril H. Hartmann, George Routledge & Sons, 1930.

Luttrell: Narcissus Luttrell, *A Brief Historical Relation of State Affairs from September 1678 to April 1714*, 6 vols., Oxford, 1857.

Macaulay: Thomas Babington Macaulay, *The History of England from the Accession of James II*, ed. Charles H. Firth, 6 vols., Macmillan & Co., 1913–15.

Macky: *Memoirs of the Secret Services of John Macky*, ed. Spring Macky, 2nd ed., 1733.

Macpherson, *History:*   James Macpherson, *The History of Great Britain, from the Restoration to the Accession of the House of Hannover*, 2 vols., 1775.

Macpherson, *Original Papers:*   James Macpherson, *Original Papers; Containing the Secret History of Great Britain from the Restoration, to the Accession of the House of Hannover*, 2nd ed., 2 vols., 1776.

Miège: Guy Miège, *The Present State of Great Britain*, 1707.

Moore: John R. Moore, *A Checklist of the Writings of Daniel Defoe*, Bloomington, Indiana University Press, 1960.

Moore, *Daniel Defoe*:   John R. Moore, *Daniel Defoe Citizen of the Modern World*, Chicago, University of Chicago Press, 1958.

Morgan: William T. Morgan, *A Bibliography of British History (1700–1715)*, 5 vols., Bloomington, Indiana University Press, 1934–42.

N&Q: *Notes and Queries*, ed. W. J. Thoms, and others, 218 vols., George Bell, 1849–.

New Dictionary: B. E., *A New Dictionary of the Terms Ancient and Modern of the Canting Crew* [1699].

Nichols, *Anecdotes*:   John Nichols, *Literary Anecdotes of the Eighteenth Century*, 9 vols., 1812–15.

Nichols, *Illustrations*:   John Nichols, *Illustrations of the Literary History of the Eighteenth Century*, 8 vols., 1817–58.

Nicolson, *Diary*:   William Nicolson, Bishop of Carlisle, *Diary*, Carlisle Public Library.

NLI: National Library of Ireland, Dublin.

NLS: National Library of Scotland, Edinburgh.

Noble: Mark Noble, *A Biographical History of England, from the Revolution to the End of George I's Reign*, 3 vols., 1806.

Noorthouck: John Noorthouck, *A New History of London, Including Westminster and Southwark*, 1773.

Numerical Calculation: *A Numerical Calculation of the Honourable Mem——rs As were Elected for the Ensuing Parl——nt*, 1705 [folio half-sheet].

OED: *The Oxford English Dictionary*, ed. James A. H. Murray and others, 13 vols., Oxford, Clarendon Press, 1933.

Ogg, *1–2*:   David Ogg, *England in the Reign of Charles II*, 2nd ed., 2 vols., Oxford, Clarendon Press, 1956.

Ogg, *3*:   David Ogg, *England in the Reigns of James II and William III*, 2nd ed., Oxford, Clarendon Press, 1957.

Oldmixon, *History*:   John Oldmixon, *The History of England during the Reigns of King William and Queen Mary, Queen Anne, King George I*, 1735.

Oldmixon, *Maynwaring*:   John Oldmixon, *The Life and Posthumous Works of Arthur Maynwaring, Esq; Containing Several Original Pieces and Translations, in Prose and Verse, never before Printed*, 1715.

Original Letters: *Original Letters of Locke, Algernon Sidney, and Anthony Lord Shaftesbury*, ed. T. Forster, 1830.

Osborn MSS.:   The James Marshall and Marie-Louise Osborn Collection in the Yale University Library.

Parl. Hist.:   *Cobbett's Parliamentary History of England,* 36 vols., 1806–20.

Partridge: Eric Partridge, *A Dictionary of Slang and Unconventional English,* 4th ed., New York, Macmillan, 1951.

Pepys, *Diary:*   *The Diary of Samuel Pepys; A New and Complete Transcription . . . ,* ed. Robert Latham and William Matthews, 7 vols., Los Angeles, University of California Press, 1970–72.

Phil. Trans.:   *Philosophical Transactions of the Royal Society of London,* 29 vols., London, 1665–1716.

Pittis, *Proceedings:*   William Pittis, *The Proceedings of Both Houses of Parliament, In the Years 1702, 1703, 1704, upon the Bill to Prevent Occasional Conformity, Interspers'd with Speeches for and against the Bill, Most of which were Never before Printed,* 1710.

Plas Newydd MS.:   The Manuscripts of George C. Paget, Lord Anglesey, Plas Newydd, Anglesey.

Plomer: Henry R. Plomer, *A Dictionary of Printers and Booksellers . . . 1668–1725,* Oxford, Bibliographical Society, 1922.

POAS: *Poems on Affairs of State,* 1697–1716 (Case 211).

POAS, Yale: *Poems on Affairs of State,* ed. George deF. Lord and others, 7 vols., New Haven, Yale University Press, 1963–75.

Pope, *Corr.:*   *The Correspondence of Alexander Pope,* ed. George Sherburn, 5 vols., Oxford, Clarendon Press, 1956.

Portland MSS.:   Manuscripts of the Duke of Portland on deposit in the Department of Manuscripts, Nottingham University Library.

Prior, *Works:*   *The Literary Works of Matthew Prior,* ed. H. Bunker Wright and Monroe K. Spears, 2 vols., Oxford, Clarendon Press, 1959.

Private Correspondence of Sarah, Duchess of Marlborough: *Private Correspondence of Sarah, Duchess of Marlborough, Illustrative of the Court and Times of Queen Anne,* 2 vols., 2nd ed., 1838.

PRO: Public Record Office, London.

PRSA: *A New Collection of Poems Relating to State Affairs, from Oliver Cromwell to this Present Time: By the Greatest Wits of the Age,* 1705.

Ralph: [James Ralph], *The History of England during the Reigns of King William, Queen Anne, and King George the First,* 2 vols., 1744–46.

RCP, *Annals:*   Royal College of Physicians, *Liber Annalium Collegii Medicorum Lond.,* vols. I–VIII [1518–1722].

Rosenberg: Albert Rosenberg, *Sir Richard Blackmore, A Poet and Physician of the Augustan Age,* Lincoln, University of Nebraska Press, 1953.

Roxburghe Ballads: The *Roxburghe Ballads,* 9 vols. in 10, vols. 1–3 ed. William Chappell, vols. 4–9 ed. J. W. Ebsworth, Hertford (Ballad Society), 1871–99.

Rymer, *Critical Works:*   *The Critical Works of Thomas Rymer,* ed. Curt A. Zimansky, New Haven and London, Yale University Press, 1956.

Saint-Simon: Louis de Rouvroy, duc de Saint-Simon, *Mémoires,* ed. Gonzague Truc, 7 vols., Librairie Gallimard, Paris, 1947–61.

Shaw: William A. Shaw, *The Knights of England,* 2 vols., Sherratt and Hughes, 1906.

Shrewsbury Corr.:   *Private and Original Correspondence of Charles Talbot, Duke of Shrewsbury,* ed. William Coxe, Longman, Hurst, Rees, Orme, and Brown, 1821.

Simpson: Claude M. Simpson, *The British Broadside Ballad and Its Music,* New Brunswick, New Jersey, Rutgers University Press, 1966.

SND: *The Scottish National Dictionary,* ed. William Grant, 9 vols., Edinburgh, Scottish National Dictionary Association, 1931–.

Somerville: Thomas Somerville, *The History of Great Britain during the Reign of Queen Anne,* 1798.

Speck: William A. Speck, *Tory & Whig The Struggle in the Constituencies 1701–1715,* Macmillan, St. Martin's Press, 1970.

Spence: Joseph Spence, *Observations, Anecdotes, and Characters of Books and Men Collected form Conversation,* ed. James M. Osborn, 2 vols., Oxford, Clarendon Press, 1966.

Steele: *A Bibliography of Royal Proclamations of the Tudor and Stuart Sovereigns,* ed. Robert Steele, 2 vols., Oxford, Clarendon Press, 1910.

Strype: John Stowe, *A Survey of the Cities of London and Westminster,* ed. John Strype, 2 vols., 1720.

Survey of London: Charles R. Ashbee and others, *The Survey of London,* 37 vols., London County Council, 1900–.

Swift, *Corr.:*   *The Correspondence of Jonathan Swift,* ed. Harold Williams, 5 vols., Oxford, Clarendon Press, 1963–65.

Swift, *Discourse:*   Jonathan Swift, *A Discourse of the Contests and Dissentions between the Nobles and the Commons in Athens and Rome,* ed. Frank H. Ellis, Oxford, Clarendon Press, 1967.

Swift, *Journal:*   Jonathan Swift, *Journal to Stella,* ed. Harold Williams, 2 vols., Oxford, Clarendon Press, 1948.

Swift, *Poems*: *The Poems of Jonathan Swift,* ed. Harold Williams, 3 vols., Oxford, Clarendon Press, 1937.

Swift, *Prose*: *The Prose Writings of Jonathan Swift,* ed. Herbert Davis, 13 vols., Oxford, Basil Blackwell, 1939–62.

TCD: Trinity College, Dublin.

Texas: Miriam Lutcher Stark Library, University of Texas, Austin, Texas.

Thoresby: *Letters of Eminent Men, Addressed to Ralph Thoresby, F.R.S.,* 2 vols., 1832.

Tilley: *A Dictionary of the Proverbs in England in the Sixteenth and Seventeenth Centuries,* ed. Morris P. Tilley, Ann Arbor, University of Michigan Press, 1950.

Tindal: Nicholas Tindal, *The History of England by Mr. Rapin de Thoyras. Continued from the Revolution to the Accession of King George II,* 3rd ed., 4 vols. in 5, 1743–47.

Trevelyan: George Macaulay Trevelyan, *England under Queen Anne,* 3 vols., Longmans, Green, 1930.

Tryal of Dr. Henry Sacheverell: *The Tryal of Dr. Henry Sacheverell, before the House of Peers, for High Crimes and Misdemeanors; Upon an Impeachment by the Knights, Citizens and Burgesses in Parliament Assembled,* 1710.

Venn: *Alumni Cantabrigienses, Part I, From the Earliest Times to 1751,* ed. John Venn and J. A. Venn, 4 vols., Cambridge, Cambridge University Press, 1922–27.

Verney Letters: *Verney Letters of the Eighteenth Century from the MSS. at Claydon House,* ed. Margaret Maria Lady Verney, 2 vols., London, Ernest Benn, 1930.

Vernon: *Letters Illustrative of the Reign of William III from 1696 to 1708 Addressed to the Duke of Shrewsbury by James Vernon,* ed. G. P. R. James, 3 vols., 1841.

Walcott: Robert Walcott, *English Politics in the Early 18th Century,* Cambridge, Harvard University Press, 1956.

Wentworth Papers: *The Wentworth Papers 1705–1739 selected from the Private and Family Correspondence of Thomas Wentworth, Lord Raby, Created in 1711 Earl of Strafford,* ed. James J. Cartwright, 1883,

Wing: *Short-Title Catalogue . . . 1641–1700,* ed. Donald Wing, New York, Index Society, 1945–51.

Wood: Anthony à Wood, *Athenae Oxonienses. An Exact History of All the Writers and Bishops who have had their Education in the University of Oxford.*

To which are added the Fasti, or Annals of the said University, ed. Philip
Bliss, 4 vols., 1813–20.

Wood, *Life and Times:*   *The Life and Times of Anthony Wood,* ed. Andrew
Clark, 5 vols., Oxford, Clarendon Press, 1891–1900.

Zedler: Johann Heinrich Zedler, *Groszes Vollständiges Universal-Lexicon
aller Wissenschaften und Künste,* 64 vols. and 4 supplements, Halle and
Leipzig, 1732–54.

INTRODUCTION

I. 1704–1714

It is not only distance that lends enchantment to our view of the age of Queen Anne. It was known at the time to be a brilliant age. "Historians will always be fond of this part of the *English* History," it was said, for "it shines so bright it wants no Ornament, and it is not in the Power of Envy or Ingratitude to transmit it to Posterity in any other Colours but what are dazling and amazing."[1] Alexander Pope agreed that these were "*Albion*'s Golden Days."[2] It was a time when Jonathan Swift was (unacknowledged) minister of information, and "a Mr. Prior was Ambassador, and a Mr. Addison Secretary of State."[3] Even the vices of 1704–14 were known to be more than life-size:

> Blush Christians now, and Blush Posterity,
> At such black Sins, who reads the History
> Of these curst Times.[4]

Such a rich soil as this could yield not one, but four mixed crops of satire a year, in Hilary, Easter, Trinity, and Michaelmas terms.[5]

Until the imposition of a tax on printed papers in August 1712, the crop could be harvested without hindrance. But not, of course, without danger. It is probable, but not certain, that John Tutchin, said to be the first editor of *Poems on Affairs of State,* was beaten to death by the victims of his "scurrility."[6] Other writers, both those whose work is known to be included in this volume—Swift, Daniel Defoe, William Shippen, Joseph Browne—and those whose work may not be—William Pittis, George Ridpath—lived in varying degrees of sustained flight from the law.

The greatest number of state poems of the last ten years of the Queen,

1. *The History and Defence of the Last Parliament,* 1713, p. 153; cf. *POAS,* Yale, *6,* 449.
2. *Windsor-Forest,* 1713, p. 18.
3. James Boswell, *London Journal 1762–1763,* ed. Frederick A. Pottle, New York, McGraw-Hill, 1950, p. 91.
4. *Some Gold Truths Out at Last* ("Influenced by the Vile Unchristian Jars"), 1711.
5. Arber, *passim.*
6. [William Pittis], *Heraclitus Ridens,* 26–30 October 1703; Defoe, *Review,* 13 July 1708; Noble, *2,* 312.

like those of 1697–1704, sprang up in a few, particularly fertile histori-
cal watersheds: failure of the Tack in November 1704; negotiation of
the union with Scotland; the dismissal of Harley in February 1708;
the Sacheverell affair—the Great Divide—in 1709–10; negotiation of
the peace with France, August 1711–April 1713; and the Hanoverian
succession in August 1714. Of the 75 poems in this volume, nearly 50
are involved with these six subjects. The remaining poems are scattered
among more than 20, providing numerous verse on such unpoetic
subjects as the election of a Speaker of the House of Commons, Tory
rhetoric, "our Soveraign Lord the People," the presentation of a
Jacobite medal to the Faculty of Advocates, and the refusal of the gov-
ernment to allow a pope-burning procession in London.

During the exclusion crisis of 1678–81, England had been polarized
into Whig and Tory. But in the reign of Queen Anne, the poles them-
selves were splintered into old Whigs and new Whigs, Harley's men
and lord treasurer's men, junto Whigs and country Whigs, country
Tories and court Tories, and October Club and March Club, so that it
became difficult "under all these Masks to see the true Countenance
of any Man," including that of Defoe who made the complaint.[7] The
age was essentially and intrinsically double. Everyone who needed to,
took the oaths to support a Protestant succession and registered at St.
Germain to support a second restoration of Catholic Stuarts. A long,
expensive, and bloody war waged for simple economic advantage was
variously misrepresented to the millions of Englishmen who could not
conceivably profit from it, as a cool exercise in geopolitics or as a hot
religious war. And this particular mixture of doubleness and confusion
—that can never be reduplicated—produced a unique and wildly
exuberant crop of satirical verse:

> The Arts of Priest-Craft and the Tricks of State
> Did for the angry Muse large Themes create.[8]

II. The Genre

The doubleness of the age found its perfect reflection in the doubleness
of satire, with its requirement that it be true (like history) and ordered
by the imagination (like art). In satire, Dryden said, "no Impression
can be made where there is no Truth for the Foundation."[9] In practice

7. Edinburgh *Review*, 4 February 1710.
8. *The Baboon A-la-Mode. A Satyr against the French* ("Speak Thou sweet Solace of my vacant
Hours"), 1704, p. 1.
9. Dryden, *Works*, *13*, 84.

the satirists made a big distinction between libel (or lampoon) and sat-
ire. Swift knew "the wonderful Delight of libelling Men in Power and
hugging yourself in a Corner with mighty Satisfaction for what you
have done,"[10] but he knew that this was not satire. "The Satyr," as
Defoe had said, "lyes in the Truth, not the ill Language."[11] If Marl-
borough had not been insatiably greedy, or if Wharton had not been an
insatiable lecher, to say that they were might have constituted grounds
for legal action but not for satire. Libel does not become satire until it
becomes true. Conversely, falsehood in satire, like the charge that
Karoline Wilhelmine of Ansbach would not marry Prince Georg
August of Braunschweig-Lüneburg until her own brother was dead,
loses its satirical (but not its libellous) force and becomes a critical
defect in the poem.[12]

   The satirist's claim of impartiality is wholly conventional, like the
Petrarchan lover's claim of sincerity, and cannot be taken seriously.
But the Augustan satirist's claim of "representing Things as they really
are"[13] must be taken seriously, for it is the Augustan quest. It is the
humanistic counterpart of the thrust of the new science, and the great
intellectual adventure of 1660–1800. All the major Augustans, from
Dryden and Rochester to Johnson and Goldsmith, thought they were
engaged in it.

   Satire has long been known to be double in two other ways. It is
double in the way that it imitates reality. And it is double in its effects
on its audience. Dryden, translating Daniel Heinsius's definition in *De
Satyra* (1629), explains that satire is projected "partly dramatically,
partly simply [narratively], and sometimes in both kinds of speaking."
The effects of satire are similarly double: "either hatred, or laughter,
or indignation is moved." Corresponding to the tragic emotions of pity
and fear, are the satiric emotions of hatred, laughter, and indignation.
Satire is a mixed genre. And what it is that is mixed is entertainment
and seriousness. Dryden, for one, insisted that there be more entertain-
ment than seriousness. So the best satire is like a juicy libel suit inter-
spersed with a good sermon and transmogrified into "a most elegant
and complete poem."[14]

10. *The Examiner*, 1 February 1710/11.
11. Defoe, *The Dissenter's Answer to the High-Church Challenge*, 1704, p. 3.
12. *Pasquin to the Queen's Statue*, 16n., below.
13. [Arthur Mainwaring], *The Medley*, 7 May 1711; cf. Samuel Johnson: "Let us endeav-
our to see things as they are" (James Boswell, *The Life of Samuel Johnson, LL.D.*, ed. G. Birk-
beck Hill and L. F. Powell, 6 vols., Oxford, Clarendon Press, 1934–50, *1*, 339.
14. Dryden, *Works, 13*, 107, 65.

The satirists knew that their mandate was moral. "Satyr was first introduced into the World," Swift said, "whereby those . . . might be with-held by the Shame of having their Crimes exposed to open View in the strongest Colours, and themselves rendered odious to Mankind."[15] Defoe concurred. "Satyr can scourge," he said, "where the Lash of the Law cannot."[16] The genre was handed down from pagan poets, but the form that it took in the Augustan Age derives from its Christian context. Ultimately it is the fall of man that justified satire for the Augustans. Not only the major figures like Swift and Defoe, but the minor ones like Thomas Phillips were agreed on this:

> When men grew vicious, and enclin'd to Hell,
> They did the Lash of pointed Satyr feel.[17]

Samuel Johnson even insisted that "false Satire ought to be recanted . . . lest the Distinction between Vice and Virtue should be lost."[18]

This is how satire became, in John Updike's words, "an instrument for piecemeal correction,"[19] an instrument for fulfilling the satirist's moral mandate. "We pretend to be all Travelling to Heaven," Defoe said, "tho' we fall out by the Way; and we fall out about the Way too: But if every Man disturb'd himself less about the Course his Neighbour Steers, and concern'd himself more about his own, there would more find the right Way thither."[20] Piecemeal correction, in fact, was the only alternative to root and branch correction, which had broken England in two and almost destroyed it. "Correct yourself, for others you cannot correct," is a theme not only of Defoe's modest pamphlet of 1704, but of *Religio Laici* (1682), *Gulliver's Travels* (1726), and *The Good Natur'd Man* (1768).

The requirement that it be true imposed upon Augustan political satire the fatal necessity to be occasional, topical—and transitory. "Although the present Age may understand well enough the little Hints we give, the Parallels we draw, and the Characters we describe," Swift said, "yet this will all be lost to the next."[21] This is where "the Restorers of Antient Learning from the Worms, and Graves, and Dust

---

15. *The Examiner*, 26 April 1711.

16. Defoe, *Conjugal Lewdness: or, Matrimonial Whoredom*, 1727, p. 362.

17. [Thomas Phillips], *An Epistle to Sr. Richard Blackmore* ("Not that you need Assistance in your Wars"), 1700, p. 5.

18. [Samuel Johnson], *An Account of the Life of Mr. Richard Savage*, 1744, pp. 55–56.

19. *(London) Times Literary Supplement*, 63 (4 June 1964), 473.

20. Defoe, *The Dissenter's Answer to the High-Church Challenge*, 1704, p. 48.

21. *The Examiner*, 7 December 1710.

of Manuscripts"[22] come in. Like dancing or acting, the art of political satire must be fixed. "Unless elucidated by commentation," Alexander Campbell said, "[it] must in a short time, become obsolete, or altogether unintelligible."[23]

In this respect, however, political satire is only a special case of the general embarrassment caused for literary criticism by the bare existence of topical allusions. Samuel Johnson, for example, can hardly conceal his exasperation at Shakespeare's insistent allusiveness:

> Whatever advantages he might once derive from personal allusions, local customs, or temporary opinions, have for many years been lost; and every topick of merriment or motive of sorrow, which the modes of artificial life afforded him, now only obscure the scenes which they once illuminated.[24]

If the darkened scenes can again be illuminated, however fitfully, something of the original merriment or sorrow may be preserved, even though our words only mediate between the little that we know and the vastness of our ignorance of the past.

Ever since Selden said it, everyone has agreed that "the colouring," "the Complexion," "the Humour" of an age is reflected in the occasional literature of the period more perfectly than in "More solid things":

> Tho' some make slight of *Libels*, yet you may see by them how the wind sits: As take a straw and throw it up into the Air, you shall see by that which way the Wind is, which you shall not do by casting up a Stone. More solid things do not shew the Complexion of the times so well, as *Ballads* and *Libels*.[25]

The advantages and disadvantages of the art are summarized in this dilemma: political satire supplies some of the coloring that is lacking in official history, but the colors fade.

The best political satire, therefore, is the most topical, the most crammed with obscure, unlikely, but verifiable details. These details, in turn, must constitute a credible "secret History" at some variance

---

22. Swift, *Prose*, *1*, 57.

23. Alexander Campbell, *An Introduction to the History of Poetry in Scotland*, Edinburgh, 1798, p. 140.

24. Samuel Johnson, *The Plays of William Shakespeare*, 8 vols., 1765, *1*, sig. A2r.

25. John Selden, *Table Talk*, 1689, p. 31, quoted in *London Lampoon'd*, 1703, p. 30, and in Thomas Percy, *Reliques of Ancient English Poetry*, 3 vols. 1765, *2*, iv.

from official history. "Universals, *say the School-men,* draw no Blood."[26]
In Blake's words, "To Particularize is the Alone Distinction of Merit,"[27]
in political satire as in painting.

The requirement that it be art imposed upon Augustan political
satire the necessity to be witty, ironical, and almost endlessly resource-
ful in the improvisation of new subgenres and stanza forms. If it was
agreed that "Historians . . . should write the naked Truth,"[28] then
the poets were expected to write the adorned truth. Abel Boyer, the
historian, need not have worried that his *Annals* were, as he said,
"destitute of the Ornaments."[29] The only requirement was that they be
true. But "the World expects we should make every thing agreeable,"
the poet complained, "even Correction itself."[30]

So there are examples, among the poems in this volume, of nearly all
the satirical subgenres: the hymn (*On the Greatest Victory Perhaps that
Ever Was*), the vision (*A New Ballad Writ by Jacob Tonson*), the epistle
(*An Epistle to Sir Richard Blackmore, Kt.*), the prophecy (Shippen?, *Duke
Humphrey's Answer*), the paradox (Defoe, *The Age of Wonders*), the litany
(Mainwaring?, *A New Protestant Litany*), the farewell (*A Farewell to the
Year 1714*), the pasquinade (*Pasquin to the Queen's Statue at St. Paul's*).
But there is neither an advice-to-the-painter poem (but see p. 177) nor
a session-of-the-poets. None of the half-dozen examples of the former
that were written in 1704–14, including two by Sir Richard Blackmore,
seem to be worth reprinting. And the spavined verses of John Sheffield,
duke of Buckingham, *The Election of a Poet Laureat in 1719* ("A Famous
Assembly was summon'd of late"), occurred too late even to be consid-
ered for this volume.

There is an even greater selection of mock-genres here than in
volume six, including some exotic new ones: a mock-campaign speech
(Defoe, *Declaration without Doors*), a mock-address-from-the-throne
(*Switch and Spur*), a mock-Calves-Head-Club-hymn (*Leviathan*), a mock-
doxology (*The Thanksgiving*), and a mock-parliamentary-speech (Swift,
An Excellent New Song). There are several soliloquies that almost assume
the form of dramatic monologues in the manner of Tennyson or

26. *Moderation Display'd, The Second Part* (" 'Twas Night, as on my Bed I waking lay"),
1705, sig. A2v.
27. William Blake, *The Complete Writings,* ed. Geoffrey Keynes, New York, Random
House, 1957, p. 451.
28. John Cockburn, *A Specimen of Some Free and Impartial Remarks on Publick Affairs,* 1724,
pp. [74–75 misnumbered] 66–67.
29. Boyer, *Annals,* 1703, sig. A4r.
30. Thomas Brown, *Amusements Serious and Comical,* 1700, p. 139.

Browning. These are Tutchin, *The French King's Cordial*; Joseph Browne, *The Humble Memorial*, in which Defoe is the imagined soliloquist; and *The British Embassadress's Speech to the French King*. The last is the closest to dramatic monologue, for it ends in dramatic action. But the anonymous poet could not assimilate the action into the structure of the soliloquy and so had to switch into narrative to end the poem.

There are also several examples of mock-panegyric (Defoe, *A Reply to the Scots Answer to the British Vision*, and Mainwaring?, *A Panegyrick upon the English Catiline*). These, when "read backward like a Witch's Pray'r,"[31] produce satire. It is this same principle, of course, that creates irony. And there are several examples in this volume of that most dangerous of all satirical forms, total irony: *Leviathan*, Defoe?, *A Welcome to the Medal*, and Thomas D'Urfey, *The Peace in View*. Sir Harold Williams doubted that Swift's audience could understand the total irony of *It's Out at Last*, one of Swift's seven penny papers of August 1712.[32] And it is true that Augustan satirists did occasionally overestimate their audience's capacity or willingness to understand them. *The Shortest-Way with the Dissenters* (December 1702) and *A Tale of a Tub* (April 1704) both testify to this fact. But the frequency with which total irony occurs in works of the last ten years of the queen indicates that the audience had learned to read correctly ironical works in which there is almost no hint of their true political orientation.[33]

Finally, there have been included in this volume two works of pure panegyric: Prior, *An Ode, Humbly Inscrib'd to the Queen*; and *The Save-Alls*. This was done for two reasons: first, to illustrate total irony by showing its reverse, and second, to complete the documentation of irony. For *The Save-Alls*, a work of total panegyric, turns out not to be lacking in irony, of the unconscious variety, of course.

The necessity for political satire to be ordered by the imagination, however, was crossed by another tradition that required *satiric* art to be rough and low. "In an occasional performance," Dr. Johnson warned, "no height of excellence can be expected." "Sir, it is intended to be low: it is satire. The expression is debased to debase the character."[34] A satire was so strongly felt to be a satyr, that when the mythological creatures were meant, it was necessary to distinguish them as

31. *POAS*, Yale, *6*, 152.
32. Swift, *Journal*, *2*, 554.
33. Defoe?, *A Welcome to the Medal*, headnote, p. 493 below.
34. Johnson, *Lives*, *1*, 424; James Boswell, *Journal of a Tour to the Hebrides*, ed. Frederick A. Pottle, New York, McGraw-Hill, 1936, p. 58.

"Satyrs of the Woodland Sort."[35] "Satyr and ill-sounding Rhymes" were judged to be perfectly compatible,[36] and some of the best sound effects in this volume are achieved by the jarring jangles of half-rhyme, forced rhyme, and no-rhyme. Not even *"Prosaic Lines"* were proscribed, for in satire "you only ought to bite."[37]

The apparent artlessness of the genre, the despair of systematizing critics today, was one of its main appeals to the age of Queen Anne. It gave its readers the sense that what was shown was close to reality. Addison attributed the success of *Absalom and Achitophel* to "the delight which the mind feels in the investigation of secrets."[38] The voyeuristic effect of the best satire of the period, the delicious sense of possessing inside knowledge, was noted in the previous volume,[39] but more importantly, this effect can now be seen to satisfy one of the great compulsions of the Augustans: to see things as they are.

III. The Poets

The reward that the Augustan satirists gained for achieving these effects was, in the overwhelming majority of cases, oblivion. Of the 75 poems in this volume, 37 remain totally anonymous and 14 can be only tentatively attributed to an author. Less than one third of the best political satire of the great age of satire, therefore, can be attributed with any degree of certainty. And even here the evidence is mainly circumstantial and "Circumstances will not amount to a Proof, said the Prisoner."[40] Johnson had the greatest scorn for "Writers who take advantage of present incidents or characters which strongly interest the passions and engage universal attention . . . [and in whom] all the motives of interest and vanity concur,"[41] but he neglected to say that vanity is not much promoted by anonymous publication. Prior, for one, came to doubt that it was worth the candle. "Satyr," he said, "however agreeable for the present to the Writers or Incouragers of it

35. *POAS*, 1703, *2*, 102; cf. "good modern Satyrists, tho' not like those of old, whom Painters represent with Asses Ears, and Goats Legs" (*A Pacquet from Wills*, 1701, p. 45).

36. Samuel Cobb, *Poems on Several Occasions*, 1707, p. 205; cf. "was it Lucilius's own genius or the harsh nature of his material that denied him verses more finished and smooth?" (Horace, *Sat.*, I, x, 57–59)

37. Samuel Wesley, *An Epistle to a Friend concerning Poetry* ("As Brother *Prynne* of old from Mount *Orgeuil*"), 1700, p. 27.

38. Johnson, *Lives*, *1*, 373.

39. *POAS*, Yale, *6*, xxx.

40. [William Pittis], *The Whipping Post*, 10 July 1705.

41. *The Rambler*, 23 March 1751.

does in time do neither of them good, considering the uncertainty of Fortune, and the various change of Ministry."[42]

Anonymous publication and the resort to allegory were imposed upon the satirists for the same reason: to evade the force of libel laws and privilege of parliament. "How can a Body tell what it means by *H——se of C——ns*," Tutchin drolled.[43] But "*the Dread of Authority*" imposed itself equally upon nameless satirists who discoursed "*of Birds and* Beasts"—and even of vegetables, in *A Tale of a Nettle*—upon Defoe who resorted to allegory to protect "the innocent Printers, Publishers and Dispensers" of his work, and upon Swift, who ransacked "History for some Character bearing a Resemblance to the Person we would describe" and then attacked Wharton as Verres and Marlborough as Crassus.[44]

It is difficult to judge how effective the satirists believed their work to be. Defoe pretends to be amazed that "Libellers . . . dare to affront the Government with Ballads and Balderdash," but this is exactly what he did himself.[45] And he argues very convincingly that *The True-Born Englishman* had reduced the incidence and virulence of xenophobia in England.[46] One of his most persistent detractors laughed at Defoe's assumption that his "ridiculous Half-sheets will have an Influence upon Parliaments in their Choice of Measures,"[47] but there is no other reason why Harley should have continued to pay him to write the *Review*. And while it was Swift (in large part) who brought down Marlborough, it was Defoe, six years before, who had conceived that a public idol could be deflated so completely:

> For when the bloated Monster's once pull'd down,
> The *Soul deserts*, the Bubble's broke and gone.[48]

Defoe, however, does not dominate this volume the way he dominates the preceding volume in this series. It is not that he wrote less in 1704–14

---

42. Prior, *Works, 1*, 583.

43. *The Observator*, 14–18 April 1705.

44. *Chaucer's Whims*, 1701, sig. A2r; *Review*, 1 June 1710; *The Examiner*, 30 November 1710.

45. Defoe, *And What if the Pretender Should Come?*, 1713, p. 38; Defoe?, *A Welcome to the Medal*, headnote, p. 493 below.

46. Defoe, *Conjugal Lewdness: or, Matrimonial Whoredom*, 1727, pp. 400–01. Walter Scott believed that Swift's, *The Last Speech and Dying Words of Ebenezer Elliston* (1722), "operated for a long time" to keep down the crime rate in Dublin (*The Works of Jonathan Swift,* ed. Walter Scott, 2nd ed., 19 vols., 1883, *6*, 298).

47. [William Pittis], *The Whipping Post*, 2 November 1705.

48. *The Dyet of Poland* (July 1705), 485–86, below.

than he did in 1697–1704, for of course he wrote more. *Jure Divino: A Satyr. In Twelve Books* ("Nature has left *this Tincture in the Blood*") has 7,620 lines, and there are 1,047 more in *A Hymn to Peace* ("Hail Image, of th'Eternal Mind") and 1,273 more in *Caledonia, A Poem in Honour of Scotland* ("In Northern Hights, where Nature seldom Smiles"). All three of these poems were published in the same year, 1706, but there was no compelling reason to include them in the present volume. Although Defoe continued to write prose and verse on the same subject as late as November 1706,[49] according to "the rule of transversion, or regular duplex: changing verse into prose, or prose into verse,"[50] the truth seems to be that he began to tire of turning prose into verse in 1704–06 and that after *The True-Born Britain* ("Hail! mighty *Genius* of this fruitful Isle") in 1707, he wrote no more long poems. This may be reflected, whether consciously or not, in Defoe's own baseless complaints that "the Satyrs of this part of our Age are . . . mean, in comparison of the last."[51]

In the present volume Defoe is rivalled by Arthur Mainwaring, whose evolution from Jacobite to Junto Whig was complete by 1704.[52] Alongside of five poems known to be Defoe's and two tentatively attributed to him here for the first time, there appear in this volume two poems known to be Mainwaring's and five attributed to him here for the first time. Besides these verses, Mainwaring wrote a reply in *The Medley* to nearly every number of *The Examiner* and thus became the principal antagonist of Swift.

Six of Swift's poems are included in the present volume. Swift was opposed not only by Mainwaring on the Whiggish left, but also on the Jacobite right by William Shippen, one of whose poems and four more attributed to him are also included in the present volume. And by one of the quaint ironies of literary history, Swift was also joined by What's his Name Defoe, "the Fellow that was *pillory'd*,"[53] in defending the "moderate" center, where Harley positioned his government of 1710–14. In church politics, however, Swift trooped with Shippen, defending the Church of England against Defoe the dissenter and the libertine Mainwaring.

Behind the regulars, Mainwaring and Defoe, Swift and Shippen,

49. Defoe, *The Vision* (November 1706), headnote, p. 212 below.
50. *POAS*, Yale *4*, 118.
51. *Review*, 31 March 1713.
52. *POAS*, Yale, *5*, 57.
53. Swift, *Prose*, *2*, 113.

marched the volunteers, paid and unpaid, famous and unknown:
William Congreve, Matthew Prior, Thomas D'Urfey, William Walsh,
John Tutchin, Charles Darby, Joseph Browne, William Atwood,
George Duckett. Next came a camouflaged rout of known writers of
state poems none of whose work of 1704–14 can now be identified:
Charles Montagu, Lord Halifax, Charles Mordaunt, Lord Peter-
borough, Henry Mordaunt, John Toke, and a dozen more. Bringing
up the rear, but in fame only, are the nameless figures who wrote some
of the best verse in the present volume: the Master of *Switch and Spur*,
the *Leviathan* poet, the Angry Epigrammatist. Some day it may be
possible to determine that an academic piece like *A Tale of a Nettle*,
although not the work of Francis Atterbury, may have originated in
Atterbury's studio.

The Master of *Switch and Spur* shows a remarkable facility for fitting
the rhythms of colloquial speech to the harness of decasyllabic couplets,
"changing prose into verse":

> *Spain* is quite lost; and *Portugal* in danger
> Unless the last Extreamity make her change her
> Resolves, and quit th'Alliance, which once shaken
> Will soon dissolve: and should *We* be forsaken
> By one *Confederate* of the *Roman Church,*
> The rest would Flinch and leave *Us* in the Lurch.[54]

But this was an age in which a bellman could turn out a first line
worthy of Yeats:

> I Am not Eagle-ey'd to face the Sun,[55]

and poems worthy of Blake were printed anonymously in songbooks:

> In Summer time when Flowers do spring,
>   And Birds sit on a Tree,
> Let Lords and Knights say what they will,
>   There's none so Merry as we:
>   There's *Will* and *Moll,*
>   Here's *Harry* and *Doll,*
>   With *Brian* and bonny *Betty;*
>   Oh, how they did Jerk it,

---

54. *Switch and Spur*, 31–36, below.
55. *Some Verses Inscrib'd to the Memory of the Much Lamented John Dolben, Esq;*, 19n., below.

Caper and ferk it,
Under the Green-wood Tree.[56]

IV. The Texts

For 65 of the 75 poems in this volume an early printed copy was available. So it was decided to retain the accidentals of the copy text, leaving "to every Authour, his own practice unmolested."[57] The 75 copy texts themselves derive from a variety of sources:

manuscripts	10
newsprints	3
folio half-sheet editions	33
other separate editions	8
printed anthologies	17
collected editions	1
other printed books	3

Not all of the manuscript copies came into existence in the same fashion, of course. The largest number of them are products of a scriptorium,[58] but commonplace-book copies (p. 633 below) and separate manuscript copies (p. 627 below) are also represented. Newsprint copies were almost certainly set up from the latter. Some of the folio half-sheet editions may also be the work of "piratizing Printers, who lie upon the Catch,"[59] but others are the product of routine collaboration between writer, publisher, and printer, such as that between Jonathan Swift, John Morphew, and John Barber.

State poems found almost as many ways to be disseminated as they did to come into the world. Some "very valuable *Poems* and *Songs,* written by some of the greatest Wits of the last and present Age," the editor of one printed anthology complained, "are now . . . handled about only in Manuscript."[60] Ten such poems, in fact, are printed for the first time in the present volume. The commonplace-book manuscript copy (*Am*) of *The British Embassadress's Speech to the French King* is subscribed, "privately dispers'd just after the peace of Utrecht," and the gentlemanly prejudice against publishing persisted for a long

56. *Wit and Mirth: Or, Pills to Purge Melancholy. . . The Second Part,* ed. Henry Playford, 1700, p. 122.
57. Samuel Johnson, *A Dictionary of the English Language,* 2 vols., 1755, *1,* sig. A2v.
58. *POAS,* Yale, *5,* 528.
59. [Edward Ward], *The Second Volume of the Writings of the Author of The London Spy,* 1709, sig. A4r.
60. *Deliciae Poeticae; Or, Parnassus Display'd,* 1706, sig. A2v.

time. Sir Benjamin Backbite thought it was "very vulgar to print." He distributed his own lampoons in separate manuscript copies. "I find they circulate more," he said, "by giving copies in confidence to the friends of the parties" lampooned.[61] There may even have been something like an oral tradition in state poems. The commonplace-book manuscript copy (G) of Shippen?, *The Character of a Certain Whigg* bears strong evidence that it was a memorial reconstruction, and the duchess of Marlborough had an entertaining repertoire of state poems that she sang to the accompaniment of Arthur Mainwaring on the harpsichord.[62]

But most state poems were printed and sold in the streets by ballad-singers. The literate were also reached by mail. Peter Wentworth received some verses sent him "by the penny post by an unknown hand." He did not say whether these verses were printed or in manuscript, but obviously both could be posted. A separate manuscript copy (B) of Tutchin, *The French King's Cordial*, was mailed to Sir John Lowther, the retired Whig member of parliament for Cumberland. And a broadside copy (Ah) of *The Country Parson's Advice to Those Little Scribblers*, folded as a letter and sealed, was sent from London to "Mrs Proger att Gwerndee near Abergaveny" by the Monmouthshire courier.

The illiterate were provided with readers. "They will Gather together about one that can *Read*, and Listen to an *Observator* or *Review* (as I have seen them in the Streets) where all the Principles of Rebellion are Instill'd into them."[63]

The 75 poems in this volume were chosen from more than 1,000 possibilities on principles laid down in *POAS*, Yale, *4*, xli. All available witnesses to the text of these 75 poems have been collated and the substantive variants recorded, "however trifling and unimportant they may appear to blockheads," as Edmond Malone deposed.[64] For Prior's *An Ode, Humbly Inscrib'd to the Queen*, Defoe's *A Scot's Poem*, and a few shorter poems, accidental variants have been recorded as well.

As in the preceding volume of this series, no attempt was made to provide "objective" commentary. "The writing of explanatory notes" is said to be "like no other species of literature,"[65] and one way that it is

---

61. *The Plays and Poems of Richard Brinsley Sheridan*, ed. Raymond C. Rhodes, 3 vols., Oxford, Blackwell, 1928, *2*, 33.

62. Arthur Mainwaring?, *A New Ballad: To the Tune of Fair Rosamund*, headnote, p. 306.

63. [Charles Leslie], *A View of the Times*, 1708, sig. π2v.

64. James M. Osborn, *John Dryden: Some Biographical Facts and Problems*, New York, Columbia University Press, 1940, p. 131.

65. *Ancient Ballads and Songs*, ed. Peter Buchan, 2 vols., Edinburgh, *1*, ix.

unique is in its deliberate bias. The purpose of the commentary is not to balance the books, or to set the record straight, but to make a political satire intelligible in its own terms.

The wild beasts of the desert shall also meet with the wild beasts of the island, and the satyr shall cry to his fellow.

ISAIAH 34:14

1704

ARTHUR MAINWARING

The History and Fall of the Conformity-Bill.
Being an Excellent New Song, to the Tune of *Chivy-Chase*
(January 1704?)

This "merry Ballad," as John Oldmixon called it (Oldmixon, *Maynwaring*, p. 40), conceals an unexpected seriousness of purpose. The purpose, most simply, was to defend the unpopular case of toleration in England. The so-called Toleration Act of 1689 granted the nonconformists freedom of worship at the price of their continued exclusion from the civil life of the nation. It exempted them from the penalties for nonattendance at the services of the Church of England, but reimposed the Test Acts of 1673 and 1678 that required attendance at the services of the Church of England as the condition for holding civil or military office. So the nonconformists were able to participate in civil life only by "a legal evasion of the law" (Trevelyan, *1*, 279). They could hold office in a municipal corporation or under the crown only if they were willing to conform occasionally—once a year in most cases—to the rites of the Church of England as by law established. The bills to *prevent* occasional conformity provided that anyone who took the sacrament required by the Test Act to qualify himself for public office and then resorted to "any Conventicle, or Meeting under Colour of any Exercise of Religion, in other Manner than according to the Liturgy and Practice of the Church of *England*" (Calamy, *Abridgement*, *1*, 624–25), should be removed from office and fined.

This, as Defoe saw, deprived the nonconformists, not of a legal right, but of a legal evasion of a civil disability. "The Act of Toleration," he said, "is an Exempting the Dissenters from all Penalties . . . for Dissenting; this [bill to prevent occasional conformity] lays a . . . Penalty on their Dissenting again" (*A Serious Inquiry into This Grand Question: Whether a Law to Prevent the Occasional Conformity of Dissenters, Would Not Be Inconsistent with the Act of Toleration*, 1704, p. 12).

More particularly, the purpose of this "merry Ballad" was to defend the low church bishops who had come under violent attack (*POAS*, Yale, *6*, 506) when they provided the votes to defeat the bills to prevent occasional conformity (lines 17–24 below). The bill at issue in the

3

present poem was the second, introduced in the Commons on 25 November and sent up to the Lords on 7 December 1703. There it was rejected during the second reading on 14 December by 71 votes to 59; 14 negative votes were cast by low church bishops (Luttrell, *5,* 369; *Parl. Hist., 6,* 170). Gilbert Burnet, bishop of Salisbury and the most eminent of the low churchmen on the episcopal bench, knew exactly why he was so unpopular. "I am perhaps one of the clergymen in the world," he said, "that am most against all severity on the account of religion" (*A Supplement to Burnet's History of My Own Time,* ed. Helen C. Foxcroft, Oxford, Clarendon Press, 1902, p. 250). But most conforming Englishmen felt that this was indefensible. They feared that toleration would "pull downe the Church of England" (Wood, *Life and Times, 3,* 439).

Officially it was said that "no Church, *but that of Rome,* professes Persecution" and that "the Church of *England,* has no persecuting Inclination of her self" (Defoe, *Jure Divino: A Satyr,* 1706, p. xviii; *Review,* 12 June 1705), but in fact, as Defoe had leisure to reflect while he stood in the pillory, one faction in the church was eager "to persecute for Conscience Sake" (*A Serious Inquiry into This Grand Question: Whether a Law to Prevent Occasional Conformity of Dissenters, Would Not Be Inconsistent with the Act of Toleration,* 1704, p. 27). What was really at stake in the bills to prevent occasional conformity was the principle of toleration, or the right of the Church of England to exclude non-conformists from civil life.

The impudent, teasing tone of the present poem can be misleading. We cannot be certain—at least upon first reading—that we are supposed to laugh at the charge that the church has been left in the lurch by its bishops (15–16). If the poem, very playfully, confirms that the occasional conformist's "Godliness is Gain" (52), it also confirms, very seriously, the "Right" (56) of occasional conformity, even against the "Might" (66) of a majority in the House of Commons. And since mythopoeia is not the stock in trade of minor Augustan poets, it may be said that the inventiveness—as well as the impudence—of the present poem is remarkable. The account it provides of the origins of the persecuting spirit in the House of Commons would not be surprising in Blake.

Although Alexander Pope recorded in his copy of *PRSA,* 1705, now in the British Museum (C.28.e.15), that *The History and Fall of the Conformity-Bill* was "Certainly written by Mr. Congreve," there can be little doubt that it was written by Arthur Mainwaring. Mainwaring's literary executor recalled that "some said it was Lieutenant General *Mordaunt's,* others father'd it on the Lord H[alifax?], but Mr. Maynwaring was the Author of it" (Oldmixon, *Maynwaring,* p. 40).

In three copies (*Aghj*) the poem is dated 1703 or 1703/4, but one (*Ap*) narrows it down to January 1703/4, which agrees very well with the events of November–December 1703 described in the poem.

The tune that Mainwaring adopted to celebrate the death of the second bill to prevent occasional conformity was the same that Thomas Deloney had chosen to celebrate the death of fair Rosamond, mistress to Henry II. Variously called *Flying Fame, Chevy Chase,* or *The Lady's Fall,* it was the most popular ballad tune of the period (Simpson, pp. 96–101, 370).

The popularity of Mainwaring's ballad is attested by the imitations and continuations that it generated. Two of these are *The High Church Lamentacion to the Tune of Chevey Chase or the 3 Children in the Wood* ("That God does bless our Soveraigne Lady Anne") preserved in Harvard MS. Eng. 606, and *The Managers: A Ballad. To the Tune of Chivy-Chase* ("God bless our Gracious Sovereign *ANN!*") in *A Collection of New Songs. Adapted to the Times.* Printed for T. Poet, n.p., n.d.

The History and Fall of the Conformity-Bill.
Being an Excellent New Song,
to the Tune of *Chivy-Chase*

God bless our gracious Sovereign *ANNE*,
    For so I shall her call,
Who ruleth in our *English* Land,
    An *English* Heart withal.

The Prince, her Turtle Mate I trow,   5

1. *ANNE:* Anne Stuart (1665–1714) was the daughter of James II by his first wife, Anne Hyde. In 1683 she married George, prince of Denmark. After William of Orange had landed his troops in England in November 1688, Anne deserted her father and made her way from London to Nottingham. The Bill of Rights of 1689 made her heiress to the English throne in the event of Mary and William dying childless. She lived aloof from court during the 1690s, being estranged from her sister and brother-in-law, and cultivated her own circle, which included John and Sarah Churchill, the future duke and duchess of Marlborough. On William's death in March 1702, Anne became queen. Physically she was far from being a regal figure. When Sir John Clerk of Penicuik saw her in 1706, "Her majesty was labouring under a fit of the Gout, and in extream pain and agony, and on this occasion every thing about her was much in the same disorder as about the meanest of her subjects. Her face, which was red and spotted, was rendered something frightful by her negligent dress, and the foot affected was tied up with a pultis and some nasty bandages" (*Memoirs of the Life of Sir John Clerk of Penicuik, Baronet, Baron of the Exchequer extracted by himself from his own Journals 1676–1755*, ed. John M. Gray, Edinburgh, 1892, p. 62). Her physique had not been helped by 17 confinements, most of them miscarriages, nor her temperament by the death in July 1700 of the duke of Gloucester, the only one of her children to survive infancy. She was slow and obstinate—Henry St. John was to refer to "that fatal irresolution inherent to the Stuart race [which] hung upon her" (*A Letter to Sir William Windham*, 1753, p. 70). Although in William's reign "She was not made acquainted with publick Affairs" (Burnet, *2*, 312), Anne evolved some simple but firm ideas about the English constitution which she clung to all her life. One was that the status and privilege of the Church of England must be strongly supported. Another, even more deeply held, was that the prerogatives of the crown must at all costs be preserved. To some degree these principles were incompatible. The first inclined her toward the Tories; the second led her to seek a place between, or rather above, the two parties.

4. *English Heart:* In her first speech to parliament, delivered on 11 March 1702, just three days after the death of "Dutch William," Queen Anne said, "as I Know *My own heart to be Entirely English* [see illustration, p. 6], I can very Sincerely Assure you, There is not any Thing you can expect or Desire from Me, which I shall not be ready to do for the Happiness and Prosperity of *England*" (Boyer, *Annals*, 1703, p. 7). As Burnet (*2*, 310) noted, "This was looked on, as a reflection on the late King."

5. *The Prince:* Prince George, the royal consort (1653–1708), was the second son of King Frederick III of Denmark. James II called him "Est-il possible?" and William III took no more notice of him "than if he had been a page of the back stairs" (*The Life of James the Second*, ed. James S. Clarke, 2 vols., 1816, *2*, 227; *Account of the Conduct*, p. 38). Upon the accession of Anne, however, "He was unhappily prevailed with, to take on him the Post of

Queen Anne's Entirely English Heart, the reverse of an accession medal executed by John Croker

I also pray God bless:
And eke the Duke of *Marlborough,*
Both his and her good Grace.

And now I think within this Realm
I need pray for no more;   10
For they who do sit at the Helm,
Are two out of these four.

And yet I mayn't omit the Church,
To pray for in my Pray'rs,
Which has of late been left i'th'lurch   15

High-Admiral, of which he understood little" (Burnet, *2*, 515). This post required him, as a Lutheran, to become an occasional communicant. So when the first bill to prevent occasional conformity reached the House of Lords, "the PRINCE of Denmark (though himself an occasional conformist) was persuaded to vote for it" (Burnet, *2*, 337; *Account of the Conduct,* p. 140). Anne allowed him to absent himself when the House of Lords voted on the second bill in 1703.

Turtle Mate: true love. When George died Burnet (*2*, 515) noted that "The Queen had been, during the whole course of her Marriage, an extraordinary tender and affectionate Wife." Her affection led her in 1702 to seek for him the title of king and the honor of succeeding William III as captain general of the confederate forces, but she was frustrated in both attempts (Burnet, *2*, 339).

7. *the Duke of Marlborough:* John Churchill (1650–1722) was created duke of Marlborough by Queen Anne in December 1702. "The Duke of *York*'s Love for his Sister (by whom he had the Duke of *Berwick,* and other Children) first brought him to Court" (Macky, p. 4). When York became James II he advanced Churchill to the post of major general in his army. Consequently Churchill's desertion of James in 1688 was one of the main reasons why the Glorious Revolution was bloodless. William rewarded him with the title of earl of Marlborough, but subsequently the two men became estranged. Marlborough then attached himself to Princess Anne, and on her accession was made captain general of all the forces and master of the ordnance.

8. *her good Grace:* Sarah Churchill, née Jennings (1660–1744) was married to Marlborough in 1678. She shared Princess Anne's isolation from court under William, whom they called "Caliban" in letters addressed to each other as "Mrs. Morley" (Anne) and "Mrs. Freeman" (Sarah). When Anne became queen, in Sarah's own words, "This elevation of my mistress to the throne brought me into a new scene of life . . . Hitherto my favour with her ROYAL HIGHNESS . . . had been of no moment to the affairs of the nation . . . But from this time, I began to be look'd upon as a person of consequence" (*Account of the Conduct,* pp. 121–22). She was made privy purse and groom of the stole to the queen.

12. *two:* The lines apparently refer to the belief that the duke and duchess of Marlborough really governed England, while Anne and her consort were cyphers (Swift, *Prose, 3,* 225). But Sarah's influence was greatly exaggerated: she confessed herself that she could not make even minor ministerial appointments (Coxe, *Memoirs, 1,* 82–83). And Anne's power and influence were greatly underestimated (Holmes, pp. 194–216).

13–14. *Church, | To pray for:* Not failing to pray for is a ballad commonplace. Cf. *The Boy and the Mantle* (Child 29): "And the goodly Queene Guenever! / I canott her fforgett."

15. *left i'th'lurch:* The bill to prevent occasional conformity, Burnet (*2*, 338) said, "seemed to favour the Interests of the Church, so hot men were for it: and the greater number of the Bishops being against it, they were censured as cold and slack in the concerns of the Church."

By her own Sons and Heirs.

Ah Bishops! Bishops, you I mean!
　　They say you were possess'd,
As one may say, like Birds unclean,
　　To foul thus your own Nest.   20

For unto you a choice Bill came,
　　Sent from the Commons House,
And yet you did reject the same,
　　As if not worth a Louse.

And now to tell I do intend,   25
　　How they this Bill did bring in,
By that you'll find the very end
　　Of this my Tale's beginning.

Few happy in this World there are,
　　And fewer in the next;   30
The first Experience does declare,
　　The last the Gospel-Text.

And therefore some Great Men of Note,
　　Whom I shall name anon,
Did in the Senate stoutly vote   35
　　For Christian Union.

Now Conscience is a thing we know
　　Like to a Mastiff Dog,
Which if ty'd up so fierce he'll grow,

21–23. *a choice Bill . . . reject:* See headnote, above.

26. *Bill did bring in:* William Bromley, Henry St. John, and Arthur Annesley were ordered to bring in a second bill to prevent occasional conformity on 25 November 1703 (*CJ, 14,* 230).

32. *the Gospel-Text:* The text is Matthew 7:13–14: "wide is the gate, and broad is the way, that leadeth to destruction, and many there be which go in thereat: Because strait is the gate, and narrow is the way, which leadeth unto life, and few there be that find it."

34. *anon:* lines 99 and 109 below.

36. *Union:* In her speech at the opening of the session on 9 November 1703 the queen had expressed her earnest desire of seeing all her subjects "in perfect Peace and Union among Themselves" (Boyer, *Annals,* 1704, p. 163). The high churchmen promptly turned the phrase to their own advantage and Sir Humphrey Mackworth pointed out that "*Peace and Union* both in *Church and State*" could be achieved only by an act to prevent occasional conformity (*Peace at Home: Or, A Vindication of the Proceedings of the Honourable the House of Commons on the Bill for Preventing Danger from Occasional Conformity,* 1703, p. 11).

37. *Conscience:* Cf. *The Dyet of Poland,* 630n. below.

He'll bite his very Clog. 40

Wherefore some wiser Men than some,
        Thought they could give good Reason,
How that this Bill just now did come
        A little out of season.

Dissenters they were to be press'd 45
        To go to Common-Prayer,
And turn their Faces to the East,
        As God were only there:

Or else no place of Price or Trust
        They ever could obtain, 50
Which shews that Saying very just,
        That Godliness is Gain.

Now some I say did think this hard,
        And strove with all their Might,
That Subjects might not be debar'd 55
        Of Freedom, nor of Right.

For who can think our Lord can care
        From whence the Voice does sound,
Tho we should pray as Seamen swear,
        The Compass Points around? 60

Sure he, I say, our Pray'rs can hear,
        Whence ever we do call;
For if so be the Heart's sincere,
        Oh that is all in all.

But yet to see how the World goes, 65

44. *out of season*: It was Lord Haversham who warned the Lords that "this Bill . . . could never have come in a more unseasonable and more dangerous Juncture" (Boyer, *Annals*, 1704, p. 186).

45. *press'd*: The bill provided that anyone who attended a dissenting service after taking the sacrament according to the rites of the Church of England in order to qualify for public office, should be fined £50 and removed from office (ibid., p. 26).

55–56. *Subjects . . . debar'd | Of . . . Right*: This was precisely the ground on which Defoe, for example, switched from supporting to opposing the bill to prevent occasional conformity: "It takes from the Dissenters," he said, "what they enjoyed before by Law" (*The Case of the Dissenters as Affected by the Late Bill Proposed in Parliament, for Preventing Occasional Conformity*, 1703, p. 19).

57–58. *care | From whence*: Cf. Samuel Johnson, *The Prince of Abissinia*, 2 vols., 1759, *1*, 76: "That the Supreme Being may be more easily propitiated in one place than in another, is the dream of idle superstition."

Right is by Might devour'd;
And they who did this Bill oppose,
     Alas! were overpow'r'd.

St. *Stephen* first was in degree,
     That Persecution felt;   70
And persecuted so was he,
     He better had been gelt.

Oh! better had it been for he,
     I'll say while I have breath,
Ten times unstoned for to be,   75
     Than stoned unto Death.

But let that pass, and mark me well;
     For things unknown before,
And strange and true I now shall tell,
     Or ne'er believe me more.   80

How *Stephen* stoned was you've heard;
     Now to atone that Guilt,
A Chappel of those Stones is rear'd,
     By which his Blood was spilt.

St. *Stephen*'s Chappel is it hight,   85
     And stands in *Westminster*,
Near to that place where want of sight
     Makes Justice sometimes err.

Now how these Stones make hard the Heart
     Of Burgess, or of Knight;   90
And do by Influence impart
     Their persecuting Spight;

It's hard to tell the Cause thereof,
     Like other Mysteries;
Nor would I aim at that, although   95
     That I were ne'er so wise.

69. *Stephen:* St. Stephen the proto-martyr was stoned to death in Jerusalem for speaking against the temple and the Law (Acts 6:11–14, 7:58). Mainwaring may have known the ballad of *St. Stephen and Herod:* "And ledyt Stevyn out of this town and stonyt hym wyth ston . . . And therfore is his evyn on Crystes owyn day" (BM MS. Sloane 2593, f. 23).

     in degree: of importance.
85. *St. Stephen's Chappel:* the House of Commons.
88. *Justice:* The law courts in Westminster Hall were adjacent to the House of Commons.

But yet 'tis true, or tell me now,
     How could such Zeal inspire
Sir *Edward Seymour*, or *John How*
     Of *Gloucestershire* Esquire;   100

With divers Men of lesser Note,
     Tho equal in Desert;
Who did their Voices for to Vote,
     With Clamours loud exert.

None of whose Lives I think can boast,   105
     That they have much Religion;
Or value more the Holy Ghost
     Than *Mahomet* his Pigeon.

Ev'n *Harley*'s self, I say, would scarce

99. *Seymour:* Sir Edward Seymour of Berry Pomeroy, Devonshire, fourth baronet (1633–1708), an "old Prostitute of the exploded Pension'd Parliament in *Charles* the Second's Reign" (*A Collection of State Tracts*, 3 vols., 1705–07, *2*, 653), continued to sit in parliament as a member for Exeter (1698–1708). Seymour had been one of the few Tories to oppose James II from the first, and he joined William of Orange in 1688. During William's reign, however, he "was at the Head of those who opposed the Measures of the Court, in the *House of Commons*" (Macky, p. 111):

> Pretending for his Countreys good,
> He since has acted all he cou'd,
>   To keep his Prince in Pain.
>   (*POAS*, Yale, *6*, 347)

"On the Queen's Accession to the Throne, he was made Comptroller of the Houshold, and of the Privy Council. He is believed to be the prudentest Man in *England*; of great Experience in the Affairs of his Country, but extremely carried away by Passion" (Macky, p. 112). He was particularly passionate in his zeal for the bill against occasional conformity.

John How: John Grubham Howe (1657–1722) sat for Cirencester from 1689 to 1698, and for Gloucestershire from 1698 to 1701. After losing his election there in 1701 he insured against defeat in 1702 by standing in no fewer than four constituencies, including Gloucestershire, where he was successful. In 1705, however, he lost again and never sat in parliament thereafter. In William's reign he was "the most violent and open Antagonist King *William* had in the House" (Macky, p. 117). "On the Queen's Accession to the Throne, he was made a Privy-Counsellor, and *Pay-master* of the *Guards* and *Garrisons*" (ibid., p. 118). According to Lord Dartmouth, "Mr. John How moved in the house of commons to bring in a bill to prevent hypocrisy in religion; without further design, as he told me, than to expose the dissenters, and shew what rogues they were" (Burnet, 1823, *5*, 49*n.*).

108. *Mahomet his Pigeon:* "The *Impostor* [Muhammad] . . . bred up *Pigeons* to come to his Ears to make show thereby, as if the *Holy Ghost* conversed with him" (Humphrey Prideaux, *The True Nature of Imposture Fully Displayed in the Life of Mahomet*, 1697, p. 48).

109. *Harley:* Robert Harley (1661–1724) was educated in dissenting academies and the Inner Temple, but was not called to the bar. He entered parliament in a by-election for Tregoney in April 1689 and represented New Radnor from 1690 until his elevation to the

Be made a *Smithfield* Martyr;　　　　　　　　110
For proof, clap Faggots to his A——,
　　You'll find you've caught a Tartar.

Now this same Bill compleatly cook'd,
　　To the Peers House is follow'd;
And they who brought it thither look'd　　　　115
　　It forthwith should be swallow'd.

But as a hasty Pudding's spoilt,
　　If there do fall some Soot in't;
Or if burnt to: So this was spoil'd
　　By Bishop *Burnet's* Foot in't.　　　　　　120

For he with Toe Episcopal
　　Thereto gave such a Zest,
Their Lordships strait grew squeamish all,
　　Nor could the same digest.

In vain brisk *Nottingham* did speak,　　　　　125

---

peerage as earl of Oxford in May 1711. After having opposed the court for most of William's reign, he was elected Speaker of the House of Commons in February 1701 and occupied the chair until 1705. It was said that "No Man understands more the Management of that *Chair* to the Advantage of his Party, nor knows better all the Tricks of the House" (Macky, pp. 115–16). He was secretary of state from May 1704 until his downfall in February 1708 (cf. *Abigail's Lamentation for the Loss of Mr. Harley*, below). He rose again in 1710 to become chancellor of the exchequer and virtual head of the ministry, a status that was recognized in May 1711 when he became lord treasurer. He remained prime minister until Anne dismissed him a few days before her own death on 1 August 1714.

110. *Smithfield Martyr:* Protestants burned at Smithfield in the reign of Catholic Mary Tudor (1555–58).

112. *caught a Tartar:* "in stead of catching, to be catcht in a Trap" (*New Dictionary*). Harley had been born and "bred a *Presbyterian*" (Macky, p. 116) and was hardly likely to risk political suicide for a high church cause. He had opposed bringing in the second bill to prevent occasional conformity, and behind the scenes he was working to defeat it. On 8 December 1703 Godolphin, the lord treasurer, wrote to him: "every body sees too late we were in the right that would have kept this bill at a distance. Like an unruly musket it might serve to frighten those against whom it was presented, but not hurt any but those who give fire to it" (Longleat MS. Misc. Portland, f. 151).

119. *burnt to:* burnt to (the) pot, burnt up; presumably a bad pun on Burnet; cf. 132*n*. below. *OED* (s.v. Pot, *sb.* 13j) cites [Prior and Montagu], *The Hind and the Panther Transvers'd* (1687), p. 12: "Burn'd . . . to th'Pot."

120. *Burnet:* Gilbert Burnet (1643–1715), the cashiered chaplain of Charles II and *éminence grise* of the revolution, was one of the bishops to whom Sir John Pakington attributed the loss of the second bill to prevent occasional conformity. Burnet himself agreed that "I had the largest share of Censure on me, because I spoke much against the Bill" (Burnet, *2*, 363–64). One of his speeches is preserved in Boyer, *Annals,* 1704, pp. 175–85.

125–28. Quoted in [Mainwaring], *The Medley,* 16 October 1710.

Daniel Finch, second earl of Nottingham, from a portrait by Jonathan Richardson, c. 1726

Who is so tall and slim;
In vain did *Guernsey* silence break,
Who is so like to him.

Their Words alas! went for no more
Than does the News of Grubster,   130
Or than in Commons House before
Went *Hedges* Voice the Shrubster.

The wise and valiant Lord of th'North,

---

125. *Nottingham:* Daniel Finch (1647–1730), second earl of Nottingham, was leader of the high church party in the House of Lords. Anne had appointed him secretary of state in May 1702, but Nottingham's great obsession was religious conformity. It was he who first conceived of a bill to prevent occasional conformity in 1689, and it was he who encouraged William Bromley to introduce such a bill in the House of Commons in November 1702 (Roger Thomas, "Comprehension and indulgence," *From Uniformity to Unity*, ed. G. F. Nuttall and Owen Chadwick, S.P.C.K., 1962, pp. 247–50; *The Reformer Reform'd*, 1703, p. 5; Horwitz, p. 186). Finally, at the price of apostasy from the Tories, Nottingham was able to secure passage of a bill to prevent occasional conformity in December 1711. Thereafter he remained in the opposition until the accession of George I when he became president of the council. Far from being "brisk," he was "an endless Talker" (Swift, *Prose*, 5, 258).

126. *tall and slim:* Nottingham was "a tall, thin, very black Man, like a *Spaniard* or *Jew*" (Macky, p. 26); see illustration, p. 13.

127. *Guernsey:* Nottingham's younger brother, Heneage Finch (1647?–1719), or "silver-tongued Finch" (GEC, *1*, 364), is Polytropos in *An Essay upon Satire* (1679) (*POAS*, Yale, *1*, 408). He had been solicitor general (1679–86) and a member of parliament for Oxford University (1678, 1689–98, 1701–03) and Guildford (1685–87). He was chief counsel to the seven bishops in June 1688, but held no office under William III and refused to subscribe to the association to defend the king in 1696. In 1703 he was created Baron Guernsey. Upon the Hanoverian succession he became earl of Aylesford.

128. *like to him:* Guernsey was also "a tall, thin, black Man" (Macky, p. 90).

130. *Grubster:* apparently a nonce word like "Grubstreetian" (*OED*), for an inhabitant of Grub Street.

132. *Hedges:* Sir Charles Hedges (c. 1650–1714) graduated B.A. from Magdalen Hall, Oxford, in 1670 and D.C.L. in 1675. In 1689 he was appointed a judge of the admiralty court and knighted. In the Commons, where he represented Dover (January–November 1701), Malmesbury (1701–02), Calne (1702–05), West Looe (1705–13), and East Looe (1713–14), he was said to be "a better Companion, than a Statesman . . . [but] very zealous" for the Tory party (Macky, pp. 127–28). In November 1700 he was appointed secretary of state, but according to the duchess of Marlborough he had "no capacity, no quality" and had to be asked to resign in December 1701. "The first Remarkable Occurrence . . . after the Queen's Coronation, was, the Choice"—at the insistence of the earl of Nottingham—of Hedges to be secretary of state. He now became a great favorite at court and accompanied the queen to Bath in August 1702 (*Account of the Conduct*, pp. 168, 170; Boyer, *Annals*, 1703, p. 28; Luttrell, *5*, 124, 207). In order to keep his place, however, "he tried to block the introduction of the second Occasional Conformity bill in November 1703" (Holmes, p. 256). He was replaced by the earl of Sunderland in December 1706.

Shrubster: a pun on Hedges apparently based on an obsolete meaning of "shrub": "A mean, inferior, insignificant person" (*OED*).

133. *North:* William North, sixth Lord North and Grey (1678–1734), left Magdalene Col-

With little better Luck,
In windy Words did bluster forth;   135
    So did his Grace of *Buck*.

For to tell Truth, some Peers did smoke,
    That this same Bill's Progression
Might by degrees at length have broke
    The Protestant Succession.   140

Such Snakes in Grass were for to bite
    Those who could not discern 'em;
Wherefore this Bill was kick'd out quite
    Pro nunc & sempiternum.

Now God preserve our Queen, I say,   145
    And grant her long to reign;
And God keep Popery, I pray,
    On t'other side the Main.

And grant Presbytery may stay,
    And all the canting Breed,   150
For ever, and also for ay,
    On t'other side the *Tweed.*

---

lege, Cambridge, in 1694 without taking a degree. Five years later he took his seat in the
House of Lords. In the next reign he became "a great courtier" and a distinguished soldier.
Although a Tory, he does not appear to have voted for the second bill to prevent occasional
conformity (Holmes, p. 430). Subsequently he involved himself in Jacobite intrigue and the
Whigs were alarmed when he became governor of Portsmouth in 1711. In 1722 he was
committed to the Tower on charges of high treason. When released on bail, he retired to Paris
and died in Madrid (GEC, *9,* 658–60).

136. *Grace of Buck:* John Sheffield (1648–1721), third earl of Mulgrave, had been banished
from the court of Charles II for presuming to make love to Princess Anne, then 17. Upon
Anne's accession, "to the admiration of all men" (Burnet, *2,* 314), he was made lord privy
seal, sworn to the privy council, and on 23 March 1703 created duke of Buckingham and
Normanby. He was "Violent for the *High-Church*" (Macky, p. 20).

140. *The Protestant Succession:* "Lord M[ohu]n . . . did not stick to say, that *if they pass'd
this Bill, they had as good Tack the pretended Prince of* Wales *to it*" (Boyer, *Annals,* 1704, p. 189).

English Gibraltar, an anonymous engraving

On the Greatest Victory
Perhaps that ever Was or Ever Will Be
by Sir George Rooke.
In Imitation of Sternhold and Hopkins.
To the Tune of *Hey boys up go we*
(September? 1704)

William Walsh's prediction that "Pacifick Admirals . . . Shall fly from Conquest, and shall Conquest meet" (*POAS*, Yale, *6*, 494–95) was amply fulfilled by Admiral Sir George Rooke's defense of Gibraltar in the summer of 1704.

The fortress (see illustration, p. 15) had been taken in July 1704, and although its strategic significance was not immediately perceived by the English, the French considered it important enough to warrant a counterattack to recapture it. Accordingly, on 13/24 August 1704, Louis-Alexandre de Bourbon, comte de Toulouse, engaged Sir George Rooke in the battle of Málaga. In the preliminary manoeuvering for position, Rooke allowed Toulouse to come between the English Fleet and Gibraltar. "Our Fleet was one more in number," James Lowther reported to his father, "but the French much bigger Ships . . . they fought from 10 in the morning till seven at Night when the French bore away. There was no Ship lost or taken in the engagement but they say 4 of the French Ships that were disabled sunk the next day as they were towing off . . . We had 700 Men kill'd & 1500 wounded [and] severall Ships much Shatter'd" (Carlisle R. O. MS. D/Lons, James Lowther to Sir John Lowther, 14 September 1704). Both sides claimed victory, but the truth seems to be, as Godolphin observed, that it was "a sort of a drawn battle where both sides had enough of it" and Peter Le Neve conceded that Sir George Rooke "fought the french in the Mediterranean sea but I cannot say beat them" (HMC *Bath MSS.*, *1*, 62; Le Neve, p. 444).

Although not quite the farce that it is represented to be in *On the Greatest Victory*, the battle of Málaga could by no means bear comparison with the victory at Blenheim in terms of strategic importance. Yet this was exactly the comparison that the high flying Tories were now intent to enforce. In September 1704 Defoe reported to Harley from Bury St. Edmunds that "the High Church party look on [Rooke] as their own. The victory at sea they look upon as their victory over the

Moderate party, and his health is now drunk by those here, who won't drink the Queen's, nor yours. I am obliged with patience to hear you damned, and he praised, he exalted, and Her Majesty slighted, and the sea victory set up against the land victory; Sir George exalted above the Duke of Marlborough" (HMC *Portland MSS., 4*, 137). When parliament met in the fall, the Tories in the House of Commons voted an address on the queen's speech congratulating Anne upon "the great and glorious Successes, with which it hath pleased God to bless your Majesty . . . under the Command, and by the Courage and Conduct, of the Duke of *Marlborough,* and . . . under the Command, and by the Courage and Conduct, of Sir *George Rooke*" (*CJ, 14,* 392).

The Whigs responded to these odious comparisons by belittling the achievement of Rooke. "Some people are very ill natured to Sir George Rooke," one of his sympathizers complained in September, "and there is hardly a coffeehouse where his battle is not fought over againe, and 'tis believed by all the accounts we recieve that we never had more occasion for a day of thanksgiving not for a victory but an escape" (HMC *Bath MSS., 2,* 178). And the duchess of Marlborough was indignant that her husband's "*complete victory* at Blenheim was, in the address of congratulation to the QUEEN, ridiculously paired with Sir GEORGE ROOK's *drawn battle* with the French at sea" (*Account of the Conduct,* p. 146). The address from the Whiggish House of Lords made no mention of Málaga.

Two poems published in *POAS*, 1707, reflect the Whig attitude to the battle. The first, *On the Sea Fight between Sir G. R. and Tolouse, 1704,* begins:

> Who does not extol our Conquest Marine?
> Courage and Conduct, *Rook* and *Tolouse,*
> 'Twas the sharpest Engagement that ever [was] seen,
> Courage, &c.
> Where no Ship was taken, and no Trophy won,
> Courage, &c.

The second, *On the Greatest Victory,* was written "in Imitation of Sternhold and Hopkins," the sixteenth century versifiers of the Psalms. It is here printed in full.

The poem is dated 1704 in four manuscripts (*ABFK*), but there is unfortunately no evidence of authorship. The very un-hymn-like tune, *Hey, boys, up go we,* to which in one copy (*H*) the song is designated to be sung, has an interesting history dating from the Smectymnuan controversy of 1641. It was, apparently, Thomas D'Urfey's use of the tune for a song in his play, *The Royalists* (1682), that created its great popularity. Simpson records that it was subsequently used in at least five ballad operas and more than 50 broadsides (Simpson, pp. 3C4–08). "The clean contrary way," the reading of line 8 in *FGH*, is the name of an even older tune, but Simpson also points out that several songs with "The clean contrary way" refrain every eighth line, were designated to be sung to *Hey, boys, up go we* (Simpson, p. 109).

On The Greatest Victory
Perhaps that ever Was or Ever Will Be
by Sir George Rooke.
In Imitation of Sternhold and Hopkins
To the Tune of *Hey boys up go we.*

As brave Sir *George, Thoulouse* did beat,
So brave *Thoulouse* beat him;
But whensoe'er again they meet,
George will his Jacquet trim.

They both did fight, they both were beat,   5
They both did run away;
They both did strive again to meet
The quite contrary way.

Title. *Sternhold and Hopkins:* Thomas Sternhold (d. 1549) and John Hopkins (d. 1570) collaborated to produce a metrical version of the psalms (c. 1547) which survived into the next age as a standard for bad poetry (*POAS,* Yale, *3,* 301; Thomas Brown, *The Works,* 4 vols., 1711, *4,* 163; *Political Merriment: Or, Truths Told to Some Tune,* Part II, 1714, p. 164).

1. *Sir George:* Sir George Rooke (1650–1709) was knighted by William III for his action off La Hougue in May 1692. Thereafter "He was unsuccessful in all the Expeditions wherein he commanded" (Macky, p. 119). His most conspicuous failure came only a year later when 100 vessels of a merchant fleet, of which he commanded the convoy, were destroyed by the French in Lagos Bay, "And the disgrace of it," as Burnet (*2,* 116) observed, "was visible to the whole World." In parliament, where he sat for Portsmouth (1698–1708), Rooke was a high church courtier who "signalized" himself in the impeachment proceedings against the Junto lords in 1701. Upon the accession of the queen, he was made admiral of the fleet and given a place under the lord high admiral, Prince George, on the unusually-constituted commission of admiralty known as the Prince's Council (Luttrell, *5,* 172, 177). In July 1702 "Queen Anne and the prince were godfather & godmother" to his only son (Le Neve, p. 444) and in November Rooke returned to London as the hero of Vigo (*POAS,* Yale, *6,* 467– 84) to receive the "Favour of her Majesty, and . . . the loud Acclamations of the People." On the 21st, when he resumed his seat in the Commons, Harley read a unanimous resolution of the House thanking him for the great and signal services he had performed for the nation (*CJ, 14,* 39). On the same day he was sworn of the privy council (Luttrell, *5,* 239).

Thoulouse: Louis-Alexandre de Bourbon, comte de Toulouse (1678–1737), the third son of Louis XIV and Mme. de Montespan, was made admiral of France at the age of five. The campaign of 1704 was his first in full command of a fleet and from this dubious victory over Rooke the French king drew what consolation he could for the disaster at Blenheim (Saint-Simon, *2,* 366–68).

Moderation Display'd
(December 1704)

Moderation Display'd is a country Tory response to the ministerial changes of April 1704. The word "Moderation" had become a vogue word in the vocabulary of party controversy and "Moderate Men" were suddenly discovered both in church and state. In clerical circles moderates formed the bulk of the low church party, while in parliament they tended to gravitate toward the "managers," Marlborough, Godolphin, and Robert Harley, rather than toward the party leaders like the Tory earls of Nottingham and Rochester or the Whig Junto. Moderation was a dominant issue all during the years 1704–08 when the "managers" broke with the Tory leaders and tried to govern without surrendering power to the Whig Junto.

In April 1704 the queen's ministry was purged of most of its high church Tory elements. At the cabinet level Nottingham resigned the post of secretary of state while Sir Edward Seymour and the earl of Jersey were removed from their offices of comptroller of the household and lord chamberlain. They were replaced by men whose political loyalties were to the crown rather than to a party. Thus Robert Harley and his friend Sir Thomas Mansell took over from Nottingham and Seymour, while the earl of Kent got Jersey's place.

These changes were brought about as much by clashes of personality as by differences of policy. The high church ministers had been unable to agree with Godolphin and Marlborough over the men and measures which the ministry should employ. Where they wanted Tory rule to safeguard the church, the "managers" wanted moderate men to prosecute the war. As Charles Davenant, one of the new moderate men, explained it, "Tis not . . . a Change from Tories to Whiggs but from Violence to Moderation" (BM MS. Lansdowne 773, f. 29v).

The continued popularity of Marlborough with many high church Tories—even after he had broken with their erstwhile leaders—was a remarkable feature of moderation, and essential to its success. Describing the "new race of moderate men" to Lord Weymouth in August 1705, William Ettricke observed "that these are grown very numerous

. . . And for their Expressions for the D of Marlborough He is the rising Sun to whom their Adoration is (at least Seemingly) directed; and Claim Such a Share in him as not to admit any but themselves to have a real Satisfaction in his successes" (Longleat MS. Thynne XXV, f. 424v). Marlborough's smashing victory at Blenheim provided a quick stimulus for moderation, just as his slow capitulation to the Whigs eventually destroyed it. This change is reflected even in the text of *Moderation Display'd*. The first edition ended with 76 lines of unqualified praise of the duke's victory at Blenheim (pp. 630–32 below). In the second edition of 1705 these lines were replaced by 12 lines of carefully qualified praise (and uncannily accurate prophesy) (lines 266–77 below).

The poem is a disenchanted commentary on the ministerial changes of 1704 that "may give Opportunity to a *New Sett of Men*," as Shippen expressed it in the preface to the first edition, "to Ruine both Church and State with their *New* Politicks." His aim is to expose "the Principles and Practices of this *New Party*, who have Assum'd to themselves a very Specious Name and Character, and would be thought the only Patriots of their Country" (*Moderation Display'd*, 1704, sig. A2r). In 1704 he concluded that this "*New Sett of Men*" would "render themselves Odious, and cannot Subsist long" (ibid., sig. A2v). In 1705 his vision became more particular: "their *Crafty Leader* himself will in a very short time be supplanted by his *New Allies*; and if he falls unpitied by his *Old Friends*, he must consider, 'tis but the just Reward of his prevaricating deceitful Practices" (*Moderation Display'd*, 8º, 1705, sig. A7v–A8r). When Harley did fall in February 1708 and the court threw in its lot with the Whigs, that was the end of moderation.

The difference between poetry and history that Aristotle talks about (*Poetica*, 1451b) is nicely illustrated by *Moderation Display'd*. The poet, Aristotle says, has no business with the actual. It is the historian who must deal with what has happened. Poetry deals with what might happen "according to probability or necessity." As "Display'd" in the poem, moderation is conceived in hell by a female fiend called Faction and brought to earth by her favorite son, the second earl of Sunderland "newly Dead" (29). So the ghost of Sunderland rises up out of hell to astound a meeting of the Whig Junto, which he had dominated when alive, at Althorp, the Northamptonshire estate that he had so lavishly adorned (see illustration, p. 20). "Poetry universalizes more" and the universal is achieved when a man says or does what is characteristic of his temperament, probably or necessarily, under the circumstances.

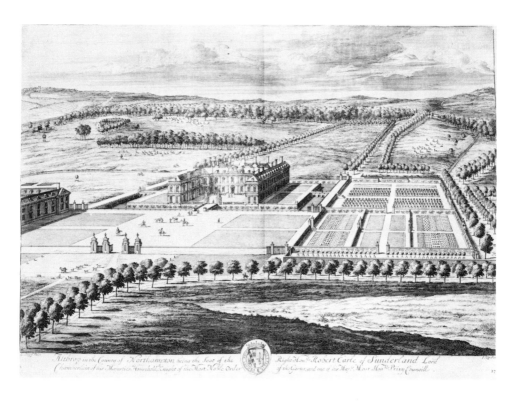

Althorp Park, Nottinghamshire, the seat of the earls of Spencer, an engraving by Jan Kip from a drawing by Leonard Knyff

Somers and Halifax and the third earl of Sunderland are struck dumb by this apparition. Tonson befouls himself. Only Wharton is able to say the words that lay the ghost. Historically the poem takes something both from *Paradise Lost* and from *Absalom and Achitophel* and contributes something to *The Dunciad*.

In addition to two answers "Paragraph by Paragraph" (pp. 629–30 below), the poem generated at least one second part and two sequels in verse:

> *Moderation Display'd, The Second Part,* ("'Twas Night,
>   as on my Bed I waking lay"), 1705 (Victoria and
>   Albert Museum copy)
> *The Sequel: Or Moderation Further Display'd, A Poem,*
>   By the Author of Faction Display'd ("Satyr once
>   more my towring *Muse* sustain"), 1705 (Yale copy)
> *The Devil upon Dun: Or, Moderation in Masquerade.*
>   *A Poem* ("While yet expecting the Returning
>   Day"), 1705 (Rylands Library copy)

One edition of the last (BM copy: 806.k.16 [67]) is brazenly advertised on the title page to be "By the Author of the *True Born Englishman,*" apparently in an effort to sell copies to unsuspecting Whigs.

The author of *Moderation Display'd* was said by Defoe to be "that Man of Fury and Satyr, Mr. D——" (*The Experiment: Or, The Shortest Way with the Dissenters Exemplified,* 1705, p. 3). Tutchin calls him "a Poor, Scandalous *Tory* . . . that has Written so many Libels upon our Right Reverend Bishops, that has so Villanously Reflected upon the Memory of King *William,* and has Prais'd the Worst and Scandaliz'd the Best Men in Church and State" (*The Observator,* 20–23 December 1704), which probably means no more than that Tutchin had read *Faction Display'd.* The author of one of the answers to *Moderation Display'd* refers simply to "our *Tory* Author" and "our Poetick *Tory*" (*Moderation Vindicated,* 1705, pp. 5, 12). It appears from this that neither Defoe, nor Tutchin, nor the anonymous answerer knew who the author was. The University of Durham copy (Routh LXIV.F.25/3) of *Aa* is inscribed, in an old hand, "By Bertram Stote Esqr. Member of Parliament for Northumberland." Stote, whose sister married William Shippen about 1695 (J. P. Earwaker, *East Cheshire: Past and Present,* 2 vols., 1877–80, *1,* 393), served only in one parliament (1702–05). The same attribution is made by William Pittis in *The Proceedings of Both Houses of Parliament, In the Years 1702, 1703, 1704, Upon the Bill to Prevent Occasional Con-*

formity, 1710, p. 56. Pittis also refers to the author of *Moderation Dis-play'd* as "a *Tacker*" (*The Dyet of Poland, a Satyr. Consider'd Paragraph by Paragraph,* 1705, p. 54), which Stote was (see illustration, p. 65) and Shippen was not (since he was not elected to parliament until 29 December 1707). But the attribution to Shippen, made by Alexander Pope and Giles Jacob (*POAS,* Yale, *6,* 650) and supported by widely scattered copies of the poem inscribed on the title page "By William Shippen Esqr.," still seems more likely.

The date of publication of *Moderation Display'd* can be estimated within narrow limits: the latest event to which it refers is the failure of the Tack on 28 November 1704 (239–40) and it was noticed by Tutchin in *The Observator* for 20–23 December 1704.

William Shippen, an engraving by Edward Harding

MODERATION DISPLAY'D

Again, my Muse—Nor fear the steepy Flight,
Pursue the Fury thro' the Realms of Night;
Explore the Depth of Hell, the secret Cause,
Whence the New Scheme of *Moderation* rose.
    Now Faction re-assum'd her Native Throne,   5
Which prostrate Fiends with awful Homage own.
A Crown of Eating Flame her Temples bound,
Darting a Blew Malignant Radiance round.
An Iron Scepter in her Hand she bore,
Emblem of Vengeance and destructive Pow'r.   10
A bloody Canopy hung o'er her Head,
Where the *Four* falling *Empires* are pourtray'd.
Monarchs Depos'd beneath her Foot-stool lie,
And all around is Hell and Anarchy.
Whilst thus she tow'ring sat, the Subject Train   15
With Shouts proclaim'd the Triumphs of her Reign.
Then they the Chaos sung, and Nature's Jars,
How the first Atoms urg'd their *Medley* Wars,
How Civil Discord and Intestine Rage
Have boil'd in ev'ry Nation, ev'ry Age.   20
They sung Divided *Albion*'s hapless State,
Her Clashing Senate's Feuds, her lab'ring Church's Fate:

Title. *Moderation:* In 1701 the word was still "a mark of Sincerity" in the Tories' political lexicon (*The Claims of the People of England, Essayed*, 1701, p. 89), but in the next year it became an obscenity when Charles Leslie fulminated against *The New Association of those Called Moderate-Church-Men with the Modern-Whigs and Fanatics to Undermine and Blow Up the Present Church and Government* (1702).

2. *the Fury:* Faction (*Faction Display'd*, 9 [*POAS*, Yale 6, 651]).

5. Cf. *The Dunciad*, 4, 17: "She mounts the Throne: her head a Cloud conceal'd. "

12. *Empires:* The "four great beasts" of Daniel's dream were interpreted to mean four succeeding "kingdoms," of which the last was to "devour the whole earth . . . tread it down, and break it in pieces" (Daniel 7:1–23).

13. *Monarchs Depos'd:* " 'Tis She [Faction], that wou'd, for ev'ry slight Offence, / Depose a True Hereditary Prince" (*Faction Display'd*, 19–20). Cf. *Absalom and Achitophel*, 782–83; "The most may err as grosly as the few; / And faultless Kings run down, by Common Cry."

   beneath her Foot-stool: Cf. *The Dunciad*, 4, 21–22: "Beneath her foot-stool, *Science* groans in Chains, / And *Wit* dreads Exile . . . . "

15. *tow'ring:* Cf. *Faction Display'd*, 224 (*POAS*, Yale, 6, 660).

17. *Chaos:* Faction is the daughter of Chaos (*Faction Display'd*, 11). Cf. *The Dunciad*, 4, 13–14: "Then rose the Seed of Chaos, and of Night, / To blot out Order."

23

And, as her coming Ruin they exprest,
A sullen Rapture swell'd in ev'ry Breast.
For such the Bent of their Distorted Will,   25
Only to know Delight in Thoughts of Ill.
But on a sudden, Lo! descending flew,
A Meagre Ghost, which soon the Fury knew,
Cethego newly Dead, her Darling Pride,
Whose Firm Unwav'ring Faith she long had try'd,   30
Long in her Secret Councels had retain'd,
By which her Empire o'er our Isle she gain'd.
No sooner was arriv'd the Welcome Guest,
But him in soothing Terms, she thus addrest:
    Hail best Belov'd of all my Sons, Receive   35
What Praise, what Joy these Gloomy Realms can give;
For 'tis to thy Successful Arts I owe
My Reign above, my Triumph here below.
    This said, th'Unbodied Shade obsequious kneel'd,
Struck with Amazement, and with Rapture fill'd: 40
    O Mighty Queen! Permit me to Adore
Thy Awful Shrine, thy all Informing Pow'r,
Whose nearer Influence my Breast Inspires
With Glorious Rage and Mischievous Desires.
'Twas in Thy Cause I sunk a mouldring Frame,   45
Unequal to the Hardy Task of Fame.
But still my Mind releas'd from Mortal pains,
Her innate Faculty of Ill retains.
    More he had said, but the surrounding Throng,
Impatient of delay, pursu'd their Noisy Song.   50
    Mean time the Fiend revolving in her Thought
The mighty Change *Cethego*'s Death had wrought,
Resolv'd at length to Summon to her Aid
Each plotting Daemon, each Seditious Shade.
She gave the Signal, and a Dreadful Sound   55

26. *Delight in . . . Ill:* The phrase recalls Satan (*Paradise Lost*, I, 160): "ever to do ill our sole delight."

29. *Cethego newly Dead:* Robert Spencer, second earl of Sunderland (1640–1702) was "the greatest Politician of our Age" (Boyer, *Annals*, 1703, p. 231). As political "manager" for both James II and William III, he was regarded by the country Tories as "A second *Machiavel*" (*Faction Display'd*, 263) who had betrayed James and brought the Whigs to power under William. He had died on 28 September 1702.

52. Cf. *Faction Display'd*, 60–61.

Shook the Infernal Dreary Mansions round.
Then thus she eas'd her anxious Soul:
  O dearest Friends! O faithful Ministers!
Ye mutual Partners of my Joys and Cares!
New Ways, new Means my restless Thoughts imploy,   60
How *Albion* to reduce, her Peace destroy.
Long have I labour'd, but alas! in vain,
For now Succeeds the Heav'nly *Anna*'s Reign;
Who watchful Guards a Stubborn Peoples Good,
By Fears not stagger'd, nor by Force subdu'd.   65
Such are the Gifts of her Capacious Mind,
Where Justice Mercy Piety are joyn'd.
As Motion Light and Heat, combin'd in one,
Make up the Glorious Essence of the Sun.
But still she Mortal is, nor will I cease,   70
Till my Revenge be Crown'd with wish'd Success.
First then, suppose we shou'd divest the Throne
Of Friends, whose Souls are Kindred to her own.
Celsus Disgrac'd, *Hortensio* next appears,
Whose Vigilance still Baffles all my Cares;   75
To whom by Right of Ancestry belong
A Loyal Heart, and a perswasive Tongue.
Now Plots are form'd, and publick Tempests rowl,
He boasts a strange unshaken Strength of Soul;

74–84. Quoted in *The Dyet of Poland, a Satyr. Consider'd Paragraph by Paragraph*, 1705, p. 56.

74. *Celsus Disgrac'd:* Laurence Hyde, earl of Rochester (1641–1711), the second son of Edward, earl of Clarendon, and thus an uncle of Queen Anne, was the hero of *Faction Display'd* (435–51). He had held high office under Charles II and James II and became a leading Tory in the reign of William III, who made him lord lieutenant of Ireland in 1700. Anne continued him in this post until February 1703. One of the replies to *Moderation Display'd* objected to the word "Disgrac'd": "saying *A la mode de France* he is *disgraced* . . . is utterly false and scandalous" (*Moderation Vindicated*, 1705, p. 10), but Rochester remained out of office until September 1710 when he was appointed lord president of the council.

Hortensio: Daniel Finch, earl of Nottingham, succeeded Rochester as leader of the ministerial Tories upon Rochester's dismissal in 1703.

76. *Ancestry:* Nottingham was the grandson of Sir Heneage Finch, Speaker of the House of Commons in the reign of Charles I, and eldest son of Heneage Finch, first earl of Nottingham, who was Charles II's lord chancellor.

78. *Plots:* Nottingham's political career was adversely affected by the Whigs' effort to implicate him in the Scotch plot of 1703. The Whig lords alleged that his investigation of the intrigues of Simon Fraser and James Boucher was insufficiently thorough, and they undertook an independent investigation. That some kind of insurrection in Scotland was planned is beyond doubt and so is Nottingham's innocence of any involvement in it (*POAS*, Yale, *6*, 615–17; Horwitz, pp. 191–96).

Fearless against her Foes the Church sustains,　　　　　　80
Alike their Friendship and their Hate disdains,
Disdains their Clamour and Seditious Noise,
Secure in the Applauding Senate's Voice.
Of Noble Stem, in whose *Collat'ral* Lines
Virtue with equal Force and Lustre shines.　　　　　　　　85
When *Suada* pleads, Success attends the Cause,
Suada the Glory of the *British* Laws.
Not the Fam'd Orators of Old were heard
With more attentive Awe, more deep Regard,
When Thronging round them, their Charm'd Audience hung　90
On the attracting Musick of their Tongue;
Nor Hell to *Laelio* can her Praise refuse,
Whose Worth deserves his own recording Muse;
Who in *Sophia*'s Court, with just Applause,
Maintain'd his Sov'reign's Rights, his Country's Cause.　　95
For 'tis in him, with Anguish that I find
All the Endowments of a Gen'rous Mind,
Whate'er is Great and Brave, whate'er Refin'd.

83. *Applauding Senate:* The Tory House of Commons defended Nottingham against the attacks of the Whig lords by resolving on 21 December 1703 "That the Earl of *Nottingham,* one of her Majesty's principal Secretaries of State, for his great Abilities and Diligence in the Execution of his Office, for his unquestionable Fidelity to the Queen, and her Government, and for his steady adhering to the Church of *England,* as by Law established, hath highly merited the Trust her Majesty hath reposed in him" (*CJ, 14,* 260).

86. *Suada:* Heneage Finch, Lord Guernsey, was said to be "one of the greatest orators in *England*" (Macky, p. 90).

92. *Laelio:* Charles Finch, fourth earl of Winchilsea (1672–1712), was Nottingham's nephew. He held no office in William's reign, having refused to subscribe to the association to defend the king, but upon the accession of Anne he was appointed lord lieutenant of Kent, governor of Dover Castle, and deputy warden of the Cinque Ports under Prince George (Luttrell, *5,* 183). Since he was "zealous for the Monarchy and Church to the highest Degree," he was removed from all his offices in 1705 (Macky, p. 85; Luttrell, *5,* 535, 539). He loved "Puns, and that sort of low Wit" and was to become a "particular Friend" of Jonathan Swift (Macky, p. 85, Swift, *Journal, 2,* 555).

94. *Sophia:* Sophie, dowager electress of Braunschweig-Lüneburg (1630–1714), was a granddaughter of James I and the daughter of Friedrich V, elector palatine of the Rhine. In 1658 she married Ernst August, who became elector of Braunschweig-Lüneburg, or Hanover, in 1692 and died in 1698. By the Act of Settlement of 1701 she became heir to the throne of England in default of issue from William III or from Anne and if she had lived two months longer she would have become Sophie I, queen of England, Scotland, and Ireland.

Court: In August 1702 Anne appointed Winchilsea an envoy extraordinary to Hanover, "to compliment the dutchesse dowager in her majesties name, [and] to acquaint her with her majesties accession to the crown." Winchilsea remained in Hanover until April 1703 (Luttrell, *5,* 209, 287).

For 'tis in him Fame doubly does Commend
An Active Patriot, and a Faithful Friend.   100
Then from his near Attendance be remov'd
Urbano, tho' by All Admir'd and Lov'd;
Tho' his sweet Temper and obliging Port
Become his Office, and Adorn the Court.
He seems by Nature form'd Mankind to please,   105
So Free, so Unconstrain'd is his Address,
Improv'd by ev'ry Virtue, ev'ry Grace.
Senato too, who Bravely does deride
Sempronia's little Arts, and Female Pride;
Whose Lofty Look, and whose Majestick Mien   110
Confess the tow'ring God-like Soul within.
A Speaker of unparallel'd Renown,
Long in the Senate, long in Council known.
Ally'd to *Celsus* by the Noblest Claim,
By the same Principles, by Worth the same.   115

101–07. Quoted in *The Dyet of Poland, a Satyr. Consider'd Paragraph by Paragraph*, 1705, p. 56.

102. *Urbano:* Edward Villiers, first earl of Jersey (1656–1711), had been master of the horse to Queen Mary and secretary of state from 1699 to 1700. In 1700 William III had appointed him lord chamberlain and Anne continued him in that post until April 1704 when he was dismissed—apparently guilty of association with the high church faction in the cabinet. His own mystification is reflected in his letter of 5 May 1704 to Richard Hill: "I do not doubt of your being informed of our late changes, what relates to my-self was so surprising that it made me unfit for sometime to give you any account of it . . . I immediately repair'd to my lord Treasurer [Godolphin] to know my crime, but could get nothing laid to my charge but my herding and protecting some that took measures contrary to the Queen's service" (Middlesex Records MS. Jersey Acc 510/154).

108–19. Quoted in *The Dyet of Poland, a Satyr. Consider'd Paragraph by Paragraph*, 1705, pp. 54–55.

108. *Senato:* Sir Edward Seymour was dismissed from the post of comptroller of the household on 22 April 1704.

109. *Sempronia:* The duchess of Marlborough (*Faction Display'd*, 430–31) pressed Anne to get rid of the high church Tories in her ministry from 1702 to 1704. Seymour appears to have been particularly objectionable to the Churchills for even Sarah's more accommodating husband wrote to her in June 1703 that "We are bound not to wish for any body's death, but if 14 [Sir Edward Seymour] should die, I am convinced it would be no great loss to the queen nor the nation" (Coxe, *Memoirs, 1*, 133).

Pride: Swift notices the duchess's "haughty Pride" in *The Examiner*, 19 April 1711 (*Prose, 3*, 134).

110–11. Seymour "hath a very erect Countenance, and is a stately Man for his Age; of a fair, sanguine Complexion, about Seventy Years old" (Macky, p. 113).

111. *tow'ring:* Cf. 15 above.

114. *Ally'd:* Francis, Seymour's second son by his second wife, married Mary, Rochester's daughter, on 17 February 1704.

Old as he is, still Firm his Heart remains,
And dauntless his declining Frame sustains.
So, pois'd on its own Base, the *Center* bears
The Nodding Fabrick of the Universe.
Nereo shall cease t'extend his *Anna*'s Reign   120
High as the Stars, unbounded as the Main.
'Tis He, whose Valour the *Batavian* Wars
Inur'd to Glory from his greener Years.
'Tis He *La Hogue*'s opposing Ord'nance bore,
Nor fear'd the Lightning's Flash, nor Thunder's Roar.   125
'Tis He (with *Scipio* darling of our Isle)
From vanquish'd *Vigo* forc'd the *Indian* spoil.
'Tis he the *Streights Defence* so lately Storm'd,
A Town by Nature Fortified and Arm'd.
'Tis He unequal far in Force, o'ercame   130
A Fleet secure of Conquest and of Fame,
A Fleet by vast expence for Fight prepar'd,

117. *declining Frame:* Besides old age, Seymour suffered from diabetes.

120. *Nereo:* Sir George Rooke extended "*Anna*'s Reign" by the capture of Gibraltar on 24 July 1704. The siege of Gibraltar was actually undertaken in the name of Charles III, the Habsburg pretender to the throne of Spain, but upon capitulation of the Spanish garrison, Rooke, on his own responsibility, caused the union jack to be raised and took possession in the name of Queen Anne.

122. *Batavian Wars:* Rooke began his career as a volunteer in the Second Dutch War (1664–67) and was a lieutenant in the Third (1672–74).

124. *La Hogue:* Rooke distinguished himself in the battle of La Hougue (May 1692) by boarding and burning 12 French ships within sight of James II and the invading French army (John Ehrman, *The Navy in the War of William III,* Cambridge, Cambridge University Press, 1953, p. 396).

126. *Scipio:* James Butler, second duke of Ormonde (1665–1745), was said to be "one of the most generous, princely, brave Men that ever was" (Macky, p. 10). His military career began at the age of 19 when he was made colonel of a regiment of horse. He supported the revolution and fought at the king's side in all of William III's campaigns. Politically however he was said to be "gouverné par Mylord Rochester son Beau Pere" (BM MS. 30000E, f. 236v). In 1702 he commanded the ground troops in the failure at Cadiz and the success at Vigo. The following year he succeeded Rochester as lord lieutenant of Ireland, a post he held until 1707 and again from 1710 to 1712, when he replaced Marlborough as captain general of the armed forces. Toward the end of Anne's reign he became lord warden of the Cinque Ports. He was implicated in the Jacobite intrigues of Bolingbroke and dismissed from all his posts at the accession of George I. In 1715 he fled to France.

127. *Vigo:* After the failure of the expedition against Cadiz in 1702, Rooke and Ormonde destroyed or captured the entire Spanish silver fleet in Vigo Bay (*POAS,* Yale, *6,* 467–84).

128. *the Streights Defence:* Gibraltar; see 120*n.* above.

129. *by Nature Fortified:* See illustration, p. 15.

130–33. On 13/24 August 1704 Rooke prevented a French fleet from retaking Gibraltar in the battle of Málaga.

At once the *Spaniards* Terror and their Guard.
'Tis he my Pois'nous baleful Breath has Born,
But with a gen'rous and Heroick Scorn.   135
For Fiends must still this just monition have;
Envy's the Coward's homage to the Brave.
Nor *Bajazet* shall Rule in favour long,
Tho' he so sweetly *Gloriana* Sung.
A Son of *Phoebus,* whose Seraphick lays   140
Were only equal to her Heav'nly Praise.
But He not claims the Muses art alone,
Whose Nobler Gifts in ev'ry Sphear have shone.
A Soul he boasts with Native Grandeur born,
That my *Volpone*'s Schemes rejects with Scorn: 145
Form'd of a brighter and diviner Mould,
Can ne'er by humbler Reason be controul'd;
Can ne'er in *Dark involv'd Designments* join,
But bravely with the Court will all his Pow'r resign.
Here as their various Virtues she confest,   150

134. *baleful Breath:* Defoe had glanced at Rooke in *The Spanish Descent* (1702) and in *The Address* (April? 1704) and Walsh had sniped at him in *The Golden Age Restor'd* (1703) (*POAS,* Yale, *6,* 472, 478, 646, 504), but the major attack was begun by Tutchin in *The Observator* of 12–15 July 1704 and continued by Defoe in the *Review,* 22 August 1704. Rooke ignored these attacks, but Charles Leslie took up his defense in *The Rehearsal,* 4–11 November 1704.

138. *Bajazet:* John Sheffield, marquis of Normanby and duke of Buckingham, became Bajazet in a poetical exchange in 1675 between Sir George Etherege and John Wilmot, earl of Rochester (*POAS,* Yale, *1,* 342–47). Buckingham, who himself wrote verse which Samuel Wesley called the "*Perfection*" of English poetry, retaliated in *An Essay upon Satire* (1679), in collaboration with Dryden (*An Epistle to a Friend concerning Poetry,* 1700, p. 6; *POAS,* Yale, *1,* 396–419). An authorized edition of Buckingham's works, "overlooked" and corrected for the press by Alexander Pope, appeared in 1723.

139. *Gloriana Sung:* Buckingham wrote these verses to Anne upon being presented with her picture (*Three New Poems,* 1721, p. 18):

> *Mistaken Zeal* was the first *Mary*'s Share,
> *Elizabeth* was form'd for *Regal Care;*
> In ANNE alone these happy Nations find
> *Prudence* and *Piety* together join'd.

145. *Volpone:* Sidney Godolphin, first earl of Godolphin (1645–1712) had become Volpone in *Faction Display'd* (408–28). After Halifax he was the leading financial genius of the period, serving as a lord of the treasury (1679, 1687–88, 1689–96, 1700–01) and as lord treasurer (1684–85, 1702–10). Although he had been a Tory and was even regarded as a Jacobite in William's reign, he served Anne as a "manager," or broker between the crown and the parties. This led the country Tories to regard him as an apostate, or even as a Whig. He was by all "allowed [to be] a very cunning man" (*Wentworth Papers,* p. 131).

Scorn: An earlier occasion on which the marquis of Normanby, as he then was, cast reflections on Godolphin's motives is recorded in Vernon, *2,* 264.

Rancour innate and Vengeance shook her Breast.
She paus'd—At length her further Mind exprest:
   Be these, and such as these, discharg'd from Court,
The *Better Genii* that the Crown support:
Then in their stead let *Mod'rate* Statesmen Reign,   155
Practice their new pretended Golden Mean.
A Notion undefin'd in Virtues Schools,
Unrecommended by her sacred Rules.
A Modern Coward Principle, design'd
To stifle Justice, and unnerve the Mind.   160
A Trick by Knaves contriv'd, impos'd on Fools,
But Scorn'd by Patriot and Exalted Souls.
For *Mod'rate* Statesmen, like *Camelions,* wear
A diff'rent Form in ev'ry diff'rent Air.
They stick at nothing to Secure their Ends,   165
Caress their Enemies, betray their Friends.
Their Medley Temper, their Amphibious Mind
Is fraught with Principles of ev'ry kind;
Nor ever can, from Stain and Error free,
Assert its Native Truth, and Energy.   170
As the four Elements so blended were
In their first Chaos, so united there,
That since they ne'er could fully be disjoyn'd,
Each retains something of each other's Kind;
Nor is this wholy Air, nor that pure Flame,   175
But still in both some Atoms are the same.
   Let *Jano,* second of this Trimming Band,
Next to *Volpone* deck'd with Honours stand.
Like him for *black Ingratitude* Renown'd,
Like him with all the Gifts of Cunning crown'd.   180
None better can the Jarring Senate guide,
Or lure the *Flying Camp* to either side.

155. Cf. "Moderation was the *Word,* the *Passpartout,* that open'd all the *Place* Doors"
([James Drake], *The Memorial of the Church of England,* 1705, p. 7).

177. *Jano:* Robert Harley was widely known as "the subtile, the crafty, the *double fac'd*
Janus" (*A Detection of the Sophistry and Falsities of the Pamphlet, Entitul'd, the Secret History of the
White Staff,* 1714, p. 8).

180. *Cunning:* "Mr. Harley is generally allowed as cunning a man as any in England"
(*Wentworth Papers,* p. 132).

181. *Senate guide:* He "knew forms, and the Records of Parliament so well, that he was
capable both of lengthening out, and of perplexing debates" (Burnet, *2,* 109).

182. *Flying Camp:* In the context "the *Flying Camp*" might be either Harley's personal follow-

Of an Invet'rate Old Fanatick Race,
Of Canting Parents, sprung this Child of Grace.
In Show a *Tory*, but a *Whig* in Heart,   185
For Saints may safely act the Sinner's part.
Once he was ours, and will be ours again,
For Art to stifle Nature strives in vain,
For ev'ry thing, when from its *Center* born,
Still thither tends, still thither will return.   190
So from its Orb a Comet glaring Flies,
With unauspicious Beams thro' distant Skies;
But soon Revolting to its Native Sphear,
Owns the attractive Force and *Vortex* there.
Let him with these Accomplishments supply   195
Hortensio's steady Faith, and Loyalty.
    Bruchus, for he has Wealth to buy a Place,
Shall wear *Urbano*'s Key, his Post disgrace.
A worthy Son, in whom collected shine

---

ing (Holmes, pp. 259–65) or moderate members of both parties whose support he attracted.

183. *Fanatick Race:* Both of Harley's parents were dissenters and he was "bred up in a Fanatick *Conventicle* and *Seminary*" in Shilton, Oxfordshire (*A Detection of the Sophistry and Falsities of the Pamphlet, Entitul'd, the Secret History of the White Staff,* 1714, p. 8).

185. *In Show a Tory:* Harley had entered politics after the revolution as a Whig, but like many other Whigs, e.g. Anthony Ashley Cooper, third earl of Shaftesbury, he had been unable to support the Whig Junto when they assumed power in 1694. The accession to power of a party which had previously existed only as an opposition party split it into two factions, the court and country Whigs. Harley led the country faction, which combined with dissident Tories into "the New Country-Party," opposed to the Junto. When the Junto fell from power and were impeached in 1701, many country Whigs rallied to their support. Harley, however, remained opposed to them, although as late as 1703 Shaftesbury could still believe that "he is ours at the bottom" (*Original Letters,* p. 192). Because he continued to collaborate with Tories, many historians regard Harley as a moderate Tory in Anne's reign. In fact it is best to regard him as a "manager," like Godolphin, "grievously misrepresented by *all Parties,* for the great Crime of *being of none*" (*A Continuation of the Review,* 1742, p. 57).

189–90. Cf. "None need a guide, by sure Attraction led, / And strong impulsive gravity of Head" (*The Dunciad, 4,* 75–76).

194. Cf. "a vast involuntary throng, / Who . . . Roll in her Vortex, and her pow'r confess" (*The Dunciad, 4,* 82–84).

196. *Hortensio:* Harley had replaced Nottingham as secretary of state on 18 May 1704.

197. *Bruchus:* Henry Grey, earl of Kent (1671–1740) "was always violent [for] the tory party and was never in any employment till he was made Lord Chamberlain on the removal of Lord Jersey as [is] said for 10000 Pounds which he gave the Duchess of Marlborough. He is one of a good estate, a very ugly figure, of but indifferent parts" (*Wentworth Papers,* p. 134). In November 1706 he was created marquess of Kent and in April 1710, upon his replacement as lord chamberlain, he was created duke of Kent and became a court Whig. Lord Hervey called him "a *yes and no* hireling to the Court for 40 years" (*Memoirs,* p. 226, cited in GEC, *7,* 178).

The Follies of his Mad and Ideot Line.   200
Lord of the woful Countenance, whose Skin
Seems sear'd without, and putrify'd within.
A Dapper Animal, whose Pigmy Size
Provokes the Ladies Scorn, and mocks their Eyes.
But Balls and Musick are his greatest Care,   205
So willing is the Wretch to please the Fair.
'Tis strange, that Men, what Nature has deny'd,
Should make their only Aim, their only Pride.
    Let *Britono,* who from the Parent Moon
Derives his *Welch* Descent directly down,   210
Succeed *Senato* in his High Command,
And bear the Staff of Honour in his Hand.
A flutt'ring empty Fop, that ev'ry Night,
Sits Laughing loud, and Jesting in the Pit,
Whilst a surrounding Crowd of Whores and Bawds,   215
His sprightly Converse, and his Wit applauds.
An *Atlas* proper to sustain the Weight
Of an Incumber'd and declining State.
    Thersites, an Apostate Brother, long

202. *putrify'd:* Kent was so malodorous that he was known as "The Bug" or even as "His Stinkingness" (Blenheim MS. E 27). He was replaced as lord chamberlain by the duke of Shrewsbury, whom Swift allowed to be "possessed of many amiable Qualities; but in the Agreeableness and Fragrancy of his Person, and the Profoundness of his Politicks, must be allowed to fall very short of [Lord Kent]" (*Prose, 3,* 79).

209. *Britono:* Sir Thomas Mansell of Trimsaran, county Carmarthen, fifth baronet (c. 1667–1723), was a neighbor of Robert Harley. He was educated at Oxford and "always made an agreeable Figure in the *House of Commons*" (Macky, p. 114), where he sat for Cardiff (1689–98) and Glamorgan (1699–1712). "A very violent tory," Mansell "refused to sign the association in King William's time and chose rather to leave his seat in Parliament than do it . . . He was made Controller of the Household upon the remove of Sir Edward Seymour; he quitted that charge with others when Mr. Harley was removed, who undoubtedly procured him this employment. He is a man of wit and gaiety and has lived much about town" (*Wentworth Papers,* pp. 133–34). He was one of the "Dozen of Peers, made all at a Start" in December 1711 to provide a Tory majority in the House of Lords. Swift admired his good nature but thought he had "a very moderate capacity" (*Prose, 5,* 260).

213. *Fop:* Mansell's reputation as "a lover of the Ladies" (Macky, p. 114) is confirmed by his letter of 11 September 1707 to Edward Nicholas, complaining of life in the country: "were you here now and saw your Goddes which was Peg: Edmunds," he wrote, "you wou'd swear time never made such an alteration for she's ful as big as my lady Delawar. I think bigger. And so great a change in al the rest they are not worth thinking off. But to you I must confess that now and then somthing comes in one's way and flesh and blood does fal upon it" (BM MS. Egerton 2540, f. 140).

219. *Thersites:* Although no contemporary reader ventured to identify Thersites in any of the copies examined, the best candidate is Thomas Coke (1674–1727), a country Tory in

For Railing fam'd, and Virulence of Tongue;   220
Who lately held in scandalous Disgrace
The fawning Courtier, and the Slave in Place;
Who vilify'd, for every slight Offence,
With equal Gall the Statesman and the Prince:
Now, soften'd by Advancement, can controul   225
The wonted Rage and Fury of his Soul:
An Advocate for *Moderation* grows,
Would heal their Breaches, and their Jars compose;
Forgets that he the Guilty Court disclaim'd,
And loudly praises what he once defam'd.   230
So Northern Mastiffs, in a warmer Sun,
Their Fierceness lose, and gentler Natures own.
   Causidico, whom fear of Want made Bold,
Barters his boasted Honesty for Gold.
Tacks and *Impeachments* once he urg'd as Law,   235
To curb the Throne, the Ministry to awe:
Witness *Sigillo* and the *Irish Grants;*

William's reign who became a court Whig in Anne's when he was appointed a teller of the exchequer in April 1704 upon the recommendation of the duke of Marlborough (HMC *Cowper MSS.*, *3,* 32). He took an active part in the debates in the Commons, on one occasion denouncing Harley as "a Presbyterian rogue" (Vernon, *2,* 444), but he failed to vote for the Tack of the third bill to prevent occasional conformity and voted *against* Bromley as Speaker in October 1705 and *for* the impeachment of Sacheverell in March 1710. In 1706 he was appointed vice chamberlain of the household, a place which he held until his death, and in 1709 he married, as his second wife, one of Anne's maids of honor, Mary Hall. For these apostasies he was put out of his seat in Derbyshire (1698–1710) and had to seek election in Grampound (1710–15).

223. *every slight Offence:* See 13*n.* above.

233. *Causidico:* Simon Harcourt (1661–1727) was educated at Pembroke College, Oxford, and the Inner Temple. His "Want" proceeded from the fact that the estates which he inherited in 1688 were "in a very embarrassed condition" (*DNB, 8,* 1206). Hearne (*9,* 334) thought he was "most certainly a very great Lawyer, tho' governed by Interest, so that he changed Principles often." Swift (*Poems, 1,* 190) called him "trimming *Harcourt*" and Arthur Onslow testified that he was "without shame" (Burnet, 1823, *5,* 48*n.*). Harcourt began his political career as a member for Abingdon (1690–1705, 1710). In William's reign he voted solidly Tory: he refused to sign the association to defend the king, voted to tack the bill revoking William's grants of forfeited Irish estates to the land tax, and "signalized" himself in the impeachment proceedings against Somers in 1701. He had been a schoolmate of Robert Harley and upon Anne's accession Harley secured his appointment as solicitor general (Holmes, p. 261). He was knighted in June 1702. In November 1704 he refused to vote for the motion to tack the third bill to prevent occasional conformity to the land tax.

234. *Gold:* In 1701 Harcourt was blacklisted as a "*Poussineer,*" overly susceptible to "*Tallard's* Gold" (*A Collection of White and Black Lists,* 4th ed., 1715, pp. 5–8; *POAS,* Yale, *6,* 337).

But cease we now, he cries, those old Complaints.
Let us restrain our too impetuous Zeal,
Nor ever *tack a* persecuting *Bill*.   240
Let us henceforth *offending Statesmen* screen;
Let Justice sleep in *Anna*'s gentle Reign.
So is the Patriot chang'd from what he was;
So solid a Conviction is a Place.
    Not rais'd for this by *Abdon*'s bounteous Hand,   245
Abdon, whose Virtues ev'ry Praise demand,
Abdon, who with his Post his Truth maintains,
Whose steady Soul a wav'ring Renegade disdains.
Thracio, who arrogantly vaunted Young,
The Politicians Art, and Poet's Song,   250
Shall now the Fame his Friends bestow'd, destroy,
Shall be the Tories Scorn as once their Joy.
An errant *Judas,* of the *Motley* Train,

240. *persecuting Bill:* It was said that Whig opponents of the bills to prevent occasional conformity had bribed "your Observators and other mercenary Pamphleteers, to raise a hideous outcry about Persecution, and represent this Design in such odious colours to the People, that if possible it may miscarry" (Thomas Brown, *Letters from the Dead to the Living,* Third Part, 1707, p. ²220). Shippen repeats sarcastically William Walsh's phrase in *The Golden Age Restor'd,* 53 (*POAS,* Yale, *6,* 497).

245. *Abdon:* Sir Nathan Wright (1654–1721) left Emmanuel College, Cambridge, without taking a degree and was called to the bar in 1677 from the Inner Temple. He argued the crown's case in the attainder of Sir John Fenwick in December 1696 and was knighted the following year. In May 1700 as a little known serjeant at law with "a fat broad Face, much marked with the Small-pox" (Macky, p. 41), he was appointed lord keeper to succeed Somers after the most distinguished jurists in England had refused the appointment (*POAS,* Yale, *6,* 212). His biblical counterpart was a judge in Israel (Judges 12:13).

249. *Thracio:* Henry St. John (1678–1751) was called "*Thracian St. John*" in William Walsh's *The Golden Age Restor'd,* 109 (*POAS,* Yale, *6,* 503). His political career began as a member for Wootton-Bassett (February 1701–08), a Wiltshire borough controlled by his father (Walcott, p. 68). His brilliance as a speaker soon earned him important assignments: in March 1702 and again in January 1703 he was elected one of the commissioners of public accounts (Luttrell, *5,* 154, 250); he was one of the managers of the first two bills to prevent occasional conformity (*CJ, 14,* 14, 238), and one of the commissioners to audit the accounts of Lord Ranelagh (300n., below). The first hint of his apostasy came in February 1704 when he declined to serve again on the commission for public accounts. In April he was rewarded with one of Blathwayt's posts and in November 1704 he was replaced by John Ward as one of the managers of the third bill to prevent occasional conformity (Luttrell, *5,* 395, 411; *CJ, 14, 419*). Like Harley (*Jano*) and Harcourt (*Causidico*), he was a Sneaker and thus earned his place in the story as a "Judas" (253).

250. *Poet:* St. John's literary career was not so brilliant. He contributed a copy of commendatory verses to Dryden's Virgil in 1697, a pindaric ode, *Almahide* ("I long have wander'd from the Muses Seat") which was published in *A New Miscellany of Original Poems,* 1701, pp. 98–114, and some other trifles (*POAS,* Yale, *6,* 503).

Perfidious, Noisy, Impudent, and Vain.
An Agent fit to propagate my Ends,   255
Who basely for a *Place* will quit his Friends.
For let but *Scriba,* that Rich Worthless Fool,
Fantastically Formal, Gayly Dull;
Let him unwillingly resign his Post,
Thracio and all his fine Harangues are lost.   260
　　Let these, as useful Tools, a while possess
The Court Preferments, and indulge their Ease.
But they shall fly, like Mists before the Sun,
When my Design's to full Perfection grown,
Exert their Pow'r, and make the ruin'd World my own.   265
　　Camillo, tho' triumphant in the Field,
Seduc'd by *Grants,* shall to his Party yield.

256. *Place:* The place for which St. John "quit his Friends" was secretary at war. He was appointed in April 1704 and hastened to explain to Sir William Trumbull that "we are far from being in a Whig interest." He acknowledged that there was "a good deal of jealousy and dissatisfaction alive among some of our friends" but contended, somewhat lamely, that "the dispute was for persons and not for things" (Berkshire R. O. MS. Trumbull Add. 133, Henry St. John to Sir William Trumbull, 16 May 1704).

257. *Scriba:* William Blathwayt (1649?–1719) is a kind of political anomaly. After one session during which he represented Newtown (1685–87), he occupied a seat for Bath (1693–1710) that was controlled by the Jacobite duke of Beaufort. He was put down as a "High Church Courtier" in 1705 (*Numerical Calculation*) and is called a court Tory by his last biographer (Gertrude A. Jacobsen, *William Blathwayt,* New Haven, Yale University Press, 1932, pp. 480–81). Yet he invariably voted with the ministry even when it was most Whiggish. He was in fact a model civil servant whose ponderous manner was the cause of much merriment (*POAS,* Yale, *6,* 351). He began his career as one of Sir William Temple's secretaries at The Hague in 1668. He became secretary to the lords of trade (1679–96), secretary at war (1683–1704), auditor general of plantation revenues (1689–1717), and a member of the board of trade (1696–1707). He finally lost his seat in parliament in 1710 for voting with the ministry rather than with the Tories in the divisions over the Sacheverell trial.

　　Rich: Defoe had already noticed Blathwayt's low resistance to "the Power of Gold" (*POAS,* Yale, *6,* 332). This enabled him to build one house at Dyrham Park, Gloucestershire, with gardens laid out by André Le Nôtre, and to fit out another to receive the queen when she visited Bath in July 1702.

258. *Dull:* "William III set a royal stamp upon [Blathwayt] by pronouncing him dull" (Gertrude A. Jacobsen, *William Blathwayt,* New Haven, Yale University Press, 1932, p. 34).

266. *Camillo:* the duke of Marlborough. Shippen had set out in the first edition of his poem to "eternize *Camillo's* Name" for his great victory at Blenheim on 13 August 1704. The present lines represent his second thoughts on Marlborough.

267. *Grants:* In December 1702 Marlborough had received a grant of £5000 a year out of post office receipts.

　　to his Party yield: In 1705 Marlborough was still regarded as a Tory, but the signs that he would yield to the Whigs were already apparent. Possibly because he is not yet willing to regard the duke as an apostate, Shippen blames his waywardness on "The Witchcraft" (275) of the duchess of Marlborough.

A Chief, to form whose mighty Mind, conspire
The *Roman* Conduct, and the *Grecian* Fire.
Germania's Stator, and *Britannia*'s Joy,   270
Whose Fame does the whole Western World imploy.
By whom (so Heav'n and *Anna* have decreed)
Tyrants are humbled, enslav'd Nations freed.
But still not all his Valour can withstand
The Witchcraft of *Sempronia*'s Golden Hand.   275
In her he shall my boundless Empire own,
And lay his purchas'd Palms and Lawrels down.
    When thus the Fury had her Scheme Display'd,
Assenting Hell a low Obeisance paid.
    Moloch, Protector of the *Papal Chair,*   280

270. *Stator:* L. sustainer. *OED* cites *The Rustic Rampant* (1657), there wrongly attributed to
Cleveland: "He was the Stator, the Saviour of the Nation."

277. *lay . . . down:* Shippen's prophecy was accomplished on 31 December 1711 when
Marlborough was dismissed from all his employments.

280. *Moloch:* Thomas Tenison (1636–1715) graduated B.A. (1657), B.D. (1667), and
D.D. (1680) from Corpus Christi College, Cambridge. His political and religious principles
had been suspect since 1683 when he published *An Argument for Union* urging the comprehen-
sion of dissenters in the Church of England. Thomas Hearne called him "a man of . . . no
Principles of Honesty and Conscience," but in fact Tenison "was always a Man of moderate
Principles" (Hearne, *5,* 153; Macky, p. 136). He embodied in his huge bulk, "With brawny
sinews & with Shoulders large, / Fitter to row than loll in Lambeth barge," the "Modera-
tion" that is exposed in the present poem and defined in Harley's remarkable letter to
Tenison of 11 August 1702: "I must tell you," Harley wrote, that "you are entirely under
the influence of those who have not only dischargd themselves from all obligations of religion,
but also have for many years been promoting, first Socinianisme, then arrianisme & now
deisme. In the state they have propagated notions wch destroy all governmt. In order to
perfect that, they set up for notions which destroy all religion & so consequently dissolve the
bonds of all society" (Berkshire R. O. MS. Trumbull Add. 18; HMC *Bath MSS., 1,* 53).
Tenison was "early in the confidence of those who planned the invasion of William III"
(*DNB, 19,* 538) and thereby acquiesced at least in the "Massacres and Christian War" waged
against the forces of James II in Ireland. William responded by making Tenison archdeacon
of London (1689), bishop of Lincoln (1691), and archbishop of Canterbury (1694). Tenison
then confirmed the reputation by which he had earned his Miltonic pseudonym, "besmear'd
with blood / Of human sacrifice, and parents' tears" (*Paradise Lost, 1,* 392–93), when he voted
in December 1696 to send Sir John Fenwick to the block (Calamy, *Historical Account, 1,* 383–
84). Tenison was hated because he stubbornly insisted upon, and exercised, the archepiscopal
right to prorogue convocation (Calamy, *Abridgement, 1,* 572–639), but he was hated even more
for his opposition to the bills to prevent occasional conformity. In one critical division of
December 1702 it was Tenison who produced the votes that defeated the first bill, 50–47
(Klopp, *10,* 222). When the second bill was sent up to the House of Lords in December 1703,
Tenison "by the assistance of fourteen other bishops, had such an influence over many of the
temporal lords, that it was rejected after the second reading" (Calamy, *Historical Account, 2,*
16). So Tenison became the "Whiggish Primate," who sided "with the Dissenters against
the Church establish'd" (*POAS,* Yale, *6,* 545; [William Pittis], *The Case of the Church of*

Author of Massacres and Christian War,
Was now Convinc'd that Sanguinary Laws
Could ne'er the *Reformation*'s Growth oppose,
Could ne'er in *Albion*'s Church advance his Cause.
He therefore, urg'd with his old constant Hate,   285
By *Mod'rate* Means consents to work her Fate.
Hopes by *Dissenting Agents* to regain
What *Zealous Missionaries* sought in vain.
He finds how soon by *Toleration*'s Aid
Her Pow'r is weaken'd, and her Rights betray'd.   290
Nor doubts *Occasional Conformity*
Will by degrees her Essence quite destroy.
   Then *Satan,* Prince of the *Fanatick* Train,
Who form'd the Conduct of their *Glorious* Reign,
Approv'd the Scheme, not hoping to Restore   295
His Subjects to their late unbounded Pow'r.
For well he knew, their Avarice and Pride
Had wean'd the Bankrupt Nation from their side.
But these Auspicious *Moderation* Times,
By not Detecting, Sanctify their Crimes,   300

England's Memorial, 1705, p. 36). Swift called him "The dullest, good for nothing man I ever knew" (*Prose, 5,* 271) and Lord Dartmouth agreed that he was "exceeding dull," but added that he "died very rich" (Burnet, 1823, *4,* 238*n.*).

282. *Sanguinary Laws:* another sarcastic reference to the bills to prevent occasional conformity (240*n.*, above).

288. *What Zealous Missionaries sought:* By "a very short Bill, 'for the utter Eradication of Bishops, Deans, and Chapters,' " parliament sought in March 1641 "to put the Ax to the Root of the Tree" (Henry Hyde, first earl of Clarendon, *The History of the Rebellion,* 3 vols., Oxford, 1702–04, *1,* 187).

289–90. Cf. Anthony à Wood, *Life and Times, 3,* 439: "The effect of toleration—instead of enjoying their religion in peace without disturbance, they endeavour to pull downe the church of England by their writings and preachings."

294. *Glorious Reign:* the Interregnum (1649–1660).

300. *Crimes:* As paymaster general of the army (1691–1702), Richard Jones, earl of Ranelagh, handled vast sums of money "and God knows where it went; but after the King's death, it was found that twenty two millions stirling was not accounted for" (Ailesbury, *1,* 241). Ranelagh resigned his post in December 1702 to avoid prosecution. He was expelled from the House of Commons in February 1703 after an audit of his accounts had been made, but he succeeded in quashing the legal proceedings against him for embezzlement. It was commonly believed that Halifax, who was auditor of the exchequer (1699–1715), and Orford, who had been treasurer of the navy (1689–99), were also guilty. The Commons had ordered Halifax to be prosecuted in January 1703, but Sir Edward Northey, the attorney general, entered a plea of nolle prosequi "so no verdict was given" (Luttrell, *5,* 262, 439). The Commons promptly ordered Halifax to be retried but again the proceedings were quashed (Luttrell, *5,* 488). Orford's case was never brought to court. In March 1704 the

By baffling Justice, and eluding Law,
Make Vice insult, and Sin Triumphant grow.
Nay such th' Effects of *Moderation* are,
The Guilty to Reward, as well as Spare.
Hence Foes to Prelacy are Clad in Lawn,   305
Hence Rebels are the Fav'rites of the Throne.
What could they more desire, than thus to pass
The blest Remainder of their happy Days,
Fatted with Plunder, and dissolv'd in ease?
    Nor *Belial,* th' *Atheist*'s Patron, could Complain,   310
For *Moderation* would enlarge his Reign,
Where all unpunish'd Talk and Live Profane.
Where Irreligion Providence denies,
Nor dreads the Laws of Earth, nor Thunder of the Skies.
Mammon, the *Trader*'s, and the *Courtier*'s God,   315
No sooner heard the Project but allow'd;
For hence his Vot'ries uncontroul'd might live,
And endless Frauds commit, and endless Bribes receive.
    But most *Cethego* the Design approves,
Who Dead and Living in *Maeanders* moves.   320
He knew how he deluded hapless *James,*
By the same wily Arts, and subtle Schemes,
Proposes then, that he alone be sent,
To execute the Fury's New Intent.
When he had ended, thus she soon replies: 325
    Blest be the Shade, that can so well advise,
On thee thy Goddess smiles, on thee relies.
Fly, nimbly to thy Native Soil repair,
Urge and Inforce the well-form'd Council there.
Occasion favours, the *Cabal* is met   330

Commons voted 60–57 that his delays in making up his accounts "may be of great Loss to the Publick" (*CJ, 14,* 375), but the Lords, after hearing all the evidence, concluded that he had made a fair account (Luttrell, *5,* 406).

305. *Foes:* These were the low churchmen whom William III raised to the episcopacy and who, because they refused to vote for the bill to prevent occasional conformity, were called "enemies to the Church" (Burnet, *2,* 338). Their names are listed in Defoe's *King William's Affection to the Church of England Examin'd,* 1703, pp. 19–21.

306. *Rebels:* like Harley, "Of an Invet'rate Old Fanatick Race" (183).

310. *Belial:* Belial "Counsell'd ignoble ease, and peaceful sloth" (*Paradise Lost, 2,* 227).

315. *Mammon:* Mammon admired "more / The riches of Heav'n's pavement, trodd'n Gold, / Than aught divine or holy" (*Paradise Lost, 1,* 681–83).

319. *Cethego:* See 29*n.* above.

At thy own Mansion, thy belov'd Retreat,
The Muses Darling Theam, the Graces Seat.
There *Clodio*'s and *Sigillo*'s anxious Thoughts,
Are brooding o'er *Imaginary Plots:*
Whilst *Bibliopolo* with his awkard Jests   335

331. *thy own Mansion:* Althorp, the Northamptonshire seat of the earls of Sunderland (see illustration, p. 20).

333. *Clodio:* Thomas Wharton, Lord Wharton (1648–1715), "born and bred a Dissenter," as he boasted in the House of Lords (Bryan Dale, *The Good Lord Wharton,* Congregational Union of England & Wales, 1901, p. 25), "early acquired and retained to the last the reputation of being the greatest rake in England" (*DNB, 20,* 1329). As a member for Wendover (1673–79) and Buckinghamshire (1679–96), he was also one of the first Whigs, voting for the exclusion of the duke of York and corresponding with the prince of Orange. William III appointed him a privy councillor and comptroller of the royal household (1689–1702), warden of the royal forests south of Trent (1697–1702), and lord lieutenant of Buckinghamshire (1702), but balked at making him secretary of state, "thinking him . . . too much a Republican to be intrusted with the Administration of State Affairs" (Macky, p. 91). In February 1696 Wharton succeeded to the peerage as fifth Lord Wharton, but upon the accession of Anne he was removed from all his offices. Wharton then became the most active manager of the Whig Junto, leading the opposition to the bills to prevent occasional conformity (Boyer, *Annals,* 1704, p. 187) and abetting Matthew Ashby in his celebrated suit against the mayor of Aylesbury (Trevelyan, *2,* 20–25). He first appears as Clodio, "Chief of all the Rebel-Race," in *Faction Display'd* (*POAS,* Yale, *6,* 658).

Sigillo: John Somers, Lord Somers (1651–1716), "the life, the soul, and the spirit of [the Whig] party," as Lord Sunderland told William III (Hardwicke, *2,* 446), was educated at Trinity College, Oxford, and the Middle Temple. As a member for Worcester (1689–93) he was chairman of the committee which drafted the Declaration of Rights and became a great favorite of William III, who appointed him solicitor general (1689), attorney general (1692), lord keeper (1693), lord chancellor (1697), and raised him to the peerage as Baron Somers of Evesham in December 1697. But Somers' decision in the most important case that came before him was overturned by the House of Lords (*POAS,* Yale, *6,* 660–61) and Sir Edward Seymour in the House of Commons "reflected on him . . . for his religion, that he was a Hobbist" (Vernon, *3,* 13). Somers never married, but his mistress is named in *Father's Nown Child* (*POAS,* Yale, *5,* 427) and his ill-cured pox was a standing joke (*POAS,* Yale, *6,* 16, 520, 629, 660). Somers was dismissed in April 1700 and narrowly escaped impeachment the following year for procuring "exorbitant Grants" for himself and for other irregularities in the conduct of his office. When the Tory back-benchers learned, for example, that Somers had affixed the great seal to a blank commission and sent it off to William so that the terms of "that curst *Partition*" treaty could be inscribed thereon, they exclaimed that he might as well have sold England outright (BM MS. Add. 30000E, f. 143v). This incident may have suggested Somers' label-name, which first occurs in *Faction Display'd* (1704) (*POAS,* Yale, *6,* 660).

334. *Plots:* See 78*n.,* above. Wharton and Somers were both members of the Lords' committee appointed in December 1703 "to consider of the *Scottish* Conspiracy" (*POAS,* Yale, *6,* 622).

335. *Bibliopolo:* Jacob Tonson (1656?–1736) began his career as a stationer's apprentice (1670–77), laid the foundation for his fortune when he bought the rights to *Paradise Lost* (1683, 1690), and ended as unofficial publisher to the Whig party. He was also the founder of the Kit-Cat Club (Edward Ward, *The Secret History of Clubs,* 1709, pp. 360–63) where Whig

Deserves his Dinner, and diverts the Guests.
Bathillo, in his own unborrow'd Strains,
Young *Sacharissa*'s Angel Form profanes:
Whilst her dull Husband, sensless of her Charms,

---

propaganda was devised and authors' copy corrected by Somers and Halifax and "recommitted to . . . their Trusty Secretary *Jacob* . . . to Babble it abroad by the Hawkers" (*A Vindication of the Whigs,* 1702, pp. 9–10). He was introduced as Bibliopolo in *Faction Display'd* (*POAS,* Yale, *6,* 667–68).

337. *Bathillo:* Charles Montagu, Lord Halifax (1661–1715), was the fourth son of a younger son of Henry Montagu, first earl of Manchester. He was educated at Westminster School (where he met Matthew Prior) and Trinity College, Cambridge, which he left without taking a degree. Montagu was a short man whom the duchess of Marlborough found "frightful." He married in 1688 his cousin's widow, who was then "about 60" (GEC, *8,* 372). When she died ten years later (Luttrell, *4,* 407), he "followed several beauties [cf. 338*n.* below] who laughed at him for it" and then formed a lasting liaison with Catherine Barton, Sir Isaac Newton's niece (Macky, p. 53; *N&Q, 8* [3 December 1853], 544; *Timon in Town, to Strephon in the Country,* Osborn MS. Chest II, No. 2 [Phillipps 8302], f. 81). In parliament, where he sat for Maldon (1689–95) and Westminster (1695–1700), he "gained such a visible ascendant over all that were zealous for the King's Service, that he gave the Law to the rest" (Burnet, *2,* 218). William appointed him a commissioner of the treasury (1692), chancellor of the exchequer and privy councillor (1694), and first lord of the treasury (1697). "It is to him," Macky said, that "the King owes the great Loans that were made to the Crown, the establishing the Paper Credit, and the Debentures; as the Nation doth the recoining our Money." But "His quick Rise made him haughty" and in November 1699, "as a Screen from all Objections against his Administration" (Macky, pp. 51–53), he resigned all his posts for the profitable sinecure of auditor of the exchequer. In December 1700 he was created Baron Halifax. Like Somers he was saved from impeachment in 1701 by a Whig majority in the House of Lords. Upon the accession of Anne he was removed from the privy council, and the House of Commons ordered him prosecuted for breach of trust in his management of the treasury. His trial ended in a nolle prosequi in June 1704 (300*n.,* above). It is as a patron of literature that Halifax figures in *Faction Display'd* (*POAS,* Yale, *6,* 664–66). Halifax continued to play a major role in the conception and execution of Whig propaganda (*The Kit-Kat C—b Describ'd. O Monstrous Moderation!,* 1705, pp. 4–5).

unborrow'd: Shippen alludes to Halifax's reputation as a literary remora ([Thomas Phillips], *An Epistle to Sr. Richard Blackmore Occasion'd by the New Session of the Poets,* 1700, p. 10; [William Pittis], *Letters from the Living to the Living,* 1703, p. 219). Cf. *The Junto,* 40*n.* below.

338. *Sacharissa:* Lady Anne Churchill (1683–1716), the second daughter of Marlborough. In January 1700 she married Charles Spencer, who succeeded his father as third earl of Sunderland in September 1702. In April 1702 the queen appointed her a lady of the bedchamber (Luttrell, *5,* 163). Halifax celebrated "the little Whig" in a Kit-Cat toast written in 1703 (*The Fifth Part of Miscellany Poems,* 5th ed., 1727, p. 68):

> All Nature's Charms in *Sunderland* appear,
> Bright as her Eyes, and as her Reason clear:
> Yet still their Force, to Men not safely known,
> Seems undiscover'd to herself alone.

339. *dull Husband:* Charles Spencer, third earl of Sunderland (1674–1722), was educated privately and entered politics as a member for Tiverton (1695–1702), a Devonshire borough which his father largely controlled (Boyer, *Annals,* 1703, p. 231; Walcott, p. 45). In parliament he became a zealous partisan of the Whig Junto and during the debate on Fenwick

Lies lumpish in her soft encircling Arms.   340
For he to Wisdom makes a Grave Pretence,
But wants alas! His Father's Depth of Sense.
Howere, supplying all Defects of Wit,
He shews a true Fanatick Zeal and Heat.
   She spoke. The Spectre in a Moment Gains   345
Altropia's Balmy Air, and Flowry Plains.
At his approach the Dome's Foundation shook,
When 'midst their Revels rushing in he broke.
Involv'd in Wreaths of Smoak awhile he stood,
Seeming at distance an unshapen Cloud.   350
But soon, the Cloud ascending to the Skies,
He manifest advanc'd before their Eyes.
Horror and Guilt shook ev'ry Conscious Breast,
But *Bibliopolo* most his Fears exprest,
Fainting he tumbled—Pass we o'er the rest.   355
Clodio alone fixt and unmov'd appear'd,
And what the Phantom said undaunted heard:
   Forbear, my Friends, your Hot pursuits restrain,
Behold your lov'd *Cethego* once again.
From *Faction*'s dark unbottom'd Cell I come,   360
Fraught with *Britannia*'s Fate and final Doom.
For, Meditating Vengeance in her Mind,
At length a Finish'd Plan she has design'd.
Nor doubts by *Mod'rate* Methods to obtain,
What she by rougher Arts has sought in vain,   365
That *Whigs* should Triumph in a *Tory* Reign.
   Thus he began, and then proceeds to tell

---

boldly proposed that the bishops be prevented from voting (Vernon, *1*, 69). "While he was Member of the House of Commons, he would often among his familiar Friends refuse the Title of Lord; [and] swear that he . . . hoped to see the Day, when there should not be a Peer in *England*" (Swift, *Prose, 7*, 9). His "rough way of treating his Sovereign" (ibid.) offended Anne, but the duke and duchess of Marlborough finally persuaded her to make him secretary of state in December 1706. Preferment, however, did not incline him to "lay Aside the violence of his Temper" (BM MS. Add. 4192, f. 112). He treated the queen "with great rudeness and neglect, and chose to reflect in a very injurious manner upon all princes, before her, as a proper entertainment for her" (Burnet, 1823, *6*, 7*n*.). So Anne was glad to dismiss him in 1710. His mother-in-law recalled that "it was thought, [he] would be a fool at two and twenty: But afterwards [he] was cried up for having parts." Swift agreed with her, however, that "His Understanding [was] at best of the middling Size" (*The Opinions of Sarah Duchess-Dowager of Marlborough*, [Edinburgh], 1788, p. 78; Swift, *Prose, 7*, 9).
   346. *Altropia*: Althorp (331*n*. above) is pronounced Althrop.

What *Faction* had before reveal'd in Hell.
　　The wellcome Narrative touch'd *Clodio*'s Heart,
Who did in Words like these his Joy impart:　　　　　　370
　　Since thy *Divided State* permits, be thou
As once a Friend, a Guardian Genius now.
Give us to execute this Grand Design,
Thine be the Conduct, and the Glory thine.
Nor can we doubt Success—*Sempronia* Smiles,　　　　375
And Hell and Faction aid the Woman's Wiles.
　　Pleas'd with this Answer, the retiring Ghost
Condens'd the ambient Air, and in a Cloud was lost.

JOHN TUTCHIN

The French King's Cordial
(December 1704?)

The Tack, the most momentous affair of state in the first half of Anne's reign, occurred when 134 Tories (actually 136 including the tellers) voted to attach the third bill to prevent occasional conformity to the land tax bill on 28 November 1704. Frustrated by the defeat of two previous bills in the House of Lords, the Tackers intended by this strategy to force the third bill through the upper house, since by tradition the Lords could neither alter nor amend a money bill, but could only pass or reject it outright. And rejection seemed unthinkable since this would sacrifice the single most important source of revenue for the war against France. Furthermore, as Burnet (*2*, 401–02) pointed out, "those in the Secret" knew that if the Lords rejected the bill, the "Money would be stopped [and] our Allies, as despairing of any help from us," would be encouraged "to accept of such terms as *France* would offer them."

It had been rumored that the Tories would undertake this measure as early as December 1703, when the second bill to prevent occasional conformity was defeated (HMC *Downshire MSS.*, *1*, ii, 818; BM MS. Lansdowne 773, ff. 12v–22v). Few in the ministry, however, took the threat seriously. The court did not believe that Bromley and his cohorts would be reckless enough to carry out the threat, much less that the attempt would succeed.

On 14 November 1704 when a motion to bring in the third bill to prevent occasional conformity was passed by a majority of only 26 votes (Luttrell, *5*, 486), compared with 43 for the previous bill, Harley was persuaded that "it will be impossible for them to tack it, if they be mad enough to attempt it" (Blenheim MS. FII 16). Four days later, however, when Sir Simon Harcourt learned that the Tack had been decided upon in earnest, he wrote to Harley immediately: "Dear Sir, Universall Madness reigns. The more enquiry I make concerning the Occasionall Bill, the more I am confirm'd in my Opinion that if much more care than has been, be not taken, that Bill will be consolidated. I find the utmost endeavours have been us'd on one side, and little or none on the other" (BM MS. Loan 29/138, Bundle 5).

44THE FRENCH KING'S CORDIAL

This was enough to jolt Harley into action. On the back of Harcourt's letter he scribbled a list of some 90 Tories who might be persuaded to oppose the Tack, or at least to abstain. Against these names he placed others, apparently of those whom he hoped would do the persuading (*BIHR, 34* [1961], 95–97). Godolphin too began to mobilize against the Tack. "I find Mr. Boyle also much alarmed," he told Harley, "and have agreed with him to meet tomorrow in the evening about 7 at Mr. Secretary Hedges with those gentlemen of the House of Commons, to consider if anything can be proposed to defer it in that House, and at the same time to think what course can be taken to stop it in the other" (William A. Speck, *The House of Commons 1702–1714,* D. Phil. thesis, Oxford University, 1965, p. 124).

The motion to tack the bill to the land tax was debated after its second reading on 28 November 1704. One of the court speakers argued "That the English nation was now in the highest consideration abroad: That all Europe was attentive to the resolutions of this parliament; and that, if any divisions should happen between the two Houses, it would cast a damp upon the whole confederacy, and *give the French king almost as great advantage, as we had gained over him at Blenheim*" (*Parl. Hist., 6,* 361, italics added).

The words in italics provide not only the point of departure for the present poem but also an interesting example of historical statement short-circuiting into poetical statement. For the belief that the Tackers were indirectly assisting Louis XIV is easily twisted into a claim that they were deliberately helping him. And in the utterance that becomes the poem, Louis XIV is imagined to be taking comfort in his defeat at Blenheim from the action of the 134 Tackers.

In two replies to the poem, *The Tackers Vindicated; Or, An Answer to the Whigs New Black List,* 1705, p. 6, and *A Cordial for the French King* ("Thô my Spirits are brought very low") (BM MS. Add. 21094, f. 156), *The French King's Cordial* was attributed to John Tutchin. This attribution is also supported by internal evidence (1*n.*, 22*n.*, 74–75*n.*). Tutchin, indeed, would have had every reason in December 1704 to conceal his authorship of the poem. He had been subject since July 1703 to almost continual legal harassment for publishing *The Observator.* The bill which a grand jury brought in against him for publishing *The Observator* of 2–5 June 1703 was eventually returned ignoramus, but in December 1703 the House of Commons ordered an investigation to determine the author of *The Observator* of 8–11 December (*CJ, 14,* 248). On 3 January 1704 Tutchin was ordered into the custody of the sergeant at arms. He had already absconded and a £100 reward was offered for his arrest. Even in his "Exile" as he called it, Tutchin continued to publish *The Observator* and to claim that he was being prosecuted for his claims of "gross Mismanagement" in the victualling of the navy.

In May 1704 Tutchin surrendered himself to the queen's solicitor, Sir Simon Harcourt, and was released on £1,000 bail. Each of the seven articles in the charges drawn up against him cited paragraphs in *The Observator* that were alleged to be seditious, libellous, or false. Tutchin himself was identified as "one *John Tutchin* of the City of London, Labourer," a *déclassement* that he bitterly resented (*The Observator*, 7–10, 10–14, 14–17 June, 21–24 October 1704).

In November 1704 Tutchin was tried by a jury at the queen's bench and found guilty on all counts. But objections were raised and on 28 November 1704, the same day that the Tack was defeated in the House of Commons, the verdict was set aside "by a strange *Hocus Pocus*" and Tutchin walked out of the Guildhall a free man (*DNB, 19,* 1310; *An Account of the Birth, Education, Life and Conversation of that Notorious and Bold Scribbler the Observator,* 1705, p. 5).

One copy (*D*) of the first revised state of the poem is subscribed "Dec. 1704," a date which agrees well enough with the fact that Dame Sarah Cowper entered the "Second Part" of the poem (the addition of which was part of the first revision) in her diary (*G*) on 23 January 1705. In other copies the poem is dated 1704 (*E*) and 1705 (*AM*).

The tune indicated for the song in two copies (*DG*), *Old Simon the King,* is an old one, "probably known to Elizabethans" (Simpson, p. 546). D'Urfey adopted it for *The Newmarket Song* ("The Golden Age is come") in 1684 (*POAS,* Yale, *3,* 493). Gay used it for an aria in *The Beggar's Opera* (1728) and it was a favorite tune of Squire Western.

THE FRENCH KING'S CORDIAL

I Think I shall never Dispair
Tho' Beaten at *Blenheim* full sore,
Since I have gotten else where
One Hundred and Thirty Four.

Tho' *Marlborough* Ruin'd my Cause,   5
I'll soon the Matter Restore,
For amongst the Makers of Laws,
I've One Hundred and Thirty Four.

The *Cub* that I've Nourish'd so long,
In Time will pay off his Score,   10
For I find his Party is Strong,
'Tis One Hundred and Thirty Four.

I'll send him Home to his Throne,
Which his *Father* abandon'd before,
Where he'll be Supported and own'd   15

1. *never Dispair:* "The *French* Kings . . . chief Dependance has been on the *Tacking* Party in *England*" (*The Observator*, 11–14 April 1705).

2. *Tho' Beaten:* "One such Vote from our Parliament had made [Louis XIV] sufficient Amends for all the Prejudice our Armies had done him" (*A Brief Account of the Tack*, 1705, p. 4).

4. *One Hundred and Thirty Four:* On 28 November 1704 the Commons ordered the third bill to prevent occasional conformity to be read a second time. "A Motion being made, and the Question being put, That the [occasional conformity] Bill be committed to the Committee of the whole House, to whom the Bill, for granting an Aid to her Majesty by a Land Tax, and otherwise, is committed:

> The House divided:
> The Yeas go forth:
> Tellers for the Yeas, *Mr. Bromley*
>   *Mr. Freeman*   134
> Tellers for the Noes, *Lord Coningsby*
>   *Sir Cha. Hotham*   251
> So it passed in the negative" (*CJ, 14,* 437).

9. *The Cub:* James Francis Edward (1688–1766), the product of the warming pan in Whig mythology and the Jacobites' Prince of Wales, had been exiled at St. Germain since December 1688. By the Act of Settlement of June 1701 he was excluded from the succession, but upon the death of his father in September 1701 he was recognized by Louis XIV as James III of England.

13. *Throne:* "All these *Tackers* have a Design to De-Throne Queen *Ann,* and to bring in *Perkin*" (*The Observator*, 19–23 May 1705).

By the One Hundred and Thirty Four.

The *Scotch* will no longer Deceive him.
The Channel is Guarded no more;
The *Party* which is to Receive him
Is One Hundred and Thirty Four.   20

St. *Poll* with an *English Fleet,*
To the Number of Half a Score,
Shall Guard him if it's thought meet
By the One Hundred and Thirty Four.

The Land-Tax had surely miscarried,   25
And I had had All in my Power,
Had but the Question been Carry'd
By One Hundred and Thirty Four.

My Grandson to Spain had been Tack'd
Much faster than ever before,   30

17. *Scotch . . . Deceive him:* James' hope that the Scotch plot (*POAS,* Yale, *6,* 615–17) would place him on the throne of his half-sister, Anne, must have been dashed by the end of 1704.

18. *Channel . . . Guarded no more:* French privateers cruised in the Channel unmolested in the summer of 1704 (Luttrell, *5,* 450, 459, 488).

21. *St. Poll:* Marc-Antoine, chevalier de Saint-Pol-Hécourt (c. 1665–1705), commanded the French privateers based at Dunkirk. Saint-Pol's sallies against English shipping in the Channel were particularly successful in the summer and autumn of 1704 since most of the English navy was deployed in the Mediterranean (J. H. Owen, *War at Sea under Queen Anne 1702–1708,* Cambridge, Cambridge University Press, 1938, p. 277). Saint-Pol was killed in October 1705 while capturing three English men-of-war and ten of the eleven merchant ships which they were convoying (ibid., p. 125). His squadron at this time numbered six men-of-war and four large privateers (Luttrell, *5,* 606).

an English Fleet: "I cannot tell you the Exact Number of our Men of War that have been Taken by the *French,* or have been Deliver'd up to them by Cowardly Commanders," Lord Haversham reported to the House of Lords, "But I can tell you the Numbers of such Ships as are now Employ'd as Privateers against us." Haversham then named "Half a Score" of ships (*The Observator,* 13–16 December 1704).

25. *Land-Tax:* By far the most important direct tax of the period was a rate on an assessment of the rental value of land made in 1693. In war time the rate was fixed at four shillings in the pound, and brought in about £2,000,000 per annum. Acts were required annually to raise this revenue, and it was to this bill that the Tackers wished to attach the occasional conformity bill. Failure to vote the land tax would have made it impossible for England to continue the war (Burnet, *2,* 401–02).

29. *Grandson:* Philippe, duc d'Anjou (1683–1746), was the son of the dauphin, Louis, and the second grandson of Louis XIV. Upon the death of Carlos II in October 1700 and the extinction of the Habsburg dynasty, Philippe was named successor to the Spanish throne. In April 1701 before his 18th birthday he assumed at Madrid the government of a bankrupt and demoralized empire that could only be defended and maintained by French arms and subsidies (William Coxe, *Memoirs of the Kings of Spain,* 2nd ed., 5 vols., 1815, *1,* 98, 121).

29–30. *Tack'd | Much faster:* established more securely.

Had the Vote succeeded as Pack'd
By the One Hundred and Thirty Four.

But they have put some of my Friends
Into Places of *Profit* and *Power,*
Which spoil'd for this Session the Ends   35
Of the One Hundred and Thirty Four.

There's *Hammond,* and *Harcourt,* and *How,*

33–34. *Friends | Into Places:* "Several of the most considerable Men of that side having been taken off by the Ministers, and gratify'd with good Places, they left their Party in the Lurch, and voted against the Tack. And thus this Noisy, Mischief-making, Party-driving, Good-for-nothing Bill came to be utterly lost" (*Faults on Both Sides,* 1710, p. 27). The same point is made in *The Lamentation of High-Church* ("Thus God does bless our Sovereign *Anne"*) (*POAS,* 1707, *4,* 120–21):

> And now they take the Sons of the Church,
>   And put them into Places,
> Which makes them leave us in the lurch,
>   Oh! this the very Case is.
>
> Our rich and constant *M[anse]ll* now,
>   Since they a Place have gave him,
> He votes not as he us'd to do,
>   But just as they would have him.
>
> Our Bully-back Jack *H[o]w,* alas!
>   Since he is made Pay-Master,
> What my Lord *Sly* will have him do,
>   He'l do it in all hast Sir.
>
> Young *H[ammon]d* too, that talkt so much
>   To bring the Lords to Trial,
> He minds not Us, nor Them, nor Church,
>   But minds the Navy-Royal.
>
> Our prating *Ar[thu]r M[oo]re,* whom we
>   Always rely'd on still,
> For seven hundred Pounds a Year
>   Does vote against the Bill.

37. *Hammond:* Anthony Hammond (1668–1738) was educated at St. John's College, Cambridge, and became a member of parliament for Huntingdonshire (1695–98), Cambridge University (1698–1701), Huntingdon (1702–05), and Shoreham (1708). He was, as Dr. Johnson said, "a man of note among the wits, poets, and parliamentary orators in the beginning of [the eighteenth] century" (*Lives, 2,* 313). He was particularly noted for "his noisy Tory eloquence" (Hearne, *9,* 264), but he also wrote amatory verse and political pamphlets. He ran with the high church "Herd" (*POAS,* Yale, *6,* 348) which was hot to enforce the penal laws against dissenters and to "make the Bishops less dependent upon the Crown" (Vernon, *2,* 428; Bodl. MS. Rawl. A.245, f. 83v). But he left the herd in May 1702 when he was appointed a commissioner of the navy. His conversion was so complete that he could write in his memoirs that "In Publick Affairs He is naturally moderate, & somthing

And St. *John*, and *Mansell*, and *Moore*,
Who like Rogues have Forsaken now
The One Hundred and Thirty Four.   40

But I think my Affairs at Sea
Go Better than ever Before,
Since they are Employ'd who obey
The One Hundred and Thirty Four.

Their Captains Surrender with Ease   45
Their Convoy and Ships of War,
Which shews they are all of a Piece
With the One Hundred and Thirty Four.

I'll not value the *Whigs* of a Louse,
Tho' a Check be given to my *Power*,   50

---

uncertain in his oppinions, from wch two Causes he has been thought to be of both sides or somtimes of one & somtimes of the other, tho' as to the jacobites in his Heart he never was inclined to them" (Bodl. MS. Rawl. D.174, f. 87). Thus he failed to vote for the Tack, although his name does not appear in the very incomplete list of Sneakers (*A Health to the Tackers*, 2n.) in *A Numerical Calculation*.

Harcourt: Of the six defectors mentioned here, only two of them, Harcourt and St. John, are included in the list of Sneakers in *A Numerical Calculation*.

38. *Moore:* Arthur Moore (1666?–1730), "the Jaylor's Son . . . from the North of *Ireland* came," according to the words of a popular song (*Political Merriment: Or, Truths Told to Some Tune*, 1714, p. 14). An "eminent . . . instance of extraordinary rise from mean beginnings, by the mere force of natural genius," he proceeded "from being a footman, without any education, to be a great dealer in trade" (Burnet, 1823, *6*, 151–52). He made his money at first in foreign trade, becoming a director of both the East India Company and the South Sea Company, and at last "by every method," including bribery (*CJ*, *13*, 382–83) and fraud (*An Historical Essay on Mr. Addison*, 1783, p. 8). He was a member of parliament for Great Grimsby (1695–1700, December 1701–15). His appointment, in June 1704, as one of the comptrollers of the army accounts (Luttrell, *5*, 434) had a remarkable effect on his voting record. He had been one of those Tories who had "signalised" themselves in the impeachment proceedings against the Junto lords in 1701 and had voted for an extension of time for taking the abjuration oath in 1703. In November 1704, however, he failed to vote for the Tack and in 1705 he was described as a "High Church Courtier" (*Numerical Calculation*). In October 1705 he voted against Bromley for Speaker and by 1709 he appeared in *A List of Moderate Patriots* who voted to repeal the Tory place clause in the Act of Settlement.

41. *Affairs at Sea:* "A Clandestine Trade . . . whereby the *French* Fleet has been supply'd with Provisions and Ammunition of War from *England*" was under investigation in the House of Lords in November 1704 (*The Observator*, 4 November–6 December 1704).

45. *Captains Surrender:* Captain John Evans lost the *Fowey* to Saint-Pol in July 1704 when the English frigate accidentally parted company with the fleet coming home from Virginia (J. H. Owen, *War at Sea under Queen Anne 1702–1708*, 1938, Cambridge, Cambridge University Press, p. 107). Captain Thomas Kenny commanded the *Falmouth*, which Saint-Pol captured in August (ibid., pp. 111–13) and Captain William Crosse surrendered the *Elizabeth*, a new ship of 70 guns, in November 1704 (Luttrell, *5*, 488).

I'm Secure in a *Protestant* House
Of One Hundred and Thirty Four.

Am I not a politique Prince,
That have ruin'd Mankind by my Power,
To have in a *Protestant* Land   55
One Hundred and Thirty Four.

The Second Part

Cabals I have had in that Nation,
These *Fourty Five Years* and more;
I find they are not out of Fashion
With the One Hundred and Thirty Four.   60

With Wenches I doz'd an Old *Stallion*
Who *Flanders* did Sell for a *Whore.*
I'll now Play a Game of *Rebellion*
With One Hundred and Thirty Four.

I Govern'd and Gull'd Brother *Jemmy*,   65
Whilst he firmely believ'd what I Swore,
Till they Banish'd him hither to see me
From the One Hundred and Thirty Four.

I maintain now their Sham Prince of *Wales*
As I did Banish'd *Jemmy* before,   70
Tho' I wish he was gone from *Versailes*
To the One Hundred and Thirty Four.

Now to keep the Brave Allies in Heart,
I'm glad their Friend *Tallard*'s gone o're;

61. *Stallion:* Charles II.
62. *Sell:* Charles sold Dunkirk to France in 1662 (*POAS,* Yale, *1,* 419). Tutchin revives the claim that Charles diverted the proceeds of the sale to his mistresses, though there is no evidence that the money obtained from this source was so spent (Ogg, *1,* 204–05).
65. *Jemmy:* James II.
69. *Sham Prince:* Swift quotes the duke of ——— who called "*that Person, not the Pretended Prince, but the Pretended Impostor*" (Swift, *Prose, 3,* 164).
74. *Tallard:* Camille d'Hostun (1652–1728), eldest son of the comte de Tallard began his military career as a 15-year old guidon and became a marshal of France in 1703. He came to England first as the ambassador of Louis XIV (March 1698–April 1701) and returned to England in December 1704 as a prisoner of war (Luttrell, *4,* 349; *5,* 35, 498). He commanded the right wing at Blenheim, but his extreme myopia made it difficult for him to use the

I hope he'll again do his part   75
With the One Hundred and Thirty Four.

Tho' he Sheath'd his *Sword* with Disgrace,
Yet he knows how to draw a *Loui' d'ore;*
And that Weapon will always take place
With the One Hundred and Thirty Four.   80

Anjou would be left in the Lurch,
That Most *Catholick* Son of a *Whore,*
Were it not for such Sons of the Church
As the One Hundred and Thirty Four.

When my Troops from *Bavaria* were Packing,   85
No *Plaister* so fitted my Sore
As the *brawling* and *wrangling* and *TACKING*
Of the One Hundred and Thirty Four.

The *Kings* of the *Spaniards* and *Romans*
Will be humbled and turn'd out of Door,   90
If I get but a New House of Commons
Like the One Hundred and Thirty Four.

Nor shall my Firm Hopes ever faulter,
Tho' my People and I are grown poor,

---

terrain to the best advantage and he forgot apparently to call up his reserves. His positions
were overrun by Marlborough's troops, his eldest son was mortally wounded at his side, and
he himself captured in his coach fleeing from the battlefield. He remained at Nottingham,
intriguing against the government, until November 1710 (Luttrell, 6, 650), when he was
released without ransom. Louis created him duc de Tallard in March 1712.

75. *again do his part:* During Tallard's first visit to England he was alleged to have spent so
much money for bribery and intelligence that French louis d'ors became as common in Lon-
don as gold guineas (*POAS,* Yale, *6,* 337). Cf. "*Observator:* Count *Tallard,* and the other
French General Officers . . . are at *Nottingham* and *Litchfield. Country-man:* . . . can you tell
me whether Count *Tallard* has brought so many Pistoles with him this Bout as he did t'other?"
(*The Observator,* 20–23 December 1704).

81. *Anjou:* See 29n. above.

85. *Troops . . . Packing:* After Blenheim the French never seriously threatened the
Empire again.

89. *Kings:* The archduke Charles of Habsburg (1685–1740) was the second son of the
emperor Leopold I and both a cousin and a nephew (by marriage) of the last Habsburg king
of Spain, Carlos II. He was proclaimed Charles III, king of Spain, in Vienna on 1/12
September 1703 and sent off to Lisbon to seize the Spanish throne by the force of Portuguese
and English arms (*POAS,* Yale, *6,* 609–12). His elder brother, the archduke Joseph (1678–
1711), king of the Romans, succeeded his father as emperor in May 1705.

94. *poor:* The French were feeling the strain of 15 years of almost uninterrupted warfare.

'Till *Justice* has Tack'd to an Halter   95
The One Hundred and Thirty Four.

Louis had to resort to various devices to raise enough money for the war effort, including
stringent economies at court and even taxes on baptisms and marriages (Saint-Simon, *2*,
765–66).

1705

A New Ballad Writ by Jacob Tonson
and Sung at the Kit Kat Clubb on the
8th of March 1705
(March 1705?)

Three failures within three years to enact a bill to prevent occasional conformity (Luttrell, 5, 498) was a bitter defeat for the country Tories. And since they had been unswerving in their opposition to the court in the previous reign, it was not difficult to imagine the third defeat of the country Tories in the new reign as a posthumous victory for William III. William had not been a year in his grave when he was resurrected in another vision poem, *The Mitred Club* (*POAS*, Yale, 6, 506), to embolden the low church bishops to vote against the first bill to prevent occasional conformity and here he is again resurrected to exult in the failure of the third bill.

Nor was it inappropriate to imagine this exultation as "*A New Ballad Writ by Jacob Tonson and Sung at the Kit Kat Clubb on the 8th of March 1705*," the third anniversary of the death of William III. Jacob Tonson, whom the duke of Somerset was proud to call "Dear Jacob," was anathema to the Tories:

> *With leering Looks, Bullfac'd, and Freckled fair,*
> *With two left Legs, and Judas-colour'd Hair,*
> *And Frowsy Pores, that taint the ambient Air.*
> (*Faction Display'd*, 377–79, *POAS*, Yale, 6, 667)

Not only was he a poet in himself (Harry M. Geduld, *Prince of Publishers*, Bloomington, Indiana University Press, 1969, pp. 175–83), but the cause that poetry was in other men. "Jacob creates Poets," as young Alexander Pope was to discover (Nichols, *Anecdotes, 1,* 295). Tonson did not simply print and disseminate Whig propaganda; as "Secretary" and host of the Kit-Cat Club—which did not meet during his absences from London—he was at least present during discussions that determined Whig policy (Yale MS. Transcripts of Letters to Jacob Tonson, pp. 31, 40; *A Vindication of the Whigs*, 1702, pp. 8–10; *The Secret History of Clubs*, 1709, pp. 360–63).

In a kind of verse counterpart to *The Shortest-Way with the Dissenters* (1702) the poem proposes—ironically of course—a final solution to the Tory problem, *The Shortest-Way with the Tories*, a Jacobean "Scheme" (28) of fire and sword.

There is no external evidence for the date of composition, the author, or the tune of this impudent song, which is printed here for the first time.

A New Ballad Writ by Jacob Tonson and Sung at the Kit Kat Clubb on the 8th of March 1705

Let my Brittons now boast,
Cryes our Dutch Monarch's Ghost,
Of the good they Received from old Sorrell,
They the Court still shall find,
Prove Catt after kind   5
And the Herring's the same in Each Barrell.

Mother Jennings's Race,
And the Spawn of her Grace,
Shall hold Nanny fast in their clutches.
Is it not the same Thing,   10
As when I was King,
Albemarle was as good as the Dutchess.

Tho' Sunderland's dead,
Old Crawley shall Tread
In his Steps, and bring things to Perfection.   15

3. *Sorrell:* the horse William III was riding when he had his fatal fall on 21 February 1702.

5. *Catt after kind:* proverbial (Tilley, C135).

6. Also proverbial (Tilley, B94). Cf. [Francis Grose], *A Classical Dictionary of the Vulgar Tongue*, 2d ed., 1788: "HERRING. The devil a barrel the better herring; all equally bad."

7. *Mother Jennings's Race:* The duchess of Marlborough, née Sarah Jennings, had five children: four daughters, and a son who died in February 1703. Both Sarah and her second daughter, Anne, countess of Sunderland, were ladies of the bedchamber and the queen liked to have both of them with her on state occasions. *The London Gazette*, 12–16 November 1702; Luttrell, *5*, 585). Cf. *The Golden Age Revers'd*, lines 102–03: "Sarah . . . now surrounds the Throne / With her Innumerable Pigmy-spawn" (*POAS*, Yale, *6*, 526).

9. *Nanny:* Queen Anne.

12. *Albemarle:* Arnold Joost van Keppel (1670–1718) was created earl of Albemarle in February 1697 and supplanted Willem Bentinck, earl of Portland, as William's favorite Dutch courtier about the same time. This was the relationship that precipitated those rumors of "Unnatural Vice which some said [the king] was addicted to." Despite the assurance of one of William's apologists that "he was as free from it, as *Lot* when he left *Sodom*," there were many, including Jonathan Swift, who believed the rumors (*A Satyr upon King William*, 3rd ed., 1703, sig. Blv; Swift, *Prose*, *5*, 259); cf. *POAS*, Yale, *6*, 18.

   the Dutchess: In a letter of remarkable frankness the duchess mentions Anne's "having noe inclenation for any but of [her] own sex" (Blenheim MS. GI 7).

13. *Sunderland:* See *Moderation Display'd*, 29n. above.

14. *Old Crawley:* "Sir William Crawley" was a kind of code name for Godolphin. On Godolphin's death in 1712 John Aislabie observed to Colonel James Graham (or Grahme) that "Sr Wm Crawley is much lamented among the Whigs" (Levens MSS.).

Dull Church men shall Fool,
And let my Whiggs rule;
As you'l see before the next Election.

For the Body is Broke,
That Resisted my yoke,   20
Their Slavish Complyance disclosing;
And the few that are left
Of their Leaders Bereft,
Have no longer the Power of Opposing.

Thus after three years,   25
Past betwixt hopes and Fears,
I and Sunderland rise with fresh glory.
If St. James's Scheme,
Be the Cabinett's Theme,
We'll Root out the name of a Tory.   30

18. *next Election:* The Triennial Act required a new election before July 1705.

19. *Body is Broke:* The reference may be to the division in the House of Commons on 28 November 1704 when the Tory party split on the question of tacking the third bill to prevent occasional conformity to the land tax bill. "The Sticklers for the Bill were strangely disappointed, above a Hundred of those who before used to Vote with them, having deserted them on this critical Occasion; so that the Negative prevail'd by a Majority of *251* Voices against *134*" (Boyer, *Annals,* 1705, p. 173).

20. *Resisted:* William "came at last to be persuaded, that the Tories were irreconcilable to him" (Burnet, *2,* 305).

22. *the few:* presumably the 134 tackers.

23. *Of . . . Leaders Bereft:* These include the high church Tories who had been bought off by being appointed to "Places of *Profit* and *Power*" (Tutchin, *The French King's Cordial,* 34n.) and the Sneakers (*A Health to the Tackers,* 2n.).

27. *Sunderland rise:* cf. Shippen, *Moderation Display'd,* 345–46, 360.

28. *St. James's Scheme:* St. James's scheme was to make converts to Christianity by commanding "fire to come down from heaven, and consume them," but Jesus reminded him that "the Son of Man is not come to destroy men's lives, but to save them" (Luke 9:54, 56). James, and his brother John, the sons of Zebedee, were called Boanerges, which means "the sons of thunder." James, who met his death by the sword, is represented in art with sword in hand.

29. *Cabinett:* By the end of the seventeenth century most of the functions of the privy council had been taken over by a smaller group of ministers, chosen more for their political than for their administrative importance. Under Anne this inner group was known as the lords of the committee when they met in the monarch's absence, and the cabinet council, or merely the cabinet, when the queen presided (*Transactions of the Royal Historical Society,* 5th series, *7,* 137–57).

Here's a health to the Tackers, an anonymous drawing

A Health to the Tackers
A New Song
(March? 1705)

Anne's first parliament was prorogued on 14 March 1705 and although the writ for a new election was not signed until 5 April, the Triennial Act required a new election before July 1705 in any case. So *A Health to the Tackers* is probably an election song for the two Tory members for Coventry, Sir Christopher Hales and Thomas Gery. The success of the song as political propaganda can be estimated by guessing how important it may have been in raising the Tory mob that seized the town hall in Coventry, beat up Whigs who attempted to vote, and thus secured large majorities for Hales and Gery (*Review*, 10 May 1705).

Besides the Tack, the poem mentions another issue raised in the election of 1705. This was the case of *Ashby* v. *White*, which in the previous parliament had polarized not only Tory and Whig, but commoner and peer. The case had begun in January 1701 when Matthew Ashby, a Whig voter in Aylesbury, Buckinghamshire, had been prevented from voting in a parliamentary election by the Tory mayor, William White. Ashby sued White at the assizes on the grounds that he had been denied a legal right. The judge upheld his claim, but White appealed to the court of queen's bench, which reversed the judgment. Then, backed by Wharton, who managed the Whig interest in Aylesbury, Ashby took his case to the House of Lords. There it became a party cause: while the Whig majority in the House of Lords easily set aside the decision of the queen's bench, the Tory majority in the Commons denied the jurisdiction of the Lords and insisted that the Commons alone could adjudicate franchise and election disputes. The Commons backed up this claim on 5 December 1704 by ordering Ashby and the others who had brought suit against White to prison for breach of privilege (*CJ, 14,* 444–45).

Tory propagandists seized on the intervention of the Lords in *Ashby* v. *White* as an example of peers interfering in the rights of commoners and this argument appears to have swayed voters. Henry St. John wrote to the duke of Marlborough on 18 May 1705, summarizing election results to date: "Most of the changes I hitherto observ'd on the lists, are against the Torys; and it is not to be conceiv'd what a prejudice they have done their interest in all places by attempting the Tack. There is nothing checks the tide that runs against 'em, but their opposition to your Lordships proceedings in relation to the Ailesbury business, which is very far from being popular" (Blenheim MS. AI 20).

The health suddenly became a popular sub-genre during the election of 1705 and the consistently high church Tory orientation of all of them suggests the possibility of common origin. Besides the present poem, there was published *The Suffolk Health* ("Here's a Health to the *Tackers,* about let it pass"), *The Northamptonshire Health* ("Let's [or "We'll"] Remember the Men that go with us again"), *The Welch Health* ("He that Owns with his *Heart,* and Helps with his *Hand*"), *A Catch on the Election for Middlesex* ("Come my Boys, a Good Health to our *Middlesex Men*") (Copies: *Bibliotheca Lindesiana,* uncatalogued).

The health of course generated replies, or counterhealths: *The Northamptonshire Health* was reprinted with a new title, *A Health to the Northamptonshire Sneakers,* and followed on the same side of the sheet by *The Reply* ("Here's a Health to the *Knight*") (of which there are copies at Harvard and Huntington); the present poem was answered by *A Health to the Lords, in Answer to that to the Tackers* ("Here's a Health to our *Patriots,* the *Lords*") published in *The Diverting Post,* 7–14 April 1705.

The appearance of *A Health to the Tackers* in *The Diverting Post* of the week before, 31 March–7 April 1705, provides a *terminus ad quem* for the date of composition of the song, but its author unfortunately remains anonymous.

The nameless tune printed in *Aab* and *C* appears to be original, i.e. written for this song. Claude M. Simpson, in a private communication, points out that "The Tackers" appears as a tune direction (without music) in *The New Loyal Health* ("You brave Loyal Hearts ev'ry where") of which the Luttrell copy (BM: 1871.e.9 [152]) is dated 28 November 1710, and that the tune called *A Health to the Tackers* appears in *The Dancing Master,* 3d ed., 1718, *2,* 223, and in *The Compleat Country Dancing-Master,* 1719, *2,* 245.

A HEALTH TO THE TACKERS
A NEW SONG

Here's a Health to the Tackers, my Boys,
But mine Arse for the Tackers about,
May the brave *English* Spirits come in,
And the Knaves and Fanaticks turn out:
Since the Magpyes of late are confounding the State,   5
And wou'd pull our Establishments down,
Let us make 'em a Jest, for they Shit in their Nest,
And be true to the Church and the Crown.

Let us chuse such Parliament Men
As have stuck to their Principles Tight,   10
And wou'd not their Country betray
In the Story of *Ashby* and *White,*
Who care not a Turd for a Whig or a Lord,
That won't see our Accounts fairly Stated,
For *Churchill* ne're fears the Address of those Peers   15
Who the Nation of Millions have Cheated.

The next thing adviseable is,

2. *Tackers about:* On 28 November 1704 when the Commons divided on the question of
whether to tack the third bill to prevent occasional conformity to the land tax, about thirty
members, according to one Tory account, "hung down their Heads and Cowardly Deserted
the *Cause* of their *Creator*" by withdrawing from the House (*The Tackers Vindicated,* 1705, p.
4). Most of these Sneakers, as they came to be called, were the followers of Robert Harley: his
brother Edward Harley, his cousin Thomas Harley, Sir Simon Harcourt, George Granville,
and Henry St. John, plus a few opportunists like Sir Francis Child and Sir Charles Dun-
combe (*Numerical Calculation*).
3. *come in:* be elected.
5. *Magpyes:* The Tackers were equally outraged by Whiggish bishops who fouled their own
dioceses by voting against the bill to prevent occasional conformity: "a Bp. . . . read a long
Speech, and that before *Her Majesty* . . . in order to kick it out of the House" (*The Tackers
Vindicated,* 1705, p. 4).
12. *Ashby and White:* See headnote.
14. *Accounts fairly Stated:* See *Moderation Display'd,* 300n. above. In the last parliament a
bill to continue the commission to audit the public accounts had been lost. On 16 March
1704 the Lords objected to one of the names on the Commons' list and proposed to add two
more, but before these differences could be settled parliament was prorogued on 3 April
1704 (*LJ, 17,* 483, 562; *CJ, 14,* 387–88).
15. *Churchill:* The implication seems to be that although Marlborough is guilty of pecu-
lations as great as those of Halifax or Orford (Shippen, *Moderation Display'd,* 300n. above),
he need not fear investigation by the Lords, for the Lords themselves are equally guilty.

Since Schism so strangely abounds,
    To oppose ev'ry Man that's set up
By Dissenters in Corporate Towns,   20
For High Church and Low Church has brought us to no Church,
    And Conscience so Bubbl'd the Nation,
That who is not still for Conformity Bill
    Will be surely a Rogue on Occasion.

CHARLES DARBY?

The Oxfordshire Nine
April 1705

Like the two preceding poems, *The Oxfordshire Nine* is an election piece urging the Oxfordshire electors "at last to grow wise" (line 83, below) and vote Whig. "It is the Misfortune of the *English Nation* to be imposed upon by *Words*: And I doubt not," William Shippen had prophesied, "but the Name of a *Tacker* will be represented at the next *Elections* . . . as more odious than that of an *Atheist*" (*Moderation Display'd*, 1705, sig. A6v). This became the main propaganda line of the Whigs in the election of May 1705.

Lists of the Tackers began to be noticed in the newsprints in March and one was advertised for sale in *The Observator* for 5–9 May 1705, just as the general election was getting under way. Not all the lists were published by Whigs, however. Some, like the one published at Oxford (see illustration, p. 65), urged the election of "those Worthy Patriots, who [undertook] to prevent the Church of *England* from being undermined by the Occasional Conformists." Nor were all the lists printed. One, "in large Golden Capital Letters," was set into "a very large Table" at the Mitre Tavern in Fleet Street (Hearne, *1*, 59).

Worst of all, the list even produced its martyr. A Scotsman, Michael McClellan, who was campaigning for Sir John Jennings, the successful Whig candidate for Queensborough, Kent, by distributing the list of the Tackers, was beaten to death by a soldier on behalf of the Tory incumbent, Colonel Robert Crawford (Luttrell, *5*, 561, 577; [Defoe], *A Collection from Dyer's Letters*, 1706, p. 18).

The present poem, however, is an election piece in a very different register. It is low-keyed, gentle, bemused—almost a regretful exposé of the naked inconsistencies of Tackers. It exhibits the moderation that Harley had adopted as a tactic and that Defoe was publicizing: "Men of Peace . . . are the Men we ought to Choose, to represent us in Parliament," Defoe said, "Men of Moderation in the Abstracted Sence" (*Review*, 28 April 1705).

The author of *The Oxfordshire Nine* may be a Cantabrigian. In Narcissus Luttrell's manuscript note on the copy of *Aa* now in the

National Library of Scotland, the poem is "said to be writ by Mr Darby a Con: Minister in Suffolk." This is Charles Darby, born in Bramford, Suffolk, and educated at Jesus College, Cambridge. He became a fellow of Jesus College (1657–66) and then, for 45 years, the rector of Kedington, Suffolk (1664–1709) (Venn, *2*, 9). He is the author of *Bacchanalia: Or A Description of a Drunken Club*, which achieved three editions during Darby's lifetime and one after his death (*BM Catalogue, 9*, 615), *An Elegy on the Death of the Queen*, 1695, and *The Book of Psalms in English Metre*, 1704. Luttrell also attributed *The Tackers. By a Church of England Minister* ("In vain of the Battel we boast") to "Mr Darby of Suffolk" and dated it "Aprill 1705" (NLS copy). These are some doggerel verses imitative of Tutchin's *The French King's Cordial* (1704). They were also attributed to Defoe (*Daniel the Prophet No Conjurer: Or His Scandal Club's Scandalous Ballad, Called The Tackers; Answer'd Paragraph by Paragraph*, 1705), who repeatedly denied the attribution (*Review,* 5 May 1705, 12 May 1705).

The date of *The Oxfordshire Nine* is also indicated by Luttrell's gloss: "Aprill 1705."

A LIST of those Worthy Patriots, who to prevent the Church of England from being Undermined by the Occasional Conformists, did, like truly Noble Englishmen, Vote that the Bill to prevent Occasional Conformity might be Tack to the Land-Tax Bill, to secure its Passing in the House of Lords; so that this their Zeal does appear (to all Wise Men) as Conspicuous for the Interest, as their Lives are Ornaments to that Church of which they are Members.

The Names.	Places.	County.	The Names.	Places.	County.
John Anstis, Esq;	St. German,	Cornwal.	Sir Richard Howe, Bar.		Wilts.
James Anderton, Esq;	Ilcester,	Somerset.	Sir James Howe, Bar.	Hindon,	Wilts.
Hon. Arth. Annesly, Esq;	Cambridge University,	Cambridge.	Robert Hyde, Esq;		Wilts.
Sir Edward Alton, Bar.	Bridgnorth,	Salop.	William Harvey, Esq;	Old Sarum,	Wiltshire.
Hon. Thomas Bulkely, Esq;		Carnarvan.	Sir Thomas Hanmer, Bar.		Flint.
Robert Byerley, Esq;	Knaresborough,	York.	Sir Willoughby Hickman, Bar.	East Retford,	Nottingham.
Hon. Robert Bertie, Esq;	Westbury,	Wilts.	John James, Esq;	Brackly,	Northampton.
Hon. Charles Bertie, Esq;	Stamford,	Lincoln.	Sir Robert Jenkinson, Bar.		Oxon.
Hon. James Bertie, Esq;	New-Woodstock,	Oxon.	Robert Kemp, Esq;	Dunwich,	Suffolk.
Sir Edmund Bacon, Bar.	Oxford,	Suffolk.	Wilfred Lawson, Esq;		Cumberland.
Sir Charles Blois, Bar.	Dunwich,	Suffolk.	Sir Francis Leigh,		Kent.
John Bence, Esq;	Ipswich,	Suffolk.	Tho. Leigh of Lime, Esq;	Newton,	Lancaster.
Leonard Bilson, Esq;	Petersfield,	Southampton.	William Levenz, Esq;	East Retford,	Nottingham.
Sir Jacob Banks, Knt.	Minehead,	Somerset.	Henry Lloyd, Esq;	Cardigan,	Cardigan.
William Bromley, Esq;	Oxon University,	Oxon.	Warwick Lake, Esq;		Middlesex.
Sir George Beaumont, Bar.	Leicester,	Leicester.	Sir Roger Mostyn, Bar.		Chester.
Orlando Bridgman, Esq;	Wiggan,	Lancaster.	Thomas Mostyn, Esq;	Flint,	Flint.
Sir Charles Barrington, Bar.		Essex.	John Manly, Esq;	Bossiney,	Cornwal.
Sir Henry Bellasis, Kat.	Durham City,	Durham.	Sir John Mordaunt, Bar.		Warwick.
John Banks, Esq;	Corff-Castle,	Dorset.	Sir Humphrey Mackworth,	Sandwich,	Cardigan.
Sir Henry Bunbury, Bar.	Chester,	Chester.	John Mitchell, Esq;		Kent.
Richard Bingham, Esq;	Bridport,	Dorset.	Sir Edward Norreys,		Oxon.
James Buller, Esq;		Cornwal.	Francis Norreys, Esq;	Oxon City,	Oxon.
William Cage, Esq;	Rochester,	Kent.	Hon. Charles North, Esq;	Banbury,	Oxon.
William Cary, Esq;	Launceston,	Cornwal.	Hugh Parker, Esq;	Evesham,	Worcester.
John Curzon, Esq;		Derby.	Sir John Packington, Bar.		Worcester.
Thomas Coulson, Esq;	Totness,	Devon.	Sir Henry Parker, Bar.	Alisbury,	Backs.
Arthur Champney, Esq;	Dunstable,	Devon.	Granado Pigot, Esq;		Cambridge.
John Comyns, Esq;	Malden,	Essex.	William Pole, Esq;	Camelford,	Cornwal.
Charles Cæsar, Esq;	Hertford,	Hertford.	Henry Poley, Esq;	Westlow,	Cornwal.
Robert Crawford, Esq;	Queenborough,	Kent.	James Praed, Esq;	St. Ives,	Cornwal.
Hon. William Cecill, Esq;	Stamford,	Lincoln.	Thomas Price, Esq;	Webley,	Hereford.
Sir Walter Clarges, Bar.	Westminster,	Middlesex.	Thomas Polsgrave, Esq;	Norwich,	Norfolk.
William Coward, Esq;	City of Wells,	Somerset.	Henry Portman, Esq;	City Wells,	Somerset.
Henry Chivers, Esq;	Calne,	Wilts.	Sir John Parsons,	Rygate,	Surrey.
Thomas Cassin, Esq;		Dorset.	Henry Pennet, Esq;	Wotton Basset,	Wilts.
Sir William Drake, Kt. Bar.	Honiton,	Devon.	John Roll, Esq;	Salt Ash,	Cornwal.
George Dashwood, Esq;	Sudbury,	Suffolk.	Thomas Rowney, Esq;	Oxon City,	Oxon.
John Drake, Esq;	Agmondesham,	Backs.	John Snell, Esq;		
Jos. Lewis Dimmocke, Esq;		Lincoln.	Sir Edward Seymour, Bar.	Exeter,	Devon.
Richard Dyott, Esq;	Litchfield,	Stafford.	Sir John Stonehouse, Bar.		Berks.
Earl of Dysert,		Suffolk.	Peter Shackerly, Esq;	Chester,	Chester.
Sir Robert Davers,	St. Edmundsbury,	Suffolk.	Charles Seymour, Esq;	Westlow,	Cornwal.
James Darcy, Esq;	Richmond,	York.	Sir Henry Seymour, Bar.	Eastlow,	Cornwal.
Sir James Etheridge,	Great Marlow,	Backs.	Hon. William Seymour, Esq;	Totness,	Devon.
William Elson, Esq;	Chichester,	Sussex.	Francis Scobel, Esq;	Grampound,	Cornwal.
Richard Fownes, Esq;	Corfe Castle,	Dorset.	Joseph Sawle, Esq;	Tregony,	Cornwal.
William Fitch, Esq;	Malden,	Essex.	John Spark, Esq;	Newport,	Cornwal.
Ralph Freeman, Esq;		Hertford.	Hugh Smithson, Esq;		Middlesex.
Hon. Heneage Finch, Esq;	Maidstone,	Kent.	William Stephens, Esq;	Medena,	Southampton.
Charles Fox, Esq;	New Sarum,	Wilts.	Sir Bryon Stapleton, Bar.	Boroughbridge,	York.
Sir Samuel Gerard, Bar.	Agmondesham,	Backs.	Bertram Stote, Esq;		Northumberland.
Henry Gorges, Esq;		Hereford.	Thomas Strangeways, Esq;		Dorset.
Richard Gulston, Esq;	Hertford,	Hertford.	Hon. Henry Thyn, Esq;	Weymouth,	Dorset.
John Gape, Esq;	St. Albans,	Hertford.	Sir Edward Turner,	Orford,	Suffolk.
Sir William Glyn, Bar.	New Woodstock,	Oxon.	Sir John Thorold, Bar.		Lincoln.
Francis Gwinn, Esq;	Christ-Church,	Southampton.	John Toke, Esq;	East Griested,	Sussex.
Joseph Girdler, Esq;	Tamworth,	Stafford.	Sir Richard Vivian, Bar.		Cornwal.
Thomas Gery, Esq;	Coventry,	Worcick.	George Vernon, Esq;	Haslemer,	Surrey.
Hon. Francis Grevile, Esq;	Warwick,	Warwick.	John Vaughan, Esq;	Montgomery,	Montgomery.
Hon. Algernoon Grevile, Esq;	Warwick,	Warwick.	Edward Vaughan, Esq;		Montgomery.
Frederick Hern, Esq;	Hardness,	Devon.	Sir George Warburton, Bar.		Chester.
Nathaniel Hern, Esq;			Sir John Williams,		Hereford.
Richard Halford, Esq;		Rutland.	James Winstanly, Esq;	Leicester,	Leicester.
Henry Holmes, Esq;	Yarmouth,	Hampshire.	Sir William Whitlock,	Oxon University,	Oxon.
Thomas Heath, Esq;	Haslemere,	Surrey.	Leonard Wyssel, Esq;		Surrey.
Sir Christopher Hales, Bar.	Coventry,	Warwick.	John Ward, Esq;	Newton,	Lancashire.
John Hallyn, Esq;	Bodmyn,	Cornwal.	Sir John Wynn, Kt. Bar.	Canarthan,	Canarvan.

The List of the *Tackers* in Print

The Oxfordshire Nine

Perusing the List of the *Tackers* in Print,
And carefully marking what Members were in't,
Some Names I observ'd to most Counties did fall:
But *Oxford* afforded no fewer than All.
Nine Members, Nine Tackers. And more had there been,   5
And their Number as great as their Spirits were keen:
Or had this small County, more fierce than the rest,
But sent up as many as some in the West:
A desperate Risque we had presently run
Of the League being broke, and the Nation undone.   10
Then let us be grateful, and thank Heaven for't,
Since their Heads were so hot, that their Hands were so short.
But will this agree with their Courtship, thought I,
When the Queen was harangu'd and extol'd to the Sky,
In Her way to the *Bath,* by the Litterate Fry?   15

1. *the List:* See illustration, p. 65. As Defoe says (*Review,* 20 March 1705), none of the lists were entirely accurate.

8. *as many as some:* Cornwall returned 44 members to parliament, Devon 26, and Wiltshire 34.

10. *League:* the Grand Alliance between England, the Netherlands, and the Empire, which William III concluded just before his death. Lord Cutts, one of England's military heroes, argued in the Commons that the Tack "would cast a damp upon the whole Confederacy" (Boyer, *Annals,* 1705, p. 173).

14. *Queen . . . harangu'd:* The queen visited Oxford on her way to Bath on 26 August 1702, and stayed overnight. "Her Majesty was met by the Vice Chancellor, Doctors and Masters, in their Robes on Horseback at some distance from *Oxford,* whither the Earl of *Abingdon,* Lord Lieutenant of *Oxfordshire,* with the High-Sheriff and Principal Gentlemen had conducted Her Majesty from the Borders of the County. Dr. *Maunder,* the Vice Chancellor, in the Name of the University, having harangued Her Majesty, they all waited on Her to her Court at *Christ-Church.* As Her Majesty entred into the Lodgings, Dr. *Aldridge* the Dean, at the head of the Canons, paid his Duty to her Majesty in *English,* and to his Royal Highness in *Latin.* When her Majesty came into her Room of State, she was complimented in *English* Verse by Mr. *Harcourt,* Son to the Sollicitor General; and his Royal Highness by Mr. *Cowslade.* At Supper Mr. *Finch,* Son to the Honourable and Eloquent *Heneage Finch,* Esq; one of the Burgesses for the University, paid the Queen the like Compliment; and when her Majesty was retired to her Bedchamber the same was done by Mr. *Pultney,* all Gentlemen Commoners of that Society. The next Day the Queen was pleased to grace the University by her Royal Presence in Convocation. . . . From the Convocation-House the Queen went to the Theatre, where a fine Consort of Vocal and Instrumental Musick was performed, and Poems recited by Mr. *Oately* and Mr. *Restoff,* Gentlemen Commoners of *Baliol College,* and Mr. *Bilson,* Gentleman Commoner of *New College* . . . " (Boyer, *Annals,* 1703, pp. 76–77). The verses composed by Harcourt, Cowslade, Finch, and Pultney were published in *POAS,* 1716, *2,* 411–15.

Or can we imagine it mightily sutes
With Thanks for Her Gift of the Tenths and First-fruits?
Unless it be grateful in Sons of the Church
Their best Benefactress to leave in the Lurch;
And when for their sakes she had lessen'd Her Store,   20
To shut up the Purse and supply Her no more.
    For clogging it so as she cannot comply,
Is just the same thing as quite to deny.
And *Tantalus*'s Story again to revive,
By giving Her that which She cannot receive.   25
    For if a good Bill with another be join'd,
It should be with One of a sutable Kind:
But to yoak it with what is not proper to pass,
Is next to the yoaking an Ox with an Ass;
Or to imitate Him, who in Story is said   30
To couple together the Quick and the Dead.
    Or will it agree with their *Blenheim* Address,

17. *Gift:* "The 'first-fruits and tenths' of [all] benefices, originally exacted by the Pope, had, after the Reformation, been annexed by the Crown. Nominally, the incoming clergyman had to pay his whole first year's income and the tenth of every year's income; but, in fact, the 'first-fruits and tenths,' like so many old English taxes, had become a fixed charge of a much less onerous character, estimated at about £16,000 a year for the whole country . . . Queen Anne was persuaded to act a part worthy of her special love of the Church, at the instance partly of Burnet, partly of her ecclesiastical adviser, the prudent Sharp, the Tory archbishop of York. Accordingly, in February 1704 the announcement of Queen Anne's Bounty was made, and an Act of Parliament was passed that year to give it effect. She not only remitted all arrears of first-fruits and tenths to poor clergymen in debt to the government on that head, but she made over the fund itself for the increase of inadequate stipends" (Trevelyan, *1*, 47–48).

21. *shut up the Purse:* "Some Lords," Burnet said (*2*, 402), "told myself that they would never pass the Bill with this Tack, so by this means Money would be stopped."

29. *yoaking an Ox with an Ass:* forbidden in Deuteronomy 22:10.

30. *Him:* An Egyptian embalmer, who is said by Herodotus (II, 89) to have been caught in the act with a female corpse, making "love . . . the Ægyptian way," as Dryden put it: "Or as a Rhyming Authour would have sed, / Joyn the dead living, to the living dead" (Dryden, *Poems, 1*, 141).

32. *Blenheim Address:* The address at Oxford University thanking Anne for her bounty to the clergy was printed in *The London Gazette*, 7–10 August 1704. Although this address congratulated "the success of your Majesty's arms," these words could scarcely refer to the battle of Blenheim, news of which did not reach England until 10 August. Cambridge University also thanked the queen for the bounty on 20 August in an address which included an overt reference to Blenheim (ibid., 17–21 August 1704). It was not until 1 January 1705 that the dons of Oxford got round to congratulating Anne on the victory at Blenheim, and then in true Tory fashion they linked it with the battle of Málaga (p. 15 above). Indeed they contrived to make Rooke's failure to be defeated sound as impressive as Marlborough's greatest victory, describing both battles "as Beneficial as they are Glorious" (*The London Gazette*, 4–8 January 1705).

Of Speeches and Verses sent Post from the Press;
Out-running poor *Cambridg* in Loyal Pretence,
And before her in Haste, as behind her in Sense?   35
Will not this make their Poetry backward to chime,
And turn to Burlesque all *Addison*'s Rhyme?
Extolling our Valor, and mighty Success,
When they shew by their Tacking they wish it were less.
Or commending our Cause, when with the same Breath   40
By stopping our Mony they starve it to Death.
    Unless they suppose the Nine Muses alone
Would ballance the Hurt the Nine Members had done:
Or the Queen were so weak as to wink at the Wrong,
Forget the Affront, and be pleas'd with a Song.   45
    But still I was poring, and sought to Divine
What Mystery lay in the Number of Nine:
I thought the Nine Muses might serve for the feat,
Since there they have chosen their antient Seat.
But I found my Mistake e're I went very far: 50
For Tacking tends only to Discord and Jar.
    The famous Nine Worthies ran next in my Mind;
But little Agreement in this I could find:
Since nothing less worthy could ever be seen,
Than to fetter a Just and a Generous Queen.   55
Nor trust Her with Mony to manage the Sword,
But on the Condition of breaking Her Word.
    Or what could they offer less Worthy and Brave,
Than to hazard a Land they were chosen to save?

---

37. *Addison's Rhyme:* Addison, who had been a fellow of Magdalen College, Oxford, until 1703 or 1704, published *The Campaign, A Poem, To His Grace the Duke of Marlborough* ("While crouds of Princes your deserts proclaim") on 14 December 1704 (Peter Smithers, *The Life of Joseph Addison*, Oxford, Clarendon Press, 1954, pp. 89, 93).

49. *there:* Oxford.

52. *Nine Worthies:* "It is notoyrly knowen thorugh the unyversal world that there been nine worthy and the best that ever were, that is to wete, thre Paynyms, thre Jewes, and thre Crysten men," Hector, Alexander the Great, Julius Caesar, Joshua, David, Judas Maccabeus, Arthur, Charlemagne, Godefroi de Bouillon (William Caxton's preface, Sir Thomas Malory, *Le Morte Darthur*, ed. Eugene Vinaver, 3 vols., Oxford, Clarendon Press, 1967, *1*, cxliii). Cf. *Love's Labours Lost,* 5.1.113.

57. *breaking Her Word:* In her speech proroguing parliament in May 1702 Anne had promised to "be very careful to preserve and maintain the Act of Toleration" and she repeated her promise in February 1703 (*LJ, 17,* 150, 321), but Burnet (*2,* 337) saw immediately that it was "The Toleration itself" that was "aimed at" in the bill to prevent occasional conformity.

Or dangerous Tricks, and Experiments try,   60
Exposing us all to the Chance of a Die,
And venture at once both the Church and the State,
When they saw the *French Hannibal* stand at the Gate?
   But still may our *QUEEN* twice a Conqueror prove;
Of Her Foes by Her Arms, and Her Subjects by Love.   65
The last is the noblest we know of the two;
But I fear she will find 'tis the hardest to do.
   Yet let not Her Majesty wholly despair,
Tho bravest Attempts the most difficult are:
For as in Eighth *Henry* our Roses combin'd,   70
And in our First *James* the two Kingdoms were join'd:
Who knows but our *ANNE* may by Heav'n be decreed
To close the wide Wounds of a Nation that bleed?
An Union that is of Importance so high:
Nor that of our Roses, nor Realms can out-vie.   75
A Victory equal to *Blenheim* Success;
And justly deserving a Triumph no less.
And what from Her Reign we must hope for alone:
For She by her Sweetness must do it, or None.
   Let us hope then and pray our next Senate may be   80
As zealous for Peace and Agreement as She.
And that our Electors may open their Eyes;
And think it no shame at the last to grow wise.
Or if some of that List to the House should be sent;
Let us pray they may see their Mistake, and repent.   85
And the powerful Charms of her Excellent Reign

60. *dangerous . . . Experiments:* In her speech at the conclusion of the session, in March 1705, Anne warned the parliament against any such "dangerous Experiments" as the Tack for the future (*LJ, 17,* 720).

74. *Union:* For the failure of an attempt in 1702–03 to negotiate a treaty of union between England and Scotland, see p. 208 below. During the winter of 1704–05, however, amidst the crisis created by the Tack and the case of the Aylesbury electors, and with England and Scotland on the verge of war, an act empowering the queen again to appoint commissioners to negotiate a treaty of union was passed in December 1704 and received the royal assent in March 1705 (*LJ, 17,* 596, 606, 717).

81. *Peace and Agreement:* Anne concluded her speech on 14 March 1705 by exhorting the parliament to "Peace and Union" and urging them to proceed to the election of new members "with the greatest Prudence and Moderation" (*LJ, 17,* 720).

85. *repent:* Only 90 of the 134 Tackers survived the 1705 election (Speck, p. 108), and all of those present at the opening of parliament in October 1705 voted impenitently against the court in the division over the speakership between the Whig, John Smith, and the Tory, William Bromley, member for Oxford University and leader of the Tackers.

May sweeten their Tempers, and fetch them again.
Until, with a Blush, they reflect on that Vote,
As a taking three Kingdoms at once by the Throat:
And the only Unkindness that ever was shown   90
To the Kindest of Queens, since she sat on the Throne:
And may so regret the Indignity past,
That as 'twas the first, so it may be the last.

The Tack
(April–May? 1705)

The Tack was no nine days' wonder. It marked the momentary triumph of moderation over high church extremism. It split the Tory party and was a major issue at the polls in May 1705, as the two preceding poems attest. The notorious 134 were subjected to the most vitriolic Whig abuse. Tutchin railed at them in *The Observator*. Defoe rebuked them in the *Review*, on one occasion describing a Tacker as "a Man of Passion, a Man of heat, a Man that is for ruining the Nation upon any hazards, to obtain his ends . . . A Man that to gratifie his Passion, foolishly call'd Zeal, would run us upon the most dangerous Experiment that ever this Nation Escap'd" (*The Moderation, Justice and Manners of the Review*, 1706, p. 17). *The Character of a Tacker* made even more exaggerated claims: "A *true Tacker* is a true *Jefferys;* that is to say, An abandon'd Slave to the Popish Interest . . . A *Tacker* is a *Jacobite* in Disguise . . . A *Tacker*, in fine, is one who denying that we ought to live by Law, ought by his own Rule to be *HANG'D without Law*" (*A List of Those Worthy Patriots*, n.d., pp. 5–6).

The paper war over the Tackers was one of the most bitter of Anne's reign. In response to the overheated rhetoric of the Whigs, the Tories undertook to represent the Tackers as honest patriots and loyal churchmen. The following poem is one of the best of these Tory coolants. It gaily elevates the Tack into a principle of universal application, like sympathetic magic or gravitation, and then in transcendent innocence asks: What's all the fuss about tacking the bill to prevent occasional conformity to the land tax bill?

Dated 1705 in two manuscript copies (*BM*), *The Tack* apparently was first printed by William Pittis in *The Whipping Post* for 21 August 1705. But this date seems rather late. In two commonplace books (*HM*) *The Tack* occurs next to *The Welch Health*, an election song (p. 60 above), and it was during the election of May 1705 that excitement about the Tack reached its apogee.

There is no evidence to identify the author or the tune.

THE TACK

The Globe of Earth on which we dwell
    Is Tack'd unto the Poles.
Those little Worlds our Carkasses
    Are Tack'd unto our Souls.

The Parsons Work is Taylor like,   5
    To Tack the Soul to Heaven,
The Doctor's is to keep the Tack
    'Twixt Soul and Body Even.

The Priest besides, by's Office Tacks
    The Husband to the Wife,   10
And that's a Tack, God help 'em both,
    That often lasts for Life.

The Lawyer studys, how to Tack
    His Client to the Laws;
The Atturney Tacks whole Quires and Rheams   15
    To lengthen out the Cause.

The Commons, Lords, and *English* Crown
    Are all three Tack't together
And if they chance e'er to Untack,
    No good can come to either.   20

The Crown is Tack'd unto the Church,
    The Church unto the Crown.
The Whiggs are slightly Tack'd to both,
    And so may soon come down.

Since all the World's a general Tack,   25
    Of one thing to another,
Then why about one honest Tack,
    Do Fools keep such a Pother?

9–10. *Tacks | The Husband to the Wife:* Cf. Goldsmith, *The Good Natur'd Man* (1768), ed. Arthur Friedman, Oxford, Clarendon Press, 1966, *5,* 80: "if the two poor fools have a mind to marry, I think we can tack them together."

The Dyet of Poland,
A Satyr
(July 1705)

It is clear that what Poland meant to Defoe was a country divided and almost destroyed by party conflict. "We are at present the most divided Nation in *Europe,*" he complained in May 1705, "The *Polanders* are Fools to us" (184*n.* below). Lurking in the background of the poem, however, and nowhere stated but everywhere implied, is another analogy between Poland and England—or a cautionary tale about succession to the throne and foreign invasion. Most Englishmen had been delighted when the Protestant Charles XII of Sweden had driven Catholic Friedrich August from the throne of Poland, because it seemed like a parallel to Protestant William of Orange driving Catholic James II from the throne of England. But Defoe found the parallel specious (*Review,* 12 August 1704), so in *The Dyet of Poland* he recast Charles XII as Louis XIV and Friedrich August as Queen Anne. In the new interpretation, the fable runs like this: in 1697 Friedrich August, elector of Saxony [Queen Anne], secured election by the diet of Poland [the bill of rights] as successor to Jan Sobieski [William III]; in January 1702, however, Charles XII [Louis XIV] invaded Poland; the country was mercilessly ravaged and Friedrich August forced to flee; in July 1704 the diet was forced to elect Charles XII's nominee, Stanislaus Leszczynski [James Francis Edward, the pretended Prince of Wales] as king of Poland [England]. "Strange and wonderful News from *Poland,*" Defoe exclaimed (*The Master Mercury,* 25 September 1704). And when he called Admiral Sir George Rooke, "Rokosky," and the country Tories, "Rookites," Defoe may have known that there was a faction opposed to Friedrich August called "Rokosians" (493*n.* below; Defoe, *Letters,* p. 61; Luttrell, *4,* 387). But in any case the moral of the fable is clear: the divisive policies of the Tories in the first parliament of Anne could have led, as they did in Poland, to foreign invasion and a puppet king. "England," as Defoe summed it up, "*has made a very Narrow Escape*" (*Review,* 5 May 1705).

These are some of the reasons that may have led Defoe to cast his most ambitious party satire in Polish terms. There were both traditional and practical reasons for projecting the satire "in other terms." A tradition reaching down from Aristophanes, through Lucian and Cyrano de Bergerac, encouraged the invention of imaginary or foreign settings for satire. Swift had attacked the country Tories in terms of classical Roman analogues in *A Discourse of the Contests and Dissentions* in 1701 and in 1709 Delariviere Manley would invent New Atalantis to attack the Churchills. And the use of "covert names" to avoid prosecution for libel or *scandalum magnatum* was simply a matter of prudence (*POAS*, Yale, *6*, 226).

In her speech at the opening of the session in November 1703, which had been written by Godolphin and Harley, Anne enjoined her parliament to "perfect Peace and Union" (Feiling, p. 371; *CJ*, *14*, 211). The strategy of the duumvirs was to win support from "the Moderate Men of both Partyes," in Defoe's phrase. Harley called them "men in the public interest" (*Letters*, p. 53; HMC *Portland MSS.*, *2*, 188). In practice this meant splitting both parties and winning the support of moderate men of each. Harley did this when he brought into the government Henry St. John, a country Tory, and John Holles, duke of Newcastle, a court Whig. Defoe's advice to Harley to split the Whigs, "they are Easy to be divided," must have been most acceptable, for this is exactly what Harley was doing. And on 28 November 1704 the Tories split themselves when about a hundred of them deserted "The wild faction in the House," as Harley called them (HMC *Portland MSS.*, *2*, 188), and voted against the Tack.

By this time Defoe was hearing people say (correctly) that Harley "Loves Neither Side" (*Letters*, p. 67). Neither did Defoe. There can be no doubt that mutual distrust and rejection of the emerging party system (Vernon, *3*, 91; 139*n*. below) provided a base for collaboration between Harley and Defoe. Defoe's theory can serve equally well for a description of Harley's practice: " a just Ballance of Parties must preserve the Peace of *England*, as the Ballance of Power preserves the Peace of *Europe*" (*Review*, 12 June 1705). But even this is slightly misleading, because moderation for Defoe as well as for Harley was a strategy, a practical response to a political stimulus, not a philosophy of politics. "Govern, as That Every Party shal believe you Their Own," was Defoe's advice to Harley (*Letters*, p. 42).

Harley and Defoe certainly disagreed on how wide the moderate band of the spectrum should be. Defoe would have included the more conservative members of the Whig Junto. In his letters to Harley he urged the inclusion of Somers: "Such a Man Can Not be bought too Dear," he said (*ibid.*, p. 69). But Defoe's retrospective praise of Halifax, Orford, and Somers:

> Satyr look back, Survey the Glorious Roll,
> The Life of *Polish* Power, the Nations Soul,
> (203–04)

must have sounded hollow to Harley who had worked tirelessly to secure their impeachment in 1701.

So the satire in *The Dyet of Poland* is really directed agains the extremists of both parties, "the Men of Fury, let them be of what Party they will," as Defoe called them, or "the merciless men of both parties" in Queen Anne's words (*Review*, 2 June 1705; *Letters of Queen Anne*, p. 172). This explains why—in spite of the violence of the attack against Nottingham, Seymour, Rooke, and the rest—the tone of the poem is conciliatory. Defoe undoubtedly believed that the extremists in both parties were beyond redemption: "till the Leprosie of Strife, which is upon them, is Cur'd, *Let them be shut out of the Congregation*" (*Review*, 1 May 1705). But for the rest, whom Defoe and Harley considered "the Substantiall part of the Nation"—both in number and estate—the poem is saying, "Come in, Come, and joyn with us to . . . make a firm Peace of Partys" (*Review*, 8 May 1705).

The political purpose of the poem, therefore, is ecumenical. It is not to gloat over the fall, but to put Humpty together again. Defoe had high hopes for this poem: "I am Sure of its being Very Usefull," he told Harley, "I Expect strange Effects from it as to the house" (*Letters*, p. 19). It may be surmised that these "strange Effects" were the "perfect Peace and Union" that the queen desired. *The Dyet of Poland* begins with "furious Tempests" and "worse Storms," works its way through some of Defoe's most reckless personal satire, and ends in calm and safety while "*Moderation* Guides the Helm of State" (1325).

The earliest reference to *The Dyet of Poland* occurs in a letter that was probably written in June 1704. This is the letter quoted above in which Defoe mentions the poem to Harley for the first time and importunes him to let Defoe "Perfect it and Turn it abroad into the World." Defoe was just about to undertake his first assignment for Harley, that incredible junket through East Anglia, "Spreading Principles of Temper, Moderation, and Peace," as he said, "Thro' Countrys [i.e. counties] where I go." He wanted to take the manuscript of *The Dyet of Poland* with him, "As I am Sure of its being Very Usefull." By 7 July 1704

Defoe was eagerly awaiting Harley's verdict, of which, unfortunately, there is no trace beyond the fact that the poem was published (*Letters*, pp. 60, 19, 26).

After the first phase of its prepublication existence, the poem entered a second stage of private circulation in print. Here the source is a hostile witness, William Pittis, but the circumstantiality of the story makes it sound convincing: *The Dyet of Poland*, Pittis says, was "Printed in *Bartholomew Close* . . . dispers'd secretly and clandestinely . . . left at particular Coffee-Houses and Taverns . . . shewn about publickly, and the Meaning of it explain'd, for some Months before it was pub-lish'd, by the Author of it" (*The Case of the Church of England's Memorial Fairly Stated*, 2d ed., 1705, p. 39; cf. *The Whipping Post*, 10 July 1705; Hearne, *1*, 4–5). The printer in Bartholomew Close was John Darby, Jr. (*The Observator*, 23–26 May 1705), whose father probably published the "true" edition of *The True-Born Englishman* for Defoe in 1700 (*POAS*, Yale, *6*, 763).

The first reference to the printed poem may be that of René L'Her-mitage, the Dutch resident in London, who reported on 20 July 1705 that "la Diette de Pologne . . . une espèce de satyre du Parlement" had been published a few days ago, "depuis peu" (BM MS. Add. 17677AAA, f. 375v). This date agrees well enough with the notices of the poem in *The Whipping Post* for 17 July and 24 July 1705. Defoe set out from London to Brentford on his second assignment for Harley on 16 July 1705, presumably without having proofread the poem (cf. p. 638 below). Demand for copies was so great that three editions were required in six months.

In addition the poem was twice reprinted as the basis for an answer by William Pittis of which there were two editions in 1705. Pittis, who also wrote *The True-Born Englishman: A Satyr, Answer'd* (1701), must have worked from a prepublication copy, for *The Dyet of Poland, A Satyr. Consider'd Paragraph by Paragraph* was said to have been "Just publish'd" on 15 July (Hearne, *1*, 7). Pittis of course was well-ac-quainted with Defoe's earlier verse (154*n.*, 826–27*n.* below), but on other subjects strangely uninformed (470*n.*, 897*n.*). He even confuses Francis Gwyn, a country Tory, with Sir Rowland Gwyn, a court Whig (*The Dyet of Poland, A Satyr. Consider'd Paragraph by Paragraph.*, 1705, p. 51), just as anyone might do today. His comments are designated (*D*) in the footnotes that follow. The Key included in the third edition of the poem is cited as *Key*.

THE DYET OF POLAND,
A SATYR

In Northern Climes where furious Tempests blow,
And Men more furious raise worse Storms below,
At Nature's Elbow, distant and remote,
Happy for Europe *had She been forgot,*
The World's *Proboscis,* near the Globe's Extremes,   5
For barb'rous Men renown'd, and barb'rous Names,
There *Poland* lies too much her Maker's Care,
And shares the mod'rate Blessings of the Air,
Just as far off from Heav'n as we are here:
    Under the Artick Circle of the Sky,   10
Where Vertues Streams run Low, and Natures high,
For Heat of Clime too far, of Blood too nigh,
Temper'd for Plenty, plenteously supply'd
With Men advanc'd in ev'ry Grace *but Pride.*
    A mighty Nation throngs the groaning Land,   15
Rude as the Climate, num'rous as the Sand:
Uncommon monstrous *Vertues* they possess,
Strange odd prepostrous *Polish* Qualities;
Mysterious Contraries they reconcile,
The *Pleasing Frown* and the *Destroying Smile;*   20
Precisely gay, and most absurdly grave,
Most *humbly high,* and *barbarously brave;*
Debauch'dly Civil and *Prophanely Good,*
And fill'd with *Gen'rous* brave *Ingratitude,*
By *Bounty disoblig'd,* by *Hatred won,*   25
Bold in their Danger, Cowards when 'tis gone;
To their own Ruin they're the only Tools,
Wary of Knaves, and eas'ly chous'd by Fools;

---

3. *Nature's Elbow:* "Natures *Backside* would have done as well every Jot, but it's a *Paw
Word,* as the Observator tells his Countryman *Roger* [*The Observator,* 30 May–2 June 1705],
and must be flung aside for being Uncourtly" (*D*).

8. *mod'rate:* See p. 19 above.

19. *Contraries:* "A *True-Born Englishman*'s a Contradiction" (Defoe, *The True-Born English-
man,* 372, *POAS,* Yale, *6,* 277).

24. *Ingratitude:* "*Ingratitude,* a Devil of *Black Renown,* / Possess'd her [England] very early
for his own" (ibid., 159–60).

Profoundly empty, yet *declar'dly wise,*
And fond of blind Impossibilities;   30
Swell'd with Conceit, they boast of all they do,
First praise themselves, then think that Praise their Due:
So fond of flatt'ring Words, so vain in Pride,
The World *Mocks* them, and they the World *Deride;*
Value themselves upon their Nations Merit,   35
In Spight of all the Vices they inherit;
So wedded to the Country where they dwell,
They think that's Heav'n, and all the World's a Hell.
Their frozen *Vistula* they'd not forgo
For fruitful *Danube,* or the flow'ry *Po.*   40
Rapid *Boristhenes* delights them more
Than pearly Streams, or a *Peruvian* Shore:
And *Russian Dwina* dwells upon their Song,
Hurried by barb'rous Steeps and Hills, and pusht along.
    The Land too happy would the People bless,   45
Could they agree to know their Happiness;
Nature with very liberal Hand supplies
Her Situation-Insufficiencies:
The temperate Influence revolves of Course,
And Spight of Climate Nature works by Force.   50
The bounteous Spring the Winters Wast repairs,
And makes the World grow young in Spight of Years.
The fruitful Earth uncommon Freedom shows,
And foreign Wealth by foreign Commerce flows.
    But Peopl'd with a hard'ned Thankless Race,   55
Whose Crimes add Horror to the milder Place,
The Bounties by indulgent Heav'n bestow'd
Corrode the Mischief and debauch the Blood.
That Native Fierceness which in Christian Lands
Makes Heroes, and their Poets Praise commands,   60
Here 'tis a Vice, which rankles up to *Fewd,*
And nourishes the Gust of vile Ingratitude.

32. *praise themselves:* "*An* Englishman *ne're wants his own good word*" (ibid., 581).
    43–44. "Neither are the two last Lines the most sensible Mr. *Foe* has written in his Life, though they are very Musical to the Ear" (*D*). Cf. "The Trumpeter's out of Tune at the first Note; that is, he has no manner of Musick in the first Line" ([William Pittis], *The True-Born Englishman: A Satyr, Answer'd,* 1701, p. 67).
    59. *Fierceness:* "Fierce as the *Britain*" (*The True-Born Englishman,* 431).

Pride, Plenty's Hand-maid, deeply taints their Blood,
And Seeds of Faction mix the Crimson Flood.
Eternal Discords brood upon the Soil,   65
And universal Strifes the State embroil.
In every Family the Temper reigns,
In every Action Seed of Gall remains.
The very Laws of Peace create Dispute,
And makes them quarrel who shall execute.   70
Their valu'd Constitutions are so lame,
That Governing the Governments inflame.
Wild Aristocracy torments the State,
And People their own Miseries create.
    In vain has Heav'n its choicer Gifts bestow'd,   75
And strives in vain to do *a Wilful* Nation Good:
Such is the Peoples Folly, such their Fate,
As all Decrees of Peace anticipate.
Immortal Jarrs in ev'ry Class appear,
Conceiv'd in Strife, and Nurs'd to Civil War.   80
    Such, *Poland,* is thy People, such thy Name,
Yet still thy Sons our Panegyricks claim,
Because their partial Genius is inclin'd
To think they merit more than all Mankind.
    Imaginary Happiness will do   85
For near as many Uses as the true:
And if the *Poles* in their own Plagues delight,
Wise Heaven's too just to let them thrive in Spight.
    Great *Sobieski* had their Crown obtain'd,
With steady Glory thirteen Years he Reign'd,   90
And none *but who some Mischief meant,* complain'd.
His Conqu'ring Sword made all Men think it fit,
That he who sav'd the Land should Govern it.
The Field of Battle he had first possest,
By Sixty Thousand slaughter'd *Turks* confest.   95

63–64. *Pride . . . And . . . Faction:* "*Pride,* and *Strife,* are Natives of our Soil" (Defoe, *The Pacificator,* 21, *POAS,* Yale, *6,* 160).

84. *merit more:* "And think whate're they have, they merit more" (*The True-Born English-man,* 623).

89. *Sobieski:* "Now he begins to fall into Particulars, and by Great *Sobieski* must be meant *K. W*[*illiam*], who Reign'd over us Thirteen Years" (*D*).

91. *Mischief meant:* The "Mischief" was the intent to restore James II to the throne.

95. *Sixty Thousand slaughter'd Turks:* King William "Conquer'd *Ireland* . . . after the Loss of Sixty Thousand *French* and *Irish* that sided with the Unfortunate King *James*" (*D*).

The fatten'd Frontiers felt the reeking Flood,
And dy'd the Soil with *Asiatick* Blood.
The weeping *Neister* half the Host receives,
Hurries them down to darker *Euxine* Graves:
And *Mahomet*'s insulting Banners lay 100
Beneath the Cross, his Valour's easie Prey.
    With mild and gentle, but with steady Hand,
He rather led than rul'd th'uneasie Land.
Fill'd with Important Cares, he saw their Fate,
And all the growing Mischiefs their own Feuds create; 105
Which made him less repine, and less deplore
To quit the Crown with such Concern he wore.
    Tell us, ye Sons of Policy and Fraud,
Whose vast Intrigues your selves alone applaud;
Who always plot too deep, and soar too high, 110
And Damn the Nations Peace you know not why.
What ail'd the *Poles,* with Peace and Plenty blest,
To change for Years of Blood their Days of Rest?
Describe the Men of Avarice and Pride,
With all Ambition's dark Disguise array'd; 115
How, for the Nation's Liberty, they Cant
Till those *they say abuse it* they supplant,
And then the mock pretended Sham lay by,

98. *Neister:* the Boyne River, 25 miles north of Dublin, which William crossed against the opposition of James II's army on 1 July 1690. The casualty figures are subject to epic heightening: instead of "half" of "Sixty Thousand," "between 1000 and 1500 Men" of James II's army and "nigh four hundred" of William's army were killed in the fighting (George Story, *An Impartial History of the Wars of Ireland,* 1691, p. 85).

100. *Mahomet:* James II. This detail too is subject to epic heightening: it was "Some of Duke *Schonberg*'s . . . Horse," not William III, who "took one or two of King *James*'s Standards" (ibid., p. 83).

101. *his:* William's.

103. *rather led than rul'd:* William told Antonie Heinsius, the Dutch pensionary, in November 1700 of his refusal to dragoon the English, "not being able," he said, "to play any other game with these people than engaging them imperceptibly" (Grimblot, *2,* 479).

109. *Intrigues:* In another letter to Heinsius of April 1700 William described the late session of parliament in these terms: "The members have separated in great disorder, and after many extravagances. Unless one had been present, he could have no notion of their intrigues; one cannot even describe them" (ibid., *2,* 398).

112–13. Cf. *Absalom and Achitophel* (1681), 165–66: "Else why should he, with Wealth and Honours blest, / Refuse his Age the needful hours of Rest?"

117. *supplant:* "*I have seen* the same Persons . . . being receiv'd into Places and Preferments . . . cry up those Men for Patriots of their Country, who before, they Reproach'd as Betrayers of the Nation" (*Review,* 9 September 1712).

Pleas'd with the Profits of Authority.

    Statesmen are Gamesters, Sharp and Trick's the Play,   120
Kings are but Cullies, wheedl'd in to Pay;
The Courtiers' Foot-balls, kick'd from one to one,
Are always Cheated, oftentimes Undone;
Besieg'd with Flatt'ry, false Report, and Lies,
And sooth'd with Schemes of vast Absurdities.   125
The jangling Statesmen clash in their Designs,
Fraud fights with Fraud, and Craft to Craft inclines;
Stifly engage, quarrel, accuse and hate,
And strive *for Leave* to help undo the State;
For all the strong Contention ends in this,   130
Who shall *the Pow'r of doing Ill* possess:
Envy and Strife are only rais'd so high,
Because a Man's a greater Knave than I:
But if I can his Place and Wealth succeed,
He rails of Course, and I'm the Knave indeed.   135
Places and Pensions are the *Polish* Spoil
Which all sides please, and all sides reconcile.
'Tis natural to all the Sons of Men,
To *Rail* and *Plot* when out, be *Quiet* in.

    Long had Divided *Poland* felt the Smart   140
Of vast Intrigues and Politicians Art:
As many Men of Character and Blood,
So many Thieves about the Scepter stood;
As many Gifts th'Exhausted Prince could give,

---

119. "If he would fasten upon any one of the Country Party, for taking of Places, after they had rail'd at Men in Offices, we can give him two of the C[ourt] side . . . for one, by way of Exchange" (*D*).

129. *for Leave:* Defoe is quoting the formula by which bills are introduced in parliament. Cf. "the Parliament had not sat long, before Mr. *William Bromley* moved in the House of Commons, *That Leave be given to bring in that Bill* [to prevent occasional conformity]" (Boyer, *History*, p. 161).

139. *out . . . in:* The phrase is a Defoe commonplace: "The Grand Contention's plainly to be seen, / To get some men put out, and some put in" (*The True-Born Englishman*, 13–14; cf. "really, at the bottom, the whole Quarrel is guided by the Interests of Parties, Places, Preferments, to get Some in, and Some out" (*A Challenge of Peace, Address'd to the Whole Nation*, 1703, p. 5); "I have seen the Bottom of all Parties . . . *All is a meer Show, Outside, and abominable Hypocrisie,* of every Party, in every Age, under every Government, in every Turn of Government; when they are OUT to get IN, when IN, to prevent being OUT" (*Review*, 9 September 1712).

144. *Gifts:* In the 1690s William made lavish grants of the estates of English and Irish Jacobites that had fallen to the crown under judgments of outlawry: 135,820 acres to Willem

So many Friends he only seem'd to have: 145
The craving Wretches hang about the Throne,
He gave them all the Nation's Wealth, and all his own.
    Not all the Conquer'd Lands the *Turk* resign'd,
Not all the World, had he the World obtain'd,
Wou'd their insatiate Avarice suffice,   150
Supply their Hands or satisfie their Eyes;
Who shall unhappy sinking *Poland* save,
What Gifts can close the Hands that always crave,
Unsatisfi'd as Death, and greedy as the Grave?
At every just Refusal Discontent,   155
And rave *for Want of Bribes* at Government.
    The valiant *Sobieski* had bestow'd
Moldavian Lands he conquer'd by his Sword.
He thought it just *that Province* to bestow
On those whose Valour helpt to make it so;   160
But all the wiser Men who had no Share,
Against the Justice of the Gift declare,
Oblige the yielding Hero to recant,

Bentinck, earl of Portland; 108,633 acres to Arnold Joost van Keppel, earl of Albemarle; 77,290 acres to Richard Coote, earl of Bellamont; and 70-odd more grants. To Portland he also gave the manors of Denbigh, Bromfield, and Yale, traditionally reserved for the Prince of Wales (HMC *Lords MSS.*, New Series, *4*, 34–35, 46) and the manor of Swaden, worth £2,000 a year (Luttrell, *3*, 472). As a result, Portland was "supposed to be the richest Subject in *Europe*" (Macky, p. 62).

148. *the Turk:* James II. In May 1695 William gave 95,649 acres, "all the private estate of the late King James," to Elizabeth Villiers, his discarded mistress (HMC *Lords MSS.*, New Series, *4*, 54).

154. "But this I have to say for him, when he turns Plagiary, he makes bold with his own Works . . . Witness *Unsatisfied as Death, and Greedy as the Grave,* which are apply'd to . . . Sir R[obert] Cl[ay]ton in his Satyr call'd the *Reformation* [*of Manners*, 233, *POAS*, Yale, *6*, 409]" (*D*).

158. "By *Moldavia* is meant *Ireland*" (*D*)

159. *thought it just:* Defoe paraphrases William's address to the Commons in February 1699: "I was not only led by Inclination, but thought myself obliged in Justice, to reward those who had served well, and particularly in the Reduction of *Ireland,* out of the Estates forfeited to me by the Rebellion there" (*CJ, 13,* 228).

163. *recant:* Although property forfeited under a judgment of outlawry reverts to the crown, the country Tories had been trying since 1689 to divert the income into the public treasury to defray the costs of William's war. Finally in April 1699, by tacking it to a money bill, they were able to pass a bill for an account to be taken of the forfeited estates in Ireland and a year later, after the report of the commissioners had been heard, the Tory majority in the Commons succeeded in tacking to the land tax a bill resuming all of William's grants of Irish estates. To avert a financial panic William reluctantly gave his assent to the bill and prorogued the parliament (Luttrell, *4*, 632–33).

And re-bestow the hasty envy'd Grant.
But tell us, now, ye Men of *Polish* Wit,   165
How the *Moldavian* feels the formal Cheat;
Let *Annesleski* reimburse the Bribes,
Ravisht to wrong, instate the *Polish* Tribes.
Let all the sham Conveyances appear,
The Phantosme Sales, and Fancy'd Purchaser.   170
Let some true Satyr all that Grievance lash,
Lands without Title, Buyers without Cash.
Under the weighty Fraud *Moldavia* bleeds,
And private Cheat the publick Cheat succeeds;
Retrieving Laws by vast Designs Push'd on,   175
Cover Great Sobieski'*s Errors by their own.*

With all these Frauds and Feuds and Millions more,
Which rack'd the injur'd *Poles,* and kept them poor,
Wise *Sobieski,* with strong Cares opprest,
Dismist the Throne, and chose to be at Rest;   180
Embroil'd he left them, whom embroil'd he found,
And Great *Augustus,* with his Pow'rs Enthron'd.
In vain the new Crown'd Monarch strives to please,

166. *Cheat:* One pamphleteer called the resumption of William's grants of Irish estates "a great Blow to the Protestant Interest in *Ireland*" (*Short Remarks upon the Late Act of Resumption of the Irish Forfeitures,* 1701, p. 14) and another added that "nothing could have been devised more Injurious and Detrimental to the *English* Protestant Interest in *Ireland,* than that fatal Bill" (*The Popish Pretenders to the Forfeited Estates,* 1702, p. 3).

167. *Annesleski:* Francis Annesley was a grandson of Francis Annesley, Viscount Valentia, and a half nephew of Arthur Annesley, first earl of Anglesey. He became some kind of agent for the duke of Ormonde and a seat in the Irish House of Commons was obtained for him in Ross, "a town of the Earl of Anglesey's" (HMC *Ormonde MSS., 8,* 40, 56, 291). He was one of the original directors of the new East India Company (Chamberlayne, 1700, p. 597). As chairman of the commission for the Irish estates that had been resumed in 1700 (163*n.* above), he assured Simon Harcourt that "the Trustees are very unwilling to do anything to displease the least of their masters" (HMC *Ormonde MSS., 8,* 41). But in spite of this complaisance, one paragraph in his report of February 1702 was voted false and scandalous by the Irish Commons and Annesley was expelled the House (Luttrell, *5,* 345, 346). Subsequently he sat in the English parliament for Preston (1705–08) and Westbury (1708–15, 1720–34) as a member of the October Club and Hanoverian Tory.

167. *Bribes:* "The Trustees for managing the *Irish* Forfeitures . . . lived in great State . . . being much hated, and openly charged with partiality, injustice, and corruption" (Walter Harris, *History of the Life and Reign of William-Henry, Prince of Nassau and Orange,* Dublin, 1749, p. 493).

176. *Sobieski's Errors:* "[William's] greatest Infirmity was too much Bounty" (*Review,* 22 March 1707).

182. *Augustus:* Queen Anne.

Or Cure th'Hereditary vile Disease,
In vain Confed'rates with the Nations Friends,   185
In vain their Laws and Freedom he defends.
The Parties joyn, in Grand Cabals they meet
The Monarch's healing Projects to defeat;
Grasp at his Gifts, and share the high Reward,
But not his Honour or Commands regard.   190
Not Sacred Oaths can their Allegiance bind
Farther than by their Int'rest they're inclin'd;
Prompted by Avarice and deep Revenge,
With Fawning Face, and awkward Zeal they Cringe;
But all *that can no Royal Bounty share,*   195
Their factious Thoughts and strong Disgusts declare;
No Bounds their feign'd Alleg'ance can secure,
To Day they'll swear, *to Morrow they'll abjure.*
    The Monarch willing to dissolve the Feud,
That spread too fast in their infected Blood,   200
Summons the General Dyet to appear,
The Nations and his own Demands to hear.
    Satyr look back, Survey the Glorious Roll,
The Life of *Polish* Power, the Nations Soul,
Poland's Collection, all the Peoples Breath,   205
The Monarch's Safety and the Tyrant's Death.
The antient Lords of the JAGELLAN Line,

184. *th'Hereditary vile Disease:* faction. "We are at present the most divided Nation in *Europe*," Defoe said, "The *Polanders* are Fools to us" (*Advice to All Parties*, 1705, p. 2). His cure for the disease was coalition government: "a Union of Parties is the only step to this Nations Settlement" (ibid.).

187. *Parties joyn:* not with each other, but in party caucuses; cf. p. 133 below.

197–98. The first meaning of the lines is that politicians out of office and courtiers out of favor will take the oaths of allegiance to Anne today and abjure them tomorrow if the pretender is brought in. But the word "abjure" recalls the last act that received the assent of William III (13 William III c. 6). It required officeholders and members of parliament to abjure the pretender. Many Tories hesitated to take the oath and the time for taking it had to be extended to 1 August 1703 by another act of parliament (1 Anne Stat. II c. 17).

201. *Summons:* Anne addressed parliament on 11 March 1702, three days after William's death (Boyer, *Annals*, 1703, pp. 6–7).

206. *the Tyrant's Death:* "*The TYRANT'S DEATH,* Squints . . . at their Old Practice of Decollation, which the Party [Defoe] is Advocate for, has no small Veneration for the Memory of, at their Cruel Festivals on the Anniversary of Her Majesty's Royal Grand-Fathers Martyrdom [the calves' head feasts on 30 January]" (*D*).

207. *JAGELLAN:* Jagiello, or Jagellon (1350–1434), as Wladislaus II, was the first of the Jagiellonic kings (1386–1572) who transformed Poland from a parcel of petty principalities

Here in their representing Glory shine,
With Loyal Hearts, and strong Industrious Hands,
Ready to hear *Augustus* great Commands.   210
The antient *Polish* Greatness to restore,
Assist with Council, and support with Power;
    What tho' among th' Illustrious Troop there's found,
Some less Polite than some, and some unsound.
The Devil among *the sacred Twelve* appear'd,   215
But Devils *once known* are no more to be fear'd;
The General Votes to Loyalty encline,
And Mischief sinks beneath her own Design.
Satyr, if there's a *Pole* among the Tribes,
Less true than Truth it self, *'tis him* thy Verse describes.   220
    Here Great *Taguski* first in Order came
Of bright, unspotted, tho' suspected Fame.
Youth had supply'd his Head with parent Wit,
In Judgment solid, and in Sense compleat;
The Muses him with early Garlands Crown'd,   225
Sublime in Verse, and in his Phrase profound;
Polite in Language, in his Satyr strong,
Yet kills with all the Softness of a Song:
To steady Justice all his Thoughts encline,
Faithful in Council, able in Design;   230
Rais'd by due Merit to the highest Trust,
The *Captious Senate* own'd that Merit just.
What cannot high Exalted Vertue do?
He shows this strange unusual Wonder true,
The Monarch's Fav'rite, and the Peoples too;   235
His Enemies to his just Praise submit,

---

into a modern state. In line 723 below the representative of "the old *Jagellan* Race" is James Francis Edward, the Stuart pretender, who by the basic law of inheritance through the eldest son was the *de jure* king of England. In the present context, therefore, "JAGELLAN" probably means "hereditary."

215. *The Devil among:* "Then entered Satan into Judas surnamed Iscariot, being of the number of the twelve" (Luke 22:3).

221. *Taguski:* "[Charles Montagu] the L[ord] H[alifa]x" (*D*).

232. *Merit just:* In February 1698 the House of Commons voted a resolution, "That the Honourable *Charles Mountague* Esquire, Chancellor of the Exchequer, for his good Services to this Government, does deserve his Majesty's Favour" (*CJ, 12,* 116).

235. *The Monarch's Fav'rite:* Halifax was excluded from the privy council upon Anne's accession: "What he means by calling his L——p the *Monarch's Favourite* is unknown to me" (*D*).

Fly from his Satyr, and adore his Wit;
In vain they form Impolitick Designs,
Envy lies bury'd in her Deepest Mines.
For both Sides own this Character's his Due   240
Always to *Poland,* and *Augustus* true.
　　There *Ruski* with his early Trophies stood
Won from the *Swedes* upon the *Baltick* Flood.
When *Conti strove to snatch the* Polish Crown,
And all *the Gen'rous* Poles *his Conduct own.*   245
　　Rigatski next, our just Applause Commands,
The *Polish* Peace on his wise Conduct stands;
High Chancellor in *Sobieski*'s Reign;
And all true Poles *would have him so again.*
In Law upright, and prudent in the State,   250
In Council deep, in Execution great;
But by the Faction of the *Swedes* opprest,
And to make way for Fools and Knaves dismist.
　　Amongst the *Polish* Prelates there appear'd
Cujavia, lov'd for Piety, for Prudence fear'd;   255
Careless of Faction, or of Party-hate,
He firmly fixt to *Sobieski*'s Fate;
Follow'd his Fortune, and his Favour shar'd,
And had the Miter for his just Reward.
What tho' the *Metropolitan* declin'd,   260
And more for *Conti*'s Monarchy design'd;

242. *Ruski:* Edward Russell, earl of Orford (1653–1727), was the leading naval com-
mander of the last reign. His "early Trophies" included the crushing defeat of the French
invasion fleet in the English Channel off La Hougue in 1692.
244. *Conti:* "K James" (Yale copy of *Aa*). Just as James II was the unsuccessful candidate
of Louis XIV for the throne of England, Francois-Louis de Bourbon, prince de Conti (1664–
1709), was the unsuccessful candidate of Louis XIV for the throne of Poland left vacant by
the death of Jan Sobieski in June 1696.
246. *Rigatski:* "by whom [John Somers] the Lord *S[omers]* is Personated; (King *William*)
having invested him with Large Demains at *R[e]igate* in *Surrey*" (*D*).
253. *dismist:* Somers' removal as lord chancellor in April 1700 was demanded by Rochest-
er, Godolphin, and Harley as the price of forming a government of Tories, "the Faction of
the *Swedes* [i.e. French]." Somers was replaced by Sir Nathan Wright, a nonentity with "a
fat broad Face" (Macky, p. 41) who was "despised by all parties, [and] of no use to the
crown" (*Account of the Conduct,* p. 147).
255. *Cujavia:* Thomas Tenison, archbishop of Canterbury. Garth mentioned Tenison's
"celestial Piety" in *The Dispensary, 2,* 51 (*POAS,* Yale, *6,* 73).
260. *the Metropolitan:* William Sancroft (1617–93), archbishop of Canterbury, was de-
prived in 1690 for refusing to take the oaths of allegiance to William and Mary, because he
"design'd" more for "*Conti*'s [James II's] Monarchy."

Cujavia, all the Primates Place supply'd;
And *Poland,* her intended Prince enjoy'd;
Culm, and *Posnania,* Ecclesiastick Peers,
And *Patcherouski,* old in Zeal as Years;   265
With Thirteen Sacred *Polish* Miters who
Are *Polish* Lords, and *Polish* Prelates too,
Were all to *Poland* and *Augustus* true.
    These wore the *Polish* Lawrels to the last,
And fixt the *Polish* Liberties so fast,   270
That Fate it self cou'd not the Band destroy;
But what they once possest, they still enjoy.
These were the *Columns* which so long sustain'd
The *Load of State* when *Sobieski* Reign'd;
Who all the Lines of Government restor'd,   275
And held the Scepter while *he drew the Sword.*
When he encampt on the *Moldavian* Plains,
And freed the *Poles* from *Mahomet's Servile Chains,*
The *Turkish* Banners to his Sword submit
Abroad his Valour, and at home their Wit;   280
They fought with *Equal* Enemies at home,
And *Equal* Trophies to their Conduct come;
The Conquer'd Difficulties of the State
Make all Men own their Conduct to be Great;
And they that seek to blame their Management,   285
And charge on them what they could not prevent,
Should tell us in what Age it shall be known
No Faults attend the State, no Knaves the Crown.
    Ungrateful *Poland,* never will be blest

263. *her intended Prince:* Queen Anne.

264–65. *Culm, and Posnania . . . And Patcherouski:* "By *Culm, Posnania, Patcherousky* and Thirteen Mitres more, are meant some very Good E[cclesiastica]l Peers, who were against the Bill to prevent *Occasional Conformity*" (*D*). Fourteen bishops voted against the second bill to prevent occasional conformity in December 1703 (Boyer, *Annals,* 1704, p. 229). Patcherouski suggests Simon Patrick (1626–1707), bishop of Ely, who was 79 in 1705.

269–76. *These . . . held the Scepter:* After the death of Queen Mary in 1694 William appointed lords justices to rule England during his absences on the continent. Until 1700 these included Thomas Tenison, archbishop of Canterbury, and some of the leading Whig politicians: Somers, Shrewsbury, and Devonshire.

278. *Mahomet:* James II.

279. *Turkish:* Jacobite.

285. *they:* country Tories.

their Management: "Past Mismanagements" was a Tory cant phrase for the Whig governments of William III (*The Art of Governing by Partys,* 1701, p. 154).

Till *Sobieski*'s Management's confest;   290
Till some of his forgotten Rules restor'd,
Such Statesmen wield the Scepter, *such the Sword;*
Till some such Heads in *Polish* Council sit,
And some such Hero shall for *Poland* fight.
    Finski, an Upright *Lithuanian* Peer,   295
Sets up for sinking *Poland*'s Prime Visier;
For Application and Impertinence
No Man has half so much with half his Sense;
With Formal Step, and *high Majestick Grin*,
Is *Polander* without, and *Swede* within.   300
Envy and awkward Spleen sit on his Face,
In Speech precise, but always thinks apace;
In *Earnest Nonsense* does his Hours divide,
Always to *little* Purpose, *much* employ'd.
Strong in Opinion, in his Judgment Weak,   305
And thinks himself exceeding politick.
The Musick of his Tongue is his Disease,
Conceives absurdly what he speaks with Ease.
The Discord of his Faculties is plain,
He talks with Pleasure, what he thinks with Pain;   310
And there 'tis own'd he shows some Policy
To make his fluent Tongue his Brain supply.
So Men are pleas'd with Shadows, so from hence
The World mistakes his jingling Tongue for Sense.
A busie trifling Statesman, *Proud and Dull*,   315
A thinking, plodding, *wise,* substantial *Fool;*
In all vast *Poland*'s far extended Round,
No Man was known so *emptily profound.*
Polite in Words, a stiff and formal Tongue,
And speaks to little Purpose, very long.   320
    To him *Augustus* gave the *Polish* Seal,

---

295. *Finski:* As secretary of state (1702–04) Nottingham tried to function as "Prime Visier" (prime minister) and to dictate appointments to the cabinet, but it was actually Godolphin who played this role (1702–10). Defoe overestimated the power of the secretaryship. He told Harley in July–August? 1704 that "The Secretaryes Office Well Discharg'd Makes a Man Prime Minister of Course" (*Letters*, p. 31). Actually it was the office of lord treasurer that was evolving into prime minister.

301. *Face:* See illustration, p. 13.

320. Quoted in the *Review*, 26 February 1713. Swift parodies Nottingham's labored style of oratory in *An Excellent New Song* (below).

And made him *Grieffier* to the Common-weal.
They that cou'd not his License first obtain,
Might not go out of *Poland* or come in;
The Publick Safety was the just Pretence   325
To keep the *Sweeds* from true Intelligence;
But the more Genuine Reason *was the Pence*.
For in his time the *Sweeds* themselves obtain'd
His Blanks to pass their Spies to *Polish* Land.
   The slow unsteady Mannager appears   330
Too *hot* for Peace, too *cold* for *Polish* Wars;
While charm'd with Foreign *Margueritta*'s Song,
His sleeping Orders he delays too long.
Whole Fleets attend the *Minstrels* softer Notes;
By her the Statesman *steers*, the Member *votes*.   335
Well might the *Syren* be compar'd to him

322. *Grieffier:* Nottingham was Queen Anne's first secretary of state (May 1702–April 1704).

328–29. *Sweeds . . . obtain'd | His Blanks:* Apparently while still in the Queen's Bench prison for fabricating the warming-pan legend of the origins of the pretended Prince of Wales, William Fuller, "the Evidence," who "practiced many cheats under pretence of being employed in the service of the government" (*CSPD 1698*, p. 382), signed an affidavit of irregularities in Nottingham's issuance of passports to "*French* Discontented Natives of *England*" (*D*), who were not of course allowed to travel to France in wartime.

332. *Margueritta:* Margherita Francesca de L'Epine (d. 1746) was an Italian operatic soprano who made her debut at Drury Lane in January 1704. While the Whigs continued to patronize the reigning English soprano, Katherine Tofts, the Tories took up the new Italian. Her singing is said to have so inflamed the sober earl of Nottingham

> That careless of his Soul & Fame
> To Play-house ev'ry night he came
> And left Church undefended.

(*Hor. Lib. 2d Ode 4th Imitated. From the Ld. Granville to the Ld. Scarsdale* ["Do not most fragrant Earl disclaim"], University of Leeds MS. Brotherton Lt. 11, pp. 53–54).

333–34. Defoe may have seen the verses in *The Diverting Post*, 9–16 June 1705, that are attributed to John Hughes:

> . . . fam'd *L'Epine* does equal Skill employ
> While list'ning Peers Crowd with Extatick Joys,
> B[edfor]d to hear her Song his *Dice* forsakes,
> And *N[ottingha]m*'s transported when she Shakes;
> Lull'd Statesmen melt away their drowsy Cares
> Of *England*'s safety in *Italian* Aires.

Cf. *The Dunciad, 4,* 618: "And Navies yawn'd for Orders on the Main."

336. *the Syren:* Orpheus. His poetry tamed wild animals, moved rocks, "And Trees unrooted left their Place; / Sequacious of the Lyre" (Dryden, *Poems, 2,* 539).

That *doz'd old Nature* with his Touch Sublime.
The lofty Cedars danc'd *his softer Airs*,
And *lofty Stupid Statesmen* bow to hers.
    Of all the *Polish* grave Nobility,   340
None acts *so low* that e'er was born *so high;*
So fond of Liberty, he ne'er endur'd
The Name of Slave, no, not to his own Word.
    Augustus saw, and soon mislik'd the Man,
And found him to the *Swedish* Cause incline;   345
With eazy Skill he read his well-known Fate,
A useless, unregarded Tool of State.
What tho' the *Polish* Dyet was Possest,
And blindly in his Favour *once Addrest;*
The publick Banter all the Kingdom knew,   350
It mov'd their *Mirth* and *Indignation* too:
The general fixt Dislike *Augustus* saw,
Laid by the haughty Thing, and left him to the Law.
The *Quacking, Mountebanking Tool of State,*
That neither could be *little* or be *great,*   355
Retir'd to give us time to let him know,
No Knave's above b'ing told that *He is so.*
    Lawrensky next, of *Prussia*'s Royal Breed,
To *Ladislaus* by Marriages allyed;
Tho' Int'rested in *Sobiesky*'s Line,   360
Yet to the *Swedes* he always did incline:

340–43. "This Paragraph, is the Product of a Complaint that this Incendiary [Defoe] vents in all Companies, about his L[ordshi]p's not keeping his Word with him, when in Newgate" (*D*). Defoe had vented this complaint most recently in *The Consolidator: Or, Memoirs of Sundry Transactions from the World in the Moon,* which was published in March 1705. Here (p. 212) he recalled that Nottingham and John Sheffield, duke of Buckingham, the lord privy seal, "took such a low Step as to go to him *to the Dungeon* where they had put him, to see if they could tempt him *to betray his Friends.*"

349. *Addrest:* The Tory House of Commons passed a vote of confidence in Nottingham in December 1703 (*Moderation Display'd,* 83n.).

358. *Lawrensky:* Laurence Hyde, earl of Rochester.

359. *Ladislaus:* "P[rince] of W[ales]" (Indiana University copy 2 of *Ab*). Since Rochester's sister was James II's first wife, Rochester was a kind of stepuncle to James Francis Edward, the son of James II and Mary of Modena.

361. *to the Swedes . . . incline:* In March 1701, while at the head of the Tory ministry, Rochester was offended by some reflections on Louis XIV in the House of Lords. He said, " 'All Men ought to speak respectfully of Crown'd Heads. . . . ' He was seconded in his Complement to the *French* King by another Earl, who said, 'The King of *France* was not only to be respected, but to be fear'd' " (Oldmixon, *History,* p. 223).

He kept the *Polish* Cash in Days of yore,
When Kings grew Rich, and made the People Poor,
And fain would now our *Polish* Treasurers teach
To make their Monarchs Poor, the People Rich.   365
   If Stories known of Old, should be reviv'd,
Of Leaves torn out, and horrid Facts conniv'd;
Of Crimes too Black for Satyr to reveal,
Which Kings ha' Dy'd, on purpose to Conceal:
Were but the black Record again Review'd,   370
When the false Peer his Master's Fate pursued,
His Picture would too low for Satyr lye,
And sink the Wretch beneath Authority;
Whether the *French*, the *Sax*, or *Polish* race,
He ever Fawn'd, and lookt with *Janus* Face.   375
When *Sobieski* did the Throne obtain,
He Grudg'd the Crown, tho' his own *Race* should Reign:
But when in *Vice-Roys* Dignity went Halves,
He stoopt to Rule *Moldavian Western* Slaves.
   Now he Repines the Management supreme   380

362. *kept the . . . Cash:* Rochester was first lord of the treasury (1679–1685) and lord high treasurer (1685–87).

367. *Leaves torn out:* Rochester was widely believed to have incurred a loss for the treasury of £40,000 in letting the contracts for collecting the hearth money in 1682, which he tried to conceal by cutting three pages out of the tax collectors' accounts (*Memoirs of Sir John Reresby*, ed. Andrew Browning, Glasgow, Jackson Son & Co., 1936, p. 291; *The True Patriot Vindicated, or, A Justification of His Excellency, The Earl of Rochester*, 1701, verso; Vernon, *3*, 156–57; "An Inscription Intended to be set up for the Earle of R[ocheste]r . . . 1701," Berkshire R. O. MS. Trumbull Add. 17).

368–69. *Crimes . . . Which Kings . . . Dy'd . . . to conceal:* An investigation of Rochester's alleged peculations, due to commence in February 1685, was forestalled by Charles II's death (*The True Patriots Vindicated: Or, A Justification of the Late Earl of Rochester*, 1711, p. 11).

377. *Grudg'd the Crown:* Rochester opposed offering the crown to William and Mary (his niece) in 1689: "*Nottingham, Clarendon,* and *Rochester,* were the men that managed the debates in favour of a Regent" (Burnet, *1*, 810). Henry Hyde, earl of Clarendon, Rochester's elder brother, remained a nonjuror, but Rochester finally accepted William as king de facto.

378. *in Vice-Roys Dignity went Halves:* In December 1700 Rochester was appointed lord lieutenant of Ireland and "went Halves" with William III in the government of the two kingdoms. The latter phrase may also have been intended to recall one of the failures of Rochester's administration of Ireland. "That which gave the greatest disgust in his Administration there, was, his usage of the reduced Officers, who were upon half pay . . . The Earl of *Rochester* called them before him, and required them to express under their hands their readiness to go and serve in the *West-Indies;* They did not comply with this: So he set them a day for their final Answer, and threaten'd, that they should have no more appointments, if they stood out beyond that time . . . the King ordered a stop to be put to it" (Burnet, *2*, 255, 291).

Is not, as he contriv'd, resign'd to him:
For this his *Vice-Roy*'s Office he laid down,
Again to Govern, and Amuse the Crown;
But wiser Councils laid him gently by,
And left him to bewail his lost Authority.   385
     Now he Cabals, the Parties to *Unite*,
And strives to bring us all to *Peace* in *Spite;*
Courts ev'ry Side to his absurd Design,
And thinks to make the *Swedes* and *Cossacks* joyn;
My Soul, his slye, pretended Peace abhor,   390
The Brooding *Union*'s Big with *Civil War;*
Rouze ev'ry Loyal *Pole* to Self-Defence,
Give them for *Arms*, their *Eyes*, for *Swords* their *Sense*,
For all Men see the empty sham Pretence.
     Old *Seymsky* was of this intrieguing Band,   395
A *Polack* born, on *Neiper*'s Golden Strand;
Antient in Crimes bred up to Fraud and Feud,
His Int'rest at his Master's Cost pursu'd;

382. *Vice-Roy's Office . . . laid down:* William dismissed Rochester in February 1702 but
Anne promptly reappointed him. He delayed returning to Ireland however until Godolphin
and Marlborough prevailed upon the queen to ask him either to assume his post or to resign.
Rochester resigned in February 1703.

384. *gently:* Cf. [Defoe], *Advice to All Parties*, 1705, p. 14; Anne, "a gentle Mistress . . . let
you fall softly."

386. *Cabals:* Rochester seems to have spent most of 1702 in trying to put together a coali-
tion government (in opposition to Godolphin and Marlborough) based on the high church
interest, peace, and the Protestant succession. He courted both the "angry men" in the lower
house of convocation (Burnet, *2*, 317) and the dissenters, whom, as Defoe said, "we know he
hates." Defoe had summarized Rochester's efforts in his earlier poem, *A Hymn to Victory*,
[August] 1704, p. 13:

          In vain he'd *Whig* and *Tory* reconcile:
          He courts th'Extremes of Parties, and in spight,
          That he may more Divide, wou'd some Unite . . .
          And strives to League with those we know he hates.

Three months later Defoe warned Harley of "a Conjunction of Extreams" directed against
him (*Letters*, p. 69).

389. *Swedes and Cossacks:* Francophiles and dissenters.

394. *Pretence:* "Mr. *Review* has Preached up Peace and Union to some purpose, if at last he
turns Renegade from his own Principles, and makes it his Business to Ridicule such as are for
a Treaty between the two Contending Parties" (*D*).

395. *Seymsky:* Sir Edward Seymour.

398. *at his Master's Cost:* Seymour was £16,000 in debt to the crown in 1688 and secured a
special clause in the Act of Indemnity to release him from that debt (*A Collection of State
Tracts*, 3 vols., 1705–07, *2*, 652).

A mighty Stock of ill-got Wealth injoy'd,
When *Polish* Troops our *Polish* Lands destroy'd;   400
When his dear Country's Liberties lay low,
He Fisht in all the Troubles made them so:
When *Poland*'s Kings the *Polish* Peers opprest,
And Property was made the Monarch's *Jest*,
In those dear Days he kept the *Royal Cash*,   405
And form'd those Cheats he since *pretends* to Lash.
Now he sets up to save the Nation's Pelf,
And wou'd have no man Cheat us but himself;
Detects ill Practices with *eager Vote*,
And rails at Bribes with *mercenary Throat:*   410
That he should be Ungrateful and Unjust,
Dispise the Grace, as he betray'd the Trust;
Be Proud, be Peevish, Insolent, and Base,
Nature has painted that upon his Face;
Envy sits rampant on his tott'ring Head,   415
And *Rogue*'s wrote there so plain that every man may read.
    And now the conscious Criminal appears,
Affects to *Cant* of *Poland*'s suff'ring Years,
Reproaches little Villains with their Crimes,

399. *ill-got Wealth:* Through his influence at court Seymour was able to secure a grant from Charles II of all the forfeited estates of Edmund Ludlow, the regicide (*DNB, 17,* 1251).

402. *Fisht in all the Troubles:* proverbial (Tilley, F334) for pursuing one's private interest in times of public calamity. Seymour qualified in 1688–89 (Defoe, *England's Late Jury,* 41–50, *POAS,* Yale, *6,* 347).

405–06. In 1673 Seymour was appointed treasurer of the navy at a salary of £3,000. "In November 1680 articles of impeachment were exhibited against him for malversation in his office, but the dissolution put an end to the proceedings (cf. [BM MS.] Add. 9291, f. 1)" (*DNB, 17,* 1251). When similar charges were made in March 1704 against his successor in this office, Edward Russell, Lord Orford, Seymour was uniquely qualified to lead the attack.

409–10. Seymour, who was one of the channels by which the old East India Company bribed members of parliament (*English Historical Review, 71* [1956], 227–28), served on a committee which found several members of the new East India Company guilty of bribery in the election of February 1701. Burnet (*2,* 259) says it was Seymour himself "whom the old Company was said to have bought before, at a very high price, [who] brought before the House of Commons the discovery of some of the practices of the New Company." Defoe remarked this anomaly in *A New Satyr on the Parliament* (1701), 82; "Brib'd *Seymour* bribes accuses" (*POAS,* Yale, *6,* 325).

413. A Whig broadside of 1701 asked, "Whether there ever was a Life more uniform and of a piece, than Sir *E——— S———*'s. Alike ill-manner'd, ill-natur'd and insolent; alike corrupt, whether in or out of the Chair, whether in or out of Favour; the same Enemy to his Countrey, when pretending to the Name of a Patriot, and when ridiculing it" (*Some Queries, which May Deserve Consideration,* 1701, verso).

And rakes among the Evils of the Times.   420
    That he should *Poland*'s Liberties maintain,
Who can the wond'rous *Riddle now Explain?*
Or, who *Believe* the *Fact,* that *Knows the Man?*
Some think, *indeed,* it shou'd be Understood
A *Penitence* for *Violence* and *Blood,*   425
To Expiate his Share in *former Reigns,*
The *Stink,* if not the *Guilt* of which remains.
If that be *True,* that he should make pretence,
To *Censure* others for a past Offence,
Savours of most *prodigious Impudence;*   430
While he that ought to Blush at former *Times,*
Boldly *Condemns* contemporary Crimes.
    Immortal Brass sits on his testy Brows,
Hard'ned with Bribes, with Frauds, and broken Vows;
Infernal Feuds flame in his guilty Eyes;   435
He starts at Peace with Anger and Surprize:
Weak'ned in Wickedness, in Wishes strong,
A bribe-receiving Hand, and clamouring Tongue;
False to Himself, his Monarch, and his Friends,
But to the lowest Step of Pride descends;   440
Abject, and Mean, when Fortune's Storms appear,
Proud and Intollerable whcn 'tis Fair;
Noisy in Speech, in Manner Insolent,
And awkwardly submits to Government.
    Often the *Polish* Monarchs have essay'd,   445
So much they of his Mischiefs were afraid,
To win the Bully off with gentle Words,
And place him in the Class of *Polish* Lords;
But he that lov'd the Villanies of Life,
And chew'd the Air he breath'd to sounds of Strife,   450
That liv'd upon those Particles of Fire

443. *Noisy:* Henry St. John describes "one of Sir Chuffer's speeches" to Harley in October 1703: "There never yet was more gravity and less thought, more noise and less mirth" (HMC *Portland MSS., 4,* 73).
    447. *Bully:* A fellow Devonian observed that Seymour was "a man of . . . many passions and perturbations, and swears and swaggers amongst the seamen" (HMC *Portland MSS., 4,* 134).
    448. *Lords:* Rumors that Seymour would be raised to the peerage recur in three reigns: in August 1682 it was supposed that he would be created Baron Pomeroy; in March 1692 it was said to be Viscount Totnes; in December 1700 earl of Bristol (Luttrell, *1,* 213; *2,* 374; BM MS. Add. 17677UU, f. 360v).

Which nourish Feud, and prompt the vile Desire,
Chose all the glittering offers to despise,
Too *vain* to be made Great, too *proud* to Rise;
   Augustus try'd him with uncommon Grace,   455
Gave him his Houshold *Staff*, and Houshold *Place;*
His Robe of Peer attempted to put on,
But he put by that *Feather* to his Son;
Accepts the high Command without the *Name*,
Because he covets *Mischief* more than *Fame*.   460
The party-Zealot never could resign
His dear Speech-making, old, contentious Sin,
Resolv'd the Head of *Faction* to supply,
And as he *Liv'd* unblest, uneasy *Dye*.
   Augustus saw the sullen Wretch go on,   465
Neither by Art or Bounty to be won,
His Malice he despis'd, his Pride contemn'd,
And to his juster Fate the Wretch condemn'd;
Left him his empty Follies to pursue,
And his unvalued Favours with his *Staff* withdrew.   470
   Th'unsteady Statesman's *Temper yet untry'd*,
Left him at once, in spight of all his Pride;
Not all his swelling Spleen would give Relief,
But sunk his Spirit underneath his Grief:
The cowardly, self-condemn'd, abandon'd Wretch,   475
Saw his ambitious Ends beyond his reach;
With strong Reluctance all his Honours quits,

456. *Houshold . . . Place:* Anne made Seymour her comptroller of the household in April 1702.

458. *Son:* Even if it is true that Seymour declined a peerage for himself, he "established his Family very well" (Macky, p. 112). His second son, Francis Seymour Conway (1679–1732), was created Baron Conway of Ragley in March 1703. Francis Seymour adopted the additional surname in June 1699 when he succeeded his next elder brother in the estates (but not the title) of Edward Conway, first earl of Conway. In his first session as a member for Bramber (March 1701–03) he earned a place in the Whig blacklist (*A List of One Unanimous Club of Members,* 1701).

470. *Staff withdrew:* "The White Staff was not taken from him, but he resign'd it . . . [as] the very *Gazette* tells us" (*D*). What *The London Gazette,* 27 April–1 May 1704, says is that "Her Majesty has been Pleased to Appoint Thomas Mansell Esq; to be Comptroller of Her Majesty's Houshold, in the Room of the Right Honourable Sir Edward Seymour Bar." Seymour was dismissed on 22 April 1704.

473. *Spleen:* "When dismissed from his place of comptroller of the household by Queen Anne, [he] sent word that he should return his staff by the common carrier" (James A. Manning, *Lives of the Speakers,* 1850, p. 363).

And with his Places now resigns his Wits.
So Pride unbounded, with no Power suffic'd,
Wants Courage but to see it self Despis'd.   480
    When Men are rais'd by Fate above their Sense,
Nature must sink them in *her own defence,*
Humane Society would else Decay,
And *Mad-men* quite demolish Liberty:
For when the bloated Monster's once pull'd down,   485
The *Soul deserts,* the Bubble's broke and gone;
Abjectly Wretched, and with Shame surpris'd,
He *meanly begs* what he before *despis'd;*
The high Extreme inverts in his Distress,
Dejected to a despicable, vile Excess.   490
So *Bullies* are but *Cowards* in disguise,
Who few Men Value, all Men should Despise.
    Rokosky next fills up the spacious Rolls,
The mighty *Captain Bassa of the* Poles;
In foreign Expeditions he's employ'd,   495
And many *Polish* Millions has destroy'd;
Abortive Projects flow in his loose Brain,

478. *resigns his Wits:* Seymour's behavior after his dismissal was indeed eccentric. It was reported in August 1704 that "Sir E. Seymour did not shave his beard from the time he lost his place till last Warminster sessions" (HMC *Portland MSS.*, *4*, 108) and another correspondent described "Sir Chuffer [walking] about his courts and gardens all the morning in a batter'd gown without breeches or wastcoat" (Levens MSS., George Harbin to James Graham, 29 May 1704). His enemies were less guarded: "some suppose he is not sound in his head," Richard Duke reported to Harley on 20 September 1704 (HMC *Portland MSS.*, *4*, 134).

481. *Sense:* capability, capacity (*OED*).

482. *her own defence:* "To make Nature [dismiss Seymour] *in her own defence,* requires such Explanatory Notes from him [Defoe], as he is not at leisure to give us, being so taken up in Reading *Horace, cum Notis Variorum*" (D). In the *Little Review,* 29 June 1705, Defoe had recommended to Dr. Joseph Browne "the right Edition . . . of Horace cum notis Variorum . . . Printed at *Leyden.*"

484. *Mad-men:* In Defoe's usage the term means high church Tories in general (*Advice to All Parties,* 1705, p. 24) or Tackers in particular (*Review,* 1 May 1705, 8 May 1705).

493. *Rokosky:* Sir George Rooke. Defoe was not frightened off the attack either by the experience of his friend, William Colepeper (519*n.* below), or by the (false) report that he himself had been "ordered to be taken into custody for reflecting on admiral Rooke, in his *Master Mercury*" (Luttrell, *5*, 469). What Defoe had published in *The Master Mercury,* 21 August 1704 and 21 September 1704, was a mock vindication of Rooke that raked up failures such as the Cadiz expedition of 1702 in which Rooke, "like a true *English* Admiral, took Care . . . to go where most Money was to be got, and least Blood to be shed."

494. *Bassa:* a pasha, a high-ranking Turkish officer; a haughty, imperious man (*OED*).

496. *Millions . . . destroy'd:* "Ships [were] fitted out at the Rates of Two Millions a Year, to fight but once in Three Years" (Defoe, *The Consolidator,* 1705, p. 78).

He loves to make a *tedious Voyage in vain.*
    Abandon'd *Poland,* how art thou Betray'd!
Sold for that very Money thou hast paid!   500
The greedy Monsters that receive thy Pay,
Trifle thy Blood, and Time, and Strength away.
Rokosky Covetous, and Insolent,
On *Poland's* weightiest Errands has been sent;
Small Prophecy might those Events foretell,   505
Where he Commanded that cou'd Fight so well.
His Voyages never have been made in vain,
He took such care of *coming Home again:*
No Man cou'd ever give him a *Defeat,*
And none can *match him* at a *safe Retreat.*   510
The carefull'st Officer the *Poles* could choose,
For when they *bid him fly,* he'll ne'er *refuse:*
A *Neg'tive Soldier,* always in the Right,
Was never Beaten, and would *seldom Fight:*
Poland will ne'er her antient Glory sho'   515
While Knaves and Cowards fight her Battles so.
    Rokoski now supports the *Polish* Crown,

498. *Voyage in vain:* Rooke set sail in May 1703 in command of an invasion fleet with four regiments of foot and six regiments of marines aboard under orders to make a descent upon the French coast. He succeeded in avoiding any engagement with the French and was back in Bath "for recovery of his health" in June (Luttrell, *5,* 291, 312). Defoe observed in *An Elegy upon the Author of the True-Born-English Man* ("Satyr sing *Lachrime,* thou'rt dead in Law"), 1704, p. 9, that Rooke spent "a Seventeen Months Advance, / To take the Air upon the Coast of France."

499. *Betray'd:* In June or July 1704 Defoe enclosed in a letter to Harley the draft of a pamphlet calling Rooke a traitor who promoted none in the fleet but "high furious Jacobite[s]" and demanding "a Suspension at least of this Obnoxious Suspected Man" (*Letters,* pp. 18–25). Harley did not allow the pamphlet to be published, but Rooke was removed from his command in January 1705 (Luttrell, *5,* 505).

508. *coming Home again:* The unexpected return to Spithead in January 1704 of the formidable fleet under Rooke's command that was under orders to convoy the archduke Charles to Lisbon and then to continue into the Mediterranean to bombard and destroy all the maritime towns in Andalusia that refused to recognize Charles III as king of Spain was remarked by Defoe in *The Address,* 134–35: "And all men own the Happiness, / That he's come home again" (*POAS,* Yale, *6,* 642).

510. *safe Retreat:* Rooke's disengagement from the French fleet commanded by the comte de Toulouse after the indecisive battle on 13/24 August 1704 is the subject of *On the Greatest Victory,* above.

517. *supports the . . . Crown:* Rooke was a court Tory who distinguished himself in the impeachment proceedings against the Junto lords in 1701 and was designated a high church courtier in 1705 (*Numerical Calculation*). Although he sat for Portsmouth, Hampshire (1698–1708), he was known as "the Flower of *Kent,*" one of the Tory bosses in the county who "gets

And Fights the Quarrels of his Master's Throne,
But Fights by Proxi when he Fights his Own.
   Poland, how past Retrieve must be thy Fate,   520
When Cowards guide thy Arms, and Knaves thy State!
Can they the braver *Swedish* Squadrons meet,
That stoop to Bully those they dare not Fight?
Courage and Crime can never dwell so near,
For where there's *Guilt,* there always will be *Fear.*   525

Part II

In *Polish* Dyet now they all appear,
In *Polish* Dyet all men free from Fear,
May all their most malicious Thoughts declare.
Augustus calls them to the place Supreme,
There first they Swear to *Poland,* then to Him,   530
That they will *both* Support, and *both Defend,*
And *All* Profess what very *Few* intend.
There from the *Throne,* He tells them of the *State,*

Offices and Preferments for his Friends" (*A True State of the Difference between Sir George Rook, Knt. and William Colepeper, Esq.,* 1704, p. 14). He managed somehow to avoid voting either for or against the Tack or to be called a Sneaker, but in January 1705 he was dismissed as vice admiral of England and in June 1705 he was removed from the prince of Denmark's council (Luttrell, *5,* 505, 562). He remained a privy councillor.

  519. *Fights by Proxi:* In July 1703 William Colepeper, one of the Kentish petitioners (*POAS,* Yale, *6,* 322, 334) and Defoe's lawyer in his trial for publishing *The Shortest-Way with the Dissenters* (1702), travelled to Windsor to petition the queen for a remission of Defoe's sentence. While he was waiting in the anteroom a postbag arrived from the fleet, and Colepeper inquired "whether Sir *George* be at the Fleet, or gone to the *Bath*" (*A True State of the Difference between Sir George Rook, Knt. and William Colepeper, Esq.,* 1704, p. 6; cf. 498n. above). Then, in gross violation of the privilege of a royal palace, Colepeper was violently beaten with a cane by Rooke's friend, Sir Jacob Banks. In the next month Colepeper was again set upon, challenged to a duel, and assaulted by three bullies acting on Rooke's behalf. Colepeper brought suit in the queen's bench and the jury found two of his assailants guilty and imposed heavy fines (ibid., p. 42; Luttrell, *5,* 392; cf. *Review,* 20 May 1704).

  523. *dare not Fight:* Colepeper accepted Sir George's challenge to fight him "upon the Coast of *Holland,*" but Sir George's note to Colepeper summoning him aboard the admiral's yacht neglected to name the port where the yacht was anchored (*A True State of the Difference between Sir George Rook, Knt. and William Colepeper, Esq.,* 1704, pp. 14, 39).

  530. *first . . . to Poland:* "Would Mr. *Foe* give himself the Trouble of perusing the Oaths the Members of Parliament take, he would not have occasion to be told he is in an Error on that Account, since they swear to be true to their *Queen* and *Country,* not *COUNTRY* and *QUEEN*" (D). "Country" is not mentioned in the oath (1 Anne Stat. I c. 22).

What things occur, and prompts their *calm Debate;*
Tells them his steady Thoughts due Peace to give,   535
And antient *Polish* Honour to Retrieve;
How he by *Law* came there, by *Law* would Reign,
And all their *Polish* Liberties maintain:
But lets them know, he finds to his surprize,
Some *Poles* are *ev'n for this* his Enemies.   540
Informs them of a deep *Livonian* Plot,
And prompts them all to Search it farther out.
Tells them the real Danger of the State,
And *asks* them to prevent their Monarch's Fate,
But presses them to *Peace* and *Calm Debate.*   545
    Its all *in vain,* for *Faction* had possest
Some Members, all the *Dyet* to molest;
In *vain* the sullen Deputies Debate,
In *vain* they weakly prop the sinking State,
In *vain* to Oathes and Loyalty pretend;   550
They *Sell* that Prince whom faintly they *Defend.*
    Satyr, with gentle Strokes the *Mischiefs touch,*

534. *calm Debate:* In her speech at the opening of parliament in November 1703, Anne expressed her "earnest Desires of seeing all [her] Subjects in perfect Peace and Union among themselves" and urged the legislators "carefully [to] avoid any Heats or Divisions" (*CJ, 14,* 211).

536. *antient . . . Honour to Retrieve:* The phrase occurs, not in an address of Anne's, but in the Commons' address of thanks to the queen for her speech at the opening of parliament in October 1702: "the Conduct of the Earl of *Marlborough* [has] signally retrieved the ancient Honour and Glory of the *English* Nation" (*CJ, 14,* 8). There was a division on the word "retrieve," a transparent slur on William III, but the motion to let it stand was carried 180–80 (*POAS,* Yale, *6,* 495). Defoe alluded to the phrase in *The Address,* 6–10 (*POAS,* Yale, *6,* 634).

537. *by Law:* Anne never claimed a divine right to the throne. In her first speech to parliament in March 1702 she spoke only of "the Succession to the Crown in the Protestant Line; and the Government in Church and State, as by Law established" (*CJ, 13,* 788). Defoe reminded Harley that "Her Majesty Came to the Crown on the Foot of a Legall Settlement" (*Letters,* p. 51).

541. *deep Livonian Plot:* Anne addressed parliament on the Scotch plot on 17 December 1703. Defoe elaborates on a very bald and guarded statement (*CJ, 14,* 253). Although many readers glossed "Livonian" as "Scotch," *Key* more accurately, or more selectively, makes it "High Ch[urch] Perkenites." And Pittis characteristically observed that the plot was "so very *deep* indeed, that I never heard of any one yet that found the Bottom of it" (*D*).

546–1133. In these lines Defoe satirizes the proceedings of the Tory majority in the House of Commons during the three sessions of Anne's first parliament, in each of which a bill to prevent occasional conformity was introduced and passed. In *The Address* (April? 1704) (*POAS,* Yale, *6,* 631), Defoe had attacked in more detail the proceedings of the second session (November 1703–April 1704). Here he condenses the proceedings of three sessions into one fictional session.

How *little* some Men said, how some *too much:*
How *some* in hopes to pull the *Cossacks* down,
Slight the *Livonian* Plot, expose the Crown,   555
Cavil, Contrive, *make Speeches*, and Debate,
And Jest too much with *Poland*'s dang'rous State.
Prepost'rous *Laws*, absurd in their Design,
And, *made on purpose to be broke,* bring in;
Divide, in order to *Consolidate*,   560
And *Tack* Destruction to the wounded State.
Secure the *Polish* Freemen in a Gaol,
For fear the *Nation's Liberties should fail*.
The *Polish* dear-bought Priviledge destroy,
That *Dyets* Tyranny they might enjoy.   565
Support the *Polish* Dignity and Crown,
By pulling all her *just Defences* down,
And save the tott'ring Kingdom from her Fate,
By *Decently* Embroiling *Church* and *State*.

   Mackreski first, the *Dyet*'s Pamphleteer,   570
Stood up;—all *Poland* waited on his Chair,
For all Men look'd some wondrous thing to hear.

554. *Cossacks:* dissenters.

561. *Tack:* The reference is to the Tories' attempt to tack the third bill to prevent occasional conformity to the land tax bill in November 1704 (p. 43 above).

562. *Freemen in a Gaol:* After the five Aylesbury electors had been ordered to Newgate for breach of privilege (p. 59 above), their lawyers petitioned for writs of habeas corpus. The Commons then "carried their anger farther; they ordered . . . the Lawyers and the Sollicitors to be taken into custody [and] These," as Burnet (*2*, 409) relates, "were such strange and unheard-of Proceedings, that by them the minds of all people were much alienated from the House of Commons."

565. *Tyranny:* "It cannot be Just . . . that the People may endure the Tyrany of 500 Usurpers more than of one" ([Defoe], *Legion's Humble Address to the Lords*, 1704, p. 2).

570. *Mackreski:* Sir Humphrey Mackworth (1657–1727) entered parliament in February 1701 as a member for Cardiganshire (February–November 1701, 1702–05, 1710–13) and was immediately set down as a Poussineer, "said to have been influenc'd by M. *Poussin*, the French Agent" (*A Collection of White and Black Lists*, 4th ed., 1715, pp. 5–8). He voted for the Tack in November 1704 and then stood for Oxford University in May 1705. Although defeated there, he was returned for Totnes (1705–08).

Pamphleteer: "Mackworth was a prolific writer of pamphlets on subjects ranging from theology to the iniquities of the Whig taverns or 'mug-houses' " (*University of Birmingham Historical Journal*, *1* [1948], 234). Defoe had already written replies to two of Sir Humphrey's pamphlets: *Peace without Union. By Way of Reply to Sir H. M.'s Peace at Home*, 1703, and *Giving Alms No Charity, and Employing the Poor a Grievance to the Nation, Being an Essay upon this Great Question, Whether Work-houses, Corporations, and Houses of Correction for Employing the Poor, as Now Practis'd in England; or Parish-Stocks, as Propos'd in a Late Pamphlet, Entituled, A Bill for the Better Relief, Imployment and Settlement of the Poor, &c. Are Not Mischievous to the Nation*, 1704.

So once the *Teeming Hill in Travail Groan'd,*
Th'expecting World, the mighty Wonder own'd;
Young Mountains, Twins at least, they lookt should come,   575
When *One poor Mouse* clos'd the vast lab'ring Womb.
   The empty Orator in Florid Speech,
Told them that he was just *as Wise as Rich;*
To's Printed Books for his Design Referr'd,
Tho' that he e'er *Design'd,* no Mortal ever heard: 580
He talk't indeed sometimes of *Church* and *State,*
Of *Piety,* and of the Lord knows what;
But no man yet his vast Intentions found,
Deep as his *Mines,* and like his *Brains unsound.*
'Twas full a *Polish* Hour the *Member* spoke,   585
But *all* the Dyet *all* he said mistook:
Some said he talk'd *of this,* and some *of that;*
Just so he jumbl'd *Providence* and *Fate:*
In both, the same Intention he pursu'd,
Neither to *Understand,* or to be *Understood.*   590
Thus he Harangu'd them *Thirteen* times and more,
And still he left them *where they were before.*
He talk'd of *Crowns,* of *Property,* and *Law,*
And means to make them *keep themselves in Awe;*
Of *Persecuting Peace,* and *quiet Jars,*   595
Nations in *Nubibus* beyond the Stars.
Of *moderate Feuds,* and calm *distemper'd States,*
And mov'd to *Bleed* us, to avoid *Debates.*
Propos'd by *poverty* our *Wants* to Cure,
Starving our *Tradesmen* to Employ the *Poor:*   600

584. *Deep as his Mines:* See p. 522 below. Defoe used the phrase "deep as the Leaden Mines of [Mackworth's] Understanding" in the *Review,* 27 March 1705, and predicted the failure of his company in the *Review,* 30 April 1706.

600. *Employ the Poor:* Another of Mackworth's projects was a bill for the employment of the poor which he introduced in three sessions of parliament (1703–05). The bill, which required the poor to be put to work in parochial factories, was opposed by Defoe in *Giving Alms No Charity* (1704) and in a series of articles in the *Review,* 24 March–26 April 1705. Defoe called the bill "an Indigested Chaos, a Mass of Inconsistency and Incongruous Nonsense in Trade, big with Monsters of Amphibious Generation, Brooding Needless and Fatal Errors, and Numberless Irretrievable Mischiefs, absolutely Destructive of our Trade, Ruinous to the Poor, tending to the Confusion of our Home Trade, stopping the Circulation of our Manufactures, and Encreasing both the Number and Misery of our Poor" (*Review,* 27 March 1705). Although passed by the Tory House of Commons in each session, Sir Humphrey's bill was defeated in the House of Lords on party grounds: "My Lord Sunderland rose up and spoke against it and said it was not fit to be passed, because Sir Humphrey Mack-

Would spoil the Nation's *Trade* to make them *Rich,*
And backt his mighty Project with a Speech;
In weighty Conference propt a tott'ring Cause
To set our Priviledge above our Laws:
But as some Learned *Speeches* us'd to fail,   605
Because they'd too much *Head,* and had no *Tayl;*
So this was Hist about because they said,
'Twas all made up of *Tayl,* and had no *Head.*
Mackreski thus his *Learned Breath* bestow'd,
And as it did no *Harm* it did no *Good;*   610
And yet his *Speech* had this unlookt-for Charm,
That as it did no *Good,* it did no *Harm.*
      Packski a *Polish* Deputy stood next,
And all the *Polish* Senators perplext;
His *Zeal* was for the Church so *fiery red,*   615
His *Breath* at Distance struck the *Cossacks* Dead;
Plosko' the *Polish* Bishop he o'erthrew,
And made *Augustus* forc't Resentment shew:
The Rev'rend *Almoner* at once displace,
And aged *Vertue* bow'd to rampant *Vice.*   620
Hark how the Party-Hero Silence broke,

---

worth was the Author of it, and accordingly their Lordships rejected it" (Bodl. MS. Carte 244, f. 59).

606. *Head* . . . *Tayl:* "As for . . . his *Convertible Terms,* (which he is so famous for in his *Little Master Review*) . . . they are beneath Sir *Humphry's* Notice" (*D*). Cf. *More Reformation,* 847–49 (*POAS,* Yale, *6,* 582) and line 1028 below.

613. *Packski:* Sir John Pakington of Westwood, fourth baronet (1671–1727), was a high church Tory leader in the House of Commons where he sat for Worcestershire (1690–95, 1698–1727). He was one of the "*Boutefeu's,* Incendiaries . . . these Furious Sons of *Jehu,*" "whose Throats are a Burning Abyss, a Center of Envious Exhalations set on Fire of Hell" (*Review,* 26 June 1705, 14 July 1705) and who called forth some of Defoe's most eloquent puritan rhetoric.

615. *Zeal:* During the general election of May 1705 "Packington had a banner carried before him whereon was painted a church falling with this inscription, For the Queen and the Church Packington" (HMC *Portland MSS., 4,* 189).

617. *Plosko'* . . . *o'erthrew:* Plosko' was William Lloyd, the 78-year old bishop of Worcester (1627–1717) who unsuccessfully opposed Pakington's re-election in July 1702 on the grounds that he was "a Whoremonger, Drunkard, and Swearer," "so full of Jacobitism, that it could not be rooted out" (*POAS,* Yale, *6,* 489). As soon as parliament convened Pakington complained at the bar of the House of Commons that the lord bishop of Worcester had violated his rights and privileges. No fewer than 15 witnesses for the plaintiff were heard and without even hearing the witnesses on the other side, the Commons voted *nem. con.* that the proceedings of the lord bishop were "in high Violation of the Liberties and Privileges of the Commons of *England*" (*CJ, 14,* 37) and upon an address from the House, Queen Anne removed Worcester from his place as her lord almoner (Luttrell, *5,* 238).

And mad with *Zeal*, and mad with *Envy* spoke.
    Ye Poles (*says he*) *Regard the tott'ring State,*
And think with me, of our Fore-Fathers Fate;
The Rebel Cossacks *all their Force o'erthrew,*   625
I'd rather see the *Swedes* do so for you.
But let us all the Cossacks *first Expel,*
And Tack *their Ruine to the* Tribute-Bill:
The Poles *may then in* Peace *and* Union *thrive,*
And Ecclesiastick *Tyranny revive.*   630
Augustus *may our* Quiet *Recommend,*
But while these *Live, what* Peace *can He pretend?*
And if Augustus *Favours their Defence,*
To His Dethroning 'tis a just pretence,
I Hate a Cossack, *tho' He were my* Prince.   635
    He Spoke, and Fury choak'd his rising Spleen,
And Passion kept more dang'rous Language in.
For now he Mourns his just Designs are crost,
Complains that *Speech* the Place he talk'd for, lost;
Declares he meant no Mischief to the Crown,   640
Aim'd at no gen'ral Int'rest but his *Own,*

623–35. These lines apparently represent or parody a speech of Pakington's in favor of the Tack in November 1704, but no record of this speech has survived. Pakington's *A Speech for the Bill against Occasional Conformity* [n.d. but c. December 1703] and his speech on the church in danger of December 1705, indicate that Defoe's parody is not much exaggerated. Here is a sample from the former: "Are we afraid to disoblige a Party of Men [the dissenters], that are against the Church and Government? Whose Principle of Hatred and Malice to the Family of *Stuarts* descends to them by Inheritance? Men, Sir, that offered open violence to her Majesty's Royal Grandfather; Men that have not only the Impudence at this time to justifie that Fact, but to turn the day of his Murder into Ridicule, and keep a Calves-head-Feast in the City."

625–26. *Cossacks . . . Swedes:* dissenters . . . French.

630. *Ecclesiastick Tyranny revive:* "So that the whole Argument must Turn upon this, whether the Church, has a Right to force the Conscience, or in plain *English,* to Persecute for Conscience Sake" ([Defoe], *A Serious Inquiry into This Grand Question,* 1704, p. 27). While more extreme writers were claiming that the Church of England had been "a Persecuting-Church ever since the REFORMATION," Defoe insisted that "the Church of *England,* has no persecuting Inclination of her self" (*Moderation Display'd. The Second Part,* 1705, sig. A2r; *Review,* 12 June 1705).

639. *the Place he talk'd for:* "Sir *John* is of another Temper, than to talk for a Place, and of too large an Estate to make his Conscience truckle to his Interest, as some that have gone over from the Church-party have" (*D*). Although Pakington boasted in his monumental inscription that "he spoke his mind in parliament without reserve, neither fearing nor flattering those in power, but despising all their offers of title and preferment" (*DNB, 15,* 93), one offer that he did not despise was £800 a year charged against an assumed name on the Irish Civil List (Holmes, p. 361).

For that he spoke, and thought he should, no doubt,
Talk Himself *in, and Talk the* Cossacks *out:*
But all his Province their Resentment show,
All his *Consolidating Nonsense* know,   645
Their future *Trusts* to *Packsky* they refuse,
So Perish all that *Poland*'s *Trusts* abuse.
    When froward *Towerosky* took his place,
Zeal on his *Tongue*, and *Fury* in his *Face*.
    Ye rev'rend Poles (*says he*) *let Heav'n forbid*   650
That Words should Poland'*s Liberties decide;*
Our War's remote, but these are Foes *indeed;*
I'd rather Beat the Cossacks *than the* Swede.
Augustus *talks to Us, I hope, in vain,*
Of Peace, *while Factious* Cossacks *shall remain,*   655
The Spawn of Rebels of Tartarian *Race,*
Who Ask no Favour, and Deserve no Grace;
If first Augustus *will Destroy the Breed,*
Then Peace at Home *may probably succeed;*
But while this Vip'rous Brood the Poles *betray,*   660
I'd not Augustus, *tho' Himself were here, Obey.*
    He said, and more than Half the *Dyet* Bow'd,

646. *Packsky . . . refuse:* Pakington's enemies distributed copies of *A Speech for the Bill against Occasional Conformity* (623–35n. above) to the freeholders of Worcestershire in anticipation of a dissolution of parliament. Charles Stephens tried to assess the effectiveness of this move in a letter of 5 January 1704 to Pakington: "Mr. Amphlet . . . is affraid you have lost by your speech. I must confess I think not; that you nor your Ancestors never had more Dissenters than the Influence of prevailing friends brought for you; and if you lose any thing that way, it must be in Mr. [Edward] Foleys party: but I cannot think the Church Party all so fast asleep or quite infatuated, that they will not rouse and exert their strength for a Person that has hazarded all so far in their Service" (Worcestershire R. O. MS. Hampton 705: 349 BA4657 [iii]). After a fierce contest in the general election of May 1705, Sir John was returned, "which is an Argument, that Mr. *Foe* shot his Bolt too soon" (*D*).
    648. *Towerosky:* "The Noble Gentleman . . . personated here [is] Mr. B——, Brother to the E—— of A——" (*D*). James Bertie (1673–1735), second son to James, earl of Abingdon, was a high church Tory member for New Woodstock (1696–1705) and Middlesex (1710–34), a Poussineer, Tacker, and member of the October Club. Dryden wrote a funeral elegy to his mother, Eleonora. He is "Towerosky" because his brother, Montagu, second earl of Abingdon, was appointed constable of the Tower of London in May 1702.
    656. *Tartarian:* "Papist" (*Key*). Sacheverell had called dissenters "the *Bastard Spawn*" of papists (*The Political Union. A Discourse Shewing the Dependence of Government on Religion,* 1702, p. 55), but in the present context the equation seems too particular. "Tartarian" may be a more general term like "barbarian."
    658. *Destroy the Breed:* Cf. [Defoe], *Advice to All Parties,* 1705, p. 19: "Here are in *England* . . . above two Millions of Dissenters . . . what [shall be] done with them? *Hang'd,* all *Hang'd, says Furioso.*"

And with consenting Silence 'twas Allow'd,
A Law should pass the *Cossacks* to Suppress,
The only way to *Poland*'s Happiness.   665
Mean while th'Assembly separately repair'd
To Church, and there the famous *Bursky* heard,
Now *Stansky,* then *Marosky,* and a Third,
That always dealt in *Tropes* and *Similies* absurd;
These furious Priests the fatal Stroke excite,   670
Tell them of Kings that spar'd th'*Amalekite;*
One Grave Divine, in Pulpit-Rhetorick known,
Talk'd of the *Dyet*'s Wit to show his own,
Banter'd a *Text* or two, and talk'd some *Greek,*
And so went Home to *Drink* out all the *Week;*   675
Dooms the poor *Cossacks* from the Sacred *Text,*
And Rav'd in Zeal till he the Cause perplext.

664. *A Law:* the three bills to prevent occasional conformity, or "to prevent the Growth
of Hypocrisy" (*D*), in Tory terms.

667. *Bursky:* Peter Birch (1652?–1710) was the high flying rector of St. Bride's, Fleet
Street. Even Francis Atterbury was shocked at the violence of his sermon on 30 January
1703 (Atterbury, *Works,* 1, 155). Cf. *On Dr. Birch, POAS,* Yale, *6,* 540.

668. *Stansky:* George Stanhope (1660–1728), whom Anne appointed dean of Canterbury
in March 1704, was one of the great preachers of the day. His sermon before the House of
Commons on the anniversary of the execution of Charles I so pleased the audience that they
desired him to publish it. "If Dr. *Stanhope,* in his Sermon upon the 30th of *January* at St.
Margaret's Church, apply'd the sparing the *Amalekite* to the Subject of that Day, it was ap-
plicable enough; for the Remissness of King *Charles* the second in not taking off the Regicides,
has been the chief Cause of our home-bred civil Dissentions ever since" (*D*). Sparing the
Amalekite (1 Samuel 28:18), however, is not mentioned in the printed sermon, which is
not a "Furioso" performance.

Marosky: A gloss in the Indiana University copy 2 of *Ab* identifies Marosky as "Dr.
Marrow," of whom nothing further can be learned. The BPL copy of *Ab* has a heavily
cropped gloss which may be "[   ] marwood."

a Third: It is probably futile to speculate about the identity of the "Third," but it is
true that Sacheverell's inflammatory sermon preached at the Oxford assizes on 9 March
1704 (702*n.* below) deploys an absurd simile about the multiplicity of sects "Which are
Drawn like so many *Lines* from a *Center,* all *Uniting* in the *Same Point,* yet *Separated* and
Widening from each Other," that was widely ridiculed (*The Nature and Mischief of Prejudice
and Partiality Stated,* 1704, p. 49).

671. *spar'd th'Amalekite:* It was Samuel who "obeyed not the voice of the Lord, nor exe-
cuted his fierce wrath upon Amalek" (1 Samuel 28:18). And Sacheverell, in the assize
sermon mentioned above, both quoted Greek and reminded the grand jury that they were
the "*Ministers of God . . . Appointed as Revengers to Execute Wrath upon Those that do Evil*"
(*The Nature and Mischief of Prejudice and Partiality Stated,* 1704, p. 57).

675. *Drink:* The same innuendo occurs in Defoe, *The Consolidator,* 1705, pp. 219–20:
Sacheverell is said to be "*not Mad,* Distracted and *Raving . . .* but *. . .* in his Senses, es-
pecially in a Morning when he was a little *free from,* &c." The charge is made explicit in
William Bisset, *The Modern Fanatick,* 1710, p. 29.

676–77. *Dooms . . . And Rav'd:* For a similar confusion of tenses see lines 864–65 below.

Priests, like the Female Sex, when they Engage,
There's always something Bloody in their Rage.
He told the *Dyet* they must *Fight* and *Pray,*   680
And pull the *Cossacks* down the *Shortest Way;*
And in his Zeal, so far his *Text* forgot,
He Perjur'd his *Augustus* on the Spot;
Unchurch'd the Nation, Curst the *Polish Tribes,*
And for their Cure, the *Cossacks* Blood prescribes.   685
　　Satyr, thy just Regret with Force restrain,
With *Temper Write,* altho' thou *Think'st* with *Pain.*
When once the Pulpit-Plague Infects the Land,
And *Sermon-Readers* get the upper-hand,
The Nations Ruin'd, all the Town's Undone,   690
And Tongue-pad Evils thro' the Vitals Run;
Reason submits its Captivated Head,
And *Raging Nonsence* Governs in its Stead.
In Vain our Banish'd Libertys we seek,
Wisemen are bound to hear, when *Coxcombs* speak;   695
Reason pays Homage to Impertinence,
And *Noise* Obtains the Victory from *Sence;*
The *Clamouring* Priest, Dogmatick, Proud and *Dull,*
Assumes Dictating Right, and *calls his Master Fool.*
　　But if the Pulpit now began to Fire,   700
The Press, the Pulpits Eccho, pusht it Higher.
Bold *Sacharesky,* in a Polish Rage,
Would all the *Poles* in Civil Blood Ingage;
Prints his Exasperated Fiery Zeal,

689. *Sermon-Readers:* "The Church of *England* Clergy are *Sermon-Readers,* they don't *Preach* and *Pray* extempore, like Dissenters" (*D*).

691. *Tongue-pad:* "a smooth, Glib-tongued, insinuating Fellow" (*New Dictionary*).

702. *Sacharesky:* "By *Sachareski,* it will not be amiss to read Mr. *Sacheverel,* Fellow of *Magdalen Colledge,* a Gentleman whose Accomplishments and Zeal render him . . . an Honour to the Church and University" (*D*). Henry Sacheverell (1674?–1724) began waving "the *Bloody Flag* . . . of Defiance" at the dissenters in a sermon preached before Oxford University on 2 June 1702. After February 1703 when Anne repeated her assurance that "upon all Occasions of Promotions to any Ecclesiastical Dignity, I shall have a very just Regard to such as are eminent and remarkable for their . . . Zeal" (*LJ, 17,* 322), Sacheverell had an additional reason to be zealous. His first reward came in 1705 when he was made chaplain of the "most splendidly" repaired church of St. Savior's in Southwark. Besides parodying his rhetoric in *The Shortest-Way with the Dissenters* (1702), Defoe had attacked Sacheverell by name in *A Hymn to the Pillory* (1703) (*POAS,* Yale, *6,* 591) and in half a dozen pamphlets.

704. *Prints:* Besides his sermons (668*n.,* 702*n.* above) Sacheverell had published *The Character of a Low-Churchman* (1702), an attack on bishop Lloyd (617*n.* above), and *The*

And *Damns the Crown, for fear o'th'Common Weal.*   705
   As two Extreams, one Mischief may Prevent,
This Fury made the *Polish* Lords Relent,
And Senators, their first Resolves, Repent.
   The Dyet Reasum'd, *Cavensky* broke
The Healing Party's silence first, and spoke: 710
   The hasty Priest (says he) I understood,
The Gown, *too often* Dips *the Sleeves* in Blood:
Th'unheard of Insolence, amaz'd my Soul,
And Horrour seizes every Christian *Pole;*
I am a Northern Deputy 'tis known,   715
Where numerous *Cossacks* Dwell in every Town;
The Peaceful, and Industrious People show,
No Reason, why they should be Treated so;
What is't to us, what their Fore-Fathers were,
The *Polish* Crown's too fast for us to Fear;   720
Besides, Rebellions differ but in Name,
In future Ages Ours may be the same;
If e're the Old *Jagellan* Race should Reign,
And Damn Our Revolutions; 'Tis in Vain
To Talk of Titles where the Swords Devour;   725
They'r always Rebels who have lost their Power.
The *Cossacks* now Encorporate, and Ty'd
By Laws, by Interest, and by Blood Allied,
Are Native *Poles,* in *Poland's* Interest Bound:
To tack them now, would *Poland's* Peace Confound;   730
They'r rich and brave, and always have withstood
Th'Invading *Tartars,* with their Wealth and Blood;

Rights of the Church of England Asserted and Proved (1705), but Thomas Hearne (*1,* 11) reveals
that Sacheverell "was Author of that Part only which Reflects upon the Dedication of that
Book [*The Rights of Protestant Dissenters,* 1704–05]. The other part which is far the larger, &
much better written, was done by Mr. [Edmund] Parks of Corpus Christi Colledge."

709. *Cavensky:* William Cavendish, marquis of Hartington (c. 1673–1729), eldest son of the
duke of Devonshire, became "a considerable Figure in the House of Commons," where he
sat for Derby (November 1695–November 1701), Castle Rising (1701–02), and Yorkshire
(1702–07). He was a low churchman, a staunch Whig, and "a constant Opposer of Mr.
Howe" (Macky, p. 47). He was one of the leaders of the opposition to the occasional con-
formity bills (*CJ, 14,* 241).

719. *Fore-Fathers:* Cf. 623–35n. above.

723. *the Old Jagellan Race:* the male line of the house of Stuart (207n. above) whose claim
to the throne of Britain was set aside at the revolution (p. 409 below).

732. *Tartars:* See 656n. above.

And have undoubted Title to Pretend
T'Enjoy that Land, they helpt us to Defend;
Besides, by Laws, their Liberties remain,   735
Those Laws, *Augustus* promis'd to Maintain,
This Priest would make those Promises in Vain:
I think their Liberties their Due, t'Enjoy,
That they may help us now, the *Swedes* Destroy;
 With him, the Old Nobility Concur'd,   740
And Damn'd the Bill as Cruel and Absurd.
 The Zealous Deputies resist in Vain,
And Envy Prompts them to their strong Disdain;
With mighty Struggle, and avow'd Regret,
They only seem t'Adjourn the warm Debate;   745
Resolv'd in future Dyets to Persue
The Cossacks *Ruin, and the Nations too.*
 Augustus, how Unhappy is thy Fate?
How hardly dost thou hold the Tottering State?
In vain, of Peace, thou do'st the *Poles* Persuade,   750
Deep as Infernal Darkness, their designs are Laid.
 Let them no more, thy Soveraign Peace Abuse,
Subjects can ne're the Princes Grace Refuse;
But 'tis a certain Signal to the Throne,
They aim at no less Purchase than his Crown.   755
But still *Augustus,* his just Wrath forbears,
And Honours Load the vilest Wretch he fears;

736. *promis'd:* In her speech proroguing parliament on 25 May 1702 Anne had promised to "be very careful to preserve and maintain the Act of Toleration, and to set the Minds of all My People at Quiet" (*LJ, 17,* 150). Then she mobilized all the resources of the court to secure passage of the first bill to prevent occasional conformity that so disquieted the minds her dissenting subjects that she had to repeat her assurances at the close of this session on 27 February 1703: "I hope, that such of [my Subjects] as have the Misfortune to dissent from the Church of *England* will rest secure and satisfied in the Act of Toleration, which I am firmly resolved to maintain" (*LJ, 17,* 321). Defoe was so fond of recalling these promises (*POAS,* Yale, *6,* 563, 638) that he was accused of bantering the queen (*The Fox with His Fire-brand Unkennell'd and Insnar'd,* 1703, p. 20).

741. *Damn'd the Bill:* The first bill to prevent occasional conformity was killed in the House of Lords by loading it with amendments unacceptable to the Commons. The second and third bills were voted down upon divisions: 71–59 on 14 December 1703 and 71–50 on 15 December 1704 (*Parl. Hist., 6,* 170–71, 368).

742. *Zealous Deputies:* the Tackers.

746–47. Cf. Defoe, *Declaration without Doors,* 12n. below.

751. Defoe retorts upon Shippen, *Moderation Display'd,* 3–4 above, that the "designs" of Jacobites, not the "Scheme of *Moderation,*" are conceived in Hell.

755. *Crown:* Cf. *The French King's Cordial,* 13n.

Fain he would all their Due Allegiance Buy,
Does all his Soft Engaging Favours Trye;
To all the Charms of Kindness he's Enclin'd,   760
With Grace, would win a *Turks* more constant Mind.
Dispos'd to Pardon, all their Follies past,
And Win them to their Countries Good at last,
Heaps, Undeserv'd, his Favours on their Heads,
With gentle Hand, to their own Duty leads,   765
Shows them the way to save the bleeding State,
And Trusts them with his Own, and *Poland*'s Fate.
Till Treason, Blacken'd with Ingratitude,
Had all their Sence and Modesty Subdu'd;
Ripen'd by Royal Mercy for Reproof,   770
The Patient Prince had been Provok'd enough.
    In vain he's of *Livonian* Plots afraid,
And *Swedes* preparing *Poland* to Invade;
Intestine Feud, the *Polish* Rakes Persue,
Their King, instead of *Cossacks* to Undo;   775
Neglect the publick danger to the last,
And make the Nations real Fears, their Jest;
Willing to leave us Open to surprize,
Poland can have no greater Enemies.
    Tocoski first, a forward Southern *Pole*,   780
A Polish'd *Carcass,* and a *Burnish'd Soul;*
We cannot say, he did the silence Break,
For he did always *little else but speak:*
How vain a thing's the Empty Sound of Words
Abstracted from the meaning it affords.   785
Long Speeches from his *heated spleen* proceed,
And Nature makes him talk, to ease his Head;

768. *Ingratitude:* Ingratitude is England's national vice in *The True-Born Englishman* (*POAS*, Yale, *6,* 262–63).
    780. *Tocoski:* John Toke (1671–1746) was educated at Trinity College, Oxford, and the Middle Temple. In parliament, where he sat for East Grinstead (1702–08), he was a country Tory and a Tacker. According to a gloss in the Indiana University copy 2 of *Ab* Toke was also "a writer for the Jacks [Jacobites]," but if this is true he was a writer like Henry Mordaunt, another Oxonian whose works were unknown to Anthony à Wood. It is clear from a passage in Defoe's letter to Harley of 28 September 1704 that his "character" of Toke was written from personal experience. He tells Harley that the false report of his arrest "for reflecting on admiral Rooke" (493*n.* above) required him to return to London where he "happend of a smart Rencounter with Mr *Toke* of East Greensted" (*Letters,* p. 58).

The *Hypocondriack* Vapours, upward Fly,
And form some Words of State and Policy;
Bear with the States-man, 'twas his *flux of Gall,*   790
For all Men know, he never meant it all.
   He Dooms the *Cossacks* to *Tartarian* Shades,
Their Civil and Religious Rights Invades.
Demand no Reason Satyr, that's supply'd
With Passion, Parties, Prejudice and Pride;   795
But if his Wiser Arguments you'd know,
He heard 'twas Just, *Old Seymsky* told him so;
That Learned Oracle supports the Cause,
And Noisy Zeal supplies the want of Laws.
   The Hot Young Beau, affects the *Marshals Chair,*   800
And hopes in time to rule *the Dyet* there;
Now he's the Party Leader of the Day,
Resolv'd to teach the *Cossacks* how to Pray,
Or from the *Polish Church* to Drive 'em all away.
   A Troop of *Tackers* at his Elbow stand,   805
Ready to move at his Usurpt Command,
Who all the Image of their Captain bear,
And in his Name may Read their Character:
The Word *in Polish,* signifies *a Fool,*
A Man without a Meaning, call'd a Tool,   810
A Weighty Block-head with an Empty Scull.

788. *Vapours:* Cf. *"Vapours,* ascending from the lower Faculties . . . over-shadow the Brain" (Swift, *A Tale of a Tub* [1704], *Prose, 1,* 105).

792. *Tartarian:* hellish; cf. *Paradise Lost, 2,* 69: "*Tartarean* Sulphur, and strange fire."

797. *Seymsky:* "Sir *Ed. S[eymou]r* . . . himself would think it no Disparagement to advise with him" (*D*).

800. *the Marshals Chair:* Harley's appointment as secretary of state in May 1704 encouraged the country Tories to think they could replace him as Speaker of the Commons. The party leaders agreed to meet in caucus at the Fountain Tavern a full week before the opening of the next session (HMC *Bagot MSS.,* p. 338). Bromley was ambitious for the post himself and summoned his friends to attend the first day (Cambridge University MS. Cholmondeley Corr. 359; cf. W. Coxe, *Memoirs of the Life and Administration of Sir Robert Walpole,* 3 vols., 1798, *2,* 4–5). But there were other candidates as well. One of them was Sir Edward Seymour who had been Speaker in the cavalier parliament. But "Broomly [and] his high-flyers could not agree upon him; so he [Seymour] turned against meddling in that matter" (*State Papers and Letters Addressed to William Carstares,* ed. J. McCormick, Edinburgh, 1774, p. 730). Another candidate, on the unconfirmed evidence of the present poem, was John Toke. In the event, however, the expected attack did not materialize because "the party that intended to throw the Secretary out of the chair found themselves too weak, and did not attempt it" (BM MS. Add. 7078, f. 223).

Nor let enquiring Heads decline the Name,
Tackers and *Tookites* always are the same;
The Emblematick Title's eas'ly known,
Their *Coat of Arms* stands up in *Warsaw* Town;   815
Rampant *the Ass*, Enrob'd *in Lyons Skin*,
To make the *Bully* keep the *Block-head* in;
Quarter'd at large it lyes, *Parte-Per-Pale*,
The *Asses Ears* against the *Lyons Tayl*:
The Family from *Tartary* Descends,   820
And all the *Furioso*'s are *their Friends;*
Before the *Swedish* Conquest they came in,
And some are lately Run away again.
Their num'rous Offspring fills our *Polish* Rolls,
So close ally'd to all our Native *Poles;*   825
We hardly know from whence they came, or when,
And yet they boast they're *True-born* Polish-men.
These are the Men would pull the *Cossacks* down,
And after them, *Augustus* and his Crown,
But *Poland*'s Genius Laught in *Hissing Air*,   830
And Guilt made all the *Rakes* disclose their Fear.
The *BILL*'s thrown out, but still they push their Cause,
In future *Dyets* hope for future *Laws;*
Rail at the *Cossacks*, false Constructions draw,
And *Bully* those they cannot *Kill by Law*.   835
    Bromsky with *Polish* Air, but *Swedish* Skill,

813. *Tackers and Tookites:* Defoe had used the word "*Tookites*" in *A Hymn to Victory* ("Madam, *The Glories of Your Happy Reign*"), 1704, p. 12, to mean parliamentary obstructionists. "*The Tookites,* a Poem upon the 134" is one of the mock book titles in [Defoe], *The Consolidator*, 1705, p. 358.

818. *Parte-Per-Pale:* divided by a vertical line through the middle *(OED)*.

821. *Furioso's:* cf. 484n. above.

826–27. "He is quoting himself, and the *True-born English-man* must be brought in, though introduc'd by the Head and Shoulders" (*D*). The lines of *The True-Born Englishman* that Pittis refers to are 50–51: "*Britannia* freely will disown the Name [*True-Born Englishman*], / And hardly knows her self from whence they came."

832. *still they push:* "who is not still for Conformity Bill / [is] surely a Rogue" (*A Health to the Tackers*, 23–24, above).

836. *Bromsky:* William Bromley of Baginton (1664–1732) was educated at Christ Church, Oxford, and on the grand tour. In parliament, where he sat for his native Warwickshire (1690–98) and Oxford University (March 1701–32), he was the leading Tory high churchman until 1710. After 1710 he joined Harley and served as Speaker (1710–13) and secretary of state (1713–14).

Boasts that he was the *Father of the Bill:*
In Foreign Parts he Travell'd much in Vain,
Just made a *Book,* and so came *Home* again:
Tells us he saw a *Bridge* at *Rochester,*   840
And when he was at *Chatham,* HE WAS THERE;
So when progressively to *France* he's come,
He Gravely says, *he knew he wa'n't at Home;*
Tells us he saw at *Oyse* a sad Disaster,
The Bridge broke down, because't *could stand no faster.*   845

837. *Father of the Bill:* Although Nottingham seems to have been the first to propose a bill to prevent occasional conformity (*Moderation Display'd,* 78*n.* above), Bromley claimed to have conceived it independently: "*You may think it is a notion Lord Nottingham has put into my head,*" he said, "*but upon my word it is my own thought*" (*Account of the Conduct,* p. 155). In any case, it was Bromley who drafted the three bills and managed their passage through the House of Commons, "much to the Content of the University," as Hearne (*1,* 301) recorded.

839. *Book:* In 1692 Bromley published an account of his European tour, entitled *Remarks in the Grande Tour of France and Italy,* that Harley was able to turn to account in 1705. "Being apprehensive of [Bromley's] Rivalling him in the Speaker's Chair [800*n.* above], by a superior Interest in *High-Church*" (Oldmixon, *History,* p. 345), Harley caused Bromley's book to be reprinted with a "silly Index," as Hearne (*2,* 11) called it, directing the reader to the more fatuous or compromising passages (HMC *Downshire MSS, 1,* ii, 843). "To all that came to his House about that Time, [Harley] said, *Have you not seen Mr. Br——y's Travels?* Being answer'd in the Negative, he went into a back Parlour, where this Impression of it lay, fetch'd it out, and gave every one a Copy, 'till that Matter was made up" (Oldmixon, *History,* p. 345). Hearne (*1,* 232) believed that Bromley would have been elected Speaker in October 1705 "had it not been for the Base Arts of the Courtiers . . . one of which was to publish a Book of his Travells . . . which they turn'd into Ridicule . . . by a scurrilous Index." That Defoe was aware of Harley's stratagem is evident from a passage in *The Consolidator,* published on 26 March 1705. In a list of mock book titles is this one (p. 355): "*Les Bagatelles,* or *Brom——ys* Travels into *Italy,* a choice Book, and by great Accident preserv'd from the malitious Design of the Author, who diligently Bought up the whole Impression, for fear they should be seen, as a thing of which this ungrateful Age was not worthy." Defoe's insistence that Bromley tried to suppress the book (cf. 861 below) is difficult to reconcile with the fact that two impressions or editions of it were published in 1692 and 1693. Bromley, of course, complained that Harley's ploy was "a very malicious proceeding, my words and meaning being plainly perverted in several places; which, if they had been improper, and any observations trifling or impertinent, an allowance was due for my being very young when they were made" (*Bibliotheca Parriana: A Catalogue of the Library of the Late Reverend and Learned Samuel Parr, LL.D.,* 1827, p. 702). Bromley was 28 when he published his *Remarks.*

840. *saw a Bridge:* "When I left it [Rochester], and had passed the Bridge, I was at Chatham" (*Remarks in the Grande Tour of France and Italy,* 1692, p. 1).

843. *wa'n't at Home:* "Crosses and Crucifixes are so plentiful every where on this Road, that from them alone an *Englishman* will be satisfied he is out of his own Countrey; besides, the Roads are much better than ours" (ibid., p. 4).

845. *Bridge broke down:* "Over the river *Oyse,* by *Senlis,* an ordinary Village, I was forc'd to Ferry, the Bridge, that was broke down by the *Spaniards,* in the last Civil Wars, being not yet re-built" (ibid., pp. 4–5).

And at *Chantilly*, th'Prince of *Conde's* Town,
A Castle stood, before they *pull'd it down;*
Monstrevil's Fortify'd, but is not Strong,
Paris lyes round, and yet is two Mile long;
And, of the Buildings, this Sage *Truth* he tells,   850
They're gen'rally of *Stone, OR SOMETHING ELSE.*
Some Lands lye high, some lower still and lower,
And where the People are not *Rich, THEY'RE POOR.*
The Learned Author then proceeds to tell
How near the *Alps* he clamber'd up a Hill,   855
With many a weary Step, and many a Stride,
And so *came down again,* on t'other side.
Tells us at *Rome* he saw a swinging Church,
And reads a Learned *Lecture* on the Porch:
Inform'd the World in Print where he had been,   860
But bought the Books himself, for fear they should be seen.
   This worthy Author, warm with *Polish* Zeal,
Strives all the *Cossacks* Freedom to repeal,
Corrects the Bill, and to remove our Doubt,
The *Persecution Preamble* left out;   865

847. *Castle stood:* "Near to it, is *Chantilly,* the Seat of the *Princes* of *Conde,* whither the late
P. retired, after the Civil Wars were ended; it is a noble old Castle; part has been pull'd
down by the present P. to be built greater" (ibid., p. 5).

848. *Monstrevil:* "*Monsternil* is a little Town in *Picardy,* situate, as the Name imports, on an
Hill, fortified with inner and outer Bastions, and a dry Ditch" (ibid., p, 3).

849. *Paris:* "*Paris* lies round and compact, not above a Mile and half any way long, the
Buildings all Stone, or resembling it" (ibid., p. 7).

855. *clamber'd up:* Bromley has much to say about the ups and downs of travel in the
mountains between Marseilles and Antibes, Varazze and Genoa, Genoa and Tortona (ibid.,
pp. 40–60).

858. *at Rome . . . a swinging Church:* Bromley provides pedestrian description of more
than 30 Roman churches (ibid., pp. 155–209).

861. *bought the Books himself:* See 839*n.* above. What must have proved most damaging to
Bromley was his reference to King William and Queen Mary as the prince and princess of
Orange and the account of his audience with the pope (*Declaration without Doors.* 54*n.* below).

865. *Preamble left out:* The first bill to prevent occasional conformity, presented to the
House of Commons in November 1702, included the following preamble: "As nothing is
more contrary to the Profession of the Christian Religion, and particularly to the Doctrine of
the Church of *England,* than Persecution for Conscience only; in due Consideration where of
an Act was passed in the first Year of the Reign of the late King *William* and Queen *Mary* of
glorious Memory, entituled, [the Toleration Act]" (Pittis, *Proceedings,* p. 3). From the second
bill, introduced in November 1703, the preamble was omitted. The reasons for this are not
clear. "The Preamble was not left out, because it savour'd of *Persecution,* but because the
Dissenters, and their Friends in Parliament, exclaim'd against it as such" (*D*). One of their
friends was Burnet, who exclaimed against the bill, not against the preamble: "I miss a

A Mark of Honesty, to let us kno',
They Scorn'd to Hide *what they resolv'd to do;*
Sure of the Game, the Mask was so laid by,
And blinded *Cossacks* saw their Destiny.
    Thus fir'd with Party Zeal, he Read the Bill,   870
And ask'd the Dyet how they lik'd *his Stile,*
With many a Learned Speech and formal Face,
For *Italy* had taught him *the Grimace.*
Th'Exasperated Fop his Plot Declares,
And to the Dyet makes *Revengeful Prayers;*   875
At *Cossacks* Ruin, makes the Grand Essay,
And tacks the Church's Fall *the Shortest Way.*
    Meersky, an Ancient Mercenary *Pole,*
With Vitious Body, and a Harden'd Soul,
Grown Old in *Crimes,* as he was Lame in *Sence,*   880

Preamble here that was in the former Bill, in favour of Toleration, which is now left out," he said in his speech in the House of Lords, "I confess, I do not know how it came to be there, for it did not very well agree with the Bill . . . It put me in Mind of a Clause in the Sentence of the Inquisitors, when a Heretick is condemn'd and deliver'd to the Secular Arm, they conjure the Magistrate by the Mercies of God, and the Bowels of Jesus Christ, that no Harm be done to the Obstinate Heretick . . . But all this is but *Farce,* for he is to be burn'd immediately" (ibid., pp. 43-44). In the third bill, introduced in November 1704, the preamble was put back, with its assurance that the Toleration Act *"ought to be inviolably observ'd,* [while] the rest of the Act notoriously invaded it" (Oldmixon, *History,* p. 344).

877. *tacks the Church's Fall:* "The Danger of the Church, is from Men of Heat and Passion . . . Let all True *English* Men but consider, how shall Popery be kept out? How shall the *French* be Beaten? How our Trade be carried on? How our Taxes paid? If instead of every Man's setting his Shoulder to the Burthen, we fall out . . . Oppress, Undermine, Exclude, and Tack upon one another" (*Review,* 17 April 1705).

878. *Meersky:* Sir Thomas Meres, Knight (1634-1715), was elected to parliament in April, called to the bar in May, and knighted in June 1660 (*A Calendar of the Inner Temple Records,* ed. F. A. Inderwick, 5 vols., 1896-1936, *2,* 334; Le Neve, p. 70). He soon became a prominent figure in the Commons, where he sat for Lincoln (1660-87, 1701, 1702-10), and his oratory was much admired by Pepys (*Diary, 6,* 114). He was Charles II's candidate for Speaker in March 1679 when Seymour was again elected (*CSPD 1679-80,* p. 98) and the Whigs believed that "turncoat Meres" had been bought by the court (*POAS,* Yale, *2,* 295). He was also one of the Commons' nominees for Speaker in 1685, but James II chose Sir James Trevor instead. He held a number of minor but potentially very profitable posts in the 1670s (*CTB 1669-72,* p. 912; *CTB 1672-75,* p. 696) and was a commissioner of the admiralty from 1679 to 1684. James II was so offended by Meres' refusal to support the declarations of indulgence that he removed him not only from the commission of foreign plantations but even from the commission of the peace (HMC *Portland MSS., 3,* 406). It was not until a Tory government had been formed in William's reign that Meres was again elected to parliament, December 1700. Under Anne his solid Tory record was somewhat tarnished by his refusal to vote for (or against) the Tack in November 1704; he was in short a Sneaker (*Numerical Calculation*).

But not at all decay'd in *Impudence;*
His long since baffl'd Conscience told his Fate,
He owns he's Damn'd, and there's an end of that:
But for the *Cossacks* Bill he rav'd so loud,
And so inflam'd his Old fermented Blood,   885
That some advis'd him to go home *to Bed,*
Open a Vein or Two and Shave *his Head,*
Not knowing he had long ago been Mad.
   The *Old Buffoon,* Debauch'd in early time,
Boasts of his Vice, and Hugs himself in Crime: 890
Lewdness has Forty Years forsook the Beast,
And left his Vicious Body to its Age and Rest;
But tho' the Active part of Vice is Dead,
The Rampant Devil's Regnant in his Head,
Hurries the Lewd Distemper'd Wretch along,   895
With Vile *Blaspheming Voice,* and *Baudy Tongue.*
   Well might *an Antient Polish Bard* Decree,
Jouler the Hound, a Wiser Beast than he:
Meersky has always been *the Dyets Jest,*
Laughs loudest at himself, to Please the rest;   900
Betwixt the Extreams of Banter, and of Rage,
He made himself the Fool, *the House the Stage,*
The *Polish Merry-Andrew,* shifting Shapes
Till he's the very Block-Head which he Apes.
   Wardsky, a Deputy of Northern Race,   905

886. *some:* These include Defoe, who advised the supporters of the bill to prevent occasional conformity to "retire into the Country, *Shave their Heads*" (*The High-Church Legion,* 1705, p. 19).

897. *Antient Polish Bard:* Despite Pittis's assurance that "Mr. *Dryden . . .* is *the Antient Polish Bard* here meant" (*D*), the NLS copy of *Ac* correctly glosses the line "John Ld Rochester." The reference is to *A Satyr against Reason and Mankind* (1679):

> If therefore Jowler finds and kills his hares,
> Better than Meres supplies committee chairs,
> Though one's a statesman, th'other but a hound,
> Jowler, in justice, would be wiser found.

(*The Complete Poems of John Wilmot, Earl of Rochester,* ed. David M. Vieth, New Haven and London, Yale University Press, 1968, p. 98).

899. *the Dyets Jest:* A poem of 1673 refers to Meres' "clownish jokes and silly jeers" (*POAS,* Yale, *1,* 205).

905. *Wardsky:* John Ward (1671?–1741) was educated at Christ Church, Oxford, and Gray's Inn, whence he was called to the bar in 1693. He was a Tory member of parliament for Newton, Lancashire (December 1703–15) and Thetford, Norfolk (1715–22). In November 1701 he was said to be "entirely of the sentiments" of Robert Harley (HMC *Portland*

Weak in his Head, but very strong in Face;
Assurance many Blessings may contain,
And often times *supplyes the want of Brain;*
A *Junior Tookite,* forward in the Cause,
To Damn the *Cossacks* by unheard of Laws;   910
A Scolding Clamouring Member, Vain and Loud,
Noisy in Words, and *not a little Proud;*
His *Polish* fury ran before his Sence,
Mighty in Wit, vast in Impertinence;
The Hissing Dyet Laught, the Beau went on,   915
Mutter'd a Curse or Two, *and so sat down.*
　　Satyr, make room for Men of *Polish* Wit,
Whose Zeal as well as Learning's too Polite;
A *Polish Tookite* of Collegiate Fame,
Hight *Anneslesky,* that's his *Polish* Name.   920
　　He Learnt ill Tongues *in Cambria's Famous Hall,*
And *very Aptly* represents them all:
Down with the *Cossacks* is his Darling Word,
The Bully Tongue supplies the Tamer Sword;
He Damns the *Cossacks* with Exalted Vote,   925
And Horrid Language fills his raveing Throat;
Nor does it Check the Man's degenerate Scorn,
To think that he *himself's a Cossack Born;*
Rather than not suppress the Growing Evil,

MSS., 4, 26). In the session of 1704–05, however, he deserted Harley, joined Bromley in managing the action against the Aylesbury electors and the third bill to prevent occasional conformity, and signalized himself as a Tacker (HMC *Bagot MSS.,* p. 338; Luttrell, *5,* 529; *CJ, 11,* 419; illustration, p. 65 above). In 1713 he deserted both Harley and Bromley and joined the Whimsical or Hanoverian Tories to vote against the French commerce bill.

920. *Anneslesky:* Arthur Annesley (d. 1737), a first half-cousin once removed of Francis Annesley (167n. above), was the third grandson of Arthur, first earl of Anglesey. He was educated in "*Cambria's Famous Hall,*" Magdalene College, elected a fellow in 1700, and member of parliament for the University (1702–10). He was one of the managers of the occasional conformity bills (*CJ, 14,* 238, 459), a Tacker, and true churchman (*Numerical Calculation*). He was also "greedy, self-centred, wayward and unscrupulous" (Holmes, p. 279). In 1710 he succeeded his brother John, whom Swift called the "great support of the Tories," as fifth earl of Anglesey.

924. *Tongue supplies the . . . Sword:* Similar stories are told of Annesley's grandfather: "he was soundly cudgelled by a Major Scott with whom he had declined a duel" (GEC, *1,* 134).

928. *a Cossack Born:* Annesley's grandfather "reconciled himself so effectually to the parliament, as to be taken into their favour and confidence." He served in 1645 and 1647 on a parliamentary commission to manage Irish affairs (*Biographia Britannica, 1,* 149; GEC, *1,* 134).

He freely Votes *his Fathers to the Devil*.   930
   Never did University pretend
To *Polish* Dyet such a Wretch to send;
'Tis own'd they did not Chuse him for his Sence,
But he got in by Dint of Impudence;
A finish'd Coxcomb, with assuming Wit,   935
In all *but Sence and Manners* he's Compleat;
So furnisht with the Language of the Town,
He made *our Dunghil Rhetorick,* all his own;
All his indeavours to support the State,
H'*Expresses* in *the Stile of Billingsgate;*   940
Of Modesty and Manners very Shy,
And blest with every Gift but Honesty.
   Gransky was newly made a *Polish* Lord,
Tho' most Men thought 'twas hasty and absurd,
His Honour thus, before his Wealth, should rise,   945
But that his *other Stock,* that Want supplies.
   One farther Mischief his advancement brought,
Our Polish Mob have made the Grievance out;
May-Fair and *Hockly* suffer such a Blow,
'Twill all the *Bears* and *Back-Sword Men* Undo;   950
All things give way to Fate's eternal Doom,
The shouting Croud ha' lost their Captain *Tom.*

943. *Gransky:* John Granville or Grenville (1665–1707) was the second son of John Gren-ville, earl of Bath. In parliament, where he sat for Launceston (1685–87), Plymouth (1689–98), Newport (1698–1700), Fowey (1701), and Cornwall (1701–03), he was a country Tory "qui s'est . . . ouvertement déclaré contre la Cour" (BM MS. Add. 30000B, f. 264v). During the session of 1701 he was one of the ringleaders in the impeachment of the Junto lords, having "been lately bought / And Country left for Court" (*The Ballad; Or, Some Scurrilous Reflections in Verse, on the Proceedings of the Honourable House of Commons: Answer'd,* 1701, p. 14). Upon the accession of Anne he was promoted from a colonel of the guards to lieutenant general of the ordnance, sworn of the privy council, and made lord lieutenant of Cornwall. In March 1703 he was created Baron Granville of Potheridge.

946. *other Stock:* "He is a Gentleman . . . with an undaunted Assurance" (Macky, p. 88).

949. *May-Fair:* May Fair was the annual rite held "in a Place called *Brook-Field,*" between St. James's and Hyde Park, where young people "spent their Time and Money in Drunken-ness, Fornication, Gaming, and Lewdness" (Strype, *2,* 34).

Hockly: the bear garden at Hockley le Hole, near Clerkenwell. The program for 27 April 1702 included "a bald faced Dog of Middlesex against a fallow Dog of Cow Cross . . . five let-goes," "a great Mad Bull . . . with Fire-works all over him, and two or three Cats ty'd to his Tail, and Dogs after them," beginning at two o'clock (HMC *Cowper MSS., 3,* 7).

952. *Captain Tom:* the proverbial "Leader of . . . the Mob" (*New Dictionary,* sig. C4r). Defoe had observed in *A New Satyr on the Parliament* (1701), 89–90, that Granville "Plyes closely at the Dancing tent, / And manages *May*-Fair" (*POAS,* Yale, *6,* 326; cf. ibid., *6,* 351).

See how the *Stage of Dirty Honour fails,*
And *Warsaw* her *Street-Colonel* Bewails;
No more the *Gladiator* now appears,   955
Patron to all the *Whores,* and all the *Bears,*
The *Polish Smithfield* Butchers storm and rage,
And sable Weeds adorn the drooping Stage;
Prize-fighting Triumphs pass no more *Cheap-side,*
Nor *female Champions* in their Armour ride,   960
The *Sword* and *Dagger-Heroes* are undone,
Gransky their darling Patron, *Gransky*'s gone;
Augustus thus at one unhappy Word,
Lost the wild Gentry first to gain the Lord.

　　Yet *Gransky* once the People's Humour Crost,   965
He would be for the *Bill,* whate'er it cost;
Tho' all the *Poles* their high Dislike exprest,
And so the *Bill* and *Lord* made up the Jest.
Gransky was always Zealous for the State,
But when the *Swedes* endanger'd *Poland*'s Fate,   970
He gravely Vow'd and Swore he'd ne'er Associate.

　　Not Vows nor Oaths can *Polish* Members bind,
When latent Prospects preposses the Mind;
For when he had the *Mareschal's Chair* in View,
Thro' Forty Oaths that blessing he'd Persue.   975
Satyr, The Ambitious Wretch Comiserate,
Insult no more a Man of adverse Fate;
The Sullen Member, *Chagrin* and *Perplext,*
With high extreams of Pride, and Envy *Vext,*
Because from Speaking Office he must *Fall,*   980
For two long Years, *he'd hardly speak at all.*

　　Augustus always, *all Men's Good* Intends,
To make the Man of Mischief some Amends,
He sent him down among his *Western* Friends.

966. *for the Bill:* Granville was one of the managers of the first bill to prevent occasional conformity (*CJ, 14,* 78).

971. *he'd ne'er Associate:* Granville refused to join the association for the defense of William III, was "one of Sir *John Fenwick*'s great Advocates," and was reported to be a Jacobite in 1698 (Macky, p. 87; BM MS. Add. 30000B, f. 273v).

974. *Mareschal's Chair in View:* Granville was one of the three unsuccessful Tory candidates for Speaker of the Commons in December 1698 when it was hoped that "les grands profits qui sont annexés à la Charge d'Orateur, et l'esperance d'en obtenir de plus grands, l'addouciroient, et l'apprivoiseroient avec la Cour" (BM MS. Add. 30000B, f. 264v–265). He was reconciled to the court by other means (943*n.* above).

The *Tinners* Petty Dyet he *Prepares,*   985
Bear-Garden there, in *Minature Appears;*
The *Mobb-Assembly* healed his Discontent,
For *Rabble* always was his Element.
   In High Mock Majesty, and awkward State,
He *Apes the Prince,* and thinks himself as great;   990
The Black Assembly, in the Sulph'rous Shades,
Where Mining Hand the Glitt'ring Oar Invades,
With all the Elder Devils of the Mines,
He calls in Convocations like Divines;
Mob'd them a Speech, within their Smoaky Den,   995
Said *much of Nothing,* and came Home again.
   Banksky, a New Contemporary Lord,
An Orator at *Poland*'s *Chancery* Board,
Furnisht with *Ciceronian* Eloquence,
And mighty *flights* of Language, *none of Sence;*   1000
Speech-making was his due Paternal Fame,
And made his Voice *a Pun* upon his Name;
A Tongue-Pad Family, of Wheedling Race,
And talks of *nothing* with a Wondrous Grace.
   Augustus mov'd him, as 'twas understood,   1005
That he might do no Harm who did no Good:
The *Cossacks* at his Honour much Rejoyce,
For right or wrong, they always lost his Voice;

---

985. *Tinners Petty Dyet:* The Stannaries in Cornwall was the corporate body of the tinners, who elected representatives to a "Convocation" (994) in Truro. Granville, as lord warden of the Stannaries, presided over the convocation of September 1703 (Luttrell, *5,* 336).
. 995. *a Speech:* "The Speech which he calls a *Mobb-Speech* may be seen in the *Gazette*" (*D*). Granville managed to introduce a threadbare allusion to "that horrid Rebellion" of 1641 (*The London Gazette,* 20–23 September 1703).
   997. *Banksky:* "By *Banksky* we are to understand the *L[or]d Gu[ern]sey* who Married Sir *John Banks*'s Daughter" (*D*). Heneage Finch had married Elizabeth, daughter of Sir John Banks of London, first baronet, in May 1678.
   998. *Chancery Board:* Heneage Finch served as solicitor general from 1679 to 1686.
   1000. *none of Sence:* Burnet (*1,* 555) similarly observed that in summing up the crown's case against Lord Russell in 1683, Finch "shewed more of a vicious eloquence . . . than of solid or sincere reasoning."
   1001. *Paternal Fame:* Finch's grandfather had been Speaker of the House of Commons (1626) and his father lord chancellor (1674–82).
   1002. *Pun:* "As for his Voice being a Pun upon his Name, (*viz.*) that there is Musick in it . . . that is so sorry a Conundrum that *OWEN SWAN* [proprietor of the Black Swan tavern and a famed punster] would kick his Vinegar drawer out of Doors for it" (*D*).
   1003. *Tongue-Pad:* See 691*n.* above.

And *Finchsky*'s glad of his assistance here,
To Check sometimes the too much talking *Peer,*   1010
By Force, to stop the forward weak Effort,
Least he should make the *Dyet* too much Sport;
How oft in Pitty has he Pinn'd him down,
Whisper'd his Father's Credit, and his own;
Told him his Grandsire's old, substantial Rule,   1015
That Silence never can describe a Fool.

    Unhappy *Finsky,* had he been but Wise,
And took his Younger Brother's grave Advice,
Whartsky, Mohunsky, and a Hundred more,
Had been as Sober as they were before;   1020
The *Dyet*'s Gravity had ne'er been broke,
For no Man Laugh'd but just when Finsky *spoke.*

    Bucksky, a stalking, sharping, *Polish* Peer,
A Whoreing, Gameing, Swearing *Chicaneer;*
How just is Fate in his well-known *Disease,*   1025
To make him *Love* the *Whore* he cannot *Please;*
Strange Power of Vice, whose Fury will prevail,
Possess the *Head* where it has left the *Tail;*
Nature grown Antick and Impertinent,
Lets *this* be Leud, and *that* be Impotent.   1030
Had there been *Money* moving with the *Bill,*
Both sides knew how to purchase his *good Will;*
His *Vote*'s so sure, it never can be lost,
'Tis always to be had by *Who bids most.*

1009. *Finchsky:* Daniel Finch, second earl of Nottingham, Guernsey's elder brother.
1016. A version of the proverbial "No wisdom to silence" (Tilley, W519)?
1019. *Whartsky:* Lord Wharton.
    Mohunsky: Charles Mohun, fourth Baron Mohun (1677–1712), "the greatest Debauchee and Bully of the Age," who was twice tried for murder before he was 21, "had the Courage to repent," as Defoe said (*Reformation of Manners,* 628) and had now become "very considerable in the House [of Lords]" (Hearne, *3,* 486; Macky, p. 94). Both Wharton and Mohun spoke against the second bill to prevent occasional conformity (Pittis, *Proceedings,* pp. 52–53).
    a Hundred more: Holmes (p. 386) puts "the really active membership of the House [of Lords]" at about 120 peers.
1022. Quoted in the *Review,* 26 February 1713.
1023. *Bucksky:* John Sheffield, duke of Buckingham, "proud, insolent, and covetous, and takes all Advantages. In paying his Debts, unwilling; and is neither esteemed nor beloved" (Macky, p. 20).
1025. *his well-known Disease:* Buckingham's sexual inadequacies are retailed in *A Faithful Catalogue of Our Most Eminent Ninnies* (1688), 110–27 (*POAS,* Yale, *4,* 196).
1028. Cf. 606n. above.

Warsaw Remembers him of Old *for that,*   1035
Tho' other *Members* suffer'd *for the Cheat;*
When City Brothers, *Orphans* fund pursue,
And lost their Bill and lost their Money too.
His lofty Pallace now affronts the Park,
Lightsome the Tenement, th'Incumbent Dark;   1040
The Emblematic sides Describe *his Grace,*
This *Double Front,* and that *a Double Face.*
Sibi Molestus, on the Coyns appear,
Tho' most Men think his Lordship need not fear,
No Man can envy him *his Heaven here.*   1045
Laetantur Lares Guilds the spacious Frize,

1037. *Orphans fund:* In the session of 1693–94 a bill was passed for raising revenue to enable
the city of London to pay off its debts to the Orphans Fund. This bill received the royal
assent in March 1694. In the next session an enquiry was made into the pressures brought by
interests in the City upon individual politicians to get this bill passed. Sheffield was charged
with accepting bribes, but acquitted upon a vote in the House of Lords. Seven peers, how-
ever, who conceived that the charges against him had been "plainly made out," signed a
protest (Luttrell, *3,* 463; *LJ, 15,* 557).

1039. *lofty Pallace:* Sheffield built Buckingham House in 1703 on land given him by the
queen in the Mulberry Gardens, Westminster, the celebrated trysting-place of Sedley's
comedy, *The Mulberry Garden* (1668), to which William King alludes: "A Princely Palace on
that space does rise, / Where Sedley's noble Muse found Mulberries" (*The Original Works of
William King, LL.D.,* [ed. John Nichols], 3 vols., 1776, *3,* 73). The house, as Sheffield de-
scribed it in a letter to the duke of Shrewsbury, completely overshadowed the two royal
palaces in Westminster: "The avenues to this house are along St. James's Park, through rows
of goodly elms on one hand, and gay flourishing limes on the other . . . with the Mall lying
betwixt them. This reaches to my iron pallisade that encompasses a square court, which has
in the midst a great bason with statues and water-works; and from its entrance rises all the
way imperceptibly, till we mount to a terrace in the front of a large hall, paved with square
white stones mixed with a dark-colour'd marble; the walls of it covered with a set of pictures
done in the school of Raphael. Out of this on the right hand we go into a parlour thirty-three
feet by thirty-nine . . . with pilasters of divers colours, the upper part of which as high as
the ceiling is painted by Ricci . . . [the letter continues for seven pages]" (*London and Its
Environs Described,* 6 vols., 1761, *2,* 45–52). The house was acquired as a royal residence in
1761 and is the present Buckingham Palace.

1042. *Double Front:* "In mentioning the court at first," Sheffield goes on to say, "I forgot
the two wings in it [see illustration, p. 120], built on stone arches which join the house by
corridores supported by Ionic pillars" (ibid., *2,* 49).

1043. *Sibi Molestus:* "on . . . this Mansion are these words depensiled in Capital Gold
Letters, *&c.* . . . SPECTATOR FASTIDIOSUS SIBI MOLESTUS (on the S[outh])
i.e. The scornful Spectator is troublesome [only] to himself" (Edward Hatton, *A New View of
London,* 2 vols. 1708, *2,* 624). Cf. Catullus, 51, 12: "otium, Catulle, tibi molestum est."

    Coyns: coigns; properly friezes.

1046. *Laetantur Lares:* "The door [see illustration, p. 120] . . . is between four tall
Corinthian pilasters, that are fluted and reach to the top of the second story. Within this
compass are two series of very large and lofty windows, over which is the entablature; and in
the middle was this inscription in large gold characters . . . SIC SITI LAETANTUR
LARES. The houshold Gods delight in such a situation" (Noorthouck, p. 719).

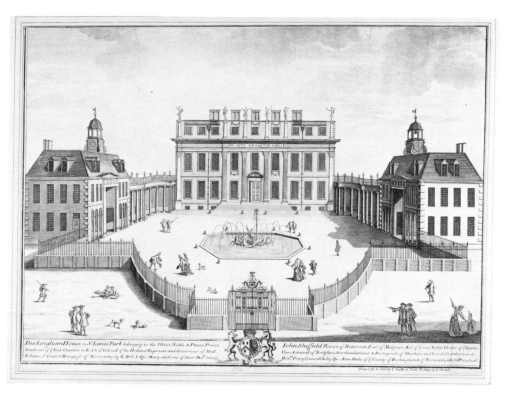

Buckingham House, St. James's Park, an engraving by Sutton Nicholls

For Houshold Gods Dwell there of every Size;
'Twas ne're for these he Built the spacious Dome,
For all his Graces Gods would lye in far less Room.
 Guinsky, a *Tartar* of *Circassian* Race,   1050
What e're he wants in Head, makes up in Face;
In spight of Title, will be call'd a *Pole*,
A *Russian* Phys, and a *Tartarian* Soul;
In Prudence Light, and in his Follies Grave,
For Nature makes the Fool suppress the Knave,   1055
A *Cossack* Bred, but grew a Coxcomb Young;
His Wits Decreasing, as his Pride grew strong;
The short Instruction had prepar'd his Mind,
But as his Vice Encreas'd, his Sence Declin'd;
Ambition now his antient Thoughts Employs,   1060
And all the little Grace he had Destroys;

1047. *Houshold Gods:* "The roof," Sheffield said, is "filled with the figures of Gods and Goddesses. In the midst is Juno, condescending to beg assistance from Venus, to bring about a marriage which the Fates intended should be the ruin of her own darling queen and people" (*London and Its Environs Described*, 6 vols., 1761, *2*, 46). Hatton records that the "Acroteria of Figures standing erect and fronting the Court . . . appear as big as the Life and look noble; the most N[orther]ly is the Figures of *Mercury* . . . *Secret* . . . *Equity* . . . *Liberty*," &c. (Edward Hatton, *A New View of London*, 2 vols. 1708, *2*, 624).

1049. *his Graces Gods:* Macky (p. 20) records that Sheffield was "Violent for the *High-Church*, yet seldom goes to it."

1050. *Guinsky:* Francis Gwyn (1648?–1734) was a successful lawyer, courtier, placeholder and Tory politician. Like Sir Humphrey Mackworth (570*n.* above), he was a high church-man, a Poussineer, and a Tacker.

of Circassian Race: By "Circassian" Defoe probably means Welsh. According to his friend Thomas Hearne (*11*, 359), however, Gwyn was "descended from the ancient Family of the Herberts, Earls of Pembroke, one of this Gentleman's ancestors having changed his name by Act of Parliament." He was also a cousin of Edward Conway, earl of Conway, and of Sir Edward Seymour (*CSPD 1679*, p. 312; *CSPD 1683*, p. 222).

1052. *In spight of Title:* One of Gwyn's titles was prothonotary and clerk of the crown for Glamorgan, Wales, and his father Edward Gwyn, was born at Llansannor, Glamorgan, so perhaps what Defoe means is that despite his (imputed) Welsh origins, Gwyn claims to be English.

1053. *Tartarian:* See 656*n.* above.

1056. *A Cossack Bred:* Whatever the religious orientation of Gwyn's father, Gwyn himself was educated at Christ Church, Oxford, and the Middle Temple, from both of which dis-senters were barred. Defoe makes a similarly unverifiable allegation about Arthur Annesley (928*n.* above).

1059. *Vice:* Gwyn's youthful vices seem almost exemplary: a mistress and a fondness for "the boxes and dice of London" (*CSPD 1679*, p. 200; *CSPD 1683*, p. 208).

1060. *Ambition:* Ambition, rather than vice, is suggested by the early references to Gwyn: in March 1676 he was appointed a commissioner to the farmers of the revenue of Ireland and a year later he was made a receiver of the special tax for shipbuilding (*CTB 1676–79*, pp. 180, 430–31).

With empty Notions Occupies his Head,
In *Seymskey*'s *Western* Empire to succeed;
Affects the antient Tyrant's vilest Part,
To fawn with Spleen, and to Insult with Art: 1065
In *Poland*'s *Western* Capital he Reigns,
Banters himself at most excessive Pains;
Seeks the Recorders Chair, and fain he wou'd,
Dispense those Laws he never understood.
A *Hackney* Deputy for every Town,   1070
But soonest Chosen where he least was known:
Full Thirty Years he did the House Molest,
The *Dyets* Banter, and the Kingdoms Jest:
In strong assuming Nonsense still goes on,
Railing at Places, but forgets his own: 1075
A Patent Broker Jobbs a great Imploy,

1063. *Seymskey's Western Empire:* Defoe also uses the phrase in a letter to Harley of 14 August 1705 (HMC *Portland MSS.*, *4,* 222). It means, of course, the extensive electoral interests of Sir Edward Seymour in Devon and Cornwall (Walcott, p. 63). Gwyn attached himself early to his cousin, became his lawyer, and was named trustee of his estate. By 1705 he was eagerly expecting Sir Edward's death. Another correspondent of Harley's told him in May 1705 that "Frank Gwyn . . . has been the fire brand of all this side the kingdom in the elections, and many gentlemen of Dorset, Somerset and Devonshire court him as Lord Rochester's representative and Sir Edward Seymour's successor in his Western Empire . . . There almost wants nothing but Sir Chuffer's death for this management of Mr. Gwyn's to take effect at Exeter" (HMC *Ormonde MSS.*, *5,* 248; HMC *Portland MSS.*, *4,* 177).

1066. *Western Capital:* Exeter. Defoe reported to Harley that the election at Honiton, adjacent to Exeter, was "a terrible mob election" in which "F. Gwyn . . . particularly distinguished himself." The losing candidate, Defoe said, was "so cowed by Sir William Drake and Francis Gwyn that he dares not petition" (HMC *Portland MSS.*, *4,,* 213, 270).

1068. *Recorders Chair:* Lord Powlett informed Harley on 2 May 1705 of Gwyn's candidacy for the recordership of Exeter, then held by Sir Edward Seymour. The campaign was unsuccessful, however, for Sir Edward did not resign the post until 2 October 1707 (HMC *Portland MSS.*, *4,* 177; Exeter City Library MS. Commissions, Pardons, &c. CXVI).

1070. *Hackney Deputy:* Gwyn represented Chippenham (February 1673–78), Cardiff (1685–87), Christchurch (1689–95, 1701–10, March 1717–22), Callington (1695–98), Totnes (January 1699–1701, 1710–15), and Wells (1722–27).

1075. *Places:* In addition to those mentioned at 1052n. and 1060n. above, some of the places which Gwyn held were clerk of the privy council (1679–85), secretary to the council committee for the affairs of Ireland (1680), commissioner of inspection for disarming Irish papists (1680), commissioner for managing the revenues of Ireland (1680), groom of the bedchamber (1683–85), commissioner of public accounts (1696), chief secretary to the lord lieutenant and member of the Irish privy council (1701), commissioner to establish a linen manufacture in Ireland (1702), deputy lieutenant of Devonshire (1703), commissioner of trade and plantations (1711–13), secretary at war (1713–14).

1076. *Patent:* Letters patent were documents constituting someone to an office in the gift of the crown (*OED*).

Broker: Gwyn bought the office of clerk of the privy council for £2,500 in 1679 and sold

That he may th'Money, *not the Post* Enjoy;
For Bear-Skin Places, Chaffers with the State,
Secures the Cash, and leaves the rest to Fate;
Enricht with Fraud, in Trick and Cheat grown Old,   1080
And Places Bought on purpose to be Sold.
Yet to Compleat himself the Nation's Jest,
He Damn'd the very Bribes that he Possest:
By his own Vote, Disgorges ill got Fees,
And so by Law Corrects his own Disease: 1085
Thus he became the *Dyets* daily Sport,
A Knave in *Council,* and a Boor at *Court:*
Learn'd without Letters, Vain without *Conceit,*
Empty of Manners, Over-grown in Wit:
Of High Tyranick Notions Prepossest,   1090
The fitter to be Monarch of the *West,*
When *Seymsky's* froward Spirit's gone to Rest.
    Powsky, a noisy *Polish* advocate,

---

it in January 1685 presumably for a profit (HMC *Ormonde MSS., 4,* 565; *CSPD 1684–85,* pp. 281–82). More recently, in May 1705, he was said to be "the person who can support men in the keeping or obtaining places in the 'Publique of their Utopia' " (HMC *Portland MSS., 4,* 177).

1077. *Money:* The commissionership for managing the revenues of Ireland had brought Gwyn £3,000 a year (HMC *Ormonde MSS., 5,* 380–81). As groom of the bedchamber he made £500 a year plus £1,500 pension. In January 1686, together with Richard Graham, Viscount Preston, George Legge, Lord Dartmouth, and James Graham, he received £10,000 for "secret service," probably in connection with the affairs of James II's illegitimate daughter, Lady Katherine Darnley, for whose estate Gwyn and Graham were trustees (*CSPD 1683,* p. 327; *CTB 1685–89,* pp. 328, 523; "The deeds of Burblethwaite Hall," *Transactions of the Cumberland and Westmorland Antiquarian and Archaeological Society,* New Series, *62* [1962], 171).

1078. *Bear-Skin:* A bear-skin sale is a short sale, the sale of borrowed stock. Defoe implies that Gwyn sells places that he does not own. Defoe uses the phrase in *A Hymn to the Pillory* (1703), 173 (*POAS,* Yale, *6,* 595).

1083. *Damn'd the . . . Bribes:* In the sessions of 1701 and 1702 Gwyn was member of a committee, of which Sir Edward Seymour (409–10n. above) was chairman, to bring in a bill to prevent bribery and corruption in elections. In neither session did the bill progress beyond a second reading.

1093. *Powsky:* Sir Thomas Powys (1649–1719) was another successful Tory lawyer. He succeeded Heneage Finch (997n. above) as James II's solicitor general in April 1685 when he was "confidently said to be a papist" (Luttrell, *1,* 375–76). Knighted in April 1686, he was promoted to attorney general in December 1687 and conducted the prosecution of the seven bishops. As Oldmixon (*History,* p. 297) says, "Sir *Thomas Powis,* who is now [January 1703] chosen a Manager against the Protestant Dissenters, is the same Man, who 14 Years before was a Manager against our Protestant Bishops." In William's reign he defended Sir John Fenwick in 1696 and was elected to parliament for Ludlow (1701-13) amid the Tory successes

Grown Rich by Law, and busy in the State;
Gravely he speaks in *Polish* Bombast Stile,   1095
And thinks the *Dyets* Pleas'd, because they Smile;
Tho' *Finsky* cou'd have laid him down the Rule,
A Wise Man's Smile's a Banter to a Fool;
But *Powsky* furnish'd with *Opinion Wit*,
None but uncommon Follies can Commit;   1100
In thought Profound, and in Contrivance vast,
Speaks best to every Question when 'tis past.
    Some Rakish *Poles*, with these at once Concur'd,
Who Peace and *Cossacks* both alike abhor'd;
Busy in Vice, but careless of the State,   1105
Thoughtless of Party-Peace, or *Poland*'s Fate;
Of these, mad *Crakerosky* was the first,

---

of January 1701. Even in his maiden session in the Commons, he earned a great reputation for oratory and Pittis said that "ev'ry Period falling from his Tongue, / Reveals a Knowledge like his Reasons strong" (*The Patriots*, 1702, p. 11). Upon Anne's accession he was made premier serjeant at law. In the Commons he was a manager both of the bill to prevent occasional conformity and of the proceedings against the Aylesbury electors (Luttrell, *5*, 529). In 1705, however, he seems to have been moving toward the moderate position of Harley: he was a Sneaker in November 1704 and also avoided voting in the election for Speaker in October 1705. His letters to Harley begging the place of attorney general (October 1710) or some other "mark of esteem" (September 1712) have survived (HMC *Portland MSS.*, *4*, 614–15; *5*, 220). He was finally promoted to a seat on the queen's bench in June 1713 but was removed the next year for his Jacobite sympathies (Edward Foss, *The Judges of England*, 9 vols., 1848–64, *8*, 56).

    1094. *Rich:* Powys "practisd the Law with great profit . . . near 4000*l*. an:" (John Campbell, Lord Campbell, *The Lives of the Lord Chancellors*, 2nd ed., 5 vols., 1846, *4*, 349).

    busy in the State: "having been Attorny General to the late K. James to his abdication, and zealously instrumental in most of the steps which ruind that Prince, and brought those great dangers on the kingdom" (ibid.).

    1095. *Bombast Stile:* In Defoe's *England's Late Jury* (1701), 127 (*POAS*, Yale, *6*, 352), Powys brings up the rear "With Rethorick Debate" and in his epitaph by Matthew Prior "Nothing equal'd His Knowledge, / Except His Eloquence" (Prior, *Works*, *1*, 528).

    1107. *mad Crakerosky:* Identified by marginalia in the University of Texas copy of *Ac* and by a manuscript key in the NLS copy of *Ac* as John Hungerford (d. 1729), another Tory lawyer, and a member of parliament for Scarborough (April 1692–March 1695, 1702–05, November 1707–December 1729). His vote against the Tory amendment to the South Sea bill in May 1711 (which was queried by the compiler) may be explained by the fact that Hungerford was counsel for the South Sea Company. Otherwise his record is solidly Tory, high church, and October Club. Like Sir George Rooke (517*n*. above), he managed to avoid voting either for or against the Tack, or being designated as a Sneaker. But he was not re-elected in May 1705. By suggesting "crack-brained," "Crakerosky" is evidently intended to reinforce "mad," and there is evidence that Hungerford was eccentric: he was expelled from Lincoln's Inn in April 1700 and ordered to vacate his chambers "for twice breaking a padlock off his door." He seems to have retained his chambers, however, for in May 1706 he was ordered to remove his dogs from the vacancy under the stairs (*The Records of the Honorable*

Of all the *Polish* Deputies the worst;
Mean to a Proverb, and below Lampoon,
Was Born too late, and may be Hung too soon.   1110
The former *Dyets* thrust him out of Doors,
And let him loose to Laws, and *Polish* Whores;
Tho' 'twas Confest, the bribe was not the Crime,
But 'twas *the Rogue that Told on't* ruin'd him.

    Cooksky, A City Knight, got out of Jayl,   1115
Stock-jobb'd the *State,* to make the Bill prevail:
The *Dantzick* Merchant's Mercenary Tool,
A Knave in Trade, and in the State a Fool,
Once he to *Warsaw*'s Castle did withdraw,
Secur'd against his Creditors by Law.   1120
The *Dyet* did his Crimes indeed persue,

Society of Lincoln's Inn. The Black Books, 3 vols., 1897–99, *3,* 204, 226). During the debate on the schism bill in 1714 Hungerford is said to have recapitulated the arguments for the bill "in his usual ludicrous way" (Tindal, *4,* 360), and on another occasion, after candles had been brought in, he interrupted the debate by offering to send for his night cap (HMC *Portland MSS., 5,* 570).

    1111. *thrust . . . out:* In March 1694 while serving as chairman of the Commons committee to which the orphans bill (1037n. above) was committed, Hungerford accepted a bribe of 20 guineas from the sponsors of the bill and was expelled the house a year later for bribery (*CJ, 11,* 283).

    1115. *Cooksky:* Sir Thomas Cooke (d. 1709) was the son of a hat maker in Lambeth who became a successful London banker, governor of the old East India Company, and was knighted in September 1690 (Le Neve, p. 434). He was also one of the original proprietors of East and West Jersey in America and was elected lord mayor of London in October 1704 but was excused for ill health (Luttrell, *5,* 82–83, 471, 472). In parliament where he sat for Colchester (November 1694–95, 1698–1705), he was a court Tory who distinguished himself in the impeachment proceedings against the Junto lords in 1701, and Harley thought he could count on him to vote against the Tack. His inclusion here, however, implies that Defoe supposed him to be a Tacker. In any case, he lost the election at Colchester in May 1705 and was defeated again at Colchester in a by-election of December 1705 (*A Collection of Several Paragraphs Out of Mr. Dyers's Letters,* 1705, p. 1; Luttrell, *5,* 626). Defoe had glanced at Sir Thomas in *Reformation of Manners* (1702,) 633 (*POAS,* Yale, *6,* 426).

    Jayl: On the same day in March 1695 that John Hungerford (1111n. above) was expelled from the House of Commons, Sir Thomas was committed to the Tower for refusing to give an account of £87,402 received from the East India Company and distributed by him. Subsequently he testified that most of it went for bribes to secure passage of the East India Company's new charter in 1693 (*CJ, 11,* 283, 316–18). Sir Thomas was released from the Tower in April 1696 (Luttrell, *4,* 51).

    1116. *the Bill:* The new charter for the old East India Company, called a bill for preserving, regulating and establishing the East India trade, was read for the first time in December 1692.

    1118. *A Knave in Trade:* In March 1700 Sir Thomas lost his appeal from the court of chancery to the House of Lords on an illegal drawback of duty on imported pepper in the amount of £14,000 (Luttrell, *4,* 626).

But fate Concur'd the Jayl that was his due,
Was Punishment, and was Protection too:
Vilely he Spent, what basely he had Won,
By Bribes Enricht, and by that Wealth Undone.   1125
    These are the Men, that Govern *Poland*'s Fate,
And pull her down, to make her very great;
With a vast Crowd that serve their Prince in Vain,
With busy Heads, but very Empty Brain,
With hasty Vote promote the *Cossacks* Fate,   1130
And to preserve the Church, undo the State.
Consolidating *Hero*'s who supply
Their want of Sence, with want of Honesty.
    But still *Augustus* in the Center stands,
And Guides the dangerous Reins with steady Hands.   1135
Supported by his People's Chearful aid,
No more at false *Livonians* he's Dismay'd,
Or of the feirce Invading *Swedes* afraid:
The *Dyet* Rises, and the King intends,
To Purge his Houshold, and reform his Friends: 1140
Dismisses from his Presence and his Pay,
The Guilty *Poles*, who hardly durst their Sentence stay,
But fled before the High Command came down,
And left him still possess'd of his long envy'd Crown.
    So *Seymsky* first dismist th'awaken'd Court,   1145
To Western *Poles* Conveys the swift report,
Tells them in what Disgust he came away,
Because h'had been too great a Rake to stay;
That all his late Proclaim'd Disgrace had been,
Because he wanted Manners to his Queen,   1150
The Case was hard, since it was always known,
He scorn'd his Birth, and Vow'd to die a Clown;
A Boor of Quality to whom it chanc'd,

1132. *Consolidating Hero's:* The Tackers.

1137. *false Livonians:* Jacobites (541n. above).

1140. *Purge:* the dismissal of Jersey, Seymour, and Blathwayt and the resignation of
Nottingham in April 1704 (Luttrell, *5*, 411, 416, 418).

1145. *first:* Defoe occasionally uses "first" simply as an expletive, as in *More Reformation*
(1703), 11, 16 (*POAS*, Yale, *6*, 552). In point of fact Jersey was dismissed on 21 April and
Seymour on 22 April 1704 (Luttrell, *5*, 416).

1147. *Disgust:* Cf. 473n. above.

That for his Anti-merit was Advanc'd.
    Villiaski follow'd, Conscious of his Crimes,   1155
Loth to account for *Sobieski*'s Times;
Augustus Sobieski's rule pursues,
This Can't Employ the Wretch cou'd that abuse;
Equal their Right, He that cou'd that betray,
It can't be fairly thought, shou'd this obey.   1160
    Finski prevented the Approaching Fates,
And wisely his own Fall Anticipates:
The Courtier with the States-man he resign'd
Guilt taught him so much of his Prince's Mind.
    Too happy *Poland,* if thy Sons but knew,   1165
How their own just Deliverance to persue:
Let the Degenerate *Palatines* Combine,
Their Prince and Liberties to Undermine;
Call in the *Swedes,* Consult, Confederate,
With the Insatiate En'mies of the State: 1170
'Tis all in vain, Heaven points the Sacred Way,
To them that dare *Augustus* still obey.
Let them but in his juster Cause Unite,
'Tis Justice and the Law make Cowards fight.
They that Advance to Liberty's Defence,   1175
Find double Vigour in their Innocence.
Invading *Swedes* will never once prevail,

1154. *Anti-merit:* "If Sir *E. S*[*eymou*]*r* was advanc'd for his *Antimerit,* what a sort of a L[ad]y must some-body be that promoted him to that Dignity? . . . A scandalous Inuendo, which the Writer ought to be called to an account for. But to answer this Paragraph in his own way, take this noble Gentleman's Character, from a very worthy Gentleman, and yet a *Tacker,* in his Poem, call'd, *Moderation display'd;* where the *Fiend,* speaking of the late Change at Cort, says [lines 108–19 above]" (*D*).

1155–56. *Villiaski . . . Loth to account:* "What the E[arl] of *I*[*er*]*sy* did in Relation to K[ing] *W*[*illiam*] after his Death, was Honourable and the Duty of his Post, and he was so very far from abusing or betraying his Master, that he had been false to his Mistress had he not secur'd that Prince's Closet" (*D*). As lord chamberlain of the household Jersey "secur'd that Prince's Closet" at William's death. "*William* was hardly cold in his Death-Bed" before the rumor began to circulate "That there were some Papers found in his strong Box, whereby it appear'd, that he had form'd the Design of Advancing the Elector of Hanover to the Crown, to the Exclusion of Queen *ANNE*" (Boyer, *Annals,* 1703, p. 33).

1167. *Palatines:* country Tories; "Patriots" (*D*).

    Combine: Cf. 386n. above.

1175–76. While it appears that Defoe is quoting himself, and the "Defence . . . Innocence" rhyme occurs frequently in his verse, the source of this couplet has not been found.

Till *Poland*'s Peace at home begins to fail.
   Long may *Augustus* wear the *Polish* Crown,
And *Poland* his Triumphant Glories own: 1180
His Council steady, and his States-men Just,
When these are happy once, *The Monarch must.*
   If there's a States-man honest and upright,
Whom neither Knaves can bribe, nor Fools Invite;
Who with unbyass't hands can hold the Reins,   1185
And seeks to save his Countries lost Remains,
That loves the People and obeys the Crown,
And seeks the Nations safety, not his own:
Unhappy Poland! find the *Hero* out,
Court him, Let Great Augustus Court him to't.   1190
Let no State Niceties prevent his Choice,
All Poland calls him with united Voice.
   'Tis done, the *Polish* Genius has prevail'd,
And Heav'n has this new Blessing just Intail'd.
Not all the *Swede*'s Invading Troops shall awe,   1195
The Loyal *Poles* their Duty to withdraw;
Confederate Lords with their disloyal Train,
Shall always make the vile Attempt in vain.
While Heaven directs *Augustus* to apply,
To Men of *Council*, Men of *Honesty*,   1200
'T's a Certain Sign there is Deliverance nigh.
   How happy is *Augustus* in his Choice,
That makes the *Swedes* repine, the *Poles* rejoyce:
See how the secret black Cabals abate,
And quit their Councils to avoid their Fate.   1205
The *Male-contents* Discern their vile Mistake,
And old degenerate Principles forsake.
See how for early Pardon now they sue,
And their Allegiance openly renew.
The Happy Monarch sees the Cloud disperse,   1210
And distant Peace shall guild the Universe;
The *Poles* their Loyalty begin to show,
But *Satyr, view the Men that made it so.*
   A Prince's Choice of Ministry and State,
Determines both his Wisdom and his Fate.   1215
Wise Councils may a weaker Prince Restore,
But none has these, but what were wise before.

Grave *Casimir* revolving and sedate,
The *Dyet*'s *Marshal* plac'd in *Finsky*'s Seat,
This Guides the Treasure, That directs the State.   1220
    Augustus has found out the *happy Two,*
That his abstracted Int'rest can pursue;
Employ their abler heads t'assist his Crown,
Regard *His Interest* and neglect their own:
With Equal Zeal, in *Poland*'s Safety joyn,   1225
May all that love Augustus thus Combine.
    No Secret crime their Personal vertue stains,
No Swedish Poyson'd Blood Infects their Veins:
Strangers to Avarice, they're well describ'd,
With *Hearts* untainted, and with *Hands* unbrib'd.   1230
The *Polish* Greatness is their true design,
How long has Poland *Mourn'd for two such Men!*
That count the Nation's Happiness their own,
Retrieve our Credit, and support our Throne;
Our *Bankrupt* Funds, and *mortgag'd Cash* restore,   1235
And make us *Rich* by *That* which made us *Poor.*
The Nation's Joy in their Advancement's seen,
And growing Triumphs Crown the peaceful Reign.
    Long may *Augustus* their just Cares enjoy,
Till their true *Measures* all his *Fears* destroy,   1240
Till all *Livonian* Plots in *Embrio*'s lye,
Abortive *Treasons* in *Conception* dye;
Traytors surrender to unerring Law,
And *Swedish Troops* from *Polish Lands withdraw.*
A universal Satisfaction shines,   1245
And coming Peace appears in their Designs.
A flowing *Cash* will due *Success* secure;
'*Tis this alone must end the* Swedish *War,*
For things are alter'd, Fighting's grown absurd,
'*Tis now the Purse that Conquers, not the Sword.*   1250

1218. *Casimir:* Lord Treasurer Godolphin.
    1219. *The Dyet's Marshal:* Harley was Speaker of the House of Commons when he replaced
Nottingham as secretary of state in May 1704. Cf. 800*n.* above.
    1235. *Funds:* The funds were public loans to the government secured by stock in the Bank
of England, East India Company, and others. In 1705 Bank stock fell below par for the first
time since 1696 and the years 1704–05 were in fact a period of economic recession (*Review*,
10 March 1705).
    1241. *Livonian:* See 541*n.* above.

And he that can the *Polish* Wealth advance,
Strikes at the *Root* of *Swedeland,* and of *France.*
    This *Casimir* has done, and *This* alone
Has chang'd so much of late the smiling Scene;
These are the Agents of the *Polish* Peace,   1255
To these we freely own our *Happiness;*
Firmly the willing *Poles* to these adhere,
Love 'em with Joy, and Trust 'em without Fear.
Fixtly the gen'ral Int'rest they pursue,
With faithful Vigour publick Business do,   1260
For *This* Belov'd by *Pole* and *Cossack* too.

The Conclusion

    Of all the needful Helps to Sov'reign Rule,
The Usefull'st Thing in Poland *is a Fool;*
Among the *Utensils* of Government,
No *Tool,* like Him, supplies the grand Intent: 1265
When he's in close *Cabal,* and *Council* set,
To turn the monstr'ous *Wind-Mill* of the State,
The huge, unweildy, tott'ring Fabrick stands
Too Solid for his Head, too Heavy for his Hands:
The Force Reverts, and with the swift Recoil,   1270
Assuming Statesmen perish in the Broil.
So, Mischief-like, the high returning Tide,
Brings sure Destruction on its Author's Head;
As *Engineers,* that ill support their Mine,
Sink in the Ruine of their own Design.   1275
    Poland, how strangely has thy Land been Blest,
By Fools Redeem'd, when e'er by Knaves Opprest:

    1253. *Casimir:* "We grant him, that the Noble *P[ee]r* represented by the borrow'd Name of *Casimir,* has done more than could be expected in a Treasury, that had been exhausted by Depre[d]ations in the late Reign" (*D*).
    1263. *Fool:* Line 316 above suggests that Nottingham may be the particular fool that Defoe had in mind.
    1267. *Wind-Mill of the State:* a comic version of another Defovian commonplace, "the Great Machine of State" (*An Elegy on the Author of the True-Born-English-Man,* 1704, p. 34; *Review,* 12 June 1705).
    1277. Pittis's sarcastic reading of this line may not be far from Defoe's meaning: "That's . . . almost as much as to say, when we were at the brink of Ruin, by a parcel of *Knaves* who shar'd the Administration in King *James*'s Reign, the Fools interpos'd . . . and brought about the late R[e]vol[utio]n" (*D*).

The Graver Blockheads of thy tott'ring State,
Protect thy Fame, and help to make thee Great.
For when they might thy Government o'erthrow,   1280
The harmless *Things themselves* alone undo.
The untrain'd Politicians court their Fate,
If *Knaves* were never *Fools,* they'd soon blow up the State.
　Here Men the *Dignity of Folly* gain,
And never live without their Wits *in vain;*   1285
The empty *Head,* and noisy *Tongue* appear,
A Step to Fame, and Dubs a *Polish* Peer.
Coxcombs of huge, uncommon Size we find,
And *Fools* beyond the Rate of Human Kind,
No Nation can such *happy Blockheads* show,   1290
Fools of *Design,* and *Fools* of *Learning* too;
With necessary *Dulness* so supply'd,
Their want of *Brains* has all their *Vice* destroy'd:
So Gravely *silly,* so Refin'dly *dull,*
So Clear the *Head,* and yet so Thick the *Skull;*   1295
So Damn'd to *Forms,* and so Ty'd up to *Rules,*
Poland shall vye with all the World for *Fools.*
In Council *Hasty,* in Performance *Slow,*
No Nation such a Breed of *Fools* can show:
Purse-proud and Fanciful they boast of Sense,   1300
A certain Sign 'tis but a vain pretence;
Loss of Discretion's their chief Happiness,
No Men that want their Brains, can want them less.
These are the Manufactures of the Land,
The Props on which our *Polish* Freedoms Stand;   1305
That many a *Polish* Province represent,
And joyn'd with *Knaves* make up a *Polish* Parliament;
That help to puzzle Causes in the *House,*
And *Hunt* a Question, as a *Fox* a *Goose:*
Strange Miracles they often-times perform,   1310
And *Calm* the *Dyet,* when 'tis in a *Storm.*
Meersky the Grand Exper'ment often made,
Has made them *Laugh* and *Rage,* be *Pleas'd* and *Mad:*
Nature made *Fools* a *Dernier* high *Resort,*

1283. Defoe quotes this line in the *Review,* 6 October 1705, as "that Verse of a Foreign Poet."

1312. *Meersky:* See 878n. above.

1314. *Dernier...Resort:* final court of appeal, hence last resource or refuge (*OED,* citing [Defoe], *A Vindication of Dr. Henry Sacheverell.* 1710, p. 73).

To *temper* men of *Sense,* and make them *Sport:*   1315
Like *David*'s Harp they can the Nation Doze,
And drive the *Devil* from the *Crazy House.*
   Satyr, forbear to Search the Wound too far,
Lest *Poland*'s latent Errors should appear;
'Ts Enough, the Nation knows the Curst Design,   1320
Has broke the Project, and has *Markt the Men,*
Augustus sees, Heav'n has his Soul inform'd,
The *Fools* are all laid by, the *Knaves* disarm'd;
Wisdom and *Temper* settles *Poland*'s Fate,
And *Moderation* Guides the Helm of State,   1325
'Tis this makes Poland *Safe, this makes* Augustus *Great.*

1316. *David's Harp:* "When the evil spirit from God was upon Saul . . . David took a harp, and played with his hand: so Saul was . . . well, and the evil spirit departed from him" (1 Samuel 16:23).

Declaration without Doors
(25 October 1705)

The general election of May 1705 created a virtual stalemate between Tories and Whigs which in turn precipitated some rude jostling for the Speaker's chair in the new House of Commons. Parliament was ordered to convene on 25 October. When the members began to return to London the week before, the Tories' chances to elect their candidate seemed much enhanced by the fact that a dozen Whig members had died during the summer and nearly a dozen more were on active duty with the armed forces. It was already known that John Smith, the Whig member for Andover and William III's chancellor of the exchequer, would be the ministerial candidate. And it was rumored that the country Tories would put up William Bromley, the high flying member for Oxford University (BM MS. Add. 17677AAA, f. 487).

The choice of John Smith was part of Harley's plan to split both the parties, for he hoped to gain support from the Whigs, who had refused to back him, and the moderate Tories, who had refused to back Sir Simon Harcourt. In mid-July, when Smith's candidacy was announced, it was made very clear that he was a court, and not merely a Whig, candidate (*BIHR*, *37*, 20–46).

As the members continued to pour into London, "the Appearance was greater than had been known at the opening of any Parliament for Fifty Years past" (Boyer, *History*, p. 209). On Monday 22 October at a caucus at the Fountain Tavern in the Strand, Bromley was nominated the Tory candidate for Speaker (Hearne, *1*, 58).

It was the report of this caucus, which could have reached Defoe in the form of Dyer's handwritten newsletter, that precipitated the present poem. *Declaration without Doors* must have been written within hours of receipt of the news, for it was carried back to London and published on 25 October, perfectly timed, one would assume, for the members to read on the morning that parliament convened (*Review*, 25 October 1705).

That afternoon, as Boyer relates, "The whole Nation was at a Gaze" (*History*, p. 209). After 457 members had taken the oaths, the first order

of business was election of a Speaker. Smith and Bromley were nom-
inated and seconded and a debate began which lasted two hours
(Luttrell, 5, 604–05). The Whigs conceded that nothing would give so
much pleasure to the courts at Versailles and St. Germain as the election
of a Tacker. Speakers on the other side argued that if Smith were
elected the church would be in danger, and Sir Edward Seymour
thundered against the election as Speaker of a member of the privy
council responsible to the court. But the Whigs recalled that Sir Edward
himself had been elected Speaker in 1673 when he was a privy council-
lor and totally dependent on the court. When the house divided, Smith
was elected by 43 votes: 249–206 (HMC *Rutland MSS.*, 2, 183). Bromley
consoled himself with the thought that "such a number [had] never
lost such a question before" (*Bibliotheca Parriana: A Catalogue of the
Library of the Late Reverend and Learned Samuel Parr, LL. D.*, 1827, p. 702).

Defoe could have read about the election in another of Dyer's news-
letters of 27 October 1705:

> There was a great contest on Thursday and a great many warm
> speeches in the House of Commons before the choice of a Speaker
> was made, each side endeavouring to lessen the abilities of
> the contrary candidate. . . Against [Bromley] they printed his
> juvenile travels with a ridiculous index made to the book . . . but
> this signified little on either side, the numbers carried the election.
> (HMC *Portland MSS.*, 4, 268)

Defoe provides in the poem what history seems to have failed to supply:
an account of Bromley's "Declaration" of his candidacy for the Speak-
ership, "without Doors," i.e. outside the House of Commons. The
poem is a dramatic monologue, or a quasi-dramatic monologue, in
which Bromley urges his own merits before the Tory caucus. It is not
caricature, but *oratio morata*, a speech in character and revealing
character.

"A Declaration without Doors; by the Author of, *&c.*" was adver-
tised as "*This Day is Publish'd*" in the *Review*, 25 October 1705. The
whole phrase, "By the author of the True-Born Englishman," is said to
appear on the title page of a quarto edition of the poem of which no
copy is known to exist (Foxon X7). In the *Review* of 30 October 1705
it was advertised that "*There will be speedily Publish'd* An Answer to that
Scurrilous and Reflecting Pamphlet, Entituled, *The Declaration without
Doors*," but no copy of this work is known either.

DECLARATION WITHOUT DOORS

O ye *Britains,* draw near,
With Attention give Ear
To my most profound Declaration:
    It may do you some good,
    Tho' I'm not understood   5
By twenty wise Men in the Nation.

I'm a Parliament Member,
Who shall sit in *November*
To settle the Nation's Affairs;
    Make Trouble and Laws,   10
    Not forgetting a Clause
About the High Church's Repairs.

The High Church's Power
Has to this very Hour,
Been of all my Caballing the true end;   15
    But I swear by my Maker,
    If you don't choose me Speaker,
The Cause will be certainly ruin'd.

I have sent Horse and Man

1. *Britains, draw near:* Bromley is to be imagined haranguing the Tory party caucus at the Fountain Tavern in the Strand on 22 October 1705 (Hearne, *1,* 58).

3. *Declaration:* Exactly when Bromley declared himself a candidate for Speaker has not been determined. The earliest reference to his candidacy that has been discovered so far occurs in a letter of 29 June 1705 from Harley to Marlborough (Blenheim MS. AI 25).

7. *Member:* Bromley had been re-elected for Oxford University in May 1705.

8. *sit in November:* On 13 August 1705 parliament had been further prorogued until 25 October, when it was convened (*CJ, 15,* 4–5).

12. *the High Church's Repairs:* Bromley is promising to introduce a fourth bill to prevent occasional conformity. The supporters of the previous bills had insisted from the beginning that they "designed nothing but the preservation of the church of England" (*Parl. Hist., 6,* 73). The attempt to tack the third such bill to the land tax suggested similar kinds of tacks (see *The Tack,* above), one of which was shoe repairing, for cobblers also use tacks. So the Tories turned out for the election in Honiton with "a little knot of shoemakers thread in their hats to shew that they were Tackers" (Bodl. MS. Ballard 21, f. 222). Bromley therefore may also be hinting that another bill to prevent occasional conformity will be tacked to a money bill.

19. *sent Horse and Man:* During the summer of 1705 Bromley and his agents sent letters throughout the country to solicit support for his election as Speaker. The following letter in a clerical hand, unsigned and undated, was received by Sir John Mordaunt, the Tory member

To do all they can,   20
To ingage all your Votes for the Chair:
Some Mony I've paid,
And more Promises made,
Of fine things I'll do when I come there.

I was sworn to the Church,   25
Both to People and Porch,
And I'm fond of the Name of High-Flyer;
I have shewn my good Will
For th'Occasional Bill,
And to set the whole Nation on Fire.   30

If I get in the Chair,
It will quickly appear,
Who is for the Church, and who not, Sir:
I'll wipe off the Paint
Made me look like a Saint,   35

---

for Warwickshire and a Tacker: "Its desired that you will take care to Engage all in your County to be in Towne some time before the Choice of the Speaker, which will certainly be the 25th of October. For its found upon the strictest Calculation that there is suffitient to place Mr. Bromley in the Chaire If those in the Interest of the Church will give their early attendance . . . and its hoped your Utmost assistance will not be wanting on this Occasion" (Warwick County R.O. MS. CR 1368/3).

21. *ingage all your Votes:* According to Tory estimates, "250 members ingaged solemnly to appear the first day of the session and to vote for [Bromley]" (Plas Newydd MS. Box 160).

27. *High-Flyer:* Bromley was "looked on as a violent Tory, and as a great Favourer of Jacobites" (Burnet, *2*, 428).

29. *Occasional Bill:* Bromley drafted and managed the passage through the House of Commons of the three bills to prevent occasional conformity (*The Dyet of Poland*, 837n. above).

35. *look like a Saint:* How Bromley managed to make himself look like a dissenter is explained by his political manoeuvering after the defeat of the Tack in November 1704. Realizing that the Tackers alone could not upset the ministry, he tried to forge an alliance with the country Whigs. The most obvious way of bringing together opposition members against the government was to sponsor a bill to reduce the number of placemen (officeholders) in the Commons. The tactic succeeded and two such bills were proposed which, as Erasmus Lewis observed, "owe their rise to the resentment of some people for the miscarriage of the bill against occasional conformity" (BM MS. Add. 4742, f. 20). By one of the bills, holders of offices created since 1687 were to be excluded from the Commons. By the other all placemen were to be excluded. The first passed, but the second was defeated (*Verney Letters, 1,* 222). Upon learning of the rejection of the second bill, Lord Fermanagh wished that "the Bill . . . had past . . . for, now the Chu[rch] of Eng[lan]d is checkt, every little Sugar-plum is pleasing to her Children" (ibid., *1,* 223). After parliament was dissolved, Bromley proposed to the country Whigs that they should continue their collaboration in the new parliament. Apparently he met with some success, for it was reported in March 1705 that "Peter King [a prominent country Whig] and . . . Bromley, etc., are reconciled, and have shaken hands to stand by each other next winter to oppose the iniquity of the times and promote the public welfare" (HMC *Frankland-Russell-Astley MSS.*, p. 176).

And Moderation shall die on the Spot, Sir.

I was chosen for the Nests
Of your Highflying Priests,
Those dainty young Sons of *Apollo;*
Now my Wit's at a head,   40
I'm appointed to lead,
And I'm sure that Sir *Humphrey* will follow.

My Learning t'advance,
I travel'd to *France,*
From *Paris* quite down to *Touloon;*   45
Where they make People pray
The Government's way,
And convert them *a mode de Dragoon.*

Before I came home,

37–38. *the Nests | Of . . . Highflying Priests:* Many of the most prominent high church and Jacobite clergymen—Atterbury, Birch, Sacheverell—who had graduated M.A. from Oxford, were enthusiastic voters for Bromley.

42. *Sir Humphrey:* Sir Humphrey Mackworth also stood for Oxford University in the election of 1705, thus creating the unique spectacle of a contest among three Tackers, since Mackworth opposed Sir William Whitlock, Bromley's high church colleague in the last parliament. It appears that Sacheverell and other fellows of Magdalen College were dissatisfied with Sir William and "unreasonably advised" Sir Humphrey to stand against him (Longleat MS. Thynne XIII, 337; HMC *Downshire MSS., 1,* 874). Since Whitlock could muster the formidable support of Lords Guernsey, Nottingham, Rochester, and Weymouth, Mackworth's defeat was a foregone conclusion (Longleat MS. Thynne XIII, 337; Bodl. MS. Rawl. Letters 92, f. 300). According to *The Doleful Complaint of Sir H. M. on the Loss of His Election at Oxford, 1705 (POAS,* 1707, *4,* 22–25),

When the Poll was declar'd,
O then it appear'd,
At which I was too much concern'd;
That Sir *William* had more
By One Hundred and Four,
Than even Sir *Humphrey* the Learned.

will follow: Despite his defeat Mackworth managed to get back into the House of Commons, finding refuge in Seymour's safe constituency of Totnes.

44. *travel'd to France:* Bromley's *Remarks in the Grande Tour* (1692) was "knavishly" republished by Harley in 1705 as part of the campaign to prevent his election as Speaker (*The Dyet of Poland,* 839n. above).

48. *a mode de Dragoon:* Before revocation of the Edict of Nantes in 1685, French Huguenots who refused to be converted were subjected to increasing harassment culminating in the quartering in their houses of dragoons under orders to mistreat them. This policy was known as "les dragonnades." More recently, in May 1703, it was reported "That the French king has ordered all the protestant inhabitants of Orange to change their religion in 3 months, otherwise [they] shal be embark'd at Thoulon and Marseilles, and transported whither he thinks fitt" (Luttrell, *5,* 293).

I travel'd to *Rome*,   50
And receiv'd the Infallible Blessing;
  I ne'er scrupled to bow
  To the Slipper or Toe,
And bestow'd a true Protestant Kissing.

I view'd the great Church,   55
And admir'd the Porch,
And I counted the Steps to the Altar;
  I went to the Mattin,
  Said my Prayers in Latin,
And I sung to her Ladyship's Psalter.   60

I bless'd the three Nations
With my wise Observations,
That they might my Learning inherit;
  But as soon as 'twas printed,
  I sincerely repented,   65
'Twas so laugh'd at I never could bear it.

Now from Popery and *Rome*,
I'm to *Coventry* come,
Where I'm quite overrun with Religion;
  The High Church and I   70
  Such Experiments try,
You wou'd swear we had *Mahomet*'s Pigeon.

The Occasional Bill
Was fram'd in our Mill,
Of true Catholick Preparation;   75
  The Warp and the Woof
  Look'd like Protestant Stuff,
But the Devil was in the Fashion.

54. *a true Protestant Kissing:* In *Remarks in the Grande Tour* (1692, p. 219), Bromley had re-counted how he was "admitted to the Honour of kissing the Pope's Slipper." The "Table of the Principal Matters" in the 1705 edition called particular attention to the incident: "*The Author kiss'd the Pope's Slipper, and had his Blessing, though known to be a Protestant; but not a Word of Religion*" (*Remarks in the Grand Tour of France and Italy,* 2nd ed., 1705, sig. a3r).

65. *repented:* Defoe mentions in *The Consolidator,* 1705, p. 355, and in *The Dyet of Poland* (861n. above) that Bromley tried to suppress *Remarks in the Grande Tour.*

68. *Coventry:* Since Bromley had been returned for Oxford University on 9 May 1705, he had nearly two weeks to campaign for the Tory candidates in Coventry. His estate at Bagin-ton was three miles south of Coventry.

72. *Mahomet's Pigeon:* See *The History and Fall of the Conformity-Bill,* 108n., above.

I huzza'd for the Tack,
For I was always a Jack,   80
And was fond of *Jure Divino;*
But with what Intent,
Or what 'twas I meant,
That's a thing neither you know nor I know.

To High-Church I'm as true,   85
As a Protestant blue,
And fain wou'd Dissenters be Mobbing;
But we had such a Defeat
In *Coventry* Street,
That we're damnably 'fraid of their drubbing.   90

I hate Moderation,
It has ruin'd the Nation,

---

79. *huzza'd for the Tack:* "The two Tacking Candidates in that Town [Coventry] had a very great Majority among the Electors" (*The Republican Bullies*, 1705, p. 4).

80. *Jack:* Jacobite. "A *Tacker* is a *Jacobite* in Disguise" (*A List of those Worthy Patriots*, n.p., n.d., p. 6; cf. 27*n*. above).

81. *Jure Divino:* "The *Hocus Pocus* of *Jure Divino*," as Tutchin called it (*The Observator*, 2–5 February 1704), was the belief that since the power of kings derived from God, no limit could be placed on it by man.

82. *Intent:* The implied intent, of course, was nothing less than to upset the present establishment in church and state and "restore" James Francis Edward, the pretended Prince of Wales, to the throne.

86. *As a Protestant blue:* as loyal to high church as the greatest fanatics are to dissent; cf. *An Elegy on the Death of Pamphlets*, 37*n*. below.

88–89. *Defeat | In Coventry:* Coventry was one of the most turbulent boroughs in England. Defoe complained in the *Review,* 10 May 1705, that "In this place, such has been the Continual Zeal and Heat of Parties, that the Division has risen up to the Greatest Animosities . . . Club-Law has been the Decider of Controversies, and on every Election, Victory in the Street, has given Victory in the Poll." Defoe's fears proved to be correct, for one of the worst election riots of the reign occurred 12 days later. "About two o'clock in the morning the disturbance began. Mr. Gery [one of the two country Tory incumbents] appeared rallying his men . . . A terrible riot ensued about five, some of the watch were knocked down and their halberds taken from them and broken. The mayor was wounded in the face by a stone thrown at him . . . The rioters then marched the streets and at nine o'clock possessed themselves of the town hall with 600 or 700 men, and continued there during the three days of the election . . . and most things were done as this rabble pleased. Many voters were beaten, knocked down, dragged along the ground by the hair and inhumanly abused" (HMC *Portland MSS.*, *4,* 188). It is not clear why Defoe represents this as a defeat for Bromley because when the dust settled the two country Tory candidates, both Tackers, were returned by large majorities. But perhaps Bromley feared that the crimes by which these majorities had been obtained were so flagrant that the elections would be overturned and the Whig candidates seated, which is indeed what happened in February 1707 (*CJ, 15,* 278).

Both the Bishops and Queen are infected;
   Do but set me i'th'Chair,
   I'll the High-Church repair,   95
And Religion shall soon be dissected.

We have made such Advances,
   You'd think them Romances,
All the Churches on Earth to unite-a;
   That *Mahomet* and We   100
   May quickly agree,
And *Rome* shall no more men affright-a.

Our true *English* Church
   Shall to Popery approach,
And Popery to her shall advance;   105
   The Sisters shall kiss,
   Pass by what's amiss,
And we shall shake hands, Sir, with *France*.

Thus the Tools of the Age
   Shall quickly grow Sage,   110
When they cant of their Union and Peace, Sir;
   This will Union convey
   The true Catholick way,
And the World shall be all of a Piece, Sir.

If the Whigs and Dissenters   115
   Should think to prevent us,
And oppose us with damn'd Moderation;

93. *Bishops and Queen are infected:* Fourteen bishops exhibited symptoms of moderation when they voted against the second bill to prevent occasional conformity (*Parl. Hist.*, 6, 171). Anne showed signs in March 1705 when she said in her speech at the dissolution of parliament, "I conclude, therefore, with exhorting you all to Peace and Union; which are . . . particularly necessary at this Time, when, the whole Kingdom being shortly to proceed to new Elections, it ought to be the Care of every body . . . to carry themselves with the greatest Prudence and Moderation" (*LJ*, *17*, 720).

95. *repair:* See 12n., above.

96. *dissected:* divided into high church and low church.

97. *Advances:* Bromley assumes that the restoration of the pretender will assure the restoration of Catholicism.

101. *agree:* Louis XIV's subvention of the infidel—creating an entente between Catholic and Muslim—was frequently remarked in Protestant England (Luttrell, *3*, 387–88; *5*, 278; cf. Swift, *The Examiner*, 12 April 1711).

109. *Tools:* "Whigs and Dissenters" (see line 115).

By unanimous Votes,
We will cut all their Throats,
And so we'll unite the whole Nation.   120

On the New Promotion
(October 1705)

The appointment of William Cowper to be lord keeper of the great seal in October 1705 was politically even more decisive than the struggle over the speakership. For although the choice of John Smith as the court candidate for the Speaker's chair marked the decision to shift the government from a Tory to a Whig basis, it was still hoped, especially by Robert Harley, that a substantial number of moderate Tories would support the ministry in the new parliament. To retain their allegiance, however, the managers had to demonstrate that by nominating Smith they had not committed themselves irrevocably to the Whigs. Thus the next major appointment became a test of the viability of moderation.

Harley was anxious to consolidate the court's interest with the moderate Tories by having a Tory promoted to the important post of lord keeper. The queen was of the same mind. But an unfortunate lack of legal talent in the Tory ranks made it impossible to find a suitable candidate. Godolphin, therefore, backed by Marlborough, urged the promotion of the brilliant Whig lawyer, William Cowper.

Whatever the reasons that led Godolphin to urge the queen to appoint a Whig as lord keeper, his decision created the first fissure in his relationship with Harley, a split which in the next three years widened into an unbridgeable gulf. For Harley realized that the appointment of Cowper would eliminate moderation as a basis for the government. His anxiety, as well as the queen's, can be detected in Anne's pleas to Godolphin "that there may be a moderate Tory found for this employment. For I must own to you I dread the falling into the hands of either party, and the Whigs have had so many favours showed them of late, that I fear a very few more will put me insensibly into their power" (*Letters of Queen Anne,* p. 172).

Failing to deflect the lord treasurer from his decision, Harley's next move was to get the announcement of Cowper's appointment delayed until after the beginning of the new session (Longleat MS. Portland VII, f. 110). The announcement in fact was made on 11 October, having, as Cowper said, been "long before proposed." This was just two weeks before the meeting of parliament and the effect, as Harley feared, was to alienate all but a handful of moderate Tories. In the division over the speakership most of the Tories who had abandoned the party in the vote on the Tack, even including 15 or 16 who had places or dependencies at court, rejoined the party to vote against the court candidate (HMC *Portland MSS.*, *4*, 268). As far as they were concerned the appointment of Cowper meant capitulation to the Whigs.

The present poem confirms that Harley was right. The anonymous poet fastens on the coincidence of Anthony Ashley Cooper, Charles II's lord chancellor, and William Cowper, Anne's lord keeper, to warn the queen of what she already knew to be the danger of falling "insensibly" into the power of wolfish Whigs.

Terminal dates for composition of the poem are established by the facts that Cowper's appointment was publicly known on 11 October (Luttrell, *5*, 601) and that Hearne (*1*, 60) entered the poem in his diary on 30 October 1705. Apparently the poem circulated only in manuscript and was not published until 1885 (Hearne, *1*, 60).

On the New Promotion

O *Anna!* thy new Friends and Prick-ear'd Court
Cannot thy Dignity and Crown support.
The Awkward Loyalty of Whigs is known
To ruine Princes whom they make their own.
Like Mastives, feed and stroke 'em, they will faun;   5
But growl and seize you, when your hand's withdrawn.
Thou art like one that has a Wolf by th'Ears;
Unsafe to hold, and if let goe he tears.
   One *Cooper* to thy Uncle was untrue.
Another, *Anna,* may be so to you: 10
Can *He thy* Honour and thy Conscience keep
Unspotted, when *his own* is fast asleep?

1. *new Friends:* Anne's new officers of state were all Whigs: the duke of Newcastle, who succeeded the Tory duke of Buckingham as lord privy seal in March 1705; William Cowper, who replaced the Tory Sir Nathan Wright as lord keeper on 11 October; and John Smith, who was elected Speaker of the House of Commons two weeks later.

Prick-ear'd: The epithet, which originally described a Roundhead, "whose Ears are longer than his Hair" (*New Dictionary,* sig. I7r), came to be applied to any dissenter or even one of "these Prickear'd, starch, sanctify'd" low churchmen like White Kennett (Hearne, *2,* 74). The immediate reference is probably to [James Drake], *The Memorial of the Church of England,* [August] 1705, p. 21, where the Whigs are set down as "a Prick-ear'd *Faction.*"

3–4. *Whigs . . . ruine Princes:* "The consistent constitutional policy of the Whigs was to reduce [William III] to complete dependence on Parliament" (*CTB 1695–1702,* Introduction, p. xxiii).

7. *Wolf:* "Th'insatiate Wolfe" was a Presbyterian in Dryden's typology (*The Hind and the Panther* [1687], I, 153). To hold a wolf by the ears is a proverb (Tilley, W603) the meaning of which is explained in the next line.

9. *One Cooper:* Anthony Ashley Cooper, first earl of Shaftesbury (1621–83) was Charles II's lord chancellor who left the court to become the first Whig: "Now, manifest of Crimes, contriv'd long since, / He stood at bold Defiance with his Prince" (*Absalom and Achitophel* [1681], 204–05).

10. *Another:* William Cowper, pronounced "Cooper" (1665?–1723), was one of the ablest Whig speakers in the House of Commons, where he sat for Hertford (1695–1700) and Beeralston (1701–05). He accepted the great seal, as he says in his diary, "on Condition I had the same Money for Equipage [£2,000] & Salary of £4000 *pr.* Annum as my Predecessor had, and a Promise of a Peerage the next Promotion" (Cowper, *Diary,* p. 1). Anne was obliged to meet Cowper's condition by raising him to the peerage in November 1706 as Baron Cowper of Wingham.

11. *thy Conscience:* Lord keeper of the great seal and lord high chancellor are simply two names for the same post which, in the Middle Ages, was frequently filled by "some dignified clergyman," for besides being the highest law officer in the kingdom, he was also "reputed the Keeper of the King's conscience" (Beatson, 1788, *1,* 227).

12. *his own:* "He is a man of . . . very bad Principles & Morals" (Hearne, *1,* 56).

Let *Cullen* witness this, whose wretched Ghost
Proclaims it—*She who trusts to him is lost.*
Think on thy *Martyr'd Grandfather,* and shun   15
That race by which *thy Father* was undone.
Th'Hereditary Hatred of that Crew
Persues the *Stewarts,* and descends to *you.*
Oh! doe not in those fatal steps proceed,
Least thy *White Neck* at last be made to bleed.   20
    No Wanton Muse does dictate this in spite;
As Vile *De Foe* and *Touchin* weekly write.
Love to my *Church* and *Monarchy* and *You*
Has arm'd my Pen with *Truth* and *Courage* too.
By Zeal, by Loyalty and Duty led   25
My Ears I hazard to secure *thy Head.*

13. *Cullen:* glossed "[Cow]pers Mistress" in *C.* Cowper is supposed to have been bigamous-
ly married to Elizabeth Culling, or Cullen, of Hertingfordbury Park, Hertfordshire, and to
have had two children by her (*POAS,* Yale, *6,* 418–19, 470n., 473n.). Swift called him Will
Bigamy (*Prose, 3,* 25).

20. *White Neck:* In *The Rehearsal* for 12–19 May 1705 Leslie reported that cries of "No
Presbyterian Rebellion. Save the Queens White Neck" had been raised in the Suffolk
election. The classical analogue is Juvenal, *Sat.* X, 345: "praebenda est gladio pulchra haec
et candida cervix."

22. *De Foe and Touchin:* "*Daniel D'Foe,* and his very worthy Fellow-Labourer in Sedition,
John Tutchin" (*The Tackers Vindicated,* 1705, p. 6) were regarded as the most loathsome Whig
journalists. "I have forborn sending the *Reviews,*" William Ettrick wrote to Lord Weymouth
in August 1705, "and I wish I were able to say every body was also weary of reading that
Poysonous author. But he with his Counterpart the *Observator* are Still the Entertainment of
most Coffee houses in Town. For tho' both are exploded by men of the best sence, and
granted by all honest men to contain nothing in 'em but the Seeds of Sedition, and a fulsom
repetition of the same thing a hundred times over, yet the Whigs, who are Generally the
greatest Coffee house mongers, joyn'd with our new race of Moderate men, support their
Credit" (Longleat MS. Thynne XXV, f. 424).

26. *Ears I hazard:* Cutting off the ears, a common punishment for libel in the reign of
Anne's grandfather (*POAS,* Yale, *6,* 589), was abandoned in Anne's reign, despite Pope's
joke (*The Dunciad* [1743], *2,* 147).

Upon the Vote that Pass'd
that the Church was Not in Danger
(December 1705?)

"The QUEEN's passion for what she called *the Church*" was so well-
known that it was accepted by the Tories as a datum (*Account of the
Conduct*, p. 6). Almost her first official words were an expression of her
"true Concern . . . for our Religion" (*CJ, 13,* 788), and in her speech
at the end of the first session of parliament Anne promised to keep
"entirely firm to the Interests and Religion of the Church of *England*"
and only "to countenance those who have the truest Zeal to support it"
(*LJ, 17,* 150). Between May 1702 and March 1705 Anne made four
appointments to the episcopal bench and all were inviolable high
churchmen (although William Nicolson, bishop of Carlisle, subsequent-
ly defected to the Whigs and George Bull, bishop of St. David's, was
more famous for "Learning" than for "Zeal").

So it was a very disillusioned high churchman who wrote the present
epigram. By April 1704 Anne was urging "Moderation" rather than
"Zeal" in her speeches from the throne (*LJ, 17,* 562, 720), and most of
the high churchmen—beginning with Rochester in February 1703—
had been turned out of her government. Worst of all, in March 1705,
she had stigmatized the Tack as a "dangerous experiment" (Charles
Darby?, *The Oxfordshire Nine,* 60*n.* above).

The present epigram must have begun to circulate before 21 July
1705 when Defoe quoted the first two lines in the *Review.* He also called
it "the common Song of the [high church] Party" (*Jure Divino: A
Satyr,* 1706, XI, 31*n.*), but no indication of a tune has survived.

The epigram acquired its present title—and a new relevance—on 6
December 1705 when the cry of the church in danger was raised by
Rochester in the House of Lords and was taken up by Sir John Paking-
ton in the Commons (Oldmixon, *History,* p. 365; *Camden Miscellany,
Vol. XXIII,* Fourth Series, *7* [1969], 33, 82–84). The government acted
quickly to stifle this cry and on 11 December 1705 passed the following
resolution through both houses of parliament: "the Church of *England,*
as by Law established . . . is now, by God's Blessing, under the happy
Reign of her Majesty, in a most safe and flourishing Condition; and
that whoever goes about to suggest, and insinuate, that the Church is in
danger under her Majesty's Administration, is an Enemy to the Queen,
the Church, and the Kingdom" (*CJ, 15,* 58). After this exercise in

thought control it seemed quite likely that Anne had abandoned the church.

Upon the Vote that Pass'd That the Church was Not in Danger

When *Anna* was the Church's Daughter,
She acted as her Mother taught her;
But now she's Mother of the Church,
She's left her Daughter in the Lurch.

1706

JOSEPH BROWNE

The Country Parson's Honest Advice
to that Judicious Lawyer, and Worthy Minister of State,
My Lord Keeper.
(30 January 1706)

This short poem provides some interesting excursions into nonsense, wit, and irony. "Brave Sir *George*" (*On the Greatest Victory,* 1) is easily read as irony. "No Man cou'd ever give him a *Defeat*" (*The Dyet of Poland,* 509) is, in the context, witty. But "Be . . . as *Somers* Brave" is true nonsense: "*Somers*" and "Brave" are totally disjunctive, like "The Wit of Cheats, the Courage of a Whore" (Pope, *Epilogue to the Satires,* I, 165). It is nonsense of a teasing kind, however, "For true No-meaning puzzles more than Wit" (Pope, *Moral Essays,* II, 114). The juxtaposition of these ridiculously inapposite terms, "*Somers*" and "Brave," arouses the fleeting thought, the footless suspicion, that Somers may, after all, be a coward. "*Devonshire's* Chastity," on the other hand, is ironical in the simple reversing sense: Devonshire was a satyr. But "*Southampton's* Wit" is ironical in a more complicated way: he was not simply unable to make witty remarks; he was witless in a more clinical sense (Robert E. C. Waters, *Genealogical Memoirs of the Extinct Family of Chester of Chicheley,* 2 vols., 1878, *2,* 487).

The poem, as Hearne (*1,* 176) said, reflects "severely . . . (but Ironically)" on 18 noble lords, 16 of whom had voted against the first and second bills to prevent occasional conformity (Holmes, pp. 425–35) and all of whom "were instrumental in promoting his lordship," William Cowper, to the post of lord keeper (Luttrell, *6,* 12). To avoid 18 actions of *scandalum magnatum,* Browne assumed the role of a naif, a "Country Parson," who would not normally be suspected of irony, and so phrased the attack that it could be defended literally as the country parson's "Honest Advice." Could his grace the duke of Bolton complain that he had been libelled, that in truth he was devoid of "Merit" (line 14)? What the parson advises Cowper to emulate are—in most cases—the virtues that he imputes to other Whig lords who were notorious—in most cases—for the opposite vice. Even the publication date, as indicated by the Luttrell copy in the Newberry Library, may have been part of the joke. If it was, the poem becomes the pious admonition of a patriotic country parson on the 57th anniversary of the martyrdom of Charles I.

Despite these precautions, the poet, Joseph Browne, was committed to Newgate three days after publication of the poem. He was indicted for libel on 12 February, tried and found guilty on 3 May, and on 30 May 1706 fined 40 marks and sentenced to stand in the pillory (Luttrell, *6, 12, 15, 43, 52*).

Joseph Browne was born c. 1673 in Sheffield, the son, apparently, of a patriotic country parson. He tells us himself that when Princess Anne reached Nottingham in December 1688, "I . . . together with my Father, and one Brother more, headed a Troop of Horse . . . and maintain'd them at our own Cost and Charges, for the Service of our Country" (*A Letter to the Right Honourable Mr. Secretary Harley, by Dr. Browne*, 1706, p. 19). Browne was educated at Lincoln College, Oxford, and Jesus College, Cambridge, whence he graduated M. B. in 1695 (*Alumni Oxoniensis, 1*, 195; Venn, *1*, 235). He was called "Dr. Joseph Brown of Jesus College" when he presented himself to the Royal College of Physicians in August 1697 as a candidate to practice medicine in London, but this degree may have been assumed rather than earned. In any case he was examined in physiology "but gave no satisfaction neither to the President nor Censors, therefore was rejected, and advised . . . to follow his studies with greater care for the future" (RCP, *Annals, 7*, 120). This, as Defoe said of Browne's effort on another occasion, was "very Unhappy" (*Review*, 8 April 1706), for Browne continued to practice medicine in London and the College continued to prosecute him for illicit practice at least until 1720 (*RCP, Annals, 7*, 174; *8*, 108, 122).

In January 1699 Browne tried again. He brought to the College some specimen sheets of an edition he was preparing of case histories recorded by Sir Theodore Mayerne, the distinguished medical innovator whose patients included the early Stuart kings and most of their courtiers, and whose portrait was painted by Rubens. The charter of the College provided that no medical works could be published in London without its license, but the president and censors did not approve of Browne's specimen sheets so he published this book, and half a dozen more medical works (BM *Catalogue, 28*, 19–20; *N&Q*, 3d series, *2* [5 July 1862], 14) without the imprimatur of the College.

Browne's literary and political interests are revealed by two publications of 1705. The first is *Specimens of a New Translation of Horace into English Verse* and the second is a country Tory answer to *The Consolidator: Or, Memoirs of Sundry Transactions from the World in the Moon*, the fanciful prose correlative to *The Dyet of Poland* that Defoe published in March 1705. Defoe might have been more favorably disposed toward Browne's proposed translation of Horace if Browne had not just published *The Moon-Calf, or Accurate Reflections on the Consolidator, Giving an Account of Some Remarkable Transactions in the Lunar World*. But under the circumstances he found no occasion "to envy [Browne] the Reputation he will get by the Poetry of it" (*Little Review*, 29 June 1705), and the project was in fact abandoned after Browne had published *A Vindication of the Specimen Designd for a General Translation of Horace, by Dr. Browne, from the Pretended Criticisms of Mr. De Foe* (1705). *The Moon-Calf* was more successful, however, and Defoe devoted most of a *Review* (31 May 1705) to defending himself.

In January 1706, by which time he was known as Dr. Joseph Browne of St. Paul's, Covent Garden, he published the present poem, with the results recounted above. He confessed to one of Harley's undersecretaries on 1 February that he had given the copy for the broadside to the printer, Hugh Mears (HMC *Portland MSS., 4,* 283), and was promptly remanded to Newgate as "the Author of a Scandalous and Seditious Libel" (*A Letter to the Right Honourable Mr. Secretary Harley, by Dr. Browne*, 1706, p. 6).

Browne responded, from Newgate, by launching a new periodical, *A Dialogue between Church and No-Church: Or, A Rehearsal of the Review*, which achieved seven numbers in April–May 1706 (*State Tracts: Containing Many Necessary Observations*, 1715, sig. A2, pp. 1–43). "To gratifie [Browne], and help make his Paper Sell," Defoe devoted most of two numbers of the *Review* (8 and 11 April 1706) to exposing the lies of Browne's party, "or . . . those we call High-Church." And Harley evidently did Browne "the Honour" to send him "friendly Advice" and "wise Instructions" to abandon "the Trade of little Scriblers" (*A Letter to the Right Honourable Mr. Secretary Harley, by Dr. Browne*, 1706, pp. 3, 4, 7, 8). Browne replied very bravely with *A Letter to the Right Honourable Mr. Secretary Harley, by Dr. Browne: Occasion'd from His Late Commitment to New-Gate. Together with His Interpretation of that Paper Call'd, The Country Parson's Advice to My Lord Keeper, laid to His Charge*, in which he reminded Harley that Mears had not said that Browne was the author of *The Country Parson's Honest Advice*, but that he had in fact

"told your under Secretary, that I was not," and that by charging
Browne with being the author (in the commitment warrant) Harley
was arrogating to himself the authority of a judge, and that "little
Scriblers," in Harley's term, "write better Sense than great Secretaries"
(ibid., pp. 6, 8). For this impudence, which contrasts sharply with
Defoe's momentary failure of nerve in *A Brief Explanation of a Late
Pamphlet, Entituled, The Shortest Way with the Dissenters* (February 1703),
Browne was again arrested, found guilty of "writing a scandalous pam-
phlet," fined 40 marks and sentenced to stand twice in the pillory
(Luttrell, *6,* 107).

Defoe took up the case in the *Review* for 8 April 1706, charging
Browne with "Bullying . . . the Secretary of State . . . Writing
Ironies, and then Expounding them *Ironically,*" exactly as Defoe had
done in *The Shortest-Way with the Dissenters* (1702) and *A Hymn to the
Pillory* (1703). Defoe makes a telling point, however, when he juxta-
poses Browne's claim that he "cou'd produce . . . the Author" of
The Country Parson's Honest Advice (p. 5) alongside his claim that he is
"ignorant of the Author to this Day" (p. 10). For there can be no
doubt that Browne wrote *The Country Parson's Honest Advice* (HMC
Portland MSS., 4, 306). Browne's career has one more parallel to De-
foe's: after having been committed to Newgate by Harley, Browne was
recruited to succeed Swift and Delariviere Manley as editor of *The
Examiner* (Noble, *2,* 232), just as Defoe was ransomed from Newgate
by Harley to edit the *Review.*

Browne's last published work may be his edition of the *Remains of the
Late Learned and Ingenious Dr. William King* (1732). Browne and his son
Marmaduke, who followed his father to Cambridge but not into medi-
cine, witnessed King's will, and Browne, according to a note in the
Yale copy of the *Remains,* purchased the manuscript from King's
sister and sole heiress. The man who began his career in November
1698 with a public lecture disproving the circulation of the blood, ran
his course without faltering. In 1732 he tells us that William King was
"naturally of a Courteous Behavior, and very obliging" (p. 9) and that
"his natural Temper . . . was sullen, morose, and peevish" (p. 15).

Besides the next two poems in this volume, *The Country Parson's
Honest Advice* was answered by *A Reply to the Parson's Advice* ("That
Lowly Vicar may in order rise"), of which a copy is preserved in the
Essex R. O. (D/DW.Z.4). This reply adopts the fiction that if the coun-

try parson would rise in the church, he must adopt the "virtues" of the high flying clergy:

> Kimberly's Sense; and Birch's Modesty:
> Smallwood's Devotion, Bink's piety;
> Stubb's Moderation, Aldrich's Sobriety.

THE COUNTRY PARSON'S HONEST ADVICE
TO THAT
JUDICIOUS LAWYER, AND WORTHY MINISTER OF STATE,
MY LORD KEEPER.

Be Wise as *Somerset,* as *Somers* Brave,
As *Pembroke* Airy, and as *Richmond* Grave;
Humble as *Orford* be; and *Wharton's* Zeal

1. *Somerset:* Charles Seymour, sixth duke of Somerset (1662–1743), began his political career as a Tory and held the office of gentleman of the bedchamber to Charles II and James II. He held no high office in William's reign until he changed his politics and became a Whig: as Shaftesbury put it, "the Duke of Somerset is a Tory, and of a Tory family, and become a zealouse and hearty man with us" (*Original Letters,* p. 193). Then he was appointed lord president of the council (January–June 1702). Anne, whom he had befriended during her estrangement from her brother-in-law, made him her master of the horse and retained him in the privy council but removed him from the presidency. As one of three Whigs in Anne's cabinet, his presence there was challenged in April 1704 by Nottingham, who demanded party rule (Blenheim MS. E 20, Sidney Godolphin to Sarah, duchess of Marlborough). Somerset, however, managed to survive both this challenge and the ministerial revolution of 1710 partly through the queen's favor and partly by his remarkable ability to trim his political sails to the court winds. But when he refused to support Harley's peace policy in 1712, he was removed from the government. Somerset was noted, not for his wisdom, but for his intolerable pride. To Macky's statement that he had "good Judgment," Swift added, "not a grain, nor hardly common sense" (Swift, *Prose, 5,* 257).

Somers: Even though Somers had been out of office since April 1700, he remained a favorite target of the Tory satirists. Browne admitted, however, that there was no evidence that Somers was a coward: "I never heard his Lordship was a Coward, but I know he was always Bold, which is a good Sign of Bravery" (*A Letter to the Right Honourable Mr. Secretary Harley, by Dr. Browne,* 1706, p. 11).

2. *Pembroke:* Thomas Herbert, eighth earl of Pembroke (1656?–1733) was "Airy" neither in his style of life, which was said to be "after the Manner of the *Primitive Christians*" (Macky, p. 22), nor his intellectual interests, which included mathematics, the Royal Society, of which he was president (1689–90), and art. "Without being of a party," it was said (ibid.), he was "esteemed by all Parties." Actually "Long Tom Herbert" was a court Tory, more court than Tory, who held public office from 1689 to 1709. In Anne's reign he was lord president of the council (1702–08), lord lieutenant of Ireland (1707–08), and lord high admiral (1708–09).

Richmond: Charles Lennox, duke of Richmond (1672–1723), was the youngest of the "Six Bastard Dukes" (*POAS,* Yale, *6,* 274), the sons of Charles II. He professed the Catholic faith in October 1685 in the presence of Louis XIV at Fontainebleau but returned to the Anglican communion in May 1692. After his marriage a year later it was said that "[il] s'y perdit de vin et de débauches" (GEC, *10,* 836–38). Although professedly "a staunche Whig" (HMC *Lonsdale MSS.,* p. 121) and a member of the Kit-Cat Club, he was suspected of being a Jacobite in 1696, and occasionally voted with the Tories (Holmes, p. 431). Swift called him "A shallow Coxcomb" (*Prose, 5,* 258).

3. *Orford:* Although Orford had been out of office since May 1699, he remained in sight because his accounts as treasurer of the navy had been audited in March 1704 (*Moderation Display'd,* 300n. above). More recently he had entertained the queen and prince consort at his

For Church and Loyalty wou'd fit thee well;
Like *Sarum* I wou'd have thee love the Church;   5
He scorns to leave his Mother in the Lurch.
For the well governing your Family,
Let pious *Haversham* thy Pattern be:
And if it be thy Fate again to Marry,
And *Seymour*'s Daughter will thy Year out tarry,   10

---

estate near Newmarket during the racing season in April 1705 (Luttrell, *5*, 542). Macky (p. 76) records that "No Gentleman was ever better beloved by the *English* Sailors than he, when he had the first command of the Fleet; but he soon lost all by his Pride."

Wharton: Wharton demonstrated his zeal for the church in 1680 by entering one in Gloucestershire, where he "made use of the pulpit in a way which even at this distance of time ought not to be described" (John Carswell, *The Old Cause*, Cresset, 1954, p. 58) but which is described below (p. 537). More recently, as Browne says, "his Zeal to the Church, was sufficiently shown in opposing the *Occasional Bill*" (*A Letter to the Right Honourable Mr. Secretary Harley, by Dr. Browne*, 1706, p. 12). Honest Tom's "Loyalty" to James II was signalized by his composition of Lilliburlero (*POAS*, Yale, *4*, 309–19) and boasting afterwards that he had "sung a deluded Prince out of Three Kingdoms" ([Delariviere Manley], *A True Relation of the Several Facts and Circumstances of the Intended Riot and Tumult of Queen Elizabeth's Birth-day*, 1711, p. 5).

5. *Sarum*: Gilbert Burnet was hated for his Scottish and Presbyterian antecedents (*POAS*, Yale, *6*, 545), his sexual prowess ("it being notorious that after threescore he married a barren widow, & impregnated her with two children at once" [Hearne, *1*, 110]), and his venality ("There . . . has been attested before a Publick Notary, a Paper containing the following words, viz. This is to certifie . . . that the Bp. of Sarum has recd 5000 libs for voting for Occasional Conformity, & that he is to receive 30000 libs more, & the Revenue of his Bpprick during Life whenever Presbytery shall be Establish'd in England, which he endeavours to have effected" [ibid., *1*, 48]).

8. *Haversham*: John Thompson, Lord Haversham (1647–1710), was an occasional conformist (*Parl. Hist.*, *6*, 564) and such a violent Whig that he was "chect'd for being Rude" in the session of 1701 ([William Pittis], *The Patriots*, 1702, p. 3). His "truly eloquent Speech" (Carlisle R. O. MS. Nicolson Diary, 23 November 1704) against the Scottish Act of Security is preserved in Boyer's *Annals*, 1705, pp. 175–78. But Haversham was "short red Faced" and "always turbulent" (Macky, p. 104), and now he was on the verge of conversion both to the Church of England and to the Tory party. His unorthodox domestic governance may have contributed something to this conversion: "In *May*, 1709 he married to his second wife Mrs. *Graham*, his House Keeper, with whom he lived in so great familiarity, even whilst his First Lady was alive, that the Rigid Presbyterian Ministers (as the Report goes) refused to administer to him the Sacrament: which is supposed to have been the occasion of his communicating with the Church of *England*" (Boyer, *Political State*, *1*, 25).

9. *again to Marry*: Browne pretended to be ignorant of Cowper's marital state: "Now, before this Information, I did not know whether my Lord Keeper was a Widower, Batchelor, or marry'd Man; but if it would insinuate he had the Misfortune of an ill Wife for his first . . . it has been many a good Man's Fate" (*A Letter to the Right Honourable Mr. Secretary Harley, by Dr. Browne*, 1706, p. 14). Presumably he knew of the death of Cowper's first wife, Judith, in April 1705 and pretended ignorance in order to recall to his readers' minds the story of Cowper's bigamous marriage (*On the New Promotion*, 13n. above). Cowper did marry again, secretly, in September 1706, to Mary Clavering.

10. *Seymour's*: "I know not who the Letters S——*y*——*r* stand for: but if they are meant for

May'st thou use her as *Mohun* his tender Wife;
And may she lead his virtuous Lady's Life.
To sum up all; *Devonshire*'s Chastity,
Bolton's Merit, *Godolphin*'s Probity,
Halifax his Modesty, *Essex*'s Sense, 15

---

the Duke of *Somerset*'s Daughter, I know no Injury is offer'd to the Lady, in tendering her a Husband, unless the Injury is sum'd up in the succeeding Lines" (*A Letter to the Right Honourable Mr. Secretary Harley, by Dr. Browne*, 1706, p. 14). By his first wife the duke of Somerset had four daughters, two of whom, Catherine and Frances, were unmarried in 1706. There seems to be no way of telling which one Browne had in mind, or why.

11. *Mohun:* Mohun's gallantry was sufficiently notorious for Macky (p. 93) to call him "one of the arrantest Rakes in Town, and indeed a Scandal to the Peerage." The reputation of Lady Mohun, who was Philippa, daughter of Arthur Annesley, first earl of Anglesey, may be estimated from Mohun's will, which left £100 to "Elizabeth, my pretended daughter by my first wife" (*DNB, 13,* 554).

13. *Devonshire:* William Cavendish, fourth earl and first duke of Devonshire (1640–1707), was one of the first Whigs and one of the signers of the invitation of 30 June 1688 to William of Orange. In Anne's reign he was lord steward of the household (1702–07) and one of the chief managers of the opposition to the bills to prevent occasional conformity. "This great Man," the owner of a dozen estates and the builder of Chatsworth, was also known on occasion as "the White Dog of Lady Fitzharding." He was "famous for Debauchery, Lewdness, &c." and was said to have seduced "more Women than any Five Keepers of Quality besides" (Portland MS. Pw V 48, p. 114; Hearne, *2,* 39–40). Three of these transactions are retailed by John Dunton, *The Hazard of a Death-Bed-Repentance, Fairly Argued from the Late Remorse of W—— late D—— of D——,* 1708, pp. 26–27.

14. *Bolton:* Charles Powlett or Pawlett, second duke of Bolton (1661–1722), was another early Whig, who landed at Tor Bay with William of Orange in November 1688. Swift found him "a great Booby" and Lady Cowper remembered him with "his Tongue lolling out of his Mouth" (Swift, *Prose, 5,* 258; Lady Cowper, *Diary,* p. 154), while "the few letters of his which . . . have survived impress one neither by their intelligence nor their literacy" (Holmes, p. 241).

Godolphin: High churchmen could not forget that Godolphin had signed the warrant that sent the seven bishops to the Tower in June 1688 (Hearne, *1,* 124) nor that he publicly voted for the second bill to prevent occasional conformity while privately instructing his dependents to vote against it (*Memoirs of the Life of the Most Noble Thomas Late Marquess of Wharton,* 1715, p. 40). He is "a cunning, sagacious Ambidexter," it was said, "And under a plain smiling Countenance, covers most profound Deceit" (*The English Theophrastus,* 2nd ed., 1706, p. 369). In July 1705 he was attacked in one of the most celebrated pamphlets of the age, *The Memorial of the Church of England,* the drift of which, as Luttrell says, was to show that Godolphin and the duchess of Marlborough were "undermining the church, by encouraging the Whiggs, and putting them into places" (Luttrell, *5,* 574). But not all the attacks came from high churchmen. In August 1704 when he advised the queen to give her assent to the Act of Security passed by the Scottish parliament, "the English Whigs threatened to impeach the Lord Treasurer Godolphin, apprehending him to act in concert with the Scots in favour of the Pretender" (Calamy, *Historical Account, 2,* 46).

15. *Halifax:* Halifax was "haughty, and . . . could not endure an Equal in Business" (Macky, p. 53).

Essex: Algernon Capel, second earl of Essex (1670–1710), whose father was a Whig martyr, held so many public offices that his death in January 1710 precipitated a crisis in

Mountague's Managment, *Culpepper*'s Pence,
Tenison's Learning, and *Southampton*'s Wit,
Will make thee for an able States-man fit.

the government (*The Civil War,* below). He was said to have had "no Genius for Business, nor will ever apply himself that Way" (Macky, p. 70). "His Mouth is always open," Macky added, and Essex may be the original of Count Drivel in Thomas Baker's comedy, *Tunbridge Wells,* which opened in January 1703.

16. *Mountague:* Ralph Montagu, first duke of Montagu (1638–1709), as Charles II's ambassador to France, "carried on the disgraceful negotiations" by which Louis XIV bought England's neutrality (GEC, *9,* 107). Then, as member of parliament for Northampton (October 1678–79, 1679–81) and Huntingdonshire (1679), he became one of the first Whigs and voted for the exclusion of James II. He succeeded as Lord Montagu in 1683 and played an important part in promoting the revolution. In April 1689 he was created first earl of Montagu. Anne did not reappoint him as lord lieutenant of Northamptonshire (1697–1702), but in April 1705 she advanced him to the honor of duke of Montagu. He may be the original of Thomas Courtine in William Burnaby's comedy, *The Lady's Visiting Day* (1701). His "Managment" is probably explained by the remark that he had one of the best estates in England, "which he knows very well how to improve." Swift called him "As arrant a Knave as any in his time" (*Prose, 5,* 258).

Culpepper: John Colepeper (1640–1719), the son of John Colepeper, first Lord Colepeper, Charles I's chancellor of the exchequer, and the younger brother of Thomas, second Lord Colepeper, Charles II's governor of Virginia, succeeded as third lord in January 1689. Despite his cavalier antecedents, he dutifully supplied a Whig vote in the House of Lords in return for an annual pension of £200 "out of the remotest malt ticquets" (*CTB 1697,* p. 78). "*Culpepper*'s Pence" qualifies as a nonexistent or imaginary entity like "*Southampton*'s Wit" because it was not renewed by Queen Anne (*CTB 1702,* p. 437).

17. *Tenison:* Hearne (*2,* 107) referred to Archbishop Tenison as "the Loggerhead at Lambeth," and Swift called him "The dullest, good for nothing man I ever knew" (*Prose, 5,* 271).

Southampton: Charles Fitzroy, first duke of Southampton (1662–1730), was the eldest of Charles II's bastards by Barbara Villiers. He married first Mary Wood, a great heiress, and then Anne Pulteney, a great Tory (p. 405 above). He was feeble-minded—"a natural Fool," according to Lady Cowper (Lady Cowper, *Diary,* p. 90)—and voted regularly with the Whigs (Holmes, p. 426). In October 1709 upon the death of his mother, he succeeded as second duke of Cleveland (GEC, *3,* 282–83).

The Lawyer's Answer
to
The Country Parson's Good Advice
to My Lord Keeper
(February? 1706)

The Tory *Country Parson's Honest Advice* evoked a Whiggish *Lawyer's Answer* that turns the tables on the country parson. But the answer is not simply a reversal of the satiric method of *The Country Parson's Honest Advice*: the lawyer does not advise the country parson to emulate the virtues of Tories notorious for the opposite vices. Instead he concentrates on the country parson's style, "so Peaceable and Wise" (line 6) and goes on to imagine what rewards await the parson for persisting in "*High-Church* Eloquence" (4). So it becomes a poem about Tory rhetoric.

The personae adopted by Joseph Browne and the unknown author of *The Lawyer's Answer* are interesting stereotypes, for the power struggle between Whig and Tory involved social and geographic antagonisms between country parsons and city lawyers. It is possible that the author of *The Lawyer's Answer* intended his lines to be read as if spoken by "*that Judicious Lawyer, and Worthy Minister of State, My Lord Keeper*," William Cowper, as he is styled in *The Country Parson's Honest Advice*, but there is no evidence for this in the lines themselves.

While the author of *The Lawyer's Answer* is unknown, he must be an unknown "Moderate-Man," because like Defoe he is equally offended by the extreme Whiggish rhetoric of "*Stephens* stile" (7) and the extreme Tory rhetoric of "*Bincks* and *Sacheverell*" (9).

It can be surmised that the poem was published shortly after 30 January 1706, when *The Country Parson's Honest Advice* appeared, but there is not even any basis for speculating about the author.

THE LAWYER'S ANSWER

TO

THE COUNTRY PARSON'S GOOD ADVICE

TO MY LORD KEEPER

Learnedly Wise, and Prudent as the Rest,
With full as much Humility and Meekness Blest,
We do at once applaud thy single Sense,
And praise thy Muse for *High-Church* Eloquence.
Fitting thy Station is the Grave Advice,   5
Who else cou'd be so Peaceable and Wise?
Not *Stephens* stile of mightier force consists,
Begun by *Shaftesbury*, and back'd by Priests.

7. *Stephens stile:* William Stephens (1647–1718) graduated B.D. from St. Edmund Hall, Oxford, in 1678 and is said to have been discharged as a schoolmaster in Bristol for "Abominable and not to be named crimes" (*BIHR, 32* [May 1959], 28). In 1690, however, he was instituted to the rectory of Sutton, Surrey, and by 1700 he had become a notorious advocate of extreme Whiggish principles, "famous for having preached a sermon before my Lord Mayor vilifieing the keeping of this anniversary day [30 January]," and called "chaplain to the Calfs-head Club" (ibid., p. 29). Of his literary style it was remarked in 1694 that "he has indeed a peculiar Knack at wounding with a Slie, Oblique, and Paltry Suggestion; at Stabbing and yet looking another way, as if he were wholly Innocent and Unconcern'd" (ibid., p. 28*n.*). In December 1705 he published *A Letter to the Author of the Memorial of the State of England,* libelling Harley, and Marlborough's conduct of the war, for which he was arrested the next month. He appeared in court "not in His Canonical Habit but in a grey Riding Coat with a Whip in His Hand & look'd very bluff," still believing that neither Harley nor Marlborough would dare to let him come to trial (ibid., p. 31). He was tried nonetheless, found guilty on 6 May 1706, fined 100 marks, ordered to provide security for his good behavior for 12 months, and to stand twice in the pillory (ibid., p. 32).

8. *Shaftesbury:* Although both witnesses read "S——rs," the association with William Stephens makes it likely that the author wrote "S——ry," the last letter of which the compositor read as a long "s." Anthony Ashley Cooper, third earl of Shaftesbury (1671–1713) began his political career as a member for Poole (1695–98). He was a country Whig with a very independent voting record: he was set down as "Doubtful" in Harley's list drawn up in anticipation of the debate on the council of trade in January 1696 and he voted with the Tories against the recoinage bill of the same year, probably in reaction against John Locke. His first book, *An Inquiry concerning Virtue in Two Discourses* was seen through the press in 1699 by John Toland while Shaftesbury spent the year in Holland. In January 1700 he took his seat in the House of Lords and soon became identified with extreme Whiggish opinion. It is not easy to discover how "*Stephens* stile" was "Begun by *Shaftesbury*," but it is true that Shaftesbury was the patron, not only of Toland, but also of William Stephens. And the copy of Stephens' pamphlet, *A Letter to the Author of the Memorial of the State of England* (1705), in the Boston Public Library, is inscribed "The Author of this pamphlet was the E. of Sh^by." With characteristic independence Shaftesbury was supporting the ministry when Stephens published his attack on it in December 1705, and he was forced to "cast off" Stephens in order to dissociate himself from the attack (*BIHR, 32* [May 1959], 36–37).

back'd by Priests: before the author of *A Letter to the Author of the Memorial of the State of*

Bincks and *Sacheverell* the Pulpit bless,
And *Stokow* makes it Ecchoe to the Press.   10
Patrons thou canst not want, where Merit shines,
Mackworth and *Pooley* will support thy Lines,
Wright for a Modern Grudge shall back thy Fame,

England was known to be the radical Whig, Stephens, it was "thought some Red hot Tory had writ the Pamphlet," or even "a Jacobite or High-Churchman" (BM MS. Add. 4291, f. 40v; Hearne, *1*, 164, 234–35).

9. *Bincks:* William Binckes (c. 1653–1712) graduated B.A. from St. John's College, Cambridge, in 1674, was instituted to prebendaries in Lincoln and in Lichfield, and in 1699 took the degree of D.D. On 30 January 1702, while proctor of the diocese of Lichfield in the lower house of convocation, Binckes preached a sermon before the house "in which he drew a Parallel between King *Charles*'s Sufferings and those of our Saviour: and, in some very indecent Expressions," as Burnet (*2*, 316) said, "gave the preference to the former." The House of Lords resolved that these "Expressions . . . give just Scandal and Offence to all Christian People" (*LJ*, *17*, 132) and ordered Binckes to be reprimanded. Instead he was appointed dean of Lichfield in May 1703 and elected prolocutor of the convocation in 1705 (Luttrell, *5*, 298, 609).

10. *Stokow:* Luke Stokoe, a London bookseller "near Spring Garden, over against the Mews at Charing Cross," appears to be the only publisher whose surname could supply a half-rhyme with "echo" (Plomer, p. 281). He was a high churchman and may have been a Jacobite (*The Examiner*, 12–19 June 1712; Hearne, *5*, 231).

12. *Mackworth:* Sir Humphrey Mackworth, Henry Pooley, and John Ward were among the suspected authors of *The Memorial of the Church of England,* as the following entry in Hearne's diary (*1*, 170) indicates: "They cannot find out the Author of the Memorial. All that affects Sr. *Humph. Mackworth*, Mr. *Poley*, & Mr. *Ward* is that 150 of 'em as soon as printed off were sent to the first as many to the 2d & 100 to the last."

Pooley: Henry Pooley, or Poley (c. 1653–1707), was educated at Jesus College, Cambridge, and the Middle Temple, whence he was called to the bar in 1678. As member of parliament for Eye (1689–95), West Looe (1703–05), and Ipswich (1705–07), he was a solid Tory, voting against making the prince of Orange king, for the Tack, and for Bromley as Speaker in October 1705. "He was a Man of a very despicable Presence," Hearne (*1*, 203) said, "being deform'd to the Highest Degree. But what made amends for this was his Admirable Parts, being endu'd with a strong Memory & most solid Judgment, insomuch that he was accounted one of the best common Lawyers in England, & for that reason suspected to have had a Hand in Penning *The Memorial of the Church of England*." The suspicion was correct: "[Dr. James Drake] writ, in concert with Mr. Poley . . . 'The Memorial of the Church of England' " (*Biographia Britannica, 3*, 1742).

13. *Wright:* "Chance more than Choice," as Macky said, brought Sir Nathan Wright into the office of lord keeper in April 1700, "The Lords Chief Justices *Holt* and *Treby* refusing to succeed so Great a Man as the Lord *Somers*" (Macky, p. 41). Wright amassed a fortune while in office through the manipulation of patronage, on one occasion selling a judgeship in the court of the exchequer for £1,000 (Burnet, 1823, *5*, 219*n*.), but he proved to be "of no use to the crown" and his "weak and wretched conduct in the court of *chancery* . . . almost brought his very office into contempt" (*Account of the Conduct*, p. 147). Accordingly, on 6 October 1705, "Mr. secretary Hedges went to Powis House, and took the seals from the lord keeper, and carried them to the queen at Windsor" (Luttrell, *5*, 599). On 11 October Anne gave the seals to Cowper.

And *Ward* for antient Hatred do the same:
Bromley his Disappointment may forgive,   15
And *Powis* is pleas'd in greater Hopes to live.
Mean time—— ——
May you, to bless your Pains, rewarded be,
With Trophies of the Party's Honesty:
Rochester's Truth, and Grace from *Normanby*,   20
Granvill's Sedateness, joyn'd with *Conway*'s Fame,
With Depth of Eloquence from *Nottingham*:
Let *Seymour*'s Peace of Mind be ever seen,

14. *Ward:* John Ward's "antient Hatred" of Cowper may go back no further than January 1704 when Cowper argued—against Mackworth, Sir Thomas Powys, and Ward—that the Commons had no right to restrain Matthew Ashby from carrying his appeal to the House of Lords (*Parl. Hist., 6*, 279–85). More recently Ward, together with Mackworth, Henry Pooley, William Bromley, and Powys, successfully opposed the Lords' effort in March 1705 to secure release of the Aylesbury electors on a writ of habeas corpus (*The Dyet of Poland*, 562n. above; Luttrell, *5*, 529).

15. *Bromley:* Bromley's disappointment was his failure to be elected Speaker of the Commons in 1704 and 1705 (*The Dyet of Poland*, 800n.; *Declaration without Doors*, headnote, above).

16. *Powis:* Sir Thomas Powys was one of the few Tories with sufficient legal ability to entertain "Hopes" of obtaining the great seal.

18. *you:* the country parson.

20. *Rochester:* See *The Dyet of Poland*, 367n. above.

Normanby: Rumor seized upon the duke of Buckingham as the author of *The Memorial of the Church of England* almost as soon as it was published, and although he assured Charles Davenant that the rumor was false, the truth seems to be that it was "written by Dr. Drake with the Assistance of Mr. *Pooley* in Matters of Law, and of one of the discarded Ministers [Buckingham] in Matters of Politics" (Hearne, *1*, 6; BM MS. Add. 4291, f. 41; Oldmixon, *Maynwaring*, p. 104). Buckingham's "Grace" shines through Johnson's lines in *The Lives of the Poets:* "His character is not to be proposed as worthy of imitation. His religion he may be supposed to have learned from Hobbes, and his morality was such as naturally proceeds from loose opinions. His sentiments with respect to women he picked up in the court of Charles, and his principles concerning property were such as a gaming table supplies" (Johnson, *Lives, 2*, 174). Macky (p. 20) called him "proud, insolent, and covetous" and Swift added that this character was "the truest of any" (Swift, *Prose, 5*, 257).

21. *Granvill:* The Smithfield tastes of Lord Granville are illustrated in *The Dyet of Poland*, 943–64, above).

Conway: The "Fame" of Francis Seymour Conway was virtually limited to being the second son of Sir Edward Seymour by the second venter. He was created Baron Conway of Ragley in March 1703 when the Tory ministry prevailed upon the queen "to create four new Peers, who had been the violentest of the whole Party; *Finch, Gower, Granvil*, and young *Seimour*" (Burnet, *2*, 344). It has been observed, however, that "The 'violence' of young Seymour must . . . have been of small moment" (GEC, *3*, 403n.).

22. *Nottingham:* The "Depth" of Nottingham's eloquence had been noticed most recently by John Toland in *The Memorial of the State of England*, 1705, p. 40: "a certain *dismal* Gentleman . . . of such unparallel'd *Eloquence* that his Speeches are never understood for the musical *chiming* of his Words."

23. *Seymour:* See *The Dyet of Poland*, 478n. above.

And *Caesar* teach thee to revere the Queen:
Be Faithful as thy Tribe was ever known,   25
And learn to Preach, and Rail of *Packington.*
May all those Blessings in the Party bred,
Fall like the Dew of *Hermon* on your Head;
Full of Church Loyalty be all your Prayers,
And all your Actions, full as wise as Theirs.   30

24. *Caesar:* Charles Caesar (1673–1741) was born in London, the son of Sir Charles Caesar, Knight, and educated at St. Catharine's Hall, Cambridge, and the Middle Temple. In parliament, where he sat for Hertford (1700–08, 1710–15) and Hertfordshire (1727–34, April 1736–41), he was a solid Tory: a Poussineer, Tacker, True Churchman, and eventually a member of the October Club. On 19 December 1705 during a debate on the regency bill, Caesar said that "a noble Lord [Godolphin], without whose Advice the Queen does nothing, . . . in the late Reign, was known to keep a constant Correspondence with the Court at St. Germans" (*CJ, 15,* 70; Luttrell, *5,* 627). These words were found to be "highly dishonourable to her Majesty's Person and Government" and Caesar was hurried off to the Tower. He survived this indiscretion to become treasurer of the navy (1711–14).

26. *Packington:* Pakington's forensic style is imitated or parodied in *The Dyet of Poland,* 623–35 above.

28. *Dew of Hermon:* "Behold how good and how pleasant it is for brethren to dwell together in unity! It is like . . . the dew of Hermon . . . for there the Lord commanded the blessing, even life for evermore" (Psalms 133:1–3). Mt. Hermon is the modern Jebel esh Sheikh, on the border between Lebanon and Syria. "The snow on the summit of this mountain condenses the vapours that float during the summer in the higher regions of the atmosphere, causing light clouds to hover around it . . . while the whole country elsewhere is parched, and the whole heaven elsewhere cloudless" (William Smith, *A Dictionary of the Bible,* 3 vols., Boston, 1860–63, *1,* 790).

29. *Church Loyalty:* The question of the loyalty of the church to the queen and to the government was raised anew by a clause in *The Memorial of the Church of England* (p. 12): "tho' the Ch[ur]ch is not to be wrought up to Rebellion, yet they may be so Alarm'd as to Secure themselves at the Peril of those M[iniste]rs who give them the Alarm." This "last Position," as Pittis said, "has rais'd such a Hurricane among the Passionate Pen-men, such as the *Review* and *Observator,* as to . . . Impugn the Church of *England*'s Loyalty with" (*The Case of the Church of England's Memorial Fairly Stated,* 1705, p. 20).

The Country Parson's Advice
to Those Little Scriblers Who Pretend to Write
Better Sense Than Great Secretaries:
Or,
Mr. Stephens's Triumph over the Pillory
(11 May 1706)

In this poem the dunces emerge from the mists of prehistory. The neolithic dunce had only come to light two years before, on 10 May 1704, with publication of *A Tale of a Tub,* of which he is the narrator. But now whole scores of scribblers, all living in manifest danger of phlebotomy and the whip, "Escape in Monsters, and amaze the town." It was in fact an Age of Scribble. Dryden had recognized this in 1667 when he enunciated the principle that "the corruption of a poet is the generation of a statesman" (*Works, 2,* 301). More recently one of them had asked, with pardonable pride, "Was there ever such a time of Scribble in *England?*" (*The Observator,* 25–28 July 1705). It was, as another had observed, "an Age when e'ery ignorant *Scribler* sets up for a Man of Authority" ([Charles Gildon], *Letters and Essays, on Several Subjects,* 1696, p. 7). And when Defoe was tried at the bar of *The Whipping Post* for writing *The Dyet of Poland,* he was made to say "*that what he had done was by a Poetical Authority,* that men of his Profession were Invested with a Licence for so doing" ([William Pittis], *The Whipping Post,* 10 July 1705). The present poem is an emphatic denial of this "Licence."

The relationship of this poem to the two preceding works in this volume is complicated. *The Country Parson's Honest Advice,* written by a Tory in the guise of a patriotic country parson, ironically exhorts William Cowper, the new lord keeper, to be like 18 other Whig lords. *The Lawyer's Answer,* written (apparently) by a "Moderate-Man" in the person of the new lord keeper, ironically exhorts the country parson to rhetorize like 18 other high church laymen and divines. *The Country Parson's Advice to Those Little Scriblers,* written (apparently) by another "Moderate-Man" in the person of William Stephens, an anomalous country parson who was also a Whig rhetorician, ironically exhorts 20 other rhetoricians, Whig and Tory, not to fear "*Fines* nor *Pillories*" (line 31).

The Luttrell copy of *A,* now in the Newberry Library, is dated 11 May 1706. The attribution of the poem to Joseph Browne (*Modern Philology, 33* [November 1935], 185) must have been made inadvertently, for no evidence of authorship is known to exist.

165

THE COUNTRY PARSON'S ADVICE
TO THOSE LITTLE SCRIBLERS WHO PRETEND TO WRITE
BETTER SENSE THAN GREAT SECRETARIES:
OR,
MR. STEPHENS'S TRIUMPH OVER THE PILLORY

Be Wise as *Addison,* as *Browne* be Brave,
As *Phillips* Airy, and as *Jones* look Grave;

Title. *Little Scriblers:* In *A Letter to the Right Honourable Mr. Secretary Harley,* 1706, p. 8, Browne congratulated Harley for having "wisely resolved, like a Great Man, as well as a Great Minister, to ruin the Trade of little Scriblers, as you are pleas'd to term such as write better Sense than great Secretaries."

Stephens's Triumph: Two months after his show of defiance in court (*The Lawyer's Answer,* 7n. above), Stephens quietly advertised in *The Flying Post* "that what he said of the Duke [of Marlborough] is false & begs his Pardon" (Hearne, *1,* 208). Dyer attributed Stephens' "Triumph" partly to this recantation. Stephens was supposed to stand in the pillory on 9 and 10 May 1706, according to his sentence, but "I concluded," Dyer said, "as soon as I saw his Recantation and heard that he made no Defence to the Information that the way was paved to his Pardon" (Hearne, *1,* 243). Stephens was saved from the pillory through the intervention of the duchess of Marlborough, even though she had not been spared the force of Stephens' "peculiar Knack at wounding" (*BIHR, 32* [May 1959], 28).

1. *Addison:* When Joseph Addison (1672–1719) returned to London from his travels about September 1703, he was—outside Oxford, where he was a fellow of Queen's College (1697–1711)—virtually unknown. But publication of *The Campaign,* that "gazette in rhyme," as Joseph Warton called it (*Essays on the Writings and Genius of Pope,* 2 vols., 1756–82, *1,* 29), on 14 December 1704, the day on which Marlborough returned in triumph to London, made Addison a public figure. The next month Defoe could still envy Addison his uninvolvement in party politics: "Envy and Party-Spleen h'has never known, / No humbling Jayls has pull'd his Fancy down" (*The Double Welcome,* 1705, p. 12). Defoe was not wholly right, for Addison had been attacked in *Faction Display'd* (*POAS,* Yale, *6,* 666), but in July 1705 the success of *The Campaign* was rewarded by Addison's appointment as undersecretary of state (Luttrell, *5,* 569), and by November Thomas Hearne (*1,* 105) was discovering that "Mr. *Addison*'s Travells is . . . very trite, being made up of nothing but scraps of verses & things wch have been observ'd over & over . . . & even some of those wch he has inserted, that have been already taken notice of are ridiculous."

2. *Phillips:* The most probable candidate is John Philips (1676–1709), "the famous Poet," as Hearne (*8,* 184) called him, who wrote *The Splendid Shilling* (1701) and who was drafted to write the Tory counterpart to *The Campaign.* "It is said that he would willingly have declined the task," but *Bleinheim, A Poem* ("From low and abject Themes the Grov'ling Muse"), written "at the house of Mr. St. John" (Johnson, *Lives, 1,* 313) and "Inscrib'd to the Right Honourable Robert Harley, Esq;" was duly published on 2 January 1705. Philips, the son of the vicar of Bampton, was educated at Winchester School and Christ Church, Oxford. According to John Dunton (p. [247 misnumbered] 241), he translated *The Present State of Europe: Or, The Monthly Mercury* and will "write you a *Design,* off in a very little Time, if the Gout (or Claret) don't stop him." Philips was tubercular and "somewhat reserved

166

Humble as *Prior* be; *Sachev'rell's* Zeal,
For Church and Loyalty, will fit you Well:
Like *Pittis*, I wou'd have you love the Church,   5

---

and silent" (Jacob, *Historical Account*, p. 134).

Jones: The most likely Jones is David Jones (1667–1720), "Author of King *William's Life with Cuts*, and printed for Mr. *Sprint* in *Little-Britain*. He's Honest and good natur'd, and writes very well. He design'd for the Ministry, but began to *teach School*, and from that Employment he turn'd Author, and Corrector for the Press" (Dunton, p. [247 misnumbered] 241). Jones also wrote *The Secret History of Whitehall* (1697), *The Tragical History of the Stuarts* (1697), *The Wars and Causes of Them, between England and France, from William I., to William III.* (1698), *The Life of James II* (1702), and from 1705 the "Yearly Account" called *The Compleat History of Europe* (Hearne, 2, 58).

3. *Prior:* Matthew Prior (1664–1721) had been taken from the bar of a tavern by the earl of Dorset, "who accidentally found him reading Horace" and sent him to Westminster School and Cambridge (Burnet, 2, 580). He achieved literary fame only a year after graduating B.A. from St. John's College when he published, together with Charles Montagu, later Lord Halifax, *The Hind and the Panther Transvers'd to the Story of the Country Mouse and the City-Mouse* (1687). By 1701 he was recognized as "one of the best Poets in *England*" whose "Genius shines thro every Page" (Macky, p. 135; *POAS*, 1707, 4, 359). Political fame, as a career diplomat, came more slowly, but by 1711 everyone was singing *An Excellent New Song, Call'd Mat's Peace* (p. 504 below). Until May 1699 it had been assumed that Prior was a Whig, but at that time he became a secretary and eventually "an intire Creature" of the Tory Lord Jersey (Luttrell, 4, 517; Macky, p. 135). In January 1701 he was elected a member of parliament for East Grinstead, a borough controlled by the earl of Dorset, a Whig. Thus Prior was enabled, when Montagu and the Junto lords were impeached during the session of 1701 to vote "against Those that had established him in the World" (Macky, p. 135) and he did not stand again for parliament. Defoe railed against his apostasy in *Reformation of Manners* (1702) and called him "Saucy Poet Prior" (*POAS*, Yale, 6, 424). Macky added that he was "very factious in Conversation" and Swift agreed that "This is near the Truth" (*Prose, 5,* 260).

4. *Church . . . Loyalty:* Cf. *The Lawyer's Answer,* 29 above.

5. *Pittis:* William Pittis (1674–1724), the second son of John Pittis, rector of St. Botolph's, Bishopsgate, in London, was educated at Winchester and New College, Oxford. While still an undergraduate he contributed verse to Peter Motteux's *The Gentleman's Journal* (July 1692), and in the same year he was elected a fellow of New College. In 1695, however, he "sold his Fellowship . . . went to *London,* [and] turn'd Quack, *Jacobite* and Libeller" (Oldmixon, *History,* p. 510). He learned to joke about "the great Advantages of being reputed a Jacobite" (*Heraclitus Ridens,* 1–5 February 1704), but in 1711 he was still signing himself "late Fellow of New College." He moved into the Inner Temple, ostensibly to study medicine under Edward Tyson, but in fact to drink with the high church literary and theatrical circle at the Rose Tavern. "I never had any great Inclination to *Dactyls* and *Spondees,*" he said, but preferred to "drudge on in the Beaten Way of *good Honest, Humble* Prose" (*The True-Born Englishman: A Satyr, Answer'd,* 1701, sig. A3v, A4r) and in the end he had published more than 50 works (*Modern Philology, 33* [November 1935, February 1936], 169–86, 279–302). A large part of his *oeuvre* was devoted to answering Defoe: he wrote *The True-Born Englishman: A Satyr, Answer'd* believing that John Toland had written it and then wrote *The True Born Hugonot* (1703) when he discovered that Defoe had written it. In the meantime he had published *The History of the Kentish Petition, Answer'd* (1701) and later he wrote *The Dyet of Poland, A Satyr. Consider'd Paragraph by Paragraph* (1705); *The History of the Mitre and Purse* (1714) in

But not like him, be by her left i'th'Lurch.
For the well-governing your *Poetry*,
Rymer and *Dennis*, let your Patterns be:

---

answer to *The Secret History of the White-Staff* (1714); and *Queen Anne Vindicated from the Base Aspersions of Some Late Pamphlets* (1714) in answer to *The Secret History of the Secret History of the White Staff, Purse and Mitre* (1715). He survived into the next reign as "one of Mr. *Curle*'s Hacks" and "*Triobularian* Scriblers" (*Memoirs of the Life of Sir Stephen Fox, Kt.*, 1717, p. vi).

6. *left i'th'Lurch:* There can be little doubt that Pittis was left in the lurch, not by the church, however, but by Harley. In July 1703, perhaps with Harley's encouragement (*State and Miscellany Poems*, 1715, p. 264), Pittis undertook to write a biweekly periodical, *Heraclitus Ridens*. "The Defence of the . . . Church establish'd, is what we are to go upon," he said in the first number, and in later numbers he provided "divers Evidences, to prove the Lawfulness or Expediency of set Forms of Prayer," the "Deduction of Episcopacy from . . . Apostolical Times," and the like (*Heraclitus Ridens*, 13–16 November, 11–14 December 1703). *Heraclitus Ridens* had to be abandoned when it was presented by a grand jury for libel ([Charles Leslie], *Cassandra. (But I Hope Not)*, No. II, 1704, p. 18; *The Observator*, 8–11 August 1705), but a year later Pittis started another biweekly periodical, *The Whipping Post* (June–November 1705). As Tories were displaced in the ministry by Whigs, Pittis's attacks grew bolder and more reckless. When *The Memorial of the Church of England* was burned by the common hangman early in September 1705, Pittis fired off a broadside, *Fire and Faggot: or The City Bonefire* ("She's dead! thanks to the Jury's pious Care") (*POAS*, 1707, *4*, 35–37). Before 17 September a warrant was issued for his arrest "for Reflecting on Dr. Willis's Sermon preached before the Queen" in *The Whipping Post* of 4 September 1705 (Hearne, *1*, 45). The next day he reprinted *Fire and Faggot* in *The Whipping Post* and on 11 October he was committed to Newgate (Luttrell, *5*, 600). Soon he found himself in Harley's office, undergoing examination for writing the "Trifling" *Fire and Faggot*. After receiving from Harley "the most solemn Assurances, that such a Confession should be of no Prejudice to him," Pittis admitted that he had also written a much more serious libel in defense of *The Memorial of the Church of England* (*The History of the Mitre and Purse*, 1714, p. 29). When Pittis was back in Newgate, "without friends, [and] without money," Harley ordered him to be prosecuted for writing *The Case of the Church of England's Memorial Fairly Stated* (HMC *Portland MSS.*, *8*, 200–01). Pittis shot back *A Hymn to Confinement*, a quarto in 2's advertised as "Fit to be stitch'd up with" the offending pamphlet. On 25 April 1706, however, he was tried at the queen's bench and found guilty. He was fined 100 marks, ordered to stand twice in the pillory "with a Paper on his Head denoting his Offence," and to give security for his good behavior for two years (Boyer, *Annals*, 1707, p. 486).

8. *Rymer:* Thomas Rymer (1643?–1713), the critic and antiquarian, left Sidney Sussex College, Cambridge, without taking a degree. In *The Tragedies of the Last Age Consider'd* (1678) he attributed the failure of Elizabethan tragedy to the fact that Aristotle had been "so little studied" (Rymer, *Critical Works*, p. 76). During the exclusion crisis Rymer, whose politics seem to have been acceptable to Thomas Hearne, published *A General Draught and Prospect of Government in Europe* (1681), tracing the encroachment of parliaments upon royal prerogative. His most important critical work, *A Short View of Tragedy*, "blaspheming Shakespeare," appeared in 1692. In the same year he was appointed historiographer royal at £200 a year and began to compile the collection of treaties which became the celebrated *Foedera*. Dryden admired Rymer's learning (although he detested "his ill-nature and his arrogance"), and Pope thought he was "on the whole one of the best critics we ever had" (Dryden, *Prose*, *1*, ii, 35; Spence, *1*, 205). Queen Anne renewed his patent as historiographer royal in July 1702 (*CTB 1702*, pp. 56–57, 478).

Dennis: John Dennis (1657–1716), "A stiff Politish Critick," was one of the *enfants*

John Tutchin, an engraving by P. Grave

And if it be at last your Scribling Fate
To Triumph o'er a Pill'ry, e'er too late,   10
Like me Recant, and be not Obstinate.
Remember *Tutchin*'s Boldness for his Cause,
That stood the fiery Tryal of the Laws.
When *sneaking Scriblers* poorly sue for Grace,

---

perdus in the armies of Wit in Defoe's *The Pacificator* (1700) (*POAS*, Yale, *6*, 167–68). His reply to Collier, *The Usefulness of the Stage to the Happiness of Mankind, to Government, and to Religion* (1698), was presented as "a libell against the government, for asserting that the people of England are the most prone to rebellion of any in the world, and alwaies quarrelling among themselves, if not diverted by playes" (Luttrell, *4*, 456), but Somers "acquainted the King with the businesse" and the proceedings were stopped (BM MS. Add. 7121, f. 21v, quoted in Hermann Lenz, *John Dennis sein Leben und seine Werke*, Halle, 1913, p. 31). In politics Dennis was a moderate Whig: he wrote *The Reverse* (1700) (*POAS*, Yale, *6*, 224) in reply to Tutchin's *The Foreigners* (1700); and *The Danger of Priestcraft to Religion and Government, with Some Politick Reasons for Toleration* (1702) in reply to one of Sacheverell's first high flying sermons, *The Political Union, a Discourse Shewing the Dependance of Government on Religion in England* (1702).

11. *me:* William Stephens. Besides his published recantation in *The Flying Post*, 21 March 1706 (Boyer, *Annals*, 1706, pp. 272–74), Stephens tried to speak "something by way of Submission" during his trial on 6 May 1706, but Judge Powell proceeded instead to pronounce sentence, which included standing twice in the pillory (Boyer, *Annals*, 1707, p. 488). "The prospect of this degrading punishment" produced another recantation, this time in a letter to the duchess of Marlborough, which secured remission of this part of Stephens' punishment (Coxe, *Memoirs*, *1*, 374–75).

12. *Tutchin:* John Tutchin (1661?–1707) was born "near *Limmington* in *Hampshire*," where his father was a dissenting minister (*The Observator*, 22 August 1705; Calamy, *Abridgement*, *2*, 349). His education at a dissenting academy in Stepney left him, like Defoe, equally confused about Latin accidence and his own status as a gentleman. He is described, in an indictment for libel, as "a seditious person, and a daily inventer and publisher of false news . . . and a perpetual disturber of the peace of this kingdom" (Howell, *14*, 1095–96), but in fact he was one of the first reform journalists, living in frequent danger of "publick Assaults [and] private Assassinations" for "discovering Publick Frauds and Cheats" (*The Fifth Volume of Observators*, 1707, sig. [A2]; cf. *The Observator*, 4–7 October 1704). And, next to Defoe, he was the most daring propagandist for "The Revolution Cause" (*The Observator*, 4 November–6 December 1704), more or less continually under indictment for libel. "I durst not so much as Piss within half a Mile of St. *Stephen*'s Chappel," he said, "for fear of a Breach of Priviledge" (ibid., 17–21 March 1705). His "fiery Tryal of the Laws" began in August 1700 when he was arrested for *scandalum magnatum* in *The Foreigners* (*POAS*, Yale, *6*, 226). On 1 April 1702 Tutchin brought out the first number of *The Observator* and kept it up twice a week for five and a half years. During his trial for libel in November 1704 the attorney general observed that Tutchin "writes magisterially, and defies all authority," and after a verdict of guilty had been set aside and Tutchin released, he was said to have "grown more Impudent than ever" (Howell, *14*, 1105; *An Account of the Birth, Education, Life and Conversation of that Notorious and Bold Scribbler the Observator*, 1705, pp. 5–6). Dunton called him "the bold Esserter of *English* Liberties [and] The Scourge of the High Flyers," but "a certain great Man call'd him *a little Scribler*" (Dunton, p. [439 misnumbered] 437; *The Whipping-Post*, 2 November 1705). At length, according to one account, "he was assaulted in the night and cruelly beaten, in consequence of which he lost his life" (Noble, *2*, 312; Howell, *14*, 1200).

He *Triumphs* o'er 'em with an *Honest* Face.   15
So *Ridpath* smiles at all *Fate*'s harsh Decrees,
But can't be pleas'd, when forc'd to pay his *Fees*.
When Parchment-Rolls, like murd'ring War appears,
Libels, that raise the trembling *Poet*'s Fears,
And set Mankind together by the Ears,   20
These to avoid, in dull Translation Trade,
Bowyer, and *Savage,* and *Oldmixon* read;

15. *Honest Face:* See illustration, p. 169. Tutchin was said to have a "Horrible" face, "much altered with the small pox" ([William Pittis], *The Last New Prologues and Epilogues, Relating to the Life of the Observator and the Death of the Royal-Oak Lottery,* 1703, p. 6; Howell, *14,* 1199).

16. *Ridpath:* George Ridpath (1660?–1726) was not only a dissenter, but a Scot, educated for the clergy at Edinburgh University. Coming to London, however, he was received into the household of Philip, Lord Wharton and "the Fate of an Author came upon him" (Dunton, p. [245 misnumbered] 239). He became both a journalist, "*notorious* to the Town for his *impudent* imposing falsities in *News,*" and a "Novelist," forwarding low-grade intelligence items to John, Lord Murray, secretary of state for Scotland (*The Stage Acquitted,* 1699, p. 2; HMC *Athol MSS.,* p. 50). John Tutchin, however, called *The Flying-Post,* which Ridpath founded in January 1695 and wrote until February 1713 when he fled to Holland, "The Honestest of all the News-Papers" (*The Observator,* 29 September–3 October 1705). In 1702–06 Ridpath wrote half a dozen books and pamphlets against the Union, allegedly for his "dark *Employers,* either Mr. [James] *J*[*ohnsto*]*n,* [James Douglas] *D.* [of] *H*[*amilto*]*n,* or others" (William Atwood, *The Scotch Patriot Unmask'd,* 1705, p. 25). The most provocative of these was *The Reducing of Scotland by Arms and Annexing it to England as a Province Considered* (1705) for which he was "bound over to appear at the queen's bench bar" (*DNB, 16,* 1179). Ridpath kept on scribbling even in exile and in 1718 received his reward: together with two booksellers he was awarded a patent for supplying the Stationery Office in Edinburgh, said to be worth £900 a year (*The Weekly Journal, or British Gazeteer,* 15 February 1718).

18. *Parchment-Rolls:* on which an indictment, e.g. for libel, might be engrossed.

22. *Bowyer:* Abel Boyer (1667–1729) was a Frenchman, born in Castres, Languedoc, and educated at the Protestant university of Franeker in Friesland. He arrived in England in 1689 and "fell into great poverty" (Baker, *1,* i, 53). But he became "a voluminous compiler of Annals, Political Collections, &c." (*The Dunciad,* II, 381*n.*), performed "some Services" for Harley (Boyer, *Annals,* 1712, p. 264), and grew rich. In 1705 Boyer took over *The Post Boy* and kept up a running battle with "Drunken *P*[*itti*]*s*" until Boyer gave over in August 1709 (Dunton, 1818, *2,* 432, 433). Among the translations that Boyer had published were: [Eustache Le Noble de Tennelière], *The Art of Prudent Behaviour,* 1701; *The English Theophrastus,* 1702; *The Theory and Practice of Architecture; Or Vitruvius and Vignola Abridg'd,* 1703.

Savage: John Savage (1673–1747) was educated at Westminster School and Emmanuel College, Cambridge. Upon graduation he became a travelling tutor to the young earl of Salisbury who made him rector of Bygrave, Hertfordshire in 1701. He was "a very jolly convivial priest," "the Aristippus of the age," and president of the Royston Club (Nichols, *Illustrations, 4,* 717; *Anecdotes, 2,* 141, 703; *POAS,* Yale, *6,* 427). Abel Boyer supplied some commendatory verses in Latin for Savage's translation of Carlo Moscheni, *Brutes Turn'd Criticks, or Mankind Moraliz'd by Beasts,* 1695. Savage in return supplied more than a thousand "new Words" for Boyer's French dictionary (*The Royal Dictionary,* 1699, sig. A3r; *Letters of Wit, Politicks and Morality,* 1701, pp. 269–72) and collaborated with Boyer in a number of other works. His translations include *Spanish Letters: Historical, Satyrical, and Moral; Of the*

Or deal in News, and write whate'er you will,
But mind you *Scrible* on the *right Side* still:
Then you may *Letters* from *Althea* bring,   25
If like *Fontvive,* 'tis with a just Design
To please the *Government,* or serve the *Queen.*
So writes *D'Foe,* an Author now in Vogue,

Famous Don Antonio de Guevara: Bishop of Mondonedo, n.d.; *The Whole Comical Works of Mons. Scarron, Translated by Mr. T. Brown, Mr. Savage and Others,* 1700; *The Art of Prudence: Or, A Companion for a Man of Sense. Written Originally in Spanish by that Celebrated Author, Balthazar Gracian,* 1705.

Oldmixon: By 1706 John Oldmixon (1673–1742) had not yet embarked on his career of "party Writer" and Whig historian. He had published several volumes of verse and one play and apparently he recognized himself in Steele's playful advertisement in *The Tatler,* 1 September 1709, for "Omicron, the unborn poet . . . [who] translates out of all languages without learning or study." Oldmixon's translations, achieved in any case without university study, included *Poems on Several Occasions, Written in Imitation of the Manner of Anacreon, with Other Poems, Letters and Translations,* 1696, and *Amintas. A Pastoral. Made out of Italian from the Aminta of Tasso,* 1698. In August 1711, however, Toland referred to him as "one of the despicable tools of the late poetical ministry" (HMC *Portland MSS.,* 5, 260).

25. *Letters from Althea:* presumably a work by De Fonvive, but not identified.

26. *Fontvive:* Jean De Fonvive or Fontvive is "an obscure Frenchman" who began his career as "a writer and translator of the lowest description" for Abel Roper, the publisher, and at length became his partner (Noble, 2, 310). It is not known when he began to write *An Account of the Publick Transactions in Christendom,* which was founded in August 1694 and became *The Post Man* in October 1695, but in November 1697 he was taken into custody and ordered to be prosecuted for "using of the King of France so disrespectfully" in *The Post Man* (*CSPD 1697,* pp. 448, 455; Luttrell, 4, 302). Defoe, who did not know him, began by complaining that *The Post Man* consisted of De Fonvive's "own Abortive Conceptions rather than Matter of Fact," but soon changed his mind and called him "the most Careful, and most Authentick of any of our Writers" (*Review,* 4 December 1708, 18 March 1704, 19 September 1704; cf. *Review,* 19 July 1712). Under Harley *The Post Man* became an unofficial government newspaper to which selected items could be leaked (HMC *Bath MSS.,* 1, 75, 81; Hearne, 2, 6). In July 1705 Harley offered De Fonvive the post of gazetteer, or official government newswriter (*POAS,* Yale, 6, 611–12), which paid £300 a year, but De Fonvive turned it down because *The Post Man,* of which he was now publisher as well as writer, brought him £600 a year (HMC *Portland MSS.,* 8, 187–88; Dunton, 1818, 2, 428), so the job went to an inexperienced and impecunious army officer, Richard Steele.

28. *D'Foe:* Defoe's experience in the pillory (*POAS,* Yale, 6, 585) so little dispirited him that Thomas Hearne (1, 238) supposed that he "glories in it to this day." Nor did Defoe temper what he wrote to avoid further prosecution: *Legion's Humble Address to the Lords* (1704) was presented to the justices of the peace of Gloucestershire as a seditious libel and a proclamation was issued on 29 May 1704 offering £100 for Defoe's arrest (*POAS,* Yale, 6, 675); in September 1704 he experienced an "Odd Alarm" when he learned that he was to be arrested for reflecting on Admiral Rooke in *The Master Mercury* (*The Polish Dyet,* 493n. above; *Review,* 4 November 1704); a year later William Pittis alleged in *The Whipping Post,* 28 August 1705, that Defoe had been "order'd to be sent down to Justice *Stafford* of *Crediton,* to be us'd by him as the Law directs." In October 1706 Defoe was again to be arrested and carried before Lord Chief Justice Holt for publishing in the *Review* of 1 October 1706 extracts from Holt's speech "pointing out the . . . Disadvantages" of the union with Scotland (Luttrell, 6, 98; Hearne, 1, 297).

Who was so lately Pill'ry'd for a Rogue;
Therefore let his Example, yours be made;   30
Neither of *Fines* nor *Pillories* be afraid.
Lesly writes on, and *Gildon* still is free
To laugh at *Ward* for writing Poetry,

32. *Lesly:* Charles Leslie (1650–1722) was born in Dublin and educated at Trinity College, Dublin. He refused to take the oaths to William and Mary in 1689 and became "the Furiosest Jacobite in *England*" (*Parl. Hist.*, *6*, 162), whose solution to all minority problems, "to use one of his witty sayings," was massacre (Dunton, 1818, *2*, 455). *The Rehearsal*, which he started to write in August 1704 in answer to Tutchin and Defoe, was said to be "full of excellent reasoning as well as wit" (Hearne, *2*, 152). The prediction that he would "make a bad martyr, and a good traveller" was fulfilled in April 1711 when Leslie fled to St. Germain to avoid arrest (Dunton, 1818, *2*, 455; Luttrell, *6*, 609).

   Gildon: The juxtaposition of Charles Gildon (1665–1724) with Leslie may not be coincidental, for Gildon was Charles Leslie's most famous convert. Gildon (1664–1724) was born in Gillingham, Dorset, and educated for the Roman Catholic priesthood at Douai. He abandoned divinity in 1684, however, and came to London. There he was admitted into the Rose Tavern circle of Brown and D'Urfey, became a deist, and published a remarkably varied series of literary works. Dunton (p. [247 misnumbered] 241) observed that "*Gildon* . . . writes with a peculiar Briskness, which the common *Hacks* can't boast of, in Regard, they want the Life and Spirit, and the same *Liberty*, and Extent of *Genius*." In 1697 Gildon was converted to orthodox Anglicanism after reading Leslie's *A Short and Easie Method with the Deists* (*The Deist's Manual*, 1705, p. 25). In 1706 Gildon was indicted for publishing *A Letter from H.R.H. the Princess Sophia, Electress of Brunswic and Luneburg, to His Grace the Archbishop of Canterbury, with Another from Hannover, written by Sir Rowland Gwynne to the Rt. Hon. the Earl of Stamford* (BM Catalogue, *226*, 62) or *A Review of Her Royal Highness the Princess Sophia's Letter to the Lord Archbishop of Canterbury, and That of Sir Rowland Gwynne to the Right Honourable the Earl of Stamford: Or, A Jacobite Plot against the Protestant Succession Discover'd* (*CBEL*, *2*, 575). Gildon may have had an opportunity "To laugh at *Ward* for writing Poetry" on 12 June 1706, for at the same time that Ward appeared before the queen's bench and pleaded guilty to writing verses "highly reflecting upon Her Majesty and the Government" (Luttrell, *6*, 57; Boyer, *Annals*, 1707, p. 489), Gildon won a continuation of his case to the next term (Luttrell, *6*, 57). In May 1707, however, Gildon's pamphlet was found to be "a Scandalous, False and Malicious Libel, tending to create a Misunderstanding between her Majesty an[d] the Princess *Sophia*," and Gildon was fined £100 (Boyer, *Annals*, 1707, p. 489).

33. *Ward:* Edward Ward (1667–1731), "of 'low extraction' and with little education" (*DNB*, *20*, 769), became a successful tavern keeper and "A Very voluminous Poet" of high church principles (Jacob, *Historical Account*, p. 225). One of his most voluminous works, *Hudibras Redivivus: Or, A Burlesque Poem on the Times*, was published in 24 parts (August 1705–June 1707). But Ward did not shrink from translating Don Quixote and Clarendon's *History of the Rebellion and Civil Wars in England* into Hudibrastic verse. He was "best known," as Jacob said (ibid., p. 226), for *The London Spy*, "a famous Piece in Prose," of which 18 numbers appeared (November 1698–April 1700). On 7 February 1706 Ward was taken into custody "for some Reflections on the Queen in *Hudibras Redivivus*" (Hearne, *1*, 179–80, 308). He had dared to accuse the queen, who boasted of a "Heart . . . entirely *English*" (see illustration, p. 6), of being in fact fainthearted (*Hudibras Redivivus. The Fifth Part*, 2d ed., 1708, pp. 6–7). He pleaded guilty and on 16 November 1706 was fined 40 marks, ordered to stand twice in the pillory and to give security for his good behavior for one year (Luttrell, *6*, 57; Boyer, *Annals*, 1707, p. 489).

Whose Prose escapes the Censure of the Times,
And Informations fall on jingling Rimes.   35
To sum up all; let *Drake*'s just Merit be
A Caution to Poetick Liberty.
Since *Ward*'s true *Genius*, and since *Gildon*'s Sense,
At last has brought them to a Dearth of Pence,
'Tis hard their Learning, and each Turn of Wit,   40
Should only make them for this *Triumph* fit.

36. *Drake:* James Drake (1667–1707) graduated B.A. "with unusual Honours," M.B. (1690) and M.D. (1694) from Caius College, Cambridge. By 1699 "the learned and ingenious Dr. Drake" was enjoying the company of Dryden (*Works, 11,* 229) and Thomas Brown and the patronage of Sir Thomas Millington, president of the Royal College of Physicians (*DNB, 5,* 1351). In 1698 he had been admitted a candidate of the College, where he met Samuel Garth and became a subscriber to the dispensary. He was also elected a fellow of the Royal Society and contributed "A Discourse concerning some Influence of *Respiration* on the *Motion* of the *Heart*," correcting some observations of Harvey and Richard Lower (*Phil. Trans.* No. 281, 1702). Drake was also an enthusiastic *littérateur.* He adapted two plays of John Fletcher as *The Sham Lover, or The Lucky Extravagant* (1697), which, he said, was "damnably acted at Drury Lane," and in 1699 he published a remarkable 367-page attack on Jeremy Collier entitled *The Antient and Modern Stages Survey'd* in which he qualified himself as the first critic of *Hamlet.* In 1700 he contributed "To Dr. *Garth,* On the Fourth Edition of His Incomparable Poem, *The Dispensary*" to *Commendatory Verses, on the Author of the Two Arthurs and the Satyr against Wit.* Drake's "Character of Mr. Tho. Brown" was published in Brown's *Legacy for the Ladies, Or, Characters of the Women of the Age* (1705). But Tory propaganda was the whore that Drake doted on. He published in rapid succession *A Short Defense of the Last Parliament* in November 1701; *Some Necessary Considerations Relating to All Future Elections of Members to Serve in Parliament* (1702); *The History of the Last Parliament* (1702), for which he was tried for libel and acquitted (*LJ, 17,* 122–23; Luttrell, *5,* 389); *The Source of Our Present Fears Discover'd* (1703); *Historia Anglo-Scotica* (1703), which was ordered by the Scottish parliament to be burnt by the common hangman (Luttrell, *5,* 315–16, 327); *The Memorial of the Church of England* (July 1705), which was presented by the grand jury of London as "a false, scandalous, and trayterous" libel, burnt by the common hangman (Luttrell, *5,* 588), deplored by the queen in her address at the opening of the session on 27 October 1705 (*LJ, 18,* 8), and publicly proclaimed as a malicious libel with £200 offered for the arrest of the author (Steele, No. 4400); and finally, 51 numbers of *Mercurius Politicus: Or, An Antidote to Popular Misrepresentations* (12 June–4 December 1705). Drake was arrested for "reflecting on the government" in *Mercurius Politicus,* No. 29 (18 September 1705), and again tried for libel (Luttrell, *6,* 16; Hearne, *1,* 186). An error was found in the indictment, however, and Drake was acquitted on 6 November 1706, whereupon the attorney general lodged a writ of error in the House of Lords (Luttrell, *6,* 105, 121). While this case was pending, Drake died on 2 March 1707.

MATTHEW PRIOR

An Ode, Humbly Inscrib'd to the Queen.
On the Late Glorious Success of Her Majesty's Arms, 1706.
Written in Imitation of Spencer's Stile.
(5 July 1706)

The case of *An Ode, Humbly Inscrib'd to the Queen* and received by the queen "very kindly," encourages some speculation on the way an English Augustan poet went to work.

The surprizing news of the victory at Ramillies reached London on the evening of 16 May 1706. In the *Review* for 18 May, printed off the very afternoon of 16 May, Defoe had scanned the prospects for the military campaign of 1706 and found them "no where promising . . . but in *Spain*." It would be "to exalt his Power to Impossibilities, and make him more than a Man," Defoe warned, to expect "something extraordinary" from the duke of Marlborough. When the impossible happened, Defoe filled up the next *Review* (21 May 1706) with "the Birth of three Hours," 128 lines of "Execrably bad" blank verse entitled *On the Fight at Ramellies* ("Say, *Britains!* felt you nothing in your Souls").

Prior presumably felt something in his soul, including the feeling that he was "indispensably obliged" to produce some verse on the subject (*Works,* 1, 232). "The Writer . . . has not always the Choice of his Subject," Samuel Johnson declared, "but is compelled to accept any Task which is thrown before him" (*The Rambler,* 29 May 1750). But instead of three hours, it took Prior nearly three months to finish his poem. It took him so long, in fact, that on 18 June he was scolded in print for his failure:

> Shall MARLBRO' still new Victories obtain?
> And shall the Muse be wanting to his Praise?
> Exert, O PRIOR! thy melodious Voice,
> Convince the World, tho' tuneful *Dryden*'s gone,
> A POET still remains, whose lofty Verse
> Can in just Numbers *Arms* and *Conquest* sing.

(*A Letter to Mr. Prior, Occasion'd by the Duke of Marlborough's Late Victory at Ramilly, and Glorious Successes in Brabant,* 1706, p. 3, of which the

Luttrell copy at the University of Chicago is dated 18 June.) It is clear that Prior was expected to write something and that it must be something "Historic and Panegyric."

It was not until the end of May, when it was learned that the French had fallen back to the Mons-Lille-Dunkirk line, that the complex magnitude of Marlborough's victory became apparent (311n. below). Prior chose to write an *ode*, he said, because "Ideas so great and numerous" as these could not properly be confined within any other genre. Then, having settled on an ode, Prior said, "I . . . set HORACE before Me for a Pattern, and particularly his Famous Ode, the Fourth of the Fourth Book" (*Works, 1*, 230).

The resemblances between *An Ode, Humbly Inscrib'd* and the fourth ode of the fourth book of Horace may seem perfunctory: both poems talk about military heroes in terms of eagles and lions; "cremato . . . ab Ilio" (53) is echoed in "From burning *Troy*" (213). But in fact the fourth ode of the fourth book of Horace *is* the "Pattern" of Prior's poem. Events of May 1706 are assimilated to Roman antitypes. Augustus becomes Anne; Decimus Claudius Drusus, who conquered Germania Inferior in 12 B.C., becomes Marlborough; the Metaurus becomes the Danube; Hannibal bewailing the defeat of Hasdrubal becomes Louis XIV bewailing the defeat of Maximilian Emanuel, elector of Bavaria.

Put in this perspective something happens to "History" in the poem. "The complicated Wonders" of Marlborough's victory (*Review*, 21 May 1706) are better able to be felt and understood by imagining them as types of victories already felt and understood by Horace. The unknown is assimilated to the known, in the normal way of poetry. In the process, however, "History" becomes a little less real, a little less unique, a little more archetypal, a little more like literature. *An Ode, Humbly Inscrib'd* is "History," but history "confused and enlarged through the mist of panegyrick" (Johnson, *Lives, 1*, 1).

Another of the "Ideas so great and numerous" that were aroused in Prior by Ramillies and its aftermath was the idea of patriotism, of intense national pride. Prior apparently was not content simply to write a Latin ode in English. He needed to Anglicize his song. And this need was met by the Spenserian stanza.

Prior's decision to employ the Spenserian stanza was more enterprising than it might seem today, for Spenser's reputation had been in decline throughout the seventeenth century. Ben Jonson's casual remark in *Timber* (1640) that, "for affecting the ancients [i.e. Chaucer]," Spenser "writ no language," had become a commonplace of criticism:

'Tis a surprizing Reflection [one critic said], that between what *Spencer* wrote last [*The Fairie Queene* (1609)], and *Waller* first [*Rex Redux* (1633)], there should not be much above twenty years distance: and yet the one's Language, like the Money of that time, is as currant now as ever; whilst the other's words are like old Coyns, one must go to an Antiquary to understand their true meaning and value.

([Francis Atterbury?], *The Second Part of Mr. Waller's Poems,* 1690, sig. A4v). Prior had committed himself to the new idiom of Waller, but Spenser delighted him and many years later he still knew much of Spenser by heart (*Works, 1,* 545). In September 1704 he had wound up *A Letter to Monsieur Boileau Despreaux; Occasion'd by the Victory at Blenheim* with the boast that England should never

> . . . want just Subject for victorious Strains,
> While MARLBRÔ's Arm Eternal Laurel gains;
> And where old SPENCER sung, a new ELISA reigns.

It may have been these lines that supplied the seed for *An Ode, Humbly Inscrib'd.*

Probably in order to avoid the necessity for finding four rhyme words for every stanza, Prior simplified the Spenserian stanza and added a line, changing it from $A^5B^5A^5B^5B^5C^5B^5C^5C^6$ to $A^5B^5A^5B^5C^5$ $D^5C^5D^5E^5E^6$. In any case, one result of Prior's use of the modified stanza was to send readers back to the original and with this result Prior was delighted:

> As to Spencer [he wrote to lord Cholmondeley on 1 August 1706], I think we have gained our point, every body acknowledges him to have been a fine Poet, thô three Months since not one in 50 had read him: Upon my Soul, 'tis true, the Wits have sent for the Book, the Fairy Queen is on their Toilette table, and some of our Ducal acquaintance will be deep in that Mythologico-Poetical way of thinking.
>
> (*Works, 2,* 896)

Thus the stage was set for James Thomson to adopt both the Spenserian idiom and the Spenserian stanza in *The Castle of Indolence* (1748) and for the rediscovery of Spenser to become almost as important a factor in the formation of the new, romantic idiom as the "rediscovery" of Ossian. It was precisely "that Mythologico-Poetical way of thinking" that appealed to Collins and Blake and Keats, and it is surprising to find Matthew Prior, a minor Augustan, at the beginning of this sucession. The major Augustans could see only the archaic diction. "The Imitators of *Spencer*," Johnson wrote in *The Rambler* for 14 May 1751, "seem to conclude that when they have disfigured their Lines with a few obsolete Syllables they have accomplished their Design . . . Life is surely given us for higher Purposes than to gather what our Ancestors have wisely thrown away."

Besides being an ode, and an "Historical Poem," like *Annus Mirabilis*, and in a very loose sense an "imitation" of Horace, the poem is also partly some other things. Lines 195–260 are a dramatic monologue spoken by Louis XIV. But Louis speaks stereotypes, for not much of Prior's imagination went into realizing Louis' character. More successful are lines 267–350, a new variety of the advice-to-a-painter genre that Prior had twice used before (*Works, 1*, 8, 257). For *An Ode, Humbly Inscrib'd* Prior devised a variant of the old genre, an advice-to-a-sculptor, the sculptor of a triumphal column to be erected for Anne, with Clio, the muse of history, providing the advice.

For besides "History," of course, the poem is also "Panegyric," the other "branch" of "Epic Poesy" in Dryden's view (*Works, 9*, 100)—or "*vile, lowsie Panegyric*," in Thomas Brown's phrase (*Familiar and Courtly Letters*, 1700, p. 213). This is a literary genre totally repellent to today's taste and Prior's phrase "sembling Art" (273) may arouse unwarranted suspicions. It is not dissembling art that Prior means, but resembling art: art that represents things as they are, that sees heroic things in heroic terms and mock-heroic things in mock-heroic terms. Swift's observation may help reconcile the modern reader to the genre: "All Panegyricks," he said, "are mingled with an Infusion of Poppy" (*Prose, 4*, 252).

As a protégé of the Tory earl of Jersey, Prior had been "very well at Court" until April 1704, when *Faction Display'd*, with its scurrilous couplet about the duchess of Marlborough, was publicly attributed to him (*POAS*, Yale, *6*, 649–50), and Jersey was removed as secretary of state (Luttrell, *5*, 416). In August 1704 when news of Blenheim reached London, Prior hastened "to shew the real respect [he] had for my Lord [Marlborough], and so vindicate [himself] for the scandal of having Lampooned him or his family" (*Works, 2*, 893), by writing *A Letter to Monsieur Boileau Despreaux, Occasion'd by the Victory at Blenheim*. As soon as the poem was printed Prior "sent 2 Copyes of it with a very civil letter to my Lady Dutchesse desiring her to do [him] the honour to give one of these copyes to the Queen . . . but was surprized some days after to find that the Dutchess sent [him] back the pacquet . . . unopen'd declaring that she would not receive anything of [his] writing" (ibid.). A copy sent to the duke, however, was politely acknowledged and Marlborough eventually spoke to Godolphin in Prior's behalf. But Joseph Addison, who wrote *The Campaign, A Poem, to His Grace the Duke of Marlborough,* was appointed undersecretary of state, which Prior had solicited in vain.

Eight days after the news of Ramillies reached London, Prior wrote to congratulate his "patron and protector" on the great victory. He wittily reminded the duke that some of his panegyrists were "so bad as to do it, only because they are ashamed or afraid to do otherwise, and that there are more Stevens's than one" (Coxe, *Memoirs, 1,* 420). He wrote again on 5 July 1706 enclosing a copy of *An Ode, Humbly Inscrib'd* and received Marlborough's "particular thanks" but nothing more, even though Prior's friends had thought it would be "strange if such a performance should not meet with more than praise expressed by words" (HMC *Bath MSS., 3,* 435).

The truth seems to be that Prior, like Swift, was a poor courtier. He said this about himself: "I was not born for a Courtier being . . . too open in my conversation" (Charles K. Eves, *Matthew Prior,* New York, Columbia University Press, 1939, p. 184), and he was not "Humble" (*The Country Parson's Advice, 3n.* above).

Neither the compulsion of the occasion, nor patriotism nor personal ambition would have been enough. It was also necessary for "one of the best Poets in *England*" to want to write a poem. Having taken Horace as the "Pattern" for the content and Spenser as the "Pattern" for the stanza and the "Stile," Prior felt free "to go off," as he said, and "to add variously, as the Subject and my own Imagination carry'd Me" (*Works, 1,* 230). Where his imagination most successfully carried him was in joining "History" to "Sculpture" (267) and elaborating the conceit of Anne's triumphal column. In the end the poem becomes a noble and pompous public monument, luxuriantly carved and cool as marble, an elegant verbal sculpture in the classical English style.

It was published on 5 July 1706 (Coxe, *Memoirs, 1,* 421) and critical opinion, with no warrant whatever from the poem itself, divided sharply along party lines. "The Whiggs . . . say'd the Imitation was of a verse now grown obsolete, the Style a little hard, &c. . . . the Tories on the other side cryed up [the] poem too much" (*Works, 2,* 896). It was answered by *A Modern Inscription to the Duke of Marlboroughs Fame,* which is reprinted below.

AN ODE, HUMBLY INSCRIB'D TO THE QUEEN.
ON THE GLORIOUS SUCCESS OF HER MAJESTY'S ARMS, 1706.

Written in Imitation of Spencer's Stile.

Te non paventis funera Galliae,
Duraeque tellus audit Iberiae
Te caede gaudentes Sicambri
Compositis venerantur Armis.

HORACE

When Great *Augustus* govern'd Ancient *Rome,*
And sent his Conqu'ring Troops to Foreign Wars:
Abroad when Dreaded and belov'd at Home,
He saw his Fame encreasing with his Years;
Horace, Great *Bard,* so Fate ordain'd, arose,   5
And bold, as were his Countrymen in Fight,
Snatch'd their fair Actions from degrading Prose,
And set their Battels in Eternal Light;
High as their Trumpets Tune his Lyre he strung,
And with his Prince's Arms he moraliz'd his Song.   10

When bright *Eliza* rul'd *Britannia*'s State,
Widely distributing her high Commands;
And boldly Wise and fortunately Great,
Freed the glad Nations from Tyrannick Bands;
An Equal Genius was in *Spencer* found,   15
To the high Theme he match'd his Noble Lays;
He travell'd *England* o'er on Fairy Ground,
In Mystick Notes to Sing his Monarch's Praise:
And telling wond'rous Truths in pleasing Dreams,
He deck'd *Eliza*'s Head with *Gloriana*'s Beams.   20

Epigraph. "[Even] the death-defying Gauls and indestructible Spaniards are wary of you.
Bloodthirsty Sugambri lay down their arms in awe of you" (Horace, *Odes,* IV, xiv, 49–52).

5–6. *Horace . . . bold:* The opinion was a commonplace (*An Essay on Criticism* [1711],
658), but a generation later Pope was able to define Horace's "sly, polite, insinuating stile"
more carefully (*Epilogue to the Satires, I* [1736], 19–20).

10. *moraliz'd his Song:* "Both [Horace and Spenser] have equally That agreeable Manner
of mixing Morality with their Story" (Prior, *Works, 1,* 231–32).

20. *Gloriana:* The "tendency of Elizabeth to become Gloriana—that is to say, her signif-
icance to her people as a supreme symbol in a total system of values, religious, national,

179

But, Greatest *Anna!* while Thy Arms pursue
Paths of Renown, and climb Ascents of Fame
Which nor *Augustus* nor *Eliza* knew;
What *Poet* shall be found to sing Thy Name?
What Numbers shall Record? What Tongue shall say   25
Thy Wars on Land, Thy Triumphs on the Main?
Oh Fairest Model of Imperial Sway!
What Equal Pen shall write Thy wond'rous Reign?
Who shall Attempts and Victories rehearse
By Story yet untold, unparallell'd by Verse?   30

Me all too mean for such a Task I weet,
Yet if the *Sovereign Lady* daigns to Smile,
.I'll follow *Horace* with impetuous Heat,
And cloath the Verse in *Spencer*'s Native Stile.
By these Examples rightly taught to Sing,   35
And smit with Pleasure of my Country's Praise,
Stretching the Plumes of an uncommon Wing,
High as *Olympus* I my Flight would raise:
And latest Times should in my Numbers read
Anna's Immortal Fame, and *Marlb'rough*'s hardy Deed.   40

As the Strong Eagle in the silent Wood,
Nor seeking Battel, nor intent on Harms,
Plays round the rocky Cliff, or Crystal Flood,
'Till by *Jove*'s high Behest call'd out to Arms,
And charg'd with Thunder of his angry King,   45
His Bosom with the vengeful Message glows:
Upward the Noble Bird directs his Wing,
And tow'ring round his Master's Earth-born Foes,
Swift he collects his fatal Stock of Ire,
Lifts his fierce Talon high, and darts the forked Fire.   50

In Council Calm and in Discourse Sedate,
Under his Vineyard in his Native Land,

---

ethical, and sociological," is noticed by Ruth Nevo, *The Dial of Virtue*, Princeton, Princeton University Press, 1963, p. 20. Cf. *The Faerie Queene*, I, i, 3; vii, 46; II, ii, 40–44; ix, 2–8.

    31. *Me all too mean:* The poet's modesty is conventional; cf. Horace, *Odes*, I, vi, 9; Spenser, *The Faerie Queene*, III, Prologue, 3. Even the phrase is Spenser's (*The Faerie Queene*, I, Prologue, i).

    41. *Eagle:* Cf. Horace, *Odes*, IV, iv, 1.

    52. *Under his Vineyard:* Despite its pointed inappropriateness to Marlborough, Prior in-

Quiet and safe thus Victor *Marlb'rough* sate,
'Till *Anna* gives Her Thunder to his Hand;
Then leaving soft Repose and gentle Ease, 55
With swift Impatience seeks the distant Foe;
Flying o'er Hills and Vales, o'er Rocks and Seas,
He meditates, and strikes the wond'rous Blow:
Quicker than Thought he takes his destin'd Aim,
And Expectation flies on slower Wings than Fame. 60

Untam'd *Bavar*, when on *Ramillia*'s Plain
Afar he did the *British* Chief behold,
Betwixt Dispair, and Rage, and Hope, and Pain,
Something within his warring Bosom roll'd:
He views that Fav'rite of Indulgent Fame, 65
Whom whilom he had met on *Ister*'s Shoar:
Too well, alas! the Man he knows, the same
Whose Prowess there repell'd the *Boyan* Pow'r,
And sent Them trembling thro' the frighted Lands,
Swift as the Whirlwind drives *Arabia*'s scatter'd Sands. 70

---

vokes the Cincinnatus myth—the military hero recalled from rustic retirement—not simply because Horace (*Odes*, I, xii, 42–44) and Marvell (*An Horatian Ode*, 29–32) allude to it, but also because it represents the ideal employment of generals between wars.

54. *Thunder:* Anne's "Thunder" broke at Ramillies on 12/23 May 1706, following the great rumble at Blenheim on 2/13 August 1704.

58. *the wond'rous Blow:* By setting out about 3 o'clock in the morning on Whitsunday, Marlborough was able to achieve an element of surprise in his attack at Ramillies, but it was by no means the "Ambush . . . [in] open Country, in the face of the Sun" that Defoe called it (*A Short Narrative of the Life and Actions of His Grace John, D. of Marlborough*, 1711, p. 29). The French are estimated to have lost 8,000 men killed and 6,000 captured (Brodrick, *1*, 150–53).

59. Cf. "The Duke of *Marlborough* . . . out-runs our Conjectures" (*Review*, 21 May 1706).

61. *Untam'd Bavar:* Maximilian Emanuel (Wittelsbach) (1662–1726), elector of Bavaria and governor-general of the Spanish Netherlands (1691–1706), concluded a treaty offensive and defensive with William of Orange and the emperor Leopold in September 1688 and commanded imperial armies against the French in all the campaigns of 1689–97. In 1702 however he defected to Louis XIV and found himself in command of a mixed French and Bavarian force at Blenheim in August 1704. The morning of the battle he issued orders that no quarter be given to his former allies, the Dutch and English (Luttrell, *5*, 455). Again in May 1706, across fields of new rye in Brabant, he found himself face to face with Marlborough.

Ramillia's Plain: The battlefield is about 20 miles southeast of Louvain.

66. *Ister:* Danube.

68. *Boyan:* Bavarian.

69. *thro' the frighted Lands:* Maximilian's flight from Blenheim did not end until his troops were safely across the Rhine and himself back in Brussels (Luttrell, *5*, 462, 472).

His former Losses he forgets to grieve,
Absolves his Fate, if with a kinder Ray
It now would shine, and only give him leave
To Balance the Account of *Blenheim*'s Day.
So the fell Lion in the lonely Glade,   75
His Side still smarting with the Hunter's Spear,
Tho' deeply wounded, no way yet dismay'd,
Roars terrible, and meditates new War;
In sullen Fury traverses the Plain,
To find the vent'rous Foe, and Battel him again.   80

Misguided Prince, no longer urge thy Fate,
Nor tempt thy Rival to unequal War;
Fam'd in Misfortune, and in Ruin Great,
Confess the Force of *Marlb'rough*'s stronger Star.
That Laurel Grove, that Harvest of thy Youth,   85
Which thou from *Mahomet* didst greatly gain,
Whilst bold Assertor of resistless Truth,
Thy Sword did Godlike Liberty maintain,
Must shed, I ween, its Honours from thy Brow;
And on another Head another Spring must know.   90

Yet cease the Ways of Providence to blame,
And Human Faults with Human Grief confess:
'Tis Thou art chang'd, while Heav'n is still the same,
In thy ill Conduct seek thy ill Success:
Impartial Justice holds Her equal Scales,   95
'Till stronger Virtue does the Weight incline;
If over Thee thy glorious Foe prevails;
He now Defends the Cause that once was Thine.
Jove's Handmaid *Pow'r* must *Jove*'s Behests pursue,

71. *former Losses:* The defeat at Blenheim "decided the Elector's Destiny, by the Loss of all his Country" (Brodrick, *1*, 107).

75. *Lion:* Cf. Horace, *Odes*, IV, iv, 13.

79. *traverses the Plain:* By riding at a full gallop, Maximilian, who was at mass in Tirlemont, was able to reach the battlefield before the confederates attacked (Frank Taylor, *The Wars of Marlborough*, 2 vols., Oxford, Basil Blackwell, 1926, *1*, 378).

83. *in Ruin:* For a month before Blenheim the confederate armies plundered and burned Bavaria "in a dreadful manner" (Luttrell, *5*, 454).

85–86. *Laurel . . . from Mahomet:* Maximilian distinguished himself in the successful defense of Vienna against the Turks in 1683 and established his military reputation by his victory over the Turks at Mohács, in Hungary, in 1687.

93. *chang'd:* See 61*n*. above.

And where the Cause is Just, the Warrior shall Subdue.   100

Hark! the dire Trumpets sound their shrill Alarms,
Auverquerque, sprung from the Renown'd *Nassau*'s
Hoary in War, and bent beneath his Arms,
With an Intrepid Hand and Courage draws
That Sword, Immortal *William* at his Death   105
(Who could a fairer Legacy bestow?)
Did to the Part'ner of his Arms bequeath:
That Sword well *Loüis* and his Captains know;
For they have seen it drawn from *William*'s Thigh,
Full oft as he came forth, to Conquer, or to Die.   110

But brandish'd high, and waving in the Air,
Behold, unhappy Prince, the Master Sword,
Which perjur'd *Gallia* shall for ever fear:
'Tis that which *Caesar* gave the *British* Lord.
He took the Gift; Nor ever will I sheath,   115
He said, (so *Anna*'s high Behests Ordain)
This Glorious Gift, unless by Glorious Death
Absolv'd, 'till I by Conquest fix your Reign.
Returns like these Our *Mistress* bids us make,
When from a Foreign Prince a Gift Her *Britons* take.   120

And now fierce *Gallia* rushes on Her Foes,

102. *Auverquerque:* Henry Nassau, Lord Ouwerkerck (1641–1708), was the third son of
Louis, count of Nassau (an illegitimate son of Maurice, prince of Orange), and thus a second
cousin of William III. He began his military career when the French invaded the Netherlands
in 1672. He landed at Tor Bay in November 1688 as captain of William's bodyguard and
fought in all of William's campaigns in Ireland and the Lowlands.

105. *That Sword:* Although the text implies that William bequeathed his sword to Ouwer-
kerck, no record of this transaction can be found. William's will, made in October 1695
(Lamberty, *2,* 121–22), does not mention Ouwerkerck, and lines 105–08 may simply refer
to the fact that upon William's death Ouwerkerck succeeded to command of the Dutch
troops committed to the confederacy.

112. *the Master Sword:* As the archduke Charles of Austria, who had been declared king of
Spain in September 1703, made his way from Vienna to Lisbon, he granted Marlborough an
audience at Düsseldorf in October 1703 and presented him with a jewelled sword (*POAS,*
1707, 4, 17). Lines 115–18 paraphrase Marlborough's words upon accepting the sword : "it
will always remind me of your just right to the Spanish crown, and of my obligation to hazard
my life and all that is dear to me, in rendering you the greatest prince of Christendom" (Coxe,
Memoirs, 1, 142).

113. *perjur'd Gallia:* See 194*n.* below.

121. *now fierce Gallia rushes:* "The Court of *France* being sensible that a defensive War,
would at last terminate in her Irrecoverable Ruin, resolv'd to make an extraordinary Effort,
and to act every where Offensively in the Year 1706 . . . The Elector of *Bavaria,* and

Her Force augmented by the *Boyan* Bands:
So *Volga*'s Stream, increas'd by Mountain Snows,
Rolls with new Fury down thro' *Russia*'s Lands.
Like Two great Rocks against the raging Tide,   125
(If Virtue's Force with Nature's we compare,)
The Two great adverse Chiefs unmov'd abide,
Sustain the Impulse, and receive the War:
Round their firm Sides in vain the Tempest beats,
And still the foaming Wave with lessen'd Pow'r retreats.   130

The Shock sustain'd, the Friendly Pair advance,
With mingl'd Anger, and collected Might,
To turn the War; and tell aggressing *France*
How *Britain*'s Sons and *Britain*'s Friends can fight.
Fix'd on Revenge, and Covetous of Fame,   135
Behold 'em rushing thro' the *Gallic* Host:
Thro' standing Corn so runs the sudden Flame,
Or Eastern Winds along *Sicilia*'s Coast.
They deal their Terrors to the adverse Nation,
Pale Death attends their Deed, and ghastly Desolation.   140

But oh! while mad with Rage *Bellona* glows,
And *Europe* rather hopes than fears her Fate,
While with large Steps to Conquest *Britain* goes,
What Horror damps the Strong, and quells the Great?
Why do those Warriors look dismay'd and pale,   145
That, ever Dreadful, never knew to Dread?
Why does the charging Foe almost prevail,

Mareschal *Villeroy*, set out early for the *Netherlands* with a Body of 70000 Men." On 25 April/
6 May Villeroi received orders to fight if he were attacked. Two weeks later, "having been
join'd by the Horse of the Mareschal *De Marcin's* Army [a fact of which Marlborough was un-
aware], and confiding in their Superiority of Number," the French crossed the Dyle and com-
mitted themselves to an engagement (Brodrick, *1*, 149–50; Frank Taylor, *The Wars of Marl-
borough*, 1921, *1*, 372; Boyer, *Annals*, 1707, pp. 77–78).

127. *The Two:* Ouwerkerck and Marlborough.

136. *rushing thro' the Gallic Host:* The confederates' main attack developed on the left flank
where Dutch and Danish cavalry under Ouwerkerck charged sword in hand against French
dragoons, of whom "most of them [were] cut in Pieces, or taken Prisoners." The Danes,
everywhere successful, "forc'd the Enemy to give Ground, and broke several of their Squad-
rons" (Boyer, *Annals*, 1707, pp. 79–80).

137–38: The allies attacked the French through fields of new rye (Trevelyan, *2*, 114).
William Walsh alludes to these lines in his *Ode for the Thanksgiving Day* ("Begin, my Muse,
and strike the Lyre"), 1706, p. 3: "Ran like a Flame through Fields of ripen'd Corn, / Or
Eastern Winds. . . . "

And the Pursuers only not recede?
Their Rage, alas! submitting to their Grief,
Behold, they weep, and croud, around their falling Chief.   150

I thank Thee, Fate, exclaims the fierce *Bavar,*
Let *Boya*'s Trumpet grateful *Io*'s sound;
I saw him fall, that Thunderbolt of War,
I saw Their *Marlb'rough* stretch'd along the Ground—
Vain Hope! short Joy! for *Marlb'rough* mounts again   155
In greater Glory, and with fuller Light:
The Ev'ning Star so falls into the Main,
To rise at Morn more prevalently bright.
He rises safe, but near, too near his Side,
A good Man's grievous Loss, a faithful Servant dy'd.   160

And lo! the dubious Battel is regain'd,
The Foe with lessen'd Rage disputes the Field,
The *Briton* fights, by fav'ring Gods sustain'd,
And *Liberty* must live, and *Gallia* yield.
Vain now the Tales which fab'ling Poets tell,   165
That wav'ring *Conquest* still desires to rove;
In *Marlb'rough*'s Camp the Goddess knows to dwell:
Long as the Hero's Life remains her Love.
The Foe retires, the Victor urges on,
And *Blenheim*'s Fame again is in *Ramillia* known.   170

150. *falling Chief:* The Dutch, not as successful as the Danes, were soon in difficulties from heavy counterattack by the *gendarmerie,* the *gardes du corps,* and other élite troops. Marlborough was bringing up reserves when he was recognized by the enemy, assaulted, and thrown by his horse at a ditch (Boyer, *Annals,* 1707, p. 80).

155. *mounts again:* Marlborough's attackers were driven off by Swiss troops commanded by Major General Robert Murray, and Marlborough himself was remounted on the horse of his aide-de-camp (HMC *Portland MSS.,* 4, 309–10).

160. *Servant dy'd:* Marlborough "had still a greater Escape, a Cannon-Ball taking off the Head of Colonel [Bringfield], his Grace's Gentleman of the Horse, as he was holding the Stirrup for the Duke to remount" (Boyer, *Annals,* 1707, p. 80). James Bringfield entered the army in December 1685 and was promoted major in 1702. He became an equerry to Prince George of Denmark and aide-de-camp to Marlborough (Dalton, *5,* 25).

165–66. proverbial; Fortune is fickle (Tilley, F606).

169. *The Foe retires:* "The Enemy, who were, at the same time, attack'd by the *English* and *Dutch* Foot with equal Bravery, gave way on all sides. Their Horse rallied again in the Plains to cover the disorderly Retreat of their Foot; but they were so closely pursued by the Confederate Cavalry, that they were forc'd to divide themselves into three small Bodies, that they might fly the faster three different Ways" (Boyer, *Annals,* 1707, p. 81).

170. In his letter to Louis XIV after the battle Maximilian called the defeat at Ramillies "as Fatal as that of *Hochstet* [Blenheim]" (Brodrick, *1,* 157).

Great Thanks, Oh Captain great in Arms! receive,
From thy Triumphant Country's publick Voice:
Thy Country greater Thanks can only give
To *Anne,* to Her who made those Arms Her Choice.
Recording *Schellenberg*'s and *Blenheim*'s Toils,   175
We wish'd Thou wou'dst no more those Toils repeat:
We view'd the Palace charg'd with *Gallia*'s Spoils,
And in those Spoils we thought thy Praise compleat;
For never *Greek,* we deem'd, nor *Roman* Knight,
In Characters like these did e'er his Acts indite.   180

Yet mindless still of Rest Thy Virtue flies
A Pitch to Old and Modern Times unknown:
Those goodly Deeds which we so highly prize,
Imperfect seem, great Chief, to Thee alone.
Those Heights where *William*'s Virtue might have staid,   185
And on the Subject World look'd safely down,
By *Marlb'rough* pass'd, the Props and Steps were made
To lift Great *Anna*'s Glory further on;
Still gaining more, still slighting what He gain'd,
Nothing was done, He thought, while ought undone remain'd.   190

When swift-wing'd *Rumour* told the mighty *Gaul*
How lessen'd from the Field *Bavar* was fled,
He wept the Swiftness of the Champion's Fall;
And thus the Royal Treaty-Breaker said:

175. *Schellenberg:* Marlborough's seizure of the Schellenberg, a strongpoint above Donau-wert on 22 June/2 July, just six weeks before Blenheim, was a costly victory, but it gave him "free Entrance into the Duke of *Bavaria*'s Country" (Boyer, *Annals,* 1705, pp. 59–61). Cf. 83*n.* above.

177. *Palace:* Westminster, "the principal Seat and Palace of all the Kings of *England* since the Conquest," became in 1224 the site of the courts of chancery, king's bench, and common pleas. "Of later Times [it was also] used for the hanging up Trophies taken from the Enemy" (Strype, 2, ³47–49). Marlborough returned to London in December 1704 and appointed 3 January 1705 "for the colours and standards taken by his grace at the battle of Hockstet . . . to be brought thro' this citty in state to Westminster Hall, where they are to be hung up as trophies of that victory; and the heralds at armes, in their proper habits, with the officers of the army, are to martial them; the horse guards are to carry the standards, and the foot guards the colours; to be attended in triumph by the kettle drums, trumpets, &c.: the like never seen before" (Luttrell, 5, 502).

184. *Imperfect seem:* Marlborough wished to "perfect" the victory at Blenheim and to end the war by an invasion of France through the Moselle Valley. Instead, he was required to conduct a pointless and frustrating campaign in 1705 which gave Louis XIV a year in which to recoup his losses (Boyer, *Annals,* 1706, pp. 61, 71, 88–91).

194. *Royal Treaty-Breaker:* Breaking treaties was an instrument of policy for Louis XIV.

And lives he yet, the Great, the Lost *Bavar*,   195
Ruin to *Gallia*, in the Name of Friend?
Tell me, how far has Fortune been severe?
Has the Foe's Glory, or our Grief an End?
Remains there, of the Fifty Thousand lost,
To save our threaten'd Realm, or guard our shatter'd Coast?   200

To the close Rock the frighted Raven flies,
Soon as he sees the Eagle cut the Air:
The shaggy Wolf unseen and fearful lyes,
When the hoarse Roar proclaims the Lion near.
Why then did we our Forts and Lines forsake,   205
To dare the *British* Foe to open Fight?
Our Conquest we by Stratagem should make,
Our Triumph had been founded in our Flight:
'Tis Ours, by Craft and by Surprize to gain;
'Tis Theirs, to meet in Arms, and Battel in the Plain.   210

The ancient Father of this Hostile Brood,

"After he had over and over given his Royal Word in several Proclamations, That he would strictly observe the Edict of *Nantz*, he broke it. After he had in the solemnest manner in the World renounced all Right to the Crown of *Spain*, and given his Faith, that he wou'd never pretend any Title to it, he broke through all this. In the Treaty of *Ryswick*, he was forced to yield up many of his Usurpations, and among the rest, forced to quit several of the Frontier Towns that he had seized on the *Rhine*, and yet soon after he broke into the Empire, and by that, broke this Treaty too" ([Thomas Burnet], *A Letter to the People, to be Left for Them at the Booksellers; With a Word or Two of the Bandbox Plot*, 1712, pp. 4–5). Burnet might have added that after undertaking, in the fourth provision of the treaty of Ryswick, not to disturb William III "en quelque Façon que ce soit" in the possession of the throne of England, Louis recognized James III as king of England upon the death of James II at St. Germain in September 1701. Cf. "Don't you hear People say, the King of *France* owes most of his Conquests to Breaking his Word?" (Colley Cibber, *The Careless Husband*, 1705, p. 14).

195–260. These lines are spoken by Louis XIV.

199. *Fifty Thousand*: Reports of enemy casualties (Luttrell, *6*, 47, 49) were as usual somewhat exaggerated, but Prior was prodigal. He congratulated Marlborough on the "defeat of sixty thousand [of] the best men that France ever saw" (Coxe, *Memoirs, 1*, 420). French losses at Ramillies are now estimated to have been fewer than 15,000 (58*n*. above).

201–10. Louis XIV is now made to regret the aggressive strategy which he had adopted for the campaign of 1706 (121*n*. above).

211. *ancient Father*: In the preface to his poem Prior wrote: "where *HORACE* praises the *Romans*, as being Descended from *AENEAS*, I have turn'd to the Honor of the *BRITISH* Nation, descended from *BRUTE*, likewise a *TROJAN*. That this *BRUTE*, Fourth or Fifth from *AENEAS*, settled in *ENGLAND*, and built *LONDON*, which he call'd *Troja Nova*, or *Troynovante*, is a Story which (I think) owes it's Original if not to *GEOFFRY* of *Monmouth*, at least to the *Monkish* Writers; yet is not rejected by Our great *CAMDEN*, and is told by *MILTON*, as if (at least) He was pleas'd with it; though possibly He does not believe it: However it carries a Poetical Authority, which is sufficient for our Purpose. It is as certain

Their boasted *Brute,* undaunted snatch'd his Gods
From burning *Troy,* and *Xanthus* red with Blood,
And fix'd on Silver *Thames* his dire Abodes:
And this be *Troynovante,* he said, the Seat   215
By Heav'n ordain'd, my Sons, your lasting Place:
Superior here to all the Bolts of Fate
Live, mindful of the Author of your Race,
Whom neither *Greece,* nor War, nor Want, nor Flame,
Nor Great *Peleides'* Arm, nor *Juno's* Rage could tame.   220

Their *Tudor's* hence and *Stuart's* Off-spring flow,
Hence *Edward,* dreadful with his Sable Sheild,
Talbot to *Gallia's* Pow'r Eternal Foe,
And *Seymour,* fam'd in Council or in Field;
Hence *Nevill,* Great to Settle or Dethrone,   225
And *Drake* and *Ca'ndish,* Terrors of the Sea;

---

that *BRUTE* came into *ENGLAND,* as that *AENEAS* went into *ITALY;* and upon the Sup-
position of these Facts, *VIRGIL* wrote the best Poem that the World ever read, and *SPENSER*
paid Queen *ELIZABETH* the greatest Compliment.
    I need not obviate one piece of Criticism, that I bring my Hero

                    From burning *Troy,* and *Xanthus* red with Blood:

whereas He was not born, when That City was destroy'd. *VIRGIL,* in the Case of His own
AENEAS relating to *DIDO,* will stand as a sufficient Proof, that a Man in his Poetical
Capacity is not accountable for a little Fault in Chronology" (Prior, *Works, 1,* 231).
    213. *From burning Troy:* Cf. "cremato . . . ab Ilio" (Horace, *Odes,* IV, iv, 53).
    215. *Troynovante:* The Troynovant myth recurs mainly in the heroic-panegyric verse of
the period, e.g. *A Congratulatory Poem to His Highness the Prince of Orange upon His Arrival at
London* (1688) ("Hail happy *Troy-novant's* Triumphant Walls"); *The Poet's Address to the
Honourable Sir Charles Duncomb* (1700) ("The fair *Augusta,* of all Lands the Pride"), p. 8:
"Old *London* is again turn'd *Troynovant.*"
    222. *Edward:* Edward, Prince of Wales (1330–76), who heads this conventional catalogue
of heroes, was the eldest son of Edward III and queen Philippa. He was called the Black
Prince supposedly because he wore black armor at Crécy (1346).
    223. *Talbot:* Gilbert Talbot, fifth Lord Talbot (1383–1418), accompanied Henry V to
France in 1415 and distinguished himself at Agincourt. John Talbot, first earl of Shrewsbury
(c. 1384–1453), led the English resistance to France in the last stages of the Hundred Years'
War. In 1439 he was styled "governor and lieutenant-general of France and Normandy"
(GEC, *11,* 698–704; *DNB, 19,* 320).
    224. *Seymour:* Edward Seymour, 1st earl of Hertford and duke of Somerset (c. 1500–1552)
fought in France in 1523 and 1544–45. On the death of Henry VIII in 1547, he became
Protector, directing the regency of his nephew, the boy king Edward VI.
    225. *Nevill:* Richard Neville, earl of Warwick and Salisbury (1428–71) was Warwick the
Kingmaker. He placed Edward IV upon the throne in 1461 and then deposed him and
restored Henry VI for six months in 1470–71.
    226. *Drake and Ca'ndish:* Francis Drake (1540?–96) was knighted by Elizabeth in 1581
upon completing his voyage around the world. He commanded a division of the English fleet

Hence *Butler*'s Sons, o'er Land and Ocean known,
Herbert's and *Churchill*'s Warring Progeny:
Hence the long Roll which *Gallia* should conceal,
For Oh! Who vanquish'd, loves the Victor's Fame to tell?   230

Envy'd *Britannia,* sturdy as the Oak
Which on her Mountain Top she proudly bears,
Eludes the Ax, and sprouts against the Stroke,
Strong from her Wounds, and greater by her Wars.
And as those Teeth which *Cadmus* sow'd in Earth   235
Produc'd new Youth, and furnish'd fresh Supplies;
So with young Vigour, and succeeding Birth,
Her Losses more than recompenc'd arise:
And ev'ry Age She with a Race is Crown'd,
For Letters more Polite, in Battels more Renown'd.   240

Obstinate Pow'r, whom Nothing can repel,
Not the fierce *Saxon,* nor the cruel *Dane,*
Nor deep Impression of the *Norman* Steel,
Nor *Europe*'s Force amass'd by envious *Spain,*
Nor *France* on Universal Sway intent,   245
Still breaking Leagues, and still renewing Wars,

against the Spanish Armada in 1588 and plundered Vigo in 1585, Cadiz in 1587, and Coruña in 1589. Thomas Cavendish (1560–92) sailed around the world in 1586–88, spoiling Spanish ports and shipping.

227. *Butler:* James Butler, twelfth earl and first duke of Ormonde (1610–1688), commanded Charles I's troops in Ireland and negotiated the restoration of Charles II. His grandson, James Butler, second duke of Ormonde (1665–1745), fought at William's side in all the major engagements of 1689–97. He was said to be "one of the most generous, princely, brave Men that ever was" (Macky, p. 10).

228. *Herbert:* Pembroke was not a military hero but he commanded the Wiltshire and Hampshire militia in the Monmouth rising (June 1685), served as first lord of the admiralty (1690–92, 1701–02), and even as lord high admiral (January–May 1702). His distant cousin, Arthur Herbert, first earl of Torrington (1647?–1716), was even less heroic. He was commissioned as admiral in 1680 and served briefly as first lord of the admiralty and admiral of the fleet (1689–90). But he was removed from his command and court-martialed in December 1690 for refusing to engage the French at Beachy Head.

Churchill: The three "Progeny" of Sir Winston Churchill (1620?–1688) were indeed "Warring": the eldest was the duke of Marlborough; the second was George Churchill (1654–1710), commissioner of the admiralty (1699–1702) and manager of all naval affairs as a member of Prince George's council (1702–08); the third was Charles Churchill (1656–1714), one of the best English regimental commanders, who was promoted lieutenant general in May 1702 and distinguished himself at Blenheim and Ramillies (Boyer, *Annals,* 1707, p. 83).

231–40. This stanza is modelled closely on Horace, *Odes,* IV, iv, 57–68.

245–46. William Atwood doubted the dramatic propriety of making Louis XIV confess

Nor (usual Bane of weaken'd Government)
Their own intestine Feuds and mutual Jars;
Those Feuds and Jars in which I trusted more,
Than in my Troops, and Fleets, and all the *Gallic* Pow'r.   250

To fruitful *Rheims,* or fair *Lutetia*'s Gate,
What Tidings shall the Messenger convey?
Shall the loud Herauld our Success relate,
Or mitred Priest appoint the Solemn Day?
Alas! my Praises they no more must Sing,   255
And to my Statue they must Bow no more:
Broken, repuls'd, is their Immortal King,
Fall'n, fall'n for ever, is the *Gallic* Pow'r—
The *Woman Chief* is Master of the War,
Earth She has freed by Arms, and vanquish'd Heav'n by Pray'r. 260

Whilst thus the ruin'd Foe's Despair commends
Thy Council and Thy Deed, Victorious *Queen,*
What shall Thy Subjects say, and what Thy Friends?
How shall Thy Triumphs in our Joy be seen?
Oh! daign to let the Eldest of the *Nine*   265
Recite *Britannia* Great, and *Gallia* Free;
Oh! with her Sister *Sculpture,* let her join
To raise, Great *Anne,* the Monument to Thee:
To Thee, of all our Good the Sacred Spring:
To Thee, our dearest Dread; to Thee, our softer King.   270

---

that "*France* was intent on Universal Monarchy, and given to break Leagues" (*A Modern Inscription to the Duke of Marlborough's Fame,* 1706, sig. a2v. Cf. 194*n.* above).

251–60. Cf. Horace, *Odes,* IV, iv, 69–72.

251. *Lutetia:* Mudville, or Paris.

252. *What Tidings:* Saint-Simon records that after the initial news of the defeat at Ramillies there was no further report from Villeroi to Louis XIV: "Les jours sembloient des années," he said, "dans l'ignorance du détail et des suites d'une si malheureuse bataille" (*Mémoires, 2,* 610). Louis, of course, is imagined to hope for good news which can be disseminated by proclamation or by public thanksgiving.

256. *my Statue:* Louis' statue, by Martin van den Bogaert *dit* Desjardins, was in the Place des Victoires (until it was pulled down during the revolution): "il se composait d'une statue de Louis XIV, couronné par la Victoire et foulant aux pieds Cerbère, symbole de la Triple Alliance. Ce groupe, en métal doré, surmontait un piédestal, flanqué aux angles de quatre statues d'*Esclaves* et décoré de quatre bas-reliefs" (*Larousse du XX*e *Siècle,* 6 vols., Paris, 1928–33, *4,* 527). It was here that Louis was "adoré en effigie" (*La Grande Encyclopédie,* 31 vols., Paris, 1886–1902, *22,* 641).

265. *Eldest of the Nine:* Clio, the muse of history.

Let *Europe* sav'd the Column high erect,
Than *Trajan*'s higher, or than *Antonine*'s;
Where sembling Art may carve the fair Effect,
And full Atchievement of Thy great Designs.
In a calm Heav'n, and a serener Air,   275
Sublime, the *Queen* shall on the Summet stand,
From Danger far, as far remov'd from Fear,
And pointing down to Earth her dread Command.
All Winds, all Storms that threaten Human Woe,
Shall sink beneath her Feet, and spend their Rage below.   280

There Fleets shall strive by Winds and Waters tost,
'Till the young *Austrian* on *Iberia*'s Strand,
Great as *Æneas* on the *Latian* Coast,
Shall fix his Foot: And this, be this the Land,
Great *Jove*, where I for ever will remain,   285
(The *Empire*'s other Hope shall say) and here

271–350. These lines constitute Clio's advice-to-a-sculptor (see headnote, above). They may have been suggested by the proposal "to erect some national monument to the glory of the Queen and her hero, the Duke of Marlborough." "Claud David of Burgundy published a large sheet-print, from the model of a fountain, with the statues of Queen Anne, the Duke of Marlborough on horseback, and several river gods, designed to be erected at the Conduit in Cheapside" (C. F. Secretan, *Memoirs of the Life and Times of Pious Robert Nelson*, 1860, p. 238; quoted in Prior, *Works*, 2, 897). Since there was no scheme to erect a permanent monument to the queen in Cheapside, the proposed monument must have been temporary, but no copy of the "large sheet-print" seems to have survived. (This information was very kindly supplied by Reginald Williams, Department of Prints and Drawings, The British Museum.)

272. *Trajan*'s . . . *Antonine*'s: Trajan's column was set up in the forum of Trajan in A.D. 113. It is 100 Roman feet (29.77 meters) high. That of Antoninus Pius was 14.75 meters high and was erected in the Campus Martius around A.D. 175 (Samuel B. Platner, *A Topographical Dictionary of Ancient Rome*, rev. by Thomas Ashby, Oxford, Oxford University Press, 1929, pp. 131, 242).

273. *sembling Art*: mimetic art.

276. *Summet*: Trajan's column and Antoninus's were both surmounted by statues of the emperors in gilt bronze.

281. *There*: Clio orders the sculptor to decorate the column with reliefs, presumably in a spiral band like that which covers the entire surface of Trajan's column and which illustrates his victories in Dacia.

282. *the young Austrian*: The archduke Charles of Austria, or Charles III, king of Spain, as he was called in England (112*n.* above), reached Lisbon on 25 March/5 April 1704 but did not set foot in Spain until July 1705, when, backed by the English fleet, he landed at Gibraltar (Boyer, *Annals*, 1706, p. 137).

285. *I*: Since Charles's older brother, the archduke Joseph, who had succeeded as emperor in May 1705, had no heir, Charles himself was heir-apparent, "The *Empire*'s other Hope," and eventually succeeded as emperor upon Joseph's death in December 1711.

Intomb'd I'll Slumber, or Enthron'd I'll Reign—
Oh Virtue, to thy *British* Mother dear!
Like the fam'd *Trojan* suffer and abide,
For *Anne* is thine, I ween, as *Venus* was his Guide.   290

There, in Eternal Characters engrav'd,
Vigo, and *Gibraltar,* and *Barcelone,*
Their Force destroy'd, their Privileges sav'd,
Shall *Anna*'s Terrors and Her Mercies own:
Spain, from the Rival *Bourbon*'s Arms retriev'd   295
Shall with new Life and grateful Joy appear,
Numb'ring the Wonders which that Youth atchiev'd,
Whom *Anna* clad in Arms, and sent to War;
Whom *Anna* sent to claim *Iberia*'s Throne,
And made him more than King, in calling him Her Son.   300

There *Ister* pleas'd, by *Blenheim*'s glorious Field
Rolling, shall bid his Eastern Waves declare
Germania sav'd by *Britain*'s ample Shield,
And bleeding *Gaul* afflicted by her Spear:
Shall bid them mention *Marlb'rough,* on that Shore   305

291. *There:* Clio orders the sculptor to engrave on the column—presumably in "Trajan," the kind of architectural lettering derived from the inscriptions on Trajan's column—the names of the sites of Anne's victories in Spain: Vigo (October 1702), Gibraltar (July 1704), and Barcelona (September 1705). While Spanish "Force" was "destroy'd" in all three of these engagements, Spanish "Privileges" were "sav'd" only at Barcelona. Catalonia had enjoyed a semi-autonomous status in Habsburg Spain; among its privileges, or *fueros,* was the right of the cortes to vote on taxation. Charles III hastened to restore the *fueros* which the Bourbon Philip V had abolished (William Coxe, *Memoirs of the Kings of Spain,* 2nd ed., 5 vols., 1815, *1,* 355).

292. *Barcelone:* From Gibraltar (282n.), the confederate flotilla under the command of Charles Mordaunt, third earl of Peterborough, and admiral Sir Cloudesley Shovel, and with five regiments and a guards battalion aboard, sailed up the coast of Spain and captured Barcelona on 23 September/4 October 1705 in an action that seemed *"miraculous"* at the time and is simply incredible today (Boyer, *Annals,* 1706, pp. 146–54).

295. *Spain . . . retriev'd:* Hatred of France was so great that Charles III was everywhere received with "great Acclamations [and] a thousand Demonstrations of Joy" (Boyer, *Annals,* 1706, pp. 138, 144–45). Four months after the fall of Barcelona nearly all of Valencia, Murcia, Cataluña, and Aragon had revolted against Philip V and accepted the rule of Charles III.

297–98. *that Youth . . . Whom Anna clad:* "The expenses of the king of Spain's voyage to Portugal . . . at her majesties charge" were already in October 1703 said to amount to £105,000 (Luttrell, *5,* 352). During his stay at Windsor, where Anne received him with "great Demonstrations of Respect and Affection," Charles publicly acknowledged her "generous Protection and Assistance" (Boyer, *Annals,* 1704, p. 226).

301. *There:* Next the sculptor is ordered to depict the Danube (Ister) at the site of the battle of Blenheim.

Leading his *Islanders* renown'd in Arms
Thro' Climes, where never *British* Chief before
Or pitch'd his Camp, or sounded his Alarms:
Shall bid them bless the *Queen,* who made his Streams
Glorious as those of *Boyn,* and safe as those of *Thames.*   310

There *Brabant,* clad with Fields, and crown'd with Tow'rs,
In decent Joy shall her Deliv'rer meet;
Shall own Thy Arms, Great *Queen,* and bless Thy Pow'rs,
Laying her Keys beneath thy *Subject's* Feet.
Flanders, by Plenty made the Home of War,   315
Shall weep her Crime, and bow to *Charles* restor'd;
With double Vows shall bless Thy happy Care,
In having drawn, or having sheath'd the Sword.
Her Sister Provinces from her shall know
How *Anne* supports a Friend, or how forgives a Foe.   320

Bright Swords, and crested Helms, and pointed Spears,
In artful Piles around the Work shall lye;
And Shields indented deep in ancient Wars,
Blazon'd with Marks of *Gallic* Heraldry:
And Standards with distinguish'd Honours bright,   325
Types of high Pow'r and National Command,
Which *Valois'* Sons, and *Bourbon's* bore in Fight,
Or gave to *Foix',* or *Montmorancy's* Hand:

310. *Boyn:* See *The Dyet of Poland,* 98*n.* above.

311–15. *Brabant . . . Flanders:* The consequences of Marlborough's victory at Ramillies were similar to those of Peterborough's victory at Barcelona (295*n.* above). Villeroi and Maximilian Emanuel withdrew in panic to Lille and all of Brabant and Flanders revolted against Philip V and accepted the rule of Charles III. "In the space of Fourteen Days, (from the 23*d* of *May* to the 6*th* of *June,* N.S.) the Duke of *Marlborough . . .* recovered the whole *Spanish Brabant;* the Marquisate of the Holy Empire, with its Capital, the famous City of *Antwerp;* the Lordship and City of *Malines,* and the Capital City [Brussels], with the best Part of *Spanish Flanders:* An Event, which can hardly be paralleled any where" (Boyer, *Annals,* 1707, p. 109). Henceforth the Spanish Netherlands was to be the Austrian Netherlands.

314. *Keys:* "On the 28th. of *May,* N.S. his Grace [the duke of Marlborough] went to *Brussels,* and was met at the Gate by the Magistrates of that City, who presented him with the Keys . . . The Duke of *Marlborough* went about Noon [22 May/2 June] to the City [of Ghent], and was met at the Gate by the Magistrates, who presented to him the Three Keys" (Boyer, *Annals,* 1707, pp. 98, 102).

327. *Valois:* The Valois dynasty ruled France from 1328 until 1589 when it was succeeded by the Bourbon.

328. *Foix:* The counts of Foix in the extreme south of France wielded power from the eleventh to the fifteenth centuries, frequently undertaking war on behalf of the Capets and the Valois, but just as frequently acting as equals of the kings of France.

Montmorancy: The lords of Montmorency, about nine miles northwest of Paris, furnished

Great Spoils, which *Gallia* must to *Britain* yield,
From *Cressy*'s Battel sav'd, to grace *Ramillia*'s Field.   330

And as fine Art the Spaces may dispose,
The knowing Thought and curious Eye should see
Thy Emblem, happy *Queen,* the *British* Rose,
Sign of sweet Pow'r, and gentle Majesty:
The *Northern* Thistle, whom no Hostile Hand   335
Unhurt too nearly may approach, I ween;
And *Ireland*'s Harp, her Emblem of Command,
And Instrument of Joy, should there be seen:
And *Gallia*'s wither'd Lillies pale, and torn,
Should, here and there dispers'd, the lasting Work adorn.   340

Beneath, Great *Queen,* Oh! very far beneath,
Near to the Ground, and on the humble Base,
To save her self from Darkness, and from Death,
That *Muse* desires the last, the lowest Place,
Who, tho' unmeet, yet touch'd the tremb'ling String   345
For the fair Fame of *Anne* and *Albion*'s Land,
Who durst of War and Martial Fury Sing;
And when thy Will appointed *Marlb'rough*'s Hand
To end those Wars, and make that Fury cease,
Hangs up her grateful Harp, to Everlasting Peace.   350

---

six constables of France, twelve marshals, besides numerous admirals, cardinals, and high officers of the crown. They were recognized by Henri IV as, next to the Bourbon, the first house in Europe.

330. *Cressy:* Clio imagines that French battle flags not captured by Edward III at Crécy in 1346 were "sav'd" to be captured at Ramillies.

331–40. The sculptor is commanded to fill up the "Spaces"—probably the four sides of the pedestal—with the traditional national symbols: the English rose, Scottish thistle, Irish harp, and French lilies (drooping).

335–36. *no Hostile Hand | Unhurt too nearly may approach:* The lines suggest the motto of the order of the thistle, *Nemo me impune lacessit,* and there had been recent examples—passage of the Act of Security (August 1704) and the execution of Captain Thomas Green (March 1705)—of how dangerous it could be to provoke the Scots. But even while Prior was writing, English and Scottish commissioners were meeting almost daily to consider the terms of a treaty of union. On 16 May, the day the news of Ramillies reached London, the Scottish commissioners demanded an account of the English national debt and annual revenue. By 22 June the commissioners had completed the treaty which was now to be laid before the parliaments of the two nations (Luttrell, *6,* 47, 59).

341–50. On the base of the column, in "the last, the lowest Place," where one would expect the quarry inscription and sculptor's name, Clio orders her own figure to be inscribed, "To save her self from Darkness, and from Death."

An Epistle to Sir Richard Blackmore, Kt.
On Occasion of the Late Great Victory in Brabant
(20 July 1706)

An Epistle to Sir Richard Blackmore provides not only a laboratory dem-
onstration of Pascal's law that "le ton de voix impose aux plus sages et
change un discours et un poème de force," but also an interesting case
of interaction between literary "form" and political "content."

The poem can be read as a serious injunction to Blackmore to cel-
ebrate in verse "the Late Great Victory" at Ramillies. Against this it
might be objected that no one would seriously urge Dr. Blackmore to
take time from hundreds of patients to celebrate one man, Marl-
borough:

> *His Fame* to Vulgar *Lives* shou'd be prefer'd
> Of the Ignoble Undistinguish'd Herd.
>
> (35–36)

But the Augustan Age was not a humanitarian age. Sympathy for the
masses was not fashionable, and even Oliver Goldsmith agreed that
"we do not so strongly sympathize with one born in humbler cir-
cumstances, and encountering accidental distress: so that while we melt
for Belisarius, we scarce give halfpence to the Beggar who accosts us
in the street" (*Collected Works, 3,* 211). Nor is this couplet by any means
so hyperbolic as dozens of others in the Marlborough hagiography.
Prior revised one of his lines, whether deliberately or not, to enable his
patron to march upon the water (*An Ode, Humbly Inscrib'd,* 57, above,
and textual note).

The claim that all the verses so far published were insufficient in
some respect (lines 37–52), would have found easy acceptance, even
by Blackmore himself (*A Letter to Mr. Prior, Occasion'd by the Duke of
Marlborough's Late Victory at Ramilly,* 1706, p. 3; Blackmore, *Advice to the
Poets. A Poem. Occasion'd by the Wonderful Success of Her Majesty's Arms,
under the Conduct of the Duke of Marlborough, in Flanders,* 1706, p. 10). The
appeal to Blackmore, therefore, seems to be freighted with credibility:

> Oh! give us a true *Specimen* of Wit,
> Thou know'st it best—*Thou Master art of it.*

> Do thou exert thy self, and let us see
> A *Poem* worthy *CHURCHILL,* worthy *Thee.*
>   (53–56)

The trouble of course is that all of this is ironical. Narcissus Luttrell was partly correct when he inscribed his copy of the poem "A Banter on Sr. Richard." It is a banter but it is directed as much at the duke of Marlborough as it is at Sir Richard. The duke is stabbed through the sides of the knight.

"A true *Specimen*" of Blackmore's "Wit" was already in existence. "Approximately one third" of *Homer and Virgil not to be Compared with the Two Arthurs* (1700) "is devoted to a series of passages culled from Blackmore's epics and exhibited as examples of ineptitude and absurdity in thought and expression" (Rosenberg, p. 61). Blackmore was "*Master*" of wit because "The Troops of Wit, Disorder'd, and O'rrun, / Are Slain, Disperc'd, Disgrac'd, and Overthrown" in *A Satyr against Wit* (1699) (Defoe, *The Pacificator,* 304–05, *POAS,* Yale, *6,* 175). A poem "worthy" of Blackmore's uncreating hand would indeed be "worthy" of Marlborough, whose "*Fame*" is defined by 9,066 "Of the Ignoble Undistinguish'd Herd" killed at Ramillies (Brodrick, *1,* 153).

> What may we not expect, when *such* a Muse
> Shall *such a Theme* and *such a Heroe* choose?
>   (67–68)

The political "meaning" of the poem depends wholly on its ironical literary form.

The Luttrell copy in the Newberry Library is dated 20 July 1706, but no evidence of authorship has emerged.

An Epistle to Sir Richard Blackmore, Kt.
On Occasion of the Late Great Victory in Brabant

Oh *Blackmore!* Why do'st *thou alone* refuse
To grace *Ramillia* with thy noble Muse,
Where *British* Valour urg'd by *CHURCHILL* on,
Has all that went before, and has it self out-done?
How canst thou answer to *thy self* and *Fame*   5
A Victory like *this*—without *thy* Name?
 Or, do'st thou still for the *Great WILLIAM* grieve,
Tho' he will *ever* in thy *Arthur* live?
Or, is *One Poet* to *One Heroe* due,
T'*AUGUSTUS Virgil,* and to *WILLIAM You?*   10
Or, is *this Age* not worthy of thy Care,
That did not thy Illustrious *Arthur* spare?
 Grieve not for *Him* whom thou hast deathless made;
Whose Laurels, like thy own, will never fade.
Thy Artful Hand, and thy Harmonious Pen   15
Can Men immortal make, and live agen.
'Tis true, *BRITANNIA* is of *Him* bereft,
But *He* his *Mantle* has to *ANNA* left;

1. *Blackmore:* Sir Richard Blackmore (1654–1729) was the leader of the "Apothecaries Physicians" in the Royal College of Physicians who for ten years prevented the College from opening a free out-patient clinic (*POAS*, Yale, *6*, 100). He was a Whig who was called a "Republican," a low churchman who was a great believer in "*the* Dictates *of our* Natural Light," and "*England's Arch-Poet,*" who, having written *Prince Arthur. An Heroick Poem. In Ten Books*" (1695) "and dedicated it to the king, his majestie . . . conferred the honour of knighthood upon him" (Hearne, *11*, 395; *A Paraphrase on the Book of Job*, 1700, sig. h2r; Pope and Swift, *Miscellanies. The Third Volume*, 1732, p. ²69; Luttrell, *4*, 199). He continued to publish in the next reign—"Never," it is said, "was a man afflicted with a *scribendi cacoëthes* more incurable" (*DNB*, *2*, 592)—and in July 1708 he was sworn one of Anne's physicians (Luttrell, *6*, 322).

8. *thy Arthur: Prince Arthur. An Heroick Poem,* of which three editions were published in 1695–96, recounts the exploits of the prince of Orange in vaguely Arthurian terms. Thus the revolution of 1688 becomes "*Prince* Arthur *with his Fleet sailing from* Neustria, *or* Normandy, *to drive the Usurper* Octa *and his Pagan* Saxons *out of* Britain *and to restore Christianity*" (*Prince Arthur,* 1714, sig. B1r). In *King Arthur. An Heroick Poem. In Twelve Books* (1697) Blackmore brought the history of William III down to the present.

12. *did not . . . Arthur spare:* In 1696 John Dennis pronounced his opinion of *Prince Arthur. An Heroick Poem:* "Mr. *Blackmore's* Action has neither Unity, nor Integrity, nor Morality, nor Universality," and Blackmore's name, as Johnson said, "became at last a bye-word of contempt" (Dennis, *Critical Works, 1*, 46; Johnson, *Lives, 2,* 252).

Who *doubly* with *his spirit* blest, has done
All that he hop'd and more—and has *ev'n Him* out-run.   20
　　So vast a *Genius* and so large a Mind
Can never to *One Heroe* be confin'd.
In *ANNA's* Reign thou hast *ELIZA's* grac't,
The *Present Age* out-shining far the *Past.*
For, whate'er Fame to *Her* advantage tells,   25
The *Copy* the *Original* excels.
　　If *Thou* and thy *Great Arthur* were condemn'd,
It was not *Thou* but *Virtue* was contemn'd;
Whose Cause thou nobly fought'st, and did'st maintain:
Oppos'd by *Sworn Confederates* in vain.   30
　　Rouze then—and reassume thy tuneful Lyre:
This CHURCHILL—This thy COUNTRY does require.
What if Ten Thousand Sick thy Absence grieve?
Let 'em grieve on, so *CHURCHILL ever* live.
His Fame to Vulgar *Lives* shou'd be prefer'd   35
Of the Ignoble Undistinguish'd Herd.
　　Tate, as in Duty bound, has somewhat said:
But He his *Office* not his *Muse* obey'd.
　　But *Prior* does in *Spencer's* Style endite,

19. *doubly . . . blest:* In addition to the biblical analogue (2 Kings 2:9–13), there may be an allusion here to the mock-epic terms that Dryden used to describe Shadwell's succession: "The Mantle fell to the young Prophet's part, / With double portion of his Father's Art" (*Mac Flecknoe,* 216–17); cf. *POAS,* Yale, *6,* 379).

23. *Eliza:* Blackmore published *Eliza: An Epic Poem. In Ten Books* in July 1705. It reads like Baker's *Chronicle* versified or a broadside ballad in couplets about the defeat of the Spanish Armada. It is not "a continued allegory, or darke conceit," like *Prince Arthur,* but it does flatter Anne as "a new *Eliza*" (pp. 93, 219).

28. *Virtue:* Blackmore "was a chaste writer; he struggled in the cause of virtue" (Cibber, *Lives, 5,* 178), but it is doubtful that he provoked the wits "*more* by his virtue than his dulness" (Johnson, *2,* 252; italics added).

30. *Sworn Confederates:* the 30–odd "Covent-Garden Wits," headed by Sir Christopher Codrington and Charles Boyle, whose epigrams "*Squibbing*" Blackmore were published in *Commendatory Verses, on the Author of the Two Arthurs and the Satyr against Wit* (1700) (*POAS,* Yale, *6,* 134, 138, 183).

37. *Tate:* Nahum Tate (1652–1715), graduated B.A. from Trinity College, Dublin, in 1672 and published his first volume of verse five years later. His version of Shakespeare's *King Lear,* with its happy ending, was first acted in 1681 and the next year he collaborated with Dryden to produce *The Second Part of Absalom and Achitophel* (*POAS,* Yale, *3,* 278). He succeeded Thomas Shadwell as poet laureate in November 1692 and ground out official verse as occasion demanded. He celebrated Blenheim in *The Triumph, or Warrior's Welcome: A Poem on the Glorious Successes of the Last Year* (1705) ("O for a Muse of Flame, the Daring Fire").

39. *Prior:* Prior's *Ode, Humbly Inscrib'd to the Queen* (1706), "in *Spencer's* Style," is reprinted above.

With the *same spirit* that the *English* Fight.   40
Thought so sublime, Expression so correct
Ever more Honour, than they give, reflect.
For tho' his *Heroe* to the Stars be rais'd,
'Tis nobler so to praise, than to be prais'd.
   Some *Minor Poets* too have done their best: 45
Tho' small their Skill, yet their good Will's exprest.
   De Foe, as ever, Execrably bad,
Throws out a Hasty *Poem*, wrote like Mad.
'Twas the first-born, and welcome in *our Mirth*,
Tho' not *One Muse* assisted at its birth.   50
   Some more, *below the dignity of Verse*,
In short-liv'd Lines wou'd glorious Deeds rehearse.
   Oh! give us a true *Specimen* of Wit,
Thou know'st it best—*Thou Master art of it.*
Do thou exert thy self, and let us see   55
A *Poem* worthy CHURCHILL, worthy *Thee.*
Thy Muse, like the fam'd Beauty of a Town,
If seen abroad, the day is all her own.
Each *Puny-Wit* draws back, and hides his Head,
And does inimitable Patterns dread.   60
   Do *you* but Write, and *All* will silent be:
For what Bold Man will dare to follow *thee?*
Do you *Ramillia's* Bloody Plains describe,
You *Distance* strait the whole *Poetic Tribe.*
Praise is the Most to which *the Best* pretend;   65
But *Wonder* and *Surprize thy* Works attend.
   What may we not expect, when *such* a Muse
Shall *such a Theme* and *such a Heroe* choose?

---

45. *Minor Poets:* Of the 20-dod copies of verse by "*Minor Poets*" celebrating Ramillies, the following were published before the present poem: [Charles Johnson], *Ramelies. A Poem* (11 June 1706) ("Hail, Goddess, to our Isle propitious"); William Wagstaffe, *Ramelies: A Poem, Humbly Inscrib'd to His Grace the Duke of Marlborough* (4 July 1706) ("*Bleinheim* e're while at ev'ry turn appear'd"); William Congreve, *A Pindarique Ode, Humbly Offer'd to the Queen, on the Victorious Progress of Her Majesty's Arms* (July? 1706) ("Daughter of Memory, Immortal Muse").

47. *De Foe:* See p. 174 above. *On the Fight of Ramellies* was also published in a folio half sheet with the title *An Essay on the Great Battle at Ramellies.*

51. *below the dignity of Verse:* The phrase, originally Dryden's (*Absalom and Achitophel*, 570), had become a favorite of Defoe's (*POAS*, Yale, *6*, 352, 574). Some of the anonymous copies of verse celebrating Ramillies are printed in *POAS*, 1707, *4*, 10, 25, 77 and in *The Poetical Works of the Honourable Sir Charles Sedley*, 1707, pp. 169, 175, 180.

By *CHURCHILL's* Actions and Examples fir'd,
Ev'n meaner Pens than thine may be inspir'd.   70
But when the *Muse* and *Subject* are compleat,
The World with justice hopes for *somewhat Great.*
Our utmost hopes, I know, (Vast tho' they be)
Of a full answer cannot fail from *Thee.*
And if *my* Poorer Muse shall waken *Thine,*   75
Some share at least of Glory will be *mine:*
As *He,* who warn'd by *me* begins to Arm,
Does owe the Victory to my Alarm.

75. *waken:* Presumably by accident, Blackmore responded three days later by publishing
767 lines of *Advice to the Poets. A Poem. Occasion'd by the Wonderful Success of Her Majesty's Arms,*
under the Conduct of the Duke of Marlborough, in Flanders (23 July 1706), of which two editions
were required. He followed up this success by publishing 517 lines of *Instructions to Vander*
Bank, A Sequel to the Advice to the Poets: A Poem, Occasion'd by the Glorious Success of Her Majesty's
Arms, under the Command of the Duke of Marlborough, the Last Year in Flanders (10 March 1709),
which, as Johnson said, "put an end" to the advice-to-a-painter genre (*Lives, 2,* 242).

WILLIAM ATWOOD

A Modern Inscription to the Duke of Marlboroughs Fame.
Occasion'd by an Antique, In Imitation of Spencer
(12 September 1706)

The present poem may owe its existence to two misconceptions and one
fact. The misconceptions are that Prior had versified "the Horse fatal
to King *William*" (12–17*n*. below) and had also written *Moderation
Display'd* (1*n*.). The fact is that Prior was a commissioner for trade and
plantations (June 1700–June 1707).

William Atwood (c. 1650–1712), in whose mind these misconceptions
seem to have existed, was the son of John Atwood of Bloomfield, Essex.
He attended Queens' College, Cambridge, and the Inner Temple,
before being called to the bar in 1674 from Gray's Inn (*The Pension Book
of Gray's Inn,* ed. Reginald J. Fletcher, 2 vols., 1901–10, *2,* 34). He
published *A Poetical Essay towards an Epitome of the Gospel* in 1674 (Wing
A4177), but it was as a lawyer, pamphleteer, and antiquary, not as a
poet, that Atwood made his reputation.

In his law practice Atwood was appointed king's counsel in March
1692 (*CSPD 1691–92,* p. 168) and successfully defended some rich and
powerful clients: Charles Gerard, earl of Macclesfield, Sir Edmund
Assheton, and Thomas Grey, earl of Stamford (HMC *Lords MSS., 3,*
29–32, 336–38; New Series, *3,* 63; *CSPD 1697,* p. 158). In politics he
was an original Whig, one of "The chief Asserters of the Antiquity of
the Commons" (in *Jani Anglorum facies nova,* 1680 [William Nicolson,
The English, Scotch, and Irish Historical Libraries, 3d ed., 1736, p. 193]), a
loyal Williamite, and so aggressive an imperialist, asserting England's
absolute dominion over Ireland (in *The History, and Reasons, of the
Dependency of Ireland* [1698]) and Scotland (in *The Superiority and Direct
Dominion of the Imperial Crown of England over the Crown and Kingdom of
Scotland* [1704]), that he was suspected of being "on the *Tory* side"
(*The Memorial of the State of England,* 1705, p. 3). As an antiquary he was
a collector of manuscripts (HMC *Inner Temple MSS.,* p. 241), a friend
of William Petyt who was keeper of the records in the Tower of London,
and an indefatigable researcher in rolls, charters, and other old docu-
ments. Even the Jacobite Thomas Hearne (*3,* 475) called him "a

learned Antiquary, & a very curious Man." His pamphlets—and the preface to *A Modern Inscription to the Duke of Marlboroughs Fame*—read like a lawyer's brief, pockmarked with marginal references and citations.

Probably through his connection with Stamford, who was president of the board of trade and plantations (1699–June 1702), but also, as he said himself, "not being unknown in Westminster Hall, or at the Bar of the House of Peers" ("Memorial of Mr. Attwood," October 1709, *Documents relative to the Colonial History of the State of New-York*, ed. Edmund B. O'Callaghan, 15 vols., Albany, 1853–87, *5*, 104), Atwood was in June 1700 appointed chief justice of the province of New York and a judge of the admiralty in New York, the Jerseys, and New England (*CSPC 1700*, p. 332; *CSPC 1701*, p. 110). He had reservations about accepting the post. It paid only £300 and Atwood was "aware how precarious such an office, dureing pleasure, in parts so remote, must needs be" (*Documents relative to the Colonial History, 5*, 104). But nothing could have prepared him for the situation in New York. What he found was a paradigm of the present: a people "miserably divided" by differences of national origin, religion, class, and politics and a strange "backwardness" in law enforcement (*CSPC 1701*, pp. 588, 589). "There is scarce a merchant," it was said, "but what is guilty of carrying on an illegal trade, and . . . the Courts protect them in it" (ibid., p. 577).

Atwood worked hard to enforce the laws and to patch up the divisions, and he seemed puzzled by his lack of success: "Tho my zeal for the Laws of England concerning trade," he said, "has occasioned great clamours, they have been far short of what had been raysed upon my interposing with the law of England to secure the peace of this miserably divided City" (ibid., p. 711). Despite assurance from the commissioners for trade and plantations in January 1702 that he would "not want such protection as they are able to give in the performance of [his] duty," they allowed Edward Hyde, Lord Cornbury, the new governor of the province of New York, to discharge Atwood on 9 June 1702 without a hearing (*CSPC 1702*, pp. 54, 391, 466). Cornbury, who was himself dismissed as governor in April 1708 for embezzlement and was a prisoner for debt in New York when he succeeded as third earl of Clarendon in November 1709 (*CSPC 1706–08*, p. 720; Luttrell, *6*, 506), simply yielded to "the universal clamour of the people" and accepted as true 33 charges drawn up by politicians and merchants who felt themselves aggrieved by Atwood's decisions (*CSPC 1702,* pp. 754, 756–59; *CSPC 1702–03,* p. 7).

In this crisis, fearing that "his regard to the *Laws* would be rewarded with *Lawless Violence*" (*The Case of William Atwood, Esqr;* 1703, reprinted in *Collections of the New-York Historical Society for the Year 1880,* 1881, p. 296), Atwood lost his nerve and fled to Philadelphia where he was able to take shipping for England.

Back in London, on 3 November 1702, Atwood tried to explain to the commissioners, including Matthew Prior, the reasons for his flight, but the commissioners, again without a hearing, decided in December to approve Lord Cornbury's unauthorized and unconstitutional action (*CSPC 1702,* p. 699; *CSPC 1702–03,* pp. 77–78, 129–31; *The Case of William Atwood, Esqr;* p. 312). Prior was also one of the commissioners who signed an order of January 1703 denying Atwood access to documents which he needed to defend himself (*CSPC 1702–03,* pp. 125–26; *The Case of William Atwood, Esqr;* p. 313).

So this may be the fact which together with two misconceptions caused Atwood to write *A Modern Inscription to the Duke of Marlboroughs Fame* in reply to Prior's "Antique" inscription "In Imitation of Spencer." As an antiquary Atwood must have smiled at Prior's efforts "to make the Colouring look more like SPENSER's, [with] *I weet . . . I ween . . . whilom . . .* and Two or Three more of that Kind" (*Works, 1,* 231). As a Whig he suspected that Prior, a Tory, "was not pleased with his Subject" and so was able to produce only "a mean, cold Performance" (*A Modern Inscription to the Duke of Marlboroughs Fame,* 1706, sig. alr). And finally, as a judge, Atwood may have resented Prior's part in a flagrant invasion of the constitutional principle of the separation of powers.

Atwood's authorship of the poem is established in the copy which he presented to Elizabeth Thomas, Dryden's Corinna (*POAS,* Yale, *6,* 206), inscribed "Ex Dono Authoris" and signed "By Wm. Atwood, Esq.," now in the library of Queen's University, Belfast. The poem was advertised in *The Daily Courant* for 29 August 1706 and the Luttrell copy, now at Harvard, is dated 18 September.

A MODERN INSCRIPTION TO THE DUKE OF MARLBOROUGHS
FAME.
OCCASION'D BY AN ANTIQUE, IN IMITATION OF SPENCER

As of his *Faction*'s Downfal *P——r* sings,
His Muse attempts to rise with broken Wings:
When he shou'd praise an envy'd Fate, he cry'd,
A Good Man's grievous Loss, a faithful Servant dy'd.
Since *Malbro'* lives to conquer, baffled *France*   5
And all her Partizans may *wayl* their Chance;
Dull antiquated Words let them pursue;
This grateful Theme inspires with something new;
As no time past a Parallel can shew.
The Cause of *Liberty*, we thought expir'd,   10
When from his glorious Toyls *William the Great* retir'd.
That Bard for *Pegasus*, then poor *Sorrel* took:
While the *more grateful Brute* stood Thunder-struck,
Thro' Sense that his indulgent Master's Grace
Had rais'd his Head above his *Vulgar Race;*   15

1. *P——r: Faction Display'd* was attributed to Prior in April 1704 (*POAS*, Yale, *6*, 650) and here apparently *Moderation Display'd* is attributed to him, for it is the latter poem (above) that sings the downfall of the country Tories. In his preface Atwood said that "Mr. Prior . . . takes the *P——r* to himself; and by threatening an Action at Law, has given occasion for something [i.e. the preface] to introduce my short Essay into the World" (*A Modern Inscription to the Duke of Marlboroughs Fame*, 1706, sig. alr).
    2. *broken Wings:* Cf. *An Ode, Humbly Inscrib'd*, 31.
    4. *Servant:* The line quoted is *An Ode, Humbly Inscrib'd*, 160; the "Servant" is Colonel James Bringfield, Marlborough's aide, who was killed while helping the duke remount on the battlefield at Ramillies.
    6. *her Partizans:* Atwood called Jacobites and Tories not enthusiastic for the war "the *French Faction*" (*The Scotch Patriot Unmask'd*, 1705, p. 59).
    7. *Dull antiquated Words:* Prior himself recorded that "The Whiggs . . . say'd the Imitation was of a verse now grown obsolete" (*Works*, *2*, 896).
    9. The line may mock *An Ode, Humbly Inscrib'd*, 29–30: "Who shall . . . Victories rehearse / By Story yet untold, unparallell'd by Verse?" "I have chosen in several Places," Atwood said, "to imitate, and apply his Expressions, possibly, with Similitudes more just than his" (*A Modern Inscription to the Duke of Marlboroughs Fame*, 1706, sig. clr).
    12. *Sorrel:* The horse that threw William III (*A New Ballad Writ by Jacob Tonson*, 3n. above) was celebrated in several epigrams (*POAS*, Yale, *6*, 364), one of which, presumably *Upon the Author of the Latin Epigram* ("Sorrell transform'd to Pegasus we see"), is here attributed to Prior. Atwood said that in the first draft of *A Modern Inscription* he had not named "the *Versifier* of the Horse fatal to King *William*," but when he heard that Prior had disowned "that lewd Satyr," he changed his mind (*A Modern Inscription to the Duke of Marlboroughs Fame*, 1706, sig. alr).

The *Poet,* mounted an unusual Height,
At *Europe*'s Loss express'd his warm Delight.
Most Nations mourn'd the want of such an Head,
As if from Earth, with him, *Astraea* fled:
But soon, in *Anna* she her self return'd,   20
And her Auspicious Pow'r Mankind discern'd:
Her conqu'ring Beams, embellishing the Throne,
Seem'd to subdue those who her Right disown.
All the *Top-Croakers* of the Sword and Gown,
T'infest the Royal Palaces were known.   25
Egyptian Magic had a *Serpent* fram'd,
For Skill in *Hieroglyphic Secrets* fam'd:
The Loyal fled, as they with Horror saw,
That *Long Thing* bred from Excrements of Law;
But soon were re-assur'd by *Malbro*'s Hand,   30
Scarce less Miraculous than *Aaron*'s Wand.
As he in *William*'s Paths of Glory goes;
He meets the same, both Home and Foreign Foes.
The many Kings of the unthinking Rout,
And the hot Bigots for *St. Germains-Lout,*   35
Like *Sampson*'s Foxes, joyning Tayl to Tayl,
His ever-verdant Laurel's Crop assail.
Intrepid and Serene, see him repel
The complicated Force of *France* and *Hell;*
Shewing the Genius which protects this Isle,   40

19. *Astraea fled:* "When she quitted Earth, Justice left her last trace here" (Virgil, *Georgics,* II, 473); cf. "Driven out of here, Astraea gradually ascended to the skies" (Juvenal, *Sat.* VI, 19).

23. *those who her Right disown:* Jacobites and republicans.

24. *Top-Croakers:* Tories in top military and civil offices under the crown (*Moderation Display'd,* 74–149), dismissed in April 1704.

24–31. "Then Pharaoh also called the wise men and the sorcerers: now the magicians of Egypt, they also did in like manner with their enchantments. For they cast down every man his rod, and they became serpents: but Aaron's rod swallowed up their rods" (Exodus 7:11–12).

34. *The many Kings:* the House of Commons. In the form, "Five Hundred Kings," the phrase was a commonplace (*POAS,* Yale, *2,* 413; *6,* 237; *A Collection of Poems on State Affairs,* 1712, p. 12).

35. *the hot Bigots:* Jacobites and Francophile Tories.
St. Germains-Lout: James Francis Edward, the pretended Prince of Wales.

36. *Sampson's Foxes:* Judges 15:4–5.

39. *Hell:* In *Moderation Display'd* (177–260) it is the collaborators of Marlborough who are Satan's minor devils; here Atwood returns the compliment and makes the opponents of Marlborough the forces of Hell.

With Joy partakes of his Victorious Toil:
And *Anne*, its Empress, Heav'n's peculiar Care,
Finds his *Heroic Deeds* Returns of Favour'd Pray'r.
The vain *Immortal Man* must now confess,
A *Woman*'s deathless Fame does his suppress;   45
Who, while He reigns o'er Multitudes of Slaves,
Far greater Numbers from Oppression saves;
With Gentle Hand her pow'rful Sceptre sways,
And the soft Influence thro' the World conveys.
Tho' *Malbro'*, in himself Wonders contains,   50
Thro' her he his *stupendious Conquests* gains:
To think for whom he fights, Vigour inspires;
In her bright Cause the *Hero* never tires,
And fresh from *Vict'ries*, still to new aspires.
Strong *Passes*, deep *Intrenchments*, mighty *Walls*,   55
Can't from his Arm protect th'experienc'd *Gauls*.
Another *Caesar;* with superiour Might,
By conqu'ring, teaches their *best Troops* to fight.
Prodigious Numbers *former Heroes* beat:
None slew so many, *manag'd* to retreat.   60
Heav'n pushes 'em so long, to try their Fate,
That to their *practis'd Arts* they fly too late.
Heav'n guides *his Hand,* and animates *his Heart,*
And with its *Blessings* crowns his high Desert.
All Precedent, and Thought he has surpass'd: 65
Who can foresee what is reserv'd at last?
The *Gallic Tyrant* gladly wou'd compound,
And give up *Kingdoms,* not to be uncrown'd;
Yet nothing but the Sword, can cure th'invet'rate Wound.
England, in peaceful Treaties, too sincere   70

44. *The vain Immortal Man:* Louis XIV refers to himself as an "immortal King" over-
mastered by a woman in *An Ode, Humbly Inscrib'd,* 257–59.

51. *Thro' her:* In July 1705 Marlborough wrote to the queen, "as I am sure I would not
only venture my life, but also sacrifice my quiet for you, so I beg you will believe that I shall
never think myself master of taking any resolution till I have first obtained your majesty's
leave" (Winston S. Churchill, *Marlborough His Life and Times,* 4 vols., Harrap, 1938, *2,* 571).

69. *nothing but the Sword:* The sword (actually a spear) was Achilles' and the victim was
Telephos, whose "invet'rate" wound was cured by scrapings from the spear (H. J. Rose, *A
Handbook of Greek Mythology,* New York, E. P. Dutton, 1959, p. 233).

70. *peaceful Treaties:* The partition treaties of 1698 and 1700, signed by England, France,
and the Netherlands, were intended to preserve the peace of Ryswick (1697) when the
childless king of Spain died.

To deal with Them who nothing future fear;
From Long Experience of unthought-of Harm,
Shou'd learn the Foes it weakens, to disarm.
This *William* saw, forc'd with regret to sheath
His pressing Sword, while *France* sought time to breath: 75
Our *Murm'rers* from that Sword did Danger feign,
That their arm'd Friend might seize unguarded *Spain*.
When the *projected Monarchy* was near,
Then was the time for *Malbro'* to appear,
Heav'n, which has mark'd him out for wondrous things,   80
The Scourge of *Tyrants*, and Support of *Kings*,
A proper Scene for such a Spirit and Conduct brings.
By Nature he was made *Conquests* to gain;
As *Anna*, over all Mankind to Reign.
That Wisdom, which her *happy Realms* unites;   85
Her equal Will to give to all their *Rights*;
Fill the submitting World with *New Delights*.
And while we're blest with such a Monarch here,
We know not what to wish, or what to fear.
                                   Ego nec tumultum,   90
Nec mori per vim metuam, tenente Caesare terras.

74–75. *forc'd . . . to sheath | His . . . Sword:* When Louis XIV failed to disarm after the treaty of Ryswick, William III wished to keep 30,000 men in arms, but the Country party in the House of Commons cut back the army first to 10,000 and then to 7,000 men. "The *Croakers* held his Hands from subduing the Enemy," as Atwood said in the preface (*A Modern Inscription to the Duke of Marlboroughs Fame*, 1706, sig. a2v).

76. *Murm'rers:* Atwood implies that the Country party only pretended to fear William III and actually wanted to help Louis XIV seize Spain; cf. "was it not pleasant to . . . observe to what End they talk'd popularly against Standing Armies, and the Partition Treaty, who were sure to make no Opposition to *France*'s Seizing the Dominions of the *Crown of Spain?*" (Atwood, *The Scotch Patriot Unmaskd*, 1705, p. 43).

78. *projected Monarchy:* In October 1700 when Carlos II finally died it was discovered that he had bequeathed the entire Spanish empire to Philippe d'Anjou, the 16-year old second grandson of Louis XIV. Louis' acceptance of the throne of Spain for Philippe, in violation of the partition treaties, raised fears that Spain and France would be united, particularly after Louis XIV declared that "il n'y a plus de pirénées" (Voltaire, *Le Siècle de Louis le Grand*, 2 vols., Berlin, 1751, *2*, 98).

79. *time for Malbro':* In June 1701 William put Marlborough in command of a new army of 10,000 men designed for Holland (Luttrell, *5*, 49, 58).

90–91. "I will not fear disorder or death by violence as long as Augustus governs in the land" (Horace, *Odes*, III, xiv, 14–16).

DANIEL DEFOE

The Vision
(27–28 November 1706)

"The conquest of Scotland," it has been said, "was a project which ambition very naturally suggested to an English king," but it remained for an English queen to realize this ambition (J. L. De Lolme, "An Essay containing a Few Strictures on the Union of Scotland with England," in Daniel Defoe, *The History of the Union*, ed. George Chalmers, 1786, p. 4). Edward I failed miserably, after wasting many years of a long reign (1272–1307) in killing Scots. James I in 1604 appointed commissioners from each kingdom to draw up articles for a treaty of union but then abandoned the project for one more compatible with his genius, *viz.* "to make himself absolute in Scotland" (Defoe, *The History of the Union*, 1786, pp. 51–53, 717–24). Cromwell succeeded momentarily in imposing a union by force. Charles II in 1666 again appointed commissioners but when they produced a treaty he dismissed them without further notice. William III in March 1689 recommended "uniting both Kingdoms into one" and on his deathbed reminded parliament that "nothing can contribute more to the present and future Peace, Security, and Happiness, of *England* and *Scotland*, than a firm and entire Union between them" (*Leven and Melville Papers*, Edinburgh, The Bannatyne Club, 1843, pp. 2–3; *LJ, 17*, 50–51).

Anne responded to this in her first speech from the throne by urging parliament "to consider of proper Methods towards attaining of an Union between *England* and *Scotland*" (*LJ, 17,* 68). Commissioners were again appointed but negotiations broke down over the issue of trading rights for the Company of Scotland and were adjourned in February 1703. Then, in August 1703, the Scottish parliament responded by passing the Act of Security, which provided that Anne's successor should be "of the Royal line and of . . . the true Protestant Religion . . . Provideing alwayes that the same be not the Successor to the Crown of England" unless England had previously conceded to Scotland "a free Communication of trade, the freedom of navigation and the liberty of the plantations" (*APS, 11,* 69, 70). The effect would have been to break the union of crowns which had existed since 1603 and to expose England to "the most extreme danger" ([James Drake], *The Memorial of the Church of England*, 1705, p. 55).

During that same summer there were rumors—of secret agents landing on the coast of Sussex and of French fleets landing arms for 16,000 Highlanders—that crystallized in December 1703 in the notorious Scotch plot (*POAS*, Yale, *6*, 615–17). The House of Lords, after hearing the evidence, concluded that the encouragement of this plotting came from not settling the succession of the crown of Scotland in the house of Hanover and urged the queen "to promote an entire Union between the Two Kingdoms, for their mutual Security and Advantage" (*LJ*, *17*, 505–06). So Anne withheld her assent to the Act of Security while Harley, her new secretary of state for the northern department, observed cynically that "the succession is to be kept unsettled for a lame arm to beg by" (HMC *Portland MSS.*, *4*, 103).

In the next session of the Scottish parliament, however, it became apparent that no supply would be voted until the Act of Security became law. Godolphin reluctantly advised the queen to give her assent to the act on 5 August 1704. The most recent historian of this period calls this decision "a critical point in the whole union episode because it placed Godolphin at the mercy of the junto" and the Junto wanted "an entire Union," or an incorporating union, as it was called at the time (*EHR*, *84* [July 1969], 507).

So, for a fourth time, commissioners were appointed: 31 for England, including Harley, Godolphin, and all the Junto lords, and 31 for Scotland, carefully excluding the *Squadrone Volante* and all Jacobites except George Lockhart of Carnwath, Wharton's nephew, who refused to sign the completed treaty and became the Jacobite historian of the proceedings. In April 1706 the two bodies opened negotiations— in separate chambers in the Cockpit in Whitehall from whence they could communicate officially only by exchange of minutes. The important horse trading of course occurred in unofficial caucus (ibid., p. 514). By 22 July 1706 the 25 articles of the treaty had been agreed upon by the commissioners and were ready to be laid before the parliaments of the two kingdoms. The second article settled the succession of the united kingdom on the electress Sophia of Hanover and the heirs of her body, being Protestants. Then the Junto lords crowded into court, demanding as their reward the ouster of Harley and Godolphin and the formation of a new Whig ministry.

Harley's attitude toward the union is hard to guess. He tried to give an impression of ignorance and indifference: "The world sufficiently knows," he said in August 1706, "how backward I have been to meddle with Northern affairs," but in fact he had been meddling with Scottish affairs at least since 1704 (HMC *Portland MSS., 4,* 324). In June 1705 he sent William Greg to Edinburgh to report on the proceedings of parliament. This was the session that passed an act to appoint commissioners for a treaty of union with England by a majority of only four votes on 1 September 1705 (HMC *Portland MSS., 4,* 194, 239). And "From this Day," as George Lockhart said, "may we date the Commencement of *Scotland*'s Ruine" (Lockhart, p. 172).

So Harley may have been one of the best informed of the 31 English commissioners and he certainly took his responsibility seriously, for he attended 39 of the 45 sessions in the Cockpit. Then, in September 1706, having vetted and tested him in two missions in England (pp. 74–75 above), Harley sent Defoe to Edinburgh. With characteristic carelessness he sent him off without instructions and without even a final interview. But Defoe, with characteristic resourcefulness, wrote instructions for himself which agreed almost exactly with Harley's when they finally caught up with him. "You are to write constantly the true State how you find things," Harley insisted, and "You must shew [the Scots], this is such an opportunity that being once lost or neglected is not again to be recovered" (Defoe, *Letters,* pp. 125–26, 132).

Defoe's response to this challenge constitutes one of the most remarkable propaganda feats in history. By adopting a dazzling array of disguises and histories, he was able to penetrate every level of Scottish society. He wrote unionist speeches (or position papers) for two noble lords: James Hamilton, sixth earl of Abercorn, who had just taken his seat in parliament, and John Gordon, sixteenth earl of Sutherland, who had served as one of the Scottish commissioners. And at the other extreme he succeeded in infiltrating a Jacobite activist group (ibid., pp. 154, 189). Then he wrote *The Rabbler Convicted: Or A Friendly Advice to All Turbulent and Factious Persons, From One of their Own Number* (1706) to dissuade the group from their violent purposes. In October he progressed from spectator, to lobbyist, to adviser in "Cases of Conscience," to the commission of the general assembly, the legislative body of the Church of Scotland, then in session. "I work Incessantly with them," Defoe said, and "They go from me seemingly Satisfyed, and pretend to be Informd." But he was not able to prevent them from declaring a day of fast to protest the union (Defoe, *Letters,* pp. 133, 139–40). Early in November he arranged to be asked to testify before a committee of parliament for calculating the equivalent on the vexed question of a drawback on salt. The members were so impressed that they invited him back to draft "a scheme of their Demands" and by the end of the month they were "Calling Every Day for me," as Defoe reported (ibid., pp. 143, 144, 163).

"I am lookt on as an English man that Designs to settle here," Defoe explained, "and I think [I] am perfectly Unsuspected." In this belief, however, he was wrong, for John Erskine, earl of Mar, the original mover of an act for a treaty of union in the Scottish parliament, reported ten days later that "Defoe . . . is still here. I'm not acquainted with him, but he really takes a great deall of pains in this affair" (ibid., p. 143; HMC *Mar and Kellie MSS.,* p. 322). Thus it came about that while Andrew Fletcher of Saltoun was foolishly arguing in parliament that "Trade to England was No advantage to them," Defoe was patiently explaining to the parliamentary committee exactly what the advantages would be. "Really I blush for them," he told Harley, "and am asham'd to Instruct men, who I thought I had not been Able to Informe of any thing" (*Letters,* pp. 153–54). Since this was the committee to which all proposed amendments to the treaty were submitted, Defoe was indirectly participating in the debates as well as recording them for history (ibid., pp. 160, 186–87).

All the time Defoe was in Edinburgh he continued to write the *Review,* three issues a week, on Tuesday, Thursday, and Saturday. About 70 numbers were devoted to the union. In addition, Defoe wrote five Essays at Removing National Prejudice, as he called them, and about 20 more essays and broadsides. He also arranged for distribution of his work: 2,500 copies of one broadside were distributed in Glasgow, Lanark, Hamilton, Stirling, and Dumfries (*Letters,* pp. 169–70). As a propagandist appealing to a mass audience Defoe knew the necessity for repetition: the ignorant, he said, hardly know whether the union is "a Man or a Horse . . . for their Sakes I repeat and repeat, and quote my self over and over" (*Review,* 5 June 1707). For the learned, and for posterity, Defoe wrote *The History of the Union* (1709), a monumental work of nearly 700 pages, with minutes of the last Scottish parliament, voting lists and other appendices. In addition Defoe wrote two long essays in verse: *Caledonia. A Poem in Honour of Scotland, and the Scots Nation,* of 1,273 lines (published in Edinburgh in December 1706 and in London on 28 January 1707), and *A Scots Poem: Or a New-years Gift from a Native of the Universe, to his Fellow-Animals in Albania,* of 1,124 lines (published in Edinburgh in January 1707 and reprinted below). And, finally, he published two short essays in verse, *The Vision* and *A Reply to the Scots Answer to the British Vision,* both of which are included here.

The immediate occasion for *The Vision* was a remarkable speech in parliament that Defoe heard on Saturday, 2 November 1706. The estates were debating the first article of the treaty of union, which was the incorporating article: "the two Kingdoms . . . shall . . . for ever after, be united into one Kingdom, by the Name of *GREAT-BRITAIN.*" The debates went on after dark and the clamor outside the Parliament House was so great that violence was feared and the guards were drawn out in readiness. The speech of John Hamilton, second Lord Belhaven was long and emotional. It began with a series of Old Testament-like prophecies of the disasters that would ensue if the kingdoms were united. When Belhaven finished speaking, Patrick Hume, earl of Marchmont and a member of the *Squadrone Volante,* "made a very short return." "He had heard a long speech, and a very terrible one," he said, "but he was of opinion, it required a short answer, which he gave in these words, 'Behold he dreamed, but lo! when he awoke, he found it was a dream' " (Defoe, *The History of the Union,* 1786, p. 328). But when the session was finally adjourned, the opponents of union had still prevented the incorporating article from coming to a vote (*APS, 11,* 312).

Defoe presumably wrote *The Vision* that night, so it could be copied out and distributed among the members before the vote was taken (and the article passed) on the following Monday, 4 November 1706. Ten days later, after Belhaven's speech had appeared in print, Defoe sent a copy of it to Harley along with "a short Comment Upon it which has made Some sport here and perhaps Done More Service than a More Solid Discourse" (*Letters,* p. 148). The "short Comment" is *The Vision,* but predictably Defoe also wrote "a More Solid Discourse," *An Answer to My Lord Beilhaven's Speech* (1706) in prose, a pedestrian job unlikely to have made sport anywhere. The interesting point is to find Defoe again working in prose and verse almost simultaneously (*POAS,* Yale, *6,* xxx–xxxi). Belhaven's speech was also versified in standard habbie measure as *Belhaven's Vision: Or, His Speech in the Union Parliament* (n.d.) ("While all the World to this Day").

Although Defoe told Harley on 28 November that "The ballad is printed" (Defoe, *Letters,* p. 162), the earl of Mar apparently had not seen a copy by 7 December 1706 when he complained that the "song on Balhaven . . . [is] not in print, which is a pittie" (HMC *Mar and Kellie MSS.,* p. 351). *The Vision,* in fact, had sold so well that a second Edinburgh edition was required, and on the day of Mar's complaint Benjamin Bragg was publishing a third edition in London (Moore, p. 51).

After so much history, the interesting literary features of the poem may be simply enumerated: 1) the speaker of the poem is a Scot (lines 15, 31), whereas the speaker of Defoe's *prose* answer to Belhaven's speech is "*an* English *Gentleman*"; 2) the verse form, which looks like Pindaric stanzas, is actually a regular stanza in anapests, rhyming $A^3B^3A^3B^3C^2C^2C^4D^4D^4$, in which the juxtaposed short and long rhyming lines at 6 and 7 produce an interesting effect like syncopation; 3) the frequent half rhymes, slant rhymes, and double rhymes—"Witches / Speeches," "adhere / secure"—reinforce the tone of withering scorn that Defoe sustains throughout the poem.

The Vision was answered by the next poem in this volume.

The Vision

Come hither ye Dreamers of Dreams,
Ye Soothsayers, Wizards and Witches,
That Puzzle the World with hard Names,
And without any meaning make Speeches:
    Here's a Lord in the North,   5
    Near *Edinburgh* Frith;
Tho little's been said of his Name or his Worth;
He's seen such a Vision, no Mortal can reach it,
I challenge the Clan of *Egyptians* to match it.

And first, in the dark it was told him,   10
Which might very well appall us,
That the World was a fighting of old time,
From *Nimrod* to *Sardanapalus;*
    That it's all Revelation,
    You may paund your Salvation,   15

1–9. Quoted in the *Review*, 22 March 1707.

5. *a Lord in the North:* John Hamilton, second Lord Belhaven (1656–1708), was one of the Scots nobles who in January 1689 invited William of Orange to take over the government of Scotland. On 27 July 1689 he commanded a cavalry troop against John Graham of Claverhouse, Viscount Dundee, and the Highlanders raised for James II, at Killiecrankie. On the same day he was appointed to the Scots privy council. Although a Presbyterian, he was "a forward, useful Member" of the Country party (Lockhart, p. 138) who adopted the eccentric practice of printing his speeches in parliament. He was also a major stockholder in the Company of Scotland Trading to Africa and the Indies, which suffered the disastrous loss at Darien in 1700. And although he had been a commissioner of the treasury from August 1704 to July 1705, he insisted, as he said, that it was "not . . . out of any Resentment that I [may] have by being turned out of a Post" that he became a violent and articulate opponent of the union (*The Lord Belhaven's Speech in Parliament, the 17th of July 1705,* 1705, p. 4). His speech of 2 November 1706 has been said to be "the best-known example of the oratory of the old Scots Parliament" (*Scots Peerage,* ed. Sir James B. Paul, 9 vols., Edinburgh, 1904–14, David Douglas, *2,* 45).

9. *Egyptians:* The Gypsies entered Scotland, from Egypt as it was supposed, early in the sixteenth century. Their reputation for prevision was based of course on their practice of fortune-telling.

10. *first:* "I think, I see *a Free and Independent Kingdom* delivering up That, which all the World hath been fighting for, since the days of *Nimrod;* yea, that for which most of all the Empires, Kingdoms, States, Principalities and Dukedoms of *Europe,* are at this very time engaged in the most Bloody and Cruel Wars that ever were; *to wit,* A Power to manage their own Affairs by themselves, without the Assistance and Counsel of any other" (*The Lord Beilhaven's Speech in the Scotch Parliament, Saturday the Second of November, on the Subject-matter of an Union betwixt the two Kingdoms of Scotland and England,* [Edinburgh], 1706, p. 3).

15. *paund:* pawn, pledge (*SND,* s.v. pawn).

For the Devil a History gives the relation,
But it's all in the Deeps, no Mortal can reach it,
We may challenge the Clan of *Egyptians* to match it.

Then *Scotland* comes next on the Stage,
For in Visions you must not be nice,   20
And a skip of three thousand Years age,
Is nothing where Men are Concise;
   I name it the rather
   Because you may gather,
How that every Man is the Son of his Father;   25
A Truth for the future no Mortal can doubt,
Whatever they might, before he found it out.

But heark, now the Wonders begin,
And take care least the Vision should fright ye;
For if it shou'd make you unclean,   30
He has not told how he would dight ye.
   First the National Church,
   Left quite in the Lurch,
Was a truckling down to the Steeple and Porch,
But what is still worse, she's affraid of her Friends,   35

16. *the Devil a:* no (*POAS,* Yale, *6,* 259, 684).

19. *next:* "I think, I see *a National Church,* founded upon a Rock, secured by a *Claim of Right,* hedged and fenced about by the strictest and pointed'st Legal Sanction that Sovereignty could contrive, voluntarily descending into a Plain, upon an equal level with *Jews, Papists, Socinians, Arminians, Anabaptists,* and other Sectaries, &c." (*The Lord Beilhaven's Speech in the Scotch Parliament* . . . , 1706, p. 3).

31. *dight:* clean (*SND,* s.v. dicht).

32. *the National Church:* the Presbyterian church, re-established in June 1690 (*EHD,* p. 640); see 19*n.* above. It was "Left . . . in the Lurch" by the treaty of union which, by failing to mention religious establishment in either kingdom, aroused fears that the Presbyterian Church of Scotland would end up sleeping in the truckle bed under the Episcopal Church of England in the high bed, or that the Scottish kirk would be governed by 26 bishops in the English parliament (Defoe, *The History of the Union,* 1786, pp. 244, 247–48). The commission of the general assembly denounced the treaty and declared a day of fast in Edinburgh on 31 October 1706 (Defoe, *Letters,* p. 140).

34. *a truckling down:* acting subserviently. The phrase is neither dialectal nor Scots, but apparently a coinage of Defoe's.

   Steeple and Porch: features of Episcopal churches but not of Presbyterian kirks.

35. *her Friends:* The "Friends" are voters *for* the union, which the Church of Scotland opposed. Again and again Defoe repeated his startling claim that the church was "Unsafe and Uneasy in [its] present Establishment" and that only the union could guarantee its liberties (Defoe, *Letters,* p. 133; *The History of the Union,* 1786, pp. 220, 244; *A Short Letter to the Glasgow-Men,* [Edinburgh, 1706], p. 2).

So Fevers make frantick Men hasten their Ends.

Was ever such Conjuring known,
Or the Church so claw'd by the Steeple;
Non-jurors are her Champions grown,
And the Prelatists vote for the People.   40
    Protesters appear
    And the *Jacques* they adhere,
And *Anti-christ* votes the true Church to secure,
O *Scotland!* Was ever such Conjuring known,
That the Mitre supports the same Church pull'd her down.   45

Then the Nation in Sack-cloth appear'd,
And the Visionist sadly bewail'd her;
For Mischiefs the like were ne'r heard,
Her priv'lege of Slavery faild her.
    For the Mob he complain'd   50
    That being born Chain'd,
Blest Bondage was lost and damn'd Freedom remain,
So with Liberty scar'd, and affraid to grow Rich,

39–40. *Non-jurors . . . Prelatists:* "Those that had really [the] least kindness for the Church, were the loudest, and appeared the most zealous for her security" (Defoe, *The History of the Union*, 1786, p. 244). Defoe's point is that the issue of security of the church was only a tactic to defeat the union, adopted by Jacobites whose *politique* would liquidate the Church of Scotland (*An Essay, at Removing National Prejudices . . . Part III,* [Edinburgh], 1706, p. 25).

41–42. *Protesters . . . adhere:* Upon an address by the commission of the general assembly a bill for securing the Church of Scotland as by law established was introduced on 4 November and rushed through parliament. Before the final vote on 12 November Lord Belhaven protested "in his own name and in name of all those who shall adhere to him That this act is no valid security to the Church of Scotland" and that the church could have no real security within the union. Twenty-three members adhered to this protest and Defoe reported to Harley the "good joke . . . that all the protestors and adherers . . . were . . . known Enemies of the Church" (*APS, 11,* 315–21; Defoe, *The History of the Union*, 1786, pp. 339–40, 671; *Letters,* p. 148).

42. *Jacques:* Jacobites.

45. The line is elliptical but the meaning seems clear: the Episcopalians, disestablished in June 1690, now pretend to be concerned for the security of the Presbyterians who displaced them.

47. *Visionist: OED* cites Defoe, *A System of Magick* (1727), p. 318: "This *Jacob Behemen* . . . was a kind of a Visionist. He pretended to see things invisible."

49. *priv'lege of Slavery:* Defoe opposed heritable offices and the heritable jurisdiction of the chiefs (which were guaranteed by article XX of the treaty of union) because "it keeps the common people and tenantry of Scotland in a condition inconsistent with the liberty of a free nation, and under an intolerable slavery to their landlords" (*The History of the Union,* 1786, p. 458).

They su'd for Repentance in a dolorous Speech.

And first our amazement t'increase,   55
The Souldiers disbanded appear,
Poor drudges put prentices to Peace,
For want of the blessings of War;
    For tho it's in the Book,
    Yet the Scripture mistook,   60
When it told us, our Swords should to Plow-shares be broke;
It might be long ago a happiness there,
But it's plain by the Vision it's otherwise here.

The Merchants are next on the Stage,
The Enchantment has circl'd them in;   65
For fear they in Wealth shou'd engage,
They resolve they'll never begin;
    The Burghs are affraid
    They shall have too much Trade,
And the Nation to Plenty be safely betray'd,   70
So they gravely Address, that to keep them Secure,
As you find them, you leave them, both Foolish and Poor.

The next is indeed a sad Sight,

56. *Souldiers disbanded:* "I think I see the *Valiant and Gallant Soldiery* either sent to learn the Plantation-Trade abroad; or at home petitioning for a small Subsistance, as the Reward of their Honourable Exploits, while their old Corps are broken, the common Soldiers left to beg, and the youngest *English* Corps kept standing" (*The Lord Beilhaven's Speech in the Scotch Parliament* . . . , 1706, p. 4).

61. *Swords . . . to Plow-shares:* Isaiah 2:4; Micah 4:3.

64. *Merchants:* "I think I see the *Honest Industrious Tradesman* loaded with new Taxes, and Impositions, disappointed of the Equivalents, drinking Water in place of Ale, eating his saltless Pottage, petitioning for Encouragement to his Manufactories, and answered by counter Petitions" (*The Lord Beilhaven's Speech in the Scotch Parliament* . . . , 1706, p. 4).

68. *The Burghs:* "I think I see the *Royal State of Burrows* walking their desolate Streets, hanging down their Heads under Disappointments; wormed out of all the Branches of their old Trade, uncertain what hand to turn to, necessitate to become 'Prentices to their unkind Neighbours; and yet after all, finding their Trade so fortified by Companies, and secured by Prescriptions, that they despair of any Success therein" (ibid., p. 4).

71. *Address:* The three estates of the Scottish parliament were lords, barons, and boroughs. Of the 66 boroughs, 24 had sent petitions to Edinburgh against the union by 26 November (Miège, 1707, p. ²148; Defoe, *Letters,* pp. 140, 142; William Ferguson, *Scotland 1689 to the Present,* Edinburgh and London, Oliver & Boyd, 1968, p. 51; *Review,* 26 November 1706).

73. *next:* "In short, I think I see the *Laborious Ploughman,* with his Corn spoiling upon his Hands, for want of Sale, cursing the day of his Birth, dreading the Expence of his Burial, and uncertain whether to marry or do worse" (*The Lord Beilhaven's Speech in the Scotch Parliament* . . . , 1706, p. 4).

The like on't has rarely been known,
'Twill ruin the Country quite,   75
It will never recover its own;
   The Plow Man's undone,
   From Father to Son;
For a terrible draw-back on Corn will come on,
In plenty they'll Ship it, be there never so much;   80
And to load us with Money, sell all to the *Dutch.*

O ye Virgins! (both Sexes) draw near,
And tho it's but in spectrum showen,
In sympathy lend us a Tear
As the Case may some time be your own;   85
   The Ladies Condition
   Deserves your Compassion;
'Tis very severe to make Beauty Petition,
Yet here his strange Tragedies turn'd to a Jigg,
That the Men want Employments, yet the Ladies shou'd Beg.   90

Then a Crew of old Sailers were brought,
At their true Benefactors to Rail;
That to fight for strange Nations were bought
And this will cut off the Entail;
   They thought it was hard   95
   The *Dutch* Ships to discard;
And to force the poor *Scots* their own Trade to regard,

79. *draw-back on Corn:* In the present context, as Defoe explains, a drawback is a "bounty for Exporting." In hearings before the parliamentary committee for examining the drawbacks and equivalents, with whom Defoe had been invited to sit (pp. 210–11] above), the northern shires were demanding an export bounty on oatmeal (which would enable them to undersell the Irish). Defoe resolved a long debate about the price to which oatmeal must fall before the bounty should be paid by proposing "an Expedient Vizt that the price should be stated in the wholl Corn," which fluctuated less wildly than the price of oatmeal. Defoe's expedient was adopted and a drawback on oatmeal was incorporated into the treaty of union (Defoe, *Letters,* pp. 156–57; *The History of the Union,* 1786, pp. 373–74).

82. *Virgins:* "I think I see the incurable Difficulties of the *Landed-Men,* fettered under the Golden Chain of Equivalents, their pretty Daughters petitioning for want of Husbands, and their Sons for want of Employments" (*The Lord Beilhaven's Speech in the Scotch Parliament* . . . , 1706, p. 4).

83. *in spectrum:* in a fantasy or vision.

89. *Tragedies turn'd to a Jigg:* Cf. *The Dunciad,* I, 69: "Tragedy and Comedy embrace."

91. *Sailers:* "I think I see *our Mariners* delivering up their Ships to their *Dutch* Partners; and what through Presses and Necessity, earning their Bread as Underlings in the Royal *English* Navy" (*The Lord Beilhaven's Speech in the Scotch Parliament* . . . , 1706, p. 4).

For Liberty claims a freedom to ill,
And it's hard to get Money against a Man's Will.

And now the Exorcist in turn   100
Like a Ghost in a Circle arises,
Without any Tears he can Mourn;
He is Extasies all and Surprises;
　　But what's wildest of all,
　　And does strangely appall,   105
Two hours he talk'd, and said nothing at all,
But let drop a few hypocritical Tears;
So the Crocodale weeps on the Carcase she tears;

Then in strange Hebrew words he bewaild ye,
Tho the Jest was by few understood,   110
　Tu quoque mi fili Squadrone,

103. *Surprises:* One surprise occurred when Belhaven fell on his knees before the Speaker,
the Lord Chancellor James Ogilvie, earl of Seafield, and begged to know whether the govern-
ment had received any proposals for "putting an End to our fatal Divisions." When the lord
chancellor made no answer, Belhaven got to his feet and continued his speech (*The Lord
Beilhaven's Speech in the Scotch Parliament* . . . , 1706, p. 12).
　106. Defoe expanded the conceit in the *Review,* 9 December, 1707:

> *Q.* But what has the noble Peer said?
> *A.* Nothing at all.
> *Q.* But what did the noble Peer think he said?
> *A.* Nothing to the Purpose.
> *Q.* But why did the noble Peer say it then?
> *A.* Because he has been used to do so.
> *Q.* But what did the noble Peer mean?
> *A.* Nothing.

107. *Tears:* "I find my Heart so full of Grief and Indignation, that I must beg Pardon not
to finish the last part of my Discourse, that I may drop a Tear, as the Prelude to so sad a
Story." Belhaven sat down and several speeches intervened before he was able to go on (*The
Lord Beilhaven's Speech in the Scotch Parliament* . . . , 1706, p. 15).
　109. *strange Hebrew words:* "But above all, *my Lord,* I think I see *our Ancient Mother* CAL-
EDONIA, like *Caesar,* sitting in the midst of our Senate, rufully looking round about her,
covering her self with her Royal Garment, attending the Fatal Blow, and breathing out her
last with a *Et tu quoque mi fili*" (*The Lord Beilhaven's Speech in the Scotch Parliament* . . . , 1706,
pp. 4–5).
　111. *Squadrone:* The *Squadrone Volante* were moderate members of the Country party, head-
ed by John Hay, second marquis of Tweeddale, to whom Godolphin had turned to form a
government for Scotland in 1704. They proved unable to govern and had to be replaced
early in 1705 by the Court party, but as a bloc of about 25 members they were able to "cast
the Balance of the contending Parties in Parliament" in favor of the union (Lockhart, p.
138; William Ferguson, *Scotland 1689 to the Present,* Edinburgh and London, Oliver & Boyd,
1968, pp. 51–52). Defoe, however, seems to have believed that Belhaven's thrust was against
the government and not against the *Squadrone.* In the *Review,* 6 December 1707, he said, "At

Or in *Scots, The Parliament*'s *wood.*
  So *Caesar* they say,
  Cry'd out in a fray,
When they kill'd him, because he'd his Country betray;   115
For *Brutus* his Country's Liberty sought;
Was a Simily e're so in happily brought?

  Thus he rumag'd the Histories old,
  Like the Tale of the Bear and the Fiddle,
For as 'twas unluckily told,   120
So the Story broke off in the middle.
  Some said my Lord Cry'd,
  Tho others deny'd;
Which matter of Moment it's hard to decide;
But here's a more difficult matter remains,   125
To tell if he shew'd us less Manners or Brains.

---

last, *this Lord,* that made *a Speech,* was for enquiring, by *what Ways and Persons,* we were brought into this miserable Condition, and where do you think he brought it all to be, *Tu quoque mi Fili Squadrone* . . . which is as much to say, being interpreted by Way of Equivalent, THE MINISTRY."

112. *wood:* insane. Cf. Defoe, *Letters,* p. 143: "in short the Kirk are *au Wood* [all insane], pardon the scotticisme."

118. *rumag'd . . . Histories:* "In Parliament [Lord Belhaven] affected long premeditated Harrangues, wherein, having a prodigious Memory, he used to be very full in citing such Passages of History, as made for what he advanced, driving Parallels betwixt preceeding and present Times" (Lockhart, p. 138).

119. *the Bear and the Fiddle:* "Th' Adventure of the Bear and Fiddle / Is Sung, but breaks off in the Middle," is the argument of *Hudibras,* I, i. The canto ends abruptly in the middle of a bear-baiting episode.

John Hamilton, Lord Belhaven

A Scots Answer to a British Vision
(27–28 November 1706)

This is another poem, like *A Modern Inscription to the Duke of Marlboroughs Fame,* that owes its existence to a misconception. The misconception in this case is that *The Vision* was written by Thomas Hamilton, Lord Haddington, and Dr. James Wellwood. "I Could not Refrain sending you a peice of my Ld Beilhavens Poetry in Answer to the Ballad," Defoe wrote to Harley on 28 November 1706, "You will also see by it I have mannagd so in the Ballad that he does not suspect it but believs it my Ld Haddington. The Dr he means [line 1*n.*] is your Next Neighbour [in York Buildings]—Dr W——d" (*Letters,* p. 162). It would be interesting to know by what details in *The Vision* Defoe "mannagd" to mislead Belhaven. Perhaps it was those lines that allude to Belhaven's name and descent, for both Belhaven and Haddington bore the Hamilton patronymic: "little's been said of his Name" (7); "every Man is the Son of his Father" (25).

For his reply, Belhaven adopted a shortened form of the stanza which Defoe had fashioned for *The Vision.* And although some obscurities remain, the poem, as Defoe said (*Letters,* p. 162), is "a meer [i.e. absolute] Originall." It is in turn witty, learned, earthy, mystifying. Perhaps its major defect is that it is not sufficiently "Scots."

Belhaven's character emerges more clearly from a surprising sequel to this poetic encounter with Defoe than it does from the facts of his career (*The Vision,* 5*n.* above) or from the highly artificial rhetoric of his printed speeches. The surprise is that Defoe succeeded in making a friend of the nobleman whom he had so rudely affronted. In the *Review* for 10 July 1708, following Belhaven's sudden death on 21 June, Defoe said, *"tho'* . . . *I never slack'd my Hand in opposing his Lordship's Opinion,* yet his Lordship knew how to differ in Opinion without Personal Resentment . . . and as I had the Honour to converse with his Lordship both by Letters and by Word of Mouth . . . I think it a Debt due to his Memory, to set his Character right in the Eyes of good Men." Then, after quoting a letter of March or April 1708 in which Belhaven said, "I confess, I thought you gave your self too much Liberty in bantering Me and my Speech in your Writings . . . yet . . . I freely forgive you all your former Sins of Ignorance," Defoe proceeded "to set his Character right": "He was a Person of Nobility, of Disposition as well as Title, of Sence, Manners and Vertue, of Honesty, Sobriety and Religion, of Courage, Learning and Loyalty . . . he had an easie Conception, a Beauty of Thought, and a Readiness of Expression." Then, in *The History of the Union,* which Defoe published the next year, he wrote a final tribute to his friend: he was, Defoe said, "a person of extraordinary parts and capacity" (*The History of the Union,* 1786, p. 328).

Belhaven must have worked from one of the manuscript copies of *The Vision* that were circulating in Edinburgh, for *The Vision* and *A Scots Answer to the British Vision* were published almost at the same time, on 27–28 November 1706.

Besides Defoe's *Reply to the Scots Answer to the British Vision,* the next work in this volume, Belhaven's poem was answered by an anonymous broadside, said, in the NLS copy, to be written "by the Court Party." The title of the work is taken from *The Second Part of Absalom and Achitophel* (*POAS,* Yale, *3,* 307): *She put her Hand upon his Scull, | With this Prophetick Blessing, Be Thou Dull, &c.* ("Ye Coblers, and Taylors draw near") n.p., n.d.

A Scots Answer to A British Vision

Quantum est Divisibile in ea quae insunt, quorum utrumque
vel unumquodque Unum quod & hoc aliquod aptum est esse.
ARISTOTLE, De Quantitate

Two *British* Wits Conspir'd,
A *Scotish* Dream to Answer,
Both equally Inspir'd
With Nonsense, Punns and Banter;
   Sense smil'd to see   5
   Them so agree
   In Bluntness and Stupiditie.

Their Plot was so well laid,
That Rhime flow'd from the North;
And what the Southern said   10
Was Cant and Noisie Froth.
   No Man Alive
   Could so Contrive
   This Bum-bee-Hive.

When your Squadrons do brake,   15

Title. *British:* The tone is scornfully sarcastic, for "British" was a dirty word in Scotland in 1706. "The people cried out, they were Scotsmen, and they would be Scotsmen still; they contemned the name of Britons" (Defoe, *The History of the Union,* 1786, p. 226). The English and Scotch did not legally become "British" until 1 May 1707 when the treaty of union took effect.

Epigraph. "Quantity means that which is divisible into constituent parts, each or every one of which is by nature some one Individual thing" (Aristotle, *Metaphysics,* V, xiii). Perhaps Belhaven's point is that quantity—"*Two . . . Wits*"—implies nothing about quality (the next term that Aristotle defines).

1. *Two British Wits:* Belhaven believed that *The Vision* had been written by his young cousin, Thomas Hamilton, sixth earl of Haddington (1680–1735) and James Wellwood (1652–1727) (Defoe, *Letters,* p. 162). Haddington was a member of the *Squadrone Volante* and a pro-unionist whose "Talent lay in a Buffoon sort of Wit and Railery" (Lockhart, p. 137). Wellwood was a more serious type: a former physician to William and Mary, member of the Royal College of Physicians, author of several important works defending the revolution, and a neighbor of Harley's in York Buildings near the Strand (*DNB,* 20, 1148). *The Vision* may be the second work of Defoe's to be attributed to Wellwood. The first was *An Answer to the Late K. James's Last Declaration* (April 1693) (Moore, p. 5).

15. *Squadrons . . . brake:* Cavalry squadrons breaking ranks and rallying suggests the recent actions of the *Squadrone Volante* (*The Vision,* 111n.). As a party out of office the *Squadrone* automatically had opposed the union and none of its members were put on the commission to frame the treaty. Gradually however they were rallied to the cause of union by promises of

Is it thus that they Rallie?
Must a Bard and a Snake
Be the first makes a Sallie?
   Can a Virgin regain
   What she's lost of her Fame,   20
   By so Foppish a Train?

Where Similies bite
Thick Sculls do not know
A Cat from a Kite,
Their Pulse beats so low.   25
   It is then no Wonder
   That their pitiful Blunder
   Pass for Lightning and Thunder.

By this the World may see
Whence the Maggot does bite,   30
Since a Rake and a Cullie,
A Doctor and a Bullie,
Must touch a Court's Fee,
And do their worst to Unite.
   Thus *Thames* and *Tine*,   35
   Without Reason or Rhime,
   Do most fondly Combine.

When Reasoning's answer'd
By Seconded Votes,
And Speeches are Banter'd   40
By Outfield Turn-Coats,

---

reimbursement of their losses in the Company of Scotland Trading to Africa and the Indies, payment of their arrears in salary, and "undue representation" among the 16 "elected" peers who were to represent Scotland in the House of Lords (William Ferguson, *Scotland 1689 to the Present*, Edinburgh and London, Oliver & Boyd, 1968, pp. 47, 51–52; *EHR, 84* [July 1969], 515–18). "Rallying" is also a pun; in the sense of "bantering" it carries on the point of line 4.

17. *a Bard and a Snake*: The Bard must be Haddington and the Snake, Dr. Wellwood, from the symbol of medical service, entwined with two serpents. Belhaven's assumption that *The Vision* was *Squadrone* propaganda may have originated in Defoe's addition of the word "*Squadrone*" to the phrase "*Tu quoque mi fili*" in Belhaven's speech of 2 November (*The Vision*, 111).

38–39. *answer'd | By Seconded Votes*: outvoted (by "Two *British* Wits," line 1)?

41. *Outfield*: second-rate, inferior; "esp. in Scotland, the outlying land which is either unenclosed or untilled moorland or pasture, or was formerly cropped from time to time without being manured" (*OED*).

Then *Sirenge* and *Condom*
Come both in Request,
While Virtuous *Quondam*
Is Treated in Jest.   45

When *Highlands* and *London*
Agrec to make Druids,
Then our Union is half done,
It wants but some Fluids,
By a full Draught of Goat-whay   50
And a Wench by the middle,
You may fall on a Way
To Decipher my Riddle.

Thus I've Rumag'd the Hulk,
To find out some Good Ware,   55
But nothing of Bulk
Appears to be there:
Since it's so, then be gone,
Consult your *Enstruther*,
And let Squadrons go on   60
To Murder their Mother.

42. *Sirenge and Condom:* contraceptive devices.

44. *Quondam:* Cf. The Wife of Bath, "I haddc the beste *quoniam* myghte be" (*The Canterbury Tales*, III[D]608). The implication seems to be that since "Virtuous *Quondam*" is laughed at in *The Vision*, 82–90, contraceptives will be much in demand.

53. *Riddle:* Perhaps the stanza means: the collaboration of a Scot (Haddington) and an Englishman (Wellwood) is an emblem of the union, which needs only a toast to seal it.

59. *Enstruther:* Sir William Anstruther of Anstruther (d. 1711), was a member of parliament for Fife (1681, 1687–1707). Like Belhaven he "spok very weill" for William of Orange and was rewarded in October 1689 by being appointed one of the ordinary lords of the session (*Leven and Melville Papers*, Bannatyne Club, Edinburgh, 1843, pp. 83, 307). Subsequently he was sworn to the privy council and knighted (GEC, *Baronetage, 4*, 366n., 387). In November 1704 he was nominated one of the lords of the justiciary and assumed the title of Lord Anstruther. He voted with the *Squadrone Volante* in 1704–05 and parted from Belhaven on the issue of the union: "Enster made a long speech," the earl of Mar reported, "and told us since wee had heard of visions he wou'd tell us of one to counter the other; but it's too long to wryt" (HMC *Mar and Kellie MSS.*, p. 324). He was also an uncle (by marriage to Lady Helen Hamilton) of the sixth earl of Haddington, whom Belhaven believed to have written *The Vision*. The text may refer to *Essays, Moral and Divine; In Five Discourses*, Edinburgh, 1701, which Anstruther published despite all his friends could do to dissuade him. After his death, his son bought up every copy that could be found, for the purpose of suppressing it (Alexander Campbell, *An Introduction to the History of Poetry in Scotland*, Edinburgh, 1798, p. 141).

60–61. *Squadrons . . . Murder . . . Mother:* See *The Vision*, 109n. above.

To Answer them all
Would Torture the Devil,
But I have at a Call
What will Conjure you Civil;   65
  For what Remains,
  Wants Words, Rhime, Sense and Brains.
                   Adieu Messieurs.

DANIEL DEFOE

A Reply to the Scots Answer to the British Vision
(November? 1706)

In the letter of 28 November 1706 in which he forwarded *A Scots Answer to a British Vision*, Defoe told Harley, "This morning I put abroad privately the Enclosed lines upon it also" (*Letters*, p. 162). These "lines" were *A Reply to the Scots Answer to the British Vision*, which presumably circulated "privately" in manuscript and then was published in two broadside editions.

In these lines Defoe put together one of his favorite genres, the mock-panegyric (*POAS*, Yale, *6*, 43), and his favorite metre, heroic couplets, to make the single point that both Belhaven's speech of 2 November 1706 and *A Scots Answer to a British Vision* were "incomprehensibly Sublime" (line 17): full of "Ampullas & sesquipedalia Verba"—in the Horatian tag which Defoe adopted as an epigraph for the second edition—but essentially meaningless.

A Reply to the Scots Answer to the British Vision

Hail noble Lord of Parts immense,
Mighty in Language and profound in Sense;
How shall an humble Muse thy Glory raise,
And in her meaner Songs attempt thy Praise.
   See in the Senate how th'Illustrious Throng,   5
Sit listning to the Musick of thy Tongue;
And when abroad thy weighty Lines are read,
What pop'lar Triumphs soon adorn thy Head;
Thy flowing Language and affecting Mein,
Moving in Phrase, in pointed Satyr keen.   10
What floods of Tears from nobler Eyes it drew,
When *Caesar*'s Words as thus apply'd by you,
Were read by those the Story never knew;
Thus for thy Prose the Crowd thy Praise rehearse,
But who shall rate the Wonders of thy Verse;   15
For when thou stoop'st to Poesie and Rhime,
'Tis all incomprehensibly Sublime;
Supream in Thought, to Grammar unconfin'd;
Thy lofty Genius soars above the Wind.
So just the Numbers, so polite the Stile,   20
So clear the Sense, and so exact the Pile;
The wondring World like Trees in *Orpheus* Wood,
Admire those Strains they never understood.
   No wonder mighty Bard thus doubly Arm'd,
Thy two edg'd Tongue has all thy Foes allarm'd;   25
Whose Squadrons by thy dreadfull Language slain,
Under th'amazement of thy Sense remain;

---

1. *immense*: Belhaven was "A rough, fat, black, noisy Man, more like a Butcher than a Lord" (Macky, p. 236).

8. *pop'lar Triumphs*: Besides being versified itself (p. 212 above), Belhaven's speech of 2 November 1706 was also defended in verse in *A Second Defense of The Scotish Vision* ("How stronge's thy Sense! How charming are thy Strains!") (n.d.) which, incidentally, identifies Defoe as the author of *The Vision*.

12. *Caesar's Words*: See *A Vision*, 109n. above.

21. *Pile*: presumably in the sense of "A heap of things [e.g. verses] . . . laid . . . one upon another in a more or less regular manner" (*OED*).

22. *Orpheus*: Orpheus, son of the muse Calliope, was able by his singing not only to charm wild beasts but to draw trees from their places and to arrest the course of rivers.

And certain Conquest shall thy Voice attend,
For all must fly what none can understand.
  What tho in mighty Parable 'twas spoke,   30
The listning Crowd thy Oracles invoke;
Charm'd with thy *Ciceronian* Eloquence,
They view the Language, thou alone the Sense;
Nor is it fit th'uncomprehending Age,
Should in abstrusest Meanings far engage.   35
  So Latine Prayers implicitely thought Good,
May edifie, tho never understood.

32. *Ciceronian Eloquence:* Belhaven's "*Ciceronian* Stile" is praised in *A Second Defense of The Scotish Vision.*

36. *Latine Prayers:* Although the exact reference has not been discovered, the general sense of the metaphor seems to be this: for those with implicit faith, Belhaven's incomprehensible speeches are as efficacious as uncomprehended prayers in Latin; or, Belhaven convinces only those who are already convinced.

1707

A Scots Poem:
Or
A New-years Gift, from a Native of the Universe,
To His Fellow-Animals in Albania.
(1–14 January 1707)

After the Scottish parliament ratified the treaty on 16 January 1707, it was easy to say, as so many historians have said, that the union of Scotland and England was inevitable. But it by no means seemed inevitable at the time.

Defoe began to write the last of his major poems shortly after parliament convened on 3 October 1706. Six weeks later he feared that the union was "yet a Dark prospect." By the end of November he was surprised by hope: " 'tis Really True," he said, that "the Union may be Carryed on." But by the end of December he saw that a crisis had been reached: "It will be Either a Union or all Confusion in a few weeks more" (Defoe, *Letters,* pp. 147, 163, 183). On 26 December the Scottish parliament began to debate "the great article of the equivalent," which, as Defoe said, "made more noise in the world than all the other articles." Unusually large numbers of strangers and High-landers already crowded the streets of Edinburgh and unusually large numbers of armed and mounted men were crowding onto the ferry boats to Leith. It was obvious that "some Secret Designs [were] on foot" and Defoe did not deny that he was afraid. Later he learned that "the Design was to have Gone in a body to the . . . parliament and Demanded Answers to their petitions—They do not Deny that if the people had taken that Occasion to have Risen, they would not have been displeased." Queensberry fired back a proclamation against "Tumultuary and Irregular Meetings" and the crisis was passed without bloodshed (Defoe, *The History of the Union,* 1786, pp. 431, 435, 658; *Letters,* pp. 182, 187–88).

It was in this crisis that Defoe finished his poem and published it as a New Year's gift to the people of Scotland. It is, of course, a propaganda piece for the union, playing on such reliable motives as greed (664) and fear (419). Of the two epic similes in the poem, one (200–45) appeals to greed and the other (586–628) appeals to fear, and both look suspiciously like poetry (or poetic devices) prostituted to propagandistic purposes. Nor does Defoe flinch from the necessity of repetition in propaganda: "What I have to say," he wrote in the *Address to the Reader* of his poem, "is, [that] There are some Subjects, that need to be repeated more than once; particularly, in such a stubborn and *prejudiced Time* as this" (*A Scots Poem*, Edinburgh, 1707, sig. A2r). But *A Scots Poem* is a propaganda piece that is redeemed and humanized and made into something more than propaganda by Defoe's admiration and affection for "a Sober, Religious and Gallant Nation" (Defoe, *Letters*, p. 187). They were also, as he found, "a Refractory, Scrupulous and Positive people" and yet he had learned too great a respect for the Scots to write *The True-Born Scotsman* (ibid., p. 176; *An Essay, at Removing National Prejudices . . . Part III*, [Edinburgh] 1706, p. 3).

Caledonia, A Poem in Honour of Scotland, and the Scots Nation, which Defoe published about the beginning of December 1706 (Moore, p. 53), is pure panegyric, high-pitched and heroic. *A Scots Poem* is not satire, but low-pitched "History." The earlier poem completely dismissed the dark side of the scene: "Let others paint the Horrid-draught," Defoe conceded, "our Pen / Shall show the bright, and wish the rest unseen" (*Caledonia, A Poem*, Edinburgh, 1706, p. 48). *A Scots Poem* shows a good deal of "the rest," which makes it much more interesting. But it does not show all, as *The True-Born Englishman* does. It holds back, even in its attacks on "the true Pretending Heir" and on Scottish Jacobites, living and dead (textual notes 469, 505, 999–1000), because the purposes of the poem are conciliatory, not corrosive. No one knows to this day why the union treaty was ratified by the Scottish parliament (T. C. Smout, *Scottish Trade on the Eve of Union*, Edinburgh and London, Oliver & Boyd, 1963, pp. 259–61), but without trying to "set out" himself, Defoe could say that he had done his share "and with better success than [he] expected" (*Letters*, p. 186).

Defoe called his poem "a *Miscellany*" and defended its miscellaneous contents by appealing to the urgency of the occasion. "In the Compiling" these verses, he said, "I was curious to inject any thing, which might be suitable for the present Juncture." And he hinted that even the "DIGRESSIONS . . . Such as that on our gracious Sovereign [314–60], the D. of A[rgyll] [38–86], the Mobb [376–403], &c." are not "so Disconnected, as that the Coherence of them, may not be discerned with small pains" (*A Scots Poem*, Edinburgh, 1707, sig. A3).

Actually the poem is something more than "a Miscellany." It is a verse essay, a Renaissance genre with English antecedents reaching back to Ben Jonson. Nor is there "any thing" in the poem—including the farsighted vision of world commerce (140–76) which anticipates so much of *The Farther Adventures of Robinson Crusoe* (1719)—that was not suitable for the crisis of December 1706. And the "DIGRESSIONS" in fact are not adventitious, as the lines on the duke of Argyll will show: the poem begins with a Scots narrator saying, "Let's unite with England; let's be rich and famous (1–30); Scots don't lack courage (31–37); look at the duke of Argyll (38–86)." Argyll of course was the leader of the majority in parliament which was voting the union treaty into existence article by article.

It is true nonetheless that *A Scots Poem* lacks the energy and high spirits of *The True-Born Englishman* (1700) or *The Spanish Descent* (1702). Occasionally there is a kind of doggedness, almost a desperation, in the verse: "But to my Story, Let me now return" (604); "Upon this Head I have no more to say" (869). The poem begins with a Scots narrator speaking (255, inter alia). Then at line 538 Defoe brings back Britannia, who had provided panegyric relief in *The True-Born Englishman* (1700) and *The Mock Mourners* (1702). But this time Britannia seems to serve no real purpose and says nothing that the narrator could not say or has not already said. "Dispel old Feuds" (8), the narrator cries, and Britannia's echo comes in pat: "Forget past Feuds" (544). By line 660 Britannia has faded into Scotia, "a sinking Kingdom" (661) that can only be revived by trade with England. "Our Parliament" (856) is the Scots parliament, not Britannia's parliament, and in line 949 it is Scotia whom no one else will marry because of England's jealousy. Scotia then fades back into Britannia, who may be speaking at line 979 and certainly is speaking in lines 1043–1105. The Scots narrator then returns to speak the epilogue (1106–25), again for no apparent reason.

It is not surprising that Defoe was tired in December 1706. From the time he had received Harley's "Ordr to Dispatch" in September 1706, he had lived a "Life of constant Hurries" (Defoe, *Letters*, p. 125; *Review*, 20 August 1706). In order to be "Entirely Confided in" by scores of Scotsmen, he had to invent and maintain a constantly-shifting series of stories and disguises. "He was . . . a Spy amongst us, but not known to be such," said Sir John Clerk of Penicuik, "otherways the Mob of Edin[burgh] had pulled him to pieces" (*Memoirs*, Edinburgh, 1892, p. 64, quoted in Defoe, *Letters*, p. 158*n*.). Besides being repeatedly in physical danger (*Letters,* pp. 134–35, 181, 184), he was almost constantly worried about money: in November he heard from his wife that she and their seven children had been "10 dayes without Money" (ibid., p. 159). On Christmas eve he was saddened by the news of his father's death (ibid., p. 180). What Defoe accomplished under these adverse conditions is still almost incredible (pp. 210–12 above). And yet his greatest cause of anxiety was none of these. It was Harley's cruel and inhuman failure to tell Defoe what to do, or to approve or disapprove of what Defoe had done on his own initiative, or even to let Defoe know whether his reports had been received. "Nothing afflicts me so much as not to hear from you," he told Harley, "[n]or [to] have the least hint what Measures to take" (*Letters,* p. 183). A heart-breaking refrain runs through all of Defoe's letters to Harley from Edinburgh. Here is the burden for December 1706 when Defoe was finishing *A Scots Poem:* "I hope you will please to approv . . . of my work," "I Entreat your Directions," "I beseech you assist me with your thoughts," "I Earnestly Entreat your Approbation of what I am doing" (*Letters,* pp. 169, 171, 174, 182).

A few weeks after he published *A Scots Poem,* "haveing Dispised sleep, houres, and Rules" too long, Defoe finally collapsed. His health, "which No Distresses, Disasters, Jails or Mellancholly Could Ever hurt before," broke in Edinburgh after parliament had ratified the final clause of the union treaty (*Letters,* p. 200). And after *A Scots Poem* Defoe wrote no more serious verse. He continued to include doggerel verse in the *Review,* such as the lines, "Happy, because confirm'd above," in the preface to Volume VIII (27 March 1711), but when he wrote an exact counterpart of his earlier verse satires on a single session of parliament (*An Encomium upon a Parliament* [1699], *A New Satyr on the Parliament* [1701], etc.), he wrote in prose (*A History of the Last Session of the Present Parliament* [June 1718]). And in the *Review* for 29 July 1708 he announced that his *"Harps are long since hung on the Willows."* As a consequence, the authorship of the few poems written after this date that have been attributed to Defoe in the present volume was carefully concealed (pp. 463, 493 below).

When the treaty of union had finally been ratified and the last Scots parliament adjourned on 25 March 1707, the Scots nobles were "posting to London for places and Honours, Every Man full of his Own Merit, and affraid of Every One Near him" (Defoe, *Letters,* p. 213). Queensberry's triumphal entrance into London is described below (1055*n.*). But Defoe was left behind in Edinburgh, with no further orders and no permission to come home. Already he may have been thinking of himself as stranded on a desert island and already he had been thinking of "a Man that is safely landed on a firm and high Rock, out of Reach of the insulting Waves, by which he was in Danger of Shipwrack" (*An Essay at Removing National Prejudices . . . Part I,* Edinburgh, 1706, p. 22).

A Scots Poem evoked a broadside reply, *A Short Satyre on that Native of the Universe, The Albanian Animal, Author of the New-year's Gift, or Scots Poem upon the Union* ("Sir, 'mong your Gifts your Candour's not the least"), n.d. Although the author seems not to have known whom he was attacking, the NLS copy is inscribed, "This seemes to be on defoe."

A Scots Poem:
Or
A New-years Gift, from a Native of the Universe,
To His Fellow-Animals in Albania.

Idem velle atque idem nolle, ea demum firma amicitia est.

Now are our Noble *Representers* met;
And boldly in their august Places set.
They carefully do treat the grand Affairs,
That may conduce to *Britain*'s future Heirs.
While they our ills endeavour to remove,   5
And for our Good, the present time improve:
Let us forget our former bloody Wars,
Dispel old Feuds, and settle ancient Jars.
Let's henceforth have a closer *Monarchie*.
May all our Votes, and Minds, in one agree.   10
Let former Foes, now as firm Friends imbrace,
So that all curse, from *Albion*'s happy Race,
May be exil'd; while nothing more we hear,
But richest Blessings, to our *Patria* dear.
Let the damn'd Plague of *Poverty* be gone.   15
For want of *Ore*, let's not our Countrey moan;
Since at our Door there lies a golden Mine;
Imploy your *Nets* then, *Fishers*, hand your Line:
Let Idleness bind up your Arms no more,
But with your *Birlins*, Coast the vacant Shore;   20

Title. *Albania*: the mediaeval name for Scotland. James Ussher, archbishop of Armagh,
claimed that before the eleventh century no one "*Scotiae* appellatione *Albaniam* unquam
designaverit" (William Atwood, *The Superiority and Direct Dominion of the Imperial Crown of
England over the Crown and Kingdom of Scotland*, 1705, p. 13). By an instructive coincidence,
Defoe also knew of a Latin *gens*, "the *Albani*, [who] transmitted their Rights to the *Romans*,
and they became one Commonwealth" (*A Fourth Essay, at Removing National Prejudices*,
[Edinburgh], 1706, p. 42).
   Epigraph: "The fastest friendship is based on an identity of likes and dislikes" (Sallust,
Bellum Catilinae, XX, 4).
   1. *Now*: The last session of the Scottish parliament was convened on 3 October 1706. The
imagined narrator is a Scot.
   15. *Poverty*: Cf. 111n. below.
   17. *a golden Mine*: "Fishing [which] the *Dutch* . . . call their Golden-Mines" ([Defoe],
A Letter from Mr. Reason, To the High and Mighty Prince the Mob, [Edinburgh, n.d.], pp. 6–7).
   20. *Birlins*: "A large barge, or rowing boat, used by the chieftains of the Western Islands

While a fair Gale, does fill your windy Sails,
And Neighbour *Dutch,* his rich *Fish-trade* bewails,
Shake off all Fears, let th'expanded World know,
That in our Land the bravest Souls do grow.
And be your Fame, to both the *Indies* known: 25
No more be huddl'd in Oblivion.
SCOT, Ah a Name that Foreigners can't find
While mixt with *English* het'rogeneous kind,
But now by Trade, inform the distant *Poles,*
That *Britain* is the World of Gallant Souls.   30
    What makes Men famous, but their grand Exploits?
Why is't that *Scotland,* then as Sluggard sits?
While other Nations plant on foreign Soil:
Their bulky Ships, make *Neptun*'s Billows boil.
Sure, Courage is not banish'd from our *Isle:*   35
Witness *Ramillies, Menin,* and the *Dyle:*
Where conquer'd *Orkney,* and the brave *Argile.*

---

of Scotland" (*OED*).

23. *World:* "let th'expand-" is an anapest and "World" is disyllabic, as in line 941 below.

36. *Menin:* Menin, a town on the Lys in west Flanders nine miles north of Lille, was one of the fortified places to which the French army had retreated after Ramillies (p. 193 above). Since "the celebrated *French* Ingenier, Monsieur *de Vauban,* had bestow'd his utmost Skill" in fortifying it, the siege was undertaken partly to "add great Reputation to the Arms of the Allies" and partly to "secure their late Acquisitions" (Boyer, *Annals,* 1707, p. 175). The town was invested on 12 / 23 July 1706 and capitulated, after "great Slaughter," a month later (ibid., pp. 175–76).

Dyle: It was from strongpoints on the left bank of the Dyle, in central Brabant, that the French had marched into battle at Ramillies, and it was supposed that they would defend these positions after their defeat. But in "a tumultuous Council of War, by Flamboy-Light, in the Market-place" of Louvain, Villeroi and Maximilian Emanuel decided to withdraw. On 14 / 25 May therefore, two days after Ramillies, the entire allied army crossed the Dyle without incident (ibid., p. 85).

37. *Orkney:* George Hamilton, earl of Orkney (1666–1737), was a younger brother of the duke of Hamilton, and "much distinguished . . . as a Souldier" (Swift, *Prose, 5,* 261). He married his cousin, Elizabeth Villiers, *maitresse en titre* to William III, in November 1695 "and got a good Estate by her" (Macky, p. 162). In January 1696 he was created earl of Orkney in the Scottish peerage. He commanded the task force that pursued Villeroi to Louvain and took possession of the city on 13 / 24 May 1706. He also commanded the left wing of the besiegers of Menin (Boyer, *Annals,* 1707, pp. 175–76).

Argile: John Campbell, second duke of Argyll (1680–1743), was commissioned a colonel in the English army in April 1694 at the age of 14 and put in command of a regiment, the Argyllshire Highlanders, which his father had raised in 1689 (Dalton, *3,* 376; *4,* 44). Early in 1702 he married a London heiress, a niece of the infamous Sir Charles Duncombe (*POAS,* Yale, *6,* 261–63) and soon established himself in London society. Colley Cibber confessed that he had stolen most of the witty dialogue in *The Careless Husband* (1705) from "Observations I have made from your Grace's manner of Conversing." Upon his father's

Worthy Great Son, of glorious Forbears;
Thou, justly all their Ancient Honours wears,
With new additions, which intitle thee *Great;*   40
And do admit thee Access to the *State,*
As well as *Camp,* where thy great Valour shone.
It's there, thou hast prodigious brav'ry show'n,
So that thy greatest Foes can ne're deny,
Thou'rt hardly equal'd in good *Chivalry.*   45
Your youthful mind such grandeur does contain,
In you, your Ancestors do live again.
Great were your *Authors,* who did still direct
Their good Intentions, boldly to protect
The true Religion and our Liberties: 50
For which they did their *All,* oft sacrifice.
'Tis such as these, that do adorn our Land,
Who do from all, Love and Respect command.
Go on, brave *Duke,* and with a Loyal Will,
The Steps of thy *great Glorious Fathers,* fill.   55
May fragrant Laurels still adorn thy Brow:
And Heav'ns best Blessings on thee always flow.
So let th'amazing World, with wonder see,
That true *Scots* Valour's lodg'd, bold *Youth,* in thee.
Briskly triumph o'er Foreign Enemies;   60
Invidious silly *Jacobite* Foes, despise.
You can't expect, brave Youth, a better Fate,

---

death in September 1703 he was sworn of the Scottish privy council and given command
of the Scots troop of life guards. In April 1705 he was appointed lord high commissioner to
the Scottish parliament, through which he was able to steer an act to appoint commissioners
for a treaty of union with England (p. 210 above). His reward followed promptly in Novem-
ber 1705 when he was created earl of Greenwich in the English peerage. In April 1706 he
resigned his commissionership and took the field with Marlborough. His regiment suffered
heavy casualties at Ramillies and Argyll himself was reported killed at Menin, where he
"distinguish'd himself very much . . . and, after the Reduction of the Place, left the Camp,
in order to repair to *Scotland*" to support the union, serve on the parliamentary committee
for calculating the equivalent (to which Defoe was summoned "Every Day"), and fight a
drunken duel with John Lindsay, nineteenth earl of Crawford (Luttrell, *6,* 48; Boyer, *An-
nals,* 1707, pp. 175–76; Defoe, *The History of the Union,* 1786, p. 298; *Letters,* pp. 143, 177).

38. *glorious Forbears:* Argyll was "Great-Grandson to that Earl who was beheaded at the
Restoration; Grandson to that Earl who was beheaded by King *James;* and Son to that Earl
who came over with King *William* at the *Revolution,* and by him created Duke" (Macky, p.
189).

61. *Jacobite Foes:* Argyll's most prominent Jacobite foe was John Murray, duke of Atholl
(Defoe, *Letters,* p. 191).

Than those same *Heroes,* who, of old, were Great.
It's always been a *Hero*'s Destiny,
To have a *Momus,* for his Enemy.   65
Yea, even good *David* had his *Shimei,*
Nor was *Achilles* from *Thersites* free.
For this is certain, nothing great appears,
But straight, Spectators are surpriz'd with Fears:
Envy and *Malice,* to their Posts they fly,   70
Strive to depress their towring Enemy.
Such are your Foes, from God a Judgment sent,
To plague the Kingdom; for they'r ne're content.
Ingracious brood, ingrain'd from Nature have
Envy and *Pique,* still 'gainst the *Good* and *Brave.* 75
'Tis not a Vice, but 'tis the *Man* they hate,
His *Name,* his *Friends,* his *Family,* and *Estate.*
    Might I but everlasting Trophies raise,
To celebrat your *House*'s lasting Praise.
I wou'd not grudge, tho it should cost my Blood,   80
To make't for ever permanent and good.
Although I must ingenuously confess,
I fail in words, such brav'ry to express;
Yet the great Subject makes my Quill digress,
Still holding for an *Axiom* just and true: 85
Merit shou'd no where be depriv'd its due.
    Such *Grandees* ever will our Kingdom grace,
Who the blest Paths of our Forefathers trace.
    We need not far search back to ancient Story,
To shew our Feats, or sound our deathless Glory.   90
No, I my Song will to these Times confine:
Only, be pleas'd, look back on *Eighty Nine,*

65. *Momus:* the son of Night, in Greek mythology, whose role was to criticize, even the gods.
66. *Shimei:* a Benjamite who threw stones at King David and called him "a man of blood" (2 Samuel 16:5–8).
67. *Thersites:* Achilles' detractor in the *Iliad,* II, 212.
68. *nothing great appears:* Cf. Swift, *Prose, 1,* 242: "When a true Genius appears in the World, you may know him by this infallible Sign; that the Dunces are all in Confederacy against him."
92. *Eighty Nine:* The revolution in Scotland was more revolutionary than it was in England. James II had governed with "an arbitrary, despotic power" and the first thing the estates did when they convened in March 1689 was to resume their exclusive control of taxation. Then they re-established a Presbyterian Church of Scotland and offered the vacant

When *Scots* did for their *Libertys* appear,
Then bravely they the *Tyrants Yoke* did tear.
To this, their Valour I may justly join,   95
Which shone at *Steenkirk, Namur,* and the *Boin.*
But *Bleinheim, Bleinheim,* sounds our Glory's Praise,
Where Fame does *Scots* eternal Trophies raise.
Ramillies next is the triumphant Field,
Where *Gallick* red did dy the *British* Shield;   100
Victorious *Scot,* as Fire and Thunder flies
Through thick Battallions to the Honour'd Prize.
Pale Death, the poor *French Gardes du Corps* appals,

---

throne to William and Mary, subject to these conditions (*EHD,* pp. 635–38; Defoe, *An Essay at Removing National Prejudices . . . Part II,* 1706, p. 22). But "the Revolution was not established" in Scotland, as Defoe said, "without a civil war, which, though it was but short, came to a decisive battle" at Killiecrankie in July 1689 (*The History of the Union,* 1786, p. 224).

96. *Steenkirk, Namur, and the Boin:* The passage of the Boyne (*The Dyet of Poland,* 98*n.* above) was the battle that secured Ireland for William III. There were no Scottish regiments there because Jacobite guerrillas were still active in the Highlands, but Orkney commanded one of the famous Inniskilling regiments that led the attack (Dalton, *3,* 7, 155). Steenkerke, 20 miles southwest of Brussels, was the site of a near-victory in July 1692 which turned into a disastrous defeat. Six of the regiments engaged there were Scottish and the commanders of two of them, James Douglas, earl of Angus, and lieutenant general Hugh Mackay, were killed (Dalton, *3,* 221, 87, 162; Defoe, *Caledonia, A Poem,* Edinburgh, 1706, p. 37). The recapture of Namur, the "impregnable" fortress on the Meuse, in August 1695, was William's greatest victory on the continent. Two Scottish regiments particularly distinguished themselves in the final assault (Dalton, *3,* 377, 395; *4,* ix–x). Orkney commanded the royal fusiliers both at Steenkerke and Namur. He distinguished himself "most eminently . . . at the siege of Namur under his Majesty's own sight and observation" (ibid., *3,* 250, 155).

97. *Bleinheim:* There were four Scots regiments at Blenheim: the Royal Scots Greys, the Royal Scots Fusiliers, the Cameronians, and the Royal Scots regiment of foot. The last, commanded by Orkney, fought its way into the village of Blenheim after Lord Cutts had been repulsed five times. "I had the good luck not to be touched," Orkney observed, "only a horse shot under me" (*EHR 19* [April 1904], 308–10).

99. *Ramillies:* The four Scots regiments which fought at Blenheim were also present at Ramillies, but "The British troops had very little hand in the action." Since the Argyllshire Highlanders had been disbanded in 1697, Argyll commanded a brigade of foot in the Dutch army. "The Duke led the Scots brigade with a battalion of the Dutch guards, and was himself the second or third man who with his sword in his hand broke over the enemy's trenches, and chased them out of the village of Ramillies pushing on into their very lines of foot. He received three shot upon him but happily all blunt." Another Scot, major general Robert Murray, organized the rescue of Marlborough (HMC *Portland MSS.,* *4,* 309–10).

103. *French Gardes du Corps:* Although the *Gardes du Corps* dragoons were heavily engaged in the battle, Defoe is probably referring to an élite regiment of foot that was overrun by the Royal Scots Greys dragoons. "Lord John Hay [second son of John Hay, marquis of Tweedsdale] did great service in the pursuit and deserves great honour, for with his own regiment alone he broke in *à la hussarde* sword in hand and at a gallop upon two battalions [of the French regiment] *du Roi* and killed or took them all prisoners" (HMC *Portland MSS.,* *4,* 311).

To each *Scots* Lance, a *French-man* Victim falls;
They tread their Corpses, and stoutly banish Fear;   105
In *Gallick* Blood, they bury each a Spear.
For that great day, they'll 'ternal Honour bear;
And never never fading Laurels wear.
    Go on, brave *Scot;* exert your vigour still,
And with your Acts, Fame's endless Records fill.   110
    Ah Poverty's the damn'd Impediment,
Marrs our Designs, our Glory, and content!
Oh *Poverty* do's th'greatest Souls oppress!
Here's one sad Source of *Caledons* distress;
A *Curse,* great hind'rance to our Happiness: 115
Yet there's not wanting, ev'n to this Disease,
A *Cure,* may bring us never failing Ease.
And that's t'obtain, from our rich Neighbour State,
Union, on terms Good, Equal, Just, and Great:
Which may revive our dying, dwindling Trade,   120
Whereby, we may be Rich and Happy made;
So live in Peace and Liberty, at home:
And who dares choose, thro' the broad Earth to roam,
Shall sail safe under *British* Ships of War;
Then no damn'd *Algerine* or *Corsaire* dare   125
Attempt our Persons, or assault our Goods.
With full blown Sails, we'll pierce the yielding Floods,
While *Neptune,* with his *Nereids,* round shall stand,
Paying Obeisance, with low Cap in hand.
The *Britons* shall be Masters of the Sea;   130
While Caitiff foes, as *Jove's* quick lightning flie.

111. *Poverty:* William Greg reported to Harley in June 1705 that poverty was "an epidemical distemper" in Scotland (HMC *Portland MSS.,* 4, 194). Crop failures and famine in 1695–98 had left an estimated "200000 People begging from door to door" (T. C. Smout, *Scottish Trade on the Eve of Union,* Edinburgh and London, Oliver & Boyd, 1963, pp. 246–49; Andrew Fletcher, *Two Discourses concerning the Affairs of Scotland,* Edinburgh 1698, p. ²24).

120. *dwindling Trade:* Some statistics are supplied in Smout, *Scottish Trade on the Eve of Union,* 1963, p. 256. "Virtually the whole period from the Revolution to the Union of Parliaments," Smout says, "was one of economic stagnation punctuated by crisis and decline." A financial crisis in 1704, in which the Bank of Scotland failed, brought the country close to bankruptcy.

125. *Corsaire:* The corsairs constituted a kind of Moslem trade guild, based in Algiers, which combined a holy war against Christianity with piracy and slave trading. The English maintained a consul there but diplomacy was not always effective. In 1683 when the French fleet shelled Algiers, the corsairs fought back by blowing the French consul from a cannon. Defoe estimated that it would cost the royal navy £1,300,000 a year "for the Defence of [Scottish] Trade" (*A Fourth Essay, at Removing National Prejudices,* [Edinburgh], 1706, p. 40).

The Immense *Ocean* shall be at Command,
To guard at Home, from Enemies, our Land.
Our Keels abroad, shall cut the yielding Main;
At Sea give Laws, to *Holland, France,* and *Spain.*   135
Our Naval Force conveys to distant Shores,
Our Native Products; and Rich Foreign Stores,
In the same *British* Bottoms, back are brought.
From outmost Limits, our Alliance's sought.

    Then, sit no more, as dreaming Fools at home: 140
But thro' th'extended World, with Boldness roam.
Surround the *Globe,* and cross the *Indian* Seas.
While *Home-Souls,* in their Northern Climate freeze,
I'd gladly breath my Air, on Foreign Shores:
Trade with rude *Indian* and the Sun-burnt *Mores.*   145
I'd speak *Chinese,* I'd prattle *African,*
And briskly cross the first *Meridian.*
I'd pass the *Line,* and turn the *Cap* about.
I'd rove, and sail th'Earth's greatest *Circle* out.
I'd fearless, venture to the *Darien* Coast;   150
Strive to retrive the former Bless we lost.
Yea, I wou'd view *Terra incognita*
And climb the Mountains of *America.*
I'd veer my Course, next, for our *Antipods,*

138. *British Bottoms:* The Navigation Act of 1660 provided that "no goods or commodities whatsoever shall be imported into or exported out of any lands, islands, plantations or territories to his Majesty belonging . . . but in such ships or vessels as do truly and without fraud belong only to the people of England or Ireland, [or] dominion of Wales" (*EHD,* p. 533).

148. *Cap:* Cape Horn.

149. *sail . . . Circle:* Great circle sailing is navigation along the arc of a great circle of the earth, i.e. a circle whose plane passes through the center of the earth (*OED,* s.v. circle, *sb.*).

150. *the Darien Coast:* Darien, in the isthmus of Panama, was the site of a settlement called Caledonia Bay, set up by the Company of Scotland Trading to Africa and the Indies, under a charter from the Scottish parliament. The first expedition sailed in 1698. A support party was sent in 1699 but in March 1700 the settlement was abandoned, "overwhelmed by famine, fever, Spanish attack, and the English refusal to lend succour even when its plight became desperate" (T.C. Smout, *Scottish Trade on the Eve of Union,* 1963, p. 252). "People there are like fools, on the subject of their colony of Darien," William III told Heinsius, and a recent historian concludes that the failure of the colony induced "a mood of political intransigence" in the Scots (Grimblot, *2,* 415; William Ferguson, *Scotland 1689 to the Present,* Edinburgh and London, Oliver & Boyd, 1968, p. 30).

151. *to retrive:* The narrator's challenge is not very practical, for article 15 of the treaty of union provided that the Company of Scotland "be Dissolved and Cease."

I'd hunt for *Monkey,* in the *Indian* Woods.   155
I'd with the *Mousons,* fairly range *Japan.*
And coast the Shores of Rich *Nouvelle Espagne.*
I'd then *entour* the *South* and *Arctick* Poles.
I'd Sail, where the cold *Northern* Ocean rolls;
And look *North-East,* to find a Passage out,   160
To *Chin',* *East Inds;* so save our tour about
Scorch't *Africk* and the *Cap Bonne Esperance;*
Towards *New Holland,* I'd my rout advance;
And know who harrows that vast *Continent,*
Where scarce e're European has been sent.   165
The greatest Dangers, n'ere shou'd make me faint.
My Course, I'd to *New SCOTLAND* then direct.
West Indian trophies should adorn my deck.
Here's a large Land, of late it was our own:
Tho' now, from *Scot,* to fickle *France,* it's gone.   170
What hinders *BRITAIN,* Colonies to Plant,
On that Rich Soil where none but *Natives* haunt,
We'll gain a Country, that's by few possest:

156. *Mousons:* monsoons. "Certain Winds which blow, in the *Indian* and *Pacifick* Oceans, &c. from one Point; at such Seasons of the Year, they sometimes continue for six Months altogether in the same Quarter, &c." (*A Scots Poem,* Edinburgh, 1707, p. 5).

160. *North-East . . . Passage:* The English quest for a northeast passage by sea to India and China began in 1525 (when Paolo Centurione proposed an expedition to Henry VIII) and was institutionalized with the chartering of the Muscovy Company in 1555.

163. *New Holland:* the name that Dutch navigators gave to Australia, the west coast of which they began to chart early in the seventeenth century.

165. *scarce e're European:* One of the few Europeans who had set foot in Australia was William Dampier. His first visit, during a buccaneering expedition, was in January–March 1688 and is described in *A New Voyage Round the World* (1697). His second, in July–September 1699, was financed by the English admiralty and is described in *Voyage to New Holland* (1703). It is likely that Defoe read both of these works before writing *The Life and Strange Surprising Adventures of Robinson Crusoe* (1719).

167. *New SCOTLAND:* Nova Scotia, or Acadie as the French called it, was disputed between Scotland and France throughout the seventeenth century. The French first settled there in 1604 but English settlers from Virginia drove them out in 1613. Then the Scots colonized it after James I had granted the entire peninsula to Sir William Alexander in 1621. Although the French regained possession a few years later, Cromwell reasserted English claims in 1654. Nova Scotia was ceded to the French by the treaty of Breda in 1667 and remained in their hands until 1713 when it was divided between France and Britain by the treaty of Utrecht. It did not become entirely a British possession until 1763.

168. *West Indian:* Defoe uses "West Indian" to mean "any place in the New World," not just "the *Caribee* Islands."

172. *that Rich Soil:* "To the *S.W.* of [Nova Scotia], and *Canada,* is a large Continent inhabited by Savages, &c." (*A Scots Poem,* Edinburgh 1707, p. 5).

We sha'nt want Trade, nor of fine Furs the best.
There, may we Plant a *New BRITANNIA:*   175
And rear a Kingdom, near *French CANADA.*
Then shall we have occasion to fulfill
Our blessed *Saviour*'s gracious Latter-Will;
Sent to far *Nations,* shal the Gospel be,
Souls to relieve, from *Satan*'s Tyranny;   180
And free dull *Indians,* from *Diabolism;*
Then in one Church initiate by Baptism.
To *Cloven-foot* they's no more grossly pray,
No more *Baw-waws,* nor *Ave Daemons* say.
This will exalt's, this will extol our Praise,   185
'Bove all, what can Rich Civil Trophies raise.
Let's then Possess that unknown Continent,
Where *BRITTONS* shal the largest Settlement
Injoy, in that immense extent of Land,
While All about, with Hairs erected stand   190
Amaz'd, to see from *Arctick* Climes to come,
So bold a Nation, and so far from home.
Surpriz'd, to know from *Frigid* Climats Sail,
So brave a People; whom an *Eastern* Gale
Do's Blow from *Europe,* for their *Indian* Coast;   195
While foes, as Snow before the winds, are lost.
    We need but some Grand Interprize begin:
Heaven will favour, sure, our good design.
Thereby will shine *Scots* Glory and their Worth;
As *Madam Moon,* who suddenly breaks forth,   200
From under black and Interposing Clouds,
Which just were ready to dissolve in Floods,
On Melancholly and dark *Earth,* below,
Which silent waits its near impending wo.
Straight, in a moment they're disperst and gone,   205

178. *Saviour's . . . Latter-Will:* "Go ye therefore, and teach all nations, baptizing them in the name of the Father, and of the Son, and of the Holy Ghost" (Matthew 28:19).

180. *to relieve, from Satan's Tyranny:* In a different context Defoe complained that the conversion of thousands of Indians to Catholicism only "made worse Devils than they were before" (*POAS,* Yale, *6,* 414).

184. *Baw-waws:* "A barbarous word [not found in the *OED*] which the Heathens in the North part of *America* repeat several times in the Worship of their Idols" (*A Scots Poem,* Edinburgh, 1707, p. 6).

Ave Daemons: a Defovian pun; "This alludes to the Papists *Ave-Maria*'s" (ibid.).

The Air grows fair, and bright our *Horizon*.
Or as the *Sun* doth send his Morning Light,
After a dark and tedious, irksom night.
Then, straight, the Vapours, which an hour before
Obscur'd our Air, now yield to bright *Aurora*. 210
His *Eastern* Rays, the Darkness do's dispel;
Night-rambling Devils skulk to Native Hell.
So Heav'ns and Skie do grow Serene and Clear,
And blessed Light do's reach our *Atmosphere*.
The World of *Beings* their homage just they pay 215
To the fair *King*, and Sovereign of the Day:
He's welcom'd by th'Obedient *Animals*:
And honour'd by the Tribe of *Rationals*.
The verdant *Heros*, their early Flow'rs do spread;
While taller *Plants*, their leaves abroad they shed. 220
The *Shrubs* in haste raise up their drouping heads.
His heat refreshes th' lower *Grass* and *Weeds*.
The *Bestial* also overspread the Plain,
While Pipe and Mirth diverts the Jolly Swain.
Birds, in shrill Notes, his happy welcome sing: 225
Their *Sonnets*, cause th'*Elastick* Air to ring.
Then are alarm'd the Savage *Brutes* of Prey,
Thro' Hills and Woods, in quest of food, they stray.
Next, the most Noble and Chief *Animal*,
Man, do's before his *Maker* daily fall. 230
Thanks for Good *Phoebus*, Guardian of the Day,
Who drives the gloomy, surly Night away.
    Just such a happy Change, our Nation finds:
If we Unite, our once Contented Minds,
With our rich Neighbour: then, doth dawn the day, 235
Which drives all Feuds and enmities away.
Let base Revenge and Damn'd Envy be gone,

226. *th'Elastick Air: OED* cites Richard Bentley's 1692 Boyle lectures: "The Air is now
certainly known to consist of elastic or springy Particles."

235. *rich Neighbour:* In order to compute the equivalent (691*n.* below) it had been neces-
sary to estimate the proportional revenue of the two kingdoms. It was agreed to be more than
40–1: £2,000,000 to £48,000 (*Articles of the Treaty of Union*, Edinburgh, [1706], pp. 6–7).

236. *Feuds and enmities:* Concerning the cost in human suffering of "Divisions" between
England and Scotland, Defoe is more eloquent in his prose: "the Destruction of so many
hundred thousand brave stout Fellows . . . the *Cries* of the Widows and Mothers . . .
Fields *over run* . . . Barns and Houses *plunder'd and burnt*" (*An Essay at Removing National Pre-
judices* . . . Part I, Edinburgh, 1706, pp. 15, 17).

And all our Int'rests be conjoyn'd in one.
No *Mastiff Devil* can our good withstand,
If as true Friends, we do join hand to hand,   240
That so no more of jealousies be known;
And in our Isle, no more Dissention sown,
And each now, more than Self, his Country mind.
So henceforth, we that Blessedness shall find,
Which, n'ere before, we luckily cou'd reach.   245
No *Wonder*. Since so damnable a breach,
Did two brave *Neighbours* fatally divide;
What cou'd but War and Poverty betide?
Yet there's no State, in the vast *Universe,*
Might more enjoy of bless or happiness,   250
Than we, the *Natives* of this admir'd Isle:
If we would banish prejudice and guile,
And let no more, our foolish ears be stunn'd,
With lies, mistakes, and fears, that have no ground.
　　'Tis true, oft *England* hath us roughly us'd,   255
And has our ruine and destruction chus'd;
Stop, *Envy*, stop, *Scotland* is guilty too;
How oft did she her Warlike hands imbrue
In *English* Blood? We can't Excuse pretend.
But let's no more 'bout former Strifes contend: 260
For if we Search, our Histories can tell,
Both have resisted one another *Well.*
　　But if we'd learn the true Cause of our ill;
What did, so oft, our Native Country fill,
With such Prodigious and unheard of wo's: 265
We can't fail know, where the foul fountain flows.
We need but over Water cast a glance;
And then we'l find th'*Originals* in *France;*
Well might they us, some empty honours give;
While, in mean time, more poor at home we live,   270
Where our Religion, Liberties and Laws,
Were still in danger, to support their cause.
'Tis to defending their long unjust Wars,
We may impute our Ancient *British* Jarrs.
Let's no more be with Names and Shadows bull'd,   275
And from our Bless, as Fops and *Boobies* gull'd.

239. *Mastiff Devil:* a big-ferocious-dog-devil, like Faust's.

But let us all in joint Concern unite;
And with true Courage and good Conduct meet
T'oppose the *Gallick* Tyrants Proud Designs;
For him no Oath nor solemn Treaty binds.   280
This *Leviathan* vastly far exceeds
The Bloody Actions and tremenduous Deeds,
Of the execrable *Dioclesian,*
Of Monster *Nero* or *Domitian.*

 Heav'ns, stand amaz'd, when *Louis's* Name ye hear;   285
And *Earth,* be clade with th'outmost *Pannick* Fear,
And let the swelling Fountains of the Deep,
Gush forth in Floods and Deluges, to weep
The unparallel'd, sad Desolation,
Caus'd by his proud, unjust Ambition.   290
Hell, stand agast, and quake ye *Daemons* all!
Your *Patron* slides, and terrible's his Fall!

 If we please search our Ancient Records,
There we find Ills can't be express'd in words;
Whereby both Nations have been ruined;   295
Two Warlike Kingdoms, near extinguished.
But let's not speak of ancient *British* Strifes.
These cost, of old, too many Gallant Lives.
Let be forgot their *Edwards* and our *James,*
And let our *Forth* incorporate with *Thames.*   300
Let *Hell, Rome, France,* and *Catholicks* unite:
And let damn'd Legions, their Conjunction greet;
But us, our Minds, with *British* Brav'ry join.
On *Tiber* plant our Banners, and the *Seine.*
So may our *Arms* make *France* and *Rome* to know,   305

280. *no . . . Treaty binds:* Cf. pp. 186–87 above.

281. *Leviathan:* "leviathan that crooked serpent" (Isaiah 27:1). Defoe's claim that Louis XIV was responsible for the deaths of more Christians than the worst of the Roman emperors is undoubtedly justifiable.

283. *Dioclesian:* Gaius Aurelius Valerius Diocletianus (245–313) was the Roman emperor (284–305) who instituted price control and systematic persecution of Christians.

284. *Nero:* Nero Claudius Caesar Drusus (A.D. 37–68), the last of the dynasty of Augustus and Seneca's most promising pupil, became Roman emperor in 54. Although he executed only a few Christians to appease the gods after the fire of Rome (A.D. 64), he was frequently identified in Christian hagiography as the true Antichrist.

Domitian: Titus Flavius Domitianus (A.D. 51–96) became Roman emperor in A.D. 81. He persecuted Christians only as part of far-reaching moral and religious reforms which he effected. He was certifiably insane during the last years of his life.

286. *clade:* clothed, a Scotticism (*SND,* s.v. cleed).

That *Britain* is a Bold and Daring Foe.
What shou'd we fear, since th'Island does produce
Brave *Generals,* who may in time conduce
To make our *Thistle* o'erspread their *Flower de Luce.*
Yes, yet remain the Noble Famous *Names*   310
Of *Stuarts, Campbells, Hamiltons,* and *Grahames.*
Our Land, some *Bruce* or *Wallace* yet contains:
And *Douglas*'s Blood yet flows in *Scottish* Veins.
Take Courage, *Scot,* for Heav'ns just be prais'd,
Upon our Throne, a *Glorious Queen* is rais'd: 315
In a blest time, our *ANN* did mount the Throne,
Fair was that day, in *Britains* Horizon.
How mildly was her happy Reign begun?
And since the mighty Valiant Faits she's done!
Her *En'mies* fear, and *Subjects* her adore,   320
Owning, that never on our Throne before
Was *Monarch* of more rare transcendant Worth,
Since Warlike *Scot* inhabited the *North.*
Our Scepter's justly lodged in her hands.
Thrice Happy *Subjects,* whom *Great ANN* Commands.   325

309. *Thistle:* The Order of the Thistle was founded by James II in 1687 and dedicated to
St. Andrew. It fell into abeyance at the revolution, but was revived by Queen Anne in 1703.
   311. In his famous speech of 2 November 1706 before the Scottish parliament Belhaven
had asked, "where are the Names of the chief Men, of the noble Families of *Stewarts, Hamiltons,
Grahams, Campbels, Gordons, Johnstons, Homes, Murrays, Kers,* &c? . . . They have certainly all
been extinguish'd, and now we are Slaves for ever" (*The Lord Beilhaven's Speech in the Scotch
Parliament, Saturday the Second of November,* 1706, p. 14). Defoe answers Belhaven by referring
to six of these ancient families which were "unextinguished," and voting for the union (*The
History of the Union,* 1786, pp. 662–67). There were five Stewarts (James, earl of Galloway;
Sir James of Coltness, lord advocate of Scotland; and three Stewarts of the second estate),
nine Campbells (John, duke of Argyll; his younger brother Archibald, earl of Ilay; and two
of his uncles, John Campbell of Mamore and Charles Campbell; Hugh, earl of Loudon;
Alexander, earl of Marchmont; Sir James Campbell of Auchinbreck, fifth baronet; Sir James
Campbell of Ardkinglass, and Daniel Campbell), one Hamilton (Thomas, earl of Hadding-
ton), and two Grahams (James, marquis of Montrose, and "Head of the H[anoveria]n, Re-
publican, Whiggish Faction in *Scotland*" [Lockhart, p. 147], and Mungo Graeme of Gorthy).
   312. *Bruce:* There were two Bruces who voted for the union: John Bruce of Kinross and
Patrick Bruce of Bunzoin.
      Wallace: There were no Wallaces in the union parliament (Joseph Foster, *Members of
Parliament, Scotland,* London and Aylesbury, 1882, pp. 349–50).
   313. *Douglas:* There were seven Douglases who supported the union: James, duke of
Queensberry, lord high commissioner to the Scottish parliament, and his cousin, William
Douglas of Dornock; James, earl of Morton, and his brother, Robert Douglas; Archibald,
earl of Forfar; Alexander Douglas of Egilshay, and Archibald Douglas of Cavers.
   319. *Faits:* feats, deeds. The spelling is an archaism (*OED*), not a Scotticism.

How has she humbl'd proud insulting *France*,
When her bright *Arms*, in *Flanders* did advance.
Her *Victories* have taught the haughty *Man*,
That Greatest *Kings* can't parallel *Our ANN*,
That none's more Glorious Sovereign than *ANN*.   330
She's show'n the *French* the weakness of their God:
She's the just Scourge of *Tyrants*, and the Rod
Of Pride and Vice, Support of Liberty,
Emblem of Vertue and Excellency.
Fame's Trumpet shall her lasting Glory sound,   335
While *Sea* do's *Earth*, or *Air* our *Globe* surround.
When future Ages shall her *Annals* hear,
In Extasie they'll cry, *A Wonder's here!*
    But my rude Lines can ne're imbalm her Name,
Her Glorious Deeds will eternize the same,   340
Her Feats shall sound her everlasting Fame.
    Let new *French* Garlands still adorn her Head;
And Bravest *Generals* her *Armies* lead.
May *Heav'n* best Blessings on our *ANN* bestow,
And may her *Name* and *Glory* daily grow.   345
Let ne're my Eyes behold that Fatal day,
When her blest Soul, to *Heav'n* wings away.
But let her Days renew as Eagle's Strength;
And may her Years be blest with endless Length;
May of her Life, each *Minut* be an *Hour*,   350
Each *Hour a Moon*, and ev'ry *Moon a Year*.
But if she must her *Government* lay down,
May She next wear an *Everlasting Crown*.
May both the *Indies* fragrant *Spices* burn,
With *Perfumes* to decore her sacred *Urn*.   355
And if we lose her, my outmost Wish is this,
Kind Heav'n with such as ANN *us always Bless!*
    We praise thee GOD! a *Woman* rules our State,

---

331. *their God:* Louis XIV. "The taking down the Image of our *Saviour,* and setting up the
French King's . . . in its Room, occasion'd this Distich, "Abstulit hinc *Jesum,* posuitq;
insignia Regis / Impia Gens alium non habet illa *Deum*" [He took down Jesus and put this
up. These people have no other god than this impious effigy] (*A Scots Poem,* Edinburgh,
1707, p. 10).
337–38. Cf. *POAS,* Yale, *6,* 394.
355. *decore:* decorate, ornament; a Scotticism (*SND*).
357. *such as ANN:* i.e. Sophie, dowager electress of Hanover.

It's the *Fair Sex* has made our *Island* great.
Women to it have *Thrice* been fortunate.   360
     Let's therefore, when our *Good Queen* do's invite
Her *Subjects* Hearts, sincerely to unite,
Obey her Good and Laudable desire,
While all the Nations round about admire;
They stand with Souls and Eyes impatient,   365
Waiting the great and singular Event.
Here's a Concern of greatest Importance,
A Grand Affair of Mighty Consequence;
A Business, did but our Fathers know,
Their *Sons* had Rich and Happy been e're now.   370
Shall we be Blind to our own Happiness?
And strengthen the Hands of all our Enemies?
No.
Think what good *Omen* to the Isle portends.
Ye'll doubtless then unite for weighty Ends.   375
And an ill-natur'd Cock-brain'd *Mob* despise,
Which always in the Face of Judgment flys;
Whose Strongest Cavil's, *Ah the Gracious Crown!*
GOD save them that and Ale, the rest goes down.
Tho (Heav'n be bless'd) they nothing have to lose,   380

360. *Thrice:* presumably Elizabeth, Mary (William's queen), and Anne.

361. *invite:* Anne twice had invited parliament to complete the "great Work" of uniting the two kingdoms (*LJ, 17,* 68; *18,* 7).

369. *Business:* trisyllabic.

372. *strengthen the Hands:* "-then the Hands" is a rare anapestic substitution.

376. *Cock-brain'd Mob:* The Edinburgh mob—"and Certainly a scots Rabble is the worst of its kind"—began to demonstrate against the union even before the debates began. "The Jacobites have wound them up," Defoe said. On the night of 23 October 1706 he heard one of them say, "There was One of the English Dogs," and later that night, before the troops were raised, he had a "great stone thrown at him, for but looking out of a window . . . and the windows below him broken by mistake" (Defoe, *Letters*, pp. 133–36, 202; *The History of the Union*, 1786, pp. 238, 239).

378. *the . . . Crown:* The crown and other regalia of the kings of Scotland were kept in Edinburgh Castle and displayed in the Parliament House during session. The mob was encouraged to fear that the crown might be taken to London. "And the boys and mob were invited by a great person, in a melancholy tone, to go in and see the ancient crown of Scotland, for that it would soon be carried away, and they might never see it any more" (Defoe, *Letters*, p. 137; *The History of the Union*, 1786, p. 227).

379. *Ale:* England had one excise tax for strong beer and a lower one for small beer. The rabble were afraid that their favorite drink, twopenny ale, would be taxed at the higher rate. "The people," Defoe explained, "are Uneasy and affraid to be left to the Mercy of the Excise Office to Construe the Law Upon them. And Indeed the Clamour of the people would be Intollerable should the strong beer Duty be Demanded on their Ale" (*Letters,* p. 157).

Yet they Stout they will conquer all our Foes.
These our Wise *Pilots* and brave *Guardians* are.
This, the poor Wretch, that fain would *Civil* War;
Whose pond'rous Thoughts, from Reason are as far,
As *Bless* is from the wretched *Camisar*,   385
Or *Worlds Center* from the *Polar Star*.
    A Mob's a Creature, never thinks, but raves,
Hodge Podge of Women, Children, Fools, and Knaves.
A Malecontent, deluded Animal.
Without Grimace, within all Spleen *and* Gall.   390
In fine, *A Chaos of* Plebeian *Skulls*,
Fill'd with some Brute's wild transmigrated Souls,
Whose daily Acts do Stigmatize them Fools.
    Yet some 'mongst th'*Rabble* seek to rear a Name,
And covet they shou'd Eternize their Fame.   395
Fame's but an airy sound, an empty Noise,
That owes its *Essence* to the vulgar Voice.
It does depend upon the giddy *Mob*,
Who praise to day, but straight to Morrow rob
Him, who was once the Subject of their Song,   400
Of a good Name, by their defaming Tongue.
What serves the *Praises of a Rascal Throng?*
Since, for Sir Devil, they'd not want a Song.
    We long have Happiness and Riches sought,
While now our *State*, to Gates of *Nothing's* brought;   405
Some would have this, and others some would that;

381. *Stout:* stubbornly persist. The word was obsolete or obsolescent in 1707 (*OED*).

385. *Camisar:* The Camisars were Protestant peasants of the Cévennes plateau in the south of France whose particular form of religious enthusiasm was the prophetic malady. They resisted Louis XIV's policy of enforced conversion to Catholicism and in July 1702 resorted to terrorism and guerrilla warfare. Their success encouraged France's enemies to consider means of supporting them (*Review*, 22 April 1704), but by January 1705 their fighting force had been exterminated and 466 of their villages burned. Some of them escaped to London where their trance-state feats continued to attract attention and to encourage local imitators (Hearne, *2, 243*). They were called French Prophets and despite their claim to the benefits which the Toleration Act extended to other dissenters (Luttrell, *6, 231*), some of them were eventually condemned to the pillory (Voltaire, *Le Siècle de Louis le Grand,* 2 vols., Berlin, 1751, *2, 258*). On 8 March 1715 Louis could proclaim the entire extinction of heresy in France.

394–403. This warning of the fickleness of the mob was directed to the duke of Hamilton, whom Defoe called "their Patron." Hamilton was everywhere "Huzza'd and followed . . . [in] his coach" by a mob shouting "God bless his Grace for standing up against the Union, . . . and the like" (Defoe, *Letters*, pp. 133, 185; *The History of the Union,* 1786, p. 236).

405. See 120*n.* above.

But neither *Belzebub* nor themselves know what.
Pray, Speak, what wou'd ye? Is't Castles in the Air?
Yea, sure no *Neighbour* shou'd enslave you there;
Nor secret Foe, shou'd e're subvert you dare.   410
Or wou'd ye build Plantations in the *Moon*?
Yes, there you'd be above a *Monarch*'s Frown.
Only but mind you take the Wing too soon.
     What Noise and Bustle's this we daily hear;
Medley of Nonsense does perplex my Ear.   415
Good Lord! What means't? *Is't th'Earths Conflagration?*
Or is the *World* to suffer *Annihilation?*
Some Mighty *Change* does certainly draw near,
That makes so many be possest with Fear.
Some rail and banter, and others some behold   420
That what no *Man* or *Devil* can unfold.
Some talk of *Visions,* some are pleas'd with *Dreams,*
While *Fustian Stuff* ejaculats in Streams.
Some cry the *Church,* and other some the *State!*
As if their Ruine were predestinate.   425
Heav'ns, what means this wondrous *Met'morphose!*
That these, who always were the *Churches Foes,*
Shou'd now its only boldest *Patrons* be.
If these our *Friends, Lord,* where's our *Enemie?*
Such as did former absolute Reigns adore,   430

419. *Fear:* "People [in Edinburgh] went up and down wandering and amazed, expecting every day strange events; afraid of peace, and afraid of war" (*The History of the Union,* 1786, p. 242).

422. *Visions:* See *The Vision,* above.

427–28. *the Churches Foes . . . its . . . Patrons:* "Twas Very odd and Diverting," Defoe said, "to find these Gentlemen Vote that the Act [for security of the church, 12 November 1706, p. 216 above] was not a Security sufficient for the Church, and Especially Sir Alexa Bruce Now E[arl] of Kincar[di]n formerly Expelld the house for sayeing the presbyterian Church was Inconsistent with Monarchy" (Defoe, *Letters,* p. 149). "This Gentleman [Kincardine] hath been *in* and *out* of the *Administration* all the Three Reigns of King *Charles,* King *James,* and King *William*" (Macky, p. 253).

429. proverbial (Tilley, F739).

430–36. These lines refer to old families, like the Douglases, Murrays, Flemings, long identified with the court, whose present representatives had gone over to the Country party to oppose the union. William Douglas, first duke of Hamilton (1634–94), served James II as a privy councillor, commissioner of the Scottish treasury, and an extraordinary lord of session, but both his sons, James, second duke of Hamilton, and Charles, earl of Selkirk, became leaders of the "Patriots" opposed to the union. John Murray, first marquess of Atholl (1631–1703), had been lord privy seal for Scotland (1672–89), an extraordinary lord of session (1673–89), and a knight companion of the Thistle (May 1687), but he played "a trimming

When Tools of *Court,* first swore and then forswore,
And th'puissent GOD then serv'd was *Louis d'Or.*
Now some of these, our Greatest Patriots are;
Now their good Heirs, with boldness (mostly) dare
Pretend, with true *Scots* Courage, up to stand,   435
For the blest Interests of our Sinking Land.
While others who our *Patriots* were before,
They're Ridicul'd, and are Caress'd no more.
O wondrous Change! Now's come that happy day,
When Silly *Children,* with the *Asp* dare play,   440
Lyon with the *Calf,* and *Leopard* with the *Kid;*
And *Reinard* does to *Lamb,* good morrow bid.
Thrice Happy *Church!* I do Congratulate
Thy long desir'd, but now attain'd to, Fate.
For *Prelat*'s now with *Presbyter* Conjoin'd;   445
And *Jack* and *Priest* are turn'd the *Clergy's* friend.
Bless me! Are who cried *Persecute* of old,
Affraid, the *Church's* Ruine to behold?

---

and shuffling part" (GEC, *1,* 316) in the revolution and Macaulay called him "the falsest, the most fickle, the most pusillanimous of mankind." His eldest son, John Murray, second marquess of Atholl, became a violent Jacobite when he was dismissed as lord privy seal in October 1704. He opposed the union and "much affected Popularity" (Lockhart, pp. 64, 66; Macky, p. 184; Defoe, *Letters,* p. 189). John Fleming, earl of Wigton (c. 1673–1744), was sent to France for a Catholic education and remained at St. Germain. Although he was an officer in the service of James II in 1692 (HMC *Stuart MSS., 1,* 74), he returned to Edinburgh, swore the oaths of allegiance to Anne, and voted against every article of the treaty of union (GEC, *12,* ii, 640).

432. *Louis d'Or:* p. 498 below.

437. *others:* like Queensberry (1050n. below), who had been a "Patriot," i.e. member of the opposition, as recently as the session of 1704, and now as lord high commissioner and leader of the Court party, was suffering "all the insults, reproaches, and indignities" of the Edinburgh mob, or Sir Patrick Johnson, "late Ld Provost [mayor of Edinburgh] and till then the peoples Darling, [who] was assaulted in his House by the Rabble" (Defoe, *The History of the Union,* 1786, p. 236; *Letters,* p. 185).

440. *Children:* "And the sucking child shall play on the hole of the asp" (Isaiah 11:8).

441. *Lyon:* "The wolf also shall dwell with the lamb, and the leopard shall lie down with the kid; and the calf and the young lion" (Isaiah 11:6).

445. *Conjoin'd:* "that monstrous conjunction of opposite and discording parties [against the union, that] brought the Jacobites to cry out for the succession [and] the episcopal people to want security for the Presbyterian church." "It was the most monstrous sight in the world," Defoe said, "to see the Jacobite and the Presbyterian, the persecuting prelatic Nonjuror and the Cameronian; the Papist and the reformed Protestant, parle together, join interest, and concert measures together" (*The History of the Union,* 1786, pp. 220, 229). Cf. *The Vision,* 37–45.

447–48. The meaning may be, "Are you who once resisted persecution now afraid to recognize that the very existence of your church is threatened?"

Sure, some Inchantment has bewitch'd the wise;
Under the *Herb,* some latent *Serpent* lies.   450
What means the *Riddle?* Can *Papists* be sincere?
They're not such fools, some other thing they fear.
The matter's this, Blest *Popery*'s to be sent
In *Mission* to some other *Continent.*
And *Jack* is displeas'd with another thing: 455
And that's, because *Hanover*'s to be King.
They'd have a Pious *Catholick* Prince, from *France,*
The *Protestant* Religion to advance.
Great Change indeed, a *Romanist* turn'd *Saint,*
And *Jacobite* to swear the *Covenant.*   460
    O Happy *Scotland,* when thy Voting *Peers,*
Are turn'd thy *Bards,* thy *Prophets,* and thy *Seers!*
Only look back to *Prophecies* of old,
You'll find, long since, there *Visioneers* foretold.
    What Airy *Phantoms* do our *Craniums* fill?   465
What Bugbear Shadows and senseless Notions will
Oppose our Good with Names and God knows what,
Of other Triffles which some fops aim at,
Hopes fixt upon a PRIGGISH WHORING BRAT.
Away, such *Jargon,* begone with *Gipsie* Dreams,   470
And Conjure not a brainless *Mob,* with Names:
Don't fool us, with ridiculous *Chimer's,*
And plague us, with *Imaginary* fears.
Is this the way to help a broken State?
Are these the means to make our Kingdom Great?   475
No. Let's, Sincere, our thinking minds apply,
To free our Nation out of Misery.
No groundless *Malice,* let your Souls possess;
But seriously consult your Happiness.

450. *Serpent:* The snake in the grass is Defoe's emblem for the persecuting faction within the Church of England who insisted upon "total Destruction of the Dissenters as a Party" (*More Short-Ways with the Dissenters,* 1704, p. 5).

452. *other thing:* settlement of the throne of Scotland upon the house of Hanover.

459. *Change:* the forlorn hope of many Jacobites that the pretender, James Francis Edward, would renounce Catholicism.

463. *Prophecies:* "And it shall come to pass afterward, that I will pour out my spirit upon all flesh; and your sons and your daughters shall prophesy, your old men shall dream dreams, your young men shall see visions" (Joel 2:28). Cf. 385*n.,* above.

470. *Gipsie Dreams:* Cf. *The Vision,* 9.

472. *Chimer's:* chimeras; the form without -a was obsolescent (*OED*).

For God knows when this hour returns again,   480
For losing it, we may attempt in vain
To 'scape sad Judgments, from just *Heaven* sent;
Then, then we may when its past time, repent.
  Let *Rattle-Brains* still chuse t'approve a *Mob*,
And all Opposers, of their Honour Rob,   485
Rather than Dictates of sound Reason hear,
Or to just Judgment or good Sense, give ear.
But these I wave, not worthy of my Song;
I wish their *Skull* were equal to their *Tongue*.
  But there are some, no living Comprehend.   490
What e're's propos'd, they'd still our Good Suspend:
Yet, they the Name of COUNTRY-MEN have got;
And that's enough to Sanctify a *Vote*.
This Name's a *Charm*, as good's a *Magick* Spell,
Enough to save a Country-man from Hell.   495
Some always grudge, and some will still repine;
But COUNTRY's *Salvo* for the worst Design.
You need but this, to sail with every wind.
Most are ill Natur'd, and are Discontent,
Because they want Place in the Government.   500
Might we not some, unto this Number add,
Who since last *Session*, Country-men are made.
I've seen at *Court*, some have the Chiefest Place;
But now turn'd *Honest*, 'cause they're in disgrace.
And who but *Annandale*'s turn'd *Honest* now;   505

480–84. Defoe virtually paraphrases Harley's instructions: "4. You must shew them this is such an opportunity that being once lost or neglected is not again to be recovered" (HMC *Portland MSS.*, *4*, 334).

492. *COUNTRY-MEN:* members of the Country party, opponents of the union.

497. *Salvo:* "A dishonest mental reservation; a quibbling evasion" (*OED*).

501. *some:* The number would include Lord Belhaven; see *The Vision*, 5n. above.

505. *Annandale:* After betraying the duke of Monmouth, James II, and William III, William Johnstone, marquess of Annandale (1664–1721), saved himself in August 1690 by betraying his fellow conspirators in the Montgomery plot to restore James II (*Leven and Melville Papers*, Bannatyne Club, Edinburgh, 1843, pp. 505–13). But for a man who was "not much to be trusted" (Macky, p. 185)—it was even said that "no Man whatsoever placed any Trust in him" (Lockhart, p. 179)—Annandale managed to be appointed to a surprisingly large number of offices in the government of Scotland: extraordinary lord of session (1693–1721), president of the council (1693–95, May 1702–February 1706), lord treasurer (1696–1705), lord high commissioner to the general assembly of the church of Scotland (1701, 1705, 1711), lord privy seal (May–December 1702), secretary of state (March–September 1705). He was even elevated from earl to marquess of Annandale (June 1701) and created a knight

Tho' he before was *Peer* and *Courtier* too.
Pray, Good Sir Country-man, then make it known
How comes King *James*'s *Courtier* to be Honest grown?
Is it because the *Court* did you Degrade?
Then Sure I am, An *Honest Man*'s soon made.   510
Yet, on both sides, I *Honest-men* allow;
Tho' still I hold, that empty *Names* won't do.
Yes, some there are, who still were *Patriots* brave,
Who, their poor *Country*, oft indeavoured have,
From *Poverty* and *Tyrrany* to save.   515
    And, above all, I chuse to mention One;
I mean, the Famous Duke of *Hamilton*,
Who, Self-inriching Offers, long withstood;

---

companion of the Thistle (February 1704). Since Annandale was "extremely carried away by his private Interest" (Macky, p. 185), it was the loss of his post as secretary of state that "induced him to oppose the Union" (Lockhart, p. 180).

    517. *Hamilton:* James Douglas, fourth duke of Hamilton (1658–1712), was one of the most enigmatic figures of his age. When the Scottish parliament failed to settle the succession on the electress Sophie upon the death of Anne's only surviving child in July 1700, Tallard (then the French ambassador) reminded Louis XIV that "les prétentions du Duc d'Hamilton par le chef de sa mère au deffaut de la maison de Stuart . . . sont publiques et connues de tout le monde" (PRO 31/3 187, f. 55v). Hamilton's pretensions to the throne of Scotland derived from his direct descent from Princess Mary Stuart, eldest daughter of James II of Scotland, who c. 1474 married as her second husband James Hamilton, first Lord Hamilton. After the murder of her only son by her first marriage, Mary's heir became James, second Lord Hamilton, created earl of Arran in 1503 (*The Scots Peerage*, ed. Sir James B. Paul, 9 vols., Edinburgh, D. Douglas, 1904–14, *1*, 20; *4*, 352–53; Sir Iain Moncreiffe of that Ilk, *The Highland Clans*, London and New York, Bramhall House, 1967, p. 49). In December 1683 Charles II sent James, fourth duke of Hamilton, to France as ambassador extraordinary to congratulate Louis XIV on the birth of his second grandchild, Philippe d'Anjou, and Hamilton remained in France to serve as an aide-de-camp to Louis in two campaigns. He commanded the Oxford regiment for James II in the revolution and accompanied him to Rochester when the king fled England. Hamilton was immediately confined to the Tower but upon his trial in April 1689 a defect in the writ enabled him to be released. He was again confined in the Tower under suspicion of involvement in Montgomery's plot, but released without trial. He swore allegiance and took his seat in parliament in May 1700 to promote the interests of the Company of Scotland, in which he was a major investor. Upon the accession of Anne, Hamilton was recognized as leader of the Country (nationalist) party in Scotland and in 1705 he led the opposition to the act for a treaty of union. On 1 September 1705, however, "without giving any reason for it," he shocked his followers by moving that the queen should have the nomination of the Scottish commissioners, "which . . . did great service to the Court" (Calamy, *Historical Account*, *2*, 48). Afterwards it was learned that he had been promised a place on the commission, which Argyll was finally unable to secure for him. He voted against every article of the treaty for which a division list was recorded and adhered to every protest (*APS*, *11*, 315–405).

    518. *Offers:* It is not known what "Self-inriching Offers" Hamilton had "long withstood." The "Offers," in fact, seem not yet to have been made: "On the Queen's Accession to the Throne, he made strong Efforts to get into the Administration, but hath not yet succeeded"

Chusing to stand up for his *Nations* Good.
May he All other things to this Postpone;   520
And be, still for a *True-born Scotsman* known,
Yea, May we never have worse *Peers* than He,
For of our *State,* to fill the first Degree.
And as 'mongst th'first, they are most justly rais'd,
So 'mongst the first, they merit to be Prais'd,   525
Who may be thought to have no bad Designs;
Yet are they caught, in the *Extended Gins;*
And by the Bait, almost *Trepanned* are;
And noos'd, into their Foes deceitful Snare.
　　Only but try, seek, search, inquire and find,   530
Who's Enemy, and who's your truest Friend,
And then I'm sure, ye'l have a Milder thought
Of those, who truly our Deliv'rance wrought.
　　Let ne're the thoughts of any such avail,
Where Discontent and Envy do's prevail.   535
Let's all *Ambition* and *Revenge* remove;
We'l yet a Happy and Blest *Nation* prove.
　　Listen then, when Old *Britannia* speaks,
While she bedews, with briny tears, her Cheeks:
　　My valiant *Sons* and *Daughters* to me dear,   540
Unto your *Parents's* good Advice give ear.
Brave *Children,* Don't your Proper Good oppose,
In Minds Unite against insulting Foes.
Forget past Feuds, I seriously Intreat;
And let old Piques be now run out of date.   545
Alas! ye have too many Enemics,
Who ready wait, your *Heritage* to Seize.
I have you long brought up and Educat,
That now you've form'd a Glorious *Ancient State;*

(Macky, pp. 177–78). Eventually, of course, the offers flew in like snowflakes: he was chosen one of the 16 Scottish representative peers (July 1708), appointed lord lieutenant of the county palatine of Lancaster (October 1710), sworn to the privy council (December 1710), elevated to the English peerage as duke of Brandon (September 1711), appointed master of the ordnance (August 1712), invested with the Order of the Garter (October 1712), and again appointed ambassador extraordinary to France. He was killed in Hyde Park in a celebrated duel with Lord Mohun in November 1712. Swift, who was his friend and admirer, said he was "very generous but of a middle Understanding" (*Prose,* 5, 261).

　　523. *For . . . to fill:* a Scotticism? Cf. "My true love for to see."
　　538. *Britannia:* Britannia had been introduced in *The True-Born Englishman* (1700) and *The Mock Mourners* (1702) to celebrate William III (*POAS,* Yale, 6, 295–97, 387–91).
　　548. *Educat:* educated; this form of the past participle is a Scotticism (*SND*).

Great Miseries have you depopulate;   550
While none, with help attend your sorry groans,
But beaten *Air* resounds your Vagrant Moans.
Ye've long Complain'd, it always was in vain;
Nothing diminish'd, nor asswag'd your Pain.
But still remain your Sores and Scarlet Wounds;   555
Your Torment yet, my ear with terrour stounds.
Are none to help, are all your *Worthies* gone?
Or are your Spirits, now exhausted, done?
Do'nt fear: A happy *Medium* I've found out:
You need not of the happy *Event,* doubt.   560
Ye want a Cure; Here, Here's the Remedy
Which will Redeem you from your Misery.
And that's, into one *State* Incorporate;
Improve th'*Occasion,* and do'nt repent too late.
It's thus, you shal my *British* Isle Secure,   565
And to your selves, Prosperity Assure.
You shal be Safe from Enemies at Home;
While Loaden'd Ships into your Harbours come,
Freighted with Forreign and *Extraneous* Goods,
They do divide the Frothy, Jarring Floods.   570
       My younger Son, I seriously advise,
Do'nt thou, thy *Elder Brother* more despise,
But Kindly do *Communicate* thy Trade
To him, whom thou hast oft Impov'rished.
Thy *High flown Courts* have stretcht their Influence   575
Him to Oppress, and broke the strongest Fence.
But Now, Let *Friendship* and true *Love* Commence;
So that thy *Candid Kindness* may excite

550. *Miseries:* see 111n. above.

   depopulate: Defoe repeatedly points to the economic consequences of emigration: "you
[Scots] have the trouble and expense of your Children till they are grown up; and then other
Nations reap the Profit of their Labour" (*An Essay, at Removing National Prejudices . . . Part
III,* [Edinburgh], 1706, p. 10); "to Export . . . People, instead of the Labour of the People
is . . . letting out the Life-Blood of a Nation" (*A Fifth Essay, at Removing National Prejudices,*
[Edinburgh], 1707, p. 15).

   569. *Extraneous:* "Of external origin" (*OED*).

   571. *younger Son:* England.

   572. *despise:* The conventional hatred of Scots memorialized in John Cleveland, *The Rebel
Scot* (1644), was still exploited in popular works like Edward Ward, *A Journey to Scotland*
(1699).

   575. *Courts:* Defoe estimated that the Scots nobility and gentry who resided in London
represented a loss of revenue to Scotland of £50,000 a year (*Review,* 14 January 1707).

Him, with both Soul and Body to Unite.
Scot, Thou'rt my *First-Born* and my *Eldest Son;* 580
Was mine before the *English Name was Known.*
My Valiant *Son,* thy Pains afflict my Soul:
For thy hard Lot, I daily do Condole.
Your Circumstances, I've thus figured:
And to my self, I've them thus fancied. 585

As to a *Ship,* who's long the Sea endur'd,
While mighty *Storms* and *Ouragans* concurr'd
To beat her down, yet still she kept her Ground:
While *Roaring Waves* do from her Sides rebound.
Then full of Terrour, She above do's spy 590
A burning Air and Melancholy Sky.
Straight, A big belli'd, furious *Cloud* appears,
Strikes the *Tarpaulins* almost dead with fears.
Nitre and *Sulphur* do its belly fill.

It's form'd by the *Aerial Princes* Skill, 595
Who counts his Chief Diversion and Delight,
To make 'gainst *Men,* the *Air* and *Clouds* to fight.
He do's apply Infernal *Chimick Arts,*
To form these *Meteors,* and such thundring Darts,
Improves his *Talent,* makes his Bullets fly, 600
With Scalding *Sulphur,* on his *Enemy.*
He on his Foes, them furious down do's send:
Their *Nitrous Parts* in *Cataracts* Descend.

But to my Story, Let me now return.
This *Brillant Cloud* did now begin to burn: 605
Then, thro' with dreadful Thunder-claps, it flies.
Its hideous Noise do's fill th'*Expanded* Skies.
Thro' lowring *Air,* as *Eolus,* it Glides;
At length it melts, and tumbling down, it slides;
And straight, the Ship in Smoak and Darkness hides. 610

586–628. This remarkable epic simile that is broken in the middle (604) and ends in a prayer (622–28)—"I Argue with the Right Revrend fathers of this Church," Defoe said, and "pass for much more of an Oracle among them than I Merit" (*Letters,* p. 140)—is the rhetorical center of the poem.

587. *Ouragans:* hurricanes, "A sort of violent and tempestuous wind, more usual on the *American* Coasts, especially the *Caribee* Islands" (*A Scots Poem,* Edinburgh, 1707, p. 16).

593. *Tarpaulins:* common sailors (*OED*).

595. *Aerial Princes:* "The Aerial Prince" who beclouds the issue of union in a suspiciously sulphurous gas, is presumably the agent of Hell's "Patron" (292), Louis XIV.

Poor *Mariners,* below, afflicted see
Proud swelling Tides and boist'rous, rising *Sea.*
On *Starboard* side, a Monstrous *Rock* they spy:
While *Larboard,* to a Sandy-bank is nigh.
They Stretch their *Lungs,* and *Heav'n* to help they call,   615
Lest 'scaping *Scyll',* they on *Charybdis* fall.
There is no way Safe to escape, but one:
Which if they Lose, for ever they're undone.
This way they seek, this the blest Path they'd have,
Lest waves their Sheets, and th'*Abyss* be their Grave.   620
    Just in such Case, we now our selves do find.
Almighty then, do thou Inlighten our *Mind!*
Shew's how to Steer, and tell us what's the Course.
And of our wo's, let's Know the distant Source.
We also pray, Discover us the Means,   625
That our Relief and Happiness contains,
And so we shall unto thy *Altars* bring
Willing *Oblations,* and just Praises sing.
    My *Son,* for thee my burden'd *Heart* do's bleed!
But do disdain, thy angry Soul to feed   630
With prejudice, against thy Neighbours State.
Do'nt in thy Head, fool whimsies *Procreate.*
Such *Maggots* and such *Frolicks* won't avail,
But cause thy *Peace* and *Priviledges* fail.
Your *Case* at Present's almost Desperate: 635
Your wisdom, then's to be *Consolidate,*
With such, as may your dying *State* revive,
And grant you may be Capable to Live.
The present *Union* will such Blessings give.
    Its whole Advantages, I can't Relate,   640

617–18. Cf. 480–84 above.

629. *My Son:* Scotland.

640. *Advantages:* In *An Essay, at Removing National Prejudices . . . Part III,* [Edinburgh], 1706, p. 8, Defoe listed the "Advantages" to Scotland of union with England under four headings:

1. Trade
2. Religion
3. Civil Government
4. Liberty and Soveraignty

Here he follows a similar scheme but in a different order: lines 642–59, Civil Government; 660–730, Trade; 835–68, Religion. Neither in the pamphlet nor in the poem can Defoe discuss "Liberty and Soveraignty" for these are "Advantages" that the union would require

Therefore, in brief, I'le some Enumerate.
And First, It brings a Solid Lasting *Peace*,
Whereby we may for ever Live at Ease,
Free from all Forreign Enemies Attempts,
And be Secured from our Civil Rents.   645
Nor shall our Strifes and former Jarrs be known,
When the whole Isle's *Incorporate* in one:
When Separate, we still in danger are
Of Home-bred Feuds and dismal Civil War:
The best Designs, we can e're undertake,   650
Our Neighbour ever, will be sure to break.
But when we're one, such things we need not fear:
For the same Interest, will to both be *Dear*.
What's *Scotland*'s Good, will then be *England*'s too:
And the same Bless will to us both Accrue.   655
Yea, when the *Two* become *One British State:*
The Isle will be so formidably *Great*,
That proudest Neighbours shal Submissive be;
And *Europe, Britain,* shal its *Umpire* see.
    And *Next,* their *Trade* to us communicate,   660
Can't fail to make our sinking Kingdom *Great;*
We's then our Home-bred *Products* all export;
And Foreign Fleets shall ride in ev'ry *Port.*
It's this that shall us Wealth and Money bring:
And make the Plague of *Poverty* take Wing.   665
Then the poor Devils that do crowd our Streets,
Shall fill our Manufactures and Fleets.
England will have, for all our Products, use;
And wo'nt our *Scots Commodities* refuse.
    Coal, Cattle, Linen, and all sorts of *Grain,*   670

Scotland to give up, if indeed it can be said that Scotland still enjoyed them in 1706. P. W. J. Riley advises us that we must "abandon almost completely the idea of England and Scotland as politically distinct" in 1706 (*EHR, 84* [July 1969], 498).

653. *Interest:* disyllabic, as in 772 below.

660. Scotia replaces Britannia as the narrator.
  communicate: communicated, a Scotticism (548*n.* above).

665. *Poverty:* Cf. 111*n.* above.

670. T. C. Smout's list of "the most valuable commodities" exported (c. 1700) is almost identical: linen goods, live cattle, wool, coal, grain (*Scottish Trade on the Eve of Union,* Edinburgh and London, Oliver & Boyd, 1963, p. 237). Defoe omits wool because the Scottish wool trade was with France, not with England, and its continuance during the war was of course unpopular in England.

  Coal: "*Scots* Coal will never want a Market at *London*," Defoe wrote in *A Fourth Essay, at*

Shall to our Nation daily Riches gain.

For then our *Linen,* from *Duty*'s be exempt;

And may be straight to their *Plantations* sent.

From these we can't but reap great Benefit,

If we with *England* presently unite: 675

For 'tis by them, they have so wealthy grown;

Why mayn't we too, since they will be our own.

Our courser Wares will yield us profit too;

And bring's what e're in *Americk* do grow.

Our Ships by *Convoys* then shall guarded be;   680

And without Fear they'll plough the Raging Sea.

'Tis such as this, that *Scotland* truly wants;

'Tis for rich *Traffick* that our Country pants.

For which we've sought long with the greatest Care:

And yet we from it truly are as far,   685

As we were known a Hundred Years before.

But to our Intrests lets be blind no more;

For we can never have a happy Trade,

Till *SCOT* and *ANGLE* be one People made.

Consider next, how much it may redound   690

T'our good, to have *Four hundred thousand Pound;*

Removing National Prejudices, [Edinburgh], 1706, p. 25, "while the Ladies keep Fires in their Nurseries and Chambers," and he could scarcely have written these words without thinking of his lady, Mary Defoe, and the seven children whom he had left behind in London.

672. *Duty's:* Defoe estimated that the duties on Scottish linen entering England amounted to £17,000 a year (ibid., p. 24) and "This being taken off," he said, "these who incline to Manufacture Linnen will be encouraged to imploy more Hands, which will take up many that are now begging or lying lautering in a starving Condition" (*A Letter from Mr. Reason, To the High and Mighty Prince the Mob,* [Edinburgh, 1706], p. 5).

673. *Plantations:* Article IV of the treaty gave Scotland free "Intercourse of Trade and Navigation," not only with England but with all "Dominions and Plantations thereunto belonging."

678. *courser Wares:* coarser linens and wool. "The Courseness of the Wool here," Defoe discovered, "is owing to the ill Husbandry of the People, not the Inclemencies of Nature" (*A Fifth Essay, at Removing National Prejudices,* [Edinburgh], 1707, p. 23).

680. *Convoys:* see 125n. above.

686. *a Hundred Years:* Cf. "Scotland . . . declining in Wealth, for above a 100 Years past" (*An Essay at Removing National Prejudices . . . Part II,* 1706, p. 10), was a commonly accepted assumption.

691. *Four hundred thousand Pound:* The exact amount was £398,085 10s. It was called the equivalent (697n. below) and it solved the gravest problem that the treaty-makers had to face. Since Scotland had no national debt and would be required by the union to assume a part of England's, estimated to be more than £17,000,000 (*The History of the Union,* 1786, p. 644), the commissioners agreed on 25 June 1706 to reimburse Scotland with an equivalent in money (ibid., p. 283). So the union has been said to be "wholly owing to the Lord *Halifax*

For tho it shou'd to them return again,
Yet still the Sum will not be lent in vain.
For who wo'nt thank another who does lend
Him, for his Stock and Fortune to amend,   695
Tho he the whole shou'd back (with int'rest) send.
 And then take notice, that th'*Equivalent*
Will (if our *Taxes*) constantly augment.
 An *English* Method to improve our *Ground,*
Will to our *Lairds* and *Tenants* Bless redound.   700
 Also we'll have a tolerable Cess,
Out of the *Verge* of *Court,* us to oppress.
 Our *Fish-trade* is a great Advantage next;
Which, if it be in *Briton*'s hands once fixt,
To the whole *Islands* good, it will concur,   705
And be a Blessing to the Rich and Poor.
Only but look what *Dutch* by this acquire;
Likewise our own Convenience inquire.
We have 'bove others, this Trade to begin;
And the great Helps to bring it forward then.   710
For now we can't Hearts, Hands, nor Stocks command,
While both the *Nations* disunited stand.

. . . who first projected the *Equivalent;* without which, that happy Agreement between both Nations, had never been accomplish'd" (*The Works and Life of the Right Honourable Charles, late Earl of Halifax,* 1715, p. 137).

697–98. *Equivalent . . . augment:* A second and smaller equivalent, "hypothecated on the increased yield of the revenue," was to be devoted to "Encouraging and Promoting the Fisheries, and . . . other Manufactories and Improvements" (William Ferguson, *Scotland 1689 to the Present,* Edinburgh and London, Oliver & Boyd, 1968, p. 48; *Articles of the Treaty of Union,* Edinburgh, [1706], pp. 9–11).

701. *Cess:* The cess was the Scots version of the land tax. It was "*a Month's Assessment,*" as Defoe explained, calculated by a method "altogether obsolete" but "peculiarly exact," of which he had never heard anyone complain. Since Cromwell's time it had been worth £6,000 so eight months' cess would have been worth £48,000 (*An Essay at Removing National Prejudices . . . Part II,* 1706, p. 18). After the union it was to be calculated as a fixed part (1/41.6) of any land tax voted by the parliament, which would put it out of the power of the Scottish court to use it as a means of oppression.

703. *Fish-trade:* Defoe's greatest enthusiasm (17 above; *An Essay at Removing National Prejudices . . . Part III,* [Edinburgh], 1706, p. 8; *Caledonia, A Poem,* Edinburgh, 1706, pp. 12–16) was the least likely of fulfillment for two reasons: 1) the failure of a similar venture, "the Royal Fishery Company of 1670, [which] was founded with great pomp and hope, and wound up in 1690, 'all turned to loss and disappointment' "; 2) the competition of the Dutch fishing industry, "an intricate and highly capitalised organisation which the whole of Europe regarded with envy" (T. C. Smout, *Scottish Trade on the Eve of Union,* Edinburgh and London, Oliver & Boyd, 1963, pp. 22, 220).

711. *Stocks:* money or capital goods (*OED*).

But *England* then will their rich Stocks advance;
That *Britain* may the *Fishing-trade* inhance.
'Tis for their Good, as well as ours they see,   715
For to establish a good *Fisherie.*
The gain will to us both accumulate,
When that we are in *One* Incorporate.
By this, vast Numbers will obtain their Bread;
They'll get for *Fish,* what e're from *North* they need;   720
They now large *Sums* for *Northern* Product spend,
But then they'll Fish in lieu of *Money* send.
Altho the *Dutch* already have the Start,
Yet if we rightly ply this Fishing Art,
Holland unto its fatal Cost shall know,   725
Upon our Coasts they's noose no *Herring* now.
Nor need they ever launch into the Main;
For there they'll see their Fishing is in vain;
'Cause they wont *Fish-Shoals* in such Numbers find,
Nor can expose their *Busses* to the Wind.   730
   I might adject unto these many more;
But won't, 'cause oft they have been told before.
   Some much have talk'd of *Foederal Union* Schemes,
But they may leave them, to be fitter *Themes*

713. *Stocks advance:* see 697–98*n.* above.

720. *what . . . from North they need:* What Defoe called the "*Norway* Trade" was in "Hemp, Pitch, Tar, Rosin, Plank, Masts, &c." (*An Essay at Removing National Prejudices . . . Part II,* 1706, pp. 30–31.

724. *this Fishing Art:* "the Dutch . . . method was to follow the fish down from Bressay Sound in Shetland with a catching fleet of several hundred, which brought their harvest to mother ships to be packed and salted and exported directly to foreign markets without touching land" (T. C. Smout, *Scottish Trade on the Eve of Union,* Edinburgh and London, Oliver & Boyd, 1963, p. 220).

730. *Busses:* "A two- or three-masted vessel . . . used esp. in the Dutch herring fishery" (*OED*).

731. *adject:* annex, add (*OED*).

733. *Foederal Union Schemes:* Almost everyone who was against the union had a favorite alternative, "Partial, Federal, Periodical or indeed Notional," as Defoe scornfully referred to them (*An Essay, at Removing National Prejudices . . .* Part III, [Edinburgh], 1706, p. 7). The Scottish commissioners had proposed a federal scheme on 24 April 1706: a single monarch, a customs union, and two parliaments—but their English counterparts declined even to consider it (*The Journal of the Proceedings of the Lords Commissioners,* Edinburgh, [1706], p. 10). "Federal union" came to mean anything that was not the treaty agreed upon in July 1706 and the debates of the union parliament made it clear "that it was not a foederal union, or a better union that those gentlemen desired, but really no union at all; and that the design was to defeat the endeavours of the Union only, in order to bring in French bondage, and King James VIII" (*The History of the Union,* 1786, p. 333).

> To be *Preachmented* to the coming *Age;*   735
> For they will be more provident and *Sage.*
> But 'tis as clear as *Suns Meridian* Light,
> That *Foederal Union* wont repair our Right.
> How can we hope, that *England* e're will give
> What we do want, and not incorporate live.   740
> Will they allow's the Profit of their Trade;
> While that our *Taxes* by our selves are made.
> That Means we'll use their *Garisons* and *Forts,*
> Their *Factories, Plantations* and their *Ports:*
> Yet we'd determine all our Duties still,   745
> That is, *Low Tax,* or any thing we will.
> So shall we with anothers *Heifer* till,
> While *English* are at all the vast Expence,
> Maintaining *Fleets* and *Forts* for our Defence.
> But certainly no Nation's so unwise,   750
> As to let others all *Monopolize.*
> But tho we shou'd in *Taxes* all agree
> We wou'd not be secur'd from Tyranny.
> Only but look to rich *Batavick Land,*
> Which (almost) does the other States Command;   755
> Because they do'nt on equal Footing stand.
> Yea, can we have more sure our *Government,*
> When none, than when some, join their *Parliament.*
> But more, such *Union's* always most unsure;
> And can't our lasting Happiness procure.   760
> For we'll be ready still to *Separate,*
> While *Faction, Pride,* or *Envy's* in the *State.*
> But here a *Mob* of *Cavillers* appear,
> For to surprize us with a World of Fear!

735. *Preachmented:* a Scotticism (*SND,* s.v. preach).
747. proverbial (Tilley, H395).
749. Cf. 125*n.* above.
754. *Batavick Land:* "*Holland,* which alwise influences the rest of the seven Provinces, tho in Foederal Union with them; because she pays more Taxes to the States, and is more powerful; So that for the most part she has the whole Honour and Name of doing all, *&c.*" (*A Scots Poem,* Edinburgh, 1707, p. 21).
758. *some:* see 792*n.* below.
761–62. These lines paraphrase some points made by William Seton of Pitmedden in a speech immediately preceding that of Lord Belhaven on 2 November 1706 (*The History of the Union,* 1786, pp. 313, 315).
763–64. Defoe attributes the unpopularity of the treaty of union in Scotland to an ef-

And first they plant a (falling) Battery   765
Of faint Objections 'gainst our Fishery.
They do bemoan the heavy *Tax* on Salt;
And never think the *Drawback* Eases that.
Whence *Britain* may sell at as easy Rates,
As any other *Commonwealths* or *States*.   770
If not: Then sure the *British Parliament*,
Will mind the Intrest of the *Government*.
They'll lower the *Duties*, if they're so severe,
As that they can have any Ground to fear,
That other Nations will us undersell: 775
The *Senate* then will regulat that well.
They next the *Tax* of *Home spent* Salt complain,
That it will grind the Faces of the *Mean*.
I own it's heavy, yet I'd them remind,
It wo'nt our Nation for two *Lustres* bind.   780
And certainly before these Years be spent,
It will be alter'd by their *Parliament*.
For *Greater Burdens* are in times of War;
Which future *Peace*, will certainly debar.
But once for all, observe *Objectors* now,   785
That there's no Nation ever will allow
Us equal *Trade, Rights, Priviledges* too
While still we have but an unequal Tax;

---

fective propaganda campaign in October 1706. "No sooner were these articles printed," he
said, "but . . . the whole nation fell into a general kind of labour, in canvassing, banding,
and cavilling at the conditions . . . The poor people were terrified with the apprensions of
insupportable taxes, loss of employment, want of all things, and large payments upon their
salt and malt" (*The History of the Union*, 1786, p. 221).

765. *(falling) Battery:* Presumably a "*Battery de Revers* . . . That . . . beats upon the
Back" of the target (*A Military Dictionary*, 3rd ed., 1708, sig. B8r).

767. *Tax on Salt:* Article VIII of the treaty provided that Scotland pay the same duty on
imported salt as England. When fish cured with imported salt were exported, however, the
import duty was reduced by means of a drawback, or refund.

768. *Drawback:* Defoe does not really answer the complaint, for as he explained himself,
"in the Salt Tax, the Draw-back allowed, is not Equivalent to the Duty paid, and therefore
the Remainder will be a Tax upon, and consequently a Discouragement to the Fishing Trade,
by hindering the Exportation" (*A Fourth Essay, at Removing National Prejudices*, [Edinburgh],
1706, pp. 30–31).

776. *regulat:* a pseudo-Scotticism.

777. *Tax of Home spent Salt:* Article VIII of the treaty provided that the duty on imported
salt which was consumed at home was not to be levied for seven years. At this time there was
to be a uniform tax on salt throughout Great Britain.

780. *two Lustres:* ten years; actually it was seven.

No. This we never can presume to ask.
By this we might the *Richest undersell;*   790
Gain but this Point, you ever will be well.
   But next, our Representative's so small,
We in our Number far below them fall.
So shou'd we; for all Mortals will confess,
According still, as the Proportion is,   795
In the supporting the *Grandeur* of the State,
So shou'd th'Share be in managing of it:
For they who most to its good do contribute,
Should surely reap the Rich and greatest Fruit.
In your own Shires this Rule is observed,   800
And shou'd it not in greater be conserv'd?
   Others exclaim, they'll never keep a Term,
So that we'll still be liable to harm.
This says, a Nation is so faithless turn'd,
As that they'll by the *Universe* be scorn'd,   805
For breach of Faith, and the most solemn Ties,
That can unite or bind Societies.
No. It's their *Honour* the Terms to observe,
And the whole *Island*'s happy Rights preserve.
For it advances the *New British* State;   810
Nor *disunited*, can they be so great.
   Yea, what Advantage cou'd they e're expect,
The *Northern* part of *Britain* for to break.

792. *Representative:* representation; obsolete and rare (*OED*). Article XXII of the union treaty fixed the Scottish representation in the parliament of Great Britain at 16 peers and 45 commoners. This was a low proportion, 1 : 11.4, relative to population, of which the ratio was estimated to be 1 : 5.5, but a high proportion relative to the wealth of the two nations, estimated to be 1 : 41.6. Most of Defoe's contemporaries, and Defoe himself (*The History of the Union,* 1786, p. 106), believed that "in the framing of a Government, a Proportion ought to be observed, between the Share in the Legislature, and the Burden [of taxation] to be born" (Burnet, *2,* 458). "Scotland was entitled by its wealth and share of taxation to thirteen members in the House of Commons; by its population to eighty-five. After a long wrangle it was agreed to compromise on forty-five" (Trevelyan, *2,* 267; cf. Defoe, *The History of the Union,* 1786, p. 165).

800. *Shires:* Barons of the shires were elected by the heretors, proprietors of estates subject to taxation (Defoe, *A Fourth Essay, at Removing National Prejudices,* [Edinburgh], 1706, p. 28).

802. *they'll never keep a Term:* This was a powerful argument against the union, e.g. [Andrew Fletcher], *State of the Controversy between United and Separate Parliaments,* 1706, p. 27. Defoe exposed the real tendency of the argument in *An Essay at Removing National Prejudices . . . Part III,* [Edinburgh], 1706, p. 31: "the *English* are Knaves, and will keep no Bargain . . . but the *French* are honest Fellows."

For when *Imbodied,* what they undertake,
We'll be enabled them for to assist;   815
But *Separate,* they can't so well subsist.
 Yea more, sufficiently it's known,
We're not so servile, nor so mean Soul'd grown,
As that, we'll e're be *Tyrannized* o'er.
No. *SCOTS* have shown their *Gallantry* before;   820
So if they'd incroach on *Church* or on the *State,*
Our willing Swords will then *Incorporate.*
They can't but see the horrible *Event,*
That might insue so damnable a Rent.
More; *England* by the *Articles* do's gain;   825
They are so equal, that they can't complain.
 What cou'd the World of such a People think,
Who wou'd from strongest Stipulations shrink?
 This fine *Objection* therefore do's conclude:
Either the *Union,* in its self is good;   830
Or if it's bad, we shou'd be satisfi'd,
That its observance be for e're denied.
But if they turn so incomparably base;
To separate, we'll then have justest cause.
 And next, our *Church* must be considered.   835
Most bellow forth, 'tis wholly ruined.
Can any thing below be more secure,
Than what so great a Body does assure?
In *British* hands, our *Church* as stable is,
As in our own; the Difference is this.   840
It's the Foundation of th'new *Government,*
Which can't be alter'd by a *Parliament.*

835–36. The final syllable of "considered" and "ruined" is accented (and rhymed).

842. *can't be alter'd:* Since religion was not mentioned in the original treaty of union, Defoe repeatedly insisted that "the Church of *Scotland* has no manner of Concern in this Treaty" (*An Essay at Removing National Prejudices . . . Part II,* 1706, p. 7; *Two Great Questions Considered,* [Edinburgh], 1707, p. 26). But the Church of Scotland found itself much concerned in this matter (*The Vision,* 32n. above). It feared being "subjected to the Legislation of Bishops" in the House of Lords and it feared that the parliament could "Erect the Episcopal Church of *England,* as the Establishment of great *Britain;* putting us off in *Scotland* with a Toleration" (*Two Great Questions Considered,* [Edinburgh], 1707, p. 24; *An Essay, at Removing National Prejudices . . . Part III,* [Edinburgh], 1706, p. 15). These anxieties were somewhat relieved when an act for securing the Church of Scotland as by law established (*The History of the Union,* 1786, p. 671) was rushed through parliament in November 1706 and subsequently added to Article XXV of the treaty of union. Defoe's assurance that "no Subsequent Parliament can make Null any Article of the Treaty" (*An Essay, at Removing National Prej-*

Our *Church* has numbers of *Well-wishers* there;
And *High-flyers* only our *Antagonists* are.
If they shou'd ought against the same design,   845
No doubt but both the Parties wou'd combine.
They're bound most solemnly it to preserve;
From which they cannot in the least dare swerve;
Or if they do, down will the Fabrick fall;
Lose but one Term, you can't but lose them all.   850
   But while *Religion* is in *Scottish* hands,
It ever in a tottring posture stands.
We're still in danger of a Major part,
Who may at once cause *Presbytrie* depart:
'Tis no unalterable *Basis* of the State: 855
Then sure our Parliament may alter it:
How oft *Religion* chang'd, and chang'd again,
Since the *One thousand five hundred fifty nine.*
First, had we *Priest,* then *Presbyter* appears,
Next is proud *Prelate* in the *Clergy*'s Ears.   860
About again; so will't for ever be,
Till 'stablish'd by more firm Securitie.
Or can we think our Neighbour turn'd so base,
As on our Ruins, for themselves to raise.
Will they their Honour and Faith Sacrifice   865
To *Malice, Pride, Revenge* and *Avarice.*
No, No. Our Isle's be govern'd by good Laws,
And *Patron* be of the *Reformed Cause.*
   Upon this Head I have no more to say;
Only I'd ask you to find out a way,   870

---

udices . . . *Part III,* [Edinburgh], 1706, p. 26), was simply wrong. Sovereignty remained with the crown in parliament and this very article of the treaty was amended in the nineteenth century to permit students who were not Presbyterians to attend the Scottish universities.

846. *both the Parties:* "*Presbyterians* here, and *Dissenters* there" (*A Scots Poem,* Edinburgh, 1707, p.23).

851–52. Defoe repeatedly argued that the Church of Scotland, which had been established in 1592, disestablished in 1612, re-established in 1639, disestablished in 1661, and re-established in 1690, was still threatened by "a Thousand Casualties and uncertainties . . . both from *England* without . . . and from a numerous and doubly Disaffected Party at Home," so that there could be no security for the Church "abstracted from this Union" (*An Essay, at Removing National Prejudices* . . . *Part III,* [Edinburgh], 1706, p. 11).

858. *One thousand five hundred fifty nine:* In May 1559 John Knox returned from exile to carry on the work of the Scottish reformation begun in May 1557 (995n. below).

859–60. *Priest . . . Presbyter . . . Prelate:* priests until 1592; then presbyters. Prelates were reimposed upon the Church of Scotland by James I in 1610.

Whereby we may our *Country* straight relieve,
Our *Rights,* our *Name,* our *Glory* may retrive.
For if you do this *Union* refuse,
It's hop'd you will some other better choose.
    First, then consider now our present State,   875
We're dwindled to a thing, *The Lord knows what.*
You'd then look back unto the days of *Yore;*
See what we were a *Century* before.
I'd likewise have you for to take a view,
How far we're chang'd, how *Miserable* now!   880
We're turn'd so poor, so silly and so mean,
So steril, bare, so wretched, and so lean,
That sure I am, there's none can ever please
To moyl and moulder in so damn'd a Case.
    Next, think how *England* has become so great,   885
So puissant, rich, so flourishing of late;
Since no so great, vast disproportion is,
In both our Soils, Products, Commodities.
No, No. Their Riches have not rose from thence:
But it's because they did a *Trade* advance,   890
Under good Laws and benign influence.
Why may'nt we hope, that we'll be wealthy made,
Having same Rights, same Privilege and Trade.
There is no Reason then for to despair,
Since the same *Growths* are here as well as there.   895
    Good God, We pray thee tell us what to do!
And grant's to choose the Noblest of the two;
Whether we'll best for ever separate;
Or with our Neighbours to incorporate.
    We either must have one same *Sovereign;*   900
Or over us Another *King* must reign;
The first's absurd, and certainly wo'nt do,
For thus we'll loyter in our *Statu quo.*
Yea, worse, since under Foreign Influence,
We'll have but Rags at length for our Defence: 905

876. *The Lord knows what:* a favorite locution of Defoe (*POAS,* Yale, *6,* 445, 600).
878. *a Century:* See 686*n.* above.
886. *rich:* see 235*n.* above.
902. *The first:* union of the crowns, which had left Scotland with a nonresident monarch since 1603.

And if an *English* Influx shou'd prevail,
Hopes of Relief wou'd then for ever fail,
Except we shou'd by Means most desperate,
Hazard our Country to *Annihilate*.
  No. We will have a *Monarch* of our own,   910
Why shall we quit our Scepter and our *Crown?*
We'll rather send straight for another *Prince;*
This will attone for all our former Sins,
Suffering so long another us inslave.
No. We'll be henceforth valiant and brave,   915
We wo'nt be *Hector'd* nor *Bravado'd* more;
But do as did our *Ancestors* before.
We'll *English Bullies* all annihilate:
And with the Dust we'll them *incorporate*.
For like bold *Scotsmen* every one will fight,   920
For's Liberty, his Privilege and Right.
Ah, were we equal in our Coin and Strength,
We might expect them to reduce at length.
Alas! How vast a Disproportion's here

906. *an English Influx:* This would not have been an impossibility in the early months of 1705 when "that famous Parliament called, *The Tacking Parliament,*" passed the Alien Act, which "in a manner declared open war with Scotland, unless by the 24th of December, the next year, they should settle the crown in the same person as now settled in England; for they appointed twenty-four men of war to be fitted out, to prevent the Scots trading with France [and] declared the Scots in England aliens" (*The History of the Union,* 1786, p. 86). Pamphlets were published with titles like [James Hodges], *War betwix't the Two British Kingdoms Consider'd,* and [George Ridpath], *The Reducing of Scotland by Arms and Annexing it to England Consider'd.*

910. *Monarch of our Own:* The monarch of course was James Francis Edward Stuart who, upon the death of his father in September 1701, had been clandestinely proclaimed James VIII in Edinburgh (BM MS. Add. 30000E, f. 357v). Scotia assumes the voice of a Jacobite to reply to [Patrick Abercromby], *The Advantages of the Act of Security, Compar'd with These of the Intended Union,* [Edinburgh], 1706, p. 4. "To pitch upon a King of our OWN," Abercromby had said, "may, perhaps, prove a *Catholicon* for all our Distempers in due time [i.e upon the death of Anne]." In *The Advantages of Scotland by an Incorporate Union,* [Edinburgh], 1706, pp. 26–28, Defoe had ridiculed the Jacobite dream of the Prince of Wales called home, marching into England at the head of an army of 60,000, plundering Lombard Street, burning London, and enslaving the English forever.

911. *Scepter and . . . Crown:* see 378n. above.

924. *Alas:* Defoe who believed that "the longest Purse Conquers" (*Review,* 29 November 1711), now resumes his Scotia voice. Cf. *The Advantages of Scotland by an Incorporate Union,* [Edinburgh], 1706, pp. 30–31: "But granting we should Unite as one Man, call Home the P——ce of W——s (for I see no other Choice *Scotland* could make) . . . and with all our Force invade *England;* For its not to be supposed, if he were King of *Scotland,* he would sit down and not urge his Pretensions to that Crown. Is it probable that we, with our Revenue

In *Men*, in *Ships*, in *Money;* That I fear;   925
Their *Navies* would demolish in few *Moons*
All our *rich Fleets* and all our *Seaport Towns.*
We've cause to dread the Event of a War.
Then, from our Isle, may't be averted far.
 But we'll with *France,* an UNION obtain;   930
Which will both Wealth and Honour to us gain.
And home we'll have the true *Pretending Heir,*
Tho' it should cost our Countrey ne're so dear.
See if your *Ancient Kingdom* can allow,
To pay the Sums, unto its *Landlord* due.   935
But this, *Religion* inconsistent makes,
For we will ne're submit our tameless Necks,
To *France* and to his *Holiness,* the *Pope.*
No, *Heav'ns* forbid! rather confound the *Fopp.*
The whole Earth knows *Gaul*'s tyrranous Design,   940
They'd the whole World, with their Fetters bind.
Tyrrants be gone; you'll not think's to bewitch
With sham Pretexts of rend'ring *Scotland* Rich.
 What other *Prince,* can we e're think upon,
Will quit his Peace, to gain so poor a Crown.   945
 Yet may we not some other State obtain,
Who will with us in *Foederal Union* joyn.
But who will e're Unite, with such as—we?
And thus have *England* for their Enemy.
 What means all this? Is it not better far,   950
T'unite with such, as *Fellow-Subjects* are?
And where there is so great Proximity,

---

of 125000 *per An.* . . . . & with our own Men, could make our Putt Good against the *English,*
who are much more Populous, can afford 3 or 4 Million *per Annum* for many years together,
have at least 80000 Men practised in War . . . which we intirely want, and a Fleet to Insult
us on every part of our Coast [since Scotland had no navy]?"

939. *Fopp:* The pretender was "reported to be handsome, and endued with an Under-
standing exactly of a Size to please the Sex" (Swift, *Prose, 8,* 33).

943. *Pretexts:* Patrick Abercromby had said, "I see no reason why we should not better our
Condition, and retrive our lost Glory, Riches and Independencie, although by the help of
a . . . *French* Allyance" (*The Advantages of the Act of Security,* [Edinburgh], 1706, p. 35).

944. *What other Prince:* In July 1705 Andrew Fletcher of Saltoun had proposed offering the
crown of Scotland to Friedrich I of Prussia (Sir David Hume of Crossrigg, *A Diary of the
Proceedings in the Parliament and Privy Council of Scotland,* Edinburgh, The Bannatyne Club,
1828, p. 167).

946. *some other State:* Defoe considers, and rejects, the candidacies of the Netherlands and
France in *The Advantages of Scotland by an Incorporating Union,* [Edinburgh], 1706, pp. 22 et seq.

In *Situation, Customs, Liberty*.
Yea, there's no People in the *Universe*,
Can's more Exalt, or can us more Depress.   955
   But if we will for ever chuse a Rent,
Where shall we have, for all our *Products* Vent?
Such as *Coal, Grain*, our *Cattle*, and our *Lint*,
Except t'*England*, or *English* Settlement.
Which if forbid, as it's no doubt they shall;   960
How many Shires, would thereby lose their *All?*
For *Holland* won't have our *Commodities;*
'Cause what they want, they'll get with greater ease.
   Since, on one hand, our Ruine's very sure;
And *Disunited*, we can't be secure,   965
Then, don't the other *Medium* refuse;
Since few deny but *It may be* of use.
We may be Happy, if we will be wise;
There's nothing hinders, but our Jealousies,
Revenge, Mistakes, Fears, and blind Prejudice.   970
But if you love still to be rul'd by *Court;*
And be your Neighbours everlasting sport,
Then hug your Chains, and don't of 'em complain:
Let ne're damn'd *Liberty* return again.
So much oblig'd will be *Posterity*,   975
To who've intail'd upon them *Slavery*.
And if ye won't be ever Undeceiv'd,
Nor from *Contempt* or *Poverty* be sav'd.
I can no more, but only bid you hear
My last Advice, my Hopes, and my Desire.   980
   No more, the name of Feud or War be known;
No more the seeds of cursed Discord sow'n.
And let not Factions, e're your Isle disturb.
Or if: May Force all foolish Tumults curb.
No more the name of Tyrany be heard;   985
Nor loss of Church or Liberty be fear'd.
Let *France*, the Hell of *Slaves* and *Tyrrants* be;
Britain, Support of *Europ*'s Liberty.

---

956. *Rent:* "A breach or dissension," a Scotticism (*SND*).

  958. *Lint:* flax; a Scotticism (*SND*). But Defoe means "linen," for flax was imported, not exported.

  979. *I:* Britannia?

To the *Western World* may she dictate Laws,
And still assert the true *Reformed* Cause.   990
Then, *Popery* dare not lift its head at *Home;*
Slavery to *France, Idolatry* to *Rome,*
Shall with disgrace, be driven to Exile.
No *Superstition* let your Land defile.
Let never former Bloody Age return,   995
When the blest *Gospel* was to kill and burn.
Too many *JAMESES* you've already had,
Too many *Papists* fill'd the Royal Bed.
And be no more of subtil *Lauderdals,*
Atholls, MONTGOMERIES, and such Rascals.   1000
DUNDEES, and other Rakes and Tools be gone.
May never such be th'plague of *Albion.*

989. *Western:* accented on second syllable.

995. *Bloody Age:* Defoe may refer to the reformation, which began in Scotland in May 1557 when a congregation was excited by Knox's preaching to set fire to the monasteries at Perth and to destroy the inmates.

997. *Too many JAMESES:* The pretended Prince of Wales was the eighth (910*n.* above).

998. *Papists:* All the Jameses except James I of England and VI of Scotland were papists.

999. *Lauderdals:* John Maitland, second earl and first duke of Lauderdale (1616–82), was "the most dishonest" member of Charles II's cabal. As secretary for Scottish affairs he "held all power and patronage in Scotland for 18 years." Toward the end of his career he advanced from mere unscrupulousness to open cruelty and was removed from all of his offices in 1680 (GEC, *7,* 489). He was succeeded by his brother, Charles, third earl of Lauderdale (d. 1691), who was removed from his posts in the Scottish mint and treasury in 1681 for perjury. Richard, fourth earl of Lauderdale (1653–95), was a papist who accompanied James II to St. Germain and was outlawed in July 1694. His younger brother John, fifth earl of Lauderdale (c. 1655–1710), was a lord of session and supported the union (*APS, 11,* 375, 379, 404).

1000. *Atholls:* Cf. 430–36*n.* above.

MONTGOMERIES: Sir James Montgomery or Montgomerie of Skelmorlie, fourth (GEC, *Baronetage, 2,* 336) or tenth (*DNB, 13,* 763) baronet (d. 1694), conspired to restore James II in 1690 (505*n.* above) but fled to France when the conspiracy was discovered and died at St. Germain (*DNB, 13,* 764) or London (GEC, *Baronetage, 2,* 336).

Rascals: accented on second syllable to make a rascally rhyme with "-derdals." In a similar case, where Defoe forces the word "Record" into an iambic foot in *Caledonia,* 1706, p. 43, he adds a footnote: "Here I make no question but to be animadverted upon for my different way of expressing the word *Record,* and changing the Quantity, making the Vowel long in the last Syllable . . . But for this, I have so good an Authority . . . as *Buchanan . . . Dies tenēbras & tenebrae Diem.*" But Defoe need have gone no further than the traditional Scots ballad in which wrenched accent—"a gude sailor . . . a braid letter . . . my deir master"— is a common characteristic.

1001. *DUNDEES:* John Graham of Claverhouse, Viscount Dundee (1649?–89), earned the sobriquet of "Bloody Clavers" by killing covenanters in Ayr and Clydesdale (October 1684). He supported James II's Romanizing policy, raised an army that defeated the forces of William III at Killiecrankie (July 1689), but was himself killed in the battle.

But in their *Vice,* true *Patriots* succeed,
Who all in Wit and Vertue shall exceed.
May never such sit at the Helm of *State,*   1005
Who spoil their *Countrey,* that themselves be great.
   Let ne're *Bizarre Cromwelian* Age return,
When did *Enthusiasts,* at your *Altars* mourn;
When *Voteries,* in Elevated Groans
Address'd their *GOD,* with *Hypocritick* Moans;   1010
By *Conquest* then they Domineer'd your *State,*
And by your fall they strove be rendr'd Great.
   Let *Absolute Model* be to *Turky* sent;
Where all must be (*maugre* themselves) content;
Where *Monarchs* proudly Tyrannize by Law.   1015
Adoring *Slaves* 'fore's *Tyrant-ship* they fall.
He plays the *Tyrant,* and won't Rule as *Rex,*
Not minding *Salus Populi's suprema Lex.*
   Be gone, *Pretenders,* in *French* maxims bred:
Too many such, almost you *Drudges* made.   1020
No Haughty *Rival* to Attempt you dare.
Your *Rampart* guards you from *Invasive* war.
   I must aver, I dread more what's within;
Your sad Divisions and *Heav'n*-daring *Sin.*
These, These, your *Enemies* and *Antagonists* are;   1025
These, often times Commence a Civil war.
   Nobles, no more to *Flatterers* give Ear;
Nor their Damn'd, fawning, fulsom, speeches hear:
Dispel all Pimping *Hackney Parasites;*
For such are always dangerous *Favourites.*   1030
   May both the *Camp* and *State* be purg'd of *Vice,*
And may *Religion* be esteem'd of Price.
Then, only then, your *Happiness* begins.
Then Prosperous *Plenty* and Blest *Justice* Reigns.

1003. *Vice:* stead or place of another; "Chiefly Scottish" (*OED*).
1007. *Cromwelian Age:* Cromwell defeated the Scots at Dunbar (September 1650) and again at Worcester (September 1651) and imposed a union on the two kingdoms by military force. He ordered the general assembly of the Church of Scotland to be turned out into the street and directed Scottish representatives to proceed to Westminster to sit for the first time in a British parliament.
1013. *Absolute Model:* model for absolutism.
1019. *Pretenders:* The courtiers of the pretender at St. Germain.
1022. *Your Rampart:* the English Channel.
1023. *within:* inside Scotland.

Your Barren *Clods* be turn'd to fruitful *Ground,*   1035
And welcome *Money* circulate around.
Your Land in *Wealth* and *People* shal increase.
And no more *Jameses* or *Charleses* shal oppress.
Then other Nations *Britain* shal Admire,
While all unto your happy bliss aspire.   1040
'Tis this, 'tis this, your Isle shal Aggrandize;
And make your *Fame* to reach the outmost Skies.
Your may, *My Sons,* then raise your drooping Eyes;
Sing Joyful *Anthems,* cant *Doxologies.*
   And may the *Union* have this blest Effect,   1045
And give you more, than any do's expect.
   In after-times, Then th'*Treaters* blest shal be,
Whom *Providence* made Instruments to free
Your Land, from Feuds and Unblest *Poverty;*
Then prais'd shal be th'Queens Representative;   1050

1036. *Money:* Coinage was in such short supply in Scotland that foreign currencies had to be allowed to circulate freely (at steep discounts). When the coinage was recalled after the union for reissue, only £411,000 was found to be in circulation.

1047. *Treaters:* The treaters, with a pun in Scottish pronunciation on "traitors," were the commissioners who drafted the treaty of union at Westminster in April–July 1706. It was fortunate that the terms of the treaty were not known when the Scottish commissioners returned home, for if they had been, Defoe said, "not many of them would have dared to have gone home, without a guard to protect them." When the treaty was published in October 1706 "the common people . . . would go about the street crying 'No Union,' and call the treaters traitors, and soon after began to threaten them openly to their faces." As late as December 1706 Defoe reported that they went in danger of their lives (*The History of the Union,* 1786, pp. 226, 229, 237; *Letters,* p. 185).

1048. *Providence:* Cf. *The History of the Union,* 1786, p. 33: "though this will . . . lead us back a great way into history, yet it will carry this advantage along with it, that we shall see all the several steps which have been taken, how Providence has led the nations, as it were, by the hand, and brought them, by the hints of their mutual disasters, to seek this treaty, as the only harbour the ship of the state could safely come to an anchor in."

1050. *th'Queens Representative:* "The D[uke] of Q[ueensberry]" (*A Scots Poem,* Edinburgh, 1707, p. 29). James Douglas, second duke of Queensberry (1662–1711), was appointed lieutenant colonel in Dundee's regiment in June 1684, upon his return from the Grand Tour. In 1688, however, he was "the first *Scots Man* that disserted over to the Prince of *Orange,* and from thence acquir'd the Epithet . . . of *Proto Rebel*" (Lockhart, p. 9). At Killiecrankie, where he commanded the sixth Horse Guards, he was defeated by his former commanding officer. He was sworn of the Scottish privy council in 1684 and again in May 1689. He was also a commissioner of the treasury (March 1692–1704, 1705–07), lord privy seal (May 1696–1702, 1705–07), an extraordinary lord of session (1696–1711), and lord high commissioner to the parliament (1700, 1702–03, 1706). In 1704 he was compromised by his attempt to turn Simon Fraser around to spy on his own political rivals and forced to resign his offices. "His . . . tricking behaviour . . . made him more odious . . . than ever" to the queen

Who long has Toiled, that our Land may thrive.
He strugles thro' worlds of Difficulties;
And for our Good, his *Peace* do's Sacrifice.
May he still mind the *Church* and *Countries* Right,
And merit e're his *Sovereign*'s Delight.   1055
Then he a *Statue* may deserve of Gold:
While others shal with *Cock* and *Pug* be roll'd
Into some fine and Honourable *Sacks,*
With *Bells* at *Skull* and *Whip* around their *Necks,*
If they shall dare, the *Kingdom* undermine: 1060
Inspir'd (from *France*) with *Gold* and *Gallick* wine.

(*Scottish Historical Review, 43* [October 1964], 101), but she was forced to reappoint him lord high commissioner, "th'Queens Representative," in 1706 to steer the treaty of union through the Scottish parliament. And Defoe agreed that it was Queensberry's "secret hand" that made the union possible (*The History of the Union,* 1786, p. 227).

1053. *Peace do's Sacrifice:* "If the Commissioner at any time staid at the parliament House later than ordinary so as to come down in the dark he was allways insulted with Stones and Dirt and Curses, the Guards hurt with stones from the tops of Houses, and once one of his Gentlemen beaten very cruelly in the Street" (Defoe, *Letters,* p. 185).

1056. *Statue:* The "Union Duke" did not get his statue until after death: "The Duke's Monument, curiously done in Marble at full Length, is . . . plac'd in the . . . Church at *Disdier* [in Dumfriesshire], where he is buried" (Defoe, *A Tour thro' the Whole Island of Great Britain* (1724–26), ed. G. D. H. Cole, 1927, *2*, 729). But he was allowed a triumph in London. On 16 April 1707 "the duke of Queensbery, with many others of the Scotch nobility," entered the city, "being mett some miles off by several coaches-and-6-horses, and upwards of 200 men on horseback with them, and two trumpetters at the head of them; and this morning his grace waited upon her majestie at Kensington" (Luttrell, *6,* 160). Queensberry's reward followed almost immediately: in May he was granted a pension of £3,000 a year and given control of all patronage in Scotland; in June he was sworn of the privy council of Great Britain, and in May 1708 he was created duke of Dover in the British peerage.

1057. *others:* Jacobites.

1057–59. *Cock . . . Whip:* Defoe refers again to Belhaven's speech (311 above). Belhaven had said "the greatest Honour that was done unto a *Roman,* was to allow him the Glory of a Triumph; the greatest and most dishonourable Punishment, was that of [a] *Paricide:* He that was guilty of *Paricide,* was beaten with Rods upon his naked Body, till the Blood gush'd out of all the Veins of his Body; then he was sow'd up in a Leathern Sack, call'd the *Culeus,* with a Cock, a Viper, and an Ape, and thrown headlong into the Sea. *My Lord, Patricide* is a greater Crime than *Paricide,* all the World over. In a Triumph, *my Lord,* when the Conqueror was riding in his Triumphal Chariot, crown'd with Lawrels, adorned with Trophies, and applauded with Huzza's . . . to his Chariot were tied a Whip and a Bell, to mind him, That for all his Glory and Grandeur, he was accountable to the People for his Administration, and would be punished as other Men, if found guilty" (*The Lord Beilhaven's Speech in the Scotch Parliament, Saturday the Second of November,* 1706, p. 6).

1061. *Gold:* The estates were indeed "inspir'd . . . with *Gold,*" but it was £20,000 of English gold, distributed by David Boyle, earl of Glasgow, the treasurer depute, mainly in the form of arrears of salary (*EHR, 84* [July 1969], 526–27).

Yea, sure that Persons Merit can't be Small,
Who has so long had access to the Hall
Of *Monarchs* of such rare discerning *Sp'rit,*
Who well have known, what *Ministers* were fit.   1065
    Let all vile sneaking, selfish Souls be gone,
Who to their *Countries* bliss prefer their own.
But let it be the sincere Sentiment
Of every *Son* that loves my *Government:*
Rather resign their Fortune, Life and Blood,   1070
A Sacrifice unto the Nations Good,
Than that for *Self* their *Countrey* should be lost.
    Brittannia, now, *Alas* can hardly boast
Of many *Curtius*'s, who the Gulf wou'd fill,
And Perish, to remove their Country's *Ill.*   1075
Many are now a Selfish invious Seed,
Unlike brave Fathers, Ugly, Spurious Breed.
Ingrate, Degen'rate, and Apostate Race,
Too many are, who wou'd the Cause Imbrace
Of their most Proud and Cruel Enemies,   1080
Rather than stand for their own *Liberties.*
Your former *Undertakings,* this have taught,
Too many *Sons* of *Belial,* Men of naught,
Are in my Bosom, wh'impudently dare,
The Name of their best *Liberators,* Tear.   1085
Such *Gratitude* can't be exprest in words!
But daily Room for Enmity affords.
How can ye hope, that these do seek your Good,
Who still for *High, Despotick* Power stood,
Who dar'd Oppose the *Service* of their *King.*   1090

1062. *Person:* Queensberry had been preferred to places of power by Charles II, William
III, and Anne.

1074. *Curtius:* Marcus Curtius rode fully armed into a crevasse that appeared in the
Roman forum after the oracle had promised that it would not close until Rome's most valu-
able possession had been thrown into it. The fissure closed immediately (Livy, vii, 6).

1076. *invious:* If this is not a printer's error, it may be an old spelling, not a Scotticism
(*OED* cites a sixteenth century "invyowse").

1083. *Sons of Belial:* A Puritan phrase for riotous courtiers (*Paradise Lost,* I, 502), but
here, as in *The Mock Mourners* (1702), lines 141, 185–93 (*POAS* Yale, *6,* 381, 383), the sons
of Belial are the English noblemen who refused to join William III in fighting the French.

1084. *my:* Britannia's.

1085. *best Liberators:* William III and his Dutch and Huguenot generals; cf. "Against the
hand that saves them they exclaim" (*The Mock Mourners,* 196).

   William inspires the Faintest *Muse* to sing
His Praise, who saved with a Mighty Hand,
Our Miserable, just Expiring *Land.*
May his blest Name never be mentioned
Without Respect: May't e're be Honoured.   1095
Heav'ns Darling, Europ's lasting *Ornament:*
Who for her Rights, his dearest Life he Spent.
At length, when call'd He with a willing Mind,
His blessed Soul to *Heav'n* content Resign'd.
   None was more worthy to ascend his *Throne,*   1100
Than whom *God, People,* and *William* pitch'd upon.
Bravest of *Queens,* and Best of *Female* Kind:
All Royal Vertues, in her Soul we find.
May she possess her *Subjects* Loyal Hearts,
And Beat her *Foes* into a thousand Parts.   1105

EPILOGUE

   I own, I'd ne're have both the *States* Conjoin'd
On Terms that are not for our Good design'd.
I bless my *Stars,* I'm not so perfect grown,
As with content my Patient Neck lay down
To have a *Slave's* and *Drudges* Yoke impos'd;   1110
But, praise to God, from such we shal be loos'd.
Yet let us think, and think on't o'er again,
That so we mayn't have e're ground to complain,
Sure All shou'd still prefer their *Countries* bliss
To other things; My daily prayers be this: 1115
   May *Heaven* to all your thoughts Propitious be,
While *Foes,* as Straw before a whirlwind flee.
May The *Almighty* all future ills divert,
Our *Priviledges* and our *Laws* assert,
Our True Religion and Just Property,   1120
The *Sovereigns* Power, and *Subjects* Liberty.

1091. *the Faintest Muse:* It was Britannia who sang William's praise in *The Mock Mourners,*
282–405.

1106. *I:* The Scots narrator resumes from line 537.

1116. *your:* Defoe addresses the "Noble *Representers*" (1) in the Scottish parliament.

In fine, May *Union* bring all Happiness:
And may't remove our present sad Distress.
Be *Churches Pillar* and *Support* of *State,*
And the blest *Mean* to make our *Kingdom* Great.   1125

JONATHAN SWIFT

Verses said to Be Written on the Union
(1707?)

Jonathan Swift was one of those unreconstructed Englishmen whose national prejudices Defoe had failed to remove. For Swift there was only "a certain Region, well known to the Antient *Greeks*, by them called, *Σkotia*, or the *Land of Darkness*," where a religious mania "of the most rank and virulent Kind" had been allowed to take root and flourish (*Prose, 1*, 97; *9*, 4).

Union with Scotland, in Swift's view, was "a monstrous Alliance," an evil necessity that had been imposed upon England by "the wrong Management of the Earl of *Godolphin*" in advising the queen to give assent to the Act of Security in August 1704 (*Prose, 3*, 95; *8*, 49, 114). It was, said Lord Haversham in a prophetic speech made in the House of Lords in the presence of the queen, "A Union, made up of so many mis-match'd Pieces, of such jarring incongruous Ingredients, *that he fear'd it would require a standing Force to keep us from falling asunder*" (*The Life and Reign of Her Late Excellent Majesty Queen Anne*, 1738, p. 325). A more recent historian has called it "the greatest of eighteenth-century jobs" (*Scottish Historical Review, 43* [October 1964], 110).

Although still "A [Whig] and one that wears a Gown"—eager to spend his credit with Somers and Sunderland for the advantage of the Church of Ireland—Swift's opposition to the union was one of the issues which divided him from his Whig friends, for the union was strongly supported by the Junto lords (p. 209 above) (Swift, *Poems, 1*, 121; *Corr., 1*, 57). And this, of course, may be one reason why he did not publish these verses in 1707.

The poem was published in 1746 when George Faulkner included it in the eighth and last volume of *The Works of Jonathan Swift, D.D.* with "other Pieces never before printed." As Sir Harold Williams has said, "the verses are in the manner of Swift, and with hardly a doubt, may be accepted as his" (*Poems, 1*, 95).

VERSES SAID TO BE WRITTEN ON THE UNION

The Queen has lately lost a Part
Of her entirely-*English* Heart,
For want of which by way of Botch,
She piec'd it up again with *Scotch.*
Blest Revolution, which creates 5
Divided Hearts, united States.
See how the double Nation lies;
Like a rich Coat with Skirts of Frize:
As if a Man in making Posies
Should bundle Thistles up with Roses. 10
Whoever yet a Union saw
Of Kingdoms, without Faith or Law.
Henceforward let no Statesman dare,
A Kingdom to a Ship compare;
Lest he should call our Commonweal, 15
A Vessel with a double Keel:

1. *lately lost a Part:* presumably the Anglo-Irish part, which Anne lost in October 1703 by her cold answer to the agitated address of the Irish parliament for "some sort of union" with England (James A. Froude, *The English in Ireland in the Eighteenth Century,* 2 vols., New York, 1881, *1,* 303–04). F. Elrington Ball supposed that the line refers to the "loss of revenue by the grant [in February 1704] of the tenths and first-fruits to the church, known as Queen Anne's Bounty" (*Swift's Verse,* London, John Murray, 1929, p. 92), but this seems unlikely.

2. *entirely-English Heart:* See *The History and Fall of the Conformity Bill,* 4n., and illustration, p. 6.

3. *Botch:* OED cites Samuel Butler, *Remains* (c. 1680, published 1759), *2,* 200: "He does not mend his Manners, but [does] botch them with Patches of another Stuff and Colour."

8. *Frize:* Frieze is a cheap, coarse woolen cloth; cf. *A Scots Poem,* 678n. above.

10. *bundle Thistles . . . with Roses:* A thistle and a rose grafted on the same stem are represented on the Scottish lion's shield in the union medal (Boyer, *History,* p. [721]). Cf. "we make a mighty Difference here [in Ireland] between suffering *Thistles* to grow among us, and wearing them for *Posies*" (Swift, *Prose, 2,* 124).

12. *Faith or Law:* By Articles XVIII and XXV of the union treaty, Scotland retained both its own form of "Laws concerning . . . Private Right" and its own established Presbyterian church. Many years later Swift acknowledged that the Scots "were united on their Conditions, which . . . they are proud enough to be ashamed of" (*Corr., 2,* 342).

16. *double Keel:* Sir William Petty (1623–87), the friend of Hobbes and a founder of the Royal Society, was also the first English political economist. He came to Ireland in 1652 as physician to Cromwell's army of occupation and settled in Dublin to become a great projector. His favorite project, to which he returned "again and again"—after each failure—was a double-hulled ship, or catamaran. "It is remarkable that the earlier trials of this class of ship—of which several were built—were more successful than the later" (*DNB, 15,* 1001).

Which just like ours, new rigg'd and man'd,
And got about a League from Land,
By Change of Wind to Leeward Side
The Pilot knew not how to guide.   20
So tossing Faction will o'erwhelm
One crazy double-bottom'd Realm.

Andrew Marvell and Sir William Temple also made poetical capital of these failures (*POAS,* Yale, *1,* 52; *Miscellanea, The Third Part,* 1701, pp. 281–82).

17. *ours:* The fourth and last of the double-hulled ships was laid down in a yard in Dublin harbor in July 1684, when Swift was 16. *Saint Michael the Archangel,* as she was christened, behaved so "abominably" in the water that the crew refused to sail beyond the bar of Dublin harbor and the project was abandoned ([George Petty-Fitzmaurice], Marquess of Lansdowne, *The Double Bottom or Twin-Hulled Ship of Sir William Petty,* Oxford, 1931, pp. xiii–xv, 132–39).

Switch and Spur:
Or
A Seasonable Prologue to the First British Parliament
(October? 1707)

1707 was the "year of *Blunders*" for the allies and for the Harley-Godolphin ministry (*The Life and Reign of Her Late Excellent Majesty Queen Anne,* 1738, p. 355). The military defeats at Almansa (line 31), Stolhofen (5), and Toulon (25), the stalemate in Flanders with Vendôme and Marlborough "striving which shal continue longest in their camps" (Luttrell, *6,* 181), and the unaccountable disaster of the fleet running aground off Land's End (41), precipitated a crisis in public confidence. The first parliament of Great Britain assembled at Westminister late in October 1707 "with a melancholy Face," as Burnet observed (*2,* 489). The opening address from the throne, in which the ministers would try to buy back public confidence, was set for 6 November.

The Tory author of the present poem imagines what the queen would say if she were allowed to tell the truth. *Switch and Spur* is a mock address *from* the throne just as *An Address to Our Sovereign Lady* (April 1704) (*POAS,* Yale, *6,* 615) is a mock address *to* the throne. And beneath the gay desperation on the surface it is not difficult to detect a current of deep loathing, not only for the compromises and the deceptions of the union with Scotland but also for the compromises, the deceptions, and above all the crushing costs of the war with France.

Since it includes nothing of what the queen actually said on 6 November 1707 (*LJ, 18,* 333–34), the poem may be assumed to have been written before that date. But there is no evidence who wrote it.

SWITCH AND SPUR

OR

A SEASONABLE PROLOGUE TO THE FIRST BRITISH PARLIAMENT

My Lords and *Gentlemen*, y'arc here Assembled
T'Assent to what (your Fathers would have trembled)
I heard propos'd so late as last November,
When *Hannibal* was at your Gates: Remember,
Villars is in the *Empire*, where this Year   5
He reap'd an early Harvest; and *We* fear
May do the like the next, Unless *We* send
Timely Supplies. The *Germans* wo'nt defend
Their Native Country at their own Expence,
The Aids that *They* expect must be from hence;   10
For they conclude unless *We* guard their *Throne*
The next *Insult* will be upon Our Own.
They'l give *Us* leave to practice on their Ground
Our Military Arts 'til *We* have found
By dear Experience (Mistress of all Fools)   15

2. *Assent:* By assembling at Westminster on 23 October 1707 the English and Scottish members enacted their assent to the parliamentary union of the two kingdoms that had been bitterly opposed both in the Scots parliament (November 1706–January 1707) and in the English parliament (February 1707).

4. *Hannibal . . . at your Gates:* The Scots members would recall Lord Belhaven's prophetic words of "last November": "*Hannibal, my Lord,* is at our Gates, *Hannibal* is come within our Gates, *Hannibal* is come the Length of this Table, he is at the Foot of this Throne, he will demolish this Throne; if we take not Notice, he'll seize upon these *Regalia* . . . and whip us out of this House, never to return again" (*The Lord Beilhaven's Speech in the Scotch Parliament, Saturday the Second of November* . . . , 1706, p. 11).

5. *Villars:* In an operation of great daring, Claude Louis Hector, duc de Villars (1653–1734), a marshal of France, threw a pontoon bridge across the Rhine at Lutterburg and broke through the German defenses at Stolhofen on 11/22 May 1707, "so that the fruits of the victory at Blenheim were lost in one night without opposition" (Luttrell, *6*, 174, 178–79). Before he was forced to withdraw in October, he burned villages and extorted huge "contributions" from the rich towns of Franconia and Swabia (Boyer, *Annals,* 1708, pp. 32–40).

8–9. *The Germans wo'nt defend | Their Native Country:* "The Empire, whose united and well-managed Strength might alone suffice to cope with the Power of *France,* did once more fall into those Misfortunes occasion'd by the usual Backwardness and Negligence of some of its Members; And the Remonstrances and Complaints that had been made to the Emperor . . . on the Part of Great Britain and Holland . . . were as ineffectual as before" (ibid., pp. 31–32).

10. *Aids:* English subsidies to German princes amounted to £147,189 in 1707–08 (*CJ, 15,* 448).

That *We*'re made Use of only as the *Tools*
To Skreen destruction from a tott'ring State
With who *We* are involv'd to risque its Fate.
Bavaria is at *Mons; Fabius Vendosme*
(Hav'ng lodg'd his Troops amongst *Us*) is gone Home   20
To Re-inforce with Fifty thousand more
Already Arm'd, and will Return before
The Circles have (tho' *Marlb'rough* do's his best
With *Han'ver*) fill'd the Military *Chest.*
Thoulon's preserv'd, and the Fam'd *Prince Eugene*   25

19. *Bavaria is at Mons:* Following his defeat at Ramillies, Maximilian Emanuel, elector of
Bavaria, moved his army into Mons (Luttrell, *6,* 54) and remained there through the winter
of 1707–08.

   Fabius Vendosme: After the defeat at Ramillies, Louis XIV recalled Louis Joseph, duc de
Vendôme (1654–1712), from Italy to replace Villeroi in June 1706. Vendôme carefully
avoided any further engagements, put his army into strongly fortified towns, and returned
to Versailles in August to beg for reinforcements (Luttrell, *6,* 79). His Fabian tactics not only
saved the French army in Flanders but induced a similar caution in the confederates. In the
campaign of 1707 the two armies "lay, for some Months, looking on one another" (Burnet,
2, 485). In September, Vendôme hastened back to Versailles where he was received "à
merveilles" (Saint-Simon, *Mémoires, 2,* 895). His classical antitype is Quintus Fabius Maxi-
mus, nicknamed Cunctator, whose delaying tactics saved Rome from Hannibal in 217 B.C.
(Livy, xxii–xxiii).

   21. *Fifty thousand:* In September 1707 it was reported "that the French intend to raise
50,000 men more" (Luttrell, *6,* 216).

   23. *The Circles:* For purposes of defense, the Empire was divided into ten circles, each of
which contributed men and money to the imperial army.

   24. *Han'ver:* Georg Ludwig, elector of Braunschweig-Lüneburg (Hanover) (1660–1727)
and the future king of Great Britain, was a "middle-siz'd" man "not addicted much to any
Diversions besides Hunting" and very careful in "laying out the public Mony" (John To-
land, *An Account of the Courts of Prussia and Hanover,* 1705, pp. 69, 71). He was placed in com-
mand of the imperial army of the Rhine following the disastrous incursions of Villars (5*n.*
above), and in October 1707 Marlborough travelled to Frankfurt "to presse his electoral
highnesse to use his best endeavours to engage the empire to augment their troops" (Boyer,
Annals, 1708, p. 45; Luttrell, *6,* 221).

   25. *Thoulon:* The major effort of the allies in 1707 was to have been the capture of Toulon,
the naval base from which the French fleet harried Dutch and English shipping in the
Mediterranean. Planned for April, it was July before 35,000 German and Savoyard troops
marched into Provence, covered by a Dutch and English fleet under the command of Sir
Cloudesley Shovell. The failure of the siege. which was opened on 15/26 July, was "attributed
to the not following prince Eugene's council, who was for attacking the French intrench-
ments . . . before they were finish't, but the duke of Savoy, &c. were against it" (Luttrell,
6, 208). Actually it was the duke of Savoy who had ordered the attack and Prince Eugene
who refused to obey the orders (Burnet, *2,* 477; Trevelyan, *2,* 307–09). The siege was aban-
doned on 11/22 August and in their frustration the retreating troops "destroyed all the
orange, olive, mulberry trees and vineyards from Toulon to the Varr" (Luttrell, *6,* 208).
"The news of Toulon," wrote Godolphin to Harley, "is extremely dejecting, and I dread
the consequences of it" (HMC *Bath MSS., 1,* 179).

   Eugene: François Eugène, Prince of Savoy-Carignano (1663–1736), was born in Paris,

Forc'd to take up with *Susa* as a Mean
To save his Credit; so th'all promising rich
Chymist has found a Med'cine for the *Itch*,
Full Recompence for all the Treasure gone
In *Fumo*, seeking the *Phylos'pher's* Stone.   30
Spain is quite lost; and *Portugal* in danger
Unless the last Extreamity make her change her
Resolves, and quit th'*Alliance*, which once shaken

---

a grandnephew of Cardinal Mazarin and a second cousin of Victor Amadeo II, duke of
Savoy. When he was repeatedly refused a commission by Louis XIV, he enlisted in the
imperial army and in thirty campaigns in the next fifty years he fought the battles of the
empire against France and the Turks. Two of his greatest successes were at Blenheim in
August 1704 and at Torino in September 1706. The latter victory had forced the French out
of Italy as completely as Ramillies had forced them out of Flanders and Brabant, and Prince
Eugene was rewarded with the governorship of the Milanese just as Marlborough had been
offered the governorship of the Spanish Netherlands. Eugene was Marlborough's choice to
undertake the siege of Toulon and he told his troops that "he would either take the town or
lay his bones under the walls." Bookmakers in London, who had been laying 3–10 that
Toulon would fall before November, suffered heavier losses than Prince Eugene, when he
abandoned the siege and marched back to Italy in August (Luttrell, *6*, 202, 204).

26. *Susa:* In their retreat toward Torino, the confederates stopped long enough to take
the town and fortress of Susa, just inside the Italian border. Susa was of importance to no one
but the duke of Savoy since it represented a French "In-let into his own Dominions" (Boyer,
Annals, 1708, pp. 112–13).

29. *the Treasure gone:* The cost of the Toulon expedition may have run as high as
£1,000,000 (*CJ, 17*, 48).

31. *Spain . . . lost:* The first disaster in the campaign of 1707 was the loss of Spain. In
April "the allies having besieged Villena, the duke of Berwick march't to its relief, and they
drawing off mett him in the plain of Almanza, where, after an hours engagement, the allies
had 8000 men killed, [and] a great number made prisoners . . . the French and Spaniards
loseing not above 800 men" (Luttrell, *6*, 167). By the end of May the armies of Philip V had
retaken Valencia and Zaragoza and confined the allies within Catalonia (Boyer, *Annals*,
1708, pp. 22–26). "For God's sake let us be once out of Spain!" St. John, the secretary at
war, wrote to Harley (HMC *Bath MSS., 1*, 194).

Portugal in danger: Relations with Portugal had been strained since June 1706 when
England demanded its money back for nonperformance of the terms of the Methuen treaty.
The Portuguese were even blamed for the debacle at Almansa: "It's said, the Portugal
horse at the beginning of the fight gave way, and put our men into disorder" (Luttrell, *6*,
53, 167). After Almansa "The Allies in *Spain* did fondly expect, that the *Portugueze* would
favor them by a Diversion, but were miserably disappointed: For, on the contrary, the Duke
of *Ossuna* on one side, and the Marquis *de Bay* on the other, enter'd their Territories" (Boyer
Annals, 1708, p. 31).

33. *quit th'Alliance:* The French faction at the Portuguese court was said to rejoice when
Pedro II, who had signed the Methuen treaty with England, died in December 1706 and
was succeeded by his 17-year old son, João V. Rumors that "the protestant princes are
apprehensive of a secret treaty between the Roman catholicks" began to reach London in
September 1707 (Luttrell, *6*, 118, 208).

Will soon disolve: and should *We* be forsaken
By one *Confederate* of the *Roman Church,*   35
The rest would Flinch and leave *Us* in the Lurch:
For They've a Common Cause as well as *We*
And (if They'd common Sense) would all agree
To carry't on, which to Prevent, *We* must
Exert our Utmost now or fall to Dust.   40
Sir Cloudsley Shovell, to our Consternation!
Is *Wreck'd* near *Scilly* in th'*Association*
By falling 'mongst the *Bishops* and their *Clarkes,*
Whereon high flying Church will make Remarks.
Ill-boding Omen, Ush'ring the first *Session*   45
Of *British Parliament!* But let no impression
Of such *Slight* acc'dents *baulk* our Resolutions
Of raising *Men* and lib'ral *Contributions*
For carrying on Our common Cause which now
Is in its *Chrysis,* and should *We* allow   50
Time for Redress of *Grievance,* or Debate
Of what might otherwise adorn the *State*
O'th'coelebrated *Union, We* might lose
The *Substance* for the *Shadow;* wherefore use
Your present time to find out ways and Means   55
To keep what We have got: *Bishops* and *Deans*

36. *The rest:* Besides Portugal, England's Catholic allies included the emperor, Joseph I; Victor Amadeo, duke of Savoy and a grandson of Charles I; and the prince-bishop of Liège.

41. *Shovell:* Sir Cloudesley Shovell (1650–1707) went to sea when he was 14, was knighted by William III in June 1689, and succeeded Sir George Rooke as commander of the fleet in May 1705. He provided powerful support for Peterborough's successful siege of Barcelona in July 1706 and covered the retreating army, after taking aboard the sick and wounded, following the failure at Toulon in August 1707. On the homeward voyage, "by an unaccountable Carelessness," his flagship, *The Association,* "struck upon the Rocks call'd, *The Bishop and his Clerks* [in the Scilly Islands, off Land's End], and was lost with all the Men in it . . . This was the fatal End of one of the greatest Sea-Commanders of our Age, or, indeed, as ever this Island produced" (Burnet, *2,* 485; Boyer, *Annals,* 1708, pp. 241–42). Since he had risen "by his personal Merit alone" from the lowest to the highest rank in the navy, Shovell was popular with ordinary seamen, who continued to call the brandy flip, with which he was regaling himself at the moment of the wreck, a Sir Cloudesley (*The Life and Reign of Her Late Excellent Majesty Queen Anne,* 1738, p. 365; Francis Grose, *A Classical Dictionary of the Vulgar Tongue,* 2nd ed., 1788, sig. L4v).

56–57. *Bishops and Deans | And Chapters Lands:* Failure of the treaty of union to effect a religious settlement aroused fears in Scotland that the kirk might be subordinated to the Anglican establishment (*The Vision,* 32n. above) and reciprocal fears in England, like those reflected in the text, that Presbyterianism might encroach upon the Anglican establishment.

And *Chapters* Lands must not be touch't As yet;
We'll talk of that when We're hereafter met
At greater Leisure; and the *Church* may stand
Although the *Church-men* ha'nt One foot of Land   60
Which does but 'Cumber 'em with Temp'ral Cares
And wast that Time which should be spent in Prayers.
    Eight Millions Sterling and Ten thousand Men
In Name (but in Reality ten times Ten)
Must be advanc'd forthwith; make no Delay   65
But (*Switch* and *Spur*) post on that all may say
Th'Addresses for the *Union* have prevail'd,
Or else the *Grand Confederacy* had fail'd,
The House of *Austria* been distress'd, tho' Subtile,
And *Charles* the third not Wedded *Wolfenbuttle,*   70
Occasional conforming Princess who
(In hopes to be a Queen) submits to doe
What ne'er before was done among the Godly,
Conform to *Rome;* which (though it looks but Odly
Yet) being in Order to promote *Our Cause,*   75
Is justifyable by the *Delphick* Laws

It was fears like these that led in February 1707 to passage of an act for securing the Church of England (5 Anne c. 5) which was appended to the treaty of union before it was passed by the English parliament (cf. *A Scots Poem,* 842n. above).

63. *Eight Millions:* Whether by coincidence or design this figure is very close to the total revenue of England from 29 September 1707 to 29 September 1708, which was £7,891,983. Of this amount £5,103,329 was actually spent for military purposes (*CTB 1708, 1,* ccxii, ccxxii).

    Ten thousand Men: On 22 November parliament authorized the raising of an additional 10,000 men to augment the 40,000 already acting with the allies (*CJ, 15,* 137).

67. *Addresses for the Union:* Addresses celebrating the enactment of the treaty of union on 1 May 1707 were presented to Anne from "most of the Cities, Towns and Corporations of *England*" (Boyer, *History,* p. 287), but these spontaneous demonstrations could be "artificially . . . procured" (Swift, *Discourse,* pp. 52–53; *Prose, 2,* 112).

70. *Wolfenbuttle:* "A Wife was to be sought for King *Charles,* among the Protestant Courts, for there was not a suitable Match in the Popish Courts: He had seen the Princess of *Ansbach,* and was much taken with her; so that great applications were made, to persuade her to change her Religion, but she could not be prevailed on, to buy a Crown at so dear a rate . . . The Princess of *Wolfenbutle* was not so firm; so she was brought to *Vienna,* and some time after was married by proxy to K. *Charles*" (Burnet, *2,* 479–80). Elisabeth Christine (Dannenberg), Princess of Braunschweig-Wolfenbüttle (1691–1750), was persuaded by her spiritual advisers (including the philosopher Leibniz, her father's librarian) that Roman Catholic rites could always be interpreted in an evangelical Lutheran fashion. She was, therefore, converted to Catholicism in May 1707 and married to Charles III in April 1708 at Barcelona (Zedler, *4,* 1162).

Of *Tolleration,* good on South side Tweed
But on *North Britain* side of Romish Breed,
Establishing iniquity by a Law;
Which the true *Kirk-Assembly* says is *Paw.*   80
For 'tis no *Rule* with *Presbyters* to do
As They'd be done by; all Dissenters too
Are alike Principl'd; Witness the *Review,*
Their *Oracle,* inspired by the *Three*
Directors of the *Whiggish Ministry,*   85
Conscience and Arms and Mammon, joyn'd as One
To finish what's so piously begun.
Avoyd all *Church* disputes; They do but hinder
The *Weightier Affairs* of *Faith's Defender.*

77. *Tolleration . . . on South side Tweed:* By an Act Exempting . . . Protestant Subjects Dissenting from the Church of *England* from the Penalties of Certain Laws (1 William & Mary c. 18) passed in May 1689 and called the Toleration Act, all Protestants were guaranteed freedom of public worship if they would take the oaths of loyalty to William and Mary (*EHD,* pp. 400–03).

78. *But on North Britain side:* When a bill similar to the Toleration Act was introduced into the Scottish parliament in June 1703, it was dropped after the second reading (*APS, 11,* 46–47). Since it would have extended toleration to "all Protestants," including "these of the Episcopal Perswasion," the commission, or permanent secretariat of the general assembly of the Church of Scotland, promptly objected that "to enact a Toleration for those of that way (which GOD in his infinite Mercy avert) would be to establish *Iniquity by a Law.*" Both the bill and the protest were reprinted by Charles Leslie in *The Wolf Stript of His Shepherd's Cloathing,* 1704, pp. ²1–3.

80. *Paw:* "Paw Words . . . *Beastly* and *Filthy Language*" (*The Observator,* 30 May–2 June 1705). Cf. Wycherley, *The Country Wife* (1675), 5.2.49.

81–82. *to do | As They'd be done by:* Matthew 7:12.

83. *Review:* Defoe mentions the kirk's refusal to grant toleration to Episcopalians in *A Short View of the Present State of the Protestant Religion in Britain* (March 1707) and in the *Review,* 6 September 1707. But he defends it at length in the ironically entitled *An Historical Account of the Bitter Sufferings, and Melancholy Circumstances of the Episcopal Church in Scotland* (October[?] 1707).

84–85. *Three | Directors:* "*The Triumvirate* who Mannage the State" were said to be Harley, Godolphin, and Marlborough (Defoe, *Letters,* p. 67), but in place of Harley, the Tory author of these verses puts William Cowper, who had been raised to the peerage in November 1706 and promoted to lord chancellor in May 1707.

86. *Conscience:* As traditional keeper of the queen's conscience, the lord chancellor "is to judge [in the court of chancery] according to Conscience and Equity, and not according to the Rigour of the Law" (Miège, 1707, p. 299).

Arms and Mammon: Marlborough, captain general of the forces, and Godolphin, lord treasurer.

89. *Faith's Defender:* For publishing a book against Luther in 1521 Henry VIII was called "fidei defensor" by the pope, a title which the monarchs of England have retained ever since.

Speed the *Supplys;* let nothing Intervene;   90
They only can present a happier *Scene*
Next Year than this: If so, We'l ride in Coaches;
If not, Then with *Sir Cloudesly, Buenos Noches.*

1708

WILLIAM WALSH

Abigail's Lamentation for the Loss of Mr. Harley.
From the Greek of Homer,
Left Imperfect by Mr. Walsh.
(February–March 1708)

Since the Harley-Godolphin ministry was by design a "moderate" or nonparty administration, it was constantly subject to attack from all sides. By 23 October 1707 when the first parliament of Great Britain convened at Westminster, the hunt was in full cry: "many of the *Whig Lords,* and most of the *Tories,* were by this Time almost equally disgusted" (Boyer, *History,* p. 309). The climax of the "year of *Blunders*" came on 31 December when William Gregg, a clerk in Harley's office and a hated Scot, was discovered to be a French spy (Luttrell, *6,* 252). Defoe had warned Harley three years before of the deplorable lack of security in the office of the secretary of state: "I have been in the Secretarys Office of a Post Night," he said, "when Had I been a French Spye I Could ha' Put in my Pockett my Lord N——ms Letters Directed to Sir Geo: Rook and to the Duke of Marlebro' Laid Carelessly on a Table for the Doorkeepers to Carry to the Post Office" (*Letters,* pp. 38–39). But Harley had done nothing to improve matters and so when Gregg's treasonable correspondence was opened at the post office in Brussels, the Whigs supposed that Harley was "a party in that business" and demanded his resignation (Boyer, *History,* p. 321; Swift, *Corr., 1,* 70).

Harley was indeed forced to resign in February 1708, but not on account of William Gregg, who is not even mentioned in the present poem celebrating that occasion. Harley's unexpected dismissal and the dramatic fashion in which it was forced upon the queen was a subject that fascinated his contemporaries. "The Spring of his Disgrace at Court," it was said, "has so many intricate Pipes which lead up to it, that we must at present lodge it amongst the Mysteries of State" (P. H., *An Impartial View of the Two Late Parliaments,* 1711, p. 117). William Walsh, however, was in a favored position to speculate upon, if not to solve, the mystery, for he was both a politician (a Junto Whig who had been returned to parliament in a by-election for the borough of

Richmond in Yorkshire in June 1705) and a courtier (gentleman of the horse, under the queen's master of the horse, Charles Seymour, duke of Somerset, an ally of the Junto). And it was Somerset who stood up at a meeting of the council on 8 February 1708 "and said, if her Majesty suffered that fellow (pointing to Harley), to treat affairs of the war without the advices of the General, he could not serve her; and so left the Council . . . [and] so did most of the Lords" (Swift, *Corr., 1,* 70).

It is remarkable, therefore, that *Abigail's Lamentation for the Loss of Mr. Harley* interprets Harley's "Disgrace" as the effect of an unsuccessful struggle with the duke of Marlborough. If Harley's "Schemes" (line 8) had succeeded, *"Ormond* had been sent to head the War" (38) and Marlborough "had been forc'd to yield" (39). Although this is a remarkable anticipation of exactly what happened on 31 December 1711, it is a startling conclusion to be drawn from the events of January–February 1708.

Harley's "Schemes" certainly included "an intrigue to alter the Ministry" (Swift, *Corr., 1,* 69). On 14 January 1708 at a meeting in the house of Henry Boyle, chancellor of the exchequer, Harley presented to Godolphin and Marlborough the "preliminaries" of a plan to include more Tories in the ministry (*EHR, 80,* [1965], 683). At this meeting or a few days later Harley and Godolphin each came to the conclusion that the other must be dropped. At this time, however, Harley seems to have had no plan to drop Marlborough and there is some evidence that Marlborough would have been willing to desert Godolphin and support Harley: "it was am[e]s ace as they say whether my Ld Treasurers old friend had not sacrificed him and given him up" (*EHR, 80,* [1965], 688–89). But on 3 February, when Harley made only a faint show of opposition to a Tory address censuring the ministry for the debacle at Almansa (*Switch and Spur,* 31*n.* above), the duke must have changed his mind (*Faults on Both Sides: Or, An Essay upon the Original Cause, Progress, and Mischievous Consequences of the Factions in this Nation,* 1710, p. 30). With the Tory back-benchers clamoring for a vote of censure, the Junto, seeking "an Opportunity to bite the Ministers . . . directed their Creatures [including William Walsh] by all means to let the Address pass as smart as the *Tories* wou'd have it . . . [and] The Ministers were frighten'd out of their Wits" (ibid.).

Harley did not learn of the duke's second thoughts until a day or two before the council meeting on 8 February. Meanwhile, on 6 February the queen proceeded to put into effect Harley's scheme for a new ministry. She sent St. John with a letter to Marlborough telling him that "she was resolved to part with Lord Treasurer" (Swift, *Corr., 1,* 69–70). Under pressure, "my Lord Treasurer's old friend" decided not to sacrifice him. Instead he replied to the queen by submitting his own resignation unless Harley were dismissed; "no consideration," he said, "can make me serve any longer with that man" (Coxe, *Memoirs, 2,* 191). The moment, on 6 or 7 February, when Harley learned of Marlborough's resignation, can have been the only time when he might have planned to replace Marlborough with James Butler, duke of Ormonde. The queen continued to hope until a few minutes before the council meeting on Sunday 8 February that Marlborough would retain his command. In a confrontation outside the council chamber, the duke insisted that his resignation be accepted so "that she might put the sword into some other hand immediately." Anne was shaken. "If you do my Lord resign your sword let me tel you you run it through my heart" (PRO 30/24/21, f. 149). While Godolphin, Marlborough, and his duchess drew off, Harley and the queen proceeded into the council chamber and in a few moments Somerset was saying, "I do not see how we can deliberate, when the commander-in-chief and the lord treasurer are absent" (Coxe, *Memoirs, 2,* 192).

Still the queen was not intimidated and now Harley may have broached to her his plan to put Ormonde in command of the British forces. "The back stairs," it was remarked, "were very much crowded for two or three days" as Harley struggled to put together a government (Trevelyan, *2,* 328). But it was too late. Parliament responded to rumors of the queen's decision to "trust to Mr. Harley's scheme for all" in a most decisive fashion. On Monday 9 February the Commons tabled the bill of supply, "tho' it was ordered for that Day" (Burnet, *2,* 496), and the Lords chose a select committee of seven Whigs to examine Gregg in Newgate and "to bring in Harley as a party in that business, and to carry it as far as an impeachment" (Swift, *Corr., 1,* 70). It was only when Harley added his entreaties to those of the prince consort and the duke of Newcastle (33*n.* below), that Anne could be persuaded to part with her secretary (Coxe, *Memoirs, 2,* 193). On Wednesday 11 February, the drama ended with the formal act of resignation described in the opening lines of *Abigail's Lamentation for the Loss of Mr. Harley.*

Walsh conceived of his poem as an epic fragment, like something out of Stobaeus: Abigail Masham looks down from "*Kensington's* high Tow'rs" (13) like Helen looking down from the walls of Troy. In sympathy with "the God-like Hero's fatal Doom" (20), the sun itself is obscured by clouds. But Harley and Mrs. Masham are blown up to epic proportions only to suffer mock-epic deflation: "the God-like Hero's" coach of state is drawn by mules (5) and Mrs. Masham's brightness (13) is in her nose.

Since Walsh had advised young Alexander Pope in July 1706 that "The best of the modern Poets . . . are those that have the nearest copied the Ancients" (Pope, *Corr.*, *1*, 20), it is interesting to observe that the opening lines of *Abigail's Lamentation for the Loss of Mr. Harley* may allude very obliquely to the lines of Horace:

> Strenuus et fortis causisque Philippus agendis
> clarus, ab officiis octavam circiter horam
> dum redit . . .
>
> [While that distinguished lawyer, bold,
> vigorous Philippus, was coming home from
> work one day about two . . .]
> (*Epistles*, I, vii, 46–48)

that Swift was to imitate more closely but in a very different tone in 1713 (*Part of the Seventh Epistle of the First Book of Horace Imitated*, 1–3):

> *HARLEY*, the Nation's great Support,
> Returning home one Day from Court,
> (His Mind with Publick Cares possest . . .)

The *end* of Walsh's poem, however, sounds more like Nostradamus than it does like Horace for it adopts the deliberately enigmatical style of the prophecy (*POAS*, Yale, *6*, 530), another genre that Swift was to turn to the purposes of political satire (in *The W——ds——r Prophecy* ["When a holy black *Suede*, the *Son* of *Bob*"], December 1711).

In August 1707 Pope visited Walsh at Abberley, his estate in Worcestershire, and it was probably on this occasion that Walsh told the 17-year old poet "that there was one way left of excelling . . . [and] that was [to be] correct" (Pope, *Corr.*, *1*, 29; Spence, *Anecdotes*, *1*, 32). A stylistic study of *Abigail's Lamentation for the Loss of Mr. Harley* might reveal what Walsh meant by "correct." For the verses were "Left Imperfect" not by Walsh's failure to correct them, but by his death on 18 March 1708 (Luttrell, *6*, 280). And "It will," as Walsh said himself, "be a very great satisfaction doubtless to a Man when he is in the Grave, to think his Verses run as smoothly as ever" (*Poems and Translations by Several Hands*, ed. John Oldmixon, 1714, p. [2]17).

Since most of the surviving copies (*BCEFGHKL*), including one at

Blenheim in the hand of Arthur Mainwaring, mention Walsh's name in the title, there cannot be much doubt that he wrote the poem. Walsh's death provides a *terminus ad quem* for the date of composition, just as Harley's resignation on 11 February 1708 provides the other limit. The popularity of the poem can be inferred from the dates of some of the copies: in November 1708 (*H*) the poem was still circulating in manuscript; it was anthologized in March 1709 (the Luttrell copy of *C* in the Folger Library is dated "24. March 1709/8"), and the poem was printed (or reprinted?) as a broadside as late as 1710 (*J*).

ABIGAIL'S LAMENTATION FOR THE LOSS OF MR. HARLEY.
FROM THE GREEK OF HOMER,
LEFT IMPERFECT BY MR. WALSH.

Now *Phoebus* did the World with Frowns survey;
Dark were the Clouds and dismal was the Day,
When pensive *Harley* from the Court return'd,
Slowly his Chariot mov'd, as that had mourn'd;
Heavy the Mules before the State's-man go,   5
As dragging an unusual Weight of Woe;
Sad was his Aspect, and he waking Dreams
Of Plots abortive and of ruin'd Schemes;
So some sad Youth, whose Griefs alone survive,
Mourns a dead Mistress, or a Wife alive;   10
Such Looks would *Russell*'s Funeral Triumphs grace,
So *Nottingham* still look'd with such a *dismal* Face.
To *Kensington*'s high Tow'rs bright *Masham* flies,

2. *the Day:* Wednesday 11 February 1708. Swift wrote to Archbishop King on 12 Febru-
ary: "Yesterday the seals were taken from Mr. Harley, and Sir Thomas Mansell gave up his
staff. They went to Kensington together for that purpose, and came back immediately"
(Swift, *Corr.*, *1*, 69).

8. *ruin'd Schemes:* "It is said that Harley had laid a scheme for an entire new Ministry,"
Swift went on to say, "and the men are named to whom the several employments were to be
given. And though his project had miscarried, it is reckoned the greatest piece of Court skill
that has been acted these many years" (ibid., *1*, 71). On 27 February Addison supplied
some of the names for Lord Manchester: "The Treasury they say was to have been in Com-
mission and Mr. Harley at the Head of it in order to have it Broken in a short time and
himself to have been Ld High Treasurer of Great Britain. Mr. St. John and the Earle Pawlett
were as it is said, to have been Secretarys of State and Harcourt Ld Chancellour. Sir T.
Hanmore too was to have come in for his share but I have forgot his Post . . . They did not
question it seems but my Ld Marlborough would have acted with them . . . How this so
much talked of scheme prov'd Abortive and came to Light before its time is still a mystery"
(Addison, *Letters*, p. 95).

11. *Russell's Funeral Triumphs:* One of the greatest triumphs of William Russell, the under-
taker in Cheapside, was the funeral of Walsh's friend, John Dryden (*POAS,* Yale, *6,* 206–08).

12. *dismal:* Nottingham's nickname (*The Lawyer's Answer,* 22n. above).

13. *bright:* "Bright" is used here to mean neither the opposite of "dismal" nor "bryghte of
ble," but "flaming red," in allusion to Abigail's countenance. Her face was so disfigured that
she was called "Carbunconella" and "that Pimplefaced Bitch" (*Letter Books of John Hervey,
1st Earl of Bristol,* 3 vols., Wells, 1894, *1,* 294; Holmes, p. 214). How Abigail Masham (d.
1734) came to live in Kensington palace is best told by the duchess of Marlborough: "Mrs.
MASHAM was the daughter of one HILL, a merchant in the city, by a sister of my father.
Our grandfather, Sir JOHN JENYNS, had two and twenty children, by which means the
estate of the family (which was reputed to be about 4000*l.* a year) came to be divided into

Thence she afar the sad Procession spies,
Where the late State's-man doth in Sorrow ride,   15
His *Welch* Supporter mourning by his Side;
At which her boundless Grief loud Cries began,
And thus lamenting, thro' the Court she ran:
   Hither, ye wretched Tories, hither come;
Behold the God-like Hero's fatal Doom.   20
If e'er you us'd with ravishing Delight,
To hear his Banter and admire his Bite;
Now to his Sorrows, yield this last Relief;
Who once was all your Hopes is now your Grief.
Had this Great Man his envy'd Post enjoy'd,   25
Tories had rul'd and Whigs had been destroy'd.
Harcourt the Mace, to which he long aspir'd,

---

small parcels. Mrs. HILL had only 500*l.* to her portion. Her husband lived very well, as I have been told, for many years, till turning projector, he brought ruin upon himself and his family." Upon discovering that her relatives were in want, Sarah sent them money. "I think Mrs. MASHAM's father and mother did not live long after this. They left four children, two sons and two daughters. The eldest daughter (afterwards Mrs. MASHAM) was a grown woman. I took her to St. Albans, where she lived with me and my children, and I treated her with as great kindness, as if she had been my sister. After some time a bedchamber-woman of the PRINCESS of Denmark's died; and . . . I thought I might ask the PRINCESS to give the vacant place to Mrs. HILL" (*Account of the Conduct,* pp. 177–78). "She learned the Arts of a Court," Burnet said (2, 487), "and observed the Queen's Temper, with so much Application, that she got far into her Heart: And she imployed all her Credit, to establish *Harley* in the supreme Confidence with the Queen, and to alienate her Affections from the Dutchess of *Marlborough.*"

16. *Welch Supporter:* "Sir T. Ma(nsell)" *DF.* Mansell quit his post as comptroller of the household "when Mr. Harley was removed, who undoubtedly procured him this employment" (*Wentworth Papers,* p. 134).

22. *Banter:* Defined as "a pleasant way of prating, which seems in earnest, but is in jest" (*New Dictionary,* sig. B3v), "banter" continued to gain currency. In September 1710 Swift acknowledged that his utmost effort "to stop the Progress of *Mob* and *Banter*" had been "plainly born down by Numbers" (*Prose, 2,* 176). Bantering Swift became one of Harley's favorite games; he particularly enjoyed calling Swift "Thomas," after the "little Parson-cousin" who had dared to claim *A Tale of a Tub* as his own (*Journal, 1,* 280n.).

Bite: "Bite" was another slang word, meaning "to put the cheat on" (*New Dictionary,* sig. B5v), or to deceive. Harley's love of deviousness and deception had already been noted by Walsh (*POAS,* Yale *6,* 494) and by Lord Cowper (*Diary,* p. 33): "that humour of his, which was, never to deal clearly or openly, but always with Reserve, if not Dissimulation, or rather Simulation; & to love Tricks even where not necessary, but from an inward Satisfaction he took in applauding his own Cunning. If any Man was born under a Necessity of being a Knave, he was."

27. *Harcourt:* Sir Simon Harcourt, who was to have been lord chancellor in Harley's projected ministry (8*n.* above), resigned as attorney general on 12 February 1708, the day after Harley's resignation.

Had now possess'd, and *Cowper* had retir'd;
And *Sunderland* his Post been forc'd to quit,
Which St. *John* had supply'd with sprightly Wit.   30
Sage *Hanmer* (passing Court-Employments by)
Had rul'd the Coffers, Tories to supply.
Gower had shin'd with rich *Newcastle*'s Seal,

28. *Cowper:* The incumbent lord chancellor was Lord Cowper, whose appointment by Godolphin in October 1705 had been opposed by Harley (p. 142 above).

29. *Sunderland:* Roger Coke "was told by a considerable Tory, but about four Days before the Discovery was publickly made, that the Earl of *Sunderland* was to be out of his Secretary's Place such a Day, he being the Person they resolved to begin with" (*A Detection of the Court and State of England*, 4th ed., 3 vols., 1719, *3*, 323).

30. *St. John:* Henry St. John was designated as secretary of state in both accounts of Harley's projected ministry that Addison sent to Lord Manchester (Addison, *Letters*, pp. 91, 95).

sprightly Wit: The same ambiguity may be involved in Belinda's "sprightly Mind" in *The Rape of the Lock*, II, 9. Walsh had already jeered at "*Thracian St. John*" in *The Golden Age Restor'd*, 109 (*POAS*, Yale, *6*, 503).

31. *Hanmer:* Sir Thomas Hanmer of Hanmer, Flintshire, fourth baronet (1677–1746) failed to take a degree from Christ Church, Oxford, but Cambridge made up for this deficiency by awarding him an honorary LL. D. in 1705. In parliament, where he sat for Thetford, Norfolk (1701–02, 1705–08), Flintshire (1702–05), and Suffolk (1708–26), Hanmer was a "True Church" Tory, a Tacker, and a member of the October Club. But he also became the leader of the Whimsicals, who criticized the peace in 1713 and emerged as Hanoverian Tories. In the parliament of 1714 Hanmer was Speaker. He was also, it is said, "distinguished in the literary world" (GEC, *Baronetage, 1*, 153). In *The Dunciad, 4*, 105, he is discovered in the act of laying his edition of Shakespeare at the feet of Dulness.

32. *rul'd the Coffers:* Addison could not remember what post Harley intended for Hanmer (8*n*. above) but this line makes it sound like chancellor of the exchequer.

33. *Gower:* Sir John Leveson-Gower of Lilleshall and Stittenham, Yorkshire, fifth baronet (1675–1709), was a Tory member of parliament for Newcastle-under-Lyme from 1692 to March 1703 when he became one of the four, "the violentest of the whole Party" (Burnet, *2*, 344), who were raised to the peerage to create a majority in the House of Lords. He was also a privy councillor (April 1702–May 1707) and chancellor of the duchy of Lancaster (1702–06).

Newcastle: John Holles, duke of Newcastle (1662–1711), was the "Protestant patron" to whom Dryden dedicated *The Spanish Friar* (1681) (*Works, 6,* 410). He was elected to the convention parliament in January 1689 but two days later succeeded his father as earl of Clare and took his seat instead in the House of Lords. In recognition of his services to the revolution, William III made him duke of Newcastle in January 1694 but appointed him to no high office. On 26 March 1705, however, Harley secured his appointment as lord privy seal, and three days later he was sworn of her majesty's privy council. It was the "Duke of Newcastle Harley's friend [who] at last prest the Q[ueen] to part with him" on 10 February 1708 (PRO 30/24/21, f. 146). With an income estimated at £40,000 a year, Newcastle was thought to be one of the richest men in England and from 1701 to 1711 he spent £225,000 buying more estates (*Renaissance and Modern Studies, 9* [1965], 44), but he was also "a stingy, close Man, & . . . a great Whigg" (Hearne, *3*, 196). Had his only legitimate child inherited all this wealth, she would have been, when she married Harley's son in October 1713, "the richest Heiress in *Europe*" (Macky, p. 35), but Newcastle left most of his estate and his title

And *Harley*'s self, to shew his humble Zeal,
Had been contented with that trifling Wand,   35
That now does Mischief in *Godolphin*'s Hand.
Our Fleet secure had been *Rooke*'s tender Care,
And *Ormond* had been sent to head the War.
Blenheim to *Radnor* had been forc'd to yield,
And *Cardiff* Cliffs obscur'd *Ramillia*'s Field.   40

---

to a nephew, Thomas Pelham-Holles, and thus "cheated" his heiress, as Swift complained (*Prose, 5,* 258).

Seal: No other evidence indicates that Harley intended to replace Newcastle as lord privy seal, let alone that Gower was his candidate for that post. It seems more probable that Harley hoped to keep Newcastle in office as a court Whig who would balance the Tory elements. It was because he prized the duke's "very great ability in moderating" that he had brought him into the government in the first place (HMC *Portland MSS., 2,* 184–89).

35. *Wand:* the lord treasurer's staff of office (see illustration, p. 475). When Godolphin threatened to resign on 8 February, Anne told him "she could find enough glad of that staff" (PRO 30/24/21, f. 150).

37. *Rooke:* Ever since Rooke's dismissal in 1705 (Luttrell, *5,* 505, 562) his friends had sought a suitable post for him, and Sir Cloudesley Shovell's death in October 1707 seemed to have created such an opening.

38. *And Ormond . . . sent to head the War:* Harley's retrospective comment on his failure to displace Godolphin and Marlborough in February 1708 may be contained in *Faults on Both Sides,* 1710, p. 31: "to think of displacing and disgracing them at that time of day, was fit for no Man in his Wits."

39. *Blenheim:* After the battle of Blenheim in August 1703, the queen rewarded Marlborough by giving him the royal manor of Woodstock, on which Blenheim palace began to be built in June 1705. In December 1706 an Act for the settling of the Honours and Dignities of *John* Duke of *Marlborough* upon his Posterity, and annexing the Honour and Manor of *Woodstock,* and House of *Bleinheim* to go along with the said Honours, was passed with remarkable speed. The bill received the necessary three readings in the House of Lords on 18, 19, 20 December. In the House of Commons it was read three times in one day, 20 December, and received the royal assent on 21 December (*LJ, 18,* 184–85; *CJ, 15,* 217, 219).

Radnor: Harley sat in parliament as the member for New Radnor, Wales, from March 1690 to May 1711 when he was elevated to the peerage.

40. *Cardiff Cliffs:* the copy of the poem at Blenheim (*G*), is endorsed by the duchess of Marlborough: "Cardiff cliffs is the name of the place where Mr Harley did live in the country. The thought is pritty, & I believe there is more of it but I only found this bit of paper" (*Huntington Library Quarterly, 33* [1970], 142n.).

A New Ballad:
To the Tune of *Fair Rosamund*
(February–July 1708)

It is possible that this is one of "the two Ballads" that Sarah, duchess of Marlborough, "had the honour," or the impudence, to show to the queen in July 1708 so that her majesty might know what people were saying about her (Blenheim MS. GI 7). It is certain that this is one of "the two Ballads of the Battle of Abigal" that the duchess offered to sing for Dame Sarah Cowper, mother of the lord chancellor: "I wish I may have the honour," she said, "of waiting upon you when you are in Hertfordshire, and that you will allow me to sing with you, for indeed I think I am much improv'd, at least in the two Ballads of the Battle of Abigal. I can sing them most rarely" (Hertfordshire County R. O. Cowper MS. Box 12, *1*, 27). The copy of *A New Ballad* (*Ab*) that follows in the manuscript is endorsed, "The Ballad the Dutchess of Marlborough mentions." And it is further possible that the duchess may have been coached for her performance by the author himself, for Arthur Mainwaring is known to have sung ballads to his own accompaniment on the harpsichord "with becoming impudence" (*Philological Quarterly,* *50* [October 1971], 616).

Whoever he was, the author took as his model for *A New Ballad* an old ballad by Thomas Deloney entitled *A Mournefull Dittie on the Death of Faire Rosamond* that was first published in *Strange Histories* (1607) and frequently reprinted. Deloney's ballad, which is also a source for Addison's opera, *Rosamond* (March 1707), begins,

> When as king Henry rulde this land,
>   The second of that name,
> Besides the quene, he dearly lovde
>   A faire and comely dame,

which *A New Ballad* deftly parodies,

> Whenas Queen Anne of great Renown
>   *Great Britain's* Scepter sway'd,

         Besides the Church, she dearly lov'd
         A Dirty Chamber-Maid.

In the transformation from old ballad to new ballad, Henry II readily becomes Anne and Queen Eleanor with only a slight strain becomes "the Church," but Rosamond, the royal mistress, does not easily translate into Abigail Masham. The duchess of Marlborough had warned the queen that "having discovered so great a passion for such a woman" was not the way to maintain her reputation (Blenheim MS. GI 7).

    Deloney's ballad was set to the tune of *Flying Fame,* which is probably an earlier name for the famous tune of *Chevy Chase.* Deloney's ballad, in its turn, supplied a new name for the old tune, and several ballads in the seventeenth and eighteenth centuries, besides the present one, call for the tune of *Fair Rosamond* (Simpson, pp. 96–99).

    The evidence that Mainwaring wrote *A New Ballad* is entirely circumstantial. The ballad reproduces phrases from Mainwaring's prose (4*n.,* 105*n.*) and locutions from his verse (83–84*n.*). More importantly it reflects the contents of the duchess of Marlborough's mind so exactly that it could have been written only by a close acquaintance. Since writing the "merry Ballad" of *The History and Fall of the Conformity-Bill* in January 1704, Mainwaring had enjoyed unusual success. In May 1705 Godolphin unexpectedly made him a present of the office of auditor of the imprest, worth about £2,000 a year (Luttrell, *5,* 548; Oldmixon, *Maynwaring,* pp. 22–23). In December 1706 he entered parliament in a by-election for Preston, Lancashire, after surviving a recount by a margin of six votes (Luttrell, *6,* 125). But more important politically than either of these positions was his special relationship with the duchess of Marlborough which began in 1707. "I am now," he said in July 1708, "in your Grace's service (in which I will die)" (*Private Correspondence of Sarah, Duchess of Marlborough, 1,* 154). Mainwaring became the duchess's informant, advisor, co-conspirator, collaborator, confidant, and accompanist on the harpsichord. It was this relationship that made it possible for *A New Ballad* to reflect the duchess of Marlborough's attitudes so exactly. And it was this relationship that propelled Mainwaring into the role of Swift's main antagonist in the propaganda battles of the last years of the reign.

    Termini for the date of composition of *A New Ballad* are Harley's dismissal on 11 February 1708, which the poem celebrates, and 18 July 1708 when the duchess of Marlborough offered to sing it for Dame Sarah Cowper. *A New Ballad* may be the "well-written" "Print" that

Addison sent to Edward Wortley on 27 April 1708. "I fancy it is Manwarings," he said (Addison, *Letters,* p. 111).

A New Ballad:
To the Tune of *Fair Rosamund*

Whenas Queen *Anne* of great Renown
　　Great Britain's Scepter sway'd,
Besides the Church, she dearly lov'd
　　A Dirty Chamber-Maid.

Oh! *Abigail* that was her Name,   5
　　She starch'd and stitch'd full well,
But how she pierc'd this Royal Heart,
　　No mortal Man can tell.

However, for sweet Service done
　　And Causes of great weight,   10
Her Royal Mistress made her, Oh!
　　A Minister of State.

Her Secretary she was not,
　　Because she could not write;
But had the Conduct and the Care   15
　　Of some dark Deeds at night.

3. *the Church:* The duchess of Marlborough testified to the queen's "most real and invariable passion for that phantom which she called *the church*" (*Account of the Conduct*, p. 270).

4. *Dirty Chamber-Maid:* On another occasion Mainwaring called Mrs. Masham "a stinking ugly chambermaid" (*Private Correspondence of Sarah Duchess of Marlborough, 1,* 392).

6. *starch'd and stitch'd:* Although the four bedchamber women ranked only third in the hierarchy of the royal household (after ladies of the queen's bedchamber and maids of honor), the queen's starcher, Mrs. Eliz. Abrahall, and the prince's seamstress of the body, Mrs. Cooper, would not have allowed Mrs. Masham to undertake very much laundry or sewing.

14. *could not write:* Nothing seems to be known about Mrs. Masham's education, but she could in fact write. Some of her letters to Harley are preserved in HMC *Portland MSS., 4,* 495–96, 499, 510–11; cf. *DNB, 12,* 1296.

16. *dark Deeds at night:* The duchess of Marlborough supposed that these were lesbian transactions between Mrs. Masham and the queen. Thus she wrote to Sir David Hamilton, the queen's physician, on 6 December 1710: " 'tis certain that the town and country are very full of prints that do Mrs Morley [the queen] great hurt because she has given so much ground for such papers, and I hear there is some lately come out which they said were not fit for me to see, by which I guess they are upon a subject that you may remember I complained of to you and really it troubl'd me very much upon my own account as well as others because it was very disagreeable and what I know to be a lye by something of that disagreeable turn there was in an odious ballad to the tune of fair Rosamund, printed a good while agoe, in which the Queen gives an account of Mr Harleys and Mrs Mashams base designs against all those that had brought them to court, and ridiculed her very justly; but that which I hated

The Important Pass of the Back-Stairs
   Was put into her hand;
And up she brought the greatest Rogue
   Grew in this fruitful Land.   20

And what am I to do, quoth he,
   Oh! for this Favour great?
You are to teach me how, quoth she,
   To be a Slut of State.

My Dispositions they are good,   25
   Mischievous and a Lyar;
A saucy proud ungrateful Bitch,
   And for the Church entire.

Great Qualities! quoth *Machiavell*,
   And soon the World shall see   30
What you can for your Mistress do,
   With one small Dash of me.

In Counsel sweet, Oh! then they sat,

---

was the disrespect to the Queen and the disagreeable expressions of the dark deeds of the night" (Blenheim MS. GI 8).

17. *the Back-Stairs:* "Those that saw the Queen that were not to be known, came in from the Park into the garden, and from thence Abigail carried them a back way to the Queen's closet" (Althorp MSS., Duchess of Marlborough to David Mallet, 24 September 1744, quoted in Trevelyan, 2, 329).

19. *the greatest Rogue:* "Mr. Harley is generally allowed as cunning a man as any in England" (Wentworth Papers, p. 132).

26. *a Lyar:* Although the duchess knew as early as June 1707 that "Mrs. MASHAM speaks of business to the QUEEN," Mrs. Masham herself continued to deny this. But "I knew for certain," the duchess said, that "she had, before this, obtained pensions for several of her friends, and had frequently paid to others, out of the privy-purse, sums of money, which the QUEEN had ordered me to bring her" (*Account of the Conduct*, pp. 185, 206).

27. *saucy:* "Particularly I remembered that . . . being with the QUEEN . . . on a sudden this woman, not knowing I was there, came in with the boldest and gaiest air possible, but, upon sight of me, stopped; and immediately, changing her manner, and making a most solemn courtesy [said], *did your* MAJESTY *ring?*" (*Account of the Conduct*, p. 185).

ungrateful: When the duchess learned the full scope of Mrs. Masham's faithlessness (*Abigail's Lamentation for the Loss of Mr. Harley*, 13n. above), she "was struck with astonishment . . . and should not have *believed*, if there had been any room left for *doubting*" (*Account of the Conduct*, p. 184).

28. *for the Church:* Mrs. Masham was "deeply imbued with the maxims of the high church party" and did not hesitate to interfere in appointments to the episcopal bench: "Last night," she told Harley in March 1710, "I had a great deal of discourse with my aunt [the queen] and much of it about the two men that are named for bishops" (Coxe, *Memoirs*, 2, 96; HMC *Portland MSS.*, 4, 536).

Where she did Griefs unfold,
  Had long her grateful Heart oppress'd.   35
    And thus her Tale she told:

From Shreds and Dirt in low degree,
  From Scorn in piteous State,
A Dutchess bountiful has made
  Of me a Lady Great.   40

Such Favours she has heap'd upon
  This undeserving Head,
That for to ease me from their weight,
  Good God, that she were dead!

Oh! let me then some means find out,   45
  This Teazing Debt to pay.
I think, quoth he, to get her Place
  Would be the only way.

For less than you she must be brought,
  Or I can never see   50
How you can pay the Boons receiv'd
  When you were less than she.

My Argument lies in few words,
  Yet not the less in weight;
And oft with good Success we use   55
  Such, in Affairs of State.

Quoth she, 'tis not to be withstood;
  I'le push it from this hour;
I will be grateful, or at least
  I'le have it in my Power.   60

Quoth he, since my poor Counsel gains
  Such Favour in your eye,
I have a small Request to make,
  I hope you won't deny.

36. *her Tale:* cf. *Duke Humphrey's Answer,* 31n., below.

47. *her Place:* The duchess was lady of the stole, lady of the robes, and keeper of the privy purse (Miège, 1707, pp. 390–91). Upon her dismissal in January 1711, Mrs. Masham succeeded to the last of these places (Luttrell, *6,* 680).

49–53. A good example of "that wonderful talent Mr. HARLEY possessed, in the supreme degree, of confounding the common sense of mankind" (*Account of the Conduct,* p. 218).

Some Bounties I, like you, have had   65
    From one that bears the Wand,
And very fain I would, like you,
    Repay them if I can.

Witness ye Heavens! how I wish
    To slide into his Place;   70
Only to shew him Countenance
    When he is in Disgrace.

Oh! would you use your Interest great
    With our most Gracious Queen,
Such things I'd quickly bring about   75
    This Land hath never seen.

Give me but once her Royal Ear,
    Such Notes I'le in it sound,
As from her sweet Repose shall make
    Her Royal Head turn round.   80

He spoke, and straitway it was done;
    She gain'd him free Access.
God long preserve our Gracious Queen,
    The Parliament no less!

Now from this hour it was remarkt,   85
    That there was such Resort
Of many great and high Divines
    Unto the Queen's fair Court,

Mysterious things that long were hid,

66. *the Wand:* Lord Treasurer Godolphin's staff of office (see illustration, p. 475).

70. *slide into his Place:* See *Abigail's Lamentation for the Loss of Mr. Harley,* 8n. above.

82. *free Access:* "By the good Offices of . . . Mrs. *Masham,* [Harley] had . . . free Egress and Regress to the Queen" (Boyer, *History,* p. 322).

83–84. Mainwaring uses a similar locution in *The History and Fall of the Conformity-Bill* (1704), 5–7 above.

87. *high Divines:* Harley's influence began to be suspected in April 1707 when Anne privately admitted two high churchmen to her closet to kiss hands for the bishoprics of Exeter and Chester (*English Historical Review, 82* [October 1967], 737) while the Whigs were being assured that low churchmen would be preferred (*Account of the Conduct,* p. 174).

89. *Mysterious things:* These seem to include the fears of high churchmen that the defeat of France would 1) destroy the hope of a second Stuart restoration (lines 105–08 below) and 2) cut off the supply of French gold (99–100 below).

Began to come to light;   90
And many of the Church's Sons
  Were in a zealous Fright.

'Twas said, with Sighs and anxious Looks,
  A General abroad
Had won more Battles than their Friends,   95
  The *French*, could well afford;

That so much Money had been sent
  Such needless things t'advance,
It sure was time, as in Reigns pass'd,
  Some now should come from France.   100

At last they spoke it out and said,
  'Twas of the last Import,
That there should be a thorough Change
  In Army, Fleet, and Court.

For wicked *Johnny Marlborough*   105
  So madly push'd things on,
That should he unto *Paris* go
  The Church was quite undone.

The wise and pious Queen gave ear
  To this devout Advice,   110
And honest sturdy *Sunderland*
  Was whipt up in a trice.

---

97. *so much Money:* Arthur Mainwaring estimated that the war was costing "Six Millions
a year" (*Four Letters to a Friend in North Britain upon the Publishing the Tryal of Dr. Sacheverell*,
1710, pp. 32–33); a more recent estimate is £8,000,000 (Geoffrey Holmes, *Britain after the
Glorious Revolution*, Macmillan, 1969, p. 22).

99. *in Reigns pass'd:* Louis XIV subsidized the Stuart kings from 1676 (*POAS*, Yale, 2,
107–08) to the death of James II in 1701.

103. *thorough Change:* "Harley had laid a scheme for an entire new Ministry" (Swift,
Corr., 1, 71).

105. *wicked Johnny Marlborough:* "His Victories are his Crimes" ([Arthur Mainwaring],
Four Letters to a Friend in North Britain upon the Publishing the Tryal of Dr. Sacheverell, 1710, p. 26).

108. *quite undone:* "When . . . the *French* Army had been beaten once again, which was
about the Eighth or Ninth time; and the dreadful News came over, that their King wou'd
make a Peace, then you may be sure it was high time for this poor Church to be at the brink
of Ruin" (ibid., p. 6).

111. *Sunderland:* Sunderland, the only Junto Whig in the Godolphin ministry, was to have
been the first to be dismissed (*Abigail's Lamentation, 29n.* above).

Avast! cry'd out the Admiral;
  No-near, you Rogues, no-near!
Your Ship will be amongst the Rocks,   115
  If at this rate you steer!

With that the Man that kept the Cash
  Slipt in a word or two,
Which made an old Acquaintance think
  This Game would never do.   120

He but one Eye had in his Head,
  But with that one he saw
These Priests might bring about his Ears
  A thing we call Club-Law.

He on his Pillow laid his Head,   125
  And on mature Debate

113. *the Admiral:* The admiral was incorrectly identified as "Orford" in one witness (*Ac*) and W. W. Wilkins (*Political Ballads of the Seventeenth and Eighteenth Centuries,* 2 vols., 1860, *2,* 80*n.*) supposed him to be "George Churchill," but it was George, prince of Denmark, the queen's consort, who was lord high admiral of England. The prince was easily drawn into Harley's scheme by being told that "he had too small a Share in the Government" (Burnet, *2,* 487), but he was just as easily "intimidated" by George Churchill, the younger brother of the duke of Marlborough, to urge the queen to drop Harley in order to avoid "a convulsion in the state" (Swift, *Prose, 8,* 113; Coxe, *Memoirs, 2,* 193).

114. *No-near:* "a command to the helmsman to come no closer to the wind" (*OED,* s.v. Near, adv., citing this line).

117–18. *the Man that kept the Cash | Slipt in a word:* On 8 February 1708 Godolphin "told the Q[ueen] he came to resign the staff, that serving her longer with one so perfidious as Mr. H[arley] was impossible" (PRO 30/24/21/149).

119 *old Acquaintance:* Charles Talbot, first duke of Shrewsbury (1660–1718), had been Godolphin's ministerial colleague and horse racing crony in the last reign (Dorothy Somerville, *The King of Hearts,* Allen & Unwin, 1962, p. 72). He had played an active part in the revolution and was twice William's secretary of state (1689–90, 1694–1700). In 1700 he was said to have been "le Chef des Whigs" (BM MS. Add. 30000D, f. 172), but now he was without office, having spent the years 1700–06 abroad, mainly in Italy. On his return to England he retired to Heythrop, his estate in Oxfordshire. Both Marlborough and Harley had sought his support for the ministry, against the Whig Junto, and had been favorably received (Cowper, *Diary,* p. 43). But lines 121–32 imply that when Harley sought to displace Godolphin, Shrewsbury abandoned him.

121. *one Eye:* The first line of a lampoon *Upon the Duke of Shrewsbury* preserved at Blenheim is "The duke with one eye" (Blenheim MS. GI 4). The text implies that even with one eye (Tilley, E239) Shrewsbury could see that Harley's scheme would have required "Club-Law," "The use of the club to enforce obedience; physical force as contrasted with argument" (*OED*).

With that, and with his Wife, resolv'd
  To play a Trick of State:

Like Dr. *Burgess* much renown'd,
  Of One he did take care;   130
Then slipt his Cloke and left the rest
  All in most sad Despair.

The Consequence of this was such,
  Our Good and Gracious Queen,
Not knowing why she e'er went wrong,   135
  Came quickly right again.

However, taking safe Advice
  From those who knew her well,

127. *that:* his pillow; "*To . . . consult with one's pillow*, etc.: to take a night to consider a matter of importance; to 'sleep upon' it" (*OED*).

his Wife: In August 1705, at the age of 45, Shrewsbury married Adelhida Paleotti, a widow from Bologna without fortune, who had abjured Catholicism in order to be married by a Lutheran minister in Augsburg (*DNB, 19*, 305). "Tis not to be conceivd," Charles Davenant said in March 1706, "what ground he has Lost in the Minds of Men by his Marriage" (BM MS. Add. 4291, f. 66).

129. *Dr. Burgess:* Daniel Burgess (1645–1713) was the most celebrated Presbyterian minister in London. He was the son of an Anglican divine who was ejected from "a very considerable Living [in Wiltshire] of about 400*l. per Annum*" by the Act of Uniformity in 1662. About the same time Burgess himself chose to leave Magdalen Hall, Oxford, without a degree, rather "than to submit to the Impositions" (Matthew Henry, *A Sermon Preach'd upon Occasion of the Funeral of the Reverend Mr. Daniel Burgess . . . With a Short Account concerning him*, 1713, pp. 32, 33). He was ordained by the Dublin presbytery and came to London in 1685. His "pop-gun way of delivery" (*DNB, 3*, 309) made him a popular preacher and in 1705 his congregation built a meeting house for him in New Court, Carey Street, Lincoln's Inn Fields. "To turn one's cloak" is, of course, proverbial (Tilley, C420) and Burgess's defection from the established church had already become proverbial. "I'll fling off my pretended Inspiration, as *Daniel Burgess* does his Cloak," William Pittis wrote in *Heraclitus Ridens*, 4–7, September 1703. Cf. *Isaac Bickerstaff's Letter to the Tongue-Loosed Doctor*, 1713, p. 13.

130. *One:* "*Number one*, one's self, one's own person and interests" (*OED*, s.v. Number, *sb.* 5b).

131. *the rest:* presumably Harley and Henry St. John, Earl Powlett, Sir Simon Harcourt, Sir Thomas Hanmer, Sir Thomas Mansell, Sir John Leveson Gower, Sir George Rooke, and the duke of Ormonde, all of whom were to have had places in Harley's ministry (*Abigail's Lamentation*, 8n.–38n. above).

133. *The Consequence:* Shrewsbury's association with the queen was of long standing. He had been "drawn into the Princess Anne's social circle" in 1691 through his friendship with Marlborough and Godolphin (Dorothy H. Somerville, *The King of Hearts*, Allen & Unwin, 1962, p. 72), and even while living in retirement at Heythrop, "the D. of Shrewsbury had found means, for 2 Years past, to come privately to the Qu." (Cowper, *Diary*, p. 43). So it

> She *Abigail* turn'd out of Doors,
> And hang'd up *Machiavell*.   140

---

is not unlikely that his example in abandoning Harley may have been one of the reasons why the queen "Came . . . right again," i.e. allowed Harley to resign.

139. *Abigail turn'd out:* There had been a rumor that "Mrs. Masham is forbid the Court" (Swift, *Corr., 1,* 70), but it was only a rumor.

140. *hang'd up Machiavell:* There was hope that Harley could be implicated in the treasonable correspondence of his clerk, William Gregg, until 28 April 1708 when Gregg was turned off. Swift was assured that there were "endeavours to bring in Harley as a party in that business, and to carry it as far as an impeachment" (Swift, *Corr., 1,* 70), while Sir John Cropley even talked of a "Bill of Attainder" (PRO 30/24/21, f. 148). But not even the promise of his life and £200 a year could compel Gregg to commit perjury (HMC *Portland MSS., 5,* 648).

Arthur Mainwaring?

Masham Display'd:
To the Tune of *The Dame of Honour*
(February–March 1708)

It is possible that this is the second of "the two Ballads of the Battle of Abigal" that the duchess of Marlborough offered to sing for Dame Sarah Cowper in July 1708 (Hertfordshire County R. O. Cowper MS. Box 12, *1,* 27). "The Battle of Abigal" was kept going after Harley's fall by rumors that the queen had promised him "a speedy Restoration" and that Mrs. Masham "was known to see him every Day" (BM MS. Lansdowne 885, ff. 62v–63). It was to prevent the first of these and to ridicule the second that *Masham Display'd* was written. As ridicule it is "A good ridicule," which as Mainwaring said, "has often gone a good way in doing a business" (*Private Correspondence of Sarah, Duchess of Marlborough, 1,* 129), but the nastiness is a reversion to good King Charles's golden days of nastiness.

The poem did enough business to generate *An Answer* ("All things went well in Court and State") that survives in more manuscript copies than the poem itself (Bodl. MS. Eng. poet. e.87, pp. 30–32; BM MS. Lansdowne 852, f. 39v; BM MS. Add. 40060, ff. 70v–71v). In *An Answer* Godolphin and the duchess of Marlborough are substituted for Harley and Mrs. Masham in the role of the guilty lovers and described in terms of the first book of *Paradise Lost:*

> She seem'd the everlasting Lake,
> He the Angel fal'n upon Her.

On 11 March 1708 when the news reached London that the pretender's invasion fleet had sailed from Dunkirk, it put "the whole Town . . . in an uproar"; stocks fell, banks closed, and the gold guinea rose three pence (*Letter-Books of John Hervey First Earl of Bristol,* 3 vols., Wells, 1894, *1,* 231). Since none of this excitement is imparted by line 49 of *Masham Display'd,* it may be assumed that the poem was written before 11 March, but after Harley's fall on 11 February 1708. The last of the three copies of *An Answer,* listed above, is dated July 1708.

John Oldmixon (*Maynwaring,* p. 326), mentions "several . . .

Satyrical Pieces" of Mainwaring's of which he could not then find a copy and *Masham Display'd* is almost certainly one of these. It is attributed to Mainwaring in the title of the earliest copy (*A*).

The tune, *The Dame of Honour*, was not an old favorite, like *Fair Rosamond*, but a current hit, "attributed to G. B. Draghi on very doubtful evidence." It was written for an entr'acte song in Thomas D'Urfey's comic opera, *Wonders in the Sun, or, The Kingdom of the Birds*, which opened in April 1706 (Simpson, pp. 155–57). Mainwaring probably thought the name of the tune was ironical, for Abigail Masham was not a maid of honor, but a bedchamber woman, or one of the queen's "dressers."

MASHAM DISPLAY'D:
TO THE TUNE OF *The Dame of Honour*

All Things are chang'd in Court and Town,
    Since *Sarah's* happy Days, Sir.
One who of late had scarce a Gown,
    Now Queen and Kingdom sways, Sir.

Poor Souldiers fight abroad in vain,   5
    And with their Blood defend Her,
Whilst sawcy Traitors of her Train
    Side with the *French* Pretender.

She'as neither Beauty, Birth nor Sense,
    Yet does controul the Nation,   10
A matchless Stock of Impudence,
    And blasted Reputation.

Four Pounds a Year was her Estate,
    Time alters her Condition,
A Lady fine she's grown of late,   15
    And a wond'rous Politician.

2. *Sarah's happy Days:* One of the most delightful scenes of the happy days before the summer of 1707 when the duchess of Marlborough discovered the perfidy of Abigail Masham is in *The Secret History of Arlus and Odolphus*, 3rd ed., 1710, p. 21, where she is described "saunt'ring alone, before the Ceremony from Church, with her Nose in the Air, her Eyes unthinkingly fix'd upon Nothing, negligently searching her Pocket for Sweetmeats."

3. *One:* Abigail Masham.

7–8. *Traitors of her Train | Side with the . . . Pretender:* In a letter to Mainwaring of March 1708 the duchess of Marlborough in anticipation of the impending general election had pointed out "the usefulness of raising a Cry upon the Jacobites." Mainwaring "took the hint," as he said, for a pamphlet, possibly his first, entitled *Advice to the Electors of Great Britain,* published 19 April 1708. The next year he reminded the duchess that they had written a book together "to prove [that] the Tories are Frenchmen, and must never rise again" (*Private Correspondence of Sarah, Duchess of Marlborough, 1,* 117, 277, quoted in *Huntington Library Quarterly, 29* [November 1965], 58–61). Here and in lines 26, 40, 49, Mainwaring makes the same identification of Tory and Jacobite.

8. *the French Pretender:* This, as James Boswell observed, "may be a parliamentary expression; but it is not a gentlemanly expression" (*The Journal of a Tour to the Hebrides,* ed. R. W. Chapman, Oxford, 1924, p. 280n.).

9. *Beauty, Birth:* Mrs. Masham's appearance and origins are described in *Abigail's Lamentation, 13n.,* above. Even Swift, who admired her, regretted that "she is not very handsome" (*Journal,* p. 412).

13. *Four Pounds a Year:* Mrs. Masham's inheritance of £500 (*Abigail's Lamentation, 13n.,* above) must have been unwisely invested.

The ugly Hag to tope retires,
   While others snore in Bed, Sir,
With Bumpers she augments those Fires,
   Which make her Nose so red, Sir.   20

Her brazen Face like Flame appears,
   With a Desire that's hearty,
I'll say it tho' I lose my Ears;
   I wish't may burn her Party.

Harley and She each Night do meet,   25
   And drink to the Pretender,
And hug and kiss, and are as great
   As the Devil and Witch of *Endor*.

The *Salamander* of her Nose,
   Which is a Publick Tax, Sir,   30
Shall be an Offering to her Foes,
   In spight of Nose of Wax, Sir.

Oh! that some truly zealous Friend
   Wou'd give the Bitch a Potion,
While *Harley*'s Mouth at lower End   35
   Were set to meet the Motion.

Or that they'd send her brawny Bum,
   As hard as *Alablaster*,
'Twou'd make a pretty Sort of Drum,
   To serve her little Master.   40

Oh! may the Queen in Safety reign,
   And *Marlb'rough* again protect her,
May he destroy the subtil Train
   Of Courtiers that infect her.

24. *burn her Party:* Mrs. Masham is endowed with a venereal disease in the hope that she will transmit it to Harley.

28. *Witch of Endor:* Saul's secret and illegal transactions with "a woman that hath a familiar spirit at En-dor" are recorded in 1 Samuel 28:7–25.

29–30. *Salamander...a Publick Tax:* cf. *1 Henry IV,* III, iii, 45–47.

38. *Alablaster:* the usual sixteenth–seventeenth century spelling of alabaster, or statuary limestone.

40. *little Master:* probably James Francis Edward Stuart, the pretended James III, then only 19 years old, but possibly Robert Harley who is "LITTLE MASTER" in *A Dialogue between Louis le Petite and Harlequin le Grand,* rptd. in [William Oldisworth], *State Tracts,* 2 vols., 1715, *1,* 181.

May he all *Robin's* Tricks defeat,   45
   However deeply laid, Sir:
And his whole Ruin to compleat,
   Turn out the Chambermaid, Sir.

Then if the *French* should send her King,
   We'll turn her Touch-hole to him,   50
With Fire and Smoak, and t'other thing,
   Oh! we shall quite undo him.

45. *Robin's Tricks:* Mainwaring wrote to the duchess of Marlborough in April 1708 minimizing the importance of Mrs. Masham: "what great feats could Mr. Harley do with his woman, that he boasts he will play against anybody[?]" (*Private Correspondence of Sarah, Duchess of Marlborough, 1,* 129).

49. *if the French should send her King:* presumably written before 9/20 March 1708 when the French did indeed send the pretended king, James III, with "about 5000 men . . . and large summs of money" to effect a landing in Scotland (Luttrell, *6,* 277).

Joseph Browne

To My Generous Friend and Worthy Patriot, Harlequin le Grand.
The Humble Memorial
Of Your Little Scribler, Spy, Champion, Closet-Counsellor,
and Poet, Daniel D'Foe
(June 1708)

For Harley's fall Abigail Masham's imagined grief can only be matched by Joseph Browne's imagined joy. Browne felt that Harley had bullied and betrayed him. And even after he was set free from Newgate a second time (p. 154 above), he felt "oblig'd to withdraw for a while" to avoid the secretary's rage (*State Tracts,* 2 vols., 1715, *1,* sig. A2v, 171, 174). So the present poem is the little scribblers' revenge against great secretaries.

The rhetorical strategy is carefully worked out. The revenge takes the dramatic form of a self-revealing "Memorial" from Daniel Defoe to his great patron, which is even more revealing of Harley because it is made to seem unconscious or inadvertent on Defoe's part. The poem establishes its credit in two ways. First, it makes Defoe speak in a whining tone not very different from the actual tone of his letter of 11 September 1707 to Harley: "The prayer of this Petition Sir is Very Brief, That I may be helped to wait, or that you will please Sir to Move my Ld T[reasure]r That Since his Ldship has thought Fitt to Encourage Me to Expect Assistance in Order to Serve the Governmt in this place;—his Ldship will be pleased . . . &c., &c." (Defoe, *Letters,* p. 243). Second, the poem is very knowledgeable about the semi-clandestine nature of the relationship between Harley and Defoe, their secret meetings (line 3), and Defoe's use of pseudonyms (43). Having thus established his credit Browne then proceeds to squander it on the apparently baseless claim that William Gregg (78) was Harley's "Agent" (67) in a treasonable correspondence with France and that Harley let Gregg hang for his own crimes (80). But this of course was exactly what most people wanted to believe in 1708.

Browne published his poem anonymously as one of the "recommendatory Poems" prefaced to *A Dialogue between Louis le Petite and Harlequin le Grand,* "a very scurrilous pamphlet" that Louis le Petite [Erasmus Lewis] told Harlequin le Grand [Harley] was in the press on 19 June

1708. "Mr. Man is I am told the author, or at least has contributed the materials," Lewis added (HMC *Portland MSS.*, *4*, 493). Browne's recollection that this volume was published in 1709 must be an error (*State Tracts*, 2 vols., 1715, *1*, sig. A2v).

TO MY GENEROUS FRIEND AND WORTHY PATRIOT,
HARLEQUIN LE GRAND.
THE HUMBLE MEMORIAL OF YOUR LITTLE SCRIBLER,
SPY, CHAMPION, CLOSET-COUNSELLOR,
AND POET, DANIEL D'FOE

Ah! Sir, before your great Deserts were known
To th'Court, the State, the Country, or the Town;
When you and I met slyly at the *Vine,*
To spin out Legion-Letters o'er our Wine,
I then foresaw your Malice and your Pride,   5
With forty more aspiring Gifts beside,
Would raise you, by some Toil, in Spite of Fate,
To be an Upstart-Prodigy of State:
But yet believ'd, when you so high had soar'd,

Title. *Harlequin:* This was becoming Harley's nickname. Mainwaring referred to "the senseless farce of Harlequin and Abigail" in April 1708 (*Private Correspondence of Sarah, Duchess of Marlborough, 1,* 129–30).
    Scribler: Defoe was among "those Little Scriblers who Pretend to Write Better Sense than Great Secretaries" (p. 171 above).
    3. *the Vine:* The Vine Tavern in Longacre was a notorious rendezvous of Jacobites:

> The faithful Club assembles at the *Vine,*
> And *French* Intrigues are broach'd o'er *English* Wine.
> (*POAS,* Yale, *6,* 500)

Harley and Defoe began their meetings in a safer rendezvous, Jones's coffeehouse in Finch Lane near the Exchange (Defoe, *Letters,* p. 13).
    4. *Legion-Letters:* Defoe wrote four of these. The first marked the beginning of his acquaintance with Harley and the last was either written at Harley's suggestion or approved by Harley for publication (Defoe, *Letters,* p. 90). The first was *The Memorial. To the K——s, C——s, and B——s in P——t Assembled,* which was delivered to the Speaker at the door of St. Stephen's Chapel on 14 May 1701 "by the very Person who wrote it, guarded with about Sixteen Gentlemen of Quality" (Defoe, *The History of the Kentish Petition,* 1701, p. 14). It claimed to come from 200,000 Englishmen—which accords very well with modern estimates of the size of the English electorate at that time (Speck, p. 16)—and it was signed, "LEGION." The second was *Legion's New Paper: Being a Second Memorial to the Gentlemen of the Late House of Commons* (November? 1701), a reply to James Drake, *A Short Defence of the Last Parliament* (1701). The third, *Legion's Humble Address to the Lords* (April 1704), was "a Libel" on the Tory majority in the House of Commons for which Defoe was ordered to be arrested ([Thomas Salmon], *A Review of the History of England,* 2 vols., 1724, *2,* 159; HMC *Portland MSS., 4,* 93, 138; Defoe, *Letters,* 65n.). The last was *The High-Church Legion* (July 1705), which William Pittis called "a silly Scurrilous Answer to the Church of *England's* Memorial" (*The Whipping-Post,* 17 July 1705).

And to the pow'rful Post you aim'd at, towr'd,   10
That you'd have stood more steady, than to fall
At once from such a lofty Pinacle:
But State-Preferments are uncertain Things,
Ruin sometimes from Royal Favour springs;
But he that robs the Bees, must never fear their Stings.   15
    I once stood fair to be a mighty Man,
You know the Time when who but Prophet *Dan;*
But I, alas! impatient of Delay,
Unwisely play'd the Fool *The Shortest Way;*
Or else to be chief *Harlequin* of State   20
Had been my Fortune, as it prov'd your Fate.
Why not? For if it's possible to rise

10. *Post you aim'd at:* Harley's "restless Ambition" had been noted by Burnet (2, 109), and soon after he had been made secretary of state in May 1704 Defoe advised him that "The Secretaryes Office Well Discharg'd Makes a Man Prime Minister of Course" (Defoe, *Letters,* p. 31).

    towr'd: mounted up, "as a hawk, so as to be able to swoop down on a quarry" (*OED*).

14. *Ruin . . . from Royal Favour:* At the same time that he was urging Harley to be "Prime Minister," Defoe warned him "That the Nation is Perticularly Jealous of Favourites" (Defoe, *Letters,* p. 29).

16. *stood fair to be a mighty Man:* Defoe's defense of William's regime in the closing years of the reign brought him into contact with the king himself. According to his own account, *The True-Born-Englishman (POAS,* Yale, *6,* 265) was "the Occasion of my being known to his Majesty; how I was afterwards receiv'd by him; how Employ'd; and how, above my Capacity of deserving, Rewarded, is no Part of the Present Case" (*An Appeal to Honour and Justice,* 1715, pp. 6–7). Defoe explained to Harley that "The late kings Bounty to me was Expended" in setting up a tile factory in Essex (Defoe, *Letters,* p. 17).

17. *Prophet Dan:* Defoe acquired this sobriquet in a pamphlet answering *The Tackers* ("In vain of the Battel we boast"), a poem which he did not write. The pamphlet was entitled, *Daniel the Prophet No Conjurer: Or, His Scandal Club's Scandalous Ballad, Called The Tackers; Answer'd Paragraph by Paragraph* (1705). But Defoe's oracular tone had been noted long before this. An anonymous pamphlet answering *The Two Great Questions Consider'd* (1700), which Defoe did write, observed that the questions were "fitter to be decided by an Astrologer than a Politician" (*Remarks upon a Late Pamphlet Intitul'd, The Two Great Questions Consider'd,* 1700, p. 4).

19. *The Shortest Way:* The Shortest-Way with the Dissenters (December 1702) was the pamphlet for which Defoe was tried and sentenced for libel. "During the Heat of the first Fury of High-Flying," he said, "I fell a Sacrifice for writing against the Rage and Madness of that High Party, and in the Service of the Dissenters" (*An Appeal to Honour and Justice,* 1715, p. 11). While he languished in Newgate, his tile business collapsed. "I was Ruin'd *The shortest way,*" he told Harley (Defoe, *Letters,* p. 17). In *A Hymn to the Pillory (POAS,* Yale, *6,* 588) Defoe began to use the phrase as a kind of identifying coda; cf. *The Paralel: Or, Persecution of Protestants the Shortest Way to Prevent the Growth of Popery in Ireland* (1705), a pamphlet that Defoe wrote to protest the imposition of the sacramental test on dissenters in Ireland.

By crafty Projects, and officious Lies;
'Tis plain, that I'm for any Station fit,
For who can doubt my Cunning, or my Wit,   25
Since I am Courtier, Poet, Prophet, and a Cit?
You know my Parts, for you have try'd 'em oft,
I've been the Tool that rais'd you up aloft;
The Offsprings of my bold unbridl'd Muse,
My Flirts and Flights, my Hymns, and my *Reviews;*   30
My Legion-Letters scatter'd up and down,
And Crys of Pop'ry to amuse the Town;
But above all, that excellent Essay,
My Step to th'Pillory, *The Shortest Way.*
These were the useful Flams and Shams, thou know'st,   35
Which made thy Passage easy to thy Post;
For my keen Wit, with your ill Nature join'd,
Blacken'd the Wise, and did the Foolish blind:
Or, by the sacred Stile of my *Review,*
There never had been Room for such as you.   40
    Have I not rhim'd and rail'd, sworn, ly'd, and spy'd,
And all to pleasure your Revenge and Pride?
Have I not chang'd, by your Advice, my Name,

26. *Courtier:* an officeholder, a supporter of the government.

    Cit: "for Citizen" (*New Dictionary*, sig. C6v), "a Word of Contempt among us" (Swift, *Prose, 4,* 252).

    30. *Hymns:* By 1708 Defoe had published five: *A Hymn to the Pillory* (July 1703), *A Hymn to the Funeral Sermon* (October 1703), *A Hymn to Victory* (August 1704), *A Hymn to Peace, Occasion'd by the Two Houses Joining in One Address to the Queen* (January 1706), and *Daniel Defoe's Hymn for the Thanksgiving* (June? 1706).

    Reviews: Defoe began writing the *Review* in February 1704, presumably under Harley's direction but "Carefully Conceal'd from all the world" (Defoe, *Letters,* p. 12). Four years later, upon his own fall, Harley turned over both Defoe and the *Review* to Godolphin (*An Appeal to Honour and Justice,* 1715, pp. 14–15), and by 24 February 1708 the *Review* was defending the reshuffled ministry on an issue that Harley had found indefensible (*Faults on Both Sides,* 1710, pp. 30–31).

    32–38. The text implies that by libelling Harley's Tory opponents ("Blackening the Wise") and pretending they were crypto-Catholics ("Crys of Pop'ry"), Defoe had made it possible for a moderate like Harley to succeed a high churchman like Nottingham as secretary of state in May 1704.

    41. *spy'd:* Harley employed Defoe to gather intelligence both in England (1704, 1705) and Scotland (1706–07); Harley "sent him to *Scotland* as a Spy, when the Treaty of Union was a Foot, and kept him in Pay ever after" (Oldmixon, *Maynwaring,* p. 168).

    43. *chang'd . . . my Name:* Browne may have known, or guessed, that Defoe assumed various pseudonyms in his work for Harley (Defoe, *Letters,* p. 62).

And us'd ten thousand Arts to spread your Fame?
Have I not travell'd *Scotland* in Disguise,   45
And fill'd the North with Reams of mighty Lies?
Dispatch'd Intelligence, that you might find
How freckl'd *Caledonia* stood inclin'd?
Did I not flatter them, and plainly prove
Their Scabs were Saint-like Blessings from above?   50
And all to serve you at a Time of Need?
'Tis true, I own, I did it for my Bread.
　　How oft have I impos'd upon the Crowd,
And whisper'd Treason, till 'twas talk'd aloud,
That you your lucky Cards might better play,   55
And win the doubtful Game *The Shortest Way?*
　　But now our Projects are at once undone;
Tho' you may stand, 'tis Time for me to run;
But I'd advise you to proceed with Care,
Since all your Hopes are in a Tuft of Hair;   60
Forget not the unhappy Fate of *Ninus,*
'Tis dangerous trusting to a Mount of *Venus.*
　　But noble Patron, e'er I take my Leave,
One special Favour I must humbly crave;
Whate'er you do, pray save me from the Fate,   65
That fell upon my Brother Spy of late;

45. *travell'd Scotland in Disguise:* see p. 210 above.

46. *Reams:* see pp. 211–12 above.

48. *freckl'd:* unstable, inconstant.

50. *Scabs:* Scab, or scabies, as an effect of poverty, was easily associated with Scotland (cf. Edward Ward, *A Journey to Scotland,* 1699, p. 13).

52. *did it for my Bread:* When Defoe entered Harley's service in November 1703 he was bankrupt and plagued by his creditors. He is said to have "had a handsome Allowance, (*viz.*) 100*l.* for the first Volume" of the *Review* (*The Republican Bullies,* 1705, p. 4), but in October 1705 he still owed £3,000 (Defoe, *Letters,* p. 106). He became totally dependent on remittances from Harley when he left for Scotland in September 1706: "Thus Sir," he said, "you have a Widdo' and Seaven Children On your hands" (ibid., p. 128).

53. *impos'd upon the Crowd:* Defoe was almost ashamed to report to Harley from Edinburgh "how Easily this People have been imposed upon" (*Letters,* p. 153).

54. *whisper'd Treason:* cf. *The Dyet of Poland,* 499n. above.

57. *now:* after Harley's fall in February 1708.

60. *a Tuft of Hair:* Abigail Masham's.

61. *Ninus:* the legendary founder of Nineveh who met his death at the hands of Semiramis, the wife of one of his officers, whom he had abducted.

66. *my Brother Spy:* William Gregg, a clerk in Harley's office, was discovered to be selling military secrets to the French in December 1707 (78n. below).

Nouns! who'd be Agent to a Scribe of State?
But sure, Great Master, you're too much my Friend,
To prove a Captain *Porter* in the End;
For tho' I'm thought to be a Saint by some,   70
I'm really unprepar'd for Martyrdom.
Besides, I vow and swear it makes me sweat,
To think so small a Volume as a Sheet,
Should all the Glories of my Life contain,
Wrote by that sad Historian, *Paul Lorrain*.   75
Therefore, if once you draw me in so far,
To make me fear a *Tyburn* Sledge or Car,
You'll find no foolish *Gregg* of Prophet *Dan*,

67. *Nouns:* a short form of Od's nouns, a corruption of God's wounds, an oath (*OED*).

69. *Captain Porter:* George Porter, "the evidence," as he was called, was a Roman Catholic officer in the army of James II who fled England when he was proclaimed guilty of treason in May 1692 (Luttrell, *4,* 245; *2,* 448–49). In December 1695 he joined Sir George Barclay and other Jacobites in a plot to assassinate William III (Abel Boyer, *The History of King William the Third. In III Parts,* 1702, *3,* 149, 153, quoted in Dalton, *2,* xxiii). Sir Thomas Prendergast (*POAS,* Yale, *6,* 708) betrayed the plot to the government and Porter was captured at Leatherhead, Surrey. He then turned king's evidence to save his life and one after another of his fellow-conspirators were hanged, drawn, and quartered on his testimony (Luttrell, *4,* 33–34, 40, 48, 51). The culmination of his career came in December 1696–January 1697 when he gave evidence against Sir John Fenwick (ibid., *4,* 155, 164).

75. *Lorrain:* Paul Lorraine (d. 1719), presumably a Frenchman and without a degree from Oxford or Cambridge, nevertheless called himself a presbyter of the Church of England and in September 1698 was appointed chaplain, or ordinary, of Newgate prison. He was a "sad Historian" (75)—Pope and Bolingbroke called him "that great Historiographer" (Pope, *Corr., 2,* 350)—because he published the lives, confessions, and dying speeches of criminals in "so small a Volume as a Sheet" (73), i.e. in a folio half-sheet or broadside.

77. *Tyburn Sledge or Car:* "Offenders of some reputation were allowed to make the journey from Newgate to Tyburn [near the present site of Marble Arch] in their own carriages which followed a hearse containing the coffin . . . The normal practice for all convicts was to be transported in carts, usually three at a time; they were manacled, seated upon their own coffins, and accompanied by a chaplain" (Leon Radzinowicz, *A History of English Criminal Law,* New York, Macmillan, 1948, pp. 170–71).

78. *foolish Gregg:* William Gregg (d. 1708), born in Scotland, became secretary of the English envoy to Copenhagen (1701–04) and chargé d'affaires in the summer of 1704 (HMC *Portland MSS., 2,* 58–63), but he was discharged for "ill qualities." Harley hired him in May 1705 to return to Scotland as a secret agent (ibid., *4,* 181) and it seems likely that he was replaced by Defoe in 1706, for by April 1707 he had become a clerk in Harley's office of secretary of state for the northern department and in "uneasy circumstances" on account of debt (ibid., *4,* 401). In October 1707 he began to sell copies of documents in Harley's office to the French. Harley discovered his practices in December (ibid., *4,* 469). Gregg made a full confession, pleaded guilty to the indictment for high treason, and was sentenced to be executed (ibid., *4,* 469; Luttrell, *6,* 252, 258). Paul Lorraine revealed that Gregg "was proffered his Life, and a great Reward if he would accuse his Master" (Swift, *Prose, 3,* 252). The convicted spy, however, was "foolish" in the poem's terms because he refused to implicate the

For I shall turn the Tables, if I can,
And hang that Master, that has hang'd his Man.   80

dismissed secretary of state and met his end on 28 April 1708 saying "Mr. Harley is perfectly
innocent and knew nothing of it" (Luttrell, *6*, 297; HMC *Portland MSS.*, *4*, 488).

WILLIAM SHIPPEN?

Duke Humphrey's Answer
(July? 1708)

The Duke Humphrey of the title is "the good Duke" of the chronicle tradition of Hall and Holinshed that Shakespeare followed in *1–2 Henry VI:*

> . . . the common people favour him,
> Calling him, *Humfrey the good Duke of Gloster,*
> Clapping their hands, and crying with loud voyce,
> *Iesu maintaine your Royall Excellence.*
>
> (*2 Henry VI,* I, i, 165–68)

The fourth and youngest son of Henry IV, he became protector of England during the minority of Henry VI and boasted that "if he had done anything that touched the king in his sovereign state he would not answer for it to any person alive, save only to the king when he came of age" (*DNB, 10,* 240–41). Upon the coronation of Henry VI he resigned the protectorship and obtained no further public employment. He was not only "a good clerk" himself but a generous patron of letters. The gift of his books first gave Oxford University an important collection of its own, and his other benefactions enabled a new library to be built over the divinity school (Richard Gough, *Sepulchral Monuments in Great Britain,* 2 vols. in 5, 1786–96, *2,* 143; *DNB, 10,* 244). He died suddenly in 1446 at Bury St. Edmunds, "not without suspicion of being strangled," and was buried in the abbey at St. Albans where he had endowed perpetual masses for his soul (Richard Gough, *Sepulchral Monuments in Great Britain,* 2 vols. in 5, 1786–96, *2,* 142).

His tomb was discovered on 20 April 1703 when workmen were digging the grave of John Gape in the floor of the abbey church of St. Albans (Robert Clutterbuck, *The History and Antiquities of the County of Hertford,* 3 vols., 1815, *1,* 72–73). The circumstances are described by Defoe:

> As some workmen were digging . . . they found some Steps which

330

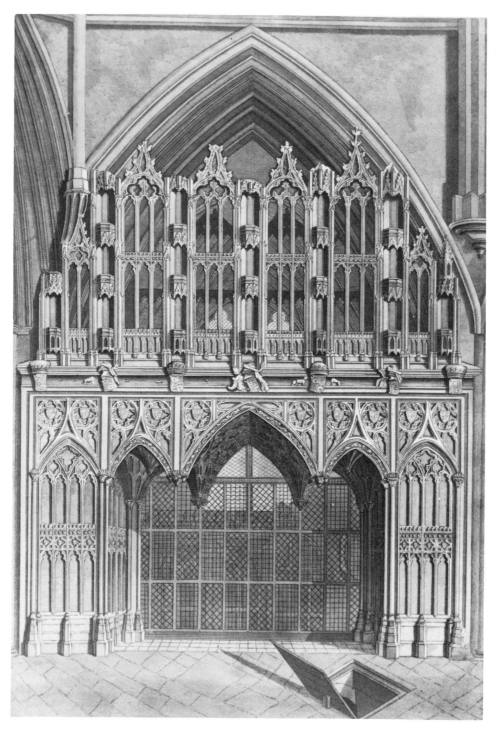

The monument of Humphrey, duke of Gloucester, an engraving by James Basire from a drawing by Jacob Schnebbelie

led to a Door in a very thick Stone Wall, which being opened, there was discover'd an arched Stone Vault, and in the middle of it a large Coffin near 7 Foot long, which being open'd, there was in it the Corps of a Man, the Flesh not consum'd, but discolor'd; by the Arms and other Painting on the Wall, it appear'd that this must be the Body of *Humphry* Duke of *Gloucester,* commonly call'd, the good Duke of *Gloucester,* one of the Sons of Henry IV

(*A Tour through the Whole Island of Great Britain,* ed. G. D. H. Cole, 1927, *1,* 389). The body, "found lying in pickle," the stairs, and the vault (see illustration, p. 331) attracted so much attention from "inquisitive persons," that only the skull (without teeth) and a few bones remain today (Richard Gough, *Sepulchral Monuments in Great Britain,* 1786–97, *2,* 142–43; *St. Albans and Hertfordshire Architectural and Archaeological Society Transactions, 2* [1903–04], 83–84).

It is not known whether these "inquisitive persons" included the duchess of the poem, her grace of Marlborough. But it is likely that they did, for Sarah Jennings had been born in St. Albans, in a house on the banks of the Ver at the foot of the abbey slope, and christened in the abbey church. After her marriage, Marlborough had built Holywell House for her in St. Albans and this "dear Hous" remained her favorite residence. It was to St. Albans that she and the duke retired after the death of their only son on 20 February 1703 (Iris Butler, *Rule of Three,* Hodder & Stoughton, 1967, pp. 18, 50, 153; David Green, *Sarah Duchess of Marlborough,* Collins, 1967, pp. 23n., 41).

The only evidence that Sarah visited the tomb, however, is in a poem of which the title puts the visit in 1707. *A Visit to Duke Humphreys Tomb* (*lately found*) *at St Albans 1707* represents that "Sarah led by Fancy, Hate or scorn, / Vouchsaf'd to visit Royal Glosters Urn" (1–2), but contemned the simple loyalty of Gloucester who, "Misled by duty and by Conscience Fool'd, / Chose to Obey the Boy he shou'd have Rul'd" (13–14). The poem goes on to imagine the "Stepps" by which Sarah planned to seize power and concludes: "Thus I this height of Glory will obtain, / *Anna* shall wear the Crown, but Sarah Reign" (27–28).

The present poem, presumably by the same Tory poet, is an "Answer" to Sarah's ambitious musings. The ghost of "the good Duke" predicts a "wretched fate" for the bad duchess.

The poem itself takes the form of a prophecy. Its sepulchral tone and riddling, arcane style show it to be a typical example of the genre

(*POAS*, Yale, *6*, 530). But since its content was unprintable, it could only be handed about in manuscript in 1708 and is now printed for the first time.

Two of the manuscripts date the poem 1708 and one of these specifies "July 1708." The author is either William Shippen or someone else intimately acquainted with Shippen's verse (11*n.*, 13–14*n.*, 23*n.*).

Shortly after publishing *Moderation Display'd* (December? 1704) Shippen, himself a lawyer of the Middle Temple, found himself in trouble with the law. According to one account he was "arrested for running [Harley] and his Messengers off the Scent" of the authors of *The Memorial of the Church of England* (July 1705) ([William Pittis], *The History of the Mitre and Purse*, 1714, p. 19). According to another he was arrested for "publishing seditious Libels" under a warrant signed by Harley on 1 Feburary 1706, and released on bail (*Copies Taken from the Records of the Court of King's-Bench, at Westminster . . . Of Warrants issued by Secretaries of State, for seizing Persons suspected of being guilty of various Crimes, Particularly, of being the Authors, Printers and Publishers of Libels*, 1763, p. 15). In June 1706 his case was postponed until next term (Luttrell, *6*, 57) and then, apparently, dropped.

Harley may not have learned that Shippen was the author of *Moderation Display'd* with its reductive exposé of himself as Jano (*Moderation Display'd*, 177–96, above). Shippen's anonymity was far more closely guarded than Swift's, for example. Shippen was "*The Muse unknown, whose strong, but factious Lay, / Pretends the Ages Vices to display*" (*A Panegyrick Epistle*, [*Wherein is given An Impartial Character of the Present ENGLISH POETS*] *to S. R—— B——* ["Permit an humble Muse to sing thy Praise"], 1706, p. 8).

Before the end of the next year Shippen had begun his long career in the House of Commons as a parliamentary Jacobite. The beginnings, however, were inauspicious. Shippen entered parliament on 29 December 1707 in a by-election for Bramber in Sussex to replace the eccentric John Asgill who had been expelled the house for blasphemy. Bramber was a borough controlled by Other Windsor, the second earl of Plymouth, whose uncle, Dixie Windsor, is said to have been Shippen's brother-in-law (J.P. Earwaker, *East Cheshire: Past and Present*, 2 vols., 1877–80, *1*, 393). The other member for Bramber was Thomas Windsor, Viscount Windsor of Blackcastle in the Irish peerage, another uncle of the earl of Plymouth. On 1 May 1708 Shippen and Lord Windsor were re-elected for Bramber, but there was a double return. On 15 January 1709 the Commons by a margin of six votes voted to throw out the incumbents and seat William Hale and Sir Cleve Moore. It was nearly two years before Shippen, in another by-election, was again returned for Bramber. For the next 33 years, however, he sat without interruption as a member for Bramber (8 December 1710–13), Saltash, Cornwall (1713–15), and Newton, Lancashire (1715–43). As one of the five "Patriots" and an unrelenting antagonist of Walpole, he "appears to have been the last M.P. to suffer imprisonment for words spoken in debate" (Peter D. G. Thomas, *The House of Commons in the Eighteenth Century,* Oxford, 1971, p. 348*n*.).

Duke Humphrey's Answer

The Royal Ghost rais'd from his peaceful Urn,
(What cannot Woman's rage?) made this return:
   Woman, who by insatiate Malice led,
Durst thus with impious scorn insult the dead;
Thou that durst thus with strong diffusive hate   5
Controll ev'n Death, and force the Laws of Fate,
As if the World was narrow, and confin'd
To the capacious rancour of thy Mind;
Prepare from Me thy wretched fate to see,
Wretched indeed! for ev'n thy due twill be.   10
Nor did the Prophet at thy *Sister*'s call,
More justly Tell th'unhappy Doom of Saul.
   Thou earthborn Meteor, that wouldst proudly vie
With those bright Stars that gild their native Sky;
Who like the Arch-Rebel giddy grown with Grace,   15
Presum'st to insult that Pow'r that gave Thee place,
Spurn'd down by injur'd Majesty, shall fall
Ev'n to that dark Abyss, thine own Original.
The Vipers which thy pois'nous Head hath bred,
Shall be the first that sting thy hated Head;   20
Blandford thy Joy, thy Blandford shall combine,
And prove the keenest Scourge of Wrath Divine
And in his Tainted Blood conclude thy bawdy Line.

11. *the Prophet at thy Sister's call:* The witch of Endor conjured up the ghost of Samuel, who prophesied that Yahweh would take the kingdom out of Saul's hands and give it to David (1 Samuel 28:7–19). The duchess's "Witchcraft" is mentioned in *Moderation Display'd,* 275 (above).

13–14. *Meteor . . . Stars:* In *Faction Display'd,* 448–51, Rochester is one of the "fixt Stars" in opposition to "wand'ring Planets" like the duchess (*POAS,* Yale *6,* 670).

15. *Arch-Rebel:* Here (and in lines 18 and 25) there may be allusions to *Paradise Lost,* I,156, 209, 357; II,405, 1027; X,371.

16. *that Pow'r:* the queen.

19. *Vipers:* The duchess's "Innumerable Pigmy-spawn" (five daughters and two sons) are mentioned in *The Golden Age Revers'd,* 103 (*POAS,* Yale, *6,* 526).

21. *Blandford:* The duchess's only surviving son, John, Lord Blandford, died of smallpox on 20 February 1703 at the age of 17.

23. *bawdy Line:* The duchess was born Sarah Jennings or Jenyns. Her "Lewd *procuring* Race" is mentioned in *Faction Display'd,* 431 (*POAS,* Yale, 6, 670).

Boast then the product of thy busy care,
Price of Damnation! Lo! anothers Heir   25
Thy gawdy Titles, and thy Wealth attends,
And what thy Lewdness gains, in Incest spends.
The black contagion from thy Spring shall flow
And Jennings Virtue in Monthermer grow.
Thus shall thy Sins in righteous Vengeance join,   30
And Churchill's Gratitude in Masham shine.
Repenting Patriots shall their worth regain,
Ev'n Harley shall seem honest once again.
From the dark Urn shall unbrib'd Justice flow,
Nor shalt Thou know the hand that gives the blow.   35
    Here, glorious Omen! here these eyes shall see
Scorn stab thy Pride, the Life and Soul of Thee.
In vain thy flattring Greatness to support,

25. *anothers Heir:* Upon Blandford's death Marlborough made a new will designating Francis Godolphin, known by his courtesy title of Viscount Rialton, as his heir. Besides being the husband of Henrietta, Marlborough's eldest daughter, Lord Rialton was the only son and heir of the lord treasurer, Sidney Godolphin. Marlborough also directed that his titles should descend through the Godolphin line and upon his death, Henrietta became duchess of Marlborough. But upon her death in 1733 without heirs, the Marlborough titles were assumed by her nephew, Charles Spencer, fifth earl of Sunderland.

27. *Incest:* Not even Thomas Hearne (*3*, 459), who calls Rialton "pitiful, mean-spirited, half-witted, whiggish, [and] snivelling," mentions incest.

29. *Jennings Virtue:* See 23n. above.

Monthermer: John Montagu (1690–1749), styled Lord Monthermer until 1709, was the third but only surviving son of Ralph Montagu, first duke of Montagu. In March 1705 he married Mary Churchill, the fourth and youngest daughter of Marlborough. Sarah's "black contagion" proved fatal to the house of Montagu. Although Mary Churchill bore three sons, none survived and the dukedom became extinct upon the death of the second duke.

31. *Masham:* See *Abigail's Lament*, 13n., above. The duchess did not know of Abigail's favor with the queen until the summer of 1707 when she heard that Abigail had been married to Samuel Masham in the queen's presence (*Account of the Conduct*, p. 182). Thereafter the two women were deadly rivals until Abigail finally triumphed in January 1711 (Luttrell, *6*, 680).

32. *Repenting Patriots:* Harley, St. John, Harcourt, and Mansell—who were regarded by the Tories as apostate "Patriots" (i.e. members of the opposition) for remaining in office while Whigs were coming into power—repented (i.e. went over to the opposition) upon Harley's failure to form a government in February 1708 (pp. 298–99 above).

worth regain: After leaving the ministry in February 1708, Harley and his colleagues "joyned with theyr friends . . . who receiv'd them with both arms as strayed sheep come into the true fold" (Bodl. MS. Ballard 39, f. 33).

34. *the dark Urn:* "the ballotting box" (*C*).

38. *flattring:* The duchess denied the charge: "I never flattered any body living" (*The Opinions of Sarah Duchess-Dowager of Marlborough, Published from Original MSS.*, [Edinburgh], 1788, p. 7).

Thou shalt to dark mysterious Arts resort;
In vain thou'lt strive thy former Crimes t'attone,   40
And right the injur'd Father in the Son;
In vain thy Treacheries alarm the Tweed,
And Northern Climes for Southern Mischiefs bleed.
    When Thames and Tweed in one fierce deluge roll,
And pour united Vengeance on thy Soul;   45
Then shall the Cordial Draught thy Sorrows heal,

40. *attone:* Duke Humphrey prophesies that Sarah will become a Jacobite and avenge James II by supporting his son, the pretended Prince of Wales.

43. *Northern Climes . . . bleed:* This apparently is a reference to the abortive Jacobite rising of March 1708. Louis XIV "concluded from the Discontent the People discovered in *Scotland* at the Terms of the Union, that they would readily join the Forces to recover their ancient Independency." Accordingly on 9/20 March the pretender and 5,000 French troops set sail from Dunkirk (Luttrell, *6,* 277), bound to Edinburgh to put a Catholic king on the throne of Presbyterian Scotland "for the benefit of the Episcopalian party" and to break the union with England. But the only Jacobites to land were a shipload of prisoners captured by Sir George Byng. The rest of the invasion fleet escaped over the route of the Spanish Armada and reached Dunkirk again on 25 March/4 April. The French troops who had "mightily huzzaed [the pretender] with *Vive le Roi*" at his first setting out, "were very mute at his coming back." A few real Jacobites, who had called out their clansmen prematurely, and some suspected Jacobites, like the duke of Hamilton and Lord Belhaven, who had done nothing, were brought to London for interrogation. But in fact no blood was shed (*The Life and Reign of Her Late Excellent Majesty Queen Anne,* 1738, pp. 403, 408; Trevelyan, *2,* 340, 345, 347–48).

44. *Thames and Tweed:* Again the prophecy is cryptic. The Tweed forms part of the boundary between Scotland and England. When it flows together with the Thames both kingdoms will unite to punish the duchess.

46. *the Cordial Draught:* The poet enforces a parallel between Rosamond Clifford (c. 1140–c. 1176), the mistress of Henry II, whose legendary death by violence occurred in a royal palace at Woodstock "wrought lyke unto a . . . mase," and the duchess of Marlborough whose death by violence is prophesied to occur in Blenheim, another curiously wrought palace under construction in Woodstock (Robert Fabyan, *The New Chronicles of England and France* [1516], ed. Sir Henry Ellis, 1811, pp. 276–77). Neither history nor legend provide any evidence that Henry's queen, Elinor, offered fair Rosamond a choice of the means of suicide. Nor do the cup of poison and the dagger (despite *DNB, 4,* 532 and *Roxburghe Ballads, 6,* 668) figure in Samuel Daniel, *The Complaint of Rosamond* (1592), Thomas Deloney, *A Mournefull Dittie, on the Death of Faire Rosamond* (*Strange Histories,* 1607), or in either of the broadside ballads derived from the latter. But they are prominently featured in a woodcut adorning the prose chapbook, *The Life and Death of Fair Rosamond, King Henry the Seconds Concubine,* which Francis Coles is said to have published c. 1640 (John Ashton, *Chap-Books of the Eighteenth Century,* 1882. p. 388), whence they were incorporated by Joseph Addison into *Rosamond, An Opera,* a libretto published anonymously in 1707 and "Inscribed to Her Grace the Dutchess of Marlborough." The stage direction for act two, scene six is "Enter . . . the Queen, with a Bowl in one Hand, and a Dagger in the other." The irony of building Blenheim on the ruins of a royal palace was not lost on Thomas Hearne. "Tho' the old Palace might exceed the New one," he said, "yet there were no such Gardens, as are now design'd to be, wch . . . seem . . . to exceed any thing of that nature in England . . . He that shall attempt the perfecting Sir Hen. Spelman's History of Sacrilege must not forget this place, the Park whereof caus'd the Destruction of several Churches" (Hearne, *1,* 202).

And the kind Bowl prevent the fatal Steel;
Then shall these Vaults with eccho'd joys resound,
And Woodstock once more boast a Rosamond.

48. *resound:* The famous echo in Woodstock Park is described in the opening lines of
Rosamond, An Opera (1707): "A hundred Eccho's round us talk: / From Hill to Hill our
words are tost." To be heard in St. Albans, however, the "eccho'd joys" of the duchess's
murderer would have to carry 45 miles.

WILLIAM CONGREVE

Jack Frenchman's Defeat:
Being an Excellent New Song to a Pleasant Tune Called,
There was a Fair Maid in the North-Country,
Come Triping over the Plain, &c.
(6–15 July 1708)

After the disasters of the year before, the allies were desperate for success in 1708. Success came, almost by accident, at the battle of Oudenarde. This was no set piece in the theatre of war, but an improvised drama. Marlborough's willingness to commit his troops to fight with their backs to an impassable river—or to commit them at all after two days of forced marches—and his consummate skill in deploying them once they were committed, paid off again. After cavalry skirmishes in the morning, the two armies drew up in the hedgerows and orchards a mile north of Oudenarde in the late afternoon of 30 June/11 July 1708 and the killing went on until dark. The first estimates of 6,000 French soldiers killed (Luttrell, *6,* 326) and another 4,700 captured (Saint-Simon, *2,* 1096), were, for once, too low (Trevelyan, *2,* 365). Only the darkness prevented Vendôme's army from being surrounded and annihilated. "If it had pleased God that we had had one hour's daylight more at Oudenarde," Marlborough wrote to Godolphin, "we had, in all likelihood, made an end of this war" (Coxe, *Memoirs, 2,* 273).

What made the battle such a popular success in England was the fact that five princes of the blood were engaged in it. Two of these, Jan Willem, prince of Orange-Nassau and stadholder of Friesland, and Georg August, heir to the elector of Braunschweig-Lüneburg and the future George II of England, particularly distinguished themselves (Brodrick, pp. 229–32). But two grandsons of Louis XIV and James Francis Edward, the pretended Prince of Wales, were supposed to have run away (see illustration, p. 338).

Considering the popularity of the poem, it is surprising that it generated no replies and only one second part. The latter, *The Second Part of Jack Frenchmans Defeat Being Another Excellent New Ballad to the Same Tune* ("You lately good People"), is preserved in Blenheim MS. GI 15 in the hand of Arthur Mainwaring. Mainwaring's poem breaks

Louis duc de Bourgogne, Charles duc de Berry, and James Francis Edward, the pretended Prince of Wales, observing (and then fleeing from) the battle of Oudenarde, 11 July 1708, an anonymous woodcut

off in the fourth stanza but not before he had made the point that the pretender's supposed flight had routed his supporters in England "From Adjutant Gwyn to old Lory."

Limits for the date of composition of the poem are 6 July when news of the victory reached London (Luttrell, *6*, 323) and 15 July when Sarah Cowper copied it into her diary (*D*).

Although it has been attributed both to Swift (*Fg; The Works of Jonathan Swift*, ed. Walter Scott, 19 vols., Edinburgh, 1814, *10*, 435; Harold Williams, *RES*, *2* [1926], 322; *RES*, *3* [1927], 212) and to Prior (Swift, *Poems*, *3*, 1078), there can no longer be any doubt that the poem was written by William Congreve. It is attributed to Congreve in three copies preserved among the Cowper manuscripts (*ACD*). Mary, Countess Cowper, wife of the lord chancellor, told Georg August in November 1714 that Congreve had called him "*Young Hanover Brave* [line 32] . . . in a ballad" (*RES*, *3* [1927], 73). The poem is also attributed to Congreve in two copies from a totally different textual tradition: the Harvard copy of John Morphew's broadside edition (*Fb*) and a manuscript in the British Museum (*Fk*). On 9 November 1708 Congreve thanked his friend Joseph Keally for an unspecified "Latin Ballad." "I think it is as well as the thing will bear," he went on to say (Congreve, *Letters*, p. 52). The next year Jacob Tonson published both "the thing," *Jack Frenchman's Defeat*, and Keally's Latin translation of it in *Poetical Miscellanies: The Sixth Part* (*Bc*). Although Congreve's name has figured in earlier volumes of this series—William Pittis parodied a song from *Love for Love* in *The Battle Royal* (1695) (*POAS*, Yale, *5*, 470) and Pope attributed to Congreve *An Address to Our Sovereign Lady* (April 1704) (*POAS*, Yale, *6*, 618), which is almost certainly by Arthur Mainwaring—*Jack Frenchman's Defeat* provides the first evidence of Congreve's involvement in poems on affairs of state.

The matter of the tune to which the verses were set is a problem even more complex than the authorship. No fewer than six tunes are indicated in surviving copies: 1) *Prithee Horace hold up thy head* (*A*) about which nothing is known; 2) *There was a Fair Maid in the North-Country, / Come Triping over the Plain* (*Ba*) on which there is "no information"; 3) *Ye Ladies of London* (*Bb*), which is "rhythmically compatible" with Congreve's verses; 4) *Ye Commons and Peers* (*BbdFh*) set by Richard Leveridge presumably for these verses; 5) *I'll tell thee Dick* (*CFabcdef*), which "does not fit the distinctive six-line stanza"; 6) *Who can but love a Seaman* (*Fa*), another tune about which nothing is known. Leveridge's tune became so popular that it was "introduced into nine ballad operas" and countless songs in the eighteenth century (Simpson, pp. 801–03).

JACK FRENCHMAN'S DEFEAT:
BEING AN EXCELLENT NEW SONG TO A PLEASANT TUNE CALLED,
There Was a Fair Maid in the North-Country,
Come Triping over the Plain, &c.

Ye Commons and Peers,
Pray lend me your Ears,
I'll Sing you a Song if I can;
How *Louis le Grand*
Was put to a Stand,   5
By the Arms of our Gracious Queen *Anne*.

How his Army so great
Had a total Defeat,
Not far from the River of *Dender;*
Where his Grand-Children twain   10
For fear of being Slain,
Gallop'd off with the Popish Pretender.

To a Steeple on High

8. *a total Defeat:* "On cacha tant qu'on put la perte qu'on fit en ce combat, où il y eut beaucoup de tués et de blessés . . . quatre mille hommes et sept cents officiers prisonniers à Audenarde, sans ce qu'on sut depuis, et la dispersion, qui fut prodigieuse" (Saint-Simon, *2,* 1096). Only darkness saved the rest of the French army, "For, had there been but two Hours more Day-light, in all probability, their whole Body of Foot, and their Right-Wing of Horse, had been entirely cut off, being almost Surrounded" (Brodrick, p. 231).

9. *Dender:* Lessines, on the Dender, a tributary of the Scheldt, and about 15 miles from Oudenarde, which the allies had only occupied the night before, was the point from which the advance guard of Marlborough's army moved out at one o'clock on the morning of 30 June/11 July 1708 (Trevelyan, *2,* 357).

10. *Grand-Children twain:* Two of Louis XIV's grandchildren, the eldest, Louis, duc de Bourgogne (1682–1712) and Charles, duc de Berry (1686–1714), were present at the battle. The duc de Bourgogne, in fact, shared command of the French army with Louis Joseph, duc de Vendôme.

12. *Gallop'd off:* "La journée avoit été fort fatiguante, la retraite étoit longue et périlleuse . . . Les princes, avec ce peu de suite qui les avoit accompagnés, prirent à cheval le chemin de Gand" (Saint-Simon, *2,* 1093–94).

Popish Pretender: The day after the battle Marlborough inquired for news of the pretended Prince of Wales who he knew had accompained the French army (Saint-Simon, *2,* 1098).

13. *Steeple:* The French princes and the English pretender observed the battle from a mill (see illustration, p. 338). As the story was told later, the pretender "made a Campaign in *Flanders,* where, by the Help of a Telescope, he saw the Battle of *Oudenarde,* and the Prince of

The Battel to Spy,
Up Mounted these gallant Young Men;   15
  But when from the Spire
  They saw so much Fire
They most gallantly came down again.

Then a Horse-Back they got
Upon the same Spot,   20
By th'advice of their Cousin *Vendome;*
  O Lord! Cry'd out He
  To Young *Burgundy,*
Wou'd your Brother and you were at Home.

Just so did he say,   25
When without more delay
Away the Young Gentry fled;
  Whose Heels for that Work
  Were much lighter than Cork,
But their Hearts were more heavy than Lead.   30

Not so did Behave
Young *Hannover* Brave
In this Bloody Field I'll assure ye;
  When his War Horse was shot
  He matter'd it not,   35
But Fought it on Foot like a Fury.

Hanover's Horse shot under him; being posted on a high Tower with two French Princes of
the Blood" (Addison, *The Freeholder,* 23 April 1716).

   21. *advice:* What Vendôme actually said to the princes was even more insulting than Con-
greve imagined: "Eh bien! s'écria-t-il, Messieurs, je vois bien que vous le voulez tous; il faut
donc se retirer! Aussi bien, ajouta-t-il en regardant Mgr le duc de Bourgogne, il y a long-
temps, Monseigneur, que vous en avez envie" (Saint-Simon, *2,* 1093).

   Cousin: Vendôme was a second cousin of the half-blood once removed of the duc de
Bourgogne.

   32. *Young Hannover:* Georg August (1683–1760), the only son of Georg Ludwig, elector
of Braunschweig-Lüneburg, by Sophie Dorothea, daughter of the duke of Lüneburg-Zell,
was placed in the order of succession to the English throne by the Act of Settlement of June
1701. In September 1705, he married Karoline Wilhelmine, daughter of the margrave of
Brandenburg-Ansbach. He was naturalized by an act of parliament in December 1705 and
raised to the peerage as duke of Cambridge in November 1706. He had joined Marlborough's
armies only a month before the battle.

   34. *Horse was shot:* "That Prince charg'd with Sword in Hand as a Volunteer, at the Head
of his Fathers Dragoons . . . His Highnesses Horse was shot under him, and Colonel *Luskey,*
who commanded the Squadron where he charg'd, was Kill'd in his Presence" (Brodrick, p.
229). The episode recalled Marlborough's unhorsing at Ramillies (Prior, *An Ode, Humbly
Inscrib'd to the Queen,* 150n. above).

While Death flew about
Aloud He called out
Hoh! You Chevalier of St. *George*.
    If you'll neither stand   40
    By Sea nor by Land,
Pretender, that Title you Forge.

Thus Firmly he stood
As became that High Blood,
Which runs in his Veins so Blue;   45
    This Gallant Young Man
    Being Kin to Queen *Anne*,
Did as were she a Man, she wou'd do.

What a Racket was here,
(I think 'twas last Year)   50
For a little ill fortune in *Spain;*
    When by letting 'em Win,
    We have drawn the Putts in
To Loose all they are Worth this Campaign.

Tho' *Bruges* and *Ghent*   55
To Monsieur were Lent,
With Interest he soon shall Re-pay 'em;
    While *Paris* may Sing

---

39. *Chevalier of St. George:* The captured French general whom Marlborough had inquired about the pretended Prince of Wales explained that in the French army he was known simply as the chevalier de Saint-Georges (Saint-Simon, *2*, 1098).

41. *By Sea:* In the intended invasion of March 1708 (*Duke Humphrey's Answer*, 43*n*.), the pretender was prevented by bad weather and bad planning even to set foot in Scotland.

42. Swift mentions "a Noble Duke who was accused of a Blunder in the House, when upon a certain Lord's mentioning the *Pretended Prince*, his Grace told the Lords, He *must be plain with them, and call that Person, not the Pretended Prince, but the Pretended Impostor*" (*The Examiner*, 31 May 1711).

47. *Kin:* Georg August was Anne's second cousin once removed.

51. *ill fortune in Spain:* See *Switch and Spur*, 31*n*. above.

53. *Putts:* "*A Country-Put*, a silly, shallow-pated Fellow" (*New Dictionary*, sig. I8v). As he formulated the notion that the defeat at Almansa in April 1707 was a trap to draw French troops into Spain to destroy them in the next campaign, Congreve may not have heard of the loss of Tortosa to the army of Philippe, duc d'Orléans, on the same day as Oudenarde, for the bad news was not known until 11 days after the news of Oudenarde reached London (William Coxe, *Memoirs of the Kings of Spain*, 2nd ed., 5 vols., 1815, *1*, 422–23; Luttrell, *6*, 323, 328).

55. *Bruges and Ghent:* The French had recaptured Ghent and Bruges only a week before Oudenarde (Brodrick, pp. 223–25). "Ce fut une joie à Fontainebleau, qui se put dire effrénée" (Saint-Simon, *2*, 1087).

With her Sorrowful King
De Profundis instead of *Te Deum*.   60

From their Dream of Success,
They'll awaken we Guess
At the Noise of Great *Marlborough*'s Drums.
They may think if they will
Of *Almanza* still,   65
But 'tis *Blenheim* where'ver he comes.

O *Louis* Perplex'd,
What General's next?
Thou hast hitherto chang'd 'em in Vain:
He has Beat 'em all round,   70
If no New ones are found,
He shall Beat the Old over again.

We'll let *Tallard* out
If he'll take t'other Bout;
And much he's Improv'd let me tell ye   75
With *Nottingham* Ale
At every Meal,
And good Pudding and Beef in his Belly.

As Loosers at Play
Their Dice throw away,   80
While the Winner he still Wins on:
Let who will Command,
Thou hadst better Disband,
For Old Bully, thy Doctors are gon.

59. *Sorrowful King:* A report reached England on 13 July that when Louis XIV read Vendôme's account of his defeat he "broke out into an extasy, Still without successe, O Spain! how much blood hast thou cost!" (Luttrell, *6*, 326).

69. *chang'd:* Louis XIV's commander in the Lowlands from 1702 to 1706 was François de Neufville, duc de Villeroi (1644–1730). After his defeat at Ramillies he was dismissed and replaced by Vendôme. After Vendôme's defeat at Oudenarde, he was replaced by Villars.

73. *Tallard:* Louis XIV's commander at Blenheim was still a prisoner in Nottingham Castle (*The French King's Cordial*, 74n. above).

85. *Old Bully:* Louis XIV was 70.

Doctors: As well as physicians (here imagined to have given up Louis XIV's case as hopeless), "Doctors" were false dice (*New Dictionary*, sig. D7r).

An Epigram on Mrs. Deborah Churchill being Hang'd
(December 1708)

On Friday 17 December 1708 "one Deborah Churchill, some time since found guilty of murther, was carried in a coach to Tyburn, and there executed" (Luttrell, *6*, 386). This unfortunate woman was born about 1678 in a village near Norwich. After her husband died she came up to London and lived with a young man named Hunt. One evening while returning from the theatre, Hunt became involved in a street brawl and killed his assailant. He made good his escape to Holland but Mrs. Churchill was arrested on the scene of the crime, tried at the Old Bailey in November 1707, found guilty, and condemned to be hanged. Her "behaviour was extremely penitent; but she denied her guilt to the last moment . . . because she did not herself stab the deceased" (William Jackson, *The New and Complete Newgate Calendar; Or, Villany Displayed in All its Branches*, 6 vols. [1795], *1*, 116–17). But her death was not wholly in vain since it provided the occasion for a splendid anonymous epigram.

AN EPIGRAM ON MRS. DEBORAH CHURCHILL BEING HANG'D

> What can the mighty *Churchills* wish for more?
> All living Places they engross'd before,
> And since one pendant *Churchill Ketch* has known,
> Perhaps they'll make the Gallows too their own.
> And that I'm sure, is now the only Place   5
> The Nation will not envy ev'n her *Grace*.

3. *Ketch:* John Ketch (d. November 1686), the eponymous hangman of London, is noticed in the *DNB*. In the first half of Anne's reign, his successor was Richard Murray, but Murray cannot have hanged Deborah Churchill since he himself died on 4 December 1708, two weeks before her execution (*Newgate in Tears. Being an Elegy on the much Lamented Death of Richard Murray, Head Hangman of England* ["Each reverend Whore and celebrated Thief"], 1708). Murray's successor, the "Jack Ketch" who hanged Mrs. Churchill, appears to have been John Price. Price was himself hanged in May 1718 for murdering a woman (*The Complete Newgate Calendar*, ed. G.T. Crook, 5 vols., 1926, *2*, 265).

1709

Leviathan,
Or, A Hymn to Poor Brother Ben
To the Tune of *The Good Old Cause Reviv'd*
(June–July? 1709)

The seventeenth century had witnessed a great debate about the origin and nature of civil government. Traditionalists, like Sir Robert Filmer, argued from the Bible and from history seen through Biblical glasses, that all authority derived from God and that patriarchal monarchy was the form of government most acceptable to God. A corollary of this concept of indefeasible hereditary right was the doctrine of passive obedience or nonresistance, that it was sinful to resist the Lord's anointed upon any pretext whatsoever.

Opposed to this religious view was a secular theory that civil government originated in a contractual arrangement for the security and benefit of the governed. In the *Leviathan,* Hobbes conceived of government as an agreement between interest groups to obey a ruler who was not party to the contract but whose function was to see that it was enforced. John Locke, on the other hand, made the ruler into one party to the contract with the ruled as the other party. Unlike Hobbes's absolute monarch, Locke's constitutional monarch was bound by the terms of the contract.

This debate survived the revolution of 1688, although the traditionalists had to exercise considerable ingenuity to square their theories with the facts of history. Some argued that God had manifested his displeasure with the head of the Stuart dynasty by transferring his blessing to James's eldest daughter and his nephew, her husband. Others maintained that there had been no resistance in 1688, that James had voluntarily abdicated and that the crown had passed to Mary by the laws of primogeniture. This, of course, required a refusal to believe in the legitimacy of the son born to James's wife in June 1688, but such incredulity was widespread, among Tories as well as Whigs. And the notion of indefeasible hereditary right actually took on a new lease of life when James died in September 1701 and his daughter Anne succeeded as queen in March 1702. "Even the more moderate Jacobites were pleased to see at least a daughter of that good but unfortunate King on the throne" (Ailesbury, *2,* 525).

Along with a new interest in divine right theories came a new insistence upon passive obedience and nonresistance. Henry Sacheverell became the most notorious spokesman for the traditional Christian ethos, though Offspring Blackall, bishop of Exeter, was a more intelligent advocate. On 8 March 1709, the seventh anniversary of the queen's accession to the throne, Blackall preached a sermon before her majesty on *The Divine Institution of Magistracy.* In its own terms, Blackall's argument is unanswerable. For, "When all's said, let all judicious Men judge, who act most for the Honour of the Church and Christianity . . . those, who after the Example of *Christ* and his Apostles recommend *Obedience* and *Patience, Meekness* and *Submission,* both by their Preaching and Practice; or those, who . . . encourage People to censure and oppose their Superiors by their Writings and Example" (*The Revolution No Rebellion,* 1709, p. 12).

Political power, Blackall argued, must derive from God, "For there is no power but of God," as St. Paul said, and "Whosoever therefore resisteth the power, resisteth the ordinance of God" (Romans 13:1–2). The magistrate's power, Blackall said, in a fine Platonic image, is "a Ray or Portion of the Divine Authority and Power . . . communicated to him by GOD" (*The Divine Institution of Magistracy, and the Gracious Design of its Institution,* 1709, p. 6). The magistrate, Blackall pointed out quite correctly, could not derive his power from the people, for the people never had it (ibid., p. 8).

When Blackall's sermon was published by royal command, Benjamin Hoadly felt compelled to write a reply, which he entitled, *Some Considerations Humbly Offered to the Right Reverend the Lord Bishop of Exeter* and published in April 1709 (*The Daily Courant,* 21 April 1709). Hoadly was the most ambitious propagandist for the contractual theory of kingship. For him, as for most of the Whigs, Anne was "the *Queen of the Revolution*" (*The Observator,* 24–26 October 1704), "a good behaviour Queen" (University of Leeds MS. Brotherton Lt. 11, p. 134), appointed by parliament *durante bene placite.*

Blackall came back with *The Lord Bishop of Exeter's Answer to Mr. Hoadly's Letter* (1709) ridiculing Hoadly's imaginary states of nature and nonexistent original contracts. The present poem catches Hoadly in the act of composing a reply to *The Lord Bishop of Exeter's Answer* (which was entitled *An Humble Reply to the Right Reverend the Lord Bishop of Exeter's Answer* [1709] when it was published on 27 July 1709 [*The Daily Courant,* 27 July 1709]).

In form the poem is a hymn, in fact a mock-Calves'-Head-Club-hymn (56*n.*). As such it celebrates, not God, but the mob, "that crooked serpent" from whom in republican theory all power is derived, "Leviathan, *our God and King*" (57). In this new application of the Biblical symbol, Leviathan is no longer the absolute monarch of Hobbes's book, "The Multitude . . . united in one Person," but "The Multitude" itself, the monster-mob taking power into its own hands. And finally, of course, the poem is another example, like *The Shortest-Way with the Dissenters* and *A Tale of a Tub*, of a work of total irony, meaning at every point the opposite of what the words say.

The Lord Bishop of Exeter's Answer to Mr. Hoadly's Letter is said to have been "Just Publish'd" in *The Daily Courant* for 20 June 1709. So *Leviathan* must have been written after this date and before Hoadly published *An Humble Reply to the Right Reverend the Lord Bishop of Exeter's Answer* on 27 July 1709 (*The Daily Courant*, 27 July 1709).

The author remains unknown.

Nor is the tune now known to which the poem is said in the title to have been set, *The Good Old Cause Reviv'd*, if indeed it ever existed. Claude M. Simpson points out (in a personal letter) that verses with this title are reprinted in *Roxburghe Ballads, 4,* 598.

LEVIATHAN,

OR, A HYMN TO POOR BROTHER BEN
TO THE TUNE OF *The Good Old Cause Reviv'd*

Why now so melancholy, *Ben?*
What, stabb'd to Death by *Blackhall*'s Pen?
Invoke old *Hobs,* and snarl again.

Title. *Leviathan:* a Biblical monster of huge size and unlimited power (Job 41:1–34; Isaiah 27:1). Hobbes used it to symbolize "the Multitude . . . united in one Person," or the absolute monarch, "that great LEVIATHAN . . . that *Mortall God,* to which wee owe under the *Immortall God,* our peace and defence" (*Leviathan Or the Matter, Forme and Power of a Commonwealth Ecclesiasticall and Civil,* 1651, p. 87).

The Good Old Cause: the parliamentary side in the civil wars. By taunting Hoadly for his "Zeal for that [good old] Cause," Blackall was accusing him of being a crypto-republican (*The Lord Bishop of Exeter's Answer to Mr. Hoadley's Letter,* 1709, p. 3; the square brackets are in the original text).

1. *Ben:* "That Rascal Ben Hoadly" (1676–1761), as Thomas Hearne (*2,* 361) called him, graduated B.A. from St. Catharine's College, Cambridge, in January 1696 and was elected a fellow the following year. He came to London in 1701 as a lecturer at St. Mildred's in the Poultry and was instituted to the rectory of St. Peter-le-Poor in Broad Street in 1704. He soon became a leading propagandist for low church and revolution principles. His most celebrated contribution to the theory of contractual kingship was a by-product of his quarrel with Blackall, whom Atterbury had undertaken to defend in a Latin sermon preached before the London clergy on 17 May 1709. Hoadly responded with *The Original and Institution of Civil Government, Discuss'd* (1710) which raised him "to the highest point in the estimation of the whig party" (*DNB, 9,* 911). His rewards had to be deferred to the next reign when he became successively bishop of Bangor (1715–21), Hereford (1721–23), Salisbury (1723–34), and Winchester (1734–61). He "did not once visit his diocese during the whole six years in which he held the Bishopric" of Bangor (*The Diary of Francis Evans,* ed. David Robertson, Oxford, 1903, p. viii*n.*).

2. *Blackhall:* Like his antagonist, Offspring Blackall (1654–1716) was both a graduate (1674–75) and a fellow (1679–87) of St. Catharine's College, Cambridge. He came to London in 1694 as rector of St. Mary Aldermary, became a celebrated preacher, and delivered the Boyle lectures in 1700. Although he had been chaplain to William III, he became one of the two high churchmen whom Anne raised to bishoprics in August 1707 (*A New Ballad,* 87*n.* above). His sermon of 8 March 1708 preached before the queen and published as *The Divine Institution of Magistracy, and the Gracious Design of its Institution* (1709) renewed the controversy on the origins of government. Hoadly responded with *Some Considerations Humbly Offered to the Right Reverend the Lord Bishop of Exeter* (1709). After "stabbing" Hoadly in his *Answer,* Blackall left him "to be mumbled by the learned and very ingenious [William Oldisworth]" (*The Lord Bishop of Exeter's Answer to Mr. Hoadly's Letter,* 1709, p. 31).

3. *Hobs:* Hoadly did not, of course, invoke Hobbes in *Some Considerations Humbly Offered to the Right Reverend the Lord Bishop of Exeter,* for the tendency of his argument is directly opposed to that of the *Leviathan.* The allusion is religious, not political. "Hobbist" had come to have a special meaning for high churchmen. In December 1699 in the House of Commons Sir Edward Seymour had "reflected on [Lord Somers] . . . for his religion, that he was a Hobbist" (Vernon, *3,* 13). Nearly a century later Samuel Johnson made the same reflection on

What, freezing nigh the Artick Pole?
Rouse, rouse thy sad dejected Soul,   5
Here's *Tom of Bedlam* with a Bowl.

Then wake, and clear the fatal Cup,
'Twill chear thy drooping Spirits up;
''Tis Faction's Bowl, leave not a Sup.

Oh, bravely drank! For this I'll raise   10
Thy Name aloft in *Milton*'s Lays,
And *Tindal*'s Rights shall sound thy Praise.

David Hume (James Boswell, *The Journal of a Tour to the Hebrides,* ed. Frederick A. Pottle and Charles H. Bennett, 1936, p. 239). "What gave a handle to some to treat [Hobbes] as an Atheist, was the Contempt he expressed for many of those scholastick Terms invented by assuming Men, who would impose their own crude Notions of the Divine Being on their fellow Creatures, as Articles of Faith" (*The Moral and Political Works of Thomas Hobbes,* 1750, p. xxii). So the implication is that Hoadly was an atheist.

 snarl: Hoadly's characteristic tone is not the snarl but an elaborate mock deferentiality: "I beseech your *Lordship* to pardon the *trouble* and *boldness* of this *Address* from *One* whom a profound *Veneration* for your *Lordship* induced seriously to consider what proceeded from so excellent and judicious a Person," etc., etc. (*Some Considerations Humbly Offered to the Right Reverend the Lord Bishop of Exeter,* 1709, 4⁰, p. 16. There were at least two editions of this work. The first, a quarto "of Three Sheets and a Quarter," was published by John Morphew. The second, an octavo that collates A⁸, is probably a piracy. A so-called second edition under Morphew's imprint, which is the edition quoted here, is evidently a second issue).

 6. *Tom of Bedlam:* Among the replies to Hoadly was one by Luke Milbourne, *Tom of Bedlam's Answer to His Brother Ben Hoadly,* dated from Bedlam, 1 June 1709. "Done in a bantering way," it was said to have been more effective "than all the serious Answers that have appear'd" (Hearne, *2,* 190).

 11. *Milton's Lays:* Milton continued to be regarded as a republican, even Whiggish, poet, particularly after 1698 when John Toland published *A Complete Collection of the Historical, Political, and Miscellaneous Works of John Milton.* Blackall had occasion to mention this work in a sermon he preached on 30 January 1699. In his preface Toland had challenged the authenticity not merely of Charles I's *Ikon Basilike* (which he attributed to John Gauden) but also of the earliest Christian documents. Blackall understood Toland to mean the New Testament. "We may cease to wonder," he expostulated, "that [Toland] should have the Boldness, without Proof, and against Proof, to deny the Authority of this Book [*Ikon Basilike*], who is such an Infidel as to doubt, and is shameless enough, even in Print, in a Christian Countrey, publickly to affront our Holy Religion, by declaring his Doubt, *That several Pieces under the Name of Christ and his Apostles . . . are suppositious*" (*A Sermon Preach'd before the Honourable House of Commons at St. Margaret's Westminster, January 30th 1698/9,* 1699, p. 16).

 12. *Tindal:* Matthew Tindal (1657–1733) graduated B.A. from Exeter College, Oxford, in 1676 and proceded D.C.L. in 1685. In November 1685 he began to practice in doctors' commons, the ecclesiastical, probate, and admiralty courts of England. Thereafter Dr. Tindal, as he was called, divided his time between Oxford, where he was a fellow of All Souls (1678–1733), and London, where he was "a noted Debauchee" (Hearne, *1,* 237). As early as 1680 he was subjected to a public "admonition" from the college because of his immoral conduct (Montagu Burrows, *Worthies of All Souls,* 1874, p. 381). "In King James's time he turn'd Papist, and upon the Revolution grew a mighty Williamite" (Hearne, *2,* 72).

Why howl the Dogs? From whence this Sound?
Why dance the Golden Tripods round?
And what is't moves the solid Ground?   15

Chorus

Great Ben *with Sacred Rage is blest,*
He foams, he swells, he is comprest,
The God sits heavy on his Breast.

Hence, hence, ye mitr'd Priests, away,
All ye who blind Obedience pay   20
To royal Monarchs' Princely Sway.

Thou, Mob, our Sov'reign Lord, appear,
With unpolluted Feet draw near,
And sit in thy imperial Chair.

Thou equal to the Gods above,   25
And scarce inferior unto *Jove;*

Intellectually he was a follower of Locke and wrote pamphlets on natural law, original contract, and freedom of the press. But the work which made him famous was one that he knew "would make the clergy mad." It was called *The Rights of the Christian Church Asserted, Against the Romish, and All Other Priests who Claim an Independent Power over it* (1706), but what it asserted was that the church has no rights, nor no power but what is granted to it by the state. More than 20 replies were made to this book, including one by Jonathan Swift, who described Tindal as "an old neglected Man, who hath long lain under the Extreams of Obloquy, Poverty and Contempt" (Swift, *Prose, 2,* 73). An attempt to prosecute the publisher of the book was unsuccessful (Luttrell, *6,* 379), but in March 1710 the House of Commons ordered *The Rights of the Christian Church Asserted* to be burnt by the common hangman (*CJ, 16,* 385).

13. *Why howl the Dogs?:* Hoadly is about to be represented as a sibyl, or priestess of Apollo, and dogs bark and tripods dance and earth quakes at the approach of the deity; cf. *Aeneid,* VI, 45–51.

17. *foams:* The sibyl in a trance state is supposed to foam at the mouth. Hoadly is being inspired (by Faction?) to write *An Humble Reply to the Right Reverend the Lord Bishop of Exeter's Answer* (1709).

20. *blind Obedience:* In his sermon of 8 March 1708 Blackall had argued that "If the Magistrate be *the Minister of* GOD, then it must needs be the Duty of Subjects . . . to yield Obedience to all . . . Laws and Constitutions of their earthly Governours . . . *Submit your selves to every Ordinance of Man, for the Lord's sake,* says St. *Peter*" (*The Divine Institution of Magistracy, and the Gracious Design of its Institution,* 1709, pp. 12–13).

22. "The *Power* of the *Magistrate* is originally derived . . . from the Contract or Concession of the People" (Benjamin Hoadly, *Some Considerations Humbly Offered to the Right Reverend the Lord Bishop of Exeter,* 1709, p. 24).

25. *equal to the Gods:* Cf. "if *Vox Populi* be *Vox Dei,* here is a plain Divine Right" (Defoe, *Some Remarks on the First Chapter in Dr. Davenant's Essays,* 1704, p. 21).

Through thee we are, we live, and move.

Thou art the universal Pole;
Round thee all other Powers rowl,
And thou dost actuate the whole.   30

From thee all Magistracy springs;
Thou giv'st the sacred Rule to Kings;
And at thy Nod they're useless Things.

What, tho' they stile themselves divine,
And would succeed by Right of Line,   35
There is no Law on Earth, but thine.

To whom thou list thou giv'st the Crown,
To *Charles* or *Nol,* to Prince or Clown;
And who sets up, may tumble down.

Thou bid'st them act the People's Good;   40
But if they rule not as they shou'd,
With Glory thou may'st let them Blood.

Like thy bold Sires in Forty-Eight,
Who neck'd their Prince, a worthy Fate!
For tyrannizing o'er the State.   45

That Prince, by Title, *Charles the First,*
Of all the Race of Kings, the worst,

27. This is a parody of what St. Paul told the Athenians: "[you] should seek the Lord . . . For in him we live, and move, and have our being; as certain also of your own poets have said" (Acts 17:27–28).

31. "The *Magistrate* hath no *Authority* . . . but what the whole . . . *Governed Society,* have in themselves" (Benjamin Hoadly, *Some Considerations Humbly Offered to the Right Reverend the Lord Bishop of Exeter,* 1709, p. 36).

36. *no Law on Earth, but thine:* Cf. "Decrees [of parliament] may be against Equity, Truth, Reason and Religion, but they are not against Law; because Law is the Will of the supreme Legislature" (Swift, *Prose, 2,* 74).

38. *Nol:* Oliver Cromwell.

42. *let . . . Blood:* "Violence is allowed to be repelled with Violence" (Benjamin Hoadly, *Some Considerations Humbly Offered to the Right Reverend the Lord Bishop of Exeter,* 1709, p. 13). Hoadly's authority is Locke: "whenever the Legislators endeavour to take away, and destroy the Property of the People, or to reduce them to Slavery, under arbitrary Power . . . the People . . . have a Right to resume their original Liberty, and, by the Establishment of a new Legislative . . . provide for their own Safety and Security" (*Two Treatises of Government,* 1690, pp. 441–42).

43. *Forty-Eight:* Charles I was executed on 30 January 1648/49.

Nor pious, great, nor good, nor just.

Therefore thy Sires could not him save,
But sent him headless to the Grave;   50
Such Honour all the Saints shall have.

And if, like them, thou wilt fulfil
Our Sov'reign Lord the People's Will,
Thou must dethrone or stab the Ill.

Chorus

Then thus great Salters-Hall *shall ring;*   55
Thus, thus the Calve's-Head-Club *shall sing,*
Leviathan, *our God and King.*

51. *the Saints:* The phrase is pointedly ambiguous. Initially the saints were the sectaries, the republicans like Milton, who cut off Charles's head. But the construction also allows Charles I to be the saint, a martyr in the eyes of the author.

55. *Salters-Hall:* "a long Presbyterian Meeting house [in Walbrook Ward in the City], handsomely fitted within, as to the Pews, &c." (Strype, *1,* ²200).

56. *Calve's-Head-Club:* This club, of which John Milton was supposed to have been one of the founders, met on 30 January to perform a kind of republican black mass to celebrate the execution of Charles I. The ceremonies included the singing of republican hymns ([Edward Ward], *The Secret History of the Calves-Head Club,* 5th ed., 1705, pp. 27–72) and "a Calfs head served up in a dish like St. John Baptists head in a charger" (HMC *Hope Johnstone MSS.,* p. 116).

Dr. Sacheverell and Benjamin Hoadly
(August? 1709)

Three weeks after Benjamin Hoadly had published *An Humble Reply to the Right Reverend the Lord Bishop of Exeter's Answer* (*The Daily Courant,* 27 July 1709), Henry Sacheverell preached a sermon at the Derby assizes. For this performance Sacheverell cast himself in the unusual role of defender of civil liberties, thundering against the societies for the reformation of manners that required neighbors "to turn *Informer,* assume an Odious and Factious Office, arrogantly intrench upon Other's *Christian Liberty,* and Innocence, and under the Shew of more *Zeal,* and *Purity* . . . turn the World upside down, and set all Mankind into Quarrels, and Confusions" (Henry Sacheverell, *The Communication of Sin: A Sermon Preach'd at the Assizes Held at Derby, August 15th, 1709,* 1709, 8⁰, p. 8). But for Henry Sacheverell, defending civil liberties could be only a pretext for attacking dissenters. The first society for the reformation of manners had indeed been founded by "Five or Six Private Gentlemen of the Church of England" (*The Post Angel,* December 1701; cf. BM MS. Add. 30000D, f. 277), but it was largely dissenters who had taken up and expanded the movement until it could disturb Sacheverell himself in the enjoyment of his favorite vices (William Bisset, *The Modern Fanatick,* 1710, pp. 28–30). And the dissenters' harping on "*thorow Reformation*" reminded high churchmen of the reformations of 1641–49 "which ended at last in the Ruin of the Kingdom" (Swift, *Prose, 3,* 47).

When Sacheverell's sermon was published "at the Request of the Gentlemen of the GRAND-JURY" of Derbyshire, the present epigram was printed on the flyleaf of the first edition, a quarto of 36 pages printed for Henry Clements, at the Half-Moon in St. Paul's Churchyard. (When the same publisher brought out a second edition in octavo, the poem was omitted).

The speaker of the epigram is a "Moderate" (line 5) and what he says about "Times" and "Principles" (8) indicates that "Moderation" is only expediency.

The author is probably Matthew Prior. Lines 7–10 of the epigram appear in two Prior manuscripts. The first of these, BM MS. Portland Loan 29/336, not foliated, is a fair copy in the italic hand of Adrian Drift, Prior's secretary. The second, Longleat MS. Prior Papers XXVIII, f. 158, is another fair copy in a secretarial hand, embodying two corrections of the text. In both copies lines 7–10 are followed by three lines that do not appear in the published epigram:

> Who knows how each Author may alter his mind
> As they or the Text other Comments may find
> Grace [——] and Sweet Burnet.

In the Longleat MS. these lines are marked "D" in the left hand margin, indicating that Alexander Pope thought that they should be excluded from an edition of Prior's works that was projected in 1723. Pope also supplied a title, "Fragment," for lines 7–10 that he accepted for publication as Prior's. The best guess, therefore, is that Drift copied into the Welbeck Abbey MS. the original rough draft of Prior's epigram. After Prior died in 1721 Drift's transcript was copied into the Longleat MS. to send to Pope. Upon the marriage in 1759 of Robert Harley's great-granddaughter, Lady Elizabeth Cavendish, to Thomas Thynne, third Viscount Weymouth and later marquis of Bath, the Prior papers passed to Longleat. The few that Lady Elizabeth left behind remained in possession of the dukes of Portland until 1950 when they were removed from Welbeck Abbey to the British Museum. But since there is no evidence that Prior (rather than someone else) wrote lines 1–6, the attribution must remain uncertain.

Equally uncertain is the date of composition of the verses, for the publication of *The Communication of Sin* sometime after 15 August 1709 provides the only evidence.

Dr. Sacheverell and Benjamin Hoadly

Among the *High Church Men,* I find there are several
That stick to the *Doctrine* of *Henry Sacheverell:*
Among the *Low Church* too, I find that as Odly,
Some pin all their Faith *on one* Benjamin Hoadly.
But We *Moderate Men* do our *Judgment Suspend,*   5
For GOD only knows where *these Matters* will End;
And *Salisbury Burnett* and *White Kennet* show,

1–3. *High Church . . . Low Church:* These terms were added to the vocabulary of political
abuse during the convocation of 1701–02 (Burnet, *2,* 347). Henry Sacheverell, who blamed
the dissenters for these *"Knavish Distinctions"* (Henry Sacheverell, *The Perils of False Brethren,
Both in Church, and State,* 1709, p. 19), may himself have been the first to use them in print:
"The first Time . . . the *Distinctions* of *High-Church* and *Low-Church* appeared in Print, was
[Sacheverell's] and *Lesley's* Printing Two *Libels;* [Sacheverell's] was call'd *The Character of a
Low Church-Man,* Printed in 1702, before either the *Observator* or *Review* made Use of the
Word" (*A Vindication of the Last Parliament, In Four Dialogues between Sir Simon and Sir Peter,*
1711, p. 257).

2. *Sacheverell:* The "Doctrine" of Henry Sacheverell was essentially theocratic, based on
the subordination of state to church, and with heavy emphasis on a holy war against dissent.

4. *Hoadly:* Hoadly's "Doctrine" was essentially Erastian, based on the subordination of
church to state, and the toleration of dissent.

5. *Moderate Men:* Between 1701 and 1710 the word "Moderation" deteriorated in the Tory
political lexicon from a term of admiration, "a mark of Sincerity" (*The Claims of the People
of England, Essayed,* 1701, p. 89), to a term of abuse. It was merely a descriptive term when
Godolphin and Harley were forming a nonpartisan ministry in January 1704 and it could be
said that "The side that desires and Promotes Moderation gets ground every day" (BM
MS. Lansdowne 773, f. 3). But by December 1710 it had become an "extremely scandalous"
word (William Bisset, *The Modern Fanatick,* 1710, sig. A4v), meaning "nothing but Getting
Money and *Preferment*" in politics (Henry Sacheverell, *The Perils of False Brethren, Both in Church,
and State,* 1709, p. 11) and "nothing but Lukewarmness in Religion" ([James Drake], *The
Memorial of the Church of England,* 1705, p. 27).

7. *Salisbury Burnett:* In 1675 Burnet "maintain'd the Doctrine of Passive Obedience &
nonResistance with great strength of argument, and carried it as high as ever any one did,
even to the suffering the most Bloudy Persecutions. But this was in a Reign when he thought
that by preaching it he might get Preferment, but afterwards when the Revolution happen'd
and the Usurper got the Crown [Burnet was consecrated bishop of Salisbury in March 1689]
he then forsook the Doctrine, as some Thousands besides did, preach'd and writ against it,
as if what he had asserted before was all Mistake" (Hearne, *2,* 325). Cf. *The History of Seven,*
10*n.,* below.

White Kennet: White Kennett (1660–1728) began his political career while an under-
graduate at St. Edmund Hall by publishing a Tory pamphlet a few days before the parlia-
ment convened at Oxford in March 1681. In the next reign, however, he opposed the
measures of James II. At the revolution he hesitated to take the oaths of allegiance and
supremacy to William and Mary (Gareth V. Bennett, *White Kennett,* S.P.C.K., 1957, pp.
11–12), but ended up as one of the strongest supporters of the revolution and the antagonist

That as the Times vary, so *Principles* go.
And Twenty Years hence, for ought you or I know,
'Twill be *Hoadly* the *high,* and *Sacheverel* the *low.*   10

---

of Atterbury in convocation. Thus he earned for himself the nickname of "weather-Cock Kennett" (Hearne, *2,* 356).

The Junto
(September 1709–April 1710)

The term junto or juncto, a corruption of the Spanish word *junta*, crept into use in England during the seventeenth century. From the beginning it was a term of abuse, used to describe cabals or cliques whose very existence generated suspicion and disapproval. At the end of William's reign, "the Junto" became the collective identity of four prominent Whig lords: Edward Russell, earl of Orford; Thomas Wharton, Lord Wharton; John Somers, Lord Somers; and Charles Montagu, Lord Halifax. It appears that these four were first called "the junto" about 1701 (Ailesbury, *2*, 534).

In Anne's reign a fifth member, Charles Spencer, third earl of Sunderland, was added and Orford was occasionally omitted. This grouping, which William Shippen adopted in *Moderation Display'd* (above), was in fact rather common: "in spight of Sodomy, Adultery, Pox or Prophaneness," it was said, "*S*——*nd*——*d* shall be a Saint, and *S*——*rs, Wh*——*n* and *H*——*x* Prophets, Martyrs, and Apostles" ([James Drake], *The Memorial of the Church of England*, 1705, p. 15). To these four the present poem adds Godolphin and Somerset, who were allies but not members of the Junto.

In December 1707 Sir John Cropley informed Lord Shaftesbury that "Juncta" was "the currant name for Ld Sommers, Ld. Hallifax, Ld Sunderland & Orford" (PRO 30/24/20, f. 141). But the omission of Wharton, "Chief of all the Rebel-Race" (*Faction Display'd*, 176, *POAS*, Yale, *6*, 658), must have been an oversight, for it was to these five that the queen referred when she complained to Marlborough in 1708 of "the five tyrannising lords" (Coxe, *Memoirs*, *2*, 292).

Anne's complaints arose because she regarded the Junto as a faction mobilized for the acquisition and manipulation of power. This was Harley's view too. According to him the term originated when the Whigs organized themselves to take advantage of Godolphin's overtures to them after the weakness of the Tories was revealed in the failure of the Tack in 1704 (p. 142 above). "Our Ministers declar'd openly for the *Whigs*, and this created a new thing call'd a *Junto*, a Ministry within a Ministry" (*Faults on Both Sides*, 1710, p. 27). As a combination seeking power the Junto was eminently successful, for by November 1709 Sunderland was secretary of state, Somers president of the council, Wharton lord lieutenant of Ireland, and Orford lord admiral. Only Halifax still remained without high office.

The poem must have been written *after* Wharton's return from Ireland in September 1709 (Luttrell, *6*, 492)—so that he could boast of the "Feats he . . . had done" (line 25) during the 1709 session of the Irish parliament—and *before* his return to Ireland in April 1710 (ibid., *6*, 575).

The author, like the author of *Duke Humphrey's Answer* (p. 332 above), is either William Shippen or an imitator of William Shippen.

THE JUNTO

At Dead of Night when peaceful Spirits sleep,
And undisturb'd, a peaceful Sabbath keep,
When only Fiends their balefull Looks display,
Impatient of Discoveries from the Day,
The JUNTO sate, in the *Northumbrian* Dome,   5
Studious of Mischeifs, and of Ills to come.
The President, as usual, fill'd the Chair,
With serious Aspect, and Malignant Air,
Diseas'd in Body, and *disturb'd* in Soul,
The one as much unclean as t'other foul.   10
On his Right Hand was Old *Volpone* plac'd,
With Wealth, and every thing but *Merit* grac'd;

1. *At Dead of Night:* Cf. "This Grand *Caball* was held at dead of Night" (Shippen, *Faction Display'd*, 64, *POAS*, Yale, *6*, 653).

2. *Sabbath:* "A midnight meeting of demons, sorcerers and witches, presided over by the Devil" (*OED*).

4. *Discoveries:* Meetings of the Junto were called to discuss what action to take in response to recent events. When, for example, news of the orders restraining the duke of Ormonde from engaging the enemy reached London in May 1712, a "Councill of Whiggs extraordinarly assembled in the morning at Lord Orford's" (*Verney Letters*, *1*, 311).

5. *the Northumbrian Dome:* Northumberland House in the Strand is also the setting of *Faction Display'd* (*POAS*, Yale, *6*, 653). It became the property of Charles Seymour, duke of Somerset, on his marriage in 1682 to Elizabeth Percy, daughter of the eleventh earl of Northumberland. Towers at the corners of the building "rise above the rest of the front . . . and terminate with a dome" (Noorthouck, p. 725)

6. *Studious of Mischeifs:* "I believe the Whigs have mischief in their heads," Sir Robert Davers wrote to Harley in November 1711, "There was lately a great meeting of them at Lord Orford's" (HMC *Portland MSS.*, *5*, 106).

Ills to come: Meetings of the Junto were also called in anticipation of important events. In September 1708 it was known that they would assemble at the Newmarket races to discuss the next session of parliament. "A Council of the Junto will be held there, and then and not till then shall we know who will be Speaker" (ibid., *4*, 505).

7. *The President:* Despite the aversion which she had to him "upon account of his having disobliged the Prince" (*Private Corr.*, *1*, 156), Anne finally capitulated and let Somers take his place as lord president of the council on 25 November 1708 (Luttrell, *6*, 377).

9. *Diseas'd in Body:* Cf. "*Somers*, tho weak in Body, strong in Mind, / No Pox can taint a Substance so refin'd!" (*The Golden Age Revers'd*, 30–31, *POAS*, Yale, *6*, 520).

disturb'd in Soul: Cf. "His restless Soul, that rends his sickly Frame, / Worn with a poys'nous and corroding Flame" (*Faction Display'd*, 235–36, *POAS*, Yale, *6*, 660).

11. *Volpone:* Godolphin; "*Volpone*, who will solely now Command / The Publick Purse, and Treasure of the Land" (*Faction Display'd*, 407–08, *POAS*, Yale, *6*, 668).

A Man whose Arts and undiscover'd Wiles
Had vested him with wrong'd *Britannia*'s Spoyls,
And whose All powerful and commanding WAND,   15
Like *Aaron*'s had distress'd and vex'd the Land.
The Mansion's *stuttering* Lord and Master next
Was on the Left on his Posteriors fixt,
And with a *Grinning* Countenance survey'd
What Schemes were drawn up, and what Plans were laid;   20
As he made Signs and Tokens all was safe,
By his *extempore* Smiles, and thoughtless Laugh.
Near him the Bully *Vice Roy* cock'd his Hat,
And prattled like a Mountebank of State,
Of Feats he o'er the Herring-Pond had done,   25
And Proselytes to Mother Faction won;
Of breaking thro' a solemn Stipulation,

14. *wrong'd Britannia:* Charges of defalcation in the treasury reached a culmination on 24 April 1711 when the House of Commons resolved "that of the Moneys, granted by Parliament, and issued for the publick Service, to *Christmas,* 1710, there are Thirty-five millions Three hundred and two thousand One hundred and Seven Pounds, Eighteen Shillings and Nine Pence, . . . whereof no Accounts have been laid before the Auditors" (*CJ, 16,* 613).

15. *WAND:* See illustration, p. 475 below.

16. *Aaron's:* Aaron's rod produced the plagues of Egypt (Exodus 7–10).

17. *The Mansion's stuttering Lord:* Cf. "(the Master of the Dome) | A Stamm'ring Hot, Conceited, Laughing Lord" (*Faction Display'd,* 67–68, *POAS,* Yale, *6,* 653). Somerset had "a great Hesitation in his Speech" (Macky, p. 17).

23. *Vice Roy:* Wharton had been appointed lord lieutenant of Ireland at the same time that Somers was sworn lord president of the council (Luttrell, *6,* 377).

24. *prattled:* Unlike Somerset, Wharton was "a ready Speaker; and content to employ his Gift upon such Occasions, where those who conceive they have any remainder of Reputation or Modesty are ashamed to appear" (Swift, *Prose, 7,* 10).

25. *Herring-Pond:* the Irish Sea. Wharton's ambition to intervene in Irish politics was mentioned in *Faction Display'd,* 221–27 (*POAS,* Yale, *6,* 660).

26. *Mother Faction:* "A restless and repining Fiend" (*Faction Display'd,* 9), she is illustrated in *POAS,* Yale, *6,* 651.

27. *a solemn Stipulation:* In February 1704 the Irish parliament had voted to adopt the provisions of the English Test Act, intending to exclude from public office anyone who would not "take the Oaths of Supremacy and Allegiance, and renounce Transubstantiation, and take the Sacrament according to the Liturgy of the Church of *England*" (*Of the Sacramental Test: To a Member of the Parliament who was for the Occasional Bill,* 1708, reprinted, Boyer, *Annals,* 1709, p. [2]126). When Wharton was appointed lord lieutenant in November 1708 the Anglo-Irish "were under great apprehensions at his first coming that He woud drive directly at repealing the Test" (Addison, *Letters,* p. 134). This was the fear that incited Swift to write and publish *A Letter from a Member of the House of Commons in Ireland to a Member of the House of Commons in England, Concerning the Sacramental Test* (December 1708) defending the test clause.

And forcing *Consciences,* by way of *Toleration.*
Nor was their Secretary from his Post;
Without his intermedling all'd be lost;   30
A Peer to be deduc'd to future Ages,
For buying *Books,* and reading *Title-Pages;*
For *Elzevirs* and *Alduses* entire,
And being full as *Honest* as his *Sire.*
The sixth and last was a presumptuous Lord,   35
More fit for *College-Crusts* than *Council-Board,*
A Pirate of a Peer, whose borrow'd praise

28. *Toleration:* An alternative to repealing the test clause in Ireland would have been to grant the Irish dissenters the same freedom of assembly and worship that English dissenters enjoyed under the Toleration Act of 1689. An order of the Irish House of Commons to bring in such a bill during the session of 1703–04 (*CJ* Ireland, *3,* 135) was not acted upon. But the issue was raised again during the session of 1709 by the eccentric James Hamilton, sixth earl of Abercorn and viscount Strabane in the Irish peerage. "The House of Lords," Addison reported in May 1709, "have had some heats on a Clause offered in their Address, to Encourage a tolleration for the Dissenters, by my Lord Abercorn who told them . . . that he did *it* to prevent something worse [repeal of the test clause]. It was rejected however by the whole Bench of Bishops" (Addison, *Letters,* p. 137).

29. *Secretary:* Sunderland.

32. *buying Books:* "The great library of Charles Spencer, third earl of Sunderland contained . . . some 20,000 printed books: it was particularly strong in incunabula (many being printed on vellum), in Bibles, in first editions of the classics, and in Continental literature of the fifteenth and sixteenth centuries" (Seymour de Ricci, *English Collectors of Books & Manuscripts,* Cambridge, Cambridge University Press, 1930, p. 38). But Swift observed that Sunderland had not "much improved . . . even in the Opinion of the World, by an overgrown Library" (Swift, *Prose, 7,* 9).

33. *Elzevirs and Alduses:* Teobaldo Mannucci, better known as Aldo Manuzio (1450–1515), founded the Aldine press in Venice in 1490. Louis Elzevier (1540–1617) established the Elzevir (as it was spelled in English) press in Leiden about 1580.

34. *Sire:* The honesty of Robert Spencer, second earl of Sunderland, is retailed in *Faction Display'd,* 251–66 (*POAS,* Yale, *6,* 662).

35. *a presumptuous Lord:* Halifax.

36. *College-Crusts:* "Ld Halifax formerly fellow of Trinity Colledge Cam." (*Ad*). Despite GEC, *6,* 246, note *c,* the scholiast seems to be correct. The Charles Montagu who became Lord Halifax received an M.A. in 1682, and became a fellow in 1683 (W. W. Rouse Ball and John A. Venn, *Admissions to Trinity College, Cambridge,* 5 vols., Macmillan, 1913, *2,* 534–35).

37–38. Cf. "Last rose [Halifax], deck'd with borrow'd Bays, / Renown'd for others Projects, others Lays" (*Faction Display'd,* 322–23, *POAS,* Yale, *6,* 664).

Proceeds from others Schemes and others Lays;
Since he now sits in Senate's Upper House
By *Murray*'s Projects, and by *Prior*'s Mouse.   40

40. *Murray's Projects:* Robert Murray (1635–1725?), like Defoe, was born in London and after serving his apprenticeship set up as projector and called himself a gentleman. One of his projects was for a credit bank, about which he wrote pamphlets in 1676–83 (Wing M3114, M3116–18). But these pamphlets are not mentioned in modern accounts of the origins of the Bank of England, which Halifax brought into existence by an act of parliament in April 1694.

Projects: Projectors were "Busybodies in new Inventions and Discoveries, Virtuoso's of Fortune, or Traders in unsuccessful if not impracticable Whimms" (*New Dictionary*, sig. I8r; cf. Swift, *Prose, 11*, 176–77).

Prior's Mouse: Halifax was accused of having contributed only his name to *The Hind and the Panther Transvers'd to the Story of the Country Mouse and the City Mouse* (July 1687), on which he is supposed to have collaborated with Matthew Prior (*POAS*, Yale, *4*, 116–45). Cf. *Moderation Display'd*, 337*n*. above.

On Dr. Sacheverell's Sermon
Preach'd at St. Paul's, Nov. 5. 1709.
To the Tune of *Packington's Pound*

(November? 1709)

What is probably the climactic episode in the reign of Queen Anne began with a sermon. It was preached in St. Paul's cathedral on Saturday 5 November 1709. The preacher was Dr. Henry Sacheverell, chaplain of St. Saviour's, in Southwark, who had been invited by the lord mayor and aldermen of the city of London to preach on the anniversary of the Gunpowder plot of 5 November 1605. This was a popular anti-Catholic holiday, usually ending up with an *auto-da-fé* in which effigies of Guy Fawkes and other hated Catholics were burned at the stake amid appropriate displays of fireworks.

Dr. Sacheverell, who was already known for "petulant Railings at Dissenters, and Low-Churchmen, in several Sermons and Libels" (Burnet, *2*, 537), chose as his text 2 Corinthians 11:26, in which St. Paul, in a moment of self-pity, complained of his "journeyings . . . in perils in the city, in perils in the wilderness, in perils in the sea, in perils among false brethren." Then Sacheverell mounted the pulpit and began his sermon. He began, of course, with appropriate expressions of gratitude for England's "Astonishing and *Miraculous . . . Deliverance*" from the Gunpowder plot of 1605. But it soon became apparent that the Gunpowder plot was to be only the vehicle of a metaphor, of which the tenor was "equally . . . Treacherous FALSE BRETHREN, *from* whom we must always expect the *utmost Perils*" (*The Perils of False Brethren, Both in Church, and State*, 1709, p. 5). The rest of the sermon was an all-out attack on low churchmen, occasional conformists, and Protestant dissenters, all of whom were alleged to be plotting to overthrow the establishment in church and state. Nothing more was said about Catholics.

The enormity of what Sacheverell had done was recognized immediately (30–31*n.* below), "dropping the *Gun-Powder* Plot, a Subject so ungrateful to [Catholics]," as Defoe said, "to employ the Day upon so much more suitable a Subject—*Viz.* The real Blowing up the Peace of Protestants" (*A Letter to Mr. Bisset, Eldest Brother of the Collegiate Church of St. Catherines; In Answer to His Remarks on Dr. Sacheverell's Sermon*, 1709, p. 14). On the other side of the political spectrum, one of

367

Thomas Hearne's correspondents, who had attended the sermon, reported that "D: Sacheverel, your mighty Boanerges thunderd most furiously at paul's against the phanaticks" (Hearne, *2*, 304).

The court of aldermen voted not to request Sacheverell to print the sermon, but print it he did, with an inflammatory dedication to the Tory lord mayor, Sir Samuel Garrard of Lamer, Hertfordshire, fourth baronet. The Tories "did so magnify the Sermon, that, as was generally reckoned, about 40000 of them were printed, and dispersed over the Nation" (Burnet, *2*, 538).

The present poem, set to the popular tune of *Packington's Pound* (Simpson, p. 564), was designed to belittle the sermon. The speaker takes up the role of *ingénu*—"We poor Folks" (24)—to warn the populace of the dangers of politicizing parsons. His homely language, designed to be understood by "Children and Servants" (2), contrasts pointedly with Sacheverell's weaseling pulpit style.

How soon after 5 November 1709 the poem was written cannot be determined. It was not published until 1715.

There is no evidence to identify the author.

ON DR. SACHEVERELL'S SERMON
PREACH'D AT ST. PAUL'S, NOV. 5. 1709.
TO THE TUNE OF *Packington's Pound*

Good People, the Words that I write now perpend,
With Children and Servants, for them too I call:
False Brethren, the *Perils* of some do pretend,
But Perils of the Pulpit are worse than 'em all;
      Then pray have a Care,   5
      Yourselves well prepare
Before you a Parson do venture to hear,
Good People keep home, and look into your Bibles,
For Sermons are now grown mere Faction and Libels.

St. *Paul's* great Cathedral was burn'd once by Fire,   10
As most Men or all have been told of, no doubt;
And since 'tis rebuilt, why what are we the nigher,
Last Fifth of *November* another broke out;
      A strange Man stept in,
      Talk'd thro' Thick and Thin,   15
Because safely wainscotted up to the Chin,
Invented such Jealousies, broached such Fears,
As Thousands of Families set by the Ears.

1. *perpend:* weigh carefully (*OED*).

3. *False Brethren, the Perils of:* Sacheverell defined "False Brethren" as "both the *Popish,* and *Fanatick* Enemies of Our *Church,* and *Government*" (*The Perils of False Brethren, Both in Church, and State,* 1709, p. 5), but in fact Sacheverell's "Enemies" were low churchmen within the establishment, occasional conformists, and Protestant nonconformists.

4. *Perils of the Pulpit:* Cf. [White Kennett], *The High Church Mask Pull'd Off,* 1710, pp. 15–16: "How have many of our Pulpits been like Mount *Aetna* and *Vesuvius,* breathing forth Flames and Sulphur? Uncharitably dooming to the Infernal Pit Protestant Dissenters."

10. *St. Paul's . . . burn'd:* Gothic St. Paul's was destroyed by fire in September 1666 in the great fire of London.

12. *rebuilt:* Work was begun on Sir Christopher Wren's new cathedral in 1675. The first service, a thanksgiving service for the peace of Ryswick, was held in December 1697, but the structure was not finally completed before 1710.

13. *another broke out:* William Bisset mentions "a Report which I heard from several, *That St.* Pauls *was on Fire a Saturday*" (*Remarks on Dr. Sach——'s Sermon at the Cathedral of St. Paul, November 5,* 1709, p. 4).

14. *strange:* Defoe summarized Sacheverell's eccentricities in an iambic verse: "A Noisy, Sawcy, Swearing, Drunken Priest" (*The Double Welcome,* 1705, p. 25).

16. *wainscotted up to the Chin:* i.e. standing in the pulpit.

17. *Jealousies:* Sacheverell "Invented . . . Jealousies" in his sermon by representing that

From School to the College these young Men are sent,
In Lectures of Mutton their Parts for to try;   20
And when under Tutors some Time they have spent,
They then commence Doctors of Divinity;
            But with half an Eye,
            We poor Folks can spy;
That they are but Doctors of Spite and Envy.   25
They tell us they're Heaven's Plenipotentiaries,
Alas! But we find 'em meer Incendiaries.

They Bell-weathers are to the Sheep of the Town,
And from their good Pastures, poor Souls they do lead;
Their Eyes they lift up, and their Text they lay down,   30
Then run away from it, and Mutiny read;

---

the dissenters claimed "a *civil Right,* as they term it . . . to *justle* the *Church* out of *Her Establishment,* by Hoisting their *Toleration* into its Place; and to . . . Demand the *Repeal of the Corporation,* and *Test Acts*" (*The Perils of False Brethren, Both in Church, and State,* 1709, pp. 18–19).

Fears: Sacheverell "broached . . . Fears" by insinuating that there was a massive plot against the establishment in church and state: "Whether these Men are not *Contriving,* and *Plotting* out our utter *Ruin,* and whether all those FALSE BRETHREN, that fall in with these *Measures,* and *Designs,* do not contribute basely to it, I leave every Impartial Man . . . to Determine" (ibid., p. 20). An eyewitness reported that "All the Congregation were shaken . . . at the terrour of his Inveterate expressions" (Hearne, *2,* 304–05).

19. *From School to . . . College:* Sacheverell went up from Marlborough grammar school, in Wiltshire, to Magdalen College, Oxford, in August 1689, at the age of 15.

20. *Lectures of Mutton:* William Bisset, *The Modern Fanatick. With a Large and True Account of the Life, Actions, Endowments, &c. of the Famous Dr. Sa——l,* 1710, p. 21, recounts more details of this episode, which apparently took place in the dining hall of Magdalen College of which Sacheverell became a fellow (1701–13): "And to add no more, what shews his *natural Temper* . . . [is] his beating one with a Shoulder of Mutton; which a Gentleman told me, he had from several of his own College."

22. *Doctors of Divinity:* Sacheverell was criticized for taking a D.D. in 1708 because at 34 he was too young, and because the £100 should have been spent to buy an annuity for his mother who was a charity patient in a hospital (ibid., pp. 15–16).

27. *Incendiaries:* William Bisset called Sacheverell "an Incendiary . . . as dangerous as a Lighted Faggot in an high Wind" (*Remarks on Dr. Sach——'s Sermon at the Cathedral of St. Paul,* 1709, p. 4).

28. *Bell-weathers . . . to the Sheep of the Town:* Sacheverell was "brought up by a popular election" to St. Saviour's in Southwark (Burnet, *2,* 537).

30–31. *Text they lay down, | Then run away from it:* "[5 November] being gunpowder treason, and the day of the landing of king William, the deliverer of Great Brittain and Ireland from popery, &c. . . . Dr. Sacheverel . . . preach't before the lord mayor at St. Pauls, his text, 2 Corinth. cap. 11. vers. 26, In perils among false brethren; and instead of speaking to the day, turn'd his discourse upon the presbyterians" (Luttrell, *6,* 507–08).

31. *Mutiny:* Despite elaborate denials to the contrary (*The Perils of False Brethren, Both in*

> God keep us at home,
> For from *France* or *Rome,*
> These Spiritual Tinkers must certainly come.
> The Pope sends them over Divisions to make,   35
> As Glaziers find Foot-balls your Windows to break.
>
> Thank God that for all this *Cuntankerous* Band,
> The brave valiant *Murlbro',* the French Men can bang;
> For Seven Years together, he has held in a Hand,
> Of Battles and Sieges of Towns each Campaign;   40
> The War soon will cease,
> And the *French* beg for Peace,
> Were it not for such vile Correspondents as these.
> So Heaven keep Queen, Lords, and Commons and all,
> From being concern'd in any Church Brawl.   45

Church, and State, 1709, p. 19), the whole purport of Sacheverell's sermon was to undermine the revolution settlement in general and the Act of Toleration (1689) in particular.

33. *from France or Rome:* "An *English Gentleman,* was at *Brussels* about the Time of the Doctor's preaching at St. *Paul's*; and the first News he heard of the Doctor or his Sermon, was from the *Pope's Nuntio,* who ask'd him . . . what News from *England?* The Gentleman answer'd, I hear none; says the *Nuntio, you have heard of the famous Docteur, that preach'd in the great Church in London?* No Sir, says the Gentleman, I know nothing of the Matter; says the *Nuntio, He's a bold honest Man, he has preach'd up the Title of the Chevalier St. George, and will stand by it.* Sir, said the Gentleman, that's impossible. *I have it,* says he, *by good Intelligence, and before you get into England, you'l find the Matter work well; it will in the End bring in the King*" (William Bisset, *The Modern Fanatick,* 1710, pp. 22–23).

44–45. This was a recurrent theme in Augustan literature. Cf. Dryden, *Religio Laici* (1682), 447–50, and more recently Defoe, *A Challenge of Peace, Address'd to the Whole Nation,* 1703, p. 21: "What has Religion to do with Politicks? . . . We should not have a tenth part of the Differences in State-Affairs, did not Church-matters and State-matters mingle so much together."

The Thanksgiving
(November 1709?)

The great victories of the war of the Spanish succession were celebrated with thanksgiving days on which church bells were rung and religious services held throughout the nation to give thanks to God, the queen, and the duke of Marlborough for the latest military success. The thanksgiving for Blenheim on 7 September 1704 was unusually splendid: The queen proceeded in state from St. James's to St. Paul's, "the streets being lin'd with the train'd bands, and the several companies in their livery gowns, the balconies hung with tapistry and crowded with spectators: . . . her majestie was drawn in a coach and 8 horses . . . the horses curiously deck't with white and red ribbons, made up like roses, and guarded by the earl of Albemarles troop richly accoutred" (Luttrell, *5*, 462–63).

On 6 October 1709, a month after the first news of the battle had arrived in London, Anne proclaimed 22 November as a day of thanksgiving for the victory at Malplaquet and the whole mechanism of celebration was cranked up again for another procession to St. Paul's, where the Whiggish Dr. White Kennett preached before the queen, and at night there were the usual bonfires, etc. (ibid., *6*, 496, 514).

But Malplaquet was not a victory like Blenheim, Ramillies, or Oudenarde. In his first report from the battlefield, near Mons, in Hainaut, Marlborough had said that the losses were "very great on both Sides" (Brodrick, p. 309) and the defeated French general, Marshal Villars, observed that "the enemy would have been annihilated by another such victory" (Coxe, *Memoirs, 2,* 459). When the full extent of the casualties became known—more than 30,000 on both sides (Trevelyan, *3,* 18)—the stock market, which had gone up on the first news of the victory, suffered great losses. What the French said was literally true: the allies had seized the battlefield, but "l'honneur de la valeur avoit demeuré aux armes de leur roy" (BM MS. Add. 17677DDD, f. 271). The allies were so weakened that a march on Paris was unthinkable and the war was soon discovered to be a stalemate.

Loss of enthusiasm for the war can be traced through Addison's *Campaign* (December 1704), Prior's *Ode Humbly Inscrib'd to the Queen* (July 1706), Congreve's *Jack Frenchman's Defeat* (July 1708), and the anonymous *Thanksgiving.* The first two poems are uncritically and unashamedly heroic; the third is still enthusiastic, but in mock-heroic terms; *The Thanksgiving* is angry and disenchanted. The emperor's nakedness has been discovered.

In one manuscript (*M*) the poem is dated 1708, which is clearly too early. In another manuscript (*R*) the date is 1710 and in a third (*Q*) it is February 1710. But these are late manuscripts and the verses presumably were written shortly before or after the thanksgiving service of 22 November 1709 which gives them point.

The poem has been attributed to Swift by Oscar Wilde's father, Dr. W. R. Wilde (*The Closing Years of Dean Swift's Life,* Dublin, 1849, p. 143), and after him by F. Elrington Ball (*Swift's Verse,* John Murray, 1929, pp. 11–13, 112), but there is no evidence that Swift wrote it (Swift, *Poems, 3,* 1061–62). Nor is there any evidence that anyone else did.

THE THANKSGIVING

In Sounds of Joy your tuneful Voices raise,
And teach the People whom to thank and praise.
Thank prudent *Anna*'s providential Reign
For Peace and Plenty, both of Corn and Grain:
Thank the *Scotch* Peers for their firm, unbought Union;   5
Thank Bishops for Occasional Communion:
Thank the Stock-Jobbers for your thriving Trade;
Thank just *Godolphin* that your Debts are paid:
Thank *Marlborough*'s Zeal that scorn'd the proffer'd Treaty;

4. *Peace:* Of the 12 years of Anne's reign 11 of them were war years.

Plenty: The disastrous winter of 1708–09, when the Thames froze over for the first time since 1682–83, was followed by such a poor harvest that the price of grain was doubled in England and "the hand of God, Famine," was lifted against the French *(Wentworth Papers,* P. 87). In September 1709 Sir Thomas Mansell wrote to Harley from Glamorganshire, "Our harvest is not near in, and the crops especially wheat but indifferent, so that our country . . . will go near to be starved before the year comes about" (HMC *Portland MSS., 4,* 527).

5. *unbought Union:* Godolphin was "shrewdly suspected of having lavish'd away near a Million *Sterling,* to bring about the *Union*" *(An Essay towards the History of the Last Ministry and Parliament,* 1710, p. 47). As a matter of fact the union was bought much more cheaply *(A Scots Poem,* 1060n. above).

6. *Occasional Communion:* The Tories held Whig bishops chiefly responsible for the three failures in 1702–04 to prevent dissenters from qualifying themselves for any civil or military post by taking communion once a year in the Church of England. Cf. *Moderation Display'd,* 280n. above, and *The Mitred Club* (1703, *POAS,* Yale, *6,* 510).

7. *Stock-Jobbers:* "*Stock-jobbing,* a sharp, cunning, cheating Trade of Buying and Selling Shares of Stock in East India, Guinea and other Companies; also in the Bank [of England], Exchequer, &c." *(New Dictionary,* sig. L6r).

thriving Trade: Loss of the Spanish trade led to an economic recession in England *(A Vindication of the Faults on Both Sides,* 1710, p. 8). "It was a time of Dearth and Scarcity," Burnet (2, 539) said, "so that the Poor were much pinched." The lowest stage of the depression occurred in 1705 when Bank stock fell below par for the first time since 1696 (George Chalmers, *An Estimate of the Comparative Strength of Great-Britain, During the Present and Four Preceding Reigns,* 1782, pp. 11, 131; *Review,* 10 March 1705).

8. *Debts:* When the treasurer's staff was finally taken from the earl of Godolphin, Harley "found the Exchequer almost empty, nothing left for the subsistence of the Army, but some tallies upon the third general mortgage of the customs; the Queen's civil list near 700,000*l.* in debt; the funds all exhausted, and a debt of 9,500,000*l.* without any provision of Parliament" (HMC *Portland MSS., 5,* 650).

9. *the proffer'd Treaty:* On 28 May the allies signed a treaty of peace with France which they had negotiated at Gertruydenberg, near The Hague, with the marquis de Torcy, Louis XIV's secretary for foreign affairs. On 4 June Louis gave his "final Answer" (Burnet, 2, 529). He agreed to all of the allied terms but one: he refused to accept Article IV which required him to use French armies to drive his grandson from the throne of Spain *(The Life and Reign of Her Late Excellent Majesty Queen Anne,* 1738, pp. 472–81). Marlborough and the

But thank *Eugene* that *Frenchmen* did not beat ye: 10
Thank your own selves, that you are tax'd and shamm'd;
But thank th'Almighty, if you are not damn'd.

Junto lords were so mesmerized by the slogan "No Peace without Spain" (Luttrell, *6*, 247), that they rejected this incredible opportunity to end the fighting with the achievement of 39 out of 40 of their war aims.

10. *Eugene:* The importance of Prince Eugene, who commanded the imperial army at Malplaquet, can be judged by the fact that "Before the arrival of Eugene's army [on 10 September 1709] the numerical odds were two to one in Villars' favour" (Frank Taylor, *The Wars of Marlborough 1702–1709*, 2 vols., Oxford, Basil Blackwell, 1921, *2*, 363).

11. *tax'd and shamm'd:* This may refer to a specific plan of the Whig money managers. "The Project of making *Land a perpetual* Fund . . . could, in time, prove . . . fatal to our Constitution. For thereby the real Property of Land would belong to the Bankers and . . . to continue *Land-Taxes* beyond the Duration of the War, would give up all our Liberties at once" (*An Essay towards the History of the Last Ministry and Parliament*, 1710, pp. 49–50).

1710

The Civil War
(February 1710)

The downfall of the duke of Marlborough was the most unpredictable event in the reign of Queen Anne. Upon the accession of the queen, Marlborough was said, in a French intelligence report, to be "le premier Ministre de la nouvelle Cour" (PRO 31/3/190, f. 48). And with his power to determine foreign policy, to wield the enormous patronage of the military machine, to appoint ministers who supported him and to force the resignation of those who disagreed with him, Marlborough was prime minister in all but name during the first half of the reign. By the end of 1708 he seemed to be at the height of his power. The victories of Blenheim, Ramillies, and Oudenarde appeared to justify his continental strategy, while the fall of Harley and the promotion of Somers and Wharton appeared to confirm his control over appointments.

But these appearances were illusory. For Anne was losing confidence in "our M[iniste]rs *He* and *She*" ([James Drake] *The Memorial of the Church of England*, 1705, p. 20). The duchess of Marlborough had already proved dispensable (*Abigail's Lamentation for the Loss of Mr. Harley*, 13n. above) but the duke was thought essential as long as Anne remained committed to the war aims of the grand alliance. After Ramillies in 1706 Harley had advised the queen to order Marlborough to march the allied armies into France (HMC *Portland MSS.*, 5, 647). During 1709, however, Harley persuaded her that she need no longer be tied to the terms of the treaties which held the allies together, and that a total victory over France was impossible in any case, particularly after the devastating losses at Malplaquet in September 1709.

Anne first demonstrated her independence of Marlborough by refusing his request in October 1709 to be appointed to the nonexistent and unconstitutional post of captain general for life (Coxe, *Memoirs, 2,* 491–92). Her next step was an indirect challenge to Marlborough's authority as commander in chief of the forces. In January 1710 the death of the earl of Essex left two military posts vacant, for Essex had been constable of the Tower of London and colonel of the fourth regiment of dragoons. Both posts, although theoretically at the disposal of the crown, were in practice part of the captain general's patronage. Marlborough in fact had in mind George Fitzroy, duke of Northumberland, for the first post, and Lieutenant General Thomas Meredith for the second.

Harley, however, persuaded Anne to exercise her prerogative to make Richard Savage, Earl Rivers, her constable of the Tower, and "*honest* JACK HILL,*" Abigail Masham's brother, colonel of the fourth dragoons, "without consulting any of her ministers" (Swift, *Prose, 8,* 117). Marlborough's agreement to the first appointment was obtained by a subterfuge. Rivers persisted in his importunities for the post until Marlborough readily agreed to let him beg this favor of the queen in order to be rid of him. The duke expected that when Anne consulted him about the post, he would secure the appointment of Northumberland.

Although Marlborough acquiesced in Rivers's appointment when Anne made it without consulting him, he dug in his heels over the promotion of Hill and precipitated the civil war of the present poem. Failing to persuade Anne to reverse her decision, Marlborough retired to Windsor Lodge. This action precipitated a palace crisis: Godolphin and Somers were anxious to compromise the differences; Marlborough himself wanted an ultimatum: either Abigail Masham must be dismissed or he would resign; his son-in-law, the earl of Sunderland, was willing to organize a parliamentary address to the queen demanding Abigail's dismissal. This was a threat that Anne took so seriously that "She sent for several persons of both houses in her service, [and] declared with great Spirit and Courage against it" (Leicestershire R.O. MS. D9.7/Bundle 23).

In the end the moderate counsels of Godolphin and Somers prevailed. Anne dropped her insistence on Hill's promotion and promoted Meredith instead. For his part Marlborough gave up the idea of an ultimatum and Abigail Masham remained. On 23 January 1710 Marlborough was granted an audience with the queen and the crisis was resolved. But the civil war ended with a truce, not with a peace. And so does the poem, which in form is a verse letter, briefly setting the stage for the audience of 23 January (1–18) and then bringing on the duke to tell his "Lies" (19–28). But the letter ends with Anne smiling to herself at the discomfiture of her "premier Ministre."

Printed here for the first time, the poem is dated "February 1709/10" in one of the two manuscripts.

The Tory author cannot be identified.

THE CIVIL WAR

Since Essex dy'd, Dear friend, 'tis rumor'd here
That strange Commotions in the State appear.
The reason's plain, because the Queen pretends
To make Distinction 'twixt her foes and friends,
And so designs, as her own Choice and Will,   5
In Lieu of Meredith to prefer Jack Hill.

1. *Essex:* Essex served in all the campaigns of 1693–1700 as colonel of the fourth dragoons and was promoted lieutenant general in 1708. He was also lord lieutenant of Hertfordshire (1692–1710), constable of the Tower of London (1706–1710), and a privy councillor (25 November 1708–10). He had the reputation of being "the lewdest young man of the town" (GEC, *5*, 146) and is said to have "contracted his [fatal] Distemper by hard drinking of bad Wine" (BM MS. Loan 29 / 321, f. [10]). He died on 10 January 1710.

2. *Commotions in the State:* On 24 January 1710 Peter Wentworth could report that " 'Tis certain there's a great Hurly burly at Court" (*Wentworth Papers,* p. 103).

6. *Meredith:* Thomas Meredith or Meredyth (d. 1719) was an Anglo-Irishman, born in Dollardstown, county Meath, and commissioned a captain in the duke of Leinster's regiment of horse in April 1691 (Dalton, *3,* 181). In March 1702 in Dublin he raised a regiment of foot which fought under his command in all of Marlborough's major engagements. Following the capitulation of Dendermonde in September 1706, Meredith was made its governor (Luttrell, *6,* 87). He was wounded at Oudenarde and finally promoted lieutenant general in January 1709 (ibid., *6,* 325; Dalton, *6,* 17). Although his parliamentary career was short—Kent (January–November 1701) and Midhurst, Sussex (1708–10)—the division lists establish Meredith as a solid ministerial Whig. He was made an equerry to the queen in November 1704, governor of Tinmouth Castle in December 1708, and in March 1708 he succeeded William Walsh as a gentleman of the horse to the queen (Luttrell, *5,* 485; *6,* 241, 284). In January 1710 he was Marlborough's candidate to succeed to the command of Essex's regiment of dragoons. In December 1710, however, Meredith was turned out of all his employments for drinking damnation and confusion to the new ministry (Swift, *Prose, 3,* 44; *Journal, 1,* 120).

Hill: Although John Hill (d. 1735) is said to have been "an indifferent soldier on horse or foot" (Dalton, *3,* 414), his family connections were impeccable. He was a younger brother of Abigail Masham, the queen's confidante, a nephew of James Stanhope, first earl of Stanhope, and a poor relation of the duchess of Marlborough. When he was only a tall ragged boy, Sarah Churchill clothed him and sent him to school at St. Albans. When a vacancy occurred she got him appointed a page of honor to the prince of Denmark. And although Marlborough "always said that JACK HILL *was good for nothing,* yet to oblige [the duchess], he made him his *aid de camp,* and afterwards gave him a *regiment*" (*Account of the Conduct,* p. 180). In November 1702 he was commissioned a captain in the Coldstream Guards (Dalton, *5,* 46). In May 1705 he was given command of Stanhope's regiment after it had been reformed following its surrender at Portalegre in Portugal (Luttrell, *5,* 572; Dalton, *5,* 66). Two years later Colonel Hill's regiment was almost destroyed at Almansa and Hill himself was captured. He was released in a prisoner exchange (Luttrell, *6,* 213) and wounded at the siege of Mons in October 1709, after his regiment, again reformed, had been sent abroad to supply the losses at Malplaquet. In January 1710 he was promoted brigadier general (Dalton, *6,* 18), and he was queen Anne's candidate to succeed to the command of Essex's regiment of dragoons.

At which Presumption John and Sarah swell
And damn that project to the Pit of Hell,
Retire from Court, and swear they'll ne'er return
'Till from the presence Mrs. Masham's torn.   10
But finding in their Absence, by their Spies,
There were some heads could full as well advise,
And knowing likewise, by Examination
Of all the Parties in their Severall Station,
How inconsiderate their Persons were   15
When by Supreme Authority left bare,
Resolve with flattery to accost the Throne.
And so reenter Sarah and her John:
    Madam, Where I have been with mighty care,
Health to preserve by taking Windsor air,   20
An odd report (as false as God is true)
Has reach'd my ears (of which I never knew),

7. *John and Sarah:* the duke and duchess of Marlborough.

9. *Retire from Court:* "On the 15th of January [1710] therefore [the duke] left the town and went to Windsor in great discontent. It was council-day [Sunday]. The QUEEN did not ask where he was, nor take the least notice of his absence. His withdrawing himself made a great noise in the town" (*Account of the Conduct,* p. 230).

10. *'Till . . . Masham's torn:* From Windsor Lodge Marlborough wrote the queen a letter which concluded, "I hope your majesty will either dismiss her [Abigail] or myself" (Coxe, *Memoirs, 3,* 8). He told Mainwaring that he would quit unless Abigail were removed "to Ireland (or rather Jamaica, which is vacant)" (Blenheim MS. E 27). The first letter, however, never reached the queen. It was sent first to Godolphin for approval by the Junto, which was withheld.

11. *Spies:* During their retreat, the Marlboroughs were kept informed of events at court by Lord Coningsby, James Craggs, Arthur Mainwaring, Adam Cardonnel, and other less imposing Whigs (*Archaeologia, 38* [1860], 9–11; Coxe, *Memoirs, 3,* 12).

12. *advise:* "Her Majesty, pursuant to Mr. Harley's advice, resolved to dispose of the first great employment that fell, according to her own pleasure, without consulting any of her ministers" (Swift, *Prose, 8,* 117).

14. *all the Parties:* from Godolphin down to Adam Cardonnel, the duke's private secretary. Godolphin was afraid that if the duke insisted upon Mrs. Masham's removal, "all the Good Men will by this step be put out of their Places and all the ill men in them" (Blenheim MS. E 27).

15. *inconsiderate:* "of no importance; inconsiderable" (*OED*).

18. *reenter . . . John:* As Peter Wentworth wrote on 27 January, "since the Duke has come to town he has been with the Queen and is all submission to her Majesty's pleasure, but cou'd not forbear telling her he had a fresh instance of his enemies imposing falsities upon her for truths against him, such was their making her believe he or any of his friends had made any interest among the members of the house of C[ommo]n's to Adress her Majesty for the removal of Mrs. Masham, wch he protested as he was an honest man he never thought of" (*Wentworth Papers,* p. 105).

That by Address I had contriv'd that she
Whom you do love shou'd ever from you be;
Which cruel consequence I did lament   25
And hasten'd quick this Mischief to prevent.
For surely, Madam, None could ever say
I cross'd your Inclination any way.
    The Sovereign smil'd within herself to hear
Such Lies delivered with so good an air,   30
But thenceforth bid him seek for no excuse;
Such Treachery ne'er should cover such abuse.

23. *Address:* It was Marlborough's son-in-law, Lord Sunderland, who "was suppos'd to have been the Promoter of the . . . Address, for Removing Mrs. M[*asham*] from Her Majesty's Bed-Chamber," which was "to be offer'd to, or rather impos'd on the House of Commons" (*An Essay towards the History of the Last Ministry and Parliament,* 1710, pp. 8, 34).

30. *Such Lies:* Although Marlborough claimed that "it never enter'd into his thoughts to Stir up the Parliament to prescrib to her [Majesty] what servants she shou'd keep about her person," Algernon Seymour, Lord Hertford, son of the duke of Somerset, was publicly saying that the duke had "pist backwards" when he "deny'd to the Queen his having any designe to stir the Commons up to address the Queen to remove Mrs. Masham" (*Wentworth Papers,* pp. 105, 108). Hertford should have known what he was talking about for he himself was involved in the crisis, being Marlborough's candidate for colonel of the duke of Northumberland's regiment if the duke had been appointed constable of the Tower (Swift, *Prose, 8,* 117).

Found on the Queen's Toilet
(February? 1710)

Defoe could complain that "*Forty One* [had been] banter'd till the Jest was lost" (*An Elegy on the Author of the True-Born-English-Man. With an Essay on the Late Storm*, 1704, p. 55), and Toland could insist that the civil wars were "much fitter to be forgot, than reviv'd on every trifling occasion" (*The Memorial of the State of England*, 1705, p. 64). But as long as there was "hardly a Family in the Kingdom, which has not had *Father, Mother, Son*, or *Near Relation, Destroy'd, Plunder'd, Imprison'd, Banish'd*, and *Undone* in that Cursed *Rebellion*" ([Charles Leslie], *The New Association of Those Call'd Moderate Churchmen, with the Modern Whigs and Fanaticks, to Under-mine and Blow-up the Present Church and Government*, 1702, p. 15), the fear of '41 remained alive. Swift's memories, for example, of his grandfather Thomas Swift, vicar of Goodrich in Herefordshire, "plundred by the roundheads six and thirty times," and of "the hardships he underwent for the Person and cause of that blessed Martyred Prince" (Swift, *Prose, 5*, 188–89), were persisting influences in his life and writing.

The present verses, pretending to have been left on the queen's dressing table on the 61st anniversary of the execution of her grandfather, revive these fears. They pick up exactly where *On the New Promotion* (October 1705) left off.

The epigram may have been written before 30 January 1710, when it was said in one witness (*G*) to have been left on the queen's dressing table, and certainly before 4 March 1710 when Thomas Hearne copied it into his diary (*N*).

The Tory author remains unknown.

FOUND ON THE QUEEN'S TOILET

O *Anna!* see, the Prelude is begun,
Again they play the Game of Forty One,
And he's the Traytor that defends the Throne.
Thus *Laud,* and thus the *Royal Martyr* dy'd,
Impeach'd by *Clamour* and by *Faction* try'd.   5
Hoadly's cry'd up (that does thy Right oppose)

2. *the Game of Forty One:* 1641 was regarded as "the Prelude" to civil war. This was the year that opposition to Charles I took a parliamentary form with the execution of Thomas Wentworth, earl of Strafford, the abolition of the prerogative courts, and the passing of the Grand Remonstrance.

3. *he:* Henry Sacheverell had recently republished *A Defence of Her Majesty's Title to the Crown,* a sermon preached at Oxford in June 1702 to which he referred in his answer to the articles of impeachment against him. In this sermon Sacheverell had said that Anne's title "Devolv'd upon Her, by a Long Succession of Her *Royal Ancestors*" and that she had been "Proclaim'd, as 'twere by the *Voice of God*" in the Universal Joy, Satisfaction, and Unanimity of Her Subjects" (*A Defence of Her Majesty's Title to the Crown, and A Justification of Her Entring into a War with France and Spain,* 2nd ed., 1710, p. 10). But now this defender of Anne's title lay under £6,000 bail awaiting trial on four charges of libel and sedition.

4. *Laud:* William Laud (1573–1645), "Admirable in his Naturalls, Unblameable in his Morals" (Thomas Fuller, *The History of the Worthies of England,* 1662, p. 93), was consecrated archbishop of Canterbury in 1633. In 1640 he was "accused . . . 'of a design to bring in Popery,' " impeached by the Long Parliament, treated "with all the rudeness, reproach, and barbarity imaginable" and finally beheaded on 10 January 1645 in the 72nd year of his life (Edward Hyde, earl of Clarendon, *The History of the Rebellion,* 3 vols., 1702–04, *2,* 440).

the Royal Martyr: Charles I was beheaded on a scaffold erected in front of his palace at Whitehall on 30 January 1649.

6. *Hoadly:* On 14 December 1709, the same day that it voted 232–131 to impeach Sacheverell of high crimes and misdemeanors, the House of Commons resolved "That an humble Address be presented to her Majesty, that she will be graciously pleased to bestow some Dignity in the Church on [Mr. Benjamin] *Hoadley,* for his eminent Services both to Church and State" (*CJ, 16,* 242). But "It was thought odd by some in the gallery that the Queen should be address'd to reward a Man for writing against the Bishop of Exeter's Sermon [p. 350 above], which very Sermon She approved and order'd to be printed" (BM MS. Add. 47025, f.145). Anne replied that she would take "a proper opportunity" to reward Mr. Hoadly (Luttrell, *6,* 525), but did nothing. "What most of all encourages [Sacheverell]," Ralph Bridges informed Sir William Trumbull on 20 December 1709, "is the Queen's refusing to assent to the Commons address in preferring Hoadly, which Her Ma[jes]ty positively refuses to do; and as we have it here, has given express orders to my Ld Chancellor to bestow no living that falls either in Her's or His guift upon Him" (Berkshire R. O. MS. Trumbull LIII). But she "ordered all Mr. Hoadly's books to be brought to her, and designs to read them" (Luttrell, *6,* 529).

thy Right oppose: i.e. Anne's right to the throne. The issue is most clearly stated by one of Hoadly's understrappers: "the main point . . . is about the Power of the Supreme Magistrate . . . whether this Power be from Heaven or of Men" (*Bess o' Bedlam's Love to Her Brother Tom: With a Word in Behalf of Poor Brother Ben Hoadly,* 1709, p. 4). Hoadly derived this power from "Men" (*Leviathan, Or, A Hymn to Poor Brother Ben,* 22*n.* above).

Because he crowns the *Mob* and arms thy *Foes.*
Stop the portentous Omen, ere too late;
View thy whole Friends', in poor *Sacheverell's* Fate.
Stated Experience bids thee now be wise,   10
Let one Rebellion in an Age suffice;
At him they strike, but *regal Right's* the Prize.

7. *the Mob:* Cf. Sacheverell, *The Perils of False Brethren, Both in Church, and State,* 1709, p. 18: "Her . . . *Hereditary Right* to the *Throne,* They have had the Impudence to *deny,* and *cancel,* to make *Her* a *Creature of their own Power,* and . . . by the same *Principles* They plac'd a *Crown* upon Her . . . [that] They (that is the Mob) may Re-assume . . . at their Pleasure."

10. *Stated:* "Definitely recognizable" (*OED*).

12. *regal Right:* Hoadly's understrappers were saying that "there was no need of an Hereditary Title" (*Dick and Tom: A Dialogue about Addresses,* 1710, p. 15).

A Tale of a Nettle
(1 March 1710)

A Tale of a Nettle is part of the high church reaction to the Sacheverell trial. One of the recurring fears of high churchmen, clergy and laity alike, was that the growth of dissent would overwhelm the Church of England as by law established. And since there was no way of measuring this growth, it could be imagined to be as rapid and uncontrolled as that of cancer—or nettle beds.

On 8 December 1705 Sir John Pakington had made a speech in parliament on this subject. "A second cause of Danger to the Church," he said, "is the great increase of dissenting schools and seminaries all over the Kingdom, in which great number of our youth are poyson'd with principles which makes them disaffected to the Church . . . [and] The third cause of danger is the great increase of the number of Conventicles. If I am rightly inform'd," he went on to say, "there are a 100 Conventicles or thereabouts in and about London, and . . . the dissenters are still building more and . . . their Conventicles are now fuller than any of our Churches, and more attendance of coaches about them. These Conventicles are as so many Garrisons of Sectaries planted against the Church" (*Camden Miscellany, Vol. XXIII*, Camden Fourth Series, Royal Historical Society, 1970, 7, 83). Pakington's fears were not imaginary. "In the years from 1691 to 1710 no less than 2,536 places were licensed [as conventicles]. Many of these would have been private houses or temporary structures, but up and down the land parsons were facing a new and disturbing phenomenon: a local dissenting congregation meeting openly and competing with them for the minds and hearts of their parishioners" (*Britain after the Glorious Revolution*, ed. Geoffrey Holmes, Macmillan, 1969, p. 163).

But after hearing Pakington's speech, the Commons voted 212–162 in favor of a resolution that "whoever goes about to suggest . . . that the Church is in danger . . . is an Enemy to the Queen, the Church, and the Kingdom" (*CJ, 15*, 58; cf. p. 146 above). So when Henry Sacheverell recalled, in his sermon of 5 November 1709, that Charles I was voted to be out of danger "at the *same Time* that his *Murtherers* were *Conspiring* his *Death*" (*The Perils of False Brethren, Both in Church, and State*, 1709, p. 20), he was charged with suggesting that the church was in danger (*Tryal of Dr. Henry Sacheverell*, p. 9) and ordered to be tried.

But this only compounded the fears of high churchmen. To be afraid that the church was in danger and then to discover that Henry Sache-verell was being prosecuted for saying so, brought about the state of mind which produced *A Tale of a Nettle*. The poem is a parable, in which the weed of dissent crowds out of England's garden the estab-lished fruits and flowers. The insistent anapestic metre, usually produc-tive of comic effects (cf. *POAS*, Yale, *6*, 619), functions here as a kind of metrical counterpart to the chronic overstatement of aureate high church pulpit rhetoric.

The verses generated both *An Explanation of the Tale of a Nettle, Para-graph by Paragraph. From the Best Edition, Printed at Cambridge, At the Re-quest of Several of the University* (1710), which is not really reliable, and *An Answer to the Tale of a Nettle* ("When the Good Man was won to so Gracious a Deed") (1710), which is not really an answer, but a con-tinuation. The latter, a folio half-sheet with an Oxford imprint, is said to be "Written by D. D'FOE," presumably to increase its sale, for there is no reason to attribute to any dissenter these feeble verses against dissent. Another sequel to the poem, said to be *"By the Author of the* Tale of a Nettle," was published in a folio half-sheet of 1710 entitled *The London Tale* ("In fickle Days, when grave Divines").

The Harvard copy of *Fa* is inscribed "by Swift" in a hand that does not seem old. Walter Scott included *A Tale of a Nettle* among "Pieces Ascribed to Swift" (*The Works of Jonathan Swift, D.D.*, 19 vols., Edin-burgh, 1814, *10*, 447) and printed it from a copy (*A*) "in the Dean's hand-writing" in the Thomas Steele manuscript that does include a poem almost certainly Swift's (*Harvard Library Bulletin, 19* [October 1971], 403–07). But in spite of this evidence, *A Tale of a Nettle* is almost certainly *not* Swift's (Swift, *Poems, 3*, 1084).

The Luttrell copy of *Fb*, now in the Rylands Library, is dated 1 March 1709/10. It also bears the instructive annotation: "Showing the dangers of the Church by the Dissenters."

A Man with Expence and infinite Toil,
By Digging and Dunging enobled his Soil;
There Fruits of the Best your Taste did invite,
And uniform Order still courted the Sight:
No degenerate Weeds the Rich Ground did produce,   5
But all things afforded for Beauty and Use;
'Till from Dunghill transplanted, while yet but a Seed,
A *NETTLE* rear'd up his Inglorious Head:
The Gard'ner wou'd wisely have rooted him up,
To stop the Increase of a Barbarous Crop;   10
But the Master forbad him, and after the Fashion
Of foolish good Nature and blind *Moderation,*
Forbore him thro' Pity, and chose as much rather
To ask him some Questions first, how he came thither.
    Kind Sir, Quoth the NETTLE, *a Stranger I come,*   15

1. *A Man:* "Queen *Elizabeth*" (*An Explanation of the Tale of a Nettle, Paragraph by Paragraph,* 1710, p. 3).

4. *uniform Order:* In April 1559, the first year of her reign, Elizabeth gave her assent to the Act of Uniformity (1 Eliz. c. 2) that ordered the adoption of the revised Book of Common Prayer (1552) and established penalties for noncompliance.

5. *No degenerate Weeds:* "*No Presbyterians in those Days*" (*An Explanation of the Tale of a Nettle, Paragraph by Paragraph,* 1710, p. 2).

7. *Dunghill:* probably Rome. The "popish dunghill" was a commonplace of anti-Catholic propaganda (G. W. Prothero, *Select Statutes and Other Constitutional Documents Illustrative of the Reigns of Elizabeth and James 1,* 4th ed., Oxford, Clarendon Press, 1913, p. 198). Cf. Henry Sacheverell, *The Perils of False Brethren, Both in Church, and State,* 1709, p. 13: "the *Republicans* Copy after the *Papists* in most of their *Doctrins* and *Practices.*"

8. *A NETTLE:* "*England* . . . [became] a Place of Refuge to People of several Nations, whose Tender Consciences compell'd them to fly their Native Country, which came flocking to her, being allowed several Places of Worship, according to their different Opinions in Religion, which since has created too many Differences among us" (*An Explanation of the Tale of a Nettle,* 1710, p. 4). Shortly after Elizabeth's accession French, Flemish, Dutch, and German Protestants were allowed to settle in London (John Strype, *Annals of the Reformation,* 7 vols. in 4, Oxford, 1824, *1,* i, 174–75).

9. *The Gard'ner:* When the foreign Protestants petitioned for leave to worship in England, "the matter being referred to her [majesty's] most honourable council and the bishops, it was refused at first" (ibid., *1,* i, 174). "*Some Bishops would have rooted them out, and have sent them from whence they came*" (*An Explanation of the Tale of a Nettle, Paragraph by Paragraph,* 1710, p. 2).

12. *Moderation:* Cf. *Dr. Sacheverell and Benjamin Hoadly,* 5n. above.

15. *a Stranger I come:* An Explanation of the *Tale of a Nettle,* 1710, p. 5, quotes Defoe, *The True-Born Englishman* (December 1700):

For Conscience compell'd to relinquish my home;
'Cause I wou'd not Subscribe to a Mystery Dark,
That the Prince of all Trees is the Jesuits Bark.
An Erroneous Tenet, I know, Sir, that you
No more than myself will allow to be true;   20
To you I for Refuge and Sanctuary Sue,
There's none so renown'd for Compassion as you:
And tho' in some Things I may differ from these,
The rest of your Fruitful and Beautiful Trees;
Tho' your Digging and Dunging my Nature much harms,   25
And I cannot comply with your Gardiner's Forms;
Yet I and my Family, after our Fashion,
Will peaceably stick to our own Education:
Be pleas'd to allow us a Place for to rest in,
For the rest of your Trees, we'll never molest 'em.   30
A kind Shelter to us, and Protection afford,
We'll do you no harm, Sir, I'll give you my Word.
    The good Man was soon won with this plausible Tale,
(So Fraud on good Nature does often prevail).
He welcomes his Guest, gives him free *Toleration*   35
In the midst of his Garden to take up his Station;

Dutch, Walloons, Flemings, Irishmen, and Scots,
Vaudois and Valtolins, and Hugonots,
In good Queen Bess's Charitable Reign,
Suppli'd us with Three hundred thousand Men . . .
Of all Professions, and of ev'ry Trade,
All that were persecuted or afraid.
                            (259–72, POAS, Yale, 6, 273)

17. *wou'd not Subscribe to a Mystery:* "*would not renounce their Religion, and turn Romans*" (*An Explanation of the Tale of a Nettle,* 1710, p. 2).

18. *Jesuits Bark:* "the medicinal bark of species of *Cinchona* [quinine] . . . (introduced into Europe from the Jesuit missions in S. America)" (*OED*). In the allegory it is simply "*Roman* Religion" (*An Explanation of the Tale of a Nettle,* 1710, p. 5).

21. *Refuge and Sanctuary:* "*See their Petition to Queen* Elizabeth *for Places of Worship for their own Use*" (ibid., p. 2).

24. *Fruitful and Beautiful Trees:* "*Ri*[te]*s and Ceremonies of the Church of* England" (ibid., p. 2).

26. *Forms:* "*Forms of Prayer in the* [Anglican] *Liturgy*" (ibid., p. 2). "The first *Puritans* . . . run down *Liturgies,* as a *Dead* Form; and set up, in Opposition to them, the *Extempore Babble* . . . for the more *Spiritual* way" (Charles Leslie, *Cassandra (But I Hope Not),* 1704, p. 86).

33. *The good Man:* Cf. Sacheverell, *The Perils of False Brethren, Both in Church, and State,* 1709, p. 19: "*Queen Elizabeth,* that was Deluded by that Perfidious Prelate [Edmund Grindal] to the *Toleration* of the *Genevian Discipline,* found it . . . an *Headstrong* and *Encroaching Monster.*"

And into his Breast do's his Enemy bring,
He little suspected the *NETTLE* wou'd Sting;
'Till flush'd with Success and of Strength to be fear'd,
Around him a numerous Off-spring he rear'd.   40
Then the Master grew sensible what he had done,
And fain wou'd have had his new Guest to be gone;
But now 'twas too late to bid him turn out,
A well rooted possession already was got:
The old Trees decay'd, and in their room grew,   45
A stubborn, rank, pestilent, poysonous Crew.
The Master who first, the young Brood had admitted,
They stung like Ingrates, and left him unpitied;
No help from Manuring or Planting was found,
The ill Weeds had Eat out the Heart of the Ground.   50
All Weeds they let in and none they refuse
That would join to oppose the good Man of the House.
    Thus one *NETTLE* uncropt, encreas'd to such store,
That 'twas nothing but Weeds, what was Garden before.

46. Such phrases were commonplaces of high church rhetoric; cf. "Obstinate, Moody, Wayward, and Self-conceited *Hypocrites,* and *Enthusiasts*" (Sacheverell, *The Perils of False Brethren, Both in Church, and State,* 1709, p. 17).

Upon the Burning of Dr. Burgess's Pulpit
(March 1710)

Since the exclusion crisis of 1679–81 the Whigs had assumed that the London mob would be on their side. So the ministry was totally unprepared when angry crowds took to the streets in support of the church and Henry Sacheverell, and Whiggish cries of self-righteous indignation were heard through the land. "This man &c. have debauched the very principles of the mob," Arthur Mainwaring complained (Blenheim MS. GI 15), and Defoe condescended to scold the rabble. "You are the first, and I hope will be the last Mobb," he said, "that ever stood up against Liberty and Property, and the Freedom of the Subject" (*A Letter from Captain Tom to the Mobb, Raised for Dr. Sacheverell,* 1710, p. 3).

On 27 February 1710 when Sacheverell's trial began in Westminster Hall, "great Numbers of the Mobility attended him thither, and conducted him back to his Lodgings in the *Temple,* with loud Huzzas . . . The next Day, the Mobb was still more numerous and louder about Dr. *Sacheverell's* Coach, and, in the Heighth of their petulant Zeal, oblig'd all Persons they met to pull off their Hats to him, and abus'd those that refus'd to comply . . . The same Evening, the Rioters went to the *Presbyterian* Meeting-House of Mr. *Burgess,* in a Court near *Lincoln's-Inn-Fields,* of which they broke the Windows; and committed several other Outrages and Disorders . . . On the 1st of *March* their Fury being encreas'd with their Numbers, they advanc'd to greater Enormities, and even *Overt-Acts* of Rebellion: For after they had attended upon Dr. *Sacheverell* as usual, they repair'd to the *Meeting-House* before-mention'd; broke it open, pull'd down the Pulpit, Pews, Benches, Wainscot, Sconces, Casements, in short, all that was combustible, and having carried all these Materials into *Lincoln's-Inn-Fields* made a Bonfire of them, with repeated Cries of *HIGH-CHURCH* and *SACHEVERELL*" (Boyer, *Annals,* 1710, p. 265). They were going to throw Burgess himself into the flames, "But they were mercifull, and only burnt his Night-cap, that he might remember what Danger he had escap'd" (Hearne, *2,* 355).

The interesting life cycle of the resultant epigram, which is really a witty rejoinder to Sir Stephen Lennard (2*n.* below), is described on p. 668. In two collateral manuscripts the verses are dated March 1710, but the author remains unknown.

Upon the Burning of Dr. Burgess's Pulpit

Invidious *Whigs,* since you have made your Boast,
That you a *Church of England* Priest would roast,
Blame not the Mob, for having a Desire
With *Presbyterian* Tubs to light the Fire.

2. *roast:* Sir Stephen Lennard (1637–1709) of West Wickham, Kent, second baronet, Whig member of parliament for Winchelsea (1681) and Kent (1698 1700, 1700–09), was the "Furious Zealot" who first proposed that Sacheverell be "roasted" (*A Letter to a Noble Lord Occasion'd by the Proceedings against Dr. Henry Sacheverell,* 1710, p. 16). But the expression became a commonplace: "nothing was in their mouths . . . but that they would roast the priest" (Ailesbury, *2,* 620) and the basis for two more poems in the period: *The Roasting of a Parson* ("May Heav'n preserve our Good *Queen* ANNE") and *A Receipt to Dress a Parson after the Newest Fashion* ("When you have a fat Parson that's fleshy and new"). Yet, as Henry St. John observed, "The Whigs took it in their minds to roast a parson, and they did roast him, but their zeal tempted them to make the fire so high they scorched themselves" (Abbie T. Scudi, *The Sacheverell Affair,* New York, Columbia University Press, 1939, p. 73).

4. *Tubs:* "a huge Bonfire was made, and the Tub in wch he us'd to hold forth was plac'd on the top of the Pile" (Hearne, *2,* 351).

The Old Pack Newly Reviv'd
(March? 1710)

The idea for this rollicking song came from the practice of giving hunting dogs political names. "You shall not meet with a Pack of Hounds," Defoe said, "but you may hear the Huntsman cry, *Hark Tory*, to him *High-Church*, Pox of that *Whig*, he's a meer Cur" (*Review*, Vol. VII, Preface, 1711, sig. A2v). It may also owe something to the "incomparable witty Jest" of Lord Wharton

> In calling Church-men *Cats*, and hurrying on
> His wide-mouth'd *Non-Con* Beagles to worry 'em

(*A Collection of Poems, For and Against Dr. Sacheverell*, 4 vols., 1710–11, *1*, 8).

The House of Commons, in which the Whigs had such a large majority that there were "few, very few of the true *English* Breed" (line 25), is reduced to a pack of hounds (33). The owner of the pack is that well-known sportsman, Lord Godolphin (38). Benjamin Hoadly is "the Huntsman" (41) and "the Leaders" (34) of the pack are the 20 members of the committee to impeach Henry Sacheverell of high crimes and misdemeanors. While the hunt is in full cry it is interrupted by the rabble: "Take heed," they say, "Sure the Devil's your Leader, and you hunt for Confusion" (52–54). Perhaps for this reason, but the point is not made explicit, the pack is now put up for sale (2). The speaker in the poem is an auctioneer, whose huckster chant is imitated in the strong anapestic rhythm of the verse and the insistent repetition of the refrain.

The internal evidence for the date of the poem is somewhat ambiguous. It would seem that the poem was written after 16 March 1710 when it became known that James Stanhope would return to Spain (83*n*.), but before 21 March 1710 when Sacheverell received an unexpectedly light sentence (*On the Sentence Passed by the House of Lords on Dr. Sacheverell*, 12*n*. below). After that the Whigs could no longer be said to be "*riding Tantivy*" (8). On the other hand, the metaphor of the public auction suggests the general election (October 1710).

There is no evidence at all to identify the Tory poet.

The Old Pack Newly Reviv'd

Come ye old *English* Huntsmen that love noble Sport,
Here's a Pack to be sold, and staunch Dogs of the Sort;
Not Sir *Sewster*, nor *Chetwynd* can match our fleet Hounds,
For breaking down Fences, or leaping o'er Bounds;
Some are deep-mouth'd and speedy, some mad, blind, and lame, 5
Most Yelpers and Curs, but all fit for the Game.
　Then to Horse, loyal Hearts, lest the Round-heads deceive ye,
　For they have the Dogs, and are riding Tantivy.

There's *Atheist* and *Deist*, and fawning *Dissenter*,
There's *Republican* sly, and old long-winded *Canter;* 10
There's *Heresy*, *Schism*, and mild *Moderation*,
That's still in the Wrong for the Good of the Nation;
There's *Baptist*, *Socinian*, and *Quaker* with Scruples,

3. *Sir Sewster:* Sir Sewster Peyton of Doddington, Cambridgeshire, second baronet (c. 1667–1717), was appointed one of the queen's masters of the buck and staghounds in June 1703 (Luttrell, *5*, 306).

　Chetwynd: Walter Chetwynd (c. 1678–1736), a Whig member of parliament for Stafford (December 1702–10, January 1712–22, November 1724–34), was the other master of the buck and staghounds from 1705 to 1711.

4. *breaking down Fences:* This phrase might have suggested the levellers to a reader of 1710, for the original levellers got their name from their "endeavour to cast down and level the enclosures of nobility, gentry and propriety, to make us all even" (*Mercurius Politicus*, 16 November 1647, quoted in H. N. Brailsford, *The Levellers and the English Revolution*, ed. Christopher Hill, Cresset, 1961, p. 309).

　leaping o'er Bounds. the archetypal Augustan sin. "This is an Observation that is found in History," Harley said during the Fenwick trial in 1697, "that those that have broke their Bounds down, it hath returned'd upon them to their Prejudice" (Oldmixon, *History*, p. 154).

5. *mad:* cf. *The Dyet of Poland*, 1107n. above.

7. *Round-heads:* "the Parliamentarian Party in the great Rebellion, that begun 1641" (*New Dictionary*, sig. K5v), but here generically for Whigs.

8. *Tantivy:* at full gallop. The word that was applied in the 1680s to Tories riding tantivy for Rome (*POAS*, Yale, *2*, illustration, p. 370) is here returned upon the Whigs riding hell-bent for a republic. "The Whigs are triumphant," Dr. Thomas Smith wrote to Hearne in March 1710, "and thinke to carry all before them" (Hearne, *2*, 352).

9–10, 13. These lines are incorporated in *The Church of England's New Hymn to the State Scaffold*, 1710, p. 14:

　　From Baptist, Socinian and scrupulous Quaker,
　　From Atheist, Deist, and fawning Dissenter,
　　From Republican Sly, and longwinded Canter,
　　　　　　　　Libera Nos Dom.

'Till kind Toleration linkt 'em all in Church-Couples.
> *Then to Horse, loyal Hearts, lest the Round-heads deceive ye,*   15
> *For they have the Dogs, and are riding Tantivy.*

Some were bred in the Camp, and some dropt in the Fleet,
Under Bulks some were litter'd, and some in the Street;
Some are good harmless Curs, without Tooth or Claw,
Some were whelp'd in a Shop, and some Runners at Law;   20
Some were poor wretched Curs, Mungrels, Starters and Setters,
'Till dividing the Spoil they put in with their Betters.
> *Then to Horse, loyal Hearts, lest the Round-heads deceive ye,*
> *For they have the Dogs, and are riding Tantivy.*

A few, very few, of the true *English* Breed,   25
Whose Noses are good, and of excellent Speed;
But what's a fine Mouth to oppose every Throat,
Where Number and Noise quite drown the sweet Note?
If he hits off a Fault, or runs the Scent right,
Honest *Tory* is worry'd for a rank *Jacobite.*   30
> *Then to Horse, loyal Hearts, lest the Round-heads deceive ye,*
> *For they have the Dogs, and are riding Tantivy.*

Five hundred stout Dogs are a brave Pack to run,
But the Leaders in chief are but old Forty One;
On hot burning Scent, when they open their Throats,   35
Then trail a Court-Place, how the staunchest change Notes!

14. *linkt 'em all:* The Whiggish idea of comprehension Sacheverell called "a *Mungril-Union of All Sects*" (*The Perils of False Brethren, Both in Church, and State,* 1709, pp. 10, 16).

18. *Bulks:* frameworks projecting from the front of shops (*OED*).

20. *Runners at Law:* strays, runaways (*OED*), outlaws(?).

21. *Starters:* dogs trained for starting game (*OED*).

29. *hits off a Fault:* to recover a lost scent (*OED*).

33. *Five hundred:* There were 558 members of the first House of Commons of Great Britain (Chamberlayne, 1708, p. 601).

34. *the Leaders:* The managers of the impeachment proceedings against Sacheverell appointed on 14 December 1709 were: Henry Boyle, secretary of state; Spencer Compton; Sir John Holland, comptroller of the household; Nicholas Lechmere; Sir Joseph Jekyll; John Dolben; Sir Thomas Parker; Sir James Montagu, attorney general; Sir Peter King; Thomas Coningsby, Lord Coningsby; Robert Eyre, solicitor general; Robert Walpole; Spencer Cowper; Lord William Powlett; John Smith, chancellor of the exchequer; William Thompson; Sir John Hawles. To this group were added on 10 February 1710: Lieutenant General James Stanhope; Colonel Henry Mordaunt, and Sir David Dalrymple (*CJ,* 16, 241–42, 305).

Forty One: See *Found on the Queen's Toilet,* 2n. above.

36. *trail a Court-Place:* throw the hounds of opposition off the scent by dragging a fat pension or office in the service of the crown across their track.

Tho' no Horn nor Voice can their Fury controul,
Yet to the *White Staff* they hunt all under Pole.
   Then to Horse, loyal Hearts, lest the Round-heads deceive ye,
   For they have the Dogs, and are riding Tantivy.   40

Crys the Huntsman, *Ben. Hoadly,* Dear Dogs I'm a *Knave,*
But you're all sov'reign Curs, and your Prince is your Slave;
This my Writings will prove, stole from *Prynn, Nye,* and *Peters,*
That all free-born Dogs may fall on their Betters;
Then away on that Scent, 'tis the *old Game* and *good,*   45
While *Peers* have fat Haunches, and *Kings* Royal Blood.
   Then to Horse, loyal Hearts, lest the Round-heads deceive ye,
   For they have the Dogs, and are riding Tantivy.

A stout orthodox Doctor fell first in the Wind;
The Pack open'd their Throats, in Hopes Mob would ha' join'd; 50

---

38. *to the White Staff:* in response to the lord treasurer's emblem of office (see illustration, p. 475 below).

    all under Pole: everything in the world.

42. *sov'reign Curs:* cf. *Found on the Queen's Toilet,* 6–7: "*Hoadly . . .* crowns the *Mob.*"

43. *Prynn:* William Prynne (1600–69), the militant Presbyterian, graduated B.A. from Oriel College, Oxford, in 1621 and in 1628 was called to the bar from Lincoln's Inn. He became an indefatigable controversialist, attacking everything in sight from long hair (*The Unlovelinesse, of Love-Lockes,* 1628) to Oliver Cromwell (*King Richard the Third Revived,* 1657). Hoadly might have been interested in such of his more than 200 published works as *A New Discovery of the Prelates Tyranny,* 1641, and *The Soveraigne Power of Parliaments and Kingdomes,* 1643.

    Nye: Philip Nye (1596?–1672), the militant independent, graduated B.A. from Magdalen Hall, Oxford, in 1619 and was ordained shortly after. But his nonconformity got him into trouble and he lived in Holland (1633–40) "that he might be free from Impositions" (Calamy, *Abridgement, 2,* 29). In 1643 he organized an independent church at Kimbolton, Huntingdonshire and in 1653 he was one of Cromwell's triers and expurgators of the clergy. Calamy called him "a Man of uncommon Depth" (ibid., *2,* 30), and Hoadly might have been interested in such of his published works as *The Lawfulness of the Oath of Supremacy* (1661) and *The King's Authority in Dispensing with Ecclesiastical Laws, Asserted and Vindicated* (1687), which he dedicated to James II.

    Peters: Hugh Peters (1598–1660), "the vicar-general and metropolitan of the independents," as he came to be called (*DNB, 15,* 957), was graduated from Trinity College, Cambridge, and ordained. But he removed himself to Rotterdam about 1629 and from thence to America in October 1635, where he became minister at Salem, Massachusetts. Upon his return to England in August 1641 he became chaplain to Sir Thomas Fairfax and the new model armies, and finally to Cromwell himself. He was tried as a regicide and executed on 16 October 1660. He is said to have been "an enthusiastical buffoon preacher" (Burnet, *1,* 162) and Hoadly may have enjoyed *The Tales and Jests of Mr. Hugh Peters* (1660) or *Hugh Peters his Figaries* (1660).

45. *the old Game:* See *Found on the Queen's Toilet,* 2n. above.

49. *Doctor:* Sacheverell.

By a strong passive Scent they ran him full Speed,
'Till the Rabble cry'd out, *You're too rank there,—Take heed;*
What, o'er leap the Church-Pales, and break thro' Constitution?
Sure the Devil's your Leader, and you hunt for Confusion!
Then to Horse, loyal Hearts, lest the Round-heads deceive ye,   55
For they have the Dogs, and are riding Tantivy.

At the Head of the Pack stupid *William's* commanding,
Who's of Quality Breed, by his deep Understanding;
If to dull worthless Whelps we may Titles afford,
His Merits confess him a Dog of a Lord;   60
Those crafty old Curs, that despise the poor Tool,
Yet only for Luck Sake they hunt with a Fool.
Then to Horse, loyal Hearts, lest the Round-heads deceive ye,
For they have the Dogs, and are riding Tantivy.

There's Blasphemy *Jack*, that was stript by Oak Royal,   65

51. *passive:* See *Leviathan*, 20*n*. above.

52. *the Rabble:* Instead of joining the Commons in the Sacheverell chase, the mob supported him (p. 392 above).

   too rank: too fast, too reckless, with the additional implication of "criminal"; *OED* cites *New Dictionary*, sig. K3r, "*Rank-rider*, a Highway-man."

53. *leap the* . . . *Pales:* "to go beyond bounds, indulge in extravagance or licence" (*OED*); cf. 4*n*. above.

54. *Confusion:* "The Truth is, the great Fundamental Principle of the *Whiggs*, is *Confusion;* . . . they hate all *Order, Clearness,* and *Regularity*" (*Most Faults on One Side,* 1710, p. 23). Sacheverell presented copies of this book, "gilded and neatly cover'd to several Members of Parliament" (*A Vindication of the Faults on Both Sides,* 1710, p. 34).

57. *William:* Lord William Powlett (c. 1666–1729) was the second son of Charles Powlett, first duke of Bolton. He was a personal friend of the Junto lords and one of their leading henchmen in the Commons, where he sat for Hampshire (1689–90), Winchester (1690–1710, 1715–30), and New Lymington (1710–15). In every division list that has survived from 1689–1714, his name appears on the Whig side. For these services he received the lucrative sinecure of farmer of the green wax. "So the Queen pays 50*l.* out of pocket to get my Lord William 100*l.* . . . . Though these grants have been usual," Harley's correspondent continued, "yet I cannot believe them to be legal" (HMC *Portland MSS., 5,* 71). Although not the chairman of the committee appointed to draw up the articles against Sacheverell—his lack of intelligence has been previously remarked (*POAS,* Yale, *6,* 23–24)—he may have sat on the front of the three benches reserved for the managers in Westminster Hall (*A Description of the High Court of Judicature for the Tryal of Dr. Henry Sacheverell* [30 March 1710]) and may have led the managers into the hall. This would account for his being at the head of the list drawn up by an eyewitness to the trial (Osborn MS. Box 21, No. 22, f. [2]).

62. For Fortune favors fools (Tilley, F600).

65. *Jack:* John Dolben (1662–1710), the second son of John Dolben, archbishop of York (1683–86), left Christ Church, Oxford, without a degree and was called to the bar from the Inner Temple in 1684. After running through his inheritance, he retired to the West Indies and married an heiress. Upon returning to London he was deflected from running through

The Republican Whelp of a Sire that was loyal;
With Gaol-Birds and Whores to Plantations he cross'd,
'Till the Sharper retriev'd what the Bubble had lost;
Now in Hopes of a Place, he still yelps and impeaches,
Tho' your pert forward Cur oft himself over-reaches.   70
    Then to Horse, loyal Hearts, lest the Round-heads deceive ye,
    For they have the Dogs, and are riding Tantivy.

There's *Woolf* the rapacious, old *Bluster* and *Thunder,*

---

his wife's fortune by Bishop Trelawny, who urged him to stand for election to parliament. In November 1707 he was returned for the borough of Liskeard, Cornwall, and was reelected in May 1708. As "a great stickle[r] for Lord Treasurer" (*Wentworth Papers,* p. 73), Dolben was "the first Accuser" of Sacheverell and chairman of the committee to impeach him (*The Life and Adventures of John Dolben, Esq.,* 1710, pp. 11, 12). He died at Epsom on 29 May 1710 "and at that *very Hour, eleven in the Forenoon,* when Dr. *Sacheverell* was order'd to attend his Tryal" (ibid., p. 16).

    stript by Oak Royal: On account of the scandals connected with their operation (*POAS,* Yale, *5,* 491, 521), all the state lotteries except "the *Royal-Oak* Lottery, where you may lose Fifty Guinea's in a moment" ([Thomas Baker], *Tunbridge-Walks; or, The Yeoman of Kent,* 1703, p. 2), were shut down at the end of the war in 1697.

    66. *a Sire that was loyal:* Dolben's father, "Him of the Western dome, whose weighty sense / Flows in fit words and heavenly eloquence" (*Absalom and Achitophel*[1681], 868–69), was one of the authentic heroes of the church. While still an undergraduate at Christ Church, Oxford, he was commissioned an ensign in the king's army and twice wounded. He was secretly ordained in 1656 and became one of the few priests who "privately maintained the service and administered the sacraments of the proscribed church of England in defiance of the penal laws" (*DNB, 5,* 1095). After the restoration he worked to repair some of the depredations which church buildings had suffered. His arms as archbishop of York are carved on the roof of the gateway to the great quadrangle of Christ Church, Oxford, which he commissioned Sir Christopher Wren to design.

    73. *Woolf:* "Ld. C[oningsb]y" (*Ba*). Thomas Coningsby (1656?–1729) was at the side of William of Orange during the crossing of the Boyne and was created Baron Coningsby of Clanbrassil in the Irish peerage in April 1692 and made a privy councillor a year later. He was himself saved from impeachment by a pardon under the royal hand in May 1694 (*POAS,* Yale, *6,* 20). He was a Whig member of parliament for Leominster, Herefordshire (1689–1710), but declined to stand in October 1710, fearing perhaps as a manager of the Sacheverell trial that he could be not re-elected (Huntington Library MS. Stowe 57, *4,* 161). He was thought to be "a meer creature of Lord T[reasure]r [Oxford] & what he said in the house of Commons was always look't upon as the sense of Lord T[reasure]r" (BM MS. Add. 31143, f. 509v). At the time of the Sacheverell trial he said himself that "all the business of the House of Commons . . . then devolved upon me" (*Archaeologia, 38* [1860], 13). His wolfish propensities are revealed by his remarkable success in place-hunting and not even his Whig friends "liked that my Lord Coningsby should be so insatiable as to have some new grant every session" (Vernon, *2,* 143–44).

    old Bluster and Thunder: The oldest of the managers was Sir John Hawles (1645–1716) of Salisbury and Lincoln's Inn. He began his parliamentary career in the Convention Parliament as a member for Old Sarum, Wiltshire (1689–90). Subsequently he was elected for Wilton, Wiltshire (1695–98), three Cornish boroughs (1698–1702), and Stockbridge, Hampshire (1705–10). Anthony à Wood (*4,* ¹527n.) called him "a great Williamite . . . but ill

Sir *Peter* the grim, and the late Speaker *Blunder;*
For your dull heavy Curs love to mount in a Chair,   75
Tho' like Monkeys that climb, they expose their Parts bare;
And *Jackall* the ill-look'd, who trains up new Comers,

natured, turbulent and inclining to a republic." Knighted in November 1695, he served as solicitor general in 1695–1702, and had Wharton's support for a judgeship in 1705 (HMC *Downshire MSS., 1*, ii, 842). Even his friends thought that he was "of a peevish, conceited temper" (*Private Correspondence of Sarah, Duchess of Marlborough, 1*, 301).

74. *Sir Peter:* Peter King (1669–1734), whose father was a grocer and whose mother was a first cousin of John Locke, "was put an apprentice to a grocer in [Exeter] and from thence came to London to study the lawe . . . he hath Published a book of divinity & is an ingenious worthy gentleman" (Le Neve, p. 500). Actually he studied law at Leyden but was admitted to the bar from the Middle Temple in June 1698. The book of divinity is *An Enquiry into the Constitution, Discipline, Unity and Worship, of the Primitive Church,* 2 vols., 1691, and it is this interest, one assumes, that made him "grim." He entered parliament as a member for Beeralston, Devonshire (January 1701–15), a rotten borough controlled by the Whig magnate, Lord Stamford. King became one of the leading country Whigs of the period, whom the Junto tried to win by making him recorder of London (July 1708), getting him knighted (September 1708), and choosing him as their candidate for the Speakership in November 1708 (Luttrell, *6,* 332, 350; Le Neve, p. 500; Holmes, p. 41).

late Speaker Blunder: John Smith (1655–1723) left St. John's College, Oxford, without taking a degree and studied law at the Middle Temple without being called to the bar. In the House of Commons, where he sat for Ludgershall, Wiltshire (1679, 1681, 1689–90), Beeralston, Devonshire (December 1691–95), Andover, Hampshire (1695–1713), and East Looe, Cornwall (1715–23), he came to be known as one of the "indefatigable Sticklers for the Whig Party" (Charles Leslie, *Querela Temporum: Or, The Danger of the Church of England,* 1694, p. 15). He was twice appointed chancellor of the exchequer (November 1699–March 1701, February 1708–August 1710) (Luttrell, *6,* 269) and twice elected Speaker of the house (October 1705, October 1707; cf. p. 133 above). In December 1700 Godolphin demanded Smith's removal from the treasury (BM MS. Add. 17677UU, f. 356v) and he was replaced by Henry Boyle. But for a while at least in 1708–09 he functioned as a "Lord Treasurer's Whig" "in opposition to the wild embroilments attempted by the Junto" (*Archaeologia, 38* [1860], 8). And in September 1710 when Godolphin was finally forced out of office, it was Smith who carried his letter of resignation (along with his own) to Queen Anne (Swift, *Corr., 1,* 174). Smith, however, was consoled with the very lucrative place of teller of the exchequer (Luttrell, *6,* 633). His "Blunder," it may be supposed, was his decision to serve on the committee to impeach Sacheverell, for it probably cost him the Speakership in November 1710. The Whigs "had intended to propose him again for the chair in the new parliament, but as [they] had dwindled down to a most insignificant minority . . . the idea was given up" (James A. Manning, *The Lives of the Speakers of the House of Commons,* 1850, pp. 411–12).

75. *heavy:* "I thought him [Smith] a heavy man" (Swift, *Prose, 5,* 260).

75–76. These lines seem to have suggested Pope's footnote to *The Dunciad,* IV, 18: "Vet. Adag. 𝕿𝖍𝖊 𝖍𝖎𝖌𝖍𝖊𝖗 𝖞𝖔𝖚 𝖈𝖑𝖎𝖒𝖇, 𝖙𝖍𝖊 𝖒𝖔𝖗𝖊 𝖞𝖔𝖚 𝖘𝖍𝖊𝖜 𝖞𝖔𝖚𝖗 𝕬——. Verified in no instance more than in Dulness aspiring. Emblematized also by an Ape climbing and exposing his posteriors."

77. *Jackall:* "Sr. *J[osep]h J[ekyl]l*" (*Ba*) (1663–1738) owed at least part of his success to his marriage with a sister of Lord Somers. He was called to the bar from the Middle Temple in 1687. In 1697 he was made lord chief justice of Chester and knighted (W. R. Williams, *The History of the Great Session in Wales,* Brecknock, 1899, p. 44; Shaw, *2,* 270). In parliament where he sat for Eye, Suffolk (November 1695–1700, 1702–13), New Lymington, Hampshire (1713–22),

And still speaks in Season, for his Wit comes from *Somers*.
Then to Horse, loyal Hearts, lest the Round-heads deceive ye,
For they have the Dogs, and are riding Tantivy.   80

There's *Hackum* and *Brass* for their deep Mouths renown'd,
Because empty Sculls have a great Strength of Sound;

---

and Reigate, Surrey (1722–38), he became a leading spokesman for the Junto. But his antics in the Commons reminded Abigail Harley of a monkey (HMC *Portland MSS.*, *4*, 531), and even the duchess of Marlborough thought him capable of "a great deal of mischief" (*The Opinions of Sarah Duchess-Dowager of Marlborough*, [Edinburgh], 1788, p. 52). "The Committee appointed by the Commons, sat several times at Sir *Joseph Jekyl*'s House, in order to draw up the Articles of Impeachment" (Boyer, *Annals*, 1710, p. 225).

81. *Hackum*: "G[enera]l [*James*] S[tanho]pe" (*Ba*) (1673–1721), the grandson of Philip Stanhope, first earl of Chesterfield, was born in Paris, where his father was secretary of the embassy. He began his military career in 1691 as an aide-de-camp to Charles, duke of Schomberg, fighting the French in the Savoy. Thereafter he served with distinction in four campaigns in the Lowlands (1694–97) and was promoted colonel in February 1702. In Anne's war he fought in Spain, where his successes finally brought him promotion to lieutenant general in 1709. His diplomatic career, in which he was to become "one of the brightest ornaments of Europe," began in 1698 when he was appointed second secretary to the embassy in Paris. In February 1706 he was appointed envoy extraordinary to Charles III of Spain (Luttrell, *6*, 14). Heavy gambling, debauchery, and duelling—he killed his opponent in a duel in 1694—occupied his leisure time. His third, or parliamentary, career began in March 1702 when he was elected for Newport, Isle of Wight. Thereafter he sat for Cockermouth, Cumberland (1702–13, 1715–April 1717), Wendover, Buckinghamshire (March 1714–15), and Newport again (April–July 1717). He was a country Whig and eventually, of course, became the only serious rival to Robert Walpole within the party. He arrived from Spain on 2 January 1710 and was added to the committee to try Sacheverell on 10 February (*CJ*, *16*, 305).

Brass: "Mr. [*Robert*] W[alpo]le" (*Ba*) (1676–1745), the future prime minister, was educated at Eton and King's College, Cambridge. His political career began when he was returned to parliament for Castle Rising, Norfolk (January 1701 02). In July 1702 he became "the invincible Brazen memb[e]r of [King's] Lynn, [Norfolk]" (*Etoniana*, *9* [22 May 1907], 130), for which he sat until 1741, except for the time (January 1712–August 1713) when he was expelled the house for bribery. And except for a time in 1707–08, he almost invariably voted with the Junto Whigs (Holmes, p. 234). In June 1705 he was appointed to the council of Prince George, lord high admiral of England, through the influence of Lord Orford. In 1708 he was able to reconcile Godolphin to the Junto lords and to embolden Godolphin to throw out the Tories. For these services he was made secretary at war (February 1708–September 1710) and then, "wholly" by the interest of the duchess of Marlborough (*Private Correspondence of Sarah, Duchess of Marlborough*, *2*, 151), advanced to the more lucrative post of treasurer of the navy (January 1710–January 1711).

for their deep Mouths renown'd: It can be assumed that Stanhope and Walpole were made managers of the impeachment committee for their forensic and not for their legal abilities. There is evidence that they were considered effective speakers. "He shines as much in the Par[liamen]t as he does in the camp," said one admirer of Stanhope (Carlisle R. O. MS. D/Lons, James Lowther to William Gilpin, 7 October 1710), "He is a man of Learning and Eloquence." And Peter Wentworth refused to repeat Walpole's sallies lest he "spoil the jokes" (*Wentworth Papers*, p. 376).

Send *Hackum* to *Spain,* what great Feats he'll atchieve,
And his Conduct's enough to make *Senates* believe;
And young *Brass* of *Corinth* can never deceive ye,   85
For he pays off the Cause just as well as the Navy.
    Then to Horse, loyal Hearts, lest the Round-heads deceive ye,
    For they have the Dogs, and are riding Tantivy.

How Honour and Honesty Dogs can unite,
For their dear Country's Sake, they'll steal, plunder, and bite;   90
Themselves and their Whelps they enrich for its Good,
And make Monarchs great by shedding their Blood;
Yet so eager for Game, the *White Staff* take away,
They'd hunt down *Vulpone* for a rank Beast of Prey.
    Then to Horse, loyal Hearts, lest the Round-heads deceive ye,   95
    For they have the Dogs, and are riding Tantivy.

Then *Tory,* poor *Tory,* never hope to prevail,
You're beat from the Pack with a Stone at your Tail;
Go learn to plead Conscience, when you cheat, lie, and cant,
And plunder the Publick with the Looks of a Saint;   100
If you'd join the old Set, with new Principles fit ye,
Stick at nothing that's base, you'll be of the Committee.
    Then to Horse, loyal Hearts, lest the Round-heads deceive ye,
    For they have the Dogs, and are riding Tantivy.

83. *Hackum to Spain:* Even before the Sacheverell trial was over, on 16 March 1710, it was said that Stanhope would return to Spain (Luttrell, *6,* 557). Since he was to proceed by way of Holland, he may have travelled with Prince Eugene, who reached The Hague on 1 April. By 11/22 June Stanhope was in Barcelona (Luttrell, *6,* 567, 600).

85. *Brass of Corinth:* cf. *New Dictionary,* sig. D2r: "*Corinthian,* a very impudent, harden'd, brazen-fac'd Fellow."

86. *pays off the Cause:* "From the time of Harley's resignation [February 1708], [Godolphin] committed to him the management of the house of commons" (William Coxe, *Memoirs of the Life and Administration of Sir Robert Walpole,* new ed., 3 vols., 1800, *1,* 39).

92. Cf. *On the New Promotion,* 15–20, above.

94. *Vulpone:* Sacheverell is said to have borrowed the name from Shippen, *Faction Display'd,* 408 (*POAS,* Yale, *6,* 668) (*A Vindication of the Last Parliament. In Four Dialogues between Sir Simon and Sir Peter,* 1711, p. 75). His catalogue of "False Brethren" includes "wily *Volpones*" who "*pretend to speak* peaceably, and *smite Us mortally under the fifth Rib*" (*The Perils of False Brethren, both in Church, and State,* 1709, p. 21), which Godolphin foolishly "applyed to himself" (Swift, *Prose, 7,* 9).

102. *the Committee:* See 34*n.* above.

To the Tune of *Ye Commons and Peers*
(March 1710?)

This is another poem, like *The Country Parson's Honest Advice* (1706), that exploits the ironies existing in the *actualités*. When the news reached Sunderland on the night of 28 February 1710 that the mob was burning down meeting houses and threatening worse violence, he went immediately to the queen, who empowered him as her principal secretary of state to call out her horse and foot guards to disperse the rabble (Boyer, *Annals*, 1710, p. 266). Inevitably several of the mob were killed (HMC *Portland MSS.*, *4*, 532). "We are come to fresh paradoxicall circumstances," as one Tory observed, "that while the rabble are pulling down houses out of zeal for passive obedience, the vile tools of the most arbitrary ministry that ever nation Groaned under are rending their throats in defense of forcible resistance" (Lincolnshire Archives Office MS. Massingberd 20/89).

Equally "paradoxicall" is the fact that Lord Sunderland, who called out the guards, was the most republican member of the ministry. It was he who told Swift (*Prose*, *7*, 9) that he "hoped to see the Day, when there should not be a Peer in *England*." Yet his action in suppressing the riots was so arbitrary that the captain of the guards demanded to have his orders in writing (Boyer, *Annals*, 1710, p. 266).

The irony of the mob demonstrating against the Whigs, the advocates of popular sovereignty, and in support of the leading exponent of the divine right of kings, was also remarked ([Edward Ward], *Vulgus Britannicus: or, The British Hudibras*, 1710, p. 24):

> So unexpectedly to find,
> The S[overeign] People thus unkind;
> Who had so long been sooth'd and flatter'd,
> H[oad]*ly'd*, *Review'd*, and *Observator'd*,
> And tempted by a Thousand Arts,
> To stamp Mod'ration in their Hearts;
> Yet that at last upon a *Pinch*,
> They from their Good old Friends should flinch.

Under these circumstances, merely to recount what was happening was enough to make ironies and this is what *To the Tune of Ye Commons and Peers* has done. Although it does so from an uncompromisingly Tory point of view, the need to score partisan points seems to be outweighed by the delight in scoring ironies. This feeling is borne out by the anapestic gallop of the metre, with its high percentage of feminine rhymes that "tickle awkwardly with a kind of pain," as Dryden said (*Works, 13,* 113).

Presumably the poem was written shortly after 20 March 1710 (3*n.* below), but there is no external evidence of this.

The only evidence of authorship, internal or external, is the fact that the unique manuscript is inscribed, in a different and later hand, "Dean Swift/undoubted—." But at the time of Sacheverell's trial Swift was still a Whig and still hoping for preferment from his friends the Junto lords. There is no evidence of what he thought about the trial *at the time.* Later, as an apologist and historian of the next ministry, Swift's opinions of Sacheverell are made very clear. He thought that the Whigs were very foolish to prosecute Sacheverell on "a Point of no Importance" (*Prose, 6,* 74; *7,* 6), that "the whole Sacred Order was understood to be concerned" in the prosecution of Sacheverell (*Prose, 7,* 3), and that the prosecution of Sacheverell finally brought down the Godolphin ministry (*Prose, 8,* 142). In January 1712 when Sacheverell asked him "to do something" for Sacheverell's brother, Swift complied with the request but assured Stella that Sacheverell "shall be none of my acquaintance" (*Journal,* p. 469). And after having dinner with him at John Morphew's, Swift put him down as "not very deep" (ibid., p. 516).

The poem is published here for the first time, from an apparently unique manuscript, with the permission of the Harvard College Library. The title of the poem may have been lost when the manuscript was cropped. The tune, *Ye Commons and Peers,* is the one that Richard Leveridge supposedly wrote for Congreve's *Jack Frenchman's Defeat* (July 1708), above.

To the Tune of *Ye Commons and Peers*

Pray Lend Me Your Ears
I'll Cut 'Em all off if I Can

Sacheverell the learned,
 Of wise men discerned,
Had fairly got off with the Peers,
 But the Bishops were cully'd
 And all the Lords bully'd,   5
And none but poor Ladies in Tears.

 Oh England awake!
 Thou hast plaid thy last Stake
And must part with old Paul to the Romans;
 Both he and St. Peter,   10
 In spight of my Metre,

2. "The Body of the Clergy, and even the greatest Men amongst them, looked upon their whole Order to be struck at in Dr. *Sacheverel*. When he was brought before the House [of Commons on 14 December 1709] therefore, Dr. *Lancaster,* Vice-chancellor of *Oxford,* accompanied him thither, and he was met by above an hundred of the most eminent Clergymen in Town in the Court of Requests; among whom were several of the Queen's Chaplains" (*The Life and Reign of Her Late Excellent Majesty Queen Anne,* 1738, p. 500).

3. *got off:* Although Sacheverell was found guilty of the four charges against him by a vote of 69–52 in the House of Lords on 20 March 1710 (*Tryal of Dr. Henry Sacheverell,* pp. 450–52), the text implies that he would have "got off," i.e. been found innocent, if he had been tried fairly.

4. *cully'd:* made fools of, deceived (*OED*). Perhaps the implication is that the bishops were cullied into staying away, for less than half of them were present at the trial and these 13 divided strictly on party lines, seven finding Sacheverell guilty and six not guilty.

5. *Lords bully'd:* Charles Fitzroy, second duke of Cleveland, was locked up in his own house by his Tory wife to keep him from voting against Sacheverell (Geoffrey Holmes, *The Trial of Doctor Sacheverell,* Eyre Methuen, 1973, p. 224).

6. *Ladies in Tears:* When Sacheverell "made his own defence . . . the poor ladies wet all their clean handkerchiefs" (HMC *Portland MSS.,* 4, 535).

9. *Paul to the Romans:* In the controversy over the origins of civil government Romans 13:1–2 was a crucial text: "For there is no power but of God," it said. On the other hand the violence of the London mob, which went on from pulling down conventicles to plundering private houses, charging the horse guard, and threatening to attack the Bank of England (Boyer, *Annals,* 1710, pp. 265–67), demonstrated "the ill Consequences of the Doctrine advanced by [the Whigs] of the Original of Government's being from the People" (Hearne, *2,* 355).

10. *St. Peter:* Peter's epistles were frequently cited in support of nonresistance and passive obedience (*Leviathan,* 20n. above). Cf. William Beveridge, *Submission to Governours. Or, The Doctrine of St. Peter, concerning Government,* 1710.

Must yeild to a vote of the Commons.

When the mobb gets up next,
Without Canon or text,
To ding down these men of resistance;   15
Then Harry the Doctor
Will prove a good Proctor
And well you deserve his assistance.

You must trust to your guards,
Who their pay and rewards   20
Will value above reputation;
Then late you'l recall
Poor Peter and Paul,
When an army commands all the Nation.

In vain you cry out   25
And keep such a rout
'Gainst Lewis, the Pope, and pretender;
'Tis obedience to laws
Must keep up the cause
Of the church and her glorious defender.   30

Then sure 'tis a jigg

12. *yeild to a vote*: The Whigs put parliament into God's place of absolute unlimited power: "*That* [i.e. the legislative power] is a Power, we know not how to disallow, or disobey. *There,* we shall see and feel the Weight of S. *Paul's* Authority, pressing Submission to the Lawful Powers, and calling for Obedience to the Rulers, that are set over us" ([William Fleetwood], *The Thirteenth Chapter to the Romans, Vindicated from the Abusive Senses Put upon It,* 1710, p. 9).

14. *Without Canon or text*: Without the authority of the Bible or the laws of the church.

15. *To ding down*: to knock down, thrust down, overthrow (*OED*).

these men of resistance: the Whigs, who advocate the people's right to overthrow the government. Benjamin Hoadly insisted that Romans 13:2, "they that resist shall receive to themselves damnation," was "only to be understood of resisting *good Governors*." "And, had this great and good Man but indulged us a little farther, and informed us who were to be Judges of a good and bad Administration, he had certainly put an End to all Disputes upon this Subject" (*The Life and Reign of Her Late Excellent Majesty Queen Anne,* 1738, pp. 506–07).

17. *Proctor*: defender, guardian (*OED*).

19. *guards*: See headnote, above.

19–24. These lines argue that dependence upon military force alone to keep order will produce a military dictatorship, or, in the words of Jesus, "they that take the sword shall perish with the sword" (Matthew 26:52).

25–30. The argument here seems to be that the attack on the church and Sacheverell encourages the Catholic enemies of the church.

30. Cf. Defoe, *The Age of Wonders,* 42n. below.

31. *a jigg*: a joke (*OED*). Cf. Defoe, *The Vision,* 89 above.

> For the court to turn Whig
> On a mystical point of expedience,
> Whilst (O monstrous story!)
> The mobb turns Tory   35
> And preacheth up passive obedience.

32. *court . . . turn Whig:* Anne attended most sessions of the Sacheverell trial incognito, "And, as [she] was one Day going to *Westminster* in a Chair, the People gathered about her, and cried out, *God bless your Majesty and the Church; we hope your Majesty is for Dr.* Sacheverel" (*The Life and Reign of Her Late Excellent Majesty Queen Anne,* 1738, p. 505). Presumably she was for Dr. Sacheverell (*Found on the Queen's Toilet, 6n.,* above), but she refused to support him. Mrs. Masham "asked her if she did not let people know her mind in the matter. She said, no, she did not meddle one way or other, and that it was her friends' advice not to meddle" (HMC *Portland MSS., 4,* 532). Since no one was neutral, Anne, by not supporting him, appeared to be against him and thus the court, on the "mystical" grounds of expedience, appeared to "turn Whig."

35. *mobb turns Tory:* See p. 392 above.

Of the 12 *"Modern Inconsistencies"* exposed in *High Church Miracles* (p. 442 below), the most paradoxical is the attempt to reconcile theories of divine right with the facts of what happened during the revolution. Not all the ingenuity of Francis Atterbury or Sir Simon Harcourt could put together Sacheverell's belief in an indefeasible divine right of succession and the detailed clauses in the Bill of Rights altering that succession. Logical consistency would require believers in divine right to be Jacobites, but high churchmen were profuse in their declarations of loyalty to Queen Anne (*High Church Miracles, 7n.* below). As a result they were attacked by nonjurors as well as by Whigs. Thomas Hearne for example (*2, 364–65*) could not believe in Sacheverell's integrity since he had "taken the Oath of Allegiance to her Majesty . . . and by consequence he contradicts what he had asserted in his Sermon namely that Resistance is lawfull upon no account whatever." Where nonjurors blamed these inconsistencies on bad logic, Whigs were apt to see them as a smoke screen to hide Jacobites. *Fair Warning* penetrates this smoke screen to expose the real intentions of "the Pretenders Churchmen" (*The Observator*, 5–8 April 1710).

The poem was so popular that it generated two replies, *The Tory's Fair Answer*, by N. F. G. (*"Monarchs* beware, your Titles they disown") (*Bc*) and *Answer to Fair Warning* ("Whilst Grave *Sacheverell* saps the Ground, we find") (*D*), and a "reverse" also entitled *Fair Warning* and with the same first line, but substituting "Ben: Hoadly" in line 2 (Osborn MS. Box 89, No. 12). The phrase got to be a slogan among the Whigs; Hoadly uses it twice in *The Jacobite's Hopes Reviv'd by our Late Tumults and Addresses*, 1710, pp. 8, 16, and William Bisset entitled a prose pamphlet *Fair Warning: Or, A Fresh Taste of French Government at Home* (1710).

The Luttrell copy of *Ba,* now at Harvard, is dated 5 April 1710. The poem was then printed in *The Observator*, 5–8 April 1710 (*A*), from another source. A third collateral copy (*C*) is also dated "Ap: 1710."

There is no evidence of the author's identity.

Madam, look out, your Title is arraign'd,
Sacheverell saps the Ground whereon you stand.
'Tis *Revolution* that upholds the Throne;
If *Non-resistance* thrive, then you are gone.
If *Passive Doctrine* boldly be reviv'd,   5
Your Crown's precarious, and your Reign's short-liv'd.
Such Notions with Impunity profest,
Will make *the Power of Parliaments a Jest,*
Their *Acts of Settlement* like Ropes of Sand,

1. *Title:* For Whig extremists, Anne's title was parliamentary only, created by statute (p. 350 above). For Tory extremists, it was hereditary only, conferred by divine right. For moderate Whigs and Tories, it was both: Anne was queen by virtue of the law of primogeniture subject to the exclusion of Catholic candidates. High churchmen like Sacheverell who insisted that her title was hereditary only (*Found on the Queen's Toilet,* 3n. above), embarrassed the queen, for they reminded her not only that she had deserted her father in November 1688 but also that her half brother had a *prior* hereditary claim if he were legitimate. And Anne had become convinced that James Frances Edward Stuart was her half brother. She showed her dislike of the hereditary claim in October 1710 when the city of London mentioned in an address that "her right was Divine." "She immediately took exception to the expression . . . having thought often of it, she could by no means like it, and thought it so unfit to be given to anybody that she wished it might be left out" (HMC *Bath MSS.,* 1, 199).

3. *Revolution . . . upholds the Throne:* The Whigs held this seeming paradox to be quite literally true. Wharton had pointed out, in the Sacheverell trial, that "If the Revolution is not lawful . . . the queen herself is no lawful queen, since the best title she had to the crown, was her parliamentary-title, founded on the Revolution" (*Parl. Hist.,* 6, 831).

4. *Non-resistance:* Hoadly explains that for the Jacobites "*Non-resistance* [means] to damn the *Revolution*" and he goes on to imagine "what glorious Times . . . we had enjoy'd" if there been no resistance to James II: "Now and then a *Martyr* burn'd, or a *rich Alderman* hang'd" (*The Jacobite's Hopes Reviv'd by our Late Tumults and Addresses,* 1710, pp. 8–9, 7). And if there had been no resistance to James II in 1688, he would have been succeeded in September 1701 by his son, James Francis Edward, who would have reigned until 1766 and Anne would have remained a younger daughter of the royal family.

5. *Passive Doctrine:* As Hearne (*2,* 374) said, *Fair Warning* is a poem "against Passive Obedience," which is another term for nonresistance.

9. *Acts of Settlement:* Succession to the throne was settled by two laws: the Bill of Rights (1689) and the Act of Settlement (1701). The first declared that only Protestants could succeed to the throne, which excluded both the Palatine line, the Catholic descendants of James I's daughter, Elizabeth, who had married Frederick V, the elector Palatine; and the Orleans line, the Catholic descendants of Charles II's sister, Henrietta, who had married Philippe, duc d'Orleans. The Bill of Rights then established the children of Mary, Anne, and William of Orange as heirs to the throne. By 1701, when the childless Mary was dead, and Anne's last surviving child was dead, and William was a widower, a further provision for the succession to the crown became necessary. By the Act of Settlement, therefore, the succession went to the Protestant descendants of James I's daughter, Elizabeth, or Sophie, the dowager

And *Hannover* may rule his Native Land.   10
When Priests affirm no Limitation's good,
No Right but in Proximity of Blood,
Who sees not the *Pretender*'s understood?
Impatient for their Rightful Chevalier,
To *Rome* and *France* they now directly steer,   15
And swear the House shan't sit another Year.
Though Loyalty and Church be their Pretence,
Inherent Birthright is the Secret Sense,
And Restauration is the Consequence.

---

electress of Braunschweig-Lüneburg, and the heirs of her body being Protestants. By the Act of Union these provisions were extended to Scotland.

10. *Hannover:* Sophie's eldest son, Georg Ludwig (*Switch and Spur*, 24*n.* above).

11. *Limitation:* The "limitation . . . of the crown" to Protestants is made in the Bill of Rights, and the Act of Settlement is entitled an Act for the Further Limitation of the Crown (*EHD*, pp. 127, 129).

12. *Proximity:* By the laws of primogeniture, the pretended Prince of Wales, the Palatine line, and the Orleans line were all elder than the Hanover line (*EHD*, pp. 133, 135).

16. *the House shan't sit:* An address from Coventry, for example, assured the queen that "When Your Majesty, in Your Great Wisdom, shall be pleas'd to call a new Parliament . . . we will use our respective Endeavours to choose such Representatives, as will dutifully comply with Your Majesty, to secure our most Holy Faith against the Designs of Atheists and Hereticks; our Excellent Church against Superstition and Schism; the Protestant Succession against all Pretensions; And the best Constitution in the World, against the dangerous Schemes of restless Innovators and levelling Republicans" (*A Collection of the Addresses which have been Presented to the Queen, since the Impeachment of the Reverend Dr. Henry Sacheverell*, 1710, p. 8).

On the Queen's Speech
(April? 1710)

The queen's speech proroguing the second session of her third parliament on 5 April 1710 was written for her, of course, by her "triumphant" Whig ministers. They wanted her to express unqualified satisfaction at the outcome of the Sacheverell trial and even hoped to get in a clause exhorting the clergy to preach against vice "and not to meddle in politics" (Hertfordshire County R. O. MS. Panshanger D/EP F207, f.6). But even without this clause the speech was hard on Sacheverell.

"My Lords and Gentlemen," Anne said, "I cannot sufficiently express to you My great Concern, that you had so necessary an Occasion of taking up a great Part of your Time towards the latter End of this Session." Most people, even many dissenters, felt that the trial of Sacheverell had been a foolish and not a "necessary" occasion (Calamy, *Historical Account, 2,* 223–24). "But," the queen went on, "it is very injurious . . . to insinuate," as Sacheverell had been found guilty of insinuating, "that the Church is in any Danger from My Administration" (*LJ, 19,* 145).

The Whigs were delighted with this and the Tories were dumbfounded. "Her Majesty's most Gracious Speech," crowed George Ridpath (*The Observator,* 5–8 April 1710), "has given the Pretender's Churchmen such a Blow that they look very silly . . . [and] we hope the Poor People who are deluded with a false Alarm of the Churches Danger, will have their Eyes open'd by this Speech, since all the World must own the Truth of what Her Majesty says." And Burnet (*2,* 546) observed that "her Speech . . . seemed to look a different way from the Whispers that had been set about" that the queen had "resolved to abandon the Whigs" (*Archaeologia, 38* [1860], 13).

But "Soon after that," Burnet went on to say, Anne "made a Step that revived [the whispers] again." "Without communicating the Matter to any of her Ministers, [she] took the Chamberlain's White Staff from the Marquis of *Kent* . . . and gave it to the Duke of *Shrewsbury.*" Anne's promotion of a man who had spoken and voted for Sacheverell (Osborn MS. Box 21, No. 22, f. 30) revealed that she did not share her ministers' satisfaction at the outcome of the trial. And at the same time it was revealed to the angry Tory who wrote the following lines, that her words in her prorogation speech were "not her own" (line 10).

It is clear, however, that the anger is directed at the queen's Whig ministers, who are "Devils" (11), and not at the queen, who is only an "artificial Thing" (8) or "guiltless" timber (13). But even so, the poem was too dangerous to be published in 1710 and is printed here for the first time in its undisguised form.

The verses are dated 1710 in *A.*

ON THE QUEEN'S SPEECH

So represented, have I seen
On Puppet-Stage, a mimick Queen;
The manag'd Engin seem'd to speak
With Voice unfeign'd, and Movements make,
But 'tis thro' an ambiguous Light,   5
The lifeless Image cheats the Sight,
Whilst secret Wire and hidden Spring
Directs the artificial Thing.
The Royal Eccho thus rebounds,
Words not her own, in borrow'd Sounds.   10
So formerly the Devils spoke
The cursed Lies thro' Heart of Oak.
Their passive Timber guiltless utter'd
Whate'er th'inchantresse Spirit mutter'd.

7–8. *Wire . . . Thing:* Cf. Congreve, *The Way of the World,* III, i, 13: "Thou wooden Thing upon Wires."

9. *Eccho:* "The Conceit of making an Echo talk sensibly, and give rational Answers" is said by Addison (*The Spectator,* 8 May 1711) to be an example of false wit.

11. *Devils spoke:* The reference has not been identified. Is it a garbled allusion to *The Tempest,* I, ii, 320–29?

The History of Seven
(March–June? 1710)

When judgment was pronounced upon Dr. Sacheverell on 20 March 1710, six bishops found him "Not Guilty" and seven voted him "Guilty," which occasioned the inevitable jest, sad but true, "that the Church lyes at 6s & 7s" (Berkshire R. O. MS. Trumbull Add. 49, ? to Sir William Trumbull, 27 March 1710). The fact that the number of bishops who voted Sacheverell guilty, "An happy Mystick number" (line 5), was the same as the number of bishops whom James II sent to the Tower of London in June 1688 for rebellion, provided further grounds for irony. The original seven had been identified with the seven golden candlesticks of Revelation 1:11–12 (*POAS*, Yale, *4*, 216). The later seven, therefore, became *The Seven Extinguishers* ("The *Calve's-Head Brawny C[haplain]* leads the Van") whose "baleful Damps *Extinguish Gospel Light*" (*A Collection of Poems, &c. For and Against Dr. Sacheverell*, 4 vols., 1710–11, *2*, 3–6), like "a sheet of *Thulè*," or, as James Drake said (*The Memorial of the Church of England*, 1705, pp. 26–27), prelates who,

> by Preaching *Indifference* to the Interests of the *Ch——ch*, under the Specious, Deceitful Name of *M[oderatio]n*, have very much *Dampt*, and in a manner *Extinguished* that *Noble Spirit*, which their *Predecessours* had Infused into the *Inferiour Clergy*.

The present poem is a catalogue of the seven "Extinguishers." This was a subgenre that had broken loose from Absalom's "Friends of ev'ry sort" in *Absalom and Achitophel*, 544–681 (*POAS*, Yale, *2*, 475) and achieved a life of its own in such works as Dorset's?, *A Faithful Catalogue of Our Most Eminent Ninnies* (1688) (*POAS*, Yale, *4*, 189) and Henry Hall's *The Mitred Club* (1703) (*POAS*, Yale, *6*, 510). Within the catalogue framework there is in the present poem an undeveloped allegorical substructure: Mother (1) is the church; Daughters (33) are Oxford and Cambridge; Sons (1) are the graduates of Oxford and Cambridge in orders, i.e. the clergy.

The verses must have been written after 20 March 1710 when the House of Lords found Sacheverell guilty and before 8 May 1710, if *The Save-Alls* (8 May 1710), 113, does indeed allude to *The History of Seven*, 93, as it may do. The author of these verses, which are printed here for the first time, has not been identified.

413

THE HISTORY OF SEVEN

How cou'd ye (*Sacred Sons*) your Mother's Fate
So Vainly dread, as in desponding State,
When Seven Champions in her Cause were Stout,
All Mitr'd Heads, who bravely bore her out,
An happy Mystick number, Venerable Crew   5
Who Voted false, to prove her Doctrine true.
   No wonder *Sarum* in her Cause was brave
(For true *Scot*-like he'd Scorn to Act the Knave),
Perfidious Son deny'd his Mother's Right,
Damns now the Doctrine, once he Preach'd so tight.   10
An o're-Grown brawny Brute, Rome's secret Friend,
Who could expect that he'd our *Church* defend?
Were but his Sleeves dy'd of another Hue,
Instead of Prelate you'd a Butcher View.

1–3. The inferior clergy—graduates of Oxford and Cambridge (33 below)—are asked, sarcastically, how they could possibly fear that the church was in danger (p. 387 above) when it had such defenders as the seven bishops who voted against Sacheverell (*To the Tune of Ye Commons and Peers*, 4n. above).

6. The seven bishops voted Sacheverell guilty of telling the truth, i.e. that the church was in danger (Article III of the charges against him), in order to support the legal fiction that the church was not in danger (*Upon the Vote that Pass'd that the Church was not in Danger* [December 1705], headnote, above).

8. *Scot-like:* Gilbert Burnet was born in Edinburgh, educated at Marischal College, Aberdeen, became a probationer in the Church of Scotland while it was still under Presbyterian government (1661), and was presented with his first living at Saltoun, in East Lothian (*DNB, 3,* 394–95). Cf. Shippen, *Faction Display'd* (April? 1704), 85–88, *POAS,* Yale, *6,* 654: "A *Scotch,* Seditious, Unbelieving Priest . . . Who . . . does that Church, he's sworn to guard, Invade."

10. *Damns now the Doctrine:* In his speech on 16 March Burnet denied "That by the Doctrine of the Church of *England,* all Resistance in any Case whatsoever, without Exception, is Condemn'd" (*Tryal of Dr. Henry Sacheverell,* p. ²3).

once he Preach'd: In December 1709 the Tories brought out two of Burnet's sermons in which he had maintained passive obedience and nonresistance with great strength of argument. In a sermon preached 30 January 1675 Burnet had insisted that the Christian was bound by conscience to "an absolute Subjection to the higher Powers" and he described the right of resistance as a "pestiferous Doctrine" that originated with the pope (*The Royal Martyr and the Dutiful Subject, in Two Sermons,* 1710, pp. 44, 45). Cf. *Dr. Sacheverell and Benjamin Hoadly,* 7n. above.

11. *brawny:* Cf. "The Brawny Chaplain of the *Calves-Head-Feast*" (Shippen, *Faction Display'd* [April? 1704], 86, *POAS,* Yale, *6,* 654).

Rome's secret Friend: This role was usually reserved for Benjamin Hoadly (see illustration, p. 414), but there can be no doubt that Burnet was "as much hated by the High Church and Jacobites, as any person whatsoever" (Calamy, *Historical Account, 2,* 310–11).

The Three False Brethren [vertically]: Daniel Defoe, Benjamin Hoadly, Oliver Cromwell, or [horizontally] Pope Clement XI, Hoadly, Satan, an engraving by George Bickham

Oxford thy Principles now well are Known,   15
A Prelate fit sure to protect the Gown.
Can ever *Rhedycina's* Sons despair
Of Safe guard, in so good a *Pastor's* Care,
Or dread *Geneva's* Wolf, thô lately bold
E're breaking in to prey upon the Fold?   20
Dost thou expect for this the old Prophet's *See?*
No Charles went Right, who first promoted thee.

15. *Oxford:* William Talbot (1659?–1730) graduated B.A. from Oriel College, Oxford, in 1677 and in April 1691 "was preferr'd by the Interest of the Duke of Shrewsbury to the Deanry of Worcester upon the turning out of [the nonjuror] Dr. [George] Hickes, and was afterwards [September 1699] made Bp. of Oxon." (Hearne, *2,* 72). He is said to have been "a very great Rake all the Time he liv'd in the University; and afterwards when in orders was very much addicted to Gaming" (ibid., *1,* 106).

Principles now . . . Known: Like Burnet, Talbot published the speech he made on 16 March against Sacheverell. He justified resistance on the grounds of self-preservation when nothing else could prevent "a total Subversion of the Constitution and Laws" (*Tryal of Dr. Henry Sacheverell,* pp. ³5, ³6, ³9). Hearne (*3,* 11) called it "a most childish, pitifull, illiterate and indeed malicious and Republican, Whiggish, Libell, &, like Burnett's of Sarum, contriv'd for . . . giving the Subjects a Liberty of deposing and turning out their lawful Magistrates, whenever it shall be thought suitable."

17. *Rhedycina:* a Latinization of Rhedychen, thought to be the Celtic name of the settlement at Oxford (*Oxoniana,* ed. [John Walker], 4 vols., 1809?, *1,* 2).

19. *Geneva's Wolf:* Cf. "th'insatiate *Wolfe . . .* More haughty than the rest . . . [who] from *Geneva* first infested *France"* (*The Hind and the Panther* [1687], 153–73) and *Review of English Studies,* New Series, *4* (1953), 331–36.

lately bold: In October 1706, the pastors and professors of Geneva accused Oxford University of entertaining an ill opinion of them (Boyer, *Annals,* 1707, p. ²192). Oxford responded in February 1707 in a letter as conciliatory as it could be while still recalling that English dissenters "shake off the Lawful Authority of Bishops, and justify their Rebellion by the Example of *Geneva"* (ibid., p. ²197). But there were still "Several honest, understanding Members of the university [who were] averse to the design of the Answer" (Hearne, *2,* 5), evidently feeling, as the writer of these lines did, that it was too conciliatory to *"the Genevian Discipline,"* as Sacheverell called it (*The Perils of False Brethren, Both in Church, and State,* 1709, p. 19).

21. *the old Prophet:* This was the nickname of William Lloyd, bishop of Worcester (Hearne, *2,* 105). Shippen called him "old *Mysterioso"* (*Faction Display'd,* 123; *POAS,* Yale, *6,* 656; cf. 48*n.* below). While it is true that translation from Oxford to Worcester would have been desirable—it would have increased Talbot's income by about £600 a year (Beatson, *1,* 211, 228)—there is no evidence that he could claim any credit for the answer to the Geneva letter. Hearne (*1,* 324) said that it was drafted by George Smalridge and approved by a full convocation of the university.

22. *No Charles went Right:* Talbot's "first preferment was the rectory of Burghfield, Berkshire (1682), a living in the gift of his kinsman, Charles Talbot, afterwards duke of Shrewsbury" (*DNB, 19,* 339). So the two Charleses are the then earl of Shrewsbury and Charles II, who would have had to give his assent to Talbot's preferment (Chamberlayne, 1708, pp. 58, 93). It is impossible to imagine how the writer supposed that Charles II went wrong, but Shrewsbury presumably went wrong by becoming a favorite of William III and a great Whig (*A New Ballad,* 119*n.* above). Shrewsbury "Came . . . right again" (*A New Ballad,* 136, below) by joining the Tories in voting Sacheverell not guilty (*Tryal of Dr. Henry Sacheverell,* p. 452).

Thy former Nuptials whoso will but View,
Will scarce think, a Thief then, could now prove true.
    Let our dear Sister *Granta* to Caress   25
Her Guardian Prelate and for's care express
Her Filial Love, with all due thankfulness.
What Secret Spring of Int'rest did Controul
And Sway the Bent of *Ely's* leaden Soul,
So Traytor-like against the Church Combine   30
T'oppose her Doctrine, Cause and Right Divine?
    Happy, thrice happy must the Mother be
O're whose two Daughters and their Progeny
Such worthy Guardian Angels thus Preside!
Can they in time of Peril want a Guide?   35
    Had *Peterborough* visited the Starry Pole
As lately did Tubthumping *Bristol's* soul,

23. *Nuptials:* Like Burnet (8n. above) and Moore (26n. below), Talbot was "a digamist," having been twice married, once after he was bishop, which "never us'd to be practis'd by the Bishops of the Church of *England*" (Hearne, *1,* 106; *2,* 72).

25. *Granta:* thought to be an ancient name of the Cam, from which Cambridge was named (G. Dyer, *A Restoration of the Ancient Modes of Bestowing Names,* Exeter, 1805, pp. 238–39).

26. *Guardian Prelate:* John Moore (1646–1714) graduated B.A. from Clare College, Cambridge, in 1666 and was elected a fellow the next year. "His fortune was made when he became chaplain to Heneage Finch, first earl of Nottingham" (*DNB, 13,* 807). After a succession of rich rectories, he was consecrated bishop of Norwich in July 1691, upon the deprivation of the nonjuror, William Lloyd. He was a chaplain to William and Mary, a low churchman, and one of "The Mitred Club" who voted against the bills to prevent occasional conformity in 1702–04 (*POAS,* Yale, *6,* 510n.). He was not, therefore, a favorite of Queen Anne, who complained that he would take away from her "that little prerogative the Crown has" (*Letters of Queen Anne,* p. 257). The queen, nonetheless, had to acquiesce in Moore's translation to the richer bishopric of Ely in July 1707. Moore's zeal for the Whig cause was demonstrated when he dismissed a chimney sweep from his service for "not voting for Sir H. Colt" in the Westminster election of May 1708 (Berkshire R. O. MS. Trumbull LIII; cf. Hearne, *2,* 110).

36. *Peterborough:* Richard Cumberland (1631–1718) was born in London and educated at Magdalene College, Cambridge, whence he graduated B.A. in 1653 and D.D. in 1680. He was a friend of Pepys, who describes him in his "plain country-parson's dress" in March 1667. In July 1691 he was consecrated bishop of Peterborough upon the deprivation of the nonjuror, Thomas White. Thereafter he could always be counted upon to give his vote on the Whig side in the House of Lords (Holmes, pp. 400, 435).

36–37. *visited the Starry Pole | As lately did . . . Bristol:* John Hall, bishop of Bristol, died on 4 February 1710 (Hearne, *2,* 343).

37. *Tubthumping Bristol:* John Hall (1633–1710), "one of the Rebell Bishops," as Hearne (*3,* 50) called him, came from a puritan family in Worcestershire, matriculated at Pembroke College, Oxford, in December 1650 and was "educated there among presbyterians and independents" (Wood, *4,* 900). After taking the oaths in 1662 he was elected master of Pembroke College (1664–1710) and appointed Margaret Professor of Divinity (1676–91). In William's reign he was consecrated bishop of Bristol (August 1691) and became "a great

Will's Creatures both, o'th'hair set he form'd of Old,
All of one Mass, Stamp'd in Fanatick Mould,
Perhaps our Church's Hero then Had gain'd   40
One Vote more to the Cause he well maintain'd.
Thou and thy Dean, both in one Sphere do move:
His Doctrine's False, and thou it true dost prove.
    Ungrate *St. Asaph* to thy Patron just,
He little thought thou'dst thus betray thy Trust.   45

Admirer & Favourer" of the Whigs (Hearne, *3,* 50). "As to Principles," Hearne (*2,* 343) said, "he was a thorough-pac'd Calvinist, a defender of the Republican Doctrines, a stout and vigorous advocate for the Presbyterians, Dissenters, &c. . . . and a strenuous Persecuter of truly honest Men."

38. *Will's . . . set:* The nonjuring schism and the deaths of several bishops made it necessary for William III to fill 16 of the 26 seats on the episcopal bench in the first three years of his reign. The men he chose (*Moderation Display'd,* 305n. above) were low churchmen who invariably voted Whig. Three of the seven bishops who voted against Sacheverell, plus John Hall who died six weeks before he could do so, were "King William's bishops" (Thoresby, *1,* 436).

40. *Church's Hero:* Sacheverell.

42. *Dean:* The Dean of Peterborough was White Kennett.

43. *His Doctrine:* "Dr. White Kennett (that notorious Republican, & preacher of Rebellious Doctrine)," Hearne said (*2,* 88), "seems to have Milton's very Principles transfus'd into him" (ibid., *1,* 311).

44. *St. Asaph:* William Fleetwood (1656–1723) was born in the Tower of London and educated at Eton and King's College, Cambridge, whence he graduated B.A. in 1679 and was elected a fellow in 1678. Although he was one of the most celebrated preachers in London, where he was rector of St. Augustine (1689–1706) and a lecturer at St. Dunstan's in the West (1689–1705), he preferred retirement, and antiquarian studies in which John Evelyn found him "learned and ingenious" (Hearne, *3,* 352). He was rector of Wexham, a parish in Buckinghamshire worth only £60 a year, in April 1708 (Luttrell, *6,* 295) when Anne, without consulting her advisors and without Fleetwood's knowledge, appointed him bishop of St. Asaph. She "called Fleetwood 'my bishop,' attended his sermons, and favoured him till her death, in spite of [his] outspoken whiggism" (*DNB, 7,* 269). Besides voting against Sacheverell on 20 March 1710, Fleetwood published *The Thirteenth Chapter to the Romans, Vindicated from the Abusive Senses put upon it,* 1710, a scathing attack on Sacheverell's sermon of 5 November 1709, and became "a great Whig in the latter Part of his Life, notwithstanding he was otherwise once" (Hearne, *8,* 105).

thy Patron: glossed "Ld. Rochester" in the copy text. This identification is confirmed by a letter of Fleetwood's written 1710–11: "I shall always be on the side of the late [Whig] Ministry," he said, "because I know they served the Queen and nation so well . . . [but] if I could shift my side I might be well accepted, considering what relations I have had to one (the Earl of Rochester) who governs all" (*Biographia Britannica, 3,* 1971–72). Rochester had once more been made lord president of the council on 21 September 1710 and died suddenly on 1–2 May 1711. The patronage of Rochester may explain why Fleetwood was not one of "William's bishops," for Rochester was anathema to William III (Burnet, *2,* 280).

45. *betray:* As Hearne said (43n.), Fleetwood was not always a Whig. In the preface to his sermon on the death of Anne's last surviving child, he had struck out in the best high church fashion against "*an impudent and clamorous Faction*" that would "*turn a Kingdom into a Com-*

Could'st thou to his Stanch Notions Counter run,
'Twas well thou ne're didst Poyson his good Son.
Once Revelation headpiece fill'd thy Chair,
Yet in its Cause more firmly did appear;
Thy Principles and Miracles alike are Sound: 50
Ambition, Avarice, Pride, in thee abound.
Let *Kings*, nor *Eton* ever boast such Spawn
As Church's Cause desert, yet wear the Lawn.

---

monwealth" (*A Sermon Preach'd August the 4th 1700*, 1700, sig. A3v). When he republished the sermon in 1712, Fleetwood omitted the preface and substituted a new one which was so widely distributed by the Whigs as a party pamphlet that the House of Commons ordered it to be burned by the common hangman (*CJ*, *17*, 263). In July 1712 Swift delightedly seized upon this evidence of Fleetwood's apostasy and turned it into an *Examiner* (*Prose*, *6*, 159–61).

47. *Son:* Rochester's only son and heir was Henry Hyde, Lord Hyde (1672–1753). The line implies that Fleetwood was his tutor, perhaps at Eton, to which Lord Hyde made a contribution to the building of the Upper School in 1689 (Sir Wasey Sterry, *The Eton College Register 1441–1698*, Eton, Spottiswoode, Ballantyne, 1943, p. 184) and of which Fleetwood, also an Etonian, was made a fellow in 1691. It was not uncommon for the sons of noblemen to come to Eton attended by a private tutor. From November 1695 until May 1711 when he succeeded as second earl of Rochester, Lord Hyde was a member of parliament for Launceston, Cornwall. The extent of his "poisoning" by Fleetwood's "Change of Principles" (*Four Sermons*, 1712, p. vi) may be judged by his voting record. An otherwise perfect Tory record is marred by the fact that he was a Sneaker in the November 1704 vote for the Tack (*A Health to the Tackers*, 2n. above) and voted to impeach Henry Sacheverell in December 1709 (*The High Church True Blue Protestant List*, 1710).

48. *Revelation headpiece:* William Lloyd, bishop of Worcester, had been bishop of St. Asaph from October 1680 to October 1692. Lloyd had "stood as in the front of the battel all King James's reign" (Burnet, *1*, 190), and when he was released from the Tower on bail in June 1688 he was unable to get through Palace Yard by reason of the crowds kissing his hands and garments (Henry Hyde, earl of Clarendon, *Correspondence*, 2 vols., 1828, *2*, 177). But now at 83 he had lost his mind trying to interpret *Revelation* "chronologically" (Luttrell, *2*, 213; Swift, *Journal*, *2*, 544).

50. *Principles:* "Dr. Fleetwood is a man of time-serving Principles" (Hearne, *2*, 104).

Miracles: In a work published in 1701 Fleetwood argued that all miraculous power, whether for good or evil, comes from God, because "no Power less than that of God, can unsettle that establish'd Course of Nature, which no Power less than his could settle and establish" (*An Essay upon Miracles. In Two Discourses*, 1701, p. 10). This assertion was challenged by Benjamin Hoadly, who insisted that the devil could perform evil miracles and that intelligent men could distinguish between the devil's miracles and God's because "some *Miracles* are *greater* than others" (*A Letter to Mr. Fleetwood. Occasion'd by His Late Essay on Miracles*, 1702, p. 6).

51. *Pride:* In the dedication to *An Essay upon Miracles* (1701) Fleetwood had boasted, "if I say I think [I have done] *better* [than other writers on the subject], it is that I may not pay You so ill a Compliment, as to present You with what I had not a good Opinion of my self." Swift made fun of this in *A Letter of Thanks from My Lord W[harto]n to the Lord Bp. of S. Asaph*, 1712: "Nor need I run riot in Encomium and Panegyrick, since you can perform that Part so much better for yourself" (Swift, *Prose*, *6*, 153).

Time-serving *Trimnell,* tho' late Nick'd the Tide,
When Faction once did *Winton's* Sons Divide,   55
Yet haply then did take the weakest side,
To distant Ages shall he branded be
And Stigmatiz'd with Note of Infamy.
Of a false Brother, retrieve his Name in vain
Hee'l strive; no time shall e're expunge the Stain   60
Cast on his *Mitre,* which one who once it wore
By suffering for't embelish'd long before.

54. *Trimnell:* Charles Trimnell (1663–1723) was another of "these degenerous Clergy-men . . . that . . . renounce the divine right of the Episcopat" (Hearne, *2,* 346). He was educated at New College, Oxford, whence he graduated B.A. in July 1681. His fortune was made when he was recommended by Thomas Tenison to be chaplain to the countess of Sunderland, He accompanied the Sunderland family to Amsterdam in August 1689 and returned with them to Althorp the next year. In 1694 Sunderland presented him with the rectory of Bodington, in Northamptonshire, "which he resign'd to one Mr. Downes [after-wards bishop of Derry] upon the score of marrying his Sister as 'twas generally believ'd" (ibid., *1,* 219). In 1701 he was appointed chaplain in ordinary to Princess Anne and publish-ed a number of pamphlets defending the rights of the crown in the convocation controversy of 1701–02. Anne presented him with the rectory of Southmere, in Norfolk, in 1704 and in October 1706 he was appointed rector of St. James's, Westminster. His appointment as bishop of Norwich in December 1707 was part of a political deal whereby the Junto acquiesc-ed in Anne's appointments of Tories to the sees of Chester and Exeter in return for Whig appointments to the see of Norwich, the deanery of Peterborough (42*n.* above), and the regius professorship of divinity at Oxford. Trimnell was Sunderland's personal choice to succeed John Moore as bishop of Norwich (*English Historical Review, 82* [October 1967], 746).

late Nick'd the Tide: caught the tide. Trimnell was consecrated bishop of Norwich on 8 February 1708.

55. *Winton's Sons:* the fellows of New College, Oxford.

56. *take the weakest side:* On the death of Richard Traffles, warden of New College, in 1703, Trimnell ran against Thomas Brathwaite for election to that office. "Upon the Election," Hearne (*1,* 219) said, "he lost it but by one Vote, and several who were against him declar'd they would have been for him if he had not been married." Trimnell's first wife was Henrietta Maria, the daughter of William Talbot, bishop of Oxford (15*n.* above).

57. *branded:* The blackest mark against Trimnell was his speech at Sacheverell's trial, which concluded with a very emotional appeal: "tho' I do not pretend to any great share of Courage," he said, "I am very free to declare to Your Lordships that I am in no Comparison so apprehensive of what may befal my self for condemning this Person, as I am of what will probably befal the Publick if Your Lordships shou'd not condemn him" (*Tryal of Dr. Henry Sacheverell,* pp. 362–63).

61. *one:* Joseph Hall (1574–1656) made a reputation as a poet, calling himself "the first English satirist," before he was consecrated bishop of Exeter (December 1627), whence he was translated to Norwich in November 1641.

62. *suffering:* Hall was one of the bishops who petitioned Charles I in 1641 to protest parliament's proceeding with business while they were debarred by the mob from entering the House of Lords. The Lords took exception to this petition and persuaded the Commons to vote the bishops guilty of high treason. The bishops were hustled off to the Tower and

His Protean forms and Janus aspect Sure
Can ne'r be thought to make our Church secure.
But *Lincoln's* Prelate, swell'd with the old Leaven   65
Of *Pharasees,* Compleats the Number Seven.
Not *Bonner,* that did *London's* Mitre wear,
Was to our Church's Worthys so severe,
Or to her Sons such Mortal hatred bore
In persecuting *Mary's* Reigne of Yore.   70
Cou'dst thou for shame in Stream with *Hoadly* run
T'oppose the Power that put thy Mitre on?
Ne'er more let *Christ-Church* foster such a Snake
In her pure Arms as Loosen'd Trimming *Wake.*

"spent the Time betwixt New-years Even and *Whitsontide* in those safe Walls" (*Bishop Hall's Hard Measure, Written by Himself upon His Impeachment of High Crimes and Misdemeanours, for Defending the Church of England. Being a Case something Parallel to Dr. S——1,* 1710, p. 10).

65. *Lincoln's Prelate:* William Wake (1657–1737) graduated B.A. from Christ Church, Oxford, in October 1676. While chaplain (1682–85) to Richard Graham, Viscount Preston, English ambassador to France, "he quickly made a distinguished figure in the learned world" (*Biographia Britannica, 6,* ii, 4084). Although he was "of nonjuring Principles, & for non-complyance with the Prince and Princess of Orange . . . Secular Interest . . . strangely byass'd him" (Hearne, *8,* 287) to take the oaths to William and Mary and to accept preferment as a chaplain in ordinary to their majesties, a canon of Christ Church (June 1689–1702), and rector of St. James's, Westminster (July 1693–October 1706). During the convocation controversy he wrote *The Authority of Christian Princes over their Ecclesiastical Synods Asserted,* 1697, to which Atterbury replied in *The Rights, Powers, and Privileges of an English Convocation, Stated and Vindicated,* 1700. He was nominated bishop of Lincoln in July and consecrated on 21 October 1705.

the old Leaven: the yeast of dissent; cf. Sacheverell, *The Perils of False Brethren, Both in Church, and State,* 1709, p. 18: "We shall be *convinc'd,* to our *Sorrow,* if We don't *apprehend* that the *Old Leaven* of their *Fore-fathers* is still *Working* in their *Present Generation,*" which Wake quoted twice in his speech against Sacheverell on 17 March 1710 (*Tryal of Dr. Henry Sacheverell,* pp. 343, 344). Most of Wake's speech was a plea for a scheme of comprehension of dissenters within the Church of England, which Sacheverell had called "a *Mungril-Union* of All *Sects*" (p. 396 above).

67. *Bonner:* Edmund Bonner (1500?–1559) served as Henry VIII's envoy to the papal court and was consecrated bishop of London in 1540. In Mary's reign he became "the chiefest instrument of this persecution" of Protestants and "undertook it chearfully, being naturally savage and brutal" (Gilbert Burnet, *The History of the Reformation of the Church of England,* 2 vols., 1679–81, *2,* 304).

68. *severe:* Wake's severity was directed against Sacheverell, "in the censure and punishment of which Divine he zealously concurred with the Archbishop of Canterbury, Dr. Tho. Tenison" (*Biographia Britannica, 7,* 4088).

71–72. Wake is asked how he could agree with Hoadly that power originates with the people (p. 350 above), when it was the queen who made him a bishop?

74. *Trimming:* Considering his views on comprehension (65n. above), it is remarkable that Wake preached before the House of Lords on 30 January 1708 "in Defence of Passive obedience" (Hearne, *2,* 92), for passive obedience was "the monstrous Absurdity" (*Review,* 10 December 1709) that kept many dissenters out of the Church of England.

These Seven Brethren false, a Viperous brood,   75
Belial-sons, oppos'd the Church's Good,
Condemn'd the true Asserter of her Cause,
Repeal'd her Doctrine and her Sacred Laws.
Republicans of *Presbiterian* dye,
Who hate all forms, e'en that of Monarchy,   80
Whose waxen Consciences take those Stamps best
Which Interest, Time, or Party shall Suggest;
Those Lukewarm Sons who fled for want of Zeal
And Courage to promote their Mother's Weal,
Who in her Rescue would not interpose,   85
But left her midst the Fury of her Foes,
Will equally of blame Convicted Stand
With those before who were her Hostile band.
For he that will not when he can defend
The Church's Cause, is sure her Foe, no Friend.   90
    Those few true Sons who firmly did adhere
And always Scorn'd to every point to Veere,
York in the Van, and *Chester* in the Rear,
To future Ages shall transmit their Name
And live Immortal in the Lists of Fame.   95

77. *true Asserter:* Henry Sacheverell.

80. *forms:* See *A Tale of a Nettle,* 26*n.* above.

83. *Lukewarm:* a synonym for "Moderate" (*Dr. Sacheverell and Benjamin Hoadly,* 5*n.* above); cf. Hearne, *2,* 360: "moderation Men in the sense that the Party take the word, that is such as are against the Church of England, Men that are lukewarm."

    Sons who fled: 14 bishops and the archbishop of Canterbury were absent on 20 March 1710 when the vote on Sacheverell's guilt was taken in the House of Lords.

88. *those before:* possibly an allusion to *The Mitred Club* (*POAS,* Yale, *6,* 510), the 12 bishops who voted against the first bill to prevent occasional conformity in December 1702 (*POAS,* Yale, *6,* 510).

91. *true Sons:* The six who voted against Sacheverell's impeachment; cf. *The Save-Alls,* below.

93. *York:* John Sharp (1645–1714), archbishop of York (1691–1714) and Anne's principal advisor on preferments in the church.

    Chester: Sir William Dawes of Bocking, Essex, third baronet (1671–1724), brought up "the Rear" because he was the most recently consecrated (8 February 1708) of the six.

The Save-Alls.
Or,
The Bishops Who Voted for Dr. Sacheverell
(8 May 1710)

Since the bishops who voted against Sacheverell had become *The Seven Extinguishers,* those who voted for him by the same metaphor became *The Save-Alls,* six contrivances for allowing the *"Gospel Light"* (p. 413 above) to "burn to the end" (Title, *n.* below). *The Save-Alls,* therefore, is pure panegyric. The tone is unremittingly serious. It is a legend of good bishops fashioned "for future Ages' use" (line 8).

But *The Save-Alls* generates a kind of irony that is not illustrated in the wholly ironical *Country Parson's Honest Advice,* for example. The fact that Henry Compton, bishop of London, had literally taken arms against James II, makes a strange contrast with the claim in the poem that there was "no Tincture" of sedition in his veins (51–52). Similarly, the fact that George Hooper had taken the oaths of supremacy and allegiance to William and Mary makes a strange contrast with the insistence in the poem that he was like Thomas Ken: "Like him . . . Like him" (91, 93). For Thomas Ken refused to take the oaths and was deprived of the bishopric to which Hooper succeeded in December 1703.

Even a phrase can betray. When the brilliant, worldly, and erratic Thomas Sprat, bishop of Rochester, is praised for "unsuspected Honesty," the reader today knows that "unsuspected" here means "above suspicion." But there were other meanings current in the eighteenth century, such as "unsuspected-to-exist Honesty," which make an ironical contrast with the rest of the praise of Sprat. This kind of unconscious irony raises problems of interpretation and criticism that can only be stated here. But it may be true that men, like events in the age of Queen Anne, are so intrinsically double that to describe them, even soberly and admiringly, is enough to make ironies.

This is the point that is made by the Whiggish author of *An Answer to the Six Save-Alls* ("Since Save-Alls are so much the Mode of the Nation"), 1710:

> without dispute,
> Should a Whiggish Brother but . . .

> . . . give a Description of all done and mist:
> How foolishly High-Church, wou'd look . . . .

The Luttrell copy of the second edition of *The Save-Alls* (*Ba*), now at Harvard, is dated 8 May 1710.

The Tory panegyrist remains anonymous.

THE SAVE-ALLS.
OR,
THE BISHOPS WHO VOTED FOR DR. SACHEVERELL

While Faction with its baleful Breath proclaims
The loud Applause of undeserving Names,
And crys up Tenets that Rebellion teach,
From *Hoadly*'s Writings and from *Sarum*'s Speech,
The Muse, obedient to her Prince, should rise   5
To bear transcendent Merit to the Skies;
And Truth's Defenders piously deduce,
From Time to Time, for future Ages use.
    O *ANNA!* couldst thou but a while regard
Some Patriots Vows, and let their Pray'rs be heard!   10
Couldst thou but once thy gracious Favours deign
To Doctrines that support thy glorious Reign,
Prelates would not the sacred Lawn disgrace
By preaching up Resistance to thy Face;
Nor in thy Court Republicans be seen   15
To wrong their Country and deceive their Queen;
But *Rochester,* restor'd from his Disgrace,
Would be thy Deputy in *Wharton*'s Place,
And fam'd *Sacheverell,* unsuspended, be

Title. A save-all is "A means for preventing loss or waste." More specifically it is "A contrivance to hold a candle-end in a candle-stick . . . so that it may burn to the end" (*OED*), another device that "the *Moderns*" had to invent because Homer failed to provide "the least Direction" for one (Swift, *Prose, 1,* 79). "Any card-matches or save-alls" was a familiar London cry (Richard Steele, *The Tatler,* ed. George A. Aitken, 4 vols., 1898–99, *1,* 41n.).

1. *Faction:* Cf. *Moderation Display'd,* 2n. above and *The Junto,* 3–4, above.

4. *Hoadly's Writings:* See p. 350 above.

Sarum's Speech: In his speech on 16 March 1710 in the House of Lords, Burnet argued that from 1558 to 1628 and from 1640 to 1688 the right of rebellion—he called it "Self-defence"—was "the Publick and Constant Doctrine of this Church" (*Tryal of Dr. Henry Sacheverell,* p. 210).

14. "The Queen sat intent during the whole debate" on 16 March 1710 when Burnet spoke (Geoffrey Holmes, *The Trial of Doctor Sacheverell,* Eyre Methuen, 1973, p. 216).

17. *Rochester:* Rochester had remained out of office since he was dismissed as lord lieutenant of Ireland in February 1703; cf. "*Celsus* Disgrac'd," (Shippen, *Moderation Display'd,* 74, above). There may have been rumors in the summer of 1710 that he would return to Dublin to replace Wharton, but on 21 September Rochester was made lord president of the council and Ormonde was appointed lord lieutenant of Ireland a month later.

19. *Sacheverell:* According to the terms of his sentence, Sacheverell was suspended from

Possess'd of some fat wealthy Bishop's See.   20
Yet tho', for some Offences yet unknown,
Heav'n bears with such as these too near the Throne;
Tho' Loyalty for some time must give place
To faithless Anarchy's triumphant Race,
And Bishops, to the scandal of their Coat,   25
Against the Apostle's Exhortation, vote;
As most of them, altho' the Cause is Heav'ns,
Have left the Church at *SIXES* and at *SEVENS*.
Justice forbids that we should Virtue wrong,
Or rob Religion's Champions of their Song,   30
Who for their own and Monarch's Rights have stood,
Lavishly Bold and desperately Good,
And, fearful of Prerogative's Invasion,
Are justly styl'd *The SAVE-ALLS of the Nation.*
Such is the dauntless *YORK,* whose silver Hairs   35
Are crown'd with Learning equal to his Years.
Of Post exalted, yet of humble Mind,
Studious of good, beneficent, and kind;
As meek as *Moses* and as *Joshua* brave,
When call'd to suffer or when call'd to save.   40
Fix'd on himself, immoveable, and true,
He treads the Steps he bids us to pursue.

---

preaching for three years (*On the Sentence Passed by the House of Lords on Dr. Sacheverell*, 12n. above). There was a rumor that he would be made a bishop in August 1711 (Swift, *Journal*, p. 342; *The High-Church Address to Dr. Henry Sacheverell*, 1710, p. 6)

22. *such as these:* "Court Republicans" (15), like Burnet and Sunderland (*To the Tune of Ye Commons and Peers*, headnote, above).

26. *the Apostle's Exhortation:* "If then ye have judgments of things pertaining to this life, set them to judge who are least esteemed in the church" (1 Corinthians 6:4).

28. *SIXES and . . . SEVENS:* See p. 413 above.

35. *YORK:* John Sharp (1645–1714) graduated B.A. from Christ's College, Cambridge, in 1663 and as the rector of St. Giles's-in-the-Fields, soon became one of the most popular preachers in London. He survived persecution by James II's court of ecclesiastical commission to enjoy "no small favour" at the court of William and Mary. He was installed archbishop of York in October 1691. He was said to be *"not absolutely attached to a party"* until the accession of Queen Anne, but then the influence of his lifelong patron, the earl of Nottingham, "brought him over to be the head of the high church party." He preached the sermon at Anne's coronation and became her principal adviser in ecclesiastical preferments. He was "*a plain-dealing man . . .* who neither disguised his sentiments on any occasion, nor feared at any time to take the liberty of following his own judgment" (*DNB, 17,* 1346–47; Thomas Sharp, *The Life of John Sharp,* 2 vols., 1825, *1,* 253, 254; *Thoresby, 1,* 436–37). He was one of the managers of the bills to prevent occasional conformity in 1702–04 and made a speech in defense of Sacheverell on 16 March 1710 (Luttrell, *6,* 558).

As undebauch'd by Courtiers Smiles or Frowns,
He stands by God's Prerogative and the Crown's.
The same his Precepts which of old he taught,   45
From Reason and from Revelation brought,
His Language copious and his Meaning strong,
His Heart not inconsistent with his Tongue;
For Alms, for Arts, for Probity rever'd,
And *Guiltless* as the Preacher he'd have *clear'd.*   50
   Such *LONDON* is, whose high descended Veins
Admit no Tincture of seditious Stains;
Loyal and Just, as was his Sire who fell
A Sacrifice to Treason and to Hell,
When Rebels their Allegiance durst disown   55
And fought against their King to guard the Throne.
Oh! had not one of this Illustrious Blood
Departed from the Paths his Father trod,
And mingled with a base Malignant Herd,

51. *LONDON:* Henry Compton (1632–1713) was the sixth and youngest son of Spencer Compton, second earl of Northampton, who was killed fighting for Charles I in 1643. Henry Compton himself was a soldier before he was ordained a priest in 1662. He was educated at Queen's College, Oxford (1649–52), and in travel abroad until after the restoration. He rose rapidly in the church, becoming a canon of Christ Church (1669), bishop of Oxford (December 1674), dean of the chapel royal (July 1675), and bishop of London (December 1675). He was made responsible for the religious education of the Princesses Mary and Anne, and officiated at both of their weddings. But when James II was encouraged to destroy the Church of England, it was the "Bishop of *London,* who first broke the Ice by refusing the Illegal Suspension of Dr. [*Sharp* (35n. above)]" (Defoe, *More Short-Ways with the Dissenters,* 1704, p. 19). Compton was the only bishop among the seven signers of the invitation to William of Orange in June 1688 (GEC, *7,* 508), and he further outraged the Jacobites by marching into Oxford in November 1688 "in a blew Cloak, and with a naked Sword" (Hearne, *1,* 304) with the Princess Anne under his protection. Anne made him her lord almoner in November 1702 in place of the Whiggish bishop of Worcester and installed him in lodgings at St. James's palace from which Burnet had been removed (Luttrell, *5,* 238, 257). Compton voted for the bills to prevent occasional conformity in 1702–04, against the motion of December 1705 that the church was not in danger (p. 146 above), and for Sacheverell in March 1710.

57. *one:* Spencer Compton (1673?–1743), the third son of the third earl of Northampton, and the bishop's nephew, was the black sheep of the family who mingled with the "base Malignant Herd." As a member of parliament for Eye, Suffolk (1695–1710), East Grinstead, Sussex (1713–15), and county Sussex (1715–27), he is not known to have cast a Tory vote. He was rewarded for his apostasy by being made chairman of the committee on elections (1705–10), treasurer to Prince George at £540 a year (Chamberlayne, 1708, p. 637), and a member of the committee appointed in December 1709 to draw up articles of impeachment against Sacheverell (*CJ, 16,* 241). On 1 March 1710 he spoke in support of the third article (*Tryal of Dr. Henry Sacheverell,* pp. 144–46).

To be to Offices of Trust preferr'd,   60
What Family could more conspicuous shine
In every Branch of its untainted Line?
  Such *DURHAM*, whose inimitable Zeal
For Church and Queen, and for his Country's Weal,
Whose early Labours and continued Care   65
Add lustre to the Coronet and Chair,
And might more noble Sentiments infuse
Than what are now received amongst the *CREWS*.
  Such *ROCHESTER*, in whose unshaken Breast,
Peace, Knowledge, Loyalty, divinely rest.   70
For unsuspected Honesty renown'd,
With Age, with Honour, and with Judgment crown'd;
His Thoughts surprising, as their Sense is sound;

63. *DURHAM:* Nathaniel Crew (1633–1721), fifth son of the first Lord Crew of Stene, graduated B.A. from Lincoln College, Oxford, in 1656 and D.C.L. in 1664. He became rector of Gray's Inn (1668–72) and a member of the Inner Temple (1674–1700). As a favorite of the duke of York he was appointed dean of Chichester (1669), bishop of Oxford (1671), whence he was translated in 1674 to the rich see of Durham that he bought from Nell Gwynne (GEC, *3,* 534), and a member of the privy council (1676–79, 1686–89). Upon the accession of James II, Crew succeeded Compton (51*n.*) as dean of the chapel royal and then served on the court of high commission that was reactivated to try Compton. Together with Thomas Sprat (69*n.*) he administered the diocese of London during Compton's suspension (1686–88). As a result he was excepted by name from the general pardon of May 1690, but no action was taken against him. In 1697 he succeeded his brother as third Lord Crew of Stene. In Anne's reign he occupied himself increasingly with charitable works in his diocese and with voting Tory in the House of Lords, where he spoke on Sacheverell's behalf on 16 March 1710 (Luttrell, *6,* 558). The "noble Sentiments" in which other Crews were deficient, may have been loyalty to the crown, for the first Lord Crew of Stene supported parliament in the civil war and the second Lord Crew voted to exclude James II from the throne.

69. *ROCHESTER:* Thomas Sprat (1635–1713) graduated B.A. from Wadham College, Oxford, in June 1654 and became a fellow (June 1657–March 1670) at the time that meetings in the rooms of the warden, Peter Wilkins, were leading to the incorporation of the Royal Society in July 1662. He also wrote enough poetry to be "known to some by the name of Pindaric Sprat" (Wood, *4,* 727), and Thomas Gray thought he might "perhaps" be the last of the metaphysicals (*The Works of Thomas Gray,* ed. John Mitford, 2 vols., 1816, *1,* lxxxix). At the restoration Sprat "turned around with the virtuosi" (*DNB, 18,* 828) and was ordained a priest in March 1661. Thereafter, with some help from George Villiers, duke of Buckingham, "Ecclesiastical benefices . . . fell fast upon him" (Johnson, *Lives, 2,* 33), until he became dean of Westminster (September 1683) and bishop of Rochester (November 1684), both of which preferments he held to his death. He served with Nathaniel Crew (63*n.*) on James II's court of high commission, but gave his "positive Vote" for the bishop of London (51*n.*) and resigned shortly thereafter (Sprat, *Two Letters Written in the Year 1689 . . . To the . . . Late Earl of Dorset,* 1711, p. 5). He was not a favorite of William for he voted against the motion to declare him king of England (Tindal, *4,* ii, 162), but he read the service for the day at the coronation of Anne and in December 1702 it was rumored that he was to be made

The Pride and Advocate of *Britains* Isle,
As well as the Refiner of its Stile: 75
Whether in Verse of *Athens' Plagues* he writes,
Or Treatises in nervous Prose endites,
Solemn when he harangues and sprightly when he bites;
As happy Periods his Descriptions close,
And Satyr mixt with Panegyrick flows,   80
Whether he points at heavy *Sorbier*'s Flegm,
Or makes a *King's Society* his Theme.
    Such *BATH AND WELLS*, the raptur'd Muse inspires
With ardent Wishes and with holy Fires,
With Vows which are incessantly preferr'd,   85
That such a Life as his may long be spar'd,

---

primate of Ireland (Luttrell, *5*, 166, 251). The post, however, went to Swift's friend, Narcissus Marsh. "When the cause of Sacheverell put the publick in commotion," Samuel Johnson said, Sprat "honestly appeared among the friends of the church" (*Lives, 2*, 37).

    74. *Advocate of Britain:* Samuel de Sorbière's *Relation d'un Voyage en Angleterre,* Paris, 1664, aroused feelings of national pride in England more intense than any until the publication of *The True-Born Englishman* (December 1700). Sprat, with some help from John Evelyn, wrote the reply, *Observations on Monsieur de Sorbier's Voyage into England* (1665), a new edition of which had just been published in May–June 1709 (Arber, *3*, 643).

    75. *Stile:* Critics from John Evelyn (*4*, 188) to Samuel Johnson (*Lives, 1*, 1) have praised Sprat's pure and plain prose style. "His Name deserves principally to be recorded in History," Abel Boyer (*History,* p. 260) said, for "his raising the *English* Language to that Purity and Beauty, which former Writers were wholly Strangers to, and those who come after him can but imitate."

    76. *Athens' Plagues:* Sprat's *The Plague of Athens . . . Attempted in English, after Incomparable Dr. Cowley's Pindarick Way* was published in 1659.

    80. *Satyr:* The duke of Buckingham "had . . . the assistance of Dr. Tho. Sprat his Chaplain . . . in the composing" of *The Rehearsal* (1671) (Wood, *4*, 209; cf. *POAS,* Yale, *1*, 328) and Elkanah Settle, "in his *Anti-Achitophel* [*Absalom Senior: Or, Achitophel Transpros'd* (1682)], was assisted by . . . Sprat, and several of the best hands of those times" (Spence, *1*, 278).

    82. *King's Society:* Sprat's *The History of the Royal-Society of London* was published in 1667.

    83. *BATH AND WELLS:* George Hooper (1640–1727), whom Thomas Madox called "incomparably learned" (Hearne, *3*, 177), graduated B.A. from Christ Church, Oxford, in 1660 and became rector of Lambeth in 1675. Upon the marriage of Princess Mary in 1677, Hooper was appointed her almoner in The Hague. It was here that the prince of Orange assured him that he would never be a bishop. Mary appointed him to the deanery of Canterbury during the king's absence in 1691, but Hooper "thought he deserved to be raised higher" (Burnet, *2*, 282). In February 1701 he was elected prolocutor to the lower house of convocation and became one of those "Angry men" whose zeal for the church led them to attack even the authority of the bishops and the crown (ibid., *2*, 338). He was finally raised to the episcopal bench himself in June 1703 as the bishop of St. Asaph, whence he was translated to Bath and Wells in December 1703 (Luttrell, *5*, 304, 368). He spoke and voted for Sacheverell in March 1710 and when he died Hearne (*9*, 349) called him "the very best on the Bench of the present Bishops."

May still adorn the Mitre which he wears,
And teach his Brethren how to fill their Chairs;
The best of Prelates and the best of Men,
A worthy Successor to Bishop *Ken*,   90
Like him by no Consideration sway'd
To see his Flocks misled or Church betray'd,
Like him, when Storms impending threaten'd, bold,
So were the Pastors of God's Church of old,
Till *Moderation* made Devotion cold: 95
A Game trump'd up by *Sectaries* of late
To veil their Malice and disguise their Hate.
    Such *CHESTER* is, from whose unerring Quill
Eternal Truths, like heav'nly Dews, distil;
As soft Persuasion dwells upon his Voice,   100
And plain Instructive Doctrines are his choice.
Atheists from his Discourses Christians turn,
And Proselites their vitious Actions mourn,

90. *Ken:* Thomas Ken (1638–1711), who was raised in the household of Izaak Walton, graduated B.A. from New College, Oxford, in 1661. He then served as chaplain to Princess Mary at The Hague and in November 1684 was appointed bishop of Bath and Wells. Although he resisted James II, he refused to take the oaths to William and Mary and was deprived of his bishopric in April 1691. Thereafter he lived mainly at Longleat, the estate of Thomas Thynne, Viscount Weymouth, again declining to take the oaths, in order to be restored to Bath and Wells, in April 1702 ([J. L. Anderdon], *The Life of Thomas Ken*, 2nd ed., 2 vols., 1854, *2*, 700). He was, as Hearne (*3*, 136) said, "a truly good and pious Man."

95. *Moderation:* See *Dr. Sacheverell and Benjamin Hoadly*, 5n. above.

98. *CHESTER:* William Dawes (1671–1724), the third and youngest son of Sir John Dawes of Roehampton, Surrey, first baronet, matriculated in July 1687 at St. John's College, Oxford, whence he transferred to St. Catharine's College, Cambridge, upon succeeding as third baronet in 1690. Before he was thirty he had been appointed a chaplain-in-ordinary to William III (1696), elected master of St. Catharine's (August 1697–1714), and vice chancellor of Cambridge (1698–99). A sermon that he preached on 5 November 1697 so impressed the king that "a few days after" he made him a canon of Worcester (*The Whole Works of the Most Reverend Father in God, Sir William Dawes, Br.*, 3 vols., 1733, *1*, xx). But another sermon that he preached before Queen Anne on 30 January 1705 prevented his appointment to the see of Lincoln. "He was not afraid to utter some bold Truths, which at that time were not so well relish'd by certain persons, that were in power, and who took occasion . . . to persuade the Queen (contrary to her inclination) to give it to [William Wake (*The History of Seven*, 65n.)]" (ibid., *1*, xxx). In May 1707, however, Anne, "of her own mere motion, named Sir *William* to succeed in the Bishoprick of *Chester*" (ibid., *1*, xxxi; cf. *English Historical Review, 82* [October 1967], 737). He was "a large personable Man," Hearne (*4*, 313) said, with "a good plausible way of preaching," and he both spoke and voted for Sacheverell.

Quill: Besides his sermons, Sir William published a long poem written before he was 18, entitled *The Anatomy of Atheisme* (1693), and several popular devotional tracts but he was "not at all learned" (Hearne, *4*, 313).

Unable their old Courses to pursue.
When he lays every Sinner's Crimes in view,   105
Horror and Dread within their Breasts instils,
And even saves their Souls against their wills.
To read him truly, is to read his Life,
All of a Piece and never known to Strife;
But when false Tenets would take place of true,   110
And old Opinions are laid by for New,
Then Zealous on a Rock God's Church to fix,
The Youngest, not the Meanest, of the Six.

104–09. The phrases, "old Courses," "Crimes in View," "All of a Piece," recall the final chorus from Dryden's *The Secular Masque*(1700).

113. *Youngest:* Of the six Save-Alls, Dawes was both the most recently consecrated (8 February 1708) and the youngest in age (39 years).

The Westminster Combat
(9 May 1710)

Seven of the yelping hounds of *The Old Pack* and four new recruits from the impeachment committee are here transmogrified into 11 epic warriors who "rudely advance" (line 87) to the attack on Sacheverell but are repelled by the "small but surprizing" (73) army of Sacheverell's defense lawyers.

Defoe had presented the Sacheverell trial as a battle between rival armies in several numbers of the *Review,* but Defoe's warriors are faceless abstractions like the Bank, the Law, Union and Toleration, who fight "under the Command of that Old General CONSTITUTION" (*Review,* 22 April 1710), whereas the warriors of *The Westminster Combat* achieve at least a shadow of individuality. Sir James Montagu "fir'd a Volley of Words without Means, / Then trembling sat himself down" (31–32). Nor is the poem totally devoid of shape: it begins and ends with "Good Principles" (4, 88) and the prorogation of parliament (2, 81). But the verse is always in danger of lapsing into metrical prose and the most that Thomas Hearne (*3,* 7) could say about it was that it was "honest, tho' not very well written."

The Luttrell copy of *C,* at Harvard, is dated 9 May 1710, but the Tory author has not been identified.

THE WESTMINSTER COMBAT

'Tis odd to conceive what a War has been wag'd
  Among the late Commons of *Britain,*
Where Whigs and Low-flyers so hotly engag'd,
  Good Principles soon to get rid on.

They Fought and did Battel a certain Divine,   5
  So furious in *Westminster-Hall,*
That the Trophies and Triumphs from *Danube* and *Rhine*
  Hung shatter'd and ready to fall.

He Preach'd, as 'tis said, at the City's St. *Paul*'s,
  With a Wicked and Vicious Intent,   10
To stir up the People to break down the Walls
  Of Peace and Just Government.

For not to resist, you know, is the Way
  To destroy the Peace of the Nation,
And not to Rebel, is truly to say   15
  You spurn at True Moderation.

2. *late:* The second session of Anne's third parliament was prorogued on 5 April 1710.

4. *Good Principles:* These, as the poem makes clear, are "Loyal Principles" (88): "not to resist" (13), "Obedience to Kings" (24), and "Loyalty Passive" (56).

5. *Divine:* Henry Sacheverell.

6. *Westminster-Hall:* Sacheverell's trial before the peers was held in Westminster Hall, adjacent to the houses of parliament. It was "esteemed the largest room in Europe unsupported by pillars; being 270 feet in length, and 74 in breadth" (Noorthouck, p. 699).

7. *Trophies:* Battle trophies were hung in Westminster Hall (*An Ode, Humbly Inscrib'd,* 177n. above). "It will, no doubt, be a mighty Comfort to our Grand-children," Swift wrote in *The Conduct of the Allies,* "when they see a few Rags hung up in *Westminster-Hall,* which cost an hundred Millions, whereof they are paying the Arrears, and boasting, as Beggars do, that their Grandfathers were Rich and Great" (Swift, *Prose, 6,* 55–56).

9. *Preach'd:* See *On Dr. Sacheverell's Sermon Preach'd at St. Paul's, Nov. 5. 1709,* above.

11. *To stir up:* The phrase is from Article IV of the impeachment charges: "as a publick Incendiary, he perswades Her Majesty's Subjects to keep up a Distinction of Factions and Parties . . . and excites and stirs them up to Arms and Violence" (*Tryal of Dr. Henry Sacheverell,* p. 10). In the poem, of course, the phrase is ironical, for in fact Sacheverell said that the "*Security* of our *Government* . . . is founded upon . . . the utter *Illegality* of *Resistance* upon any *Pretence* whatsoever" (*The Perils of False Brethren, Both in Church, and State,* 1709, p. 12).

13–16. These lines, which say the same thing twice, expose the "Modern Inconsistency" in the Whigs' argument that preaching non-violence produces violence.

16. *True Moderation:* equivalent, in the context of the irony, to the Whigs' right of revolution (*Leviathan,* 42n. above).

Therefore to prevent such a mischievous Blunder,
   Which the Parsons so often commit,
The *Posse* is rais'd, and the Commons out-Thunder
   New Votes to guard the Pulpit.   20

The Doctor's Arraign'd of High Crimes and Transgressions,
   For preaching such Damnable Things,
And the rest of the Order must hate all Expressions
   Which encourage Obedience to Kings.

And quite to suppress such a Pestilent Notion   25
   Which Scandals the Rights of the People,
Their *Armies* are Marshal'd and now upon *motion*
   To pull down the Churches with Steeples.

The first that Assaulted was valiant Sir *James*,
   A Warriour of Famous Renown,   30
Who fir'd a Volley of Words without Means,
   Then trembling sat himself down.

Then *Dolben*, his Second, quite out of his Reason

21. *High Crimes:* The articles of impeachment charged that Sacheverell had said: I. that the revolution was illegal, II. that the toleration of dissenters was a mistake, III. that the Church of England was in danger, and IV. that his books and sermons tended to incite rebellion (*Tryal of Dr. Henry Sacheverell*, pp. 8–10).

28. *Churches with Steeples:* Dissenters called churches "steeple-houses" (*OED*).

29. *Sir James:* Sir James Montagu (1666–1723), a grandson of Henry Montagu, first earl of Manchester, and younger brother of Lord Halifax, was educated at the Middle Temple and became one of the most successful lawyers in England. He defended John Tutchin against libel charges in 1704 (Howell, *14*, 1095–1200) and argued so vehemently for a writ of habeas corpus for the Aylesbury electors that he was himself committed to the custody of the sergeant at arms in February 1705. Upon his discharge he was knighted (April 1705) and made one of the queen's counsel (November 1705) (Luttrell, *5*, 519, 524, 542, 609), whence he was advanced to solicitor general (April 1707–October 1708) and then attorney general (October 1708–September 1710). It was in the latter role that he "opened the charges against Dr. Sacheverell" (Foss, *8*, 43) on the first day of the trial (27 February 1710) by delivering the Commons' replication to Sacheverell's answer to the charges against him (*Tryal of Dr. Henry Sacheverell*, pp. 24–31). In parliament where he sat for Tregoney, Cornwall (1695–98), Beeralston, Devonshire (December 1698–1700), and Carlisle, Cumberland (1705–13), Montagu invariably voted Whig.

31. *a Volley of Words:* "The Att: Gen: . . . opened the Nature of the Charge in generall, without applying himself to any particular Article" (Osborn MS. Box 21, No. 22, f. 2v). He concluded by assuring the Lords that "When we shall have . . . [proved] every Particular charged on the Doctor in the Articles of Impeachment, the Commons will not doubt of your Lordships Judgment against this Defendant" (*Tryal of Dr. Henry Sacheverell*, p. 31).

33. *Dolben:* Dolben must be imagined to second Montagu as in a duel, for it was Nicholas Lechmere (41n.) who spoke second (*Tryal of Dr. Henry Sacheverell*, p. 31). Dolben spoke to the third article on 1 March 1710.

To see the Chief act such a Buffle,

With Lyon-like Rage endeavours to seize on   35

The Doctor and's Cause in the Scuffle.

The next that appear'd was the Learned Sir *Peter*,

In Antiquity Skilful and Great,

Who pour'd out such Charges that wounded much deeper,

But yet he was woundily beat.   40

Then him to relieve, do's *Lechmere* aspire,

With *Jekyl*, a Judge in the *West*,

Who Bluster'd and Rav'd and swore they wou'd fire

The Doctrine as well as the Priest.

Lord *William* comes next, most nicely equipt,   45

34. *a Buffle:* "A fool" (*OED*, citing this line).

36. *the Scuffle:* In his peroration Dolben represented the danger to England of "such False Brethren, as are now at your Lordship's Bar," whereupon Sir Simon Harcourt, Sacheverell's counsel, "made him a very low Bow, which very much diverted the House." An explanation was demanded. "Mr D[olben] rose, and repeating My L[or]ds twice, after a considerable pause, and in a great deal of Confusion, said—I only meant the Prisoner at the Barr; which Explanation, though flat Nonsence, and a Lye, was admitted" (Osborn MS. Box 21, No. 22, ff. 8, 9).

37. *Learned Sir Peter:* "Sir Peter King . . . has written a Rhapsodical History of the Apostles Creed, and is much cry'd up by the Party for his Learning tho' he never receiv'd any Litterary Education being bred up to a Mechanical Calling" (Hearne, *2*, 328).

38. *In Antiquity Skilful:* Besides *A History of the Apostles Creed, with Critical Observations on Several Articles* (1702), King had published other learned works (*The Old Pack*, 74n. above).

39. *Charges that wounded:* King's speech on the second article of impeachment "aggravated the doctor's peevish censure of the Toleration Act into a 'malicious, scandalous, and seditious libel' " (*DNB, 11*, 144–45). Even a Tory spectator had to agree that King spoke "very well" (Osborn MS., Box 21, No. 22, f. 6v).

41. *Lechmere:* Nicholas Lechmere (1675–1727), a younger son in one of the oldest families in England, left Merton College, Oxford, without taking a degree and was called to the bar in 1698 from the Middle Temple. He was, as Hearne (*2*, 351) said, "a most vile, stinking Whigg," who owed his seat in parliament for Appleby, Westmorland (1708–10), Cockermouth, Cumberland (1710–17), and Tewkesbury, Gloucester (June 1717–October 1721), to the interest of Lord Wharton. He was made a queen's counsel in May 1708 (Luttrell *6*, 302) and was one of the youngest and most aggressive members of the impeachment committee. Even his nephew called him "violent and overbearing" (*DNB, 11*, 777). Lechmere summarized the case against Sacheverell on 2 March (Osborn MS. Box 21, No. 22, f. 10).

43. *Bluster'd:* The construction does not make clear who "bluster'd," but it was reported that Lechmere "inveigh'd with unusual Bitterness against the Christian Doctrines of Passive Obedience, and Non-Resistance" (ibid., f. 3).

45. *Lord William:* Lord William Powlett spoke to the second article on 28 February 1710 and "read (or mumbled over) every Word of his Speech, so that almost no body could hear him; it was very short, and the Word Heterodox proved something too hard for him, and he was pleas'd to make use of Pathick, instead of Passive; nothing could attone for what he said,

With Musquet and Ball in his Hand,
But alass! of his Powder and Flint he was stript,
And therefore was put to a Stand.

Stanhope impatient, no longer cou'd bear
To see his own Troops disappointed, 50
But storms and discharges and rattles in th'Air
Against Kings and all that's Anointed.

Then comes Mr. *Cowper,* as part of the Rout,
Well known in an Eminent Cause,
And fights with his Friends most brave and most *STOUT* 55
'Gainst Loyalty Passive and Laws.

But the fiercest and keenest of all the Commanders
Was Trusty Sir *Thomas* of *Darby,*
Whose Prowess and Courage surpriz'd the Bystanders

---

but his Shortness, and that he might have a better Title to our Approbation on that Score, he skip'd two Pages, though 'tis said the Connection he happen'd upon by this Mistake, was Heterodox Church" (ibid., f. 6v).

49. *Stanhope:* "Gen: Stanhope spoke with a Spirit, which in him, being a Souldier, was called Fire, in another would have been Indecent Passion" (ibid., f. 5v).

52. *Against Kings:* Stanhope disposed of kings and divine right by supposing "that there is not, at this Day, subsisting any Nation or Government in the World, whose first Original did not receive its Foundation, either from Resistance, or Compact" (*Tryal of Dr. Henry Sacheverell,* p. 106). Peter the Great would have been amused at such assurance.

53. *Cowper:* Spencer Cowper (1669?–1727) was a younger brother of the lord chancellor, William Cowper, and the grandfather of William Cowper the poet. He was educated at the Westminster School and Lincoln's Inn and succeeded his brother as a member for Beeralston, Devonshire (December 1705–10). But Lord Stamford, who controlled the borough, decided not to let Cowper stand in October 1710 (Hertfordshire County R. O. MS. Panshanger D/EP F 54, f. 79; Devon R. O. MS. 346M/F67, Francis Drake to Sir Peter King, 5 June 1711). In the next reign he was returned for Truro, Cornwall (1715–27).

54. *an Eminent Cause:* Spencer Cowper was tried in July 1699 for the murder of Sarah Stout whose body had been found floating in the river at Hertford four months before. He was acquitted, but the case created a sensation (*POAS,* Yale, *6,* 420–21) and ruined Cowper's reputation—irretrievably in Hertfordshire (*East Anglian Studies,* ed. Lionel M. Munby, Cambridge, W. Heffer & Sons, 1968, pp. 127–34).

58. *Sir Thomas:* Sir Thomas Parker (1666?–1727) was educated at Trinity College, Cambridge, and the Inner Temple, whence he was called to the bar in 1691. Like Sir James Montagu, he appeared for the defense in the famous *Reg.* v. *John Tutchin* trial in November 1704 (29n. above). In May 1705 he was returned to parliament for Derby (1705–March 1710) and voted Whig in every recorded division. He was made the queen's serjeant in June 1705 and knighted the next month (Luttrell, *5,* 560, 571).

59. *Prowess:* Parker spoke to the fourth article against Sacheverell on 1 March and then replied to Sacheverell's answer on 10 March. "The best judges say Parker spoke the best" (HMC *Portland MSS.,* *4,* 533). Thomas Hearne (*2,* 360) agreed that Parker was "a good (tho'

Because a Chief Justice was hard by.   60

For *Walpole* and *Smith* and the rest of the Clan,
    Who the Doctor so bravely accosted,
Their Exploits were so mean and their Actions so vain,
    That they all deserve to be Posted.

To these may be added another Brigade   65
    Of Bishops and Temporal Lords,
Whose *Weapons* were ready, whose *Speeches* were made,
    Full charg'd not with Sense but with Words.

These all, with a Fury becoming their Zeal
    For Liberty and Moderation,   70
Did Fight, and were Beat, their Arguments fail,
    To the Pleasure and Joy of the Nation.

The Doctor, whose Army was small but surprizing,

---

not an honest) Lawyer," a judgment that was corroborated in February 1725 when Parker himself was impeached for "enormous abuses" as lord chancellor.

60. *Chief Justice:* On 10 March the "Managers against Dr. Sacheverell . . . finish'd their Reply. The whole was clos'd by Sir Thomas Parker . . . who stands fair for being Ld. Chief Justice of England. He was very severe against Dr. Sacheverell, and us'd very ill Language upon the occasion, calling him an Impostor, a false Prophet, and said that he had forfeited his Orders, with abundance of other stuff" (Hearne, *2,* 359). The next day Parker kissed her majesty's hand to be chief justice (Luttrell, *6,* 556). "This great Promotion," Burnet (*2,* 543) said, "seemed an evident Demonstration of the Queen's approving the Prosecution; for none of the Managers had treated *Sacheverel* so severely as he had done."

61. *Walpole:* "Mr. Walpole spoke with some Fire, but very abusively, and us'd Language worthy of himself, but not at all becoming the great Judicature they were before . . . His Sp[ee]ch was all aiming at Turns, & Wit, but falling wretchedly short" (Osborn MS. Box 21, No. 22, f. 5).

Smith: John Smith, chancellor of the exchequer, made a short speech in support of Article IV on 1 March (*Tryal of Dr. Henry Sacheverell,* pp. 170–73).

the rest: The nine managers not mentioned by name in the poem are Henry Boyle, Spencer Compton, Lord Coningsby, William Thompson, Robert Eyres, Sir John Hawles, Sir John Holland, Henry Mordaunt, and Sir David Dalrymple. The last two, however, never appeared in court (Osborn MS. Box 21, No. 22, f. 2).

64. *Posted:* "To expose to ignominy, obloquy, or ridicule" (*OED,* citing this line).

66. *Bishops:* The speeches of four Whig bishops, Gilbert Burnet of Salisbury, William Talbot of Oxford, William Wake of Lincoln, and Charles Trimnell of Norwich, were published (*Tryal of Dr. Henry Sacheverell,* pp. ²3–16, ³2–63).

Temporal Lords: A paragraph of Wharton's speech of 16 March is preserved in *Parl. Hist., 6,* 831, but apparently the only published speech of a temporal lord was that by Haversham in defense of Sacheverell.

69. *with a Fury:* "our Men of *incensed Moderation,*" as Swift called them (*Prose, 3,* 98).

73. *Army . . . small:* Arrayed against the 20 managers of the Commons' case against Henry Sacheverell were the four lawyers whom he had chosen to be his counsel: Sir Simon

Did totally them Overthrow;
They smote him i'th'Arse, but still his Uprising   75
Is owing to that Lucky Blow.

The Mob's of his side, the Ladies appear
All over the Town in his Favour,
Which galls the poor Managers, hanging their Ear
Like *Garrard* or any False Brother.   80

Harcourt, the friend of Harley and former attorney general (April 1707–October 1708), Constantine Phipps, Serjeant John Pratt, and Robert Raymond (Luttrell, *6*, 535). The last two, however, "who were for a short answer to the articles against him" resigned when their advice was overruled (Luttrell, *6*, 540; Hearne, *2*, 338). The Lords then appointed Duncan Dee, common serjeant of the city of London, Samuel Dodds, and Humphrey Henchman, D.C.L., to replace them (Hearne, *2*, 345). Sir Simon spoke in Sacheverell's defense for two hours on 3 March "and came off with much Applause" (ibid., *2*, 354). On 6 March, however, Sacheverell was deprived of his assistance when Sir Simon, who had been elected a member of parliament for the borough of Cardigan, took his seat in the House of Commons (Boyer, *Annals*, 1710, p. 276). Phipps then took over as Sacheverell's chief counsel and was knighted for his efforts on 26 December 1710 (ibid., 1711, p. 280).

75. *smote him:* On 20 March Sacheverell was found guilty on all counts by a vote of 69–52 (*Tryal of Dr. Henry Sacheverell*, pp. 451–52).

his Uprising: Even before the trial it was recognized that the prosecution would make "the Doctor and his performance much more considerable than either of them could have been on any other account" (HMC *Portland MSS.*, *4*, 530).

77. *The Mob:* "As soon as 'twas known abroad what a *mild Sentence* the Lords had resolv'd to pass upon Dr. *Sacheverel*, his Friends, who look'd upon it rather as an *Absolution* than a *Condemnation . . .* could not forbear expressing their Joy: Insomuch, that, in the Evening, most of the Streets in *Westminster*, and some in the City of *London*, were full of Illuminations and Boncfircs, round which many drank the *Doctor's Health, and happy Deliverance*, and oblig'd those that pass'd by to do the like" (Boyer, *Annals*, 1710, p. 331). The next night there "were Bonfires in Oxford for Joy of Dr. Sacheverell's being delivere'd with so gentle a Punishment, and the Mob burnt a tub, with the Image of a tub Preacher, in one of them" (Hearne, *2*, 365).

the Ladies: "Secheverell will make all the Ladys turn good huswiv[e]s," it was said during the trial, for "they goe att seven every mornin" (*Wentworth Papers*, p. 113). "This concern both for the Church, and the afflicted Asserter of its Rights," Abel Boyer added (*Annals*, 1710, p. 265), "was almost universal among the Fair and Tender-hearted Sex; whose natural Compassion, might, in many, be encreas'd by the Fame of the Comeliness of his Person." Cf. *Review*, 11 May 1710.

79. *hanging their Ear:* "cowed, discouraged" (*OED*).

80. *Garrard:* Sir Samuel Garrard (c. 1651–1725), of Lamer, Hertfordshire, fourth baronet, was a prominent Tory politician, member of parliament for Agmondesham, Buckinghamshire (1701, 1702–10) and lord mayor of London (1709–10). It was in the latter role that he proved a "False Brother" to Sacheverell. He invited Sacheverell to preach in St. Paul's on 5 November 1709 and Sacheverell published the sermon with a flattering dedication to Sir Samuel and the statement that it was printed by his command. But when the sermon became the chief piece of evidence against Sacheverell, Garrard perjured himself rather than to incur the displeasure of the Whig majority in the House and violently denied that he had "commanded, desir'd or countenanc'd the printing of it" (Hearne, *2*, 328). "The Lord Mayor

Dejected and scorn'd they wander about,
    Poor Wretches, forlorn and forsaken,
Upbraided and Banter'd with Jeer and with Flout,
    Because they were happ'ly mistaken.

And may all the Managers meet with such Chance   85
    And be Laught at in Country and Town,
Who so basely intend, and so rudely Advance
    To beat Loyal Principles down.

. . . has slipt his neck out of the Collar," Peter Wentworth said, "but how honourable I can't
say, for Sacheveril affirms before the house . . . that the day he preach[ed] Sir Samuel comply-
mented him upon his Sermon and took him home with him to dinner in his own coach, and
after dinner told him *he hoped* he shou'd see it in print, wch he took for a sufficient command
from a superior to an inferior" (*Wentworth Papers,* p. 100).

81. *Dejected and scorn'd:* As they followed the court on the western circuit after parliament
was prorogued, Nicholas Lechmere was "affronted and hissed" and Sir Joseph Jekyll "had
no respect showed him but was affronted rather, and suspected somebody put aqua-fortis on
his coach braces, for it fell in Bromfield" (HMC *Portland MSS., 4,* 539). Cf. *Some Verses In-
scrib'd to the Memory of the Much Lamented John Dolben, Esq.* below).

On the Sentence Passed by the House of Lords
on Dr. Sacheverell
(1 June 1710)

The Whigs had threatened to "roast" Sacheverell (*Upon the Burning of Dr. Burgess's Pulpit, 2n.* above) and many of them, no doubt, would have been glad to see him go up in flames. So they were flabbergasted when their usual majority in the House of Lords was overturned and Sacheverell was set free on 23 March 1710 with only the mildest of punishments (*12n.* below).

Marlborough asked his wife "how were these lords influenced to be for Sacheverell; duke of Northumberland, duke of Hamilton, earl of Pembroke, earl of Suffolk, bishop of Chichester, Lord Berkeley, earl of Northesk, earl of Wemyss, Lord Lexington?" (Coxe, *Memoirs, 3,* 27). The answer appears to be that the queen changed her mind. Although she had withheld preferment from Hoadly in December 1709 (*Found on the Queen's Toilet, 6n.* above), Anne told Burnet (*2,* 543) "after the Impeachment was brought up to the Lords . . . that it was a bad Sermon, and that [Sacheverell] deserved well to be punished for it." On 27 February, however, she told Sir David Hamilton "that there ought to be a punishment but a mild one . . . and that his Impeachment had been better lett alone" (Hertfordshire County R. O. MS. Panshanger D/EP F207, ff. 5–6). Finally, just before the sentencing on 21 March 1710, Anne told the earl of Kent that "she thought the Commons had reason to be sattisfied that they had made their allegations good, and the mildest punishment inflicted upon the Doctor she thought the best" (*Wentworth Papers,* p. 146). So the wavering lords, whether inspired by self-interest or by Christian charity, did "save the Priest" (15).

The date of publication of the poem is indicated by the fact that it was advertised in *The Post Man* for 1 June 1710.

It may be assumed that the author was someone who was delighted at the defeat of the Whigs and that the trial had "had the very Reverse Effect of what their Party propos'd from it: For instead of *humbling,* it universally *spirited* the Nation into a vigorous Opposition of all their Measures" (*The Secret History of Arlus and Odolphus,* 3rd ed., 1710, p. 34). But the author was also someone who had no respect for Sacheverell and was equally delighted to imagine his fires put out by the mock-heroic means described in the poem.

On the Sentence Passed by the House of Lords on Dr. Sacheverell

Hail, pious Days! thou most propitious Time,
When hated Moderation was a Crime;
When sniv'ling Saints were cropt for Look of Grace,
And branded for a Conventicle Face.
Whole Floods of Gore distain'd the guilty Years,   5
Noses ragou'd, and Fricasies of Ears:
When rampant *Laud* the Church's Thunder threw,
His sacred Fury no Distinction knew:
The People suffer'd, and the Priesthood too.
But now behold the bright inverted Scene,   10
Mercy returns in a forgiving Queen:
Her Senate's Anger burns in milder Fires,

1. *pious Days:* The personal rule of Charles I lasted from 1629 to 1640.

2. *Moderation:* See *Dr. Sacheverell and Benjamin Hoadly,* 5n. above.

3. *Saints were cropt:* High church atrocity stories were conveniently collected by Matthew Tindal (Halkett and Laing, *4,* 66) in *The Merciful Judgments of High-Church Triumphant on Offending Clergymen, and Others, in the Reign of Charles I:* "the first Instance I shall give of the tender regard which was had to Clergymen, shall be the Treatment of *Alexander Leighton* D.D. who for reflecting on the Prelacy, and charging the Bishops with Persecution . . . was sentenc'd to a perpetual Imprisonment, to a Fine of 10000*l.,* to be degraded, to be pillory'd and whipt, to have his Ears cut off, his Nose slit, and his Face branded: all which Sentence was most severely executed upon him" (pp. 5–6).

5. *Gore:* "The Reverend Mr. *Burton,* a Divine of the Church of *England* . . . Mr. *Prynn,* a Barrister of *Lincolns-Inn;* and Dr. *Bastwick,* a Physician; for writing seditious schismatical Books against the Hierarchy of the Church . . . the Pillory, Loss of their Ears, their Faces and Foreheads branded with hot Irons, perpetual Imprisonment, and a Fine of 5000*l.* each, was their Sentence . . . This barbarous Sentence was most barbarously executed: for *Burton's* and *Bastwick's* Ears were par'd so close by the High-Church Executioner, that he cut their Arterys, and therby caus'd a great Effusion of Blood; and he not only sear'd *Prynn's* Cheeks with an exceeding hot Iron, but in taking away what was left of one of his Ears, par'd off a piece of his Cheek, and left a piece of his other Ear hanging on for some time, after he had barbarously hack'd it" (ibid., p. 6).

7. *Laud:* "But this inhuman Usage of Mr. *Prynn* did not satisfy Father *Laud,* but he mov'd the Court [of Star Chamber] then sitting to have him gagg'd, and some farther Punishment inflicted on him" (ibid., pp. 6–7). "*Laud's* chief Design was to advance the Ecclesiastical Power above the Law of the Land (one of the Articles on which he was impeach'd)" (ibid., p. 25).

8. *no Distinction:* "He provok'd Men of all Qualitys and Conditions, who agreed in nothing else but their Aversion to him" (Edward Hyde, earl of Clarendon, *The History of the Rebellion,* 3 vols., Oxford, 1702–04, *1,* 79, quoted in *The Merciful Judgments of High-Church Triumphant on Offending Clergymen, and Others, in the Reign of Charles I,* 1710, p. 26).

12. *Senate . . . milder:* Sacheverell's "sentence, which 'tis exspected will be severe,"

Proud of that Clemency which she inspires.
Calmly they try their Enemy profest,
And tho' they damn the Doctrine, save the Priest;   15
On the deluded Tool look mildly down,
And spare the factious Pedant for the Gown.
So when in sullen State, by Peasants bound,
The gen'rous Lyon walks his thoughtful Round,
Should some small Cur his Privacy invade,   20
And cross the Circle which his Paws had made,
Fir'd with Disdain, he hurls his Eyes below,
But loath to grapple with so mean a Foe,
Bestrides him shiv'ring with inglorious Fear,
And pisses on the Wretch he scorns to tear.   25

Hearne (2, 362) wrote in his diary on 20 March 1710, "is to be pronounc'd tomorrow." As soon as Sacheverell had been found guilty, the managers of the impeachment drew up their list of punishments: he was not to preach for seven years; he was not to be preferred during that period; he was to be imprisoned in the Tower for three months and until he could find sureties for his good behavior, and his sermons were to be burned by the common hangman. When the first of these was put to the House of Lords on 21 March, the managers were surprized that the term was cut from seven to three years. When the second question was resolved in the negative, the managers withdrew the third, and the fourth was carried (*LJ, 19,* 118). Cf. *The Westminster Combat,* 77n. above.

15. *damn the Doctrine:* Speaking to the first article of impeachment, Sir Joseph Jekyll said, "As that Doctrine of unlimited Non Resistance was implicitly renounced by the whole Nation in the Revolution, so divers Acts of Parliament afterwards pass'd expressing that Renunciation" (*Tryal of Dr. Henry Sacheverell,* p. 75).

16. *Tool:* On 28 February, the second day of the trial, General Stanhope called Sacheverell "an inconsiderable Tool of a Party" (ibid., p. 112).

18–25. Cf. *Advice to a Painter* (1697), 95–101; *POAS,* Yale, *6,* 20:

> Thus have I seen a Whelp of Lion's Brood
> Couch, fawn and lick his Keeper's Hand for Food,
> Till in some lucky Hour the generous Beast,
> By an insulting Lash, or some gross Fraud opprest,
> His just Resentment terribly declares,
> Disdains the Marks of Slavery he wears,
> And his weak Feeder into pieces tears.

DANIEL DEFOE?

High-Church Miracles,
or,
Modern Inconsistencies
(9 June 1710)

This spirited work singles out for obloquy a round dozen of the "Endless Intollerable Contradictions" between high church principles and high church practice that Defoe complained of in the *Review* (3 June 1710). Its 26 lines of verse are followed by *The Explanation,* or 60 lines of prose annotation. That such a high proportion of footnotes to text was found necessary in 1710 may justify to some degree the high ratio in the present volume.

The Luttrell copy of the broadside, now in Chetham's Library, Manchester, is dated 9 June 1710.

The poem is said by one authority to be "Very probably, [but] not certainly, Defoe's" and by another to be "Perhaps by Defoe" (Moore, p. 74; *The New Cambridge Bibliography of English Literature,* ed. George Watson, 5 vols. projected, Cambridge, Cambridge University Press, 1971, 2, 890). The succession of "Inconsistencies," which constitutes the structure of this poem, occurs incidentally in *The Dyet of Poland* (July 1705), 560–69, and in a series of *Reviews* (20 April, 27 April, 3 June 1710). The last of these, published the same week as *High-Church Miracles,* makes use of the same "——, yet ——" sentence structure of lines 9–10 of the poem:

> a QUEEN Reigning with justice and Mercy, and Prescribing her Self by the Laws; yet Murmur'd daily at by her Subjects, because she refuses to be a Tyrant . . .
>
> A *Queen* possess'd of the Crown by the best Title in the World, yet eagerly Address'd . . . to Abandon the Title She Claims by, and own her Self an Usurper.

So the appearance in the poem (line 26) of the proverbial impossibility of washing an Ethiopian white (Tilley, E186), during the month that Defoe was reporting a "Dispute about Coals" (*Review,* 3 June 1710), may not be a coincidence.

If *High-Church Miracles* is by Defoe, as now seems likely, it may be a study for a similar, but more important poem, *The Age of Wonders,* that he published three months later.

HIGH-CHURCH MIRACLES,
OR,
MODERN INCONSISTENCIES

That *HIGH-CHURCH* have a *Right Divine* from JOVE,
By *Signs* and *Wonders,* they pretend to Prove
They can a Mortal Soul *immortal* make:
They can, by *Pray'rs,* our Constitution shake.
Virtue and Vice, at their Command, agree;   5
And Truth can well consist with Perjury.

1. *Right Divine:* Benjamin Hoadly (writing in the person of a Tory squire) summarizes the claims that high churchmen were making for themselves: "the *Independency* of *Church,* and *Churchmen* upon the *State;* the *Royal* and *Divine Dignity* of the *Priesthood;* the entire *Dependence* of us poor *Laity* upon their *Absolutions* and *Benedictions;* not without frequent Hints concerning the *restitution* of *Church-Lands*" (*The Thoughts of an Honest Tory,* 1710, p. 10).

3. *Soul immortal make:* "This Power *Mr. Dodwel,* the Learned Tutor of High-Church, Teacheth to be in every Priest, and not one of the High-Church Faction hath writ against this Heretical Doctrine" (*The Explanation*). Henry Dodwell (1641–1711), born in Dublin and educated at Trinity College, Dublin, became a distinguished mediaeval historian and a leading lay nonjuror. He resigned a fellowship at Trinity College rather than to take orders, and the Camden Professorship of History at Oxford rather than to take the oaths to William and Mary. In February 1706 (Hearne, *1,* 193) he published *An Epistolary Discourse concerning the Soul's Immortality,* arguing that the "natural" soul was made immortal at the moment of baptism. The work was immediately and successfully attacked by a whole series of low churchmen, deists, and mystics—Samuel Clarke, Thomas Milles (Hearne, *1,* 218, 269), Edmund Chishull (assisted by Benjamin Hoadly [Hearne, *1,* 326]), Anthony Collins, and John Norris—and defended by the Jacobite Charles Leslie (*The Rehearsal,* 11, 14 February 1707). Even Thomas Hearne, Dodwell's protégé and admirer, thought that "his Failings . . . ought rather to be pitied" and William Nicolson, bishop of Carlisle, observed that "The poor Man could do well to let controversial Points alone" (Hearne, *1,* 209). But most of the inferior clergy—Hearne (*2,* 10, 131) reports on those of London and Norwich—were delighted to be endowed with thaumaturgic powers.

4. *Pray'rs:* "They *Pray'd* publickly, and Printed *Prayers* for the Doctor, as one under Persecution for Religion, tho' he was Impeach'd by the *Commons,* and found Guilty by the *Lords,* of High Crimes and Misdemeanours, in Preaching and Printing Two Sermons, *With a wicked, malicious, and seditious Intention, to Undermine and Subvert Her Majesty's Government, and the Protestant Succession as by Law Establish'd;* &c., [quoting the summary of the articles of impeachment in *Tryal of Dr. Henry Sacheverell,* pp. 8–10]. They Pray'd also for the Church as in extream Danger; and their Sermons were suited to their Prayers; whereby they Trumpetted up the *Mob* against Her Majesty and the Parliament; and the latter they omitted Praying for, during the Trial" (*The Explanation*). "Many Sermons were preached, both in *London* and in other Places," Burnet says (*2,* 540), "to provoke the People" to demonstrate for Sacheverell and one Benjamin Palmer, a chaplain in the royal household, was "suspended . . . for praying for Dr. *Sacheverell's* Deliverance from Persecution in her Majesty's Chapelle" (Hearne, *2,* 356).

They Damn all Right but of th'*Immediate* Heir;
And Reconcile it to the *Oaths* they Swear.
Passive can be, and yet *Resist* the Queen;
Loyal to *Her*, yet *Perkin* would bring in.   10
The Sovereign's Supremacy they own,
But say, the Pulpit is the Higher Throne;
To Bishops give Divine and Kingly Pow'r,
Yet Curse them first, and after would Devour.

7. *th'Immediate Heir:* "Their *Oxford-Decree,* which the Lords have Condemned to the Flames, and their other Scandalous and *Treasonable* Pamphlets, *Denyed the Legality of Precluding the next Heir to the Crown:* And on Discourse with them, you'll find, they are full of Encomiums on an *Hereditary Right;* and yet the same Persons *Abjure* the Pretender . . . by Swearing to Her Majesty and the Protestant Succession, as limited by Acts of Parliament on the House of *Hanover*" (*The Explanation*). Mainwaring makes the same point (*The Humble Address of the Clergy of London,* 24n. below). The Oxford Decree, voted by the university convocation on 21 July 1683, upheld the doctrine of indefeasible hereditary right in the most extreme form. It was ordered to be burned along with Sacheverell's sermons on 23 March 1710 (*LJ, 19,* 122).

8. *Reconcile it to the Oaths:* Cf. Defoe, *Letters,* p. 266: "some strangers have asked [Sacheverell] . . . how it was possible either that talking in that manner he could take the oath, or that taking the oath he could talk in that manner."

9. *Passive:* "They allow of no Resistance, tho' the Estates, Rights, and Liberties of the whole Nation be invaded; tho' a Tyrant should deprive you of Parliaments, and Murther the People for his Pleasure and Diversion; and yet these false Teachers *Rebel* themselves under the mildest Government of Her present Majesty, as their late Insurrections do sufficiently Witness. And tho' all their Actions are against Her Majesty's Government, yet what Solemn Professions of Love and Loyalty do they, *Judas*-like, make to her?" (*The Explanation*).

10. *Perkin:* The original Perkin was Perkin Warbeck "who professed to be the younger son of Edward IV, and as such claimed the crown in 1495" (*OED*). The current Perkin was James Francis Edward Stuart, the only son of James II, who claimed the crown in September 1701.

11. *Supremacy:* "Her Majesty's Supremacy in the *Church,* is confirm'd by divers Acts of Parliament; and tho' the *Canon* Excommunicates *ipso facto,* whosoever Speaks against it; yet all High Church Authors have the Impudence to Deny it in Print. Nay they prefer the Inferiour Priests to the Greatest Emperors and Kings; as appears by their Books, cited in a small Pamphlet, entituled, *A New Catechism, with Dr.* Hicks's *Thirty-Nine Articles.* But you may Observe yourself in Conversation, whenever they say Grace, or Toss off a Health, they Name the Church (as Superior) before the Queen" (*The Explanation*). The "small Pamphlet" consists of 89 questions answered by quotations from high church publications intended to expose the latter as "absurd and prophane"; e.g. "*Q. What think you of the Oath of Supremacy? A.* 'Tis not an Oath of Fidelity to the King, but of Unfaithfulness to the Church. *Appendix to the Rights of God's Church on Earth*" (*A New Catechism, with Dr. George Hickes's Thirty-Nine Articles,* 1710, p. 12).

13–14. *Bishops . . . Curse:* "Dr. *Atterbury* and his Friends, can Testify in what an Insolent Manner, the High Flyers have Treated the Higher House of *Convocation.* What Libels and Invectives have they Publish'd? What Indignities have they Offer'd to our Moderate and Religious Bishops? Especially to his Grace of *Canterbury,* and the Bishop of *Salisbury;* the latter of which, tho' a very great Ornament to our Church, and so Esteemed throughout all *Christendom,* was in Danger of being Massacred, in the late High-Church Insurrection" (*The*

Christ they can serve, by Churches pulling down;   15
Advance *Prerogative*, by *Insults* on the Crown.
Pop'ry they Hate, yet *Abbots* would Restore;
Abjure *Rome*'s Pow'r, yet Grasp themselves at more.
God they Profess Righteous and Just to be:
Yet God, they say, Commissions Tyranny.   20
Their Mercy, Love, and Charity are shown
In Massacres, and Persecution.
Saints they can Damn, and Devils quickly make 'em,

Explanation). Watching from the windows of his house, Burnet saw the skull of one rioter split open by another: "Before my own Door," he said (*2*, 542), "One, with a Spade, cleft the Skull of another, who would not shout [*The Church and Sacheverell*] as they did. There happened to be a Meeting-house near me, out of which they drew every thing, that was in it, and burned it before the Door of the House. They threatened to do the like Execution on my House; but . . . As the Guards advanced, the People ran away."

15. *Churches pulling down:* "They Pull'd down the Churches of Protestant Dissenters, for being profess'd Enemies to the *Pope* and *Pretender*; but not a Window did they break of either Papist or Jacobite" (*The Explanation*). Besides Burgess's meeting house near Lincoln's Inn Fields, the mob destroyed "those of Mr. *Earl* in *Long-Acre*; Mr. *Bradbury*, in *New-street*, *Shooe Lane*; Mr. *Taylor*, in *Leather-Lane*; Mr. *Wright*, in *Black-Fryars*; and Mr. *Hamilton*, in *Clerkenwell*" (Boyer, *Annals*, 1710, pp. 265–66); cf. "*High-Church is for Toleration*, yet they pull down the *Dissenters* Meetinghouses" (*Review*, 20 April 1710).

16. *Insults on the Crown:* "If undermining Her Majesty's Title, Defaming Her Government, Libelling Her Ministry, Denying and Opposing Her Supremacy, Tacking of Bills, Directing Her when to Dissolve a Parliament, and acting in Defiance of Her Royal Proclamations against *Riots,* &c. be Methods to advance *Prerogative*, then High-Church have effectually done it. So did they Serve their God, by Burning his Churches" (*The Explanation*).

17. *Abbots . . . Restore:* "Abby-Lands" (*The Explanation*). James II had to assure his loving subjects in April 1687 that he would maintain them "in all their properties and possessions, as well of church and abbey lands as in any other their lands and properties whatsoever" (*EHD*, p. 397). And the talk of high churchmen about resuming church lands secularized more than 170 years ago still made the present proprietors extremely nervous.

18. *Grasp . . . at more:* "This has been fully Demonstrated by *The Rights of the Christian Church*, whom the whole *Legion* of High-Church have in vain attempted to Answer" (*The Explanation*). Besides Swift (*Leviathan*, 12*n.* above), some of the high churchmen who wrote replies to Tindal's *The Rights of the Christian Church Asserted* (1706), making large claims for the autonomy of the church, were William Wotton, George Hickes, Charles Leslie, Samuel Hill, William Assheton, and William Oldisworth.

22. *Massacres, and Persecution:* "This is set forth in a small Treatise, *ironically* Intituled, *The Merciful Judgments of High-Church*; and is confirm'd by their late Barbarous Behaviour towards the Protestant Dissenters" (*The Explanation*); cf. *On the Sentence Passed by the House of Lords on Dr. Sacheverell*, 3*n.*, 5*n.* above.

23. *Saints they can Damn:* "This alludes to their pretended Power of Damning any Person, tho' never so Holy, by their *Excommunications* and *Anathema*'s; and on the contrary, of Absolving for a Purse of Money, the most profligate Sinner. *But, Physician, first Cure thy Self*" (*The Explanation*). Petty persecutions by the clergy are illustrated by a case in the parish of Whitechurch, Kent, of which Thomas Hearne's friend Abraham Kent was rector. Kent wrote to Hearne "about a poor woman who has been excommunicated for above sixteen years, and

Can Dev'ls Absolve, and after Consecrate 'em.
But I defy themselves, and all their Devils,   25
To wash the *Æthiop* White, and Purge *High-Church* from Evils.

---

whom he is trying to reduce to submission by stopping the contributions of the charitable"
(Hearne, *1*, 218).

Devils . . . make 'em: "The *Doctor* [Sacheverell] . . . leaves them [dissenters] *with the Devil and his Angels* (*Review*, 20 April 1710); cf. Defoe, *The Age of Wonders*, 15–16 below.

26. *To wash the Æthiop:* In the midst of the *Review* of 3 June 1710 retailing the "Endless Intollerable Contradictions" by high churchmen, Defoe evidently was asked to give an account of the action that the lightermen of the port of London were bringing against the Newcastle colliers for combinations in restraint of trade. "And here I am importunately called off from going on with this Medley of Confusion, to keep the Peace among the *black Ones* in *Billinsgate*," the coal market (*Review*, 3 June 1710). The dispute about coal is continued in the next three issues of the *Review*, while the "Medley of Confusion" is apparently concluded in the present poem.

.

Some Verses Inscrib'd to the Memory
of the Much Lamented John Dolben, Esq;
Who Departed this Life the 29th of May 1710
(June? 1710)

In the obituaries for May 1710 Abel Boyer noted that "On the 29th, *John Dolben,* Esq; Son to the late Archbishop of *York,* and Member of Parliament for *Leskard,* in *Cornwall,* who carried the Impeachment against Dr. *Sacheverell* to the Lords Bar, and distinguish'd himself in that solemn Tryal, died at *Epsum,* of a Fever, to the great Joy and Exultation of Dr. *Sacheverell*'s Friends" (Boyer, *Annals,* 1711, p. 417). The present poem is part of the "Exultation," which also included *News from the Shades below . . . or A Letter from John D—lb—n to his Friends the Whiggs* upon the arrival of Dolben's soul in hell, and two verse elegies in *A Collection of Poems, For and Against Dr. Sacheverell,* 4 vols., 1710–11, *1,* 11–13, 28–30: *An Elegy Balladwise on the Death of John Dolben, Esq.* ("Is *John Dolben* dead? Fare him heartily well") and *Another Elegy on the Death of John Dolben, Esq.* ("Weep, all you *Schismaticks,* since he is gone").

Another Elegy is attributed to "Isaac Bickerstaffe," but not even a pseudonym can be attached to the present verses.

Some Verses Inscrib'd to the Memory
of the Much Lamented John Dolben, Esq;
Who Departed This Life the 29th of May 1710

Est honor in tumulis, animas placate paternas.

Come all ye Managers, come forth and Moan,
Dolben your first Belov'd is dead and gone.
At your Expence a *Mausolaeum* raise
Large as was *Dolben's Booth,* to *Dolben's* Praise,
Where you with him did frequently resort   5
To play the *Fool* and make the People *Sport.*
    See that a Grave to put him in be made
Hard by, where *British* Kings and Queens are laid.
Mingle his Dust with theirs, for He, like You,
Always to Monarchy Loyal was and True.   10
Let your own halting Priest o're Him pronounce
A Funeral Oration—and denounce
Judgment on those who dare not Kings dethrone,
With *Comments* brought from *Calvin* and from *Rome.*

Epigraph. "Honor is paid to the dead. Propitiate the souls of the fathers" (Ovid, *Fasti,* II, 533).

1. *Come all ye:* The minstrel incipit, evidently designed to attract a crowd, became a favorite formula of the broadside ballad writers.

Managers: The 20 members of parliament who conducted the impeachment of Sacheverell are listed in *The Old Pack, 34n.* above.

2. *first Belov'd:* John Dolben was "the first Accuser" of Sacheverell in the House of Commons and chairman of the impeachment committee (*The Life and Adventures of John Dolben, Esq.,* 1710, pp. 11, 12).

dead: Dolben died on 29 May 1710 at Epsom (ibid., p. 16).

4. *Dolben's Booth:* The shows at Bartholomew Fair were housed in booths (*Wit and Mirth: Or Pills to Purge Melancholy,* Vol. IV, 1706, pp. 66, 143), but Dolben's "Booth" was the great scaffold which Sir Christopher Wren erected in Westminster Hall to accommodate the queen, all the members of both houses of parliament, and their guests at the Sacheverell trial (*CJ, 16,* 296, 336; *Wentworth Papers,* pp. 110–11).

8. *Hard by:* Westminster Abbey, "this great Magazine of Mortality," as Steele called it, provides "the Repository of [the] English Kings" (*The Spectator,* 30 March 1711). Dolben, however, was buried in Finedon church, Northamptonshire, under a grey marble tombstone (*DNB, 5,* 1098).

11. *halting Priest:* Benjamin Hoadly, who was crippled (see illustration, *POAS,* Yale, *6,* 651).

14. *Calvin . . . Rome:* The meeting of the Jesuit and dissenter extremes was a commonplace; e.g. *Two Sticks Made One: Or, The Devil upon Dun,* 1705: for the Jesuit "secular Power

Come, *Row* and *Congreve,* now adorn his Herse,   15
Vanbrugg and *Garth,* with never dying Verse:
Let *Addison* arise and *Mountague,*
(Sure something to this mighty Ghost is due)
And thou, O *Bellman,* Haste among the Throng,
Who at his *Window* once so sweetly Sung.   20
    Mourn *Whiggs!* Your *Puritanick* Looks put on,
Such as you wore in Times of *Fourty One.*
Dolben is dead; not *Holy Garth* cou'd save
The *Moderate Honest Dolben* from his Grave.
Hence, *Lechmere,* learn before it be too Late   25
A *Garret-Leap* cannot exempt from Fate.

. . . ascends from the Community to the King"; for the dissenter "Sovereign Power is more in a People than in the King"; cf. *The History of Seven,* 11*n.* above.

15–17. Nicholas Rowe, William Congreve, Sir John Vanbrugh, Samuel Garth, Joseph Addison, and Charles Montagu, Lord Halifax, were all Whig poets and all, except Rowe, were members of the Kit-Cat Club (Oldmixon, *History,* p. 479).

19. *Bellman:* Bellmen walked through the streets of London at night, ringing a bell and calling out the time and the weather (Pepys, *Diary,* 16 January 1660). Papers of doggerel verse were also part of their stock in trade (John Cornish, *A Copy of Verses Humbly Presented to All My Worthy Masters and Mistresses* ["I Am not Eagle-ey'd to face the Sun"], 1710). But the reference here is to mock-bellman's verses entitled *A Copy of Verses spoke by the Bell-Man of St. Margaret's Westminster, last Christmas under the Window of John Dolben, Esq; one of the Managers against Dr. Henry Sacheverell* (*A Collection of Poems, &c. For and Against Dr. Sacheverell,* 4 vols., 1710–11, *3,* 19).

> My Master *Dolben,* he did well
> For to impeach *Sacheverell;*
> For he was an invidious Incendiary,
> And loved not King *William,* nor Queen *Mary.*
> So *Pim* did formerly impeach Doctor *Mainwaring,*
> For he was a Man that was both obstinate and daring,
> And never would, 'till twas too late, take Warning.
> Good Morrow, Master *Dolben,* my Masters and Mistresses
>   all, good Morning.

22. *Fourty One:* Cf. *Found on the Queen's Toilet,* 2*n.* above.

23. *Holy:* Garth had the reputation of being "an Open and Profess'd Enemy to all Religion" who believed "there was neither a God nor future state" (BM MS. 47128, f. 95; cf. Pope, *Corr.,* 2, 25).

26. *Garret-Leap:* This is an incident of February 1705 in the famous case of *Ashby* v. *White* (p. 59 above). After the Commons had committed the Aylesbury electors to Newgate without bail, their counsel argued so violently for a writ of habeas corpus that they too were found to be in breach of privilege and were ordered into the custody of the serjeant at arms (*The Westminster Combat,* 29*n.* above). Nicholas Lechmere, however, was able to avoid arrest when he "got out of his Chamber in the *Temple,* Two Pair of Stairs high, at the back Window, by the Help of his Sheets and a Rope" (*CJ, 14,* 551–53).

> He fell upon the twenty ninth of *May*,
> To *England*'s Crown and Church a *glorious* Day,
> And may it Evermore Auspicious prove
> (Blest by the *Nod* of Cloud dispelling *Jove*),   30
> Frown on the Factious, on the Loyal Smile,
> And Peace and Plenty fill the *British Isle*.

27. *twenty ninth of May*: Dolben died on the fiftieth anniversary of the restoration of Charles II.

30. *Cloud dispelling*: This is a mock-epic detail, for Zeus normally gathers clouds (*Iliad*, V, 736; VIII, 38).

On My Lord Godolphin
(August 1710?)

Harley spent the whole spring and summer of 1710 doing what he had failed to do in a few days of January 1708, namely, to put together a ministry of "Queen's Friends," or "moderate men of both parties" (Klopp, *13*, 438). Shrewsbury, who had balked in 1708 (Mainwaring, *A New Ballad*, 121*n*. above), now came in gladly in April as Anne's lord chamberlain (Luttrell, *6*, 570). In June the young Lord Dartmouth was brought in to replace Sunderland, who was so obnoxious to the queen (*Letters of Queen Anne*, p. 303). For a time Harley believed it possible to keep Godolphin in the treasury, for the problems of doing without him were enormous. But on 5 August Harley decided that it was "impracticable" for the queen and Godolphin to "live together. He every day grows sourer and indeed ruder to 32 (the Queen)," Harley told Newcastle, "and will hear of no accommodation, so that it is impossible he can continue many days" (HMC *Portland MSS., 2,* 213). Anne herself made one last attempt at a reconciliation with her old friend and when this failed she was furious. On 8 August the queen wrote to Godolphin from Kensington palace:

> The uneasiness which you have showed for some time has given me very much trouble, though I have born it, and had your behaviour continued the same it was for a few years after my coming to the crown, I could have no dispute with myself what to do. But the many unkind returns I have received since, especially what you said to me personally before the lords [at a council meeting on 6 August], makes it impossible for me to continue you any longer in my service; but I will give you a pension of four thousand a year, and I desire that, instead of bringing the staff to me, you will break it, which, I believe, will be easier to us both.

(Blenheim MS. BII 32, quoted in Sir Tresham Lever, *Godolphin His Life and Times,* John Murray, 1952, p. 241). She sent the letter to him at Whitehall by a groom of the stables, and "Mr. *Smith,* Chancellor of the Exchequer, happening to come in a little after, my Lord broke his Staff, and flung the Pieces in the Chimney, desiring Mr. *Smith* to be a Witness that he had obeyed the Queen's Commands, and sent him to the Queen with a Letter . . . which Mr. Smith delivered, and at the same Time surrendered up his own Office" (Swift, *Corr.*, *1*, 174). The treasury was put in commission, under John Powlett, Lord Powlett, Robert Harley, Sir Thomas Mansell, and Robert Benson. Harley also assumed the post of chancellor of the exchequer and by 19 October the new ministry was completely constituted.

The following epigram on Godolphin's fall by an anonymous Tory is printed here for the first time.

ON MY LORD GODOLPHIN

Behold the Man who bore the powerfull Wand,
Ensign of Treasure and supreme Command
Reduc'd by an offended Monarch's Wrath
To bowl with *Hopkins* and be prais'd by *Garth*.

4. *Hopkins:* Presumably Thomas Hopkins (d. 1720), "an eminent money-scrivener who rendered himself extremely useful to the nobility and gentry of his time by supplying them with the loan of money; for which, however, he was especially careful to have good security and pretty usurious interest" ([James Caulfield], *Memoirs of the Celebrated Persons Composing the Kit-Cat Club*, 1821, p. 225). He is said to have been a descendant of Vulture Hopkins (for whom Pope supplies an edifying footnote in *Epitsle III: To Allen Lord Bathurst*), but the relationship is nowhere made clear. In June 1702 he was made comptroller of the salt tax with a salary of £500 a year (Luttrell, *5*, 182) and in May 1706 he was moved up to commissioner of the salt tax (ibid., *6*, 50). In these modest posts and without the advantage of education at either university, Hopkins is said to have amassed a fortune "worth upwards of 200,000*l*." He was not one of the 30 original members of the Kit-Cat Club (Boyer, *History*, p. 524), but he is one of the 48 whose portraits were painted by Sir Godfrey Kneller. Concerning his lack of skill at bowls, which the writer of the epigram parallels with Garth's lack of skill in panegyric, there is no record.

Garth: Although he had written no major work since *The Dispensary* (1699), Samuel Garth's reputation as a poet remained high, partly no doubt because he had become "a zealous party-man" (Noble, *1*, 240). His eulogy of Godolphin, *A Poem to the Earl of Godolphin* ("Whilst Weeping *Europe* bends beneath her Ills"), published as a broadside in August 1710 and reprinted in *A Collection of Poems, &c. For and Against Dr. Sacheverell*, 4 vols., 1710–11, *4*, 4–5, was certain therefore to be "weigh'd . . . by the unerring Balance of Party." Matthew Prior, who both coined the phrase and applied it to Garth's poem in *The Examiner* for 31 August–7 September 1710, found neither "Poetry, Grammar, or Design in the Composition," but only "*A strong unlabour'd Impotence of Thought!*" (Prior, *Works*, *1*, 389–90), thus very prettily turning Garth's phrase from the sixth edition of *The Dispensary* against Garth himself (*POAS*, Yale, *6*, 730).

ARTHUR MAINWARING?

*The Humble Address of the Clergy of London
and Westminster, Paraphras'd*
(August? 1710)

As soon as his sentence had been read and Dr. Sacheverell was free to
start his triumphal progress westward, addresses to the throne began to
pour in from all over England and Wales. Most of them came from
Tory squires in the counties and from Tory citizens in the parliamentary
boroughs and they all expressed "*a doating Fondness for a new Parliament*"
([Arthur Mainwaring], *Four Letters to a Friend in North Britain, upon
Publishing the Tryal of Dr. Sacheverell*, 1710, p. 18). Their contents were so
similar, in fact, that the suspicion arose that they had been drafted in
London and sent out to the provinces to be signed and delivered.
"Copies or Patterns of Addresses were sent down to the more dark and
ignorant Parts of the Land, such as *Wales, Somersetshire, Oxford-shire*
[Mainwaring left Oxford without a degree], &c. In which Addresses
there was a secret meaning, different from that which was express'd
. . . But to Countries [i.e. counties] more enlightned . . . they only
transmitted some particular Heads to work upon" (ibid.).

Mainwaring supposed that this was the work of "*Harlequin*" (ibid., p.
22)—or Robert Harley—and he very obligingly picked out the "Pat-
tern" for the prototypal address, which is repeated in the lines of the
present poem indicated by the numbers in square brackets:

> When the Hereditary Right has been fully display'd [23], there
> generally follows a tender Expression in favour of our present
> Settlement [24]: and then perhaps in the very same Paragraph,
> you shall find with equal wonder and delight, an utter Abhorrence
> of that Resistance [13–16] which was the Foundation of that same
> Settlement: And immediately after, you shall see a most kind and
> dutiful Tender of Lives and Fortunes to maintain that Government
> [33–34], the Foundation of which they had just before been under-
> mining (ibid., pp. 19–20).

Perhaps the height of the "Addressing Madness," as Defoe called it
(*Review*, 18 May 1710), was reached on 23 August 1710 when Henry

Compton, bishop of London, and 150 of his clergy presented an address to the queen at Kensington palace. "As a distinguishing Favour to them," Anne ordered the address to be printed the next day in *The London Gazette*. And the significance of this largess was not lost: " 'Tis the only one of all the Numerous Addresses that have been presented of late that has been printed in the Gazette" ([White Kennett], *The Wisdom of Looking Backward*, 1715, p. 65; Hearne, *3*, 44).

The pretext for the address was the need of the clergy to defend themselves against charges made by Charles Leslie in *The Good Old Cause, Or, Lying in Truth*, published in June 1710. Leslie had accused them of openly opposing the Hanoverian succession and secretly supporting the pretender. He inferred the truth of the latter "purely from their Fondness and Zeal" for this word *"Hereditary"* ([John Swinfen], *The Reasons of the Absenting Clergy for not Appearing at St. Paul's, on Monday August 21. 1710*, 2nd ed., 1710, p. 3; *The Objections of the Non-subscribing London Clergy, Against the Address*, 1710, p. 30).

Leslie's book "made a great Noise," as Hearne said, and when a warrant was issued for his arrest, he absconded and eventually made his way to St. Germain (Hearne, *3*, 36; Luttrell, *6*, 609, 615). So the London divines were told that an address was to be drawn up "only to vindicate themselves from an Aspersion . . . lately cast upon them by Mr. *Lesley*" ([John Swinfen], *The Reasons of the Absenting Clergy for not Appearing at St. Paul's, on Monday August 21. 1710*, 2nd ed., 1710, p. 3). That is why the address so indignantly repudiates the charge that the clergy's "Acknowledgment of your Majesty's Hereditary Title, and irresistible Authority, is . . . a Plain Declaration in Favour of the Pretender" (*The London Gazette*, 22–24 August 1710).

But the real occasion for the address seems to have been quite different. John Swinfen suspected that the London address was "intended as a Pattern for all the other Bishops and Clergy" of England "to copy after" (*The Reasons of the Absenting Clergy for not Appearing at St. Paul's, on Monday August 21. 1710*, 2nd ed., 1710, p. 7). Swinfen makes it clear that the address did not originate with the bishop of London, who was "in the Country for some time after this Address was forming." "There were other sort of People at the bottom of it," he added (ibid., pp. 19, 20). Benjamin Hoadly heard that George Smalridge, lecturer of St. Dunstan's-in-the-West, whom the Whigs had passed over for the regius professorship of divinity (Hearne, *2*, 88), "had a principal Hand in drawing up the . . . Address" (*Some Short Remarks upon the Late Address of the Bishop of London and his Clergy, to the Queen*, 1711, p. 3).

"The Matter of Fact was this," White Kennett discovered, "Upon the removal of my Ld Treasurer the Proposal of some Address from the City Clergy was recommended by Mr. Harley; and form'd by Dr. Atterbury, and Dr. Smallridge, and sent to Dr. Snape and Mr. Brown who prepar'd a way for it, by talking in Coffee houses and other companies, that it was only meant to clear themselves from being thought Jacobites or Enemies to the Protestant Succession, which Some People were now the more inclin'd to impute to them because of Mr. Lesley's book entitled *The Good Old Cause*" (BM MS. Lansdowne 1024, f. 219v).

Since there were irregularities in the procedure for drafting and presenting the petition, many London divines refused to sign it. Estimates of the number of beneficed London divines who refused to sign the address ran from more than one half of the total of 102 to "at least one Third" (Benjamin Hoadly, *Some Short Remarks upon the Late Address of the Bishop of London and His Clergy, to the Queen*, 1711, p. 19; [John Swinfen], *The Objections of the Non-subscribing London Clergy, Against the Address*, 1710, p. 40). In any case, the claim made in the address that it represented "the unanimous Sense and Resolution of the Clergy, not only of [London and Westminster], but of the whole Kingdom," is the kind of big lie that makes successful propaganda. And even its critics did not deny "The effect it has had in the late Elections" ([John Oldmixon], *The History of Addresses . . . Part II*, 1711, p. 273).

This, of course, is exactly the "effect" that Harley was hoping for. As much as he feared and avoided enthusiasm in his private life, he was not averse, in an election year, to its exploitation for political gain. Mainwaring, or whoever it was that wrote the following verses, understood that a sharp slap in the face is sometimes the only effective antidote to enthusiasm. *The Humble Address of the Clergy of London and Westiminster, Paraphras'd* is paraphrased in the person of a high flying London divine, like the speaker in *The Age of Wonders* but more cynical. By coming closer to the truth, the "paraphrase" reveals the big lies in the original address.

There is even less evidence that Arthur Mainwaring wrote these verses than there is that he wrote *A New Ballad: To the Tune of Fair Rosamund* (above), but it is evidence of the same kind. The verses reproduce situations from Mainwaring's prose (13–16n., 24n., 31–32n., 41n.). The verses that follow *The Humble Address of the Clergy of London and Westminster, Paraphras'd* in one manuscript (*C*), entitled *The second part to the Tune of Rosamond* ("I pray God Bless our Gracious Q——n"), are really the second part of *A New Ballad: To the Tune of Rosamund*.

And there is evidence that Mainwaring had a manuscript copy of the address of the London clergy in his possession before it was printed. "A little spirit would correct and cure all this madness," he observed to the duchess of Marlborough (*Private Correspondence of Sarah, Duchess of Marlborough, 1,* 343).

THE HUMBLE ADDRESS OF THE CLERGY OF LONDON
AND WESTMINSTER, PARAPHRAS'D

May it please your Majesty,

We, the Hundred and fifty Elect of the Gown,
The Chosen of his Lordship throughout the whole Town,
Now you've turn'd out your Friends, for which Heaven bless you,
Conceive we may safely abuse and Address you.
In the first place, we beg you'd be pleas'd to take Notice,   5
For 'tis nothing but Truth, *in verbo Sacerdotis,*
That the Hearts and the Hands of right Clergy-men never
Were known in State Matters to travell together;
This we wisely premise that from thence you may guess
What Credit is due to your Clergy's Address: 10
The Tryal was wicked, no Precedent for it,
And as Genuine Sons of the Church, we abhor it.

1. *the Hundred and fifty Elect:* This was the figure reported in the press ([John Oldmixon], *The History of Addresses . . . Part II,* 1711, p. 274), but the number is misleading. For "not one half" of the true "Elect," the 102 beneficed London clergy, signed the address ([John Swinfen], *The Reasons of the Absenting Clergy for not Appearing at St. Paul's, on Monday August 21. 1710,* 2nd ed., p. 25).
2. *The Chosen of his Lordship:* Since "a very great Majority" of the clergymen who signed the address were unbeneficed lecturers, curates, or readers, it is not surprising that the influence of their diocesan, Henry Compton, bishop of London, was assumed to be decisive. It was even said that "importunate Letters had prevail'd with some few" of the beneficed clergy ([White Kennett], *The Wisdom of Looking Backward,* 1715, pp. 65–66; [John Swinfen], *The Objections of the Non-subscribing London Clergy, Against the Address,* 1710, p. 25). But in fact "his Lordship," who was "easy and weak, and much in the power of others" (Burnet, *2,* 630), seems not to have played a decisive part; see headnote, above.
3. *your Friends:* the Whigs: Kent, Sunderland, Godolphin.
7. *Hearts:* The address began with an expression of solidarity with earlier addresses: "Our Hearts have all along accompanied our Fellow-Subjects, the Genuine Sons of the Church of England, in their dutiful Applications to your Majesty." But the word "Hearts" recalls one of the "Modern Inconsistencies" between high church principles and high church practices. Benjamin Hoadly, *Some Short Remarks upon the Late Address of the Bishop of London and His Clergy,* 1711, p. 13, chides the subscribers for imputing "irresistible Authority" to the queen: "If we believe your Hearts . . . you mean an irresistible Authority without exception in any Case whatsoever. If we believe your Words . . . then you mean by Irresistible, such an Authority, as in Cases of [James II's] *Arbitrary Power and Popery,* may be resisted."
11. *no Precedent:* The address went on to express "Indignation . . . at the unprecedented Attempts lately made to Undermine . . . all Religion and Government." "Now, if a Man were at a Loss to know what is intended by this Phrase, *Unprecedented Attempts,* he may soon satisfie himself, that it is . . . the *Impeachment, Tryal and Condemnation of Dr.* Sacheverel" ([John Swinfen], *The Objections of the Non-subscribing Clergy, Against the Address,* 1710, p. 17).

Of your Honour, no doubt, 'twas a desperate Invasion
To maintain to your Face, and that of the Nation,
That the late Revolution, by which you now reign,   15
Was free from Rebellion's most damnable Stain.
Your Majesty's Title we say's by Descent,
But we join, to support it, the Peoples Consent.
Thus the Church Bacon's sav'd, come Whig or come Tory,
We've a Meaning reserv'd, to prove we are for ye;   20
We have taken the Oaths and our Livings secur'd,
Yet ne'er heard of his Claim, whose Claim we've abjur'd.
Sometimes Right divine by Descent's our Expression,
Sometimes we cry up the establish'd Succession.
So that catch as catch can, we've engag'd the Caresses   25
Of one or the other by our two-fac'd Addresses.

13–16. Why it should dishonor Anne to say that there was no violence in "the late happy Revolution" is explained in [Arthur Mainwaring], *Four Letters to a Friend in North Britain, upon the Publishing the Tryal of Dr. Sacheverell*, 1710, pp. 7, 14: Sacheverell said "there was *no Resistance made to the Supreme Powers* at the time of the Revolution [*The Perils of False Brethren, Both in Church, and State*, 1709, pp. 12–13], and said it in the very face of the Bishop of *London*." "By asserting *the utter Illegality of Resistance,* and that the contrary Position *is damnable* [ibid., p. 12], it is obvious, what a dreadful Sentence he pronounc'd against the Queen, who was her self in actual Resistance at the time of the Revolution."

17–20. Paragraph 5 of the address said: "We have Sworn, and are steadfastly purposed to pay all Duty and Allegiance to your Majesty, as to our Rightful and Lawful Sovereign, whose Title to the Crown by Descent has been affirmed and recognized by all your Liege People in full Parliament." Hoadly pointed out that it was "imposing on the Eyes and Understandings of all Men, to affirm, That her Majesties Hereditary Title has been . . . any otherwise recogniz'd than by the same Acts, which settled the Crown on King *William* . . . and entails it on the House of *Hanover*" (*Some Short Remarks upon the Last Address of the Bishop of London and His Clergy*, 1711, p. 15).

20. *a Meaning reserv'd:* John Swinfen pointed out that this was "a *Party-Address* . . . drawn up with great Ambiguity, with such Dexterity and Artifice, as if its true Meaning was design'd to be conceal'd" (*The Objections of the Non-subscribing London Clergy, Against the Address*, 1710, p. 42).

21. *Oaths:* to abjure the pretender (p. 83 above).

22. Paragraph 6 of the address began, "We know of no other Persons who has any Claim to our Obedience."

23. *Right divine by Descent:* See 17–20n. above.

24. *the establish'd Succession:* Paragraph 7 concludes: "we acknowledge the most Illustrious House of *Hanover,* as the next Heirs in the Protestant Line, to have the only Right of ascending the Throne, and indisputable Title to our Allegiance." Mainwaring observes that they "have confounded the very Names of Persons and Things. And therefore it is not strange to find those that are *High for the Uninterrupted Succession* declare their Zeal for the House of *Hanover*" (*Four Letters to a Friend in North Britain, upon the Publishing the Tryal of Dr. Sacheverell*, 1710, p. 20).

26. *two-fac'd:* "It is shrewdly to be suspected therefore, that it was drawn up with a

We own 'tis a Sin your Power to resist,
Yet we vow to withstand it whenever we list,
For if we but fancy that Slavery's a coming,
My Lord calls, To Horse, and we fall a drumming.   30
We thought the French King was low enough long since,
And to ruin him quite, was too much in Conscience.
We therefore send up this peaceable Prayer,
Oh Lord! scatter those that delight in the War.
    To conclude, Oh thou Mother of our Mother, the Church,   35
Good Grand-mother, leave us not in the Lurch;
You see we are here in a millitant State,
And our Triumphs, God knows, are promis'd us late.
Ah do but indulge us, in next Convocation

---

direct View to this double Meaning" ([John Swinfen], *The Objections of the Non-subscribing London Clergy, Against the Address,* 1710, p. 3).

27–28. Cf. *7n.* above.

28. In paragraph 8 the subscribers "thank God . . . for the Legal Provisions . . . made to secure us from Popery and Arbitrary Power, which we once [in 1688] . . . vigorously and successfully withstood . . . nor shall we fail to manifest an equal Zeal against them whenever, and by what means so ever, they shall meditate a Return."

30. *My Lord:* See *The Save-Alls,* 51*n.* above.

31–32. Cf. [Mainwaring], *Four Letters to a Friend in North Britain, upon the Publishing the Tryal of Dr. Sacheverell,* 1710, p. 20: Marlborough "has fallen by just degrees still more and more out of their Favour, as his Conquests advanc'd nearer to their beloved Kingdom of *France.*"

33–34. The address concludes: "In the meantime we shall not cease to bow our Knees to God, and most ardently to Pray, that he would multiply and increase the Successes with which your Wise and Just Designs have been hitherto attended, and continue to bless your Arms and Counsels, 'till they have effectually subdued the restless Enemies of our Peace both at Home and Abroad . . . and scattered all the People that Delight in War." The latter, in this case, are the Whigs; cf. Mainwaring?, *The Queen's Speech,* 9*n.* below.

37. *millitant:* "all those that believ'd [Sacheverell's] Doctrine were bound in Conscience to rise in Arms for a Holy War" ([Mainwaring], *Four Letters to a Friend in North Britain, upon the Publishing the Tryal of Dr. Sacheverell,* 1710, p. 8).

38. The reference may be to Jesus' instructions to his disciples: "when men shall revile you, and persecute you . . . Rejoice, and be exceeding glad: for great is your reward in heaven" (Matthew 5:11–12; cf. John 15:18–27).

39. In paragraph 9 the subscribers made the startling claim that the address expressed "the unanimous Sense" of the clergy of the whole kingdom, "as we doubt not will appear to your Majesty, whenever they have an Opportunity of expressing it in Convocation." Anne had prorogued convocation in November 1708 to put a stop to the "illegal Practices" of the lower house that "invaded Her Majesty's Royal *Supremacy*" (Boyer, *Annals,* 1709, p. 257). Atterbury, who "form'd" the address (headnote, p. 456 above; cf. [John Swinfen], *The Objections of the Non-subscribing London Clergy, against the Address,* 1710, p. 12), was prolocutor of the lower house of convocation. So it was "a bold and forward Stroke in your Address," as Hoadly observed, "even to mention the Convocation to her Majesty. Consider how freely the Lower House dealt with her Royal Prerogative at their last Sitting, and how severe a

We'll drive your Supremacy out of the Nation,   40
And hoist up our own, and have an Ovation.

Reprimand she was pleas'd to give them for it" (*Some Short Remarks upon the Last Address of the Bishop of London and His Clergy*, 1711, p. 21).

41. *our own:* "The [high flying] Inferiour Clergy . . . claim an equal and co-ordinate Power with their Bishops, an Exemption from the Queen's Supremacy, and an absolute Independency of the Church from the State" ([Mainwaring], *Four Letters to a Friend in North Britain, upon the Publishing the Tryal of Dr. Sacheverell,* 1710, p. 18).

Ovation: "a lesser triumph characterized by less imposing ceremonies than the triumph proper" (*OED*).

DANIEL DEFOE

The Age of Wonders
To the Tune of *Chivy Chase*
(5 September 1710)

This "Most Impudt Ballad," as Defoe called it (*Letters,* p. 277), may
have had a very different meaning for him than it had for its readers,
including Robert Harley, from whom Defoe concealed his author-
ship. Publicly it is an ironical celebration of "Modern Inconsist-
encies":

> This is an Age . . . of Contradiction and Paradox [Defoe said]
> . . . Men swearing to the Government, and wishing it overturn'd,
> abjuring the Pretender, yet earnestly endeavouring to bring him
> in . . . owning the Succession, and wishing the Successors at
> the Devil . . . ; it is very hard indeed under all these Masks to see
> the true Countenance of any Man

(Edinburgh *Review,* 4 February 1710). This pattern of contradiction,
repeated in prose in a succession of *Reviews* and in verse in *High-Church
Miracles* (above), is the rhetorical model for *The Age of Wonders.* But
the tone is quite different. In the *Review* Defoe speaks in his own person,
or in the person of "Mr. *Review,*" who bears a partial likeness to Daniel
Defoe. Mr. *Review* finds the endless duplicity of the age "very hard
indeed." But the accommodating, high flying churchman through
whom Defoe speaks in *The Age of Wonders,* finds it delightful: "Such
Wonders ne'er were seen!" (10). Possibly to avoid misinterpretation of
his ironies, which happened in the case of another work written in the
guise of a high flying churchman, *The Shortest-Way with the Dissenters,*
Defoe twice lowers the high church mask to address the reader directly
(49–50, 61–64). But for the rest, the "Wonders" of the title are des-
cribed in a tone of naive satisfaction. But all the "Wonders" turn out
to be practised deceptions, "*Hocus-Pocus*" (39). Publicly, therefore, *The
Age of Wonders* becomes an exposé of "all the *High-Flying* Lunacies of
the Age" (*Review,* 22 December 1709).
Privately Defoe may have thought of it as a dramatic monologue

with Henry Sacheverell as speaker. It would be difficult to overestimate the satisfaction that Defoe derived from the Sacheverell trial. In some ways it was a vindication of himself. Sacheverell, as Defoe had said, was "the Real Author" of *The Shortest-Way with the Dissenters* (1702), "tho' another was Punish'd for it" (*More Short-Ways with the Dissenters*, 1704, p. 8). Now, after seven years, Sacheverell was tried for saying literally what Defoe had been punished for imputing to him ironically. This time Sacheverell was found guilty and Defoe was set free.

The temptation to gloat over this peripeteia must have been almost overwhelming. But Defoe resisted it. Sacheverell's fall was only a "Tragi-Comedy" (*Review*, 23 February 1710), something no one could take seriously. What was really on trial, as Defoe said, was the revolution settlement, "the present Constitution" (*Review*, 18 February 1710).

When it was all over Defoe did allow himself to refer to "the late Exploded, Silenc'd Furioso, Dr. *Sacheverell*" (*Review*, 6 June 1710). And he may have imagined that in *The Age of Wonders* he was allowing this "Exploded" priest to expose himself.

The evidence for Defoe's authorship, although wholly circumstantial, is convincing nevertheless, as in the case of *The Address* (1704, *POAS*, Yale, *6*, 634), to which *The Age of Wonders* seems to allude three times (7*n.*, 74*n.*, 86*n.*,). The *Age of Wonders* is presumably the "Most Impudt Ballad," published "To day," that Defoe enclosed in a letter to Harley of 5 September 1710 (*Letters*, p. 277). Since the poem praises Godolphin (53*n.*), whom Harley had succeeded less than a month before, and dispraises Godolphin's successor (61–64*n.*, 113–14*n.*), it is not difficult to imagine why Defoe did not tell Harley that he was the author. Defoe's remark on this occasion, "I Fancy I kno' " the printer, is paralleled by his remark upon sending Harley another of his own anonymous works, *Atalantis Major*, in December 1710: "I have Some Guess at" the author, he said (*Letters*, pp. 277, 307). Further evidence of Defoe's authorship of *The Age of Wonders* may lie in the fact that he mentions it in the *Review*, 23 November 1710, and then quotes it twice (*Review*, 2 December 1710, 27 March 1711). "At every Turn, you are quoting your own lamentable Rhymes," one of his critics complained (*The Reviewer Review'd*, n.d., p. 2).

The poem was popular enough to generate *Wonders upon Wonders. In Answer to The Age of Wonders* (1710) ("The Year of *Wonders* is arrived, / *Truth* makes a brave advance"), an engraved folio half-sheet, and *The Age of Wonders. The Second Part to the Same Tune* ("Twelve Articles of Faith we had"), which was printed in *A Merry New Year's Gift; Or, The*

Captain's Letter to the Colonel about the Late Election in Southwark, 1712 (cf. TCD MS. I.5, *3,* 130).

The NLS copy of *Bb* is dated "Sept. 1710," which is almost certainly the date of publication. Internal evidence, however, indicates that the poem was written in July 1710 before Godolphin's dismissal on 8 August (57–58) and before Defoe's "short Conference" with Harley prior to 28 July from which Defoe had to "break away So Rudely" (Defoe, *Letters,* pp. 271–72).

The stanza is a standard ballad form, $A^4B^3A^4B^3$, and the tune is that old favorite, *Chevy Chase.*

THE AGE OF WONDERS
TO THE TUNE OF *Chivy Chase*

The Year of Wonders is arriv'd,
    The Devil has learnt to dance;
The Church from Danger just retriev'd
    By Help brought in from *France*.

Nature's run mad, and Madmen rule,   5
    The World's turn'd upside down;
Tumult puts in to keep the Peace,
    And Popery the Crown.

In all the Ages of the World,
    Such Wonders ne'er were seen;   10
Papists cry out for th'*English* Church,
    And Rabbles for the Queen.

Title. In the *Review* Defoe had called it "an Age of Mysteries and Paradoxes" (*Review*, 8 December 1709) and "an Age of Riddles" (*Review*, 24 December 1709), but not apparently an age of wonders. He may have seen the phrase, however, in the title of a grubstreet production of May 1710: *The Age of Wonders: Or, A Farther and Particular Discription of the Remarkable, and Fiery Apparition that was seen in the Air, on Thursday in the Morning, being May the 11th 1710* (BM : 1104.a.24). The apparition, which was that "of a Man in the Clouds with a drawn Sword [moving] from the North West over toward *France*" and which was interpreted "to denote some sudden or strange News from that Country," is a projection of the same anxiety and expectation that is expressed in the poem.

1. *The Year of Wonders:* The phrase occurs in a popular song of 1707 called *The Duke of Marlborough's Health* ("*Marlborough*'s a brave Commander") (*A New Academy of Complements,* 1715, p 99); cf. *POAS,* Yale, *4*, 275.

5. *Nature's run mad:* "One of the first Contemplations, I had on the *Strange and Wonderfulls* of the present Age, ended in this—That there are Times and Seasons when *Nations go mad*, as well as particular Persons; that Nature has Periods and Revolutions of Time, when she suffers unusual Fermentation, fall[s] into Fits" (*Review*, 8 April 1710).

Madmen: "If Tories, if Jacobites, if High-Flyers, if Mad-Men of any kind are to stay in, or come in, I am against them" (*Review*, 12 August 1710).

6. There is a chapbook entitled *The World Turned Upside Down or The Folly of Man Exemplified in Twelve Comical Relations upon Uncommon Subjects*, n.d. (John Ashton, *Chapbooks of the Eighteenth Century*, 1882, p. 265). If Defoe had looked into this work he would have found one couplet with a striking relevance to the dreaded "*Changes at Court*" (*Review*, 25 July 1710): "No wonder then the World is found / By change of place Turn'd upside Down."

7. Cf. Defoe, *The Address* (April? 1704), 18: "How can Contention bring forth Peace" (*POAS,* Yale, *6*, 635).

11. Cf. Defoe, *A Letter from Captain Tom to the Mobb, Now Rais'd for Dr. Sacheverel*, 1710, p. 4: "how many *Irish* Papists were known to walk, and huzza, and cry *High-Church* before your Doctor?"

12. "When the Guards fell upon them [p. 403 above]—the poor Wretches were amaz'd—

The Pulpit thunders Death and War,
  To heal the bleeding Nation;
And sends Dissenters to the Dev'l,   15
  To keep the Toleration.

The High-Church Clergy mounted high,
  Like Sons of *Jehu* drive;
And over true Religion ride,
  To keep the Church alive.   20

The Furiosos of the Church
  Come foremost like the Wind;
And Moderation, out of Breath,
  Comes trotting on behind.

The Realm, from Danger to secure,   25
  To foreign Aid we cry;
With Papists and Nonjurors join,
  To keep out Popery.

The Guards! says one of the poor simple Fellows, *how can that be, the QUEEN is of our side"* (*Review*, 18 March 1710).

13. *Pulpit thunders:* The prosecution of Sacheverell did not silence high church ministers. On the contrary, on 30 January 1710, "the Anniversary for the Martyrdom of King Charles 1st . . . all the Churches in and about London . . . rang with the Hainousness of the Crime of murdering that excellent Prince" (Hearne, *2*, 340). And "during the Tryal of Dr. *Sacheverell* . . . [the clergy] preach'd the decry'd Doctrine ten times more than ever" (*Most Faults on One Side*, 1710, p. 28).

15–16. "These Church-men . . . deliver over their Fellow-Subjects, over whom they have no Authority, to the Devil" (*Review*, 21 February 1710).

17. "Peoples Eyes *do already begin . . . to see Jacobitism* Riding upon them a Gallop" (*Review*, 18 July 1710).

18. *Jehu:* Jehu, the hard rider (2 Kings 9:20), whose solution to the problem of nonconformity was genocide, was one of Defoe's favorite symbols for high flying Anglicans (*POAS*, Yale, *6*, 445, 597; *Review*, 26 June 1705; *Review*, Vol. VII, The Preface, sig. A3v).

19–20. Swift maintains the same paradox in reverse when he makes his deist spokesman in *An Argument against Abolishing Christianity* (1711) say "that the Abolishing of Christianity may perhaps bring the Church in Danger" (*Prose*, *2*, 36).

21. *Furiosos:* This was another of Defoe's symbols for persecuting Anglicans: "Here are in *England* . . . above two Millions of Dissenters . . . what [shall be] done with them? *Hang'd, all Hang'd, says Furioso*" (*Advice to all Parties*, 1705, p. 19; cf. *The Dyet of Poland* [July 1705], line 821, above; *Review*, 1 April 1707). "Dr. *Furioso*" had become Sacheverell's name (*Three Letters betwixt Dr. Furioso and Perkin*, 1710; *Review*, 6 June 1710).

23–24. J. Woodfall Ebsworth (*Roxburghe Ballads*, *8*, i, 227) glosses these lines "Bp. Hoadley," and it seems likely that they allude to the crippled defender of low church.

25–26. Cf. Defoe, *England's Late Jury* (November 1701), 3–5: "*England* need never . . . seek out for a Foreign Aid, / Our Dangers to Repel" (*POAS*, Yale, *6*, 345).

27–28. "Awake, Gentlemen . . . Can *Jacobites* and *Non-Jurors* be your Defence" (*Review*, 3 December 1709).

King *William* on our Knees we curse,
    And damn the Revolution;   30
And to preserve the Nation's Peace,
    We study its Confusion.

With treacherous Heart and double Tongue,
    Both Parties wc adhere to;
Pray for the Side we swear against,   35
    And curse the Side we swear to.

To Heaven we for our Sov'reign pray,
    And take the Abjuration;
But take it *Hocus-Pocus* way,
    With jugling Reservation.   40

Sachev'rel-like, with double Face,
    We pray for our Defender;
To good Queen *Anne* make vile Grimace,
    But drink to the Pretender.

With Presbyterians we unite,   45

29–30. "Since the Prince of *Orange* . . . was the great Cause of all our Misfortunes . . .
'twill be a great Point gain'd to . . . blacken his Memory as much as possible . . . because
if we can once make the Revolution odious and black, all that is built upon it will fall of
course" ([Defoe], *A Letter from a Gentleman at the Court of St Germains, to One of His Friends in
England*, 1710, pp. 14–15). Defoe makes his Jacobite quote Sacheverell (*The Perils of False
Brethren, Both in Church, and State*, 1709, p. 12). These words then became the basis for Article
I of the impeachment charges: "the said *Henry Sacheverell* . . . doth . . . maintain, *That
. . . to impute Resistance to the said Revolution, is to cast Black and Odious Colours upon his late
Majesty, and the said Revolution*" (*Tryal of Dr. Henry Sacheverell*, pp. 8–9).

32. *Confusion:* In April 1700 James Vernon (*3*, 3) had noticed that "our affairs . . . have
a natural tendency to confusion" and by April 1710 Anne had learned to "expect nothing
but confusion" (Coxe, *Memoirs, 3*, 61). As Defoe summed it up, "I can say nothing, nor see
nothing but *Confusion, Confusion, Confusion*" (*Review*, 3 June 1710).

35–36. *the Side we swear against . . . the Side we swear to:* the pretender . . . the Hanover
line (*The Dyet of Poland*, 197–98n. above); cf. "*High Church* . . . have *abjur'd* the Side they
fight for, and *sworn* to the Side they *fight against*" (*Review*, 15 April 1710).

38. *take the Abjuration:* In May 1708 Defoe told Sunderland that "her Majesty is in danger
from those that take the Abjuration and safe in those that refuse it" (Defoe, *Letters*, p. 258).

39–40. Cf. *Review*, 22 December 1709: "Dr. S—— . . . will take all the Oaths, Abjura-
tions, and Declarations, ten Parliaments can make."

42. *Defender:* It is the queen, of course, who is styled "Defender of the Faith," but in
1709–10 this was a role that Sacheverell increasingly took upon himself (*To the Tune of Ye
Commons and Peers*, 30 above; *A Farewell to the Year 1714*, 6n. below).

44. *drink:* "He [Sacheverell] has drunk King James's health upon his knees" (Defoe,
Letters, p. 266; William Bisset, *The Modern Fanatick*, 1710, p. 22); cf. "If ever the Church is
betray'd . . . it is by those Gentlemen who abjure King *James* on one side, and drink his
Health on the other" (*Review*, 31 December 1709).

45. Cf. *The Dyet of Poland*, 386n. above.

And Protestant Succession;
But if the Devil came for both,
    We'd give him free possession.

Our Scheme of Politicks is wise,
    Good Lord! that you'd but read it;   50
'T pulls *Marlbro'* down, to beat the *French,*
    And the Bank, to keep our Credit.

Because our Treasurer was just,
    And House of Commons hearty;
And neither wou'd betray their Trust,   55
    Or sell us to a Party:

Our Business is, that neither may
    Their Places long abide in;
But get such chosen in their room,
    As no Man can confide in,   60

Who shall deserve your mighty Praise
    For Fund, and eke for Loan;
And may the Nation's Credit raise,
    But never can their own.

46. *Protestant Succession:* "You [Jacobites in England] must appear intirely devoted to the Protestant Succession" ([Defoe], *A Letter from a Gentleman at the Court of St. Germains, to One of His Friends in England,* 1710, p. 33).

49–50. In several numbers of the *Review* (15 July, 27 July 1710) Defoe had indulged his witticism that Sacheverell's *"Grand-Tour"* through England was supplying "SPECTACLES" in aid of the *"National* Eye-sight," and here he steps out of character to urge the reader to *see* that Sacheverell's behavior has only one purpose: to put the pretender on the throne of Great Britain.

52. Cf. "Dr. *Sacheverell's* Mobb, going to pull down . . . the Bank to help Trade" (*Review,* 8 August 1710).

53. *Treasurer . . . just:* Following Sunderland's dismissal on 14 June 1710, it became apparent that Godolphin's ministry would be replaced. "It will for ever be said of them," Defoe wrote, "that a better and a more just Body of Councellors, never Prince in this Nation displac'd" (*Review,* 17 June 1710).

57. *neither:* neither Godolphin nor Anne's third parliament.

59. Cf. [Defoe], *An Encomium upon a Parliament* (1699), 44; "And get your selves put in their room" (*POAS,* Yale, *6, 53*).

61–64. Defoe steps out of character again to predict that even if the ministry-to-be and the next parliament succeed in resolving the financial crisis precipitated by Sunderland's dismissal (Boyer, *Annals,* 1711, p. 231), they will always lack popular support. If Defoe meant literally what he wrote in the *Review* of 15 July 1710, that "THE CREDIT of the Nation . . . is . . . absolutely Dependant upon the Person" of Godolphin, then these lines may be ironical, implying that the ministry-to-be and the new parliament will fail to raise "the Nation's Credit" (63).

Because declaring Rights to reign,   65
    Our Parliaments have part in;
We'll have the Queen that Claim disown,
    For one that's more uncertain.

The Restoration to make plain,
    That *Perkin* mayn't miscarry,   70
We've wisely wheedl'd up the Queen
    To Right Hereditary.

Next with our non-resisting Cheat,
    Occasion muckle laughter;
That we who turn'd the Father out,   75
    Must not resist the Daughter.

The Dignity of Parliaments,
    The stronger to imprint in's;
We hug the Priest whom they condemn,

65–66. See *Fair Warning*, 1n. above.

67. *that Claim:* parliamentary right: "the Parliament of *England,* and the Parliament of *Scotland,* have Establish'd the Crown, over the Bellies of the Hereditary Heirs, upon the Line, not as it respects Blood, but Religion" (*Review,* 11 May 1710).

68. *one that's more uncertain:* hereditary right: "possess'd of the Crown by the best Title in the World," the queen is "Address'd . . . to Abandon the Title She Claims by, and own her Self an Usurper" (*Review,* 3 June 1710).

69–70. "If the Right to the Crown be founded on Proximity of Blood, so that [princes] succeed to Dominion, as Children do to their Father's Estates . . . it clearly and unanswerably follows . . . that *James* III. is the only Prince, since the Death of the late King, who can, or ought to succeed to the Crown of *Great Britain*" ([Defoe], *A Letter from a Gentleman at the Court of St. Germains, to One of His Friends in England,* 1710, p. 25).

71. *wheedl'd up the Queen:* The high flyers "brøter their Sovereign . . . with the new-fashioned Cant, of her Hereditary Right" (*Review,* 11 May 1710).

73. *non-resisting Cheat:* See *High-Church Miracles,* 9n. above.

74. *muckle:* Cf. [Defoe], *The Address,* 1: "Muckle Power" (*POAS,* Yale, *6,* 634).

75. *turn'd the Father out:* "And when the said King *James* return'd into his own Dominions (*Ireland*) again, and drawing together an Army, possess'd himself of all the said Kingdom of *Ireland* . . . They, the Church of *England,* Nation of *England,* sent over a Church of *England* Army, Furnish'd, Rais'd, Paid, and Employ'd, by a Church of *England* Parliament, Commanded wholly by Church of *England* Officers, *for none you know may have Commissions but Members of the Church*—These Landed in *Ireland;* Fought King *James* at the *Boyn, Shot at him,* did their endeavour *to kill,* and put him to Death . . . *they Routed him,* Defeated his Forces . . . and drove him a Second Time, to save himself by flight into *France*—And all this to prove . . . that the Church of *England* has ever adhered to the Great Doctrine of NON-RESISTANCE, and that Resisting the Sovereign, may not be practised upon any pretence whatsoever" (*Review,* 30 May 1710).

79. *hug the Priest:* Immediately after he was sentenced, Sacheverell was presented with a parsonage in Selattyn, Shropshire, worth £200 a year (Hearne, *2,* 368, 384). In June 1710 he

And ridicule their Sentence.   80

In order to discourage Mobs,
    And keep the People quiet,
The Rablers we condemn for Form,
    But not a Rogue shall die yet.

The Duke of *Marlborough* to requite,   85
    For retrieving *English* Honour;
His Dutchess shall have all the Spite
    That Fools can put upon her.

For Battles fought and Towns reduc'd,
    And Popish Armies broken,   90
And that our *English* Gratitude
    May to future times be spoken,

While fighting for the Nation he
    Looks Danger in the Face,
We strive t'insult his Family,   95
    And load him with Disgrace.

Because he's crown'd with Victory,
    And all the People love him,
We hate the Man for his Success,
    And therefore we'll remove him.   100

---

left London and proceeded westward to receive, "as his due, the homage and adoration of multitudes" (*Private Correspondence of Sarah, Duchess of Marlborough, 2,* 135).

83. *The Rablers:* Of the 105 rioters arrested on 28 February–1 March (*A True List of the Names of Those Persons Committed to the Several Gaols,* 1710), 19 were brought to trial. Of these, two were acquitted, 15 fined, and two—Daniel Damere and George Purchase—condemned to death for treason. In the *Review* for 8 August 1710 Defoe complained that although "the Villains . . . were found Guilty . . . the Sentence [had not been] Executed upon them." Both the prisoners were subsequently pardoned, which "many were apt to ascribe to the Prevalency of the High-Church Party" (Boyer, *Annals,* 1711, p. 201).

86. *retrieving English Honour:* This is a reminder to the Tories that they themselves in October 1702 had voted an address to the queen to thank Marlborough for having "retrieved" England's honor ([Defoe], *The Address,* 7; *POAS,* Yale, *6,* 634). The Whigs had taken this as a slight to William III and would have substituted the word "maintained" (*CJ, 14,* 9).

87. *Spite:* After her final interview with the queen on 6 April 1710 and her departure from court, the duchess became the object of "fresh Scandal every Day . . . Invectives . . . And . . . Lampoon" (*Belisarius and Zariana. A Dialogue,* 1710, pp. 7–8).

91. *English Gratitude:* "*English* Gratitude is always such, / To hate the Hand which does oblige too much" (Defoe, *The True-Born Englishman,* 867–68, *POAS,* Yale, *6,* 294).

97–99. Cf. Mainwaring?, *A New Ballad: To the Tune of Fair Rosamund,* 105n. above.

And now we're stirring up the Mob
 Against a new Election,
That High-Church Members may be chose
 By our most wise Direction.

That Queens may Parliaments dissolve,   105
 No doubt 'tis right and just;
But we have found it out that now,
 Because she may, she must.

The Bankrupt Nation to restore,
 And pay the Millions lent;   110
We'll at one dash wipe out the Score,
 With Spunge of Parliament.

Then we can carry on the War,
 With neither Fund or Debit;
And Banks shall eat us up no more,   115

101. *stirring up the Mob:* In his progress westward, "being attended with Multitudes of People, [Sacheverell] was receiv'd with Bonefires and Ringing of Bells" (Boyer, *Annals,* 1711, p. [210 misnumbered] 206). Sacheverell's design was "to confirm the People in the High-Church Interest, in case . . . the Queen should dissolve the Parliament" (ibid., p. 202). Defoe reported the "common Vogue, [that] we are to have a New Parliament" in the *Review* for 4 July 1710. And he supposed that by "Mobbing and Bullying the *Whigs* . . . all over *England,*" the high churchmen would return a large majority in the next parliament (*Review,* 8 July 1710).

108. *she must:* See p. 454 above.

109. *The Bankrupt Nation:* See *The Thanksgiving,* 8n. above.

112. *Spunge of Parliament:* "Lord [Godolphin?]" suggested to Defoe the possibility that a new ministry might simply repudiate the national debt, "take a *Parliament Spunge* and wipe it all out." This possibility so appalled Defoe that he mentioned it repeatedly in the *Review* and called it "a Notion destructive of Parliaments and the Constitution" (*Review,* 13 July, 27 July, 12 August 1710) and in 1714 fear of "the Spunge" was revived as a Whig election slogan.

113–14. "He that proposes to carry on the War without Credit, proposes Impossibilities, and indeed talks Nonsense . . . we had given up to *France* seven Years agoe, if our Credit had sunk" (*Review,* 17 August 1710).

114. *Fund or Debit:* A fund is part of the national revenue, such as the duty on malt, that is put up as security for loans from the public. As David Ogg (*3,* 413) explains, "what we now call the national debt was then thought of, not as an aggregate, but as a series of deficiencies, of greatly varying amounts, in the funds—deficiencies which, it was thought, could eventually be made good by taxation." These deficiencies came into existence whenever the treasury overestimated the yield on new sources of revenue, such as a duty imposed on malt in 1697 that was estimated to produce £800,000 a year. On this security the public lent £1,400,000. In its first year, however, the levy yielded only £344,000, for a deficiency—which Defoe here calls a "Debit"—of £456,000.

115. *Banks . . . eat us up:* On the evening of the day that she dismissed Sunderland, Anne

Upon pretence of Credit.

If not, we'll close with Terms of Peace,
Prescrib'd by *France* and *Rome;*
That War, being huddled up Abroad,
May then break out at Home.   120

---

was waited upon by a delegation of Whig financiers and officers of the Bank of England (Luttrell, *6,* 594) to warn her that if the ministry fell "all credit would be gone, stock fall, and the Bank be ruined, which included the ruin of the nation" (HMC *Portland MSS.,* *4,* 545). Defoe adopted a very independent line on this issue in the *Review.* He refused either to support the argument of the City financiers or to abandon Godolphin. Instead, he told the "rising Party, *as they call themselves,*" exactly what they would have to do to maintain the public credit: "let them come to *Exchange-Alley,* and give Premiums to take Stock at the present Price; when the Parliament shall be Dissolv'd, let them agree to have the Stock put upon them at an Advance; when the Ministry is Chang'd, let them engage to Circulate the Exchequer-Bills at *Par,* and take off the Annuities at 16 Years Purchase; let them agree to accept the Bank-Stock at 126, and to give 1 *per Cent.* for Seal'd Bills" (*Review,* 4 July, 8 July 1710). After "a short Conference" with Harley in mid-July, Defoe began to expand these ideas in a pamphlet, *An Essay upon Public Credit,* which was published on 23 August 1710 and immediately attributed to Harley (Defoe, *Letters,* pp. 276–77).

117–18. ". . . to join in with any just Methods, for preserving Publick Credit . . . I shall a little proceed to Enquire . . . Lastly, whether . . . we had not better venture it, than see *France,* by these Breaches, Triumphing over the Confederacy, and *French* Popery, Hand in Hand with Tyranny, coming in like a Flood?" (*Review,* 17 August 1710).

JONATHAN SWIFT

The Virtues of Sid Hamet the Magician's Rod
(October 1710)

Swift arrived in London on 7 September 1710 empowered to negotiate remission of the first fruits and twentieth parts, a tax of about £1,200 a year that the Irish clergy paid into the English treasury. He was still "much inclined to be what they called a Whig in politics" (Swift, *Prose*, *8,* 120) and hoped to use his acquaintance with the Junto lords to secure this benefaction for the Church of Ireland. But he found himself in the midst of a ministerial revolution in which it seemed that "every Whig in great office will, to a man, be infallibly put out" (Swift, *Journal*, *1,* 7).

Within two days of his arrival in London, he called upon Lord Godolphin with whom he had discussed this matter in June 1708. It was only a courtesy call, for Swift could have not expected much help from a cast courtier. "I was to visit my Lord *Godolphin*," Swift reported to Archbishop King in Dublin, "who gave me a Reception very unexpected, and altogether different from what I ever received from any great Man in my Life; altogether short, dry, and morose" (Swift, *Corr.*, *1,* 173). Swift had been offended by Godolphin on the occasion of their interview in 1708 when Godolphin very cynically implied that the price of taking off the first fruits and twentieth parts was the support of the clergy for repeal of the test clause in Ireland, which Swift and ninety-nine percent of his fellow churchmen felt "would level the Church Established, with every sniveling Sect in the Nation" (Swift, *Prose, 6,* 130). On this occasion, with Godolphin at the height of his power, Swift could only bow and take his leave. But to be "received . . . with a great deal of coldness" (Swift, *Journal*, *1,* 6) by a politician out of power, put very different ideas into Swift's head. It "has enraged me so, I am almost vowing revenge," he wrote to Esther Johnson (Swift, *Journal*, *1,* 6).

Three days later at St. James's coffeehouse, Swift ran into another Whig, Charles Bodvile Robartes, second earl of Radnor, and "talked treason heartily against the Whigs, their baseness and ingratitude. And I am come home rolling resentments in my mind, and framing schemes

of revenge: full of which (having written down some hints) I go to bed"
(ibid., *1*, 13).

One of these "hints" became *The Virtues of Sid Hamet the Magician's Rod*. The first reference to it in the *Journal to Stella* occurs on 26 September and by 1 October it is "almost finished." "[I] will print it for revenge on a certain great person," Swift added. On 4 October Swift gave the copy to John Morphew to be printed (ibid. *1*, 30, 37, 41) and on 7 October Morphew entered it in the Stationers Register.

By 14 October the verses had been published and were being "cried up to the skies." People "think no-body but Prior or I could write them," Swift boasted to the ladies in Dublin. And indeed they are a remarkable display of "the faculty of imagination" in action, "which, like a nimble spaniel, beats over and ranges through the field of memory, till it springs the quarry it hunted after; or, without metaphor, which searches over all the memory for the species or ideas of those things which it designs to represent" (Dryden, *Prose*, *2*, 260). Later Swift teased the ladies in Dublin: "Do you like *Sid Hamet's Rod?* Do you understand it all?" Esther Johnson understood it "well enough." "An enemy [of Godolphin's] should like it," she said, "and a friend not." "I don't like women so much as I did," Swift had concluded on a similar occasion (Swift, *Journal*, *1*, 59, 65, 110, 127, 90).

Sidney Godolphin, first Earl Godolphin, an engraving by Jacobus Houbraken

The *Rod* was but a harmless Wand,
While *Moses* held it in his Hand,
But soon as e'er he *lay'd it down,*
'Twas a devouring Serpent grown.
    Our great Magician, *Hamet Sid,*   5
Reverses what the Prophet did;
His *Rod* was honest *English* Wood,
That senseless in a Corner stood,
Till Metamorphos'd by his Grasp,
It grew an all-devouring Asp;   10
Would hiss, and sting, and roll, and twist,
By the meer Virtue of his Fist:
But when he *lay'd it down,* as quick
Resum'd the Figure of a Stick.
    So to Her Midnight Feasts the Hag   15
Rides on a Broomstick for a Nag,

Title. *The Magician's Rod:* "The staff of lord treasurer *Godolphin* [see illustration, p. 475], which, on the 29th of *May* 1711, was given to *Robert Harley,* earl of *Oxford*" (*Bh*).

2. *Moses:* "And the Lord said unto [Moses], What is that in thine hand? And he said, A rod. And he said, Cast it on the ground, and it became a serpent" (Exodus 4:2–3).

3. *lay'd it down:* The phrase means "resigned his office," but as Swift knew, Godolphin had not resigned; he had been dismissed (p. 452 above). "Whatever word or Sentence is Printed in a different Character, shall be judged to contain something extraordinary either of *Wit* or *Sublime*" (Swift, *Prose, 1,* 28).

5. *Hamet Sid:* This nickname for Sidney Godolphin is borrowed from Sidi Hamet Benengeli, "the first Author" of *Don Quixote,* to whom Cervantes attributes the original work in Arabic. As an historian Sidi Hamet is "exact, sincere, and impartial," but he is also a Moor, and Moors, as Swift may have remembered, are "all . . . given to impose on others with Lies and fabulous Stories" (*The History of the Renown'd Don Quixote de la Mancha,* trans. Peter Motteux, 4 vols., 1700–12, *1,* 82; *3,* 658).

9–12. Cf. [James Drake], *The Memorial of the Church of England,* 1705, p. 24: "The T[reasurer] may please himself with a Dream of Power and Popularity, and fancy himself some Mighty Monarch, when he sees his Levees crowded, and half a hundred Gentlemen waiting his Orders, and watching his Nods; but 'tis his Staff they follow, not him; if his Footman bore it, they would all be as obsequiously at his Heels."

16. *Broomstick:* Broomstick was much in Swift's mind at this time. In October 1708 he had included his *Meditation on a Broomstick* in a tentative table of contents for a volume of collectanea (*The Works of Jonathan Swift, D.D.,* ed. John Hawkesworth, 14 vols., 4⁰, 1755–79, *14,* 741). But before this volume was published in February 1711, "the unspeakable" Edmund Curll had published two editions of *A Meditation upon a Broom-stick, and Somewhat Beside; of the Same Author's* from a surreptitiously obtained copy (Swift, *Prose, 1,* 237), the first in April 1710.

That, rais'd by Magick of her Breech,
O'er Sea and Land conveys the Witch;
But, with the Morning-Dawn, resumes
The Peaceful State of common Brooms.   20
    They tell us something strange and odd,
About a certain Magick *Rod,*
That, bending down its Top, divines
When e'er the Soil has Golden Mines:
Where there are none, it stands erect,   25
Scorning to show the least Respect.
As ready was the *Wand* of *Sid*
To *bend* where *Golden Mines* were hid;
In *Scottish* Hills found precious Ore,
Where none e'er look'd for it before;   30
And, by a *gentle Bow,* divin'd
How well a *Cully*'s Purse was lin'd:
To a forlorn and broken *Rake,*
Stood without Motion, like a Stake.
    The *Rod* of *Hermes* was renown'd   35
For Charms above and under Ground;

22. *a certain Magick Rod:* "The *virgula divina,* or *divining-rod,* is described to be a forked branch of a hazel or willow, two feet and a half long: it is to be held in the palms of the hands with the single end elevated about eighty degrees; and in this position is said to be attracted by minerals and springs, so as by a forcible inclination to direct where they are to be found" (*Bh*).

29–30. Swift gives further currency to the rumor that Godolphin had "lavish'd away near a Million *Sterling,* to bring about the *Union;* with no other design than to retrieve a False step [advising the queen to give her assent to the Act of Security (pp. 209 and 374 above)], for which he might have lost his Head" (*An Essay towards the History of the Last Ministry and Parliament,* 1710, p. 47). The Tories in the House of Lords in November 1704 "intended to add a severe vote against all who had advised [the Act of Security]" (Burnet, 1823, *5,* 179) and they would have been delighted to have impeached Godolphin. But "The Whigs diverted this," Godolphin "having . . . delivered himself entirely into their management, provided they brought him off" (ibid.). The Junto's first demand, union with Scotland, created the necessity for bribes. On 21 September 1706 James Johnstone reported that "225 (Duke Queensberry) . . . railed at 15 [Godolphin]; said he was not for 58 (the Union), &c. but at last 102 (a sum of money) quieted him. I believe 103 (the sum of money) is ten thousand pounds; the thing itself is no secret" (*Correspondence of George Baillie of Jerviswood,* Bannatyne Club, Edinburgh, 1842, p. 160).

35. *Rod of Hermes:* Hermes's wand, "(Lat. *caduceus*) was originally an enchanter's wand, a symbol of the power that produces wealth . . . and also an emblem of influence over the living and the dead . . . with one touch of his staff [Hermes could] close or open the eyes of mortals . . . so [was] he also the conductor of the souls of the dead in the nether-world (*Psychopompos*)" (Oskar Seyffert, *A Dictionary of Classical Antiquities,* New York, Meridian Books, 1956, pp. 288, 287).

To sleep could Mortal Eye-lids fix,
And drive departed Souls to *Styx*.
That *Rod* was just a Type of *Sid*'s,
Which, o'er a *British* Senate's Lids,   40
Could *scatter Opium* full as well,
And drive as many *Souls to hell*.
    Sid's Rod was slender, white, and tall,
Which oft he us'd to *fish* withal:
A *PLACE* was fastned to the Hook,   45
And many a Score of *Gudgeons* took;
Yet, still so happy was his Fate,
He caught his *Fish*, and sav'd his *Bait*.
    Sid's Brethren of the conj'ring Tribe
A Circle with their *Rod* describe,   50
Which proves a Magical Redoubt
To keep *mischievous Spirits* out:
Sid's *Rod* was of a larger Stride,
And made a Circle thrice as wide,
Where *Spirits* throng'd with hideous Din,   55
And he stood there to *take them in*.
But, when th'enchanted *Rod* was *broke*,
They vanish'd in a stinking Smoak.
    Achilles' Scepter was of Wood,

40. *British Senate:* Godolphin undertook to control both houses of parliament by systematic bribery (cf. *The Dyet of Poland*, 639n. above). Somers "was sure" that Lord Haversham, for example, "might be had" for £1,000 (*Private Correspondence of Sarah, Duchess of Marlborough, 1*, 277). Ten members of parliament known to be in receipt of pensions are named in *A List of Gentlemen that are in Offices, Employments, &c.*, Cambridge, [1705].

45. *PLACE:* About 20 place-holders in *A List of Gentlemen that are in Offices, Employments, &c.*, Cambridge, [1705] had been appointed by Godolphin. After the Union, 20–25 percent of the House of Commons, called "the Queen's Servants," were expected to vote with the ministry. In the House of Lords the figure was between 40 and 50 percent (Holmes, pp. 354, 387).

48. Cf. "They blame [Harley] for his slowness in turning people out; but I suppose he had his reasons" (Swift, *Journal, 1*, 298). Surely the reason is that an unfilled post can secure the votes of half a dozen hopeful candidates, whereas only one can be gained by filling it.

55. *Spirits throng'd:* Defoe observed that the scores of Scots who came to London during the reign of James I "gaping for Preferment . . . serv'd only to make the *English* jealous and uneasy" (*An Essay at Removing National Prejudices against a Union with Scotland*, Part I, 1706, p. 7).

59. *Achilles' Scepter:* The sceptre on which Achilles swore his awful oath was Agamemnon's:

    . . . this sceptre, which never again will bear leaf nor
    branch, now that it has left behind the cut stump in the mountains,

Like *Sid*'s, but nothing near so good;   60
Tho' down from Ancestors Divine
Transmitted to the Heroes Line,
Thence, thro' a long Descent of Kings,
Came an 𝕳𝖊𝖎𝖗-𝖑𝖔𝖔𝖒, as *Homer* sings,
Tho' this Description looks so big,   65
That *Scepter* was a sapless Twig:
Which, from the fatal Day when first
It left the Forest where 'twas nurst,
As *Homer* tells us o'er and o'er,
Nor Leaf, nor Fruit, nor Blossom bore.   70
Sid's Scepter, full of Juice, did shoot
In Golden Boughs, and Golden Fruit,
And He, the *Dragon* never sleeping,
Guarded each fair *Hesperian* Pippin.
No *Hobby-horse*, with gorgeous Top,   75
The dearest in *Charles Mather*'s Shop,
Or glitt'ring Tinsel of *May-Fair*,
Could with this *Rod* of *Sid* compare.

---

nor shall it ever blossom again, since the bronze blade stripped
bark and leafage . . . .
. . . Hephaistos had wrought [it] carefully.
Hephaistos gave it to Zeus the king, the son of Kronos,
and Zeus in turn gave it to the courier Argeïphontes,
and lord Hermes gave it to Pelops, driver of horses,
and Pelops again gave it to Atreus, the shepherd of the people.
Atreus dying left it to Thyestes of the rich flocks,
and Thyestes left it in turn to Agamemnon to carry
and to be lord of many islands and over all Argos.

(*The Iliad, 1,* 234–39, *2,* 101–08, trans. Richmond Lattimore, Chicago, University of Chicago Press, 1951, pp. 65, 78–79).

69. *o'er and o'er:* Is Pope referring to this line when he says, "in Opposition to some Moderns who have criticiz'd upon it as tedious, that [Homer's description of Agamemnon's sceptre (59*n.* above)] has been esteem'd a Beauty by the Ancients" (Pope, *Poems, 7,* 102)?

71–72. Godolphin "frequently had . . . vast Sums of Money from the City, upon the Strength of his own Credit" (*The Secret History of the Late Ministry,* 1715, p. 69).

74. *Hesperian Pippin:* Golden apples in the garden of the Hesperides on the river Oceanus were guarded by a dragon that never slept.

76. *Charles Mather:* "An eminent toyman in *Fleet-street*" (*Bhno*). "His shop lay over against Chancery Lane. See *The Tatler,* Nos. 27, 113, 142; *The Spectator,* Nos. 328, 503, 570" (Swift, *Poems, 1,* 135).

77. *May-Fair:* "Near *Hyde-Park,* where a Fair was annually held" (*Blm*). The fair was a rite of spring held "in a Place called *Brook-Field,* in the Parish of St. *Martin in the Fields,*" between St. James's and Hyde Park, where young people "spent their Time and Money in Drunkenness, Fornication, Gaming, and Lewdness" (Strype, *2,* 34).

Dear *Sid*, then why wer't thou so mad
To break thy *Rod* like naughty Lad?   80
You should have kiss'd it in your Distress,
And then return'd it to *your Mistress*,
Or made it a *Newmarket* Switch,
And not a *Rod* for thy own Breech.
But since old *Sid* has broken this,   85
His next may be a *Rod in Piss*.

80. *break thy Rod:* See p. 452 above.

82. *your Mistress:* "*Queen* ANNE" (*Bjklm*).

83. *a Newmarket Switch:* "Lord Godolphin is satirized by Mr. Pope for a strong attachment to the turf. See his Moral Essays [*Epistle I: To Richard Temple, Viscount Cobham,* 140–45]" (*Bno*). Godolphin was attending the races at Newmarket in April 1710 when Anne made the first move toward replacing his ministry by appointing Shrewsbury her lord chamberlain (Coxe, *Memoirs, 3,* 61–62).

86. *a Rod in Piss:* "A prospective punishment, scolding" (Partridge, p. 635).

JONATHAN SWIFT

A Dialogue between Captain Tom and Sir Henry Dutton Colt
(9 October 1710)

Swift was sitting in St. James's coffeehouse on the night of 21 September 1710 when he heard the long-awaited news that the queen had dissolved parliament.

Of the two incumbents in the borough of Westminster, one of them, Thomas Medlycott, a Tory and a protegé of the duke of Ormonde, was encouraged to run again. The other, Henry Boyle, a court Whig and one of the managers of the Sacheverell trial, who lost his post as secretary of state to Henry St. John on the day parliament was dissolved, declined to stand again (Huntington Library MS. Stowe 57, *4*, 161). Something of the confusion and cross-purposes of the new, designedly moderate, ministry are shown in the choice of a candidate to replace Boyle.

"Mr. Webb," general John Richmond Webb, was "persuaded to desist" from standing for Westminster "in order to quiet the City." Then a local brewer, Thomas Crosse, a Tory who had twice been elected for Westminster, was chosen to run with Medlycott in the high church interest. But although they were told that "all were engaged" for Medlycott and Crosse, "Some warm, inconsiderate persons . . . set up Mr. Stanhope for Westminster" (HMC *Portland MSS., 2*, 222–23; *Wentworth Papers*, p. 140). Mr. Stanhope, although he too had been one of the managers of the Sacheverell trial, was the hero of the hour to whom the poets were singing, "Whene'er you fought the Haughty Foes were broke, / The Priest more Haughty trembled when you spoke" (*To Mr. Stanhope, One of the Managers of the House of Commons, and General of Her Majesty's Forces*, 1710). Among the "warm inconsiderate persons" who had put up General Stanhope were the duke of Somerset, who complained that he had been deceived by Harley (*Wentworth Papers*, pp. 144, 145), and the duke of Newcastle, whom Harley had brought into the ministry as lord privy seal (March 1705–August 1711) and who was nominally acting as one of Harley's principal election managers. Teamed up with Stanhope was an old Whig warhorse, Sir Henry Dutton Colt, who had also been twice elected for

480

Westminster and who had polled 29 more votes than Medlycott in July 1708, but whose election had been overturned by a vote of the House. The rivalry of two such strong slates, together with such provocations as a brewer could easily provide, had, as Harley regretfully concluded, "given occasion to much heat" (HMC *Portland MSS.*, *2*, 223).

Since the demonstrations for Sacheverell in February and March, rioting and violence had never quite subsided in London. It was kept up, the Whigs said, to influence elections "on the side of the *Church* and *Monarchy*" (Boyer, *Annals*, 1711, p. 249). Electioneering, in fact, had begun long before there were writs for a new election. One of the first things that Swift noticed upon his return to London on 7 September was that "Elections are now managing with greater Violence and Expence, and more Competitors than ever was known" (Swift, *Corr.*, *1*, 174). "The Influence of the Mob," it was said, "was . . . remarkable in the Election for the City of *Westminster*" and a German eyewitness observed that "people behaved so wildly that one might have been in Poland" (Boyer, *Annals*, 1711, p. 249; *London in 1710 from the Travels of Zacharias Conrad von Uffenbach*, trans. and ed. by W. H. Quarrell and Margaret Mare, Faber & Faber, 1934, p. 146).

There was also, of course, a literary dimension to this conflict. Arthur Mainwaring devoted *The Whig Examiner* of 28 September 1710 to an election speech for Stanhope. Just as Swift had taken Alcibiades as a classical analogue for two of the Junto lords in 1701 (Swift, *Discourse*, pp. 134–35), Mainwaring made Stanhope speak in the person of the same Greek hero:

> Is it then possible, O ye *Athenians* . . . That I who have over-thrown the Princes of *Lacedaemon* [6*n*. below], must now see my self in danger of being defeated by a Brewer? . . . Let it not avail my Competitor, that he has been tapping his Liquors while I have been spilling my Blood; that he has been gathering Hopps for you, while I have been reaping Lawrels. Have I not born the Dust and Heat of the Day, while he has been sweating at the Furnace? . . . Has he any other Wound about him, except the accidental Scaldings of his Wort, or Bruises from the Tub or Barrel?

It seems fairly certain that some of these words are reflected in the following lines of the present poem: *Brewer* (8), Laurel (15), Hops (16), *FURNESE* (14), *Tub* (20). But it is not certain that Mainwaring's *Whig Examiner* by itself provided a sufficient cause for *A Dialogue between Captain Tom and Sir Henry Dutton Colt*, for Swift was literally caught up in the election riot that the German saw (6n. below). It may have taken this striking experience plus the experience of Mainwaring's *Whig Examiner* to precipitate the following verses.

What Swift wrote is essentially a fragment of dialogue, a mock-heroic confrontation between the Whig candidate, Sir Henry Dutton Colt and Captain Tom, the leader of the Tory mob. It is essentially a recruitment speech: Sir Harry, consciously adjusting his speech and manner to the level of "common folk," attempts to engage Captain Tom to demonstrate in favor of "Old *Colt* and brave General *Stanhope*" (6). He fails, of course, just as the Whigs were to fail at the polls. "Some of those who offer'd to give their Voices for . . . General *Stanhope*, and Sir *Henry Dutton-Colt*, were knock'd down, and sorely wounded, which obliged many of their Party to return Home, without Polling; whereby the [Tory] Candidates had a vast Majority" (Boyer, *Annals*, 1711, pp. 249–50).

The restoration of these amusing verses to the Swift canon was proposed by Arthur Main (*Harvard Library Bulletin*, *11* [1957], 76–77) and confirmed by George P. Mayhew in his definitive article on the poem (*Bulletin of the John Rylands Library*, *53* [1971], 397–427).

The dates of composition and publication of the verses can be established within close limits. Swift witnessed the election riot on Thursday 5 October, the day after his first meeting with Harley. When Sir Andrew Fountaine called the next morning at Swift's lodgings, he caught him "writing in bed" (Swift, *Journal*, *1*, 43). On Saturday 7 October, after his second meeting with Harley, Swift went to his publisher, Benjamin Tooke (20n. below), "to give him a ballad," presumably the "Ballad, full of puns, on the Westminster Election, that cost me half an hour," as Swift boasted to Stella on 20 October (Swift, *Journal*, *1*, 46, 65). Since the last day of polling was Monday 9 October, it may be further surmised that the poem was published then.

The next day Swift decided that he was "not fond at all of St. James's Coffee-house, as I used to be" (ibid., *1*, 48).

A Dialogue between Captain Tom and Sir Henry Dutton Colt

Come, fair Muse of *Grub-street,* the Dialogue write,
Betwixt Captain *Tom* and a goodly old Knight.
Quoth ancient Sir *Harry,* My dear Captain *Thomas,*
Sure you and your Subjects will not depart from us.

Title. Dialogue: Swift may have been influenced to use the dialogue form by its great popularity at the moment. Besides 20 titles in Morgan, *2,* 128–91, there are also *A Late Dialogue between Dr. Burgess, and Daniel d'Foe, in a Cyder-Cellar near Billingsgate* ("*Quoth Daniel* the *Doctor,* to *Daniel d'Foe*") printed in *A Collection of Poems, &c. For and Against Dr. Sacheverell,* 4 vols., 1710–11, *2,* 11; *Pulpit-War: Or, Dr. S———ll, the High-Church Trumpet, and Mr. H———ly, the Low-Church Drum, Engaged. By Way of Dialogue* . . . ("Tell me, Proud Insect, since thou can'st not Fly"), 1710, an octavo pamphlet, and *A Dialogue between Whigg and Whigg* ("There came a *Scot* of Late I hear, to wait upon *Tom Double*"), Dublin, [1710?], a folio half-sheet.

Captain Tom: the generic "Leader of . . . the Mob" (Defoe, *The Dyet of Poland,* 952n. above). Defoe had already assumed the role of a Whiggish Captain Tom in order to scold the Tory mob in *A Letter from Captain Tom to the Mobb, Now Rais'd for Dr. Sacheverel,* [March] 1710. But Swift's Tory Captain Tom, who speaks the vernacular of Tothill Fields, owes nothing to Defoe's creature, who sounds exactly like "Mr. *Review.*"

Colt: Sir Henry Dutton Colt, of St. James, Westminster (c. 1646–1731), first baronet, had long been a figure of fun. Sir Harry, as he was called, was an over-aged "Satyr" in *Tunbridge Lampoon* (1699) and in May 1708 there was thought to be something "Odd / Between his *Neice* and *him*" (University of Nottingham MS. Portland Pw V 47, f. 62; Hearne, *2,* 110). He was a Whig member of parliament for Newport, Isle of Wight (1695–98), but switched to Harley's New Country-Party and stood for Westminster against James Vernon in July 1698. "He rails at courtiers," Vernon said, "and sets up for a national interest till he makes it a jest." But Colt built up a following among "the very scum of the town," which worried Vernon. Even Patch, the duke of Shrewsbury's footman, called himself a gentleman and voted for Colt. When he was defeated, Colt immediately announced that he would enter a protest (Vernon, *2,* 126, 137, 140). His petition was "heard, and laughed at, and voted false, vexatious and frivolous." It was observed that "no man a great while has more effectually exposed himself for want of common civility and common sense" (*CSPD 1698,* p. 430). As a result the king ordered him to be put out of the commission of the peace in December 1698 (Luttrell, *4,* 465). Colt finally secured election in Westminster (December 1701–02, 1705–08) and was reconciled to the Whigs. Again in 1708 he stood at the top of the poll but lost his seat to the Tory petitioner, Thomas Medlycott. This was difficult to do in a house controlled by a strong Whig majority, but it was achieved because "environ 34 ou 35 Membres du Party des Moderes [Whigs] qui s'impatientoient d'aller a l'Opéra pour entendre chanter le Fameux Nicolino, sortirent de la chambre, et le Party des Anglicans rigides [Tories] le sentant alors le plus fort, profita de leur Absence et ayant fait mettre en Question si le Sr. Medlicot etoit düement elu, l'Affirmative l'emporta de 154 voix contre 142 . . . On remarqua aussi en cette occasion que la plus part des Membres Ecossois, se resouvenant que sous le dernier Regne, le chevalier Colt s'etoit mit a la teste de ceux qui s'opposoient a l'Etablissement de la Colonie Ecossoise a Darien, donnerent leurs voix en faveur du Sieur Medlicot" (BM MS. Add. 22202, f. 2v). Colt's state of mind in the election of October 1710 can be readily deduced from these failures in 1698 and 1708.

4. *your Subjects:* Captain Tom's subjects, "true Friends of the *Church* and *Sacheverel*" (29),

Then hold Hat and Heart, and Right-Hand ev'ry Man up,   5
And bawl out, Old *Colt* and brave General *Stanhop.*
Let the General's Merits and mine be maintain'd:
Turn off the old *Brewer,* and be not *Cross-Grain'd.*
In a Protestant Country, why are you for *Crosses?*
And *Brewers* will poison you all with Molosses.   10
Besides, Are not all the damn'd Jacobites *Brewers,*
Still brewing of Mischief, and so may be yours?
And Papists are Brewers, with Faggots to burn us;
But if you love Brewing, you may have a *FURNESE.*

---

were "for the most part common folk." The supporters of the Whigs, on the other hand, were "made up for the most part of gentlemen of quality and lords" (*London in 1710 from the Travels of Zacharias Conrad von Uffenbach,* trans. and ed. by W. H. Quarrell and Margaret Mare, Faber & Faber, 1934, pp. 146–47).

6. *Old Colt and brave General Stanhop:* On 5 October Swift took a hackney coach to pay a visit to Sir Godfrey Kneller and "In the way," he said, "we met electors for parliament-men: and the rabble came about our coach, crying A Colt, a Stanhope, &c. we were afraid of a dead cat, or our glasses broken, and so were always of their side" (Swift, *Journal, 1,* 42).

Stanhop: After a flying visit to London to serve on the impeachment committee, Stan-hope had returned to Spain to defeat the hapless armies of Philip V, from which the French had been withdrawn, almost as easily as he had defeated an impertinent priest. First on 16/27 July 1710 near Almenar in Lerida, where Stanhope killed a Spanish general with his own hands at the head of a cavalry charge, and then on 9/20 August at the gates of Zaragoza, the confederates won overwhelming victories and seemed at last on the verge of total success in Spain (Tindal, *4,* i, [2]176–78; Luttrell, *6,* 627). On 21 September the "great news" reached London that "king Charles and Stanhope are at Madrid" (Swift, *Journal, 1,* 25). Stanhope's proxy at the election was his cousin, Lieutenant General Sherington Davenport (HMC *Portland MSS., 4,* 603; Dalton, *6,* 18).

8. *the old Brewer:* Thomas Crosse (1663–1738), proprietor of a brewery in Westminster (Walcott, p. 223), was born in Westminster, educated at the Westminster School in its heyday under Richard Busby, and represented Westminster in parliament (1701, 1702–05, 1710–22). In politics he was an unreconstructed Tory and member of the October Club. He had run against Sir Henry Dutton Colt in four previous elections, winning twice (January 1701 and August 1702) and losing twice (December 1701 and May 1705). This time he won the rubber and was created baronet in July 1713.

Cross-Grain'd: Swift warned Stella that his ballad on the Westminster election was "full of puns" (Swift, *Journal, 1,* 65).

10. *poison you . . . with Molosses:* The general nature of the fraud may be inferred from the following: "Molosses or Treacle has certainly been formerly made too much Use of in . . . brewing . . . when Malts have been dear: But it is now prohibited" (*The London and Country Brewer,* 5th ed., 1744, p. 31); cf. Swift, *Prose, 3,* 138.

14. *FURNESE:* Sir Henry Furnese (1658–1712) was born in Sandwich, Kent, the son of a bankrupt butcher. He began his career as an "apprentice to a Stockin-seller in the ex-change . . . traded in poynt to Flanders by which it is said he gott an estate" (Le Neve, p. 436) and died a baronet and member of parliament. He was one of the original directors of the Bank of England in 1694 and served as receiver for the £2,000,000 loan which the New East India Company made to the government in 1696. His first attempt to secure election to parliament ended in expulsion in February 1699, but "Equipt with Leudness, Oaths, and

Then *Stanhop* shall send you each Laurel he crops;   15
And *Laurels* are sometimes as bitter as Hops.
   When comely Sir *Harry* had thus shot his Bolt,
Then reply'd Captain *Tom*, God-a-mercy, old *Colt*,
You had better have been at your *Spade* and your *Club*,
Than take up our Time with a *Tale of a Tub*.   20
You shall be *discarded*, I say't to your *Face*:
We'll play *All the Game*, and not bate you an *Ace*.
Then let me advise you no longer to stay,
But *pack* up and *shuffle*, and *cut* it away.
And tho' you have Wit, Youth, Beauty, and Parts,   25
While we keep up our *Clubs*, you shall ne'er win our *Hearts*.

Impudence" (Defoe, *Reformation of Manners*, 151, *POAS*, Yale, *6*, 406), he was elected sheriff of London the following year. Upon his installation he entertained at dinner in Drapers Hall 600 guests, including three dukes, 20 other peers, and dozens of members of parliament. His second attempt to secure a seat in parliament also ended in expulsion in February 1701, but in November 1701 he finally was elected for Sandwich and served until his death, delivering a Whig vote in all the recorded divisions. The bulk of his great fortune was made in the field of army remittances and "from Feb. 1705 to Aug. 1710 he engrossed all the valuable contracts for paying the armed forces in the Low Countries, Portugal and Spain" (Holmes, p. 156). In June 1707 he was created the first baronet of Great Britain and the following year his success was sealed by his election to the Kit-Cat Club (*Private Correspondence of Sarah, Duchess of Marlborough*, *1*, 279). "Thus it happens, that Mr. P[rio]r, by being expell'd the Club, ceases to be a *Poet;* and Sir *Harry* F[urnes]e becomes one, by being admitted into it" (Prior, *Works*, *1*, 389). At this triple pun on furnace / Furnese / Farnese ["a Sovereign Prince in *Italy*"] (Swift, *Prose*, *3*, 152), George P. Mayhew suggests "as a stage direction a guffaw upon Colt's part at his own cleverness" (*Bulletin of the John Rylands Library*, *53* [1971], 421).

   15. *Laurel he crops:* Cf. "reaping Lawrels" (*The Whig Examiner*, 28 September 1710), headnote, p. 481 above.

   16. *Laurels . . . bitter:* Cf. "General Stanhop's great services in Spain, his ingenuity and great abilitys, now the Court sun does not shine upon him, can make nothing of it against a brewer" (Carlisle R. O. MS. D/Lons, James Lowther to William Gilpin, 7 October 1710).

   19. *Spade and . . . Club:* Sir Harry was a notorious gambler, profaning even the sabbath "With wicked *Cards* and *Dice*" (*Letters from the Living to the Living*, 1703, p. 24; Hearne, *2*, 110).

   20. *a Tale of a Tub:* As a vernacular phrase meaning a cock-and-bull story (Tilley, T45) this expression is perfectly in character for Captain Tom. It also reflects some of Swift's preoccupations in 1710. On 20 June, in the midst of negotiations with Benjamin Tooke for a fifth edition of *A Tale of a Tub*, complete with *An Apology*, footnotes, and "cuts," Swift was annoyed by Edmund Curll's publication of *A Complete Key to the Tale of a Tub*, attributing the greater part of the work to Swift's "little Parson-cousin" (Swift, *Corr.*, *1*, 165–66; cf. Swift, *Journals*, *1*, 47).

   21. *discarded:* Captain Tom was prophetic, for Sir Harry stood at the bottom of the poll (*The British Apollo*, 9–11 October 1710).

   22. *bate you an Ace:* another vernacular phrase, meaning "to make the slightest abatement" (*OED*).

   26. *Clubs:* Besides carrying out the card-playing puns of lines 19–25, "Clubs" had another

Brave *Stanhop* for Fighting will have his Reward,
And the Queen, when she pleases, can make him a *Lord*.
But we are true Friends of the *Church* and *Sacheverel*;
And vote for a *Manager* surely we never will!   30
Besides, we have found too much Heat in some Rulers,
And will give them a *Brewer*, because they want *Coolers*.
If Christians love *Crosses*, why should they be blam'd?
You shall see us *bear* ours, and not be asham'd.
But we know what you aim at: you all would engross,   35
And not leave the Church or the Nation a *Cross*.
    When the Captain had finish'd, away went old *Numps*:
He had got a *Bad Game*, and could not turn up *Trumps*.
His Eggs they are addle, and Dough was his Cake;
So fairly he left them to *Brew* as they *Bake*.   40

---

meaning: "most of those . . . who behaved the most shamefully [in the election riots] had great clubs hanging to their saddles, and with these they gave each other heavy blows" (*London in 1710 from the Travels of Zacharias Conrad von Uffenbach*, trans. and ed. by W. H. Quarrell and Margaret Mare, Faber & Faber, 1934, p. 147).

28. *make him a Lord:* Again Captain Tom is prophetic, but it was George I in July 1717 who raised Stanhope to the peerage as Viscount Stanhope of Mahon, in Minorca, which he had captured from the Spanish in September 1708.

30. *a Manager:* Stanhope was one of the "Twenty brave Pleaders" who managed the prosecution of Sacheverell (*The Old Pack*, 81n. above).

32. *Coolers:* "Ale, stout, or porter taken after spirits" (Partridge, p. 178).

33. *Crosses:* another triple pun: Tory candidate / Christian symbol / coin worth about two shillings (*Bulletin of the John Rylands Library, 53* [1971], 422).

34. *bear ours:* "Cross's men . . . kept on making crosses with their hands (in allusion to his name)" (*London in 1710 from the Travels of Zacharias Conrad von Uffenbach*, trans. and ed. by W. H. Quarrell and Margaret Mare, Faber & Faber, 1934, p. 146).

37. *Numps:* "A silly or stupid person" (*OED*).

38. *a Bad Game:* This echoes a phrase from the *Journal* of 5 October 1710: "MD . . . lost four and eight-pence last night but one . . . because you played bad games" (Swift, *Journal, 1*, 43).

    turn up Trumps: proverbial (Tilley, T544). The poem ends in a virtuoso display of proverbs and puns.

39. *His Eggs . . . are addle:* proverbial: "You come in with your five Eggs a penny, and four of 'em addle" (*New Dictionary*, sig. E1v); cf. Tilley, E92; Swift, *Journal, 2*, 447: "We have eggs on the spit, I wish they may not be addle."

    Dough was his Cake: proverbial for a failure or mismanagement (Tilley, C12).

40. *to Brew as they Bake:* proverbial for suffering the effects of one's actions (Tilley, B654).

An Acrostick on Wharton
(12 December 1710)

This is the "Province" to which Dryden relegated Thomas Shadwell, but the anonymous author of the present "Acrostick" cannot have found it "Peacefull." He shares with the rioters who wanted to pull down Wharton's house during the Sacheverell trial (Boyer, *Annals,* 1710, p. 266) a rage to strike out at something incomprehensibly evil.

On 1 May 1710, after his brilliant management of the Sacheverell trial, Wharton went back to Ireland to resume his duties as lord lieutenant (Luttrell, *6,* 575). But as soon as he heard of Godolphin's dismissal, he hurried home to England to manage his interests in the coming elections. He was dismissed on 26 October and on 9 November 1710 Swift began his attack in *The Examiner.* The famous *Examiner* of 30 November attacked Wharton in terms of Cicero's diatribe against Verres. Before the end of the year Swift had published his full-scale attack, *A Short Character of His Ex[cellency] T[homas] E[arl] of W[harton]* (Hearne, *3,* 100).

An Acrostick on Wharton was printed in *The Post Boy,* 12 December 1710.

AN ACROSTICK ON WHARTON

Whig's the first Letter of his odious Name;
Hypocrisy's the second of the same;
Anarchy's his Darling; and his Aim
Rebellion, Discord, Mutiny, and Faction;
Tom, Captain of the Mob in Soul and Action;   5
O'ergrown in Sin, cornuted, old, in Debt,
Noll's Soul and *Ireton*'s live within him yet.

2. *Hypocrisy:* "He seemeth to be but an ill Dissembler, and an ill Liar, although they are the two Talents he most practiseth, and most valueth him self upon" (Swift, *Prose, 3*, 179).

3. *Anarchy:* "King William at his private parties drunk sometimes to excess . . . In one of his parties with Lord Wharton, whom he always called Thom Wharton, he said, 'Thom, I know what you wish for, you wish for a republic.' Lord Wharton answered, 'And not a bad thing' " (Dalrymple, *3*, ²182). William thought him "too popular, or too much a Republican to be intrusted with the Administration of State Affairs" (Macky, p. 91).

5. *Tom:* Wharton liked to be called Tom. Even after he succeeded as Lord Wharton in February 1696, he continued to sign his letters "T. Wharton," and he was popularly known as "honest Tom" (Burnet, 1823, *5*, 228*n.*). Tories sometimes called him "King Tom" (*Verney Letters, 1*, 242).

Captain: See *A Dialogue between Captain Tom and Sir Henry Dutton Colt*, Title, *n.*

6. *O'ergrown in Sin:* "The most dissolute cavaliers stood aghast at the dissoluteness of the emancipated precisian. He early acquired and retained to the last the reputation of being the greatest rake in England . . . to the end of his long life the wives and daughters of his nearest friends were not safe from his licentious plots" (Macaulay, *5*, 2402; cf. Swift, *Prose, 3*, 28).

cornuted: cuckolded (*OED*). "He bears the Gallantries of his Lady with the Indifference of a Stoic, and thinks them well recompenced by a Return of Children to support his Family without the Fatigues of being a Father" (Swift, *Prose, 3*, 180).

old: Wharton became 62 in August 1710. A folio half-sheet, *A Tale of My L——d Wh——on: Upon His Going for Ir——nd*, [May] 1710, mentions his "Paunch stuff'd out with Arrogance."

in Debt: Wharton spent so much money on race horses and elections that he was always in desperate financial straits. The day after he kissed the queen's hand to be lord lieutenant of Ireland in November 1708, bailiffs entered his house in Dover Street and seized all his possessions (HMC *Portland MSS., 4*, 511). "He hath sunk his Fortune by endeavouring to ruin one Kingdom," Swift said, "and hath raised it by going far in the Ruin of another . . . Since he went into *Ireland*, he . . . hath met with great Success, having gained by his Government, of under two Years, five and forty thousand Pounds by the most favourable Computation" (Swift, *Prose, 3*, 180–81).

7. *Noll:* Oliver Cromwell.

Ireton: Henry Ireton (1611–51), the great puritan and regicide, was Cromwell's son-in-law. In May 1699 the French ambassador told Louis XIV that Lord Wharton was "at the head of the Presbyterians" (Grimblot, *2*, 321).

1711

se vend a Paris chez Trouvain rüe St. Jacques au grand Monarque auec priuilege du Roy

James Francis Edward Stuart, the pretended Prince of Wales, an engraving attributed to A. Trouvain

DANIEL DEFOE?

A Welcome to the Medal;
Or,
An Excellent New Song, Call'd
The Constitution Restor'd in 1711,
To the Tune of *Mortimer's-Hole*
(September 1711)

Propaganda for the Jacobite invasion attempt of March 1708 included a medal cast by Norbert Roettier claiming the whole realm of England, Scotland, and Ireland for the youthful Prince of Wales (see illustration, p. 491)(Edward Hawkins, *Medallic Illustrations of the History of Great Britain and Ireland,* ed. Augustus W. Franks and Herbert A. Grueber, 2 vols., 1885, *2,* 312–13; but cf. Boyer, *Annals,* 1711, p. 66; 1712, p. 205). Three years later an English noblewoman resident in a Flemish convent (73*n.* below) brought a copy of this medal to Edinburgh and presented it to the Faculty of Advocates, the bar association of Scotland. On 30 June 1711, at the next regular meeting of the advocates, the dean announced receipt of the gift, proposed a vote of thanks to the duchess, and touched off a display of raw Jacobite sentiment that he could hardly have expected. James Dundas, eldest son of Lord Arniston, a judge in the court of session, brushed aside all objections as the protests of *"a few pitiful* Scoundrels *and* Mushrooms, *not worthy of our Notice"* and moved to accept the medal and return thanks to the duchess. His motion was carried (2*n.* below) and Dundas himself was delegated to convey the thanks of the faculty to the duchess.

Accordingly on 3 July 1711 Dundas waited on her grace at her lodgings in the Cannongate and spoke the following words:

> *MADAM,* We are deputed by the *Dean and the Faculty of Advocates,* in their Name, and for Our selves, to return our most hearty Thanks to Your Grace for Your Favours, and particularly for the Honour You do Us in presenting the MEDAL of Our Sovereign The King . . . .
>
> *MADAM,* I hope, and am Confident, and so do my Constituents, that Your Grace shall have very soon an Opportunity to Com-

pliment the *Faculty* with a second MEDAL, Struck upon the Restauration of the King and Royal Family, the Finishing *Rebellion*, Usurping *Tyranny* and *Whiggery*.

(Scotch-Loyalty Exemplify'd, in the Behaviour of the Dean of the Faculty, and his Brethren, at Edinburgh, in relation to the Reception of a Medal of the Pretender, presented to them by the Dutchess of Gourdon, [1711]).

"Having made some noise in *Edinburgh*," the incident was brought to the attention of the government in Westminster and Sir David Dalrymple, the queen's lord advocate, was ordered "to inquire into the whole Matter." On 18 July the Faculty of Advocates assembled in an extraordinary session to reject the offer of the said medal and to vindicate "their Duty and Loyalty to . . . the Protestant Succession, as by Law Establish'd in the Illustrious House of *Hanover*" (Boyer, *Annals*, 1712, pp. 207–08). Two weeks later, however, the alleged minutes of the meeting of 30 June were surreptitiously made available to George Ridpath and published in *The Flying Post*, 31 July–2 August 1711.

The Whigs, of course, were delighted. "Be sure to keep up the alarm about the Medal," one of Defoe's informants wrote to him from Edinburgh on 15 August (Defoe, *Letters*, p. 350). Defoe did not need to be encouraged to strike out against Jacobites: he had already published *The Scotch Medal Decipher'd, and The New Hereditary-Right Men Display'd: Or, Remarks on the Late Proceedings of the Faculty of Advocates at Edinburgh, upon Receiving the Pretender's Medal* and before the end of the month he produced *A Speech for Mr. D——sse Younger of Arnistown, If he should be impeach'd of H*[*igh*] *T*[*reaso*]*n for what he said and did about the Pretender's Medal.*

The Faculty of Advocates responded on 8 August by publishing a "Narrative of the Act of the Faculty" and sending a copy to the queen. Even though the "Narrative" did not "Give a full or True account of Matter of Fact" (Defoe, *Letters*, p. 353), the government published it, together with the minutes of the meeting of the Faculty of Advocates retracting the gift of the medal, in *The London Gazette*, 14–16 August 1711.

Sometime between 15 and 24 August James Dundas made matters worse by publishing a defense of himself entitled *The Faculty of Advocates' Loyalty.*

A few days later Defoe told Oxford that unless the government took action to dispel it, the rumor "That the Ministry is for The Pretender, will be . . . Confirm'd to the people" (Defoe, *Letters*, p. 353). On 18 September, therefore, Sir James Stewart of Goodtrees was put back in office as Anne's lord advocate and Sir David Dalrymple was left holding the medal (*The Arniston Memoirs,* ed. George W. T. Omond, Edinburgh, 1887, p. 53). Finally, on 6 October Oxford wrote the Princess Sophie assuring her that the queen had ordered James Dundas to be prosecuted (cf. 71*n.* below) "and because the Lord Advocate, (to whose care it did belong) was not very forward in putting the laws in execution upon this occasion, the Queen has thought fit to remove him, and to place Sir James Stuart in his room, who, I hope, will quickly correct the imprudence of those people" (Macpherson, *Original Papers, 2,* 257).

A few days later the ministry's side of the story was printed in *The Post Boy,* 9–11 October 1711. Defoe's side of the story, a much more compelling one, had already been set to music in the present poem. In form it is an uninhibited Jacobite song, another example of total irony, like *The Age of Wonders.* But in *A Welcome to the Medal* Defoe never seems to drop his disguise, as he does in *The Age of Wonders* (p. 462 above). Only its exaggeration gives away the anti-Jacobite intent of the poem. Not even the most credulous Jacobite can be imagined to have believed in 1711 that "Old *Lewis* is sure to succeed in the War" (38).

But this did not prevent the poem from being taken seriously as Jacobite propaganda in 1711. Thus one anonymous high churchman felt compelled to publish *Loyalty Display'd: Or, An Answer to the Factious and Rebellious Song, call'd, Welcome to the Medal; or, The Constitution Restor'd in 1711* ("Confound all the Medals of *James* the Third's Face") in order to repudiate the supposed Jacobitism of a popular song.

A *terminus ad quem* for publication of Defoe's song is 28 September 1711 when St. John signed a warrant to arrest Henry Hills and Thomas Harrison "for publishing and vending a scandalous and seditious Libel, called A Welcome to the Medal, or an excellent new Song called The Constitution restored in 1711" (*Copies Taken from the Records of the Court of King's Bench, at Westminster . . . Of Warrants issued by Secretaries of State, for seizing Persons suspected of being guilty of various Crimes, particularly, of being the Authors, Printers and Publishers of Libels,* 1763, p. 16). A month later, they were ordered to be prosecuted (Boyer, *Annals,* 1712, p. 264), but the author was never discovered.

Evidence that the author is Defoe is of the usual circumstantial kinds: parallels to his prose of the same period (7*n.,* 59*n.*), parallels to his letters (19*n.*), parallels to his verse (53*n.,* 104*n.*). What is lacking is quotation in the *Review,* but *A Welcome to the Medal* is another work, like *The Age of Wonders* (above), that Defoe would have every reason to conceal from Oxford. Even Oxford's elastic sense of humor might have been overtaxed by lines 56–65 and the ministry's prosecution of the printers of the poem indicates that Defoe's caution was not unfounded. William Wagstaffe seems to have suspected that Defoe (or George Ridpath, the writer of *The Observator*) wrote *A Welcome to the Medal*. Here is what Wagstaffe says: "*O Observator, O Review, O you Authors of the Wellcome to the Medal and Credit restor'd*, come into Court and . . . bear Testimony against Captain SILK's *Hautboys* [7*n*. below]" (*The Ballad of The King shall enjoy his own again: With a Learned Comment thereupon, at the Request of Capt. Silk, Dedicated to Jenny Man*. By The Author of Tom Thumb, 1711, p. 14).

No tune called *Mortimer's Hole* is known, but J. Woodfall Ebsworth offers an explanation of the origin and of one derisive application of the phrase: "'*Mortimer's Hole*' mockingly alludes to Harley's title of 'Baron Mortimer,' on elevation to the peerage; and less directly to Nottingham Castle, where, entering by a secret passage in the rock, King Edward III arrested Roger Mortimer, the paramour of Queen Isabella" (*Roxburghe Ballads, 8,* ii, 822).

A Jacobite medal by Norbert Roettier probably cast in
Paris to commemorate the invasion attempt of March 1708

A Welcome to the Medal;
Or,
An Excellent New Song, Call'd
The Constitution Restor'd in 1711,
To the Tune of *Mortimer's-Hole*

Let's joy in the Medal with *James* the IIId's Face
And the Advocates that pleaded for him:
Tho' the Nation renounces the whole Popish Race,
Great *Lewis* of *France* will restore him.
La, la, &c.   5

Health to the new Coll'nels and Captains so pritty,
With *Silk* and the rest of the Train, Sir,

Title. *The Constitution Restor'd in 1711:* What is implied is that by accepting the medal the Faculty of Advocates had restored the constitutional principle of succession by hereditary right set aside in 1689 (3*n.* below).

1. *Medal:* See illustration, p. 495. It was "a Silver Medal . . . having on the Right Side [the pretended Prince of Wales's] Head, and over it these Words, *Cujus Est?* Which are the same our Saviour used, when taking in his Hand the Tribute-Money, he ask'd *whose Image that was* [Mark 12:16]? The Reverse of the Medal represented the Kingdom of *Great-Britain* and *Ireland,* with this *Motto* over it, *REDDITE:* Being the first Word of our Saviour's Solution of the Question, about the Lawfulness of paying Tribute, or Obedience to *Caesar, Render* . . . *therefore* [Mark 12:17], &c." (Boyer, *Annals,* 1711, p. 66).

2. *the Advocates:* Of the 75 members of the Faculty present at the meeting of 30 June 1711, 63 voted that "Thanks should be returned to Her Grace," the duchess of Gordon, for the present of the medal (*Scotch-Loyalty Exemplify'd, in the Behaviour of the Dean of the Faculty* [1711]). Defoe supposed that "the Design of the Faction was to give a Reputation to their Cause, by bringing in so many Gentlemen of the long Robe to espouse it" (*The Scotch Medal Decipher'd, and The New Hereditary-Right Men Display'd,* 1711, p. 9).

3. The Bill of Rights of December 1689 provided that "all and every person or persons that is, are or shall be reconciled to or shall hold communion with the see or Church of Rome, or shall profess the popish religion, or shall marry a papist, shall be excluded . . . [from] the crown and government of this realm." The Scottish Claim of Right of the same year, but in much simpler language, provided "That by the law of this kingdom no papist can be king or queen" (*EHD, 8,* 127, 636).

6. *the new Coll'nels:* In October 1710, in the midst of the general election, the new commissioners of the lieutenancy (all crown appointees) turned out six Whigs (Chamberlayne, 1710, p. 635) and appointed, as commanders of the City regiments, six Tory merchants and bankers: Sir Robert Bedingfield, Sir Francis Child, Sir Samuel Garrard, Sir Richard Hoare, Sir John Parsons, and Sir William Withers (Boyer, *Annals,* 1711, pp. 245–46).

7. *Silk:* Captain John Silk commanded a company in the Yellow Regiment of the City militia from Christmas 1698 to 1711 (City of London R. O., Lieutenancy of London Minute Book, pp. 237, 262, 279–80. This reference was very kindly supplied by Dr. Eveline Cruickshanks). His offense was also retailed in the *Review,* 4 September 1711: "that Impudent Officer, unworthy of her Majesty's Commission, a Scandal to the Lieutenancy, and a Re-

Who play'd thro' the City the High-Churchmens Ditty,
  The King shall his own have again, Sir.
  La, la, &c.   10

What tho' we did swear to the Protestant Heir,
  And roundly Abjur'd the Pretender;
Our Oaths must give place to the True Royal Race,
  Or our High Faith will want a Defender.
  La, la, &c.   15

Who wou'd not rejoice at a Turn of the State,

proach to the City of *London* . . . Marching through the City on his gew-gaw Cavalcade, at the Head of the *London* Train'd Bands, caus'd his Haut-Boys to play the Tune of *The King shall enjoy his own again* . . . and by Virtue of his Commission, has taken an Oath to her Majesty, abjuring her Enemy the Pretender." Silk, a pewterer in real life, was defended by William Wagstaffe (see headnote, p. 494).

8–9. Defoe went on to explain the significance of the London trained bands marching to the tune of *The King shall enjoy his own again* in two subsequent numbers of the *Review*, 22 September, 25 September 1711: "It is . . . an *Old Song* and *a Tune to it*, was made in the Exile of King *Charles* II [Simpson, p. 764, confirms that it was written by Martin Parker in 1643] . . . this *Song* and *Tune* is constantly sung by the *Jacobites* on the 11*th* of *June*, the Birth-Night of the Pretender . . . that by it, they express . . . their Zeal for the Pretender, and their Contempt of the Queen." And he also quoted a few verses of the "more Genuine" lyric:

> Now the Tories Reign,
> Our Hopes revive again,
> And the Revolution Rogueries shall come down:
> Awa, Whigs, awa,
> For we hope to see the Da
> When *Jemmy,* bonny *Jemmy* shall recover his Crown.

> Then let the Loans run,
> As they have now begun,
> All their Tricks to recover are in vain;
> For we hope to see the Day
> When your Q——n shall run away
> And the King shall enjoy his own again.

George Ridpath was the first to infer a connection with the medal: "Our old new-vamp'd Military Song, *That the King shall enjoy his own again* . . . came too quick upon the back of the *Scottish Medal*, not to give us cause to suspect that there's a very good Understanding betwixt some military Men in the *South* and some Lawyers in the *North*" (*The Observator*, 5–8 September 1711).

11. *swear to the Protestant Heir:* The Regency Act of March 1706, extended to Scotland in 1708, required all officeholders to swear allegiance not merely to Queen Anne but also to the succession "limited to the Princess *Sophia*, Electress and Dutchess Dowager of *Hannover*, and the Heirs of her Body, being Protestants" (*Statutes at Large, 3,* 552).

12. *Abjur'd the Pretender:* See *The Age of Wonders*, 35*n*. above.

16. *a Turn of the State:* that turned out the Godolphin-Junto ministry and brought in Harley's ministry.

Which rescu'd our Old Constitution?
From that happy Period we joyfully date
The Fall of the curs'd Revolution.
La, la, &c.   20

To begin with Resistance, *Sacheverel* did say,
'Tis the Doctrine of Devils and Hell, Sir;
But Passive Obedience does now bear the Sway,
As the Wise *Irish* Bishops can tell, Sir.
La, la, &c.   25

Hereditary Right, which sav'd *James* the Just
From the damnable Bill of Exclusion,
Will bring in his Son, as High-Church-Men do trust,
To the *Hannover* House's Confusion.
La, la, &c.   30

And to shew that the *Jacobite* Interest rises,
To High-Churchmens great Consolation,
The Pretender's Medals do bear double Prizes,
And his Friends are in high Reputation.
La, la, &c.   35

While thus our brave Priesthood with vigilant Care
Our Factions and Ferments do nourish,
Old *Lewis* is sure to succeed in the War,

18. *that happy Period:* April–October 1710.

19. *the curs'd Revolution:* On 27 August 1711 Defoe complained to Harley that James Dundas had not been prosecuted for the medal scandal. "There are Unhappily a Party Among us," he said, "who Take great pains from These Things to posess the Minds of The People That the Ministry are Not in the Revolution Intrest" (Defoe, *Letters,* pp. 352–53).

21–22. Cf. *The Age of Wonders,* 29–30n. above.

24. *Irish Bishops:* The Irish House of Lords (in which the 22 ecclesiastical peers occasionally constituted a majority) moved a very high church address to the queen on the opening of the session in July 1711. It congratulated the queen on "those necessary Alterations in the Management of your Majesty's Affairs at home" and very pointedly repudiated Wharton's management of Ireland (*LJ* Ireland, *2,* 366). Archbishop King was even muttering about impeaching Wharton (Swift, *Corr., 1,* 242).

26. *James the Just:* James II.

27. *Bill of Exclusion:* The first Whigs failed in three parliaments (1679, 1680, 1681) to secure a bill to exclude the Catholic duke of York from succeeding to the throne (*POAS,* Yale, *2,* 374–79, 413–14).

33. *do bear doubled Prizes:* have doubled in price, in despite of the fact that "the intrinsick Value" of the medal did not "exceed half a Crown" (Defoe, *The Scotch Medal Decipher'd, and The New Hereditary-Right Men Display'd,* 1711, p. 7).

And his Grandson's Scepter must flourish.
La, la, &c.   40

The *Dutch* shall be ruin'd, the Whigs shall be damn'd,
    And *Austria*'s House be confounded;
The *Gauls* shall rejoice while our Allies are shamm'd,
    And our Quarrels with *France* are compounded.
La, la, &c.   45

Now *Prior* and *Moor,* with Pistoles in great store,
    From *France* are arrived at *Dover;*
And *Abel* may roar till his Lungs are quite sore,

39. *Grandson's Scepter:* Louis XIV's grandson, Philip V, reoccupied Madrid in December 1710 and his throne was never seriously threatened thereafter.

41. *Dutch shall be ruin'd:* Secret negotiations for a separate peace with France were opened in December 1710. What this finally cost the Dutch is indicated in *A New Song, Being a Second Part to the Same Tune of Lilliburlero,* 9n. below.

42. *Austria's House be confounded:* When the archduke Charles, whom the allies had been calling the king of Spain since September 1703, succeeded as emperor Charles VI upon the death of his brother on 6/17 April 1711, the Tories were confirmed in their determination to make peace with Louis XIV at the expense of the Habsburg claim to the Spanish empire. This determination was first made public in *The Examiner,* 26 April 1711, in which Swift represented the policy of No Peace without Spain as a Whig "Gasconade" to perpetuate the war (Swift, *Prose, 3,* 140). The Whigs had no difficulty in showing that this policy was in fact an obligation imposed by the terms of the Grand Alliance in September 1701 and affirmed by each succeeding ministry, Whig or Tory (*Reflections upon the Examiner's Scandalous Peace,* 1711, pp. 3–22). Charles was so aggrieved by England's betrayal that he carried on the war alone for another year before signing the treaty of Rastatt in March 1714.

46. *Prior:* By the end of August 1711 it was "known that Mr. Prior has been lately in France" (Swift, *Journal, 1,* 348–49).

Moor: After having been a Tory and a Whig, Arthur Moore tacked about again, voted against the impeachment of Sacheverell, and "to the great Surprize of many wealthy Citizens" was made one of the lord commissioners of trade and plantations in September 1710 (Boyer, *Annals,* 1711, p. 243; *History,* p. 476). He became the confidant of St. John and Harcourt (Burnet, 1823, *6,* 151n.) and a principal negotiator in the treaties with France and Spain. Although he did not accompany Prior to Paris, it is not unlikely that his role in the affair was similar to that described by Swift in *A New Journey to Paris* (11 September 1711): "Monsieur *Moore,* who had already prepared a Bark, with all Necessaries, on the Coast of *Dover,* took Monsieur *Prior* disguised in his Chariot: They lay on *Monday* Night, the 12th of *July,* at the Count de *Jersey's* House in *Kent;* arrived in good time the next Day at *Dover,* drove directly to the Shoar, made the Sign by waving their Hats; which was answered by the Vessel; and the Boat was immediately sent to take him in" (Swift, *Prose, 3,* 211).

Pistoles: or louis d'or, were gold coins worth 17*s.*

48. *Abel:* Abel Roper (1665–1726) was born in Warwickshire and apprenticed to his uncle, a London printer who was master of the Stationers' Company in 1677. Soon after he set up for himself he published the first edition of *Lilliburlero* (*Some Memoirs of the Life of Abel, Toby's Uncle,* 1726, p. 4; *POAS,* Yale, *4,* 309), but in Queen Anne's reign he published *The Memorial of the Church of England.* From May 1695 to August 1714 or thereabouts he pub-

That there can be no need of *Hanover*.
La, la, &c.   50

Great Treaties like ours must infallibly bear,
  Since the Persons employ'd are so able;
Tho' one was a Drawer and t'other, some swear,
  Was the Politick Groom of a Stable.
La, la, &c.   55

Yet they're guided by one who is very well known,
  And a thorow-pac'd Statesman is reckon'd.
In the *Radnor* Address the Whigs he knock'd down,
  With the 12*th* of K. *Charles* the Second.
La, la, &c.   60

---

lished *The Post Boy,* the Tory counterpart of George Ridpath's Whiggish *Flying Post.* The Harley ministry leaked stories to *The Post Boy;* Swift wrote paragraphs for it, and Roper was said to be "far into the Secret" of the peace negotiations in 1711 (*Wentworth Papers,* p. 212; Swift, *Journal, 2,* 446, 574; *Tory Annals Faithfully Extracted out of Abel Roper's Famous Writings,* 1712, sig. A4v). He died on 5 February 1726, the same day as his Whiggish rival, George Ridpath.

49. *no need of Hanover:* "*Roper's Famous Writings*" do not seem to yield this proposition. Perhaps the intent is simply to say that Roper was a Jacobite, as he was indeed suspected to be (*Heraclitus Ridens,* 17–21 August 1703; *An English Merchant's Remarks, upon a Scandalous, Jacobite-Paper, Publish'd the 19th of July last, in the Post-Boy,* 1716.

51. *bear:* "To hold good; to . . . stand, 'do.' " *Obs.. (OED,* s.v. Bear, *v.*1, 14).

53. *a Drawer:* cf. "A *Vintner's* Boy" (Defoe, *Reformation of Manners,* 585, *POAS,* Yale, *6,* 424); "*Prior* had been taken a Boy, out of a Tavern, by the Earl of *Dorset*" (Burnet, *2,* 580).

54. *Groom:* "*Arthur Moor* . . . had risen up from being a Footman" (ibid., *2,* 622).

56. *one who is very well known:* On 23 May 1711 Robert Harley had been raised to the peerage as Baron Harley of Wigmore, Herefordshire, earl of Oxford, and earl of Mortimer. On 29 May he was also made lord high treasurer "and Carryed the white staff before the queen this morning to the Chappell," as Defoe proudly related (Defoe, *Letters,* pp. 328–29).

58. *the Radnor Address:* On 27 April 1710 an address was presented to the queen from the high sheriff, deputy lieutenants, justices of the peace, grand jury, and other gentlemen "assembled at the Great Sessions . . . for the County of *Radnor.*" The address was presented to her majesty by Thomas Harley, member of parliament for the county of Radnor, and Robert Harley, who represented the borough of New Radnor (*A Collection of the Addresses Which have been Presented to the Queen, Since the Impeachment of the Reverend Dr. Henry Sacheverell,* 1710, p. 9).

59. *the 12th of K. Charles the Second:* The Radnor address recognized and acknowledged Anne's power and authority "as expressed and declared in a Statute made in the Twelfth Year of the Reign of Your Royal Uncle King *Charles* II" (ibid.). This is a typically Harleian obscurity for it is impossible to decide which act of 1660 was meant. Of the 37 statutes enacted in that year not one of them specifically defines royal authority (*Statutes at Large, 2,* 624–81). But Harley may have told Defoe what he meant. Defoe (in the Scots dialect which he adopts to speak for James Dundas) observes that "the Act of 12 Car. II declaires the Duty of Un-limited Obedience, and the Unlawfulness of resisting upon ony pretence whatsomever" (*A Speech for Mr. D——sse,* 1711, p. 7).

Thus bravely he fights their lewd Bill of Rights
    And baffles their damn'd Revolution,
By Statutes repeal'd, Non-Resistance he heal'd,
    And to High-Church he gave Absolution.
    La, la, &c.   65

Wide open to all a Subscription-Book stands,
    With some Advocates at *Edinborow;*
Where *Perkin*'s true Friends do set to their Hands,
    If he'll come they'll receive him to morrow.
    La, la, &c.   70

Good Mr. *Dundass* has giv'n him a Pass
    The Kingdom of *Scotland* to enter;
And the Dutchess of *Gordon,* that brave Popish Lass,
    Does swear by the Mass, he may venture.

61–64. Since the Bill of Rights (1689) and the Act of Settlement (1701) had put the throne on an entirely new, parliamentary basis (*The Fair Warning,* 9n. above), Harley's citation of superseded statutes could be construed as counterrevolutionary, reviving divine right doctrines, and providing political sanction for the claims of the high flying clergy: "one may infer," it was said, "that, that Person by quoting a Statute made so many Years before the Revolution, is a *French* Partizan, and one who denies the validity of all Laws since" (*Cursory but Curious Observations of Mr. Ab—l R—per, upon a Late Famous Pamphlet, Entituled Remarks on the Preliminary Articles Offer'd by the F. K.,* 1711, pp. 9–10).

66. *Subscription-Book:* The metaphorical Jacobite "Subscription-Book" is presumably the Minute Book of the Faculty of Advocates in which the names of the 63 who approved the vote of thanks to the duchess (2n. above) are imagined to be inscribed. But in fact the Minute Book preserves no record of this transaction (*The Arniston Memoirs,* ed. George W. T. Omond, Edinburgh, 1887, p. 53).

71. *Dundass:* James Dundas (d. before November 1726) was the eldest son of Robert Dundas, a staunch Whiggish judge of the court of session who assumed the title of Lord Arniston. Little more is known of him than the episode described in the headnote. He must have been admitted a member of the Faculty of Advocates, presumably before July 1709 when his younger brother was admitted. It was not until March 1712 that proceedings against him were instituted "for his contending to have a medal of the pretender received by the Faculty of . . . Advocats, and for his causing print a scandalous pamphlet called the *Advocats' Loyalty,*" and the case never came to trial. Dundas married in 1713, but predeceased his father without issue (ibid., pp. 53–56).

73. *the Dutchess of Gordon:* "That schismatic woman in the north," as Walter Scott called her in *The Heart of Midlothian* (ibid., p. 56), was Lady Elizabeth Howard, second daughter of Henry Howard, fifth duke of Norfolk. In October 1676 she married George Gordon, third marquess of Huntly and first duke of Gordon. In or before 1696 she escaped from an unhappy marriage into a convent in Flanders. Her husband was arrested as a Jacobite suspect after the invasion attempt of March 1708 and her son, Alexander, second duke of Gordon, led out 2,000 of his clansmen in 1715, but the duchess's moment of greatness came on 30 June 1711 when she was "prominently brought into notice by her presenting to the Faculty of Advocates a medal with the head of the Pretender on one side" (*The Scots Peerage,* ed. Sir James Balfour Paul, 9 vols., Edinburgh, David Douglas, 1904–14, *4,* 550).

 La, la, &c.   75

By such Great Examples all People will find,
 That the *Jacobites* are in no Peril
For the Prince at *St. Germains* to speak out their Mind,
 Or to drink a full Bumper to *Sorrel.*
 La, la, &c.   80

Thus *Lesley* and *Hicks* with their Politick Tricks
 Have gain'd on the Sense of the Nation;
The Dissenters are troubl'd to find themselves bubbl'd,
 For Indulgence is no Toleration.
 La, la, &c.   85

Their Barns are burnt down and their Teachers are damn'd

77. *Jacobites are in no Peril:* "They act Now [September 1711] barefaced, Furious, and Insolent" (Defoe, *Letters,* p. 355).

81. *Hicks:* George Hickes (1642–1715), the great antiquarian and hero of the nonjurors, was graduated B.A. from Magdalen College, Oxford, in February 1663, and went to Scotland in May 1677 as chaplain to the high commissioner, John Maitland, duke of Lauderdale (Hearne, *1,* 268). Upon his return, ecclesiastical preferments came in rapid succession and in August 1683 he was made dean of Worcester. He refused to take the oaths to William of Orange and was deprived in February 1690. In May 1693 he was received by James II at St. Germain and upon his return he was secretly consecrated bishop of Thetford by William Sancroft, the deprived archbishop of Canterbury. His most famous scholarly work is *Linguarum veterum septentrionalium thesaurus grammatico-criticus et archaeologicus* (1703–05).

84. *Indulgence is no Toleration:* High churchmen insisted that the so-called Act of Toleration (1689) did not confer "a *civil Right*" upon the dissenters, but was only an "*Indulgence* [that] the Government has condescended to give 'em" (Sacheverell, *The Perils of False Brethren, Both in Church, and State,* 1709, pp. 18, 19). The reason for this distinction is explained by Henry St. John: "The true reasons, I believe, why the word indulgence is used preferably to toleration are these: First, because the former is the term in law; secondly, because in truth, dissenters are not tolerated; the penalty of the law is only suspended, and they, by consequence, only indulged. And, thirdly, because some have been of late years so hardy as to assert, that being tolerated by act of parliament, amounts to a legal establishment; and that therefore they are on as good a foot as the church of England. Since people, barely indulged, are so ready to contend for a parity, it is much to be feared, that if this point were once yielded to them, they would soon struggle for a superiority" (Bolingbroke, *Letters, 1,* 43). When the queen's speech at the opening of parliament in November 1710 failed to include the usual clause about maintaining the Toleration Act, "but only the *Indulgence by Law allow'd to scrupulous Consciences,*" "this change of Phrase into *Sacheverel's* Language was much observed" and "Bank-Stock fell that very Day Three *per Cent*" (Boyer, *Political State, 1* and *2,* 31–32; Burnet, *2,* 558).

86. *Barns are burnt down:* "Thus we have it now in *England,*" Defoe complained in the *Review,* 4 August 1711, "burning one Meeting-House, plundering another, and Mobbing and Ransacking the *Dissenters.*" The meeting house that was burnt was in Westbury, Wiltshire (*Review,* 31 July 1711). In both these numbers of the *Review,* Defoe associates attacks on dissenters with "the Story of the Medal in *Scotland.*"

For preaching in Tubs without Orders;
The silly Low-Church will be left in the lurch,
And the *Scotch* Kirk drove out of our Borders.
La, la, &c.   90

Let Schismaticks pine, let Republicans whine,
And henceforth abandon these Nations;
While Tories rejoice and cry with one Voice,
Obedience without Limitations.
La, la, &c.   95

Let our Trade go to wreck, and all our Stocks sink,
While our High-Church rides safe from all Danger;
Since Land's above Money, we have reason to think
The Queen's Brother will conquer the Stranger.
La, la, &c.   100

Let the Whigs that love Trade, the *South-Seas* invade,
And there we will give 'em Debentures
For the Money they've lent, till the whole Sum be spent,

91. *Schismaticks:* accented on the first syllable (cf. *POAS,* Yale, *6,* 8).

94. *Obedience without Limitations:* "*Absolute,* and *Unconditional Obedience* to the *Supream Power* . . . and the utter *Illegality* of *Resistance* upon any *Pretence* whatsoever" (Sacheverell, *The Perils of False Brethren, Both in Church, and State,* 1709, p. 12) were those "High-Church-Idols," Defoe said, that "Tyranny create" (*Jure Divino. A Satyr,* 1706, VII, 23); cf. 59*n.* above.

96. *Stocks sink:* "The Fall of the Stocks [Mainwaring, *An Excellent New Song, Called Mat's Peace,* 19*n.* below] is now the publick News of the Town" (*Review,* 4 September 1711).

98. *Land's above Money:* No one in the age of Queen Anne doubted that the ownership of real estate conferred political power, but the Tories' belief that the power of land was superior to the power of money, both quantitatively and qualitatively (i.e. more power and more prestige), was being challenged, as it is here in this ironical phrase. "O Money, Money!" Defoe exclaimed, "All Power, all Policy is supported by Thee, even Vice and Vertue act by thy Assistance, by Thee all the great Things in the World are done" (*Review,* 16 October 1707).

99. *the Stranger:* the Hanoverian successor.

101. *South-Seas invade:* The South Seas Company was formed in May 1711, with Harley as its governor and St. John and Arthur Moore (46*n.* above) on its board of directors, to exploit trading concessions in the West Indies and Latin America that the ministry hoped to secure from Spain in the peace negotiations. Besides a public sale of stock, that began in June 1711 and raised £4,000,000 in a few days, the company also was capitalized by a grant of £576,000 from the treasury (Boyer, *Political State, 1* and *2,* 303, 447–48, 525–26; *Annals,* 1712, p. 323).

102–03. *Debentures | For the Money they've lent:* More than £9,000,000 of the existing national debt was exchanged for shares in the South Sea Company plus interest at 6 percent (Defoe, *Letters,* p. 341). Shares in the company were also issued as security for new loans (Peter G. M. Dickson, *The Financial Revolution in England,* Macmillan, 1967, pp. 65–67).

And a Spunge wipe out all their Adventures.
La, la, &c.   105

They shall have for Director their *German* Elector,
 Who certainly will not play booty;
He's too much in the Stock the Project to shock;
 Good Princess *Sophia, Adieu t'ye.*
 La, la, &c.   110

104. *Spunge:* See *The Age of Wonders,* 112*n.* above.

106. *German Elector:* Georg Ludwig, the elector of Braunschweig-Lüneburg.

107. *play booty:* proverbial: to betray the cause one pretends to support (Tilley, B539).

108. *too much in the Stock:* The elector became a large stockholder when a government debt to him of £9,375 was paid in shares of the South Sea Company (Macpherson, *Original Papers,* 2, 265).

 shock: "To run counter to, to oppose. *Obs. rare*" (*OED,* s.v. Shock *v.*² 1.c).

ARTHUR MAINWARING

An Excellent New Song, Called Mat's Peace,
Or, The Downfall of Trade,
To the Good Old Tune of *Green-sleeves.*
(September–October 1711)

The feints and fakes that finally culminated in the treaty of Utrecht
began with François Gaultier, a fat French priest, secretary to the
emperor's ambassador in London and an intimate of Edward Villiers,
earl of Jersey, whose wife was a Roman Catholic. Gaultier was a French
intelligence agent and in August 1710 he was ordered to open negotia-
tions with the earl of Jersey for a separate treaty of peace. Jersey was
almost ideal for Torcy's purposes: he was a man of "very ordinary
Understanding" (Macky, p. 28), a Jacobite, and a former ambassador
to France. During his embassy (1698–99), Matthew Prior had been
his secretary.

Even before the terrible news of Stanhope's defeat and capture at
Brihuega reached London on the day after Christmas, 1710, the
English ministers had let it be known that they were willing to make
peace "without Spain," that is, without demanding that Louis's
grandson, Philip V, be driven out of Spain. But they also let it be
known that publicly and at the conference table when negotiations
were brought out in the open, they would support the Habsburg
claimant to the Spanish succession (29n. below). They also insisted
that the preliminary articles must be made to appear to originate in
Paris (*English Historical Review, 49* [1934], 100–05).

By May 1711 the preliminary articles drafted by the English min-
isters, Jersey, Shrewsbury, and St. John, had been sent over from
Paris, approved by the English ministers and duly forwarded to their
Dutch allies. Now it became necessary to send someone back to Paris
with Gaultier to find out whether Torcy and Louis XIV would accept
the preliminary articles as the terms on which they would in fact
negotiate a treaty of peace. For this mission Matthew Prior was chosen.

Prior was fitted out with a pseudonym (3n. below) and very limited
powers that were not countersigned by a minister:

The Honorable Matthew Prior, Esq. Her late, most Sacred Majesty's Plenipotentiary to Louis the XIV. King of France, and one of the Commissioners of Her Customs.

Matthew Prior, Esq., an engraving attributed to F. Chereau after a portrait by Alexis Simeon Belle

Anne R.

Le sieur Prior est pleinement instruit et authorisé de communi-
quer à la France nos demandes Preliminaires, et de nous en
rapporter la reponse.

A.R.

(L. G. Wickham Legg, *Matthew Prior: A Study of His Public Career and
Correspondence*, Cambridge, Cambridge University Press, 1921, pp.
146–47, 149). On or about 1 July 1711 Prior left London, probably
following the itinerary described by Swift in *A New Journey to Paris* (*A
Welcome to the Medal*, 46n. above). One detail of Swift's account, Prior's
visit to Jersey at his estate in Kent, is confirmed by a document in the
Archives du Ministère des Affaires Étrangères (Charles K. Eves,
Matthew Prior Poet and Diplomatist, New York, Columbia University
Press, 1939, p. 237). Another account mentions "a Visit to his Friend,
Sir *T*[*homas*] *H*[*anmer*]" in Suffolk, which would provide a good alibi
for not being in London ([Abel Boyer], *An Account of the State and
Progress of the Present Negotiation of Peace*, 1711, p. 4).

Despite all these precautions, Prior was seen in Calais by an infor-
mant of John Macky, master of the Dover packet and a government spy.
Macky promptly reported to Bolingbroke that an English gentleman
had arrived in Calais and immediately taken post for Paris. Boling-
broke's secretary wrote back instructing Macky to look out for the
gentleman's return (Macky, p. xvi).

In the first week of August 1711, his mission accomplished (4n.
below), Prior set out from Fontainebleau in the company of Gaultier
and Nicolas le Bailiff, comte de St. Jean Mcsnager, to return to London.
But John Macky carried out his instructions more aggressively than
St. John had intended. "That officious servant employed all his people,
between the Forelands, to watch the return of Prior. He at length had
advice that a vessel had landed at Deal, three persons with Secretary
St. John's pass. He made haste to Canterbury, and met there his old
acquaintance, Matthew Prior, under a feigned name" (Macpherson,
History, 2, 494; cf. John Banks, *The History of His Own Time. Compiled
from the Original Manuscripts of His Late Excellency Matthew Prior*, 1740, p.
348).

Prior made a mistake in not admitting his true identity, for his
physical description—"a thin hollow-looked Man, turned of forty
Years old" (Macky, p. 135)—was on file in Macky's office and memory.
So Macky "look'd more fixedly upon the Gentleman, and finding him

to be Mr. *P*——*r*, expostulated with him for concealing his true Name; adding," in true Dogberry fashion, "That, in discharge of their Trust, they must keep him in Custody, till they had receiv'd further Instructions from the Secretaries" ([Abel Boyer], *An Account of the State and Progress of the Present Negotiations,* 1711, p. 4). But even before St. John's instructions had been received, Macky "dispatched immediately an express to the duke of Marlborough, then besieging Bouchain, with this important intelligence. He informed also the earl of Sunderland of what he had heard and seen; and that nobleman communicated to the Imperial and Dutch ambassadors, his fixed opinion, that negociations of peace were begun. Marlborough sent a copy of [Macky's] letter to Secretary St. John" (Macpherson, *History, 2,* 494–95).

Not only had the security of Prior's mission been compromised, but it had been compromised to the ministry's most powerful political enemies and to the allies whom the ministry was hoping to circumvent. After he issued orders for Prior's release, St. John issued further orders for Macky's arrest. Macky's creditors were "hounded out upon him" and while he lay in prison, his house and goods were seized (Macky, p. xviii; HMC *Portland MSS., 5,* 303).

On 31 August 1711 Swift told Stella "it is now known that Mr. Prior has been lately in France" (Swift, *Journal, 1,* 348–49). The secret was out and *An Excellent New Song . . . To the Good Old Tune of Green-sleeves* was written so that this breach of security could be sung in the streets. But more than that, it is a very gay song with some very bitter commentary by a dying man. Beneath the gaiety, it affords a glimpse into the tragedy of wasted effort, for Mainwaring understood that what had really been compromised was the principle of No Peace without Spain, "Spain," as he told the duchess of Marlborough, "being the thing we fight for" (*Private Correspondence of Sarah, Duchess of Marlborough, 1,* 390). Nor should the gaiety be allowed to obscure the fact that the poem judges *"Mat's Peace"* and sentences him to be whipped and to stand in the pillory (lines 70, 77) and St. John and Oxford to be impeached (55–56, 75–76, 78–79).

The poem is attributed to Mainwaring by John Oldmixon, who "was inform'd by a Person, who copied [it] from his Manuscripts, that [it was] his" (Oldmixon, *Maynwaring,* p. 326).

St. John's order for the arrest of the printer on 23 October 1711 (Boyer, *Annals,* 1712, p. 264) provides one limit for the date of publication of the poem, and the arrival in London on 11 September 1711 of the news that Bouchain had capitulated (16*n.* below) supplies the other.

"The Good Old Tune of *Green-sleeves*" was one of the most popular in the eighteenth century and is, of course, still current today. In a shortened form it is the tune to which many of the mock-litanies in the present series were sung. Mainwaring's nine-line stanza, however, "requires not only the full form of the tune, but also repetition of the two final bars" (Simpson, p. 277*n.*)

An Excellent New Song, Called *Mat's Peace,*
Or, the Downfall of Trade,
To the Good Old Tune of *Green-sleeves.*

The News from Abroad does a Secret reveal,
Which has been confirm'd both at *Dover* and *Deal,*
That on Mr. *Mathews,* once called plain *Mat,*
Has been doing at *Paris,* the Lord knows what.
But sure what they talk of his Negotiation,   5
Is only intended to banter the Nation:
For why have we spent so much Treasure in vain,
If now at the last we must give up *Spain,*
    If now we must give up *Spain.*

Why so many Battles did *Marlborough* win?   10
So many strong Towns why did he take in?
Why did he his Army to *Germany* lead,
The Crown to preserve on the Emperor's Head?

1. "Mr. *Prior*'s Journey to *Paris* was . . . mention'd, as Publick News in the Foreign *Prints,* and, after them, in the *Domestick*" (Boyer, *Annals,* 1712, p. 232).
2. *Dover:* Burnet (*2,* 580) records, incorrectly, that "upon his Return, [Prior] was stopt at *Dover.*"

    Deal: "Landing near *Deal,* about the latter End of *July,* or Beginning of *August* last, [Prior] was seiz'd by the Custom-House Officers" ([Abel Boyer], *An Account of the State and Progress of the Present Negotiation,* 1711, p. 4).
3. *Mr. Mathews:* Prior's passport was made out to Jeremy Mathews (Charles K. Eves, *Matthew Prior Poet and Diplomatist,* New York, Columbia University Press, 1939, p. 237).
4. *the Lord knows what:* "What pass'd in the private Interviews between Mr. *P——r,* and the Ministers of *France,* is still an absolute Secret" ([Abel Boyer], *An Account of the State and Progress of the Present Negotiation of Peace,* 1711, p. 37). Torcy's memoranda for Louis XIV are preserved in the Archives du Ministère des Affaires Étrangères, Correspondence Politique, 233. Prior's private journal ended up in Oxford's possession and is printed in HMC *Portland MSS., 5,* 34–42. Both are summarized in Charles K. Eves, *Matthew Prior Poet and Diplomatist,* New York, Columbia University Press, 1939, pp. 238–45.
6. *banter:* "There's Reason to believe," Abel Boyer said (*An Account of the State and Progress of the Present Negotiation of Peace,* 1711, p. 37), "that [Swift's] *Account of a Journey to* Paris . . . was design'd as a Amusement; and only to let the World know . . . That there was a Negotiation on Foot; and . . . what some People doubted, *viz.* That Mr. *P——r* insisted upon very high Terms."
8. *give up Spain:* In the preliminary articles that were published in *The Post Boy,* 13–16 October 1711, Britain agreed "That King *Philip* shall have all *Spain*" (Boyer, *Annals,* 1712, p. 250).
12. *Army to Germany:* Marlborough led the confederate army across the Rhine in May 1704.
13. *preserve . . . the Emperor:* By the defection of the elector of Bavaria and a civil war in

Why does he the Honour of *England* advance?
And why has he humbled the Monarch of *France*   15
By passing the Lines and taking *Bouchain,*
If now at the last we must give up *Spain,*
    If now we must give up *Spain.*

Our Stocks were so high and our Crcdit so good,
(I mean all the while our late Ministry stood)   20
That Foreigners hither their Mony did send,
And Bankers Abroad took a pleasure to lend.
But though all the Service was duly supply'd,
And nought was *embezled* or *misapply'd,*

Hungary, "the Emperor was reduced to the last Extremities" before the battle of Blenheim (Burnet, *2,* 381).

16. *passing the Lines:* In July 1711 the French army "lay behind Lines, that were looked on as so strong, that the forcing them was thought an impracticable thing; and it was said, that *Villars* had wrote to the *French* King, that he had put a *Ne plus ultra* to the Duke of *Marlborough:* But, contrary to all expectation, he did so amuse *Villars* with feint Motions, that at last, to the surprize of all *Europe,* he pass'd the Lines [at Arleux] near *Bouchain,* without the loss of a Man" (ibid., *2,* 576).

taking Bouchain: Bouchain, on the Scheldt, a heavily-fortified strongpoint in the *Ne plus ultra* line in French Flanders, was invested on 31 July/10 August and occupied on 3/14 September 1711 (Broderick, pp. 348–56). The presence of Villars's army of 100,000 men, "superior to ours," *The Evening Post* reported on 11 13 September 1711, "and constantly attempting to disturb us, makes the Success of this Siege the more remarkable." It was Marlborough's last victory.

19. *Stocks were so high:* From the highs of April 1710, when "the last Ministry stood," stocks declined steadily during the next four months while Harley was putting together his ministry. Bank stock went from 123 1/2 to 108 3/4; United East India Company from 137 1/2 to 121 1/4; Million Bank from 76 to 71; Sword Blades from 65 to 62 1/2 (*The Post-Man,* 13–15 April 1710, 15 17 August 1710). Nor did the slide stop there. A year later the same stocks were selling, respectively, at 104, 117 1/4, 61, and 52 3/4 (*The Evening Post,* 7–9 August 1711).

Credit so good: In February 1709 the Bank of England "open'd their books for a new subscription of 2,200,000*l.* towards next years taxes, and in 5 hours the whole was subscribed . . . and a great deal more offer'd to be subscribed, but refused" (Luttrell, *6,* 410; cf. *The Virtues of Sid Hamet the Magician's Rod,* 71–72n. above). Now, however, "every Body talks of [Credit] as dead" (*Review,* 8 September 1711).

21. *Foreigners:* "Nor was it only at Home that [Godolphin] had so glorious a Reputation; Foreigners during his whole Ministry pour'd in their Money into our Country" (*The Secret History of the Late Ministry; From their Admission, to the Death of the Queen,* 1715, p. 69; cf. Peter G. M. Dickson, *The Financial Revolution in England,* Macmillan, 1967, pp. 304–10).

24. *nought was embezled:* Godolphin had so little money upon his dismissal in August 1710 that if he had not inherited an estate from his brother in the same month (Luttrell, *6,* 623), he would have been dependent upon the Marlboroughs. Complaints were even made that "his equipage . . . was too mean and scanty" (Calamy, *Historical Account 2,* 258), and "the inconsiderable sum of money . . . which he left at his death, shewed that he had been indeed

By all that wise management what shall we gain,   25
If now at the last we must give up *Spain,*
   If now we must give up *Spain.*

We made this Alliance, as well it is known,
That *Austria's* Great House might recover their own:
King *Charles* is of part of his Kingdom possest,   30
And *Bouchain* would quickly fright *France* from the rest.
For sure the whole Nation by this time must know,
The way to *Madrid* is by *Paris* to go;
But why have we made such a glorious Campaign,
If now at the last we must give up *Spain,*   35
   If now we must give up *Spain.*

All Treaties with *France* may be sung or be said,
To morrow they'll break what to day they have made;
And therefore our Senate did wisely *address,*
That none should be made whilst they *Spain* did possess.   40
The Queen too to them did last Sessions declare,
That *Spain* ought to be their *particular* Care:
But Speeches, Addresses and *Senates* are vain,
If now at the last we must give up *Spain,*

the nation's treasurer, and not his own" (*Private Correspondence of Sarah, Duchess of Marl-
borough,* 2, 118).

29. *Austria . . . recover their own:* The treaty of the Grand Alliance concluded between
England, the Netherlands, and the Empire in September 1701 stipulated for the Habsburgs
"the procuring an equitable and reasonable satisfaction to his Imperial Majesty for his
pretension to the Spanish succession" (*EHD, 8,* 873).

30. *part:* In October 1711 the archduke Charles was in possession of Cataluña, Majorca,
Sardinia, Sicily, the kingdom of Naples, the duchy of Milan, the Spanish ports in Tuscany,
and the Spanish Netherlands.

31. *the rest:* Philip V, Louis XIV's second grandson, was in possession of all of Spain ex-
cept Cataluña, and all of Spanish America.

38. *To morrow they'll break:* "When we hear Men talk of Treaties with the King of *France,*
and of that King's acting *bona fide* . . . when we hear of Forts to be given . . . Harbours to
be demolish'd . . . we may be sure those that say these things intend only to deceive
others . . . Did ever the King of *France* perform any one thing that he promis'd by a Treaty?"
(*Remarks upon the Present Negotiations of Peace Begun between Britain and France,* 1711, p. 24;
this pamphlet is attributed to Mainwaring by Oldmixon, *Maynwaring,* p. 248).

39. *Senate . . . address:* The House of Lords resolved on 19 December 1708 "That no
Peace can be honourable or safe, for Her Majesty and Her Allies, if *Spain* and *The Spanish
West Indies* be suffered to continue in the Power of the House of *Bourbon*" (*LJ,* 18, 395).

41. *Queen . . . declare:* In her speech at the opening of parliament on 27 November 1710,
the queen declared that "The carrying on the War in all its Parts, but particularly in *Spain,*
with the utmost Vigour, is the likeliest Means, with GOD's Blessing, to procure a safe and
honourable Peace for us and all our Allies" (*LJ, 19,* 166).

If now we must give up *Spain*.   45

By giving up *Spain*, we give up all our Trade;
In vain would they tell us a Treaty is made
For yielding us Forts in the distant *South Seas*,
To manage our Traffick with Safety and Ease.
No Lyes are too gross for such impudent Fellows,   50
Of Forts in the Moon as well they might tell us;
Since *France* at her pleasure may take them again,
If now at the last we must give up *Spain*,
    If now we must give up *Spain*.

Some Lords were impeach'd for a famous Partition,   55
Which kept the Allies in far better Condition;
For then of *Raw Silk* we were only bereft,
But now neither *Silver* nor *Gold* will be left.

46. *give up all our Trade:* "the Consequences of yielding *Spain* to the Duke of *Anjou*, wou'd be . . . 1. The Loss of Three Millions and a Half of annual Income by foreign Trade; a Sum which more than ballances all our foreign Expences even during the present War. 2. The annual Expence of Half a Million, without any Income of Mony by our foreign Markets. 3. The Loss of Imployment and Subsistence for at least a Million of Souls, a sixth or seventh part of the whole People. 4. and Lastly, The Reduction of all Estates to one fourth part of their present Value, to the utter Impoverishment of all the Landholders in *Great Britain*" ([Francis Hare?], *A Letter to a Member of the October-Club: Shewing, That to yield Spain to the Duke of Anjou by a Peace, wou'd be the Ruin of Great Britain*, 1711, pp. 54–55).

48. *Forts:* A paragraph in *The Post Boy*, 21–23 August 1711, ostensibly from The Hague, reported "that to induce Great-Britain to make Peace, France has offer'd to give her Four FORTS from the Streights of Magellan, along the Coasts of Chili and Peru, for the Security of the Commerce of that Nation, in the South-Seas. But all in vain. The Britains still turn'd a deaf Ear to the melodious Accents of that deluding Syren." Boyer (*An Account of the State and Progress of the Present Negotiations of Peace*, 1711, p. 9) suspected that this paragraph was inserted by the ministry to put "a favourable Construction" on the no longer secret negotiations between France and Great Britain.

55. *Lords were impeach'd:* In April 1701 the Junto lords, Somers, Halifax, and Orford, were impeached by the House of Commons for acquiescing in the negotiation of the partition treaties of 1698 and 1700 (Swift, *Discourse*, pp. 30–32, 42–51).

56. *far better:* Cf. [Mainwaring], *Remarks on the Preliminary Articles Offer'd by the French King, in Order to Procure a General Peace*, 1711, p. 22: "even by the late Treaty of Partition for which King *William*'s Ministry was impeached . . . the House of *Austria* was to have the *Spanish* Monarchy and the *West Indies,* and the *Dauphin* and his Issue to have nothing but part of the [Spanish] Dominions in *Italy*."

57. *Silk:* By the terms of the second partition treaty, England would have lost access to Spanish possessions in Italy that were the source of raw silk for England.

58. *neither Silver nor Gold:* Without access to Spanish America, Britain would be cut off from "the Channel of Bullion . . . from the Coasts of *America*" that was such an important source of French revenue. It was, in fact, "the nightmare of Bourbon power made impregnable because constantly replenished with the wealth of the Indies" that drove the Whigs to

If that Treaty then did Impeachment require,
Sure this calls at least for the Rope or the Fire;   60
Since *Britain* had never such Cause to complain,
If now at the last we must give up *Spain*,
  If now we must give up *Spain*.

When *Pett'cum* to *Paris* did openly go,
What Doubts and what Jealousies did we not show: 65
How loudly did we against *Holland* exclaim,
Yet surely our Statesmen are now more to blame.
For how can they think our Allies will not fire
At privately sending that *Matchiavel Prior*,
Who richly deserves to be *whip'd* for his Pain,   70
If now at the last we must give up *Spain*,

---

demand No Peace without Spain. "What will this Power arise to, when [France] shall have
the whole Produce of *Gold and Silver* in the *Indies*," Mainwaring asked, "And how can any
Englishman think of this without Horror!" (*Review*, 3 January 1709/10; Henry Kamen, *The
War of Succession in Spain 1700–15*, Weidenfeld and Nicolson, 1969, pp. 167, 192–93; [Main-
waring], *Remarks upon the Present Negotiations of Peace Begun between Britain and France*, 1711, p.
20).

 64. *Pett'cum:* Hermann Petkum (d. after 1720) had long been the diplomatic representa-
tive of the duke of Holstein-Gottorp at The Hague (HMC *Round MSS.*, p. 320). He seems to
have been recruited first (c. 1708) by Antonie Heinsius, the grand pensionary of the United
Provinces, to negotiate a separate peace with France, and then by Oxford (c. 1713) as an
intelligence agent. Actually Petkum was a double agent who had been in French pay at least
since 1703 (Winston Churchill, *Marlborough His Life and Times*, 4 vols., George G. Harrap &
Co., 1938, *4*, 19). His name became well-known in London when thousands of copies of a
broadside entitled *A Letter from Monsieur Pett——m to Monsieur B——ys* (1710) were distrib-
uted in July and August 1710 (*The Examiner*, 10–17 August 1710). The letter, which probably
was forged, gave "so particular an account of the Expectations of the *French* from our fatal
Divisions in *England*" that it was supposed to be Jacobite propaganda (*The Secret History of the
Late Ministry; From their Admission, to the Death of the Queen*, 1715, p. 246). While Prior was in
Fontainebleau, Torcy showed him recent letters from Petkum to convince him of Dutch
skulduggery (L. G. Wickham Legg, *Matthew Prior: A Study of His Public Career and Correspon-
dence*, Cambridge, Cambridge University Press, 1921, pp. 152–53). Two of Petkum's intel-
ligence reports to Oxford are preserved in HMC *Portland MSS.*, *5*, 412, 422 and some of his
correspondence with Torcy is included in HMC *Round MSS.*, pp. 317–66. He survived the
peace to become the minister of Holstein-Gottorp in London and to entertain George I at
lavish dinner parties in his house on Arlington Street. In 1719, however, he was declared
persona non grata and recalled on account of his involvement in Jacobite intrigues. He is
said to have been "ein gespreitzer, auf Grossthürei und klingende Belohnung erpichter
Windbeutel" (HMC *Portland MSS.*, *5*, 538, 540, 545–46; J. F. Chance, *Notes on the Diplomatic
Relations of England and Germany*, Oxford, B. H. Blackwell, 1907, pp. 29–30).

 Paris: Petkum had made three visits to Paris. The first, in December 1706, was secret.
The second, in July 1708—exactly as in the case of Prior's—was intended to be a secret
but the secret leaked out. The third, in November 1709, was reported in the Dutch news-
prints (HMC *Round MSS.*, pp. 320, 327–29, 341–43).

If now we must give up *Spain*.
Since Matters stand thus, I am sorely afraid,
Whenever this scandalous Peace shall be made,
Our Senate for *Cato* will quickly decree   75
Some Punishment worse than *a Sting of a Bee*.
Poor *Mat* in the *Pillory* soon will be seen,
For *Mortimer* too, Oh! well had it been
That he in his *Hole* had been pleas'd to remain,
If now at the last we must give up *Spain*,   80
    If now we must give up *Spain*.

74. *scandalous Peace:* The phrase also occurs in *Reflections upon the Examiner's Scandalous Peace*, Mainwaring's reply to Swift's trial balloon for a peace "without . . . *Spain*" (*The Examiner*, 26 April 1711).

75. *Cato:* The reference is to the post-Swift *Examiner* of 19–26 July 1711: "Methinks I behold the Younger *Cato* in Mr. *St. J——n*; All that Love for His Country, that Contempt of Danger, and Greatness of Soul, of whom it is said, *'Twas not for Honour or Riches, nor rashly, or by chance, that He engaged Himself in the Affairs of State; but He undertooke the Service of the Publick, as the proper Business of an honest Man; and therefore He thought Himself obliged to be as diligent for the Good of That, as a Bee for the Preservation of her Hive.*" Since Mainwaring had "a very mean Opinion not only of Mr. *St. John's* Honesty, but of his Capacity" (Oldmixon, *History*, p. 456), this must have seemed to him a particularly distorted vision.

78–79. *Mortimer . . . Hole:* Mortimer, of course, is Oxford (*A Welcome to the Medal*, 56*n.* above). *Mortimer's Hole* is the name of a tune of which neither words nor music have survived. "Hole," in Mainwaring's fancy, is a complicated and reiterated pun on small dingy abode or prison cell (Partridge, p. 397) / anus / stock in the South Sea Company. This last meaning is primary in another poem by Mainwaring, *An Excellent New Song, Call'd Credit Restor'd, in the Year of our Lord God, 1711* ("All *Britains* rejoyce at this Turn of the State") (Oldmixon, *Maynwaring*, p. 336); cf. p. 494 above.

The Procession:
A New Protestant Ballad. To an Excellent Italian Tune
(November 1711)

To celebrate the 153rd anniversary of the accession of Queen Elizabeth on 17 November 1558, the Whigs planned a party that the Protestant queen would have thoroughly enjoyed. It was to have been a mass spectacle, entitled *The March of the Chevalier de St. George* (see illustration, p. 514) and unequalled since the great pope-burning processions of November 1679, 1680, and 1681.

The Tories said that Wharton was "the first Inventor of the Design" for the procession of 1711 ([Delariviere Manley], *A True Relation of the Several Facts and Circumstances of the Intended Riot and Tumult on Queen Elizabeth's Birth-day*, 1711, p. 10). And if this is true, Wharton was a worthy successor to the first earl of Shaftesbury. For he boldly appropriated as much of Shaftesbury's procession as he could use (see illustration, *POAS*, Yale, *2*, 506), including "Six Beadles with Protestant Flails," and then introduced innovations of his own: "Twenty four Bagpipes marching four and four, and playing the memorable Tune of *Lillibullero*," together with allusions to current events: "A Figure representing Cardinal *Gualteri*, lately made by the Pretended Protector of the *English* Nation, looking down on the Ground in a sorrowful Posture" (*Political Merriment: Or, Truths Told to Some Tune*, 4 vols., 1714–15, *2*, 212–13). Every detail of the procession was designed to lead to a single conclusion: an overwhelming rejection of peace "on the Foot of the Proposals made by *France*" (Boyer, *Annals*, 1712, p. 278; cf. p. 504 above).

Swift explained the whole thing to Stella on 17 November: "the Whigs designed a mighty procession by midnight, and had laid out a thousand pounds to dress up the Pope, Devil, Cardinals, Sacheverell, &c. and carry them with torches about, and burn them . . . But they were seized last night, by order from the secretary [Dartmouth] . . . The Militia was raised to prevent it, and now, I suppose, all will be quiet" (Swift, *Journal*, *2*, 415–16). All was quiet indeed and there was no celebration for the Protestant queen.

The government was "apprehensive." There was fear that "a dangerous Conspiracy" might lurk beneath this antic pageantry (Swift, *Prose*, *7*, 28; [Delariviere Manley], *A True Relation of the Several Facts and Circumstances of the Intended Riot and Tumult on Queen Elizabeth's Birth-day*,

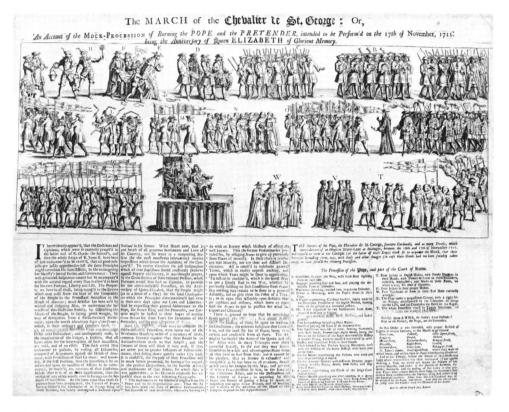

The Mock-Procession of Burning the Pope and the Pretender, intended to be perform'd on the 17th of November, 1711

1711, p. 4). Yet the spectacle of a secretary of state "arresting" 15 card-
board dummies was the best joke of the year. "The *Devil*, the *Pope*, and
the *Pretender*" were not impounded, the earl of Wharton insisted, "*Their
Disciples came by Night and stole them away*" (Oldmixon, *History*, p. 478).
And even some of Swift's favorite ladies insisted upon turning "all this
affair of the pope-burning into ridicule" (Swift, *Journal*, *2*, 417). These
are the delights that are explored and exploited in the present poem.

Even from The Hague, Hermann Petkum was able to see that the
supposedly "moderate" new ministry was "too violent" and uncon-
fident. It "betrays its want of experience and of tact," he said (HMC
Round MSS., p. 357). The "dangerous Conspiracy" that the government
feared was partly at least a projection of its own conspiratorial state of
mind. "Those People who make such an Out-Cry of a Design, and a
Plot," it was recognized, "must needs be in great Necessity of a *Plot*"
(*The Protestant Post-Boy*, 22–24 November 1711).

Neither the date of publication nor the author has been discovered.

THE PROCESSION:
A NEW PROTESTANT BALLAD. TO AN EXCELLENT ITALIAN TUNE.

Let's sing the New Ministry's Praise
With Hearts most thankful and glad,
For the Statesmen of these our Days
Are the wisest that ever we had.

But not to wander too far   5
In the Maze of their endless Merit,
I'll give you an Instance most rare
Of their Vigilance, Wisdom and Spirit.

They heard on Queen *Bess*'s Birth-Day
The Prentices had an intent,   10
Th'old Protestant Gambol to play,
Which *Churchmen,* they thought, should prevent.

The Frolick, it seems, was no less
Than to carry about in Procession
A *Pope* in ridiculous Dress,   15

9. *Queen Bess's Birth-Day:* The 17th of November, or Queen Elizabeth's Day, as it is called, is not the anniversary of Queen Elizabeth's birthday, but "the Anniversary of Queen ELIZABETH's Accession to the Crown" (Boyer, *Annals,* 1712, p. 278).

10. *Prentices . . . intent:* It had been the "constant Practice" of London apprentices "from Generation to Generation, for about 150 Years" to celebrate Queen Elizabeth's Day by making straw figures of "the great Dragon," Satan and the minor devils, and the pope, "Old *Antichrist,* the *Scarlet Whore,*" and burning them in bonfires (*Political Merriment: Or, Truths Told to Some Tune,* 4 vols., 1714–15, *2,* 215; cf. J. E. Neale, *Essays in Elizabethan History,* New York, St. Martin's Press, 1958, pp. 9–20).

11. *Th'old Protestant Gambol:* The minutes of the Green Ribbon Club for 1 November 1679 record "that it is the opinion of this club that a Pope shall be burnt according to custom" (*History, 44* [1959], 19).

12. *Churchmen, they thought, should prevent:* "The Court," Swift said, "apprehensive of a Design to inflame the Common People, thought fit to order that the several Figures should be seized as Popish Trinkets; and Guards were ordered to patrole for preventing any tumultuous Assemblies" (Swift, *Prose, 7,* 28). But "it appear'd very strange, that a Popular Rejoycing so grateful to this PROTESTANT City, which was never attempted to be quash'd but in King *James* the Second's Reign, should, at this Juncture, be interrupted" (Boyer, *Annals,* 1712, p. 279; "never" is wrong, for the procession scheduled for 17 November 1682 was also prohibited by the government).

15. *A Pope:* The procession was to have been brought to a close by figures of "the *Pope,* the *Pretender,* and the *Devil,* seated under a . . . Canopy [of] Scarlet Stuff trimmed with deep Silver Fringe . . . This *Machine* was designed to be born upon Men's Shoulders; the

And to burn it by way of Diversion.

Besides these turbulent Fo'ke
(Than their Ancestors much more uncivil)
To their Pageant had added the Joke
Of a *Perkin*, and eke of a *Devil*,   20

With Cardinals, Jesuits, Fryers,
A Cartload together at least,
Intended to crown their Bonefires,
A very unseas'nable Jest.

For sure there cou'd be no Sense,   25
When a Peace is coming upon us,
T'affront such a powerful Prince
As the *Pope;* why it might have undone us.

Then if the Most Christian King
Should have taken it ill at our hand,   30

---

long Train dependant from the *Figures,* were to conceal those that carried them" ([Delari-viere Manley], *A True Relation of the Several Facts and Circumstances of the Intended Riot and Tu-mult on Queen Elizabeth's Birth-day,* 1711, p. 6). "After the proper Ditties were sung, The Pretender was to have been committed to the Flames . . . And then the Devil was to jump into the Flames with his Holiness in his Arms" (*Political Merriment: Or, Truths Told to Some Tune,* 4 vols., 1714–15, *2,* 214).

20. *a Perkin:* The figure of the pretender was to have been "habited in Scarlet laced with Silver, a full fair long Periwig . . . a Hat and Feather . . . [and] white Gloves" ([Dela-riviere Manley], *A True Relation of the Several Facts and Circumstances of the Intended Riot and Tumult on Queen Elizabeth's Birth-day,* 1711, p. 6).

a Devil: "I am assured," Swift said, "that the figure of the Devil is made as like lord treasurer [Oxford] as they could" (Swift, *Journal, 2,* 416–17).

21. *Cardinals, Jesuits, Fryers:* Preceding the pope were to have been (*Political Merriment: Or, Truths Told to Some Tune,* 4 vols., 1714–15, *2,* 213):

. . . four fat Friars in their Habits, Streamers carried over their Heads, with these Words, *Eat and Pray.*

Four *Jesuits* in *English* Habits, with bloody Daggers in their Hands, with Flower-de-Luces on their Shoulders, inscrib'd, *Indefeasible;* and Masks on their Faces, on which is writ, *The House of* Hanover. . . .

Four Cardinals of *Rome* in their Red Hats curiously wrought.

26. *Peace is coming:* "At their several Bonefires, where the *Parade* was to make a Stand, the Preliminary Articles [*An Excellent New Song, Call'd Mat's Peace,* 8n. above] were to be burnt, with a Cry of, *No Peace*" ([Delariviere Manley], *A True Relation of the Several Facts and Cir-cumstances of the Intended Riot and Tumult on Queen Elizabeth's Birth-day,* 1711, p. 10). According to another report the cry was to have been "*No Peace on the present Terms*" (Berkshire R. O. MS. Trumbull LIII, Thomas Bateman to Sir William Trumbull, 19 November 1711).

29. *Most Christian King:* The style and title of the kings of France included the phrase, "Rex Christianissimus."

Such a very unmannerly thing
Might have put the Peace to a stand.

The *Jacobites* next, to be sure,
Would have ris'n to defend their Master;
And who could have told where a Cure   35
Could be found for such a Disaster.

Besides it would bear a doubt,
Whether burning the *Pope* and the *Devil*
Might not be designed to flout
At High-Church and Dr. *Sacheverell*.   40

Furthermore in these Days of Sin,
'Twas fear'd by Folks that were hearty,
A numerous Mob might have been
Ev'n rais'd for the *Devil* and's Party.

'Twas therefore expedient found   45
To send the Foot Guards on the Scout,
To search all the Suburbs around,
And find the bold Pageant out.

They took it, and as it was fit,
A Magistrate Wise and Great   50
The Criminals strait did commit,

40. *Sacheverell:* The Tories claimed that a figure representing Henry Sacheverell, "which the Work-woman was ordered to make as like his Picture as possibly she could," was to have been included in the procession ([Delariviere Manley], *A True Relation of the Several Facts and Circumstances of the Intended Riot and Tumult on Queen Elizabeth's Birth-day,* 1711, p. 7), but Sacheverell was not included in the Whigs' published "Intention" (see illustration, p. 514).

46. *Foot Guards:* "Accordingly, on *Friday* the 16th, about Twelve a Clock at Night, some of Her Majesty's Messengers, sustain'd by a Detachment of Grenadiers of the Foot Guards, with their Officer, were order'd to go to an Empty House in *Angel Court* in *Drury-Lane,* which being broke open, they found in it the Effigies" (Boyer, *Annals,* 1712, pp. 278–79; cf. *Wentworth Papers,* p. 221).

50. *A Magistrate:* The "Magistrate" was the secretary of state, the newly-created earl of Dartmouth. He was William Legge (1672–1750), the only son of the first Baron Dartmouth. Educated at Westminster and King's College, Cambridge, he was appointed a commissioner of the board of trade and sworn to the privy council upon the accession of Anne and was said to be "in a fair way of rising at Court" (Macky, p. 89). In June 1710 he replaced Sunderland as secretary of state for the southern department and on 5 September 1711 was created Viscount Lewisham and earl of Dartmouth.

51. *The Criminals:* The "Criminals" are the effigies found in the empty house off Drury Lane. They were "put on several Carts . . . about Two a Clock in the Morning, carry'd to the *Cock-Pit,* and there lodg'd in a Room between the Council-Chamber, and the Earl of *Dartmouth's* Secretary's Office" (Boyer, *Annals,* 1712, p. 279).

That the Law might determine their Fate.

Then for fear of a Rescue by Night,
At which we should all ha' been troubled,
'Twas order'd (and sure that was right)   55
That the Guards should be everywhere Doubled.

Besides that no harm might come nigh us,
The Bands so well Train'd were drawn out,
And as long as those Heroes stand by us
The *Devil* himself we may rout.   60

What tho' some People did sneer,
And call 'em the *Pope*'s Life Guard;
They stood to their Arms and their Beer
All Night, and kept Watch and Ward.

So God save our Gracious Queen,   65
And Her Ministers every one,
And he that don't say *Amen*,
Is a Churl, and may let it alone.

The *Hanover* House God preserve,
And blast the Pretender's Hope,   70
The Protestant Cause let's serve,
And give to the *Devil* the *Pope*.

58. *Bands so well Train'd:* "Moreover, on *Saturday, Sunday* and *Monday* [17–19 November] the Trained-Bands of *London* and *Westminster* were under Arms" (ibid., p. 279). The trained bands were the militia of the city of London and the county of Middlesex (Chamberlayne, 1716, pp. 647–48, 660). "To make a Man out of love with Soldiery," said Thomas Brown, "let him see the Train-bands exercise" (Thomas Brown, *The Works,* 3 vols., 1707–08, *1,* 175).

ARTHUR MAINWARING?

A Panegyrick upon the English Catiline
(December 1711?)

Generically, *A Panegyrick upon the English Catiline* makes the point that satire is mock-panegyric and vice versa. The difference is simply one of tone: satire is ironical panegyric.

A Panegyrick upon the English Catiline is also an example of false wit, because it is not consistently conceived as panegyric: "no Man thy Word could ever trust" (line 12). It is essentially a fragment, something that Pope would have kept by him "nine Years" and then assimilated into a dramatic structure like *An Epistle to Dr. Arbuthnot*.

It is also a lampoon, depending for its effects on the stock responses of Whig readers. Its rhetoric is limited to a kind of guilt by association. Oxford is *like* Nero, or Catiline. He is not the leader of a government of "Queen's Servants" who are above party. His party is defined by Francis Atterbury, Sir Humphrey Mackworth, and Henry Sacheverell. By association, therefore, it is high church, bankrupt, and crypto-Jacobite.

What little evidence there is (11*n.*, 12*n.*, 14*n.*), suggests that *A Panegyrick upon the English Catiline* may be another of the "Satyrical Pieces" that Oldmixon failed to recover (*Maynwaring*, p. 326). Mainwaring is known to have considered Oxford and his brother Edward Harley as "a Couple of ———— with whom no Measures of Decency or Delicacy were to be kept" (ibid., p. 340).

Whoever the anonymous writer was, he succeeded in gaining the attention of Oxford. "Lord Treasurer," Swift reported on 5 December 1711, "gave me a scurrilous printed paper of bad verses on himself, under the name of the *English Catiline,* and made me read them to the company. It was his birth-day, which he would not tell us, but lord Harley whispered it to me" (Swift, *Journal, 2,* 430–31).

Presumably the verses were published shortly before Oxford's 50th birthday on 5 December 1711.

A Panegyrick upon the English Catiline

Hail Mighty Hero of the *British* Race,
Famous for Cunning now, as once for Grace;
Whate'er the Arts of former Times could do,
Is, to your Glory, far out-done by you.
Nero rejoyc'd to see his Flaming *Rome,*   5
But you at once whole Kingdoms can consume;
And owing 'tis to your Great Arts alone,
That they are better pleas'd to be undone.
If you gainsay, they dare not trust their Eyes;
They know no Truths, if you but say they're Lyes: 10
So Sinking Credit they believe does rise.
And tho' no Man thy Word could ever trust,
Yet they believe that thou art True and Just.
The Plunder'd Treasury thou wilt Restore,

1. *British Race:* This may be an allusion to Oxford's Welsh connections. The Harleys were originally a Shropshire family with estates in the marches of Wales (Collins, 1812, *4,* 44, 53). Harley himself sat in parliament for New Radnor (1690–1711), a Welsh borough about a dozen miles from the family estate at Brampton Bryan, Herefordshire. Cf. *Abigail's Lamentation for the Loss of Mr. Harley,* 39–40 above.

2. *Cunning:* "He was a cunning and a dark man" (*Account of the Conduct,* p. 261). "He hoped by cunning to varnish over his want of faith and of ability" (Henry St. John, Viscount Bolingbroke, *A Letter to Sir William Windham,* 1753, p. 57).

Grace: Oxford's grandfather, Sir Robert Harley, was a puritan, "earnest for presbytery" and eager to demolish idolatrous monuments. His father, Sir Edward Harley, commanded a regiment of foot under Cromwell. So Henry Aldrich could refer to Harley himself as "that spawn of a Presbyterian" (Feiling, p. 421).

6. *whole Kingdoms can consume:* As lord treasurer, Oxford could burn up the wealth of England, Scotland, and Wales in tax levies.

7. *your Great Arts:* Oxford was said to be "eminent in the Arts of deluding those that hearken to him" (Burnet, *2,* 614).

10. *Truths . . . 're Lyes:* "Could any one but an idiot call him honest," Mainwaring asked (*Private Correspondence of Sarah, Duchess of Marlborough, 1,* 238).

11. *Credit . . . rise:* Mainwaring includes the same sarcasm in *An Excellent New Song, call'd Credit restored, in the Year of our Lord God, 1711:* "From this happy Year you for ever may date / Of Credit the Restoration" (Oldmixon, *Maynwaring,* p. 334); cf. Mainwaring, *An Excellent New Song, Called Mat's Peace,* 19n. above.

12. *no Man thy Word could ever trust:* "No man alive believes [him]," Mainwaring said, "any more than an Oates or a Fuller" (*Private Correspondence of Sarah, Duchess of Marlborough, 1,* 392).

14. *The Plunder'd Treasury:* The House of Commons voted on 24 April 1711 that there was £35,000,000 "whereof no Accounts have been laid before the Auditors" and four days later resolved "that of late Years . . . the Management of the Treasury [had been] an high

And so thou must, if those that made it Poor   15
Should put it in the State it was before.
Bless'd with a Noble and a Clear Estate,
Thou only mean'st to make the Nation Great,
And free it from the Plagues it felt of late,
Just as thy *Atterbury* will set free   20
The Church from Pestilential Heresy,
And Ancient Rights restore to Prelacy.
That Church and Nation may with Splendor shine,
Is sure as much thy long contriv'd Design,
As it was good Sir *Humphry*'s in the Mine.   25

Injustice to the Nation" (*CJ, 16,* 613, 619). But in fact Godolphin's management of the treasury was "so unexceptionable, that it was not possible to fix any Censure on his Administration" (Burnet, *2,* 568). Mainwaring (with help from Robert Walpole) wrote a folio pamphlet, *A State of the Five and Thirty Millions Mention'd in the Report of the Committee of the House of Commons,* defending Godolphin (Oldmixon, *Maynwaring,* pp. 298–300).

17. *a Noble and a Clear Estate:* According to St. John, Oxford's "estate was very mean" (Henry St. John, Viscount Bolingbroke, *A Letter to Sir William Windham,* 1753, p. 61).

20. *Atterbury:* Francis Atterbury (1660–1728), the high church controversialist and crypto-Jacobite, began his career in 1687 while a tutor at Christ Church, Oxford, by publishing an essay opposing James II's attempt to Romanize the university. He was appointed to his first important ecclesiastical post in February 1701 for writing *The Rights, Powers, and Privileges of an English Convocation* (Luttrell, *5,* 15), which made extravagant claims for the autonomy of the lower house of convocation. In 1704, after Atterbury had been installed dean of Carlisle, Harley supported him in his quarrels with William Nicolson, the Whiggish bishop of Carlisle (HMC *Portland MSS., 4,* 139). Atterbury collaborated in drafting the controversial address of the London clergy of August 1710 (p. 456 above) and about the same time Mainwaring heard that Harley had "retained Dr. Atterbury to write a justification of his actions" (*Private Correspondence of Sarah, Duchess of Marlborough, 1,* 393), which became the pre-Swiftian *Examiner.*

22. *Ancient Rights:* Atterbury's opposition to the attempts of Bishop Nicolson to visit Carlisle cathedral in 1707 led to the passage of an Act for the avoiding of Doubts and Questions touching the Statutes of divers Cathedral and Collegiate Churches (6 Anne c. 21), which unequivocally re-affirmed the ancient right of episcopal visitation.

24. *Design:* St. John came to wonder whether Oxford "ever had any determined view besides that of raising his family" (Henry St. John, Viscount Bolingbroke, *A Letter to Sir William Windham,* 1753, p. 51).

25. *Sir Humphry's in the Mine:* The "Design" of Sir Humphrey Mackworth's Company of Mine Adventurers, a lead mining and smelting enterprise at Melincryddan, Wales, was simply to make money: £26,490 was subscribed the first day that the stock was sold in October 1698 (Luttrell, *4,* 434). The price of the shares rose until 1707, but "the whole undertaking was riddled with dishonesty, for most of which Mackworth . . . was personally responsible" (*University of Birmingham Historical Journal, 1* [1948], 234). When the company went bankrupt in 1709, "Widows and Orphans" were left holding the bag (*Review,* 4 April 1710). And although the House of Commons unanimously voted Mackworth guilty of "many notorious and scandalous Frauds" in March 1710 (*CJ, 16,* 391), Harley's new government, of which Mackworth was an articulate supporter, failed to prosecute.

> *Harcourt* in fine Harangues, thy Praises tells;
> Just so he did the Great *Sacheverell's.*
> Had he but Liv'd in Days of *Catiline,*
> Those Praises had been his, which now are thine,
> And like Success attended his Design.   30

26. *Harcourt . . . thy Praises tells:* Harcourt's opportunity came in the court of exchequer on 1 June 1711 when Oxford was sworn lord treasurer. "You have been the great Instrument," he said, "of restoring Publick Credit [line 11 above], and relieving this Nation from the heavy Pressure and Ignominy of an immense Debt, under which it languish'd [line 14 above]; and you are now entrusted with the Power of securing us from a Relapse into the same ill State [line 19 above], out of which you have rescued us" (Boyer, *Annals,* 1711, p. 385).

27. *so . . . Sacheverell's:* Harcourt was chief defense counsel for Sacheverell in the impeachment trial and his summing up was said to have "at least equal'd any thing we yet know of the Grecian, or Roman Oratory, both in exactness according to their Rules of Delivery, the Cadences, and the Strength the justness, and the Beauty of the Expression" (Osborn MS. Box 21, No. 22, f. 11v).

28. *he:* Harcourt—instead of Cicero perhaps (*POAS,* Yale, *6,* 628).

Catiline: After multiple crimes and conspiracies, Lucius Sergius Catilina (c. 108–62 B.C.) was killed leading revolted legions in an unsuccessful coup d'état (Sallust, *Bellum Catilinae,* xiv–xv).

29. *his:* Catiline's.

30. *his:* Catiline's.

JONATHAN SWIFT

An Excellent New Song,
Being
The Intended Speech of a Famous Orator against Peace
(6 December 1711)

Daniel Finch, second earl of Nottingham, was the leading Anglican layman of his day, the *"Don Quixote* of the *Church"* ([John Toland], *The Memorial of the State of England,* 1705, p. 53). Thus his defection to the Whigs in November 1710 was not only a surprise in itself, but it tied together an outstanding event of the early years of Anne's reign—the triple failure of the Tories to pass a bill against occasional conformity—and the outstanding event of the last years of the reign—the enactment of the treaty of Utrecht.

Although he had done nothing to bring down the Godolphin ministry, Nottingham expected to share with Harley and Shrewsbury in the spoils (Horwitz, p. 221; Swift, *Prose, 7,* 15). And although he was violently opposed to Harley's "wild and unwarrantable scheme of balancing parties," as he called it, he expected to be included in this scheme (Horwitz, p. 228; 3*n.* below). Early in the session of November 1710–June 1711 his resentment took the form of demands for criminal prosecution of the late ministers that were certain to appeal to the October Club Tories, just organizing themselves in the House of Commons in opposition to Harley.

Harley made three attempts, short of taking him into the government, to regain Nottingham's support. The first, in February 1711, ended with Nottingham walking out of the meeting muttering strange threats that "if we did not act in concert with the whigs, we should soon find the effects of our good-nature" (Burnet, 1823, *6,* 37*n.*). The second, in October 1711, was a letter, to which Nottingham returned a very chilly answer (HMC *Portland MSS., 5,* 101). But very soon after this, Oxford learned the meaning of Nottingham's threat: he had joined with the Whigs to bring down the ministry on the question of peace without Spain (Horwitz, pp. 230–31).

Oxford responded by postponing the opening of parliament until 7 December 1711 (Swift, *Journal, 2,* 421) to give the Scots lords time to

reach London to secure his majority in the House of Lords. Then he
made a final attempt to engage Nottingham in the court interest, but
was for the third time rebuffed (Boyer, *History,* p. 525). Oxford also
begged the queen to "speak to a certain Lord who was looked upon as
Dubious" (Swift, *Prose, 8,* 147). Then, counting the pensionary lords
who "were only kept in awe by the fear of offending the Crown" (ibid.,
7, 17), he concluded that he had a majority of ten in the House of Lords
and decided not to ask for a further prorogation (ibid., *8,* 146).

At the last minute Oxford caused to be inserted in *The Post Boy,* 4–6
December 1711, the following public notice:

> Whereas a very tall, thin, swarthy complexion'd Man, between 60
> and 70 Years of Age, wearing a Brown Coat, with little Sleeves and
> long Pockets, has lately withdrawn himself from his Friends, being
> seduc'd by wicked Persons to follow ill Courses. These are to give
> Notice, That whoever shall discover him, shall have 10s. Reward;
> or if he will voluntarily return; he shall be kindly receiv'd by his
> Friends, who will not reproach him for past Follies, provided he
> give good Assurances, that, for the future, he will firmly adhere to
> the Church of England, in which he was so carefully educated by
> his Honest Parents.

At the same time he hinted to Swift at dinner on 5 December "as if he
wished a ballad was made" on Nottingham. Swift sent off to the printer
the next day the present ballad, "two degrees above Grubstreet," and
copies were available that night for the meeting of the Brother's Club
(Swift, *Journal, 2,* 430–31). In this work of pure imagination and a few
facts supplied by Oxford and Dartmouth (37–38*n.,* 46*n.*), Swift not only
brings to life the second earl of Nottingham, but writes the speech that
he will deliver tomorrow in the House of Lords.

The poem was answered in an unusually feeble "reverse," *The Not-
tinghamshire Ballade, An Excellent New Song, Being the Intended Speech of a
Famous Orator* (1711) ("*An Orator was found in* Nottinghamshire"), of
which there are copies at NLS and Harvard.

AN EXCELLENT NEW SONG,

BEING

THE INTENDED SPEECH OF A FAMOUS ORATOR AGAINST PEACE

An Orator *dismal* of *Nottinghamshire*,
Who has forty Years let out his Conscience to hire,
Out of Zeal for his Country, and *want of a Place*,
Is come up, *vi & armis*, to *break the Queen's Peace*.
He has vamp't an old Speech, and the Court to their sorrow,   5
Shall hear Him harangue against PRIOR to Morrow:

1. *dismal:* "So they call him from his looks," Swift explained (*Journal, 2,* 430); for his looks see *The History and Fall of the Conformity-Bill,* 126*n.* above and illustration, p. 13.

2. *forty Years:* Finch entered parliament in a by-election for the borough of Great Bedwin, Wiltshire, in February 1673. Before the election he took care to provide a new town hall for Great Bedwin (Horwitz, p. 7).

3. *want of a Place:* Although rumors had made him secretary of state in June, first lord of the admiralty in September, and lord privy seal in December 1710 (Burnet, 1823, *6,* 7–8*n.*; Luttrell, *6,* 633, 667), Nottingham had been carefully excluded from Harley's "balanced" government. "Upon the Earl of *Rochester's* Decease [21 May 1711], he conceived, that the Crown would hardly overlook him for President of the Council; and deeply resented that Disappointment. But the Duke of *Newcastle* Lord Privy Seal dying some time after [15 July 1711], he found that Office was . . . disposed of to [John Robinson] the Bishop of *Bristol*" (Swift, *Prose, 7,* 16). Harley thought he was an "old woman" (Horwitz, p. 222) and he was "disagreeable personally to the Queen" (Bolingbroke, *Letters, 1,* 281). Since he had been out of office since May 1704 (when Harley replaced him as secretary of state), he was "as sour and fiercely wild as . . . anything . . . that has lived long in the desert" (HMC *Portland MSS., 5,* 119).

4. *vi & armis:* with force and arms. A legal phrase for "direct and immediate force or violence against the plaintiff or his property" (Henry C. Black, *Black's Law Dictionary,* 4th ed., St. Paul, Minnesota, West Publishing Co., 1968, p. 1675).

the Queen's Peace: "the general peace and order of the realm as provided for by law" (*OED,* s.v. Peace, *sb.* 9b). In the context, however, "the Queen's Peace" means a treaty with France on the basis of the six preliminary articles that Prior had brought back from France in August 1711. Since Somerset was industriously spreading the rumor that the preliminary articles were not acceptable to the queen (Swift, *Prose, 8,* 147), it was important by this phrase to suggest that they were. And now, or shortly hereafter, "The Queen's Peace" became a favorite Tory toast (*A Detection of the Sophistry and Falsities of the Pamphlet, Entitul'd, The Secret History of the White Staff,* Part II, 1714, p. 17).

5. *an old Speech:* On 19 December 1707 Nottingham had opened an attack in the House of Lords on the Godolphin ministry for the failures in Spain. He proposed sending 20,000 men there from Flanders where "he thought it worth being upon the defensive for the regaining of Spain." He was joined in the attack by the Junto lords and when Marlborough conceded their criticism, Somers "took an occasion to propose a question that he thought all would agree in, viz., that no peace could be safe or honourable, till Spain and the West Indies were recovered from the House of Bourbon" (Vernon, *3,* 300–01; *Huntington Library Quarterly, 15* [1951–52], 38–39; HMC *Egmont MSS., 2,* 219–21).

5–6. *the Court . . . Shall hear Him . . . to Morrow:* Oxford had known of Nottingham's

526

When once he begins, he never will flinch,
But repeats the same Note a whole Day, like a *Finch*.
I have heard all the Speech repeated by *Hoppy*,
And, *mistakes to prevent, I have obtain'd a Copy*.   10

The SPEECH.

Whereas, Notwithstanding, I am in great Pain,
To hear we are making a Peace without *Spain*;
But, *most noble Senators*, 'tis a great Shame
There should be a Peace, while I am *Not in game*.
The Duke shew'd me all his fine House; and the Dutchess   15
From her Closet brought out a full Purse in her Clutches:

---

general disaffection since February 1711 (p. 524 above). And even of his specific intention to "offer a Vote in the House of Lords [on 7 December] against any Peace while Spain continued in the Hands of the Bourbon Family . . . the Ministers had early Notice" (Swift, *Prose, 8,* 146).

6. *PRIOR:* See pp. 504–06 above.

8. *a whole Day:* Nottingham's "talkative . . . manner" was considered an "Impediment to the Publick Business" (Swift, *Prose, 7,* 15). In the actual debate on 7 December he "spoke long for the question" (HMC *Polwarth MSS., 1,* 3).

Finch: Nottingham's family name.

9. *Hoppy:* Hoppy may be Edward Hopkins (1675–1736), a nephew of Thomas Hopkins (*On My Lord Godolphin, 4n.* above) and son of Sir Richard Hopkins (Le Neve, p. 108). He was educated at Eton, Trinity College, Oxford, and on the grand tour, wherein he both "Intrigu'd with Glory and with Spirit whor'd" (HMC *Bath MSS., 3,* 240) and thus became both a member of the Kit-Cat Club (Oldmixon, *History,* p. 479) and a member of parliament for Coventry, Warwickshire (December 1701–1702, February 1707–10) and Eye, Suffolk (1713–27). He went to Vienna as Sunderland's secretary in 1705 and in November 1709 was appointed envoy to Hanover to succeed Emanuel Scrope Howe (Luttrell, *6,* 507) but seems not to have been posted (J. F. Chance, *Notes on the Diplomatic Relations of England and Germany,* Oxford, B. H. Blackwell, 1907, pp. 8–10). Swift mentions him in January 1723 as someone "whom I have long known" (*Corr., 2,* 445; cf. *Prose, 10,* 58; *English Historical Review, 34* [1919], 493–95, 504). His portrait is reproduced in [James Caulfield], *Memoirs of the Celebrated Persons Composing the Kit-Cat Club,* 1821, p. 227).

12. *Peace without Spain:* See 5–6n. above.

14. *Not in game:* "We all pun here sometimes," Swift told Esther Johnson (*Journal, 1,* 153). To Archbishop King he explained that Nottingham "would be against any Peace without *Spain;* and why? Because he was not Privy Seal" (*Corr., 1,* 340).

15. *The Duke:* Swift imagines that Nottingham's recruitment to Whiggery took place at Blenheim. Actually it took place in London during an interview with Marlborough and Godolphin late in November or early in December 1711 (Horwitz, p. 231).

16. *a full Purse:* Swift believed at the time that "Nottingham has certainly been bribed" and later he recorded that "The Earl of *Nottingham* became a Convert for Reasons already mentioned. Money was distributed where Occasion required" (Swift, *Journal, 2,* 432; *Prose, 7,* 108).

I talk'd of a *Peace*, and they both gave a start;
His Grace swore by ———, and her Grace let a F——t:
My *long old-fashion'd Pocket* was presently cramm'd;
And sooner than Vote for a Peace I'll be d——n'd.   20
But some will cry, *Turn-Coat*, and rip up old Stories,
How I always pretended to be for the *Tories*:
I answer; the *Tories* were in my good Graces,
Till all my *Relations* were put into *Places*.
But still I'm in Principle ever the same,   25
And will quit my best Friends, while I am *Not in game*.
When I and some others subscribed our Names

17. *both gave a start:* In the actual interview Marlborough and Godolphin "fully declar'd against this Peace, hoped that I was of the same mind," Nottingham wrote to his wife, "for that the Success wou'd depend upon me, who might do what they cou'd not, that is persuade some Tories to concurre in this opinion, without which this Matter must miscarry and we shou'd be undone" (Northamptonshire R. O. MS. Hatton-Finch 281, Nottingham to Lady Nottingham, 16 December 1711).

19. *long . . . Pocket:* Since a "long stomach" was "a voracious appetite" (Francis Grose, *A Classical Dictionary of the Vulgar Tongue,* 1785, p. 105), "long . . . pockets" must indicate a voracious appetite for money.

21. *Turn-Coat:* "I should [wonder] at any that knew me," Nottingham protested to Lady Dorchester, "if they cou'd think a place wou'd change my opinion" (Horwitz, pp. 233–34).

24. *Relations . . . put into Places:* A disappointed candidate for the bishopric of Carlisle in June 1703 complained that Lord Nottingham "lays his hand on all church preferment. His brother, his chaplains, and his favourites are all taken care of" (HMC *Bagot MSS.,* p. 337). Nottingham had already succeeded in getting his brother, Henry Finch, promoted to the deanery of York, and his "favourites," Humphrey Prideaux to the deanery of Norwich, and William Nicolson to the bishopric of Carlisle (Luttrell, *5,* 164, 171). More recently, two of his nephews, the earl of Dartmouth and Sir Thomas Benson, had been appointed secretary of state and commissioner of the treasury, respectively. His friend John Annesley, fourth earl of Anglesey, had been appointed paymaster of Ireland, and a prebendal stall at Canterbury had been added to his brother's benefices. In June 1711, his nephew, Heneage Finch, had been made master of her majesty's jewel house, his indigent cousin, Charles Finch, earl of Winchilsea, was put at the head of the new commission for trade and plantations, an office worth £1,500 a year, and another "favourite," John Ward, was made a Welsh judge. Finally, in July 1711, his son-in-law, Sir Roger Mostyn, was made paymaster general of the marines (Boyer, *History,* pp. 500, 514–15). By this time St. John could hope that "his relations are so well provided for, that . . . he ought to be contented" (Bolingbroke, *Letters, 1,* 281).

27. *subscribed our Names:* Nottingham had been approached in June 1688 to join the conspiracy to send an invitation to William of Orange to seize the English throne. "Upon the first proposition [he] entertained it, and agreed to it. But at their next meeting he said, he had considered better of that matter" (Burnet, *1,* 764) and his name is not included among the "Immortal Seven" (GEC, *7,* 508) who signed the invitation in cipher. His own account of this episode written many years later says nothing about a blotted signature: "This was the greatest difficulty that ever I was plung'd into in my whole life . . . I was indeed asham'd to quitt the Company who had admitted me into their Secrets and on the other hand I did not dare to proceed in an affair of which the next step would be high treason" (Leicestershire Record Office MS. Finch Political Papers 148, p. 10, quoted in Horwitz, p. 52).

To a Plot for expelling my Master King *James;*
I withdrew my Subscription by help of a *Blot,*
And so might discover, or gain by the Plot: 30
I had my Advantage, and stood at Defiance,
For *Daniel* was got from the Den of the Lions.
I *came in* without Danger; and was I to blame?
For rather than *hang,* I would be *Not in game.*

I swore to the *Queen* that the *Prince* of *Hanover* 35
During Her Sacred Life, should never come over:
I made use of a *Trope;* that *an Heir to invite,*
Was like keeping her Monument always in sight.
But when I thought proper, I alter'd my Note;
And in Her own hearing I boldly did Vote, 40
That Her *Majesty* stood in great need of a *Tutor,*
And must have an *old,* or a *young Coadjutor:*
For why; I would fain have put all in a Flame,
Because, for some Reasons, I was *Not in game.*

Now my new *Benefactors* have *brought me about,* 45
And I'll Vote against Peace, *with Spain,* or *without:*
Tho' the *Court* gives my *Nephews,* and *Brothers,* and *Cousins,*
And all my whole Family, Places by Dozens;
Yet since I know where a *full Purse* may be found,
And hardly pay Eighteenpence Tax in the Pound: 50

35. *swore to the Queen:* While he was still secretary of state (May 1702–May 1704), Nottingham told the queen, according to Lord Dartmouth, "that whoever proposed bringing over her successor in her life-time, did it with a design to depose her" (Burnet, 1823, *5,* 227n.).

37–38. The italicization of lines 37b–38 may indicate that they are the *ipsissima verba* of Nottingham in his audience with the queen (35n. above). Since Dartmouth was an intimate friend of Swift, he could have provided the quotation. Cf. [Edmund Gibson?], *Memoirs of Queen Anne: Being a Compleat Supplement to the History of Her Reign,* 1729, p. 277: "Some of the Ministry . . . [told the queen that] for the Electoral Prince . . . to sit in the House of Peers . . . was all one as setting her Coffin before her Eyes."

39. *alter'd my Note:* Having made these assurances to the queen while he was secretary of state, Nottingham turned around in November 1705, after he had been dismissed, and voted to invite the dowager electress of Hanover to reside in England (Horwitz, p. 205).

40. *in Her own hearing:* "The Queen heard the Debate, and seemed amazed at the Behaviour of some, who when they had Credit with her . . . had possessed her with deep Prejudices against it" (Burnet, *2,* 430). Dartmouth records that "This made an impression upon the queen to lord Nottingham that could never be overcome" (Burnet, 1823, *5,* 227n.).

46. *against Peace, with Spain, or without:* Oxford recognized that "the outcry against a peace at this time is raised by the art and cunning of some who are against any peace" (HMC *Portland MSS., 5,* 120).

49. *a full Purse:* See 16n. above.

50. *Eighteenpence Tax in the Pound:* This is intended to outrage Tory squires who were paying the wartime tax on their estates of four shillings, or forty-eight pence, in the pound.

Since the *Tories* have thus disappointed my Hopes,
And will neither regard my *Figures* nor *Tropes;*
I'll *Speech* against *Peace* while *Dismal*'s my Name,
And be a *true Whig,* while I am *Not in game.*

52. *Figures nor Tropes:* Nottingham indeed lived up to expectations. In his speech he referred to France, "our enemy" as "a loose card" that we ought not "to be put to our trumps" to take (HMC *Lords MSS.*, New Series, *9,* 369).

The Queen's Speech.
To the Tune of *Packington's Pound*
(December 1711?)

The following song of four stanzas set to the tune of *Packington's Pound* is a remarkably close parody in a difficult stanza form of the queen's words at the opening of the second session of her fourth parliament on 7 December 1711.

More remarkable is the great economy of means used to generate irony in the poem. Even the feeble non sequitur, as in "By which" (line 12) and "therefore" (21), generates potent ironical effects. The slight mistake of saying "ally" (10) for "enemy" seems to induce a disproportionately large ironic jolt. And the introduction of such prickly words as "Pain" (4) and "ruin" (36) into the bland and windy discourse that governments assume to address their constituents, brings about a remarkable reductive effect.

The discourse that is parodied was one of the most important that Anne had to make. She and her servants were now irreversibly committed to peace on terms that had been negotiated, separately and secretly, with the enemy. They "were willing," therefore, in James Macpherson's words that are not without their own ironies, "to have some account of the progress of that important measure to lay before the two houses, when they should first assemble. The speech with which the Queen opened the session, was more suitable to the known design of her servants, than in itself sincere" (Macpherson, *History,* 2, 506).

It is understood, of course, that Anne's address was "not her own" (*On the Queen's Speech,* 10, above). It was drafted for her by her ministers, revised in council meeting, and submitted for final polishing to the ranking Tory littérateur, old Bajazet of good King Charles's golden days, now the duke of Buckingham and absent from the last council meeting. Buckingham found it "so very good," as he said in his letter returning it to the lord treasurer, "that I believe it out of anybody's power to mend it" (HMC *Portland MSS.,* 5, 120). But this time Oxford's "budget full of miracles upon all occasions" (ibid., 5, 119) failed to work.

As soon as Anne had spoken her part, taken off her royal robes, and come back to the House of Lords incognito to hear the debate and by her presence to "moderate any Heats that might arise," Lord Nottingham was launched into "a long and laboured speech" (Boyer, *Annals,* 1712, p. 284; Macpherson, *History, 2,* 508). He was moving a clause to be inserted in the usual address of thanks for the queen's speech, "That no Peace can be safe or honourable to *Great Britain* or *Europe,* if *Spain* and *The West-Indies* are to be allotted to any Branch of the House of *Bourbon*" (*LJ, 19,* 336). Five hours later Nottingham's clause had been carried in the affirmative by a vote of 61–55 and the Oxford ministry and peace without Spain were both in high jeopardy (Boyer, *Annals,* 1712, p. 288; HMC *Polwarth MSS., 1,* 2–3).

The Queen's Speech can be assumed to have been written shortly after 7 December 1711, but there is no external evidence for this.

The suspicion that Arthur Mainwaring wrote the poem might not be worth recording were it not for the fact that it was first printed in *Political Merriment: Or, Truths Told to some Tune. Faithfully Translated from the Original French of R.H. S.H. H.S. F.A. G.G. A[rthur] M[ainwaring] M.P. . . . ,* 1714–15 (Case 280), like so many poems known (*The History and Fall of the Conformity-Bill, An Excellent New Song, Called Mat's Peace*) or suspected (*A New Ballad: To the Tune of Fair Rosamund, Masham Display'd*) to be his. The manuscript copy at Blenheim is endorsed in the duchess of Marlborough's hand: "A very pritty poem which repeats in ridicule one of the queen's own speeches." The genre, mock-address, is one of Mainwaring's favorites (*POAS,* Yale, *6,* 615; *7,* 454). The poem itself includes some of his current preoccupations, like French bribes (7*n.* below), and some of his comic nonrhymes (lines 33–34 below; cf. *The History and Fall of the Conformity-Bill,* lines 121, 123). "But Circumstances will not amount to a Proof, said the Prisoner" (*The Whipping Post,* 10 July 1705).

THE QUEEN'S SPEECH.
TO THE TUNE OF *Packington's Pound*

As soon as I could I have call'd you together,
Tho' twice I've prorogu'd you, since first you came hither;
My Council 'tis true, who with *France* have been treating,
Were somewhat in Pain, when they thought of your Meeting.
　　　　But since it is known,　　　　　　　　　　　　　5
　　　　Our Commons have shewn
A Decent regard to *French* Coyn, and our own,
To take your Advice I'm no longer afraid,

1. *As soon as I could:* Anne's actual words were, "I have called you together as soon as the Public Affairs would permit" (*LJ, 19,* 335).

2. *twice . . . prorogu'd:* After the usual series of prorogations during the summer, parliament was twice prorogued after most of the peers and members had returned to London in the fall, once on 13 November and again on 27 November 1711. On the latter occasion Swift reported that "The parliament is again to be prorogued for eight or nine days; for the Whigs are too strong in the house of lords: other reasons are pretended, but that is the truth" (Swift, *Journal, 2,* 421).

3. *Council:* Yet another prorogation was proposed at a meeting of the privy council on the night of 5 December, "but some Members . . . represented the Fears and Jealousies which such an Adjournment, after so many Prorogations, might create in the Minds of the People" (Boyer, *History,* p. 525).

France: The preliminary articles were signed for France by Mesnager on 27 September 1711 and published in *The Post Boy,* 13–16 October 1711. A great outcry went up when it was learned that Spain and Spanish America had been abandoned to Louis XIV's grandson and that the only guarantee that the two crowns would not be united under a Bourbon monarch was Louis XIV's *bona fide,* which had long been a joke (*An Ode, Humbly Inscrib'd to the Queen,* 194n. above; cf. Mainwaring, *An Excellent New Song, Called Mat's Peace,* 39n. above). When the published terms seemed so unfavorable, there were dark suspicions that even greater concessions to France had been made in secret articles. It was in fact "a Peace of the Ministry, to whom . . . it was absolutely necessary," as even Swift agreed (*The Secret History of the Late Ministry,* 1715, p. 346; Swift, *Journal, 2,* 429).

treating: negotiating, treatying. But to treat with the enemy in time of war is, of course, high treason. The poet also felt (10–11) that the Tory treaty-makers were "treating" France in the sense of entertaining them at Britain's expense.

7. *French Coyn:* Mainwaring had read "the Rumour dispers'd in foreign Prints of great Sums of Money remitted from *France* to other Places" (*Remarks upon the Present Negotiations of Peace Begun between Britain and France,* 1711, p. 28) and he may have heard that in January 1711 the earl of Jersey had accepted a pension of £3,000 a year from France (Trevelyan, *3,* 179). Cf. Mainwaring?, *A New Ballad: To the Tune of Fair Rosamund,* 97–100 above.

8. *Advice:* Although the conduct of foreign affairs was still the exclusive prerogative of the crown (Boyer, *Annals,* 1712, p. 287), there was also a tradition that war was declared and peace concluded with the advice and consent of parliament. The implication, however, is that Anne is willing to accept this "Advice" because peace "already is made" (9).

Concerning a Peace, which already is made.
The *French*, our Allies, their Concurrence express,   10
The *Indies* and *Spain* for themselves to possess;
By which I establish your Freedom and Laws,
The *Protestant* Church, and the *Hanover* Cause.
            By this too your Trade
            So large will be made,   15
That in Future Times it of me shall be said;
For such Loyal People my Love was no other,
Than that of a tender affectionate Mother.

The Princes and States that engag'd in the War,
I wisely have left of themselves to take Care;   20

9. *Peace . . . made:* "And I am glad that I can now tell you," Anne went on, "that, notwithstanding the Arts of those who delight in War, both Place and Time are appointed for Opening the Treaty of a General Peace" (*LJ, 19,* 335). The place was Utrecht, the time 1 January 1712, but again the implication is that the negotiations will be mere window dressing because peace "already is made." "The Arts of those who delight in War" was understood to be "levelled at the Duke of *Marlborough*" (Burnet, *2,* 583).

10. *The French, our Allies:* Mainwaring uses the same phrase in *Remarks upon the Present Negotiations of Peace Begun between Britain and France,* 1711, p. 15. It was a daring transposition to create a shocking phrase, for France had been the enemy since 1689 and Englishmen had died fighting the French only three months before this in the siege of Bouchain. What Anne actually said was, "Our Allies (especially *The States General*), whose Interest I look upon as inseparable from My own, have, by their ready Concurrence, expressed their entire Confidence in Me" (*LJ, 19,* 335). "Her saying, that the Allies reposed an entire Confidence in her, amazed all those who knew, that neither the Emperor [as the Habsburg claimant to the throne of Spain] nor the Empire had agreed to the Congress, but were opposing it with great Vehemence [Johann Wenzel, count de Gallas, the Austrian ambassador, had protested against the preliminary articles so violently that he had been declared persona non grata and expelled the month before]; and that even the *States* were far from being cordial or easy, in the steps that they had made" (Burnet, *2,* 583; Boyer, *Annals,* 1712, pp. 252–53).

12–13. "My chief Concern," the queen went on to say, "is, that the Protestant Religion, and the Laws and Liberties of these Nations, may be continued to you, by securing the Succession to the Crown, as it is limited by Parliament, to the House of *Hanover*" (*LJ, 19,* 335). The irony is produced by the "By which," which derives these benefits most implausibly from peace without Spain.

14–18. "I shall endeavour," Anne said next, "that, after a War which has cost so much Blood and Treasure, you may find your Interest in Trade and Commerce improved and enlarged by a Peace, with all other Advantages which a tender and affectionate Sovereign can procure for a dutiful and loyal People" (*LJ, 19,* 336). In these lines of the text the goddess Dulness struggles to be born.

19–22. "The Princes and States, which have been engaged with us in this War, being by Treaties entitled to have their several Interests secured at a Peace," the queen said, "I will not only do My utmost to procure every one of them all reasonable Satisfaction; but I shall also unite with them, in the strictest Engagements for continuing the Alliance, in order to render the general Peace secure and lasting" (ibid.).

20. *left of themselves to take Care:* Even Shrewsbury was afraid that "it may look suspiciously,

And therefore our Friendship sure never can cease,
But all will unite for securing the Peace.
    And since as you find
    The *French* are so kind,
To take the poor Lot that for them is design'd,   25
I hope none will envy *Great-Britain* or me,
The Glory of making such Terms as you see.

All former Abuses I now will redress,
And hang up the Men that have serv'd with success;
This Notice I give you, that you may confound   30
All those that have made me so great and renown'd;
    And this I propose
    To shew all my Foes,
That we are a People most unanimous;
So may God direct you in your wise Consultations,   35
To ruin these Happy and Flourishing Nations.

as if her [Majesty's] party had had no consideration but of what concerns Britain; and, having settled that with France, would leave her friends to shift for themselves" (Bolingbroke, *Letters, 1,* 335–36).

23–27. In these lines "the *French*" are substituted for parliament. "My Lords, and Gentlemen," Anne said, "As I have had your chearful Assistance for the carrying on this long and chargeable War; so I assure Myself, that no true Protestant, or good Subject, will envy *Britain,* or Me, the Glory and Satisfaction of ending the same, by a just and honourable Peace for us and all our Allies" (*LJ, 19,* 336).

28–31. "I shall do My utmost," the queen continued, "to encourage our Home Manufactures . . . and to correct and redress such Abuses as may have crept into any Part of the Administration during so long a War" (ibid.). Although Mainwaring may not have known that the ministry was ready to proceed against Marlborough, General William Cadogan, and Robert Walpole, he did know that a commission for examining the public accounts had been voted during the previous session (Boyer, *Annals,* 1711, pp. 354, 360) and that six of the seven commissioners were members of the October Club (Boyer, *Political State, 3,* 117–21).

32–36. "I cannot conclude," the queen said, "without earnestly recommending to you all Unanimity; and that you will carefully avoid every Thing which may give Occasion to the Enemy to think us a People divided amongst ourselves, and consequently prevent our obtaining that good Peace, of which we have such reasonable Hopes, and so near a View. I pray God direct your Consultations to this End, that, being delivered from the Hardships of War, you may become a happy and a flourishing People" (*LJ, 19,* 336).

WILLIAM SHIPPEN?

The Character of a Certain Whigg
(31 December 1711)

This is the Tory counterpart of *A Panegyrick upon the English Catiline*. It depends for its effectiveness on the stock responses of its Tory readers. Artistically, however, it is more successful than *A Panegyrick upon the English Catiline*.

The genre of *The Character of a Certain Whigg* is announced in its title. It is a "character"—of Thomas Wharton, fifth baron, first earl, and eventually (February 1715) first marquess of Wharton. Its announcement as a character probably implies that it will not be impartial, which is fulfilled in the opening couplet, and that it will have a theme. The second expectation is fulfilled in Wharton's "joined Contradictions" (line 4) that are carefully built up through lines 5–17 to achieve a climax in line 18, where the perverted trope of a sane madman, like a broken watch that is still running, is a sufficient analogue for Wharton's compulsive personality.

If this is the work of William Shippen, its evolution can be traced from *Faction Display'd* (April? 1704) (*POAS*, Yale, *6*, 658), through *Moderation Display'd* (December? 1704) (p. 39 above) and *The Junto* (September 1709–April 1710) (p. 364 above), with each stage adding something to the finished character.

Evidence that it is Shippen's work exists only in the similarity of its form and content (2n., 5n., 8n., 18n. below) to Shippen's known verses.

The Luttrell copy of *B*, now in the Newberry Library, is dated 31 December 1711.

The Character of a Certain Whigg

Industrious, unfatigu'd in Faction's Cause,
Sworn Enemy to God, his Church, and Laws:
He doats on Mischief for dear Mischief's Sake;
Joins Contradictions in his wond'rous Make;
A flattering Bully, and a stingy Rake;   5
Joins Depth of Cunning with Excess of Rage,
Leudness of Youth with Impotence of Age;

1. *FACTION's Cause*: Wharton's style as an election manager may be judged from the following: a trial in Yorkshire in which he was defendant opened at ten o'clock in the morning on 7 May 1708 and the court sat all night (Luttrell, *6*, 300–01). "As soon as the Judge began to Summon up the Evidence to the Jury, [Wharton] left the Court, went into his Coach and six Horses, and order'd his Coachman to drive him directly to *Woburn* [his seat in Buckinghamshire] where he got about Twelve at Night, and rose at Five next Morning, set out at Six for *Malmesbury*, where, having Rode thirty Miles of the way a Horseback, he arrived at Night. The next Day [10 May 1711] was the Election for Members for that Borough, which he manag'd with that Dexterity and Dispatch as to carry it for both of his Friends [Henry Mordaunt and Thomas Farrington], and on the Morrow took Coach for London" (*Memoirs of the Life of the Most Noble Thomas, Late Marquess of Wharton*, 1715, pp. 43–44).

2. *Enemy to GOD*: "As long as he was talked of," Wharton was called "an atheist grafted on a presbyterian" (Burnet, 1823, *5*, 228n.). There was a total eclipse of the sun during his burial on 22 April 1715 (*A Miscellaneous Collection of Poems*, 2 vols., Dublin, 1721, *1*, 8n.).

his CHURCH: Although he called himself "*a Churchman by Choice*" (*Memoirs of the Life of the Most Noble Thomas, Late Marquess of Wharton*, 1715, p. 37), Wharton's benefactions took strange forms. In 1680 he was arrested and fined £1,000 for desecrating the cathedral in Gloucester (Swift, *Prose, 3*, 57). Then, during a debate in the House of Lords in December 1705 on whether the church was in danger, when Wharton ridiculed the notion, the old duke of Leeds stood up and said, "If there were any that had pissed against a communion table, or done his other occasions in a pulpit, he should not think the church safe in such hands. Upon which lord Wharton was very silent for the rest of that day" (Burnet, 1823, *5*, 236n.).

LAWS: One law to which Wharton was particularly inimical was the Irish test clause (Shippen?, *The Junto*, 27n. above).

5. *A flattering BULLY*: Wharton was frequently engaged in duels and discovered "a dextrous way" of disarming his opponents, "which never fail'd of giving him an Opportunity to shew his forgiving as well as his Heroick Temper" (*Memoirs of the Life of the Most Noble Thomas, Late Marquess of Wharton*, 1715, pp. 31–33; Vernon, *2*, 324; cf. "The Bully Vice Roy," Shippen?, *The Junto*, 23 above).

a stingy RAKE: Swift mentions "Love of Money, and Love of Pleasure" as two of Wharton's three ruling passions (Swift, *Prose, 3*, 180–81).

6. *Cunning*: "As for Business, he is said to be very dextrous at that Part of it which turneth upon Intrigue, and he seemeth to have transferred those Talents of his Youth for intriguing with Women, into public Affairs" (ibid.).

Rage: "He will rattle his Coachman in the Middle of the Street" (ibid., *3*, 179).

Descending, though of RACE Illustrious born,
To such vile ACTIONS as a Slave wou'd scorn.
A Viceroy once, by unpropitious FATE,   10
The RULER and the ROBBER of the STATE.
His DIGNITY and HONOUR he secures
By OATHS, PROFANENESS, RIBALDRY, and WHORES;
Kisses the Man whom just before he BIT,
Vends Lies for JESTS and Perjury for WIT.   15
To great and small alike extends his FRAUDS,
Plund'ring the CROWN and bilking ROOKS and BAUDS.
His *Mind* still working, *Mad*, of PEACE bereft,
And *Malice* eating what the Pox has left.
A MONSTER, whom no VICE can bigger swell,   20
Abhorr'd by HEAV'N and long since due to HELL.

8. *RACE Illustrious:* "Although the Whartons appear to have been at Wharton [Westmorland] since the time of Edward I [1272–1307], the pedigree begins with Thomas [Wharton] who was M.P. for Appleby, 1436–37" (GEC, *12*, ii, 594*n*.); cf. "antient Stock" (Shippen, *Faction Display'd*, 61, *POAS*, Yale, *6*, 628).

10. *Viceroy:* The "unpropitious *Fate*" that let Wharton rule and rob Ireland was the death on 28 October 1708 of Prince George, the royal consort. In her grief Anne was unable to hold out any longer against the Junto's demands for a post for Wharton and on 15 November 1708 she allowed him to kiss her hand as the lord lieutenant of Ireland (Luttrell, *6*, 373). Wharton also "Urg'd his active Star" by blackmailing Godolphin (Burnet, 1823, *5*, 381*n*.). Then, during the short time that he was in Ireland (April–September 1709, May–August 1710), he was able to steal at least £45,000 (Swift, *Prose*, *3*, 181). According to another source he found over £70,000 in the Irish treasury and "left but 29 shilens and 6 penc" (BM MS. Add. 31143, f. 595v).

14. "He will openly take away your Employment To-day . . . To-morrow he will meet or send for you as if nothing at all had passed, lay his Hands with much Friendship on your Shouldiers . . . with the greatest Ease and Familiarity" (Swift, *Prose*, *3*, 179).

15. *Lies:* "Are you such a simpleton," Wharton said, "as not to know, that a lie well believed is as good as if it were true" (Burnet, 1823, *5*, 228*n*.).

18. *Mind . . . working:* Cf. Shippen, *Faction Display'd*, 178, *POAS*, Yale, *6*, 658: "Working, Turbulent, Fanatick Mind."

Arthur Mainwaring?

A New Song.
Being a Second Part to the Same Tune of *Lillibullero*
(November–December 1711?)

This may be one of the few cases in English literary history where the "Second Part" by *The Author of the First* is not delinquent. The first, *An Excellent New Song, To the Memorable Tune of Lillibulero,* begins:

> Oh! Brother *Tom,* dost know the Intent,
> *Lillibulero Bullen a la,*
> Why they prorogue the Parliament?
> *Lillibulero Bullen a la,*
> *Lero, Lero, Lero, Lero, &c.*

and rattles along like this for 12 more stanzas.

The present poem is superficially just as merry. It is easily sung to the tune of *Lillibullero,* but there is an unmistakable undertone of seriousness. The seriousness was generated partly by fears for what was happening: addresses pouring into London from all over England upholding hereditary right (p. 454 above), open demonstrations of Jacobitism in Scotland (p. 491 above), and peace negotiations that seemed incomprehensible unless they were to include another restoration of Catholic Stuarts (43*n.* below).

But the seriousness in the poem is equally generated by fears for what was not happening— the feeling that everything that had been won in the war was being lost in the peace: "Thus when our Army had advanc'd so far, that one Battel, or even one Siege more wou'd in all probability have put a good End to the War," Mainwaring said, "a secret Negotiation was set on foot between *Britain* and *France*" (*Remarks upon the Present Negotiations of Peace Begun between Britain and France,* 1711, p. 7)—the feeling that peace was a trap: "We are so inchanted, or rather poison'd with the Name of Peace, that we do not see the Mischief which the *French* have speciously cover'd under it" (ibid., p. 29).

There can be no doubt that these fears and frustrations were felt and were not something assumed for rhetorical effect. "The Cause we are engag'd in," Mainwaring said, "is great and just: 'Tis the Cause of

Truth and Liberty; then let us not basely desert or betray it . . . an ill Peace is worse than War it self" (ibid., pp. 34–35).

Since the first part of the poem mentions prorogation of parliament, which occurred on 13 and 27 November 1711 (*LJ, 19,* 331, 334), and the prevention of the pope-burning procession on 17 November (p. 514 above), the most likely date for the second part may be November–December 1711.

The suspicion that Arthur Mainwaring is the author of *A New Song* is aroused mainly by parallels between the song and Mainwaring's prose pamphlet, *Remarks upon the Present Negotiations of Peace Begun between Britain and France,* published both in folio and octavo editions, in 1711 (Oldmixon, *Maynwaring,* p. 248).

The *Lillibullero* tune, as well as the words of *A New Song,* continues to have a life of its own. It is probably the antipapist associations of the original ballad that suggested to the pipers of a Highland regiment in June 1944 to play *Lillibullero* in St. Peter's Square, "gieing Popie a blaw" (Simpson, p. 455).

A New Song.
Being a Second Part to the Same Tune of *Lillibullero*

A Treaty's on foot, look about *English* Boys,
Stop a Bad Peace as soon as you can,
A Peace which our *Hanover*'s Title destroys,
And shakes the high Throne of Our Glorious Queen *ANNE*.
  Over, over, Hanover, *over,*   5
  Haste and assist our Queen and our State;
  Haste over, Hanover, *fast as you can over,*
  Put in your Claim before 'tis too late.

A Bargain our Queen made with her good Friends
The *States*, to uphold the Protestant Line;   10

1. *A Treaty's on foot:* When "the Secret broke out" in September 1711, Burnet was so alarmed that he "plainly" told the queen that "any Treaty by which *Spain* and the *West-Indies* were left to King *Philip*, must in a little while deliver up all *Europe* into the hands of *France;* and, if any such Peace should be made, she was betrayed, and we were all ruined; in less than three Years time, she would be murdered, and the Fires would be again raised in *Smithfield*" (Burnet, *2*, 580, 583).

2. *a Bad Peace:* a peace without Spain. "This was then the Chief End of the War, *To recover* Spain *and the* Indies *for the House of* Austria: And there is but one Reason in the World which should make us submit to an Ill Peace, and that is the being beaten every Campaign, and unable to succeed in the Field: But this, I thank God, is the Condition of our Enemies, not our own" ([Mainwaring], *Remarks upon the Present Negotiations of Peace Begun between Britain and France,* 1711, pp. 6–7).

3. *Hanover's Title destroys:* The elector "saw clearly, that if *Spain* and the *West Indies* were left to King *Philip*, the *French* would soon become the superiour Power to all the rest of *Europe;* that *France* would keep *Spain* in subjection, and by the Wealth they would fetch from the *Indies*, they would give Law to all about them, and set what King they pleased on the Throne of *England*" (Burnet, *2*, 581); cf. Mainwaring, *An Excellent New Song, Called Mat's Peace,* 58n. above. Torcy, at any rate, believed that the ministry intended to restore the pretender (*Journal inédit de Jean-Baptiste Colbert, Marquis de Torcy,* ed. Frédéric Masson, Paris, 1884, p. 442).

5. *Hanover, over:* The poem probably anticipates, rather than reflects, the proposal made by Prince Eugene to the Whig leaders in January 1712 "that to strengthen the Whigs, the Electoral Prince should pass into England, to awe the ministry, by appearing at the head of their enemies" (Macpherson, *History, 2,* 531–32).

9. *Bargain:* The "Bargain" was the Barrier Treaty with the Netherlands, negotiated by the Whigs and signed by Charles Townshend, Viscount Townshend, in October 1709. In return for 20 garrisoned towns and forts in the Spanish Netherlands and northern France, and 400,000 crowns a year to maintain them as "a Barrier to keep *France* at a distance," the Dutch undertook to guarantee "par Mer & par Terre" the succession of the crown of Great Britain in the Protestant line of Hanover (Lamberty, *5,* 464–69). Mainwaring began *A Short Account and Defence of the Barrier Treaty* but never finished it (Oldmixon, *Maynwaring,* pp. 227–47).

If a Bad Peace is made, that Bargain then ends
And spoils her good Majesty's gallant Design.
   Over, over, Hanover, *over,*
   Haste and assist our Queen and our State;
   Haste over, Hanover, *fast as you can over,*   15
   Put in your Claim before 'tis too late.

A Creature there is that goes by more Names
Than ever an honest Man cou'd, shou'd or wou'd,
And I wish we don't find him an arrant King *James*
Whenever he peeps out from under his Hood.   20
   Over, over, Hanover, *over,*
   Haste and assist our Queen and our State;
   Haste over, Hanover, *fast as you can over;*
   Put in your Claim before 'tis too late.

The *Dauphin* of *France* to a Monast'ry went   25
To visit the Mother of him aforesaid;
He wish'd her much Joy, and he left her Content
With a dainty fine Peace about to be made.
   Over, over, Hanover, *over,*
   Haste and assist our Queen and our State;   30
   Haste over, Hanover, *fast as you can over,*
   Put in your Claim before 'tis too late.

What kind of a Peace, I think we may guess,
So welcome must be to her and her Lad:
And let any Man say it, if we can do less   35
Than be very sorry when they're very glad.

17. *A Creature:* James Francis Edward Stuart, the titular Prince of Wales, was recognized
by Louis XIV as James III of England and VIII of Scotland and called the chevalier de St.
George in France. In England he was occasionally called Perkin and eventually the "Old
Pretender."
   20. *his Hood:* Since Sunderland and Halifax had "boldly affirmed, that the chief view of
the present administration, was to restore the Pretender" (Macpherson, *History, 2,* 501), the
hope expressed here seems to be that he will never take time enough from his devotions to
made himself another Catholic king of England.
   25. *The Dauphin:* "What other meaning [than restoring the pretender] cou'd there be in
the Compliment, that was made by the *Dauphin* [Louis, duc de Bourgogne, dauphin since his
father's death in April 1711] to the *late Queen* of England [Mary of Modena]? The Paris
Gazette it self mentions the Joy he was pleas'd to wish her upon the News of our approaching
Peace. What Joy cou'd that be to her, but as it laid a Foundation for her Son's Advance-
ment?" ([Mainwaring], *Remarks upon the Present Negotiations of Peace Begun between Britain
and France,* 1711, p. 34).

Over, over, Hanover, *over,*
Haste and assist our Queen and our State;
Haste over, Hanover, *fast as you can over,*
Put in Your Claim before 'tis too late.   40

Whoe'er is in Place I care not a fig,
Nor will I decide 'twixt High-Church and Low;
'Tis now no Dispute between *Tory* and *Whig,*
But whether a Popish Successor or No.
    Over, over, Hanover, *over,*   45
    Haste and assist our Queen and our State;
    Haste over, Hanover, *fast as you can over;*
    Put in your Claim before 'tis too late.

Our Honest Allies this Peace do explain,
Of which our *French* Foes so loudly do boast;   50
But I hope, if they reckon on *India* and *Spain,*
They'l reckon without consulting their Host.
    Over, over, Hanover, *over,*
    Haste and assist our Queen and our State;
    Haste over, Hanover, *fast as you can over;*   55
    Put in your Claim before 'tis too late.

Or else we must bid farewel to our Trade,
Whatever fine Tales some People have told;

43. *no Dispute between Tory and Whig:* "Surely it is now time to think of other Matters, than whether *Tories* or *Whigs* shall prevail in the Court or in the Parliament: Things shou'd surely now be regarded, and not Men: This is not a Party—but a National Concern . . . Is this a Time to dispute about Resistance and Revolution Principles, when we have reason to dread another Conquest?" ([Mainwaring], *Remarks upon the Present Negotiations of Peace Begun between Britain and France,* 1711, p. 31).

49. *Allies this Peace do explain:* Johann Wenzel, count de Gallas, the emperor's ambassador in London, "printed the Preliminaries in one of our News-Papers . . . [and] was ordered . . . out of *England*" (*The Daily Courant,* 13 October 1711; Burnet, *2,* 580; Boyer, *History,* p. 520). Then Johann Caspar, baron von Bothmer, the elector of Hanover's ambassador, printed the elector's *mémoire* representing "the pernicious Consequences . . . if Spain and the Indies were left to the Duke of Anjou." Bothmer was not expelled, but was called in for an "*Éclaircissement*" with St. John (*The Daily Courant,* 5 December 1711; Boyer, *History,* pp. 523–24).

50. *Foes . . . boast:* "We have lately been inform'd from all hands how well the *French* Agents were satisfied with their Reception here: What Transports their Countrymen express'd when they came home, and how extreamly happy and good-humour'd their King has been ever since" ([Mainwaring], *Remarks upon the Present Negotiations of Peace Begun between Britain and France,* 1711, p. 8).

57. *farewel to our Trade:* See Mainwaring, *An Excellent New Song, Called Mat's Peace,* 46n. above.

58. *fine Tales:* "Whosoever shall advise the giving [Spain] up for a Peace; and the certain

For whenever a Peace of that nature is made,
We shall send out no Wool, nor bring home no Gold.   60
    Over, over, Hanover, *over,*
    Haste and assist our Queen and our State;
    Haste over, Hanover, *fast as you can over;*
    Put in your Claim before 'tis too late.

Then wage on the War, Boys, with all your Might;   65
Our Taxes are great, but our Danger's not small;
We'd better be half undone than be quite,
As half a Loaf's better than no Bread at all.
    Over, over, Hanover, *over,*
    Haste and assist our Queen and our State;   70
    Haste over, Hanover, *fast as you can over;*
    Put in your Claim before 'tis too late.

Income of three Millions and an half *per Annum,* for the uncertain Advantages of a *South-Sea* Trade, deserve[s] to be impeach'd by the general Voice of the Kingdom" (*A Letter to a Member of the October-Club: Shewing, That to yield Spain to the Duke of Anjou by a Peace, wou'd be the Ruin of Great Britain,* 2nd ed., 1711, pp. 23, 25–26, 30, quoted in [Mainwaring], *Remarks upon the Present Negotiations of Peace Begun between Britain and France,* 1711, p. 17).

60. *send out no Wool:* It was feared that if Louis XIV controlled Spain, he would prohibit "the Exportation of their unwrought Wool to us" and the import of English cloth (*A Letter to a Member of the October-Club,* 2nd ed., 1711, p. 10, quoted in [Mainwaring], *Remarks upon the Present Negotiations of Peace Begun between Britain and France,* 1711, p. 16). Cf. "Is it not plain that the Duke of *Anjou* and his Frenchifyed Subjects will be more inclinable to take the *French* Linsey Woolsey's, and other Beggarly Stuffs, than our West Country Serges, or *Colchester* Bays" (*A Caveat to the Treaters: Or, The Modern Schemes of Partition Examin'd,* 1711, p. 36).

bring home no Gold: See Mainwaring, *An Excellent New Song, Called Mat's Peace,* 58n. above.

65. *wage on the War:* Cf. "Let us therefore chearfully prosecute the War . . . I cannot have the least Fear, or Doubt, but the Parliament will effectually provide for the publick Service, till such Concessions are granted by *France,* as shall appear just and reasonable to the whole Confederacy" ([Mainwaring], *Remarks upon the Present Negotiations of Peace Begun between Britain and France,* 1711, pp. 32, 34–35).

66. *Danger's not small:* Cf. "The present Negotiation is dangerous to the Confederacy . . . and wou'd be destructive to *Europe* if it should end in an ill Peace" (ibid., p. 35).

68. Proverbial (Tilley, H36); cf. "Whatever Estate I had in the World, I would freely give half of it to secure the rest, rather than yield up *Spain* to the House of *Bourbon;* because I do in my Conscience believe that I should lose the whole by such a Treaty" ([Mainwaring], *Remarks upon the Present Negotiations of Peace Begun between Britain and France,* 1711, p. 18).

1712

A New Protestant Litany
(February 1712?)

In these verses the new wine of 1712 is poured into bottles that had been in use at least since 1672 (*POAS*, Yale, *1*, 190). The vintage of 1712 was heady stuff: "a Dozen of Peers, made all at a Start" (line 1)—Wharton asked "whether they voted by their foreman"—a discarded duke (4), and the lord treasurer's "*Catholick Whore*" who was a Jacobite spy (22).

The old bottles into which this new stuff is poured are the litany stanzas with their apotropaic refrain, *Libera nos domine*. And although no tune is indicated in any of the witnesses, the litanies "often call for such tunes as *Cavalilly Man* or *The Queen's Old Courtier* or *When Jockey first the Wars began*" and can be sung to any of these (Simpson, p. 88).

The date of *F*, 1713, seems too late, but February 1712, the date of *B*, seems just right.

Some of the evidence for Mainwaring's authorship is included in the footnotes.

A New Protestant Litany

From a Dozen of Peers, made all at a Start,
To save *Harley* from Scaffold, and St. *John* from Cart,
Libera nos Domine.

From Discarding the Duke, whereas no Mortal knows
Any Cause of Demerit, but beating our Foes,   5
Libera nos Domine.

From a General (God knows) Silly, Lavish and Poor,

1. *a Dozen . . . at a Start:* After its defeat on Nottingham's amendment to the address of thanks to the queen (p. 532 above), the Oxford ministry—even with a 2-1 majority in the House of Commons—was regarded as doomed. "As far as I can judge," Swift said, "the game is lost." But on Saturday night 29 December 1711 Swift broke open his letter to say that "we are all safe; the queen has made no less than twelve lords to have a majority" (Swift, *Journal, 2,* 436, 449–50). Oxford had moved so secretly that not even his colleagues knew what he was doing. "I was never so much surprised," Dartmouth recalled, "as when the queen drew a list of twelve lords out of her pocket, and ordered me to bring warrants for them; there not having been the least intimation before it was to be put in execution. I asked her, if she designed to have them all made at once" (Burnet, 1823, *6,* 87n.). The Whigs were flabbergasted and complained that "my Ld Oxford pack'd Jurys to carry Causes" (Hertfordshire County R.O. MS. Panshanger D/EP F207, f. 37). Cowper, the late lord chancellor, while acknowledging that "the Step of Chusing 12 Lords . . . is a legal Act of her M[ajest]y," still pointed out that it was "Us'd to an Extravagant Excess, and to a bad End; viz. the Modelling one of the Houses of Parliament, and that while Sitting which makes it Still worse . . . not to reward Merit . . . but to make Votes and Numbers . . . It's done to Save a Ministry" (ibid., f. 38).

2. *Harley . . . Scaffold:* The fears that are reflected here were at least real enough to be joked about: "I told lord treasurer" on 8 December, Swift said, that "I should have the advantage of him; for he [as a peer] would lose his head, and I [as a commoner] should only be hanged, and so carry my body entire to the grave" (Swift, *Journal, 2,* 435).

4. *Discarding the Duke:* The second phase of Oxford's counterattack was directed against Marlborough. The decision to dismiss him was taken at a council meeting on Sunday 30 December 1711 and that night the queen wrote a letter "so very offensive that the Duke flung it into the fire, though he was not a man of passion" (HMC *Marlborough MSS., 1,* 16b) and *The London Gazette* of 3–5 January 1712 announced that "Her Majesty hath been graciously pleased to Constitute his Grace the Duke of Ormonde Commander in Chief of all Her Majesty's Land Forces in . . . England and Colonel of Her Majesty's First Regiment of Foot-Guards."

5. *beating our Foes:* Cf. Mainwaring?, *The Humble Address of the Clergy of London,* 31–32n. above.

7. *a General:* J. Woodfall Ebsworth identified the general as Ormonde (*Roxburghe Ballads, 8,* 828), who may have been "Silly," was certainly "Lavish," and had kept a whore (*POAS,* Yale, *6,* 440–41). And even with £25,000 a year from his estates in Ireland, Ormonde was hopelessly in debt. "He will have the honour of running farther into debt by being made a General," it was observed (*The Letters of Thomas Burnet to George Duckett,* ed. David Nichol Smith, Roxburghe Club, 1914, p. 5).

Whose Courage and Wit lies in keeping a Whore,
> *Libera nos Domine.*

From a Peeress of Merit for handling a Broom, 10
For sweeping down Cobwebs and scrubbing a Room,
> *Libera nos Domine.*

From a Masculine Dutchess' preposterous Fate,
From Bauding for Whores grown chief Baud of State,
> *Libera nos Domine.* 15

Whose Husband at *Rome* our Faith did Surrender,
And swore to the Pope and his Godson Pretender,
> *Libera nos Domine.*

From a Treasurer us'd to Drink, Lie, Swear and Pray,
And to bribe *Scottish* Peers with Civil List pay, 20
> *Libera nos Domine.*

10. *a Peeress:* Abigail Masham's husband, Samuel, only a second choice for one of the 12 new peerages, had been created Baron Masham of Oates on 31 December. "Sir *Miles Wharton,* to whom it was [first] offered, refused it" (Burnet, *2,* 589). When a second choice was proposed the queen complained that "she never had any design to make a great lady" of Abigail Masham, or to "lose a useful servant about her person . . . but at last consented, upon condition she remained a dresser" (Burnet, 1823, *6,* 33n.). Cf. Mainwaring?, *A New Ballad: To the Tune of Fair Rosamund,* 10, above.

13. *a Masculine Dutchess:* The duchess of Shrewsbury "étoit une grande créature et grosse, hommasse" (Saint-Simon, *4,* 128).

14. *Bauding for Whores:* Mainwaring called her "a common strumpet" (*Private Correspondence of Sarah, Duchess of Marlborough, 1,* 392).

   Baud of State: Cf. "Slut of State" (Mainwaring?, *A New Ballad: To the Tune of Fair Rosamund,* 24, above). In the next reign it was complained that the duchess's "deluding airs Corrupt our virgins" at court (*The Letters and Works of Lady Mary Wortley Montagu,* ed. James A. Stuart-Wortley-Mackenzie, Lord Wharncliffe, 2nd ed., 3 vols., 1837, *3,* 352).

16. *Rome:* Shrewsbury had been raised a papist and converted to the Church of England in May 1679. During his residence in Rome from November 1701 to the spring of 1705, "he was accused of caballing with the papal court" and the rumors that he had been reconciled to Catholicism were so insistent that he had to publish a denial (*Shrewsbury Corr.,* pp. 639–49). Mainwaring still called him "a papist in masquerade" (*Private Correspondence of Sarah, Duchess of Marlborough, 1,* 392).

19. *Treasurer us'd to Drink, Lie:* Two of the reasons that Anne gave for dismissing Oxford in July 1714 were that "she could not depend upon the truth of what he said . . . [and] that he often came drunk" (Swift, *Corr., 2,* 86).

   Swear and Pray: Wharton used to enjoy reminding Oxford of their common dissenting background and "how often we have been together at *Pinner's-Hall,*" a Presbyterian meeting house in London (*Memoirs of the Life of the Most Noble Thomas, Late Marquess of Wharton,* 1715, p. 104).

20. *bribe Scottish Peers:* According to Oxford the "real inducement" for creating twelve new peers was that "the Scotch lords were grown so extravagant in their demands, that . . .

Whom St. *Germains* Equipt with a *Catholick Whore*,
And old *Lewis* retain'd with his Image *en Or*,

Libera nos Domine.

Who sacrific'd *Gregg* to save his own Neck,   25
And may serve *Prior* too another such Trick,

Libera nos Domine.

From St. *John* the Bloody, and *Poulet* the Cat,
From *Brydges* the Sharper, and *Beaufort* the Brat,

Libera nos Domine.   30

---

they were now come to expect a reward for every vote they gave" (Burnet, 1823, *6*, 87*n*.). Bribery of the Scots lords was so notorious that when Oxford sent £1,000 to Henry Somerset, duke of Beaufort, his grace sent it back, saying "'Twas certainly meant for some Scotch Lord" (*Wentworth Papers*, p. 216).

22. *a Catholick Whore:* Ebsworth's guess, "Oglethorpe?" (*Roxburghe Ballads, 8*, 828), is almost certainly right. Anne Henrietta Oglethorpe (c. 1683–after 1752) was one of the nine children of Brigadier General Sir Theophilus Oglethorpe, a Jacobite who returned to England in 1698 and took the oaths to William III. Anne Oglethorpe, however, received a Catholic education at St. Germain and was arrested when she entered England illegally during the Scots plot (1704). "By her Wit and Beauty, improv'd by the *French* Gayety and Politeness," she is said to have won the hearts of both Harley and Godolphin and to have been the ultimate cause of the "irreconcileable Enmity" between them (Boyer, *History*, p. 127). What is certain is that Harley procured her discharge in June 1707 when she was again arrested, this time for converting a young woman to Catholicism and decoying her into a nunnery in France (HMC *Portland MSS., 4*, 417; Luttrell, *6*, 182). And in November 1713 baron von Schütz, the envoy from Hanover, refers to "Miss Oglethorpe" as "the lord treasurer's mistress" (Macpherson, *Original Papers, 2*, 513).

23. *Image en Or:* a miniature portrait of Louis XIV in a gold frame imagined as a reward for Oxford's good services; cf. *The British Embassadress's Speech to the French King*, 2*n*. below.

25. *sacrific'd Gregg:* Joseph Browne made the same charge in *The Humble Memorial*, 78, 80 above.

26. *serve Prior . . . another such Trick:* for Prior's part in the peace negotiations, see pp. 504–06 above.

28. *St. John the Bloody:* the blood may be that of the more than 800 men who were lost in the ill-fated Quebec expedition, which St. John pushed through the privy council against the opposition of the other ministers (HMC *Portland MSS., 4*, 656).

Poulet the Cat: John Poulett, fourth Baron Poulett of Hinton St. George (c. 1668–1743) deployed his extensive electoral influence in the west country in support of Harley and was rewarded in December 1706 when he was created Earl Poulett. He served as privy councillor (December 1702–September 1714), commissioner for the union (1706), and first lord of the treasury (August 1710–May 1711), but "first in form" only, for Harley ran the treasury (Burnet, *2*, 552–53) and in June 1711 he was removed to the safe post of lord steward of the household. He had also been Harley's candidate to replace Sunderland as secretary of state in June 1710, until St. John succeeded in elbowing his way into the job. Since Poulett's usual nickname was "Swallow" (*Private Correspondence of Sarah, Duchess of Marlborough, 1*, 349–51), it is hard to explain "the Cat." Perhaps the implication is that Poulett was a Sacheverellite, for Wharton had called them "Cats" (p. 394 above) and Prince Eugene observed that Poulett was "much bigoted to the Church of England" (GEC, *10*, 620).

29. *Brydges the Sharper:* James Brydges (1674–1744) was the son and heir of the eighth

From all who would sell our Religion and Laws,
And betray our good Queen to advance *Perkin*'s Cause,
Libera nos Domine.

Give them Gibbets and Halters, and Axes in store,
And from the *French* Harpy preserve us once more,   35
We beseech thee to hear us, Amen.

Baron Chandos of Sudeley. As a member of parliament for Hereford (1698–1714) he was neither Whig nor Tory but "a great complyer with every Court" (Swift, *Prose, 5,* 260). He "signalized" himself in the impeachment proceedings against the Junto lords in 1701 (Luttrell, *5,* 39, 59) and earned a place in the Whig blacklist of that year. But from October 1705 he voted consistently with the Whigs, including a vote for the impeachment of Sacheverell in December 1709. When Harley resumed power, Brydges switched back and voted for the French commerce bill in June 1713 and still managed to get himself represented to George I as a Whig. He served on Prince George's admiralty council (April 1704–April 1705) and as paymaster general of the forces abroad (May 1705–August 1713). Brydges was already on the way to becoming "Princely Chandos" (GEC, *3,* 130), for £200,000 of the money he was able to amass in the latter post went into building "Timon's Villa," the palace of Canons, near Little Stanmore in Middlesex. One of his minor sharp practices was to use his inside knowledge of events on the continent to win bets on the progress of sieges (*Huntington Library Quarterly, 15,* [1951–52], 21–44).

Beaufort the Brat: Henry Somerset (1684–1714) succeeded as second duke of Beaufort in January 1700 and took his seat in the House of Lords in October 1705. He absented himself from court, however, until the accession of the Tory ministry in 1710, when he is said to have told Anne that "he could then call her Queen in reality" (Collins, 1812, *1,* 239). He was made lord lieutenant of Hampshire and warden of New Forest in September 1710 (*Wentworth Papers,* p. 140) and a privy councillor in December 1710. There was a rumor in January 1712 that he was to succeed Shrewsbury as lord chamberlain (Luttrell, *6,* 710), but it proved false and he had to content himself with the lesser posts of captain of the band of pensioners and lord lieutenant of Gloucestershire (ibid., *6,* 714, 715). In February 1714 he was admitted a member of St. John's Brothers' Society (Swift, *Journal, 2,* 493) and he died just after his 30th birthday following a debauch in the country (*Wentworth Papers,* p. 384). He may be "the Brat" because he is the youngest of the four courtiers mentioned in these lines.

JONATHAN SWIFT

The Fable of Midas
(14 February 1712)

The Fable of Midas is a perfect example of mock-heroic, which raises up
its victims to superhuman heights,

> Whene'er he chanc'd his Hands to lay,
> On Magazines of *Corn* or *Hay*,
> *Gold* ready Coin'd appear'd,
>
> (15–17)

only to split them off from common humanity and to let them drop
still further into comic depths, alone:

> And *Midas* now neglected stands,
> With *Asses Ears*, and *dirty Hands*.
> (81–82)

Harley had tried twice to salvage Marlborough for a bipartisan
ministry and had failed both times (p. 298 above; 30*n.* below). And St.
John predicted correctly what would be the result: "the moment he
leaves the service, and loses the protection of the court, such scenes
will open, as no victories can varnish over" (Bolingbroke, *Letters, 1,* 81).
But even before Harley's second attempt, Swift had begun, presumably
with the ministry's consent, his own attack on Marlborough in *The
Examiner,* 23 November 1710. This was followed up by *The Examiner* of
8 February 1711 in which Marlborough, in the guise of Crassus the
triumvir, was accused of "that odious and ignoble Vice of *Covetousness*"
(Swift, *Prose, 3,* 84). These attacks, however, were not irreversible, for
they also found praise for Crassus's "Gracefulness," "Understanding,"
and "subduing of [his] Anger."

But Marlborough's "Understanding" seems to have failed him when
he came home from the victorious campaign of 1711 to throw himself
into frantic and discreditable attempts to overturn the Oxford ministry
(74*n.* below). His vote against the peace preliminaries on 7 December
1711 sealed his fate. *The Fable of Midas* is irreversible in its monumental
scorn.

The disgrace of Marlborough was one of the most difficult decisions taken by the Oxford ministry. It could not fail to have dangerous repercussions, both at home where Fighting John was worshipped as a legendary hero, and abroad where he was feared as the monster Malbrouk (Swift, *Journal, 2,* 453). That it succeeded without violence may be attributed in part to a careful plan of propaganda. Oxford, who believed that in propaganda the only defense is a good offense, was delighted with *The Fable of Midas:* "Mr Secty [St. John]," Swift said, "read it before me tother night to Ld Tr. [Oxford] at Ld Mashams, where they equally approved of it" (Swift, *Journal, 2,* 488).

"To day I published the Fable of Midas, a Poem printed in a loose half sheet of Paper," Swift reported on 14 February 1712 (ibid.). On the same day Narcissus Luttrell bought the copy of *Aa*² now in the Newberry Library and wrote on it the date and "On the Duke of Marlborough."

The Fable of Midas

MIDAS, we are in Story told,
Turn'd ev'ry thing he touch't to *Gold:*
He *chip't* his *Bread,* the Pieces round
Glitter'd like Spangles on the Ground:
A Codling e'er it went his Lip in,   5
Would strait become a *Golden* Pippin:
He call'd for Drink, you saw him Sup
Potable Gold in *Golden Cup.*
His empty Paunch that he might fill,
He suck't his Vittels thro' a Quill;   10
Untouch't it pass't between his Grinders,
Or't had been happy for *Gold-finders.*
He cock't his Hat, you would have said
Mambrino's Helm adorn'd his Head.
Whene'er he chanc'd his Hands to lay,   15
On Magazines of *Corn* or *Hay,*
Gold ready Coin'd appear'd, instead

1. *MIDAS:* "For the fable of Midas, king of Phrygia, to whom Dionysus granted the power of turning all he touched to gold, see Ovid, *Met.* XI, 85ff." (Swift, *Poems, 1,* 156).

4. *like Spangles on the Ground:* Cf. the Lilliputian court drawn up at Gulliver's feet like "a Petticoat spread on the Ground, embroidered with Figures of Gold and Silver" (Swift, *Prose, 11,* 31).

5. *Codling:* "A variety of apple, in shape elongated and rather tapering toward the eye . . . not suitable to be eaten raw . . . [but] cooked while still unripe" (*OED,* quoting this line).

6. *Golden Pippin:* Cf. Swift, *The Virtues of Sid Hamet the Magician's Rod,* 74 above.

11. *Grinders:* This bit of vulgar bathos—cf. "*The Cove has Rum Grinders,* c. the Rogue has excellent Teeth" (*New Dictionary,* sig. F4r)—makes a fine contrast with the pomp and elegance of Midas / Marlborough. "The expression is debased to debase the character" (Boswell's *Journal of a Tour to the Hebrides with Samuel Johnson, LL.D., 1773,* ed. Frederick A. Pottle and Charles H. Bennett, new ed., New York, McGraw-Hill, 1961, p. 58).

12. *Gold-finders:* Here the bathos reaches even deeper—into the privy. "*Gold-finders* [are] Emptiers of Jakes or Houses of Office" (*New Dictionary,* sig. F3r).

13. *cock't his Hat:* turned up the brim. But the action may be petulant or defiant. *OED* quotes Luttrell, *2,* 204: "sir John Fenwick, sir Theophilus Oglethorp, and others, behaving themselves indecently as her majestie past by, looking her in the face and cocking their hats."

14. *Mambrino's Helm:* "*Orlando Furioso,* Canto i, st. 28. See also *Don Quixote,* chap. 36" (Swift, *Poems, 1,* 156).

16. *Magazines:* storehouses, especially for the military. *OED* cites *Samson Agonistes,* 1281: "Thir Armories and Magazins."

17. *Gold ready Coin'd:* Marlborough too turned bread into gold. The commissioners of

Of paultry *Provender* and *Bread:*
Hence we are by wise Farmers told,
Old Hay *is equal to Old* Gold;   20
And hence a Critick deep maintains,
We learn't to weigh our *Gold* by *Grains.*
 This *Fool* had got a *lucky Hit,*
And People fancy'd he had *Wit:*
Two Gods their Skill in Musick try'd,   25
And both chose *Midas* to decide;
He against *Phebus* Harp decreed,
And gave it for *Pan*'s oaten Reed:
The God of Wit to shew his Grudge,
Clap't *Asses* Ears upon the Judge,   30
A goodly pair, erect and wide,
Which he could neither *Gild* nor hide.
 And now the Virtue of his *Hands,*

---

public accounts reported to the House of Commons on 21 December 1711 that between 1702 and 1711 Antonio Alvarez Machado and Sir Solomon Medina paid Marlborough £63,000 for the contract to supply bread to the army (*CJ, 17,* 15–16).

 20. If this is proverbial, it has not found its way into the dictionaries of proverbs. Thomas Gray makes it "old words are old gold" (*Correspondence of Thomas Gray,* ed. P. Toynbee and Leonard Whibley, 3 vols., Oxford, Clarendon Press, 1935, *1,* 194).

 21. *Critick deep:* The one cited by *OED* is Robert Recorde, *The Ground of Artes* (1575), p. 202: "the least portion of waight is commonly a Grayne, meaning a grayne of . . . wheat drie, and gathered out of the middle of the ear."

 24. *People fancy'd he had Wit:* "The high sphere in which he moved, rendering him the object of envy, as well as of applause" (Macpherson, *History, 2,* 514).

 25. *Two Gods:* "In a musical contest between Apollo and Pan, Midas decided for the latter, whereupon Apollo changed his ears to those of an ass, which the king attempted to conceal beneath a high Phrygian cap" (Swift, *Poems, 1,* 156). The allegory requires the two gods to be Oxford (Apollo) and Godolphin (Pan). Marlborough "decreed" against Oxford "And gave it" for Godolphin in February 1708 (pp. 298–99 above).

 30. *Asses Ears:* Harley may have decided to fit Marlborough for his disgrace during their meeting on 29 December 1710 at Harley's house in York Buildings. The purpose of the meeting was to determine whether Marlborough would continue to serve as captain general of the forces abroad and sit at the council board with the new ministers. "He made great professions of compliance," Harley said. But Marlborough earned his asses' ears by choosing this moment to plead that his wife be kept in her posts at court (£7,500 a year). "That was the rock which all would break upon," Harley concluded, for he knew that the queen would not even allow the duchess's name to be mentioned (HMC *Portland MSS., 2,* 224; Elizabeth Hamilton, *The Backstairs Dragon. A Life of Robert Harley, Earl of Oxford,* New York, Taplinger Publishing Company, 1970, p. 172). By the time the meeting was over Harley had decided that there could be no place in a moderate ministry for the duke of Marlborough. "Certainly he has advisers who will ruin him," he told Newcastle, "and while we are keeping all things in temper, they will drive it to extremity" (HMC *Portland MSS., 2,* 224).

Was lost among *Pactolus* Sands,
Against whose Torrent while he Swims,   35
The *Golden* Scurf peels off his Limbs:
Fame spreads the News, and People travel
From far, to gather *golden* Gravel;
Midas, expos'd to all their Jears,
Had lost his *Art*, and kept his *Ears*.   40
    This Tale inclines the gentle Reader,
To think upon a certain Leader,
To whom from *Midas* down, descends
That Virtue in the Fingers ends:
What else by *Perquisites* are meant,   45
By *Pensions, Bribes,* and *three per Cent?*

34. *Pactolus:* "Midas washed away his fatal gift in the Pactolus [in Iran], whose sands were ever after rich in gold" (Swift, *Poems, 1,* 157).

37. *People travel:* The gold rush began even before Marlborough was dismissed. (The annual salaries attached to his offices are included in parentheses). In November 1711 John Robinson, bishop of Bristol and lord privy seal, was made first plenipotentiary at The Hague (£7,000) (Boyer, *Annals,* 1712, p. 269). After Marlborough was dismissed, Ormonde was made captain general of the British forces (£10,000) and colonel of the first regiment of foot guards (£2,000) and George Fitz-roy, duke of Northumberland, replaced Ormonde as colonel of the second troop of horse guards. Rivers was made master general of the ordnance (£3,000) and replaced Northumberland as colonel of the royal regiment of horse guards (*The London Gazette,* 3–5 January 1711).

39. *Jears:* "The birth-day of the Queen [6 February 1712], the duke of Marlborough was in a chair in St. James's park, with the curtains drawn; the mob, that believed it to be the prince Eugene, huzza'd the chair; but the duke modestly drew back the curtains and put himself out, and with a sign shewed his dislike to the salutation. The mob, finding their mistake, and that it was he, cried out, 'Stop thief' " (Macpherson, *Original Papers, 2,* 270).

40. *lost his Art:* Marlborough was dismissed from all his employments on 30 December 1711 (Boyer, *Annals,* 1712, p. 301).

42. *Leader:* The old meaning of the term, a military commander, identifies Marlborough, but the word was taking on political overtones, viz. "*Leaders* . . . Men of most sway in great Councils or Assemblies" (*New Dictionary,* sig. G8r).

45. *Perquisites:* The commissioners of public accounts (including William Shippen), who investigated the bread contracts, reported that "the great Sums, which appear to have been Annually paid to the Duke on Account of these Contracts, can never be esteemed Legal or Warrantable Perquisites" (Boyer, *Annals,* 1712, p. 280).

46. *Pensions:* In December 1702 when he was raised to a dukedom, Marlborough was also granted a pension of £5,000 a year out of the post office revenue (*CJ, 14,* 78).

Bribes: See 17n. above.

three per Cent: Besides the kickback on the bread contracts, Marlborough had a warrant to deduct, not 3 percent but 2 1/2 percent from the pay of foreign troops on the English establishment without any accounting therefor. From 1701 to 1711 this amounted to £282,366 9s. 7d. and Marlborough defended the arrangement on the ground that it did "not properly relate to the Public Accompts, being a Free Gift of the Foreign Troops" (Boyer, *Annals,* 1712, pp. 277, 279, 283).

By *Places* and *Commissions* sold,
And turning *Dung* it self to *Gold?*
By starving in the midst of Store,
As t'other *Midas* did before?   50
    None e'er did modern *Midas* chuse,
Subject or Patron of his Muse,
But found him thus their Merit Scan,
That *Phebus* must give Place to *Pan:*
He values not the Poet's Praise,   55
Nor will exchange His *Plumbs* for *Bays:*
To *Pan* alone rich Misers call,
And there's the Jest, for *Pan* is *ALL:*
Here *English* Wits will be to seek,
Howe'er, *'tis all one in the* Greek.   60
    Besides, it plainly now appears,
Our *Midas* too has *Asses* Ears;
Where every Fool his Mouth applies,
And whispers in a thousand Lies;
Such gross Delusions could not pass,   65
Thro' any Ears but of an *Ass.*
    But *Gold* defiles with frequent Touch,
There's nothing *fouls* the Hands so much:
And Scholars give it for the Cause,
Of *British Midas* dirty Paws;   70
Which while the *Senate* strove to scower,

47. *Commissions sold:* The poem anticipates the charges made by Earl Poulett on 28 May 1712 during the debate on the restraining orders. Ormonde, Poulett said, "was not like a certain General, who led troops to the slaughter, to cause a great number of officers to be knocked on the head in battle, or against stone walls, in order to fill his pockets, by disposing of their commissions" (*Parl. Hist.*, 6, 1137).

49. *starving in the midst of Store:* The duke was parsimonious as well as avaricious. "This mean passion of that great man operated very strongly in him in the very beginning of his life, and continued to the very end of it." On one occasion when he won sixpence at picquet, he insisted upon being paid even though this meant changing a guinea, on the ground that he needed the change for a sedan chair. The loser "did at last get change, paid the Duke his sixpence, observed him a little after he left the room, and declares that (after all this bustle that had been made for his sixpence) the Duke actually walked home" (Spence, *1*, 163–64).

56. *Plumb:* "A Cant Word for 100,000*l.*" (*Alqrst*).

64. *a thousand Lies:* Public flattery of Marlborough had long been a minor industry. *The British Warriour. A Poem* ("The *British* Muse in *Chaucer* first began") (n.d. but published 30 October 1706) is a good example; cf. p. 195 above.

65. *gross Delusions:* Marlborough may not have discounted all the flattery, for "He told the queen, he was neither covetous nor ambitious" (Swift, *Journal*, *1*, 145).

71. *strove to scower:* The House of Commons elected commissioners to examine the public accounts in March 1711 (Boyer, *Annals*, 1711, p. 354).

They washt away the *Chymick* Power.
While He his utmost Strength apply'd,
To Swim against this *Pop'lar Tide,*
The *Golden* Spoils flew off apace,   75
Here fell a *Pension,* there a *Place:*
The *Torrent,* merciless, imbibes
Commissions, Perquisites, and *Bribes,*
By their own Weight sunk to the Bottom;
Much good may do 'em that have caught 'um.   80
And *Midas* now neglected stands,
With *Asses Ears,* and *dirty Hands.*

72. *washt away the Chymick Power:* The commissioners for examining the public accounts reported to the House of Commons on 21 December and on 31 December 1711 the following entry was made in the minutes of the privy council: "Being informed that an information against the Duke of Marlborough was laid before the House of Commons, by the commissioners of the public accounts, her majesty thought fit to dismiss him from all his employments, that the matter might undergo an impartial investigation" (Boyer, *Annals,* 1712, p. 298; Coxe, *Memoirs, 3,* 280).

73. *utmost Strength apply'd:* Marlborough's "conduct, since his arrival from Holland [18 November 1711], was full of offence and liable to suspicion . . . He threw his whole weight into the scale against the ministry. He caballed with Buys. He courted Bothmar. He herded with the discontented of all nations. Neglecting that government of his passions, for which he had been admired by the world, he fell into all the impotencies of rage and resentment, upon every party-debate. He left to the Queen her choice of two alternatives. To stop the progress of the peace, to dismiss the ministry, and to dissolve the parliament, or to rid herself of a person, who, from a servant, was likely to become a tyrant. She determined to adopt the latter measure" (Macpherson, *History, 2,* 512–13).

81. *Midas now neglected stands:* "The duke of Marlborough was at Court today [30 December 1711], and no body hardly took notice of him" (Swift, *Journal, 2,* 452).

JONATHAN SWIFT

Toland's Invitation to Dismal
To Dine with the Calves-Head Club
(26 June 1712)

The second session of the fourth parliament of Anne, which began on 7 December 1711 with the Oxford ministry teetering on the brink of dissolution, ended on 21 June 1712 with the ministry safely restored to its base. Nottingham had failed to bring over more Tories to vote Whig in the House of Lords and Marlborough had failed in *his* "Design of ruining the Ministry" (Swift, *Prose, 7,* 21, 29). In Oxford's words, "The second Session ended the 21st of *June,* 1712, and notwithstanding *Bothmer's* memorial [p. 543 above], and all other attacks both from abroad and at home, Supplies were provided, and every thing relating to the Public put upon a good foot, and the Malecontents began to despair, as appeared by the Duke of *Marlborough's* retiring abroad, and other particulars" (Tindal, *4,* ²386). And since Swift had written *An Excellent New Song, Being the Intended Speech of a Famous Orator against Peace* (above) to avert the evil omens in December 1711, it was appropriate that he should celebrate the deliverance from evil in June 1712.

The note of exultation lies just beneath the surface of these impudent verses so "strangely adapted," as Deane Swift said, "to the proceedings and outrage of the WHIGS at that particular juncture" (Deane Swift, *An Essay upon the Life, Writings, and Character, of Dr. Jonathan Swift,* 1755, p. 227). In Swift's fantasy Nottingham pays the price of his defection to the Whigs by being accepted by the Whigs.

Swift moves the time of the action of his poem back to 29 January, on the eve of the day solemnized by high churchmen as the anniversary of the martyrdom of Charles I, and by republicans at calves' head feasts "in contempt of the memory of the B[lessed] Martyr" (Hearne, *1,* 337). The logic of Nottingham's defection now demands that he be invited to a calves' head feast. And etiquette requires that the invitation be sent by the imagined secretary of the Calves' Head Club, the republican and deist, John Toland.

As form for his fantasy Swift remembered Horace's invitation to his friend Torquatus to dine with him and a few friends on the eve of Caesar's birthday (*Lib. I, Ep. v*). "Have you seen Toland's Invitation to Dismal?" Swift asked his Dublin ladies on 1 July 1712, "How do you like it? but it is an Imitation of Horace, and perhaps you don't understand Horace" (Swift, *Journal*, 2, 544). The "Imitation" genre requires the matter as well as the language of the original to be translated into the vernacular. Thus Horace's Sabinus, who may be detained by "cena prior potiorque puella," becomes Wharton, "unless prevented by a Whore" (line 35). And Swift finds the perfect modern instance of Horace's "olidae . . . caprae" in the malodorous duke of Kent (38). The form of lines 23–26 also suggests that Swift had read Joseph Browne, *The Country Parson's Honest Advice* (above).

The Luttrell copy of *Aa* now in the Newberry Library is dated 26 June 1712. Thomas Creech's translation of Horace's *Lib. I, Epist. v* (*The Odes, Satyrs, and Epistles of Horace Done into English by Mr. Creech*, 5th ed., 1720, pp. 280–81) is printed alongside the "Imitation," as Samuel Johnson insisted that it should be, to make it easier to enjoy "the beauty of the performance" (James Boswell, *The Life of Samuel Johnson, LL.D.*, ed. G. Birkbeck Hill and L. F. Powell, 6 vols., Oxford, Clarendon Press, 1934–50, *1*, 122).

Horace, *Lib. I, Ep. v.*

If you can sit upon a paultry Seat,
My Friend *Torquatus,* and endure to Eat
A homely Dish, a Sallad all the Treat:
Sir, I shall make a Feast, my Friends invite,
And beg that you wou'd Sup with me to Night.   5
My Liquor flow'd from the *Minturnian* Vine,
In *Taurus' Consulship,* 'tis common Wine;
If you have better, let your Flasks be sent;
Or let what I, the Lord, provide, content.
My Servants sweep and furnish ev'ry Room,   10
My Dishes all are cleans'd against you come;

Toland's Invitation to Dismal
To Dine With the Calves-Head Club

If, dearest **Dismal,** you for once can Dine
Upon a single Dish, and Tavern Wine,

Toland to you this Invitation sends,
To eat the *CALVES-HEAD* with your trusty Friends.

Title. *The Calves-Head Club:* See *Leviathan,* 56n., above.

1. **Dismal**: Nottingham's nickname (Swift, *An Excellent New Song, Being the Intended Speech of a Famous Orator against Peace,* 1n. above).

for once: Nottingham, who spent £5–6,000 a year and whose allowance for "Diet" as secretary of state had been £1,102 3s. 10d., was not accustomed to frugality (*Studies in Social History,* ed. J. H. Plumb, Longmans, Green & Co., 1955, pp. 165–66).

3. *Toland:* John Toland (1670–1722), the deist, was born in Londonderry, the "Son of an *Irish* Priest by a *French* Cook" ([Luke Milbourne], *A Letter from Tom o'Bedlam to the B—— of B——r's Jesuit,* 1717, p. 5). Raised a Catholic, he became a Protestant before he was 16, and was sent by some "eminent dissenters" to the University of Glasgow. There he became a student activist, "a Principal Man at Heading the Mob, and *Hallooing* them at the Clergy" ([Charles Leslie], *Cassandra. (But I Hope not),* No. II, 1704, p. 64; cf. *Original Letters of Eminent Literary Men,* ed. Sir Henry Ellis, The Camden Society, 1843, p. 227). From Glasgow he proceeded to Leyden for two years and then to Oxford, where his behavior was "so publick and notorious" that he was ordered to depart. "Evidence was . . . offered upon Oath, of his Trampling on the Common prayer book, talking against the Scriptures, commending Commonwealths, justifying the murder of K. C[harles] 1st, railing against Priests in general, with a Thousand other Extravagancys" (*N&Q,* 3rd series, *1* [4 January 1862], 7). In September 1697 he was banished from Ireland and his most famous book, *Christianity not Mysterious* (1696), was ordered to be burned by the common hangman (HMC *Portland MSS., 3,* 586). Harley put him to work writing against a standing army and sent him on a diplomatic mission to Hanover in the summer of 1701 (Swift, *Discourse,* pp. 36–42). In 1705, with Harley's "encouragement," he wrote *The Memorial of the State of England* in reply to James Drake's *The Memorial of the Church of England* (1705) (*A Collection of Several Pieces of Mr. John Toland,* 2 vols., 1726, *2,* 228). He returned to England in 1710 after several years on the continent, wrote against Sacheverell, and tried unsuccessfully to be employed again by Oxford as a secret agent or propaganda writer. In the latter role he rated himself superior to Swift, whom he characterized—not inaccurately—as "remarkable . . . for his levity" (ibid., *2,* 222).

Forbear thy wanton Hopes, and Toyl for Gain,
And *Moschus'* Cause; 'tis all but idle Pain.
To Morrow *Caesar*'s Birth-day comes, to give
Release to Cares, and a small Time to live.   15
Then we may sleep 'till Noon, and gay Delight

And merry Talk prolong the Summer's Night.
What is my Wealth, if I must always spare?
He that lives Poor, to leave a wealthy Heir,
Is near a-kin to Mad. I'll Drink and Play,   20
Enjoy my self, and fling my Gold away.
I'll frolick (let the sparing be thought wise)
Content to be esteem'd a Fool for this:
What Wonders cannot Wine effect? 'tis free
Of Secrets, and turns Hope to Certainty;   25

---

5. *vain ambitious Hopes:* See Swift, *An Excellent New Song, Being the Intended Speech of a Famous Orator against Peace,* 3*n.* above. Mainwaring had predicted that Nottingham would break with the Tories if he were not appointed lord president of the council to succeed Rochester, who died in May 1711 (*Private Correspondence of Sarah, Duchess of Marlborough, 2,* 71).

6. *Bribes:* See Swift, *An Excellent New Song, Being the Intended Speech of a Famous Orator against Peace,* 16*n., 49n.* above.

Tropes: See ibid., 52*n.* above.

7. *To morrow:* 30 January, the anniversary of the execution of Charles I.

Mystick Feast: "Their Bill of Fare, was a large Dish of *Calves-Heads* dressed several ways; a large *Pike* with a small one in his Mouth, as an Emblem of Tyranny; a large *Cods-head,* by which they pretended to represent the Person of the *King* singly, as by the *Calves-head* before, they had done him, together with all them that had suffer'd in his Cause; a *Boars-head* with an *Apple* in its Mouth, to represent the King by this as *Bestial,* as by the others they had done *Foolish* and *Tyrannical*" (Edward Ward, *The Secret History of the Calves-Head Club,* 1703, p. 18).

8. *latest:* Nottingham's defection to the Whigs became publicly known on 7 December 1711 (Boyer, *Annals,* 1712, p. 284).

9. *Signs and Symbols:* "An Ax hung up in the Clubb-Room . . . was reverenced, as a Principal Symbol in this *Diabolical Sacrament* . . . After the Repast was over, one of their Elders presented an *Eikon Basilike,* which was with great solemnity Burn'd upon the Table, whilst the *Anthems* were Singing. After this, another produc'd *Milton's Defensio Populi*

Suspend a while your vain ambitious Hopes,   5
Leave hunting after Bribes, forget your Tropes:
To morrow We our *Mystick Feast* prepare,

Where Thou, our latest *Proselyte*, shalt share:
When We, by proper Signs and Symbols tell,
How, by *Brave Hands*, the *Royal TRAYTOR* fell;   10
The Meat shall represent the *TYRANT*'s Head,
The Wine, his Blood, *our Predecessors* shed:
Whilst an *alluding* Hymn some Artist sings,
We toast Confusion to the Race of Kings:
At Monarchy we nobly shew our Spight,   15
And talk *what Fools call Treason* all the Night.

Who, by Disgraces or ill Fortune sunk,
Feels not his Soul enliven'd when he's Drunk?
Wine can clear up *Godolphin*'s cloudy Face,
And fill *Jack Smith* with Hopes to keep his Place;   20

Anglicani, upon which all lay'd their Hands, and made a Protestation in form of an Oath, for ever to stand by, and maintain" (Edward Ward, *The Secret History of the Calves-Head Club,* 1703, p. 18).

12. *Predecessors:* "*Milton* [whose prose works Toland edited and published in 1698] and some other Creatures of the Commonwealth . . . instituted this *Clubb*" (ibid., p. 17).

13. *Hymn:* Some true Calves' Head Club hymns are collected in *The Secret History of the Calves-Head Club,* 1703, pp. 27–70 and a mock-Calves'-Head-Club-hymn is included above, p. 350.

18. *enliven'd when he's Drunk:* "Wine makes a man better pleased with himself," Johnson said, and "To make a man pleased with himself, let me tell you, is doing a very great thing" (James Boswell, *The Life of Samuel Johnson, LL.D.,* ed. G. Birkbeck Hill and L. F. Powell, 6 vols., Oxford, Clarendon Press, 1934–50, *3,* 327, 328).

19. *Godolphin's cloudy Face:* Lord Raby noticed Godolphin's "severe countenance" about the time of the change of ministry, and Swift had looked upon it at the same time (*Wentworth Papers,* p. 131; p. 473 above).

20. *Jack Smith:* Smith was removed from the post of chancellor of the exchequer to make room for Harley in August 1710 (Luttrell, *6,* 616), but "what surprises the town is that Mr. Smith," the former Whig Speaker of the House of Commons, was made one of the tellers of the exchequer, at £750 a year (*Wentworth Papers,* p. 144). He held onto this post until July 1712 (Boyer, *Political State, 4,* 31).

It pushes on the unarm'd Man to Wars;
It frees the troubled Mind from weighty Cares;
It teaches Arts, it teaches how to Think,
And what Man is not Eloquent in's Drink?

And who tho' cramp'd in narrow Want's not free?   30
   Now I'll provide (pray leave that Task to me)
I'm willing, and I'm fit for such a Care,
Your Seats shall be as clean as any are;
Your Napkins good, no Spot shall foul the Cloth,
Whose Sight might make you snuff your Nose, and loath.   35
The Cups well scour'd, the modest Table grace,
The Dishes shine that you may see your Face.
None shall be there that shall have treach'rous Ears,
And carry o'er our Threshold what he hears:
And that thy Boon Companions may be fit,   40

21. *Scarborow:* Richard Lumley (c. 1650–1721), another Anglo-Irishman, was the grandson and heir of the first Viscount Lumley of Waterford. "He was bred up in the Religion of his Family, which had been always *Roman Catholick,* and turned *Protestant* at the Time of the Popish Plot, in the Reign of King *Charles* the Second" (Macky, p. 74). He commanded the cavalry troop that captured Monmouth in July 1685 and his regiment of horse was one of those that James II ordered to be deployed on Hounslow Heath. But Lumley had already signed the invitation to William of Orange and used those same troops to seize Newcastle for William in December 1688. Accordingly he was made a gentleman of the bedchamber and privy councillor in February 1689, colonel of the first troop of horse guards in April 1689, and created earl of Scarbrough—as GEC (*11,* 508) spells it—in the English peerage in April 1690. He retired from active military duty after the treaty of Ryswick and sold his colonelcy for £12,000 in March 1699 (Luttrell, *4,* 492). In the new reign he was retained on the privy council and his wife was again made a lady of the bedchamber. In the House of Lords Scarbrough voted to acquit Sacheverell but otherwise his record was impeccably Whiggish. It was he who discovered the Scotch plot in December 1703 (*POAS,* Yale, *6,* 616, 627) and on 7 December 1711 he seconded Nottingham's motion to include a No Peace without Spain clause in the address of thanks to the queen (Swift, *Prose, 7,* 17). Swift thought "He was a knave and a coward" (ibid., *5,* 288).

22. *Hal——:* Despite Deane Swift and Sir Harold Williams (*The Works of the Reverend Dr. Jonathan Swift,* 19 vols., Dublin, 1762–68 [Teerink 53], *13,* 359; Swift, *Poems, 1,* 163), "Hallifax," Luttrell's gloss (Newberry Library copy of *Aa*), is almost certainly what Swift intended. "Pert" meant "unbecomingly ready to express an opinion . . . cheeky . . . uppish or forward" (*OED*) and Shippen called Halifax "presumptuous" in *The Junto,* 35 (above).

Sommers: "He is of a grave Deportment" (Macky, p. 50). Swift said "the formality of his nature" was "the only unconversable fault he has" (Swift, *Prose, 8,* 119).

23. *Portland:* William Henry Bentinck (1682–1721) was the son of William III's Dutch favorite. His tutor (1693–1703) was Paul de Rapin, sieur de Thoyras, who was to become the most distinguished French historian of England. As Lord Woodstock, Bentinck became a Whig member of parliament for Southampton borough (1705–08) and Southampton County (1708–09). He succeeded as second earl of Portland in November 1709. Appointed colonel of

By Force of Wine ev'n *Scarborow* is Brave,
Hal—— grows more Pert, and *Sommers* not so Grave:
Wine can give *Portland* Wit, and *Cleveland* Sense,
Montague Learning, *Bolton* Eloquence:
Cholmondeley, when Drunk, can never lose his *Wand*,   25
And *Lincoln* then imagines he has Land.
   My Province is, to see that all be right,

Glasses and Linnen clean, and Pewter bright;
From our *Mysterious Club* to keep out Spies,
And *Tories* (dress'd like Waiters) in Disguise.   30
You shall be coupled as you best approve,

the first troop of horse guards in July 1710, he managed to hang on until July 1713, when he had to make way for John Ashburnham, Lord Ashburnham, Ormonde's son-in-law, whose regiment had been disbanded (Dalton, *6*, 225). Swift called Portland's father "As great a Dunce as ever I knew" (Swift, *Prose*, *5*, 258).

24. *Montague:* John Montagu (1690–1749), heir to the first duke of Montagu, married Mary, fourth daughter and coheiress of the first duke of Marlborough in March 1705. In March 1709 he succeeded to his father's title and hereditary post of master of the wardrobe, a sinecure that was abolished upon the second duke's death. Montagu became a very active Whig peer, member both of the Kit-Cat and Hanover clubs (Holmes, p. 299). But his mother-in-law observed that "All his talents lie in things only natural in boys of fifteen" (*Private Correspondence of Sarah, Duchess of Marlborough, 2*, 184).

25. *Cholmondeley:* Hugh Cholmondeley (c. 1662–1725), Viscount Cholmondeley of Kells, was educated at Christ Church, Oxford, and was one of the first Anglo-Irishmen to take up arms for William of Orange (GEC, *3*, 201). He was, accordingly, created Baron Cholmondeley in the English peerage in April 1689 and Anne made him a privy councillor in March 1705 and the earl of Cholmondeley in the English peerage in December 1706. Godolphin appointed him treasurer of the household in November 1708 and Cholmondeley was able to hold onto his "*Wand*" in Oxford's "motley" administration (Swift, *Prose*, *8*, 124) and to continue to deliver a Whig vote, until April 1713 (*Wentworth Papers*, p. 330), "though these times are as dangerous and uncertain for those that set their hearts upon holding places as perhaps ever were," as he wrote to his friend Matthew Prior (HMC *Bath MSS.*, *3*, 438). Swift thought he was "Good for nothing as far as I ever knew" (Swift, *Prose*, *5*, 260).

26. *Lincoln:* Henry Clinton (1684–1728) succeeded as seventh earl of Lincoln in September 1693. He was a "poor Lord," with "nothing but a pension [of £500 a year] to depend on" (*The Correspondence of Sir James Clavering*, ed. H. T. Dickinson, Gateshead, Surtees Society, 1967, p. 108). But he was also a member of the Kit-Cat Club and with no post to worry about losing, he could provide "active opposition to the Tory ministry" (GEC, *7*, 699). Oxford responded by keeping his pension in arrears (Holmes, p. 388).

27. *My Province:* Cf. Pope, *The Rape of the Lock*, II, 91: "Our humbler Province is to tend the Fair."

Septimius too, and *Brutus* I'll invite:

And if no dearer Miss, or better Feast,
Holds *Sabin,* he shall make another Guest:
I've Room enough, and each may bring his Friends,
But Sweat at Tables too much throng'd offends.   45
Pray, send Me word what time you will be here,
How many Friends you'll bring; forget thy Care.

And whilst thy Clients throng about thy Hall,

Creep forth thro' the back Door, and bilk 'em all.

---

32. *next the Men you love:* Whigs had been anathema to Nottingham before his defection to them in 1711. In April 1704 he had resigned from the government rather than to serve with Whigs.

33. *Orford:* Lord Orford, another member of the Whig Junto, was finally reinstated as first lord of the admiralty in November 1709. Upon his resignation in September 1710, it was said erroneously that Nottingham would succeed him (Luttrell, *6,* 508, 633).

Boyl: Henry Boyle (d. 1725), third son of Charles Boyle, Baron Clifford of Lanesborough, and the grandson of William Seymour, second duke of Somerset, and of Richard Boyle, second earl of Cork and first earl of Burlington, made "a considerable Figure in the *House of Commons*" where he sat for Tamworth, Staffordshire (1689–90), Cambridge University (1692–1705), and Westminster (1705–10). Although nominally a Tory in William's reign, he subscribed to the association to defend the king in 1694, voted against disbanding the army, and became in Anne's reign totally Whiggish. He was appointed a commissioner of the treasury (1699–1701), privy councillor (March 1701–14), and chancellor of the exchequer (1701–08). The prediction (Macky, p. 126) that he "obliges every Body in the *Exchequer;* and in Time may prove a Great Man," was fulfilled when Boyle was appointed lord treasurer of Ireland (1704–10), lord lieutenant of the West Riding of Yorkshire (1704–15), and secretary of state (February 1708). Swift was "almost shocked" by his removal from the last post in September 1710 to make way for St. John. "I never remember such bold steps taken by a Court," Swift said, "though I did not care if they were all hanged" (Swift, *Journal, 1,* 24).

Seated at Table next the Men you love.
Sunderland, Orford, Boyl, and *Richmond*'s Grace
Will come; and *Hampden* shall have *Walpool*'s Place.
Wharton, unless prevented by a Whore,   35
Will hardly fail, and there is room for more:
But I love Elbow-room whene'rc I drink,
And honest *Harry* is too apt to stink.

Let no Pretence of Bus'ness make you stay,
Yet take one Word of Counsel by the way: 40
If *Guernsey* calls, send word you're gone abroad;
He'll teaze you with King *Charles* and Bishop *Laud,*
Or make you Fast, and carry you to Prayers:
But if he will break in, and walk up Stairs,
Steal by the Back-door out, and leave him there;   45
Then order *Squash* to call a Hackney Chair.

January 29.

34. *Hampden:* Richard Hampden the younger, of Buckinghamshire (d. 1729), was the son of John Hampden the younger, one of the first Whig politicians. He was also a kinsman of Wharton and Robert Harley (Walcott, pp. 40, 86). In parliament, where he sat for Wendover, Buckinghamshire (January 1701–08, 1722–27), Buckinghamshire (1708–10, 1715–22, 1727–29), and Berwick-on-Tweed, Northumberland (December 1711–15), he was a client of Wharton's and an unexceptionable Whig. Since his father called himself a free thinker, it is not surprising that Hampden herded under "No Church" (*Numerical Calculation*). And although he was represented to George I as a Whig who occasionally voted Tory, there is no Tory vote recorded for him in surviving division lists. But in December 1712 Peter Wentworth heard the crowd at White's teasing Mr. Hampden "that he was no Whig." "He affirm'd he was a Whig still, but he was for peace" (*Wentworth Papers,* p. 310).

Walpool's Place: Walpole's place would have been vacant on 30 January 1712 because Walpole had been expelled from the House of Commons and committed to the Tower on 17 January 1712 for "a high Breach of Trust, and notorious Corruption" in his office as secretary at war (*CJ, 17,* 30). He was not released until July 1712 when he "met with a disappointment, for he had no musick nor dinner prepared for him by the Hanover Club" (*Wentworth Papers,* p. 291).

38. *Harry:* Henry Grey, duke of Kent. See Shippen, *Moderation Display'd,* 197n., 202n. above.

41. *Guernsey:* "The Earl of Nottingham's brother" (*Afghjklm*), Heneage Finch, Lord Guernsey. Toland reminds Nottingham that his brother may call on him tomorrow to take him to a conventional 30th of January Anglican service, amid fasting and prayer (43).

46. *Squash:* Dick Squash, Nottingham's negro servant (*POAS,* Yale, *6,* 543–44).

An Elegy on the Death of Pamphlets
(September 1712?)

"Do you know, that Grubstreet is dead and gone last Week," Swift asked his Dublin ladies on 7 August 1712, "No more Ghosts or Murders now for Love or Money . . . now, every single half Sheet pays a halfpenny to the Qu——. The Observator is fallen, the Medleys are jumbled together with the Flying-post, the Examiner is deadly sick, the Spectator keeps up, and doubles it price. I know not how long it will hold" (Swift, *Journal, 2,* 553–54).

What was responsible for this premature report of the death of Grubstreet was an Act for laying several Duties upon all Soap and Paper . . . and upon certain printed Papers, Pamphlets, and Advertisements (10 Anne c. 19), which received the royal assent on 22 May 1712 (*CJ, 17,* 234). Besides the half-penny tax on broadsides, the new statute levied a penny tax on pamphlets no larger than a folio sheet, and two shillings a folio sheet for larger pamphlets (*Statutes at Large, 3,* 812).

The new taxes were to take effect on 1 August 1712 and were confidently expected to reduce the attacks on the ministry. Oxford, who probably understood better than any of his contemporaries the importance of propaganda in the constitutional monarchy that had been established by the revolution, was also more subject to the temptation to control the press. "I wil always be ready to contribute the utmost I can to . . . allaying those heates and animosities which are greatly increasd by the many Scandalous Lying Pamphlets which are dayly propagated by designing Knaves," he wrote to the archbishop of Canterbury in January 1702, and he enclosed the draft of a bill "to have a Printer or Author answerable for everything which is published" (Lambeth Palace MS. 930, f. 25).

Now that he was at the head of the government, Oxford could yield to this temptation. And he was reminded to do so by the flood of pamphlets that almost washed his ministry out of existence. From the 493 included in Morgan for 1709, the number of pamphlets leaped to 822 for 1710. And the worst of it, as one of Oxford's correspondents told him, was that "Whiggish libels sell best" (HMC *Portland MSS., 5,* 94). "So much Licentiousness," Swift exploded in *The Examiner,* "would not be suffered in any other Country of Christendom" (Swift, *Prose, 3,* 135–36). The secretary of state simply could not keep ahead of the flood: on 23 October 1711 "Fourteen Booksellers, Printers, or Publishers, who had been lately taken up . . . by Warrants from Mr. Secretary St. *John,* for Printing, and Publishing Pamphlets, Libels, and Ballads, some of which were, indeed, Scandalous Invectives against the Ministery . . . appear'd, at the Bar of the Court of *Queens-Bench*" (Boyer, *Annals,* 1712, p. 264). Clearly there was a problem, and it was hoped that the solution was a tax on printed papers.

On 17 January 1712 the queen sent a message to the Commons pointing out what "great Licence is taken in publishing false and scandalous Libels . . . This Evil seems to have grown too strong for the Laws now in force: It is therefore recommended to you to find a Remedy equal to the Mischief" (*CJ, 17,* 28). The Commons promptly undertook to find a means "to put a Stop to the publishing . . . false and seditious Libels" (*CJ, 17,* 28). There was indeed no general agreement that the press should be free. Neither Swift nor Defoe believed in freedom of the press. "As the Press is now used," according to a typical opinion, "it is a Paper-Inquisition; by which any Man may be arraign'd, judg'd, and condemn'd (ay, and broad Hints given for his Execution too) without ever knowing his Accusers" (*An Essay for the Press,* 1712, p. 7).

Oxford was so interested in the new legislation to control the press that he had weekly reports sent to him of the yield of the new tax and its effects on newspaper circulation. Newspapers were indeed "deadly sick," as Swift said. "In the first seven weeks of the tax, the average weekly issue of stamps was about 67,441; in . . . five weeks in mid-1713, the weekly average was only about 39,341" (*Bulletin of the Institute of Historical Research,* 31 [November 1958], 218). The number of pamphlets fell back to 720 in 1713 (Morgan, *2,* 361–443; *5,* 78–80) and if the tax of two shillings a sheet on larger works had been enforced, it would indeed have meant the death of pamphlets.

The anonymous Whig who wrote *An Elegy on the Death of Pamphlets* does not attack the new law on the ground that it violates a civil right, but accepts it on the ground that it will hurt the Tories more than the Whigs, because a good cause needs not the "Crutches" of propaganda, just as Godolphin had said.

A date of composition in September 1712 is suggested by the apparent reference in line 4 to two pamphlets that appeared in that month (Boyer, *Political State, 4,* 164, 170).

AN ELEGY ON THE DEATH OF PAMPHLETS

What, shall whole Reams of Breathless Pamphlets die
And no one Living sing their Elegy?
O *Barber,* deal the dismal News around,
No *Conduct* now must rise from *Fairy Ground;*
No dull *Tom Double,* or *John Bull* appear, 5

3. *Barber:* John Barber (1675–1741) was born—not in Newgate, according to the scandal—but "in a small House in *Gray's-Inn-Lane, Holborn,*" and christened in St. Andrews, Holborn, by Edward Stillingfleet, with Elkanah Settle standing as his godfather. Although his father was a journeyman barber—"or (as the Barbers choose to call it) . . . a Barber-Surgeon"—he was apprenticed to "Mrs *Clark,* a Printer and a Widow, in *Thames-Street*" and "long before he was out of his Time, he was reckoned one of the best Compositors of the Trade." The secret of his "uncommon Success in the World," said his first biographer admiringly—before the publication of *Tom Jones* (1749)—was that he "always kept the main Chance in View." In 1705, for example, he met Henry St. John and Delariviere Manley. Some years later Mrs. Manley became his mistress and died in his house on Lambeth Hill in July 1724. And in 1710, after Barber had "huzza'd" Sacheverell through the streets, St. John made him printer of the votes of the House of Commons. Through Swift, he was made printer of *The London Gazette* in place of Jacob Tonson, printer of *The Examiner* and *Mercator,* and stationer to the ordnance. In the next reign, Barber made a fortune in South Sea stock and became alderman (1722), sheriff (1730), and lord mayor of London (1732–33) (*The Life and Character of John Barber, Esq.,* 1741, sig. Π2r, pp. 2–5, 17, 19; *An Impartial History of the Life, Character, Amours, Travels, and Transactions of Mr. John Barber,* 1741, pp. xiv, 1, 2vii; Swift, *Journal, 1,* 320, 343, *2,* 455, 464).

4. *Conduct: The Conduct of the Allies* was published on 27 November 1711. Within two months it had sold 11,000 copies and Barber was talking about a seventh edition (Swift, *Journal, 2,* 422, 474).

Fairy Ground: This is probably a reference to a Whig pamphlet published in September 1712 in which Swift is ticked off as "a *Witty Parson* (but without Wisdom)" (*The Present State of Fairy-land. In Several Letters from Esquire Hush, An Eminent Citizen of Fickle-borough, To the King of Slave-onia,* 1713, p. 41).

5. *Tom Double:* The uncommon success of Tom Double, "a Modern Whig," for some of whose characteristics Daniel Defoe sat as model, is pursued through four works by Charles Davenant: *The True Picture of a Modern Whig, Set Forth in a Dialogue between Mr. Whiglove and Mr. Double, Two Under-Spur-Leathers to the Late Ministry* (1701); *Tom Double Return'd out of the Country: Or, The True Picture of a Modern Whig, Set Forth in a Second Dialogue between Mr. Whiglove and Mr. Double, at the Rummer Tavern in Queen Street* (1702); *The True Picture of a Modern Whig Reviv'd. Set Forth in a Third Dialogue between Whiglove and Double, at Tom's Coffee-House in Covent-Garden* (1707); and *Sir Thomas Double at Court and in High Preferments. In Two Dialogues between Sir Thomas Double and Sir Richard Comover, alias Mr. Whiglove, on the 27th of September 1710* (1710). Barber printed the first of these while he was still a journeyman printer and "under a Necessity of borrowing Money to defray the Expences." But the demand was so great that he cleared about £300 and used the money to go into business for himself. According to the same source, it was Davenant who introduced Barber to Swift (*An Impartial History of the Life, Character, Amours, Travels, and Transactions of Mr. John Barber,* 1741, p. 2), but Swift thought that the last part of the Tom Double series was "foolish" (Swift, *Journal, 1,* 83).

John Bull: England's national stereotype was born on 6 March 1712 with the publi-

> To make us what in Truth we never were;
> No Mother *Haggy,* nor St. *Alban*'s Ghost,
> To recommend an *Atheist* to a Post.
> All, all the Scandal which thy Press has born,
> That yet remains unwip'd, or yet untorn,　　　　10
> Martyr'd, on Pies shall stick, or Plumbs shall wrap,
> A Sacrifice to every Grocers Shop,

---

cation of John Arbuthnot's *Law is a Bottomless-Pit. Exemplify'd in the Case of the Lord Strutt, John Bull, Nicholas Frog, and Lewis Baboon. Who Spent all they had in a Law-Suit.* Four parts followed: *John Bull in His Senses: Being the Second part of Law is a Bottomless-Pit* (18 March 1712); *John Bull Still in His Senses: Being the Third Part of Law is a Bottomless-Pit* (17 April 1712); *An Appendix to John Bull Still in His Sense: Or, Law is a Bottomless-Pit* (9 May 1712), and *Lewis Baboon Turned Honest and John Bull Politician: Being the Fourth Part of Law is a Bottomless-Pit* (31 July 1712). Barber may be the "Friend in the City" with whom Swift dined on 10 March 1712 and talked "about a little Business of printing; but not my own." In the next sentence Swift assured the Dublin ladies that there would be "a second Part" of *Law is a Bottomless-Pit,* which was in fact published a week later. "The Commons," Swift went on to say, "are very slow in bringing in their Bill to limit the Press, and the Pamphleteers make good use of their Time for there come out 3 or 4 every day" (Swift, *Journal, 2,* 510).

　　6. *us:* The speaker is a chorus of Whig scribblers: Jean de Fonvive, George Ridpath, and Daniel Defoe. "What in Truth [they] never were" is "Money-Men," which Davenant represents them to be in the Tom Double series. Tom Double began life as "Corrector of a private Press in a Garret, for three Shillings a week," but by 1710 he was worth £250,000 (*The True Picture of a Modern Whig,* 1701, pp. 5, 17; *Sir Thomas Double at Court and in High Preferments,* 1710, p. 12).

　　7. *Mother Haggy . . . St. Alban's Ghost:* Mother Haggy is a character in *The Story of the St. Alb——ns Ghost, or The Apparition of Mother Haggy* (19 February 1712). She is Frances Jenyns or Jennings, wife to Richard Jenyns of Sandridge, near St. Albans, and mother of Haggite, or Sarah Jenyns, duchess of Marlborough. Frances Jenyns was suspected to be a witch and her portrait at Althorp helps explain why. *The Story of the St. Alb——ns Ghost, or The Apparition of Mother Haggy,* a kind of prose version of Shippen, *Faction Display'd* (*POAS,* Yale, *6,* 648) or *The Junto* (above), imagines a meeting of the Junto at "Avaro's House," the Marlboroughs' mansion at Holywell, on the Jenyns estate, during which the ghost of Mother Haggy materializes to predict Avaro's fall, a sacrifice to "Avarice and Ambition."

　　8. *Atheist:* The Story of the St. Alb——ns Ghost, or The Apparition of Mother Haggy was attributed to Swift (Swift, *Journal, 2,* 494) but was written by William Wagstaffe "in his younger Years." Wagstaffe (1685–1725) graduated B.A. (1703) and M.A. (1707) from Lincoln College, Oxford, and came up to London to study medicine with "his Relation," Thomas Wagstaffe, the nonjuror. Since medical students are traditionally atheists and necessarily unemployed, it would not have been difficult to imagine that Wagstaffe wrote *The Story of the St. Alb——ns Ghost, or The Apparition of Mother Haggy* to recommend himself "to a Post" in the Oxford ministry (*Miscellaneous Works of Dr. William Wagstaffe, Physician to St. Bartholomew's-Hospital, Fellow of the College of Physicians, and of the Royal Society,* 1726, pp. v–vi, xiv).

　　10. *unwip'd . . . untorn:* unwashed formes or uncut pages, that will remain unsold on account of the paper tax.

　　11. *Martyr'd, on Pies shall stick:* the traditional fate of unsold copies; cf. *MacFlecknoe,* 101: "Martyrs of Pies, and Reliques of the Bum" (*POAS,* Yale, *1,* 382); cf. *The Dunciad* (B), I, 144, 156.

Though thou methinks might'st greater Merits plead,
Be tolerated longer to be read;
Since but for Loads of Scandal from thee thrown,   15
An Infamy by Purchase made thine own:
Some Men who carry Things so wondrous high,
Would have experienc'd what it was to die.
And others with Impostumated Power,
Been told there are Apartments in the Tower.   20
    But what has *Abel* done to be thus trick'd?
Han't he been Can'd, been Buffetted and Kick'd?
From *Coffee House* to *Coffee House* expos'd,
Like a blown *Deer* for *Calumny* been nos'd?
Been beat into Repute, and render'd Famous,   25
Ev'n for subscribing *Abel* Ignoramus;
For empty Periods full of Noise and Scandal,
And for Untruths that never had a Handle?
Such Persecutions one would think might save
Him and his *Tory-Paper* from the Grave.   30
Prevail for a Reprieve, at least till he
Might Speak to those with whom he is in Fee:

16. *Infamy by Purchase:* Presumably Barber bought "Infamy" by taking money to print Davenant, Arbuthnot, Wagstaffe, Swift, et al.

17–18. The lines may mean: Were it not for Barber's printed smoke screen, Oxford and his colleagues would have been found guilty of treason (in the peace negotiations?).

19. *Imposthumated:* formed an abscess; cf. Arbuthnot, *Law is a Bottomless-Pit,* 1712, p. 15: "The Bruise imposthumated, and afterwards turn'd to a stinking Ulcer."

21. *Abel:* Abel Roper.

22. *Can'd . . . and Kick'd:* "I have not been free from Prosecutions in *Westminster-Hall,*" Roper is made to say, "frequent Showers of *Cane-shot* have pour'd on my Shoulders in Coffee-Houses and the open Streets; And, upon any turn of Weather, my aching Shin-Bones still renew in me the sad Remembrance of the many Kicks and Bruises they have receiv'd" (*Tory Annals Faithfully Extracted out of Abel Roper's Famous Writings. Vulgarly Call'd Post-Boy and Supplement,* 1712, sig. A2v–A3r). Roper was also thrashed in the lobby of the House of Commons by an outraged Whig member, Lord William Powlett (Bodl. MS. Ballard 20, ff. 75–76).

24. *blown:* out of breath. *OED* cites Marvell, *The Rehearsal Transpros'd: The Second Part,* 1673, p. 35: "and chase the blown Deer out of their Heard."

26. *subscribing Abel Ignoramus:* Roper was arrested on the complaints of the envoys of Portugal and Savoy that *The Post-Boy* of 10 November 1711 included "Invectives against Sovereign Princes and Crowned Heads in the Grand Alliance," but when his case came up on 28 November, "he escap'd any further Punishment, upon his begging Pardon of the Two Envoys, and inserting a Recantation in the *Post-Boy* of the 4th of *December*" (Boyer, *Annals,* 1712, p. 280).

32. *those with whom he is in Fee:* Roper's escape from further punishment on 28 November 1711 "encreased the Suspicion of many that he was, underhand, favour'd and countenanc'd by some Great Men" (ibid.).

Plead on his Knees for Pitty and for Grace,
And beg some Scavenger's or Dustman's Place,
Since he in Filth has hitherto been dabbling,   35
And nothing but the Party's Nonsense babbling.
As for our Parts, we *Protestants* true blew,
The *Post-Man, Observator,* and *Review,*
With all profound Humility submit
To any *Tax,* on *Noise,* or *News,* or *Wit,*   40
Well knowing, that if Strength of *Tory,* such is,
To go without his *Leading-Strings* and *Crutches,*
The *Whigs* whose *Cause* could ever go alone,
Must still be said to stand in need of none.

37. *Protestants true blew :* During the exclusion controversy of 1679–81, the loyalists began to call their adversaries "*True Blues,* because such were not satisfied to be Protestants, as the Churchmen were, but must be *true* Protestants, implying the others to be false ones, just not Papists" (Roger North, *Examen,* 1740, p. 321).

The Plotter Found Out:
Or,
Mine Arse in a Band-Box.
To the Tune of *Which No Body Can Deny*
(November 1712?)

Since Oxford had been attacked before (45*n*.) and that "Accident" had proved of such great use to him (Burnet, *2*, 567), now that he was in trouble again, the attempt to assassinate him on 4 November 1712 seemed too well-timed to be true. For there could be no doubt that Oxford was in trouble. In May 1712 he had defended the infamous restraining orders in the House of Lords on the grounds that they would bring peace within a few days (*Parl. Hist.*, *6*, 1136). Nearly six months later there was still no treaty.

One trouble, of course, was that by disengaging its armies and abandoning its allies on the battlefield, Britain had lost the initiative in its negotiations with the enemy: "we are in a Manner pinned down," Swift explained, "and cannot go back an Inch with any good Grace: So that if the *French* play us foul, I dread the Effects" (Swift, *Corr.*, *1*, 300).

The other trouble was internal. The ministry was in danger of "breaking into pieces" (Swift, *Journal*, *2*, 556). St. John was outraged on 7 July 1712 when he was raised to the peerage as viscount, not as earl, of Bolingbroke. In September 1712 Oxford made a half-hearted attempt to replace him as chief negotiator with France (Trevelyan, *3*, 223) and in October Bolingbroke was further outraged when he was not chosen of the garter. A few days later Swift managed "to patch up these people together once more" (Swift, *Journal*, *2*, 568), but it must have been evident to everyone by now that Bolingbroke was out to get Oxford's job.

Furthermore, it was widely believed that St. John had contrived the screw plot in November 1710 (46*n*. below) to discredit the Whigs (Oldmixon, *History*, p. 452). So, for all these reasons, it was easy to believe that Swift had contrived the bandbox plot in November 1712. This is the theme that is developed in the present song.

The author may be George Duckett (46*n*., 50*n*. below), but the evidence is insufficient.

The poem must have been written after 11–13 November 1712 when

Swift's account of the incident, which it follows closely, was published in *The Evening Post* and *The Post Boy*.

The tune, *Which Nobody Can Deny*, "consists of the first strain of *Greensleeves* . . . lengthened from eight to ten measures to accommodate a repetition of the refrain line" (Simpson, p. 274).

The Plotter Found Out:
Or,
Mine Arse in a Band-Box.
To the Tune of *Which No Body Can Deny.*

Come listen ye *Britons,* the whilst I relate,
A Plot in a Band-box that happened of late;
As *Abel* hath wisely set forth in great State.
Which no Body can deny, &c.

Unto a Lord's Porter was sent a small Packet,   5
About which the *Tories* have made a great Racket;
But the School-boy that made it has not had it back yet.
Which no Body can deny, &c.

This *Westminster* Rogue a Pistol had stole,
Nay, fill'd it with Powder, and cramb'd it with Ball;   10
Resolving to Fire it in *Mortimer*'s Hole.
Which no Body can deny, &c.

This Pistol a Stock had, but yet not two Locks,

Title. *Band-Box:* "A slight box of card-board or very thin chip covered with paper, for collars, caps, hats, and millinery; originally made for the 'bands' or ruffs of the 17th c." (*OED*).

3. *Abel:* Abel Roper's account in *The Post Boy*, 11–13 November 1712, follows the account that Swift wrote for *The Evening Post* of the same date (Swift, *Prose, 6,* 196–97).

5. *Porter:* The bandbox was addressed to Oxford's porter, so famous for "denying" his lordship (BM MS. Lansdowne 852, f. 51v; Swift, *Prose, 6,* 196; *Journal, 1,* 126).

7. *School-boy:* On 3 November 1712 "a tall, slender Boy, having on a Gray Coat and a brown bob Peruke, delivered a Band-Box, (directed to the Lord Treasurers Porter) at a Penny-Post House behind Ludgate, which the next Morning was carried to the [penny post] Office in Chichester Rents, Chancery Lane, and from thence to the Lord Treasurers" (Swift, *Prose, 6,* 196). The line implies that the plot was in reality a Guy Fawkes Day prank.

11. *Mortimer's Hole:* See Defoe?, *A Welcome to the Medal,* Title *n.* above; Mainwaring, *An Excellent New Song, Called Mat's Peace,* 78–79*n.* above.

13. *Pistol a Stock had:* "The Box was carry'd up to my Lord's Bedchamber, and deliver'd to his Lordship, who lifting up the Lid as far as the Pack-thread that ty'd it would give way, said, He saw a Pistol; whereupon, a Gentleman in the Room [Swift] desired the Box might be given to him; he . . . open'd it, by cutting with a Penknife the Packthreads that fasten'd the Lid. The first Thing that appear'd was the Stock and Lock of a Pocket-Pistol" (ibid., pp. 196–97).

not two Locks: Since the first account of the incident had described "*a Band-box with Three Pistols charg'd and cock'd,*" Swift's "true account" "did not much promote the Belief of a PLOT against the Lord Treasurer; not only because it contradicted the first Report . . . by reducing Three Pistols to a Steel set on a Pistol-stock to strike Fire only, and two Ink-horns, &c. but

Which the mischievous Dog clapt in a Band-box;
With a meaning as wicked as ever had *Vaux*.   15
    Which no Body can deny, &c.

For this Band-box he loaded just like a Petard,
With two Linnen Barrels of black Gun-powder;
To blow up two Goose Quils, as sure as you're there.
    Which no Body can deny, &c.   20

Two Ink-horns did steal too this Rogue, a shame on 'm,
Which in this dire Engine he us'd for a Cannon;
From the Devil no doubt, this Thought came upon 'm.
    Which no Body can deny, &c.

With Touch-holes behind, and not at their Noses,   25
These Pot-guns stood Cross-ways, as *Abel* supposes;
To batter down Palaces, Churches and Houses.
    Which no Body can deny, &c.

Nay, to shew that this Plot went yet still a deal higher,
In the Band-box were also two Quils of Wild-fire;   30
Which were to go off too, when need should require.
    Which no Body can deny, &c.

Thus loaded with Mischief was this Box of *Pandore*,
And sent by a Porter, as I told you before;
Nay unto *Bob Presbyter*'s House too, what's more.   35
    Which no Body can deny, &c.

---

also . . . because no great Pains were taken to trace out the Persons that sent the Band-Box" (Boyer, *Annals*, 1713, pp. 294–95).

15. *Vaux:* Guy Fawkes (1570–1606), whose "meaning" was to assassinate James I by blowing up the House of Lords on the opening day of parliament, 5 November 1605, when King, Lords, and Commons would all be assembled there.

18. *two Linnen Barrels:* The pistol was fastened to the inside of the bandbox with nails and "on each side of the Fire-lock were laid the Middle-pieces of two large Ink-horns charg'd with Powder and Ball, and Touch-holes bored at the Butt-ends of 'em, to which were fasten'd two Linnen Bags of Gunpowder, and at the other end of the Bags were two Quils fill'd with Wildfire" (Swift, *Prose, 6,* 197).

21. *Ink-horns:* "A Gentleman told me," Swift said, "that if I had been killd, the Whigs would have called it a Judgmt, because the Barrells were of Inkorns, with which I had done them so much mischief" (Swift, *Journal, 2,* 573).

26. *Pot-guns:* pop-guns, children's toys (*OED*).

Cross-ways: "These two artificial Barrels [inkhorn-bag-quill] were plac'd with the Muzzels contrary-ways" (Swift, *Prose, 6,* 197).

30. *two Quils of Wild-fire:* See 18n. above. Wildfire was the name given to various highly inflammable substances, easily ignited and very difficult to extinguish (*OED*).

35. *Bob Presbyter:* See Mainwaring?, *A Panegyrick upon the English Catiline,* 2n. above.

House: Oxford's London residence was in York Buildings in the Strand.

But by *Bob*'s usual Luck the Mischief was mist all,
For he knew where to look for't, and soon spy'd the Pistol;
And then gave the Box to a Wit, that was his Tool.
    Which no Body can deny, &c.   40

Swift Gogled and Star'd, and turn'd up his Whites,
And ran with the Box to the Window to Rights;
Where he found out, what put us all into sad Frights.
    Which no Body can deny, &c.

How lucky 'twas *Guiscard* ne'er knew this Machine,   45
Nor the Rogues that would *Paul*'s have let down on the Queen;
For then a good Peace we should never have seen.
    Which no Body can deny, &c.

---

39. *a Wit:* Swift.

42. *ran with the Box to the Window:* Swift "desired the Box might be given to him; he took it to the Window, at some Distance from my Lord, and open'd it." "I wonder how I came to have so much presence of mind," he said, "which is usually not my talent" (Swift, *Prose, 6,* 196; *Journal, 2,* 572–73).

45. *Guiscard:* Antoine de Guiscard was a younger brother of the comte de Guiscard, a marshal of France. To avoid prosecution for multiple crimes, he fled first to the Cevennes and finally to England, where he represented himself as a political refugee. In April 1706 he was "with much Discretion raised at first Step from a profligate *Popish Priest* to a Lieutenant-General and Colonel of a Regiment of Horse" (Swift, *Prose, 3,* 108). Although he was "wholly ignorant of a Camp," his incompetence was only exposed when his troops refused to serve under him, and soon thereafter "his Pension [was] ill paid, and himself reduced to Extremity" (*A True Narrative of What Pass'd at the Examination of the Marquis de Guiscard, at the Cock-Pit, the 8th of March, 1710–11,* 1711, pp. 10, 12; Luttrell, *6,* 47). He resorted to espionage, but his treasonable correspondence with France was discovered and on 8 March 1711 he was arrested in St. James's Park and brought immediately to the Cockpit to be examined by members of the privy council. He must have recognized that the game was up, for "he stepp'd towards the Table, as if he design'd to say something to Mr. *Harley;* and stooping down, said, *J'en veux donc à Toy, Then have at thee,* so stabb'd him about the middle of the Breast: But by a singular Providence, lighting on the Bone, the Pen-knife broke about half an Inch from the Handle" and so the second blow did not prove fatal. In the ensuing mélée, Guiscard himself was fatally wounded (Boyer, *Annals, 1711,* pp. 338–41).

46. *Paul's have let down:* On 9 November 1710 it was discovered that several iron bolts had been removed from the great timbers of the west roof of St. Paul's. Since the queen had been scheduled to attend divine services in the cathedral on 7 November, it was assumed that a plot had been discovered "to destroy the Queen and the Court, by the Fall of the Roof of the Cathedral of St. *Paul*" (Boyer, *Annals, 1711,* pp. 253, 254–55). The screw plot, as it was called, was fastened upon the Whigs, but it turned out "That the missing of the Iron-Pins, was owing to the Neglect of some Workmen, who thought the Timbers sufficiently fasten'd without 'em" (ibid., p. 255). Thus the bandbox episode was promptly represented in a prose broadside by George Duckett as *A Great Plot! The Second Part of St. Paul's Screw-Plot! Or, Mine A—rse in a Ban-Box!* (*The Letters of Thomas Burnet to George Duckett 1712–1722,* ed. D. Nichol Smith, Oxford, The Roxburghe Club, 1914, pp. 225–26).

And whoever hereafter shall of this vile Act read,
Will give Thanks for this peeping and stretching the Pack-Thread; 50
And pray that his Honour for to stretch may ne'er lack Thread.
Which no Body can deny, &c.

50. *Thanks:* cf. "But thanks to the Stars, my L — is escap'd;—Thanks too to Parson
S . . . t, whose peeping into *Ban boxes* has sav'd the Nation" (ibid.).

1713

THOMAS D'URFEY?

The Peace in View.
A Song to the Tune of *A Health to the Constitution*
(December 1712–January 1713?)

This is another exercise in total irony: a Whiggish speaker pretending to be a Jacobite delighted with the progress of events in 1712 and looking forward to a Stuart restoration in 1713. The speaker's real orientation, however, is given away in his admiration of "brave *Eugene*" (line 10) and his scorn for "the High-Church Crew" (19).

Both the content, adjusted to the political situation at the end of 1712, and the stanza form, derive from a song written by Thomas D'Urfey in May 1709 for the end of the third act of his comedy, *The Modern Prophets: Or, New Wit for a Husband* (1709). There is no reason, in fact, to suppose that anyone else made the adjustments.

D'Urfey, whose best songs were written for Charles II (*POAS*, Yale, *3*, 493), was alive and well in 1712, or, in Addison's words, "still living, and in a blooming old Age . . . the Delight of the most Polite Companies and Conversations from the beginning of King *Charles* the Second's Reign to our present Times" (*The Guardian*, 28 May 1713). D'Urfey's song, *The King's Health: Set to Farinel's Ground* ("Joy to Great *Caesar*"), written in 1681, "gave the Whigs such a Blow as they were not able to recover that whole Reign" (ibid.). But at the revolution, D'Urfey became a Whig and one of the "vatum . . . turba" who sang the praises of Charles Montagu, as Halifax was then (*The Comical History of Don Quixote. The Third Part*, 1696, sig. A2).

In the next reign he "Once got fifty guineas (according to tradition) for singing a single song to queen Anne in ridicule of 'the princess Sophia, electress and duchess dowager of Hanover,' . . . naturally no great favourite with the then reigning monarch:

> The crown's far too weighty
> For shoulders of eighty;
> She could not sustain such a trophy;
> Her hand, too, already
> Has grown so unsteady

> She can't hold a sceptre;
> So Providence kept her
> Away.—Poor old Dowager Sophy."

(William Hone, "Tom Durfey," *The Table Book*, 2 [1828], 650). And "He also satirized the Harley-Bolingbroke ministry, for he took the true refugee view of the Peace of Utrecht as a bad bargain for Britain and for the Protestant interest:

> A ballad to their merit may
> Most justly then belong,
> For, why! they've given all (I say)
> To Louis for *a song*."

(David C. A. Agnew, *Protestant Exiles from France in the Reign of Louis XIV*, 2nd ed., 3 vols., London and Edinburgh, 1871–74, *3*, 130).

The present poem makes exactly the same point, but makes it indirectly, by irony. In fact, the main adjustment made between D'Urfey's act-song for *The Modern Prophet* and the present song is in the tone. The tone of the former is enthusiastic and totally innocent of irony:

> Now, now comes on the Glorious Year,
> *Britain* has Hopes and *France* has Fear,
> *Lewis*, the War, has cost so dear,
>   He slily Peace does tender;
>
> But our Two Hero's [Marlborough and Eugene] so well know
> The Breach of his Word some Years ago,
> They resolve they will give him the other Blow,
>   Unless he *Spain* surrender,

and so on for two more stanzas (*The Modern Prophets: Or, New Wit for a Husband,* n.d., p. 45). The advantage of irony is that it gives an edge to the present song that is totally lacking in the original. Presumably the irony might also attract unwary Jacobites and expose to them the naked foolishness of their position.

Limits for writing the poem seem to be 23 November 1712, when Shrewsbury's appointment as ambassador to France (13) became known (Boyer, *Annals*, 1713, p. 312) and 18/29 January 1713 when the Dutch "bowed" to the ministry and signed a new barrier treaty (7).

The tune is also known as *Now, Now Comes On the Glorious Year* and *Guiscard* (Simpson, pp. 521–23).

THE PEACE IN VIEW.
A Song to the Tune of *A Health to the Constitution*

Now, now comes on the *Tory* Year,
France has new Hopes and *Britain* fear,
Perkin intends to govern here,
   And be our Faith's Defender:
For *France* is become our good Ally,   5
The *Dutch* and *Emperor* too must fly,
Unless they will bow to our Ministry,
   And *Flanders* and *Spain* Surrender.

A Health to our General then begin,
Who left in the Lurch the brave *Eugene;*   10

---

1. *the Tory Year:* Cf. Bolingbroke, *A Letter to Sir William Windham,* 1753, p. 60: "the peace was to be . . . the period at which the millenary year of toryism should begin."

2. *fear:* "Mr. *Prior* . . . was sent over privately into [France], Which gave no small Umbrage to many . . . who . . . were afraid of some underhand Practices" (*Memoirs of Queen Anne,* 1729, p. 133).

4. *Faith's Defender:* See *Switch and Spur,* 89n. above. Under the pretender the Church of England would have been once again at the mercy of a Catholic, as it had been under James II

5. *France . . . our good Ally:* Cf. "The *French,* our Allies" (Mainwaring?, *The Queen's Speech,* 10n. above).

6. *The Dutch:* For their "Barrier" against France, the Dutch had to settle for the best that Bolingbroke could get from Torcy, which was far less than they were entitled to by the barrier treaty of October 1710 (*A New Song,* 9n. above). Bolingbroke later acknowledged that he had given away too much (Bolingbroke, *Letters on the Study and Use of History,* 2 vols., 1752, 2, 123–24). A new barrier treaty between Britain and the Netherlands was signed on 18/29 January 1713 in Utrecht (Lamberty, *8,* 34–42).

   Emperor: See Defoe?, *A Welcome to the Medal,* 42n. above.

7–9. *our Ministry . . . our General:* Cf. Trevelyan, *3,* 218: "On the day the Restraining Orders [10n. below] were written, Torcy's London agent, Gaultier, wrote to him of Bolingbroke as 'our Secretary' and of Ormonde as 'our General.' " But the first meaning of "our" in the poem is "Jacobite."

10. *left in the Lurch the brave Eugene:* With 40 battalions and 12 squadrons of cavalry under his command, Ormonde joined up with Prince Eugene at Tournai on 25 April/6 May 1712, in order to lay siege to Cambrai or Arras (HMC *Portland MSS., 5,* 165). About two weeks later he received new orders: "it is . . . the Queen's positive command to your Grace, that you avoid engaging in any siege, or hazarding a battle, till you have farther orders from her Majesty" (Bolingbroke, *Letters, 2,* 320). On the same day Gaultier asked St. John what Villars should do if Eugene were to take the offensive without Ormonde's 12,000 troops. "Il m'a repondu," Gaultier reported to Torcy, "qu'il n'auroit point d'autre chose à fair qu'à luy tomber desous et la tailler en pièces, luy et son armée" (Archives du Ministère des Affaires Étrangères MS. 238, f. 73, quoted in Trevelyan, *3,* 230). Trevelyan observed that this was

With him let *Oxford* too come in,
   Who brought about this Wonder:
Let *Shrewsbury*'s Duke next him take place,
And *Bolingbroke* with his handsome Face,
Whose Courage and Wits are all of a piece,   15
   To make the *Whiggs* knock under.

Let *Prior* and *Swift* now receive their Due,
With *Gautier* their Brother *Protestant* Blue,

"little short of a plot . . . to give Villars the opportunity to defeat Eugene" (ibid., *3*, 218). Accordingly, on 5/16 July 1712, Ormonde marched off with his 12,000 troops in the direction of Ghent. And a week later Villars fell with overwhelming force on a part of Eugene's army encamped at Denain and in a few hours killed 300 Dutch and German officers and 2,500 men (Boyer, *Annals*, 1713, pp. 189–90). "Oh it will sound nobly in the Ears of after Ages, when they shall be told, that the brave . . . *English* . . . basely deserted and betray'd their Friends and Confederates" (*The Secret History of the Late Ministry*, 1715, p. 158).

11. *Oxford*: "Lord Bolingbroke used to say, that the restraining orders to the duke of Ormond were proposed at the cabinet council, in the queen's presence, by the earl of Oxford, who had not communicated his intention to the rest of the ministers" (Burnet, 1823, *6*, 119n.). But the truth seems to be that it was Bolingbroke who devised the orders without communicating his intention to the rest of the ministers (Trevelyan, *3*, 217).

12. *this Wonder*: The restraining orders were called "this Lunacy" in *Military and Other Poems*, 1716, p. 65.

13. *Shrewsbury's Duke*: After resisting Harley's overtures in 1708 (Mainwaring?, *A New Ballad: To the Tune of Fair Rosamund*, 119n. above), Shrewsbury was made lord chamberlain and a privy councillor "by the sole Interest of Harley" in April 1710 (BM MS. Lansdowne 885, f. 67). He became a Whiggish makeweight to Bolingbroke in Oxford's coalition government and in the last stages of the peace negotiations he was sent ambassador extraordinary to France (November 1712–August 1713). Then he was appointed lord lieutenant of Ireland (September 1713–October 1714) and finally succeeded Oxford as lord treasurer (30 July–11 October 1714).

14. *Bolingbroke . . . his handsome Face*: Among the characteristics of "the greatest young man I ever knew," that Swift reeled off to his Dublin ladies, was "beauty" (Swift, *Journal*, *2*, 401).

15. *Courage and Wits*: Swift mentions St. John's "wit, capacity . . . [and] quickness of apprehension" (ibid.), but says nothing about his "Courage." Marlborough, however, observed that St. John "speaks more boldly to the Queen in Council than anyone else" (Winston S. Churchill, *Marlborough His Life and Times*, 4 vols., Harrap & Co., 1938, *4*, 372).

16. *knock under*: short for "*knock under board, under (the) table*, succumb in a drinking-bout; acknowledge oneself beaten, give in, yield," submit (*OED*).

17. *Prior and Swift*: Cf. *Private Correspondence of Sarah, Duchess of Marlborough*, *2*, 129–30: "The Rev. Mr. Swift and Mr. Prior quickly offered themselves to sale . . . both men of wit and parts ready to prostitute all they had in the service of well-rewarded scandal . . . The former of these had long ago turned all religion into a Tale of a Tub, and sold it for a jest. But he had taken it ill, that the ministry had not promoted him in the Church for the great zeal he had shown for religion by his profane drollery; and so carried his atheism and humour into the service of their enemies."

18. *Gautier*: François Gaultier (d. 1720), born in Rabodange, near Falaise, was an unbeneficed priest when he came to London in November 1700 as chaplain to Camille d'Hos-

And all the rest of the High-Church Crew,
    Who are against *Hannover;*   20
With Hands and with Hearts, let us all now join
Against the *Whiggs,* and their Friends combine,
Until we have settled Right Divine,
    Upon our own *Come-over.*

---

tun, duc de Tallard, the French ambassador. When Tallard was recalled, Gaultier stayed behind (Mainwaring, *An Excellent New Song, Called Mat's Peace,* p. 504 above). In the early stages of the peace negotiations, he acted as a secret intermediary between France and England (Swift, *Prose, 7,* 34–36; Macpherson, *History, 2,* 490–91), and after August 1711 as a recognized diplomatic agent (*Journal inédit de Jean-Baptiste Colbert, Marquis de Torcy,* ed. Frédéric Masson, Paris, 1884, pp. 347–48). He was also a Jacobite courier (ibid., p. 426).

Protestant Blue: See *An Elegy on the Death of Pamphlets,* 37n. above. Since Gaultier was a Catholic priest, the implication is that Prior and Swift were his coreligionists.

23. *Right Divine:* The pretender's "Right Divine" to the crown of Britain had been set aside by the Bill of Rights and the Act of Settlement (*Fair Warning,* 9n. above).

24. *Come-over:* The Whigs were urging the electoral prince, Georg August, to "come-over" to England to insure the Hanoverian succession (Macpherson, *Original Papers, 2,* 389). In the context, "our own *Come-over*" is the restoration of the pretender; cf. the expressed hope that even if the pretender were converted to Protestantism, there would be "no Experiment try'd hereafter, to run the hazard of making use of a COMEOVER" (Boyer, *Annals,* 1712, p. 213).

The British Embassadress's Speech to the French King
(March 1713)

Swift and Defoe were shocked by this poem. "Here is the cursedest Libel in Verse come out, that ever was seen," Swift said, "it is very dull, too. It has been printed in 3 or 4 different ways, & is handed about, but not sold; it abuses the Qu—— horribly" (Swift, *Journal*, 2, 644). "Abuses the Qu—— horribly" is accurate enough, but "very dull" the poem is not. It revives for a moment something of the inspired, pre-reformation-of-manners nastiness of the earlier volumes in the present series. It is, as Defoe called it, an "insolent and unmannerly Libel" (*Review*, 7 May 1713).

Its abuse of the queen takes the form of an interesting psychological paradigm that is not inherently improbable, namely, that Anne's guilt for withholding from her half brother the throne of England transferred itself into her willingness to allow Louis's grandson to occupy the throne of Spain. The nastiness takes the form of a fantasy that is manifestly improbable. The poet imagines the impeccable duke of Shrewsbury ceremoniously conveying his "Masculine Dutchess," a more than middle-aged woman who still pretended to have love affairs (*A New Protestant Litany, 13n.* above; *Wentworth Papers*, pp. 214, 283), to be enjoyed in bed by the 74-year old French king.

On 25 March 1713 an informant told Oxford that this "scandalous and treasonable paper" was "being dispersed by one Robins a shoemaker in Bell Yard near Temple Bar" (HMC *Dartmouth MSS., 1*, 315). Dartmouth, the secretary of state, wasted no time in tracking down the printer, William Hurt, and bringing him to court on 27 June, where he was sentenced to stand twice in the pillory, to pay a fine of £50, and to be imprisoned for two years until he should pay the fine (Swift, *Journal*, 2, 644n.). But the author was never discovered.

On 23 March 1713 Defoe was arrested for debt and imprisoned for 11 days. On 11 April he was arrested again, this time for publishing three mock-Jacobite pamphlets: *Reasons against the Succession of the House of Hanover* (February 1713); *And What if the Pretender Should Come* (March 1713); and *An Answer to a Question that No Body Thinks of, Viz. But What If the Queen Should Die?* (April 1713). On 22 April Defoe was ordered back to prison for protesting in the *Review* against the lord chief justice Sir Thomas Parker's deliberate misinterpretation of these ironical pamphlets as Jacobite literature. Defoe insisted that they must be read "*as . . . all Ironical speaking must be,* just contrary," as "Satyr upon the Pretender" (*Review,* 16 April 1713). On 2 May, after writing letters of apology to Justice Parker, Defoe was released from prison. About the same time, it was "very maliciously . . . *written in News Letters,* and even printed in the North of *Britain,* that the Trouble I have been lately in, was for being the Author of . . . *The Ambassadresses Speech, &c.* To which my Answer is in short this, *viz.* That it not only *is false,* but not *rational;* and that it is not possible that I can be either such a Villain to Her Majesty, or such a Fool to my self" (*Review,* 7 May 1713).

The date of publication is indicated by Swift's notice of the poem on 23 March 1713 and R. W.'s report to Oxford of 25 March enclosing a copy (Swift, *Journal,* 2, 644; HMC *Dartmouth MSS., 1,* 315).

THE BRITISH EMBASSADRESS'S SPEECH TO THE FRENCH KING

Hail Tricking Monarch! more successful far
In Arts of Peace, than Glorious Deeds of War.
As *Anna*'s Great Embassadress I come
With News that will rejoyce both you and *Rome*.
Ne'er did the *French* Affairs so gayly smile   5
These Hundred Years, as now in *Britain*'s Isle:
For there the Spirit of Blind Delusion reigns,
And spreads its Fury o'er the stupid Swains.
The Lords, the Commons, and the Priests conspire
To raise your Power, and their own Ruin higher.   10
Nay even the Queen, with Qualms of Conscience prest,
Seems to advance your Cause above the rest.
Her generous Temper can't forget so soon
The Royal Favours you have always done

1. *Tricking Monarch:* Louis XIV, "finding that he had less to fear from the court of England than from any of the confederates, began to draw back from his promises to it" (Somerville, p. 493).

2. *Arts of Peace:* "The scene of business was now transferred from Utrecht to Paris, where the duke of Shrewsbury resided as ambassador; and acted in conformity to the instructions he received from lord Bolingbroke. The correspondence between the ambassador and the secretary exhibits a curious specimen of the chicane and treachery of the French court, and of the inconsistency and distraction of the English ministry. Amidst all the blustering and recrimination affected by the latter, we discern a progressive concession to the court of France; so that, in the result, she modelled every thing that remained undecided, agreeably to her own interest" (ibid., p. 494). Besides the particular concessions, like Cape Breton Island, that Louis was able to wring out of the English, it is true in general that he gained more by the peace (Spain and the West Indies) than he gained by the war (a few market towns in Flanders); cf. 31n. below. Thus it is not surprising that, at the conclusion of Shrewsbury's embassy in August 1713, Louis favored him with his portrait in miniature, set in diamonds (Dorothy H. Somerville, *The King of Hearts, Charles Talbot, Duke of Shrewsbury,* Allen & Unwin, 1962, p. 303; Michael Foot, *The Pen and the Sword,* McGibbon & Kee, 1957, p. 69).

3. *Embassadress:* Adelida Paleotti, duchess of Shrewsbury, accompanied her husband on his embassy to Paris. "The Duke of *Shrewsbury,* with his *Dutchess,* embark'd at *Greenwich* for *France*" on 14 December 1712 (Boyer, *Annals,* 1713, p. 398).

4. *Rome:* Although the duchess of Shrewsbury was "an Italian Papist, who had upon . . . marriage professed herself a Protestant" (*Private Correspondence of Sarah, Duchess of Marlborough, 2,* 123), she was suspected to have retained her Catholic faith.

7. *Delusion reigns:* Cf. "the multitude [were] running headlong down the precipice after the fascinating name of peace" (Cunningham, *2,* 399).

11. *the Queen:* Anne's imputed "Qualms of Conscience" may have arisen from her guilt for usurping the throne of her brother, whom Louis XIV had protected since infancy and recognised as James III in September 1701.

Both to her Father and his injur'd Son.   15
And therefore is contriving every Day,
Her mighty Debt of Gratitude to pay.
For you she has ceas'd the Thunder of the War,
Laid up her Fleet, and left her Chanel bare;
For you the Fighting *MARLBOROUGH*'s disgrac'd,   20
And in his Room a Peaceful General plac'd;
For you she broke her Word, her Friends betray'd,
With Joy look'd on, and saw them Victims made.
That Pious Princess, when I left her Court,
The Place where none but Friends to you resort,   25
Bid me to greet you in the kindest Words,
That the most Sacred Tye of Love affords:
And tell you that she mourns with secret Pains,
The mighty Loss you've born these Ten Campaigns.
And therefore now resolves to give you more,   30
By this last Treaty than you had before,
And to its former Height raise your declining Power.

15. *Father and . . . Son:* James II and the pretender.

18. *ceas'd the Thunder of the War:* An armistice between Britain and France was proclaimed on 8/19 August 1712 and extended in December until April 1713, by which time the treaty of Utrecht had been signed (Lamberty, *8,* 1–2).

19. *Chanel bare:* On 12 July 1712 a squadron under Sir John Leake that had been patrolling the Channel was recalled to the Downs, leaving the English garrison at Dunkirk unprotected and English shipping defenseless against French privateers (Stephen Martin-Leake, *The Life of Sir John Leake,* ed. G. Callender, 2 vols., Navy Records Society, 1920, *2,* 388–91).

21. *a Peaceful General:* Ormonde (D'Urfey?, *The Peace in View,* 10n. above). Swift puts these words into the mouth of Prince Eugene (*TLS,* 10 May 1974). Was it Eugene's phrase?

22. *broke her Word:* "The withdrawing the *English* Forces in this manner, from the Confederate Army, was censured, not only as a manifest Breach of Faith and of Treaties, but as treacherous in the highest and basest degree. The Duke of *Ormond* had given the *States* such Assurances, of his going along with them thro' the whole Campaign, that he was let into the Secrets of all their Counsels, which by that Confidence were all known to the *French* . . . by this open Breach of Faith . . . the Confederates could no longer trust or depend on us" (Burnet, *2,* 610).

23. *Victims:* After his victory at Denain in July 1712 (D'Urfey?, *The Peace in View,* 10n. above), Villars was able to recapture Douai, Le Quesnoy, and Bouchain in the next three months (Boyer, *Annals,* 1713, pp. 196, 248, 256).

24. *Pious Princess:* See p. 146 above.

31. *this last Treaty:* By the terms of the treaty of Utrecht, which Shrewsbury was sent to Paris to bring to "an immediate conclusion," the House of Bourbon was left in possession of France, Spain, and the West Indies. "The House of *Bourbon*," Steele wrote, "is at this Juncture become more formidable, and bids fairer for an Universal Monarchy, and to engross the whole Trade of *Europe,* than it did before the War" (*Tracts and Pamphlets by Richard Steele,* ed. Rae Blanchard, Baltimore, Johns Hopkins Press, 1944, p. 174).

She knows she has no Right the Crown to wear,
And fain would leave it to the Lawful Heir.
In order to effect this grand Design   35
And baffle all the *Hanoverian* Line,
A Set of Ministers she lately chose,
To Honour and their Country equal Foes:
Wretches, whose Indigence has made 'em bold,
And will betray their Native Land for Gold.   40
Oxford's the Chief of this abandon'd Clan;
Him you must court, for he's your only Man.
Give him but Gold enough, your Work is done,
He'll bribe the Senate, and then all's your own.
Dartmouth and *Bolingbroke* are Friends to you,   45
Tho' 'tis not in their Power much Harm to do.
But *Oxford* reigns Prime Minister of State,

34. *the Lawful Heir:* the pretender. According to the Jacobites, "The Queen herself, eager for the eventual succession of her brother," was ready "to permit him to remain, during her own life in Scotland, under the character of presumptive heir of the crown" (Macpherson, *Original Papers, 2,* 364).

36. *baffle . . . the Hanoverian Line:* "Her Majesty had . . . the Hannoverian family and succession in utter abhorrence" (*Memoirs of the Life of Sir John Clerk of Penicuick, Baronet,* ed. John M. Gray, Edinburgh, 1892, p. 81).

39. *Indigence:* Before his return to office in August 1710, Harley "was in very ill circumstances . . . there was a great Clamour against him . . . for Debts to common Tradesmen" (Blenheim MS. E 27). In May 1712 Shrewsbury "had to remind the Treasurer that half a year of his personal pension of £3,000 was due" (Dorothy N. Somerville, *The King of Hearts, Charles Talbot, Duke of Shrewsbury,* Allen & Unwin, 1962, p. 293) and when urged to accept the ambassadorship, Shrewsbury "seem'd not much pleas'd with it, [and] spoke of the expence it would be to him" (*Wentworth Papers,* p. 305; cf. HMC *Bath MSS., 1,* 224).

42. *your only Man:* As long ago as February 1702 Shaftesbury had come to the same conclusion about Harley: " 'Tis he and he alone that wounds us; for all the strength of the Tories or Church party is nothing, but by that force which he brings over to them from our side" (*Original Letters,* pp. 174–75).

44. *bribe the Senate:* By August 1710 "so much mony" had been spent in bribes that the Court party could expect a huge majority in the House of Commons even before the election writs were issued (*Wentworth Papers,* p. 136).

45. *Dartmouth:* Dartmouth may have been appointed secretary of state in June 1710 because he was "a servile Creature of Harley's" (BM MS. Lansdowne 885, f. 66v), but he was not a Jacobite (HMC *Dartmouth MSS.,* p. 329). He is probably a "Friend" to Louis XIV because on 27 September 1711 he signed the preliminary articles of the treaty that left Spain and the West Indies in the hands of Louis's grandson.

Bolingbroke: The other secretary of state boasted that his restraining orders to Ormonde (D'Urfey?, *The Peace in View,* 10n. above) saved the French army from being beat. During his embassy to Paris in August 1712 he was imprudent enough to be seen "at the Play with the Pretender" (Hertfordshire County R. O. MS. Panshanger D/EP F207, f. 45).

47. *Prime Minister:* Although Walpole is conventionally recognized as the first prime minister of Britain, the term was applied to him "as a term of reproach by a generation which

Ruling the Nation at a mighty Rate;
And like a Conjurer with his Magick Wand,
Does both the Parliament and Queen command.   50
Keep but that wily Trickster still your Friend,
He'll crown your Wishes with a prosperous End.
Now is your time to push for *Britain*'s Crown,
And fix King *James* the Third upon the Throne:
A powerful Fleet prepare, you need no more,   55
But only land him on his Native Shore;
They'll soon depose the present reigning Thing,
And in her Stead proclaim your Favourite King.
    Thus spoke the Gay Embassadress; when strait
Up rose the Tyrant from his Chair of State,   60
With Love transported and a joyous Air,
Within his trembling Arms he clasp'd the Fair;
That Night, as Fame reports, and some have heard,
A pompous Bed was instantly prepar'd,
In which the Monarch and the Heroine lay,   65

saw in the prime ministers of France, such as Dubois, Orléans, Bourbon and Fleury, subjects who were exercising in their own person all the royal functions" (*Handbook of British Chronology*, ed. Sir F. Maurice Powicke and E. B. Fryde, Offices of the Royal Historical Society, 1961, p. 106) and it is in this pejorative sense that the term is used here. But in a neutral, technical sense, meaning head of a government under the monarch, the term was used at least as early as September 1697 (Vernon, *1*, 359) and in July–August? 1704 Defoe was urging Harley to use his office of secretary of state to become "Prime Minister" (Defoe, *Letters*, p. 44). "When Harley became Chancellor of the Exchequer and second Commissioner of the Treasury in August 1710 James Brydges, the Paymaster, judged that he was 'now premier Minister', and Joseph Addison, after giving himself a week or so to size up the new situation . . . came out with the unequivocal statement that 'Mr. H——ly is first Minister of State' " (Holmes, p. 440).

49. *his Magick Wand.* Cf. Swift, *The Virtues of Sid Hamet the Magician's Rod,* Title *n.* above.

51. *wily Trickster:* A Jacobite reported that "the great man Harle[y] . . . [is] so cuning and close a man, that wan shod not despayre of him" (Macpherson, *Original Papers, 2*, 378).

52. *your Wishes:* Another Jacobite agent reported in February 1713 "That Mr. Harley and his brethren would call home the [pretender] . . . That Mr. Harley manages [i.e. amuses] the Low Church and Hannover, until he can get the peace settled. Believes him hearty to the [pretender's] interest . . . though few Jacobites believe him to be so" (ibid., *2*, 387–88).

56. *his Native Shore:* Scotland "would be hearty for [the pretender] to get rid of Mr. Underhill [the Union], whom he hates mortally, and believes . . . will be his ruin" (ibid., *2*, 386).

57. *the present reigning Thing:* Anne is a "*Thing*" in *On the Queen's Speech*, 8, above.

59. *the Gay Embassadress:* Cf. "that Coquetilla, whose deluding airs Corrupt our virgins, still our youth ensnare" (*The Letters and Works of Lady Mary Wortley Montagu*, ed. James A. Stuart-Wortley-Mackenzie, Lord Wharncliffe, 2nd ed., 3 vols., 1837, *3*, 352). The gossip in London was that the duchess was "mightily liked in France" (*Wentworth Papers*, p. 321).

And spent their Hours in Politicks and Play.
The Duke o'erjoy'd, that his *Italian* Dame
Could in so Old an Hero raise a Flame,
With an ambitious Pleasure, as 'tis said,
Led her himself unto the Royal Bed.   70

68. *so Old an Hero:* Louis XIV had his 74th birthday in September 1712.

1714

The Country Squire's Ditty.
A Ballad. To the Tune of *To you Fair Ladys*
(April–June? 1714)

The origin of the March Club on 24 March 1712 is described in the report of a Dutch diplomatic agent in London. "La société de Mars s'assembla hier [Monday, 31 March 1712]," he said, "et se trouva a ce qu'on dit au nombre de plus de 50 . . . Le. Sr. [George] Pit, qui est un membre des communes pour la province de Hamshire s'est mis a leur teste, et est riche a ce qu'on dit de plus de 10 a 12000 £ St. de rente. Et la plus part des autres sont aussy des plus riches de la chambre. Ils ont pris le Lundy pour le jour de leur assemblée et ce fut hier le second jour . . . Tous les membres de cette société estoient de celle d'Octobre . . . ils s'en sont separés parce qu'un ministre d'état y etoit entré et s'estoit fait elire president, et qu'ils ne veulent pas estre gouvernés par la cour" (BM MS. Add. 17677FFF, ff. 138v–139).

In the next two years the March Club enjoyed two great triumphs: in June 1713 it joined the Whigs to vote down the ministry's commercial treaty with France and in the last session of the reign (February–July 1714) the Hanoverian Tories, or the Whimsicals, as their enemies called them, again joined with the Whigs to defeat a second Stuart restoration.

It is in the midst of this second triumph that the imagined member of the March Club composed *The Country Squire's Ditty* and the note of celebration is everywhere apparent in the song. The singer has not yet learned of a momentary setback: the queen has defeated his most daring ploy, which was to bring Georg August, the dashing electoral prince of Hanover, to Westminster to assume his rightful seat in the House of Lords.

The *Ditty* must have originated *after* the writ summoning Georg August was delivered to the Hanoverian ambassador on 14 April 1714 (Macpherson, *Original Papers, 2,* 590–92) but *before* the news of Anne's letters of 19 May 1714 forbidding the prince to come, was known to the author (8*n.* below).

The music for *Shackley Hay, or To All You Ladies Now at Land,* which may have originated as a dance tune, was first printed in 1613. The "fa-la-la" refrain was originally repeated after the sixth and eighth lines of each stanza, but the seven-line version of the present *Ditty* is also the one that Pope used for *The Court Ballad* (1717) (Simpson, pp. 647–51).

THE COUNTRY SQUIRE'S DITTY.
A BALLAD. TO THE TUNE OF *To you Fair Ladys.*

To you dear Topers at the Court,
   We Country *Tories* write:
We will no longer make you Sport,
   Nor with such Fools unite.
We are no Sheep for you to fleece,   5
Nor will be gaul'd by such a Peace;
With a fa, la, la, la, la, la, la.

The Duke of *Cambridge,* whom God bless,

Title. *Country:* in the sense of "opposition." The narrator is not writing *from* the country, but *as* a Tory opposed to the court.

1. *Topers at the Court:* The leaders of the Court party, Oxford and Bolingbroke, were both heavy drinkers. "Robin's red Nose" had long been a joke in Whig circles (Blenheim MS. GI 15; *A New Protestant Litany,* 19n. above) and Swift scolded Bolingbroke "like a dog" for drinking too much (Swift, *Journal, 1,* 240).

2. *Country Tories:* The October Club was formed in January 1711 when a dozen country squires who were also Tory members of parliament met at the Bell Tavern in King Street, Westminster, to canvas ways of expressing their dissatisfaction with the new ministry. The club soon numbered 159 members (Boyer, *Political State, 3,* 117–22), all men of "good estate and not one in the government" (John Rylands Library MS. Legh of Lyme, F. Legh to P. Legh, 20 February 1711). Altogether they constituted as formidable an opposition to the ministry as the Whigs. Harley and Bolingbroke met this opposition by joining it and in March 1712 St. John got himself elected president of the October Club. This so infuriated some of "the Primative October men," as they called themselves, that they formed the March Club (*Wentworth Papers,* pp. 283–84). The October Club, "weary of the taxes," had supported the ministry in its policy of peace at any price, but the March Club began to demand "a good Peace, An Equitable Peace—A Peace that answers all our Treaties" (*March and October: A Dialogue,* 1712, p. 7). This, of course, proved to be impossible, for the ministry had thrown away all means of obtaining better terms. So the speaker rejects the treaty that the ministry had signed on 11 April 1713.

3. *no longer make you Sport:* The founding members of the October Club are said to have "gone blindfold into all the Measures of the present Ministers" in the first session of Anne's fourth parliament (1710–11) because they were "amused and deluded with vain Promises of Preferment" (Boyer, *Political State, 3,* 122).

6. *gaul'd:* abraded, injured. *OED* cites Sir Walter Raleigh, *The History of the World,* 1614, p. 232: "gawled with the yoke of forraine dominion."

8. *Duke of Cambridge:* Georg August, the electoral prince of Braunschweig-Lüneburg, had been created duke of Cambridge in the English peerage in November 1706 and given precedence over all the nobility of Great Britain by an act of parliament of January 1712 (Boyer, *Annals,* 1712, pp. 331–32). On 12 April 1714, application was made for a writ summoning the prince to take his seat in the House of Lords. The writ was issued and rumors began to fly that the duke was on his way to London (HMC *Portland MSS., 5,* 419). On 19 May, however, the queen wrote personal letters to the dowager electress, the elector, and the electoral prince

Comes in the Nick of Time;
And *Oxford* ev'ry Day grows less   10
    In Grandeur, not in Crime:
While others' Ruin he debates,
His Head shall crown the City Gates;
With a fa, la, la, la, la, la, la.

Or since his fav'rite *South-Sea-Trade*   15
    He would pretend to love;
We'll thither send that wise Lord's Head,
    Their Projects to improve:
And when he's once remov'd so far,
Who doubts the Stock will be at Par?   20
With a fa, la, la, la, la, la, la.

Friend *Harry* next we would advance
    To some unlucky Hap:
I think we'll send him back to *France*,
    To get another Clap.   25
And howe'er bitter be the Pill,
He'll take it, if 'tis gilded well;

---

making it perfectly clear that she would not tolerate the prince's presence in England. Copies of these letters were handed about in manuscript and finally printed on 1 July 1714 (Boyer, *Political State, 8,* 599–602).

10. *grows less:* Upon his dismissal in July 1714 Oxford told Swift that he had "had no power since July 25: *1713*" (Swift, *Corr., 2,* 85).

13. *Head:* Cf. *A New Protestant Litany,* 2n. above. The prophecy was partially fulfilled in July 1715 when Oxford was impeached on 16 charges of high treason and committed to the Tower, where he remained for two years.

15. *South-Sea-Trade:* See *A Welcome to the Medal,* 101n. above.

20. *Par:* Stock in the South Sea Company, issued at £100, sold below £80 all during 1712. "Although by the end of 1713 it had risen to 94, it only reached and stayed at par at the end of 1716" (Peter G. M. Dickson, *The Financial Revolution in England,* New York, Macmillan, 1967, pp. 216–35).

22. *Harry:* Bolingbroke.

24. *back to France:* Bolingbroke went to France in August 1712 to discuss the peace terms with Torcy; cf. *The British Embassadress's Speech to the French King,* 45n. above. He returned to England on 7 September 1712.

25. *another Clap:* "Lewd *Harry*," as Bolingbroke was called, lived at "th' Centre / Of . . . Pimps, Surgeons, and Whores" (*Political Merriment: Or, Truths Told to Some Tune,* [Part I], 1714, p. 22; Part IV, 1715, p. 61). He boasted that he spent Sunday 6 June 1714 "very agreeably; for (said he) in the morning I went to the Queen and ruin'd the Dog, meaning the Ld Treasurer; at dinner I got drunk with Champagne, and at night was put to bed to the prettiest whore in England, and two Lords tuck'd up the Sheets" (BM MS. Add. 47027, f. 127; cf. *Wentworth Papers,* p. 395).

27. *if . . . gilded:* an allusion to Bolingbroke's resourcefulness in using his public office

With a fa, la, la, la, la, la, la.

For *Phipps*, who has nor Law nor Sence,
　　But hew'ds in *Dublin* Town,   30
That there was *English* Impudence
　　Far greater than their own.
To the wild *Irish* let him fly,
And be one of their Ministry:
With a fa, la, la, la, la, la, la.   35

But let all *Protestants* combine
　　Against a Bastard Race:
Bring in the *Hanoverian* Line,
　　And slavish *Jacks* disgrace.
And send the present *Ministry*   40
To sing out, *Heigh Boys up go we;*
With a fa, la, la, la, la, la, la.

---

for private gain, most successfully in the supply contracts for the Quebec expedition (1711) and the negotiations for the commercial treaty with Spain (1713–14) (HMC *Portland MSS., 5,* 655, 661).

29. *Phipps:* Constantine Phipps (1656–1723), the third son of a counrty squire, was educated at St. John's College, Oxford, and the Middle Temple, whence he was called to the bar in 1684. He was a Jacobite and defended Sir John Fenwick in September 1696 (Luttrell, *4,* 112), but he made his reputation as Sacheverell's chief counsel in March 1710 (*The Westminster Combat,* 73n. above). In December 1710 he was knighted and made lord chancellor of Ireland (Luttrell, *6,* 664, 675). In December 1711 he undertook to reduce the overwhelming Whig majority in the Irish House of Commons by appointing Tory sheriffs in the counties and securing the election of Tory mayors in the towns. "The city of Dublin led the opposition, and elected a whig mayor, whom the government refused to recognize. The catholic mob were for the castle; the well-to-do citizens and freemen were for the corporation. Both sides were obstinate, and for nearly two years Dublin was without a municipal government" (*DNB, 15,* 1115). Phipps further showed his "Impudence" by prejudging cases in litigation, protecting Jacobite printers from the operation of the libel laws, and cramping the annual ceremonies honoring William III. By December 1713 he had made himself so unpopular that the House of Commons addressed the queen to remove him (Boyer, *Political State, 6,* 364–75).

33. *the wild Irish:* the Catholic mob in Dublin.

37. *a Bastard Race:* on the assumption that James Francis Edward Stuart was not the son of Queen Mary of Modena, but a product of the warming pan.

39. *Jacks:* Jacobites.

41. *Heigh Boys up go we:* the name of the tune of a popular song, with the refrain, "Then Hey Boys up go we," which Thomas D'Urfey reworked in 1682 from a song of Francis Quarles. It became a very popular tune for political songs (Simpson, pp. 304–08).

The Fall of the House of Stuart

One hundred and eleven years of Stuart rule were ended a little after seven o'clock on Sunday morning, 1 August 1714, when an ugly, 49-year-old woman died in her bed in Kensington palace. But the death of Queen Anne released no tear-floods of elegy such as the deaths of James II and Willaim III had evoked in 1701–02 (*POAS*, Yale, *6*, 353). It was noticed at the time "that few Princes ever died so little regretted and lamented by the Generality of their Subjects . . . On *Saturday* Morning, July the Thirty-First, when Her Majesty was reported to be dead, the Publick Funds immediately rose Three or Four *per Cent.* but, in the Afternoon, when 'twas known she was still alive, they fell again to their former Value" (Boyer, *Political State, 7*, 640).

What was not noticed at the time was that few princes ever died so little celebrated in verse. "The reign of queen Anne [was] the most propitious and brilliant recorded in the annals of Britain" (Somerville, p. 571). It was an age in which "a Mr. Prior was Ambassador, and a Mr. Addison Secretary of State" (James Boswell, *London Journal 1762–1763*, ed. Frederick A. Pottle, New York, McGraw-Hill, 1950, p. 91). But Queen Anne's elegist was not Prior, Swift, or Gay, not Addison, Pope, or Garth, not Wycherley, Congreve, or Vanbrugh, but George Tollet, aged 17, who had matriculated at Christ Church, Oxford, only a few months before writing *A Ballad in Imitation of Habbie Simson the Piper of Kilbarchan* ("Ald England now may say alace, / For *Anne*'s Dead who was her Grace"), which has yet to find a publisher (BM MS. Harleian 7316, ff. 38–39).

Of five anonymous elegies on the death of Anne that *were* published:

> *On the much Lamented Death of the most Pious and Illustrious Princess, her late Majesty Queen Anne* ("From joyous Songs, and from the vocal Groves"), n.d.
>
> *Song in Commemoration of Royal Nann* ("My Nan she was good"), n.d.
>
> *A Mournful Copy of Verses on the much lamented Death of our late most Glorious Majesty Queen Anne, of Ever-Blessed Memory* ("What Joy did *England* once receive"), n.d.
>
> *The Mourning Court; Or, A Tribute of Tears, for the*

> *much Lamented Death of our Pious Queen Anne* ("With
> bleeding Heart and weeping Eyes"), n.d.
> *The Weeping Church-Men: Being a Mourning Copy of
> Verses on the Departure of our late Soveraign Queen Anne*
> ("You loyal Church-men far and near"), n.d.

only the first makes any pretensions whatsoever. The others are two
degrees *below* Grubstreet about on the level of bellman's verses, and
the last two in the list are set to the same tune of *Queen Dido,* or *Troy
Town* (Simpson, p. 587).

Nor were there any mock-elegies of the sort that sprang up after the
death of William III and provoked Defoe's angry outburst in *The Mock
Mourners.* Instead there are the two following poems, neither of them
elegies, but both of them embodying sophisticated literary responses to
"the *Greatest Revolution,* that, perhaps, ever happen'd . . . : *viz.* The
Prime Minister and Favourite disgraced; a Queen dead; and an ab-
sent Successor, against whom there was a great Party who began to
declare for his Competitor, proclaim'd in the Cities of *London* and
Westminster, with such Tranquility as can scarce be believ'd but by
them who were Eye-Witnesses of that *memorable Event*" (Boyer, *Political
State, 8,* 119).

An Excellent New Hymn,
Compos'd by the Priests of the Order of St. Perkin,
For the Use of High-Church, upon Their Approaching
Day of Humiliation, Being the Coronation-Day of
His Truly Protestant Majesty King George
(October? 1714)

Anne herself finally assured the Protestant succession and the exclusion of the pretender when, on her deathbed, she placed the white rod of the lord treasurer, which she had taken from Oxford only four days before, in the hands of Shrewsbury instead of Bolingbroke. She may have told Shrewsbury to *"use it for the Good of her People,"* according to the legend, but it is not even certain that she was fully conscious when she effected this symbolic transfer of power (Boyer, *Political State, 7,* 630; Trevelyan, *3,* 304).

Neither the Jacobites in London nor the Jacobites in Bar-le-Duc were ready with a plan to seize power (4*n.* below), but Shrewsbury acted quickly:

> letters were expressed to the Judges, to the Lords Lieutenant, to the Lord Mayor of London and the Lord Provost of Edinburgh, to all Mayors of Corporations, to Ormonde the Captain-General, to the Governors of garrisoned towns and forts, and last but not least to the commanders of the fleet on which all depended . . . An embargo was laid on all shipping in the ports; the Tower, Edinburgh Castle and other strongholds were revictualled and the garrisons increased; the troops were fetched home from Dunkirk and Flanders; the London militia were called out; horse and dragoons were concentrated round London; all over England and Scotland the horses and arms of Roman Catholics were ordered to be seized.

As a result, "Not a mouse . . . stirred" against the 54-year old elector of Hanover as he proceeded unhurriedly to London (Trevelyan, *3,* 305, 315). He was proclaimed George I, King of Great Britain, France, and Ireland, on 1 August. He entered London on 20 September, and was crowned in Westminster Hall on 20 October 1714. "One may easily conclude," as Lady Cowper put it, that the last "was not a Day of real Joy to the Jacobites" (*Diary of Mary Countess Cowper,* 1864, p. 5).

It is this lack of "real Joy" in the coronation of George I that is explored in *An Excellent New Hymn*. The Whig who wrote it "personates the Style and Manner of other Writers, whom he has a mind to expose" (Swift, *Prose, 1*, 3). And the exposure is total, for by the end of the antihymn, the Jacobite has lost his faith in Jacobitism: "Nature Rebels, and Fact declares / Our Principles are Lies" (71–72).

No external evidence has been discovered to determine either the author or the date of publication of this poem, reprinted here for the first time since 1714.

An Excellent New Hymn,

Compos'd by the Priests of the Order of St. Perkin, for the Use of High-Church, upon Their Approaching Day of Humiliation, Being the Coronation-Day of His Truly Protestant Majesty King George

Part I.

Oh! Why dost thou forsake us thus?
  Must thy griev'd *Zion* mourn?
Unto our dwindling Thousands soon,
  O *Lucifer*, return.

Proud *Hermodactyl*'s lofty head   5
  Is humbl'd to the Dust:
Lord *Gambol* now is laugh'd to scorn,
  In whom we plac'd our Trust.

And eke his Grace of *Mobington*,

4. *Lucifer*: The pretender was only six-months old when he forsook England in December 1688, and in the invasion of March 1708 he failed even to make a landing in the British Isles. Now there were rumors that he had turned Protestant, or been brought to London in disguise and would seize power after the queen had been assassinated and London burned (*The Present State of Fairy-Land*, 1713, p. 8; Macpherson, *History*, *2*, 530–31).

5. *Hermodactyl*: Oxford is Dr. Hermodactyl, the quack, in *The Enigmatical Court: Or, A Key to the High-German Doctor* (1714). He prefaces his mountebank speech by insisting that he will not address his audience "in a suppliant way" (ibid., p. 5).

6. *humbl'd to the Dust*: "The Q. has told all the Lords the reasons of her parting with him," Erasmus Lewis reported to Swift on 27 July 1714, the day that Oxford was dismissed, "viz. that he neglected all business, that he was seldom to be understood, that when he did explain himself, she could not depend upon the truth of what he said; that he never came to her at the time she appointed, that he often came drunk, that lastly to crown all he behav'd himself towards her with ill manner indecency & disrespect" (Swift, *Corr.*, *2*, 86). He was further humiliated on 19 September 1714 when he was introduced to George I at Greenwich as "le comte Oxford dont V. M. aura entendu parler" and "received with the most distinguishing contempt" (Klopp, *14*, 665; Bolingbroke, *A Letter to Sir William Windham*, 1753, p. 67).

7. *Lord Gambol*: Dr. Hermodactyl introduces Bolingbroke as Harry Gambol, "the smartest Fellow which belongs to my Stage [and] the prettiest Tumbler" (*The Enigmatical Court: Or, A Key to the High-German Doctor*, 1714, p. 10). Bolingbroke's flight to France in March 1715 to avoid answering questions about the treaty of Utrecht is recounted in *The Scamperer: Or Gambol's Gallop to France, To Save him from the Ax in Great Britain; with His Diary since His Departure*, 1715.

9. *his Grace of Mobington*: the London mob.

Full sore we do lament;   10
Who, in the Day of Tryal, stood
All Dangers to prevent:

That dreadful Day, when *Damere*'s Arm
Salvation for us wrought;
And *Purchas* at the Head of Mob,   15
'Gainst *Whiggish* Squadrons fought.

When Canting *Presbyterian* Tubs
Were made a Sacrifice,
And costly Flames in *Lincoln-Fields*,
Rose to the wond'ring Skies.   20

Whose interposing Interest did
Our Generals save from death,
And cheating *Tyburn* of its due,
Preserv'd their precious Breath.

Spitfire no more can do us good,   25

---

10. *we do lament:* The London mob had been uniformly high church in March 1710 during
the demonstrations for Sacheverell. But it was unpredictable in the weeks following the
queen's death on 1 August 1714. Upon the proclamation of George I, Oxford "was hiss'd all
the way by the mob, and some of them threw halters into his coach. This was not the effect of
Party, for the D: of Or[mon]d was huzza'd throughout the whole city . . . [and] an attempt
to affront [Bolingbroke] in the Calvacade . . . did not succeed" (Swift, *Corr., 2,* 102–03).

11. *the Day of Tryal:* 1 March 1710; see 17–18*n.* below.

13–15. *Damere . . . And Purchas:* Daniel Damere, one of the queen's watermen, and
George Purchase, "a Bailiff, who had before been a Life-Guard-Man, but was dismissed upon
some Misdemeanour," were the most notorious leaders of the mob raised for Sacheverell
(Boyer, *Annals,* 1710, p. 267; Luttrell, *6,* 559).

14. *Salvation . . . wrought:* "Being Drunk," Damere said, "I scarcely knew what then I
did" (*The Sorrowful Lamentation and Confession of Daniel Damere, The Queen's Waterman* ["Dear
Friends and Countrymen give Ear"], 1710).

16. *'Gainst Whiggish Squadrons:* "One of their Ringleaders, *George Purchase* by Name . . .
crying out to the Guards, *Damn ye, who are you for, High-Church or Low-Church* . . . ran res-
olutely with his Sword in his Hand, and made a full Pass at Captain *Hansberg*" (Boyer,
Annals, 1710, p. 267).

17–18. *Tubs . . . made a Sacrifice:* See p. 393 above; *High-Church Miracles,* 15*n.* above.

21. *interposing Interest:* Damere and Purchase were tried for high treason, found guilty, and
sentenced to be hanged (Luttrell, *6,* 572, 606). But both received the queen's most gracious
pardon, which was as inexplicable to Defoe (*The Age of Wonders,* 81–84, above) as it is to the
present poet. So it is explained here that it was the pretender who interposed to procure a
pardon for his "Generals" (who were called "*Admiral Damarie,* and *General Purchas*" in Wil-
liam Bisset, *The Modern Fanatick,* 1710, p. 10).

25. *Spitfire:* Sacheverell; cf. *A Character of Don Sacheverellio, Knight of the Firebrand,* Dublin,
[1710]; *On Dr. Sacheverell's Sermon Preach'd at St. Paul's, Nov. 5, 1709,* 13*n.* above.

The *Schismaticks* prevail:
And trusty *Rummer,* in disgrace,
May set up selling Ale.

For why, the Matter's very plain,
French Claret's out of Season: 30
Then who wou'd Factor be in *France,*
That hath or Sense or Reason?

Now honest *Brogue* to native Land,

26. *Schismaticks:* (accented on the first syllable) dissenters.

27. *Rummer:* There were two Rummer taverns, one between Charing Cross and Whitehall and the other in Queen Street, Cheapside. The latter, since it was known to Thomas Brown and William King, D.C.L., is more likely to have served "*French* Claret" (30) to high church-men (*Some Memoirs of Abel, Toby's Uncle,* 1726, p. 42; Thomas Brown, *Letters from the Dead to the Living,* 2nd ed., 1702, p. 15; William King, *The Original Works,* 3 vols., 1776, *2,* 304).

28. *set up selling Ale:* Ale (and port) were the Whig drinks. The Whig hostess Jenny Man boasted that she was "No Friend to Right Divine, / Therefore she must not sell French Wine" (*The Flying Post,* 6–8 November 1712).

31. *Factor:* a commercial representative, or commission merchant. English factors had long been resident in Spain, Portugal, and Italy, but not in France. Bolingbroke's attempt to reorient English trade toward France had been defeated by the Whigs and Hanoverian Tories in the House of Commons in June 1713 (Trevelyan, *3,* 254–58).

33. *Brogue:* Atty Brogue is Arthur Moore (*The Enigmatical Court: Or, A Key to the High-German Doctor,* 1714, p. 16). During 1712 John Robinson, bishop of Bristol, lord privy seal, and British plenipotentiary at Utrecht, had negotiated a reciprocal trade agreement with France "by the Lights he received from Mr. *Arthur Moore*" (Boyer, *History,* p. 556). Articles eight and nine of the commercial treaty signed on 11 April 1713 (Lamberty, *8,* 82–83) were wholly of Moore's drafting (*DNB, 13,* 788). Moore next undertook, as Bolingbroke's agent, to negoti-ate three explanatory clauses to the treaty of commerce with Spain. On 18 June 1713 when the Hanoverian Tories joined with the Whigs to vote down the commercial treaty with France, "the Member, who spoke most in favour of the bill, was the same, who had been chiefly employed in that treaty, Mr. *Arthur Moore;* but, some of his arguments being strained and precarious, the majority even of his own party adhered to the opinion of Sir *Thomas Hanmer*" (Tindal, *4,* i, 320*n.*). In February 1714 the South Sea Company began its own investigation of Moore. Whereas the directors believed that the commercial treaty with Spain had procured for the Company the entire Assiento de Negroes, they now discovered that half had been reserved for Queen Anne and Philip VI and 7 1/2 percent for "an *unknown Person,*" strongly suspected to be Bolingbroke, Lady Masham, and Arthur Moore (Boyer, *History,* pp. 666, 710). Moore sold out his stock in the South Sea Company on 11 June 1714 so that it could not be seized, but he could not prevent the company's censure of him for breach of trust on 7 July. Meanwhile the House of Lords had taken up the commercial treaty with Spain and discovered that the explanatory articles "(made at *Madrid,* after signing of the Treaty at *Utrecht*) [made] it impossible for our Merchants to carry on that Trade without certain Loss" (ibid., pp. 709–10). Under examination by the Lords, Moore "gave such con-tradictory answers relative to this transaction . . . that it became more mysterious and suspected" (Somerville, pp. 562–63) and evidence was offered that he had accepted a bribe of 2,000 louis d'ors a year from the French and "a sallery from the King of Spain, and the Grant from him of some Duties to the Queen" (Boyer, *History,* p. 710; *Wentworth Papers,* p.

Must Lacquey home again,
If that a Martyrdom by Hemp,   35
Does not his Flight restrain.

But if that trusty *Con* shou'd 'scape
Their *Whiggish* Cruelty,
O send him back, that he may write
Our Martyrologie.   40

Part II.

Why dost thou thus thy Slaves requite,
And not regard our Cry?
Lo! in the bitter Pangs of Death
Does thy lov'd *High-Church* lie.

Her worthy Sons (hard Fate!) from all   45
Employments are displac'd;
No hopes to rise again: And *Whigs*
Are with their Honours Grac'd.

Strangers do Lord it over us;
Oh hopeful Reformation!   50

---

398). Her Majesty put an unexpected end to her last parliament on 9 July. Moore "was to have been Chancellor of the Exchequer in Lord Bolingbroke's administration, if the Queen had not died" (*An Historical Essay on Mr. Addison*, 1783, p. 8).

34. *Lacquey home:* run alongside the master's [Swift's?] horse, like a footman, back to Ireland. Swift appears in *The Enigmatical Court: Or, A Key to the High-German Doctor*, 1714, p. 15, as Smut, "the Wittiest Knave" in the doctor's troupe.

37. *Con:* conformist, churchman.

42. *Cry:* "The avowed Partisans of the *Pretender* . . . by their dismal Countenances betray'd the Agony and Confusion they were in, to see their Hopes dash'd of a sudden" (Boyer, *Political State, 7,* 633).

46. *displac'd:* Bolingbroke was dismissed on 31 August 1714 even before George I reached England. Within a few days of his arrival on 20 September, the king had "begun to change all the Ministers, & to put in the Whiggs, every Post bringing us News of this Alteration, to the Grievous Mortification of that Party called Tories. The Duke of Marlborough is made Captain General of all the Forces in Room of the Duke of Ormond . . . The first Kt. that King George made is one Vanbrugh, a silly Fellow, who is the Architect at Woodstock" (Hearne, *4,* 409).

49. *Strangers:* foreigners. In his proclamation of November 1714 the pretender maintained "That the Revolution ruined the *English* Monarchy, laid the Foundation of a Republican Government, and devolv'd the Sovereign Power on the People; *and that* we are exposed to Arbitrary Power, and become a Prey to Foreigners [i.e. the Hanover dynasty]" (Boyer, *Political State, 8,* 552).

But where's a Prince to bless us with
    A second *Restoration?*

Thy Martyr'd Sire and thou, great *James,*
    Were wretchedly trapan'd,
And exil'd Pensioners, thy Race,   55
    Are in a Foreign Land.

Was it for this thy Servants strove
    With so much Care and Toil,
And Peace past Understanding made,
    For this their native Soil?   60

Was't all Religion Catholick
    And the Right Line t'exclude,
They ventur'd Neck and all, and shall
    Brunswick on us intrude?

Quickly arise to our relief,   65
    Our Faith begins to fail us:
For now the *Hanoverian*'s come,
    We fear the Rogues will Jail us.

Passive-Obedience backward shrinks,
    And *Non-Resistance* dies;   70
Nature Rebels, and Fact declares
    Our Principles are Lies.

55. *Pensioners:* The first questions that the pretender addressed to Louis XIV on the subject of his removal from France were, "Who is to provide for my maintenance? How much is it to be, and how shall it be paid?" (Macpherson, *Original Papers, 2,* 294).

57. *thy Servants:* Oxford, Bolingbroke, Arthur Moore, Matthew Prior, and the others who drafted and negotiated the treaty of Utrecht.

59. *Peace past Understanding:* the peace of Utrecht, "the peace of God, which passeth all understanding" (Philippians 4:7).

61–62. *Religion Catholick . . . t'exclude:* "The Succession . . . has been settl'd by Law on the Illustrious House of *Hanover,* not as their being *next A-Kin,* but purely on Account of their being *Protestants*" (*The Reasons and Necessity of the Duke of Cambridge's Coming To, and Residing In, Great Britain,* 1714, p. 14).

64. *Brunswick:* The electors of Hanover were a junior branch of the house of Braunschweig-Lüneburg.

69–70. *Passive-Obedience . . . And Non-Resistance dies:* With the accession of a king who owed his throne to acts of parliament, the reciprocal dogmata of divine-hereditary-indefeasible-right on the one hand and passive-obedience-non-resistance on the other were "as dead as Queen Anne the day after she dy'd" (Partridge, p. 676).

A Farewell to the Year 1714
(December 1714?)

The farewell genre probably was appropriated from the oral tradition, where it is represented by such examples as *Johny Armstrong's Last Goodnight*. It was recognized to be a genre at least as early as the 1680s in Samuel Woodforde's phrase, "Far[e]wells, Droll[s], and Shredds of Verse" (Johannes Prinz, *Rochesteriana*, Leipzig, 1926, p. 67). The literary tradition of the farewell is illustrated in the present series by eight examples, beginning with *The Banish'd Priests' Farewell to the House of Commons* (1673), and including *The King's Farewell to Danby* ("Farewell, my dear Danby, my pimp and my cheat") (1679), *Sir Thomas Armstrong's Last Farewell* (1684), *The Salamanca Doctor's Farewell* (May 1685), and *Farewell to England* ("Farewell false friends, farewell ill wine") (1697), to which the present poem may owe something of its form—the repetition of "Farewell"—as well as its genre (*POAS*, Yale, *1*, 204; *2*, 111; *3*, 563; *4*, 15; *5*, 521).

But the elegiac tone of *A Farewell to the Year 1714*, which contrasts so sharply with the flippancy and cynicism of the earlier examples, is all the contrivance of its anonymous Tory author. "After the melancholy scene at Kensington, and the hurry at London," there was time for reflection. John Berkeley, Lord Berkeley, who was no poet, was so stunned that he could "hardly fix to doe anything" (*Wentworth Papers*, p. 409). Henry St. John, Lord Bolingbroke, who *was* a poet—"the greatest Libeller and State Ballad-maker in *Britain*" (Oldmixon, *History*, p. 476), none of whose libels or state-ballads can now be identified—was equally sobered. "The Earl of Oxford was remov'd on Tuesday," he wrote, "the Queen dyed on Sunday . . . what a world is this, & how does fortune banter us?" (Swift, *Corr.*, *2*, 101).

What was, for the Whigs, "the *Greatest Revolution*, that, perhaps, ever happen'd" (p. 604 above), was, for the Tories, the greatest anticlimax. For these feelings of emptiness and loss the author of *A Farewell to the Year 1714* was able to find expression as effective as Goldsmith's in *The Deserted Village* (line 31–34):

> These were thy charms, sweet village; sports like these,
> With sweet succession, taught even toil to please;
> These round thy bowers their chearful influence shed,
> These were thy charms—But all these charms are fled.

No external evidence has been found to determine either the author or the date of composition of this poem, published here for the first time.

A FAREWELL TO THE YEAR 1714

Farewell old year, for Thou canst ne're return,
No more than the great Queen for whom we mourn;
Farewell old year, with thee the Stuart race
Its Exit made, which long our Isle did grace;
Farewell old year, the Church hath lost in Thee   5
The best Defender it will ever see;
Farewell old year, for Thou to us did bring
Strange changes in our State, a stranger King;
Farewell old year, for thou with Broomstick hard
Hast drove poor Tory from St. James's Yard;   10
Farewell old year, old Monarch, and old Tory,
Farewell old England, Thou hast lost thy glory.

2. *the great Queen:* Not even Prior could make of Queen Anne another Gloriana, but not even the duchess of Marlborough could reduce her to "a cypher" (*Account of the Conduct*, p. 229). It was Harley who understood the truth: "The Queen," he said, "is the centre of power" (Hardwicke, *2*, 487).

6. *The best Defender:* This answers the question that John Smith asked at the Sacheverell trial, "I would desire to know who the Doctor takes to be the Defender of the Faith" (*Tryal of Dr. Henry Sacheverell*, p. 171).

9. *Broomstick:* with a pun on "Brunswick" (see textual notes, p. 696 below, and *An Excellent New Hymn*, 64n. above).

10. *St. James's Yard:* The royal palace is "an irregular brick building, without one single beauty on the outside to recommend it . . . in the front next St. James's-street there appears little more than an old gatehouse; and on passing through the gate we enter a little square court, with a piazza on the west side of it leading to the grand stair case" (Noorthouck, pp 718–19). Through this court that was always crowded and up this grand staircase poor Tories had passed to the presence chamber on levee days to solicit royal favor (James P. Malcolm, *Londinium Redivivum*, 4 vols., 1803–07, *4*, 238). One of the places where George I had been proclaimed on 1 August was before the gate of St. James's palace (Boyer, *Political State, 8*, 118).

11. *Farewell . . . Tory:* "The grief of my soul is this," Bolingbroke wrote a few days after he had been dismissed in August 1714, "I see plainly that the Tory party is gone" (Macpherson, *Original Papers, 2*, 651).

1715

Pasquin to the Queen's Statue
at St. Paul's, during the Procession, Jan. 20. 1715
(January 1715?)

The 20th day of January 1715 "being appointed as a Thanksgiving for K. George's safe Arrival & his quiet taking Possession of these Kingdoms," Mr. Atkinson of Queen's College, Oxford, preached a flattering sermon on the text, *"By me Kings reign & Princes decree Justice"* (Hearne, 5, 18). But the application was false, for George I reigned not *gratia dei,* but by two acts of parliament (p. 409 above), and the heir to the throne of Britain by divine right waited in the wings to make his entrance on 22 December 1715.

It is only fair to let the Jacobites have the last word on the subject of the Hanoverian succession celebrated on 20 January 1715, for they stood to be the chief losers by it. The Whigs, who had carefully cultivated Georg Ludwig since 1701 (*POAS,* Yale, *6,* 659), could hope that a dynastic revolution and the impending election would sweep them back to power. The moderate Tories, one of whose leaders, Sir Thomas Hanmer, had been Speaker in the parliament that had been dissolved only 15 days before, and another of whose leaders, the admirable Shrewsbury, had been lord treasurer until October 1714, could still hope for a share of power in another bipartisan government. But the Jacobites had nothing to hope for.

Their frustration is expressed in a large body of verse and prose of which *Pasquin to the Queen's Statue* is a good sample. "Nothing coud be grosser," Horace Walpole recalled, "than the ribaldry that was vomited out in lampoons, libels, & every channel of abuse against the Sovereign and the new court, and chanted even in their hearing about the public streets" (*Reminiscences Written by Mr Horace Walpole in 1788,* ed. Paget Toynbee, Oxford, Clarendon Press, 1924, p. 30). *Pasquin to the Queen's Statue* supplies good evidence that Horace Walpole's memory was not at fault.

Although there is no external evidence for the date of publication of the poem, it cannot have been very far from 20 January 1715, the date of the event it celebrates.

Nor would there be any point in mentioning that line 26 repeats a favorite locution of William Shippen, were it not for the fact that Shippen was sent to the Tower on 2 March 1718 for making the same complaint on the floor of the House of Commons that is made in line 65 below. He urged the triumphant Whigs to advise the king "that our government does not stand on the same foundation with his German dominions, which . . . are obliged to keep up standing armies in time of peace" (*Reliquiae Hearnianae: The Remains of Thomas Hearne, M.A.*, ed. Philip Bliss, 2 vols., Oxford, Oxford University Press, 1857, *1*, 384–85).

The Statue of Our Sovereign Lady QUEEN ANNE, being of y finest Marble, erected in Honour of Her Majesty at the West end of St PAULS CATHEDRALL London.

The Statue of Queen Anne by Francis Bird erected in 1712 in St. Paul's Yard, an anonymous engraving

Pasquin to the Queen's Statue
at St. Paul's, during the Procession, Jan. 20. 1715

Behold he comes to make thy People groan,
And with their Curses to ascend thy Throne;
A Clod-pate, base, inhuman, jealous Fool,

Title. *Pasquin:* "The . . . Statue of *Pasquin* at *Rome,* is grown famous, not half so much for the Performances of the Person who it Represented, as for the use made of it since it was set up; under this Figure were always Posted Libels and Satyrs, Papers of Personal Scandal, and all manner of Sarcasms, either on the *Roman* Government, or on the Actions of other Princes and Nations; from hence, a Lampoon in a Modern Dialect, is new-Christen'd, and now call'd Pasquinade" (*Review,* 13 May 1712). The archetypal pasquinade is a dialogue between Pasquin and another statue, found in the Campo Martio and christened Marforio, *a foro Martis.*

the Queen's Statue: In this poem the other statue is that of Queen Anne by Francis Bird, erected in 1712 in St. Paul's Yard, facing Ludgate Hill. "A public statue in London," it has been said, "needs to be very bad [see illustration, p. 619] to attract to its demerits any special attention" (*DNB,* 2, 535), but Anne's statue provided the occasion for the following popular verses:

> Brandy Nan, Brandy Nan,
> You're left in the lurch
> With your face to the gin shop,
> And your back to the Church.

Coincidentally, it was in June 1712 that Swift reported, "the Qu—— has done with Braces . . . and nothing ill has happend to her since; so she has a new Lease of her Life" (Swift, *Journal,* 2, 542).

the Procession: "On *Thursday,* the 20th of *January* [1715], being the Day appointed for a General Thanksgiving to Almighty *GOD,* for the King's happy and peaceable Accession to the Throne, His Majesty, with their RR.HH. the Prince and Princess of *Wales,* attended by the chief Officers of State, Privy Counsellors, others of the Nobility, and some of the foreign Ministers, was pleased to go from St. *James's* Palace to the Cathedral Church of St. *Paul's,* where after Divine Service, and the Singing of *Te Deum* set to excellent Musick, by Dr. *Crofts,* an excellent Sermon was preach'd by the Right Reverend Dr. *Richard Willis* Lord Bishop of *Glocester.* The Lord Mayor and Court of Aldermen of *London* gave their Attendance in the accustomed Manner; the City Companies in their Liveries were in their respective Stands, the Streets being lined by the Militia: The Guns in the Park were fired on a Signal at the Singing of *Te Deum* in the Cathedral, as they were also at his Majesty's Setting out from, and Return to his Palace: And at Night there were Illuminations, Bonefires, and other Publick Demonstrations of Joy" (Boyer, *Political State, 9,* 59).

2. *Curses:* What these were may be inferred from the demonstrations on 20 October 1715, upon the coronation of George I. In Bristol a mob kicked out the bonfires, *"crying out,* Down with the *Roundheads,* God bless Doctor *Sacheverel."* In Birmingham the cry was "Down with the *Whigs."* The Reading mob was even more explicit, crying, "No *Hanover* . . . No Foreign Government" (Boyer, *Political State, 8,* 363, 367–68). The most explicit were those who "added, 'D——m King *George!*' " (*Diary of Mary Countess Cowper,* 1864, p. 19).

3. *Clod-pate:* "The King's character may be comprised in very few words. In private life

The Jest of *Europe,* and the Faction's Tool.
Heav'n never heard of such a Right Divine,   5
Nor Earth e'er saw a Successor like thine:
For if in Sense or Politicks you fail'd,
'Twas when his lousy long Succession you entail'd.
    Let the ungrateful Wretch think what you've done,
For all his beggar'd Race, and Bastard Son.   10
See his mock Daughter and her Offspring shine
In all those blazing Brilliants that were thine:
Drunk with incestuous Lust, the cunning Jilt
Pretends Religion to conceal her Guilt.

---

he would have been called an honest blockhead" (*The Letters and Works of Lady Mary Wortley Montagu,* ed. James A. Stuart-Wortley-Mackenzie, Lord Wharncliffe, 3 vols., 1837, *1,* 107).

inhuman, jealous: "Whether guilty or not (and no known evidence of her guilt exists, except in a correspondence of disputable authenticity), the Electoral Princess Sophia Dorothea was accused of a criminal intrigue with Count Philip von Königsmark, a Swedish adventurer . . . in the Hanoverian military service . . . Against the princess . . . sentence of divorce was pronounced [on 28 December 1694] on the ground of malicious desertion, and she was detained a prisoner at Ahlden, near Celle, till her death, 3 Nov. 1726" (*DNB,* 7, 1026; Zedler, *4,* 1164).

4. *the Faction's Tool:* See 26n. below.

5. *Right Divine:* In the words of a Jacobite broadside, it was James Francis Edward Stuart "To whom the Crown belongs by Right Divine" (*Let Each have their Own* ["When his Lov'd *Germans* GEORGE was forc'd to leave"], n. p., n.d.).

7. *you:* "the Queen's Statue."

10. *Bastard Son:* Doubts about the legitimacy of Georg August (Hearne, *9,* 317) were raised by his mother's alleged liaisons with Cosmo III de Medici, grand duke of Tuscany, as well as with Königsmark in 1694.

11. *mock Daughter:* The real daughter of George I, Sophie Dorothea, did not come to England because she had married in 1705 the crown prince of Prussia, who succeeded as Friedrich Wilhelm I in 1713. The context makes it clear that George's "mock Daughter" is his daughter-in-law, Karoline Wilhelmine of Ansbach (1683–1737), who married Georg August in 1705. George I called her *"Cette Diablesse"* (*Reminiscences Written by Mr Horace Walpole in 1788,* ed. Paget Toynbee, Oxford, Clarendon Press, 1924, p. 27).

Offspring: By the time they came to England, Caroline and Prince George had four children: Frederick, born in January 1707, who remained in Hanover, and three daughters who were brought to England: Anne, born 1709; Amelia, born 1710; and Caroline, born 1713.

12. *blazing Brilliants:* "The new King . . . instantly distributed what he found amongst his German Favourites . . . [but] Caroline never obtained of the late Queen's jewels but one pearl-necklace" (*Reminiscences Written by Mr Horace Walpole in 1788,* ed. Paget Toynbee, Oxford, Clarendon Press, 1924, p. 23n.).

14. *Pretends Religion:* Karoline refused in 1703 to marry the archduke Charles, later the emperor Charles VI, on the grounds that she could not abandon her Protestant faith (Ruby L. Arkell, *Caroline of Ansbach, George the Second's Queen,* Oxford University Press, 1939, pp. 8–14); cf. *Switch and Spur,* 70n. above.

Kings cou'd not draw her from her Brother's Bed;   15
Till he was slain, she wou'd not yield to wed.
See how her Hen-peck'd Stripling struts with Pride,
To *George* alone in little Sense ally'd:
With Head-piece fram'd miraculously thin,
All Brush without, and Emptiness within.   20
See his fantastick Air and foreign Mein,
His aukward Gesture, and affected Grin,
Which apish *Bullock* imitates in vain.

15. *Brother:* Karoline's brother, Wilhelm Friedrich, was born in 1685. When their father died in 1686, the children were taken to live first in Eisenach, and then, when their mother married the elector of Saxony in 1692, to Dresden, where manners and morals are said to have been "extraordinary." Upon the death of their mother in 1696, the children lived in Berlin with their guardians, the elector of Brandenburg and his wife, Sophie Charlotte of Hanover. Upon the death of Sophie Charlotte in 1704, Karoline and her brother lived in Triesdorf until her marriage in September 1705 to Georg August of Hanover, which she made conditional upon Wilhelm Friedrich's approval (ibid., pp. 5–26).

16. *slain:* Wilhelm Friedrich in fact survived until January 1723 (Zedler, *2*, 474).

17. *Hen-peck'd:* Karoline's "first thought on her marriage was to secure to herself the sole and whole direction of her spouse" and Georg August remained "entirely under the government of his wife" until her death in 1737. (*The Letters and Works of Lady Mary Wortley Montagu*, ed. James A. Stuart-Wortley-Mackenzie, Lord Wharncliffe, 3 vols., 1837, *1*, 118, 119). Even when he became king he was taunted in a popular rhyme, "You may strut, dapper George, but 'twill all be in vain, / We know 'tis queen Caroline not you does reign."

Stripling: This may be ironical, for Prince George was 31 years old. "Stripling" may refer to his small size (William Coxe, *Memoirs of the Life and Administration of Sir Robert Walpole*, new ed., 3 vols., 1800, *2*, 3).

Pride: "His pride told him that he was placed above constraint . . . [and] he looked on all the men and women that he saw as creatures he might kick or kiss for his diversion; and, whenever he met with any opposition in those designs, he thought his opposers insolent rebels to the will of God" (*The Letters and Works of Lady Mary Wortley Montagu*, ed. James A. Stuart-Wortley-Mackenzie, Lord Wharncliffe, 3 vols., 1837, *1*, 117).

18. *To George . . . ally'd:* Since Georg August believed in his mother's innocence and on one occasion at least tried to force his way past the guards to see her (3*n*. above), and since he had been invited in 1711 to live in England "without the knowledge, or against the inclination of George the First" (William Coxe, *Memoirs of the Life and Administration of Sir Robert Walpole*, new ed., 3 vols., 1800, *1*, 134), he was always at odds with his father. In January 1718, George I ordered the prince and his family to remove themselves from St. James's palace.

little Sense: Prince George was "unhappily under the direction of a small understanding" (*The Letters and Works of Lady Mary Wortley Montagu*, ed. James A. Stuart-Wortley-Mackenzie, Lord Wharncliffe, 3 vols., 1837, *1*, 117).

19. *Head-piece:* skull or cranium (*OED*). Prince George had a remarkably high, receding forehead.

23. *Bullock:* William Bullock (1657?–1740?) was an actor who specialized in low comedy roles. He played at Drury Lane from 1696 to 1706 and at that theatre and the Haymarket from 1706 to 1715. He was said to be "the best Comedian that has trod the Stage since *Nokes*

Had you, great Queen, ne'er broke the Nation's Laws,
And wrong'd your Brother, and your Brother's Cause: 25
Ne'er by the Hell-born Faction been dismay'd,
By Fools deluded, or by Knaves betray'd;
Brunswick a petty Prince had still remained;
By Mercenary Troops his Court maintain'd,
And over Slaves and *German* Boobies reign'd: 30
On Leeks and Garlick still regal'd his Taste;
In dirty Doulas Shirts and Fustian drest:
Been once a Month from Bugs and Lice made clean,
The only Free-born Subjects of his Reign.
　　Was it for this your Ashes are abus'd,   35
Your Servants libell'd, and the Peace accus'd?
You to the Church distributed your Store;
Gave to the Distress'd, the Innocent, and Poor:
But now your vast Revenue's all bestow'd
On Punks at home, and Managers abroad.   40
Legions of Pimps, and Whores they scarce can score,
Infest this Island and the Land devour;

---

and *Lee*" and his asparagus-eating routine was much envied (*A Comparison between the Two Stages*, 1702, p. 199; *The Tatler*, 20–22 June 1710).

　24. *broke the Nation's Laws:* Anne broke the law of primogeniture by succeeding to the throne to the exclusion of the heir male (*5n.* above).

　26. *the Hell-born Faction:* the Whigs. "The *King* is as we wish upon the Subject of Parties" (*Diary of Mary Countess Cowper*, 1864, p. 31) and none but Whigs were appointed to the new ministry. Cf. Shippen, *Moderation Display'd*, 3–4, 360–66, above.

　32. *dirty Doulas:* "A coarse kind of linen" (*OED*, citing *1 Henry IV*, III.3.79: "filthy Doulas").

　Fustian: "a kind of coarse cloth made of cotton and flax" (*OED*).

　35. *Ashes are abus'd:* Anne's death was openly celebrated by the Whigs: "Ipswich Aug 21 [1714]. Altho' we are deeply concernd for the Loss of the Queen we can't forbear giving some Account of the indecent & disrespectful Behavior of our Whigs upon the News of the Death of the Queen which was brot the 2d instant. The next morning Orders were sent to the Church wardens to command them to ring their Bells . . . so that we had ringing in most Churches all day long" (Exeter City Library MS. Ancient Letters 471).

　36. *Servants libell'd:* See p. 605 above, and *The Enigmatical Court: Or, A Key to the High-German Doctor* (1714), in prose.

　Peace accus'd: Besides in the verse of Mainwaring and D'Urfey above, the attack on the treaty of Utrecht was kept up in such prose pamphlets as Steele's *The Importance of Dunkirk Consider'd* (September 1713), *The Crisis* (January 1713), and *The French Faith Represented in the Present State of Dunkirk* (July 1714).

　37. *to the Church:* See Charles Darby?, *The Oxfordshire Nine*, 17n. above.

　40. *Punks:* Cf. *The Blessings Attending George's Accession and Coronation* ("The golden Age is now again restor'd"), n.p., n.d.:

But this insatiate Brood still gape for more:
More than for Native Kings was e'er decreed:
But Beggars hors'd will to the Devil speed.   45
Pigburgh and *Kilmanseck,* the modest Toast,
Will soon have Pensions at the Nation's Cost,
Beyond what *Portland,* or what *Orkney* boast.
    But since on Knavish Models *George* is split,
By *Townshend* cully'd, and by *Churchill* bit;   50

Hither he brought
. . . *Himself,* his *Pipe, Close-stool* and *Louse;*
Two *Turks,* three *W——es,* and half a dozen *Nurses:*
Five hundred *Germans,* all with empty Purses.

At the time of his death in 1727 it was said that George 1 was "quite rotten & eat up with whoring" (Hearne, *9,* 332).

45. Proverbial (Tilley, B239).

46. *Pigburgh:* Johanna Sophie (1673–1743), daughter of Heinrich Friedrich, Count Hohenlohe-Langenburg, became the countess of Schaumburg-Lippe, called the countess of Bückeburg (Picquebourg), when she married Friedrich Christian, Count Schaumburg-Lippe-Bückeburg, from whom she was separated in 1702. She was a *dévote,* who published *Gottschallenden Hertzen Music* at Nürnberg in 1703. In October 1714 she came to England as "Hofmeisterin" in the household of Caroline, princess of Wales (Zedler, *17,* 1530, 1545; *Briefe der Gräfin Johanna Sophie zu Schaumburg-Lippe,* ed. Friedrich-Wilhelm Schaer, Rinteln, C. Bösendahl, 1968, pp. 1, 31; Ruby L. Arkell, *Caroline of Ansbach,* Oxford, London, 1939, pp. 66–67).

Kilmanseck: Sophie Charlotte, Countess von Platen and Hallermund, and *jure mariti* Baroness von Kielmannsegge (c. 1673–1725), whom "time and very bad paint had left without any of the charms which had once attracted him," arrived in London in September 1714 with George I. This "was enough to make her called his mistress, or at least so great a favourite that the whole court began to pay her uncommon respect" (*The Letters and Works of Lady Mary Wortley Montagu,* ed. James A. Stuart-Wortley-Mackenzie, Lord Wharncliffe, 3 vols., 1837, *1,* 109, 111). What Horace Walpole chiefly remembered was her great bulk—she became known as the Elephant and Castle (GEC, *4,* 80–81)—and the paint: "two acres of cheeks spread with crimson, an ocean of neck that overflowed & was not distinguished from the lower part of her body, and no part restrained by stays" (*Reminiscences Written by Mr Horace Walpole in 1788,* ed. Paget Toynbee, Oxford, Clarendon Press, 1924, p. 30).

47. *soon have Pensions:* The prophecy was generously fulfilled. Kielmannsegge "had two gallons of beer a day for herself and servants in 1714. In June 1715 she requested and was given four and a half gallons; by April 1717 she had twelve barrels a month, increased on 17 April to fourteen, and on 6 June to sixteen. Her allowance of sherry, claret, bread and candles grew correspondingly." By 1718 it was decided to give her £3,000 a year and a kitchen in lieu of board and other allowances (J. M. Beattie, *The English Court in the Reign of George I,* Cambridge, Cambridge University Press, 1967, p. 80).

48. *Portland:* William III lavished such grants on his favorite, Willem Bentinck, earl of Portland, that he made him "the richest Subject in *Europe*" (Macky, p. 62).

Orkney: William settled on his mistress, Elizabeth Villiers, in May 1695 "nearly all the Irish estates of King James," said to be worth £25,995 13s. a year (GEC, *10,* 108). She then married her cousin, George Hamilton, who was created earl of Orkney in January 1696.

50. *Townshend:* Charles Townshend, second viscount Townshend and Horace Walpole's

Take it from me that his Destruction's sure,
Nor can his ill-got Monarchy endure:
For when known Villains at the Helm preside,
And Kings against themselves with Faction side;
When impious Rage against the Church they boast,   55
Her Sons oppress'd, the Constitution lost;
Then soon abandon'd by the Rabble Rout,
Despis'd and hiss'd, and trampled under Foot,
A King becomes a vile detested Name,

---

brother-in-law (*POAS*, Yale, *6*, 627*n*.), signed the notorious barrier treaty with the Dutch in October 1709 (p. 541 above). In February 1712 he was accused in parliament of exceeding his instructions and voted an enemy to his country (*DNB, 17*, 1037). But through his friendship with Andreas Gottlieb von Bernstorff, Hans Caspar von Bothmer, and Jean de Robethon, the Hanoverian "Managers abroad," he was appointed George I's first secretary of state in September 1714. Lord Hervey called him "violent, haughty, cruel, impatient, &c., and . . . 'more tenacious of his opinion than of his word.'" The princess of Wales called him "the sneeringest, fawningest Knave that ever was" (GEC, *12*, i, 805*n*.). One of the things he deceived the king about was the merit of his rivals: "If my Lord Halifax said anything," Townshend told the king that he spoke "in favour of the Tories; if any other spoke," Townshend said "he was of my Lord Halifax's party; so that no one could have a fair hearing but himself" (*The Letters and Works of Lady Mary Wortley Montagu*, ed. James A. Stuart-Wortley-Mackenzie, Lord Wharncliffe, 3 vols., 1837, *1*, 122–23).

 Churchill: Upon Anne's death, Marlborough hastened to reach England before the king arrived and was received "amidst the unanimous Acclamations of the People, by above 50 Coaches of the Nobility, Gentry, and Aldermen of this City, and attended by several Hundred of the Citizens on Horseback" (*The Flying Post*, 3–5 August 1714). Upon George's arrival, one of his first acts was to sign a warrant reinstating Marlborough as captain general of the forces, master general of the ordnance, and colonel of the first regiment of foot guards. But the old leaven of avarice still worked within him and Marlborough's demands for more and more finally disgusted even the Whigs, including Sir John Perceval: "The Italian says, Se non é vero e ben trovato, and here I may well apply that proverb to the D of Marlborough who craves after Imployments, and tho' consider'd in the following manner by the King, viz. One Son in law Ld. L[ieutenan]t of Ireland, another Ld. Chamberlain to the princess, the 3d Cofferer, his Nephew Comptroller of the household, his Brother in law Clark of the Green-Cloth . . . yet notwithstanding these, and twice as many more which he has procured for his more remote relations and Creatures, he is yet dissatisfied, and resolves to be so, unless he gains to himself also the important place of Groom of the Stole to his Majesty" (BM MS. Add. 47027, f. 178).

 51. *Destruction's sure:* One of the mistresses of George I refused at first to come to England, "fearing that the people of England, who, she thought, were accustomed to use their kings barbarously, might chop off his head in the first fortnight" (*The Letters and Works of Lady Mary Wortley Montagu*, ed. James A. Stuart-Wortley-Mackenzie, Lord Wharncliffe, 3 vols., 1837, *1*, 108).

 55. *against the Church:* George I, a Lutheran, knew that most of the lower clergy of the Church of England, by promoting indefeasible hereditary right, had opposed the Hanoverian succession. So he did not favor the church. In December he issued "Directions," signed by Townshend, which commanded, among other things, that the clergy not "intermeddle in any Affairs of State" (Boyer, *Political State, 8*, ii, 536–40).

And quits his Life as well as Crown with Shame. 60
Be this that bold usurping Upstart's Fate,
Who on another's Throne would fain look Great:
Sworn to maintain, yet laughs at all the Laws,
And by Tyrannick Rule supports his Cause:
By Redcoats and by Arms enforcing Sway, 65
By hungry Bloodhounds, and by Birds of Prey.
He said; and strait the curs'd Usurper's Soul,
Like *Ætna* heav'd, his Eye-balls wildly rowl:
Such is his Rage, and so the Monster stares,
When the dread Ghost of *Coningsmark* appears. 70
And *Mahomet* and *Mustapha* prepare
To stem by Force his Madness and Despair.

65. *Redcoats:* In September 1714 there was a rumor that "some Great Men discourst lately in their Merryment that there is a design to form the militia next sessions into a standing body and to place the half pay officers over them" (Bodl. MS. Ballard 31, f. 129). In the election of January–February 1715, therefore, the Tories campaigned for "No Standing Army" and against the Whigs' "Augmentation of Troops for the better Suppressing of Mobs and Riots" ([Francis Atterbury?], *English Advice to the Freeholders of England,* 1714, pp. 26, 31).

70. *Coningsmark:* Philipp Christoph, count of Königsmark (1665–94) was a Swedish soldier of fortune who fought bulls in Spain, murdered or procured the murder of Thomas Thynne of Longleat (Luttrell, *1,* 164), and became the lover or the supposed lover of Sophie Dorothea, the electoral princess of Hanover (3n. above). When Georg Ludwig heard the rumors, he ordered Königsmark "to quit his dominions the next day. The Princess, surrounded by Women too closely connected with her Husband, & consequently enemies of the Lady they injured, was persuaded by them to suffer the Count to kiss her hand before his abrupt departure; & he was actually introduced by them into her bedchamber the next morning before She rose. From that moment He disappeared, nor was it known what became of him, till on the death of George 1st, on his son the new King's first journey to Hanover, some alterations in the palace being ordered by him, the body of Konismark was discovered under the floor of the Electoral Princess's dressingroom" (*Reminiscences Written by Mr Horace Walpole in 1788,* ed. Paget Toynbee, Oxford, Clarendon Press, 1924, p. 21).

71. *Mahomet and Mustapha:* Two Turks whom Georg Ludwig had taken prisoner at Buda in 1686 and who had become his most trusted servants, accompanied him to England. The suspicion that they had strangled Königsmark fed the rumors that the king "keeps two Turks for abominable uses" (BM MS. Add. 47028, f. 7v).

72. *Madness:* There were also rumors that George was "frantick often times and walks about in his Shirt" (ibid.).

In the textual notes, sigma, Σ, stands for the sum of the unspecified witnesses (W. W. Greg, *The Calculus of Variants,* Oxford, Clarendon Press, 1927, p. 14). A line number (or numbers) followed immediately by the lemma, indicates that the variants to the right of the lemma replace the whole line (or lines). Letters in parentheses, e.g. *F———(ch),* stand for letters that are found in some unspecified witnesses but not all.

TEXTUAL NOTES

The History and Fall of the Conformity-Bill

Copy text: Aa

Collation: Besides the printed copy text (*Aa*), three more printed texts and 18 manuscript copies have been recovered, all collaterally derived from the copy text:

POAS, 1704, *3,* 425–31 (Yale copy)	*Aa*
PRSA, 1705, pp. 557–61 (BM copy)	*Ab*
University of Chicago MS. PR1195.C72, pp. 136–40	*Ac*
Osborn MS. Chest II, No. 58	*Ad*
Hertfordshire County R. O. MS. Cowper Box 46, Lampoons	*Ae*
Staffordshire R. O. MS. Dartmouth D.1778. V.1117	*Af*
Berkshire R. O. MS. Trumbull Add. 17	*Ag*
Portland MS. Pw V 42, pp. 443–53	*Ah*
Bodl. MS. Firth b.21 (51)	*Aj*
Political Merriment: Or, Truths Told to Some Tune, 1715, pp. 313–19 (Case 280[3]) (Yale copy)	*Ak*
Hertfordshire County R. O. MS. Cowper Box 11	*Al*
Worcestershire R. O. MS. Lechmere Box 40	*Am*
Osborn MS. Chest II, No. 18, pp. 48–54	*An*
Bodl. MS. Rawl. poet. 169, f. 28r	*Ao*
BM MS. Add. 40060, ff. 41–45	*Ap*
Bodl. MS. Rawl. D.360, ff. 62–63	*Aq*
Carlisle R. O. MS. D/Lons	*Ar*
BM MS. Stowe 305, ff. 280–81	*As*
Carlisle R. O. MS. D/Lons	*At*
Harvard MS. Eng. 834 (18)	*Au*
Harvard MS. Eng. 834 (19)	*Av*
The Life and Posthumous Works of Arthur Maynwaring, Esq;, 1715, pp. 40–41	*Aw*

Afgh appear to be products of a scriptorium. *Afg* are separate copies. *Af* has been folded in a letter fold, and *Ag* in a legal fold and endorsed "Ballad on Conformity Bill. 1703/4." *Ah* is part of a factory anthology. *Aq* includes only lines 1–64 and *Aw* only lines 37–64, 137–40.

Title: The History and Fall of the Conformity-Bill. Being an excellent new Song, to the Tune of Chivy-Chase *Aab*   The History and Fall of the Conformity Bill

627

Ach   The History (and Fall) of the Conformity Bill, being an Excellent New Song to the Tune (of the) Ladies Fall (&c.) *Adfgjklmnopq*   The History (and Fall) of the Conformity Bill being a(n) (Excellent) new Ballad to the tune of the Ladys Fall *Aer*   The (History and) Fall of the Conformity Bill; Being an Excellent New Song to the Tune of the Ladyes fall or Chevy Chase *Astu*   To the Tune of Chivy Chase *Av*   [none] *Aw*

11–14 *omitted Au*   53–56 *follows* 60 *Aj*   61–64 *omitted Ar*   62 Whence ever] Whenever *Aabcdgjksu*   Where-ever *Aw*   65–152 *omitted Aq*   69–76 *omitted Al*   69–80 *omitted Ap*   69–84 *omitted Ag*   85 St. *Stephen's*] And Stephen's *Aabc*   Oh *Stephen's Ak*   As Stephens *Ap*   This chappell *As*   hight] height *Aabcefghkpsv*   Light *Adt*   99 *Edward Seymour . . . John How*] *E(d)——(d) S(ey)——(r) . . . J——(n) H——(w) Aabcekrt*   109 *Harley's*] *H(ar)——y's Aabckt*   120 *Burnet's*] *B——ts Aabckr*   125 *Nottingham*] *N(ott)——(g)——(m) Aabcdekrt*   127 *Guernsey*] *G(uern)——(y) Aabcdekr*   130 Grubster] Grub-street *Aju*   131–32 *omitted Au*   132 *Hedges*] *H——(ge)s Aabcr*   140 Succession] Suc——on *Aabc*   149–52 *enclosed in square brackets Aabc omitted Σ Aabdeghpr adds:* Sic cecinit R(obert) Wis(e)dom(e)   *Ar further adds:* I doe appoint Timothy Goodwin &c to print this ballad and that no other do presume to print the same   R. H.

On the Greatest Victory

Copy text: D
Collation: The text survives in nine widely-varying manuscripts as well as in the printed copy text:

Folger MS. M.b.12, p. 304	*A*
Portland MS. Pw V 44, p. 432	*B*
Essex R. O. MS D/DW.Z.4	*C*
POAS, 1707, *4*, 113 (Yale copy)	*D*
Univ. of Chicago MS. PR1195.M73, p. 141	*E*
NLS MS. 3807, p. 286	*F*
BM MS. Portland Loan Arundell 11, f. 36	*G*
Carlisle R. O. MS. D/Lons	*H*
Hertfordshire County R. O. Cowper MS. Box 46	*J*
Harvard MS. Eng. 606, p. 51	*K*

Of these, *AB* are assumed to represent the archetype most closely. *J* includes ten lines, in a different stanza form, presumably by another hand.

Title: On the Greatest Victory Perhaps that ever was or ever will be by Sir George Rook. In Imitation of Sternhold and Hopkins *AB*   On the Sea-fight *C*   A Song on the same [The Sea Fight between Sir G. R. and Tolouse, 1704] *D*   On the Sea-fight Anno *E*   On the Navale Ingadgment in the Mediterr: betwixt the

English & Dutch & the French anno 1704 *F*   Another *G*   To the Tune of hey boys up go wee *H*   A Tarpawlins account of the late Sea fight. A more true & full account of the late great Battel at Sea than has been hitherto published *J*   On the Sea Fight off Malaga 1704 *K*

Before 1 *J adds:*

> Sir George did meet With the French Fleet
>   And boldly did look at 'em
> He stay'd so long till he could see
> Sir Cloudsly beat the Enemy
>   And how the Duke did thwack 'em
>
> Quoth he anon I must be gone
>   Tholouse inrag'd may venture
> To come, in spight of wind and sea
> And unprovok'd fall foul on me
>   And Swinge us in the Center.

1] As Bold Sr George beat brave Thoulouse *C*   As brave Sir *Rooke Thoulouse* did beat *D*   The great Sir George Tholouse did beat *EFGH*   The Brave Sr George Tholouse did beat *J*   Rooke did as bravely Tholouse beat *K*   2 So brave *Thoulouse*] So Bold Thoulouse *C*   The brave Tholouse *EF*   The great Thoulouse *CJ*   Toulous again *H*   As bravely hee *K*   3] And if they e're do meet againe *C*   But whensoe-'er they meet again *D*   But if they chance to meet again *EF*   For which when next he does him meet *G*   But if they chance again to meet *H*   But when agen they chance to meet *J*   But when Geo· do's him meet againe *K*   1 *George* will his Jacquet] Rooke will his Jackett *C*   He will his Jacket *G*   his Jackett hee will *K*   5 fight, they] fight and *K*   were] did *CDFK*   6 They] And *FJK*   7 They] Yet *F*   And *K*   strive again to meet] for each other Seeke *C*   strive to meet again *DEFJ*   8 quite] clean *FGH*

Moderation Display'd

Copy text: B
Collation: The following copies have been recovered:

> *Moderation Display'd: A Poem.* By the Author of *Faction*
>   *Display'd,* 1704 (Yale copy)   *Aa*
> *Moderation Display'd: A Poem.* By the Author of *Faction*
>   *Display'd,* 1705 (NLS copy: 1.265 [22])   *Ab*
> BM MS. Add. 21094, ff. 147v–151v   *Ac*
> *Moderation Vindicated, in an Answer, Paragraph by Para-*
>   *graph, to a Late New Poem, Intituled, Moderation Dis-*
>   *play'd,* 1705 (Victoria & Albert Museum copy)   *Ad*
> *Moderation Display'd: A Poem.* By the Author of *Faction*

> *Display'd. Answer'd Paragraph by Paragraph* (B. Bragg),
>   1705 (University of Michigan copy)   *Ae*
> *Moderation Display'd: A Poem. By the Author of Faction*
>   *Display'd* (H. Hills), 1709 (Yale copy)   *Af*
> *POAS*, 1707, *4*, 98–109 (Bodl. copy: Thorn-Drury
>   d. 27)   *Ag*
> *Moderation Display'd. A Poem.* By the Same Author, 1705
>   (Yale copy)   *B*

Of these only two, *Aa,* a quarto, and *B,* an octavo volume, are substantive. The latter, advertised on the title page as "Now first Correctly Published, with large Amendments, and the addition of several Characters omitted in former Editions," is not an earlier and more correct copy of *Aa,* but a later revision. It is *Aa* "with Improvements," as Thomas Hearne (*1,* 31) surmised. "The Addition of several Characters" added 75 lines to the poem, but "large Amendments" cut out the final 104 lines (of which Shippen salvaged only 18, lines 120–37). Most of these 104 lines were devoted to a strained panegyric of Marlborough which Shippen himself admitted to be "wholly uninspired." Most of the 75 lines that were added, however, are satire, at which even Shippen's detractors acknowledged that he had "a better Talent" (*Moderation Vindicated,* 1705, p. 22). So *B* is printed here because it is a better poem and better represents Shippen's final attitude toward the duke of Marlborough.

Ab, the second edition, is another quarto volume, reset from *Aa. Acdef* also derive independently from *Aa. Ag,* in turn, was set up from *Ae.*

54 Daemon] Devil *A*   56] Ran Bellowing thro' all th'Abyss profound *A*   58 Friends] Friend *B*   101 his] this *B*   106 is] in *A*   120 *Nereo* shall cease t'extend his] 'Tis he extends the Heav'nly *A*   124 *La*] *Acg   Le AabdefB* 125 Flash] blasts *A*   126 our] their *B*   134 my Pois'nous] Detraction's *A* 135 gen'rous] Noble *A*   136 Fiends must still] let his Foes *A*   138–52 *omitted A*   149 his] its *B*   179 *black Ingratitude*] secret Policy *A*   191–94 *omitted A*   219–60 *omitted A*   232 lose] loose *B*   265 the ruin'd World] the World *B*   266–77 *omitted A*   267 his] this *B*   287–88 *omitted A* 315 *Trader's*]*Aeg   Traders   Aabcdf   Trader   B*   352 advanc'd] was seen *A* 369–70]

>   *Clodio* was Raptur'd, and in Terms like these,
>   His Joy and Approbation did express   *A*

375–76]

>   Attempts that often Baffle Humane Care,
>   By aiding Spirits soon effected are;
>   Their Knowledge in immediate *Intuition* lies,
>   Nor does, like ours, from long Deductions rise   *A*

378 *A adds:*

>   Here cease thy Satyr, Muse, and form thy Tongue
>   To louder Numbers and Heroick Song:
>   Here Celebrate, unbyass'd as thou art,
>   The Triumphs of *Sempronia*'s other Part,
>   Nor let her Stain the Hero's High Desert.

Now the *Imperial Eagle* hung her Head,
Drooping she Mourn'd her wonted *Thunder* fled.
Now was she fitted for a foreign Yoke,
Her Sceptre nodded, her Dominion shook.
Such was the tott'ring State of Antient *Rome*,
When Conqu'ring *Hannibal* pronounc'd her Doom,
When yet the fatal *Capua* was unknown,
That blasted all the Laurels *Cannae* won.
Where shall she Succour seek? Or whither fly?
Shall she for ever in Confusion lie?
Shall the first Kingdom of the *Christian World*
Be un-reliev'd in endless Ruine hurl'd?
Not so? her Aid Auspicious *Anna* brings,
Anna the Angel of unhappy Kings.
She sends *Camillo* with an *English Force,*
To stem the Ravaging *Invader*'s Course.
France and *Bavaria* now in vain Combine,
In vain their Fierce unnumber'd Legions joyn,
In vain the Thunderbolts of War oppose:
Eugenio and *Camillo* are their Foes.
Like *Caesar,* Both for Stratagems Renown'd,
Like *Alexander,* both with Martial Fury crown'd.
    At length the Great Decisive Day drew near,
On which alone depended all the War.
At length the Fight began, the Canon roar'd,
Nor knew *The Empire* yet her Sov'reign Lord.
But soon *Camillo* with resistless Arms,
With doubled Rage, the Hostile Troops alarms.
The Troops, that thought no Valour match'd their own,
Till *English* Courage bore them headlong down.
Before his Conqu'ring Sword they vanquish'd fly,
Or in the Field, or in the *Danube* die.
The *Danube* reeking ran a Purple Flood,
Swell'd and distain'd with Deluges of Blood.
O were I Poet equal to my Theam!
The *Future World* should wond'ring read this Stream;
Where many Thousand Warriors more were slain,
Or than on *Xanthus* Banks, or the *Pharsalian* Plain:
Tho' these to all Exploits are far preferr'd,
One by the *Grecian,* one the *Roman* Bard.
Hence is the *Empire* to it self restor'd,
Revolting Nations Recognize their Lord.
Lewis no more shall God-like Titles Claim,
Nor *Europe* aw'd and Trembling dread his Name.
Hence a new Scene of Happiness appears,
A long Successive Train of Golden Years.
So sav'd *Demetrius* the *Athenian State,*

Oppress'd by Foes, and sunk with adverse Fate.
No sooner was the Bloody Battle won,
But all his Fame with Adoration own;
But on the Mighty Victor they bestow'd,
The Sacred Stile and Honours of a God.
But tho' no Altars we profanely raise,
But tho' a less, we pay a juster Praise,
All but the Blind Idolatry intend,
Which ridicules the Glorious Worth it would commend.
    When with his *Eastern* Spoils, returning home,
Augustus enter'd his applauding *Rome,*
Virgil and *Horace* waited on his Fame,
Glad to record the Muses Patron's Name;
And well could they in everliving Strains,
Describe his Triumphs, and Reward his Pains.
But Modern Heroes, tho' as truly Brave
As those of Old, not equal Poets have.
No *Virgils* now, nor *Horaces,* to raise
Trophies proportion'd to their Deathless praise.
An *Addison* perhaps, or *Tate* may write;
Volpone pays them for their *Venal* Wit.
But since my Muse, warm'd with a *Gen'rous* Flame,
Unbrib'd would eternize *Camillo*'s Name;
Let him accept such Homage as she brings,
Nor think that wholly uninspir'd she Sings.
    But, Goddess, still one Labour more remains,
Still *Nereo* claims thy Tributary Strains;
Tune thy Harmonious Voice to *Nereo*'s Praise,
A Subject pregnant with immortal Lays.
            [see lines 120–33, above]
For what can *English* Bravery withstand,
When *Nereo* or *Camillo* do Command?
It vindicates the Sea, and Triumphs ore the Land.
            [see lines 134–37, above]
So *Aristides* long with Malice strove,
Nor could his Vertue win a Factious People's Love.

The French King's Cordial

Copy text: C
Collation: Ten manuscript and three printed copies have been recovered:

    Harvard MS. Eng. 606, pp. 115–17   *A*
    Carlisle R. O. MS. D/Lons   *B*
    The Tackers Vindicated; Or, An Answer to the Whigs New

> *Black-List: Which has been Dispers'd Abroad since the*
> *Rising of both Houses of Parliament, To Misrepresent*
> *such Members As have Shewn Themselves Worthy*
> *Patriots in Defence of the Church Established; In Order to*
> *Render 'em Suspected to the People of England at the*
> *Ensuing Elections. With A Word to Mr. John Tutchin,*
> *About his Scandalous Ballad, that goes to the Tune of One*
> *Hundred Thirty Four, On the same Subject,* London,
> 1705 (BM copy: 8122. cc. 17)   *C*
> BM MS. Add. 40060, ff. 56v–58v   *D*
> Folger MS. M.b.12, ff. 255v–57   *E*
> BM MS. Add. 32096, f. 187   *F*
> Hertfordshire County R. O. MS. Cowper Box 9,
>   Diary, *2*, 367–68, *3*, 14–16   *G*
> Bodl. MS. Top. Oxon. C.108, pp. 75–78   *H*
> BM MS. Add. 27408, f. 74   *J*
> Osborn MS. Chest II, No. 18, pp. 93–95, 114–15 *K*
> *A List of those Worthy Patriots, who to prevent the Church of*
>   *England from being Undermined by the Occasional*
>   *Conformists, did, like truly Noble Englishmen, Vote that the*
>   *Bill to prevent Occasional Conformity might be Tack'd to*
>   *the Land-Tax Bill, to secure its Passing in the House of*
>   *Lords; so that this their Zeal does appear (to all Wise*
>   *Men) as Conspicuous for the Interest, as their Lives are*
>   *Ornaments to that Church of which they are Members* [n.p.,
>   n.d.], pp. 7–8 (TCD copy)   *L*
> *POAS*, 1707, *4*, 109–11 (Yale copy)   *M*
> Bodl. MS. Tanner 306, f. 481   *N*

The manuscripts *AB* are preserved in quite different forms. *A* is an addition, in a nonclerical hand, to a factory-produced anthology; *B* was copied out by a correspondent of the Tory Sir John Lowther and mailed to his seat at Whitehaven, Cumberland. No broadside version of the poem has been recovered. It seems first to have been printed at the end of a Tory election pamphlet of 1705 (*C*). The manuscripts *DE* are also preserved in quite different forms: *D* is an extract from a commonplace book, while *E*, which lacks lines 57–96, is a factory product. *FGHJKN* all derive from commonplace books. *J* lacks lines 57–96 but supplies the "names of the Tackers 134 spoken of in the song." *L*, the second edition, is appended to another Tory election pamphlet. *M*, an anthology copy, is collateral with *L*.

Wide variance in the text and length of the witnesses suggests the possibility of authorial revision, in several phases, as well as conflation between the phases. Assuming *A* to represent the first stage of composition, the first revision may have included:

1. switching lines 50 and 54
2. reordering the stanzas, putting lines 13–24 after line 48
3. adding lines 57–96, called the "Second Part" in *G* and "the remainder" in *K*

The second revision apparently included:

    4. restoring lines 13–16 to follow line 12
    5. omitting lines 17–20
    6. revising lines 21–48

Evidence of conflation may be seen in the following examples:

    7. *CD* have the revised stanza-order of *B* (2, above), but the unrevised reading of line 54 (1, above)
    8. *FGHJKLMN* have the revisions of 4–6, above, but line 50 in *FGH* and line 54 in *JKLMN* both preserve the unrevised reading of *A*

Title: The French King's Cordiall, or verses on the attempt made to tack the bill to prevent occasional conformity to the Land tax Bill 1704 *A*   [none] *BCH*   The French Kings Cordial (or 134) To the tune of Old Simon the King *DG*   The Consolidators Or The French King's Cordiall *E*   The French Kings Cordial, or . . . 134 *F*   The French King's Cordiall *JKN*   The French King's Consolation *L*   The French King's Lamentation for the Loss of the Occasional Bill, 1705 *M*

1 shall] need *FGH*   2 *Blenheim*] *ACFGH* Hochstead Σ 3 else where] *AL* some-where Σ 5 Ruin'd] has Ruin'd *CFGHKM*   6 the] that *LMN* 7 the] their *CFGHK*   9 *Cub* that] Cubb *A*   Club (that) *BDEJ*   *C——b C* Bratt (that) *FGH*   Nourish'd] cherish'd *BDEJKLMN*   nursed *H*   10 his] their *BCDEK*   the *FGHJ*   11 his] their *BDE*   the *J*   12 'Tis] they'r *B*   They are *D*   They're a *E*   There's a *J*   By the *L*   13–24 *follow* 48 *BCDE* 13 him] their King *BCDE*   Perkin *J*   his] the *BDEFGHJ*   13] Such constancy to him is showne *F*   Already his party is grown *GH*   (For) I'm sure he will be maintain'd *JKLMN*   14 Which his] His *FGHK*   abandon'd] deserted *FGH*   16 *By the*] By *BCK*   To *GH*   17–20 *omitted FGHJKLMN* 21–24 *follow* 48 *FGHJKLMN*   21 St. *Poll* with] St. Paul leads *F*   I can sett out *GH*   I can fitt (out) *JK*   I'll Fit out *LMN*   23] Shall guard him if tis thought fitt *B*   Shall guard him if this is thought fitt *DE*   That he rul'd the whole Navy twere fitt *F*   And this is Approv'd and (Thought) Meet *GH*   And they shall all be imployed *JL*   And these shall be all employd *K*   And these shall all be employ'd *MN*   24 *By the*] By *C*   Say the *F*   For the *LMN*   25 Land-Tax] Allyance *FGJKLMN*   Villains *H*   surely miscarried] been dissolv'd *FN*   quite been Dissolv'd *GH*   all been dissolv'd *JKLM*   26 I had had All] I'de had all *A*   all had been *F*   all had been now *GH*   I had got all *JLM*   27 Had but the] Had the *FGHKLN*   Had then the *M*   been Carry'd] but been resolv'd *FGH*   but been carry'd *K*   been Carried *then L*   28 *By*] *ABCDK*   By the Σ 29–32 *omitted C*   29] My Grandson had tack'd been to Spain *F*   My son had been Tackt to Spain *GHJK*   My *Son* had been *Tack'd* unto *Spain LM*   My Son had been tacked into Spaine *N*   30 Much faster] Much sooner *H*   Faster *JKN*   31] Were the Votes not abortive and vain *FGH*   Had but the design a gone on *J*   Had the design gone on *KN*   Had the *Great Designe* gone on *L*   Had the great Design but gone on *M*   33 But they have] Tho' the foe has *FG*   Tho my

foe has *H*   34 Into] In *BDEKL*   Out of *F*   35] Which Spoyld for this
Season my Ends *E*   Yet Still my party extends *FGH*   or else the Question had gone
JKLMN   36 *Of the*] Of *BC*   Of my *D*   To (an) *FGH*   With the *JKLM*   For
the *N*   37 *Hammond*] H(a)——(mon)d *CKM*   *Harcourt*] H(ar)l(e)y *BDEK*
H——ty *C*   Hartcott *F*   H——t *M*   39] like Rogues have forsaken their
Freinds *A*   (They) Have now Forsaken their *Friends CJKLM*   Have deserted our
Party now *FGH*   Have now deserted their Friends *N*   41 But I think] I think
BDEJKLMN   Yet when *F*   But then *GH*   42 Go] *BCN*   look *Σ*   ever
Before] heretofore *G*   43] since they are imployed who are of the mind *A*   Since
they are Employ'd that way *C*   Great officers there agree *FGH*   (for) some officers
are of the mind *JKMN*   Since *Officers are of the Mind L*   44 *The*] Of the
AJKLMN   Of *C*   With the *FH*   With *G*   45 Their] Those *FGH*   Some
JKLMN   Surrender with Ease] that did me Present *FGH*   have made me a
present *JKLMN*   46 Their Convoy and] Their Convoys and *BDE*   With some
of their *FGH*   Of some of their *JLMN*   Of some of Your *K*   47] To Shew
they are all of a peicc *BE*   Did act with the full Consent *FGH*   They surely are
all of a piece *J*   And these are all of a peice *KMN*   And They are all of a piece *L*
48 *With the*] With *BC*   Of (the) *FGHN*   49–52 *follow* 24 *BCDEFGH   omitted*
JKLMN   49] (But) My pollicy's not at a Stand *FGH*   50 Tho' a Check be
given to] I'le ruin Mankind by *BD*   And Ruine Mankind by *E*   51] And
Secure in a Protestant House *BDE*   For I gove(r)n in old England *FGH*
53–56 *omitted CDEFGH*   53] My Policy's not at a Stand *B*   54 That
have ruin'd Mankind by] Tho' a Check be given *B*   Who have Ruin'd Mankind
with *LMN*   55] for I govern in old England *B*   Yet have in a Protestant
Land *N*   57–72 *omitted CD*   57–96 *omitted AEJN*   57 *Cabals* I have
had] I have had my Caballs *KLM*   59 they are not] I'm not yet *KM*   I am
not *L*   62 *Flanders* did Sell] Dunkirk resign'd *KLM*   63 I'll now Play
a] I'le play a new *F*   And I play a new *KLM*   64 *With*] By the *FGH*   With
the *KM*   65–68 *omitted K*   66 Whilst he] He *LM*   69 Sham] dear
KLM   70 Banish'd *Jemmy*] his old Father *KLM*   73 the] their *C*
these *DLM*   those *FGH*   our *K*   74 their Friend *Tallard*'s] my freind
Tallard's *DFKM*   my *Tallard*'s *L*   79 And that] That *CK*   take] have
DKLM   81–84 *omitted C*   81 would be] must be *DKLM*   had bin *H*
82 That] The *KLM*   83 Were it not for] Till he's rais'd by *DKLM*   85
Troops] forces *D*   from *Bavaria* were] were sent (all a) *DKLM*   89–92 *omitted*
D follow 84 *L*   89 *Kings*] King *CFHK*   90 Will] Must *KLM*   91
but a New] the next *K*   another *L*   but another *M*   93–96 *omitted C*   93
Firm Hopes] tongue *DL*   Strong hopes *KM*   94 my People and I are grown]
I'me squez'd and draind very *DKLM*   95 has Tack'd to] is tackt with *DKLM*
does tack to *F*   96 *The*] To the *DKLM*

A New Ballad Writ by Jacob Tonson

Copy text: BM MS. Add. 21094, f. 140v.
Collation: Since no other witness to the text has been discovered, the copy text is

reproduced *verbatim et literatim* with the addition of some punctuation and a possibly superfluous "the" in line 18.

A Health to the Tackers

Copy text: Aa
Collation: The following witnesses to the text have been recovered:

A Health to the Tackers. A New Song . . . Oxford: Printed, 1705 (Huntington Library copy)	*Aa*
Wit and Mirth: Or, Pills to Purge Melancholy, 4 vols., 1699–1706, *4,* 70 (Yale copy)	*Ab*
The State Garland of Antient and Modern Loyal Songs and Catches, Part I, Dublin, [1715?], p. 13 (Case 477) (Yale copy)	*Ac*
BM MS. Add. 21094, p. 395	*B*
A Health to the Tackers, n.p., n.d. (Harvard copy, Julian Marshall Collection)	*C*
The Diverting Post, 31 March–7 April 1705 (BM copy)	*D*
The Coventry Ballad, &c. To an Excellent New Tune. The Second Edition. Norwich, Printed MDCCV (Copies: Clark Memorial Library, Harvard)	*E*
Bodl. MS. Eng. poet. e.87, p. 94	*F*
Osborn MS. Chest II, No. 18, pp. 116–17	*G*
Bodl. MS. Tanner 306, f. 476	*H*
Cambridge University Library MS. Mn 6.42	*J*

Aa is a folio half-sheet printed in a single column on one side only. The two anthology copies, *Abc*, derive from *Aa. BDE* localize the song in Coventry. *C* is an engraved song sheet that also provides the music for a flute accompaniment. The copy in *The Observator,* 11–14 April 1705 was reprinted from *D. E,* another folio half-sheet printed in a single column on one side only, appears not to have been set up from *Aa. FGHJ* are inferior and presumably later manuscripts. *H* is both illuminated (see illustration, p. 59) and annotated: "Rogue" (line 24) is incomprehensibly glossed "Walpole Tacker."

Title: A Health to the Tackers. A New Song *Aa*   A Health to the Tackers *AbcC*   A Health to the Tackers on Election at Coventry 1705 *B*   A Health to the Tackers, or the Coventry Ballad *D*   The Coventry Ballad, &c. To an Excellent New Tune *E*   A Song on the Tack 1705 *F*   The Health *G*   [none] *H*   A Health *J*

1 my] brave *FHJ*   2 for the Tackers] to the Sneakers *J*   6 pull] put *DHJ* peck *E*   Establishments] Establishment *CDEFGHJ*   7 Shit in their] S(h)——t in their *AaCD*   Shit their own *E*   defile their *F*   8 and the Crown] and Crown *AcJ*   9 us chuse] us now choose *E*   14 our] their *J*   18 Schism]

Faction *HJ*   strangely] strangly *BC*   strongly *EGJ*   21 has] have *CDEFGH*
22 so Bubbl'd] does bubble *J*   23 That] For *Aabc*   And *B*   Conformity]
Conformity's *D*

The Oxfordshire Nine

Copy text: Aa
Collation: The following copies have been recovered:

The Oxfordshire Nine . . . London, Printed in the Year MDCCV	*Aa*
Hertfordshire County R. O. MS. Cowper Box 9, Diary, 2, 361–64	*Ab*
Oxfordshire . . . Printed in the Year MDCCIV	*Ac*
POAS, 1707, *4*, 1–4 (Yale copy)	*Ad*

Aa (Carlisle R. O. and NLS copies) and *Ac* (Bodl. copy) are broadsides printed in a
single column on both sides of the sheet. Although there are no substantive variants
among the copies, *Abcd* appear to derive collaterally from *Aa*.

Title: The Oxfordshire Nine *Aab*   Oxfordshire *Ac*   The Oxfordshire Nine
April 1705 *Ad*

The Tack

Copy text: G
Collation: The following copies have been recovered:

Chicago University MS. PR1195.M73, pp. 68–69	*A*
BM MS. Add. 40060, f. 62v	*B*
BM MS. Egerton 924, f. 29	*C*
Hearne, *1*, 54	*D*
Bodl. MS. Rawl. poet. 173, f. 1	*E*
Deliciae Poeticae; or Parnassus Display'd. In a Choice Collection of Very Valuable Poems and Songs, 1706, p. 149 (Case 240) (Yale copy)	*F*
The Whipping-Post, 21 August 1705 (BPL copy)	*G*
Osborn MS. Chest II, No. 16, p. ³19	*H*
Whig and Tory: Or, Wit on Both Sides, 1712, p. ⁴42 (Case 254[c]) (Yale copy)	*J*
BM MS. Add. 21094, f. 156	*K*
Essex R. O. MS. D/DW Z.4	*L*
Bodl. MS. Eng. poet. e.87, p. 55	*M*

Although they represent the earliest manuscripts, *ABCD* have already broken down into two separate traditions. The Scottish origins of scribe *A* are revealed by his spelling of "Rimms and Quairs" for "Quires and Reams" of line 15. *EFGHJ* are printed versions of 1705–1712 and manuscripts closely related to them. *KLM* are later and corrupt versions of *ABCD*. The copy in *Tory Pills to Purge Whig Melancholy . . . The Second Edition*, 1715, p. 83, was set up from *J*.

Title: The Tack *ABCKM*   On the Tack *D*   The Grand Tack in Queen Ann's Reign, on occasion of the Occasional Conformity Bill *E*   The Grand Tack *FGHJ*   [none] *L*

1 The] This *AEF*   of] on *KLM*   dwell] move *LM*   3 Those] The *BDEFGHJ* These *CK*   Worlds our] World of *GHJ*   Globes our *LM*   5 Work is Taylor like] *ACKLM*   chiefest businesse is *Σ*   6 the Soul] our Souls *ALM*   our Soul *E*   7 Doctor's] Doctor *ABCEF*   8 'Twixt] 'Tween *D*   of *EFGHJ* 9 by's] by *BCDGHK*   the *JL*   his *M*   10 to] and *A*   12 That often lasts for] that sometimes lasts for *B*   That always holds for *CD*   that holds them for their *EF*   will hold them during *GHJ*   may hold for Eithers *K*   will serve for eithers *LM*   13–16 *omitted J*   13 Lawyer studys] Lawyers study *LM*   14 His Client] His Clients *AEF*   the Client *H*   Their Client *M*   Laws] Cause *GH*   16] as He the Breviate draws *GH*   17] The Queen, the Lords, the Commons *GHJ*   18] are in Senate Tack'd together *GHJ*   19 they chance e'er to Untack] they e're chance to untack *CDGHK*   they chance to be untackt *EF*   by any Means untack'd *J*   they should chance to untack *L*   you should chance to untack *M*   20 to] of *M*   24 And so may soon come] And may as Soon come *A*   would feign pull both of 'em *G*   would pull both of them *H*   And fain would pull both *J*   so may soon be *K*   25 Since all the World's] Since then we see *K*   And since wee see *L*   Now since we see *M*   27 Then why about one honest] Why then a Pox about the *A*   Then was a P——x about the *CK*   Why then about one honest *DEF*   Then why a pox about the *LM*   28 keep] *ABK*   make *Σ*

The Dyet of Poland

Copy text: Aa (Yale copy: NZ.Z682d [9]).
Collation: Of the five editions of the poem in 1705 only the first (*A*) is substantive. This is a carelessly printed quarto in which there is even an error in the errata list (p. 22 for p. 27). Five states of this edition can be distinguished:

The uncorrected state:
p. 16	line 10:	"Which"
	line 15:	"*doz'dold*"
	line 21:	"no not"
p. 32	line 5:	"The"
	line 6:	"their"
p. 54	line 3:	"et"

Copies: BPL (*Defoe 27.10 no. 12), Rosenbach

Foundation, Yale (NZ.Z682d [9])   *Aa*

p. 32   line 5:   "The" corrected to "One"
        line 6:   "their" corrected to "his"
Copies: BPL (*Defoe 21.D88.1705), Indiana copy 2,
Newberry, Princeton   *Ab*

p. 32   line 5:   "The"
        line 6:   "their"
p. 54   line 3:   "et" corrected to "Let"
Copies: Cornell, Clark Memorial, Morgan, NYPL
(C p.v.203 [12]), Texas, NLS (NG.1559.c.30)   *Ac*

p. 16   line 10:   "Which" corrected to "While"
        line 15:   "*doz'dold*" corrected to "*doz'd old*"
        line 21:   "no not" corrected to "no, not"
p. 32   line 5:   "The"
        line 6:   "their"
p. 54   line 3:   "et" corrected to "Let"
Copy: Indiana copy 1   *Ad*

p. 16   line 10:   "Which" corrected to "While"
        line 15:   "*doz'dold*" corrected to "*doz'd old*"
        line 21:   "no not" corrected to "no, not"
p. 32   line 5:   "The" corrected to "One"
        line 6:   "their" corrected to "his"
p. 54   line 3:   "et" corrected to "Let"
Copies: Cincinnati, Huntington, Illinois   *Ae*

The second edition (*B*) (Foxon D9) is an octavo of which the Yale copy (Z78.51d) has been collated. It incorporates the corrections of the errata list in the first edition, but introduces dozens of new errors. The Boston Public Library has a large paper copy.

The third edition (*C*) (Foxon D10) is another octavo of which the Yale copy (Ik.D362.C700 v.1) has been collated. It has a new title page: *The Dyet of Poland, A Satyr. To which is Added A Memorial to the Tantivy-High-Flyers of England. The present Disturbers of that Government, as Their Wise Predecessors were, when the Lord Essex, Russel, and Sydney fell. Printed at Dantzick, in the Year 1705.* The *Memorial* is 22 lines of verse plus one line signed *Hudibras*. This edition, which is even less carefully printed than the first two, adds a short Key.

The fourth edition (*D*) (Foxon D11), of which the Yale copy (Ik.D362.705D) has been collated, is an octavo published by Ben. Bragg. It was reset from the first edition (ignoring the errata, however) as the basis for an answer to the poem. The title page, *The Dyet of Poland, A Satyr. Consider'd Paragraph by Paragraph. To which is added A Key to the whole, with the Names of the Author, and the Nobility and Gentry, that are Scandalously Pointed at, in it,* is misleading, for there is no real key, although a few characters in the poem are identified in the paragraphs of reply interspersed between the verse paragraphs of the poem. Of this volume there was a so-called second edition (*E*) (Foxon

D12) of which the BPL copy has been collated. Actually only H4 was partly reset to correct some errors in the order of the text, while the rest was reprinted from standing type after a few desultory corrections had been made.

The relation between these editions, therefore, may be illustrated as follows:

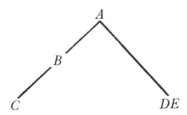

The accidentals of the copy text have been amended in the following cases: commas have been deleted where their presence would cause confusion today, namely between an adjective and the noun it modifies (line 161), between a verb and its adverbial modifier (lines 666, 1060, 1253), between a verb and its object (lines 731, 746, 1098), between the subject and verb (lines 777, 815, 949), and between two parts of a compound verb (line 931). A semicolon between a prepositional phrase and the verb has been deleted at line 1062.

On the other hand, commas and semicolons have been supplied where their omission seems to be an error, namely at the end of lines 31, 171, 194, 242, 267, 291, 334, 479, 678, 774, and within lines 343, 698, 764, 909, 945.

122 Courtiers'] Courtiers *ABCDE*   137 Which] Will *ABCDE*   167 *Annesleski*] *A——leski ABCDE*   280 *his*] *C* their *Σ*   332 While] Which *Aabc*   342 fond of Liberty] fond Liberty *Aabc*   383 Amuse] *Errata list BC* Abuse *Σ*   416 *Rogue's*] *R——e's ABCDE*   473 Spleen] *Errata list BC* Pride *Σ*   601–602] *Errata list BC order reversed Σ*   671 Tell] *DE* Tells *Σ*   672 One] *Errata list AbeBC* The *Σ*   673 show] shown *A*   his] *Errata list AbeBC* their *Σ*   789 form] forms *ABC*   791 it] at *ABCDE* 848 *Monstrevil*] Montrevil *DE*   868 Mask] *Errata list BC* Mark *Σ*   896 *Blaspheming*] Blasphemous *ADE*   1110 Hung] H—— *ABCDE*   1114 *Rogue*] *R——e ABCDE*   1118 Fool] F——l *ABCDE*   1148 Rake] R——ke *ABCDE*   1150 Queen] Qu——n *ABCDE*

Declaration without Doors

Copy text: Ab (Yale copy).
Collation: Besides a folio half-sheet, carelessly printed in two columns on one side only (*Aa*) (Foxon X7), of which the Harvard copy (Ec65.A100.B675p) has been collated, only the anthology copies, *POAS*, 1707, *4*, 18–22 (*Ab*) and *Political Merriment*, 1714, pp. ²202–06 (*Ac*), have been recovered. As Foxon deposes, Walter Wilson,

William Lee, and Paul Dottin "list an untraced quarto with this title and 'by the author of the True-Born Englishman.' " But only Wilson claims to have seen this volume and it remains untraced. The compositor of *Aa* found it necessary to make large abbreviations in his text, setting lines 7–9 as follows:

> I'm a P——t M——r
> Who shall sit in *N*——*er*,
> To settle the N——'s Affairs.

Title: Declaration without Doors *Aac*   A Declaration without Doors, 1705 *Ab*
10 Trouble] T—— *Aabc*   Laws] L—— *Aac*   29 for th'Occasional] For
Occasional *Aac*   30 to] so *Ac*   42 *Humphrey*] H—— *Aac* H—— *Ab*
47 Government's] Government *Ac*   93 Bishops and Queen] B——s and Q——
Aabc

On the New Promotion

Copy text: A
Collation: The seven manuscripts that preserve the text of the poem derive collateral-
ly from the archetype. They are:

> Hearne, *1,* 60   *A*
> Bodl. MS. Rawl. D.383, f. 89v   *B*
> Osborn MS, Box 37, No. 16   *C*
> Osborn MS. Chest II, No. 16   *D*
> BM MS. Add. 21094, f. 161v   *E*
> BM MS. Lansdowne 852, f. 132v   *F*
> BM MS. Harleian 6914, f. 110   *G*

AB appear to reproduce the archetype most closely, but *B* is fragmentary, lacking
lines 21–26.

Title: Verses on the New Promotions. Sent to the Queen *A*   On the New Pro-
motions made by the Queen *B*   Advice to the Queen *C*   On the late promotion
To the Queen 1705 *D*   Verses on the Late Promotion 1705 *E*   Verses on the
late Promotion by the Queen. 1708 *F*   Verses on the New Promotion, Sent to the
Queen *G*

2 Dignity and Crown] Crown and Dignity *BC*   3 Awkward] Antient *E*
5 and stroke] and strike *A* *omitted F*   6 hand's withdrawn] hand is Gonn
C   7 one that has] him that has *BCD* him that hath *EG* him who hath
F   8 and if] If you *C* but if *F*   9 thy] your *ACEF*   14 Proclaims it]
Proclaims this *A* Proclaims, that *B* Prophetick is that *G*   who] that *CD*
15 on] of *ACE*   16 thy] your *D*   19 Oh!] Ah *BE*   those] these
CD   20 at last be made] be made *B* be made at last *D* at last is made *F* be

likewise made *G*   21–26 *omitted B*   22 Vile] Wise *G*   23 *Church* and]
Country *C*   Church to *G*   26 *thy*] your *CDE*   my *G*

Upon the Vote that Pass'd
That the Church was Not in Danger

Copy text: B
Collation: Of the many copies of this epigram that may have circulated in 1705, only three in print and five in manuscript have been recovered:

[Defoe], *Review,* 21 July 1705	*A*
[Defoe], *Jure Divino: A Satyr,* 1706, XI, 31*n.* (Yale copy 1)	*B*
Osborn MS. Chest II, No. 16, p. ³19	*C*
TCD MS. I.5, *1,* 206	*D*
Harvard MS. Eng. 606, p. 69	*E*
POAS, 1707, *4,* 17 (Yale copy)	*F*
BM MS. Lansdowne 852, f. 122v	*G*

A prints only the first two lines. In a doggerel version preserved in BM MS. Add. 21094, f. 153, the original tetrameter line has been expanded to admit a feeble hexameter in the last line: "By Sid—— and Sarrah forc't, she leaves it in the Lurch."

Title: [none] *ABE*   A: R: *C*   The Tory's Opinion of Q: Ann An Epigram *D*   Suppos'd to be writ by a Dignify'd Clergyman *F*   Upon the vote that pass'd that the Church was not in danger *G*

1 *Anna*] She *ABC*   2 acted as] practiced what *E*   did what ere *G*   3 now she's] since she's *C*   now she is become the *E*   4 she's left] She leaves *FG*

The Country Parson's Honest Advice

Copy text: Aa
Collation: The text is preserved in 12 manuscripts and three printed broadsides. One edition of the latter, of which the copies at NLS, Harvard, and the Essex R. O. have been collated, is *The Country Parson's Honest Advice to That Judicious Lawyer, and Worthy Minister of State, My Lord Keeper,* n.p., n.d., printed in a single column on one side only (*Aa*). Another edition with the same title, of which the Harvard, Newberry Library, and Bodl. (Vet. A.3c.123) copies have been collated, is printed in a single column on both sides (*Ab*). A third edition, of which the Texas copy has been collated, bears the same title with an addition, *With a Reply, How to become a Bishop.* Both the text and *The Reply* ("That Lowly Vicar may in order rise") are printed in a single column on the same side of the sheet (*Ac*). These three editions exhibit no substantive variants. Thomas Hearne copied one of them into his diary on 5 February 1706 (*1,* 178).

Three of the manuscripts with the same title as *Aab* and two more with shortened versions of the title appear to be copies of the printed broadsides, but positive evidence is lacking, for again there are no substantive variants. These manuscripts are the following:

Hertfordshire County R. O. MS. Cowper Box 11, Vol. of Poems, no fol.	*Ba*
Harvard MS. Eng. 834, no fol.	*Bb*
Harvard MS. Eng. 606, f. 114v	*Bc*
BM MS. Add. 21094, f. 161v	*Bd*
Osborn MS. fc75	*Be*

The remaining manuscripts are these:

Bodl. MS. Eng. misc. c.116, f. 6	*C*
Osborn MS. Box 37, No. 16, no fol.	*D*
Cambridge University Library MS. Mn 6.42, f. 10	*E*
Osborn MS. Chest II, No. 16, p. 20	*F*
BM MS. Harleian 6914, f. 109	*G*
BM MS. Lansdowne 852, f. 33	*H*
Bodl. MS. Rawl. poet. 203, f. 49	*J*

Title: The Country Parson's Honest Advice to that Judicious Lawyer, and Worthy Minister of State, My Lord Keeper *AabBabc*   The Country Parson's Honest Advice to that Judicious Lawyer, and Worthy Minister of State, My Lord Keeper, With a Reply, How to become a Bishop *Ac*   The Country Parson's Honest Advice To Lord Keeper C——p——r *Bd*   A Country Parsons Advice to that Judicious & Worthy Minister of State the Lord Keeper Cowper. 1706 *Be*   The Country Parsons advice to my Ld Keeper Cooper *C*   Country parsons advice to my Lord Keeper *D*   The Country Parsons advice To Wm Cowper Esq: Ld Keeper of the Great Seal of England *E*   The Country Parsons Advice to the Ld Keeper, Cooper *F*   Advice to the Ld. K——r *G*   The Countrey Parsons Advice to my [Ld] Keeper 1706 *H*   The Country Clergy Mans Advice to that Judicious Lawyer and worthy Minister of State William Lord Cowper, Lord Chancellour of Great Britain *J*

4 wou'd] will *GHJ*   7 well governing] good Ruling of *F*   well guiding of *G*   your] his *C*   thy *EFG*   8 thy] your *DH*   10 *Seymour*'s Daughter] *S——y——r*'s Daughter *ABabcdCE*   that Miss Seymour *FG*   14 *Bolton*'s] And Bolton's *F*   *Godolphin*'s] Ld Treasurer's *F*   16 Managment] Honesty *FG*

The Lawyer's Answer

Copy text: Ab

Collation: There appear to be two states of the broadside edition, both entitled *The Lawyers Answer to the Country Parson's Good Advice to My Lord Keeper,* London, 1706, and both printed in a single column on one side only. Of these the Harvard copy represents the uncorrected state (*Aa*): it prints "Ann" for "And" in line 10, "is is" in line 16, and "the" for "thee" in line 24. There are copies of the corrected state (*Ab*) in the Bodl. and BM.

7 *Stephens*] *S——ns Aab*   8 *Shaftesbury*] *S——rs Aab*   Priests] Pr——sts *Aab*   9 *Bincks*] *B——ks Aab*   *Sacheverell*] *S——l Aab*   10 *Stokow*] *St——w Aab*   12 *Mackworth*] *M——h Aab*   *Pooley*] *P——y Aab*   13 *Wright*] *W——ght Aab*   14 *Ward*] *W——d Aab*   15 *Bromley*] *B——y Aab* 16 *Powis*] *P——is Aab*   to] may *Aab*   20 *Rochester's*] *R——rs Aab*   *Norman-by*] *N——by Aab*   21 *Granvill's*] *G——ls Aab*   *Conway's*] *C——y's Aab* 22 *Nottingham*] *N——m Aab*   23 *Seymour's*] *S——rs Aab*   24 *Caesar*] *C——r Aab*   26 *Packington*] *P——n Aab*   29 Church] Ch—— *Aab*

The Country Parson's Advice to Those Little Scriblers

Copy text: Aa
Collation: Only three witnesses are known: *The Country Parson's Advice to Those Little Scriblers, Who Pretend to Write Better Sense Than Great Secretaries: Or, Mr. Stephens's Triumph over the Pillory,* n.p., n.d., a folio half-sheet printed in a single column on both sides, of which the Newberry Library copy has been collated (*Aa*); another folio half-sheet with the same title and no imprint, but printed in a single column on one side only, of which the University of Michigan copy was collated (*Ab*); and *POAS,* 1707, *4,* 63–64, with "1706" added to the title (*Ac*). *Abc* appear to derive collaterally from *Aa.*

1 *Addison*] *Ad——n Aabc*   *Browne*] *Br——ne Aabc*   8 Patterns] Pattern *Ab* 22 *Oldmixon*] Old Mixon *Aab*   25 *Althea*] Altea *Aabc*   26 *Fontvive*] Fontville *Aab*   27 or] and *Ac*   29 Rogue] R—— *Aabc*   31 nor] or *Aab*

An Ode, Humbly Inscrib'd to the Queen

Copy text: A
Collation: No more witnesses to the text of the poem have been recovered than those known in 1959 to Wright and Spears (Prior, *Works,* 2, 895). There were three of these and the Yale copy of each has been collated for the present edition:

[Matthew Prior], *An Ode, Humbly Inscrib'd to the Queen. On the Late Glorious Success of Her Majesty's Arms. Written in Imitation of Spencer's Stile,* London (Jacob Tonson), 1706   *A*
[Matthew Prior], *Poems on Several Occasions,* London (Jacob Tonson), 1709, pp. 275–96   *B*

[Matthew Prior], *Poems on Several Occasions,* London
(Jacob Tonson and John Barber), 1718, pp. 248–65   *C*

A is a separate folio edition, carefully proofread and machined. *B* includes extensive revision, presumably authorial. Cancels in a second issue of *B* (Yale copy: Ik. P938.C707Bb) do not affect the text. *C,* which Wright and Spears adopted for their copy text, is the result of a very slight revision of *B.*

2 Conqu'ring Troops] Legions forth *B*   Conqu'ring Bands *C*   5 *Horace,*] *Horace*
AB   13 Great,] Great *A*   19 And telling] Reciting *BC*   24 sing] Sing
AB   29 Victories] Feats of Arms *BC*   30 By Story yet untold, unparallell'd]
Not yet by Story told, nor parallel'd *BC*   32 daigns] daign'd *B*   33 I'll]
I'd *B*   37 Wing,] Wing *A*   38 would] will *C*   39 should] shall
C   42] Mindless of warlike Rage, and hostile Care, *BC*   44 Arms] War
BC   51] Sedate and calm thus Victor *Marlbrô* sate, *BC*   52 Under his
Vineyard] Shaded with Laurels, *BC*   53] 'Till *Anna* calls him from his soft
Retreat, *BC*   54 'Till *Anna* gives Her] And gives Her Second *BC*   55 soft]
sweet *BC*   Ease,] Ease *A*   56 swift Impatience] ardent Speed he *BC*   57
Flying] Marching *BC*   59–61]

> Our Thought flies slower than Our General's Fame,
> Grasps He the Bolt? we ask, when He has hurl'd the Flame.
> When fierce *Bavar* on *Judoign*'s spacious Plain   *BC*

62 Afar he did] Did from afar *BC*   77 dismay'd,] dismayd *A*   82 thy Rival]
the Hero *BC*   85 That . . . Grove, that Harvest] Those . . . Groves (the
Merits *BC*   87 Whilst] While *BC*   89–90]

> Must from thy Brow their falling Honours shed,
> And their transplanted Wreaths must deck a worthier Head.   *BC*

94 Conduct seek] Councils date *BC*   99–100]

> Righteous the War, the Champion shall subdue;
> For *Jove*'s great Handmaid *Power*, must *Jove*'s Decrees pursue.   *BC*

102 sprung] branch'd *BC*   *Nassau*'s] *Nassaws BC*   104 With an Intrepid Hand
and] His Glorious Sword with Dauntless *BC*   105 10]

> When anxious *Britain* mourn'd her parting Lord,
> And all of *William* that was Mortal Dy'd,
> The faithful Hero had receiv'd this Sword
> From His expiring Master's much lov'd Side.
> Oft from its fatal Ire has *Louis* flown,
> Where-e'er Great *William* led, or *Maese* and *Sambre* run.   *BC*

111 and waving in the Air,] in an ill-omen'd Hour *BC*   112–13]

> To Thee, proud *Gaul*, behold thy justest Fear
> The Master Sword, Disposer of thy Power;   *BC*

114 Lord] Peer *BC*   116 He said] This Steel *BC*   117 This Glorious Gift]
The General said *BC*   118 I by Conquest fix] Conquest has confirm'd *BC*
127] Unmov'd the Two united Chiefs abide, *BC*   131 Shock sustain'd, the
Friendly] Rage dispers'd, the Glorious *BC*   135 Fix'd on Revenge] On Conquest fix'd *BC*   140 Deed] Arms *BC*   141 Oh! while mad with Rage]
while with fiercest Ire *BC*   143] While *Britain* presses Her afflicted Foes:

BC   145 Why do those Warriors look] Whence look the Soldiers Cheeks
BC   146 That] Erst *BC*   never knew] know they now *BC*   147 Why
does the charging Foe] The Hostile Troops, I ween, *BC*   149 Their Rage, alas!
submitting to] Alas! their lessen'd Rage proclaims *BC*   150 Behold, they weep,
and] For anxious, lo! they *BC*   153 that] their *BC*   154 I saw Their *Marl-
b'rough* stretch'd along] Ever to Vengeance sacred be *BC*   155 Hope] Wish
BC   for *Marlb'rough*] the Hero *BC*   161 And lo! the dubious] Propitious
Mars! the *BC*   162 Rage] Wrath *BC*   164 And *Liberty . . . Gallia*] Free-
dom . . . lawless Power must *BC*   169–70]

> Again *France* flies, again the Duke pursues,
> And on *Ramillia*'s Plains He *Blenheim*'s Fame renews.   *BC*

171 receive] receive, *AB*   176 wish'd Thou wou'dst no more] dreaded lest Thou
should'st *BC*   177 *Gallia*'s] *Gallic BC*   181 Rest] Ease *BC*   182 Pitch]
Pitch, *AB*   183 prize,] prize *AB*   187 pass'd] past *A*   188] Sublimer
yet to raise his Queen's Renown: *BC*   190 Nothing was done, He thought]
Nought done the Hero deem'd *BC*   193 Fall;] Fall, *AB*   194 said:] said.
AB   197 me,] me *AB*   202 he sees the Eagle cut] the rising Eagle cuts
BC   203 fearful] trembling *BC*   205 Why then] Ill-starr'd *BC*   206
the . . . Foe] our . . . Foes *BC*   222 *Edward,*] *Edward AB*   Sable] azure
A   224 *Seymour,*] *Seymour AB*   225 *Nevill,*] *Nevill AB*   226 *Ca'ndish,*]
Ca'ndish AB   227 Sons,] Sons *A*   230 vanquish'd,] vanquish'd *AB*   Vic-
tor's] Victors *AB*   244 *Spain,*] *Spain; AB*   246 Still . . . still] Oft. . . oft
BC   Wars,] Wars: *AB*   247 usual] frequent *BC*   248 Jars;] Jars.
A   Jars: *B*   256 And . . . they] They . . . now *C*   258 fall'n for ever,]
fall'n, for ever, *AB*   fall'n for ever *C*   267 *Sculpture,*] *Sculpture ABC*   join] join,
AB   270 Dread;] Dread, *A*   280 spend] spread *BC*   286 *Empire's*]
Empires A   287 Intomb'd I'll Slumber, or Enthron'd] Vanquish'd Intomb'd
I'll lye, or Crown'd *BC*   288 Virtue,] Virtue *AB*   295 the Rival] th'Usurp-
er *BC*   299 claim] Claim *AB*   300 King,] King *A*   305 Shore] Shore,
AB   311 There *Brabant*] *Brabantia BC*   314 her] the *C*   315 *Flanders*]
Flandria BC   319 Her Sister Provinces from her] From These their Sister
Provinces *BC*   320 or] and *C*   324 Marks] Signs *BC*   326 Types]
Marks *BC*   332 should] shall *C*   333 happy] Gracious *BC*   334
Sign . . . Pow'r] Type . . . Rule *BC*   336 nearly . . . approach] rudely . . .
provoke *BC*   337 And *Ireland*'s . . . her Emblem of] *Hibernia*'s Device of her
BC   338 Instrument of Joy, should] Parent of her Mirth, should *B*   Parent of
Her Mirth, shall *C*   339 And *Gallia*'s wither'd Lillies pale,] Thy vanquish'd
Lillies, *France,* decay'd *BC*   340 Should, here and there dispers'd] Should, with
disorder'd Pomp *B*   Shall with disorder'd Pomp *C*   348 appointed *Marl-
b'rough*'s] and when Thy *Marlbrô*'s *B*   and when Thy Subject's *C*   349 To end]
Had quell'd *BC*   make] bid *BC*   350 Everlasting] Conquest, and to *C*

An Epistle to Sir Richard Blackmore, Kt.

Copy text: [drop head title] An Epistle to Sir Richard Blackmore, Kt. On the Occa-

sion of the Late Great Victory in Brabant. [colophon] *London*, Printed for *John Chantry*, at the Sign of *Lincoln's-Inn-Square*, at *Lincolns-Inn* Back Gate, 1706. Price 2d. (*Copies:* Bodl., Rylands Library, Newberry Library).
Collation: Since the poem is known only in the 1706 quarto the copy text has been reproduced *verbatim et literatim* with one correction: *CHURCHILL* for *CHUCHILL* in line 32.

A Modern Inscription to the Duke of Marlboroughs Fame

Copy text: A Modern Inscription to the Duke of Marlboroughs Fame. Occasion'd by an Antique, in Imitation of Spencer. With a Preface Unveiling Some of the Beauties of the Ode, Which has Pass'd for Mr. Prior's [motto], 1706 (Rylands Library copy).
Collation: Since the poem is known only in the 1706 folio, the copy text has been reproduced *verbatim et literatim* with the exceptions noted below.

5 conquer, baffled *France*] conquer; baffled *France*, Sense, . . . Grace,   24 Sword and] Sword, and He,   60 manag'd] manag'd,   64 its] it's   14 Sense . . . Grace] 46 while He] while,

The Vision

Copy text: The The Vision, A Poem [n.p., n.d.] (Foxon D93) (Yale copy: Ik.D362.706v).
Collation: Although the poem is known to have circulated in manuscript (HMC *Mar and Kellie MSS.*, p. 351; Defoe, *Letters*, pp. 148, 162), no manuscript copy has been recovered. Foxon D93 and D94 appear to be two states of the first edition (*Aa*). Copies of D94 in the BPL and Rylands Library differ from the Yale, NLS (1.505 [25a]), and Huntington copies of D93 only in the correction of three errors: elimination of the first "The" in the title and the first "h" in "Withches" (line 2) and deletion of a semicolon at the end of line 106.
    Foxon D95 is the second edition (*Ab*) presumably produced by the same Edinburgh printer. A few errors are corrected in the standing type of pages 1–2, but pages 3–4 are reset. The presswork is careless, however, and the number of new errors introduced equals the number of old ones eliminated. Thus "Her's" (line 5) is corrected to "Here's," but in line 125 "here's" relapses to "her's." And as Foxon notes, the BM copy "has a variant position of the page number 4."
    Foxon D96 is the third edition (*Ac*), "Reprinted at *London* for *Benjamin Bragg*, at the Black Raven in *Pater-noster-Row*. 1706," as the imprint reads. It was set up from *Aa*.

Title: The Vision, A Poem *Aab*   The Vision, A Poem. Being an Answer to the Lord Beilhaven's Speech *Ac*

2 Wizards] Vizards *Aabc*   7 little's] little has *Aabc*   15 paund] pawn

Ac   47 Visionist] Visionest *Aabc*   53 scar'd] scarr'd *Aab*   55 amazement t'increase] amazement 'lincrease *Aab*   Amazement'll increase *Ac*   62 might] must *Ab*   93 That to fight] Their Freight *Ac*   were] was *Ac*   94 off] of *Aa*   117 e're so in] e're-soon *Ac*

A Scots Answer to a British Vision

Copy text: A Scots Answer to a British Vision . . . n.p., n.d. (*Copies:* NLS, Harvard [two copies]).
Collation: The copy text, a folio half-sheet in two columns on one side only, is reprinted *verbatim et literatim.*

A Reply to the Scots Answer to the British Vision

Copy text: A Reply to the Scots Answer to the British Vision . . . n.p., n.d. (Foxon D58) (NLS copy).
Collation: The copy text (*Aa*) represents the uncorrected state of the first edition. A later state (Foxon D57) (*Ab*), of which the copy in the Huntington Library has been collated, exhibits minor corrections: elimination of an extraneous comma after "Answer" in the title and others at lines 11 and 37.

The second edition (Foxon D59) (*B*), of which the Harvard copy has been collated, was set up from *Ab*. It appears to have been corrected by the author: the emendations at lines 1 and 28 do not seem to be those of a press corrector.

Title: A Reply to the Scots Answer to the British Vision *Aab*   A Poem to the Author of the Scots Answer to the Brittish Vision. *Projicit Ampullas & sesquipedalia Verba,* Hor. *B.*

1 Lord] Orator *B*   11 Eyes] Eye, *Aa*   27 th'amazement] the Amazement *B*   28 Voice] Force *Aab*   37 May edifie] Edifie *Aa*

A Scots Poem

Copy text: A Scots Poem: Or A New-Years Gift from a Native of the Universe, to His Fellow-Animals in Albania [motto] Edinburgh, Printed Anno Dom. M,DCC,VII (Foxon X34) (NLS copy).
Collation: Since no other witness remains, the copy text, a quarto pamphlet, has been reproduced *verbatim et literatim* with the following exceptions: commas separating subject and verb ("*Britain,* is" line 30), verb and object ("protect, The true Religion" lines 49–50), compound nouns ("Fire, and Thunder" line 101), compound adjectives ("Rich, and Happy" line 121), and the parts of prepositional phrases ("about,

Scorcht *Africk*" lines 161–62), have been deleted without record; other editorial emendations, substantive or accidental, are recorded in the apparatus.

2 august Places] August places   12 So that] That so   15 Plague] Plague, 18 then,] then   28 kind,] kind   31 Exploits?] Exploits: 55 Steps] Steps,   60 triumph] triumph,   61 *Jacobite*] *J——te*   66 Yea,] Yea   67 *Achilles*] *Achilles,*   69 straight,] straight   72 God] God, 76 but] but,   *Man*] *Man,*   79 *House*'s] *Houses*   85 true:] true   92 *Nine,*] *Nine;*   105 Corpses] Corps's   114 Source] Source,   146 African,] African.   148 *Line*] Line,   154 *Antipods*] *Antipod's*   161 *Inds*] *Ind's*   164 know] know,   165 sent.] sent   172 haunt,] haunt 182 initiate] initiate,   183 *Cloven-foot*] *Cloven-foot,*   184 say.] say   196 Snow] Snow,   202 ready] ready,   203 below,] below;   204 waits its] waits, it's   209 before] before,   217 welcom'd] welcom'd,   221 *Shrubs*] *Shrubs,*   223 *Bestial*] *Bestial,*   227 alarm'd] alarm'd,   238 Int'rests] Interests,   242 sown,] sown   244 find,] find;   250 happiness,] happiness: 252 we] we,   guile,] guile;   257 Stop,] Stop 258 she] she,   259 Excuse] excuse   262 another] another's   264 What did,] What, did   267 Water] Water,   268 then] then,   287 Fountains] Fountains,   289 Desolation,] Desolation;   294 There] There, 298 These cost,] These, cost   301 *Catholicks*] *Catholicks,*   304 *Tiber*] *Tiber,* 308 conduce] conduce,   314 Courage,] Courage   322 *Monarch*] *Monarch,* 326 *France,*] *France:*   333 Vice,] Vice;   337 hear,] hear;   340 same,] same   352 down,] down;   355 *Perfumes*] *Perfumes,*   362 unite,] unite;   369 did . . . know] had . . . knew   372 Enemies?] Enemies. 374 *Omen*] *Omen,*   376 despise,] despise: 377 flys;] flys.   383 War;] War.   390 *Grimace,*] *Grimace:*   413 Only but] Only, but,   431 forswore,] forswore.   437 While] While,   440 *Asp*] *Asp,*   play,] play; 444 to,] to   455 *Jack* is] *Jack's*   457 *France,*] *France*   458 Religion] Religion,   advance.] advance   459 *Saint,*] *Saint?*   460 *Jacobite*] *Jacobite,*   Covenant.] C——t   463 back] back,   467 Good] Good?   468 Triffles] Triffles——   469 PRIGGISH WHORING BRAT] P—— H W——G B——T   474 way] way,   476 Let's, Sincere,] Let's Sincere   477 Nation] Nation,   480 knows] knows,   481 vain] vain,   483 time,] time   484 *Rattle-Brains*] *Rattle-Brains,*   485 Rob,] Rob;   486 hear,] hear;   492 COUNTRY-MEN] C——Y-M—N,   493 enough] enough, 495 Country-man] C——n,   Hell] H—l   497 COUNTRY's] C——Y's 500 Place] P——   502 Country-men] C——n   made.] made   505 *Annandale*'s] A—— is   506 before] before,   *Peer*] ——   507 Pray] Pray,   Country-man,] C——n;   508 King *James*'s *Courtier*] K—— *Courtier,* Honest] H——st   510 Then] Then,   512 Tho'] Tho',   517 Duke of *Hamilton,*] D. of H——n.   520 May] May,   525 Prais'd,] Prais'd. 526 thought] thought,   Designs;] Designs,   532 thought] thought,   534 ne're] nere   538 speaks] bespeaks   539 Cheeks:] Cheeks.   543 Unite] Unite,   552 But] But,   559 *Medium*] *Medium,*   561 Remedy] Remedy;   562 you] you,   565 Secure,] Secure;   567 Safe] Safe, 571 *Son,*] *Son:*   573 Trade] Trade,   578 So that] That so   580 *Son;*]

Son:　　581 mine] mine,　　586 endur'd,] endur'd;　　592 furious]
furious,　　appears,] appears:　　593 *Tarpaulins*] *Tarlaupins,*　　595 form'd]
form'd;　　Skill,] Skill:　　598 *Arts,*] *Arts:*　　608 Glides;] Glides,
610 Ship] Ship,　　620 Lest] Lest,　　623 Course.] Course?　　625 Means,]
Means.　　630 feed] feed,　　633 avail,] avail:　　635 *Case*] *Case,*
640 Its] It's　　642 *Peace,*] *Peace:*　　643 Whereby] Whereby,　　Ease,]
Ease:　　644 Attempts,] Attempts:　　645 Secured] Secured,　　656 Yea,]
Yea　　662 then] then,　　664 this] this,　　666 Streets,] Streets;
674 Benefit,] Benefit;　　695 Fortune] Fortune,　　amend,] amend:　　696
Tho] Tho,　　697 *Equivalent*] *Equivalent,*　　701 Cess,] Cess;　　704 fixt,]
fixt;　　723 Start,] Start;　　724 Art,] Art;　　725 know,] know;　　734
Themes] *Themes,*　　743 *Forts,*] *Forts:*　　745 still,] still;　　746 is,] is
747 till,] till.　　748 Expence,] Expence.　　757 *Government,*] *Government;*
758 some,] some　　790 *undersell;*] *undersell,*　　792 next,] next　　small,]
small;　　796 State,] State;　　800 observed] observ'd　　802 Term,]
Term;　　808 the] th'　　812 Yea,] Yea　　818 grown,] grown;
821 *State,*] *State;*　　823 *Event,*] *Event.*　　835 considered.] considered,
840 Difference is] Difference's　　856 *Parliament*] Parliament　　865 Sacri-
fice] Sacrifice.　　873 *Union* refuse,] Union refuse;　　875 State,] State;
882 lean,] lean:　　883 please] please,　　890 it's] it's,　　897 grant's]
grants　　904 Influence,] Influence:　　906 shou'd] shoud　　907 fail,]
fail.　　918 *English*] E——sh　　922 Strength,] Strength!　　924 here] here?
925 fear;] fear,　　926 *Moons*] *Moons;*　　930 But] But,　　931 Which]
Which,　　932 home] home,　　933 Countrey] Countrey,　　934 See]
See,　　935 its] his　　939 No,] No　　Fopp] Fope　　940 *Gaul's*] *Gauls*
942 bewitch] bewitch,　　943 Pretexts] Pretexts,　　944 e're] er'e
945 quit] quite　　947 Who] Who,　　948 But] But,　　e're] er'e
956 if] if,　　Rent,] Rent;　　972 sport,] sport.　　974 *Liberty*] Liberty,
981 War] Wars　　991 its] it's　　996 was] was,　　997 *JAMESES*]
J——S,　　998 *Papists*] P——ts,　　999 *Lauderdals*] *L——ls*　　1000 *Atholls,*
MONTGOMERIES] *A——ls, M——S's*　　*Rascals*] *R——ls*　　1001 *DUNDEES*]
D——S,　　1005 such] such,　　*State,*] *State;*　　1007 Let] Let,　　1011
Conquest] *Conquest,*　　1014 content;] content.　　1015 *Monarchs*] *Monarchs,*
1017 *Rex,*] *Rex;*　　1018 minding] minding,　　1022 guards] Guards
1024 *Sin.*] *Sin*　　1038 *Jameses* or *Charleses*] J——s or C——s　　1039 Then]
Then,　　1042 *Fame*] Fame,　　1043 may,] may　　1045 And] And,
1047 be,] be　　1052 worlds] world　　1055 *Sovereign's*] *Sovereigns*　　1057
roll'd] roll'd,　　1059 *Necks,*] necks　　1064 *Sp'rit,*] *Sp'rit:*　　1066 gone,]
gone:　　1068 But] But,　　1069 *Son*] *Son,*　　1070 Blood,] Blood
1072 Than] Than,　　*Self*] *Self,*　　1073 boast] boast!　　1076 Seed,] Seed.
1078 Race,] Race.　　1079 Imbrace] Imbrace,　　1081 stand] stand,　　1084
Bosom,] Bosom:　　1085 Tear] *Tear*　　1087 Room] Room,　　Enmity]
Enmity,　　1088 Good,] Good;　　1090 *King.*] *King*　　1091 *William*]
William,　　1094 May] May,　　Name] Name,　　1099 Soul] Soul,　　*Heav-*
'n] *Heavens,*　　1100 worthy] worthy,　　1103 Soul] Soul,　　1104 Hearts,]
Hearts:　　1105 *Foes*] Foes,　　1106 Conjoin'd] Conjoin'd,　　1107 Terms]
Terms,　　1109 content] content,　　down] down:　　1114 Sure] Sure,

bliss] bliss, 1116 May] May, 1118 May] May, divert,] divert: 1120 Property,] Property: 1124 *Support* of *State,*] Support of *State.* 1125 And] And, *Mean*] *Mean,*

Verses said to be Written on the Union

Copy text: Aa
Collation: This may have been one of "several original Poems" which Swift gave George Faulkner "in his Life Time" and which Faulkner published the year after Swift's death (*The Works . . . In Eight Volumes,* Dublin, 1746, "The Preface by the Dublin Bookseller," *8,* sig. Π4v), but Faulkner provides no further evidence of the provenance or authenticity of this poem. No manuscript has been recovered and the eighteenth-century printed copies are the following:

The Works of Jonathan Swift, D.D, Dublin, 1746, *8,* 314 (Teerink 44) (Smith College copy)	Aa
Miscellanies, 1746, *11,* 242–43 (Teerink 66) (U. of Pennsylvania copy)	Ab
Miscellanies, 1749, *11,* 242–43 (Teerink 68) (Smith College copy)	Ac
Miscellanies, 1751, *14,* 216–17 (Teerink 82) (U. of Pennsylvania copy)	Ad
The Works of Jonathan Swift, D.D., Dublin, 1751, *8,* 152–53 (Teerink 45) (U. of Pennsylvania copy)	Ae
The Works of Jonathan Swift, D.D., Dublin, 1752, *8,* 222–23 (Teerink 45A) (U. of Pennsylvania copy)	Af
The Works of Jonathan Swift, D.D., ed. John Hawkesworth, 1755, *4,* i, 283–84 (Teerink 87) (Smith College copy)	Ag
The Works of the Reverend Dr. Jonathan Swift, Dublin, 1772, *8,* 222–23 (Teerink 48) (U. of Pennsylvania copy)	Ah
The Works of the Rev. Dr. Jonathan Swift, ed. Thomas Sheridan, 17 vols., 1784, *7,* 39 (Teerink 119) (U. of Pennsylvania copy)	Aj
The Works of the Rev. Jonathan Swift, D.D., ed. John Nichols, 19 vols., 1801, *7,* 37 (Teerink 129) (U. of Pennsylvania copy)	Ak

Teerink (p. 35) calls *Ae* "the same printing" as *Aa,* but the University of Pennsylvania copy of *Ae* is an entirely different setting of type, and the title page,

Volume VIII. / Of The / Author's Works. / Containing / Directions to Servants; / And / Other Pieces in Prose and Verse, / published in his Life-time, with several / Poems and Letters never before printed. / [monogram] / *Dublin:* / Printed by George Faulkner, in *Essex-street,* / M,D,CC,LI.

differs from the title pages of both issues of *Aa. Ah* on the other hand is the same setting of type as *Af.*

What appears to be contamination in *Af*—both *Ad* and *Af* read "Poesies" for "Posies" in line 9—is more likely to be a remarkable example of coincidental error. John Hawkesworth corrected the error in his edition of 1754–55 (*Ag*).

Hawkesworth took his text directly from *Ad* and did not, in this case, collate it with the Dublin editions (Swift, *Discourse,* p. 187).

The relationship of these copies can be shown in a diagram:

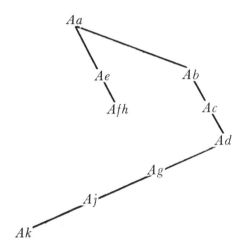

Title: no variants.

13 Statesman] Statesmen *Abcdg*

Switch and Spur

Copy text: BM MS. Lansdowne 852, f. 131.
Collation: Since no other copy has been recovered, the copy text is reproduced *verbatim* with the following emendations:

1 *Gentlemen,*] Gentlemen   2 what (. . . trembled)] what . . . trembled   3 I heard] I have heard   4 was] 's ev'n   Remember,] Remember   7 next,] next   8 Supplies.] Supplies;   22 Arm'd,] Arm'd;   35 *Church,*] *Church*   37 They've] Th'ave   42 near] nere   53 lose] loose   55 and] a   63 *no paragraph in MS.*   67 prevail'd,] prevail'd   70 *Wolfen-*

buttle,] *Wolfenbuttle;*   73 *Godly,*] Godly   75 *Cause,*] *Cause*   83 *Review,*]
Review   84 *Oracle,*] *Oracle;*   85 *Ministry,*] *Ministry.*   86 Mammon,]
Mammon   90 *no paragraph in MS.*   92 *so,*] so   Coaches;] Coaches
93 *Cloudesly, Buenos*] *Cloudesly bonos*

Abigail's Lamentation for the Loss of Mr. Harley

Copy text: C
Collation: The following copies have been recovered:

Hertfordshire County R. O. MS. Cowper Box 12, Family Book, *1,* 25–26	*A*
Bodl. MS. Ballard 47, ff. 85–86	*B*
Poetical Reflexions, Moral, Comical, Satyrical, &c., Part the Eleventh, B. Bragge, 1709 (Folger copy)	*C*
Abigal's Lamentation For the Loss of Secretary *H——y. Translated from the Greek of* Homer. [n.p., n.d.] (Harvard copy)	*D*
Clark Memorial Library MS. uncatalogued (formerly Phillipps MS. 3824), f. 63	*E*
NLI MS. 10244 Townley Hall Papers [no fol.]	*F*
Blenheim MS. GI 15	*G*
BM MS. Add. 40060, ff. 79v–80	*H*
The Prophesy: Or, *M—— m'n* Lamentation for *H——y. Translated from the* Greek *of* Homer . . . Printed for Abel Roper, at the *Black Boy* in *Fleetstreet,* 1710 (Bodl. copy: Firth b.21 [79])	*J*
BM MS. Lansdowne 852, f. 148	*K*
Longleat MS. Portland XI, f. 43	*L*

ABC are assumed to represent the archetype most nearly. The first half-sheet edition (*D*), printed in a single column on one side only, and the manuscripts *EFGH*, derive collaterally from a source different from the source of *ABC*. The second broadside edition (*J*), also printed in a single column on one side of the sheet, and the manuscripts *KL*, derive from the source of *DEFGH* but show evidence of conflation with *ABC*. Another copy, BM MS. Portland Loan Arundell v. ll, f. 43, similar to KL, was found too late to be included in the apparatus.

Title: [none] *A*   Asgills lamentation for the losse of Mr. Harley. From the Greek of Homer left imperfect by Mr. Walsh *B*   Abigail's Lamentation for the Loss of her Mistress's Secretary. From the Greek of Homer; left imperfect by Mr. Walch *C*   Abigal's Lamentation For the Loss of Secretary H——y. Translated from the Greek of Homer *D*   Abigls lamentation for the loss of H——ly translated from the Greek of Homer left unfinished by the Welsh *E*   A(bigail's) lamentation for the loss of (Mr.) H(a)——(ly) Translated from the Greek of Homer left by Mr. Walsh imperfect *FGHKL*   The Prophesy: Or, M——m's Lamentation for H——y. Translated from the Greek of Homer *J*

1 the World with Frowns] *AB* with Frowns the World *Σ*   3 *Harley*] *ABKL*
H(a)——(ly)Σ   7–8 *omitted E*   7 he] his *C* the *D*   9 So] *A* Like
BC As *Σ*   11 *Russell's*] *R——l's C*   12 So *Nottingham* still] Since nothing
C So *N(otting)(ham) still DFGHJ* So Nottingham *E*   look'd] looks *CGHKL*
13 Tow'rs] Tower *BCGH*   *Masham*] *M——m CJ*   15 doth] does *BCDE*
17 loud] sad *A* and *C*   20 the] *A* Your *Σ*   fatal] wretched *E*   21
us'd] *A* went *Σ*   23 Sorrows] *ABC* Sorrow *Σ*   this] *A* your *Σ*   24
Hopes] Hope *DEH*   now your] now become your *GHJKL*   27 *Harcourt*]
H——t CJ Hart——t *E*   28 *omitted E*   28 *Cowper*] *C——r CJ*   29
Sunderland] *S——d CJ* his Post been forc'd to] *A* had been forced his Place to
BDE by Force his Place must *C* been forced his Place to *Σ*   30 St. *John*]
S(t). *J(ohn's) CEHJ*   sprightly] mighty *B* ready *J*   31 *Hanmer*] *H——r(e)*
CJ   33 *Gower*] *G——r CJ*   *Newcastle's*] *N——(w)——(C)——(l)e's*
CJ   34 *Harley's*] H——(l)y's *CEJ*   36 That now] *A* Which now *BCJ*
Which yet *Σ*   *Godolphin's*] *G(od)——n's* CEJ   37 Fleet] Fleets *ABGH*
38 *Ormond*] Bellasis *B* *O——(n)d CDJ*   head] lead *EFGH* Rule *JKL*   40
Ramillia's] Ramil(l)ie's *BEH* Ramelly's *C* Ramelies *D* Ramilly's *J*

A New Ballad:
To the Tune of *Fair Rosamund*

Copy text: Aa
Collation: The following copies have been recovered:

A New Ballad: *To the Tune of* Fair Rosamund [n.p., n.d.] (BM copy: 1850.c.10 [12])	*Aa*
Hertfordshire County R. O. MS. Cowper Box 12, Family Book, *1*, 28–32	*Ab*
Hertfordshire County R. O. MS. Cowper Box 9, Diary, *5*, 33–38	*Ac*
A New Ballad. To the Tune of *Fair Rosamond* [n.p., n.d.] (Copies: BM[162.m.70 (11)], Bodl. [Firth b.21 (94)], Harvard)	*Ba*
A New Ballad. To the Tune of *Fair Rosamond* [n.p., n.d.] (BM copy: CUP.645.c.1 [26])	*Ca*
University of Leeds MS. Brotherton Lt.11, pp. 155–60	*BCb*
Political Merriment: Or, Truths Told to Some Tune, 1714, pp. 274–81 (Case 280[2]) (Yale copy)	*BCc*
A Pill to Purge State-Melancholy: . . . The Third Edition, 1716, pp. 29–35 (Case 288[c]) (Yale copy)	*BCd*
TCD MS. I.5, *4*, 224–26	*BCe*

AaBaCa are folio half-sheet editions printed in two columns, *AaBa* on both sides of the sheet and *Ca* (pirated?) on one. Since *BaCa* display no substantive variants and no certain accidental variants, priority cannot be established by collation.

The two Cowper manuscripts (*Abc*) are copies either of *Aa* or of a closely related text. The Brotherton manuscript (*BCb*) and the two anthology texts (*BCcd*) derive from *BaCa*. The TCD manuscript in turn is almost certainly a copy of *BCc*.

Variants are recorded only for *Aabc, Ba,* and *Ca.*

Title: [no variants]

1 Queen *Anne*] *Abc*   Q——— *A*——— *Aa*   Qu——— *A*——— *Σ*   5 *Abigail*] *Abc* *Ab* ———
Aa *Abi*——— *Σ*   16 at] of *Ac*   19 Rogue] *Ac* *R*——— *Σ*   27 Bitch] *Abc*
B———ch *Aa* B——— *Σ*   43 from] of *Ab*   52 were] *Aabc* are *Σ*
53 Argument lies] *Aabc* Arguments lies *Ba* Arguments lie *Ca*   74 Queen]
Abc Q———n *Aa* Q——— *Σ*   91 Church's] Churches *Aab*   127 with his]
Ac what his *Σ*   134 Queen] *Ac* Q——— *Σ*   138 who] *Aabc* what *Σ*

Masham Display'd

Copy text: B
Collation: Three copies have been recovered:

        Bodl. MS. Eng. poet. e.87, pp. 28–30   *A*
        Political Merriment: Or, Truths Told to Some Tune, 1715,
            pp. 19–20 (Case 280 [3]) (Yale copy)   *B*
        A Pill to Purge State-Melancholy, 3d ed., 1716, pp. 35–36
            (Case 288[c]) Yale copy)   *C*

A is both corrupt and fragmentary but still retains readings of undoubted authority. The independence of the three copies is established by the fact that each of them retains lines of undoubted authority not preserved in the other two, viz. *A* (5–8), *B* (21–24), *C* (45–48). The three copies are derived from the archetype in the following fashion:

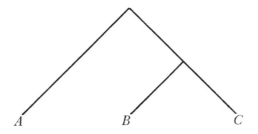

Title: A Ballad by Mr Manwaring upon Mr Secretary Harley & Mrs Massam *A*
Mass——m display'd: *To the Tune of* The Dame of Honour *B*   *A Ballad to the Tune*
of the Dame of Honour *C*

1 Town] State *A*   4 Queen] Q——(n) *BC*   Kingdom] K——d——m *B*
5–8 *omitted BC*   9 Birth] Wit *A*   10 does] would *A*   11 matchless]
mighty *A*   15] It was the Devil sure, not Fate *A*   26 And a wond'rous]
Made Her turn *A*   17 Hag] Beast *B*   Jade *C*   retires] aspires *A*   18 in
Bed] abed *AC*   21–24 *omitted AC*   25–28 *omitted C*   25 Harley] Ox——d
B   26 Pretender] Pr——r *B*   30 Which is] Which has been *B*   That has
been *C*   32 spight of] spight of her *A*   spite of the *C*   33–52 *omitted A*
35 *Harley*'s] *Ox——d's BC*   41 the] our *C*   42 *Marlb'rough*] *Marl——h*
B   44 Of Courtiers that infect] And *Mass——m* who infects *B*   45–48
omitted AB   45 *Robin*'s] *R——n's C*   49 should send her] will send their *B*

The Humble Memorial

Copy text: *Aa*
Collation: Only three copies have been recovered:

> [Robert Mann?], *A Dialogue between Louis le Petite, and*
> *Harlequin le Grand. Containing, Many S——e Riddles,*
> *C——t Intrigues, Welch Witticisms, Pedagogue Puns, S——y*
> *Quibbles, and Occasional Conundrums. Publish'd for the Benefit*
> *of all True Patriots, to Direct their Choice in an Able*
> *S——r. To which is added, Some Recommendatory Poems,*
> *by some Favourites of the Two Esquires,* [1708], pp. v–vii
> (Yale copy).   *Aa*
> [William Oldisworth], *State Tracts: Containing Many*
> *Necessary Observations and Reflections on the State of our*
> *Affairs at Home and Abroad; with Some Secret Memoirs.* By
> the Author of the *Examiner,* 2 vols., 1715, *2*, 142–46
> (Harvard copy)   *Ab*
> TCD MS. I.5, *3*, 178–80   *Ac*

Ab and *Ac* derive successively from *Aa.* The copy text is reprinted with the following
emendations:

2 State] S——e *Aab*   8 State] S——e *Aab*   10 Post] P——t *Aab*   Point
Ac   13 State] S——e *Aab*   14 Royal] R——l *Aab*   20 *Harlequin*
of State] *H——quin* of S——e *Aab*   34 Pillory] P——y *Aab*   39 *Review*]
R——w Aab   45 *Scotland*] S——nd *Aa*   46 North] N——th *Aab*   48
Caledonia] C——nia *Aa*   Cameronia *Ac*   50 Scabs] S——bs *Aa*   Swabs *Ac*

54 Treason] T——n *Aab*   60 Tuft . . . Hair] T——ft . . . H——r *Aab*
62 *Venus*] V——us *Aab*   69 *Porter*] P——r *Aa*   75 *Lorrain*] L——in *Aab*
77 *Tyburn*] T——n *Aa*   78 *Gregg*] G——g *Aa*   80 hang . . . hang'd . . .
Man] h——g . . . h——d . . . M—— *Aa*

Duke Humphrey's Answer

Copy text: A
Collation: The text survives in four manuscripts, all derived collaterally from the archetype:

Bodl. MS. Eng. poet. c.87, pp. 34–36	*A*
BM MS. Lansdowne 852, f. 23	*B*
Bodl. MS. Firth b.21 (71)	*C*
BM MS Add. 40060, f. 76	*D*

Title: Duke Humphr(e)y's Answer *AD*   Duke Humphreys Answer: 1708 *B*
The Duke of Gloucesters Ghost *C*

4 Durst] Dares *BCD*   5 durst] dost *BCD*   6 Fate,] Fate; *A* Fate *BC* Fate: *D*
12 th'unhappy Doom] the unhappy Doom *ABC* th'unhappy fate *D*   13
Meteor] Monster *D*   14 those] the *C*   their] the *AB*   15 Arch-
Rebel] Arch-Angel *A*   16 Thee] the *BCD*   18 Abyss,] Abyss *ABCD* 19
hath] has *BCD*   20 sting] taint *A*   23 Blood] death *BCD*   24
care,] care *ABCD*   27 gains] gaind *BC* got *D*   28–29 *omitted A*
29 Jennings] J(e)n——gs *BC*   Monthermer] m——h——r *B* M——s——m
D   30 Thus] Then *C*   34–35 *follow* 31 *A*   35 gives] gave *CD*
37 Scorn stab thy] Scorn'd stabb'd by *A*   38 flattring] totering *CD*   42
thy] with *B*   44 deluge] torrent *D*   48 Vaults] Vales *D*

Jack Frenchman's Defeat

Copy text: Ba
Collation: The following copies have been recovered:

Hertfordshire County R. O. MS. Cowper Box 46 Lampoons	*A*
Jack French-Man's Defeat: Being an Excellent New Song, to a Pleasant Tune, called, *There was a Fair Maid in the* North-Country, *Came Trip⸱ ʊg over the Plain,* &c. [n.p., n.d.] (BM copy: C.40.m.10[102])	*Ba*
A Ballad on the Battle of Audenarde [n.p., n.d.] (Copies: Chetham's Library, Halliwell-Phillipps No. 1836;	

Harvard, Julian Marshall Collection)   *Bb*
Poetical Miscellanies: The Sixth Part, 1709, pp. 250–54
   (Case 172[6]a) (Yale copy)   *Bc*
The State Garland of Antient and Modern Loyal Songs and
   Catches, Part II, Dublin: Printed by Daniel Tompson,
   1715, pp. 49–52 (Case 477) (Yale copy)   *Bd*
Hertfordshire County R. O. MS. Cowper Box 12,
   Family Book Vol. 2, pp. 27–30   *C*
Hertfordshire County R. O. MS. Cowper Box 9, Diary,
   4, 7–10   *D*
A Pill to Purge State-Melancholy: Or, A Collection of
   Excellent New Ballads, The Third Edition, with
   Additions, 1716, pp. 5–8 (Case 288[c]) (Yale copy)   *Ea*
The Hive. A Collection of the Most Celebrated Songs, 4 vols.,
   1732, *4,* 219–22 (Case 331 [4]) (Harvard copy)   *Eb*
Jack Frenchman's Lamentation, An Excellent New Song.
   To the Tune of, *I'll tell the Dick,* &c. Or, *Who can but*
   love a Seaman, &c. [n.p., n.d.] (BM copy: 1876.f.1
   [40])   *Fa*
Jack Frenchman's Lamentation. An Excellent New
   Song, To the Tune of *I'll tell thee Dick, &c.*
   . . . *London:* Printed, and are to be Sold by *John*
   Morphew, near *Stationers-Hall,* 1708 (Harvard copy:
   pEB65.C7605.708j)   *Fb*
Jack Frenchman's Lamentation, *An* Excellent New
   Song, To the Tune of *I'll tell thee Dick, &c.* . . .
   Edinburgh Re-printed in the Year 1708 (BM copy:
   12350.m.18 [3]).   *Fc*
The Battel of Audenard. A Poem . . . *Also A New Copy*
   of Verses of Jack Frenchman's Lamentation, London
   (H. Hills), 1708 (Bodl. copy)   *Fd*
Essex R. O. MS. D/DBy.Z5   *Fe*
TCD MS. I.5, *3,* 112–13   *Ff*
BM MS. Add. 30381, pp. 247–50   *Fg*
The Merry Musician: Or, A Cure for the Spleen, Part I,
   1716, pp. 247–50 (Harvard copy)   *Fh*
University of Leeds MS. Brotherton Lt.11   *Fj*
BM MS. Add. 40060, ff. 71v–73v   *Fk*

A is a fragmentary manuscript which omits lines 25–30 and 67–84 but which appears to have circulated before *Ba* was published and which preserves several unique readings of obvious authority. It also preserves a unique refrain, "With a fa la &c.," which concludes every stanza. *Ba,* a folio half-sheet printed in two columns on one side only and illustrated with "a fair Representation of the Battle curiously Engraven" (*The Daily Courant,* 17 July 1708), is assumed to be the first edition. *Bb,* a song sheet engraved in two columns on one side only, was set up from *Ba.* It omits the woodcut and includes, at the top of the page, the music to *The Ladies of London* and, at the bottom of the page, "Another tune," which is Richard Leveridge's *Ye Commons and Peers* (Simpson, p. 801). Of the two anthology copies, *Bcd, Bc* appears to have been set up from *Ba,* and *Bd* from *Bb.* *C* was copied from a manuscript similar to *A* but set to a different tune. The copyist of *C* supplied lines 37–42 from "the printed ballad," presumably *Ba.* Here is what he wrote: "the following verse [37–42] is in the printed ballad. I suppose was forgot in the coppy from wch I writ it." *D,* Dame Sarah Cowper's copy, omitting lines 37–42, may derive from the same source. *Ea,* since it includes lines 37–42 but inserts them after line 48, may also derive from the source of *CD* and have added lines 37–42 from another copy. *Eb* was set up from *Ea.*

Fa, the second folio half-sheet edition is printed in two columns on one side only and omits no lines, but it represents a separate tradition which is slightly inferior to *B.* It is illustrated with a simple woodcut of soldiers marching. *Fb,* the third broadside edition, was set up from *Fa* in two columns on one side only, but omitting lines 37–42. Of this edition there are two states or issues: the second (Bodl. copy: Firth b.21[67]) corrects in the standing type an error ("perlexed") in line 67 of the first and adds "The Second Edition" to the publisher's imprint. *Fc,* a fourth broadside edition, *Fd,* Henry Hills' piracy, tacked onto a blank page at the end of another work, and three more manuscript copies, *Fefg,* all derive collaterally from *Fb.* *Fh,* another anthology copy, was set up from *Fb* but seems to have improvised its title from *Ea.* *Fjk,* at last, are two more manuscript copies derived from *Fb.* *Fk* however shows evidence of contamination from *ABC.*

Title: A Ballad made upon the battle of Audenarde: by Mr. Congreve. to the tune of prithee Horace hold up thy head *A*   Jack French-Man's Defeat: Being an Excellent New Song, to a Pleasant Tune, called, There was a Fair Maid in the North-Country, Come Triping over the Plain, &c. *Ba*   A Ballad on the Battle of Audenarde *Bb*   A Ballad: On the Victory at Audenarde *Bc*   A Ballad on the Battle of Audenarde. Set by Mr. Leveridge *Bd*   Song By Mr. Congreve To the Tune of, You tell me Dick &c. *C*   15 July. 1708. A New Ballad by Mr Congrave *D*   An Historical Account of the Battel of Audenarde *Ea*   The Battle of Audenarde. 1708 *Eb*   Jack Frenchman's Lamentation, An Excellent New Song. To the Tune of, I'll tell the Dick, &c. Or, Who can but love a Seaman, &c. *Fa* Jack Frenchman's Lamentation. An Excellent New Song, To the Tune of I'll tell the(e) Dick, &c. *Fbcef*   Jack Frenchman's Lamentation. A New Copy of Verses, To the Tune of I'll tell thee Dick, &c. *Fd*   Jack Frenchman's Lamentation *Fg*   Monsieur thwack'd; or, an Historical Account of the late Battle of Audenard. To a Tune of Mr. Leveridge's *Fh*   Jack Frenchman's Lamentation. To the Tune of I'll tell the Dick *Fj*   The Frenchman's Lamentation An Excellent New Song to the Tune of I'll tell the Dick *Fk*

1 Ye] You *A*   7 How his] This *A*   8 total] fatal *A*   9 Not far from the River of] *BFh*   close by the river *A*   All close by the River *CD*   And close by the River *Σ*   14 The] This *A*   15 gallant] *A*   clever *Σ*   16 But] And *B*   18 They most gallantly] *A*   They cleverly *B*   Most cleverly *Σ*   19 Then a] *B*   On *A*   Then on *Σ*   20 Upon] *A*   All upon *BCD*   All on *Σ*   21 th'advice] *A*   advice *Σ*   23 To] *A*   Unto *Σ*   25–30 *omitted A*   25 Just so did he] *B*   While thus he did *CD*   While this he did *Σ*   26 When with-

out] *B* Without *Σ*   30 But] *B* Thô *Σ*   more heavy than] *B* much
heavier than *CD* as heavy as *Σ*   32 Young] The Young *BD*   33 I'll]
A I *Σ*   ye] you *BacCDFh*   35 He] Yet he *BD* matter'd *B* valu'd *Σ*
36 Fought it] Charg'd still *B* Fought still *CD*   37–42 *omitted DFbcdefghjk*
follow line 48 *Eab*   37 While] Whilst *A* When *Bbd*   43 Thus Firmly]
A Thus Boldly *B* Full firmly *Σ*   44 that] *BabcCD* this *A* his *Σ*   45
Which] That *A*   46 This] *AB* For this *Σ*   47 Kin] a-kin *EF*   48
Did] Fought *B*   49 What a Racket] What racket *CD*   51 ill fortune]
Misfortune *EF*   52 When] For *EF*   56 To Monsieur] To the Mounsier
BabdFk   were] *A* we *Σ*   57 he soon shall] we soon did *D* they shall *EF*
58 While] Whilst *AFk*   60 *De Profundis*] *AB* Nunc dimittis *Σ*   61 their]
BCD this *Σ*   63 Noise] *A* Sound *Σ* Drums] *ABCEFghk* Drum *Σ*
64 think] dream *A*   65 Of] On *Fk*   67–84 *omitted A*   68 General's]
General *EFabcdefgjk*   69 chang'd 'em in] *BC* changed in *Σ*   71 New
ones are] new one is *Eb* new ones *Fabceg* new one, *Fd* new ones be *Ff* new
Fj new be *Fk*   72 the Old] 'em *Fabcdefghj* 'em all *EbFk*   78 Pudding and
Beef] Beef and Pudding *EaF*   81 Winner he . . . Wins] Winners do . . . win
EF   83 Thou hadst] You had *D*

An Epigram

Copy text: A
Collation: The poem is preserved in three manuscripts collaterally derived from
a common source:

> BM MS. Lansdowne 852, f. 137   *A*
> BM MS. Lansdowne 852, f. 23v   *B*
> Longleat MS. Portland XI, f. 47   *C*

A fourth copy, BM MS. Portland Loan Arundell v. ll f. 47r, similar to *C*, was found
too late to be included in the apparatus.

Title: An Epigram occasion'd by Madam Churchill's being hang'd last Friday. 1708
A   On Mrs. Deborah Churchill hang'd at Tybourn *B*   [none] *C*

1 wish for] now do *A*   2 engross'd] had all *C*   4 Perhaps they'll make the
Gallows too] It's hop'd they'l make the Gallows too *B* They'l make the gallow's
too perhaps *C*   5 And that I'm sure, is now] Then be it so, for that's *C*   *After* 6
A adds:

> Or any of th'Illustrious *Blacksmith*'s Race.
> Would they engross that Place, they'd be forgiven
> By all the Brittish Earth perhaps—by Heaven
> But if they will not be so Just and Civil
> Then Heaven and Earth must leave them to the Devil.

*A certain Blacksmith near Dorchester had a Duke to his Grandson &c. but those who do not approve this line may leave it out, and read in the following *She* for *they,* and it may prove both Rhime: and Reason to every one.

Leviathan

Copy text: Ad

Collation: The following copies have been recovered:

Leviathan, Or, A Hymn to Poor Brother Ben. To the Tune of *the Good Old Cause Reviv'd,* London, 1710 (Harvard copy)	*Aa*
Leviathan, Or, A Hymn to Poor Brother Ben. To the Tune of *the Good Old Cause Reviv'd,* London, 1710 (Bodl. copy: Firth b.21[75b])	*Ab*
A Collection of Poems, &c. For and Against Dr. Sacheverell, 4 vols., 1710–11, *3,* 31–33 (Case 254[3]) (Yale copy)	*Ac*
Tory Pills to Purge Whig Melancholy . . . The Second Edition, 1715, pp. 78–80 (Case 254[f]) (Harvard copy)	*Ad*

Of two almost identical folio half-sheet editions, the Harvard copy has been designated *Aa* because it reads "the Rule not" at line 41, which the Bodl. copy (*Ab*) corrects to "they Rule not." *Ac* was set up from *Ab,* and *Ad* from *Ac.*

Title: Leviathan, Or, A Hymn to Poor Brother Ben. To the Tune of the Good Old Cause Reviv'd *Aabcd.*

7 wake] awake *Acd*

Dr. Sacheverell and Benjamin Hoadly

Copy text: C

Collation: The text survives in a printed copy and ten manuscripts, all derived collaterally from a common source:

Hearne, *2,* 352	*A*
BM. MS. Lansdowne 852, f. 27v	*B*
The Communication of Sin: A Sermon Preach'd at the Assizes held at Derby, August 15th, 1709. by Henry Sacheverell, D.D., 1709, 4⁰, sig. Alv (Madan copy)	*C*
Berkshire R. O. MS. Trumbull Add. 17	*D*
Osborn MS. Chest II, No. 16	*E*

BM MS. Egerton 1717, f. 53   *F*
Osborn MS. Box 37, No. 16   *G*
BM MS. Add. 21094, f. 176   *H*
BM MS. Egerton 924, f. 32   *J*
Northamptonshire R. O. MS. I.L. 4381   *K*
TCD MS. I.5, *2*, 209   *L*

Title: [none] *ACDEFK*   (On) Dr. Sacheverel(1) & Ben: Hoadl(e)y *BJ*   On
the Humours of the Age *G*   Interest governs Conscience *H*   Nothing Certain
L

1 Among] Amongst *FGHJK*   *Church Men*] Church *EH*   2 That stick to the
Doctrine of] Do swear to the *Merit(s)* of *CDEFG*   Dare stand to the merits of *H*   That
will stand by the merits of *J*   That will stand to the merrit of *K*   Who loudly declare
for *L*   *Henry*] Harry *AGH*   Honest *K*   3 Among] Amongst *FGHJK*   Church
too] Church I *D*   Churchmen *FKL*   Church *J*   I find] do see *D*   I see *EFGJ*   I
think *K*   are some *L*   4 *Some pin all their*] some pin their *H*   Pinn their whole
L   *on one*] on *ABCEL*   to one *F*   upon one *G*   5 *Men* do] Men *EF*   Men
will *HJ*   Folks *K*   Churchmen *L*   *Judgment*] *Judg(e)ments CFGHK*   Opinions
E   6 where *these*] where those *B*   how *these CDG*   where this *L*   *Matters*]
matter *L*   will] may *CDG*   7 And *Salisbury*] For Sal'sbury *ABDEGH*   Since
Salisbury CJ   Salsbury *F*   There's Salsberry *K*   *Burnett* and *White Kennet*]
(Burnett) and Kennet(t) White *ABCDFHJKL*   Kennet and West do *E*   8
That as the Times vary] That Doctrines *may Change CDEFGHJ*   that Religion may
Change *K*   That Principles alter just *L*   so *Principles* go] as *Preferments* do (go)
CDEFGHJ   as preferment does go *K*   as the Times go *L*   9 And] But *B*
So that *J*   Some *K*   you or I] I or you *B*   as we *C*   you and I *DFGJK*   I and
you *E*   that you *L*   10 'Twill] *ABK*   It may *E*

The Junto

Copy text: Aa
Collation: The text survives in three folio half-sheet editions, one manuscript, and two
anthologies, none of which include substantive variants:

The Junto [n.p., n.d.] (Harvard copy)   *Aa*
The Junto [n.p., n.d.] (University of Indiana copy)   *Ab*
The Junto [n.p., n.d.] (BM copy)   *Ac*
BM MS. Add. 21094, f. 173   *Ad*
A Collection of Poems, For and Against Dr. Sacheverell, 4 vols.,
   1710–11, *1*, 31–32 (Case 254[1]) (Yale copy)   *Ae*
Tory Pills to Purge Whig Melancholy, 2nd ed., 1715, pp.
   22–23 (Case 254[f]) (Harvard copy)   *Af*

The only relationship that can be deduced among these six copies is that *Af* appears to have been set up from *Ae. Ab* and *Ac* are both printed in italic. The folio half-sheet editions may be distinguished as follows: *Aa* reads "foul" in line 10; *Ab* reads "*Counteance*" in line 19, and *Ac* reads "Wiles" in line 13.

Title: The Junto *Aabcdef*

5 *Northumbrian*] *N——th——rian Aabcdef*   17 *stuttering*] *fluttering Aef*   26 won;] won. *Aabc* won, *Ad*   29 Secretary] *Se——ry Aabcdef*   33 *Elzevirs*] *Elzivirs Aa Elzivers Aef*

On Dr. Sacheverell's Sermon

Copy text: Political Merriment: Or, Truths Told to Some Tune, Part III, 1715, pp. 42–43.
Collation: Although it can hardly be doubted that the poem circulated in manuscript in the closing months of 1709, only one witness has been discovered. It is reproduced *verbatim* with half a dozen unrecorded changes in accidentals.

The Thanksgiving

Copy text: K
Collation: The text survives in 16 manuscript copies and two printed anthologies, of which the following are collaterally derived from a common source:

Essex R. O. MS. D/DW Z.3	*A*
BM MS. Add. 21094, f. 174v	*B*
Osborn MS. Chest II, No. 16	*C*
Northamptonshire R. O. MS. I.L.4381	*D*
Hearne, *2,* 352	*E*
Portland MS. Pw V 41, p. 91	*F*
Staffordshire R. O. MS.	*G*
University of Leeds MS. Brotherton Lt.13, f. 41v	*H*
Hertfordshire County R. O. MS. Cowper Box 9, Diary, 5, 9	*J*
Whig and Tory: Or, Wit on Both Sides, 1712, p. 441 (Case 254[c]) (Yale copy)	*K*
BM MS. Egerton 924, f. 32	*L*
Bodl. MS. Eng. poet. e.87, p. 28	*M*
Interleaved copy of James Harward, *A Prognostication for the Year of Our Lord God 1666,* Dublin, 1666, p. 92 (Swift, *Poems, 3,* 1058, 1061, 1083–84)	*N*
University of Leeds MS. Brotherton Lt.11, p. 80	*O*
Berkshire R. O. MS. Trumbull Add. 17	*P*

BM MS. Lansdowne 852, f. 29v   *Q*
Bodl. MS. Firth b.21 (73)   *R*

Osborn MS. Box 37, No. 16 is textually identical with *D* and *Tory Pills to Purge Whig Melancholy*, The Second Edition, 1715, p. 67 (Case 254[f]) was set up from *K*.

It appears that the title and eight lines of the poem originated in *The Thanksgiving* ("Republicans, your tuneful Voices raise"), 38 lines of witty but tendentious verse which were published in *A Collection of Poems, For and Against Dr. Sacheverell*, 4 vols., 1710–11, *1*, 8–9 (Case 254[1]b). To these borrowed lines four new ones (3–4 and 9–10) were added to produce the present epigram, of which it is assumed that *AB* most nearly represent the archetype. In the process of transmission this pointed and spirited Jacobite complaint against Queen Anne was worn down to a conventional Tory attack on "the Three": Lord Godolphin and the duke and duchess of Marlborough (textual notes 3, 5, and 12).

Title: The Thanksgiving *ABCDEHJKNOP*   [none] *FG*   Directions for a Thanksgiving Day *L*   The Thanksgiving for 1708 *M*   The Thanksgiving February 1709/10 *Q*   On the Thanksgiving *R*

1 Sounds] Songs *H*   2 teach] learn *J*   whom] when *C*   how *M*   3 prudent *Anna*'s] Anna's prudent *C*   Prudent Zara(h)'s *LM*   Humble Sarah's *NOPQ* humble Zara's *R*   4 both of Corn and] both of Coyn & *EFGHJKMNOQR* and all sorts of *L*   5–6 *omitted B   follow* 8 *L*   5 Thank the Scotch Peers] Thank(s) to Volpone *MNOPQR*   their firm] the firm *C*   your firm *DFGHJ* your *KMNOPQ*   firm and *L*   the *R*   7 Stock-Jobbers] Banks and Brokers *NO*   8 Thank just *Godolphin*] & just G——d——n *G*   And thank Godolphin *H*   Once more thank Volpe *MNOPQR*   your] the *C*   all *DEGJKLPQ* our *R*   10 But thank] And thank *ALN*   Thank *O*   that   Frenchmen] the Frenchmen *DEGHJKMNPQR*   the French *L*   that the Frenchmen *O*   *After* 10 *L adds:*

> Thank Whigs that vote the Church need fear no Ruin:
> As plain appears by what those Whigs are doing.

11 that you are] if you are *DJKNOPQR*   for beeing *G*   for that you're *H*   that you're so *L*   that you're still *M*   12 But thank] And thank *AEH*   And sing *MNO*   Thank *P*   th'Almighty] Te Deum *MNO*   if you are not] that you are not *BCL*   when the Three are *MNOPQ*   when these Three are *R*

The Civil War

Copy text: A
Collation: The poem survives in two manuscripts, Berkshire R. O. MS. Trumbull Add. 17 (*A*) and BM MS. Lansdowne 852, f. 25 (*B*). Since both manuscripts are virtually unpointed, the necessary punctuation has been supplied.

Title: The Civil War *A*   The Civil War: February 1709/10 *B*

10 Masham's] Messams *A*   M——ms *B*   15 their Persons were] the Persons
are *AB*   31 thenceforth] henceforth *A*

Found on the Queen's Toilet

Copy text: A
Collation: The text survives in the copy text and 13 collateral manuscripts:

A Collection of Poems, For and Against Dr. Sacheverell, 4 vols., 1710–11, *1*, 3 (Case 254[1]b) (Yale copy)	*A*
Bodl. MS. Rawl. poet. 173, f. 2	*B*
Osborn MS. Box 37, No. 16	*C*
Osborn MS. Chest II, No. 16	*D*
Essex R. O. MS. D/DW Z. 3	*E*
University of Leeds MS. Brotherton Lt. 11, p. 80	*F*
BM MS. Add. 21094, f. 174v	*G*
Bodl. MS. Firth b.21 (73)	*H*
Staffordshire R. O. MS. Bagot D.1721/3/246	*J*
Northamptonshire R. O. MS. I. L. 4381 (2)	*K*
Bodl. MS. Ballard 27, f. 56	*L*
Berkshire R. O. MS. Trumbull Add. 17	*M*
Hearne, *2*, 352	*N*
BM MS. Lansdowne 852, f. 27v	*O*

Title: Said to be found upon a Great Lady's Toylet *A*   Said to be found upon a great Lady's Toylet about the same time [i.e. as the time of Sacheverell's trial] *B*   A Copy of Verses found on the Q⁵ Toylett *C*   Found in the Qn's Twilight *D*   Found on the Qu(ee)n's Toilet(t) *EF*   Laid on The Q——'s Toylet on the 30th Jan: 1710 *G*   Left on the Queens Toilet *HO*   Said to be found on the Queens Toylet *J*   [none] *KLM*   A Poem Found on the Queen's Toilet *N*

Before 1 *G adds:*

The best of Prelates in a factious Age
Unjustly fell by the mad Senate Rage
Not Long unhappy Charles surviv'd his Fate
And with the Church Expir'd the Regal Race.

3 the Throne] thy Throne *CGN*   the Crown *F*   4 *Martyr*] *AB*   Gran(d)sire *Σ*   5 by *Clamour*] with Clamors *F*   with clamour *GHJ*   by Clamors *KLMNO*   Faction] Traytors *A*   Factions *KMO*   6 that does] *AB*   who does *C*   who dares *DLNO*   that dares *Σ*   Right] Rights *AJK*   8 Stop] O stop *LMNO*   portentous Omen] dire proceedings *LMNO*   ere too] ere it be too *A*   9 View thy whole Friends'] And View thy own *CDEFGHJK*   And see thy own *LMNO*   10 Stated] Fatall *CDEGHJKLMNO*   Woful *F*   bids thee now] now bids all *AB*   11 *follows* 12 *NO*   11 Rebellion in an Age] *A*   Rebellion in one Age *B*   bless'd

Martyr of thy race *Σ*   12 At him they strike] They strike at him *F*   *regal*
Right's the Prize] *regal Right's* their Prize *A*   want that Sacrifice *C*   thou'rt the
sacrifice *DEFJKLMNO*   your the sacrifice *GH*   *After* 12 *J adds:*

> Fools, at the other house to try the preist
> What! is your own Authority a Jest
> Try him your Selves like Rump, without more words
> You that can make the King, can make the Lords

A Tale of a Nettle

Copy text: Fa
Collation: The text is preserved in the following copies:

The Works of Jonathan Swift, D.D., ed. Walter Scott, 19 vols., Edinburgh, 1814, *10*, 447–48	*A*
BM MS. Lansdowne 852, ff. 90v–91	*B*
Bodl. MS. Rawl. D.383, f. 61	*C*
Bodl. MS. Rawl. D.376, f. 199v	*D*
BM MS. Add. 27408, f. 23	*E*
The Tale of a Nettle . . . Cambridge, Printed in the Year, 1710 (Harvard copy: fEc75.A100.B775C vol. I)	*Fa*
The Tale of a Nettle. Written by a Person of Quality. . . . Cambridge, Printed in the Year, 1710 (Copies: University of Texas, Rylands Library)	*Fb*
The Tale of a Nettle. Written by a Person of Quality. . . . Cambridge, Printed in the Year, 1710 (Copies: University of Leeds Brotherton Collection, University of Pennsylvania)	*Fc*

A is printed from a copy "in the Dean's handwriting" in the Thomas Steele manuscript (*Harvard Library Bulletin, 19* [October 1971], 403–07), but the present location of the manuscript is not known.

Of the three broadside copies, *Fa* and *Fb* seem to be the first and second impressions, respectively, of the first edition, while *Fc* is apparently a later edition, correcting most of the printer's errors in *Fab*, but introducing numerous new ones. *Fb* and *Fc* can be distinguished as follows:

line 26	*line 34*	
with the	on	*Fb*
withe	and	*Fc*

Title: A Tale of a Nettle *AD*   Upon a Nettle *B*   The Tale of a Nettle *CEF*

1 and infinite] and wonderfull *CD*   of wonderfull *EF*   2 Digging] *A*   Planting

Σ 3 There] Where *B* your] *A* the *Σ* 5 Weeds] *A* Weed *Σ* the Rich Ground] the ground *BC* did produce] produce *A* 6 But] And *EF* for] *BD* both *Σ* 8 rear'd] rais'd *D* 13 chose as] chose the *B* chooseth *D* 14 Questions first, how] Questions how *B* 16 *For Conscience compell'd to relinquish*] A Wanderer thrô Convenience I relinquisht *B* By conscience compell'd to relinquish *D* 18 *is*] *A* was *Σ* 21 *omitted D* 24 *your Fruitful*] the fruitfull *C* the faithfull *DEF* 25 *Tho' your*] As your *B* Tho' by *D* 26 *your Gardiner's Forms*] your garden in forms *A* your Gard'ner in Forms *B* the Gardiners Forms *C* your Gard'ner in form *D* the Gard'ner in form *E* the Gard'ner in Forms *F* 27 *my*] *AC* our *Σ* 29 *rest in*] rest *C* 30 *For*] And *C* 'Mongst *DEF* *the rest of your Trees*] we none of your Family *C* the rest of the Trees *D* *we'll never*] we will not *B* ere will *C* *molest 'em*] molest *C* 32 *harm, Sir, I'll*] *AB* harm I'll *Σ* 33 won with this] mov'd with a *B* won by this *DEF* 35 free] full *C* 37 Breast] *A* Bosom *Σ* 38 little] *AB* never *Σ* 39 'Till] *AC* Still *Σ* and of] and *B* of *CDEF* 41 sensible what] sensible of what *BC* 46 stubborn, rank, pestilent] stubborn, pestilent *A* 47 the young] that young *DEF* 49 or] and *DEF* 50 The ill Weeds] *A* the Weeds *Σ* out] up *B* 51–52 *omitted CDEF*

Upon the Burning of Dr. Burgess's Pulpit

Copy text: Ba
Collation: Ten copies, varying more widely in title than in text, have been recovered:

Fire and Faggot, Or; An Ellegy on Dr. S——ch——ls	
Two Sermons, Which were Burnt on Monday the 27th of	
March, 1710, n.d., p. 7 (Newberry Library copy)	*A*
A Collection of Poems, For and Against Dr. Sacheverell, 4	
vols., 1710–11, *1,* 7–8 (Case 254[1]b) (Yale copy)	*Ba*
Whig and Tory: Or, Wit on Both Sides, 1712, pp. 7–8	
(Case 254 [c]) (Yale copy)	*Bb*
Whig and Tory: Or, Wit on Both Sides, 2nd ed., 1713, pp.	
7–8 (Case 254 [d]) (Yale copy)	*Bc*
Tory Pills to Purge Whig Melancholy, 2nd ed., 1715, pp.	
67–68 (Case 254 [f]) (Harvard copy)	*Bd*
Northamptonshire R. O. MS. I.L. 4381	*C*
BM MS. 40060, f. 82v	*D*
Osborn MS. Box 89, No. 13, f. 110 (Phillipps 17695)	*E*
University of Leeds MS. Brotherton Lt. 11, p. 79	*F*
Osborn MS. Box 89, No. 12	*G*
Berkshire R. O. MS. Trumbull Add. 17	*H*
BM MS. Add. 21094, f. 181	*J*
BM MS. Lansdowne 852, f. 30	*K*

This is another epigram (p. 664 above) which was detached from a longer poem and given a life of its own. It is assumed that the epigram began its life as the last four lines of some undistinguished verses on the burning of Sacheverell's sermons (A) of which lines 4–11 are plagiarized from some equally undistinguished verses on the burning of *The Memorial of the Church of England*, a folio half-sheet of 1705 entitled *An Elegy on the Burning of the Church Memorial* ("No! Sacred Pages, never more repine"). Onto these four lines were then engrafted nine new lines of witless verse on the burning of Burgess's meeting house and the result was thrice reprinted in the eighteenth century (*Babcd*) and once in the nineteenth century (*Roxburghe Ballads, 8,* 242). At last the nine-line tail was removed and the liberated epigram could sport and flutter in manuscript copies.

Title: [none] *ACDE*   Upon the burning of Mr. Burges(s)'s Pulpit *Babcd*   An Epigram *F*   2 disticks writ over Dr: Burgess meeting House *G*   On the mobs pulling down several meeting houses *H*   On the Mob for Dr. Sacheverell *J* Dropt in Westminster Hall March 1709/10 *K*

1 your] the *DEF*   2 Priest would] priest will *G*   Priesthood *K*   3 a] their *A*   4 Tubs] Tub *F*

The Old Pack Newly Reviv'd

Copy text: Ea
Collation: The following copies have been recovered:

The Old Pack Newly Reviv'd [n.p., n.d.] [on verso: *A New Copy of Verses on the Present Times Relating to the Church and Dr. Sacheverell*] ("Come ye Old English Huntsmen, that love noble sport") (Huntington copy)	*A*
The Pack of Bear Dogs, Dublin (E. Waters), 1713 (Cambridge University copy)	*Ba*
The State Garland of Antient and Modern Loyal Songs and Catches, Part I, Dublin [1715?] (Case 477) (Yale copy)	*Bb*
BM MS. Add. 21094, ff. 171–72	*C*
The Old Pack [n.p., n.d.] (BM copy: Lutt.II.156)	*Da*
The Old Pack. With Additions [n.p., n.d.] (Harvard copy: *pEB7.A100.715oc)	*Db*
The Old Pack [n.p., n.d.] (Harvard copy: *pEB7.A100. 715ob)	*Dc*
The Old Pack [n.p., n.d.] (BM copy: C.20.f.4)	*Dd*
University of Leeds MS. Brotherton Lt. 11, pp. 126–31	*De*
A Collection of Poems, For and Against Dr. Sacheverell, 4 vols., 1710–11, *1,* 19–22 (Case 254[1]) (Yale copy)	*Ea*
Tory Pills to Purge Whig Melancholy, 2nd ed., 1715, pp. 8–12 (Case 254[f]) (Harvard copy)	*Eb*
The Old Pack. With Additions [n.p., n.d.] (*Bibliotheca*	

    Lindesiana, uncatalogued)   *Fa*

    The Old Pack [n.p., n.d.] (Bodl. copy: Firth b.21 [83])   *Fb*

A simplified version of the relationships among these copies is represented in this diagram:

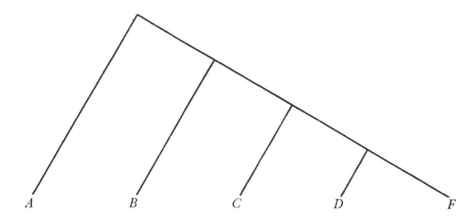

What appears to be the first edition (*A*) is a folio half-sheet printed in two columns with almost incredible carelessness, *e.g.,* "he'll Active" for "he'll Atchieve" (83) and "the which staff" for "the *White Staff*" (103). Some of the errors, "stickwin'd" for "*Chetwynd*" (3), "Whose" for "who's" (58), and "*Jack* call" for "*Jackall*" (77), suggest that the copy may have been taken down from dictation. On the other hand, *A* preserves unique readings of undoubted authority (17, 98, 102).

Although published three years later than *DEF* and apparently set to a different tune (textual note 8), *Ba* derives from a better copy than *DEF*. *Bb* was set up from *Ba*.

The manuscripts *C* and *De* have no independent authority.

Da, Db, and *Fa* seem to derive from a common source different from the source of *ABC*.

Ea appears to have been set up from *Da* and in turn is the source of *Eb*. As well as being included after line 80, lines 65–72 of *Ea* have been detached from *The Old Pack,* supplied with a feeble couplet to replace the refrain, and printed on p. 14 as a separate epigram with the title, *On Mr. Dolben's Voyage to, and Return from the Indies.*

Da, Db, and *Fa* are three folio half-sheet editions, distinguishable by the spelling "Woolf," "Wolf," and "Wolfe," respectively, in line 65. Corresponding to these three 13-stanza editions, there are three 12-stanza editions, *Dc, Dd,* and *Fb,* distinguishable in the same way by the spelling "Woolf," "Wolf," and "Wolfe," but omitting lines 65–72. Although the 13-stanza editions more closely represent the original than the 12-stanza editions, it appears from the subtitle, "With Additions," in two of them (*Db* and *Fa*), that they were published after *Dc, Dd,* and *Fb.*

Of *Dd* two states can be distinguished. The first state prints the numeration of stanza XI as IX (BM copy: C.20.f.4 [156]) and the second corrects this error (copies: Harvard [pEB7.A100.715od], Princeton).

Of *Fb* there are also two states, one reading "Noe" in line 43 (Bodl. copy: Firth b.21 [83]) and a second corrected to "Nye." Two substates of the latter may be further distinguished: the first, with a broken letter, reading "hor" in line 35 (Harvard copy: 10488.4 PF) and the second corrected to "hot" (Harvard copy: *pEB7.A100.715o; University of Leeds Brotherton copy).

Title: The Old Pack Newly Reviv'd *A*   The Pack of Bear Dogs *Bab*   The Old Pack *CDacdeEaFb*   The Old Pack. With Additions *DbFa*

3 *Sewster . . . Chetwynd*] Suller . . . stickwin'd *A*   *Suster . . . Chetwind B*   match] watch *DcdeF*   4 or] and *DEF*   Bounds] *B*   *Mounds Σ*   6 Most] Some *DEF*   8] *For they have the Dogs, for they have the Dogs; And are Riding* Tantive, Tive, Tive. *B*   9 Atheist . . . Deist] *AB* Atheists . . . Deists *Σ*   10 old long-winded] *AB*   long-winded *Σ*   13 *Quaker*] *ADe* Quakers *Σ*   14 kind] blind *B*   17 Camp, and] *AB* Army *Σ*   dropt in] *A*   drop in *B*   dropt from *Σ*   19 are good harmless] were *poor senseless B*   were good harmless *F* Tooth or Claw] Teeth or Claw *C*   Teeth or Claws *DEF*   20 whelp'd] *bred B* Law] Laws *E*   21 poor wretched] *B*   wretched poor *Σ*   Mungrels, Starters] Mungrel Starvers *CDEF*   25 the true] true *A*   a true *B*   the *F* 26 are] *AC*   were *Σ*   27 every Throat] such Throats *CDF*   such vile Throats *E*   28 Number] *B*   Numbers *A*   Hunters *Σ*   Note] *AB*   Notes *Σ*   29 off] of *ABCDEF*   33 are] is *B*   35 Throats] Throat *B*   36 Notes] Note *B*   41 *Hoadly*] *Ho——ly E*   Dogs] *AB*   Whelps *Σ*   43 Writings] Writing *C*   stole] *AB* stol'n *Σ*   45 that] the *DEF*   49 the] their *B* 51 By a strong] On a hot *B*   ran] *B*   run *Σ*   52 too rank] rank *DEF*   53 break thro'] break *DEF*   54 Sure] Here *DEF*   57 of the] of a *E*   *William's*] *William DEF*   58 Breed] bred *CDE*   62 they] *AB* they'll *Σ*   65–72 *follow* 80 *DabEab*   omitted *DcdeFb*   *follow* 104 *Fa*   65 There's] *DE*   Loud *Σ* 66 that was] truly *DabEFa*   67 Gaol-Birds] Goal-Birds *ABDabEFa*   Jayle birds *C*   70 your] the *B*   this *E*   73 the rapacious] rapacious *DEF*   old] loud *B*   and *DEF*   74 Sir] *B*   And *Σ*   75 your] these *B*   the *DEF* 76 they expose their Parts] *B*   they expose the part *A*   th'expose that Part *Σ* 77 *Jackall*] *Jack* call *A*   *Jack,* call'd *B*   78 *Somers*] *S——ers E*   81 Mouths] Mouth *A*   84 his Conduct's] it's Conduct *DE*   its Conduct *F*   85 can] will *B*   86 the Cause just as] *AB*   a Cause as *Σ*   the Navy] *AB*   a Navy *Σ* 90 their dear Country's] their Countrey's *Da*   their Country's *DbcdeEF*   91 they] they'll *B*   its] *AB*   their *Σ*   93 Game] *AB*   Gain *Σ*   94 They'd] They'll *B*   They *DEF*   down] Dr. *B*   dear *Σ*   98 Stone] *A*   Shoe *Σ* 101 you'd] you *E*   102 of the] *A*   of their *B*   o'th' *Σ*

To the Tune of *Ye Commons and Peers*

Copy text: Harvard bMS Am 1622 (189).
Collation: Since no other witness is known, the copy text is reproduced *verbatim,* with a minimum of punctuation supplied, four precautionary blanks (e.g. "B-ps" in line 4) filled in, and abbreviations expanded.

Fair Warning

Copy text: A
Collation: The text survives in the following copies:

The Observator, 5–8 April 1710 (Yale copy)	*A*
Fair Warning . . . *London, Printed for, and Sold by* John Baker, *at the Black Boy, in Pater-Noster-Row,* 1710 (Harvard copy (pEB65.A100.B675b vol. 5, p. 74)	*Ba*
A Collection of Poems, &c. For and Against Dr. Sacheverell, 4 vols., 1710–11, *3,* 22 (Case 254[3]) (Yale copy)	*Bb*
The Whiggish Fair Warning to the Q——n, upon the Late Change of the Ministry; With the Tory's Fair Answer . . . Printed in the year MDCCXI (Harvard copy)	*Bc*
Political Merriment: Or, Truths Told to Some Tune, [Part III], 1715, pp. 54–55 (Case 280[3]) (Yale copy)	*Bd*
BM MS. Add. 40060, f. 83	*C*
BM MS. Add. 21094, f. 176v	*D*
BM MS. Add. 14854, f. 153	*E*
Hertfordshire County R. O. MS. Cowper Box 9, Diary, *5,* 14	*F*
Bodl. MS. Firth b.21 (72)	*G*
BM MS. Lansdowne 852, f. 132	*H*
BM MS. Add. 28253, p. 55	*J*
TCD MS. I.5, *2,* 213	*K*

Since it retains one line (15) of apparent authority that is omitted in all other witnesses, *A* is assumed to represent the archetype more nearly than *Ba,* which probably was published three days earlier. The broadside, *Ba,* printed in script type on one side of the sheet only, is the source in turn of two anthology copies and the second broadside edition (*Bbcd*). The manuscripts *CDEFGHJK* also derive from *Ba* or a collateral manuscript.

Title: Fair Warning *ĀBabdCDE*   The Whiggish Fair Warning to the Q——n, upon the late Change of the Ministry; With the Tory's fair Answer *Bc*   In a Letter to the Queen by the D——s of M——l——h *F*   To the Queen *G*   The Warning *HJ*   To her Majesty Queen Ann *K*

3 'tis *Revolution* that] The Revolution's what *HJ*   upholds the] upholds your *BCDEF*   Supports the *K*   4 If . . . then you are gone] *A*   Let . . . and you're undone *Σ*   5 *Doctrine . . .* be] *A*   Doctrines . . . are *Σ*   6 Reign's] Reign *BCDEHJK*   Right's *F*   8 *Parliaments*] parliment *FH*   9 *Settlement*] Settlements *AJ*   11 Priests affirm] *A*   Pulpits sound *Σ*   12 No] Nor *EFGHJ*   Or *K*   14 Rightful] *A*   darling *Σ*   15 *omitted BCDEFGHJK*   16 And swear the House shan't sit] *A*   You're in their Mercy for *BCDE*   You'r att their Mercy for *F*   You're att their mercy in *GHJK*   17 be] *AEGK*   are *BCDF*   is *HJ*   18 the] their *BCD*

On the Queen's Speech

Copy text: E
Collation: Besides the printed text, four manuscript copies have been recovered:

BM MS. Lansdowne 852, pp. 50–51   *A*
Northamptonshire R. O. MS. I.L 4382   *B*
Berkshire R. O. MS. Trumbull Add. 17   *C*
BM MS. Add. 21094, p. 355   *D*
A Collection of Poems, For and Against Dr. Sacheverell,
    4 vols., 1710–11 *1,* 33 (Case 254[1]) (Yale (copy)   *E*

When the poem was published (*E*), Anne was displaced by Louis XIV as the ma-
nipulated monarch, but the text, which may have been set up from *C*, was enclosed
between the conjurer's cant words "BUZ" and "MUM" to alert the reader to some
secret significance.

Title: [none] *AB*   On the Q——ns Speech *C*   A Simile on an Eccho, in St.
James's Parke *D*   On the French King *E*

2 Queen] King *E*   4 make] Meeke *B*   9 rebounds] Resounds *B*   10
her] his *E*   11 Devils] Devil *E*   12 Their] His *E*   Heart] Hearts *A*
14 th'inchantresse] th'Enchanting *BCE*   within The *D*

The History of Seven

Copy text: BM MS. Lansdowne 852, ff. 128v–29.
Collation: Since no other witness has been recovered, the copy text is reproduced with
a minimum of punctuation added at the ends of lines (which are almost unpointed in
the manuscript), in compounds like "*Scot*-like" (8) and "o're-Grown" (11), and
in possessives which otherwise might be read as plurals: "Mother's" (1, 9) and
"Church's" (40, 53, 76). The copy text has been amended as follows:

3 were] was   4 who] so   27 Her] Their   60 the] his   74
Loosen'd] Lowsun'd

The Save-Alls

Copy text: Ba
Collation: The text survives in six closely related printed copies:

The Save-Alls. Or, *The Bishops who Voted for Dr.*

Sacheverell . . . Edinburgh, *Printed by* James
Watson *and Sold at his Shop opposite to the* Lucken-
booths, 1710 (Copies: NLS [Ry III. c.34 (31)],
Clark Memorial Library)   *A*
The Save-Alls (n.p., n.d.) (Copies: Harvard,
University of Cincinnati)   *Ba*
The Six Save-Alls [n.p., n.d.] (Bodl. copy)   *Bb*
The Save-Alls . . . Printed in the Year, MDCCX
(Bodl. copy: Firth b.21[76a])   *C*
A Collection of Poems, For and Against Dr. Sacheverell,
4 vols., 1710–11, *1,* 33–36 (Case 254[1]b) (Yale copy)   *Da*
Tory Pills to Purge Whig Melancholy, 2nd ed.,
1715, pp. 23–27 (Case 254[f]) (Harvard copy)   *Db*

A, lacking lines 1–28 and possibly a piracy, is a folio half-sheet printed on both sides. *Ba* is a very careless impression (four obvious errors in lines 96–111) of another folio half-sheet edition printed on both sides. *Bb* is a second impression of *Ba,* with emendations and corrections (including three of the four errors in lines 96–111) made in the standing type, and a new title.

C, a third folio half-sheet edition, is printed in two columns on one side only. It was reset from *Ba* with some (but not all) of the corrections made in *Bb.* Since *Da* is a resetting of *Bb,* only two of its variants are included in the apparatus: line 18 where the right word seems finally to be indicated, and line 32 where the compositor's emendation, if not simply an accident, may be an effect of sectarian malice. *Db,* in turn, was reset from *Da.*

Title: The Save-Alls. Or, The Bishops who Voted for Dr. Sacheverell *A*   The Save-Alls *BaCDab*   The Six Save-Alls *Bb*

1–28 omitted *A*   4 Sarum's] S——m's *Ba*   S—— *Bb*   S——'s *C*   11 thy gracious Favours] a gracious Freedom *BaC*   15 Court] Courts *BaC*   C—— *Bb*   17 *Rochester*] R——er *BabC*   18 Deputy] Delight *Ba*   D——te *Bb*   Delegate *C*   D——ty *Da*   Wharton] Wh——n's *BaCDa*   W—— *Bb*   20 some fat wealthy Bishop's] T——n's Archbishops *BaC*   22 bears with . . . too near] suffers . . . to Gaurd *BaC*   32 Lavishly] Knavishly *Da*   56 the] his *BabC*   58 Departed] Lately departed *BabC*   his Father] he *BbC*   96 *Sectaries*] S——ries *A*   Secretaries *Ba*   104 Courses] Tenets *ABabC*   110 Tenets] Notions *Bb*

The Westminster Combat

Copy text: A
Collation: The text survives in four folio half-sheet editions, all printed in two columns on one side only, and in two anthologies:

The Westminster Combat [n.p., n.d.] (BM copy:
    1876.e.20[34])   *A*
The Westminster Combat [n.p., n.d.] (Bodl. copy: Firth
    b. 21 [75a])   *B*
The Westminster Combat [n.p., n.d.] (Copies: BM
    [112.f.44 (22)], Harvard [*pEB65.A100.B675b]   *C*
The Westminster Combat [n.p., n.d.] (*Bibliotheca*
    Lindesiana, uncatalogued)   *D*
A Collection of Poems, For and Against Dr. Sacheverell,
    4 vols. 1710–11, *1*, 25–28 (Case 254[1]b) (Yale copy)   *E*
Tory Pills to Purge Whig Melancholy, 2nd ed.,
    1715, pp. 16–19 (Case 254[f]) (Yale copy)   *F*

A reads "Valley" for "Volley" (31), "know" for "known" (54), "Who" for "Whose" (59), and "Post" for "Posted" (64). *B* corrects these errors (but introduces a new one in line 80). *C* prints the title in two banks of type and adds "*FINIS.*" *D* omits lines 13–16. *E* was set up from *A*, and *F* from *E*. *EF* are not included in the textual apparatus.

Title: [no variants].

2 Commons] C——ns *ABCD*   3 Whigs] Whig *ABCD*   9 *Paul's*] *Paul ABCD*   13–16 *omitted D*   19 Commons] C——ns *ABCD*   24 Kings] K——s *ABCD*   28 Churches] C——es *AC* Ch——es *BD*   29 *James*] *J—— ABCD*   31 Means] mean *ABCD*   33 *Dolben*] *D——n ABCD*   34 act] Art—— *A* Att—— *BCD*   37 *Peter*] *P—— ABCD*   39 pour'd out such] pour'd such *ABCD*   41 *Lechmere*] *L——re ABCD*   42 *Jekyl*] *J——l ABCD*   45 *William*] *W——m ABCD*   49 *Stanhope*] *St——e AB* *St——pe CD*   52 Kings] K——s *ABCD*   53 *Cowper*] *C——r ABCD*   56 Laws] L——s *ABCD*   58 *Thomas* of *Darby*] *T——s* of *D——y ABCD*   60 Chief Justice] C—— J—— *ABCD*   61 *Walpole* and *Smith*] *W——le* and *S——h ABCD*   66 Bishops . . . Lords] B——ps . . . L—ds *ABCD*   72 Nation] N——n *ABCD*   77 Mob's] Mobb *AB* Mob *CD*   79 Managers] M——r(s) *ABCD*   80 *Garrard*] *G——r——d ABCD*   any] a *BCD*   85 Managers] m——r(s) *ABCD*

On the Sentence Passed by the House of Lords on Dr. Sacheverell

Copy text: B
Collation: The text survives in four copies:

On the Sentence Passed by the House of Lords on Dr.
    Sacheverell . . . London: Printed in the Year. 1710
    (Cincinnati copy)   *A*
A Collection of Poems, &c. For and Against Dr. Sacheverell,

4 vols., 1710–11, *2,* 20 (Case 254[2]) (Yale copy)   *B*
Hertfordshire County R. O. MS. Cowper Box 9, Diary, *5,*
   26–27   *C*
TCD MS. I.5, *2,* 216–17   *D*

Title: On the Sentence Passed by the House of Lords on Dr. Sacheverell *AB*   On
Sacheverel's Sentence *C*   A Poem On the Mercy Shown to the Revd: Villain
Saccheverell *D*

3 sniv'ling] snuffling *D*   8 *omitted C*   21 Paws] Chains *D*

High-Church Miracles

Copy text: High-Church Miracles, Or, *Modern Inconsistencies* . . . London, Printed and
Sold by *A. Baldwin,* at the *Oxford Arms* in *Warwick-Lane.* 1710 (*Copies:* Harvard
[*EB7.A100.710h2], BM, Bodl. [G Pamph 1680 [31]).
Collation: The poem seems to have survived only in the copy text. This is a folio
half-sheet, printed on both sides, and including *The Explanation* in prose. The text is
reproduced here *verbatim et literatim* except that commas are substituted for semicolons
at the end of lines 11 and 13, a semicolon is substituted for a period at the end of line
12, a full stop is omitted at the end of line 2, and one substantive emendation is intro-
duced:

5 Vice] Wit

Some Verses Inscrib'd to the Memory
of the Much Lamented John Dolben, Esq;

Copy text: Some Verses Inscrib'd to the Memory of the much Lamented *John Dolben,*
Esq; who departed this Life the 29*th* of *May* 1710 [n.p., n.d.] (Bodl. copy: Firth b.21
[88]).
Collation: Since no other copy has been recovered, the copy text, a folio half-sheet
printed in a single column on one side only and enclosed in broad funereal border, is
reproduced here with the punctuation normalized in perhaps a dozen instances and
the following emendations:

1 ye] the   6 *Fool . . . Sport*] *F——l . . . Sp——t*   19 Haste] Hast

On my Lord Godolphin

Copy text: BM MS. Lansdowne 852, f. 35

Collation: Since the apparently unique copy in Lansdowne 852 is without punctuation, it is reproduced here *verbatim et literatim* with punctuation supplied.

The Humble Address of the Clergy of London
and Westminster, Paraphras'd

Copy text: B

Collation: One textual tradition is represented by two manuscripts and a folio half-sheet edition (the copy text):

Bodl. MS. Rawl. poet. 81, f. 45v	*A*
The Clergy of the City of London *and Liberty of*	
Westminster's *Address to the Queen, Presented on the 23d*	
of Aug. 1710. Paraphras'd. A Poem [n.p., n.d.]	
(Copies: Chetham's Library; Indiana University)	*B*
Hertfordshire County R. O. MS. Cowper Box 9, Diary,	
5, 47–48	*C*

Three (pirated?) folio half-sheet editions and three anthologies represent an inferior tradition:

The London Address [n.p., n.d.] (Harvard copy:	
Eb7.A100.710l)	*D*
The London Address [n.p., n.d.] (*Bibliotheca Lindesiana,*	
uncatalogued)	*E*
The London Address [n.p., n.d.] (Harvard copy:	
Eb7.A100.710lb)	*Fa*
A Collection of Poems, &c. For and Against Dr. Sacheverell	
4 vols., 1710–11, *3,* 23–25 (Case 254[3])	
(Yale copy)	*Fb*
Political Merriment: Or, Truths Told to Some Tune,	
1714, pp. ²200–02 (Case 280[2]) (Yale copy)	*Fc*
Tory Pills to Purge Whig Melancholy, 2nd ed.,	
1715, pp. 73–75 (Case 254[f]) (Harvard copy)	*Fd*

The author of what is assumed to be the original poem (*ABC*) is characterized first by his frequent substitution of an iamb in the third foot of an anapestic tetrameter line: for which (3), and that (14), come Whig (19), to prove (20), whose Claim (22), and we (30), was low (31), was too (32) this peace- (33), us not (36), and have (41), and second by his willingness to force words that are natural trochees into the anapestic meter: Chosen (2), *verbo* (6), other (26), Power (27), carry (34)—in fact the poem cannot be properly read without accenting these words on the second syllable.

    The reviser of the poem (presumably the author, but possibly someone else) eliminated six of the eleven iambic substitutions: (30), (31), (32), (33), (36), (41), and four of the five wrenched accents: (2), (26), (27), (34).

On two occasions (11–12, 34) the revised reading (*DEF*) has been adopted to restore the wording of the actual Address of 23 August 1710.

DEF may be distinguished as follows:

> address (4) . . . in next (39)   *D*
> Address (4) . . . in next (39)   *F.*
> Address (4) . . . in the next (39)   *Fa*

Title: The Clergy's Address in plain English Meeter *A*   The Clergy of the City of London and Liberty of Westminster's Address to the Queen, Presented on the 23d of Aug. 1710. Paraphras'd. A Poem *B*   The Bishop and Clergy of London Address *C*   The London Address *DEFabcd*

Salutation] May it please &c. *A*   [none] *BC*   *Madam, DEF*   2 The Chosen of his Lordship throughout the whole] By his Lordship conven'd from all Parts of the *DEF*   3 Heaven] *C*   Heavens *Σ*   4 abuse] mislead *DEF*   6 Truth, *in verbo*] Truth, *Verbo DEF*   7 right Clergy-men] High-Church-men were *DEF* 8 Were] Yet *DEF*   10 your Clergy's] our Loyal *DEF*   11 The Tryal was wicked, no Precedent for] As for the late Tryal, we all do abhor *ABC*   12 And as Genuine Sons of the Church, we abhor] We say 'twas quite Wrong, they'd no Precedent for *ABC*   13 Honour] Power *B*   desperate] horrid *DEF*   18 But we join, to support it] Tho we swear 'tis *confirm'd* by *DEF*   20 ye] *A*   you *Σ*   23 Right divine by Descent's] in our Works *Right Divine's DEF*   25 So that catch] *A*   So catch *Σ*   26 Of one or the other, by our two-fac'd] Of *St. Germains* and *Hanover* by our *DEF*   27 your Power] your just Pow'r *DEF* 28 to] wee'l *A*   withstand it] withstand *B*   29 Slavery's a coming] Slavery's coming *DEF*   30 calls] *A*   cries *Σ*   and we] and we all *DEF*   31 low] reduc'd *DEF*   32 much] cruel *DEF*   33 send up] put up *BC*   all join in *DEF*   34 that delight in] that carry on *A*   who carry on *B*   that wou'd carry on *C*   35 Mother, the Church] Mother-Church *CDEF*   36 leave us not] now leave us not *B*   leave us not now *CDEF*   39 us, in] your *C*   us in the *F* 41 and have an Ovation] and have an Oblation *B*   till the next Restoration *DEF*

The Age of Wonders

Copy text: Ba

Collation: The text survives in the following copies:

> Hertfordshire County R. O. MS. Cowper Box 12,
>   Family Book, *2*, 50–54   *A*
> The Age of Wonders: To the Tune of *Chivy*
>   *Chase* . . . Printed in the Year M.DCC.X
>   (Copies: BPL, BM, Bodl., Harvard)   *Ba*
> The Age of Wonders. To the Tune of *Chivy*

Chase . . . London Printed, and *Edinburgh* Reprinted by *John Reid Junior.* MDCCX (Copies: NLS, BM)	*Bb*
The Age of Wonders: To the Tune of *Chivy Chase . . .* Printed in the Year M.DCC.X (University of Cincinnati copy)	*C*
The Age Wonders: To of the Tune of *Chivy Chase . . .* Printed in the Year M.DCC.X (Indiana University copy)	*D*
A Collection of Poems, &c. For and Against *Dr. Sacheverell,* 4 vols., 1710–11, *4, 7*–10 (Case 254[4]) (Yale copy)	*E*
Political Merriment: Or, Truths Told to Some Tune, 1714, pp. ²103–08 (Case 280[2]) (Yale copy)	*F*
A Pill to Purge State-Melancholy, 1715, pp. 51–56 (Case 288) (Yale copy)	*G*
TCD MS. I.5, *3,* 133–37	*H*

There is so little evidence that some of the inference concerning relationship of the witnesses must remain provisional. The three folio half-sheet editions of 1710, all printed in two columns on one side only, may be distinguished as follows:

line 10	*line 59*	
ne'er	such	*Ba*
ne'er	some	*C*
ne'ere	some	*D*

The Cowper MS. (*A*) retains one stanza of evident authority (73–76) which is found in no other witness. The BPL copy of *Ba* is an uncorrected state, with "Cleargy" in line 17, "keeb" in line 82, and other errors. *Bb* was set up from *Ba* and *F* from *C* or *D. G,* in turn, derives from *F,* and *H* from *G. E,* which omits lines 101–20, may have been set up from a folio half-sheet edition different from *BCD.*

Title: [no variants]

25 Danger] dangers *A*   59 such] some *CDFGH*   s—— *E*   73–76 *omitted*
BCDEFGH   79 whom] who *BCDEF*   87 Dutchess] *AG* D——ss *Σ*
92 May to future] May t'future *BCDEF*   95 t'insult] to insult *CDEFGH*
99 his] *GH*   the *Σ*   100 we'll] *A*   will *Σ*   101–20 *omitted E*

The Virtues of Sid Hamet the Magician's Rod

Copy text: Aa
Collation: The following copies have been collated:

The Virtues of *Sid Hamet* the Magician's Rod . . .
   London, Printed: for John Morphew, near
   Stationers-Hall, MDCCX (Teerink 524) (Copies:
   BM, Harvard, U. of Pennsylvania)   *Aa*

The Virtues of *Sid Hamet* the Magician's Rod . . .
   London *Printed: And Re-printed at* Edinburgh *by*
   James Watson, *and sold at his Shop next Door to the*
   Red-Lyon *opposite to the* Lucken-booths. 1710
   (NLS copy)   *Ab*

The Virtues of *Sid Hamet* the Magician's Rod . . .
   London Printed, and Re-Printed in Dublin, 1710
   (Teerink 524) (Copies: Bodl. [Firth b. 21 (85)],
   Texas, Huntington)   *Ac*

Miscellanies in Prose and Verse, 1711, pp. 411–16
   (Teerink 2[1]) (Smith College copy)   *Ad*

Miscellanies in Prose and Verse. The Second Edition,
   1713, pp. 409–14 (Teerink 2[2]) (Smith College
   copy)   *Ae*

TCD MS. I.5, *1,* ²44–46   *Af*

Miscellanies. The Last Volume, 1727, pp. 81–86
   (Teerink 25[3a]) (Copies: Trinity College,
   Cambridge [Rothschild No. 1421]), Smith
   College)   *Ag*

Miscellanies. The Last Volume, 1728, pp. 81–86
   (Teerink 25[3e]) (U. of Pennsylvania copy)   *Ah*

Miscellanies. The Last Volume, 1731, pp. 184–88
   (Teerink 26) (U. of Pennsylvania copy)   *Aj*

The Works of J.S. D.D, Dublin, 1735, *2,* 44–48
   (Teerink 41) (Smith College copy)   *Ba*

The Works of J.S, D.D, Dublin, 1735, *2,* 34–37
   (Teerink 49) (U. of Pennsylvania copy)   *Bb*

Poems on Several Occasions. By J.S, D.D, Dublin, 1735,
   pp. 34–37 (Teerink 55A) (U. of Pennsylvania copy)   *Bc*

Miscellanies. The Last Volume, 1736, pp. 177–80
   (Teerink 28) (U. of Pennsylvania copy)   *Ak*

The Works of J.S, D.D, Dublin, 1737, *2,* 35–38
   (Teerink 42, pp. 28, 30) (U. of Pennsylvania copy)   *Bd*

The Works of J.S, D.D, Dublin, 1737, *2,* 32–35
   (Teerink 50) (U. of Pennsylvania copy)   *Be*

Miscellanies. The Last Volume, 1738, pp. 156–59
   (Teerink 30) (U. of Pennsylvania copy)   *Al*

Miscellanies. The Fourth Volume, 1742, pp. 82–85
   (Teerink 66) (U. of Pennsylvania copy)   *Am*

The Works of Jonathan Swift, D.D, Dublin, 1744, *2,*
   35–38 (Teerink 44) (U. of Pennsylvania copy)   *Bf*

Miscellanies. The Fourth Volume, 1747, pp. 82–85
   (Teerink 67) (U. of Pennsylvania copy)   *An*

The Works of Jonathan Swift, D.D, Dublin, 1747, *2*,
   32–35 (Teerink 51) (U. of Pennsylvania copy)   *Bg*
Miscellanies. The Fourth Volume, 1751, pp. 79–82
   (Teerink 68) (U. of Pennsylvania copy)   *Ao*
Miscellanies. The Fourth Volume, 1751, pp. 79–82
   (Teerink 69) (U. of Pennsylvania copy)   *Ap*
The Works of Dr. Jonathan Swift, 1751, *7,* 75–77
   (Teerink 82) (U. of Pennsylvania copy)   *Aq*
The Works of Jonathan Swift, D.D., ed. John
   Hawkesworth, 1755, *3,* ii, 71–74 (Teerink 87)
   (Smith College copy)   *Bh*
The Works of the Reverend Dr. Jonathan Swift, Dublin,
   1762, *2,* 38–40 (Teerink 53) (U. of Pennsylvania copy) *Bj*
The Works of the Reverend Dr. J. Swift, Dublin, 1763,
   2, 33–35 (Teerink 52) (U. of Pennsylvania copy)   *Bk*
The Works of Dr. J. Swift, Dublin, 1763, *2,* 37–40
   (Teerink 45A) (U. of Pennsylvania copy)   *Bl*
The Works of the Reverend Dr. Jonathan Swift, Dublin,
   1772, *2,* 37–40 (Teerink 48) (U. of Pennsylvania copy) *Bm*
The Works of the Rev. Dr. Jonathan Swift, ed. Thomas
   Sheridan, 17 vols., 1784, *7,* 65–68 (Teerink 119)
   (U. of Pennsylvania copy)   *Bn*
The Works of the Rev. Jonathan Swift, D.D., ed. John
   Nichols, 19 vols., 1801, *7,* 62–65 (Teerink 129)
   (U. of Pennsylvania copy)   *Bo*

Of the broadside editions, *Aa* and *Ab* (the latter unknown to Teerink or Williams) are printed in a single column on both sides of the sheet, while *Ac* is printed in two columns on one side only. The manuscript *Af* probably was copied from *Ae.*

    Swift's copy of *Ag* (now in the Rothschild Collection, Trinity College, Cambridge), which was used as copy text for *Ba,* makes no corrections in the text of *The Virtues of Sid Hamet the Magician's Rod,* but Swift did pencil a large S in the margin, confirming his authorship of the poem (*The Rothschild Library,* 2 vols., Cambridge, 1954, *1,* 367; *2,* 570) and subsequently he did make substantive changes in the text of the poem, presumably on the proof sheets of *Ba.*

    Bc is the same setting of type as *Bb* and *Ah* is the same setting as *Ag.* John Hawkesworth, the first editor of the poem, took *Ap* as his copy text but introduced several readings from *Bg.*

    The relationships among this unusually large number of witnesses are shown in the diagram on p. 681 (cf. Swift, *Discourse,* p. 183).

8 That senseless] That(,) senseless, *Aabcdef*   15 Hag] Hag, *AabcdefBbc*   23 its] it's *Aabcd*   37 fix,] fix *Aabcd*   45 *PLACE*] Plaise *AlmnopqBhn*   46 many a Score] many Score *AabcdefghjklmnopqBhno*   59 *Achilles'*] *ACHILLES*'s *Aabcdef*   61 Tho'] That *AghjklmnopqBhno*   85 *indentation added*   But] For *Aabcdefghjklmnopq*   86 may] will *Aabcdefghjklmnopq*

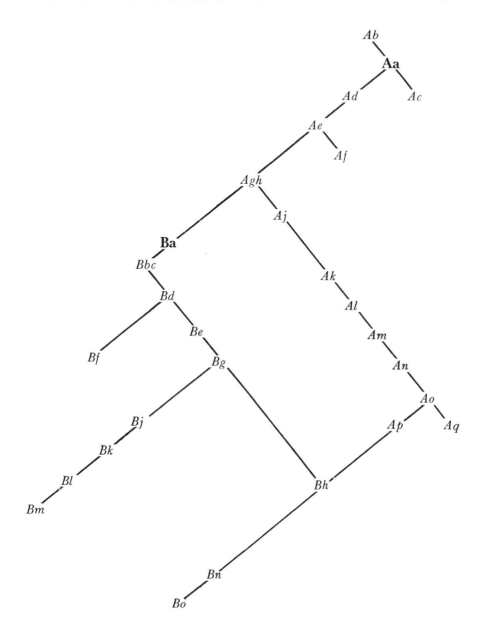

A Dialogue between Captain Tom and Sir Henry Dutton Colt

Copy text: Aa
Collation: The text survives in two broadside editions, both printed in two columns on one side of the sheet and in half-lines (possibly to imitate ballad stanza, but more probably simply to economize):

> A Dialogue between *Captain* Tom *and Sir* H——y
> D——n C——t . . . *Printed for the Consolation of those*
> *who can bear a* Cross *in the Year 1710* (Copies:
> University Library Cambridge [Syn.3.71.4], Trinity
> College, Cambridge [Rothschild No. 276], BM
> [C.121.g.9 (159)]   *Aa*
> A Dialogue between *Captain* Tom, *and Sir* H——y
> D——n C——t . . . *Re-Printed for the Consolation of*
> *those who can bear a* Cross *in the Year,* 1710 (Copies: Uni-
> versity Library Cambridge [Hib.3.740.2], Dublin Public
> Library Pearse St. Branch [Sir John T. Gilbert
> Collection, Newenham Pamphlets, III, 58],
> Huntington [HEH 355350])   *Ab*

The BM copy represents an earlier uncorrected state of *Aa. Ab*, set up from *Aa* in a different font of type, may be a Dublin piracy.

6 *Colt* . . . *Stanhop*] C——t . . . *St—nh—p Aab*   15 *Stanhop*] *St—nh—p Aab*
18 *Colt*] C——t *Aab*   27 *Stanhop*] *St—nh—p Aab*

An Acrostick on Wharton

Copy text: H
Collation: All of the following copies seem to derive collaterally from a common source:

> Osborn MS. Chest II, No. 53   *A*
> Bodl. MS. Rawl. poet. 155, p. 112   *B*
> BM MS. Add. 21094, f. 165   *C*
> Hertfordshire County R. O. MS. Cowper Box 9, Diary,
>   5, 63   *D*
> University of Leeds MS. Brotherton Lt. 13, f. 41   *E*
> Hearne, *3*, 89   *F*
> Bodl. MS. Eng. poet. e.87, p. 53   *G*
> *Whig and Tory: Or, Wit on Both Sides*, 1712, p. 442
>   (Case 254[c]) (Yale copy)   *H*
> BM MS. Lansdowne 852, f. 31r   *J*
> BM MS. Egerton 924, f. 38   *K*

In addition, the poem was printed in *A Collection of Poems, &c. For and Against Dr. Sacheverell*, 4 vols., 1710–11, *4*, 19 (Case 254[4]) in a feebly expanded form of which the first lines are:

> *WHIG*'s the first Word that swells his odious Name;
> *Hypocrisy*'s the second, good Mens Shame.

Title: [none] *A*   An Anagram on Wharton *BC*   (An) Anagram *DE*   A-crostique upon old Ld Wharton *F*   An Acrostick on the Ld Wharton *G*   (An) Acrostick *HJ*   1710 *K*

1 Whig's] Whig *JK*   his odious Name] his name *EHK*   2 Hypocrisy's] *ABH*   Hyppocrate *CK*   Hypocrisy *Σ*   3 Anarchy's] *ABC*   Anarchy *Σ*   5 in] I'ts *J*   6 Sin] vice *C*   Sins *K*   cornuted] corrupted *B*   old] basc *A* and *F*   7 Soul and *Ireton*'s live within] Soul and Ireton's reign in *B*   & Iretons line, is in *C*

A Welcome to the Medal

Copy text: Ac

Collation: The text survives in two folio half-sheet editions, both printed in two columns on one side only, and one anthology:

> A Welcome to the Medal; Or An Excellent New
>   Song; Call'd *The Constitution Restor'd*, in 1711. To
>   the Tune of *Mortimer's-Hole* . . . Oxford at the
>   Theatre. M.DCC.XI (Copies: Society of Antiquaries
>   of London; *Bibliotheca Lindesiana*, I, 271)   *Aa*
> A Welcome to the Medal; Or An Excellent New
>   Song; Call'd *The Constitution Restor'd*, in 1711. To the
>   Tune of *Mortimer's Hole* . . . Oxford, at the Theatre.
>   M.DCC.XI (Copies: Bodl. [Firth b.21 (107)], Texas)   *Ab*
> *Political Merriment: Or, Truths Told to Some Tune*, 1714,
>   pp. ²35–40 (Case 280 [2]) (Yale copy)   *Ac*

There are no substantive variants among the three copies and only a few printer's errors. Thus it is impossible to determine whether *Aa* is a careless (pirated?) resetting of *Ab* or whether *Ab* is a corrected edition of *Aa*. *Ac* was chosen as copy text because *Aab* are a typographical gallimaufry in which roman, italic, black letter and upper case type are mixed almost indiscriminately.

3 Popish] Popist *Aa*   7 *Silk*] S——lk *Aabc*   24 *Irish*] *I*——sh *Aabc*   43
shamm'd] sham'd *Ac*   46 *Prior* and *Moor*] Pr——r and M——r *Aabc*   58
Radnor] Rad——r *Aabc*   91 whine] Wine *Aab*

Mat's Peace

Copy text: Aa
Collation: The following copies have been recovered:

> An Excellent New Song, Called, Mat's Peace, or the
> Downfal of Trade. To the Good Old Tune of
> *Green-Sleeves* . . . Printed in the Year M.DCC.XI
> *(Copies:* Texas, Library Company of Philadelphia,
> Bodl. [Firth b.21 (102)], NLS)   *Aa*
> *Political Merriment: Or, Truths Told to Some Tune,* 1714,
> pp. ²61–65 (Case 280 [2]) (Yale copy)   *Ab*
> [John Oldmixon], *The Life and Posthumous Works of
> Arthur Maynwaring, Esq.,* 1715, pp. 327–30   *Ac*
> *A Pill to Purge State-Melancholy: Or, A Collection of
> Excellent New Ballads.* The Third Edition, with
> Additions, 1716, pp. 61–64 (Case 288 [c]) (Yale copy)   *Ad*
> An Excellent New Song, Called, Mat's Peace: Or, The
> Downfal of Trade. To the Good Old Tune of
> *Green-Sleeves* . . . Printed in the Year, MDCCXI
> (Harvard copy)   *B*
> Hertfordshire County R. O. MS. Cowper, Box 46,
> Lampoons, no pag.   *C*

AaB, folio half-sheets printed in two columns on one side only, and the manuscript *C* appear to derive from a common source. *Abd* derive collaterally from *Aa,* while *Ac* in turn derives from *Ab.*

Title: An Excellent New Song, Called, Mat's Peace, or the Downfal of Trade. To the Good Old Tune of *Green-Sleeves AB*   A Ballad made on the Treaty of Peace in the Year 1711 to the tune of green sleeves *C*

9 now we] now at the last we *B*   10–18 *follow* 27 *C*   19–27 *follow* 9 *C*
20 our late] the late *C*   34 have we made] shou'd we have *B*   such a glorious]
this successful *C*   40 should] might *C*   41 Queen too to] Queen to *B*
46 By] In *C*   up all our] up our *B*   68 how can they] who is't can *C*   69
that] his *B*   *Prior*] P——r *AB*   70 deserves] deserv'd *AB*   76 a . . . a]
the . . . the *C*   78 *Mortimer*] M——r *AB*   79 in his *Hole* had been pleas'd]
had been pleas'd in his *Hole AB*

The Procession

Copy text: Aa
Collation: The text is preserved in the following copies:

The Thanksgiving: A New Protestant Ballad. *To an Excellent Italian Tune* . . . Printed in the Year MDCCXI (University of Cincinnati copy)   *Aa*

The Thanksgiving: A New Protestant Ballad. *To an Excellent Italian Tune* . . . *London*, Printed in the Year 1711 (Copies: BM [Rox. III, 556], Harvard, BPL, Texas)   *Ab*

The Thanksgiving: A New Protestant Ballad. *To an Excellent Italian Tune* . . . *London*, Printed in the Year 1711 (Copies: BM [112.f.44 (28)], Bodl. [Firth b.21 (109)], Pierpont Morgan Library)   *Ac*

Political Merriment: Or, Truths Told to Some Tune, 1714, pp. ²128–31 (Case 280 [2]) (Yale copy)   *Ad*

BM MS. Add. 30381, ff. 277–81v   *Ae*

There is not sufficient evidence to determine priorities among the three broadside editions, all of which are printed in two columns on one side of the sheet only. *Aa* prints lines 37–72 in italics, which are not reproduced above. The three broadside copies can be distinguished as follows:

line 31	*line 54*	
unmanerly	been	*Aa*
unmannerly	beed	*Ab*
unmannerly	been	*Ac*

Title: The Thanksgiving: A New Protestant Ballad. To an Excellent Italian Tune
Aabcd   The Procession. To an Excellent Italian Tune *Ae*

1 the New] to the *Aa*   Ministry's] M——y's *Aabcd*   3 Statesmen] S——smen *Aabcd*   47 around] round *Aabcde*   62 call] call'd *Ae*

A Panegyrick upon the English Catiline

Copy text: Ca
Collation: The following copies have been recovered:

Hertfordshire County R. O. MS. Cowper, Box 9, *Diary, 6,* 1–2   *A*

Hertfordshire County R. O. MS. Cowper, Box 9, *Diary, 6,* 31–32   *B*

A Panegyrick upon the English Catiline . . . Printed in the Year MDCCXI (Copies: BM, *Bibliotheca Lindesiana,* uncatalogued)   *Ca*

Political Merriment: Or, Truths Told to Some Tune, 1714, pp. ²229–30 (Case 280 [2]) (Yale copy)   *Cb*

TCD MS. I.5, *1,* 261–62   *D*

After transcribing *A* into her diary, Dame Sarah Cowper appears to have found a better copy which she transcribed as *B*. *Ca*, a folio half-sheet printed on one side in a single column, is almost certainly the source of the anthology copy, *Cb*, and possibly the source of the manuscript *D* as well.

Title: A poem *A*   A panegerick upon the Tr——r. Janu: 4th 1711 *B*   A Panegyrick upon the English Catiline *CabD*

1 the *British*] old Brittish *A*   4 far out-done] now outdone *A*   14 Treasury] T——ry *Cab*   16 State it was before] State, they found it in before *A*   19 it from the] of those *A*   20 *Atterbury*] A—— *A*   At——bury *Cab*   25 in the Mine] in His Mine *A*   26 *Harcourt*] H——t *A*   Ha——t *Cab*   27 the Great] before *A*   the Vile *D*   30 And] Had *A*

An Excellent New Song,
Being
The Intended Speech of a Famous Orator against Peace

Copy text: Aa
Collation: The following copies have been collated:

An Excellent New Song. Being The *Intended Speech of a famous Orator against Peace* [n.p., n.d.] (Teerink 554) (Copies: Harvard, Bodl.)	*Aa*
An Excellent New Song. Being *The Intended Speech of a Famous Orator against Peace* [n.p., n.d.] (TCD copy)	*Ab*
Portland MS. Pw V 413	*Ac*
TCD MS. I.5, *1,* ²31–32	*Ad*
A Supplement to the Works of the Most Celebrated Minor Poets (F. Cogan), 1750, pp. 89–90 (Teerink 81) (Yale copy)	*Ae*
A Supplement to Dr. Swift's Works (J. Nichols), 1779, pp. 554–55 (Teerink 87) (Smith College copy)	*Af*
A Supplement to Dr. Swift's Works . . . In Three Volumes (J. Nichols), 1779, *3,* 200–02 (Teerink 90) (Yale copy)	*Ag*
The Works of the Rev. Dr. Jonathan Swift, ed. Thomas Sheridan, 17 vols., 1784, *7,* 74–76 (Teerink 119) (Yale copy)	*Ah*
The Works of the Rev. Jonathan Swift, D.D., ed. John Nichols, 19 vols., 1801, *7,* 71–73 (Teerink 129) (Yale copy)	*Aj*

Abcdef derive collaterally from *Aa*. *Ab*, which was unknown to Teerink or to Williams, may be a Dublin piracy of *Aa*. Both are printed in a single column on both sides of the sheet.

Ag was set up from *Af,* and *Ah* from *Ag. Aj* appropriated both the text and footnotes of *Ah,* but adopted the reading of *Ag* for line 10. *Roxburghe Ballads, 5,* 109 reprints lines 1–10, 53–54, and F. Elrington Ball (*Swift's Verse,* John Murray, 1929, p. 117) reprints lines 45–54, both from *Aj.*

The "Paper, intituled, '*The Earl of* Nottingham's *Speech to the Honourable House of Lords*' " (*LJ, 19,* 343, 349) that Sir Harold Williams supposed to be a pirated edition of *An Excellent New Song* (Swift, *Poems, 1,* 142) apparently is part of the speech that Nottingham delivered in the House of Lords on 7 December 1711. It is reprinted in HMC *Lords MSS., New* Series, *9,* 368–69.

4 *Queen's*] *Q——'s Aabc*   9 *Hoppy,*] *Hoppy. Aa*   Hoppy *Acd*   10 *I have obtain'd*] I've Obtained *Adfgj*   I have gotten *Ah*   15 Duke . . . Dutchess] D—— . . . D——s *Aabc*   16 Clutches:] Clutches *Aabc*   Clutches, *Ae*   18 Grace . . . Grace] G—— . . . G(race) *Aabc*   19 *Pocket*] Pocket, *Aabde*   21 But] But, *Aabefg*   28 King] K. *Aab*   35 *Queen . . . Prince* of *Hanover*] *Q——(n) . . . Pr——* of H——*r Aabc*   41 *Majesty*] *M——* *Aab*

The Queen's Speech

Copy text: B
Collation: Only two copies have been recovered:

> Blenheim MS. GI 15   *A*
> *Political Merriment: Or, Truths Told to Some Tune,* 1714,
>   pp. 55–56 (Case 280 [1]) (Yale copy)   *B*

The manuscript is not in the hand of Arthur Mainwaring.

Title: A New Song to the Tune of Packington's Pound *A*   *The Qu——ns Speech. To the Tune of* Packington'*s Pound B*

4 somewhat] something *B*   10 *French,* our Allies,] french our Allies *A*   French our Ally's *B*   25 the . . . that] that . . . which *A*   26 or] and *B*   31 All those that have made] The people that make *A*   35 you in your] your all *A*

The Character of a Certain Whigg

Copy text: A
Collation: The following copies have been recovered:

> The Character of A Certain Whigg . . . Printed in the
>   Year 1712 (Copy: Bodl. [Firth b.21 (24)])   *A*
> The Character of A Certain Whigg . . . Printed in the

Year 1712 (Copies: Newberry Library, Bodl. [Rawl.
  poet. 207, p. 57], University of Cincinnati, Harvard)   *B*
University of Leeds MS. Brotherton Lt.11, p. 139   *C*
Bodl. MS. Rawl. poet. 203, f. 34   *D*
Bodl. MS. Rawl. poet. 181, f. 67   *E*
Bodl. MS. Eng. poet. e.87, p. 83   *F*
Bodl. MS. Rawl. poet. 155, p. 102   *G*

What little evidence there is (line 15) indicates that *A* is the earlier of the two broad-side editions, both of which print the poem in a single column on one side of the sheet. *CD* may be copies of *B*. *DE* are defective, lacking lines 3, 8–9, 12–15. *FG* derive from a source similar to *ABC*. *G* appears to be a memorial reconstruction.

Title: The Character of a Certain Whig(g) *ABC*   Character of Tho(mas) late Marquiss of Wharton *DE*   The Lord Wharton's Character *F*   A Character of Wharton *G*

3 *omitted DE*   3 He doats] Doating *G*   4 Joins Contradictions] Tom's Contradicting *F* Joyn'd contradictions *G*   wond'rous] monstrous *F*   6 Joins] Tom 'as *F* Mix'd *G*   8–9 *omitted DE*   8 Descending] Descended *G*   10 Viceroy] Vice——y *AB*   unpropitious] impropitious *FG*   12–15 *omitted DE*   12] Secur'd his honour and his dignity *G*   13 By . . . RIB-ALDRY and WHORES] With . . . Ribaldry, & Whores *F* By . . . Whores and Ribaldry *G*   14 Kisses] Would Kiss *G*   15 Vends] Takes *BCF* Us'd *G* Perjury] Ribaldry *C*   16 To great and small alike extends] Extended to both great and small *G*   17 Plund'ring] Plunder'd *G*   bilking ROOKS] bilking whores *DEF* bilk'd his Whores *G*   18 His *Mind* still working] Still work'd his mind tho *G*   19 Pox] P——x *ABC*   has] had *FG*   20 can] could *DG*   21 by] of *DE*   and long since due] and long since doomed *E*   is hurry'd now *F* injustly gone *G*

A New Song

Copy text: Ad
Collation: The following copies have been recovered:

Bodl. MS. Rawl. D.992, ff. 23v–24   *Aa*
Hertfordshire County R. O. MS. Cowper Box 12,
  Family Book, *2*, 33–34   *Ab*
A New Song. Being a Second Part to the same Tune of
  Lillibullero, &c. [n.p., n.d.] (Copies: NLS, Bodl.
  [Firth b.21 (103)], Texas, Library Company of
  Philadelphia, Harvard [EBB7])   *Ac*
A New Song. Being a Second Part to the same Tune of
  Lillibullero, &c. [n.p., n.d.] (Harvard copy [EBB7

       In memory of Lionel de Jersey Harvard])   *Ad*
    A New Song. Being a Second Part to the same Tune of
       Lillibullero, &c. [n.p., n.d.] (Harvard copy [Kress
       S.2594])   *Ae*
    A Pill to Purge State-Melancholy: Or, A Collection of
       Excellent New Ballads, 1715, pp. 57–58 (Case 288)
       (Yale copy)   *Af*

There is not sufficient evidence to establish priorities among *Aabcde.* The three folio half-sheet editions, all of which are printed on one side only in a single column, may be distinguished as follows:

line 49:	*line 57:*	
does	farewel	*Ac*
do	farcwel	*Ad*
do	farewell	*Ae*

George Ridpath "new vamp'd" the song and printed it in *The Flying Post,* 30 September–2 October 1712, with the title, *The Song* ("A Plot's now on foot, look about *English* Boys") (*Political Merriment: Or, Truths Told to Some Tune,* Part II, 1714, p. 219). The variants, which are slight, are not included below.

Title: [none] *Aa*   Song Being a Second Part to the same tune of Lillibullero
Ab   A New Song. Being a Second Part to the same Tune of Lillibullero, &c. *Acdef*

19 arrant] Errand *Aa*   errant *Af*   20 Whenever] *Aa*   Whene'er *Σ*   49 do] does *Ac*   52 They'l] *Aa*   They *Σ*   59 whenever] *Aab*   whene'er *Σ*

A New Protestant Litany

Copy text: A
Collation: The following copies have been recovered:

Political Merriment: Or, Truths Told to Some Tune, 1714,	
pp. 53–54 (Case 280[1]) (Yale copy)	*A*
BM MS. Add. 40060, f. 88	*B*
Bodl. MS. Firth c. 3, f. 1	*C*
University of Leeds MS. Brotherton Lt.11, pp. 154–55	*D*
A New Litany . . . *Cambridge,* Printed in the Year 1712	
(Copies: Harvard, Bodl. [Firth b.21 (125)]).	*E*
Hertfordshire County R. O. MS. Cowper Box 9,	
Diary, 6, 67	*F*

Although it is later than the other copies, *A* derives from a source anterior to the source of *BCDE. F* may be transcribed from the broadside (*E*), which is printed in a single column on one side only. The copy in *Roxburghe Ballads, 8,* 828, was set up from *A.*

Title: A New Protestant Lit(t)any *AB*　　A New Litany *CDE*　　A New Litany. 1713 *F*

2 *Harley*] H——y *AB*　Har——y *C*　H—— *E*　H——ly *F*　　St. *John*] St. J——n(s) *ABCF*　S. *J*—— *E*　　3] *Libera nos AB*　omitted *F*　　4 whereas no Mortal] when nobody *BCDE*　which nobody *F*　　5 of . . . but . . . our] of . . . but by . . . our *A*　of . . . but . . . his *B*　or . . . but . . . our *F*　　7 (God knows) Silly, Lavish and] *A*　O(rmon)d as silly as *Σ*　　8 Whore] W(h)——re *AE*　　10 of Merit] *A*　advanced *Σ*　　for] from *ABCDEF*　　handling] *A* Working *B*　trundling *Σ*　　11 sweeping] *A*　brushing *Σ*　　scrubbing] rubbing *A*　　13 a Masculine . . . preposterous] *A*　S(hrewsbur)y's . . . exalted by *Σ*　　14 for . . . grown] *A*　for . . . to be *BCDE*　of . . . to be *F*　　Whores] W——res *A*　　17 Godson] Gran(d)son's *DEF*　　19 Treasurer] Tr——r *ABC*　T—— *E*　us'd to] *A*　that will *Σ*　　20 to bribe] *A*　bribe *Σ*　　*Scottish* Peers] *A*　Scottish Lords *B*　the Scotch Lords *Σ*　　List] Lords *D*　L——'s *E*　　22 Whom] *AC*　Who *B*　From *Σ*　　Whore] W——re *A*　　23 *en Or*] in O're *A*　en Dor(e) *BC*　on D'ore *DEF*　　26 too] *A*　so by *Σ*　　28 St. *John*] St. *J*——n(s) *ABC*　S. *J*—— *E*　　Poulet] P——t *ABE*　Pol——t *C*　　29 *Brydges*] B——s *A*　M(ulgra)ve *BCDEF*　　Beaufort] B——f——t *A*　Beau——t *BC*　B——t *DE*　　31 all] *A*　those *Σ*　　who] that *CDE*　　34 in] good *F*　　35 Harpy] *A*　Harp(e)y(e)s *Σ*

The Fable of Midas

*Copy text: Aa*¹

Collation: The following copies have been collated:

(Teerink 42, p. 30) (U. of Pennsylvania copy)   *Af*

Miscellanies, In Prose and Verse, 1738, *5,* 1–4 (Teerink 30)
(U. of Pennsylvania copy)   *Ag*

Miscellanies, 1742, *5,* 1–4 (Teerink 66) (U. of
Pennsylvania copy)   *Ah*

The Works of Jonathan Swift, D.D, Dublin, 1744, *2,*
74–77 (Teerink 44) (U. of Pennsylvania copy)   *Aj*

Miscellanies, 1745, *5,* 1–4 (Teerink 67) (Yale copy)   *Ak*

The Works of Jonathan Swift, D.D, Dublin, 1747, *2,*
67–70 (Teerink 51) (U. of Pennsylvania copy)   *Al*

Miscellanies, 1749, *5,* 1–4 (Teerink 67A) (U. of
Pennsylvania copy)   *Am*

Miscellanies, 1751, *5,* 1–4 (Teerink 69) (U. of
Pennsylvania copy)   *An*

The Works of Dr. Jonathan Swift, 1751, *10,* 1–4
(Teerink 82) (U. of Pennsylvania copy)   *Ao*

The Works of Jonathan Swift, D.D., ed. John
Hawkesworth, 1755, *4,* i, 2–5 (Teerink 87) (Smith
College copy)   *Ap*

The Works of the Reverend Dr. Jonathan Swift, Dublin,
1762, *2,* 41–43 (Teerink 53) (U. of Pennsylvania copy)   *Aq*

The Works of Jonathan Swift, D.D., Dublin, 1763, *2,*
75–78 (Teerink 45A) (U. of Pennsylvania copy)   *Ar*

The Works of the Reverend Dr. J. Swift, Dublin, 1763, *2,*
64–66 (Teerink 52) (U. of Pennsylvania copy)   *As*

The Works of the Reverend Dr. Jonathan Swift, Dublin,
1772, *2,* 75–78 (Teerink 48) (U. of Pennsylvania copy)   *At*

The Works of the Rev. Dr. Jonathan Swift, ed. Thomas
Sheridan, 17 vols., 1784, *7,* 71–74 (Teerink 119) (U.
of Pennsylvania copy)   *Au*

The Works of the Rev. Jonathan Swift, D.D., ed. John
Nichols, 19 vols., 1801, *7,* 69–71 (Teerink 129) (U.
of Pennsylvania copy)   *Av*

Teerink called *Aa*[1] a piracy of *Aa*[2] but in fact *Aa*[2] is a reimpression of *Aa*[1] with a new imprint. The text is printed in a single column on both sides of the sheet. In the remaining witnesses there is no evidence of authorial revision.

27 *Phebus*] *Aab   Phoebus Acdeg   Phoebus'* Σ

Toland's Invitation to Dismal

Copy text: Aa
Collation: The following copies have been collated:

T——l——nd's Invitation to *DISMAL,* to Dine with

the Calves-Head Club. Imitated from Horace,
Epist. 5. Lib. 1 . . . January 29 (Teerink 580)
(Copies: University of Leeds Brotherton Collection,
Bodl., Harvard, Newberry Library, Texas)   *Aa*
T——l——nd's Invitation to *DISMAL,* to Dine with
the Calves-Head Club. Imitated from Horace, Epist.
5. Lib. 1. . . . *January,* 29 (Teerink 580) (Copies:
NLS, Harvard)   *Ab*
Bodl. MS. Eng. poet. e.87, pp. 164–66   *Ac*
BM MS. Add. 37683, f. 2   *Ad*
Deane Swift, *An Essay upon the Life, Writings, and
Character of Dr. Jonathan Swift,* 1755, pp. 227–30
(Teerink 1345) (Smith College copy)   *Ae*
*The Works of Dr. Jonathan Swift, Dean of St. Patrick's,
Dublin. Volume XIII. Collected and Revised by Dean
[sic] Swift,* Dublin, 1765, pp. 357–61 (Teerink 47)
(U. of Pennsylvania copy)   *Af*
*The Works of Dr. Jonathan Swift, Dean of St.
Patrick's, Dublin. Volume VIII. Part I. Collected and
Revised by Deane Swift,* London, 1765, pp. ²230–32
(Teerink 87) (Smith College copy)   *Ag*
*The Works of Dr. Jonathan Swift, Dean of St. Patrick's,
Dublin. Volume XVI. Collected and Revised by Deane
Swift,* London, 1765, pp. 357–61 (Teerink 88) (U.
of Pennsylvania copy)   *Ah*
*The Works of Dr. Jonathan Swift, Dean of St. Patrick's,
Dublin. Volume XVII. Collected and Revised by Deane
Swift,* London, 1765, pp. 211–14 (Teerink 90) (U. of
Pennsylvania copy)   *Aj*
*The Works of Dr. Jonathan Swift, Dean of St. Patrick's,
Dublin, Volume XIII. Collected and Revised by Deane
Swift,* Dublin, 1765, pp. 244–46 (Teerink 52) (U. of
Pennsylvania copy)   *Ak*
*The Works of Dr. Jonathan Swift, Dean of St. Patrick's,
Dublin, Volume XIII. Collected and Revised by Deans
Swift,* Dublin, 1765, pp. 282–85 (Teerink 53) (U.
of Pennsylvania copy)   *Al*
*The Works of the Reverend Dr. Jonathan Swift, Dean of St.
Patrick's, Dublin . . . Collected and Revised by Deane
Swift . . . Volume XIII,* Dublin, 1772, pp. 357–61
(Teerink 48) (U. of Pennsylvania copy)   *Am*
The Works of the Rev. Dr. Jonathan Swift, ed. Thomas
Sheridan, 17 vols., London, 1784, *7,* 79–81 (Teerink
119) (U. of Pennsylvania copy)   *An*
The Works of the Rev. Jonathan Swift, D.D., ed. John
Nichols, 19 vols., London, 1801, *7,* 77–79 (Teerink
129) (U. of Pennsylvania copy)   *Ao*

Ab is reset from *Aa* in the same font of type. Both *Aa* and *Ab* are printed in a single column on one side of the page with Horace's Latin at the foot. They can be distinguished, as Teerink discovered, by an erroneous comma after "January" in *Ab*. Neither *Ab* nor any of the later copies show evidence of authorial revision.

Deane Swift's text (*Ae*) was set up from *Aa*. *Am* is the same setting of type as *Af*. Thomas Sheridan's text (*An*) was set up from the copy of *Aa* in the Lambeth Palace Library. *Ao* was set up from *An*.

Title: T(o)l(a)nd's Invitation to Dismal, to Dine with the Calves-Head Club. (Imitated from Horace, Epist. 5. Lib. 1) *Aabcdeno*   Toland's Invitation To Dismal To dine with the Calf's-Head-Club. Imitated from Horace, Epist. V. Lib. 1. A Ballad *Afghjklm*

3 *Toland*] T——l——nd *Aabe*   19 *Godolphin's*] G——d——lph——n's *Aabe*
20 *Jack Smith*] J——ck Sm——th *Aabe*   21 *Scarborow*] Ac Sc——rb——r——w
Aab Scarbor——w *Ad* Sc——rb——r——gh *Ae* Scarborough Σ   22 *Hal*——]
Hal *Aefghjklmno*   *Sommers*] S(o)m(me)rs *Aabcde*   23 *Portland* . . .
Cleveland] P——rt——d . . . *Cl*——v——nd *Aabe*   24 *Montague* . . . *Bolton*]
M——t——g——e . . . B——lt——n *Aabe*   25 *Cholmondeley*] Ch——ly *Aabe*
26 *Lincoln*] L——nc——n *Aabe Linc*——ln *Ad* L——n *Afghjklm*   33 *Sunderland,*
Orford, Boyl . . . *Richmond's*] S(u)nd——(l)——(n)d, Or(f)——rd, B(o)——l(e)
. . . R(i)ch——d's *Aabde*   34 *Hampden* . . . *Walpool's*] H(a)mp(d)——n . . .
W(al)p——l(e)'s *Aabde*   35 *Wharton*] W(hart)——n *Aabde*   41 *Guernsey*]
Gu——rn——y *Aabe*   calls] call *Aefghjklm*

An Elegy on the Death of Pamphlets

Copy text: Political Merriment: Or, Truths Told to Some Tune, Part II, 1714, pp. 158–59 (Case 280 [2]) (Yale copy).
Collation: Since only the copy text has been recovered, it is reproduced above with the following emendations:

1 What,] What   3 *Barber,*] B——b——r   11 Martyr'd,] Martyr'd   20
Tower] T——r   26 Ev'n] Even   31 he] be

The Plotter Found Out

Copy text: Political Merriment: Or, Truths Told to Some Tune, 1714, pp. 46–48 (Case 280 [1]) (Yale copy).
Collation: The copy text is reproduced *verbatim et literatim* with the following exceptions:
Title: Arse] A——e   21 Rogue,] Rogue   on 'm] on'n   23 upon 'm]
upon'n   35 what's] that's

The Peace in View

Copy text: A
Collation: Only two copies of the poem have been recovered:

> *Political Merriment: Or, Truths Told to Some Tune*, 1715,
>   pp. ³45–46 (Case 280[3]) (Yale copy)   *A*
> *A Pill to Purge State-Melancholy*, 1715, pp. 143–44
>   (Case 288) (Yale copy)   *B*

Title: The Peace in View. A Song. To the Tune of A Health to the Constitution
A   A New Ballad *B*

1 *Tory*] Tories *B*   2 *France* has new] *Frenchmen* have *B*   *Britain*] Britons
B   6 *Dutch* and *Emperor* too] Emperor too and the *Dutch B*   11 *Oxford*]
Ox——d *AB*   12 brought] wrought *B*   13 *Shrewsbury's*] Sh——s——b——ys
A *B*——*k's B*   14 *Bolingbroke*] Bol——b——ke *A* *B*——ke *B*   15 all
of] of *B*   17 *Prior . . . Swift*] Pr——r . . . Sw——t *A*   18 their Brother
Protestant] their Protestant *B*   22 Friends combine] Cause combin'd *B*   24
Come-over] come over *A*

The British Embassadress's Speech to the French King

Copy text: Ab
Collation: The following copies have been recovered:

> The Br——sh Embassadress's Speech to the French
>   King [n.p., n.d.] (Copy: Hertfordshire County
>   R. O. MS. Cowper Box 46 Lampoons)   *Aa*
> The Br——sh Embassadress's Speech to the French
>   King [n.p., n.d.] (Copy: Society of Antiquaries of
>   London)   *Ab*
> *Political Merriment: Or, Truths Told to Some Tune*, 1715,
>   pp. ³71–73 (Case 280[4]) (Yale copy)   *Ac*
> Bodl. MS. Firth b.21 (113)   *Ad*
> Bodl. MS. Tanner 306, f. 474v   *Ae*
> Hertfordshire County R. O. MS. Cowper Box 9
>   *Diary, 6,* 56–58   *Af*
> Osborn MS. Box 22, No. 7   *Ag*
> University of Leeds MS. Brotherton Lt.11, pp. 170–72   *Ah*
> University of Nottingham MS. Portland Pw V 41, f. 163   *Aj*
> Bodl. MS. Rawl. D.383, f. 112   *Ak*
> Bodl. MS. Rawl. D.383, f. 67   *Al*
> University of Leeds MS. Brotherton Lt.q.3   *Am*
> TCD MS. I.5, *1,* 246   *An*

Liverpool University Library MS. (on end papers of
   [Charles Mowbray], *The Lives of the Two Illustrious*
   Generals, 1713)   *Ao*
NLS MS. 5330, f. 324   *Ap*
Bodl. MS. Eng. misc. c.116, f. 2   *Aq*
Bodl. MS. Rawl. C.986, ff. 23–24   *Ar*
NLS MS. 2935, f. 110   *As*
Folger MS. M.a.187, f. 169   *At*
MS. copy in end papers of *POAS,* 1716, *4* (editor's copy)   *Au*
Chetham's Library MS. Halliwell-Phillipps 2055   *Av*
Bodl. MS. Fol. θ665, f. 218   *Aw*

The manuscript copies appear to be collaterally derived from the edition printed on a slip, of which *Aa* represents the uncorrected state. *Ab* corrects typographical errors in lines 50, 57, and 60 of *Aa. Ac,* an anthology copy, was set up from *Aab. Ajkl* appear to be factory products, and the poem is acknowledged in *Am* to have been "privately dispers'd." The original editors of *POAS* may have found it too scandalous to print, but it was written into some copies (*Au*) nevertheless.

Title: The Br(itti)sh Embassadress's Speech to the French King *Aabcdefhjklmnqr* [cropped?] French King *Ag*   [none] *Ao*   The British Ambassadres to the frensh King *Ap*   The Brittish Ambassador's Lady's Speech To the King off France *As*   The Dutchess of Sommerset The British Ambassadress To the French King. 1713 *At*   The Br———sh Embass (Dutchess of Shrews:) Speech to the French King *Au*   The Embassdress Speech to the French King *Avw*

3 *Anna's*] *A———'s Ab*   5 *French*] *F———h Ab*   6 *Britain's*] *B———n's Ab*
8 *omitted Ag*   9 *Lords*] *L———s Ab*   Commons] *C———s Ab*   11 Queen,]
Q——— *Ab*   16–70 *omitted Av*   36 *Hanoverian*] *H———n Ab*   Line,] Line.
Aabc   37 chose,] chose *Ab*   41 *Oxford's*] *Ox———d's Ab*   Clan;] Clan,
Ab   42 court,] court; *Ab*   44 Senate!] Se———te *Ab*   45 *Dartmouth*]
D———th *Ab*   *Bolingbroke*] *B———ke Ab*   47 *Oxford*] *O———d Ab*   50
Parliament] P———t *Ab*   Queen] Q——— *Ab*   53 *Britain's*] *B———n's Ab*
54 King *James*] K———g *J———s Ab*   59–70 *omitted Am*

The Country Squire's Ditty

Copy text: A
Collation: The following copies have been recovered:

The Country Squire's Ditty. A Ballad. To the Tune of
   To you fair Ladys, &c. [n.p., n.d.] (*Bibliotheca*
   Lindesiana, 2, 434–35)   *A*
BM MS. Lansdowne 852, f. 152   *B*
Hertfordshire County R. O. MS. Cowper Box 12,
   Family Book, *2,* 43–44   *C*

A is printed on one side of a strip ballad on which *The First Psalm* ("The Man is blest that hath not lent") is printed on the reverse. It is probable that *BC* are collaterally derived from *A*.

Title: The Country Squire's Ditty. A Ballad. To the Tune of To you fair Ladys, &c. *A*   (The) Country Squire's Ditty *BC*

6 gaul'd] gull'd *C*   10 *Oxford*] *O——d AB*   12 other's] others *AB*   17 that] the *AB*   20 the Stock] that Stocks *C*   29 *Phipps*] *P—— AB   Ph——ps C*   nor Law] no Law *B*   37 Bastard] Bastard's *B*   40 *Ministry*] *M——y A*

An Excellent New Hymn

Copy text: An Excellent New Hymn, Compos'd By the *Priests* of the Order of St. *Perkin,* for the Use of *High-Church,* upon their approaching Day of *Humiliation,* being the Coronation-Day of his *truly Protestant* Majesty King *George* [n.p., n.d.] (*Bibliotheca Lindesiana,* uncatalogued).

Collation: The copy text is a strip ballad with Part I printed on one side and Part II on the other. Since no other copy has been recovered, the copy text is reproduced *verbatim et literatim,* except that commas have been deleted within lines 32 and 45 (and at the end of line 61), moved in lines 3 and 53, and added at the end of line 62.

A Farewell to the Year 1714

Copy text: A
Collation: Two copies of the poem have been recovered:

Bodl. MS. Eng. poet. e.87, p. 161   *A*
BM MS. Lansdowne 852, f. 161   *B*

Title: On the old year. 1714 *A*   A Farewell to the Year 1714 *B*

3 Stuart] Stuart's *A*   6 it will ever] that She e're will *B*   7 did] dost *A*
9 Broomstick] Brunswick *A*   10 Tory] High Church *A*

•   *Pasquin to the Queen's Statue*

Copy text: Aa
Collation: Besides the printed copy text (*Aa*), the poem survives in 12 manuscripts and

a second printed edition (*Ag*), all derived collaterally (with one possible exception) from the copy text:

PASQUIN to the Queen's Statue at St. *Paul's* during the Procession, *Jan.* 20. 1714 [n.p., n.d.] (Copies: Huntington, Harvard, Bodl. [MS. Rawl. poet. 207, p. 53], PRO Sp/35/3)	*Aa*
Kent R. O. MS. U442 Z26/6	*Ab*
BM MS. 14854, p. 115	*Ac*
Osborn MS. Box 95, No. 7, p. 118	*Ad*
BM MS. Add. 29981, f. 61v	*Ae*
Bodl. MS. Top. Oxon. c.108, f. 157	*Af*
Pasquin to the Queen's Statue at St. Paul's, during the Procession, Jan. 20. 1714 (Copy: Hertfordshire County R. O. Cowper MS. Box 46 Lampoons)	*Ag*
Bodl. MS. Rawl. poet. 155, p. 128	*Ah*
BM MS. Add. 32463, f. 10v	*Aj*
Bodl. MS. Hearne, Diaries 62, p. 7c	*Ak*
Bodl. MS. Rawl. poet. 203, f. 27v	*Al*
Bodl. MS. Rawl. poet. 173, f. 3	*Am*
BM MS. Lansdowne 852, f. 186	*An*
Bodl. MS. Eng. poet. e.87, p. 99	*Ao*

Al may be a copy of *Ak*.

Title: Pasquin to the Queen's Statue at St. Paul's, during the Procession, Jan. (the) 20(th). 1714(/5) *Aabcdefgmo*   Pasquin to the Queens Statue at St Pauls During the Procession on the Thanksgiving Jan^{ry} 20th *Ah*   Pasquin to Queen Ann's Statue at St. Paul's London, during the Procession on the Thanksgiving day for King George's Accession to the Throne. 20th January 1714/5 *Aj*   Pasquin to the Statue of Queen Anne at St Pauls during the Procession on Jan. 20. 1714/15 *Ak*   Pasquin's Speech to the Statue of Queen Anne during the procession on the thanksgiving day on Jan 20. 1714/5 *Al*   A Pasquin to the Queens Statue at St. Pauls during the Procession Jan. 29th. 1714 *An*

18 *George*] G——(*e*) *Aabefgk*   Sire *Al*   28 *Brunswick*] B(*r*)——(*ic*)*k Aabefgkl*   Bruns——k *Ao*   43 this] *Afkln*   his *Σ*   46 modest] modish *Ackl*   49 *George*] G——(*e*) *Aabefgkl*   50 *Townshend*] T——(*en*)*d Aabcefgk*   Townsend *Adjmno*   Churchill] C(*h*)——(*i*)*ll Aabcefgk*   70 *Coningsmark*] C(*on*)——(*arc*)*k Aabefgko*

INDEX OF FIRST LINES

Poems printed in this volume are in italics

699

INDEX

Italicized pages refer to the footnotes